HANDS ON AUTOCAD®
RELEASE 12

Jim Boyce
Jeff Beck
David Byrnes
B. Rustin Gesner
Kurt Hampe
Alex Lepeska
Randy Maxey
Larry Money
John Moran
Richard Stotts
William Wyatt

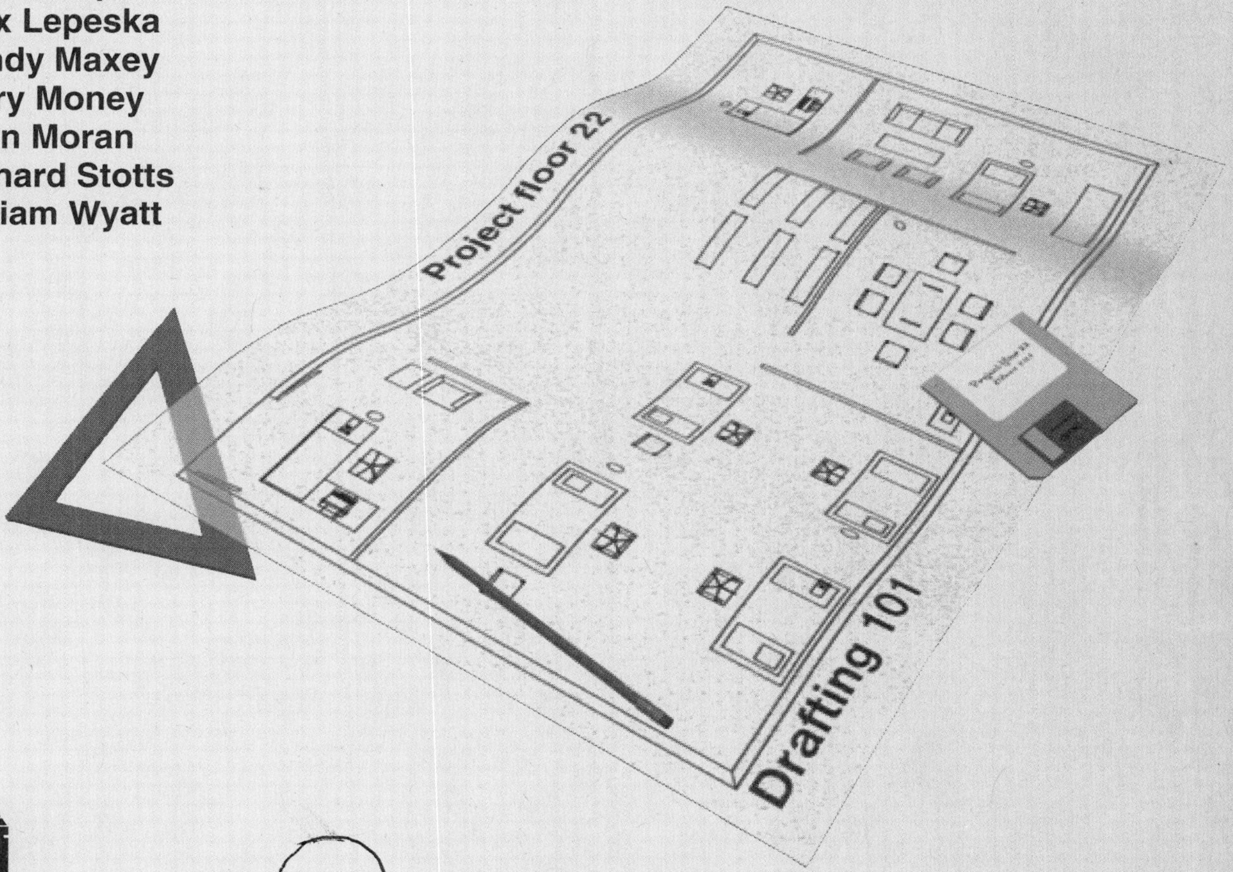

Project floor 22

Drafting 101

NRP
NEW RIDERS
PUBLISHING

New Riders Publishing,
Indianapolis, Indiana

© 1994

Hands On AutoCAD® Release 12

By Jim Boyce, Jeff Beck, David Byrnes, B. Rustin Gesner, Kurt Hampe, Alex Lepeska, Randy Maxey, Larry Money, John Moran, Richard Stotts, and William Wyatt

Published by:
New Riders Publishing
201 West 103rd Street
Indianapolis, IN 46290 USA

Printed in the United States of America 2 3 4 5 6 7 8 9 0

Hands on AutoCAD release 12 / Jim Boyce … [et al.].
p. cm.
Includes index.
ISBN 1-56205-227-1 : $24.95
1. Computer graphics. 2. AutoCAD (Computer file) I. Boyce, Jim, 1958-
T385.H333 1994 94-1446
620'.0042'02855369--dc20 CIP

Warning and Disclaimer This book is designed to provide information about the AutoCAD Release 12 program. Every effort has been made to make this book as complete and as accurate as possible, but no warranty or fitness is implied.

The information is provided on an "as is" basis. The author and New Riders Publishing shall have neither liability nor responsibility to any person or entity with respect to any loss or damages arising from the information contained in this book or from the use of the disks or programs that may accompany it.

Publisher	Lloyd J. Short
Associate Publisher	Tim Huddleston
CAD Publishing Director	B. Rustin Gesner
Acquisitions Manager	Cheri Robinson
Acquisitions Editor	Rob Tidrow
Managing Editor	Matthew Morrill
Marketing Manager	Gregg Bushyeager
Product Director	Jim Boyce
Project Leader	Peter Kuhns
Editors	Steve Weiss Geneil Breeze Richard Limacher Phil Worthington
Technical Editors	Tom Bledsaw Gary Sobczak
Book Design	Roger S. Morgan

Production

Nick Anderson	Juli Cook
Lisa Daugherty	Stephanie Davis
Rich Evers	Dennis Clay Hager
Angela P. Judy	Stephanie McComb
Jan Noller	Shelly Palma
Kim Scott	Michelle M. Self
Susan Shepard	Ann Sippel
Elaine Webb	Alyssa Yesh
Angela Bannon	Danielle Bird
Ayrika Bryant	Kim Cofer
Terri Edwards	Kim K. Hannel
Jamie Milazzo	Wendy Ott
Linda Quigley	Ryan Rader
Beth Rago	Kris Simmons
Tonya R. Simpson	SA Springer
Becky Tapley	Suzanne Tully
Dennis Wesner	Donna Winter
Indexer	Rebecca Mayfield
Acquisitions Coordinators	Stacey Beheler Alicia Krakovitz
Editorial Assistant	Karen Opal
Publishing Assistant	Melissa Lynch

About the Authors

Jim Boyce is a Contributing Editor of *WINDOWS Magazine*, and a regular contributor to *CADENCE Magazine* and other computer publications. He has been involved with computers since the late seventies, and has used computers in one way or another as a structural designer, production planner, systems manager, programmer, and college instructor. He has a wide range of experience in the DOS, Windows, and UNIX environments. Jim is the author and co-author of numerous books published by New Riders Publishing. You can contact Mr. Boyce via e-mail at the Internet address 76516.3403@compuserve.com.

Jeff Beck attended Pulaski Area Vocational Technical School for Drafting, and received State Certification as drafter/detailer. Jeff was a CAD drafter for IDI Technical Services and Attended Columbia State Community College. He has also taught AutoCAD classes for Pulaski Area Vocational Technical School. Mr. Beck also freelances in computer training, computer set-up and customization, and CAD drafting.

David Byrnes is a consultant in architectural conservation and historic preservation planning in North Vancouver, British Columbia. He also owns a CAD service bureau, providing drafting, plotting, scanning, and drawing conversion services to the local architectural and engineering community. He teaches facilities management planning software for an AutoCAD third-party developer. Mr. Byrnes also does freelance writing. He worked "on the board" for seven years before learning AutoCAD.

B. Rustin Gesner is publishing director of New Riders Publishing in Gresham, Oregon. Prior to joining New Riders, he was founder and president of CAD Northwest, Incc., in Portland, Oregon. Mr. Gesner is a registered architect and formerly practiced the profession in Oregon and Washington after attending Antioch College and the College of Design, Art, and Architecture at the University of Cincinnati. Mr. Gesner is co-author of the New Riders books *Maximizing AutoCAD Volume I* (formerly titled *Customizing AutoCAD*) and *Volume II* (formerly titled *Inside AutoLISP*), *AutoCAD for Beginners, Inside AutoCAD*, and *Inside AutoCAD for Windows.*

Kurt Hampe has worked as a programmer for a brief period before becoming a teacher for Kentucky Polytechnic. Mr. Hampe taught at the Marion County Adjustment Center, teaching inmates to use computers. After a seven month stint at the Adjustment Center, he began teaching for Corporate Computer Training Center.

While at the Training Center, Kurt began writing and editing technical manuals and books. This led to his present goal of becoming a full time author/editor. In addition to writing, Kurt also consults, programs, and drafts in AutoCAD. Hobbies include guitar, cooking, and driving much too fast.

Alex B. Lepeska is an Instrumentation Designer and CAD Coordinator/LISP Programmer for Chiyoda International Corporation of America in Seattle, Washington. Mr. Lepeska has worked in Electrical and Instrumentation for five years and worked with AutoCAD since version 2.5. Alex teaches Intermediate and

Advanced Engineering Graphics at Pierce College of Puyallup in Washington. He spends time on the side helping set up CAD Coordination and menu programming for small businesses.

Randall A. Maxey is the founder of R.A. Maxey and Associates, a consulting firm located in Westerville, Ohio. Mr. Maxey attended Ohio State University, Franklin University and Marion Technical Colleges. His consulting firm, started in 1989, provides technical knowledge and expertise to firms seeking to improve the proficiency of their engineering and design efforts.

Larry L. Money received a Bachelor of Architecture degree from the College of Architecture and Design at the University of Michigan and has over 28 years' experience in the architecture and construction business. He is an associate professor in the Technical Education Department at Del Mar College and serves as the program director for Architectural Technology. His teaching experience spans over 18 years including more than 13 years of CAD instruction for college credit, as well as four years of professional development workshops in AutoCAD.

John Moran has been using AutoCAD since version 2.18. He is currently employed as a Business Systems Programmer/Analyst for a manufacturer of large, numbered aircraft in the Seattle, Washington area. He is also an instructor of AutoCAD programming at Clover Park Technical College, Tacoma, Washington, a tutor in their Adult Literacy Program and owner of a small programming company. He was formerly employed as an electrical engineer in New Jersey, New York and Washington.

Richard L. Stotts graduated from Kilgore College in Kilgore, Texas; and Brigham Young University in Provo, Utah; North Texas State University, East Texas State University. Richard has been a drafting instructor at Grayson Community College, drafting and CAD instructor at North Harris College. He has also worked in industry at Hughes Tool, Texas Instruments, and General Electric.

William O. Wyatt is Professor of Drafting at John Tyler Community College, Chester, Virginia. He has taught architectural and mechanical drafting for eleven years and chaired the Division of Engineering Technologies for ten years. He received his Doctor of Education from Virginia Tech and his Masters of Science and Bachelor of Science degrees in Industrial Technology from Eastern Kentucky University. He is a certified engineering technician and has experience in architectural and mechanical design.

Acknowledgments

The authors are grateful to all the editors at New Riders who worked on this project, especially Steve Weiss, Phil Worthington, Geneil Breeze, and Rich Limacher. Special thanks to Peter Kuhns for keeping track of hundreds of pieces and making sure everything flowed smoothly. Special thanks also to Cheri Robinson for managing the seemingly endless process of acquisitions for the book.

Jim Boyce offers a special thanks to Rusty Gesner for his help in developing the book and for offering other direction; Kevin Coleman for his help in developing the illustrations; Randy Maxey for taking on so much more than he bargained for and still maintaining a sense of humor; Alex Lepeska, Kurt Hampe, and Larry Money for agreeing to handle some of the overflow of work; and Margaret Berson for tips on macros and other writing mechanics.

Trademark Acknowledgments

Contents at a Glance

Table of Contents

New Riders Publishing

The staff of New Riders Publishing is committed to bringing you the very best in computer reference material. Each New Riders book is the result of months of work by authors and staff, who research and refine the information contained within its covers.

As part of this commitment to you, the NRP reader, New Riders invites your input. Please let us know if you enjoyed this book, if you had trouble with the information and examples presented, or if you have a suggestion for the next edition.

Please note, however, that the New Riders staff cannot serve as a technical resource for DOS or DOS application-related questions, including hardware- or software-related problems. Refer to the documentation that accompanies your DOS or DOS application package for help with specific problems.

If you have a question or comment about any New Riders book, please write to NRP at the following address. We will respond to as many readers as we can. Your name, address, or phone number will never become part of a mailing list or be used for any other purpose than to help us continue to bring you the best books possible.

New Riders Publishing
Paramount Publishing
Attn: Associate Publisher
201 West 103rd Street
Indianapolis, IN 46290

If you prefer, you can FAX New Riders Publishing at the following number:

(317) 581-4670

We also welcome your comments in the PHCP forum on CompuServe.

Thank you for selecting *Hands On AutoCAD Release 12*!

Introduction

AutoCAD is a very popular CAD application, and AutoCAD users far outnumber the users of any other CAD system. Since the introduction of AutoCAD, the program has grown from being relatively simple to large and complex. Even if you are new to AutoCAD, however, you do not need to be intimidated by its size and complexity. Over a million designers and drafters have learned to use AutoCAD; *Hands On AutoCAD Release 12* will help you learn AutoCAD too.

Hands On AutoCAD Release 12 is your guide to a significant step in the evolution of AutoCAD. Release 12 has been dubbed "the user's release." Like most of the previous releases of AutoCAD, Release 12 adds many new features. The most noticeable new feature of Release 12 is the more productive design environment that results from enhancements to the user interface. Release 12 provides a more comprehensive set of pull-down menus and dialog boxes, an integrated screen menu, and several improvements in input and editing that make AutoCAD easier and more intuitive to use.

Hands On AutoCAD Release 12 helps you take advantage of the many new or improved features AutoCAD Release 12 offers over previous versions of AutoCAD, including:

- ☞ **More dialog boxes**. Release 12 includes easy-to-use dialog boxes for many kinds of operations and for virtually all settings. The enhanced dialog boxes make AutoCAD easier to learn and use than ever before.
- ☞ **Better menus**. The main menu is gone, replaced by a File pull-down menu. The pull-down menu is better organized and more complete

than the old main menu, and features nested child submenus for related sets of commands and options. The screen menu automatically displays pages of options for every command, whether you enter the command by menu or from the keyboard.

☞ **Enhanced object selection**. You can use several new methods to select objects more quickly, easily, and precisely for editing. These methods include automatic windowing and selecting objects crossing irregular lines, or selecting windows with irregular boundaries.

☞ **Noun/verb editing**. You can now select entities, then specify the command to edit them with. In *Hands On AutoCAD Release 12*, this new selection method is called *pick-first* selection.

☞ **Grips editing**. You can select entities and then pick geometric points (like object snap points) on them called grips to drag them around and modify them by, using several of the most common editing operations.

☞ **Locked layers**. You can lock layers to leave them visible, while preventing object selection or editing on them.

☞ **Plotting**. Plotting is greatly improved in Release 12, with dialog-box control, your choice of any number of alternative plotters or plot configurations, and optional plot preview.

☞ **PostScript**. You can use, plot, and export PostScript fonts and fills for publishing-quality graphics.

☞ **Graphics file formats**. AutoCAD Release 12 can import PostScript, TIFF, GIF, and PCX graphics files; and can export these and other common graphics-file formats.

☞ **Dimensioning**. AutoCAD Release 12 makes dimensioning fast and easy through a new set of submenus (which give you fast access to dimensioning commands) and a dialog box (for setting variables and managing styles). You no longer need to remember all those cryptic variable names.

☞ **Linetypes**. Broken linetypes now display with polylines of all types.

☞ **Automated boundary and hatch generations**. You can automatically generate complex boundary polylines defined by multiple entities, and you can then hatch those boundaries.

☞ **Regions.** You can create editable, single-entity flat objects from polylines and circles, and then extract properties such as area, perimeter, centroid, bounding box, moment of inertia, products of inertia, principal moments, and radius of gyration.

☞ **Rendering and shading**. Release 12's built-in rendering and shading features enable you to create presentations in AutoCAD, without using another program, such as AutoVision.

The Benefits of this Book to New AutoCAD Users

This book requires no previous AutoCAD experience; it takes you from the beginning level through intermediate level. The drawing exercises teach you how to use the program's interface, commands, menus, and dialog boxes. This book requires no previous DOS experience, but it does provide a minimal background in using files and disks. If you need more information on the basics of DOS before you start working with AutoCAD, ask your instructor for help. *Hands On AutoCAD Release 12* also focuses on the use of the menus and dialog boxes, which reduce the amount of typing you will have to do to use AutoCAD.

The Benefits of this Book to All Readers

No matter how proficient you are with AutoCAD or your computer, and no matter how you read this book, you will revisit it again and again as a reference manual for the basic functions that you perform most often in AutoCAD. You will find *Hands On AutoCAD Release 12* indispensable as you use it to find explanations and examples of specific commands and techniques.

How this Book Is Organized

Hands On AutoCAD Release 12 is separated into many small units, each covering a specific topic in AutoCAD. Drawing lines, for example, is treated in its own unit. Drawing circles and arcs is treated in another unit. Because the book is broken down into these small units, you can concentrate on one area at a time, becoming proficient with each topic before moving on to the next.

Because the unit topics are narrowly defined, you do not necessarily have to work through the units in order. For example, you can skip from Part Two to a unit in Part Five if you prefer. Even so, the arrangement of the units has been structured to follow one another in a logical manner. It is recommended that you work through the units in order as much as possible.

At the end of each unit is a Unit Review, which provides a brief overview of what you have learned in the unit. The Unit Review provides a variety of questions to test your knowledge of the material covered in the unit. Many of the units also include exercises in the Unit Review that you can work through to gain additional experience with the commands and techniques explained in the unit.

Part I: Getting Started

Part One serves as an introduction to computers and to AutoCAD. In Part One you learn about computer hardware and software, and learn the role each hardware item plays in your computer. Part One also takes you through a brief AutoCAD session to create a simple drawing. You learn about AutoCADs *interface*, which you use to interact with AutoCAD (entering commands and other input, for example).

Part II: Using Basic CAD Techniques

Part Two explains basic commands and CAD techniques. In Part Two you learn to set up a new drawing, learn what graphic entities are in AutoCAD, and learn to draw basic entities such as lines, arcs, and circles. Part Two also teaches you how AutoCAD's display works and covers commands you can use to zoom in and out, pan, and work with multiple views of your drawing. Part Two finishes with an introduction to *editing*, which is the process of modifying existing entities.

Part III: Intermediate Drafting and Editing

Part Three introduces the remaining graphic entities not covered in previous units. In Part Three you learn to draw ellipses, donuts, rectangles, and polygons. You also learn to edit polylines, a special type of entity that is covered in Part Two.

Part IV: Drawing Accurately

A primary benefit of CAD over manual drafting techniques is its accuracy. Part Four introduces many different commands and techniques you can use to ensure that your drawings are accurate. You learn in Part Four how to set units, calculate scale factors, work with grid and snap settings, use object snap modes to lock on to points on entities, and define your own coordinate system.

Part V: Using Advanced CAD Techniques

Part Five takes you beyond simple drawing creation to more complex *editing* tasks. You learn to use existing lines, arcs, circles, and other entities in the drawing as a basis for new entities. By copying entities, for example, you can draw duplicate or repetitive parts of a drawing very quickly. You also learn in Part Five how to compose and plot a drawing.

Part VI: Advanced Editing

Part Six expands on the editing skills you learn in Part Five. Part Six explains selection sets and teaches you how to use them when creating a drawing. You learn how to modify existing entities by trimming, breaking, extending, and stretching them. You also learn how to apply chamfers and fillets, and how to change some of the characteristics of many entities.

Part VII: Organizing a Drawing

Actually drawing lines and other entities is just a small part of preparing a drawing. Your drawing will be useful only if you organize the information on it properly. Part Seven introduces layers, colors, and linetypes, and teaches you to use these characteristics to organize the information in a drawing. Part Seven also introduces *blocks* and *external references* (Xrefs), which make it possible for you to create symbols and standard details in your drawing.

Part VIII: Annotating a Drawing

The process of annotating a drawing includes adding text and dimensions to the drawing. Part Eight teaches you to add text to the drawing with various sizes, rotations, and font styles. Part Eight also explains in detail the many different commands that AutoCAD provides for adding dimensions to a drawing.

Part IX: Working with Boundaries, Inquiry, and Area

As you work with a drawing, you will often need to determine area, distance, and other basic information. Part Nine teaches you to use a selection of commands to determine the distance and angle between two points, as well as the area and perimeter of a boundary. You also learn in Part Nine how to add cross-hatching to an area of your drawing.

Part X: Using Symbols

Part Ten expands on the information you gain in Part Seven about symbols, blocks, and external references. You learn to create symbols that contain textual information called *attributes.* Attributes are useful for extracting information from your drawing to use in bills of materials, parts schedules, and other documents. Part Ten also teaches you to edit blocks and external references.

Part XI: Working in 3D

Part Eleven provides a very basic introduction to three-dimensional drawings. You first bridge the gap between 2D and 3D drawings by creating a two-dimensional isometric drawing. You then learn about 3D coordinates and planes in preparation for drawing a simple 3D wireframe.

How To Use the Tutorials

Each unit is divided into a series of exercises, each of which teaches one or more AutoCAD commands. Explanatory text accompanies each exercise, putting commands and techniques into context, explaining how commands behave, and showing you how to use different options. If you just read the text and exercises, and look at the illustrations, you will learn a great deal about the program. But if you want to gain a greater mastery of AutoCAD Release 12, you need to sit down at a computer that is equipped with AutoCAD Release 12 and work through the exercises.

Using the HOA DISK

The best way to use *Hands On AutoCAD Release 12* is to work through every exercise in sequence. You can work through selected exercises to cover topics of particular interest, but most exercises require drawings that were created in earlier exercises or chapters, or which already contain lines or other entities. To simplify the exercises, the Instructors Guide includes a disk of *prototype drawings* that you will use in each exercise as a starting point for the exercise.

Your instructor will have set up the prototype drawings on your system to accommodate your system configuration. Unit 9 explains the use of prototype drawings, but your instructor will also give you specific information about how to find and use the prototype drawings that are provided with *Hands On AutoCAD Release 12.*

Following the Book's Conventions and Exercises

The conventions used for showing various types of text throughout this book are, insofar as possible, the same as those used in the *AutoCAD Reference Manual.* These conventions are shown in this section. Some conventions, such as the use of italics to introduce a new term, are very simple. Others, such as those used in the exercises, are worth a closer look.

Exercises

A sample exercise follows. You do not need to work through it, but you should study the format so that you know what to expect from the exercises throughout the book. Most exercises are preceded or followed by one or more illustrations, which were captured from the screen during an actual exercise. Exercises are arranged in two columns, with direct instructions on the left and explanatory notes on the right. Lengthy explanations sometimes extend across both columns. The numbers shown in circles refer to points in the illustrations.

A Sample Exercise

Continue in the SAMPLE drawing from the previous exercise.

1. `Command:` *Press* F9	Activates snap mode
2. `Command:` *Choose* Draw, *then* Circle, *then* Center, Radius	Issues the CIRCLE command
3. `_circle 3P/2P/TTR/<Center point>:` *Pick point at* ①	Specifies the circle's center point
4. `Diameter/<Radius>: 3 ↵`	Draws a 6" circle

continues

Exercises

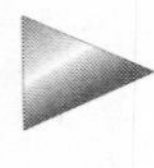

5. `Command:` *From the screen menu, choose* DRAW, *then* LINE:	Issues the LINE command
6. `From point:` *From the popup menu, choose* Center	Specifies the CENter object snap mode
7. `center of` *Pick the circle at* ②	Starts the line at the circle's center
8. `To point:` *Pick at* ③	Draws the line
9. `To point:` **`3,5`** ↵	Specifies the coordinates that you type
10. `To point:` *Press* Enter	Ends the Line command

The AutoCAD Release 12 interface uses many of the elements used by other modern programs with a GUI (Graphical User Interface). When you see an instruction such as "`Command:` *Choose* Item" in an exercise, it means to move the pointer to the top of the screen, which displays a menu bar, then move the pointer to the item on the menu bar, and click the left mouse button (or button 1 on the digitizer puck). This displays a pull-down menu—a list of menu items from which you can choose commands and options. When you move your pointer to an item and choose it, a command is issued, or a child submenu or a dialog box appears.

When the exercise tells you to "*Choose* Draw, *then* Circle," you should choose the Draw pull-down menu, then the Circle item from it. If a pull-down menu or dialog box is currently displayed, *Choose* refers to an item on it.

The *screen menu* is the menu that appears at the right side of the drawing area. All instructions to choose from the screen menu are prefaced with "*From the screen menu, choose....*" Instructions to use the popup menu (which appears at the pointer's location when you press a certain pointer button) are prefaced with "*From the popup menu, choose....*" Otherwise, the exercises assume that you use the pull-down menu. See unit 6 for more information on using menus and dialog boxes. You can choose any menu or dialog box item, whether it is text or an icon, by moving the pointer to the item and clicking the left mouse button. If you are not already familiar with the AutoCAD interface, Part One introduces you to it.

In some cases, you will see the symbol ↵ in the exercises. Your computer may have a key labeled Enter, or one labeled Return, or one with an arrow symbol. In any case, ↵ means that you need to press the key that enters a return (generally by using the little finger of your right hand).

You often enter commands from the keyboard. Similarly, point coordinates, distances, and option keywords often must be typed. The exercise text generally indicates when typed input is required by showing it in blue text following a prompt, such as `Command:` **`UNITS`** ↵ or `To point:` **`3,5`** ↵. You should type the input as it appears, and then press Enter.

Early in the book, you will notice that exercises contain copious prompts and explanations of what is (or should be) happening as you enter commands. Later exercises often omit prompts that are issued by commands that have become routine and explanations of familiar effects.

Many exercises end with an instruction to end or save the drawing. You may not want to end a drawing, because most units can be completed in one or two sittings. You should save your drawings when instructed, however, because doing so helps you build a habit of saving drawings at regular intervals. If you want to proceed at a leisurely pace, you can end your drawing whenever you see the Save instruction, and reload it later. If you want to take a break where a save or end instruction is not shown, just close and save or end your drawing and reload it later.

Notes, Tips, and Warnings

Hands On AutoCAD Release 12 features many special "sidebars," which are set apart from the normal text by icons. The book includes three distinct types of sidebars: "Notes," "Tips," and "Warnings." These passages have been given special treatment so that you can instantly recognize their significance and easily find them for future reference.

A note *includes "extra" information that you should find useful, but which complements the discussion at hand instead of being a direct part of it. A note may describe special situations that can arise when you use AutoCAD Release 12 under certain circumstances, and may tell you what steps to take when such situations arise. Notes also may tell you how to avoid problems with your software and hardware.*

A tip *provides you with quick instructions for getting the most from your AutoCAD system as you follow the steps outlined in the general discussion. A tip might show you how to conserve memory in some setups, how to speed up a procedure, or how to perform one of many time-saving and system-enhancing techniques.*

A warning tells you when a procedure may be dangerous—that is, when you run the risk of losing data, locking your system, or even damaging your hardware. Warnings generally tell you how to avoid such losses, or describe the steps you can take to remedy them.

Exercises and Your Graphics Display

The authors created this book's illustrations by capturing screen displays during the process of performing the exercises. All screen displays were captured from systems using standard VGA display controllers set for the 640×480-pixel resolution. Text-font settings were customized to produce pleasing printed illustrations. If your system has a super-VGA or EGA card, or another high-resolution display controller, your screen displays may not exactly match the illustrations. Menus and screen elements may appear larger or smaller than they do in the illustrations, and you may want to zoom in or out further than the instructions indicate. You should learn from the outset, in fact, that you must adjust to the task at hand and the resources available. You may find that entities are easier to see if you use different colors than instructed in the exercises, especially if you are working with a white background rather than a black background.

You probably will find the drawing image clearer if you use the AutoCAD Release 12 CONFIG command to set your video display to use a black drawing background. See your Interface, Installation, and Performance Guide for more information on configuration, or consult your instructor.

What You Need To Use this Book

To use *Hands On AutoCAD Release 12*, you need the following software and hardware, at the least. This book assumes the following:

- You have a computer with both AutoCAD Release 12 and PC DOS/MS-DOS 3.0 or later installed and configured. DOS 6.2 or later is highly recommended.
- You have at least 3M of free hard disk space left after you have installed and configured AutoCAD Release 12.
- You have a graphics display and pointing device configured to work with AutoCAD.

Handling Problems

As you work through the exercises in *Hands On AutoCAD Release 12*, you may experience some problems. These problems can occur for any number of reasons, from input errors to hardware failures. If you have trouble performing any step described in this book, take the following actions:

- ☞ Try again. Double-check the steps you performed in the previous exercise(s), as well as earlier steps in the current exercise.
- ☞ Check the settings of any AutoCAD system variables that were modified in any previous exercise sequences.
- ☞ Check the *AutoCAD Reference Manual* or the AutoCAD Release 12 on-line help.
- ☞ Ask your instructor for help.

Contacting New Riders Publishing

The staff of New Riders Publishing is committed to bringing you the best in computer reference material. Each New Riders book is the result of months of work by authors and staff, who research and refine the information contained within its covers.

As part of this commitment to you, New Riders invites your input. Please let us know if you enjoy this book, if you have trouble with the information and examples presented, or if you have a suggestion for future editions.

Please note, however, that the New Riders staff cannot serve as a technical resource for AutoCAD Release 12 or any other applications or hardware. Refer to the documentation that accompanies your programs and hardware for help with specific problems. Your AutoCAD dealer can provide general AutoCAD support.

If you have a question or comment about any New Riders book, please write to NRP at the following address:

New Riders Publishing
Prentice Hall Computer Publishing
Attn: Associate Publisher
201 W. 103rd St.
Indianapolis, IN 46290

We will respond to as many readers as we can. Your name, address, or phone number will never become part of a mailing list or be used for any other purpose than to help us continue to bring you the best books possible.

Thank you for selecting *Hands On AutoCAD Release 12*!

PART I

Getting Started

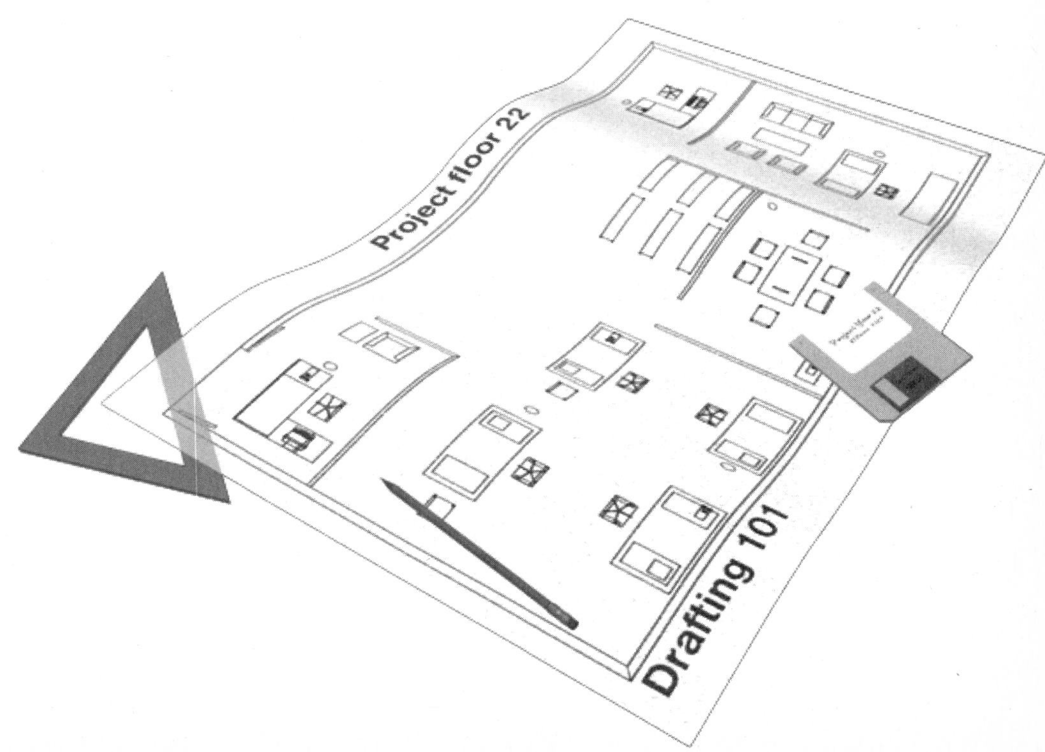

UNIT 1

Introduction to CAD

CAD is an acronym for computer-aided design (also computer-assisted design and computer-aided drafting). Sometimes you see the acronym spelled CADD, which stands for Computer-Aided Design and Drafting. This unit helps you understand just what CAD is and how it significantly improves the design and drafting process.

The objectives for this unit are to:

- Understand some of the uses for CAD
- Describe the advantages of CAD over manual design and drafting techniques
- Understand how CAD techniques differ from manual drafting techniques
- Describe applications for CAD in different design disciplines

What Is CAD?

The proliferation of personal computers and the dramatic improvement in performance of today's computers has had an impact on virtually all areas of business. Engineering and drafting are certainly no exception. In fact, science, engineering, and drafting are some of the fields in which computers were first put to commercial use.

You just read that CAD stands for Computer-Aided Design, or Computer-Aided Drafting. This describes what the term means, but it does not explain what CAD is in practical terms. Essentially, CAD encompasses the use of computers to automate and simplify the design and drafting process. The term *CAD software* refers to software (computer programs) that engineers, architects, designers, and drafters use to prepare drawings electronically by computer instead of manually by pencil, ink, and vellum. Figure 1.1 shows a typical CAD workstation.

Figure 1.1

A typical CAD workstation.

In past years, CAD was used almost exclusively by large companies that could afford the expensive hardware and software CAD required. At one time, you needed a room-sized computer to run even the simplest CAD software. Today, personal computers are just as powerful—yet relatively inexpensive—which makes it possible for virtually any sized business to take advantage of even the most sophisticated CAD software.

How Is CAD Different from Manual Drafting?

In manual drafting, you use a pencil or pen to draw lines, arcs, text, dimensions, and other graphical symbols on vellum or mylar. With a CAD program such as AutoCAD, you use a computer to create an electronic representation of a design or drawing. This drawing is stored on a disk in the computer while you create and modify it. When you complete the drawing, you can make a copy of it on paper using a *plotter* or *printer.* (Hardware used with CAD systems, including plotters and printers, is described in unit 2.) This paper drawing can then be used for distribution and manufacturing just like a drawing that was created manually.

In some situations, hard copies of drawings are not required. After the drafter or engineer completes the drawing, a checker or supervisor examines the drawing on another workstation for errors or changes. After the drawing has been checked and corrected, it is released for production electronically. Instead of sending a paper copy of the drawing to the manufacturing department, the engineering department sends the drawing *file* (an electronic copy of the drawing) to the production department's computer system through a network connection, phone line or a removable hard disk. The production department can then use the electronic drawing data to create programs to drive cutting machines, lathes, robotics, and other manufacturing equipment to produce the part.

Drawing with AutoCAD

A manual drafter uses scales, triangles, and other standard drafting tools to prepare a drawing. Plastic templates of standard symbols and parts help speed the drawing process by enabling the drafter to reproduce symbols quickly on the drawing. Unfortunately, templates and other tools cannot speed up the tedious process of adding notes, dimensions, and other items of information to the drawing.

AutoCAD provides tools similar to those used in manual drafting for preparing a drawing. These tools in AutoCAD, however, are not physical tools like triangles and templates. Instead, AutoCAD mimics many standard drafting tools with its various program functions. To mimic a straightedge, for example, AutoCAD provides a function that draws straight horizontal or vertical lines (see fig. 1.2). To mimic the function of a circle template, AutoCAD provides a command for drawing circles of any radius (see fig. 1.3).

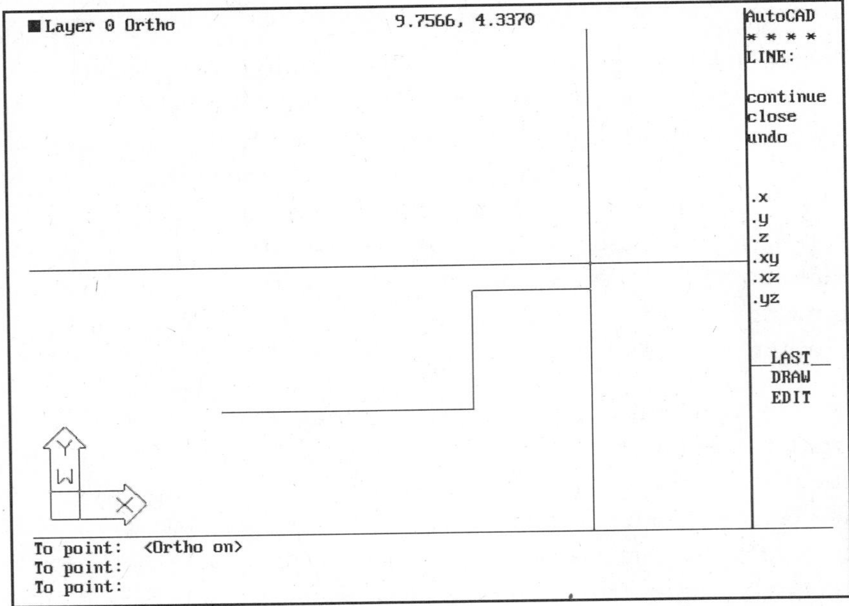

Figure 1.2

AutoCAD includes a function that automatically draws straight lines.

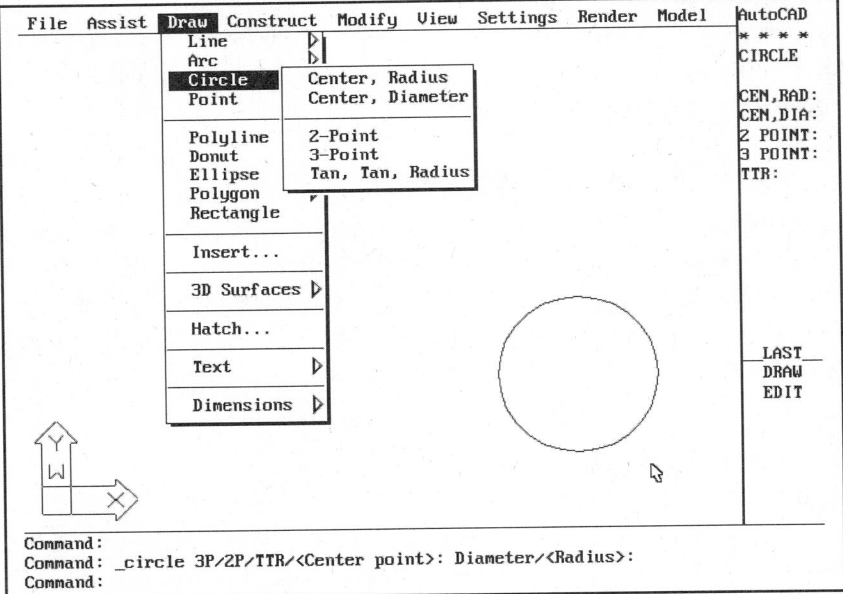

Figure 1.3

AutoCAD includes functions for drawing many basic shapes, such as circles.

Understanding the Advantages of CAD

CAD programs like AutoCAD offer a number of advantages over manual drafting techniques. Some advantages derive from AutoCAD's improvements over manual drafting methods. Still others derive from new design methods that are possible with CAD but not with manual design and drafting.

Drawing Quickly

One of the most obvious CAD advantages is the speed at which a skilled user can prepare a drawing versus the time required to produce the same drawing manually. This is due to a number of reasons, some of which are listed as follows:

☞ **Electronic drawing tools.** Many of the software tools that AutoCAD provides are an improvement over similar manual drafting methods, and others are unique to the CAD environment. These tools make it easier to prepare a drawing, which makes it possible to complete a drawing in less time. For example, AutoCAD includes automated dimensioning. Instead of manually calculating a dimension and drawing the extension lines and other graphic entities that make up a drafted dimension, an AutoCAD user can pick a few points on the drawing, and AutoCAD calculates and places the dimension automatically—complete with all extension lines, arrowheads, and so forth. Figure 1.4 shows AutoCAD placing a dimension on a drawing.

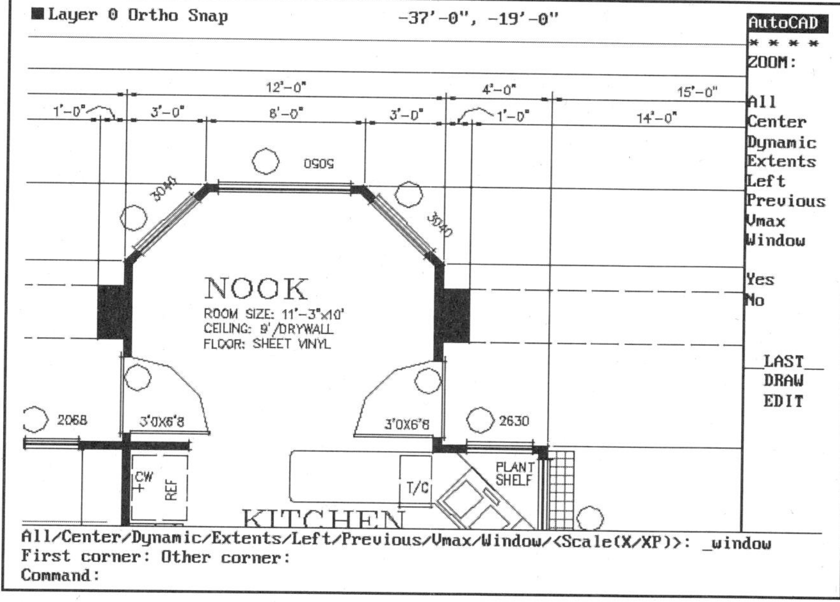

Figure 1.4

Placing a dimension in AutoCAD is a simple task.

☞ **Copying and modifying information.** AutoCAD makes it possible to modify existing portions of a drawing and reuse those portions elsewhere in the drawing. Instead of drawing both halves of a symmetrical part, for example, AutoCAD makes it possible to draw just one half, and then in a few seconds produce a mirror-image copy for the second half. Figure 1.5 shows an existing portion of a drawing being mirrored to produce a symmetrical part.

Figure 1.5

Mirroring is one example of how easy it is to modify a drawing with AutoCAD.

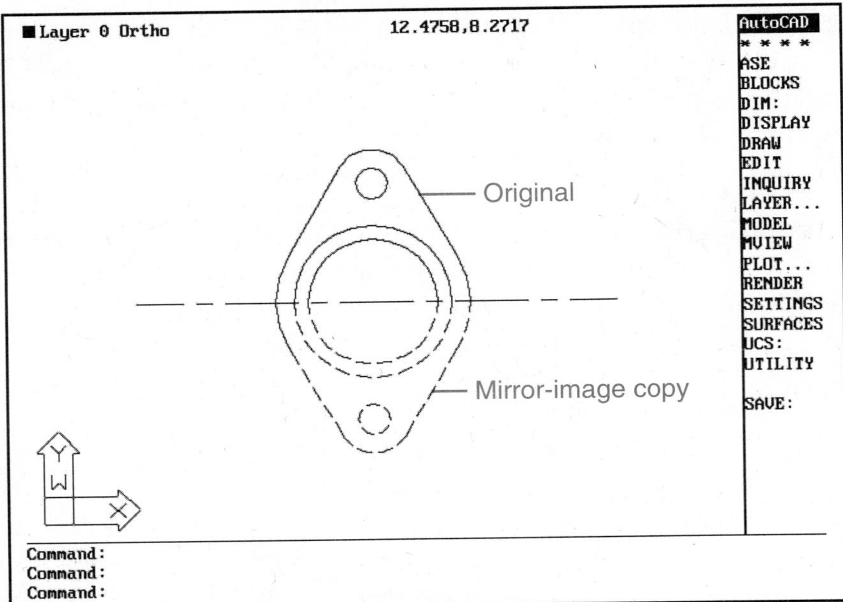

- **Reusing drawings.** Although it is possible to use old manually-prepared drawings to develop new drawings, AutoCAD makes this task much easier. You can load an existing drawing, modify it as needed, and save it as a new drawing.

- **Symbols and standard parts.** AutoCAD enables you quickly to insert any drawing into any other drawing. This makes it possible to develop libraries of standard symbols and parts. You can insert these symbols and parts into a drawing with a few simple commands. In a manually-prepared drawing, copying symbols in this way is not possible. Figure 1.6 shows symbols being inserted into a drawing.

Drawing and Dimensioning Accurately

One of the most important advantages for many AutoCAD users is the accuracy that CAD in general brings to the design and drafting process. The accuracy of a manually-prepared drawing depends on many factors: the skill of the drafter, the quality of the tools used, the width and wear of pen and pencil tips, and more. A skilled manual drafter can prepare a drawing that is accurate to within about .02". An AutoCAD drawing is accurate to fourteen decimal places, or .00000000000001", making the drawing database extremely accurate. A typical plotter is accurate to approximately .005", making a plotted hard copy of a drawing considerably more accurate than a manually-prepared drawing.

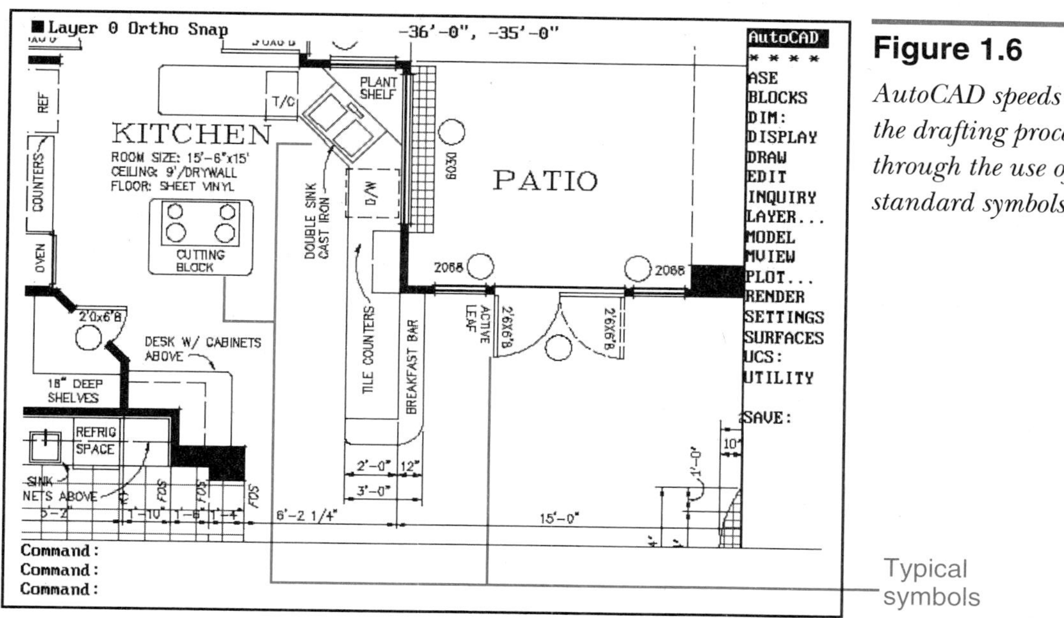

Figure 1.6

AutoCAD speeds the drafting process through the use of standard symbols.

The other benefit derived from AutoCAD's accuracy is the ability to determine dimensions automatically. In a manually-prepared drawing, the drafter must manually calculate dimensions based on the geometry of the part. In AutoCAD, you can pick the points you wish to dimension, and AutoCAD calculates that dimension for you. This capability makes it much easier to derive dimensions directly from the drawing's geometry, which often eliminates lengthy manual calculations.

Modeling and Testing Designs

Another important advantage offered by CAD, particularly in mechanical and electronic design, is the capability to model and test a design prior to manufacturing prototypes or beginning a production run. A mechanical design can be modeled in three dimensions, producing an accurate representation of the part. A designer or engineer can then subject the part to stress analysis, production review, or even put the part into simulated use to test its function—all without ever producing the part itself.

The capability to test a design in this way helps eliminate design errors or production difficulties before expensive tooling or other manufacturing processes are begun. In the electronics field, CAD enables electronics designers to test a circuit prior to building any prototypes of the design.

Developing 3D models of a design using AutoCAD also offers another advantage: AutoCAD enables you quickly and automatically to produce two-dimensional drawings of a design from a 3D design database. Once a design is modeled in 3D, it is a relatively simple process to develop a full set of 2D manufacturing drawings from that 3D model, further speeding the design and drafting process.

Driving the Manufacturing Process

For companies that use CAM (computer-aided manufacturing) to automate production and manufacturing, CAD offers a significant improvement over manual design methods. The same 3D model that you use to develop 2D drawings of a design, for example, can be used with CAD/CAM programs (CAM stands for Computer Aided Manufacturing) by the manufacturing staff to drive lathes, cutting machines, robotic assembly machines, and other automated manufacturing equipment. Using the same design model in both engineering and manufacturing eliminates errors that can be introduced to the design during manufacturing.

Becoming Productive with AutoCAD

An important point to keep in mind, particularly if you are experienced with manual drafting methods, is that it takes some time to become productive with AutoCAD. It takes time to learn to use any new tool effectively, and a program as complex and as powerful as AutoCAD is no exception.

Experience has shown that it can take as little as two weeks or as much as six weeks of intensive CAD use after completing AutoCAD training to become as productive with AutoCAD as you are with manual drafting techniques (to reach a productivity level of 1:1). In other words, it takes some time for you to be able to complete a drawing as fast with AutoCAD as you could prepare the drawing manually.

Once you reach that 1:1 ratio, however, your productivity begins to improve rapidly. The advantages that AutoCAD offers over manual drafting methods can improve your productivity from as little as 2:1 to as much as 20:1 or more, depending on the types of drawings you prepare. As you build libraries of standard reusable symbols and parts, your productivity can improve even more.

Unit Review

What You've Learned

- What CAD is
- How CAD differs from manually drafting techniques
- The advantages AutoCAD brings to the design and drafting process over manual techniques
- A few ways in which CAD is applied to design and manufacturing in some disciplines

Review Questions

True or False

1.01 T F Science, engineering, and drafting are some of the fields in which computers were first put to commercial use.

1.02 T F Today, CAD hardware and software are so expensive that only large companies can afford to use CAD.

1.03 T F It sometimes is not necessary to make a copy of a CAD drawing on paper because the drawing file can be used directly in manufacturing.

1.04 T F AutoCAD exactly mimics the way a drawing is prepared manually by providing electronic triangles, compasses, and other drafting tools.

1.05 T F The ability to model a part before manufacturing it is an important advantage to using CAD.

Multiple Choice

1.06 AutoCAD is accurate to ______________ decimal places.

(A) 7

(B) 12

(C) 3

(D) 14

Student: ______________________________ Date: ______________

Instructor: ______________________ Course: ____________ Section: __________

1.07 A skilled drafter can prepare a drawing that is accurate to only about __________.

(A) .0003"

(B) .02"

(C) .5"

(D) None of the above

Short Answer

1.08 You can make a paper copy of a drawing on __________ or __________.

____

____

1.09 AutoCAD makes it easy to insert __________ and standard parts into a drawing.

____

1.10 The acronym CAM stands for __________ __________ __________.

____

____

____

Student: __________ Date: __________

Instructor: __________ Course: __________ Section: __________

UNIT 2

An Overview of Computers and Hardware

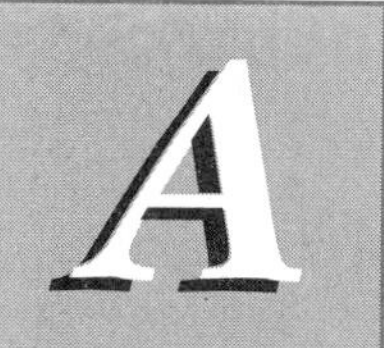

A cabinetmaker must understand how his tools work in order to build a piece of fine furniture, just as a surgeon must understand his tools to perform surgery. A computer is the tool you use with AutoCAD to prepare drawings. Although you do not have to understand the inner workings of a computer to use AutoCAD, you must have a basic understanding of each of the parts of a typical CAD workstation to use AutoCAD effectively.

This unit provides an overview of the equipment, or hardware, in a typical AutoCAD workstation, and helps you learn how to use that hardware.

The objectives for this unit are to:

- ☞ Understand, in general terms, how a computer functions
- ☞ Describe the hardware items, as well as their functions, in a typical CAD workstation
- ☞ Describe the purpose of a computer network

A computer system, such as a CAD workstation, consists of two main components: hardware and software, which are very different from one another. This unit describes the different hardware items in a CAD workstation. Unit 3 explains software.

Understanding Computer Hardware

The term *hardware* refers to the physical components included in a computer system. A typical CAD workstation contains a number of different hardware components, each performing a unique but necessary function. At the heart of every computer, for example, is a CPU.

The CPU

The acronym CPU stands for *central processing unit*. The CPU in a computer is the "brains" of the computer—where all of the computing takes place. Essentially, the CPU *is* the computer. All the other hardware in the computer supports the CPU, providing input and output functions for the CPU. The hardware also provides data storage for the CPU as well as for programs that run on the CPU. Figure 2.1 shows the CPU in a typical PC workstation.

Figure 2.1
A CPU in a typical PC workstation.

Unless you are responsible for selecting and purchasing CAD workstations for your company, you do not have to worry about the differences in CPU types and capabilities from one computer to another. The CPU is an integral part of the system, and often is not something you, as an average user, can enhance in any way.

Even though you cannot change your CPU, you may be curious about where it is located. Your CAD workstation contains a large circuit board called a *motherboard*. The CPU is located in a socket on the motherboard. The motherboard also contains all of the other support microchips and other circuitry required to support the CPU as a functioning computer. The motherboard and other components are located in a *system unit*. Figure 2.2 shows a typical desktop PC system unit.

Figure 2.2

A typical desktop PC system unit.

Memory

A computer requires *memory* to store programs and data. (Programs are discussed a little later in this unit.) A computer's memory stores information on a short-term basis, usually only while the computer is actually using the programs or data. When the programs or data are not being used, they reside on a long-term storage device called a *disk.* Types of disk systems are explained later in this section. Figure 2.3 shows the memory installed in a typical PC workstation.

A computer's primary memory often is referred to as its RAM, which is an acronym for *random-access memory.* To understand how much RAM is contained in a typical workstation, you have to understand how memory is measured. A computer recognizes *bits* of data, with a bit being equal to a 1 or 0. Bits are organized into storage units called *bytes.* A byte is eight bits, which is enough space to store the equivalent of one character, such as the letter T, for example.

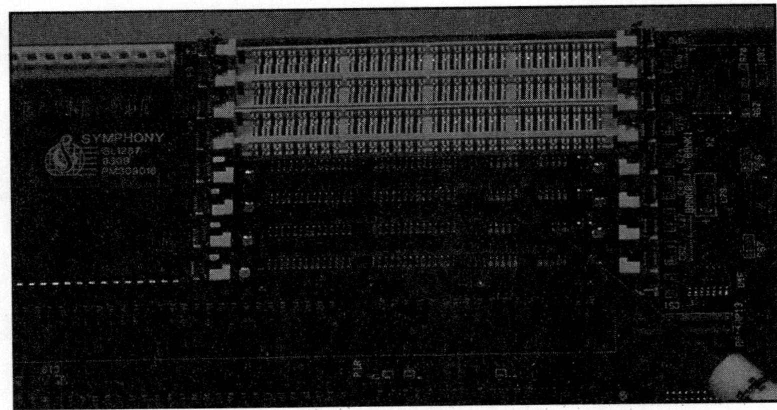

Figure 2.2

The memory installed in a typical PC workstation.

A *kilobyte* is 1,024 bytes, which is enough space to store roughly one document page. A Kilobyte is usually abbreviated with a K; 1,024 bytes are often referred to as 1K of RAM.

One thousand twenty-four kilobytes are called a *megabyte,* which is equal to over 1 million bytes (1,024 kilobytes ×1,024 bytes in a kilobyte = 1,048,576 bytes). A megabyte, which is usually abbreviated with an M, is therefore the equivalent of about 1 million characters.

The total amount of RAM in a computer workstation is measured in megabytes. Today's CAD workstations generally contain as little as 4M to as much as 32M or more of RAM (the recommended amount is 8M). Often, the more RAM a computer contains, the faster it can perform. This speed is not related to the speed at which the CPU operates, however (which is called the CPU's *clock rate*). More memory helps a CPU perform its job faster because it gives it more resources to work with, but adding more memory to a computer does not make the CPU run faster.

Disks and Disk Drives

The computer's RAM is for short-term data storage; the system's *disks* and *disk drives* are used for long-term data storage. Data and programs that are not being used generally are stored on a *hard disk.* Figure 2.4 shows a hard disk and a floppy disk (discussed next). The hard disk is contained inside the computer's case, and usually is not designed to be removed from the system. A hard disk offers a large storage capacity which, like RAM, is measured in megabytes. A typical workstation may contain as little as 40M of hard disk storage space, or it may contain much more. Workstations that function as central *servers* for other systems often have more than a gigabyte (1,024M) of hard disk storage. As you work in AutoCAD and create drawings, you store them on the computer's hard disk.

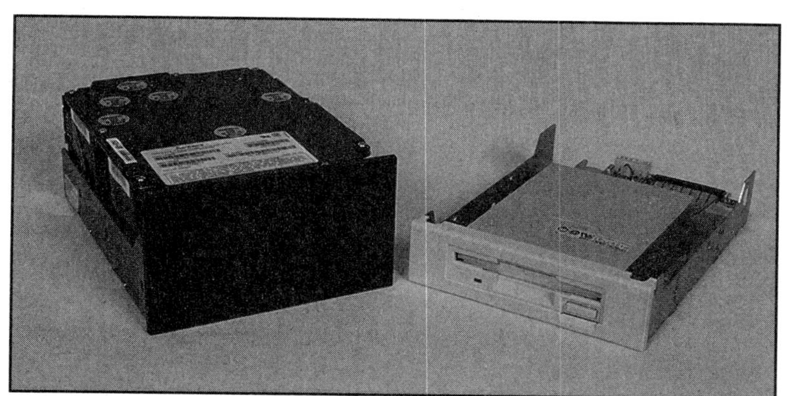

Figure 2.4

A hard disk and a floppy disk drive.

In addition to hard disks, CAD workstations often contain one or two *floppy disk drives* that accept removable disks called *floppy disks*. These are similar in some ways to a hard disk, except that the actual disk recording material is made from a thin sheet of flexible plastic encased in a hard plastic holder. A floppy disk holds much less data than a hard disk is capable of holding. A typical floppy disk in a PC workstation holds up to 1.44M of data.

Although you store most of your drawings on the workstation's hard disk while you are creating a new drawing, you should make backup copies of your work on floppies for safekeeping. Storing your drawings on a floppy disk makes it possible for you to move your drawings between workstations that are not connected via network. Having backup copies of your work on floppy disk also ensures against losing your data if the hard disk is damaged in some way or you accidentally erase your drawings from the hard disk. Unit 30 explains in more detail the use of disks for storing drawings.

The Monitor

The computer requires some external *peripherals* to function as a complete system. These peripherals usually connect to the back of the computer's system unit by cables. The *monitor* is one of the computer's peripherals and is also an output device.

The monitor is the TV-like display on which AutoCAD appears. The monitor is a sort of "window" to what the computer is doing. The monitor works in conjunction with a *video adapter* inside the system unit to create the picture you see when you work with AutoCAD.

The Keyboard, Mouse, and Digitizer

The keyboard is one of the main *input* devices you use when you work with AutoCAD. The keyboard includes all of the keys you normally find on a typewriter, and it also includes a numeric keypad and special function keys.

Although you use a mouse or digitizer to pick many of the points in a drawing and to select menu options, you use the keyboard to enter commands, command options, numeric values, and to turn on and off many of AutoCAD's functions. (The ability to type is very helpful when using AutoCAD, but not a necessity.)

In addition to a keyboard, you also need a *mouse* or *digitizer* to enter coordinates, select commands, and otherwise interact with AutoCAD. A mouse (see fig. 2.5) is a small hand-held device with two or three buttons on it (sometimes more). As you slide the mouse along a pad or tabletop, a *cursor* moves on the display. The cursor is used to locate points in a drawing and to select menu items in AutoCAD. Unit 5 explains the use of the mouse in more detail.

Instead of a mouse, your CAD workstation may use a digitizer. Digitizers are available in different sizes, but the most common size used with AutoCAD workstations is roughly 12"×12". The digitizer consists of a *tablet* and *puck* or *stylus*. The tablet is a flat unit that rests on the desk. The puck is a hand-held device much like a mouse that rides on the surface of the tablet. Some digitizers use a stylus instead of (or in addition to) a puck. The stylus is much like an electronic pen. A digitizer puck often has four or more buttons on it that you can use to perform various functions in AutoCAD. A stylus usually has a selection of buttons on it also.

A digitizer serves much the same function as a mouse to enable you to provide input to AutoCAD, but it also offers a number of advantages over a mouse. AutoCAD includes a menu that can be placed on the digitizer's tablet. Instead of choosing commands and command options from the AutoCAD display, you can choose them from the digitizer. This enables you to access nearly any AutoCAD command or function quickly without having to search through different menus to find it. The digitizer also can be used to trace a paper drawing and copy it into AutoCAD (a process known as *digitizing*).

Printers and Plotters

While the keyboard, mouse, and digitizer serve as input devices to AutoCAD, *printers* and *plotters* serve as output devices. You often need to prepare a hard copy of your AutoCAD drawings on paper or mylar for checking or distribution. There are a number of different types of printers available for today's CAD workstations. Most reproduce a copy of your drawing on regular paper, but some can also print on mylar.

Printers are usually limited to 8.5"×11" paper size, but some can print on slightly larger paper. To prepare a large drawing (size C or larger, for example), you need to use a plotter. CAD systems utilize two main types of plotters: pen plotters and electrostatic plotters. A pen plotter mechanically produces a copy of the drawing with a combination of pen and paper movements (like a robot drafter). An electrostatic plotter uses an electrostatic process to deposit (spray) ink onto the drawing media to produce the drawing image.

Units 48 and 49 explain plotting and printing in detail.

Network Interface

In addition to all of the other devices installed at your workstation, the computer may also contain a *network interface adapter.* This adapter connects it to a *network* of other computers by a cable. Special software, called a *network operating system,* allows your computer to access resources located on one or more other computers. For example, many of your drawings may actually be stored on another computer instead of your workstation. A workstation that is connected to a network often is referred to as a network *node.*

In addition to enabling users to share disk storage space, another important use for a network is to enable users to share printers and plotters. When you plot or print a drawing, the commands to plot the drawing travel across the network to the computer to which the plotter or printer is connected. The printer or plotter does not have to be connected to your workstation.

Another common use for a network is to enable users to communicate with one another via *electronic mail,* or *e-mail.* If you want to send a message to another user, you compose the message at your workstation, then use the network to deliver the message to the other user. E-mail is extremely useful in situations where you must work with other designers or drafters on a project, because it provides a means for all users within a group to communicate with one another, and to share drawings and other information as well.

Unit Review

What You've Learned

- ☞ What the term *hardware* means
- ☞ The function of each of the main hardware components in a typical CAD workstation
- ☞ How memory and disk space are measured
- ☞ What a CPU does in a computer system

Review Questions

True or False

2.01 T F The term *hardware* refers to the physical components that make up a computer workstation.

2.02 T F A CPU is used only to hold information for long-term storage.

2.03 T F A floppy disk can store much more information than a hard disk.

2.04 T F The amount of primary memory in a computer is measured in megabytes.

2.05 T F Disk storage space is measured in megabytes.

Multiple Choice

2.06 A typical floppy disk in a typical PC workstation can store ______________ megabytes.

(A) 2.88

(B) 1.00

(C) 1.44

(D) None of the above

2.07 A ___________ disk is used mainly for backup storage, and not for primary storage.

(A) hard

(B) floppy

(C) rigid

(D) storage

Student: ______________________ Date: __________

Instructor: ______________________ Course: __________ Section: __________

2.08 A workstation connected to a network often is referred to as a _______________ on the network.

(A) PC

(B) site

(C) node

(D) None of the above

Short Answer

2.09 The two main types of plotters are ____________ plotters and _______________ plotters.

2.10 Briefly described the difference between a pen plotter and an electrostatic plotter.

____

____

____

Student: ________________________ Date: ____________

Instructor: ________________________ Course: ____________ Section: ____________

UNIT 3

An Overview of Software

nit 2 described the hardware that comprises a workstation's physical components—the system unit, disk drives, plotter, printer, and other equipment. This unit describes *software*, which is very different from hardware but still a very necessary part of any computer.

The objectives for this unit are to:

- Understand how software differs from hardware
- Describe what function software serves
- Describe different types of software

Understanding Software's Role

By itself, the hardware in a computer system is absolutely useless, except perhaps as a very large doorstop. To make it a useful tool, a computer needs *software*, which is a set of step-by-step electronic instructions that directs the computer to act and react in certain ways. Software typically is stored on a hard disk, either locally on your workstation's hard disk or on a server located elsewhere in the network. Software is loaded into the computer's memory, where the CPU can access it and execute the instructions it contains.

A number of different types of software exist in a typical computer. The computer's operating system is one type of software.

Operating System Software

A computer's *operating system software* is what enables the computer to perform basic functions such as accepting input from the keyboard, using the computer's RAM, reading from a disk, storing information on a disk, and other basic system-level functions. The operating system software is what enables the computer to function.

In an IBM-compatible personal computer (PC), the operating system software is generically referred to as DOS, which stands for *disk operating system.* You might also see DOS referred to as MS-DOS, which stands for *Microsoft DOS.* (Microsoft Corporation developed the original version of DOS for the IBM PC, and still markets DOS today.) A few other companies also market their own versions of DOS, although these different "varieties" of DOS are all very much the same.

Many AutoCAD workstations use a UNIX operating system. UNIX and DOS are very different in capability and function, but they both serve as operating system software for their respective computer systems.

There are other common operating systems available for today's computers. These include OS/2, Windows NT, and others. Autodesk markets versions of AutoCAD to run under the OS/2 and Windows environments.

Application Software

If you have used computers, you probably are at least somewhat familiar with *application software,* more commonly known as *programs.* AutoCAD is an example of application software, which is usually stored on hard disk (sometimes on floppy disks) just like the operating system software. Like the operating system, application software is loaded into the computer's memory so the CPU can execute instructions that the software contains.

The main difference between operating system software and application software is its function. Operating system software is designed to execute general tasks; application software is designed to perform specific *application* tasks. AutoCAD's application, for example, is to perform the tasks of designing and drafting. Other application software includes word processors for creating and modifying text documents; spreadsheets, for manipulating numbers; databases, for sorting and evaluating large quantities of data; and graphics programs, for creating and modifying graphic art. Figure 3.1 shows a spreadsheet program. Figure 3.2 shows a word-processing program.

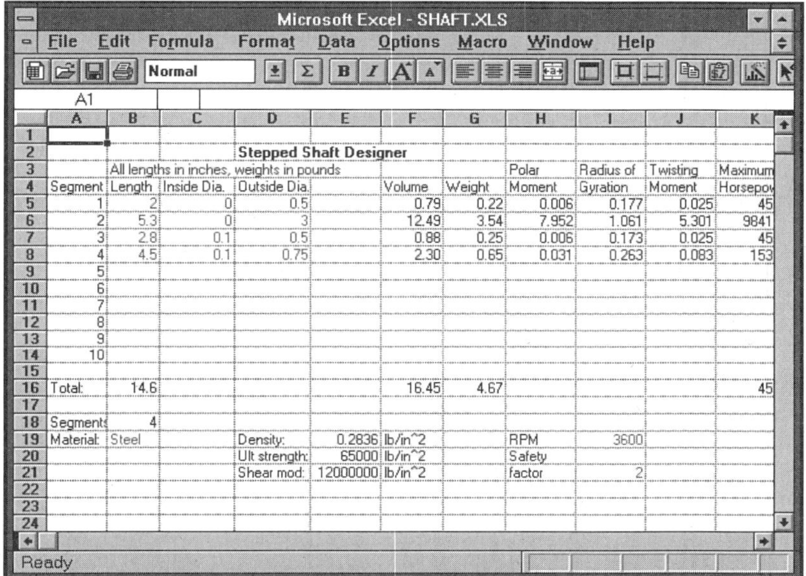

Figure 3.1

A spreadsheet program is used to manipulate and analyze numbers.

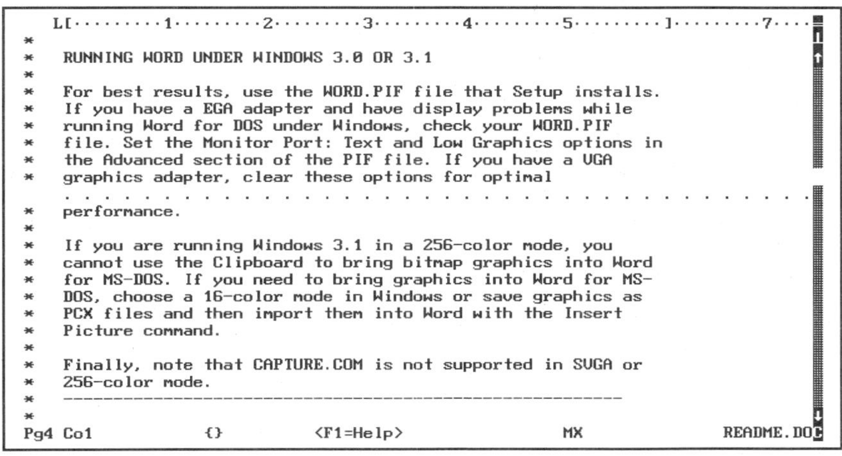

Figure 3.2

A DOS-based word-processing program.

As an AutoCAD user, you work mainly with application software. You also work to a limited degree with the operating system. AutoCAD duplicates some of the tasks—such as managing your drawings stored on disk—that you can perform with operating system commands outside of AutoCAD. Having at least a little experience with your system's operating system commands is helpful, however, and Unit 4 explains some of the most commonly used commands.

Utility and Driver Software

In addition to operating system and application software, your computer system probably includes other types of software. A number of special-purpose utility programs exists for a wide variety of tasks. AutoCAD also has many add-on utility programs, for example, that help tailor AutoCAD to specific design and drafting disciplines.

Your computer also uses *driver* software. A driver is a program that enables your computer to access the various types of peripheral hardware connected to it. AutoCAD, for example, uses drivers to access and control the video display, digitizer, and plotter. In addition to the drivers supplied with AutoCAD, your operating system uses its own drivers.

Unit Review

What You've Learned

- What the term *software* means
- What the difference is between hardware and software
- The functions that different types of software perform on a computer

Review Questions

True or False

3.01 T F A computer can function without any software at all.

3.02 T F Software is loaded into the computer's memory, and the CPU then executes the instructions in the software.

3.03 T F AutoCAD is an example of application software.

3.04 T F AutoCAD is available only for the MS-DOS operating system.

3.05 T F UNIX and DOS are operating systems.

Multiple Choice

3.06 Application software that is designed for creating and modifying text documents is called a ________________.

(A) database

(B) spreadsheet

(C) word processor

(D) None of the above

3.07 A(n) ______________ is a program that enables your computer to access and control specific types of hardware.

(A) application

(B) database

(C) utility

(D) driver

Student: ________________ Date: ________

Instructor: ________________ Course: ________ Section: ________

Short Answer

3.08 Explain briefly how software differs from hardware.

____

____

____

3.09 Describe how operating system software differs in function from application software.

____

____

____

3.10 Describe what function driver software performs.

____

____

____

Student: ______________ Date: ______________

Instructor: ______________ Course: ______________ Section: ______________

UNIT 4

A Tour Around Your Computer

Although it is not necessary for you to understand in detail how your computer or operating system works in order to use AutoCAD, you do need to understand a few basic concepts about your system in order to use it effectively. You must also know a number of things you should and should not do when using your workstation. This unit explains how to turn on your computer, log on to your network (if applicable), and work with a small selection of operating system commands. It also includes a list of tips and procedures for using the computer system.

The objectives for this unit are to:

- ☞ Turn on the computer and log on to the network, if applicable
- ☞ Understand basic procedures for operating a computer
- ☞ Understand basic file system concepts
- ☞ Use operating system commands to activate and navigate directories

Starting the Computer and Logging On

It is very possible that during most of your lab work in this course, you might never have to turn on your workstation. It may already be on and ready to run AutoCAD when you enter the lab. But you are not likely to have this situation forever, so you do need to know how to start the computer and possibly log on to a network before starting AutoCAD. Naturally, the first step is to start your computer.

Starting the Computer

Use the following procedure to turn on your computer:

1. **Turn on the monitor.** You should turn on the monitor before turning on the computer to prevent a surge to the CPU. Most monitors have a power switch either on the front of the monitor near the bottom of the screen, or on the back of the monitor near the bottom-right side. When the monitor is on, but the computer is still off, you do not see any text or other information on the screen. Generally, your only indication that the monitor is on is a small indicator light on the front panel of the monitor (but your monitor may not have such an indicator).
2. **Turn on the digitizer.** After turning on the monitor, turn on the digitizer—if one is attached to the computer. If your system uses a mouse instead of a digitizer, you do not have to turn on the mouse. Like the keyboard, the mouse functions automatically when the computer is on.
3. **Turn on the computer.** The last item that should be turned on is the computer itself. The power control might be a toggle switch near the right-rear corner of the system unit (as you face its front panel) or a push-button switch located on the front panel.

A few seconds after you turn on the computer, you should see a variety of start-up messages beginning to appear on-screen. The types of messages that appear depend on your type of system. In general, it is not important for you to monitor these start-up messages until you receive a prompt from the system for your input, which is described in the following sections.

Reaching a Command Prompt

You are likely to see a *DOS prompt* after the system completes the boot process and is ready for your input. The DOS prompt varies according to the way the workstation has been configured, but should look something like the following examples:

```
C:\>
C:>
```

The `C:` portion of the prompt represents the ID of the current drive. This usually is a `C`; but on some systems it might be a different letter, particularly if your workstation is connected to a network. Drive letters identify one drive from another (drives are discussed in more detail later in the unit). When the DOS prompt appears, DOS is indicating that it is ready to accept your commands.

On most systems you do not need to do anything other than turn on the computer to get a DOS prompt—although it might take as long as 30 seconds for the prompt to appear. If your workstation has been configured with a menu system, you may need to select a menu option before you can get a DOS prompt. Your instructor should explain this to you if it pertains to your system.

If you are working on a UNIX system, the first prompt you see is a `login:` *prompt, followed by a* `password:` *prompt. After you enter your login name and password, you receive a command prompt that varies according to the way your user account has been configured. Most often, though, the prompt is a dollar sign* (`$`).

Logging On to the Network (DOS Systems)

If your DOS workstation is on a network, you need to log on to the network in order to be able to use the network's resources, which may include a network disk where AutoCAD is located, a remote plotter, and other devices. The log-on process varies according to the network operating system being used. One of the most commonly used network operating systems for DOS-based networks is Novell NetWare. The following log-on examples use NetWare commands. If your system uses a different network operating system, the log-on commands are probably still quite similar, but check with your instructor for the proper commands.

1. At the DOS prompt, type **LOGIN** and press Enter.

NetWare displays the prompt `Enter your login name:`.

2. If your network has only one file server (check with your instructor), enter the user account name that has been assigned to you by your instructor. For example:

   `Enter your login name:` **`FRED`** ↵

3. If your network has more than one file server, enter the name of the file server you want to attach to, followed by a backslash character (\) and your login name. For example:

   `Enter your login name:` **`SERVER1\FRED`** ↵

4. If your user account has been set up to require a password, NetWare prompts you to enter your password, which you should do without delay. To prevent other users from learning your password, NetWare does not display the password as you type it.

After entering your password correctly, you are logged on to the network. Then you are ready to start AutoCAD or execute other operating-system commands.

Understanding the DOS File System

You read earlier in this unit that the DOS prompt shows the *active drive,* and that drive disks are identified by letters. The first floppy drive in a PC is assigned the letter A. The second floppy drive, if one is present, is recognized as drive B. The first hard disk in the system is drive C. Other local hard drives, network drives, CD-ROM drives, and other storage devices are identified with other letters, such as D, E, F, and so on.

Usually, the disk that is active when the system boots is drive C. The first of the following two prompts indicates that drive C is the active drive; the second prompt indicates that drive A is the active drive:

```
C:\>
A:\>
```

The active drive is significant for two main reasons. First, if you attempt to execute a program by entering its name at the DOS command prompt, DOS looks to the active drive's disk for the program unless you specify otherwise. Second, most DOS commands actually are programs that are stored on the system's disk; if you enter the name of one of these commands at the DOS prompt, DOS searches the active disk for the command (just as it searches for any other program). When you want to execute a program or perform some other operation on data stored on a disk, it is important to have that disk in the active drive.

To make a drive active, type its drive letter followed by a colon (:), and then press Enter, as follows:

```
C:\> D: ↵
D:\>
```

The drive letter and colon are referred to as the drive's *ID*. For example, `A:` is the drive ID for drive A. Note in the previous example that the DOS prompt changed to reflect the new active disk (drive D).

Understanding Directories

Each disk can be organized into different storage areas called *directories*. Think of the disk as a file cabinet, and each of the directories as a file drawer capable of holding many folders, or files. Figure 4.1 illustrates the concept of computer "filing." It shows the Windows File Manager displaying a disk and its directories.

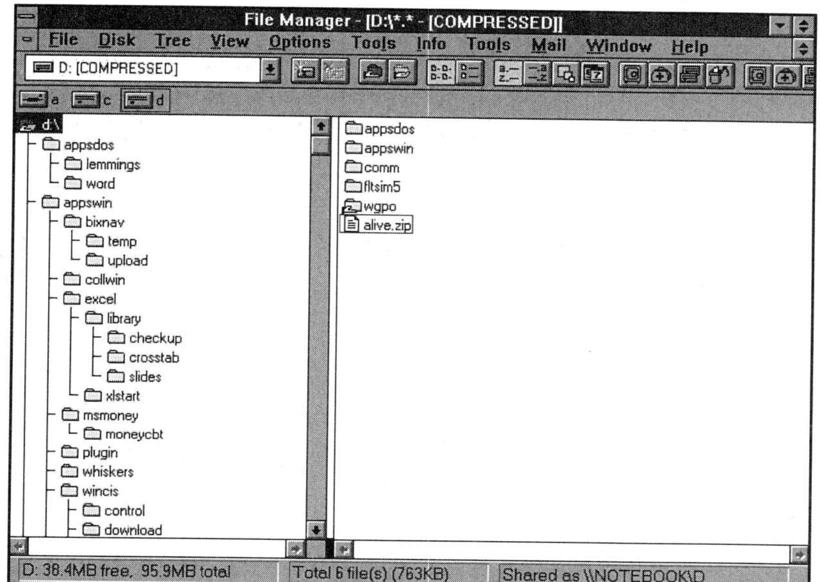

Figure 4.1

A drive and its directories displayed in the Windows File Manager.

Every disk has a main directory called the *root directory*. The root directory can contain other directories, which often are referred to as *subdirectories*. Each directory and subdirectory can contain files (such as programs, AutoCAD drawings, and so forth), other subdirectories, or both. As figure 4.1 illustrates, directories enable you to organize a disk into many different logical storage areas for data and programs. For example, you might store all your drawings in a directory that has been assigned to you by your instructor.

Changing the Active Directory

Not only can you make a disk in a drive active, but you also can make a specific directory active. If a program is contained in a directory and you want to execute that program, you can make that program's directory active, and then enter that program's name at the DOS prompt to execute that program.

To make a directory active, use the DOS CD (change directory) command. At the DOS prompt, enter the CD command followed by the directory name that you want to make active, as in the following example:

```
C:\>CD \ACAD\SAMPLE
C:\ACAD\SAMPLE>
```

This example makes active the directory SAMPLE, which is a subdirectory of the directory ACAD. The backslash character (\) is used as a separator between the directory names. If your system is set up to display the current directory as part of the DOS prompt, your prompt changes as shown on the second line of the example.

If \ACAD\SAMPLE specifies the name of a particular subdirectory, what would you enter to change to the root directory of the active drive disk? Just specify a backslash character without any text:

```
CD \
C:\>
```

The combination of drive ID and directory/subdirectory specifications is called a *path*, or *path name*. This is because it specifies a path to make some directory or subdirectory active, much like you would give directions to someone: "Go to drive C, then to the ACAD directory, and then to its SAMPLE subdirectory."

To move up one level in a subdirectory structure, use two periods (..) as the path name in a CD command:

```
CD ..
```

This causes the parent directory, which is one level higher than the current level, to become the active directory.

Viewing the Contents of a Directory

AutoCAD has commands that enable you to view the contents of a directory (sometimes called a *directory listing*). You may find times, however, when you need to do this in DOS. To do so, use the DIR (directory) command. The following illustrates this command for listing the active directory (which in this example is ACAD's SAMPLE subdirectory):

```
C:\ACAD\SAMPLE>DIR

 Volume in drive C has no label
 Volume Serial Number is 1300-3046
 Directory of C:\ACAD\SAMPLE

ave_xmpl lsp      5785 05-31-92   7:09p
acad     mnd     90328 06-15-92  11:31a
adesk_b  dwg     34175 06-09-92  12:19a
alias    lsp      5854 04-13-92   7:17p
(other lines)
stlsup   lsp      8147 06-17-92   8:13p
```

```
solmaint lsp      5824 06-17-92   8:13p
.            <DIR>      09-25-93   3:44p
..           <DIR>      09-25-93   3:44p
       74 file(s)    4648495 bytes
                    49020928 bytes free
```

Information displayed as the output of the DIR command includes the name and extension of a file, the size of the file, the date it was last modified, and the time it was last modified. Unit 9 explains files in more detail.

Now that you know what disks and directories are, you are ready to start AutoCAD. Unit 5 explains how to start AutoCAD and provides a hands-on tour of some of AutoCAD's features and capabilities.

Working in the CAD Lab

To ensure that your computer continues to function properly for you and for the other students who may be using the same workstation, you should follow some basic rules when working in the CAD lab. The following list offers some tips about things you should and should not do when working with your computer:

- ☞ Avoid touching the display screen on the monitor. Touching this leaves smudges on the screen and builds up static charges in your body.
- ☞ Leave the computer turned on when you are finished using it, because it is better to leave a computer on all day than to turn it off and on. If you are working in the lab at the very end of the day, check with your instructor about whether you should turn off the computer overnight.
- ☞ If you do turn off the computer, make sure you always exit AutoCAD before turning it off. If Windows is running on your computer, exit Windows too before turning off the computer.
- ☞ Keep food and drinks out of the CAD lab and away from the computer and keyboard.
- ☞ Do not pound on the keyboard. Use a firm but gentle stroke on the keys.
- ☞ Do not touch the exposed portions of a floppy disk, and do not write on a floppy disk—write on the label before you place it on the disk.
- ☞ Keep floppy disks from extreme heat or cold.
- ☞ Push your chair in when you leave your workstation.

Unit Review

What You've Learned

- ☞ What function a disk ID serves
- ☞ How directories and subdirectories are used to organize available disk storage space
- ☞ How to make a drive active
- ☞ How to make a directory active
- ☞ How to view the contents of a directory

Review Questions

True or False

4.01 T F The first floppy disk drive is assigned the letter C.

4.02 T F The first hard disk drive is assigned the letter C.

4.03 T F The second floppy disk drive is assigned the letter B.

4.04 T F The CD command makes a drive active.

4.05 T F C is the highest drive letter you ever see on a system.

Multiple Choice

4.06 To make a disk active, type its ____________ at the DOS prompt and press Enter.

(A) directory name

(B) path name

(C) drive ID

(D) none of the above

4.07 To make a directory active, use the ____________ command.

(A) CD

(B) change

(C) activate

(D) CC

Student: ____________________ Date: ________

Instructor: ____________________ Course: ________ Section: ________

Short Answer

4.08 Write the command you would use to change to (make active) the subdirectory \ACAD\DRAWING.

____

4.09 Write the command you would use to change to (make active) the root directory.

____

4.10 Briefly describe why directories are important.

____

____

____

Student: ____________________ Date: ________

Instructor: ________________ Course: ________ Section: ______

UNIT 5

A Hands-On Introduction to AutoCAD

You have no better method for learning how to use a program than to start actually using it. This unit plunges you right into working with AutoCAD by means of sample exercises, designed to give you a hands-on "guided tour" of some of AutoCAD's features and capabilities. The unit does not intend to teach you the concepts behind any of these commands or exercises. Instead, the exercises should give you a feel for how easy it is to create drawings with AutoCAD. You also learn how to select commands by using the mouse or digitizer, and how to enter your input by using the keyboard.

The objectives of this unit are to:

- Start AutoCAD
- Understand the functions of the mouse and digitizer buttons
- Use the mouse and digitizer to pick points and select commands
- Enter input by using the keyboard

Starting AutoCAD

To start AutoCAD, make the AutoCAD directory active, and then enter the command **ACAD** at the DOS prompt. The following exercise helps you start AutoCAD. If AutoCAD is located on a drive other than C, you must first make that drive active before continuing with this exercise.

Starting AutoCAD

1. Turn on the computer and, if necessary, log onto the network. Then, make active the drive that contains AutoCAD. Drive C is used in this example.

2. `C:\>`**`CD \ACAD`** ↵	Makes the ACAD directory active
3. `C:\ACAD>`**`ACAD`** ↵	Starts AutoCAD

The method provided in this exercise is not the only way to start AutoCAD. Your instructor may have created a batch file *for you to use to start AutoCAD. A batch file is a computer file that contains any number of commands. When you enter the name of a batch file at the DOS prompt, DOS executes all the commands in the file. Check with your instructor to see if a batch exists for you to use in starting AutoCAD.*

Your First Session with AutoCAD

Figure 5.1 shows what the AutoCAD display looks like when it starts up on the computer. The list that follows explains the purpose of each labeled item in the figure.

- **Cursor (crosshairs).** When you move the mouse or digitizer puck, the cursor moves across the display in a corresponding motion. Use the cursor to pick points in a drawing, select menu items and commands, and provide other input to AutoCAD.
- **Screen menu.** The screen menu is just one of the ways you can access AutoCAD's many commands. The screen menu is described in more detail in unit 8. Select commands from the screen menu by placing the cursor on the desired command, and then pressing the select button on the mouse or digitizer puck.

- **Drawing area.** This area of the AutoCAD display is where your drawing appears. As you learn in other units, you can work with multiple views of your drawing at one time.
- **Command prompt area.** You can type commands using the keyboard, and these typed commands appear in the command prompt area as you type them. AutoCAD always prompts you to provide the necessary information for a command, and it lists in the command prompt area the available options for the command.

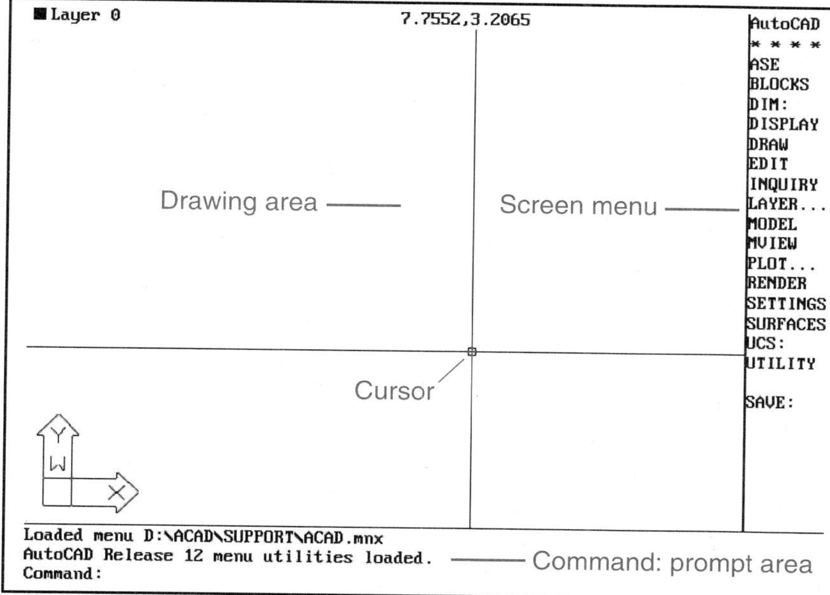

Figure 5.1

The AutoCAD start-up display.

AutoCAD Release 12 opens the drawing editor automatically when AutoCAD starts, which means you can begin drawing immediately. Before you begin experimenting with AutoCAD commands, however, you need to learn about the cursor and how you can provide input with the mouse or digitizer.

Using the Cursor

You use the cursor, which is shown in figure 5.1, to pick points on a drawing, select menu items and commands, and provide other types of input to AutoCAD. You control the cursor by moving the mouse or digitizer puck—depending on which of these input devices your workstation uses.

Your mouse or digitizer puck probably has at least two buttons. Many mice have three buttons, and most digitizer pucks have at least four. Each of these buttons has a specific function in AutoCAD. The list that follows describes each function of a typical four-button digitizer puck and a three-button mouse.

- **Pick.** Use this button to pick points on a drawing. You also use this button to select menu items and commands from AutoCAD's menus and dialog boxes. Place the cursor on the menu item or command, and then press the pick button.
- **Enter.** Pressing this button is essentially the same as pressing the Enter key on your keyboard.
- **Popup.** Pressing this button displays a menu of *object snap modes.* These object snap modes, which are described in detail in unit 38, enable you to pick existing points on entities, such as the endpoints of lines, centers of circles, and so forth.
- **Cancel.** Pressing this button is the same as pressing Ctrl+C on the keyboard. Either action cancels the command currently in progress.

Experiment a little with moving the cursor and using the mouse buttons in the following exercise. Use figure 5.2 as a guide.

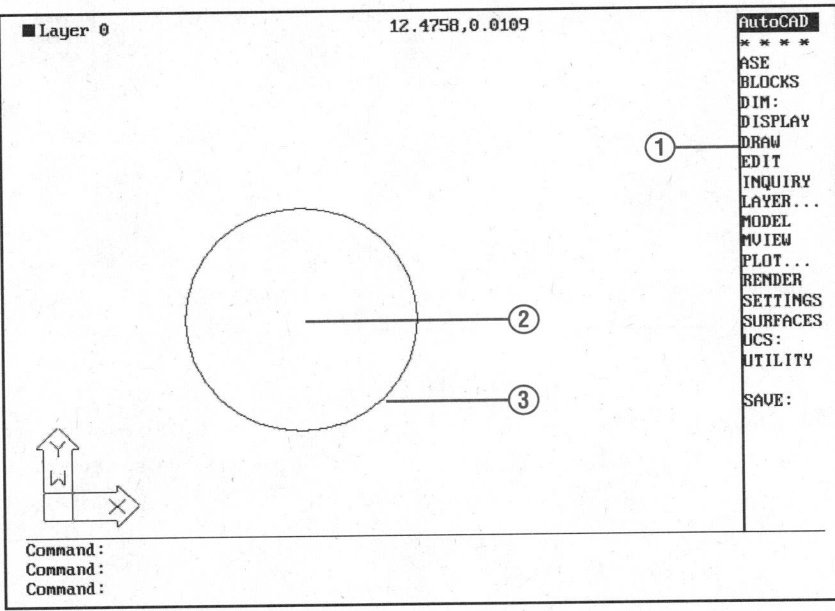

Figure 5.2

Selection points for the cursor.

Working with the Cursor and Mouse

1. `Command:` *Move the mouse or digitizer puck within the drawing area*	Moves the cursor on the display
2. `Command:` *Move the cursor to* ① *(see fig. 5.2)*	Activates the screen menu and highlights the DRAW menu item
3. `Command:` *Click the pick button on the mouse or digitizer puck*	Displays the DRAW screen menu

4. `Command:` *From the* DRAW *screen menu, choose* CIRCLE	Displays the CIRCLE screen menu
5. `Command:` *From the screen menu, choose* CEN,RAD:	Starts the CIRCLE command
6. `_CIRCLE 3P/2P/TTR/<Center point>:` *Place the cursor at* ② *and click the pick button (see fig. 5.2)*	Specifies the center point for the circle
7. `Diameter/<Radius>: DRAG` *Move the cursor to* ③ *, and then click the pick button (see fig. 5.2)*	Specifies a radius point and draws the circle
8. `Command:` *Move the cursor all the way to the top of the display*	Displays the pull-down menus
9. `Command:` *Place the arrow cursor on the* View *menu, and then click the pick button*	Displays the View menu
10. `Command:` *Choose* Redraw	Redraws the drawing (refreshes the display)

From the previous exercise you can see that the pick button serves two purposes: picking points on the drawing, and choosing menu items and commands.

Exploring Drawing Commands

Now that you have some experience picking points and choosing menu items, you can draw another circle and a few lines. Use figure 5.3 as a guide for picking points. If you make a mistake when picking a point or clicking a button, press Ctrl+C to cancel the command, and then try the command again.

Exploring Drawing Commands

Continue with your drawing from the previous exercise.

1. `Command:` *Move the cursor to the top of the display*	Displays the pull-down menus
2. `Command:` *Click on* Draw, *and then* Circle, *and then* Center, Radius	Starts the CIRCLE command and specifies a center point
3. `_circle 3P/2P/TTR/<Center point>:` *Pick point* ① *(see fig. 5.3)*	Specifies a 1" radius
4. `Diameter/<Radius> <2.1051>: 1 ↵`	

continues

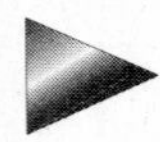

5. `Command:` *From the* Draw *pull-down menu, choose* Line, *and then* 1 segment	Starts the LINE command

Try the CANCEL command by canceling the LINE command.

6. `line From point:` *Click the* Cancel *button or press* Ctrl+C *on the keyboard*	Cancels the LINE command
7. `Command:` *From the* Draw *pull-down menu, choose* Line, *and then* 1 segment	Starts the LINE command for one segment
8. `line From point:` *Click the* Tools *button on the mouse or digitizer puck, and then choose* Tangent	Opens the Tools object snap menu and chooses the Tangent object snap mode
9. `_tan to` *Pick point* ② *(see fig. 5.3)*	Specifies start point of line
10. `To point:` *Click the* Tools *button, and then choose* Tangent	Chooses Tangent object snap mode
11. `_tan to` *Pick point* ③ *(see fig. 5.3)*	Specifies end point of line
12. `Command:` *From the* Draw *pull-down menu, choose* Line, *and then* 1 segment	Starts the LINE command for one segment
13. `line From point:` *Click the* Tools *button on the mouse or digitizer puck, and then choose* Tangent	Opens the Tools object snap menu and chooses the Tangent object snap mode
14. `_tan to` *Pick point* ④ *(see fig. 5.3)*	Specifies start point of line
15. `To point:` *Click the* Tools *button, and then choose* Tangent	Chooses Tangent object snap mode
16. `_tan to` *Pick point* ⑤ *(see fig. 5.3)*	Specifies end point of line

You have just experimented with AutoCAD's capability to locate automatically specific types of points within a drawing, such as tangents and end points. You learn in later units that this capability is a very powerful CAD technique for creating accurate drawings and simplifying the drafting process.

Modifying Your Drawing

In addition to creating new geometry in a drawing, you also can modify a drawing. In the following exercise, you use one of AutoCAD's many editing commands to remove a piece of each circle and to complete your first simple drawing. You also use the keyboard to execute an AutoCAD command. Use figure 5.4 as a guide to complete the exercise. When you have completed the exercise, your drawing should look like the one shown in figure 5.5.

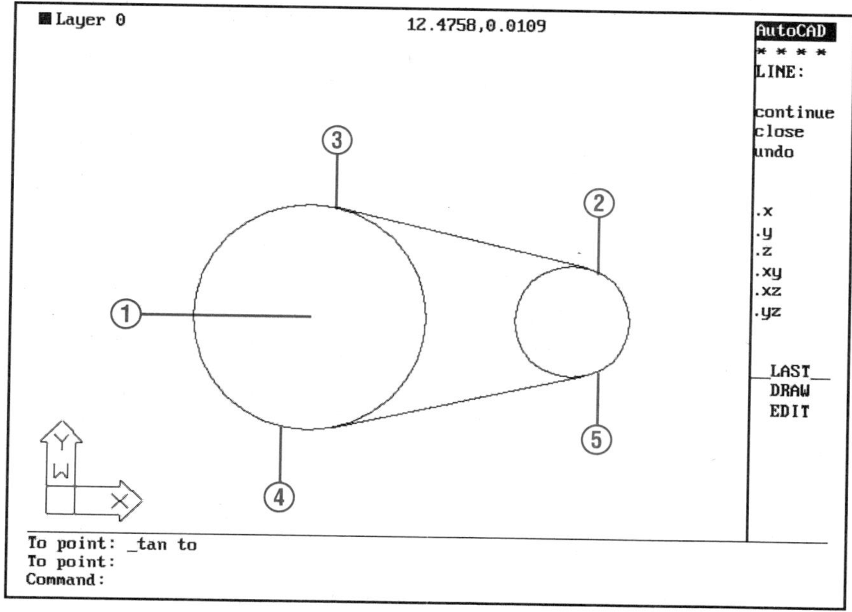

Figure 5.3

Pick points for a circle and lines.

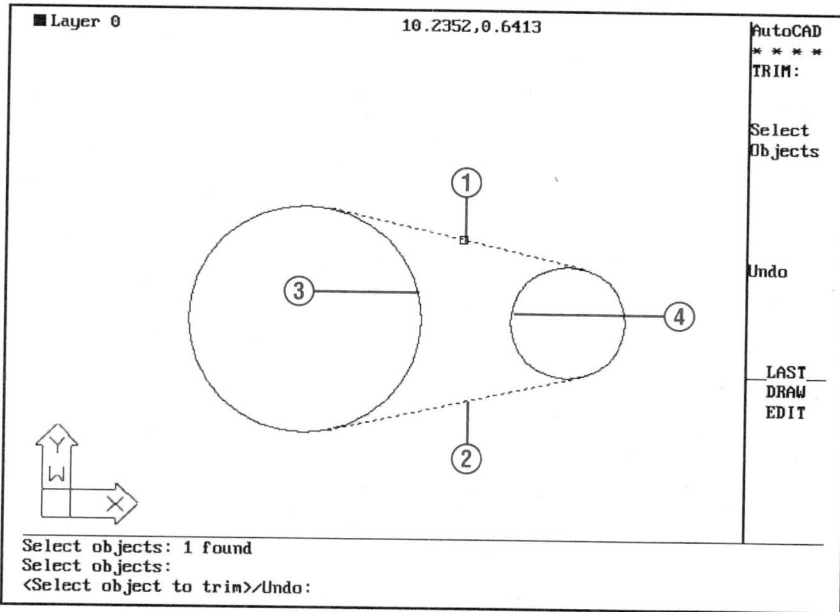

Figure 5.4

Selection points for modifying a drawing.

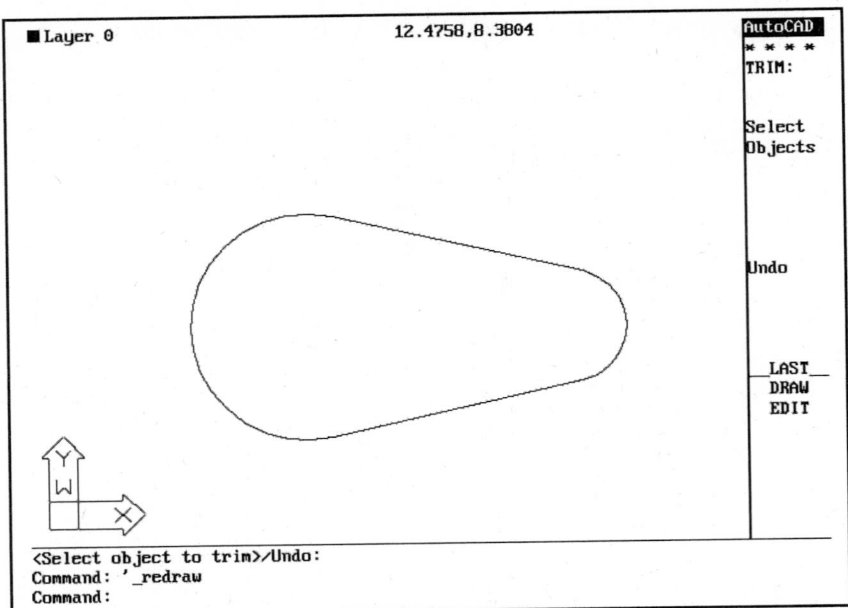

Figure 5.5

A complete drawing.

Modifying a Drawing

1. `Command:` *From the* Modify *pull-down menu, choose* Trim `_trim`	Starts the TRIM command
2. `Select cutting edge(s)...`	
3. `Select objects:` *Place the square cursor on the top line at* ① *(see fig. 5.4) and then click the pick button* `1 found`	Selects the line (see fig. 5.4)
4. `Select objects:` *Place the square cursor on the bottom line at* ② *(see fig. 5.4) and click the pick button* `1 found`	Selects the bottom line
5. `Select objects:` ↵	Ends selection of cutting edges
6. `<Select object to trim>/Undo:` *Pick the left circle at* ③ *(see fig. 5.4)*	Trims the circle
7. `<Select object to trim>/Undo:` *Pick the right circle at* ④ *(see fig. 5.4)*	Trims the circle
8. `<Select object to trim>/Undo:` ↵	Ends the TRIM command
9. `Command:` **REDRAW**	Issues the REDRAW command from the keyboard

You have now completed your first drawing with AutoCAD! In the process of preparing this drawing, you learned to use the cursor and mouse, selected commands from some of AutoCAD's menus, and entered commands and other input from the keyboard. You also have experienced a small fraction of AutoCAD's editing capabilities.

Although this unit did not cover any of the commands in detail, other units in *Hands On AutoCAD Release 12* provide thorough explanations of how each command works and how to apply it.

Unit Review

What You've Learned

- How to start AutoCAD
- The function of the mouse and digitizer buttons
- The function of the cursor
- How to pick points and choose menu items in AutoCAD
- How to enter input using the keyboard
- How to cancel a command

Review Questions

True or False

5.01 T F The pick button is used to cancel a command.

5.02 T F The mouse or digitizer puck includes a button that, when clicked, is the same as pressing Enter on the keyboard.

5.03 T F Pressing Ctrl+C on the keyboard cancels the current command.

5.04 T F To display the pull-down menus, you must move the cursor all the way to the left edge of the display.

5.05 T F The `Command:` prompt displays command options that you can use with the current command.

5.06 T F When you select a line or circle that you have already drawn, it becomes highlighted (dotted).

5.07 T F The screen menu is located at the bottom of the display.

5.08 T F The pull-down menus remain hidden until you move the cursor all the way to the top of the display.

5.09 T F Most digitizer pucks have only one button.

5.10 T F The pick button is used to pick points and choose menu items.

Student: ____________ Date: ____________

Instructor: ____________ Course: ____________ Section: ____________

Multiple Choice

5.11 The ____________ ____________ is the area where your drawing appears in AutoCAD.

(A) drawing area

(B) screen menu

(C) digitizer area

(D) pull-down menu

5.12 When you move the mouse or digitizer puck, the ______________ moves on the display.

(A) menu

(B) drawing

(C) cursor

(D) none of the above

5.13 You use the cursor to pick ______________ in a drawing.

(A) entities (like circles and lines)

(B) points

(C) commands

(D) all of the above

Short Answer

5.14 Describe the function of the cursor in AutoCAD.

____

____

____

5.15 Describe what happens when you press Ctrl+C during a command.

____

____

____

Student: ______________ Date: ______________

Instructor: ______________ Course: ______________ Section: ______________

UNIT 6

A Tour Around the AutoCAD Display

The AutoCAD display (on-screen) provides a number of different ways for you to choose commands and provide other types of input to AutoCAD. In addition, the AutoCAD display provides information about your current drawing and current AutoCAD settings. Becoming familiar with AutoCAD's display is an important part of learning to use the program. This unit provides a brief overview of the different areas within the AutoCAD display and their functions.

The objectives of this unit are to:

- ☞ Recognize and describe the function of the drawing area, the `Command:` prompt, the screen menu, the pull-down menu, and the status line
- ☞ Show how AutoCAD's dialog boxes speed your work

Understanding the Parts of the Display

The different areas of the AutoCAD display serve different purposes. The area in which you work most often is called the *drawing area.*

Working in the Drawing Area

The *drawing area* is the rectangular area of the AutoCAD display in which views of the current drawing appear. In effect, the drawing area gives you a "window" to your drawing. Figure 6.1 identifies the drawing area.

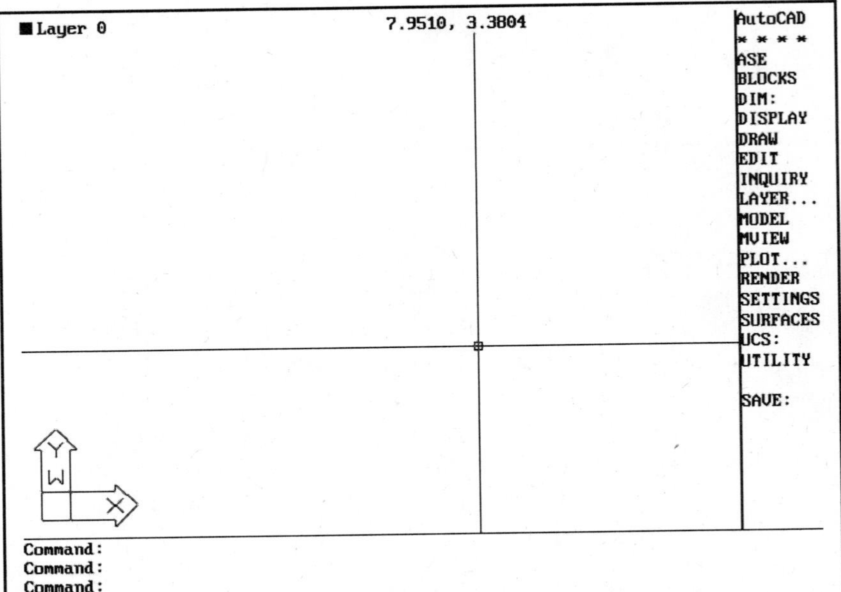

Figure 6.1

The drawing area is where your drawing appears.

As you learned in unit 5, moving the mouse or digitizer puck also moves the cursor in the drawing area. The cursor normally appears as *crosshairs* (joined horizontal and vertical lines) when it is in the drawing area. You generally use this type of cursor to pick points in the drawing. Figure 6.1 shows this type of cursor. Sometimes the cursor has a small box attached to the center of the crosshairs, depending on how AutoCAD is configured on your system. The function of this box is described in later units.

The cursor also can appear as just a small box, called a pickbox. The cursor changes from crosshairs to a small box whenever AutoCAD is prompting you to select a graphic entity, such as a line, arc, circle, and so on. Figure 6.2 shows this type of cursor.

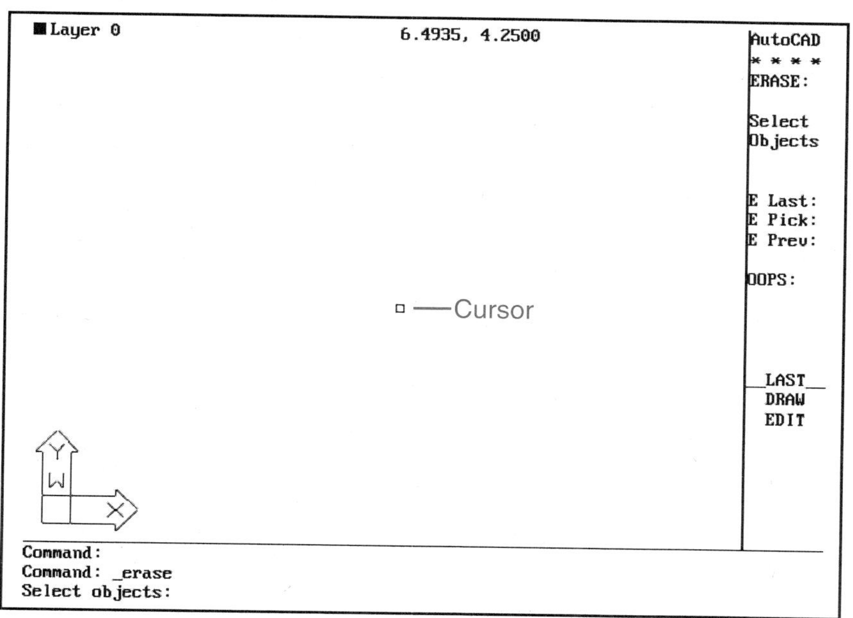

Figure 6.2

The cursor as a box, prompting for a selection.

As you work on a drawing, adding and erasing information, the display can become "dirty" with fragments of lines and circles, small *blips* (crosses) where you have selected points, and other non-drawing information. To refresh the display and "clean it up," use AutoCAD's REDRAW command.

The following exercise helps you become familiar with the AutoCAD drawing area, the cursor, and the REDRAW command. Use figure 6.3 as a guide for picking points.

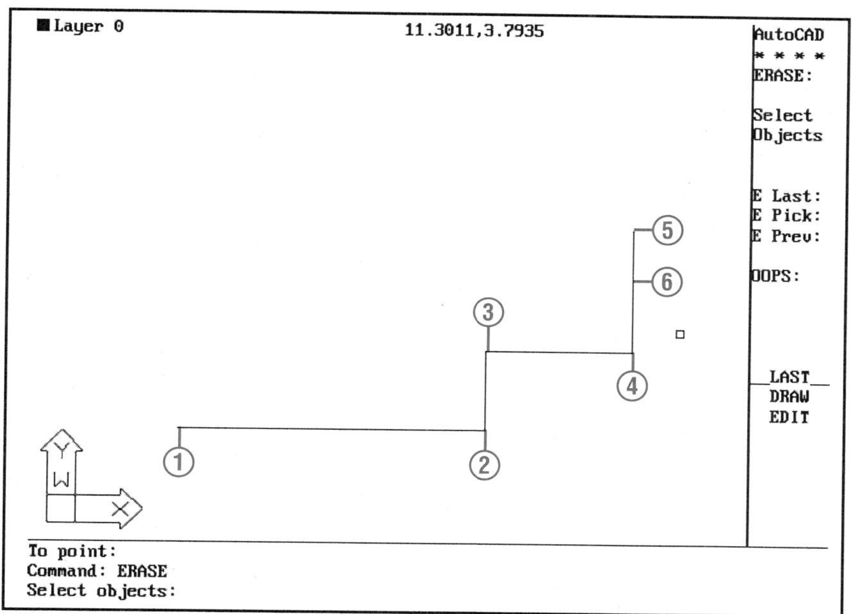

Figure 6.3

Drawing area pick points.

Becoming Familiar with the Drawing Area

Start AutoCAD and notice that the cursor first appears as crosshairs.

1. `Command:` **`_LINE`** ↵	Issues the LINE command
2. `From point:` *Pick a point at* ① *(see fig. 6.3)*	Draws a line segment
3. `To point:` *Pick a point at* ②	
4. `To point:` *Pick a point at* ③	
5. `To point:` *Pick a point at* ④	
6. `To point:` *Pick a point at* ⑤	
7. `To point:` *Press* Enter	Ends the LINE command
8. `Command:` **`ERASE`** ↵	Issues the ERASE command

Notice that the cursor has changed to a small box.

9. `Select objects:` *Select the line at* ⑥	Highlights the line
`1 found`	
10. `Select objects:` *Press* Enter	Erases the line and ends the ERASE command
11. `Command:` **`REDRAW`** ↵	Refreshes the display

Now that you are familiar with the cursor and drawing area, you are ready to learn about some of the other parts of the display.

Working with Pull-down Menus

AutoCAD provides two different areas for menus that you can use to enter commands, called the *pull-down menu* and the *screen menu.* By default, the screen menu appears along the right side of the AutoCAD display. The pull-down menu does not appear until you move the cursor to the very top of the display. Figure 6.4 identifies both menus.

Two types of *menu items* can appear in a pull-down menu. The following list explains each type:

- **Cascading menu item.** Cascading menu items have a small arrowhead at the right edge of the menu item. A cascading menu does not execute a command. Instead, it opens a secondary menu when it is chosen called a *CHILD MENU.* To open a cascading menu, click on the menu item or place the arrow cursor on top of the arrowhead.
- **Command menu item.** Command menu items execute an AutoCAD command when you select the menu item. Some items have an ellipsis

(...) at the ends of their names. When you select a menu item that includes an ellipsis, AutoCAD prompts you for additional information before carrying out the command. If the command menu item does not include an ellipsis, AutoCAD immediately executes the command.

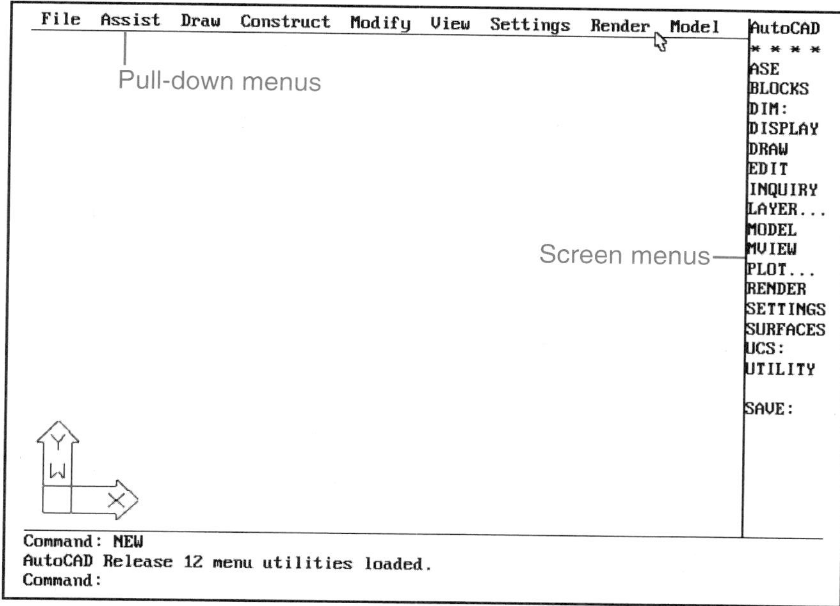

Figure 6.4

The pull-down menu and the screen menu.

Experiment with pull-down menus in the following exercise.

Using Pull-down Menus

1. `Command:` *Move the cursor all the way to the top of the display* — Displays the pull-down menus
2. `Command:` *Click on* Draw — Displays the Draw pull-down menu
3. `Command:` *From the* Draw *pull-down menu, choose* Line, *and then* Segments — Displays the Line cascade menu and then starts the LINE command
4. `line From point:` *Press* Ctrl+C — Cancels the LINE command
5. `Command:` *From the pull-down menus, choose* Draw — Displays the Draw pull-down menu

Next, experiment with opening a cascading menu by placing the cursor on the cascading menu's arrowhead.

6. `Command:` *Place the cursor on the arrowhead beside* Polygon — Displays the Polygon cascade menu
7. `Command:` *Press* Esc — Closes the menu

At the top of the AutoCAD graphics screen is the status line. *The status line disappears when you move the cursor to the top of the display to choose from among the pull-down menus. The status line displays information about your drawing environment settings. Information contained in the status line is described in other units, wherever such description is appropriate.*

In addition to using the pull-down menus, you can also use AutoCAD's screen menu to choose commands.

Using the Screen Menu

The menu along the right side of the AutoCAD display is called the *screen menu* (see fig. 6.4). The screen menu gives you access to all of AutoCAD's commands. (The pull-down menus give you access to the majority of AutoCAD commands, but not to all of them.) To select a menu item from the screen menu, position the cursor on the item you want to select. The item automatically highlights. Click the pick button to select the highlighted screen menu item.

The screen menu changes as you pick items from it, and it also changes when you select commands from the pull-down menus (the screen menu provides options for the current command). The screen menu shown in figure 6.4 is the *root screen menu.* You can access all other screen menus from the root screen menu. To return to the root screen menu from any other screen menu, choose the menu item AutoCAD, located at the top of the screen menu.

Experiment with the screen menu in the next exercise.

Using the Screen Menu

1. `Command:` *From the screen menu, choose* AutoCAD	Displays the root screen menu
2. `Command:` *From the screen menu, choose* DRAW	Displays the DRAW screen menu
3. `Command:` *From the screen menu, choose* ARC	Displays the ARC screen menu
4. `Command:` *From the screen menu, choose* LAST	Displays the last, or previous menu
5. `Command:` *From the screen menu, choose* CIRCLE	Displays the CIRCLE screen menu
6. `Command:` *From the* CIRCLE *screen menu, choose* CEN,RAD:	Issues the CIRCLE command using center point and radius

7. `_CIRCLE 3P/2P/TTR/<Center point>:` *Press* Ctrl+C	Cancels the CIRCLE command
8. `Command:` *From the screen menu, choose* previous	Displays the last LAST menu
9. `Command:` *From the screen menu, choose* next	Displays the second page of the DRAW screen menu
10. `Command:` *From the screen menu, choose* previous	Displays the previous page of the DRAW screen menu
11. `Command:` *From the screen menu, choose* AutoCAD	Displays the root screen menu

You can see from this exercise that some screen menus, such as the DRAW screen menu, have more than one page. You can switch between these pages by using the last and previous screen menu items.

Using the `Command:` Prompt

The `Command:` prompt is located at the bottom of the AutoCAD display. Instead of choosing commands from the pull-down or screen menus, you also can type them at the `Command:` prompt. You have already used this method in the first exercise of this unit. Figure 6.5 shows the options for a command at the `Command:` prompt.

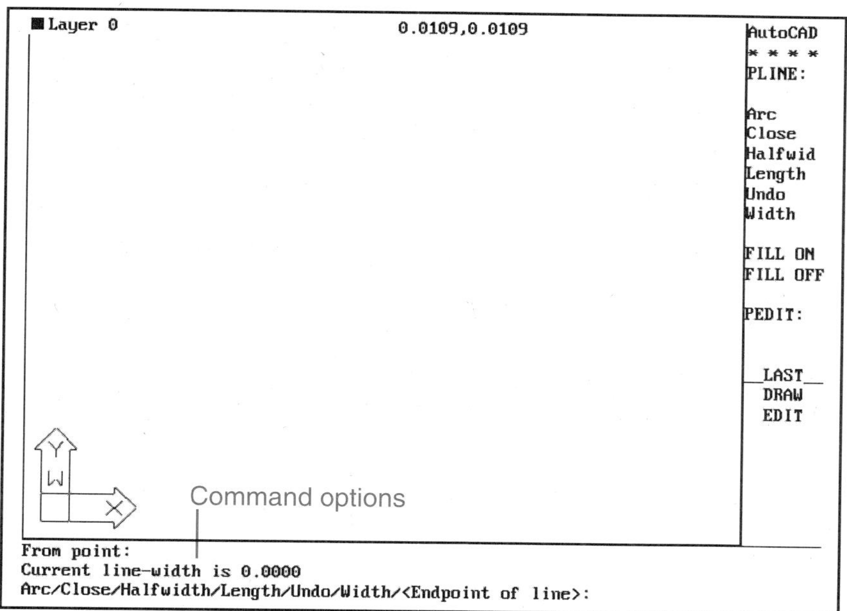

Figure 6.5

Command options appearing at the `Command:` *prompt.*

AutoCAD uses the `Command:` prompt to display the available options for the current command. As you can see from the example shown in figure 6.5, one of the characters in each option is in uppercase. To select an option by typing, you need only enter the uppercase letter and not the entire option name. (Type L for Length, for example.) Also, the last option at a `Command:` prompt is always enclosed in angle brackets < >. This option is always the *default option*, which is the option AutoCAD uses if you do not specify any other option.

Look at the `Command:` prompt often when you are first learning to use AutoCAD. In addition to displaying command options at the `Command:` prompt, AutoCAD also displays information about the current command and prompts you to supply input for the command. If you are ever unsure of what input you are supposed to enter, check the `Command:` prompt—it always indicates what input AutoCAD expects from you.

Using Dialog Boxes

Some pull-down menus and screen menus have an ellipsis (...) at the end of the menu item description. Usually, selecting one of these menu items causes AutoCAD to display a *dialog box*. AutoCAD uses dialog boxes to prompt you for settings and other options. Depending on the dialog box, these settings and options may apply to the entire drawing environment or to just the command associated with the dialog box. Figures 6.6, 6.7, and 6.8 show typical AutoCAD dialog boxes.

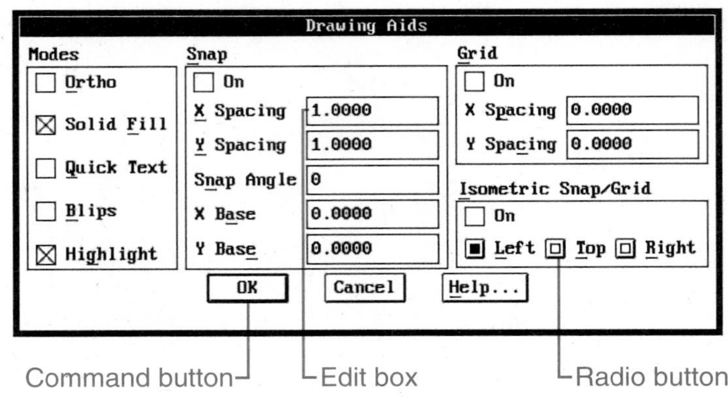

Figure 6.6

The Drawing Aids dialog box contains some typical dialog box controls.

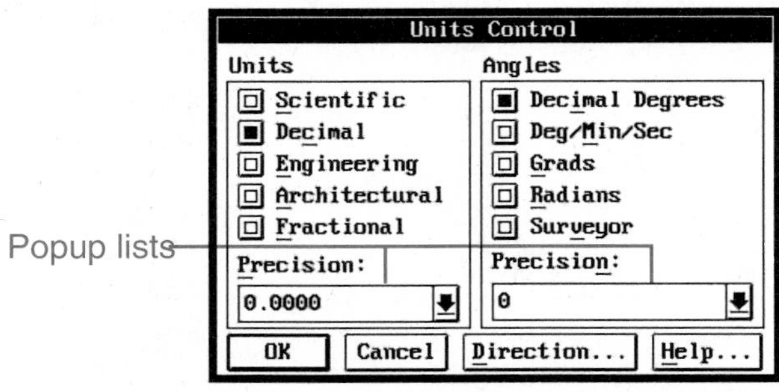

Figure 6.7

The Units Control dialog box contains popup lists.

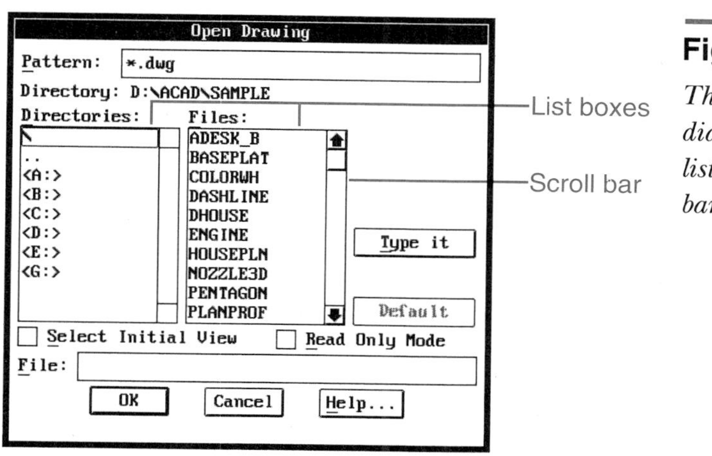

Figure 6.8

The Open Drawing dialog box contains list boxes and scroll bars.

The following list describes the types of controls you find in AutoCAD dialog boxes. (Refer to figures 6.6, 6.7, and 6.8 to identify these controls.)

- **Check box.** Check boxes turn on and off certain AutoCAD options. If a check box has a check in it, the associated option is turned on. If the check box is clear (no check), the option is turned off. Click in a check box to turn it on or off. Check boxes are usually used as a group—you can check more than one check box in any group.

- **Edit box.** Use edit boxes to enter numbers or text. Click in an edit box, and then begin typing. Double click in a text box to highlight everything in it, and then begin typing to replace the existing highlighted text or numbers with new characters.

- **Radio button.** Like check boxes, radio buttons turn on and off certain AutoCAD options. The difference is that radio buttons in a group are mutually exclusive—if you select a radio button in a group, all other radio buttons in the same group are deselected (turned off).

- **Command button.** Command buttons execute commands or activate options. The OK and Cancel buttons are examples of command buttons.

- **Scroll bar.** Scroll bars enable you to scroll through long lists of possible selections. AutoCAD also uses them as *slider controls* to specify settings that can vary through a range of possible values. (This is somewhat like a sliding volume control on a stereo.)

- **List box.** List boxes display lists from which you make selections. If the list is too long to fit in the box, the list box includes a scroll bar to enable you to scroll through the list.

☞ **Popup list.** Popup lists are like list boxes except they display only one selection. To view the rest of the list and to choose a different selection, click on the item in the list or on the small down-arrow at the right side of the list.

As you work with AutoCAD, you become more familiar with these types of dialog box controls.

Using the Text Screen

In addition to the graphics screen described in the first part of this unit, AutoCAD also includes a *text screen.* As you work with AutoCAD, you should realize that AutoCAD sends all command output to the text screen, as well as to the `Command:` prompt at the bottom of the graphics screen. Whenever you need to see more of your previous command entries than what you see in the `Command:` prompt area, switch to the text screen. To display the text screen, press the F1 key. To return to the graphics screen, press F1 again.

Unit Review

What You've Learned

- ☞ The parts of the drawing editor screen
- ☞ How to use the pull-down menus and screen menus
- ☞ How to use the `Command:` prompt
- ☞ How to use dialog boxes
- ☞ How to switch between the graphics and text screens

Review Questions

True or False

6.01 T F The cursor can appear as crosshairs or as a small box.

6.02 T F The screen menu is located at the top of the AutoCAD display.

6.03 T F The pull-down menu is located at the top of the AutoCAD display.

6.04 T F When AutoCAD is chosen from the screen menu, the root screen menu displays.

6.05 T F The F2 function key switches between the graphics screen and the text screen.

Multiple Choice

6.06 A ____________ ____________ in a dialog box is used to select only one option within a group of options.

(A) radio button

(B) command button

(C) scroll bar

(D) grid box

6.07 A menu item that includes an ellipsis (...) usually opens a ____________ ____________.

(A) command button

(B) text screen

(C) dialog box

(D) list box

Student: ____________ Date: ____________

Instructor: ____________ Course: ____________ Section: ____________

6.08 You can switch to the __________ __________ to view more of your previous command's input and output than is shown in the `Command:` prompt area.

(A) list box

(B) text screen

(C) dialog box

(D) graphics screen

6.09 A cascading menu, when selected, displays another __________.

(A) menu

(B) list

(C) drawing

(D) screen

Applying the AutoCAD Environment

6.10 In figure 6.9, identify the following items:

(A) pull-down menu

(B) screen menu

(C) `Command:` prompt area

(D) drawing area

(E) cascading menu

Figure 6.9

Components to identify within the AutoCAD display.

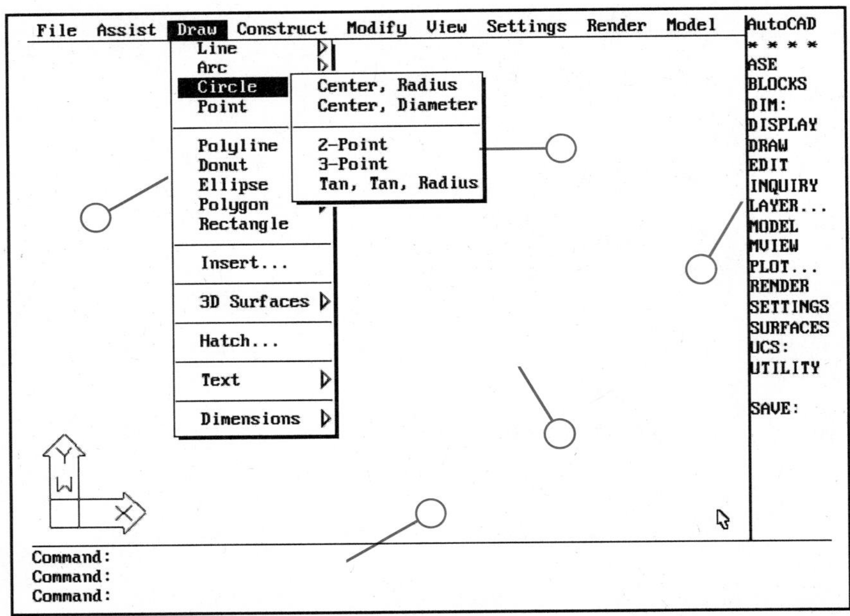

Student: __________ Date: __________

Instructor: __________ Course: __________ Section: __________

UNIT 7

Introduction to Files

When you use manual drafting methods to prepare a drawing, you typically store the drawing in a flat file drawer or on a stick file. When you use AutoCAD to prepare a drawing, you store the drawing in an electronic file on the computer's hard disk or on a floppy disk. The computer also uses many other types of files, and you need to understand files and how to use them to be able to store and manage your drawing files. This unit introduces the concept of files.

The objectives for this unit are to:

- ☞ Understand the function of an electronic file
- ☞ Open existing drawing files
- ☞ Begin new drawings and save new drawings from existing drawings
- ☞ Use the Autosave function

Understanding Electronic Files

A *computer file* is a collection of data stored on a storage device such as a hard disk, floppy disk, or tape. The files are stored magnetically, similar to the way music is stored on audio tape. When you prepare a drawing and save it, AutoCAD stores all the drawing information in a file on whichever disk you specify. If you save the file on disk, you can open the file later to edit the drawing or plot it on paper or other hardcopy media. You also can place the file on a floppy disk to send to someone else or transfer the file electronically over a phone line using a modem. If your workstation is connected to a network, other users can access the file.

In addition to drawing files, your computer has many other types of files. AutoCAD has hundreds of files, including program files, data files, and other types of files. When you run a program such as AutoCAD on your computer, the computer reads the program from its file into memory, then executes the program.

The average computer workstation often contains thousands of files. You need some way to organize and keep track of so many files. Disks and directories are the primary tools for managing files. If you have not read unit 4—"A Tour Around Your Computer"—and learned about disks and directories, do so before you continue with this unit.

Unit 4 teaches that drives are identified by a drive ID. The first hard disk in a PC, for example, is drive C. The first floppy drive is drive A. You also learned in unit 4 that directories have names that differentiate them from one another.

Your files are stored in directories, and also have names. A file name in DOS can have as many as eight alphanumeric characters (letters and numbers). You also can use the following symbols as part of a file name:

^ $ ~ ! # % & - { } ( ) @ ` '

These names are examples of valid file names:

FRED

FRED123

86BARNEY

ABC-123

In addition to a file name, files often have an extension. The *extension* has from one to three characters and serves to identify file type. An AutoCAD drawing file, for example, has the file extension DWG. Program files typically have the file extension EXE or COM. The extension is separated from the file name by a period (.). The following are examples of some typical AutoCAD drawing file names, including their extensions.

ROOFPLAN.DWG

012PLATE.DWG

NEW-PLOT.DWG

213.DWG

PCB_3312.DWG

When you save a drawing file, AutoCAD automatically adds the DWG extension to the file for you. When you open a drawing file to continue working on it, AutoCAD also automatically adds the DWG extension to the file. Therefore, you do not have to specify the file extension when you want to save or open a file—you only have to specify the file name.

In some cases, however, you need to specify a path to a file. A path consists of the disk ID, directory, and file name. If a file named PLANE.DWG is stored on drive C in a directory called \DRAWINGS, the path to the file is as follows:

```
C:\DRAWINGS\PLANE.DWG
```

Usually, you can use AutoCAD's dialog boxes to choose a file from a specific disk and directory. You generally do not have to enter the entire path to locate or save a file. You instead change the directory shown in the dialog box, which makes the directory active.

To associate disks, directories, and files with something a little easier to understand, think of a disk as a file cabinet. Each drawer in the file cabinet is a directory, and each of the items in the file drawer are your files.

Storing and Opening Your Files

In many of the exercises in *Hands On AutoCAD*, you are instructed to begin a new drawing in your assigned directory. Your assigned directory is the directory that your instructor assigns you to store your drawing files. This directory might be on the hard disk on your workstation, or it might be on a network server. Depending on how your instructor configures the system, you might have to share the directory with other users. The important point is that when you save a drawing, you must save it to a specific directory. Ask your instructor for the name and location of your assigned directory.

You are also instructed to use a prototype drawing in many exercises (unit 9, "Introduction to Drawing Setup," introduces prototype drawings and drawing setup). *Prototype drawings* serve as a "starting point" for your exercises. These prototype drawings are stored in a specific directory. If your workstation is networked, the prototype drawings are probably on a shared directory on the network, to which you have *read-only access* (you can open files from the directory, but you cannot save files to it). If your workstation is not networked, your prototype drawings are in a directory on your hard disk or on a floppy disk that your instructor gives you.

Unit 9 provides specific instructions for beginning a new drawing and using a prototype drawing.

Saving a New Drawing

AutoCAD provides three primary commands that you can use to store a drawing on disk: SAVE, SAVEAS, and QSAVE. When you work on a new drawing that does not have a drawing name and has never been saved, all three function much the same. Each one prompts you to supply a file name for your drawing by displaying the Save Drawing As dialog box shown in figure 7.1.

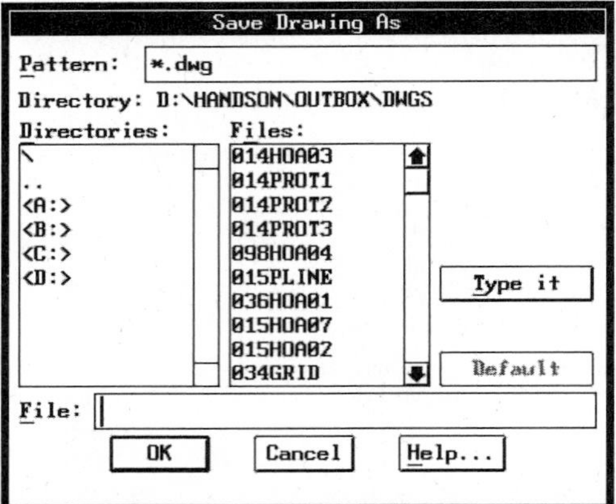

Figure 7.1

The Save Drawing As dialog box.

In the following exercise, you use the SAVEAS command to save a drawing to a file. You use the Save Drawing As dialog box to choose a disk and directory for the file. To choose a disk, double-click on the disk's drive ID in the Directories list box. To choose a directory, double-click on the directory name. To choose the root directory of a drive, double-click on the \ symbol. To choose the parent directory of the current directory, double-click on the double dots (..).

Saving a New Drawing

1. `Command:` *Choose* Draw, *then* Rectangle `rectang`	Issues the RECTANG command
2. `First corner:` *Pick a point near* ① *(see fig. 7.2)*	Specifies first corner of rectangle

3. `Other corner:` *Pick a point near* ② *(see fig. 7.2)*	Specifies other corner of rectangle and draws rectangle
4. `Command:` *Choose* File, *then* Save As	Issues the SAVEAS command and displays the Save Drawing As dialog box
5. *Use the* Directories *list box to choose the disk that contains your assigned directory, then choose your assigned directory*	Makes your assigned directory active
6. *Click in the* File *edit box, then type* **007???01**, *substituting your initials for the ??? in the file name*	Specifies the name of the drawing file
7. *Choose* OK	Saves the drawing file and sets the current drawing name

Your drawing, which should look similar to figure 7.2, is now stored on disk.

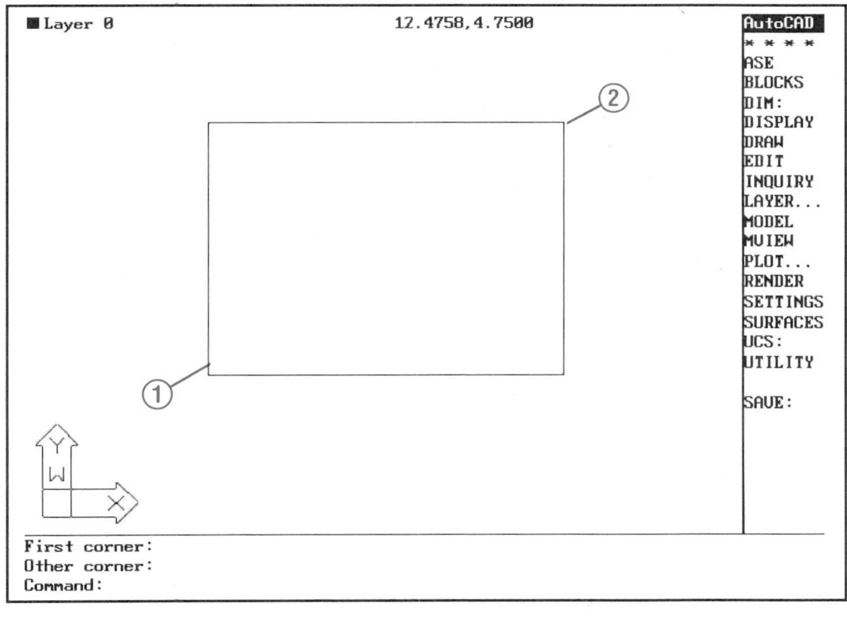

Figure 7.2

A rectangle added to the drawing.

Saving an Existing Drawing

As you edit a drawing, you should save it periodically (every 10 minutes or so). If your workstation fails for some reason, you only lose a few minutes worth of work. The QSAVE command is the command you should use to save an existing drawing. QSAVE saves your drawing using the current drawing name—it does not prompt you for any additional information. To issue the QSAVE command, enter QSAVE at the command prompt or choose File, then Save from the pull-down menu.

You can also save the current drawing with a different file name. This is a quick way to copy a drawing to a different file. If you use SAVE, AutoCAD displays the Save Drawing As dialog box and the current file name appears in the File edit box. Press Enter to save the drawing with the same name, or enter a new name. If you enter a new name, AutoCAD saves the current drawing using the new file name. The original file is not affected.

The SAVE command does not change the current drawing name. If you open the file 007THIS, then use SAVE to save the drawing to the file 007OTHER, the current drawing name remains 007THIS. If you then use the QSAVE command, AutoCAD saves the drawing as the file 007THIS. The SAVEAS command, however, changes the current file name. The SAVE command is useful if you want to save the current drawing to one or more other files, but want to continue working with the drawing under its original name.

Opening a Drawing File

As in manual drafting, you usually cannot finish a new drawing or complete revisions to an existing drawing in a single session. The OPEN command enables you to open an existing drawing file that has previously been saved to disk. You can modify the drawing, then resave it.

Use the OPEN command to open an existing drawing file at the command prompt or choose File, then Open. If the current drawing has been modified, but not saved, AutoCAD displays the Drawing Modification dialog box shown in figure 7.3.

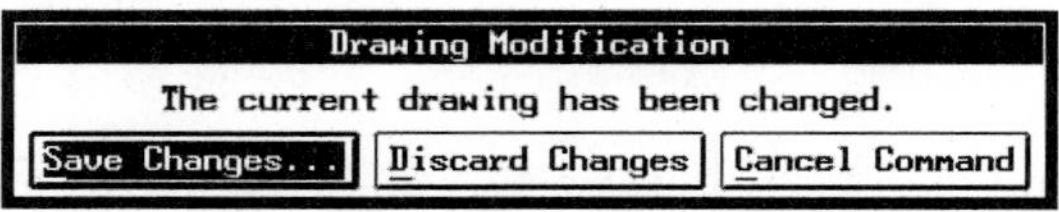

Figure 7.3
The Drawing Modification dialog box.

To save the drawing, click on the Save Changes button. If the drawing has been saved before, AutoCAD saves it under the current file name. If it is a new drawing, AutoCAD displays the Save File As dialog box so that you can specify disk, directory, and file name. To discard the drawing without saving, click on the Discard Changes button. To cancel the process and return to editing, click on the Cancel Command button.

After you specify which action to perform on the current drawing (discard, save, or cancel), the Open Drawing dialog box appears (see fig. 7.4). Use the Directories and Files list boxes to find the drawing you want.

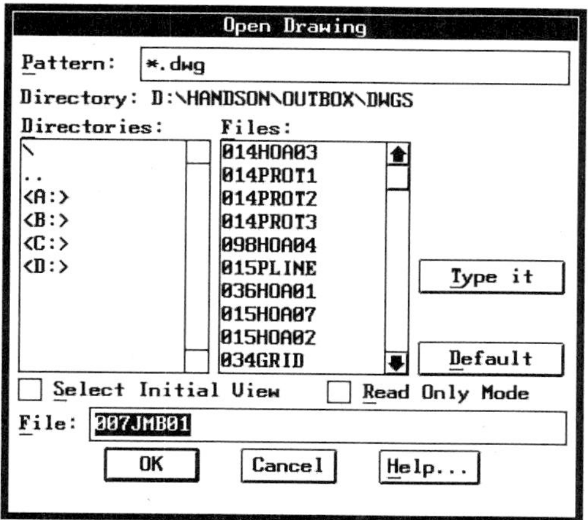

Figure 7.4

The Open Drawing dialog box.

The Open Drawing dialog box has two features that make it different from the standard File dialog box. You can open a drawing file with an initial view or open it in read-only mode or both.

Selecting an Initial View

The Select Initial View check box in the Open Drawing dialog box enables you to select a named view or the last view in a drawing. If you place a check in this check box, AutoCAD displays the Select Initial View dialog box (see fig. 7.5), which lists the view names currently saved with the drawing. You can choose `(last view)` to open the drawing with the view that was current when the drawing was last saved. Another option is to choose a view by name. When AutoCAD opens the drawing, it displays the view you select.

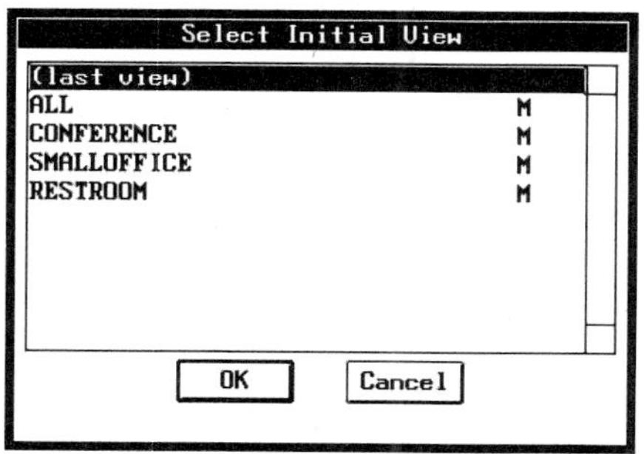

Figure 7.5

The Select Initial View dialog box.

Unit 20, "Working with Multiple Views," explains how to store and retrieve multiple views of your drawing while you work.

Using Read-Only Mode

If you check the Read Only Mode check box in the Open Drawing dialog box, AutoCAD opens the file in read-only mode. This means that you can open and view the file, but you cannot save modifications to the existing file. This protects the file from change. You can, however, save the file under another file name. If you try to save the read-only file, a dialog box displays informing you that the file is write-protected.

Use read-only mode if you want to make sure you don't make any changes to the original file.

Using SAVETIME and AUTOSAVE

AutoCAD has an option that enables it to save your drawing automatically as you work with the drawing. The SAVETIME system variable controls the time interval at which AutoCAD automatically saves your drawing. By having AutoCAD save your drawing automatically, you can reduce the possibility of losing changes to the drawing if your PC locks up or the power goes out while you work on a drawing. You can set SAVETIME so that AutoCAD saves your drawing every ten minutes, for example. To set the SAVETIME variable, enter **SAVETIME** at the command prompt, then the time, in minutes, to elapse between automatic saves.

AutoCAD saves the drawing automatically to a file named AUTO.SV$ in the current directory. The automatic save timer starts when the first change is made to a drawing file. The timer resets every time you issue a SAVE, QSAVE, or SAVEAS command. You can turn SAVETIME off by setting the interval to zero (0).

AUTOSAVE is a safety feature that lets you salvage revisions made during a given editing session in which a problem occurs. Nevertheless, you should not rely on AUTOSAVE as a substitute for saving your drawing regularly. Get in the habit of saving your drawing regularly during an editing session.

To recover the AUTO.SV$ drawing file if a mishap does take place, rename AUTO.SV$ to a new file name that has the DWG file extension. Then, open this new drawing to determine whether it is more up-to-date than the previous version of your drawing.

Unit Review

What You've Learned

- Commands: OPEN, SAVE, SAVEAS, and QSAVE
- How AutoCAD stores a drawing
- How to open and save drawings in drawing files
- How you can use SAVETIME to aid in drawing backup
- How the Read Only Mode and Select Initial View options affect the process of opening a drawing

Review Questions

True or False

7.01 T F SAVE enables you to resave a file that you have opened using read-only mode.

7.02 T F SAVEAS enables you to save a drawing with a new name.

7.03 T F The initial view can be the last view.

7.04 T F All AutoCAD drawings have a DWG file extension.

7.05 T F The QSAVE command saves the drawing without prompting you for a name, disk, or directory in which to save the file.

7.06 T F You cannot use the SAVE command to save a drawing with a new file name.

7.07 T F The SAVETIME system variable controls the length of time that passes between automatic saves.

7.08 T F You must specify a file name when you save a new drawing.

7.09 T F To save a file quickly with the same name, you can use the QSAVE command.

7.10 T F You cannot save the same drawing file in two different files with different names.

Student: ______________ Date: ______________

Instructor: ______________ Course: ______________ Section: ______________

UNIT 8

Managing Files

ou must perform certain tasks quite often to manage the files you use AutoCAD to create, such as copying, deleting, renaming, and backing up files. This unit teaches you how and why to perform these tasks in AutoCAD.

The objectives for this unit are to:

- Understand the purpose and scope of managing files
- Erase, copy, and rename existing drawing files
- Understand why and how to back up drawing files

Overview of File Management

The drawing files that you create using AutoCAD are an important asset to your company or organization. Not only must the drawings be maintained for future reference, but you can use drawing files to create new, similar drawings in short order. If a new product or design is very similar to an old design, you can copy the original drawing files and modify them to emerge with a new design.

Copying files is just one aspect of file management. You also may need to erase old drawing files, make archive copies of drawings on floppy disk or tape, or change the name of a drawing file. All these tasks fall under the description of file management.

You can perform virtually any file management task by using operating system commands. AutoCAD provides functions for managing files, however, and these AutoCAD functions are often easier to use than the corresponding operating system commands. Instead of using the DOS COPY command to copy a file, for example, you can use one of AutoCAD's file utilities to copy the file. To access AutoCAD's file utilities, choose File, then Utilities. AutoCAD displays the File Utilities dialog box shown in figure 8.1.

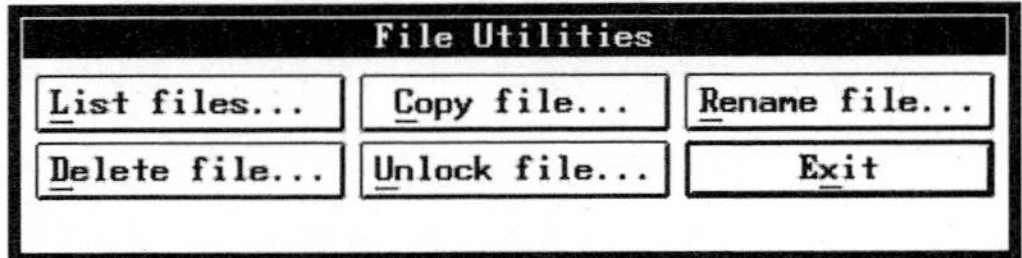

Figure 8.1
The File Utilities dialog box.

The following sections describe the functions available in the File Utilities dialog box.

Listing Files

If you choose the List files button in the File Utilities dialog box, AutoCAD displays the File List dialog box shown in figure 8.2. This dialog box is almost identical to the Save Drawing As dialog box. The difference is that only the Directories, Files, and Pattern controls are functional. You can use the File List dialog box to view the files on any disk, in any directory. This is useful when you need to find a file or determine if a particular file name has already been used.

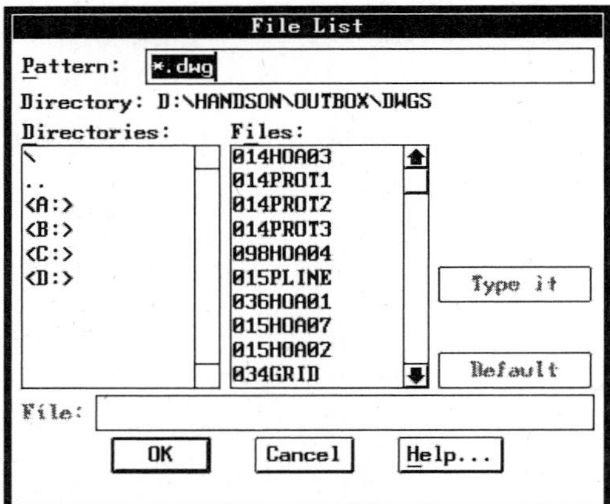

Figure 8.2
The File List dialog box.

Copying Files

Clicking on the Copy file button in the File Utilities dialog box enables you to select a source file, then specify a destination file. The *source file* is the file that you want to copy. The *destination file* is the new file in which you want to store the drawing. When you copy a file, you create a duplicate of the source file.

Copying a file in this way is a good method for duplicating a file to make an archive copy. It also is one method you can use to start a new drawing based on an existing drawing.

In the following exercise, you copy a drawing file.

Copying a File

1. `Command:` *Choose* File, *then* Utilities	Issues the FILES command and displays the File Utilities dialog box
2. *Choose the* Copy file *button*	Displays the Source File dialog box (see fig. 8.3)
3. *Locate in your assigned directory the drawing file* 007???01 *that you saved in unit 7, choose it from the* Directories *list box, then choose* OK	Specifies the file to copy and displays the Destination File dialog box (see fig. 8.4)
4. *In the* File *edit box, type* **`008???01.DWG`**, *then choose* OK	Copies the file 007???01 to new file named 008???01
5. *Choose* Exit	Closes the File Utilities dialog box

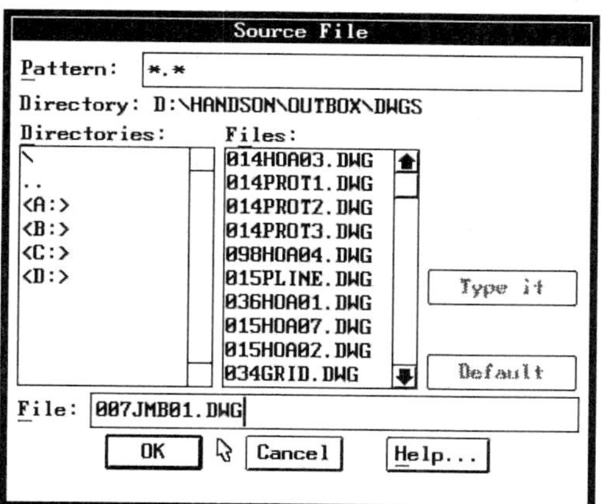

Figure 8.3

The Source File dialog box.

You must specify the drawing file extension DWG as part of the destination file name. AutoCAD does not automatically add the DWG file extension to the new file when you use the File Utilities. AutoCAD does add the DWG extension to the file name, however, when you save the file.

Figure 8.4

The Destination File dialog box.

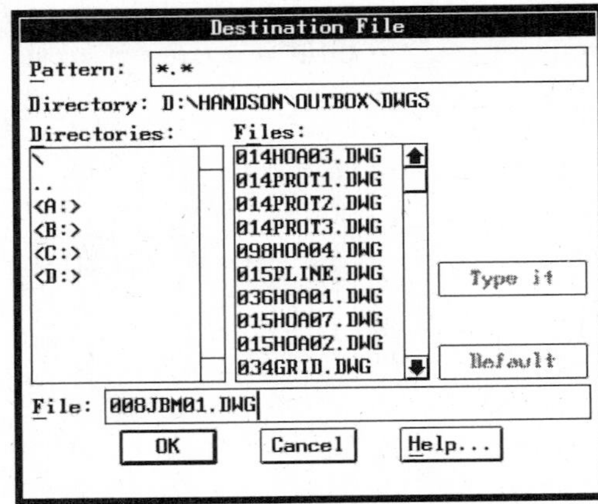

Now that you have copied the file, you can open 008???01 and edit it just like any other drawing file.

Renaming a File

Sometimes you have to rename a file. You might have saved a drawing with the wrong name, for example, and need to change it. *Renaming* a file does just what you might think: it changes the file's name without changing the contents of the file.

To change a file's name, click on the Rename file button in the File Utilities dialog box. AutoCAD then displays a dialog box labeled Old File Name, which is identical to the File List dialog box. Choose the file you want to rename, then choose OK. AutoCAD then displays a New File Name dialog box in which you specify the new file name. You must specify the file extension in both dialog boxes.

In the following exercise, rename the file 008???01 that you recently created.

Renaming a File

1. `Command:` *Choose* File, *then* Utilities	Issues the FILES command and displays the File Utilities dialog box
2. *Click on the* Rename file *button*	Displays the Old File Name dialog box
3. *Locate and choose the file* 008???01.DWG *in your assigned directory, then choose* OK	Specifies the file to be renamed and displays the New File Name dialog box (see fig. 8.5)

4. *In the* File *edit box, type* **008???02.DWG**, *then choose* OK	Specifies the new name for the file and renames the file
5. *Click on the* Exit *button*	Closes the File Utilities dialog box

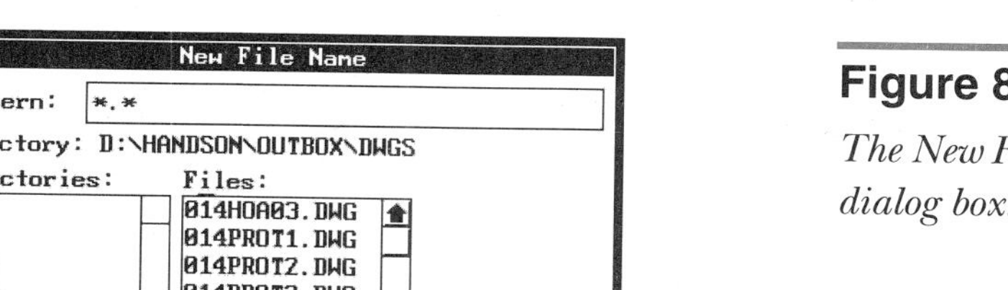

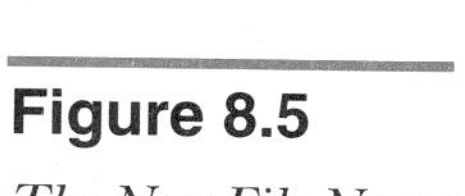

Figure 8.5

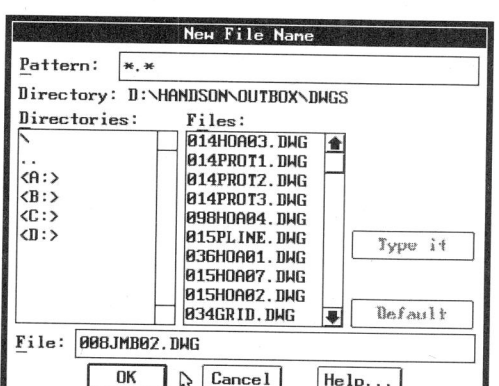

The New File Name dialog box.

The file 008???01.DWG no longer exists. It has been renamed 008???02.DWG.

Deleting a File

Occasionally you must delete a file. *Deleting* a file removes it permanently from the disk. For example, you might need to copy a selection of drawings onto a floppy disk or tape for archival purposes. After you copy the drawings, you can delete them from your hard disk to make more storage space available for new drawings.

The Delete file button in the File Utilities dialog box displays the File(s) to Delete dialog box (see fig. 8.6), which you can use to delete one or more files. You can select more than one file in the File list box. You also can click on the Select all button to choose all the files in the directory. Choosing the Clear all button clears file selection completely (deselects all files).

When you delete a file, it is permanently removed from the disk. It is unlikely for you to be able to recover a deleted file. If you accidentally delete a file that you should not have deleted, immediately ask your instructor to determine if it is possible to restore the file.

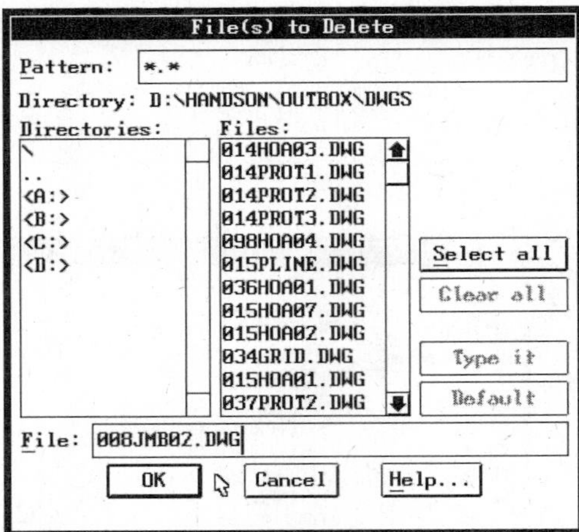

Figure 8.6

The File(s) to Delete dialog box.

In the following exercise, you delete the file 008???02.DWG that you renamed in the previous exercise.

Deleting a File

1. `Command:` *Choose* File, *then* Utilities	Issues the FILES command and displays the File Utilities dialog box
2. *Choose the* Delete file *button*	Displays the File(s) to Delete dialog box
3. *Locate and choose the file* 008???02.DWG *in your assigned directory, then choose* OK	Deletes the file
4. *Click on the* Exit *button*	

Be very careful about deleting files. It is easy to select the wrong file accidentally. After you delete the files, chances are that you will not be able to undelete the files, although in a limited number of situations you can.

Understanding Backups

Drawing files represent a very valuable investment. You might spend hours preparing a drawing. If you accidentally delete a drawing file, it could represent a major loss for the company. Assume that a designer spends 100 hours on a complex drawing. The designer earns $10 an hour. The loss of the drawing represents $1000 in labor alone that must be duplicated just to re-create the file. Therefore, make backup copies of your drawings. A backup is just a duplicate of a file. If a file is deleted or lost, you can use the backup copy in its place.

Methods for backing up files abound. One of the simplest methods is to save a duplicate copy of a drawing during a drawing session. At the end of the day, for example, save your current drawing to the hard disk as you normally do when you work on a drawing. Then, use the SAVEAS command to save the drawing to a floppy disk as a backup. Or, if you prefer, copy the file using AutoCAD's File Utilities.

Using Other Backup Methods

In many companies in which the CAD workstations are networked, backing up files is the responsibility of a network administrator or the person who is responsible for managing the CAD system. In a networked environment, working drawings are often kept on a local workstation during preparation. It is the responsibility of the user to copy his or her drawings to a centralized network server at the end of the day so the network administrator can back up the files to tape. In other situations, the working drawings are kept on a network drive, and you do not need to worry about backups.

You should remember that having current backups of your drawing files is extremely important. If, as a student, you are responsible for creating backup copies of your work, and you lose one or more important drawings because you failed to back up, you might have to re-create the drawings or possibly fail the course. If you have the responsibility of backing up your files when you work for a company and you lose drawings that are not backed up, you might lose your job. Always be aware of the importance of maintaining backup copies and make a habit of routinely backing up your files.

Unit Review

What You've Learned

- The importance of file management
- How to copy, rename, and delete files using AutoCAD's file utilities
- How to create backups using AutoCAD commands
- The purpose and usefulness of backing up drawing files

Review Questions

True or False

08.01 T F Deleting a file usually erases it for good.

08.02 T F Copying a file creates a duplicate that has the same name.

08.03 T F Renaming a file changes the name of the file without changing the contents of the file.

08.04 T F Backing up files is important only in some situations.

08.05 T F An archive copy is a copy of a file usually placed on a floppy disk, central network server, or tape.

Multiple Choice

08.06 You can __________ an existing drawing file when you need to use it for a new project.

(A) copy

(B) rename

(C) delete

(D) none of the above

08.07 Which of the following buttons in the File Utilities dialog box should you use if you need to display the names of all the files in a directory? __________

(A) Rename file

(B) Copy file

(C) List files

(D) Delete file

Student: ____________________ Date: __________

Instructor: ____________________ Course: __________ Section: __________

08.08 You can use AutoCAD's __________ command to make a backup copy of a file onto a floppy disk.

(A) COPY

(B) BACKUP

(C) SAVEAS

(D) STORE

Short Answer

08.09 How do directories and subdirectories aid in file management?

____

____

____

08.10 Explain how to back up a drawing file quickly to a floppy disk.

____

____

____

Student: ______________________ Date: __________

Instructor: ____________________ Course: __________ Section: __________

PART II

Using Basic CAD Techniques

UNIT 9

Introduction to Drawing Setup

Many of the drawings you prepare with AutoCAD will have similar settings or will include the same data, such as a standard title block. Setting up these common items in each new drawing can be very time consuming. Fortunately, AutoCAD provides a means to automate the process. In this unit, you learn how to use a *prototype drawing* to automate drawing setup. Prototype drawings save you the work of reestablishing your drawing settings whenever you start a new drawing. You can even include entities such as borders and title blocks in your prototype drawings so that you do not have to redraw them every time.

The objectives of this unit are to:

- ☞ Understand the concept of prototype drawings
- ☞ Understand how to start a new drawing using a prototype
- ☞ Understand the prototype drawing options
- ☞ Understand what type of entities to include in a prototype drawing

Prototype drawings are used throughout *Hands On AutoCAD Release 12* to set up the drawings for many of the exercises. Understanding how to use prototype drawings will make it possible for you to work through the drawing exercises in the rest of the units.

Understanding Prototype Drawings

A prototype drawing is any drawing file that you want to use as a template whenever you start a new drawing. A prototype drawing can contain settings for such things as snap increment and grid size, drawing components such as layers and dimension styles, and drawing entities such as borders and title blocks.

Any step that you find yourself doing every time you start a new drawing is a likely candidate to become part of a prototype. Any settings or data in a prototype drawing are added automatically to your new drawing, eliminating the need for you to add the settings or data to the new drawing yourself.

AutoCAD comes with a minimal prototype drawing called ACAD.DWG, which AutoCAD uses by default. If you use this as your own prototype drawing, you'll soon find yourself making the same initial settings over and over again. Fortunately, it is easy to modify the prototype drawing, and to use a different drawing as your prototype. You can select any drawing to be your prototype drawing when you open the Create New Drawing dialog box.

There is nothing unique about a drawing that becomes a prototype. Any AutoCAD drawing can be used as a prototype for any other drawing.

In the majority of the exercises in *Hands On AutoCAD Release 12*, you will use prototype drawings to provide a starting point for the exercises. In many cases, the prototype drawings provide a partially complete drawing to which you will add new information or modify existing information in the drawing. Whenever you need to use a prototype drawing in an exercise, you will see an instruction similar to the following as the first step in the exercise:

`Begin a new drawing name 009???01 in your assigned directory, using the file 009LAYER as a prototype.`

For the new drawing name, substitute your initials, or a code assigned to you by your instructor, in place of the question marks in the instruction. If your name is Mary Jane Doe, for example, the new drawing file name should be 009MJD01. In addition, you must specify the disk and directory in which AutoCAD will create the new file.

Where you locate your drawing files depends on the type of system you are using, whether the system is networked, and how your instructor has set up your AutoCAD environment. Your assigned directory may be a directory on your local hard disk, or a directory on a remote network server. Check with your instructor if you are not sure where your drawings should be located. In the next exercise, you learn how to specify the directory where your drawing should be created.

It is important that you place your drawing files in the proper location. If you place your drawing files in the wrong directory or on the wrong disk, someone else may overwrite them or erase them. In addition, your instructor may have configured your system so that your assigned directory will be backed up on a regular basis. If your drawings are not in the proper location, they will not be backed up. This increases the risk that you could lose a drawing.

The file name specified in the instruction as the prototype file will be located somewhere on your system where you can access it. As with your own drawing files, the location of your prototype drawings will vary according to your system's configuration. Your instructor will explain to you where your prototype drawings can be found. In the next exercise, you learn how to specify the location of the prototype drawing.

Avoid overwriting a prototype drawing with your own drawing, or modifying a prototype drawing. Other students may be using the same prototype; if you change it, you will affect your own drawings and those of other students.

Starting a New Drawing

When AutoCAD starts, it opens the drawing editor and displays a new, blank drawing. You can begin drawing immediately without giving your new drawing a name. To begin working on a new drawing and to assign a prototype to it, use the NEW command (type it at the keyboard, or pick it from the pull-down menus).

Starting a New Drawing

1. `Command:` *Choose* File, *then* New *(see fig. 9.1)*	Displays the Create New Drawing dialog box

continues

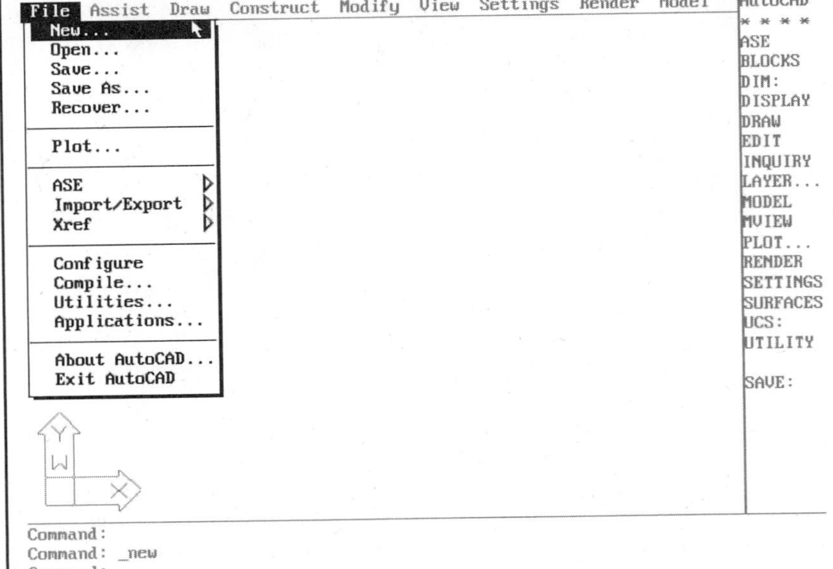

Figure 9.1

Select New from the File pull-down to start a new drawing.

Figure 9.2

The Create New Drawing Dialog Box.

The Create New Drawing dialog box appears (see fig. 9.2). The upper box, beside the Prototype button, is already filled in with the file name ACAD, AutoCAD's default prototype drawing.

2. *Choose the* Prototype *button*	Displays Prototype Drawing File dialog box (see fig. 9.3)

A list of potential prototype drawings appears in the list box (see fig. 9.3). AutoCAD first assumes that your prototype drawings will be stored in AutoCAD's SUPPORT subdirectory because that is the default location for ACAD.DWG. When you choose a prototype drawing in a new directory, that directory becomes the directory that is automatically displayed in the dialog box. The Pattern box filters out all file names that do not have a DWG extension.

3. *Use the* Directories *and* Files *list boxes to locate the prototype file* 009PROTO *(in the directory assigned for prototype drawings by your instructor), then choose OK*	Specifies the prototype drawing to use for your new drawing

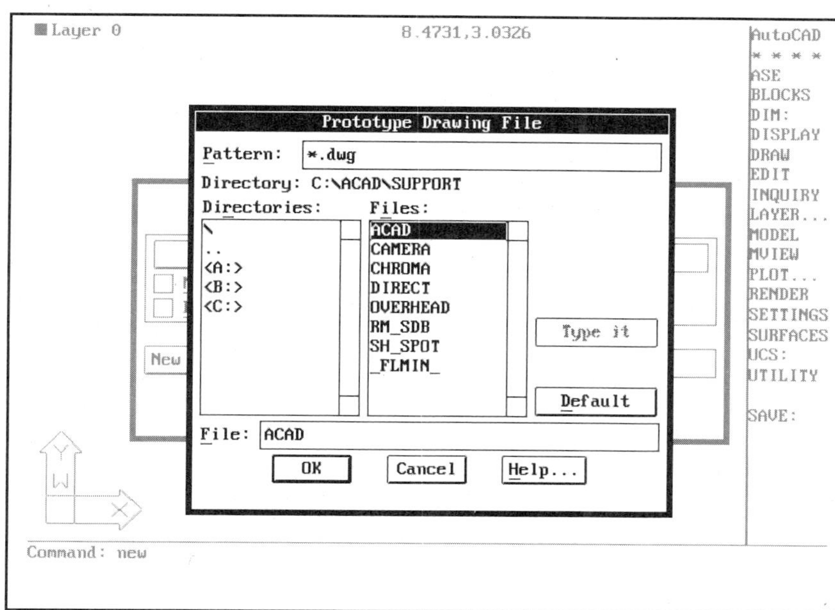

Figure 9.3

The Prototype Drawing File Dialog Box.

4. *In the* Create New Drawing dialog *box, enter* **009???01** *in the* New Drawing Name *edit box, (substituting your initials or code in place of ???) then choose* OK

   Specifies the name of the prototype drawing to use and returns to the drawing editor

5. `Command:` *Choose* File, *then* Save

   `_qsave`

   Saves your new drawing using the name you specified in the previous step

It is not necessary to enter a drawing name in the Start New Drawing dialog box. AutoCAD will let you create and edit a drawing with or without a drawing name. You will be prompted for a name the first time you save the drawing.

Setting Prototype Drawing Options

Two options that are set by controls in the Create New Drawing dialog box are No Prototype and Retain as Default. Most of the time you probably will want to start a new drawing using settings you already have specified, but occasionally you will need to start a new drawing using AutoCAD's default settings. Most often you do this if you want to bring a DXF file made by AutoCAD or another graphics program into the drawing editor. The No Prototype option is useful in this situation.

DXF is short for Drawing Exchange Format *and is the extension for a special type of text file that represents drawing geometry using text. AutoCAD's drawing file format (DWG). A DXF file contains all the information found in a drawing file, but in a format that can be read by other CAD, graphics, and illustration programs. In addition, DXF files enable data from other graphics programs to be imported into AutoCAD. AutoCAD must have its default settings current to be able to read in a DXF file completely. It therefore is important that you specify no prototype drawing when importing a DXF file into AutoCAD.*

Using No Prototype Drawing

1. `Command:` *Choose* File, *then* New	Displays the Create New Drawing dialog box
2. *In the* Create New Drawing *dialog box, check the* No Prototype *check box*	Dims the Prototype button and file name edit box (see fig. 9.4)
3. *Choose the* Cancel *button*	Starts a new drawing without a prototype

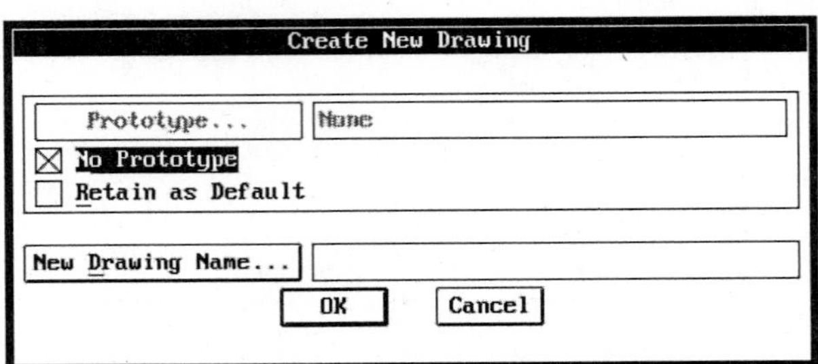

Figure 9.4
The Create New Drawing Dialog Box set to No Prototype.

You do not have to start a new drawing using ACAD.DWG as the default prototype. You can use the Retain as Prototype check box in the Create New Drawing dialog box to configure AutoCAD to use any drawing you like as the default prototype whenever you start a new drawing.

Establishing a New Prototype Drawing

1. `Command:` *Choose* File, *then* New	Displays the Create New Drawing dialog box
2. *Choose the* Prototype *button*	Displays the Prototype Drawing File dialog box

3. *Locate and choose the file* 009PROT2 *in your assigned prototype directory, then choose* OK	Chooses a new prototype drawing
4. *Check the* Retain as Default *check box, then choose* OK	Sets new drawing as prototype for all future new drawings (see fig. 9.5)

Verify your new setting by invoking the NEW command again.

5. `Command:` *Choose* File, *then* New	The Prototype edit box displays the new drawing name (see fig. 9.5)

Next, reset ACAD as the default prototype drawing.

6. `Command:` *Choose* File, *then* New	Displays the Create New Drawing dialog box
7. *Choose the* Prototype *button*	Displays the Prototype Drawing File dialog box
8. *Locate and choose the file* ACAD *in your assigned prototype directory, or in the AutoCAD SUPPORT directory, then choose* OK	Chooses ACAD as the new prototype drawing
9. *Check the* Retain as Default *check box, then choose* OK	Sets new drawing as prototype for all future new drawings

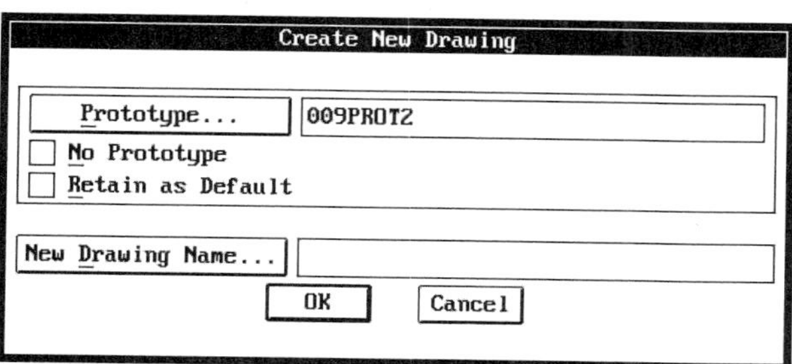

Figure 9.5

The Create New Drawing Dialog Box.

To place entities in a prototype drawing, or to configure a prototype drawing with specific settings, simply create the drawing as you would any other AutoCAD drawing, adding the common entities and settings. Then, save the drawing to disk. When you want to use the drawing as a prototype, simply choose it in the Create New Drawing dialog box.

Unit Review

What You've Learned

- What a prototype drawing is
- How to start a new drawing using AutoCAD's default settings
- Where to place your new drawings
- How to make any drawing a default prototype drawing
- How to add settings and entities to a prototype drawing

Review Questions

True or False

9.01 T F A prototype drawing is different from a standard AutoCAD drawing file.

9.02 T F Prototype drawings may not contain entities.

9.03 T F Any drawing can be used as a prototype for any other drawing.

9.04 T F Settings for grid and snap can be stored in a prototype drawing.

9.05 T F Title blocks and other standard data often are contained in prototype drawings.

Multiple Choice

9.06 The default location for prototype drawing storage is ____________.

(A) the AutoCAD directory

(B) the AutoCAD SUPPORT directory

(C) the DRAWING directory

(D) none of the above

Student: ____________ Date: ____________

Instructor: ____________ Course: ____________ Section: ____________

9.07 The Retain as Default check box in the Create New Drawing dialog box: ____________________.

(A) establishes a new prototype drawing until you exit AutoCAD

(B) establishes a permanent new prototype drawing

(C) saves the last change you made in the current prototype drawing

(D) resets the prototype drawing to the default AutoCAD settings

Short Answer

9.08 Describe a situation when it is necessary to start a new drawing with the No Prototype check box selected.

____

____

____

9.09 Explain how a prototype drawing can be used to automate the creation of a title block.

____

____

____

9.10 Briefly explain the process for creating a new prototype drawing.

____

____

____

Student: ____________________ Date: ____________________

Instructor: ____________________ Course: ____________________ Section: ____________________

UNIT 10

Understanding Graphic Entities

This unit examines two methods that computer graphics programs can use to draw and store graphic entities—*vector graphics* and *raster graphics*. To use AutoCAD efficiently, you need to understand how AutoCAD uses and stores graphic information. Nearly every action you perform in AutoCAD is affected by vector graphics because AutoCAD uses these types of graphics. Every decision you make about how and why you draw an entity is based on an understanding of vector graphics.

The objectives for this unit are to:

- ☞ Define vector-based graphics
- ☞ Define the AutoCAD drawing database
- ☞ Define raster graphics
- ☞ Understand the differences between vector and raster graphics and the implications of those differences
- ☞ Recognize the AutoCAD graphic entities

Understanding Vector and Raster Graphics

AutoCAD uses both vector and raster graphics. As a drafter or designer, however, you will use AutoCAD's vector graphics almost exclusively. The following section explains vector graphics and how AutoCAD uses them to store and display graphic entities.

Understanding Vector Graphics

A *graphic entity* in AutoCAD is any singular element of a drawing such as a line, circle, arc, ellipse, line of text, or dimension. AutoCAD recognizes each of these drawing elements and considers the element a unique piece of data that it can manipulate and display.

The term *vector graphics* refers to a process in which graphic entities are stored and drawn by a program. In a program that uses vector graphics to draw geometry, many entities are defined by their *vectors.* A vector describes the direction and magnitude of a graphic entity. For instance, a line in AutoCAD has a start point and an end point. These two points define the line's vector by controlling the line's length, location in space, and direction. Different types of entities have different types of information associated with them. A circle, for example, has a center point and radius; an ellipse has a major and a minor axis and a center point.

In AutoCAD, you draw entities by specifying information about the entity. For example, you can draw a line by specifying the line's start point and end point. You can draw a circle by specifying its center and radius.

Understanding Raster Graphics

Raster graphics define a graphic image in terms of *pixels* rather than entities. Think of a pixel as a single point of light on your screen. Each pixel in a raster image is defined separately. The only information that is required to define a raster image is the coordinates of each pixel and its color. Figure 10.1 shows an example for a very small 9×9 raster image. Each point in the grid represents a pixel. Notice that each point is drawn individually and is not related to any other point.

Although the pixels in figure 10.1 define what appears to be a line, the image actually is just a collection of dots (pixels) that happen to line up with one another to form the *appearance* of a line.

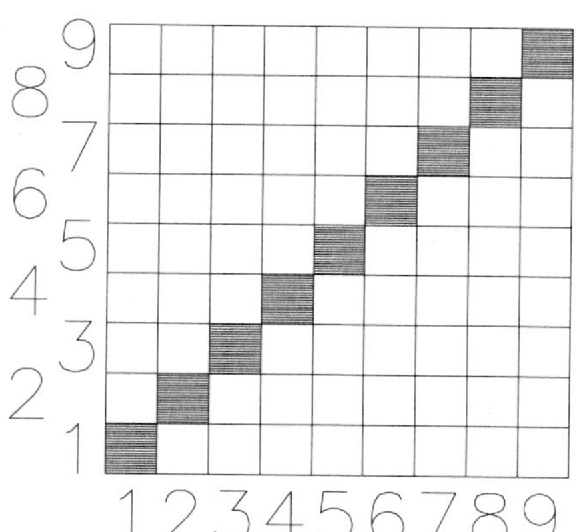

Figure 10.1

A sample raster image.

Raster graphics are often used when the image being drawn is a two-dimensional visual representation, such as a digitized photograph. Actual models or objects are created using vector graphics. For example, the photographs in a newspaper are raster graphics made up of small dots of ink.

Comparing AutoCAD's Vector Graphics with Raster Graphics

Figure 10.2 shows two lines. The left line is a vector graphic; the right line is a raster graphic. Consider how rough the raster line looks compared to the vector line, even though the amount of data required to store the raster line is much greater than that of the vector line.

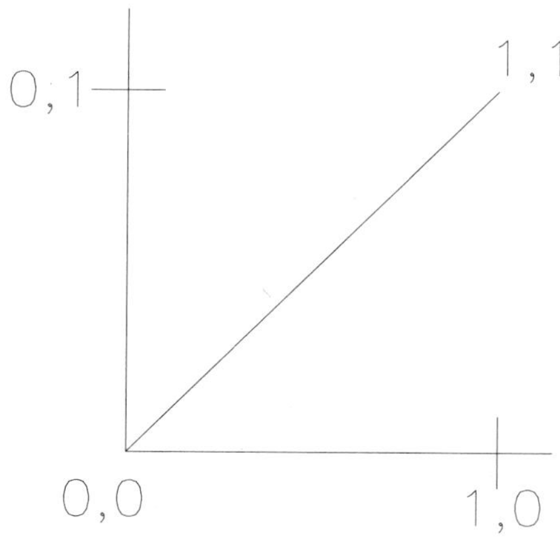

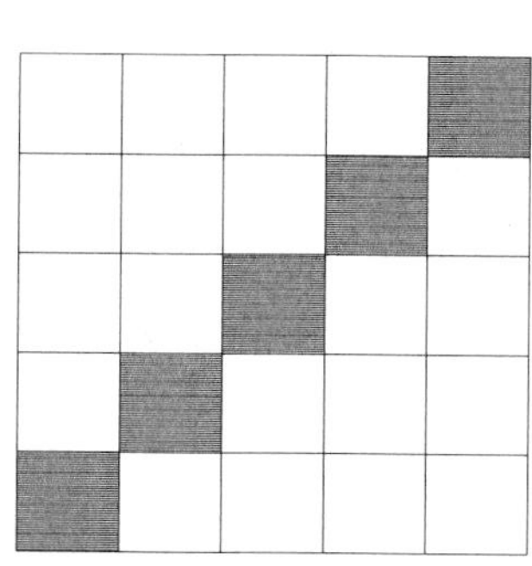

Figure 10.2

A vector graphic of a line and a raster graphic of a line.

Vector data defines an entity rather than a series of unrelated points, enabling AutoCAD to offer you a number of useful features. AutoCAD can find the exact start point, end point, and midpoint of the line. AutoCAD can also find points relative to other entities, such as intersections and tangent points. You can select the entire entity by selecting any one point on the entity.

Edit functions enable you to trim and erase entire entities with a minimum of effort and a maximum of accuracy. These types of operations are not possible with raster graphics; for this reason, vector graphics are sometimes referred to as *intelligent graphics.* The main advantages of vector graphics over raster graphics, therefore, are improved image quality and the ability to edit easily graphic entities that make up the image or drawing.

Understanding the Drawing Database

Each entity in an AutoCAD drawing is defined by various types of information about the entity. To store the entities, AutoCAD creates a *drawing database.* The drawing database stores all the information that AutoCAD needs to reproduce and edit each graphic entity, such as the entity's type, color, linetype, and a unique name to identify the entity. The drawing database also stores the information necessary to reproduce a specific entity. For example, the entry in the drawing database for a line includes the line's start point and end point, as well as general information, such as color and linetype.

Figure 10.3 shows two lines drawn in AutoCAD and the vector definitions that were used to draw the lines. Figure 10.4 shows similar information for two circles.

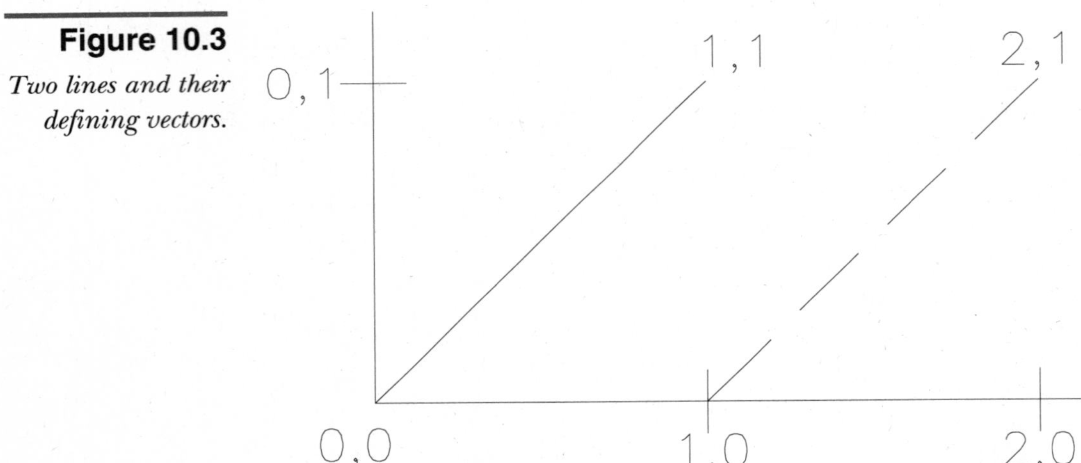

Figure 10.3

Two lines and their defining vectors.

Table 10.1 shows selected information from the drawing database for each of the entities in figures 10.3 and 10.4. The entities listed in Table 10.1 were created using different methods, but the resulting types of data in each entry are the same. AutoCAD provides many methods to draw a particular type of entity, even though the way the entity is stored is identical in each case.

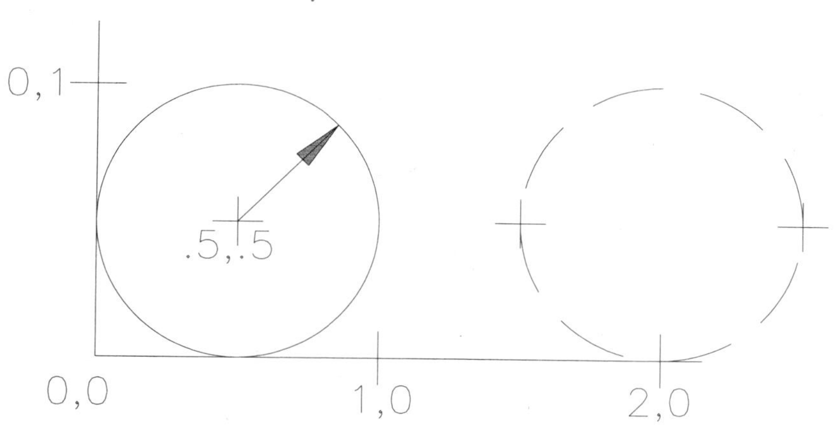

Figure 10.4

Two circles and their defining vectors.

Table 10.1
Entries in a Drawing Database

Name	Type	Start Point	End Point	Color	Linetype
0001	Line	0.0,0.0,0.0	1.0,1.0,0.0	0	Continuous
0002	Line	1.0,0.0,0.0	2.0,1.0,0.0	0	Hidden
Name	**Type**	**Center Point**	**Radius**	**Color**	**Linetype**
0003	Circle	0.5,0.5,0.0	0.5	0	Continuous
0004	Circle	2.0,0.5,0.0	0.5	0	Hidden

An important concept to understand is whenever you create a drawing in AutoCAD, you really are building a database list of the entities in the drawing, rather than actually generating a drawing on-screen. The AutoCAD drawing display simply serves as a representation of the drawing database to make it easy for you to work with the data in a drawing.

AutoCAD's Graphic Entities

The AutoCAD database stores eighteen different types of entities. Of these eighteen, eight are true graphic entities, such as lines and circles. The others include such non-graphic features as text, dimensions, and the start and end points of complex entities. Figure 10.5 shows each of the graphic entities. Table 10.2 lists all of AutoCAD's graphic entities and some of the vector information that is stored in the AutoCAD drawing database for each entity. You learn about AutoCAD's other types of entities in later units.

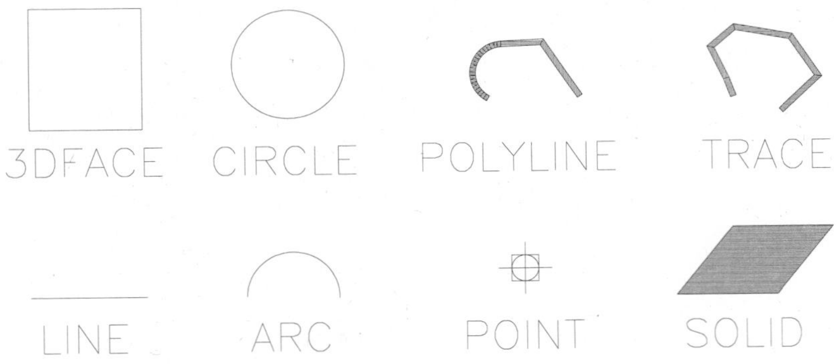

Figure 10.5
The AutoCAD Graphic Entities.

3DFACE CIRCLE POLYLINE TRACE

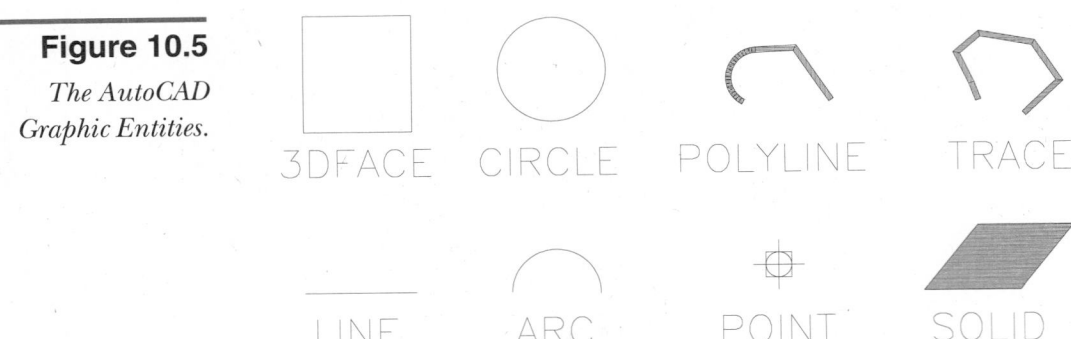

LINE ARC POINT SOLID

Table 10.2
The AutoCAD Graphic Entities

Entity	Unique data
3DFACE	Four Corners, Edge Visibility ON/OFF
ARC	Center, Radius, Start Angle, End Angle
CIRCLE	Center, Radius
LINE	Start Point, End Point
POINT	Point in Space , Orientation in Space
POLYLINE	Points in Space, Curve, Width
SOLID	Four Corners
TRACE	Four Corners

The following exercise takes you through the steps of drawing a graphic entity and displaying some of its stored data. Do not worry if you do not understand the exact process of producing the line or exactly what all the data means. The purpose of this exercise is to show you a vector graphic and some of its variables.

Creating a Vector Graphic

1. Begin a new drawing named 010???01 in your assigned directory, using the file 010PROTO as a prototype.

2. `Command:` *Choose* Draw, *then* Line, *then* 1 Segment — Begins the LINE command

3. `From point:` **`0,0`** ↵ — Specifies the beginning of the line segment

4. `To point:` **`1,1`** ↵ — Specifies the end of the line segment

   `To point:`

5. `Command:` *Choose* Assist, *then* Inquiry, *then* List — Begins the LIST command

   _list

6. `Select objects:` *Place the small cursor square (called the Pickbox) on the line you just drew and press the select button on the mouse or digitizer puck* — Selects the entity to list

7. `Select objects:` *Press* Enter — Ends object selection

The Graphics screen flips to the Text screen to list the line's data.

```
LINE   Layer: 0
       Space: Model space
from point, X=  0.0000 Y=  0.0000 Z=  0.0000
 to point, X=  1.0000 Y=  1.0000 Z=  0.0000
Length =  1.4142, angle in XY Plane =   45
Delta X =  1.0000, Delta Y =  1.0000, Delta Z = 0.0000
```

8. `Command:` *Press* F1 — Flips the Text screen back to the Graphics screen

9. `Command:` **`QUIT`** ↵ — Informs AutoCAD that you want to quit working with the Program

10. *Choose the* Discard Changes *button* — Quits AutoCAD without saving changes to the drawing

---

The main concept to understand about AutoCAD's entities is that entities are stored based on their defining data, such as end points, center points, and radii. Because the entity data is stored in this way, the entities can be edited easily. To change the linetype of a circle, for example, you simply use an AutoCAD command that enables you to change the linetype name stored with the circle in the drawing database. Although AutoCAD makes changes to a database, you only see graphical changes. You select the circle, and AutoCAD applies the new linetype to the circle. Changing the linetype of a circle drawn in a raster graphics image would require that you erase each of the dots (pixels) that makes up the image, then redraw the circle.

Unit Review

What You've Learned

- What are graphic entities in AutoCAD
- What is a vector graphic
- What is a raster graphic
- What is the drawing database and why it exists
- The advantages of vector graphics over raster graphics

Review Questions

True or False

10.01 T F The drawing database stores information about each entity in the drawing.

10.02 T F Raster images make it possible to calculate the midpoint of a line.

10.03 T F Raster Graphics are typically used for three-dimensional modeling.

10.04 T F Raster graphics define a graphic image in terms of pixels rather than entities.

10.05 T F A pixel is a single point of light on your monitor.

Multiple Choice

10.06 Because they allow advanced features and calculations, vector graphics are sometimes called ________________.

(A) functional

(B) intelligent

(C) graphic

(D) points

10.07 A vector shows ______________ and ______________.

(A) Magnitude

(B) Color

(C) Force

(D) Direction

Student: ____________________ Date: __________

Instructor: ____________________ Course: __________ Section: __________

10.08 The drawing database stores ____________ different graphic entities.

(A) 8

(B) 14

(C) 18

(D) 24

10.09 The unique vector data for a circle includes the __________ and the ______________.

(A) End point

(B) Radius

(C) Center

(D) Width

10.10 Vector graphics enable you to select an entity by picking ________________.

(A) Any point on the entity

(B) A pixel

(C) An entity

(D) A raster

Student: ______________ Date: ______________

Instructor: ______________ Course: ______________ Section: ______________

UNIT 11

Drawing Lines

The most common entity created in any form of drafting is a line segment. Lines are used for everything from borders to object lines. In addition, lines are often used in construction geometry to help you find the points for other entities. The use of lines is so important—lines are in almost every facet of drafting—that lines are introduced before any other AutoCAD entity.

The objectives for this unit are to:

- Access the LINE command
- Draw single and multiple line segments
- Draw continued line segments
- Draw double lines with DLINE

Drawing Line Segments

As you will learn in this unit's exercises, you can access the LINE command from the pull-down menu, the screen menu, or by entering **LINE** at the `Command:` prompt. You also can enter **L** at the `Command:` prompt as a shortcut to start the LINE command.

Regardless of how you access the LINE command, you always are prompted for two pieces of information. The first is the beginning of the line, and the second is the end of the line. In most cases, you are repeatedly prompted for the end point of the next segment in the series of lines.

The next three exercises introduce you to the LINE command and show you how to use the pull-down menu to access the LINE command. Do not worry about picking points exactly; precision is covered in units 12 and 13.

Using the Pull-down Menu To Access LINE

1. Begin a new drawing named 011???01 in your assigned directory, using the file 011PROTO as a prototype. Figure 11.1 shows the completed exercise.

2. `Command:` *Choose* Draw, *then* Line, *then* Segments	Starts the LINE command
3. `_line From point:` *Pick a point at* ① *(see fig. 11.1)*	Specifies the beginning of the line segment

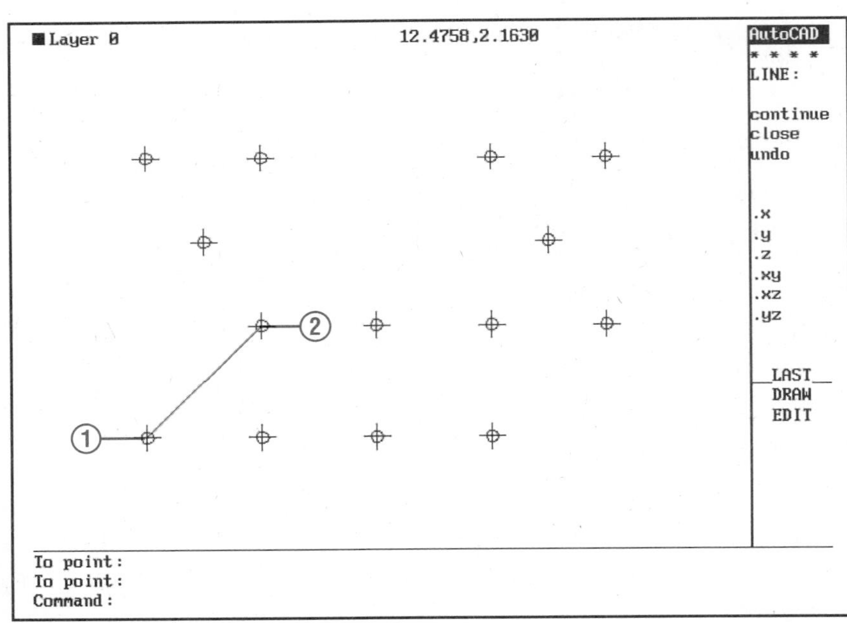

Figure 11.1

A line drawn with the LINE command.

4. `To point:` *Pick a point at* ② *(see fig. 11.1)*	Specifies the end of the line segment
5. `To point:` *Press* Enter	Ends the LINE command

As you saw in the previous exercise, the LINE command continues to prompt you for successive end points with the `To point:` prompt. The LINE command continues to prompt you for the end points of new segments until you end the LINE command by pressing Enter or Ctrl+C. The next exercise shows you how to use the LINE command to draw a series of connecting line segments.

Drawing a Series of Line Segments

Continue with your drawing from the previous exercise.

1. `Command:` *Choose* Draw, *then* Line, *then* Segments	Starts the LINE command
2. `Command: _line From point:`*Pick a point at* ① *(see fig. 11.2)*	Specifies the beginning of the line segment

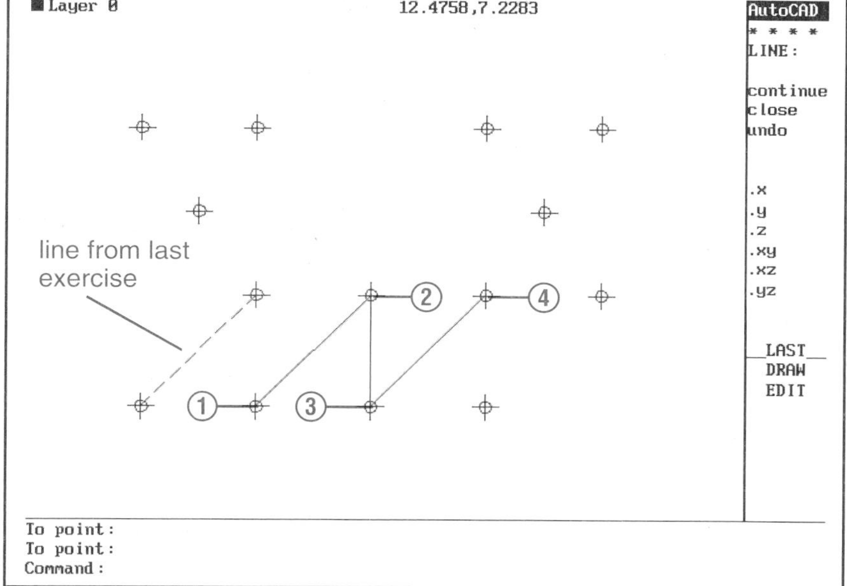

Figure 11.2
A series of contiguous line segments.

3. `To point:` *Pick a point at* ②	Specifies the end of the first line segment
4. `To point:` *Pick a point at* ③	Specifies the end of the second line segment

continues

5. `To point:` *Pick a point at* ④ — Specifies the end of the third line segment

6. `To point:` *Press* Enter — Ends the LINE command

The dashed lines in figure 11.2 are from the last drawing exercise and are not lines drawn with a different linetype.

There are times when you may want to draw a single line segment. The following exercise shows you how to use the 1 Segment option of the Line cascading menu to draw a single segment. Notice that the final `To point:` prompt is automatically filled with an Enter. The screen menu and `Command:` prompt do not offer this feature.

Drawing a Single Line Segment

Continue with your drawing from the previous exercise.

1. `Command:` *Choose* Draw, *then* Line, *then* 1 Segment — Starts the LINE command to draw a single segment

   `line`

2. `From point:` *Pick a point at* ① *(see fig. 11.3)* — Specifies the beginning of the line segment

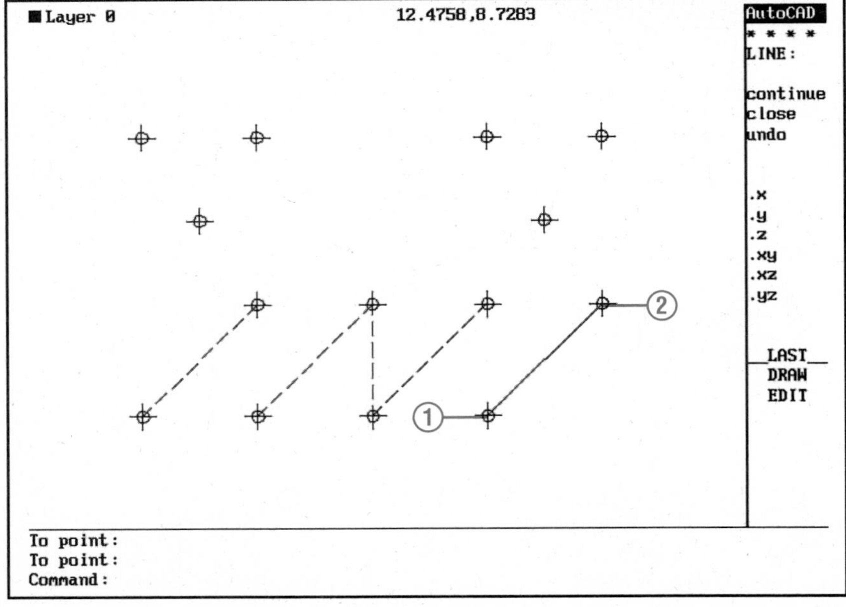

Figure 11.3

A single line segment drawn with the 1 Segment option.

3. `To point:` *Pick a point at* ② *(see fig. 11.3)* — Specifies the end of the line segment

   `To point:`

The LINE command offers three options in addition to entering coordinates: Continue, close, and undo. Close and undo are described next and shown in the following exercise.

Using the Close and Undo Options

The close option sets the `To point:` to the same value as the first `From point:` in the chain of segments creating a polygon. Close also ends the LINE command. Because a polygon must have at least three sides, you must have at least two contiguous line segments before you can use the close option to create the final line segment. To use the close option, you can choose close from the LINE screen menu or enter C or Close at the `Command:` prompt.

The undo option removes the last point picked and the associated line segment. You can use undo after picking your `From point:` if you do not like your starting point or after picking any `To point:` if you do not like the last line segment drawn. To use the undo option, choose undo from the LINE screen menu or enter U or Undo at the `Command:` prompt.

The next exercise shows you how to use the close and undo options.

Using Close and Undo

Continue with your drawing from the previous exercise.

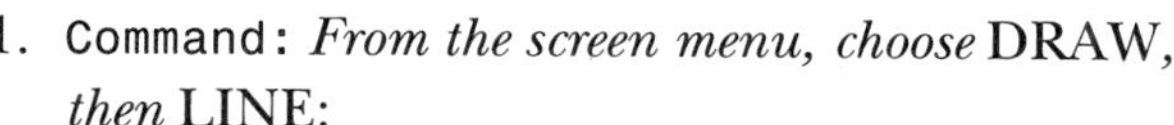

1. `Command:` *From the screen menu, choose* DRAW, *then* LINE: — Starts the LINE command command
2. `_LINE From point:` *Pick a point at* ① *(see fig 11.4)* — Specifies the beginning of the line segment
3. `To point:` *From the LINE screen menu, choose* undo — Undoes the previous point selection
4. `To point: _U`

   `All segments already undone.`
5. `From point:` *Pick a point at* ② *(see fig 11.4)* — Specifies the beginning of the line segment
6. `To point:` *Pick a point at* ③ *(see fig 11.4)* — Specifies the end of the first line segment

continues

7. `To point:` *Pick a point at* ④ *(see fig 11.4)* — Specifies the end of the second line segment

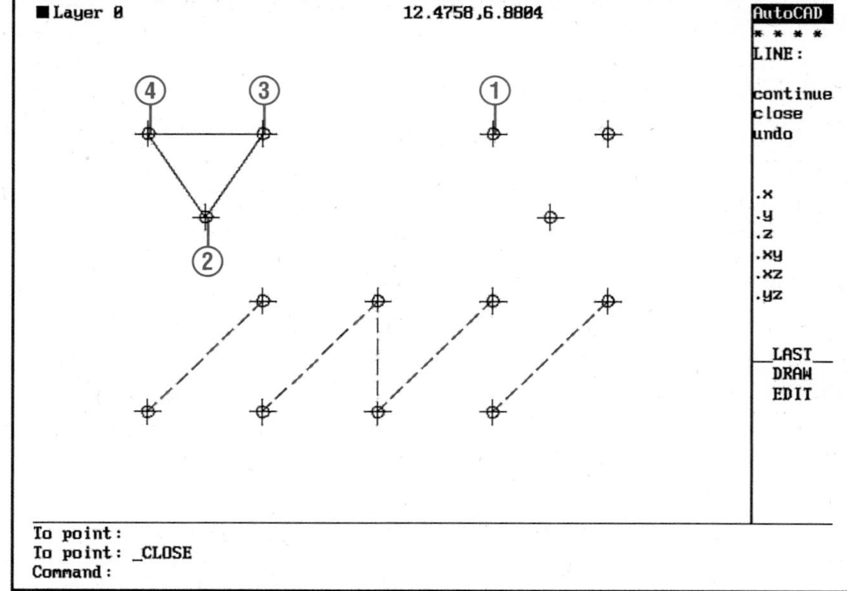

Figure 11.4
A polygon drawn with the close option.

8. `To point:` *From the LINE screen menu, choose* close — Selects the close option

9. `To point: _CLOSE` — Closes the polygon and ends the LINE command

Drawing Continued Line Segments

The LINE command offers an option called Continue. Continue causes a line to begin at the last point picked or entered. This allows you to create contiguous line segments without drawing all of the line segments with one LINE command.

You can press Enter *or the spacebar at the* `From point:` *prompt to continue a LINE segment from the last point picked.*

The following exercise shows you how to use the Continue option.

Using the Continue Option of the LINE Command

Continue with your drawing from the previous exercise.

1. `Command:` *Choose* Draw, *then* Line, *then* Segments	Starts the LINE command for multiple line segments
2. `_line From point:` *Pick a point at* ① *(see fig. 11.5)*	Specifies the beginning of the line segment
3. `To point:` *Pick a point at* ② *(see fig. 11.5)*	Specifies the end point of the first line segment
4. `To point:` *Pick a point at* ③ *(see fig. 11.5)*	Specifies the end point of the second line segment
5. `To point:` *Press* Enter	Ends the LINE command
6. `Command:` *From the LINE screen menu, choose* continue	Begins the LINE command and automatically selects starting point of the line
`From point:`	Automatically specifies the last point entered
7. `To point:` *Pick a point at* ① *(see fig. 11.5)*	Specifies the second point of the line segment

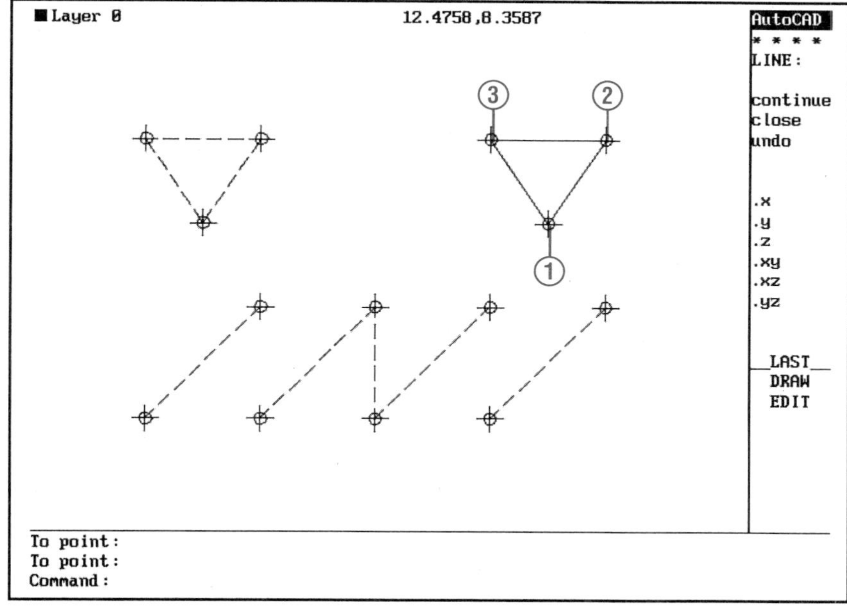

Figure 11.5

A series of contiguous line segments drawn with the continue option.

8. `To point:` *Press* Enter	Ends the LINE command

Drawing Double Lines

AutoCAD Release 12 introduced a new command called DLINE. The DLINE command draws two contiguous parallel lines or arcs (or both) from a starting point to an ending point like the LINE command. The parallel lines are offset from the temporary line created by the points you pick. The temporary line is called a *dragline.*

To access the DLINE command from the pull-down menu, choose Draw, then Line, then Double Lines. To access the Double Line command from the `Command:` prompt, enter **`DLINE`**.

Double Line is very useful for drawing perimeters such as walls as well as any two-line image such as a stud or pipe.

Options of the Double Line Command

The DLINE command displays the following prompt and has these options:

```
Break/CAps/Dragline/Offset/Snap/Undo/Width/<start point>:
```

Figure 11.6 shows some of these options at different settings.

- **Break.** Determines whether AutoCAD automatically creates a gap in any line that exactly intersects with the start or end point of the double line.
- **Caps.** Determines if there should be caps at the start, end, or both ends of the double line. The Auto option of Caps creates a gap in any line that exactly intersects the start or end point of the double line and places caps on all other start or end points.
- **Dragline.** Dragline determines the location of the dragline relative to the parallel lines. The dragline can be set to the left parallel line, the center of the lines, or the right parallel line. You can also set a distance to offset from each of those points.
- **Offset.** Determines the start of a double line based on a specific distance and direction from a base point. This lets you set the double line's beginning point relative to another point in the drawing.
- **Snap.** Determines if the double line should be continued to exactly intersect with a nearby line. In addition, you can set how close a line must be before Double Line snaps to it.
- **Undo.** Removes the last point selected. This works just like the undo option of the LINE command.

- **Width.** Determines the distance between the parallel lines.
- **<start point>.** Locates the beginning of the parallel lines.

After you have picked a starting point, Double Line displays the following prompt.

```
Arc/Break/CAps/CLose/Dragline/Snap/Undo/Width<next point>:
```

The new options that appear include:

- **Arc.** Draws parallel arcs rather than lines. The options presented by Arc are not covered here. For more information on drawing arcs, see unit 14.
- **Close.** Draws a final double line segment from the current point to the first point picked in the current double line segment. This works exactly like the close option of the LINE command.
- **<next point>.** Locates the end point of the next double line segment.

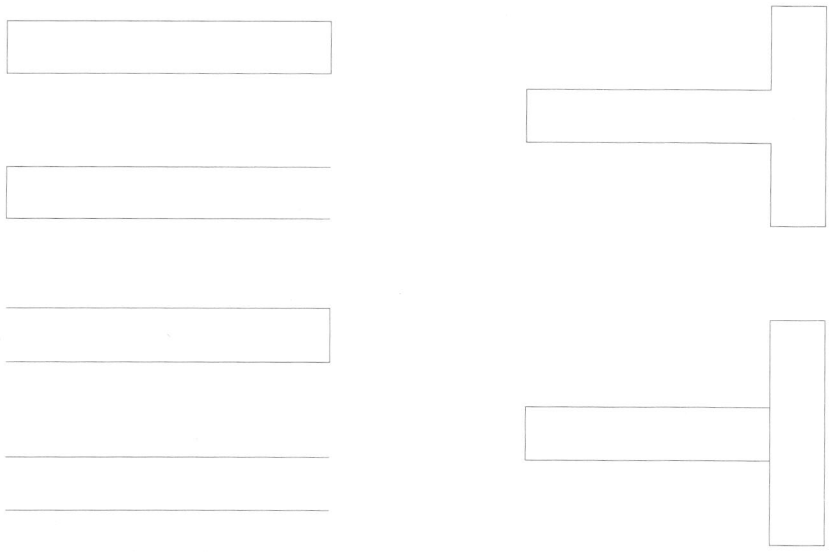

Figure 11.6

Examples of the DLINE command options.

The following exercise teaches you how to draw an exterior wall using the DLINE command. All of the options are used at their default setting except width, which is reset to nine units to approximate an exterior wall.

Drawing Double Lines

1. Begin a new drawing named 011???02 in your assigned directory, using the file 011PROT2 as a prototype.
2. `Command:` *Choose* Draw, *then* Line, *then* Double Lines — Starts the DLINE command

continues

`dline`

`Initializing... DLINE loaded.`

`Dline, Version 1.11, (c) 1990-1992 by Autodesk, Inc.`

3. `Break/CAps/Dragline/Offset/Snap/ Undo/Width/<start point>:` **`W`** ↵	Chooses the width option
4. `New DLINE width <0.0500>:` **`9`** ↵	Sets the width of the double line to nine units
5. `Arc/Break/CAps/Dragline/Offset/Snap/ Undo/Width/<start point>:` *Pick a point at* ① *(see fig 11.7)*	Selects the starting point point of the double line
6. `Arc/Break/CAps/CLose/Dragline/Snap/ Undo/Width/<next point>:` *Pick a point at* ②	Selects the next point of the double line
7. `Arc/Break/CAps/CLose/Dragline/Snap/ Undo/Width/<next point>:` *Pick a point at* ③	Selects the next point of the double line
8. `Arc/Break/CAps/CLose/Dragline/Snap/ Undo/Width/<next point>:` *Pick a point at* ④	Selects the next point of the double line

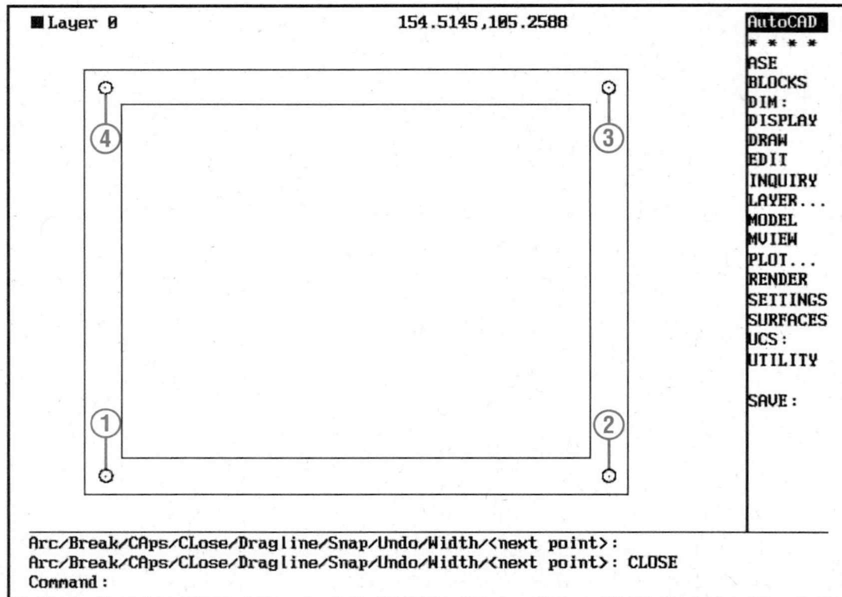

Figure 11.7

Exterior walls drawn with the Double Line command.

9. `Arc/Break/CAps/CLose/Dragline/Snap/ Undo/Width/<next point>:` **`CLOSE`** ↵	Closes the double line

Experiment on your own with the options of the DLINE command.

Unit Review

What You've Learned

- How to access the LINE command
- The options of the LINE command and how to access the options
- How to use the options of the LINE command
- How to access the DLINE command
- How to use a few options of the DLINE command

Review Questions

True or False

11.01 T F The LINE command can be accessed from the pull-down menu, the screen menu, and the `Command:` prompt.

11.02 T F You can type L at the `Command:` prompt as a shortcut to start the LINE command.

11.03 T F The LINE command draws only one line segment before returning you to the `Command:` prompt.

11.04 T F DLINE can be accessed from the screen menu.

11.05 T F The Close option of the LINE command completes a series of line segments to make a polygon.

11.06 T F A dragline determines where the parallel lines of the DLINE command are drawn.

11.07 T F The LINE command draws double lines.

Multiple Choice

11.08 The undo option of the LINE command removes ________________.

(A) the last line drawn

(B) the last point selected

(C) the close option only

(D) a continued line only

Student: ____________________ Date: __________

Instructor: ____________________ Course: __________ Section: __________

11.09 You can enter __________ or __________ at the `Command:` prompt to access the DLINE command.

(A) DLINE

(B) Double Line

(C) L

(D) DL

Additional Exercises

11.10 Using the LINE and DLINE commands, draw figure 11.8.

Figure 11.8

Exercise with LINE and Double Line.

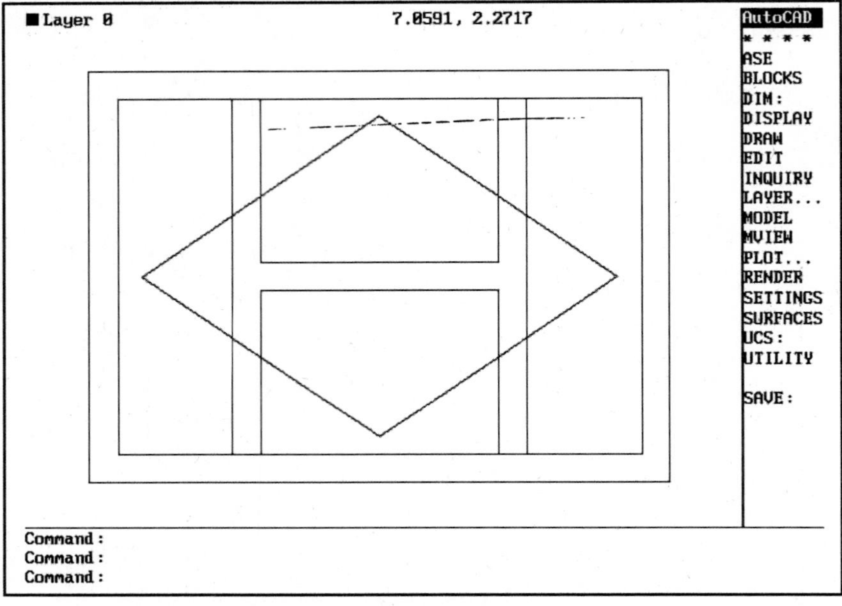

Student: __________ Date: __________

Instructor: __________ Course: __________ Section: __________

Introduction to Coordinates and Points

ou learn in later units that you can set up AutoCAD to use a snap increment and grid to help you accurately locate points in a drawing. Most often, however, you use coordinates to specify exact points and create accurate drawings. AutoCAD uses a Cartesian coordinate system for locating exact points in a drawing. This unit helps you understand the two-dimensional coordinate system in locating points and drawing lines using four different methods—absolute, relative, absolute polar, and relative polar.

The objectives for this unit are to:

- Understand the two-dimensional coordinate system
- Use absolute coordinates
- Use relative coordinates
- Use relative and absolute polar coordinates

Understanding Cartesian Coordinates

The two-dimensional coordinate system is composed of two perpendicular axes. The horizontal axis is called the X axis, and the vertical axis is called the Y axis. The origin is the point at the intersection of the X axis and the Y axis.

You can specify the location of a point in a drawing by specifying its coordinates. A two-dimensional coordinate includes two ordinate values that identify a coordinate based on its distance from the X and Y axes. The coordinate consists of two numbers separated by a comma, such as 2.5,2.75. The first ordinate value is the location of the point along the X axis, and the second ordinate value is the location of the point along the Y axis.

Measuring horizontally to the right of the origin are positive X values; to the left of the origin are negative X values. Measuring vertically above the origin are positive Y values, and below are negative Y values. At the origin, the X and Y values are both zero. Therefore, the coordinate of the origin is 0,0.

There are four quadrants, with Quadrant I in the upper right. Moving from Quadrant I in a counterclockwise direction around the origin, Quadrant II is upper left, Quadrant III is lower left, and Quadrant IV is lower right. Figure 12.1 is an illustration of the two-dimensional coordinate system.

Figure 12.1

The two-dimensional Cartesian coordinate system.

Locating a point using X and Y coordinates specifies its exact location relative to the origin. Using coordinates, you can locate a point with precision at the necessary location in the drawing. The accuracy of the drawing is limited only by the rounding off factor of the coordinate values. AutoCAD itself is accurate to 14 decimal places. Figure 12.2 shows examples of points and their coordinate values.

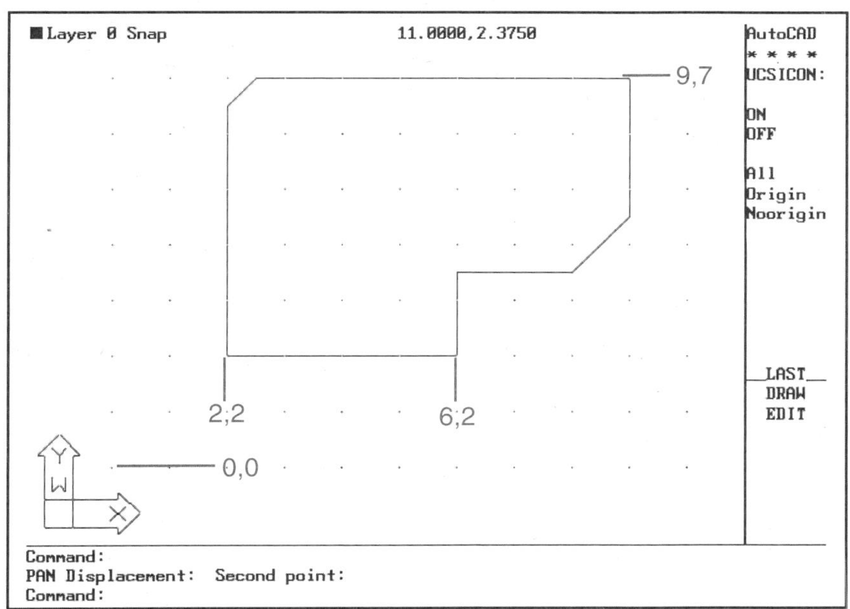

Figure 12.2

Locating points in the coordinate system.

When you begin a drawing, AutoCAD starts with the origin at the lower left corner of the display, but you can pan and zoom the display to move the location of the origin. These display-control commands are explained in units 18, "Using ZOOM to Control the Display" and 19, "Using PAN to Control the Display."

You can use the cursor to pick points, but to accurately specify a point, you often must enter its coordinates using the keyboard. The next section explains the two main methods for specifying points in AutoCAD.

Using Coordinates in AutoCAD

The two methods for specifying rectangular coordinate points are absolute and relative. An *absolute coordinate* is always measured from the origin (coordinate 0,0). A *relative coordinate* is always measured from the last point input. The last point is most often set by picking a point with the cursor or entering a coordinate at the keyboard.

Entering Absolute Coordinates

To specify an absolute coordinate in response to a prompt by AutoCAD to specify a point, enter the X ordinate, followed by a comma, and then the Y ordinate, such as 4,2. Then press Enter to input the value to AutoCAD.

The AutoCAD status line contains a coordinate display that, when you turn it on, shows the coordinate location of the cursor as it moves. To turn on coordinate display, press F6. You can switch the coordinate display from absolute readout to relative readout, which shows the current distance and angle from the last point. To change coordinate display mode, press F6 again.

In the following exercise, draw a few lines using absolute point specification. After you finish the exercise, your drawing should look similar to figure 12.3.

Absolute points work well when you know the absolute coordinates of the

Drawing Lines Using Absolute Coordinates

1. Begin a new drawing named 012???01 in your assigned directory using ACAD as the prototype.

2.	`Command:` *Choose* Draw, *then* Line, then Segments _line	Issues the LINE command to draw multiple segments
3.	`From point:` **`2,2`** ↵	Starts line at ① (see fig. 12.3)
4.	`To point:` **`6,2`** ↵	Draws line to ②
5.	`To point:` **`6,3.5`** ↵	Draws line to ③
6.	`To point:` **`8,3.5`** ↵	Draws line to ④
7.	`To point:` *Press* Enter	Ends LINE command
8.	`Command:` *Press* Enter	Repeats previous command
9.	`LINE From point:` **`2,2`** ↵	Starts line at ①
10.	`To point:` **`2,6.5`** ↵	Draws line to ⑤
11.	`To point:` *Press* Enter	Ends LINE command

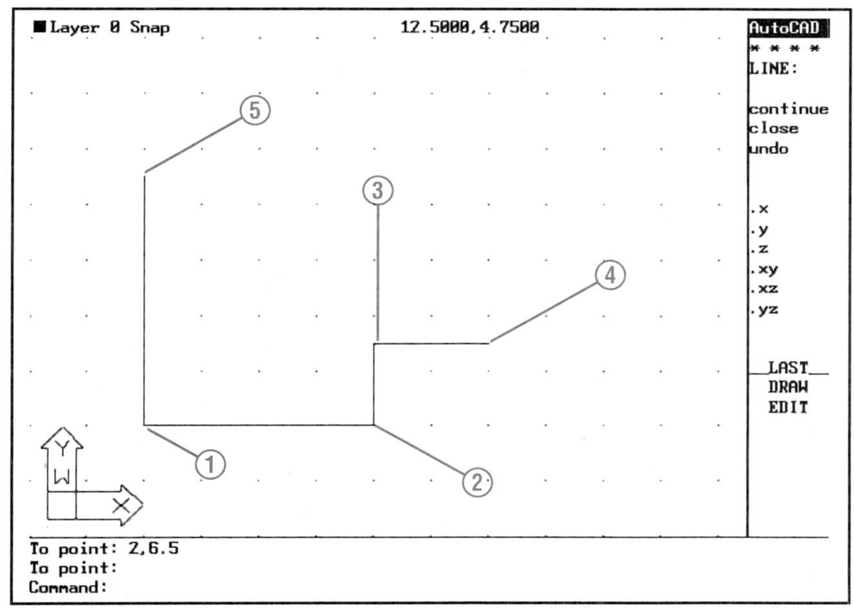

Figure 12.3

Lines drawn using absolute coordinates.

points you need to specify. Often, however, you know the relative distance between two points, but not the absolute coordinates of the points. In such situations, you can enter a relative coordinate.

Entering Relative Points

A *relative point* specifies a distance from the last point you enter. If you need to draw a line that extends six inches to the right of the current point, for example, you can specify a relative point to draw the line without knowing its absolute coordinates. To specify a relative point, precede the X and Y offset with the @ symbol. To draw a line six units to the right, for example, enter @6,0. To specify a point that is two units to the right and three units below the current point, enter @2,-3.

In the following exercise, start with an absolute point, then draw more lines using relative point specification. Figure 12.4 helps for this exercise.

You can see from the preceding exercise that relative points are based on the

Drawing Lines Using Relative Coordinates

Continue with your drawing from the previous exercise.

1. `Command:` *Choose* Draw, *then* Line, *then* Segments	Issues the LINE command to draw multiple segments
_line	

continues

2. `From point:` **`8,3.5`** ↵	Starts the line at ① (see fig. 12.4)
3. `To point:` **`@1,1`** ↵	Draws line to ②
4. `To point:` **`@0,2.5`** ↵	Draws line to ③
5. `To point:` **`@-6.5,0`** ↵	Draws line to ④
6. `To point:` **`@-.5,-.5`** ↵	Draws line to ⑤
7. `To point:` *Press* Enter	Ends the LINE command
8. `Command:` *Choose* File, *then* Save	Saves the drawing

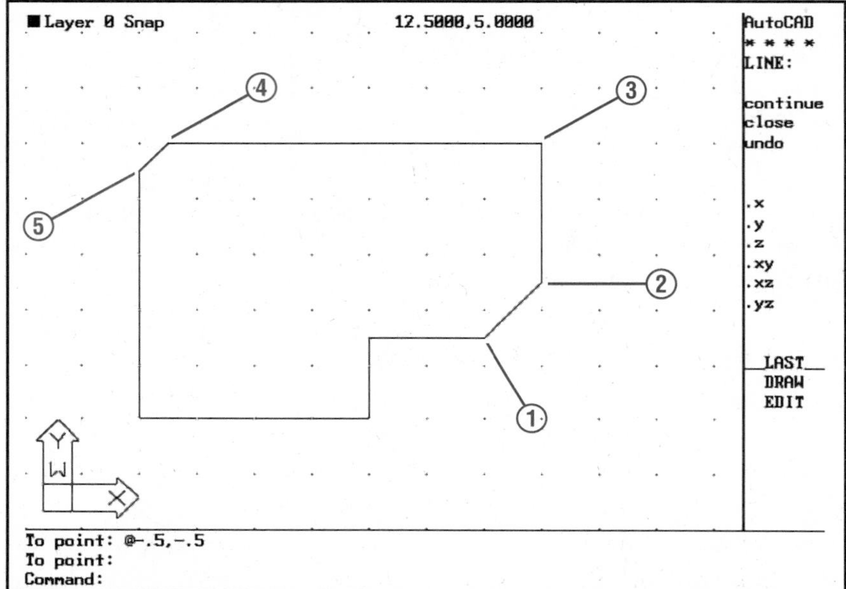

Figure 12.4

Drawing lines using relative coordinates.

last point, which constantly changes as you enter new points. In some situations, you might need to set the last point by setting the LASTPOINT variable or by using the ID command. The ID command is explained briefly in unit 13, "Using Absolute and Relative Coordinates," and in more detail in unit 90, "Using ID and Dist."

Understanding Polar Coordinates

Polar coordinates are defined as a distance and angle from a point. By default, AutoCAD measures angles counterclockwise, with zero degrees toward the postive X axis. In the default AutoCAD coordinate system, this means that zero degrees is to the right on the display. 90 degrees is straight up, 180 degrees to the left, and 270 degrees straight down. Figure 12.5 shows an example of angle measurement in a two-dimensional coordinate system.

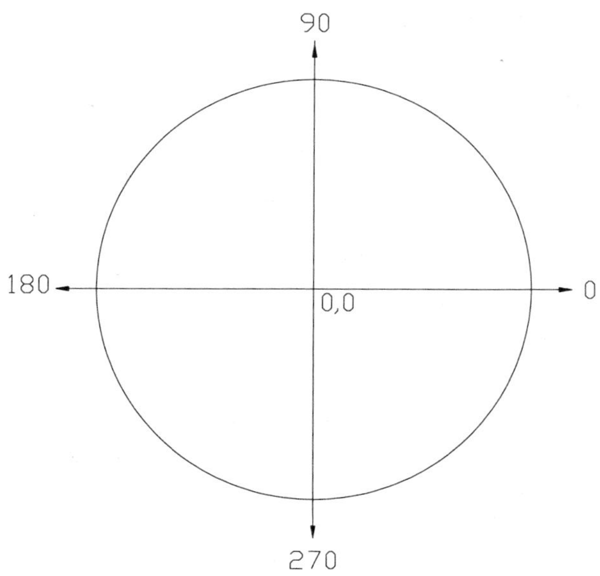

Figure 12.5

Angles in a two-dimensional coordinate system.

To specify a polar coordinate, enter the distance, followed by the < sign, followed by the angle. To specify a three-unit line at an angle of 60 degrees, for example, enter 3<60 as the coordinate. AutoCAD locates the point at a distance of three units along an angle of 60 degrees from the current point or from the origin, depending on whether the polar coordinate is relative or absolute.

Absolute polar coordinates are measured from the origin, just like rectangular absolute coordinates. Relative polar coordinates, like relative rectangular coordinates, are based on the last point entered. To enter a relative polar coordinate, precede the polar point with the @ sign.

Using Absolute Polar Coordinates

In the following exercise, you draw a selection of lines using absolute polar coordinates. The prototype drawing for the exercise contains a circle with its center point located at the origin. The quadrant points of the circle are marked with the angle from the origin to help you understand AutoCAD's system for measuring angles.

Drawing Lines Using Absolute Polar Coordinates

1. Begin a new drawing named 012???02 in your assigned directory using 012POLAR as the prototype.

2. `Command:` *Choose* Draw, *then* Line, *then* Segments	Issues the LINE command
_line	
3. `From point:` **`0,0`** ↵	Starts a line at the origin
4. `To point:` **`6<45`** ↵	Draws a line to ① (see fig. 12.6)
5. `To point:` **`6<90`** ↵	Draws a line to ②
6. `To point:` **`0,0`** ↵	Draws a line to ③
7. `To point:` **`6<-45`** ↵	Draws a line to ④
8. `To point:` **`6<270`** ↵	Draws a line to ⑤
9. `To point:` **`0,0`** ↵	Draws a line to the origin
10. `To point:` **`-6<45`** ↵	Draws a line to ⑥
11. `To point:` *Press* Enter	Ends the LINE command

Your drawing should resemble figure 12.6.

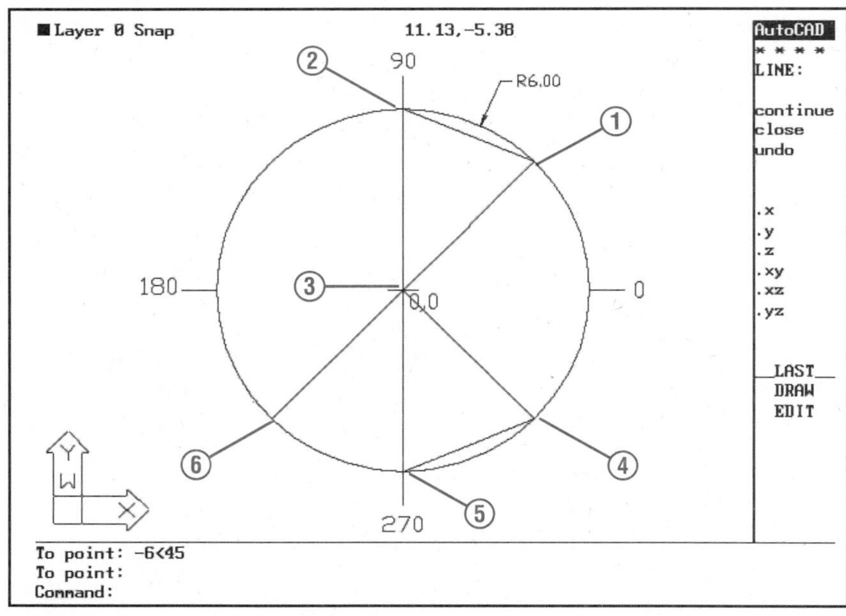

Figure 12.6

Lines drawn using absolute polar coordinates.

You can see from the exercise that you can enter negative values for the distance and for the angle in a polar coordinate.

Using Relative Polar Coordinates

To specify a relative polar coordinate, precede the coordinate with the @ symbol. In the following exercise, add some more lines to your drawing using relative polar coordinates.

Drawing Lines Using Relative Polar Coordinates

Continue with your drawing from the previous exercise.

1. `Command:` **`L`** ↵ — Issues the alias for the LINE command

   `LINE`

2. `From point:` **`6<225`** ↵ — Starts the line at ① (see fig. 12.7)
3. `To point:` **`@2<0`** ↵ — Draws line to ②
4. `To point:` **`@6<45`** ↵ — Draws line to ③
5. `To point:` **`@2<180`** ↵ — Draws line to ④
6. `To point:` *Press* Enter — Ends the LINE command

Your drawing should look similar to figure 12.7.

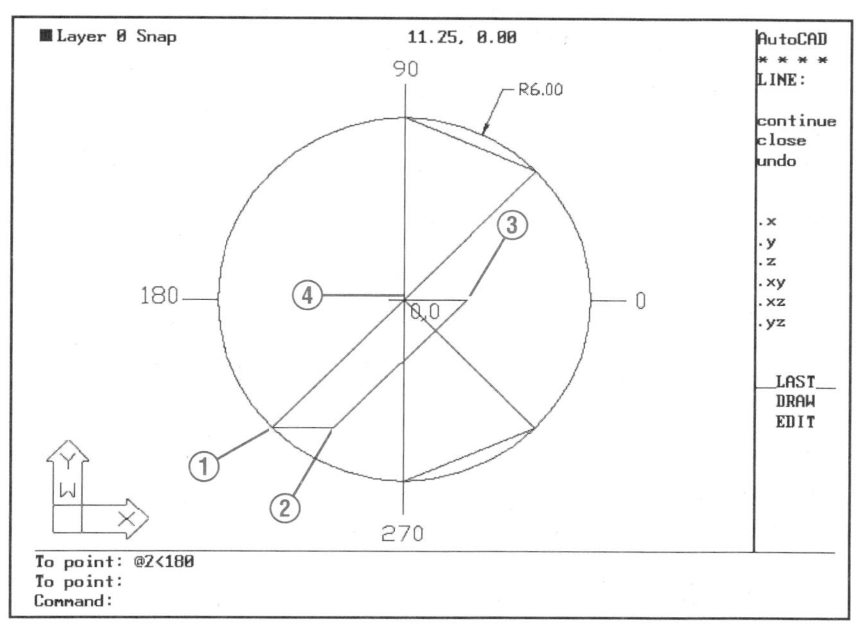

Figure 12.7

Lines drawn using relative polar coordinates.

Relative polar coordinates are useful when you know the distance and angle from the current point to the new point, but do not know the absolute rectangular or absolute polar coordinates of the new point.

Each entity in AutoCAD has special points to which you can snap. Lines have two endpoints and a midpoint, for example. Circles have a center point and quadrant points. You can use AutoCAD's object snap modes to snap to these types of points. Object snap modes are discussed in units 36 and 37.

Unit Review

What You've Learned

- ☞ How to locate points on the Cartesian coordinate system
- ☞ How to specify absolute and relative rectangular coordinates
- ☞ How to specify absolute and relative polar coordinates

Review Questions

True or False

12.01 T F The Cartesian coordinate system makes it possible for you to locate specific points using an X axis and a Y axis.

12.02 T F The Y axis runs horizontally, positive to the right and negative to the left, of the origin.

12.03 T F When you specify a point as an absolute rectangular coordinate, you must enter the X ordinate first, followed by a comma, then the Y ordinate.

12.04 T F With absolute point specification, all distances are measured from the origin.

12.05 T F Use the @ key before entering numbers to indicate relative coordinates.

12.06 T F Relative coordinates are measured from the origin.

Multiple Choice

12.07 The __________ function key turns on the coordinate display.

(A) F1

(B) F3

(C) F6

(D) F7

12.08 When the LINE command is active, the __________ key on the keyboard removes a line that is drawn incorrectly.

(A) D for delete

(B) R for remove

(C) U for undo

(D) X for X-out

Student: ______________________ Date: __________

Instructor: ______________________ Course: __________ Section: __________

Short Answer

12.09 Explain how absolute coordinates are measured.

____

____

____

12.10 Explain how relative polar coordinates are measured.

____

____

____

Student: ________________ Date: ________

Instructor: ________________ Course: ________ Section: ________

UNIT 13

Using Absolute and Relative Coordinates

A solid understanding of the Cartesian coordinate system helps you save time and produce exact drawings. Unit 12 explained absolute and relative rectangular and polar coordinates. In this unit, you gain more experience drawing with coordinates and also learn about other techniques and commands that you can use to prepare exact drawings.

The objectives for this unit are to:

- Use the coordinate display in status line
- Use point filters to locate points
- Use the ID command to locate points

Using the Coordinate Display

The AutoCAD status line, located at the top of the display, contains a coordinate display. When you turn on the coordinate display, AutoCAD shows the current coordinate location of the cursor in the current unit of measure. Figure 13.1 shows the coordinate display in the status line.

The coordinate display offers two modes. In the default mode, the coordinate display shows the absolute coordinate of the current cursor location. As you move the cursor, the coordinate display always changes to show the current cursor coordinate. The second mode that the coordinate display can use is relative mode. In relative mode, the coordinate display shows the current cursor position as a relative polar coordinate based on the last point entered.

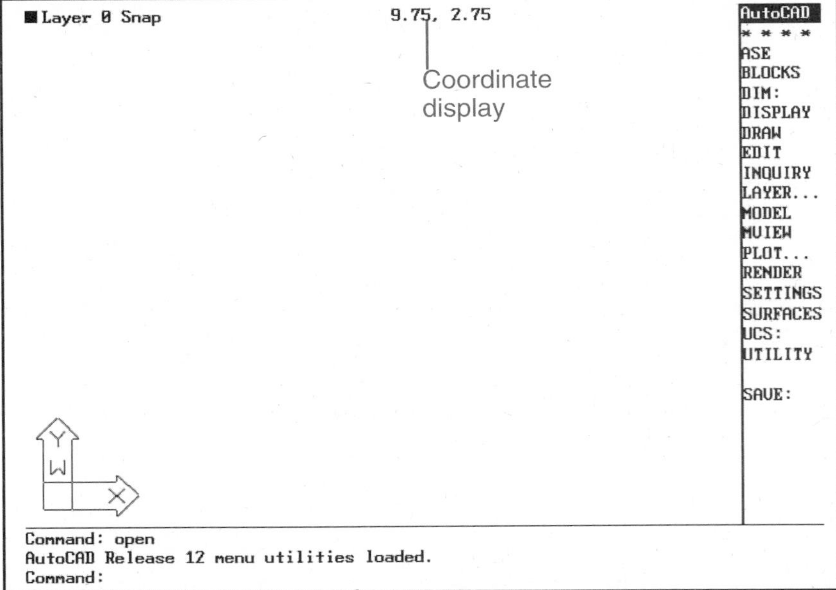

Figure 13.1

The coordinate display in the status line.

You can use the coordinate display as a guide to help you pick points and locate specific coordinates. Combined with other tools such as snap and AutoCAD's grid, the coordinate display can help speed up your drawing time dramatically.

Using a grid is explained in unit 34. Using a snap increment is explained in unit 35.

To turn on coordinate display, press the F6 function key. To switch from absolute mode to relative mode, press the F6 key again.

In the following exercise, use the coordinate display to pick points in the drawing to draw a few entities. The prototype drawing has a snap increment set, so the cursor moves in .25" intervals. This helps you locate exact points easily.

Using the Coordinate Display

1.	Begin a new drawing named 013???01 in your assigned directory using 013COORD as a prototype.	
	Move the cursor and notice that the coordinate display in the status line changes to constantly show the current cursor coordinate.	
2.	`Command:` *Press* F6	Turns off coordinate display
	Move the cursor and note that the coordinate display no longer updates.	
3.	`Command:` *Press* F6	Turns on coordinate display
4.	`Command:` *Choose* Draw, *then* Line, *then* Segments	Issues the LINE command to draw multiple segments
	`_line`	
5.	`From point:` *Locate the cursor at absolute coordinate* 0,0 *by using the coordinate display as a guide, then pick the point*	Starts the line at 0,0
	Notice that the coordinate display has changed to relative mode automatically.	
6.	`To point:` *Using the coordinate display as a guide, pick a point at* 4.50<0	Draws a line to ①
7.	`To point:` *Pick a point at* 3.00<90	Draws line to ② (see fig. 13.2)
8.	`To point:` *Press* F6	Changes coordinate display to absolute mode
9.	`To point:` *Pick a point at absolute coordinate* 2.00,3.00	Draws line to ③ (see fig. 13.2)
10.	`To point:` *Press* F6, *then press* F6 *again*	Turns off coordinate display, then changes coordinate display to relative mode
11.	`To point:` *Pick a point at* 1.00<270	Draws line to ④ (see fig. 13.2)
12.	`To point:` *Pick a point at* 1.00<180	Draws line to ⑤ (see fig. 13.2)
13.	`To point:` *Press* Enter	Ends the LINE command

Your drawing should look similar to figure 13.2.

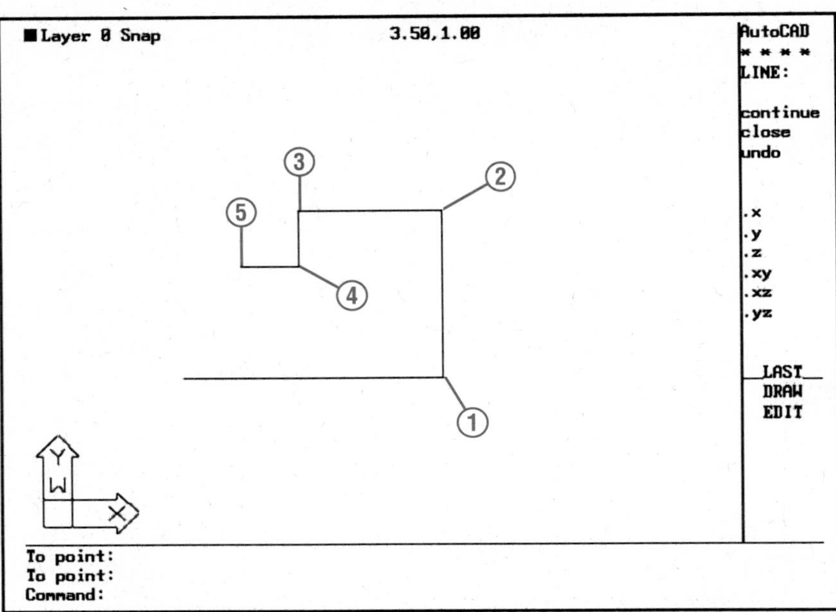

Figure 13.2

Lines drawn using the coordinate display.

When you exit the LINE command, the coordinate display changes automatically from relative mode to absolute mode. Pressing F6 when no command is active simply turns absolute coordinate display on and off. If you press F6 repeatedly when a command is active and prompting you to specify a point, the coordinate display changes modes from absolute, to relative, to off. When you need to change the coordinate display mode during a command, just press F6 until the mode you want is active.

Using Point Filters

You also can specify points based on the X and Y ordinates of other points by using point filters. Point filters give you a means of "putting together" a coordinate using the X and Y ordinates of other points. You can access the point filters from the popup menu or by entering them with the keyboard.

AutoCAD's point filters include Z ordinates, which are for 3D coordinates. In 2D drawings, the Z coordinate is always zero. Unit 99 introduces 3D coordinates and 3D drawings.

In the following exercise, use point filters to complete the outline of the simple block you started in the previous exercise.

Locating Coordinate Points Using Filters

Continue with your drawing from the previous exercise.

1. `Command:` **L** ↵	Issues the alias for the LINE command
2. `LINE From point:` *Press* Enter	Starts the line at the last point ① (see fig. 13.3)
3. `To point:` *Press* F6	Switches coordinate display to absolute mode
4. `To point:` *From the popup menu, choose* Filters, *then* .YZ	Chooses a point filter
5. `.YZ of` *Pick a point at* 2.00,3.00	Specifies the Y and Z ordinates of the point
6. `(need X):` *Pick a point at* 1.00,2.00	Specifies the X ordinate and draws a line to ② (see fig. 13.3)

The new point ② consists of the Y and Z ordinates of ③ (3.00 and 0.00) and the X ordinate of ① (1.00).

7. `To point:` *From the popup menu, choose* Filters, *then* .XZ	Chooses a point filter
8. `.XZ of` *Pick a point at* 0.00,0.00	Specifies the X and Z ordinates of the point
9. `(need Y):` *Pick a point at* 1.00,2.00	Specifies the Y ordinate of the point and draws the line to ④ (see fig. 13.3)
10. `To point:` *Pick a point at* 0.00,0.00	Draws line
11. `To point:` *Press* Enter	Ends LINE command

Your drawing should resemble figure 13.3.

Point filters are useful when you need to draw to a point that is even with another point in one axis, but has a different ordinate value in the other axis. You also can use the .X and .Y filters to locate points. AutoCAD prompts you for the missing X or Y ordinate and the Z ordinate. You can pick a point or enter a value using the keyboard. If you enter the X or Y value at the keyboard, specify a Z value of zero as in the following example:

`(need XZ):` **2,0** ↵

The first value specifies the X ordinate and the second value specifies the Z ordinate.

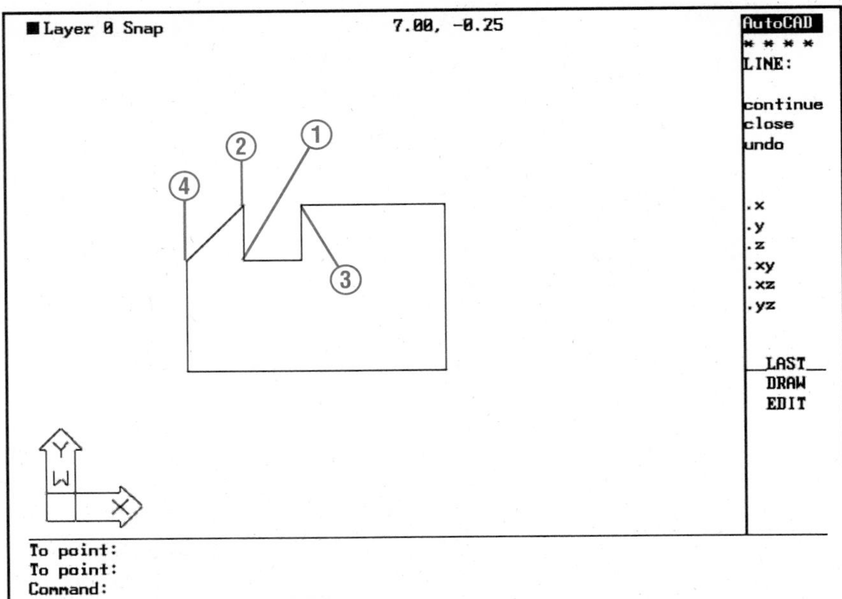

Figure 13.3

Lines drawn using point filters.

Using ID to Locate a Point

The ID command identifies the X and Y coordinates of any point and displays the coordinates in absolute value in the command prompt area. The point does not need to be the last point entered. You can use the ID command to identify the coordinates of a point. When you use ID, the point you pick becomes the last point entered. You can access the ID command by choosing Assist, then Inquiry, then ID Point. You also can enter the ID command at the command prompt or choose it from the INQUIRY screen menu.

You can use the ID command as a transparent command when another command is active. If the LINE command is active, for example, you can use ID to identify the coordinate of a point without exiting the LINE command. If you use ID in this way, however, the selected point does not become the last point entered.

In the following exercise, use the ID command to identify the coordinates of a point.

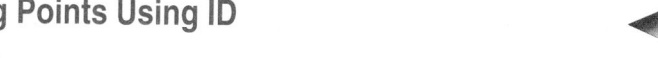

Locating Points Using ID

Continue with your drawing from the previous exercise.

1. `Command:` *Choose* Assist, *then* Inquiry, *then* ID Point	Issues the ID command
`'id`	
2. `Point:` *Pick a point at* 4.50,0.00	
`X = 4.50    Y = 0.00    Z = 0.00`	
3. `Command:` **`L`** ↵	Issues the alias for the LINE command
`LINE`	
4. `From point:` **`@0.5,0`** ↵	Starts the line .5" to the right of the point you picked for ID
5. `To point:` *Pick a point at* 5.00,3.00	Draws a vertical line
6. `To point:` *Press* Enter	

Not only does the ID command display the coordinates of a point, but it also gives you a way to begin a line or specify a point relative to an existing point.

The ID command and its use are covered in more detail in unit 90, "Using ID and Dist."

Unit Review

What You've Learned

- Commands: ID
- How to use the coordinate display
- How to use point filters when you locate points
- How to identify the coordinate of a point using ID

Review Questions

True or False

13.01 T F Absolute coordinates must be entered from the keyboard.

13.02 T F Relative coordinates can be displayed on the coordinate display in the status line.

13.03 T F Relative coordinates are measured from the last point entered.

13.04 T F The F6 key turns coordinate display on and off and switches its display mode.

13.05 T F The coordinate display is located in the command prompt area.

Multiple Choice

13.06 The coordinate display will show __________ coordinates in the status line.

(A) absolute

(B) relative polar

(C) polar

(D) Both A and B

13.07 To switch the coordinate display from absolute to relative polar mode, press __________.

(A) F5

(B) SW

(C) F6

(D) F7

Student: __________ Date: __________

Instructor: __________ Course: __________ Section: __________

Short Answer

13.08 Explain the difference between absolute and relative points.

____

____

____

13.09 What information does the ID command display?

____

____

____

13.10 If no command is active, what effect does repeatedly pressing the F6 key have?

____

____

____

Student: ____________________________ Date: __________

Instructor: ____________________ Course: __________ Section: ________

UNIT 14

Drawing Arcs and Circles

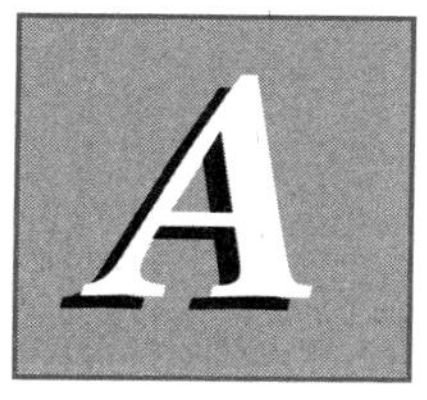

Arcs and circles are as much a part of a typical drawing as are lines. AutoCAD enables you to create perfect arcs and circles based on a wide variety of criteria. You can use many different techniques and constructions based on your personal preferences and drawing requirements. This unit teaches you to create arcs and circles in AutoCAD.

The objectives for this unit are to:

- Access the CIRCLE command
- Draw circles using all of the CIRCLE command options
- Access the ARC command
- Draw arcs using the most common ARC command options

Regardless of the method used to define a circle, AutoCAD always draws the circle counterclockwise. This is important only for later units that address editing circles.

Drawing Circles

You can access the CIRCLE command from the pull-down menu, the screen menu, or the `Command:` prompt. Regardless of how you access the CIRCLE command, you have five options for drawing the circle:

- **Center Point, Radius.** You are prompted for the center of the circle and then the radius of the circle.
- **Center Point, Diameter.** You are prompted for the center of the circle and then the diameter.
- **Two Point.** You are prompted for two points that define the diameter of the circle.
- **Three Point.** You are prompted for three points on the circumference.
- **Tangent, Tangent, Radius.** You are prompted for two entities tangent to the circle and the circle's radius.

*You can type **C** at the* `Command:` *prompt to enter the CIRCLE command.*

The next two exercises introduce you to the CIRCLE command and show you how to use the pull-down menu to access this command.

Using the Pull-down Menu To Access CIRCLE

1. Begin a new drawing named 014???01 in your assigned directory, using the file 014PROT1 as a prototype.

2. `Command:` *Choose* Draw, *then* Circle, *then* Center, Radius	Starts the CIRCLE command with the Center, Radius option
3. `Command: _circle 3P/2P/TTR/ <Center point>:` *Pick a point at* ① *(see fig. 14.1)*	Specifies the center of the circle
4. `Diameter/<Radius>:` *Pick a point at at* ②	Defines the radius of the circle
5. `Command:` *Choose* Draw, *then* Circle, *then* Center, Diameter	Starts the CIRCLE command with the Center, Diameter option
`_circle`	
6. `3P/2P/TTR /<Center point>:` *Pick a point at* ③	Specifies the center of the circle

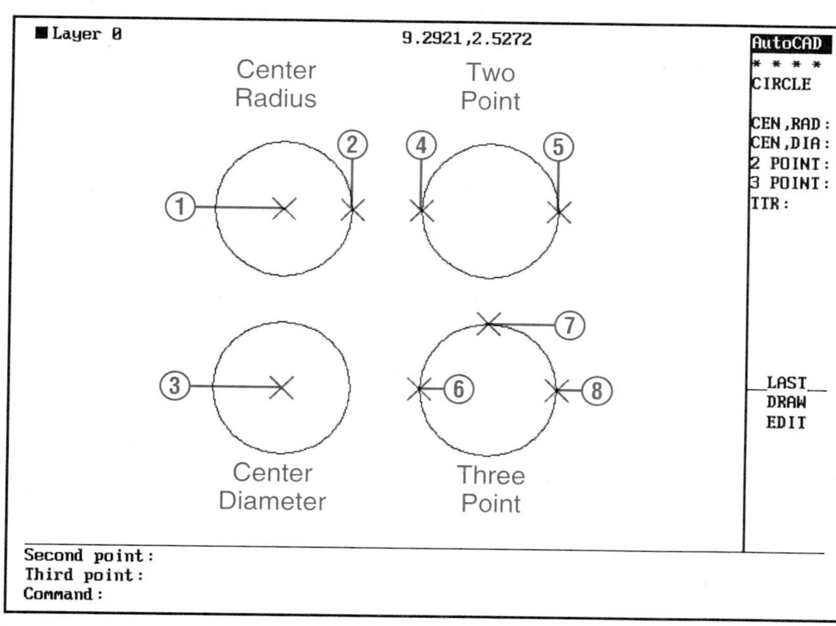

Figure 14.1

Four circles drawn using the Radius, Diameter, 2-Point, and 3-Point options.

7. `Diameter/<Radius> <1.0000>:` **D**	
8. `_diameter Diameter <2.0000>:` *Press* Enter	Accepts last diameter value

9. `Command:` *Choose* Draw, *then* with Circle, *then* 2-Point
`_circle`
`3P/2P/TTR /<Center point>:`
	Starts the CIRCLE command with the 2-Point option

10. `_2p First point on diameter:` *Pick a point at* ④	Specifies the first point on the circle's diameter
11. `Second point on diameter:` *Pick a point at* ⑤	Specifies a second point on the circle's diameter 180 degrees from the first point
12. `Command:` *Choose* Draw, *then* Circle, *then* 3-Point `_circle`	Starts the CIRCLE command with the 3-Point option
13. `3P/2P/TTR /<Center point>:_3p First point:` *Pick a point at* ⑥	Specifies the first point on the circle's circumference
14. `Second point:` *Pick a point at* ⑦	Specifies the second point on the circle's circumference
15. `Third point:` *Pick a point at* ⑧	Specifies the third point on the circle's circumference and draws the circle

As you saw in the previous exercise, the CIRCLE command retains the previous radius and diameter measurements and presents them as the defaults the next time a radius or diameter prompt is displayed.

The following exercise shows you how to use the Tangent, Tangent, Radius option to draw circles. This option is particularly useful when you have a minimum of information about the circle.

It is possible to enter values for the Tangent, Tangent, Radius option that do not create a circle. When this happens, AutoCAD prompts you with:

`Circle does not exist.`

Drawing a Circle Using the TTR Option

Continue with your drawing from the previous exercise.

1. `Command:` *Choose* Draw, *then* Circle, *then* Tan, Tan, Radius	Starts the CIRCLE command with the Tangent, Tangent, Radius option
2. `Enter Tangent spec:` *Select the circle at* ① *(see fig. 14.2)*	Selects the first entity to which the circle is tangent
3. `Enter second Tangent spec:` *Select the circle at* ②	Selects the second entity to which the circle is tangent
4. `Radius <1.0000>:` *Press* Enter	Accepts the default radius

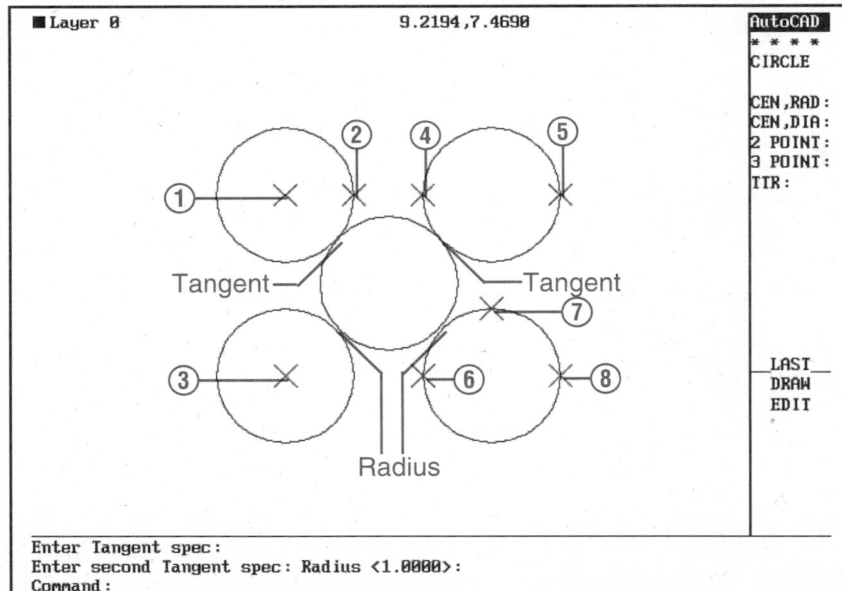

Figure 14.2

A circle drawn with the Tangent, Tangent, Radius option.

Angles and Arcs in AutoCAD

Arcs are partial circles. They can be drawn based on start points, start directions, center points, included angles, end points, lengths of chord, and radii. To make these measurements, you need to know how AutoCAD measures angles and draws arcs.

Figure 14.3 shows the angle and direction measurements used in AutoCAD. Positive angle measurements create arcs that are drawn counterclockwise, and negative angle measurements create arcs that are drawn clockwise. The direction in which an arc is drawn is not only important for creating the desired arc; it is also important when editing the arc. Commands for editing entities are discussed in later units.

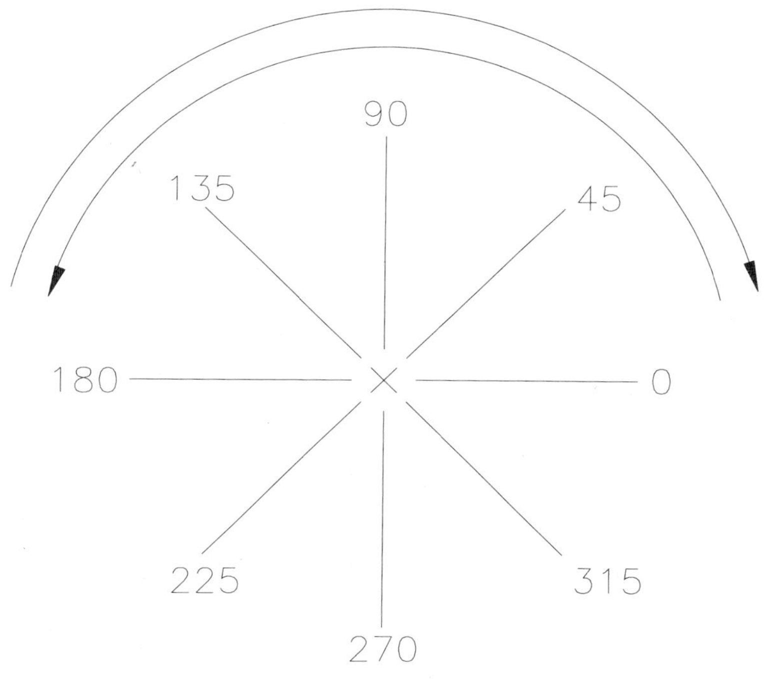

Figure 14.3

Arc angle measurements and direction.

Drawing Arcs

Arcs are drawn using the ARC command. You can access the ARC command from the pull-down menu, the screen menu, or the `Command:` prompt. Eleven variations of the ARC command use combinations of six different variables and pick points. These options are listed in Table 14.1:

Table 14.1
Arc Creation Methods

3-point
Start, Center, End
Start, Center, Include Angle
Start, Center, Length of Chord
Start, End, Angle
Start, End, Radius
Start, End, Direction
Center, Start, End
Center, Start, Include Angle
Center, Start, Length
Continue from the last point picked

*You can enter **A** at the* `Command:` *prompt to start the ARC command.*

The three most common ARC options are explained as follows and are demonstrated in the next exercise.

- **3-point.** Three-point arcs are typically used when you are drawing an arc freehand or when you know the start point, a point on the arc, and the end of the arc.
- **Start, Center, End.** This option is used any time the center, start point, and end point of the arc are known, such as for a door swing.
- **Start, End, Radius.** These arcs typically are used like a fillet or round when you know the exact end points of the arc and its radius.

Drawing Arcs Using the Pull-down Menu

1. Begin a new drawing named 014???02 in your assigned directory, using the file 014PROT2 as a prototype.

First, use the 3-point option to draw an arc.

2. `Command:` *Choose* Draw, *then* Arc, *then* 3-point — Starts the ARC command with 3-point option

3. `_arc Center/<Start point>:` *Pick a point at* ① *(see fig 14.4)* — Specifies the first point on the arc

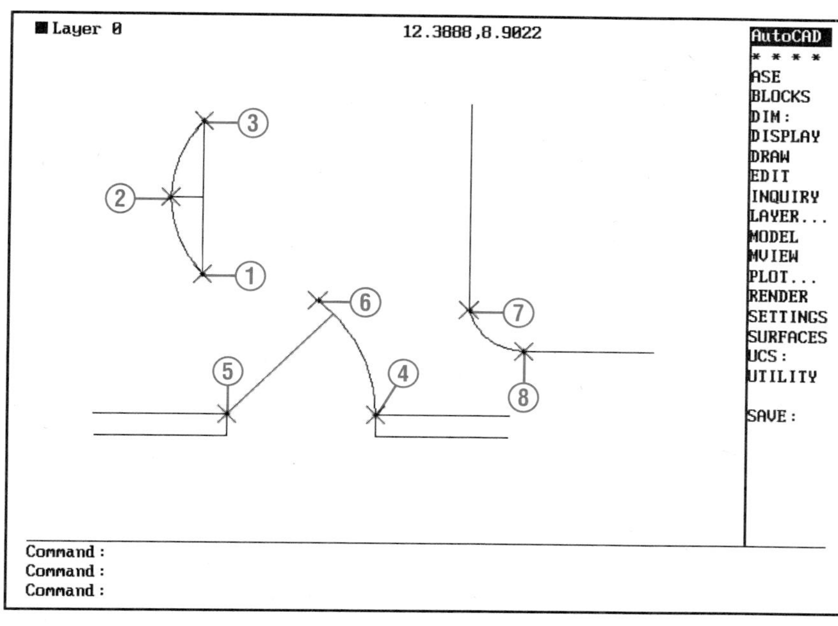

Figure 14.4

Arcs drawn using the 3-point; Start, Center, End; and Start, End Radius options.

4. `Center/End/<Second point>:` *Pick a point at* ② — Specifies the second point on the arc

5. `End point:` *Pick a point at* ③ — Specifies the third point on the arc and draws the arc

Use the Start, Center, End option to draw a door swing.

6. `Command:` *Choose* Draw, *then* Arc, *then* Start, Center, End — Starts the ARC command with the Start, Center, End option

   `_arc`

7. `Center/<Start point>:` *Pick a point at* ④ — Specifies the start point of the arc

   `Center/End/<Second point>:`

8. `_c Center:` *Pick a point at* ⑤ — Specifies the center of the arc

9. `Angle/Length of chord/<End point>:` *Pick a point at* ⑥ — Specifies the end point of the arc

Use the Start, End, Radius option to draw a round.

10. `Command:` *Choose* Draw, *then* Arc, *then* Start, End Radius — Starts the ARC command with the Start, End, Radius option

continues

11. `Center/<Start point>:` *Pick a point at* ⑦	Specifies the start of the arc
`Center/End/<Second point>: _e`	
12. `End point:` *Pick a point at* ⑧	Specifies the end of the arc
13. `Angle/Direction/Radius/<Center point>: _r Radius:` **1** ↵	Specifies the arc radius

Unit Review

What You've Learned

- How to access the CIRCLE command
- The options of the CIRCLE command and how to use them
- How to access the ARC command
- Selected options of the ARC command and how to use them

Review Questions

True or False

14.01 T F Arcs are always drawn counterclockwise.

14.02 T F The ARC command retains radius values for subsequent ARC commands.

14.03 T F It is possible to enter values for the CIRCLE command that cannot create a circle.

14.04 T F The CIRCLE command retains radius and diameter values.

14.05 T F Angles are measured counter-clockwise.

Multiple Chioce

14.06 Circles are a;waus draw ____________.

(A) throug h three points

(B) clockwise

(C) counterclockwise

(D) None of the above

14.07 Which of the following is not an option of the ARC command? ___________

(A) Start point

(B) End point

(C) Radius

(D) Diameter

Student: ______________________________ Date: __________

Instructor: ______________________________ Course: ______ Section: ______

14.08 Which of the following is not an option of the CIRCLE command? ____________

(A) Radius

(B) 2P

(C) 3P

(D) End Point

Short Answer

14.09 In figure 14.5, identify the following items and write their numbers beside each item:

(A) A Tangent, Tangent, Radius circle ____________

(B) A 3-Point arc ____________

(C) A Start, Center, End arc ______________

(D) A 2-point circle ______________

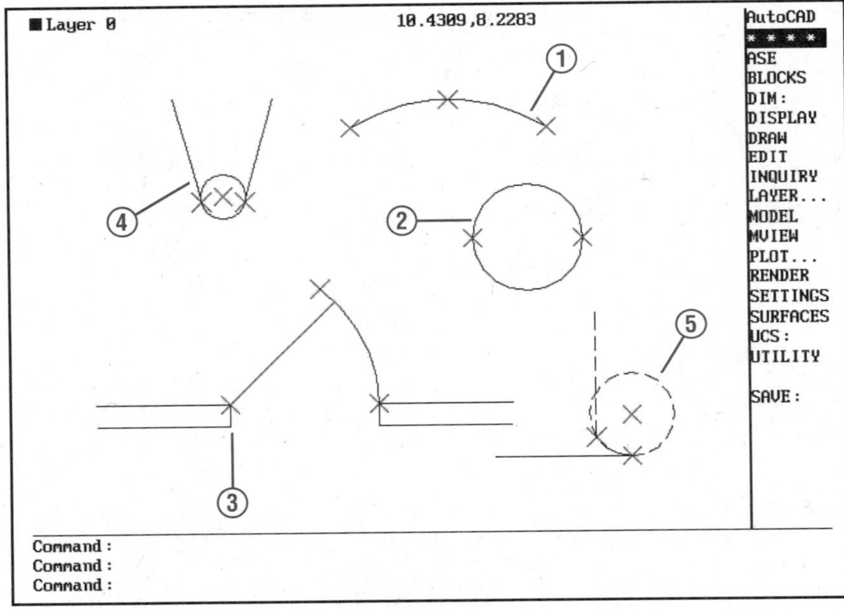

Figure 14.5

Identify arcs and circles.

Student: ______________ Date: ______________

Instructor: ______________ Course: ______________ Section: ______________

14.10 Which option of the ARC command is useful for drawing door swings?

____

14.11 Which screen menu contains the ARC command?

____

14.12 Which option of the ARC command is useful for drawing fillets and rounds?

____

Additional Excercises

Complete the following exercises on your own.

14.13 Create the door swing shown in figure 14.6.

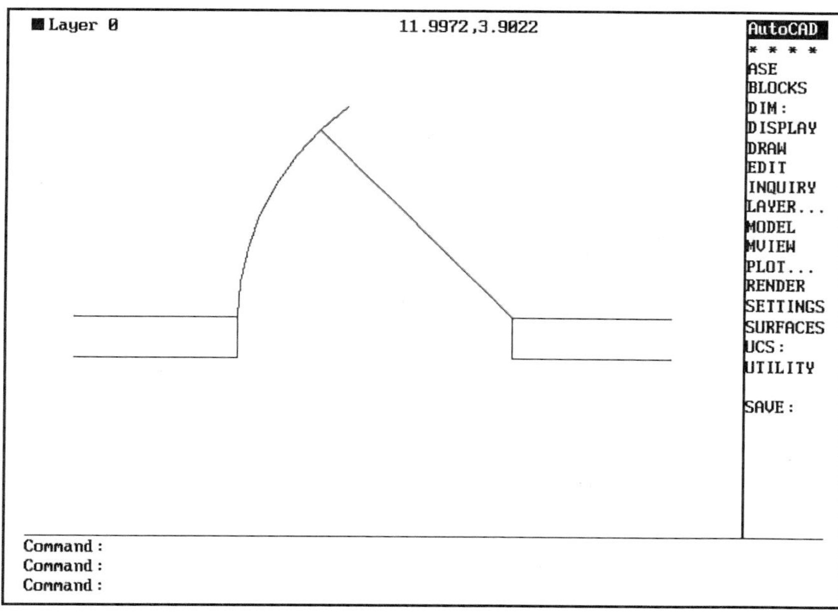

Figure 14.6

A door swing.

Student: ______________ Date: ______________

Instructor: ______________ Course: ______________ Section: ______________

14.14 Use the following information and 014PROT3.DWG to draw the object in figure 14.7:

- ☞ All arc radii are 1.0
- ☞ The circle radius is 1.0

Figure 14.7

Exercise with arcs and circles.

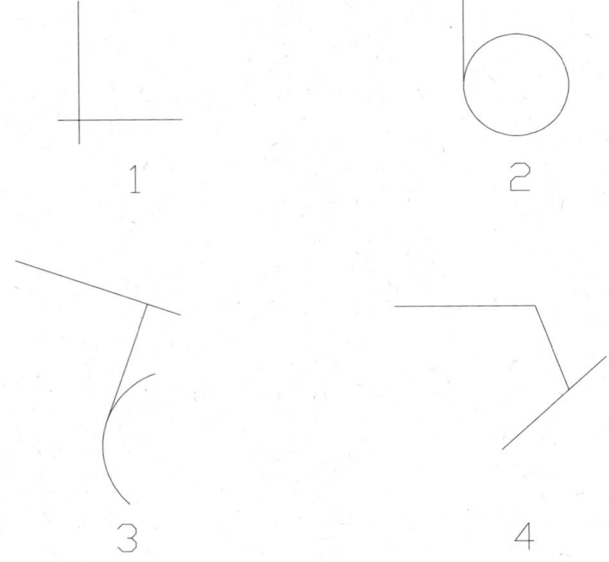

Student: ____________ Date: ____________

Instructor: ____________ Course: ____________ Section: ____________

UNIT 15

Drawing Polylines

By now, you probably are familiar with how to draw single lines with the LINE command and double lines with the DLINE command. Lines and arcs typically make up much of the geometry in a drawing. Another entity that you will use often in a drawing is a *polyline*. Working with polylines is an important part of creating an AutoCAD drawing. This unit will help you understand how to use polylines in your drawings.

The objectives for this unit are to:

- ☞ Understand how polylines differ from lines and arcs
- ☞ Draw polylines composed of linear segments
- ☞ Draw polylines that contain arc segments
- ☞ Draw polylines with varying widths
- ☞ Draw a closed polyline boundary

Understanding Polylines

Unlike lines and arcs, which can consist of only one segment, a polyline can comprise many segments. AutoCAD recognizes these multiple segments as a single entity—the polyline.

You can draw the segments in a polyline with a zero width, which makes the segments look much like line and arc segments. You also can specify a width for individual polyline segments. Figure 15.1 shows a polyline drawn with varying width segments.

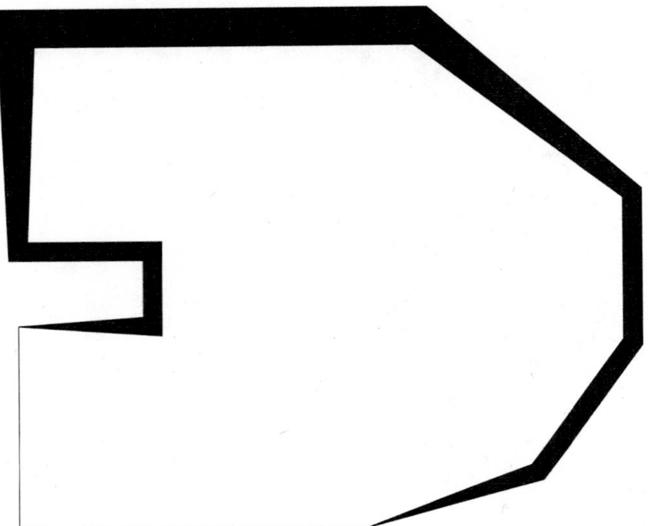

Figure 15.1

A polyline drawn with varying width segments.

Polylines are useful for drawing any complex shape that you later may need to edit or manipulate as a single entity. You can use a polyline to draw the outer perimeter walls of a building, for example, the conductive traces on a printed circuit board, contour lines on a plat, or the outline of a complex-shaped mechanical part. Polylines also are useful for smaller objects, such as polygons.

You can draw polylines yourself with the PLINE command. You will learn in other units that AutoCAD also creates polylines for you when you use some of its other drawing commands.

Drawing a Polyline

After you select the command to draw a polyline, AutoCAD prompts you for the starting point of the polyline, just as it does for line segments when you use the LINE command. After you supply the starting point, AutoCAD provides a number of options for controlling the way the polyline will be drawn.

Use figure 15.2, which shows the dimensions for the outer perimeter of a cap plate, as a guide for completing the following exercise.

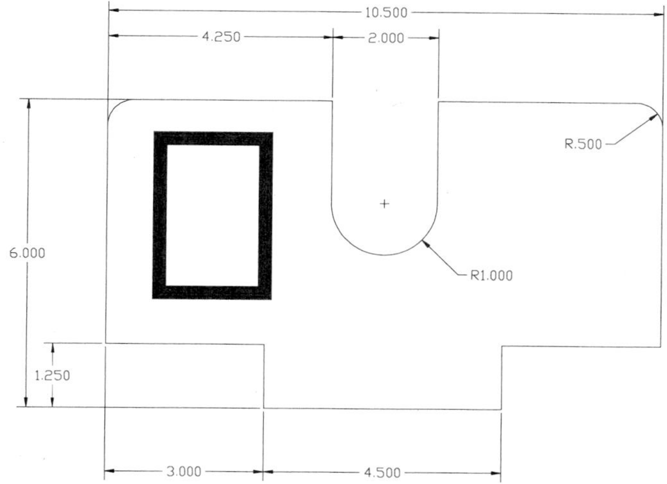

Figure 15.2

Dimensions for the CAPPLATE drawing.

Drawing a Simple Polyline

1. Begin a new drawing named 015???01 in your assigned directory, using the file 015PLINE as a prototype drawing. Use the coordinate display in the status line as a guide for picking points in this exercise.

2. `Command:` *Choose* Draw, *then* Polyline, *then* 2D — Starts PLINE command

   `_pline`

3. `From point:` **`1,2`** ↵ — Begins polyline at coordinate 1,2

   `Current line-width is 0.0000`

4. `Arc/Close/Halfwidth/Length /Undo/Width/<Endpoint of line>:` *Pick a point at* 4,2 — Draws a linear polyline segment

5. `Arc/Close/Halfwidth/Length /Undo/Width/<Endpoint of line>:` *Pick a point at* 4,.75 — Continues polyline

6. `Arc/Close/Halfwidth/Length /Undo/Width/<Endpoint of line>:` *Pick a point at* 7.5,.75

7. `Arc/Close/Halfwidth/Length/Undo /Width/<Endpoint of line>:` **`U`** ↵ — Undoes the previous segment

continues

8. `Arc/Close/Halfwidth/Length/Undo /Width/<Endpoint of line>:` *Pick a point at* 8.5,.75 — Draws a new segment

9. `Arc/Close/Halfwidth/Length/Undo /Width/<Endpoint of line>:` *Pick a point at* 8.5,2 — Draws a new segment

10. `Arc/Close/Halfwidth/Length/Undo /Width/<Endpoint of line>:` *Pick a point at* 11.5,2 — Draws a new segment

11. `Arc/Close/Halfwidth/Length /Undo/Width/<Endpoint of line>:` *Press* Enter — Ends the PLINE command

Figure 15.3 shows how the polyline should appear on your display.

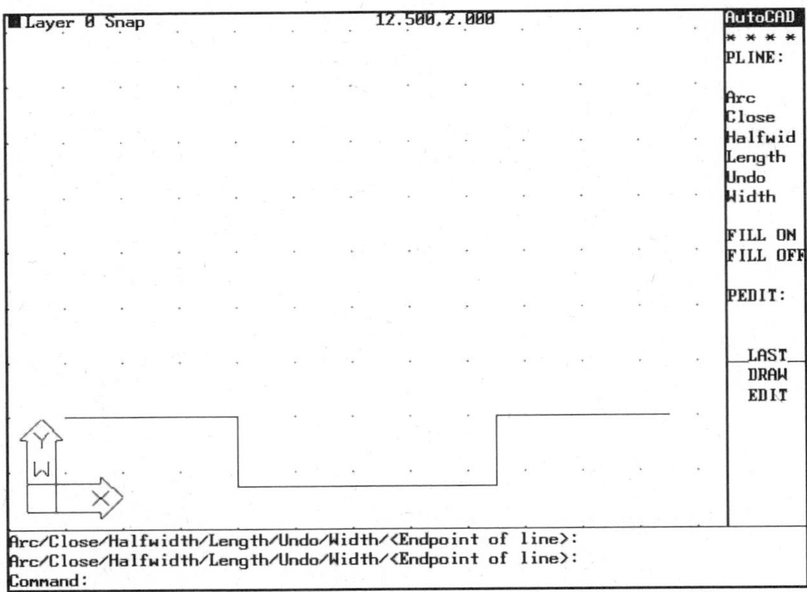

Figure 15.3 *The first few segments of the polyline.*

In the previous exercise, you used the U (Undo) option to undo the previous segment. Any time you make a mistake in creating a polyline segment and want to remove it without exiting the PLINE command, just use the Undo option.

Drawing Polylines with Arcs

Polylines often contain only straight segments, but they also can contain arc segments. Even though a polyline may include both linear and arc segments, AutoCAD still recognizes all of the segments as belonging to a single polyline entity.

The following exercise shows you how to draw polylines that contain both linear and arc segments. Continue to use figure 15.2 as a guide to complete the exercise.

Drawing Polyarc Segments

Continue with your drawing from the previous exercise.

1. `Command:` *Choose* Draw, *then* Polyline, *then* 2D. `_pline`	Starts PLINE command
2. `From point:` **`@`** ↵	Begins polyline at the last point
3. `Arc/Close/Halfwidth/Length /Undo/Width/<Endpoint of line>:` *Pick a point at* 11.5,6.25	Draws a linear segment
4. `Arc/Close/Halfwidth/Length /Undo/Width/<Endpoint of line>:` *From the screen menu, choose* Arc	Enters the polyarc mode
5. `Angle/CEnter/CLose/Direction /Halfwidth/Line/Radius/Second pt /Undo/Width/<Endpoint of arc>:` *Pick a point at* 11,6.75	Draws a polyarc segment
6. `Angle/CEnter/CLose/Direction /Halfwidth/Line/Radius/Second pt /Undo/Width/<Endpoint of arc>:` **`L`** ↵	Returns to Line mode
7. `Arc/Close/Halfwidth/Length/Undo /Width/<Endpoint of line>:` *Pick a point at* 7.25,6.75	Draws a linear segment
8. `Arc/Close/Halfwidth/Length /Undo/Width/<Endpoint of line>:` *Pick a point at* 7.25,4.75	
9. `Arc/Close/Halfwidth/Length/Undo /Width/<Endpoint of line>:` *Press* Enter	Ends the PLINE command

NOTE

You can switch between line and arc modes in the PLINE command as often as necessary. Often, you will only to pick a point to define the arc. In some cases, however, you will have to use other options and methods to draw the polyarc. PLINE options are explained later in this unit.

Next, complete the outline of the part by drawing another polyline. Use figure 15.4 and the coordinate display in the status line as a guide for picking points.

Completing the Outline of the Part

1. `Command:` *Choose* Draw, *then* Polyline, *then* 2D. `_pline`	Starts PLINE command
2. `From point:` **@** ↵	Begins polyline at the last point
3. `Arc/Close/Halfwidth/Length/Undo /Undo/Width/<Endpoint of line>:` **A** ↵	Enters Arc polyline mode
4. `Angle/CEnter/CLose/Direction /Halfwidth/Line/Radius/Second pt /Undo/Width/<Endpoint of arc>:` *Pick a point at* 5.25,4.75	Draws arc segment
5. `Angle/CEnter/CLose/Direction /Halfwidth/Line/Radius/Second pt /Undo/Width/<Endpoint of arc>:` **L** ↵	Returns to Line mode
6. `Arc/Close/Halfwidth/Length/Undo /Width/<Endpoint of line>:` *Pick a point at* 5.25,6.75	Draws linear segment
7. `Arc/Close/Halfwidth/Length/Undo /Width/<Endpoint of line>:` *Pick a point at* 1.5,6.75	
8. `Arc/Close/Halfwidth/Length/Undo /Width/<Endpoint of line>:` **A** ↵	Enters Arc polyline mode
9. `Angle/CEnter/CLose/Direction /Halfwidth/Line/Radius/Second pt /Undo/Width/<Endpoint of arc>:` *Pick a point at* 1,6.25	
10. `Angle/CEnter/CLose/Direction /Halfwidth/Line/Radius/Second pt /Undo/Width/<Endpoint of arc>:` **L** ↵	Returns to Line polyline mode
11. `Arc/Close/Halfwidth/Length /Undo/Width/<Endpoint of line>:` *Pick a point at* 1,2	Draws the last segment
12. `Arc/Close/Halfwidth/Length/Undo/Width /<Endpoint of line>:` *Press* Enter	Ends the PLINE command

Figure 15.4 shows how the polyline should appear after completing the previous exercise.

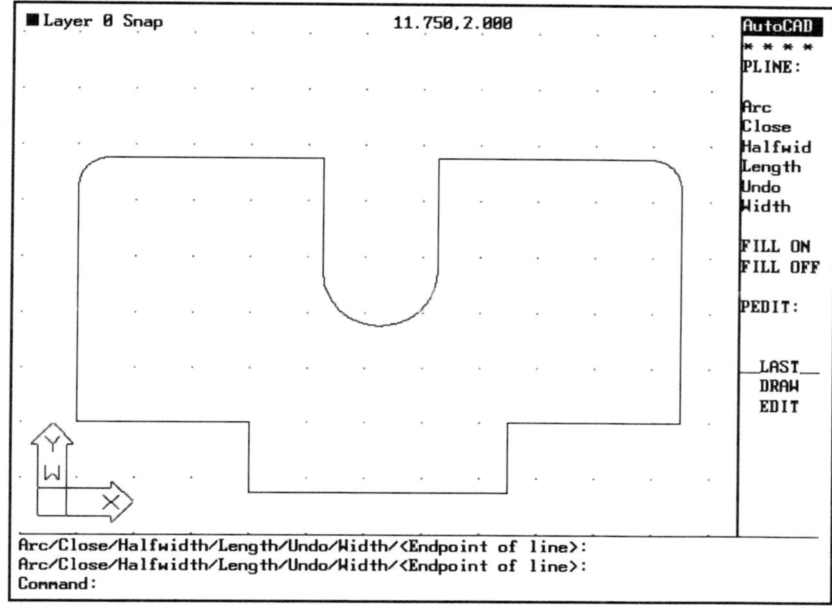

Figure 15.4

Final segments added to the polyline.

Using PLINE Command Options

The polylines you have drawn in the previous exercises have had a width of zero. You also can draw polylines with width by using the Width option to specify the width of segments in the polyline. A segment can have a continuous width or a tapered width (the starting and ending widths are different). The next exercise shows you how to use this option and the Close option to close a polyline automatically.

Using the Width and Close PLINE Options

Continue with your drawing from the previous exercise.

1. `Command:` **`PLINE`** ↵	Starts the PLINE command
2. `From point:` **`2,3`** ↵	Specifies start point
`Current line-width is 0.0000`	
3. `Arc/Close/Halfwidth/Length/Undo /Width/<Endpoint of line>:` **`W`** ↵	Specifies the Width option
4. `Starting width <0.0000>:` **`.25`** ↵	Sets segment starting width
5. `Ending width <0.2500>:` ↵	Sets segment ending width equal to starting width

continues

6. `Arc/Close/Halfwidth/Length/Undo/Width/<Endpoint of line>:` *Pick a point at* 4,3 — Draws a polyline segment

7. `Arc/Close/Halfwidth/Length/Undo/Width/<Endpoint of line>:` *Pick a point at* 4,6

8. `Arc/Close/Halfwidth/Length/Undo/Width/<Endpoint of line>:` *Pick a point at* 2,6

9. `Arc/Close/Halfwidth/Length/Undo/Width/<Endpoint of line>:` **C** ↵ — Closes the polyline

Figure 15.5 shows the wide polyline added to the CAPPLATE drawing.

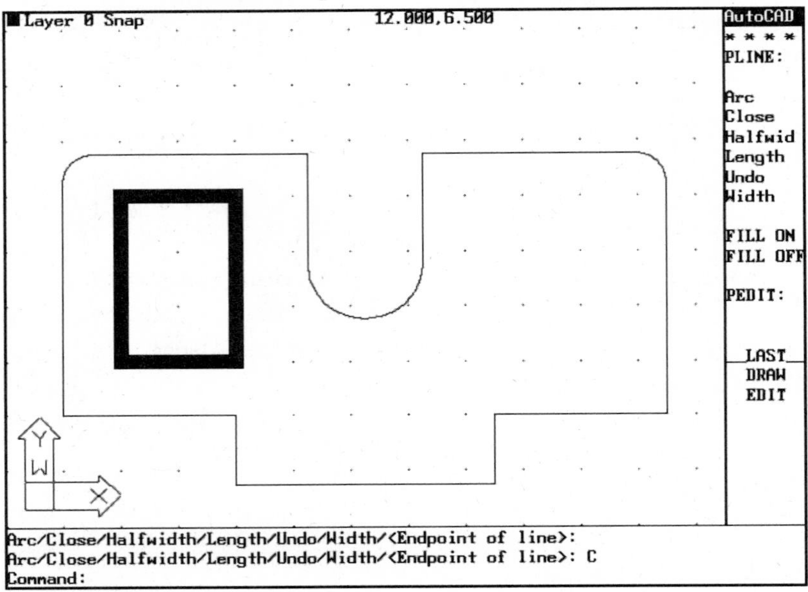

Figure 15.5
A wide polyline added to the CAPPLATE drawing.

To draw a tapered polyline, specify unequal values for the starting and ending widths.

The command FILLMODE controls whether the inside of wide polyline segments are filled. To turn off fill, specify a value of 0 in the FILLMODE command. Specify a value of 1 to turn on fill of wide polylines. This setting affects all wide polylines in the drawing.

Other PLINE Command Options

A number of command options are available for the PLINE command. The options for Line mode in the PLINE command include:

- **Arc.** AutoCAD stops drawing polylines and begins drawing polyarcs. The polyarc options prompt appears.
- **Close.** This option closes the polyline by drawing a segment from the last endpoint to the start point. The PLINE command then ends.
- **Length.** AutoCAD prompts you to specify the length of the next polyline segment. The segment is drawn at the same angle as the last polyline segment, or tangent to the last polyarc segment.
- **Width.** AutoCAD prompts you to specify the starting and ending width for subsequent segments.
- **Halfwidth.** AutoCAD prompts you to specify half the width of subsequent segments. The width of the segments will be twice this value.
- **Undo.** This option undoes the last segment that you drew.
- **Endpoint of line.** This option is the initial default. You must pick a point to specify the endpoint of the current line segment.

A number of options are available for Arc mode:

- **Angle.** AutoCAD prompts you to specify (by picking or by entering a value) the included angle of the arc segment. This does not cause AutoCAD to draw the segment because you must also specify an end point for the segment.
- **CEnter.** AutoCAD prompts you to specify the center point of the polyarc segment.
- **Direction.** AutoCAD prompts you to specify the direction for the segment, relative to the last point.
- **Line.** Returns to Line mode.
- **Radius.** AutoCAD prompts you to specify the radius of the segment.
- **Second pt.** AutoCAD prompts you to specify a second point for the arc segment, then an endpoint, enabling you to draw a polyarc segment through three points (start point, second point, and ending point).

Unit Review

What You've Learned

- Commands: PLINE
- Options: Line, Arc, Close, Width
- How to draw polylines containing line and arc segments
- How to draw wide polylines

Review Questions

True or False

15.01 T F A polyline can include many segments.

15.02 T F Polylines can only contain linear segments; they cannot contain arc segments.

15.03 T F The starting and ending widths for a polyline segment must be equal.

15.04 T F The Close option draws a segment to the beginning point of the polyline and ends the PLINE command.

15.05 T F Wide polylines are always filled; you cannot turn off the fill.

Multiple Choice

15.06 The ________ option is used to specify the width of polyline segments.

(A) Thickness

(B) Line

(C) Width

(D) None of the above

15.07 You can access the PLINE command from the ________ pull-down menu.

(A) Draw

(B) Modify

(C) Construct

(D) Edit

Student: ____________________ Date: ________

Instructor: ____________________ Course: ________ Section: ________

Short Answer

15.08 Explain a few practical uses for polylines in a drawing.

15.09 How does the Halfwidth option differ from the Width option of the PLINE command?

Applying the AutoCAD Environment

15.10 In figure 15.6, identify the polyline segments drawn with a width of zero.

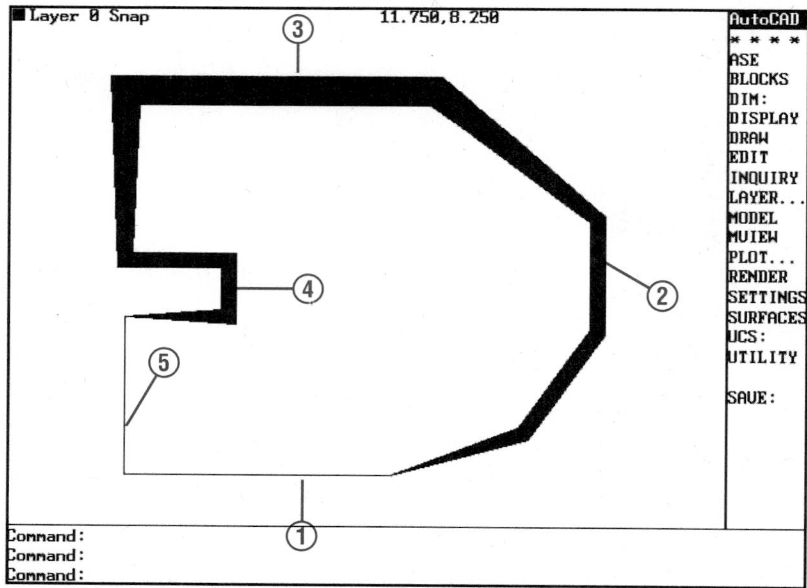

Figure 15.6

Examples of polylines.

Additional Exercises

15.11 Draw the outline of the gasket shown in figure 15.7 as a closed polyline. Remember to use the Undo option of the PLINE command if you make a mistake while drawing a segment. When the gasket outline is complete, experiment with the OFFSET command to create another polyline inside the first at a distance of .25" away.

Student: ______________ Date: ______________

Instructor: ______________ Course: ______________ Section: ______________

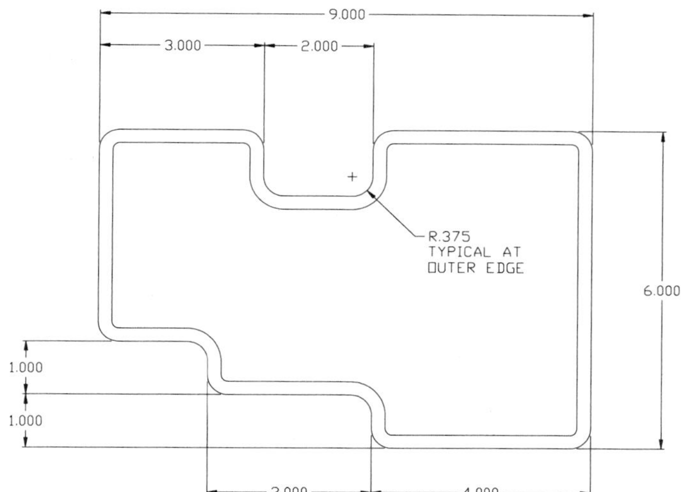

Figure 15.7

Outline of a gasket to be drawn as a polyline.

Student: ____________________ Date: ________

Instructor: ____________________ Course: ________ Section: ________

Adding Text to a Drawing

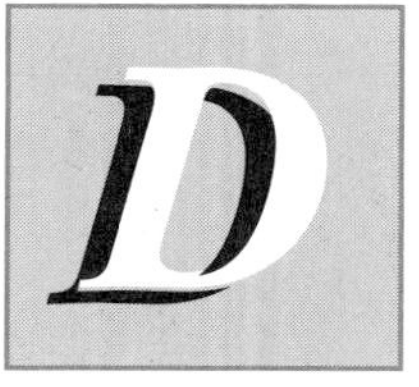

Drawings typically require text that describes material characteristics, specifies manufacturing procedures, defines bills of material, or defines other non-graphical information. This unit teaches you how to add descriptive notes and leaders to a drawing.

The objectives for this unit are to:

- Insert notes and other text into a drawing
- Control the justification of notes with the Center, Right, and default Left options of the DTEXT command
- Set the height and rotation of the text as each text entity is added to the drawing
- Use special characters and symbolic text in a note that is unavailable on the alphanumeric keyboard of the computer
- Turn QTEXT on to display text as a simple rectangle to speed up display activities
- Draw an arrow leader and insert text beside it as a note

Adding Text to a Drawing

The most common way to add text to a drawing is to use the DTEXT command. You can start the DTEXT command by choosing Draw, then Text, then Dynamic. You also can enter the command directly at the `Command:` prompt, or choose DTEXT from the DRAW screen menu. The following exercises teach you how to set the text's height, rotation, and justification.

In the following exercises, use the DTEXT command to place text for the sheet number (1 of 1) and scale (FULL) in the title block with a text height of .1 inch. Insert your name in the space between the sheet number and scale. Then repeat the DTEXT command to place a note along the left end border line establishing that this drawing sheet is an ANSI A-size sheet. Rotate the text 90 degrees and reset the text height to .05 inch. By default, the text will be placed left-justified. Figure 16.1 shows how your drawing should appear as you start the exercise.

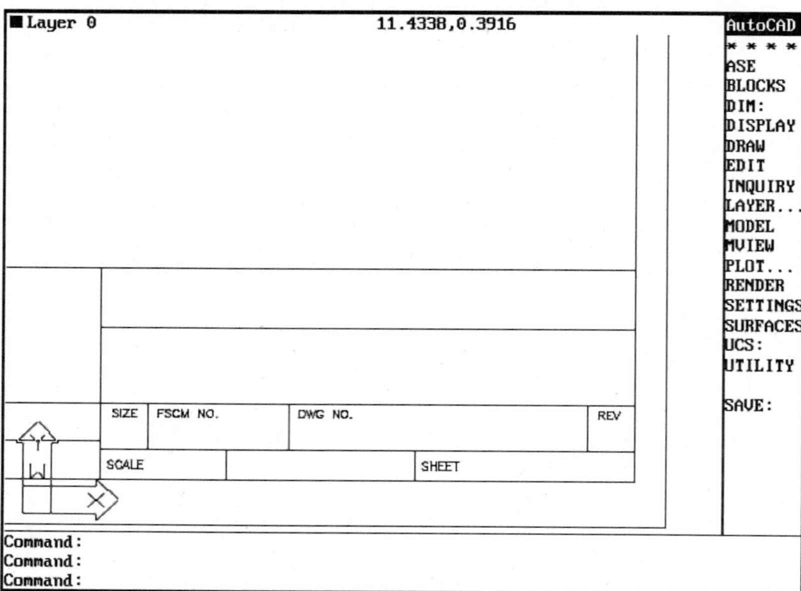

Figure 16.1

A new title block drawing.

Placing Text in a Drawing

1. Begin a new drawing named 016???01 in your assigned directory, using 016TBLOK as the prototype.

2. `Command:` *Choose* Draw, *then* Text, *then* Dynamic	Starts the DTEXT command
3. `dtext Justify/Style/<Start point>:` *Pick a point near* ① *(see fig. 16.2)*	Locates the start point of the text
4. `Height <0.2000>:` **`3/32`** ↵	Specifies a new text height
5. `Rotation angle <0>:` ↵ `Text:` **`FULL`** ↵	Accepts the default rotation Enters one line of text
6. `Text:` ↵	Ends the DTEXT command
7. `Command:` *Press* Enter	Repeats the DTEXT command

8. DTEXT Justify/Style/<Start point>: *Pick a start point at* ②	Locates the start point of the text
9. Height <0.0938>: *Press* Enter	Accepts the default text height
10. Rotation angle <0>: *Press* Enter	Accepts the default rotation
11. Text: **1 of 1** ↵	Enters one line of text
12. Text: *Press* Enter	Ends the DTEXT command
13. Command: *Press* Enter	Repeats the DTEXT command
14. DTEXT Justify/Style/<Start point>: *Pick a start point at* ③	Locates the start point of the text
15. Height <0.0938>: *Press* Enter	Accepts the default text height
16. Rotation angle <0>: *Press* Enter	Accepts the default rotation
17. Text: *(enter your name)* ↵	Enters one line of text
18. Text: *Press* Enter	Ends the DTEXT command
19. Command: *Press* Enter	Repeats the DTEXT command
20. DTEXT Justify/Style/<Start point>: *Pick a start point at* ④	Locates the start point of the text
21. Height <0.0938>: **.0625** ↵	Enters a new text height
22. Rotation angle <0>: **90** ↵	Resets the text rotation
23. Text: **ANSI A-SIZE** ↵	Enters one line of text
24. Text: *Press* Enter	Ends the DTEXT command

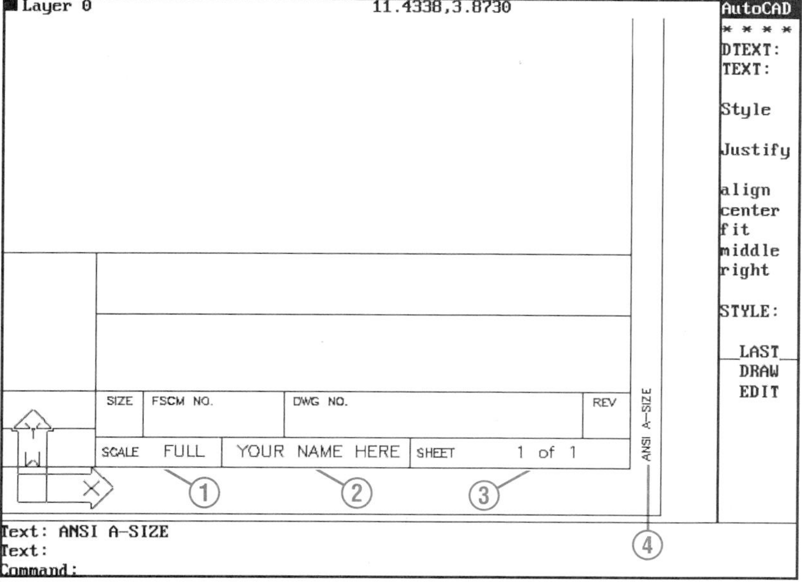

Figure 16.2

Text placement.

Next, place center-justified text for the drawing name (TEXT EXERCISE), and your school or company name and address. Then place right-justified text for the drawing number (015???01).

Controlling Text Justification

1.	Command: *From the* DRAW *screen menu, choose* DTEXT:	Starts the DTEXT command
2.	DTEXT Justify/Style/<Start point>: **C** ↵	Sets the text justification to be centered
3.	Center point: *Pick a point at* ① *(see fig. 16.3)*	Locates the centered start point for the text
4.	Height <0.0625>: **.25** ↵	Enters a new text height
5.	Rotation angle <90>: **0** ↵	Enters a new rotation angle
6.	Text: **TEXT EXERCISE** ↵	Enters one line of text
7.	Text: *Press* Enter	Ends DTEXT command
8.	Command: **DTEXT** ↵	Starts the DTEXT command
9.	Justify/Style/<Start point>: **C**	Sets the text justification to be centered
10.	Center point: *Pick a point at* ②	Locates the centered start point for the text
11.	Height <0.2500>: **.125** ↵	Enters a new text height
12.	Rotation angle <0>: *Press* Enter	Accepts default rotation
13.	Text: *(enter your school or company name, followed by* ↵*)*	Enters one line of text
14.	Text: *(enter your city and state, followed by* ↵*)*	Enters one line of text
15.	Text: *Press* Enter	Ends DTEXT command
16.	Command: *Press* Enter	Repeats DTEXT command
17.	DTEXT Justify/Style/<Start point>: *From the screen menu, choose* right	Sets the text justification to be on the right
18.	End point: *Pick a point at* ③	Locates a right end start point for the text
19.	Height <0.125>: **.1875** ↵	Accepts the default text height
20.	Rotation angle <0>: *Press* Enter	Accepts default rotation

21. `Text:` **`016???01`** ↵	Enters one line of text
22. `Text:` *Press* Enter	Ends DTEXT command

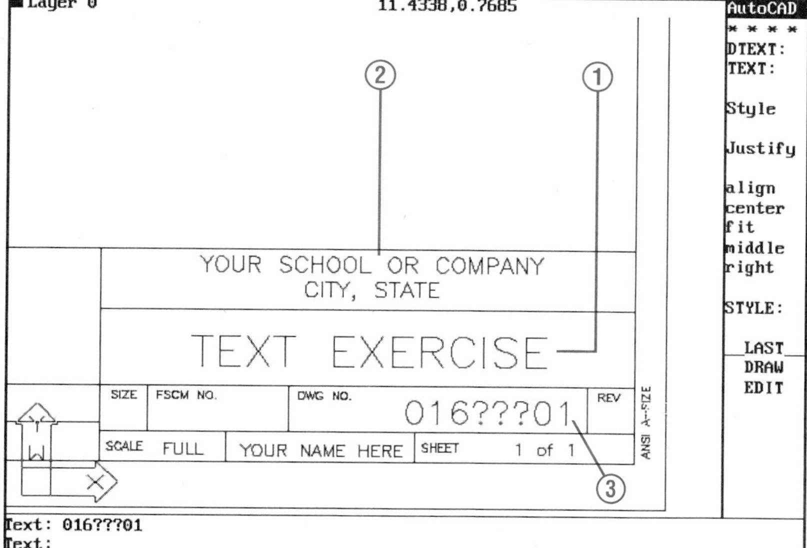

Figure 16.3

Text justification.

There are other options for justification of text that will be discussed in detail in unit 72, "Setting Text Options."

NOTE

DTEXT stands for "Dynamis Text." In addition to the DTEXT command, AutoCAD includes a TEXT command. Unlike the DTEXT command, which enables you to enter multiple lines of text with a single command, the TEXT command enters only one line of text. In most other respects, the TEXT command is the same as the DTEXT command.

Using Special Characters and Symbols

You often need to enter special symbols or characters in a drawing, such as the character for angular degrees, the symbol for diameter, and the plus or minus symbol. These characters do not appear on the keyboard. To use them in a drawing, enter these character combinations:

%%C	diameter symbol
%%D	degrees symbol
%%P	plus or minus symbol

%%U underscore symbol

%%% percent symbol

In the following exercise place general notes in the lower-left of the sheet that utilizes these character combinations to produce special characters in the text.

Using Special Characters as Symbols

1. `Command:` *Choose* Draw, *then* Text, *then* Dynamic	Starts the DTEXT command
2. `_dtext Justify/Style/<Start point>:` *Pick a point at* ① *(see fig. 16.4)*	Locates the start point for default left-justified text
3. `Height <0.1875>:` **3/32** ↵	Enters new text height
4. `Rotation angle <0>:` *Press* Enter	Accepts default text rotation
5. `Text:` **HOLES ARE %%C1/2"** ↵	Enters one line of text
6. `Text:` *Press Space* ↵	Enters one blank line
7. `Text:` **CHAMFERS ARE 45%%D** ↵	Enters one line of text
8. `Text:` *Press Space* ↵	Enters one blank line
9. `Text:` **TOLERANCE IS %%P1/32"** ↵	Enters one line of text
10. `Text:` *Press Space* ↵	Enters one blank line
11. `Text:` **%%UNO EXCEPTIONS** ↵	Enters one line of text
12. `Text:` *Press Space* ↵	Enters one blank line
13. `Text:` **DESIGN DRAFTING IS 90%%% COMPLETE** ↵	Enters one line of text
14. `Text:` *Press* Enter	Ends DTEXT command

Controlling Text Display

Drawings frequently become cumbersome when text, blocks, hatching, and other complex entities are added. ZOOM, REDRAW, and REGEN take more time to complete as a drawing becomes more complex. To reduce the time required for these commands to execute, use the QTEXT: command. The QTEXT command turns QTEXT on and off. By default, QTEXT is off, which displays all the text. If QTEXT is turned on, all text is represented by rectangles of size equal to the text. This reduces the complexity of the drawing and allows ZOOM, REDRAW, and REGEN to execute more quickly.

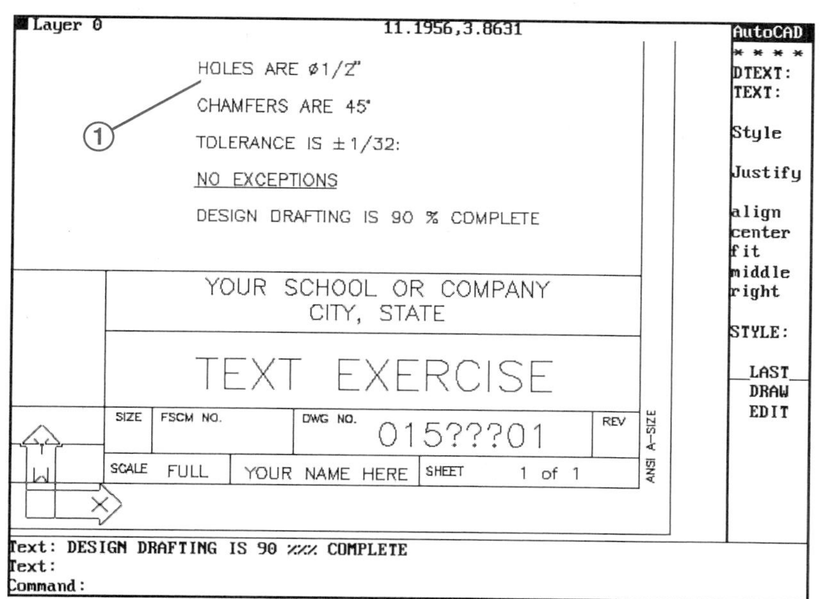

Figure 16.4

Special characters as symbols.

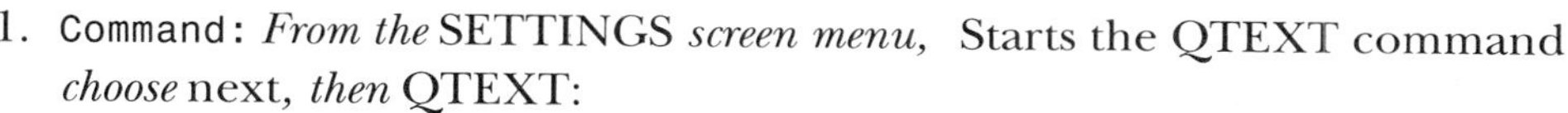

Using QTEXT To Speed Up Zoom, REDRAW, and REGEN

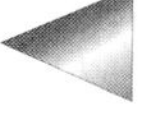

1. `Command:` *From the* SETTINGS *screen menu, choose* next, *then* QTEXT: — Starts the QTEXT command
2. `_QTEXT ON/OFF <Off>:` *From the screen menu, choose* ON — Turns on QTEXT
3. `Command:` *From the* QTEXT *screen menu, choose* REGEN:

   `REGEN Regenerating drawing.` — Regenerates the drawing with text indicated by rectangles (see fig. 16.5)
4. `Command:` *From the screen menu, choose* QTEXT:
5. `_QTEXT ON/OFF <On>:` **OFF** ↵ — Turns off QTEXT
6. `Command:` **REGEN** ↵ — Regenerates the drawing with text fully displayed
7. `Command:` *Choose* File, *then* Save — Saves your drawing to disk

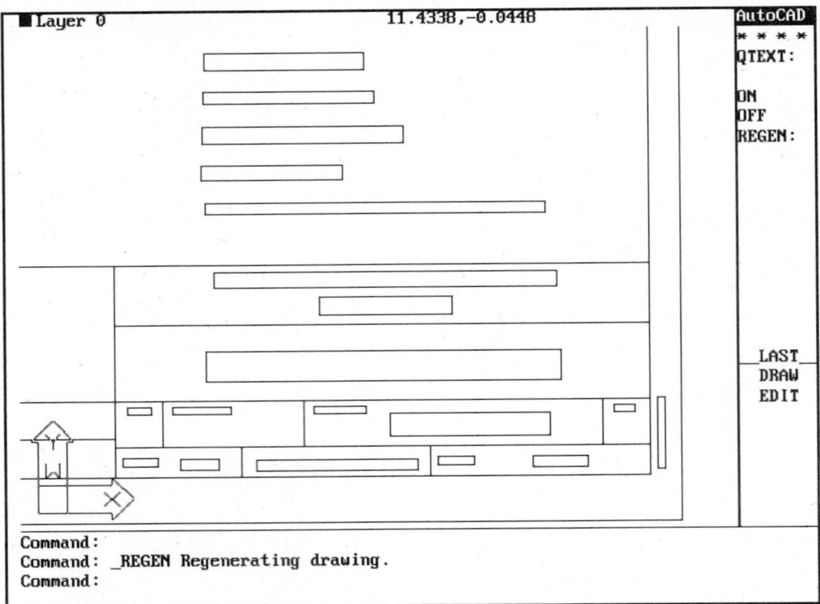

Figure 16.5

Text displayed with QTEXT turned on.

Drawing Leaders

Technical notes are frequently added to a drawing with leader arrows that point to the entity being described. You can add notes with leader arrows to your drawing by using one of AutoCAD's many dimensioning mode commands. The following exercise teaches you to add leaders to a drawing. Add notes with leader arrows to the title block sheet that point to and explain the revision table in the upper-right corner of the sheet. Use figure 16.6 as a guide to complete the exercise.

Adding Notes with Leader Arrows

Continue with your drawing 016???01 from the previous exercise.

1. `Command:` *Choose* View, *then* Zoom, *then* All	Displays the entire drawing
2. `Command:` *Choose* Draw, *then* Dimensions, *then* Leader `_dim1`	Starts the DIM:LEA command
3. `Dim: _leader Leader start:` *Pick a start point for the arrow at* ① *(see fig. 16.6)*	Locates the point of the arrowhead
4. `To point:` *Pick a point at* ②	Draws line segment
5. `To point:` *Pick a point at* ③	Draws line segment

6. `To point:` *Press* Enter	Ends line segment input and adds final horizontal segment
7. `Dimension text <>:` **DRAWING REVISIONS ARE LISTED HERE** ↵	Enters one line of text and ends LEA command

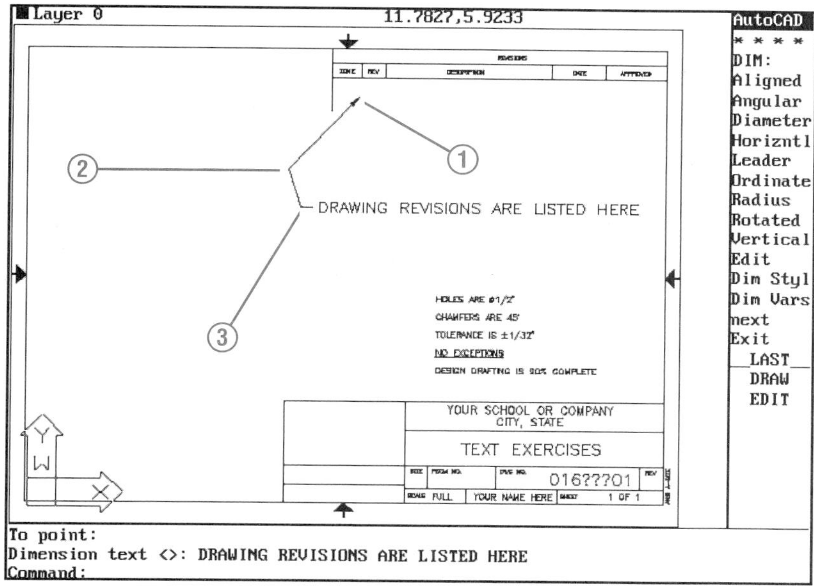

Figure 16.6

A note with an arrow leader.

Unit Review

What You've Learned

- ☞ Commands: DTEXT, QTEXT, DIM:LEA
- ☞ How to add text to your drawing
- ☞ How to control the text height and rotation
- ☞ How to control right, center, and left text justification
- ☞ How to include special characters and symbols in your text
- ☞ How to control the display of text
- ☞ How to add notes with arrows called leaders

Review Questions

True or False

16.01 T F QTEXT is an option of the DTEXT command.

16.02 T F The justification of text may changed each time a text entity is added to a drawing.

16.03 T F Special characters (symbols for degrees, percent, plus or minus, etc.) are available on the computer's keyboard.

16.04 T F Notes with arrows, called leaders, are usually created using one of AutoCAD's dimensioning commands.

16.05 T F With default standard text, the height and rotation of text may be reset each time the DTEXT command is used.

16.06 T F DTEXT selected from the Draw pull-down menu works like the DTEXT command selected from the screen menu.

Multiple Choice

16.07 Justification of text may be ____________.

(A) ON or OFF

(B) Right or Left

(C) QTEXT or DTEXT

(D) Height or Rotation

Student: ______________________ Date: __________

Instructor: ______________________ Course: __________ Section: __________

16.08 A __________ is an arrow with a line of text attached to it.

(A) special character

(B) QTEXT

(C) leader

(D) DTEXT

16.09 The proper syntax to include a degree symbol in the text of a note is __________.

(A) %%P

(B) %%D

(C) %%A

(D) %%O

16.10 The proper syntax to include a plus/minus symbol in the text of a note is __________.

(A) %%P

(B) %%D

(C) %%A

(D) %%O

Student: __________ Date: __________

Instructor: __________ Course: __________ Section: __________

Understanding the Display

UNIT 17

To use AutoCAD effectively, you need to understand the relationship between the computer display and the subject drawing being viewed. This unit shows you how AutoCAD uses the display as a "window" onto your drawing.

The objectives for this unit are to:

- Practice viewing a large drawing on a screen of limited size
- Understand the relationship between drawing file data and the display data (the AutoCAD virtual screen)
- Recognize the difference between the REDRAW and REGEN commands
- Understand the need for regeneration of the display data
- Learn to control BLIPMODE and VIEWRES

A Small Window on a Large Drawing

Most design drawings are considerably larger than the display viewing "window" for the drawing. For example, a typical floor plan drawing for a school would be plotted on a 24 × 36" sheet, but when viewed on the computer display it would be displayed in a "window" of about 6 " × 8 1/2 ". That represents a reduction of more than 75 percent of the drawing's original size. Important drawing details are difficult to understand when reduced to that extent. Notes and dimensions also are difficult to read. Figure 17.1 shows a large object displayed in the small AutoCAD drawing area.

When you use display control commands discussed in units 18 and 19, you can view small parts of a drawing close up so that you can edit them. You can move this close-up display "window" to any location in the drawing. Figures 17.2 and 17.3 show in detail the area of the drawing in figure 17.1 that is marked by ① and ②.

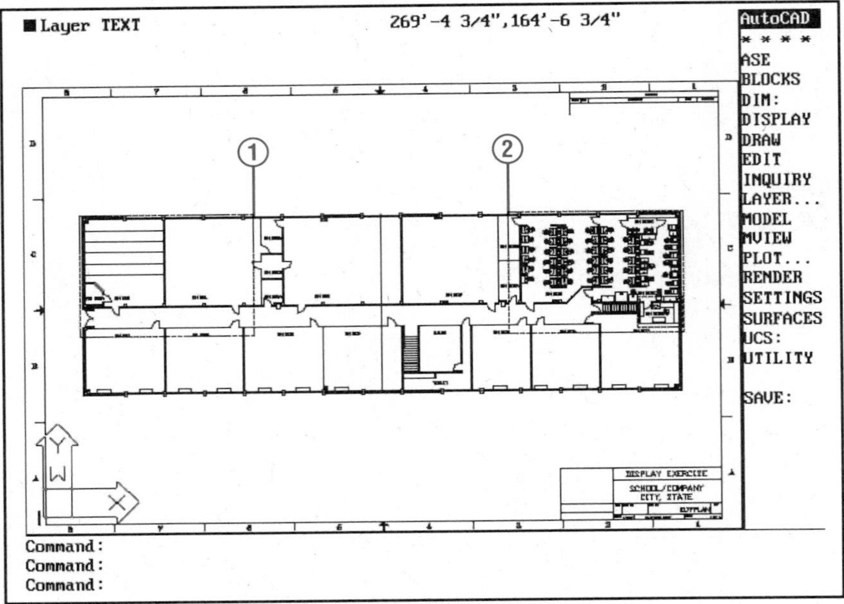

Figure 17.1

Floor Plan at display window size.

You also can select a small window on a drawing and view it in great detail—even larger than it would be on the paper drawing (see fig. 17.4). You can view small detail (only a thousandth of an inch across, for example) on your display. The capability to control the display also enables you to view large drawings on a small screen at any magnification or at actual size.

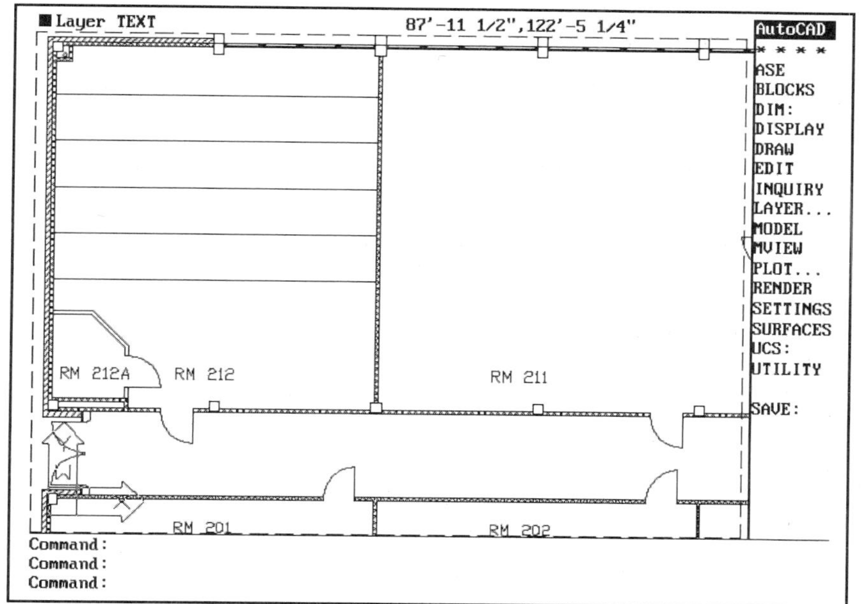

Figure 17.2

Close-up window at ①.

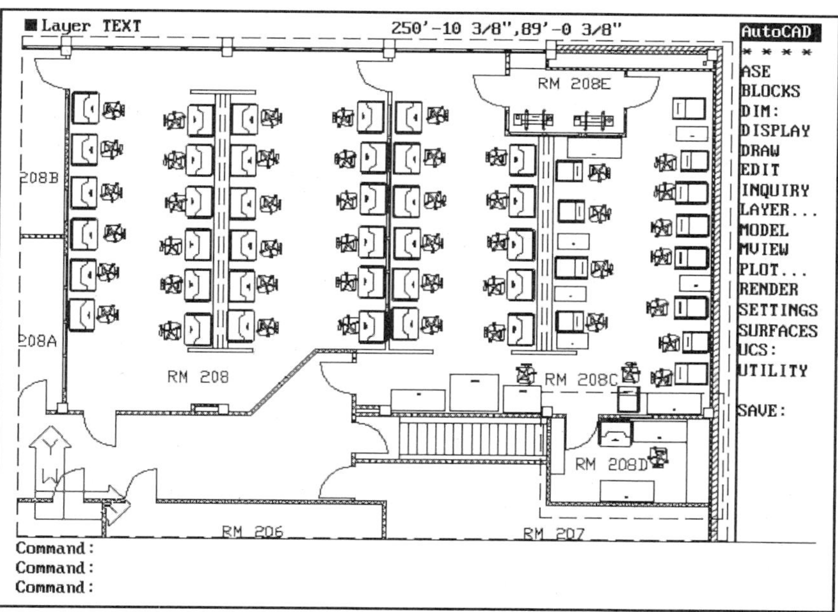

Figure 17.3

Close-up window at ②.

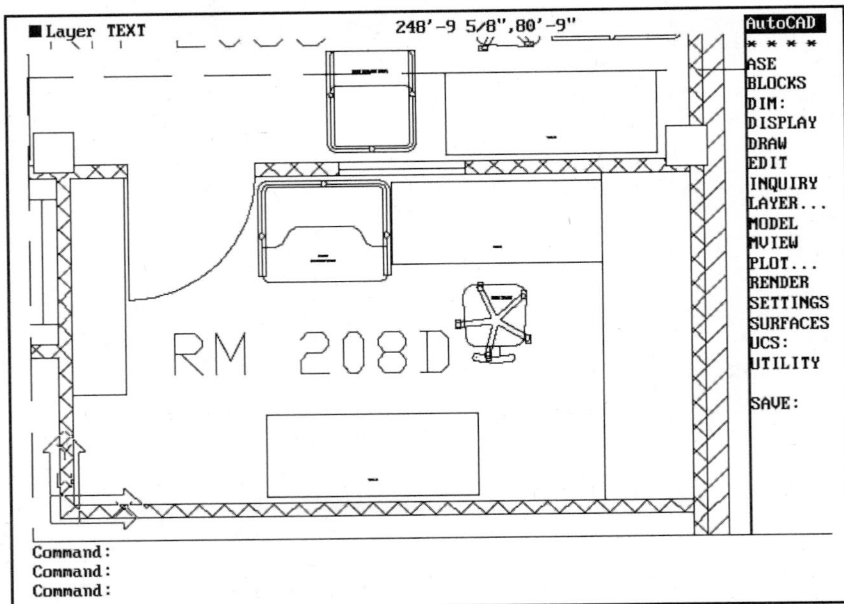

Figure 17.4

Detail of close-up window.

Understanding the Virtual Screen

When you work on a drawing in AutoCAD, AutoCAD maintains the drawing information in more than one format. Unit 10 explains how AutoCAD stores the drawing's entities in the drawing database. In addition, AutoCAD must maintain a *representation* of the drawing database so that it can display the drawing on-screen. This representation is called the *virtual screen.* Think of the virtual screen as a huge pixel map of the drawing database (unit 10 explains pixels). Whenever AutoCAD needs to display a portion of the drawing on the physical screen, it copies the representation of the drawing from the corresponding portion of the virtual screen.

When you move your view of the drawing from one point to another, AutoCAD must read the virtual screen and change the physical screen accordingly. The integer-to-integer translation from virtual screen data to physical screen data is quite fast—AutoCAD can recalculate changes in the physical screen from the virtual screen rapidly.

As the drawing changes, AutoCAD must update both the drawing database and the virtual screen so that they match one another. This process is called a *drawing regeneration.* AutoCAD regenerates the drawing automatically whenever necessary; you can force AutoCAD to perform a drawing regeneration by using the REGEN command.

When AutoCAD regenerates the drawing, it must convert the real numbers used in the drawing database to the integer representation in the virtual screen. For a complex or large drawing, this recalculation can be time-consuming. When you work with large drawings, avoid unnecessary drawing regenerations to speed up your drawing time.

Refreshing the Display

As you work on a drawing—adding, moving, and modifying entities—the physical screen can become corrupted, or "dirty." Portions of entities may disappear because an overlying entity was removed, or small crosses called *blips* may appear on the display where you picked points.

The use of the REDRAW command after editing cleans up the computer display. REDRAW restores the image on the display quickly, shows the results of editing, removes blips, and restores missing pieces of entities. Other display commands such as ZOOM and PAN also cause a redraw of the display. REDRAW essentially forces AutoCAD to recopy the current drawing area from the virtual screen to the physical screen.

In the follow exercise, draw some entities, then erase them. Clean up the corrupted display that you just edited by using the REDRAW command.

Cleaning Up the Display after Editing

1. Begin a new drawing named 017???01 in your assigned directory, using 017FPLAN as a prototype.

2. `Command:` *Choose* Draw, *then* Text, *then* Dynamic	Starts the DTEXT command
3. `dtext Justify/Style/<Start point>:` **`C`** ↵	Sets the text justification to be centered
4. `Center point:` *Pick a point at* ① *(see fig. 17.5)*	Locates the centered start point for the text
5. `Height <0'-0 1/4"">:` **`1'3"`** ↵	Enters a new text height
6. `Rotation angle <0.0>:` *Press* Enter	Accepts default rotation
7. `Text:` **`DOS-PC 486/PENTIUM`** ↵	Enters one line of text
8. `Text:` **`CAD LABORATORY`** ↵	Enters one line of text
9. `Text:` **`24 SEATS`** ↵	Enters one line of text
10. `Text:` *Press* Enter	Ends DTEXT command

continues

11. `Command:` *Choose* Modify, *then* Erase, *then* Select	Starts the ERASE command
`_erase`	
12. `Select objects:` *Place the square cursor on the text you just added, then click the select button*	Selects and erases the text but leaves the drawing area corrupted where the text was located (see fig. 17.5)
`1 found`	
13. `Select objects:` *Select the other two lines of text you just added*	
14. `Select objects:` *Press* Enter	Ends the ERASE command
15. `Command:` *Choose* View, *then* Redraw	Starts REDRAW command
`'_redraw`	Redraws the display

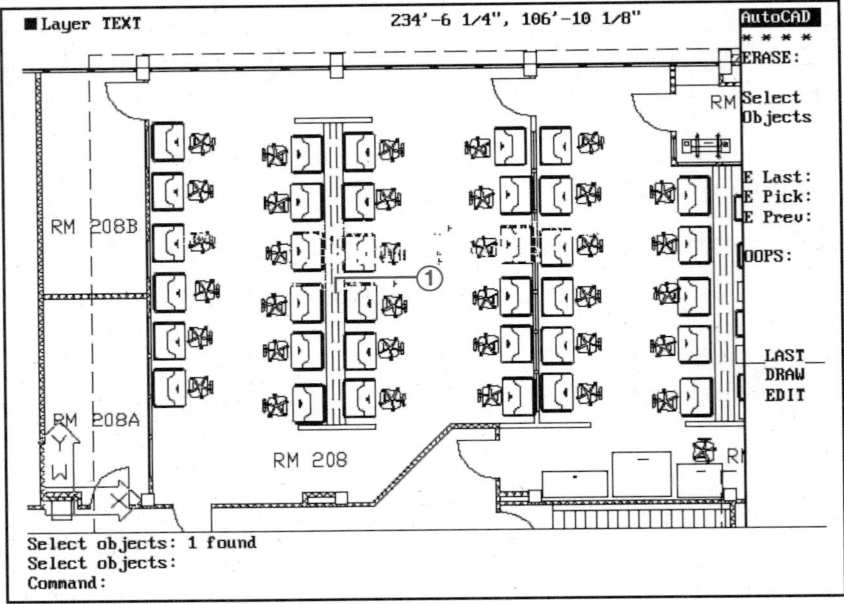

Figure 17.5

Edited drawing before clean up with REDRAW.

After using the REDRAW command, the missing portions of the symbols in the drawing return.

A quick and convenient way to redraw the display is to press F7, which toggles the grid ON or OFF and causes a REDRAW in the process. (For this to work, the grid spacing must be set to a value

that you can see.) Also, the REDRAW command can be issued as a Transparent command by preceding it with an apostrophe ('). Transparent commands can be entered while another command is active, for example. The ZOOM and PAN commands also can be issued as transparent commands as can other selected AutoCAD commands.

Redraw Using QTEXT

The QTEXT command, which is explained in unit 16, can be used to display text as rectangular boxes instead of as actual text to speed up the redraw and regeneration process. Some AutoCAD commands, including QTEXT, regenerate the drawing using the drawing data file and update the virtual screen data. The use of the QTEXT command in the following exercise illustrates this point.

Using REGEN To Show Results of QTEXT

1. `Command:` *From the* SETTINGS *screen menu, choose* next, *then* QTEXT:	Starts the QTEXT command
2. `_QTEXT ON/OFF <Off>:` *From the screen menu, choose* ON	Turns on QTEXT
3. `Command:` *From the* QTEXT *screen menu, choose* REGEN:	
4. `_REGEN Regenerating drawing.`	Regenerates drawing with text indicated by rectangles (see fig. 17.6)
5. `Command:` *From the screen menu, choose* QTEXT:	
6. `_QTEXT ON/OFF <ON>:` **OFF** ↵	Turns off QTEXT
7. `Command:` **REGEN** ↵	Regenerates the drawing with text fully displayed
8. `Command:` *Choose* File, *then* Save	Saves your drawing to disk

From the previous exercises, you can see that drawing regeneration is much slower than simply executing a redraw of the screen. When AutoCAD redraws a screen, it does not have to recalculate the entire database to redraw the screen—necessary when a drawing is regenerated.

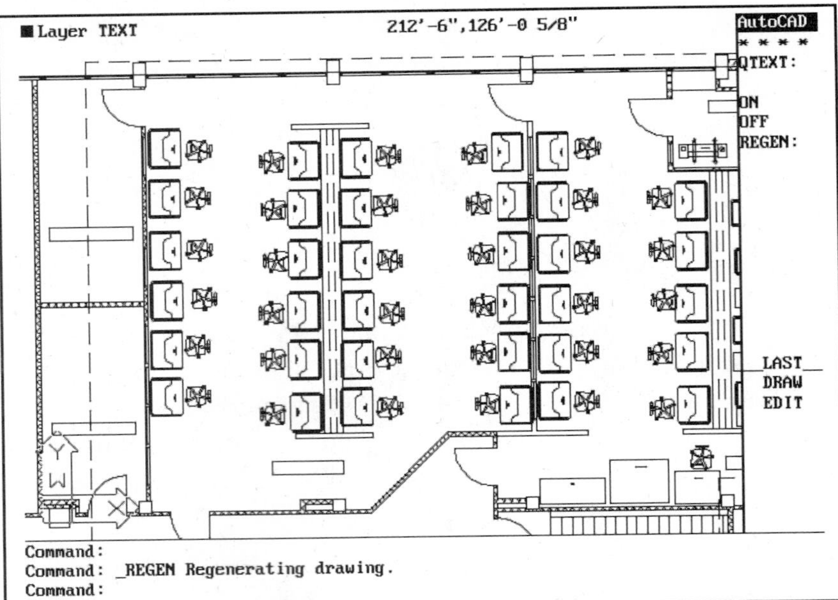

Figure 17.6
Regenerated drawing after QTEXT command.

Controlling Display Options

You can make the display environment eliminate small marks, called *blips*, that occur on the display when you select entities or pick-points. The variable BLIPMODE controls blips. The BLIPMODE setting is ON by default so that blips are produced on the display. You can turn off BLIPMODE to prevent AutoCAD from creating blips. Although blips can clutter an image on the display, they are useful indicators of former entity pick-points.

In addition to using the BLIPMODE command to control blips, you also can use the Drawing Aids dialog box to turn blips on and off.

Another display environment command is VIEWRES, which controls two parts of the display environment. First, VIEWRES controls whether display commands cause a redraw or always require a regeneration of the display from the drawing database. Second, VIEWRES controls the displayed smoothness of polyline curves, arcs, and circles.

The following exercise demonstrates the control of the display with BLIPMODE and VIEWRES.

Display Control with BLIPMODE and VIEWRES

1. Begin a new drawing without a name in your assigned directory, using 017BLIPS as a prototype.

2. `Command:` *Choose* Modify, *then* Move `_move`	Starts the MOVE command
3. `Select objects:` *Select circle at ① (see fig. 17.7)* `1 found`	Selected text is highlighted and blip is added to display
4. `Select objects:` *Press* Enter	Completes selection set
5. `Base point or displacement:` *Pick a location on the circle*	Circle attached to cursor with blip added to display
6. `Second point of displacement:` *Pick any point to place the circle*	Circle relocates to new point with blip added to display

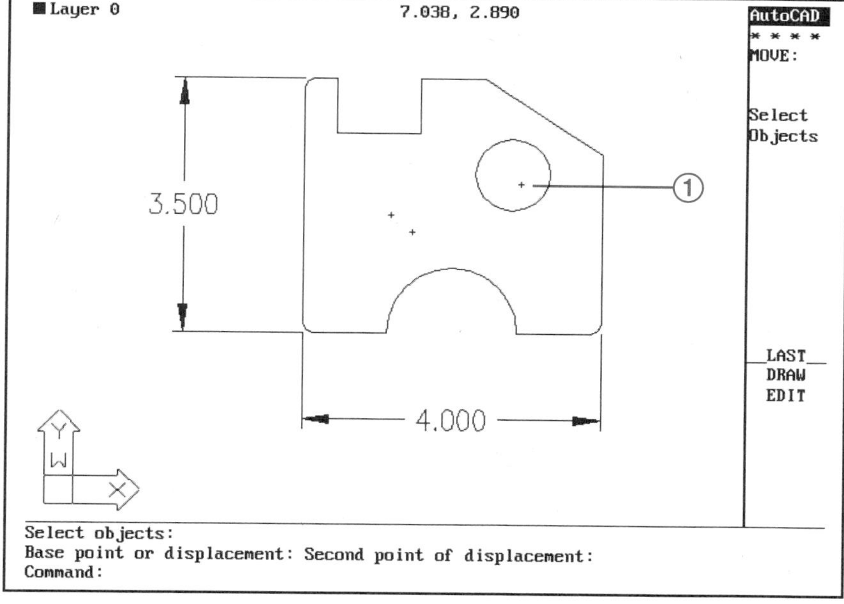

Figure 17.7

Blips on the display.

7. `Command:` **`R`** ↵	Issues the shortcut key for the REDRAW command
8. `Command:` *From the* SETTINGS *screen menu, choose* BLIPS:	Start the BLIPMODE command
9. `'_BLIPMODE ON/OFF <On>: _OFF` *From the screen menu, choose* OFF	Turns off BLIPMODE

continues

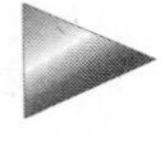

10. `Command:` *Choose* Modify, *then* Move	Start the MOVE command
`_move`	
11. `Select objects: 1 found` *Select the circle*	Selected circle is highlighted without a blip
12. `Select objects:` *Press* Enter	Completes Selection set
13. `Base point or displacement:` *Pick a location near the circle*	Circle attached to cursor without a blip
14. `Second point of displacement:` *Pick a point anywhere on the part*	Circle relocated without blips
15. `Command:` *From the* DISPLAY *screen menu, choose* VIEWRES:	Starts the VIEWRES command
`_VIEWRES`	
16. `Do you want fast zooms? <Y>` **N** ↵	Turns off fast zooms
17. `Enter circle zoom percent (1-20000) <100>:` **10** ↵	Resets arc/circle resolution
`Regenerating drawing.`	

Regenerates drawing to display drawing with new resolution (see fig. 17.8).

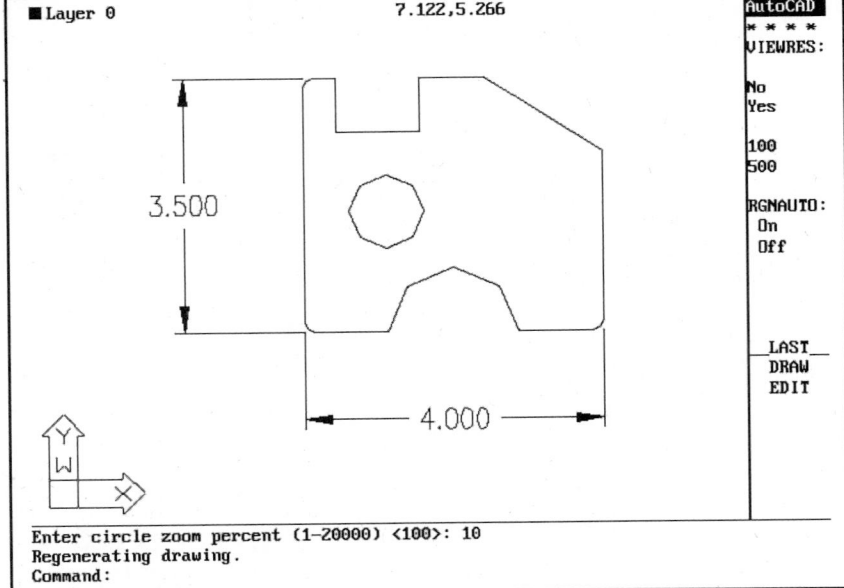

Figure 17.8

Plan with VIEWRES circle zoom set at 10.

Increasing the value for VIEWRES increases the resolution of arcs, circles, and polylines, but also increases drawing regeneration time. A reduced VIEWRES value decreases the resolution of these entities, but decreases regeneration time.

Unit Review

What You've Learned

- The limitations of viewing a drawing on a relatively small computer display
- The concept of viewing a limited part of a drawing in more detail and closer up
- The relationship of drawing file data to computer display data
- How and when to use REDRAW
- When REGEN is needed
- How to control BLIPMODE
- How to control VIEWRES

Student: ______ Date: ______

Instructor: ______ Course: ______ Section: ______

Review Questions

True or False

17.01 T F The virtual screen is the display of data from the AutoCAD drawing file.

17.02 T F The VIEWRES command can be set to require regeneration of the drawing display each time a display command is executed.

17.03 T F Regeneration of the drawing display is needed to clean up a drawing.

17.04 T F The virtual screen and the physical screen are the same.

17.05 T F Regeneration of a drawing display is faster than a redraw of a drawing display.

17.06 T F Floating-point drawing data is converted to integer data during a regeneration of a drawing display.

Multiple Choice

17.07 Fast ZOOM is possible because of the __________ of AutoCAD.

(A) physical screen

(B) virtual screen

(C) drawing display

(D) floating point

17.08 The quickest way to clean up the drawing display window after editing is the __________ command.

(A) REGEN

(B) ZOOM

(C) REDRAW

(D) VIEWRES

17.09 The __________ is much like a large pixel map in the memory of the drawing.

(A) physical screen

(B) virtual screen

(C) drawing file

(D) floating point

Short Answer

17.10 How can a drawing that is 30 " × 42 " be viewed in sufficient detail for editing in a computer display window that is only approximately 6 " × 8 1/2 "?

____

____

____

Student: __________ Date: __________

Instructor: __________ Course: __________ Section: __________

UNIT 18

Using ZOOM To Control the Display

Unit 17 explains how the AutoCAD display provides a "window" onto a large drawing. This unit explains how you can control the display with the ZOOM command to edit minute detail, view the entire drawing, or increase the available area around the current drawing. The ZOOM command is used often in AutoCAD.

The objectives of this unit are to:

- Use the Window option of the ZOOM command
- Use the Dynamic option of the ZOOM command
- Use the All and Extents options of the ZOOM command, and understand the difference between them
- Use the Previous and Vmax options of the ZOOM command
- Use scale factors to zoom in and out
- Use the Center option of the ZOOM command

Controlling a Small "Window" on the Drawing

The Window option of the ZOOM command allows you to specify opposite corners of an area to be viewed in the drawing display. AutoCAD magnifies the selected area to fill the display area. Window is the ZOOM command's default option.

As soon as you start the ZOOM command, you can pick two points to define the zoom window—you do not have to select the Window option. You also can specify the size of the window by using relative keyboard input in drawing units to locate the opposite corner.

Figure 18.1 shows the drawing you will be working with in the following exercise.

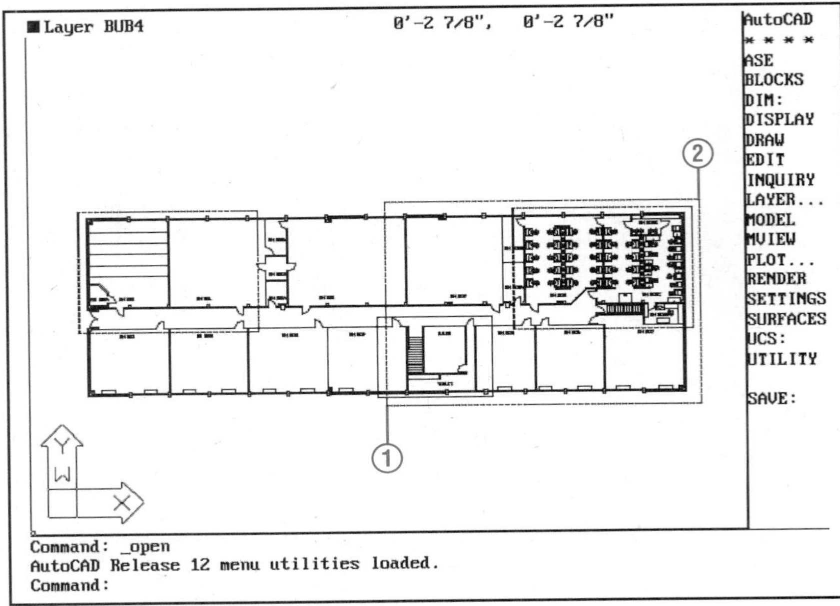

Figure 18.1
Drawing 018???01.

Using the ZOOM Window Option

1. Begin a new drawing named 018???01 in your assigned directory, using 018FPLAN as a prototype.

2. `Command: Z ↵` — Issues the shortcut key to start the ZOOM command

`ZOOM`

3. `All/Center/Dynamic/Extents/Left/Previous/Vmax/Window/<Scale(X/XP)>:` *Pick first corner at ① (see fig. 18.1)* — Picking the first corner invokes the Window option by default

4. `Other corner:` *Pick other corner at ② (see fig. 18.1)* — Displays the selected window

5. `Command:` **`Z`** ↵ — Issues the shortcut key to start the ZOOM command

   `ZOOM`

6. `All/Center/Dynamic/Extents/Left/Previous/Vmax/Window/<Scale(X/XP)>:` *Pick first corner at ① (see fig. 18.2)* — Picking the first corner invokes the Window option by default

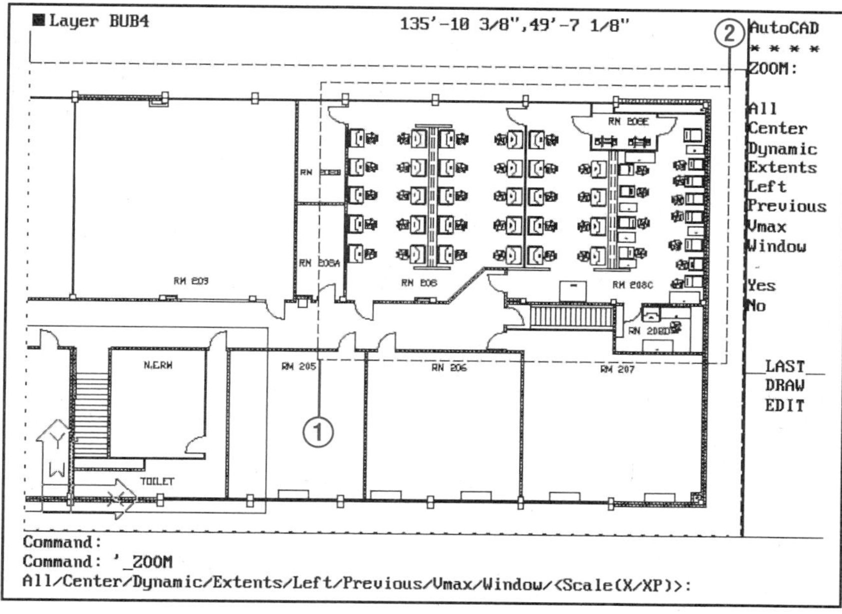

Figure 18.2

Zoom to half of plan.

7. `Other corner:` **`@-68',-48'`** ↵ — Specifies the other corner point at ②, displays the 68' × 48' window (see fig. 18.3)

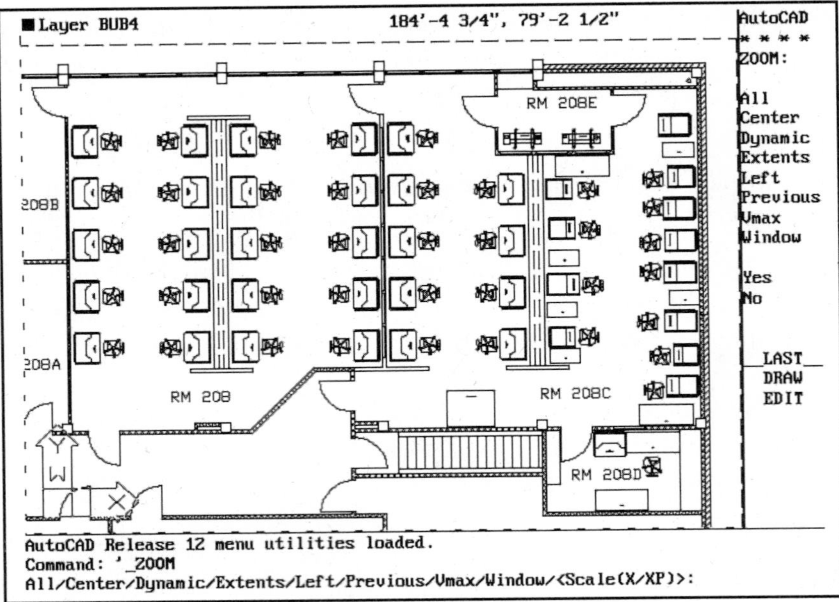

Figure 18.3

A 68' × 48' ZOOM Window.

Using the Dynamic Option

You can move your display window around the drawing with the Dynamic option of the ZOOM command. The Dynamic option allows you to reposition the window from one location to another at the same size or adjust the size of the window to zoom in or out relative to the current view.

Using the ZOOM Dynamic Option

1. `Command:` *Choose* View, *then* Zoom, *then* Dynamic — Starts the ZOOM command with the Dynamic option

   `'_zoom`

2. `All/Center/Dynamic/Extents/Left/Previous/Vmax/Window/<Scale(X/XP)>: _dynamic` *Move the* Dynamic *box to new location* ① *(see fig. 18.4), then press* Enter *or click on the* Enter *button* — Displays same window size at new location

3. `Command:` *Choose* View, *then* Dynamic — Repeats the ZOOM command with the Dynamic option

   `'_zoom`

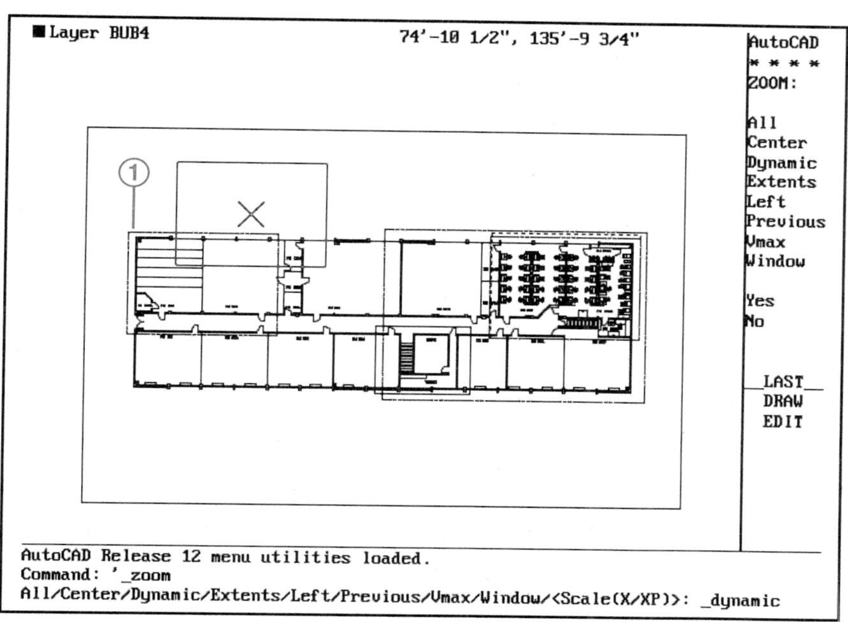

Figure 18.4

Relocate the 68' × 48' ZOOM window.

4. `All/Center/Dynamic/Extents/Left/Previous/Vmax/Window/<Scale(X/XP)>: _dynamic` *Move the* Dynamic *box to new location* ②, *(see fig. 18.5), then click on select, then adjust the size of the box to match the outline at* ③, *then click the* Enter *button*

   Displays adjusted window at new location (see fig. 18.5)

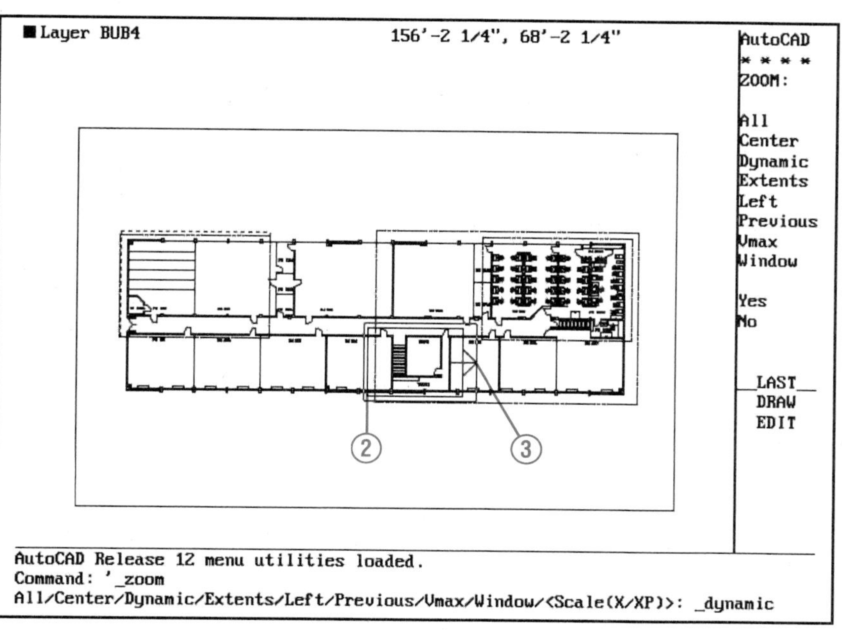

Figure 18.5

Relocate and adjust the size of the ZOOM window.

Using the Display Environment for Zoom Control

The ZOOM command has options that relate to the LIMITS of the current drawing, the drawing area occupied by entities, the current virtual screen, and the previous ZOOM windows.

The Previous option of the ZOOM command will step back through as many as ten prior views produced by ZOOM command options or other commands that produce views, including Pan, VIEW Restore, DVIEW, and PLAN all. These commands are discussed in later units.

Using ZOOM Previous

1. `Command:` *Choose* View, *then* Zoom, *then* Previous — Starts the ZOOM command with the Previous option

   `'_zoom`

   `All/Center/Dynamic/Extents/Left/ Previous/Vmax/Window/<Scale(X/XP)>: _PREVIOUS` — Displays the previous view (see fig. 18.4)

2. `Command:` *Press* Enter — Repeats the ZOOM command

   `'ZOOM`

3. `All/Center/Dynamic/Extents/Left/ Previous/Vmax/Window/<Scale(X/XP)>:` **P** ↵ — Enter the Previous option and display next previous view (see fig. 18.3)

4. `Command:` *Press* Enter — Repeats the ZOOM command

   `'ZOOM`

5. `All/Center/Dynamic/Extents/Left/ Previous/Vmax/Window/<Scale(X/XP)>:` **P** ↵ — Enter the Previous option and display next previous view (see fig. 18.2)

6. `Command:` *Press* Enter — Repeats the ZOOM command

   `'ZOOM`

7. `All/Center/Dynamic/Extents/Left/ Previous/Vmax/Window/<Scale(X/XP)>:` **P** ↵ — Enter the Previous option and display the original view (see fig 18.1)

The Vmax option of the ZOOM command returns the display to the last translation of the drawing data to the virtual screen. In other words, the Vmax option displays the last regeneration of the display.

The All option of the ZOOM command displays the drawing limits and all drawing entities, even if the entities are outside the limits. The Extents option of the ZOOM command displays only the area occupied by drawing entities. Extents will ignore the limits of the drawing and zoom as needed to display the drawing entities as large as possible.

Using ZOOM Vmax, Extents, and All Options

1. `Command:` *Choose* Settings, *then* Drawing Aids — Displays Drawing Aids dialog box, (note 10' grid spacing)

2. `'_ddrmodes` *Check the* Grid *check box* — Turns on GRID so that you can see the drawing limits

3. `Command:` *Choose* View, *then* Zoom, *then* Vmax — Starts the ZOOM command with the Vmax option

   `'_zoom`

   `All/Center/Dynamic/Extents/Left/Previous/Vmax/Window/<Scale(X/XP)>: _vmax` — Displays the virtual screen (see fig. 18.6)

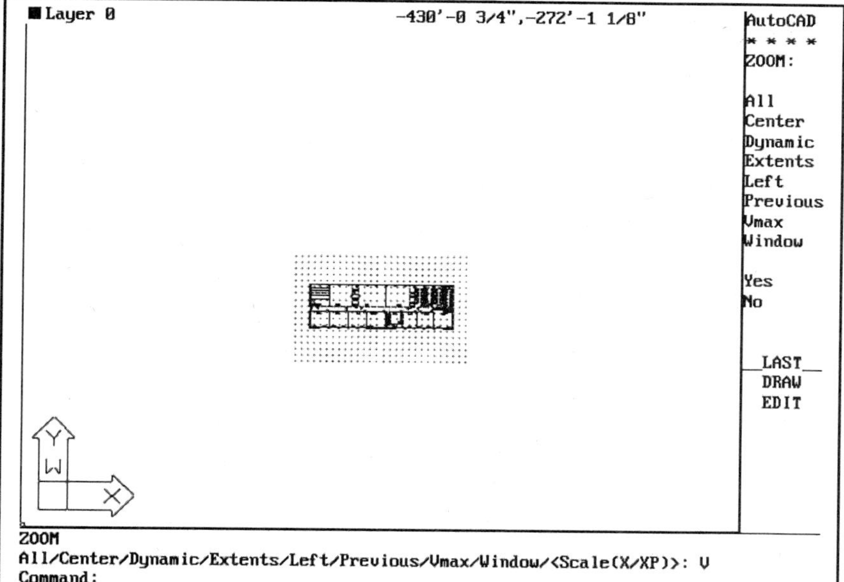

Figure 18.6

View after the Vmax option.

continues

4. `Command:` *Choose* View, *then* Zoom, *then* Extents

   Starts the ZOOM command with the Extents option

   ```
   _zoom
   ```

   ```
   All/Center/Dynamic/Extents/Left/
   Previous/Vmax/Window/<Scale(X/XP)>:
   _extents
   Regenerating drawing.
   ```

   Displays all entities in your drawing as large as possible starting at the lower left (see fig. 18.7)

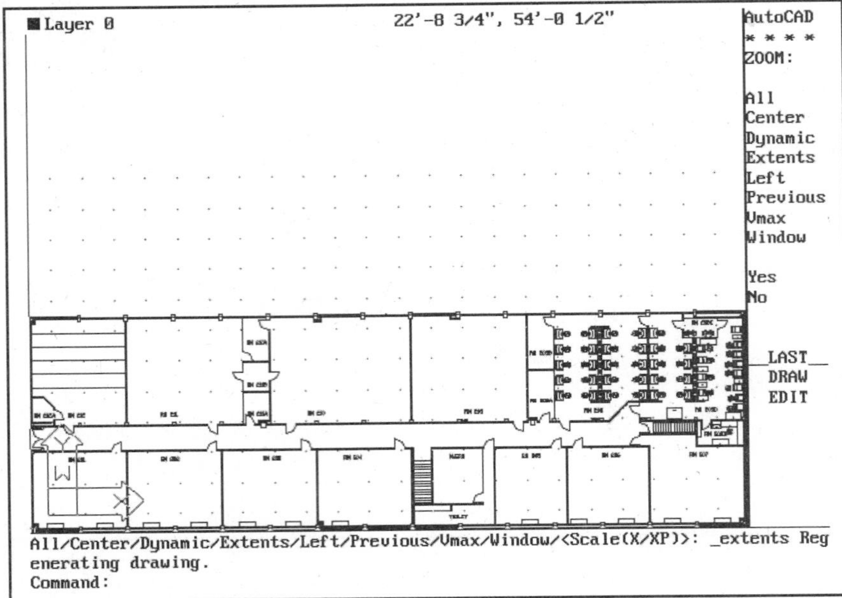

Figure 18.7

View after the Extents option.

5. `Command:` *Choose* View, *then* Zoom, *then* All

   Starts the ZOOM command with the All option

   ```
   _zoom
   ```

8. ```
   All/Center/Dynamic/Extents/Left/
   Previous/Vmax/Window/<Scale(X/XP)>:
   _all
   Regenerating drawing.
   ```

   Displays the limits and all entities in your drawing as large as possible, starting at the lower left (see fig. 18.8)
   ```

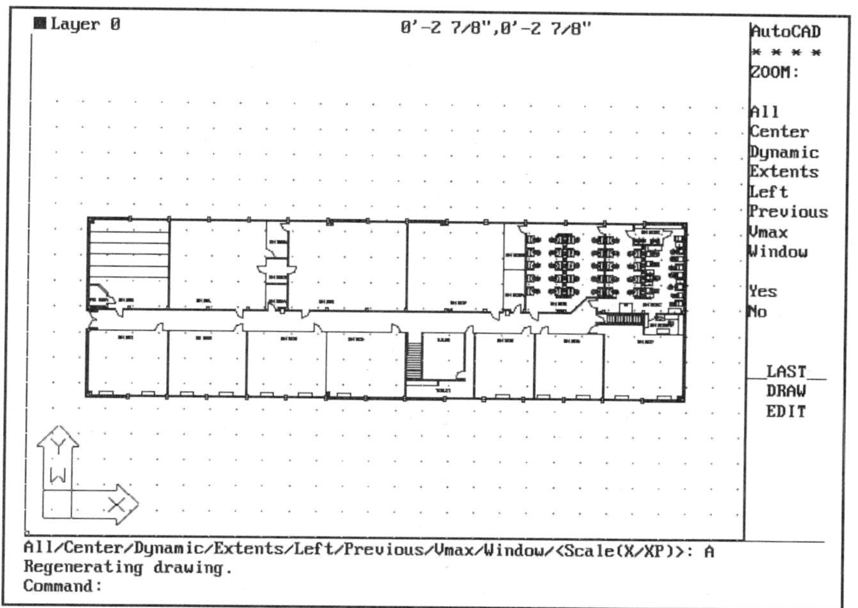

Figure 18.8

View after the All option.

Using Scale Factors for Zoom Control

The simplest way to alter the view of the current drawing is to enter a numeric scale factor at the ZOOM command prompt. The default scale factor for the full view is 1. If you enter 2, the object in the view will appear twice as large as in the full view. If you enter the numeric value of 0.25, the object will be reduced to one-quarter of its full size.

If you include an "X" following the numeric value, the zoom in or out will be relative to the current view rather than the full view. Therefore, 2X will make the object twice as large as it is in the current view, and 0.5X will make the object half its current size.

Using Scale Factors

1. `Command:` *From the* DISPLAY *screen menu, choose* ZOOM: — Starts the ZOOM command

   `'_ZOOM`

2. `All/Center/Dynamic/Extents/Left/Previous/Vmax/Window/<Scale(X/XP)>:` **2** ↵ — Doubles the size of the plan in drawing units (see fig. 18.9)

3. `Command:` *Press* Enter — Repeat the ZOOM command

   `'ZOOM`

continues

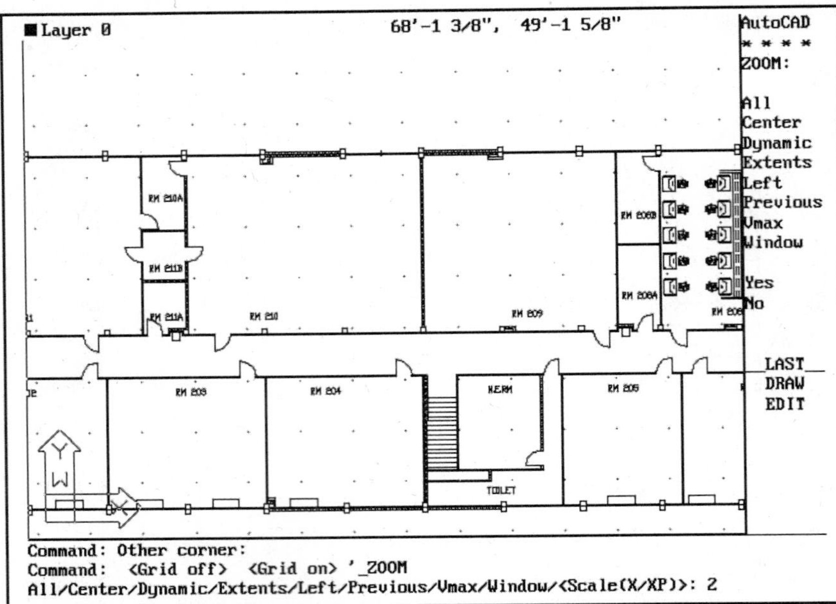

Figure 18.9

Display the plan twice as large with Scale Factor of 2.

4. `All/Center/Dynamic/Extents/Left/Previous/Vmax/Window/<Scale(X/XP)>:` **2X** ↵ — Doubles the size of the plan relative to current display (see fig. 18.10)

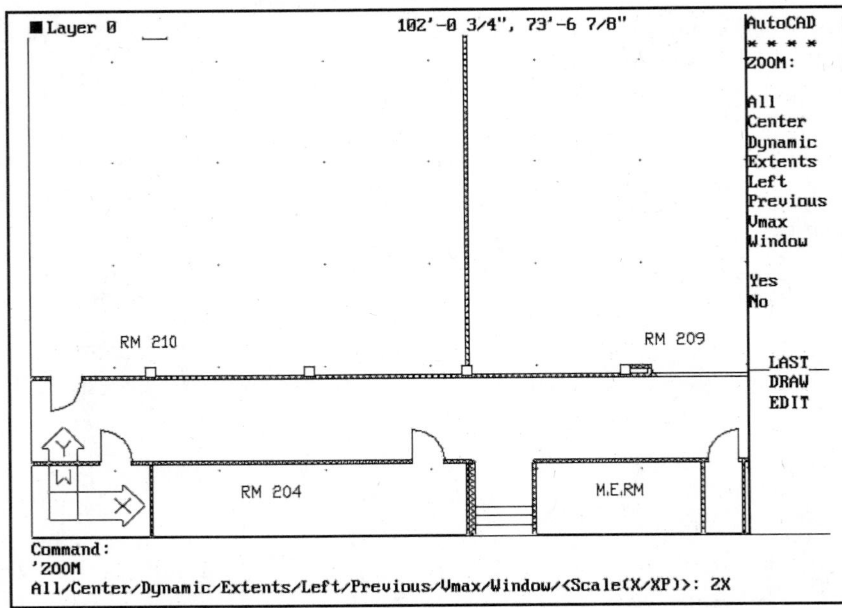

Figure 18.10

Double the current size with Scale Factor of 2X.

5. `Command:` *Press* Enter — Repeat the ZOOM command

   `'ZOOM`

6. `All/Center/Dynamic/Extents/Left/Previous/Vmax/Window/<Scale(X/XP)>:` **`0.25X`** ↵ — Displays the plan at 1/4 size relative to current display (see fig. 18.11)

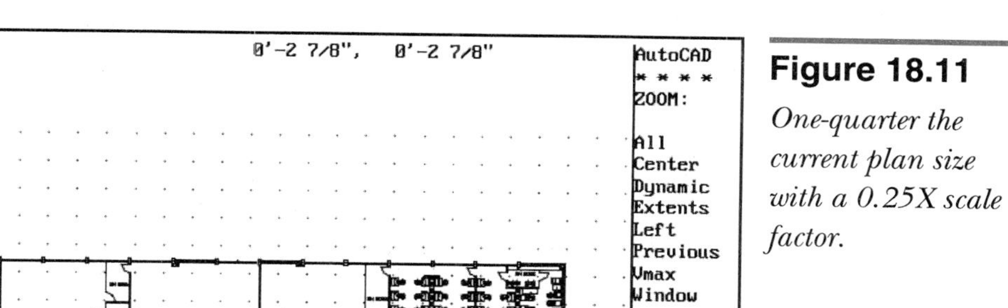

Figure 18.11

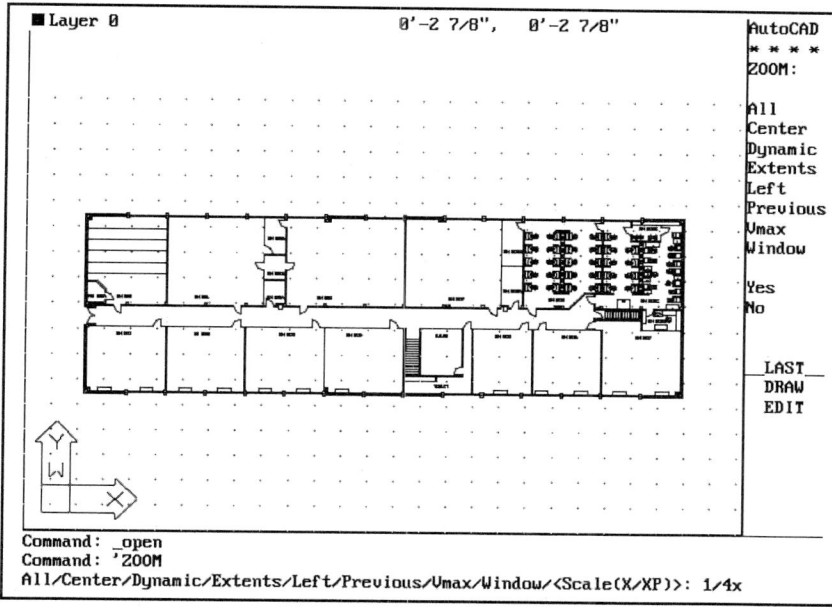

One-quarter the current plan size with a 0.25X scale factor.

The Center and Left options enable you to select a point to locate the center or left edge of the view, then specify the size of the view in drawing units. The Center option uses a point at the center of the view as a base location; the Left option uses the lower left as the base location. By adding "X" to the numeric value, the new view can be sized relative to the current window height rather than the drawing units. The addition of "XP" to the numeric value for paper space will be discussed in later units.

Unit Review

What You've Learned

- The Window, Dynamic, Center, All, Extents, Previous, and Vmax options of the ZOOM command
- How to zoom in and out of a drawing by specifying scale factors
- How to use the Dynamic option to move a scaled view window from one location to another on your drawing
- How to use the Previous option to recall the last several views produced by the ZOOM command
- How to restore a full view of the current virtual screen
- How to view the limits of the current drawing with all entities visible
- How to view all the entities in a drawing as large as possible on the display

Review Questions

True or False

18.01 T F The Vmax option alway restores a view that includes all entities in the current drawing.

18.02 T F You may view a small window of the current drawing at the scale it will be plotted on paper.

18.03 T F The last several views of the current drawing may be recalled with the Previous option.

18.04 T F The Vmax option may cause the current drawing to be regenerated.

18.05 T F The All option may cause the current drawing to be regenerated.

18.06 T F The 2X scale factor will produce a view that is two times as large as the current view.

Student: ______________________ Date: ________

Instructor: ______________________ Course: ________ Section: ________

Multiple Choice

18.07 The ______________ options will produce a view that includes all visible entities of the current drawing.

(A) Vmax and Extents

(B) Vmax and All

(C) Extents and All

(D) All of the above

18.08 The All option will always display ____________ of the current drawing.

(A) the limits

(B) the limits or more

(C) less than the limits

(D) the virtual screen

18.09 The Vmax option always displays ____________ of the current drawing.

(A) the limits

(B) the limits or more

(C) less than the limits

(D) the virtual screen

18.10 The Extents option always displays ____________ of the current drawing.

(A) the limits

(B) the limits or more

(C) all visible entities

(D) the virtual screen

Student: ____________ Date: ____________

Instructor: ____________ Course: ____________ Section: ____________

UNIT 19

Using PAN To Control the Display

In addition to the ZOOM command, AutoCAD includes other commands that enable you to change your view of the current drawing. The PAN command, for example, enables you to move the drawing "window," called a *viewport*, over the drawing from one location to another. When you need to work on a different area of the drawing, you can use the PAN command to display that new area without having to zoom in or out with the ZOOM command. PAN is very useful when you want to move the viewport slightly to see a part of the drawing that is just outside of the viewport. This unit teaches you to use the PAN command.

The objectives of this unit are to:

- ☞ Move the viewport without changing the size of the view
- ☞ Move the viewport a specified distance, outside of the current view
- ☞ Understand the advantages and limitations of PAN vs. ZOOM

Moving the Viewport with PAN

The PAN command enables you to move the viewport very quickly. You simply pick the initial point of displacement, then pick the second point to determine the amount and direction of displacement of the viewport as it pans over the drawing. In simpler terms, you move the viewport from the first point to the second point, and the view of the drawing in the viewport changes accordingly.

The use of PAN usually is faster than using the ZOOM command to change views because you often must use the ZOOM command two or more times to display the necessary viewport. In addition, the PAN command does not cause a drawing regeneration, which the ZOOM command occasionally requires.

The three exercises in this unit set up a view of your drawing at 1/4"=1'-0" in the drawing viewport using the ZOOM command. PAN is used to pan the drawing through to the various locations shown in figure 19.1, maintaining the size of the viewport and therefore the scale of the drawing as you view it in the viewport.

NOTE

In this unit, any references to moving the viewport mean moving the viewport relative to the drawing. *You are not actually moving the viewport from one point to another on the display. Instead, you are moving the viewport's location relative to the drawing to view a different part of the drawing in the viewport.*

Figure 19.1

34' x 24' viewport panned to several drawing locations.

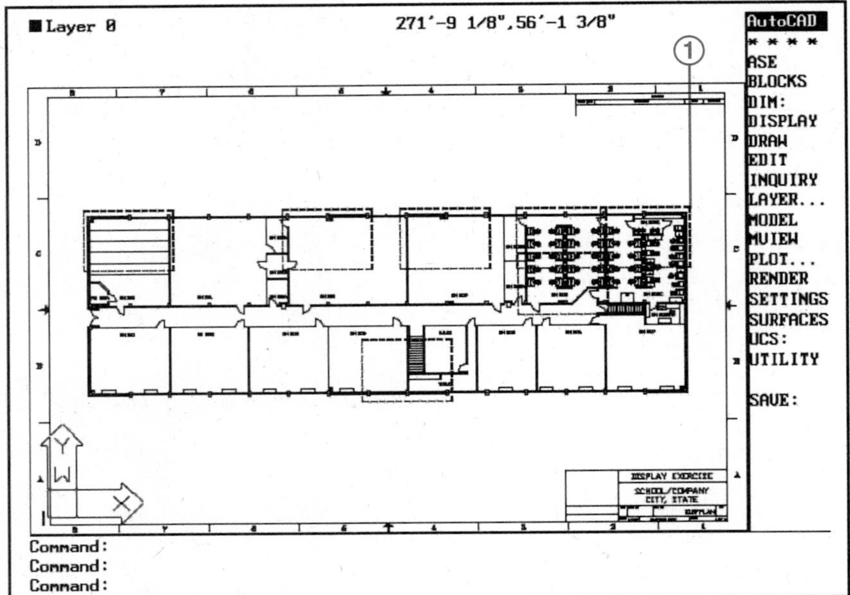

In the following exercise, use the ZOOM command to set your initial view size, then use PAN to move the view.

Panning Around in Your Drawing

1. Begin a new drawing named 019???01 in your assigned directory, using 019FPLAN as a prototype.

2. `Command:` *Choose* Display, *then Zoom then* Window — Issues the ZOOM command with the Window option

   ```
   '_zoom
   All/Center/Dynamic/Extents/Left/
   Previous/Vmax/Window/<Scale(X/XP)>:
   _ window
   ```

3. `First corner:` *Pick upper right corner at ① (see fig. 19.1)* — Specifies first window point

4. `Other corner:` **`@-34',-24'`** ↵ — Specifies second window point and displays a viewport 34"×24"

5. *Choose* Display, *then* Pan — Issues the PAN command

6. `'_pan Displacement:` *Pick displacement point at ② (see fig. 19.2)* — Locates the point on the drawing to be displaced

7. `Second point:` *Pick second point at ③ (see fig. 19.2)* — Sets the direction and distance of the displacement and changes the display

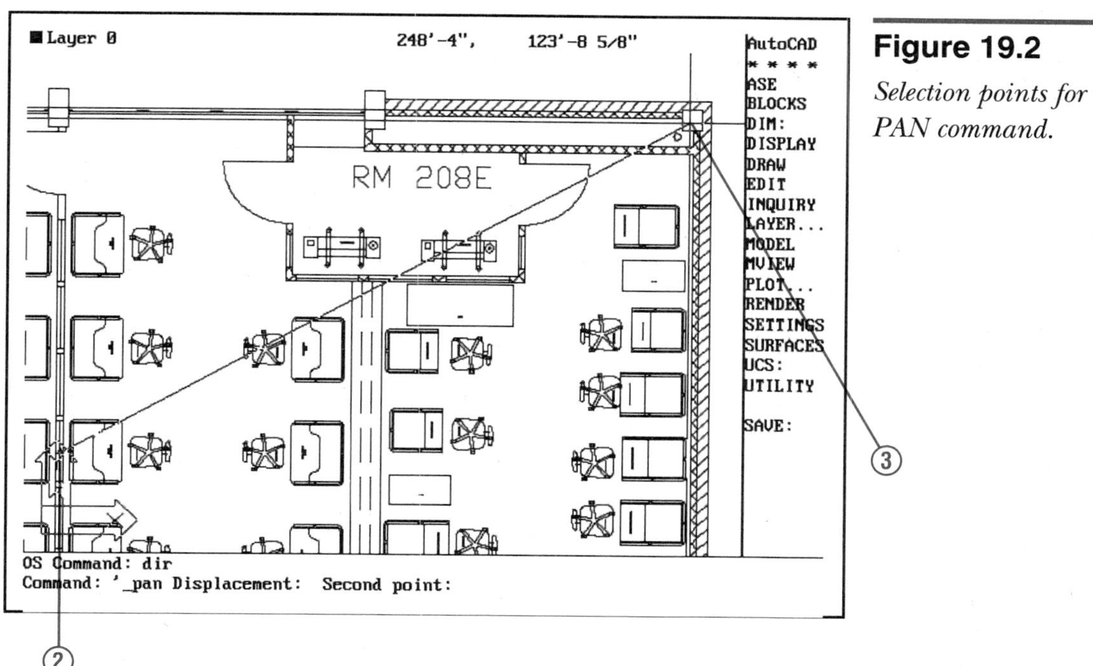

Figure 19.2

Selection points for PAN command.

8. `Command:` *Press* Enter	Repeats the previous command
9. `'PAN Displacement:` *Pick displacement point at* ④ *(see fig. 19.3)*	Locates the point on the drawing to be displaced
10. `Second point:` *Pick second point at* ⑤ *(see fig. 19.3)*	Sets the direction and distance of the displacement and pans the display

Your drawing should look similar to figure 19.4.

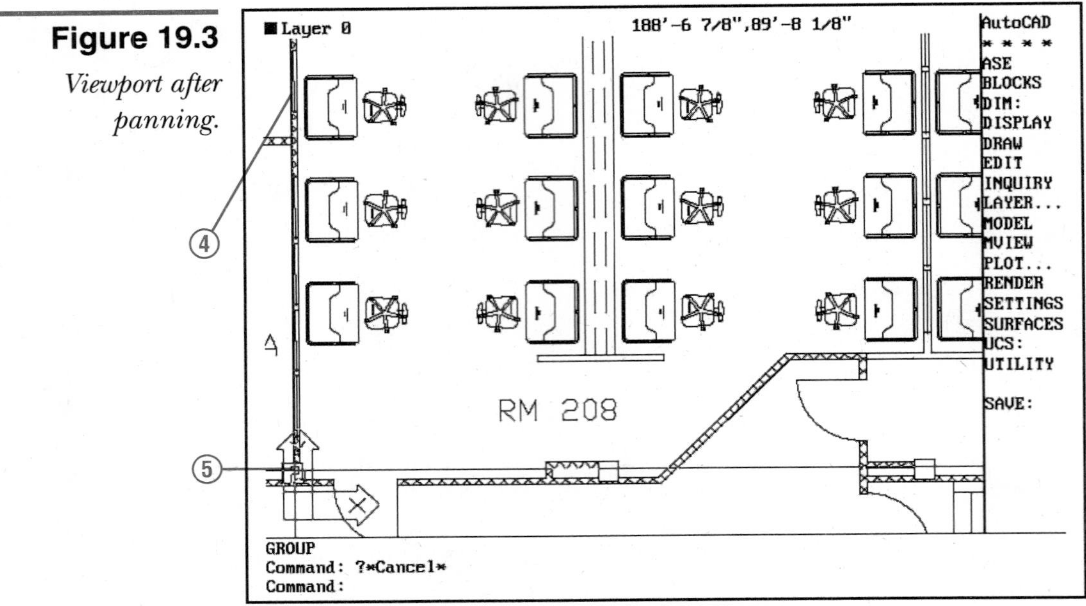

Figure 19.3
Viewport after panning.

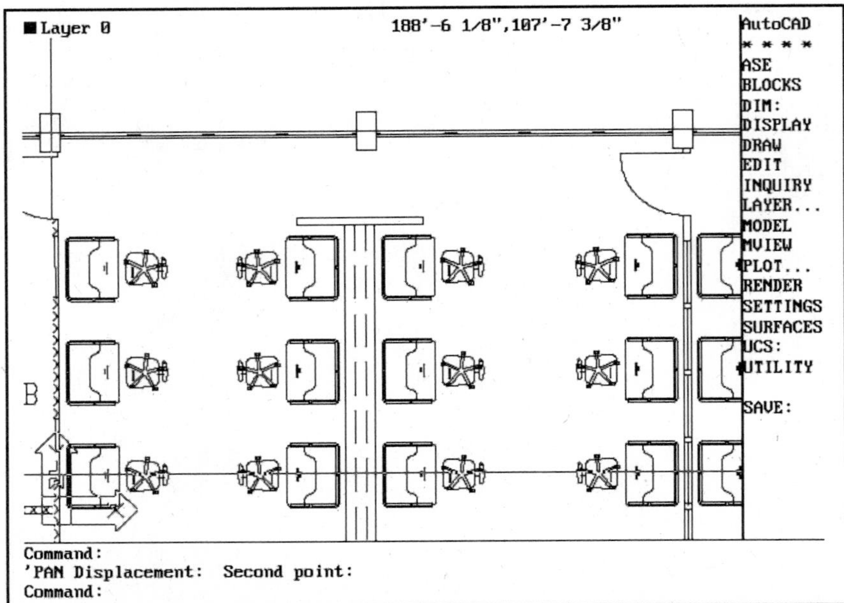

Figure 19.4
Relocated Viewport at ⑤.

Moving the Viewport a Specific Distance

Often, when you are editing a large or complex drawing, the location to which you want to pan the viewport is not within the current view on the viewport. You often know the horizontal and/or vertical distance necessary to pan to the new location (the *displacement*), although the desired point is not visible on the screen. PAN enables you to pan using a displacement.

In addition to picking points to pan the viewport, you also can enter coordinates to specify points in response to the PAN command's prompts. For example, you can enter a coordinate as the initial displacement point and then a null entry as the second point (by pressing Enter without any other input). The coordinate specifies a relative distance that the viewport will move. A negative value in the X axis will move the drawing through the viewport to the left. A negative value in the Y axis will move the drawing down through the viewport. Positive values will move the drawing to the right or up in the X or Y axis respectively.

In the following exercise, move the viewport 45' to the right, then repeat the command to move the viewport another 45' to the right.

Panning a Specific Distance

Continue with the drawing from the previous exercise.

1. `Command:` *Choose* Display, *then* Pan	Issues the PAN command
2. `'_pan Displacement:` **`45',0`** ↵	Specifies displacement
3. `Second point:` *Press* Enter	Specifies null entry and moves the viewport 45' to the right (see fig. 19.5)
4. `Command:` *Press* Enter	Repeats the previous command
5. `'PAN Displacement:` **`45',0`** ↵	Specifies displacement
6. `Second point:` *Press* Enter	Specifies null entry and moves the viewport 45' to the right (see fig. 19.6)

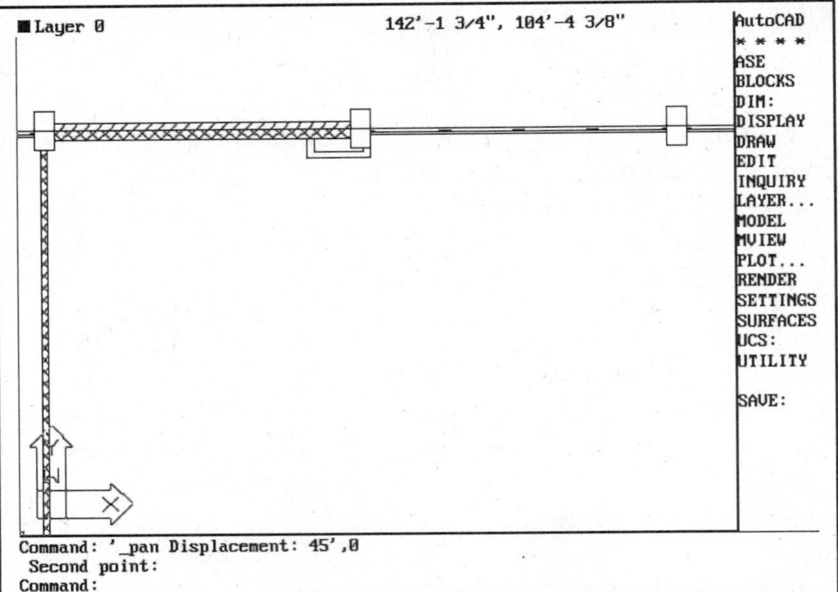

Figure 19.5

Drawing panned 45' from left to right.

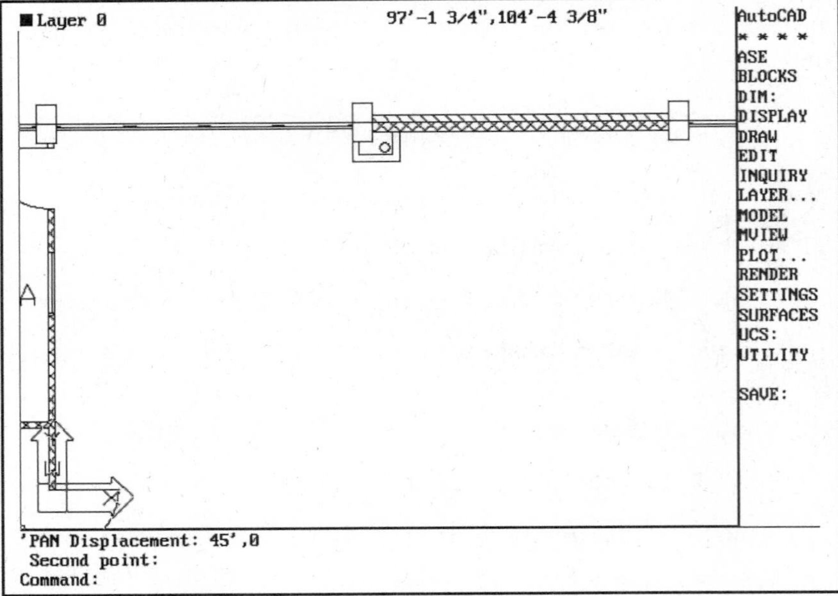

Figure 19.6

Drawing panned another 45' to the right.

If you prefer, you can pan the viewport a specific amount using a different technique. Instead of specifying a displacement, you can pick a point, then enter a relative coordinate to move the viewport. Do so in the following exercise.

PAN to a Remote Location on the Drawing

Continue with the drawing from the previous exercise.

1. `Command:` *Choose* Display, *then* Pan	Issues the PAN command
2. `'_pan Displacement:` *Pick a point anywhere on the display*	Specifies the first point
3. `Second point:` **`@-30',50`** ↵	Specifies a relative point and moves the viewport accordingly (see fig. 19.7)

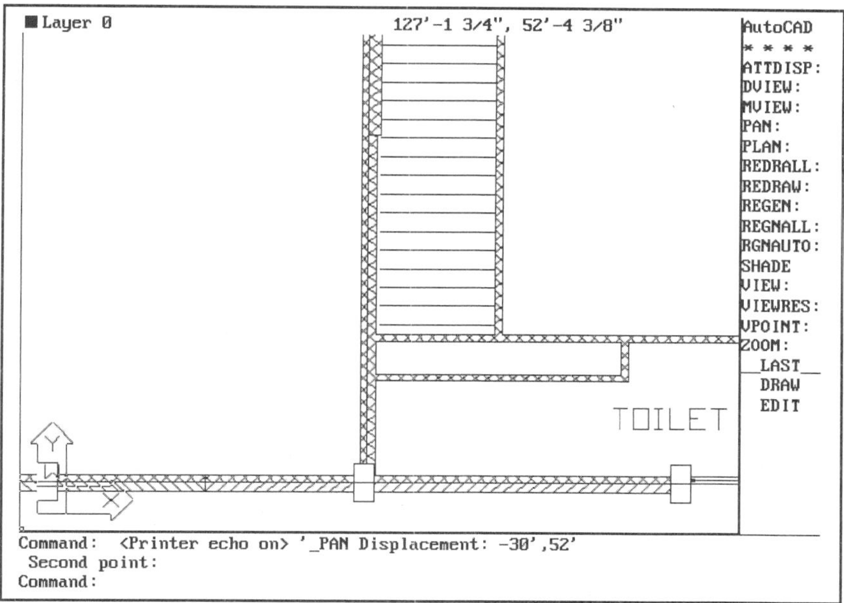

Figure 19.7

Viewport moved by specifying a relative point.

4. `Command:` *Press* Enter	Repeats the previous command
5. `'PAN Displacement:` *Pick a point anywhere in the viewport*	Specifies the first point
6. `Second point:` **`@105',0`** ↵	Pans the viewport 105' to the right (see fig. 19.8)

Figure 19.8

Drawing panned to the top left corner of the building.

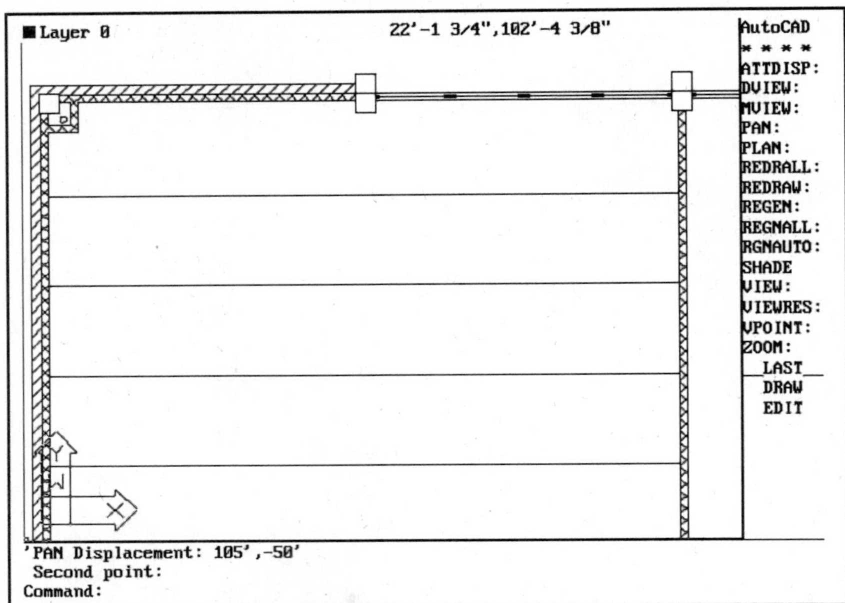

As you edit drawings, you will use the PAN command often to move the viewport around on the drawing, particularly when working with complex drawings. When combined with the ZOOM command (see unit 18, "Using ZOOM To Control the Display"), PAN gives you complete control over the position of the viewport relative to the drawing itself. When you need to simply relocate the viewport but do not need to change the relative scale of the viewport to see a larger or smaller area, use PAN. When you need to view a larger or smaller area, use ZOOM.

Unit Review

What You've Learned

- ☞ Commands: PAN
- ☞ How to move the drawing viewport
- ☞ How to relocate the viewport a specified distance
- ☞ When to use PAN instead of ZOOM

Review Questions

True or False

19.01 T F The relative size of the viewport does not change after you use the PAN command.

19.02 T F The PAN command occasionally requires a drawing regeneration (REGEN).

19.03 T F The use of PAN to move around in your drawing is usually much faster and simpler than using a ZOOM command option.

19.04 T F You can pan the viewport a specified distance by entering a coordinate at the displacement prompt and entering a null response at the second point prompt.

19.05 T F You can change the size of the viewport by using an option of the PAN command.

19.06 T F Left and Center are options of the PAN command.

19.07 T F PAN is an option of the ZOOM command.

Multiple Choice

19.08 The PAN command is listed in the __________ screen menu.

(A) VIEW

(B) DISPLAY

(C) SETTINGS

(D) EDIT

Student: ______________________________ Date: __________

Instructor: ____________________________ Course: __________ Section: __________

19.09 The PAN command is listed under the __________ pull-down menu.

(A) VIEW

(B) DISPLAY

(C) SETTINGS

(D) MODIFY

19.10 The PAN command causes a __________ of the drawing viewport.

(A) regeneration

(B) redraw

(C) Vmax

(D) Window

Student: __________ Date: __________

Instructor: __________ Course: __________ Section: __________

UNIT 20

Working with Multiple Views

You can use the ZOOM and PAN commands to control the size and location of the viewport on your drawing. With many drawings, you probably will zoom or pan to the same views over and over again for repeated editing. To avoid performing the same ZOOM and PAN operations again and again, you can name views and restore them to the display by name. You also can configure the display so that more than one viewport appears on the drawing simultaneously. You can work in any of these viewports, switching quickly between them.

The objectives for this unit are to:

- Name and store views of the drawing for future use
- Restore named views of a drawing
- Divide the drawing display into two or more viewports
- Restore named views into each viewport
- Understand the difference between views and viewports

Understanding Views and Viewports

Unit 6 introduced the area in which you draw as the *drawing area.* In reality, the drawing area is a *viewport.* A viewport is simply a rectangular area on the AutoCAD display that contains a view of your drawing. AutoCAD provides this single viewport by default when you begin a new drawing. As you will learn later in this unit, you can create additional viewports and use these multiple viewports at the same time.

A viewport is not the same thing as a *view*. A view is an image of a portion of a drawing. A view might show the entire drawing, or it might show a small portion of it. When you use the ZOOM command and zoom in on the drawing, the resulting image is a zoomed-in *view* of the drawing.

To put it simply, views are displayed inside of viewports. If you have one viewport on the display, you see a single view of your drawing. If you are using multiple viewports, however, you see multiple views of your drawing at the same time.

Saving and Restoring Views

You can save a view by name at any time. You can then later restore the viewport by name to display it quickly so that you can work with the drawing within that view. In fact, you can save several views by name so that you seldom need to use ZOOM or PAN to select a drawing viewport for editing. This capability to save and restore views is extremely convenient and can save a lot of time that you would otherwise spend repeatedly panning and zooming the display.

The View pull-down menu provides access to the View Control dialog box, which offers an easy method for working with named views. You also can use the VIEW command and its various options to save and restore views. The VIEW command is discussed in other units.

In the following exercise, size and locate several views and save each one by name. Figure 20.1 shows your prototype drawing.

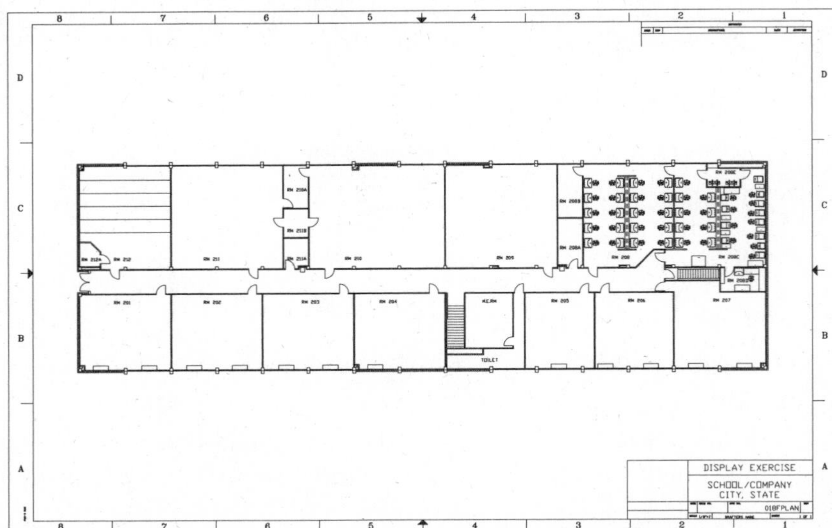

Figure 20.1

Drawing 020FPLAN.

Naming the Current View

1. Begin a new drawing named 020???01 in your assigned directory using 020FPLAN as a prototype.

2. Command: *Choose* View, *then* Set View, *then* Named View — Displays the View Control dialog box (see fig. 20.2)

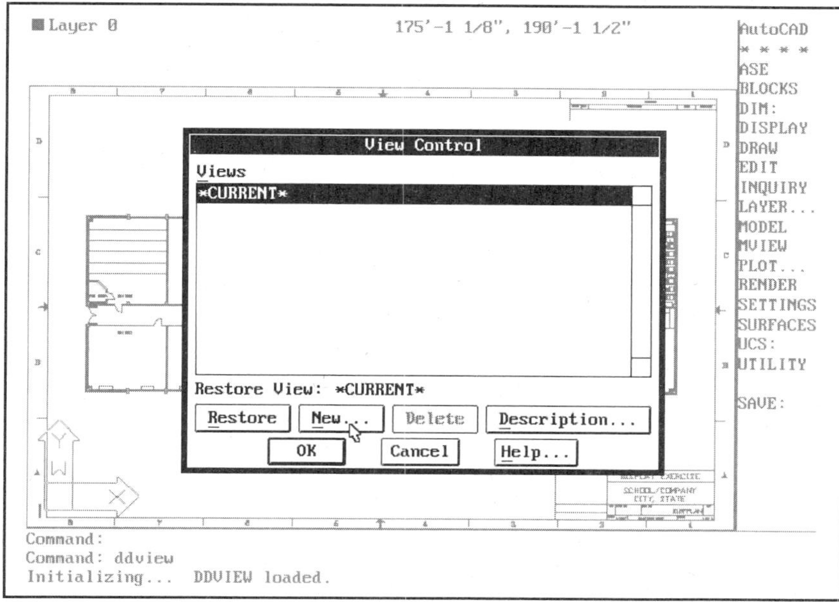

Figure 20.2

The View Control dialog box.

3. *Choose the* New *button* — Displays the Define New View dialog box (see fig. 20.3)

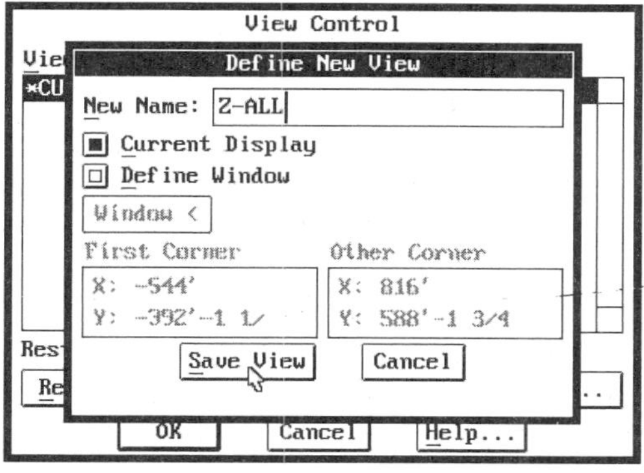

Figure 20.3

The Define New View dialog box.

4. *Click in the* New Name *edit box, then type* **Z-ALL**, *then choose the* Save View *command button* — Enters the new view name and returns to the View Control dialog box

5. *Choose the* OK *button* — Closes the View Control dialog box

You have just saved the current view with a name. If you later want to work with this view, you can simply restore it without having to use the ZOOM or PAN commands.

It is a good practice to save a view of the entire drawing by issuing ZOOM with the All option, then saving the view by name. You can restore this view without experiencing a drawing regeneration, which otherwise would occur if you issued ZOOM All a second time. This can save quite a bit of drawing-regeneration time, particularly with complex drawings.

In the next exercise, zoom the display to a specific location and save the resulting view.

Storing a Second View

Continue with your drawing from the preceding exercise.

1.	`Command:` **`Z`** ↵	Issues the alias for the ZOOM command
2.	`ZOOM All/Center/Dynamic/Extents/Left /Previous/Vmax/Window/<Scale(X/XP)>:` *Pick the first corner at* ① *(see fig. 20.1)*	Picking the first corner invokes the Window option by default
3.	`Other corner:` **`@-68',-48'`** ↵	Specifies the other corner and displays the 68' × 48' viewport
4.	`Command:` *Choose* View, *then* Set View, *then* Named View	Displays the View Control dialog box
5.	*Choose the* New *button*	Displays the Define New View dialog box
6.	*Click on the* New Name *edit box, then type* **`CAD-LABS`**, *then Choose the* Save View *button*	Enters the new view name and returns to the View Control dialog box
7.	*Choose the* OK *button*	Saves the new view name and closes the View Control dialog box

You now have saved view names for the current view. You probably noticed that moving between the dialog boxes and the ZOOM command to set up a new view is time consuming. You can avoid using the ZOOM command by using Define Window instead of Current Display when naming new views in the Define New View dialog box.

The following exercises help you locate, size, and name several views using Define Window in the Define New View dialog box. You also will restore named views from the list box in the View Control dialog box.

Restoring a Named View

Continue with your drawing from the preceding exercise.

1. `Command:` *Choose* View, *then* Set View, *then* Named View	Displays the View Control dialog box
2. *Choose* Z-ALL *from the* View *list box, then the* Restore *button, then the* OK *button*	Highlights the Z-ALL view name, identifies Z-ALL as the view to be restored (see fig. 20.4), and restores the view

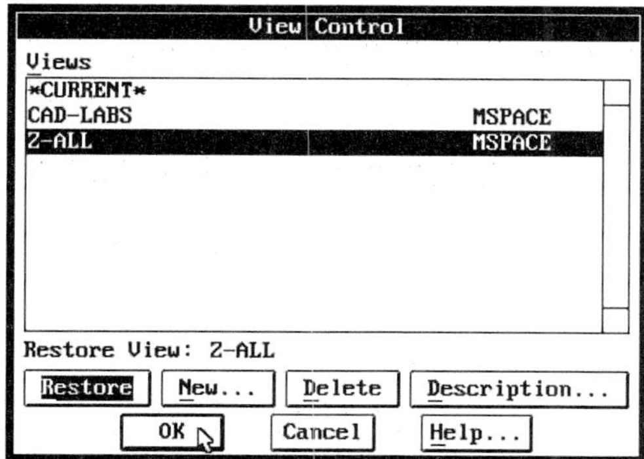

Figure 20.4

View Z-ALL.

By restoring the Z-ALL view, you have displayed the entire drawing but avoided using ZOOM All, which would have caused a drawing regeneration. With the entire drawing displayed, you now can define other views using a window.

Defining a View with a Window

Continue with your drawing from the preceding exercise.

1. `Command:` **`DDVIEW`** ↵	Issues the DDVIEW command and displays the View Control dialog box
2. *Choose the* New *button, then the* Define Window *radio button*	Displays the Define New View dialog box and enables all of the controls in the dialog box (see fig. 20.5).
3. *Click in the* New Name *edit box, then type* **`FUL-PLAN`**	Enters the new view name

continues

Figure 20.5

The Define New View dialog box with coordinates enabled.

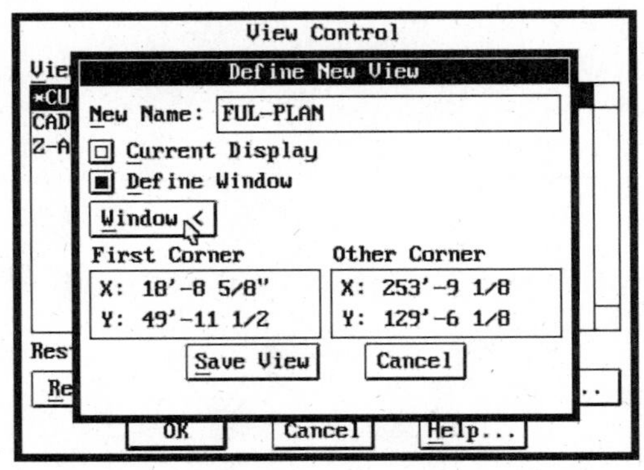

4. *Choose the* Window *button* — Temporarily displays your view without dialog boxes, enabling you to pick the window you have named (see fig. 20.6)

5. `First Corner:` *Pick the lower left corner of the Floor Plan at* ① (see fig. 20.6) — Specifies first corner of the window being named

6. `Other Corner:` *Pick the upper corner of the Floor Plan at* ② (see fig. 20.6) — Specifies second corner of the window being named and redisplays the dialog boxes

7. *Choose the* Save View *command button* — Returns to the View Control dialog box with the new view name listed

---

Figure 20.6

Temporary view of drawing with window from ① *to* ②.

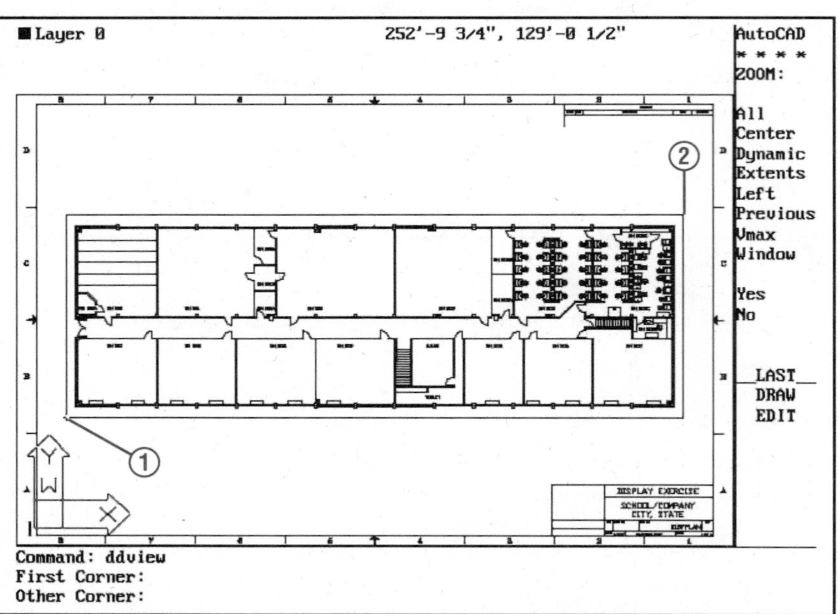

Next, create another view using a window. Name this new view RM-208D.

Defining View RM-208D

Continue with your drawing from the preceding exercise.

1. *Choose the* New *button, then type* **`RM-208D`**	Displays the Define New View dialog box with the Window button enabled and enters the new view name
2. *Click on the* Window *button*	Temporarily displays your drawing without dialog boxes, enabling you to pick the window you have named
3. `First Corner:` *Pick the lower left corner at* ③ *(see fig. 20.7)*	Specifies first corner of the window being named
4. `Other Corner:` *Pick the upper corner at* ④ *(see fig. 20.7)*	Specifies second corner of the window being named and redisplays the dialog boxes
5. *Choose the* Save View *command button*	Returns to the View Control dialog box with the new view name listed
6. *Choose the view named* RM-208D *from the* View *list box (see fig. 20.8)*	Highlights RM-208D in the list
7. *Click on the* Restore *button, then choose the* OK *button*	Restores view RM-208D and closes the View Control dialog box

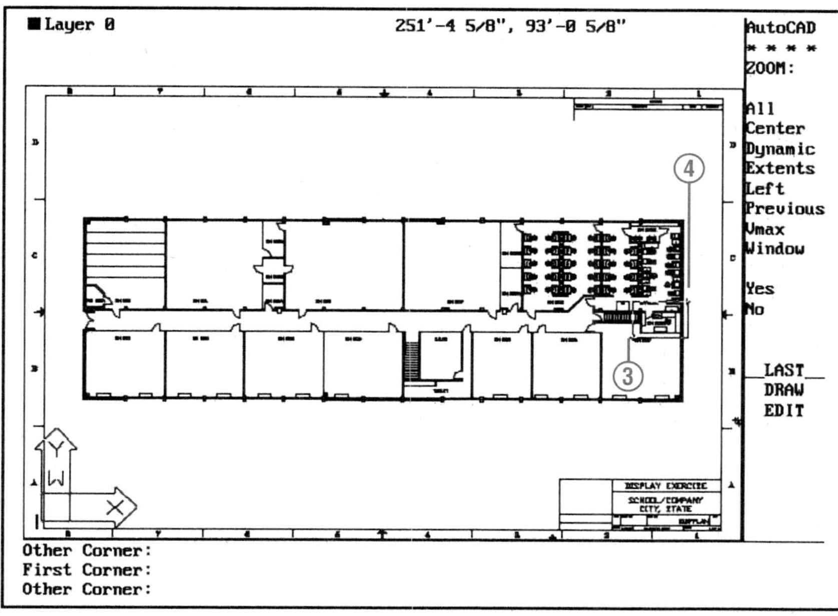

Figure 20.7

Temporary view of drawing with window from ③ *to* ④.

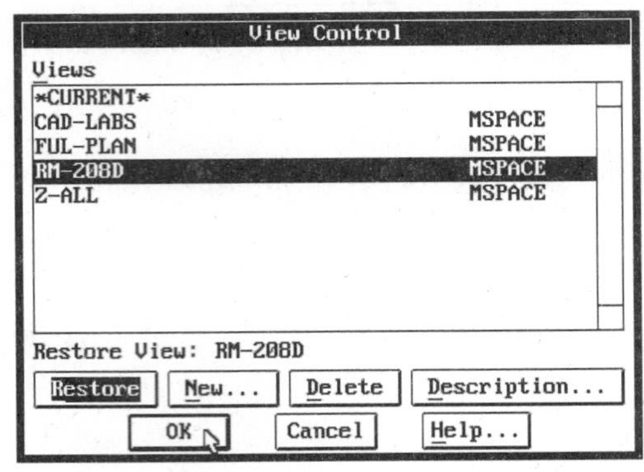

Figure 20.8
View RM-208D highlighted in the View Control dialog box.

You can repeat step number 5 to name close-up views of several additional rooms. If the list of view names exceeds 10, the scroll bar activates on the right side of the list box.

You can repeat these steps to make any of the listed views current without requiring a time-consuming ZOOM and regeneration of your drawing. Another advantage of saving different views is when you restore views, it does not interrupt the current command. Named views also are useful when configuring the display with viewports or composing a drawing for plotting (explained in units 46, "Introduction to Paper Space," and 47, "Composing a Drawing").

Using Tiled Viewports

The ability to recall views by name to make particular areas of the drawing available one at a time is a great convenience, but you must change the current view each time you want to view or edit another area of the drawing. Fortunately, you can have more than one area visible on the display simultaneously to speed up the editing process. You can display both ends of a long mechanical component, for example, and work on both ends of the part at the same time.

To do this, you configure your display to contain more than one viewport at a time. Each viewport is independent of the others and can be zoomed or panned individually without affecting the other viewports. Only one of the viewports on the display is active for editing, but you can make any one of the viewports active by picking it.

In the following exercises, set up a three-view viewport configuration and restore three of your new named views to the three viewports.

Setting Up Tiled Viewports

Continue with your drawing from the preceding exercise.

1. `Command:` *Choose* View, *then* Layout, *then* Tiled Viewports — Displays the Tiled Viewport Layout dialog box (see fig. 20.9)

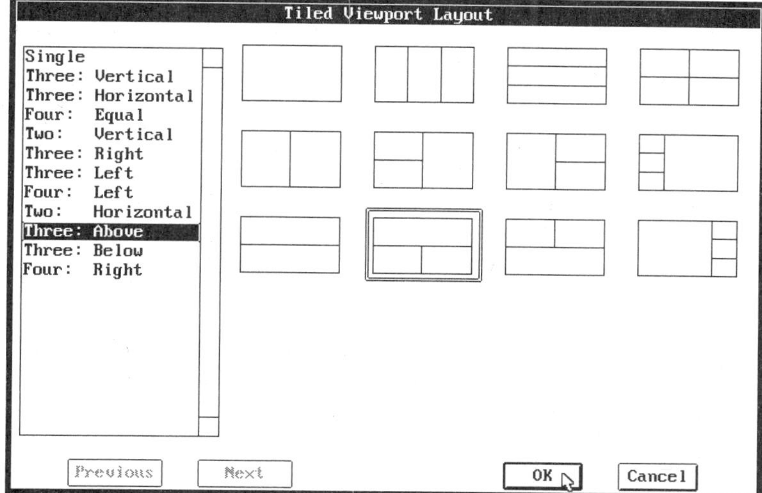

Figure 20.9

The Tiled Viewport Layout dialog box.

2. *Choose* Three:Above *from the list box, then the* OK *button* — Displays a pattern of three viewports with the current view displayed in each (see fig. 20.10)

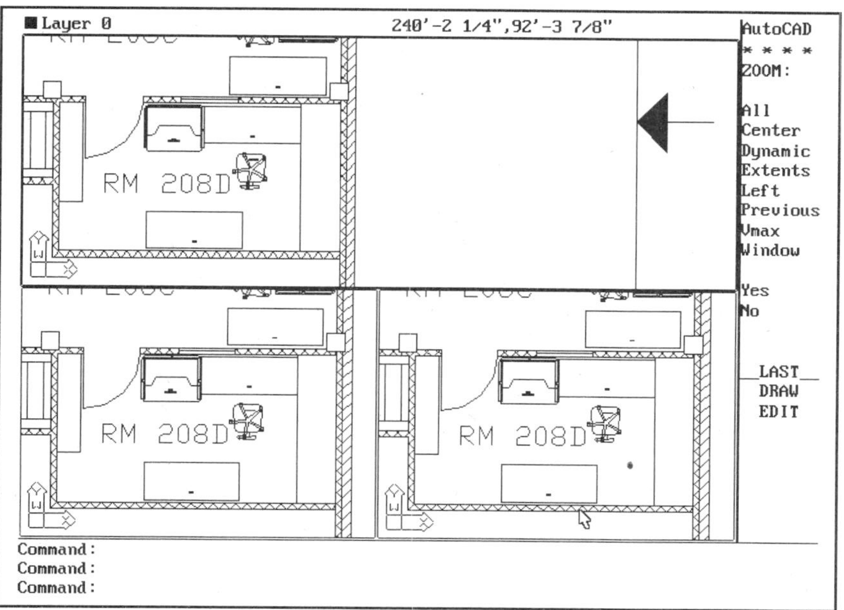

Figure 20.10

The Three Above viewport configuration.

continues

3. `Command:` *Choose* View, *then* Set View, *then* Named View	Displays the View Control dialog box
4. *Choose* FUL-PLAN *from the* View *list box, then the* Restore *button, then the* OK *button*	Highlights the FUL-PLAN view name, identifies FUL-PLAN as the view to be restored, and restores the view
5. `Command:` *Click in the lower left viewport*	Makes the lower left viewport the active viewport
6. `Command:` *Choose* View, *then* Set View, *then* Named View	Redisplays the View Control dialog box
7. *Choose* CAD-LABS *from the* View *list box, then the* Restore *button, then the* OK *button*	Highlights the CAD-LABS view name, identifies CAD-LABS as the view to be restored, and restores the view

As the title of the previous exercise indicated, the viewports you configured on your display are called *tiled viewports*. Tiled viewports always fill the display and always touch one another at the edges; they cannot overlap.

Tile viewports are particularly useful during the design stage. You can configure up to 16 concurrent tiled viewports, switching from one to another simply by clicking in the desired viewport. Depending on the size and resolution of your display, multiple viewports can make it almost unnecessary to use ZOOM or PAN.

When you work in a tiled viewport (or in AutoCAD's default single viewport), you are working in *model space*. Tiled viewports only exist when you work in model space. Model space is ideal for creating 2D drawings or 3D models, but when you need to develop different views for plotting, model space and tiled viewports are not very useful. AutoCAD provides another drawing environment called *paper space*, which uses a different type of viewport. Paper space and paper space viewports are explained in units 46, "Introduction to Paper Space," and 47 "Composing a Drawing."

Unit Review

What You've Learned

- The use of the View Control, Define New View, and Tiled Viewport Layout dialog boxes
- How to name the current view
- How to define a selected window and name it
- How to restore views by name
- How to configure more than one viewport on the display
- How to restore named views into each viewport
- The difference between views and viewports

Student: ____________ Date: ____________

Instructor: ____________ Course: ____________ Section: ____________

Review Questions

True or False

20.01 T F Views and viewports are the same.

20.02 T F Views are displayed in viewports.

20.03 T F There can be more than one view in a viewport.

20.04 T F There can be more than one viewport on the display.

20.05 T F Several viewports can be active at the same time for editing.

20.06 T F You can have only 10 views named at one time in your drawing.

20.07 T F You can delete views that are no longer useful.

20.08 T F You can name a view by defining a window.

20.09 T F Only the current view can be named.

Multiple Choice

20.10 You can access the Tiled Viewport Layout dialog box from the __________ pull-down menu.

(A) View

(B) Display

(C) Settings

(D) Modify

20.11 The __________ command displays the View Control dialog box.

(A) DDVIEW

(B) VIEW

(C) SETTINGS

(D) MODIFY

20.12 You can name views using __________.

(A) the View Control dialog box

(B) the Tiled Viewport Layout dialog box

(C) the Define New View dialog box

(D) Restore

Student: ____________________ Date: __________

Instructor: ____________________ Course: __________ Section: __________

UNIT 21

Introduction to Selection and Editing

Drawing entities is only a small part of creating a drawing in AutoCAD. You also will *edit* entities. Editing entities includes selecting the entities, then issuing various editing commands to modify the entities. Erasing entities, which you may have done in previous units, is an example of editing. In this unit you learn about selecting and editing entities.

The objectives for this unit are to:

- ☞ Understand the function of selection sets
- ☞ Understand how to select entities
- ☞ Understand the basics of editing
- ☞ Create selection sets using pick-after and pick-first selection methods

Selecting Entities

Many commands in AutoCAD require you to select entities. When you issue the ERASE command, for example, AutoCAD prompts you to select the entities to erase. Other editing commands enable you to stretch, copy, move, trim, extend, and break entities (these functions are explained in detail in other units). Before you can use any of these commands, you must first select entities.

When you select one or more entities, you create a *selection set.* As its name implies, a selection set is simply a set, or group, of entities that you have selected. You then can perform an editing function (such as erasing) on all the entities that are part of the selection set.

A small square box called the *pickbox* indicates when you can select entities. The pickbox sometimes appears at the junction of the crosshair cursor, and always appears by itself whenever you enter a command that requires you to select entities. Figure 21.1 shows the pickbox at the junction of the crosshair cursor. Figure 21.2 shows the pickbox by itself.

To select entities, place the pickbox on the entity and click on the pick button on the mouse or digitizer. When you select an entity, AutoCAD highlights the entity (changes its linetype to be dashed lines) to inform you that the entity has been added to the selection set. If you remove an entity from a selection set, AutoCAD changes its linetype back to the entity's original linetype. Figure 21.3 shows entities that have been highlighted and placed in a selection set.

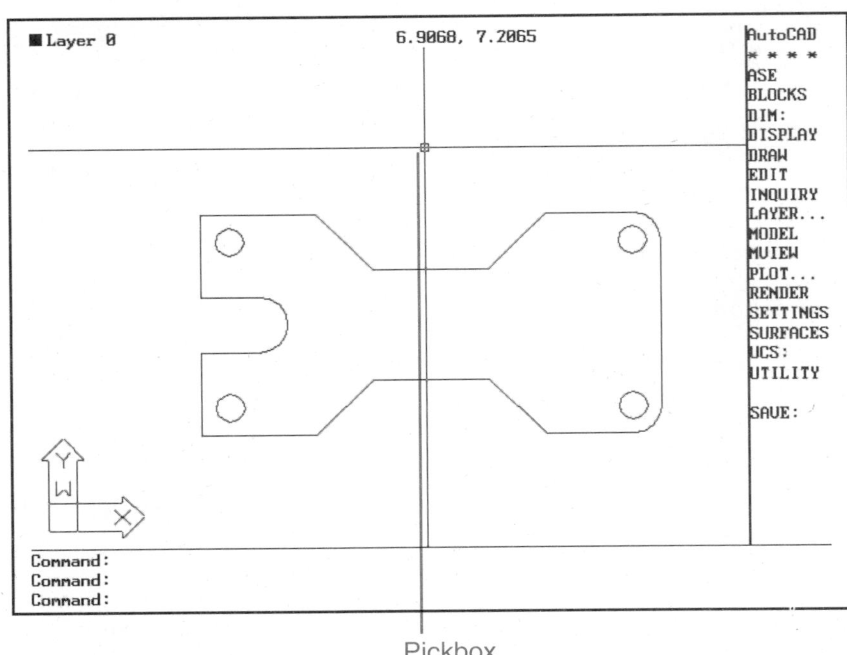

Figure 21.1

The pickbox at the junction of the crosshair cursor.

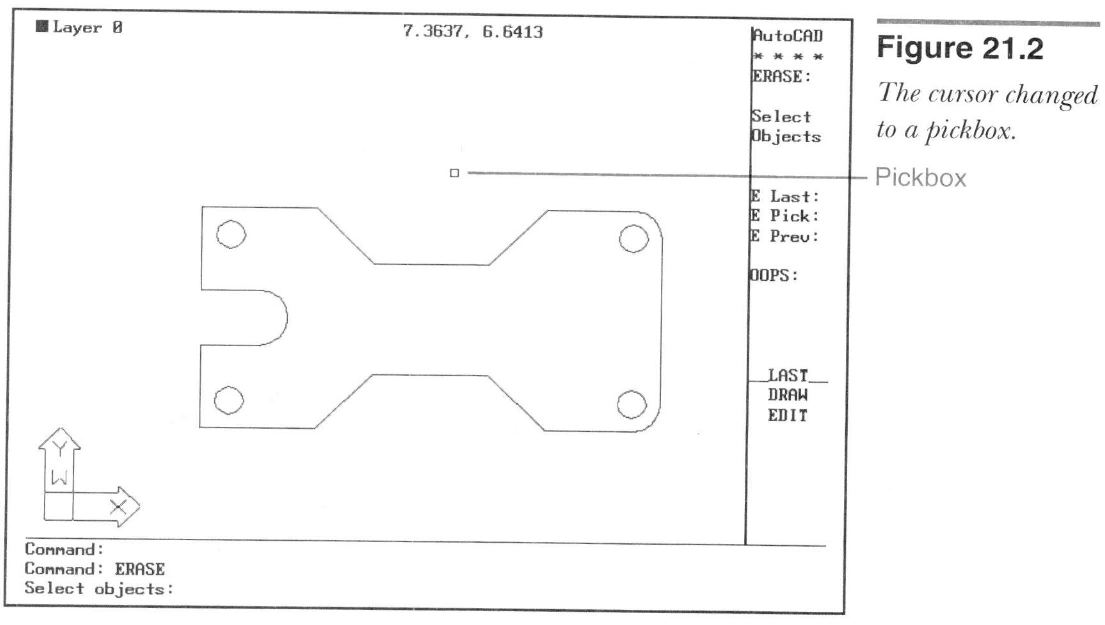

Figure 21.2

The cursor changed to a pickbox.

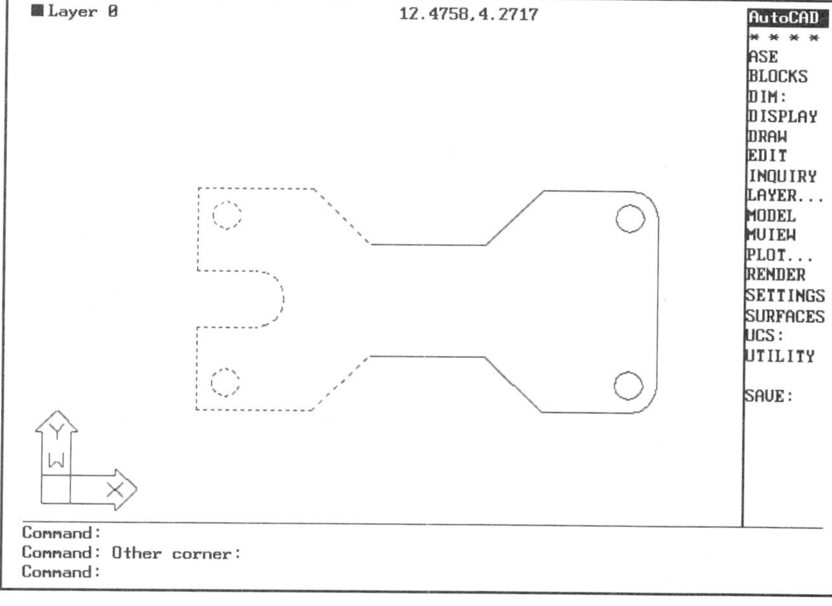

Figure 21.3

Entities in a selection set.

Using Pick-First Selection

AutoCAD offers two methods for building a selection set. By default, AutoCAD enables *pick-first* selection, which is the first of the two methods. Essentially, pick-first selection means that you can build the selection set first, then issue the appropriate editing command. The command operates on the selection set without prompting you for any additional selection. This method of selection also is referred to as noun/verb selection.

In the following exercise, use pick-first selection to build a selection set of entities and erase them. The first step in the exercise is to turn off grips. Turning off grips will make it easier for you to recognize the way selection sets work. Grips are not explained in this unit—an explanation of grips and their purpose is reserved for unit 22, "Introduction to Grips and Autoediting."

Using Pick-First Selection

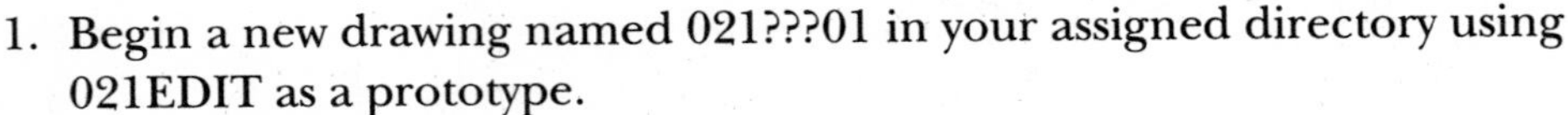

1. Begin a new drawing named 021???01 in your assigned directory using 021EDIT as a prototype.

2. `Command:` **`GRIPS`** ↵	Issues the GRIPS command
3. `New value for GRIPS <1>:` **`0`** ↵	Sets GRIPS to 0
4. `Command:` *Place the pickbox on the small circle at* ①, *then click the pick button (see fig. 21.4)*	Selects the circle, highlights the circle, and adds it to the selection set
5. `Command:` *Select the other three circles using the same method as in the previous step*	Selects the circles, highlights the circles, and adds them to the selection set
6. `Command:` *Choose* Modify, *then* Erase, *then* Select	Issues the ERASE command and erases the existing selection set
`_erase 4 found`	
7. `Command:` **`U`** ↵	Issues the UNDO command and undoes the previous command
`GROUP`	

8. Save your drawing.

As you can see from the exercise, you selected the entities first, then issued the ERASE command. AutoCAD erased the entities in the current selection set without prompting you for any other selections.

You can create only one selection set at a time in AutoCAD. You cannot create multiple selection sets or save selection sets by name.

Picking entities at an intersection can produce unexpected results. Be sure to pick the entities away from intersections for better control.

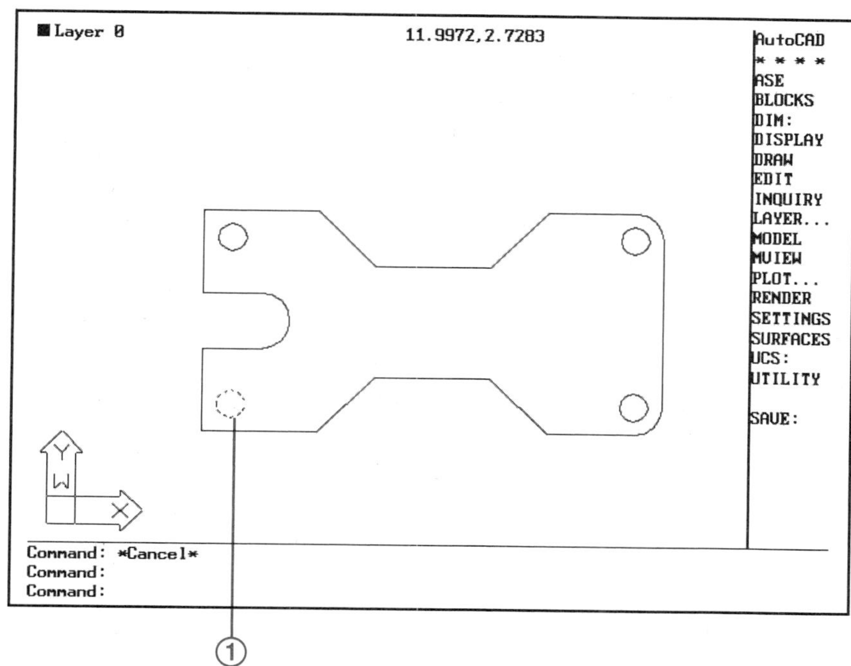

Figure 21.4

A circle highlighted and added to the selection set.

Using Pick-After Selection

In addition to selecting objects before issuing an editing command, you can issue the command first, then select the objects to be edited. This is referred to as pick-after selection. If you have not established a selection set using pick-first selection, AutoCAD automatically uses pick-after entity selection.

In the following exercise, use pick-after selection to erase the circles once again from your drawing.

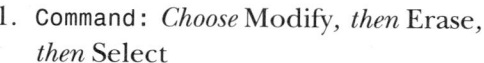

Using Pick-After Selection

Continue with your drawing from the preceding exercise.

1. `Command:` *Choose* Modify, *then* Erase, *then* Select — Issues the ERASE command to prompt you to select entities

   `_erase`

2. `Select objects:` *Select the circle at ① (see fig. 21.5)* — Selects the circle and adds it to the selection set

   `1 found`

3. `Select objects:` *Select the circle at ② (see fig. 21.5)* — Adds another circle to the selection set

   `1 found`

continues

4. `Select objects:` *Select the circle at ③ (see fig. 21.5)* `1 found`	Adds another circle to the selection set
5. `Select objects:` *Select the circle at ④ (see fig. 21.5)* `1 found`	Adds another circle to the selection set
6. `Select objects:` *Press* Enter	Ends selection and erases the entities in the selection set
7. `Command:` **`U`** ↵ `GROUP`	

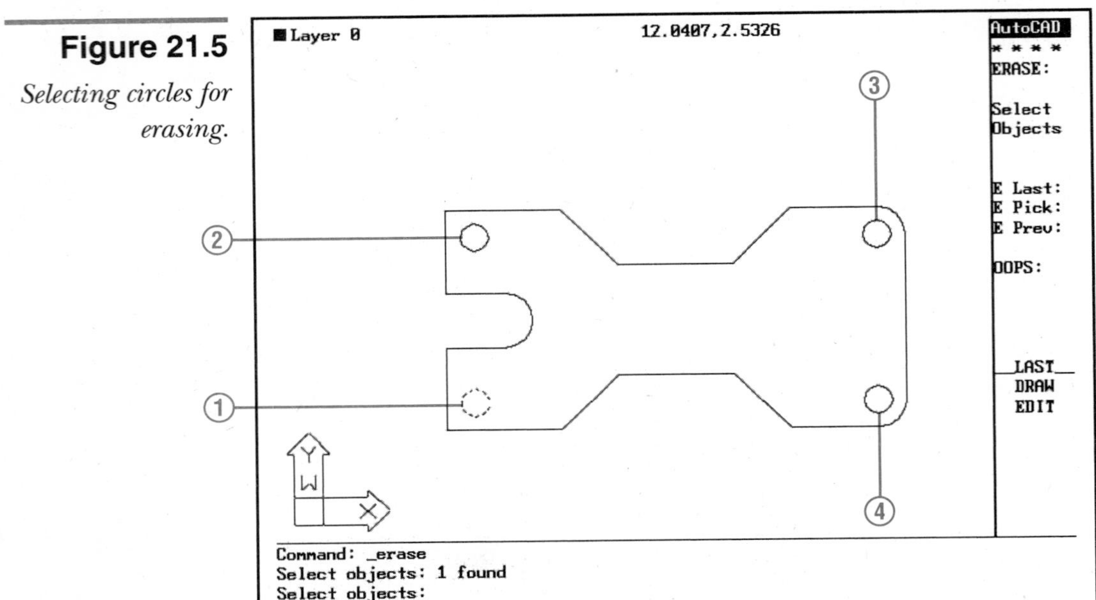

Figure 21.5
Selecting circles for erasing.

You can see that the result of this exercise is the same as the previous exercise. The only difference is the time at which you created the selection set.

Pick-first selection is useful for many editing tasks, and as you will learn in unit 22, it's necessary when working with grips. Pick-after selection, however, is sometimes more versatile because AutoCAD provides more options for selecting entities through pick-after selection. Some of these options are explained in the next section. Pick-after selection also is sometimes referred to as verb/noun selection.

Some commands cannot use pick-first selection. If a selection set exists when you issue these commands, the commands ignore the existing set and prompt you to create a new set. Use the Previous option (explained later) to restore the previous selection set.

Controlling the Selection Set

When you are using either type of selection method (pick-first or pick-after), you are not limited to just selecting entities one at a time. With both methods, you can use a window to select entities. A selection window enables you to select many entities quickly because AutoCAD selects all the entities that lie completely within the window. If an entity is only partially inside the window, it is not selected.

In the following exercise, use a window to select entities. The pick-first and pick-after methods are explored in the exercise.

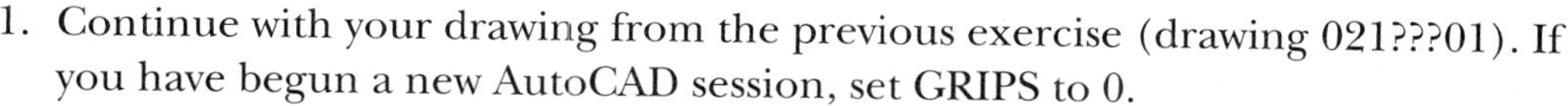

Using a Window to Select Entities

1. Continue with your drawing from the previous exercise (drawing 021???01). If you have begun a new AutoCAD session, set GRIPS to 0.

2. `Command:` *Pick a point at* ① *(see fig. 21.6)*	Causes AutoCAD to begin a window selection
3. `Command:` *Pick a point at* ② *(see fig. 21.6)*	Defines a window and selects all entities that are completely within the window
4. `Command:` *Press* Ctrl+C	Clears the selection set
5. `Command:` *Choose* Modify, *then* Erase, *then* Select	Issues the ERASE command with the option to select objects
`_erase`	
6. `Select objects:` **`W`** ↵	Starts window selection mode
7. `First corner:` *Pick a point at* ① *(see fig. 21.6)*	Specifies first point of window
8. `Other corner:` *Pick a point at* ② *(see fig. 21.6)*	Specifies second point of window and selects all entities within the window
`11 found`	
9. `Select objects:` *Press* Ctrl+C	Cancels the ERASE command

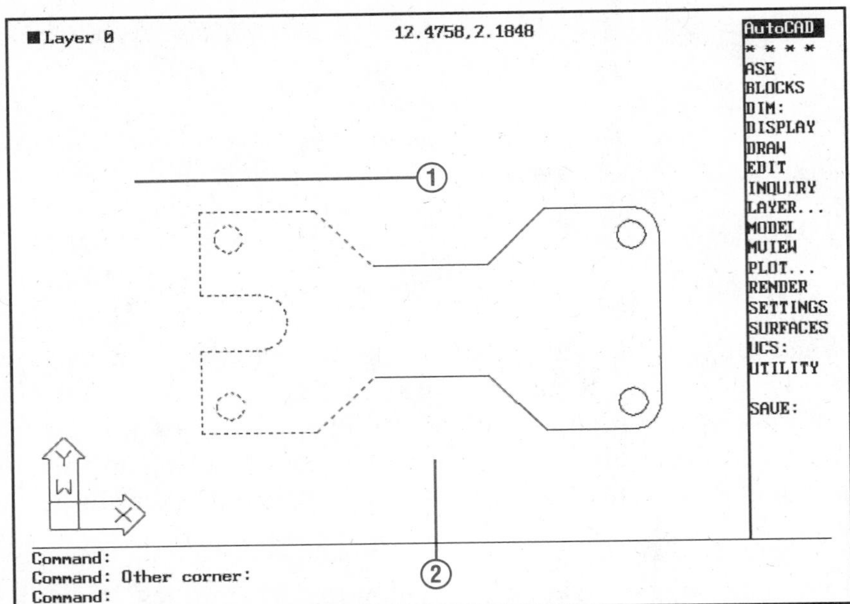

Figure 21.6

A selection set created with a window.

You also can use a *crossing window* to select entities. With a crossing window, any entity that is inside or crosses the window is selected. Use crossing selection in the following exercise.

Using Crossing Selection

1. Continue with your drawing from the previous exercise. If you have begun a new AutoCAD session, set GRIPS to 0.

2. `Command:` *Pick a point at* ① *(see fig. 21.7)*	Causes AutoCAD to begin a crossing window selection
3. `Command:` *Pick a point at* ②	Defines a window and selects all entities that are inside or cross the selection window (see fig. 21.7)
4. `Command:` *Press* Ctrl+C	Clears the selection set
5. `Command:` *Choose* Modify, *then* Erase, *then* Select `_erase`	Issues the ERASE command with the option to select objects
6. `Select objects:` **C** ↵	Starts window selection mode
7. `First corner:` *Pick a point at* ① *(see fig. 21.7)*	Specifies first point of window

8. `Other corner:` *Pick a point at* ② *(see fig. 21.7)* `6 found`	Specifies second point of window and selects all entities within the window
9. `Select objects:` *Press* Ctrl+C	Cancels the ERASE command

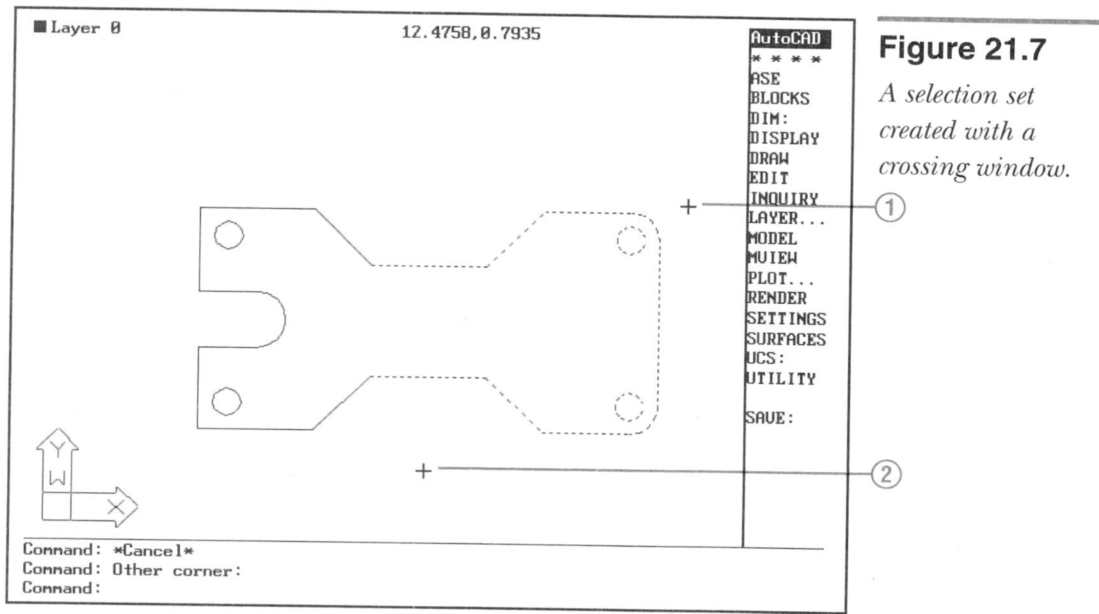

Figure 21.7

A selection set created with a crossing window.

When pick-first selection is enabled, you can start a window or crossing selection simply by picking a point that is not on an entity. AutoCAD then automatically begins either a window or a crossing selection box, depending on the location of your second point pick. If you pick a point to the right of the first point, AutoCAD uses the window method of selection. If the second point is to the left of the first point, AutoCAD uses the crossing method of selection.

Remember this rule: left-to-right for window, right-to-left for crossing.

If you enter **W** (for *W*indow) or **C** (for *C*rossing) in response to the `Select objects:` prompt when selecting entities, the relationship of your point picks has no effect on the Window/Crossing state. If you enter **C** to begin a window selection box, for example, you can pick the two window points left-to-right or right-to-left; either action will result in a crossing selection.

Removing and Adding Entities

As you build a selection set, you occasionally will make a mistake by selecting the wrong entity or will want to remove the entity from the selection set.

AutoCAD provides options that let you remove entities from the selection set. The method you use to remove an entity from the selection set depends on whether you are using pick-first selection or pick-after selection.

Use the shift key to remove entities from the set when you are using pick-first selection. Use the Add and Remove options when using pick-after selection. The following exercise shows you how to use both methods.

Using Shift-Pick

1. Continue with your drawing from the previous exercise (drawing 021???01). If you have begun a new AutoCAD session, set GRIPS to 0.

2. `Command:` *Pick points at* ① *and* ② *(see fig. 21.8)*	Creates a selection set
3. `Command:` *Hold down the Shift key and select the lines at* ③ *and* ④ *(see fig. 21.8)*	Removes the lines at ① and ② from the selection set
4. `Command:` *Release the Shift key, then select the lines at* ③ *and* ④ *(see fig. 21.8)*	Adds the lines back into the selection set
5. `Command:` *Press* Ctrl+C	Clears the selection set
6. `Command:` *Choose* Modify, *then* Erase, *then* Select `_erase`	Issues the ERASE command and prompts to select objects
7. `Select objects:` *Pick the lines at* ③, ④, ⑤, *and* ⑥ *(see fig. 21.8)*	Builds a selection set of four lines
8. `Select objects:` **R** ↵	Issues the Remove option and changes selection to Remove mode
9. `Remove objects:` *Pick the line at* ⑥ *(see fig. 21.8)* `1 found, 1 removed`	Removes the line at ⑥ from the selection set
10. `Remove objects:` *Pick the line at* ⑤ *(see fig. 21.8)* `1 found, 1 removed`	Removes the line at ⑤ from the selection set
11. `Remove objects:` **A** ↵	Issues the Add option and changes selection to Add mode
12. `Select objects:` *Pick the line at* ⑦ *(see fig. 21.8)*	Adds the line at ⑦ to the selection set
13. `Select objects:` *Press* Ctrl+C	Cancels the ERASE command and clears the selection set

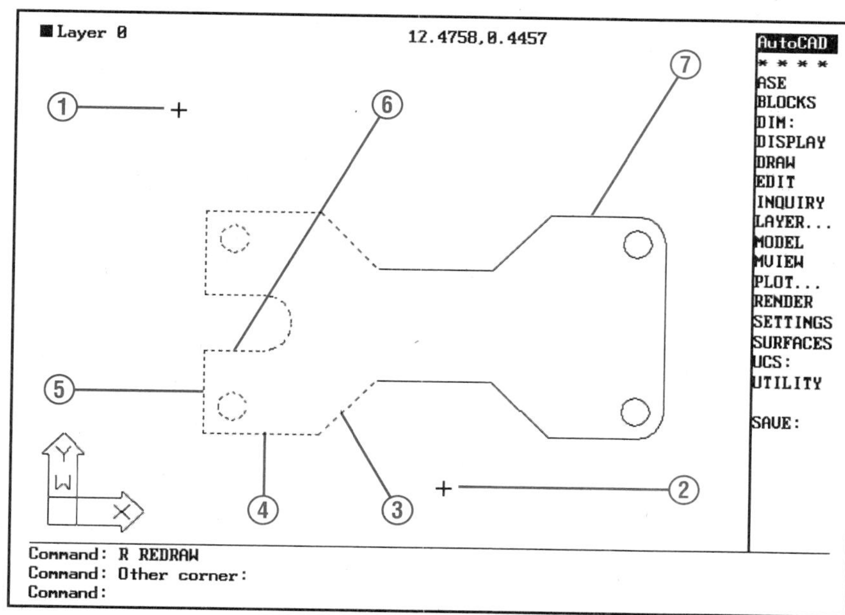

Figure 21.8

Selection points for shift-pick exercise.

Using Selection Options

Many options can be used in response to the `Select objects:` prompt to alter the way AutoCAD selects entities. Many of the more complex options are explained in unit 50, "Creating Advanced Selection Sets." The following list summarizes the few most commonly used options that you can enter at the keyboard in response to the `Select objects:` prompt:

- **Window** or **W.** Causes AutoCAD to prompt you to specify the corners of a window. Any visible entities fully enclosed by the window will be selected. If the entity extends outside of the window, AutoCAD does not add it to the selection set.
- **Crossing** or **C.** Causes AutoCAD to prompt you to specify the corners of a window. Visible entities fully enclosed by the window and entities that cross the perimeter of the window are selected.
- **Last** or **L.** Selects the very last entity created. Only one entity can be selected using Last in any selection set.
- **Previous** or **P.** Selects the entities that were included in the previous selection set (such as the selection set you created during a previous editing command).
- **Remove** or **R.** Switches object selection to Remove mode. Selecting entities when Remove mode is active removes the entities from the selection set.
- **Add** or **A.** Switches object selection to Add mode. Use this option to switch from Remove mode to Add mode.

- **Undo** or **U.** Undoes the previous entity selection. If Add mode is active, the last entity selected is removed from the set. If Remove mode is active, the last entity selected is added to the set.

The options described here are used in a number of unit exercises throughout this book.

Many more advanced options are available for creating a selection set. These options are explained in unit 50, "Creating Advanced Selection Sets."

Changing Selection Settings

There are a few settings you can use to control AutoCAD's selection methods and features. If you select Settings, then Selections Settings, AutoCAD displays the Entity Selection Settings dialog box (see fig. 21.9). You also can issue the command DDSELECT to display this dialog box.

Figure 21.9

The Entity Selection Settings dialog box.

Controls in the Entity Selection Settings dialog box include:

- **Pick-first Selection.** When this check box is enabled, you can select entities before issuing an editing command to modify the entities. If this check box is disabled (no check), you must issue the editing command first, then select entities when prompted to do so. As unit 22, "Introduction to Grips and Autoediting," explains, this option must be enabled to use grips.
- **Use Shift to Add.** When this check box is enabled, selecting an entity replaces any existing selection set with the selected entity. To add an entity to the set rather than replace the set, you must hold down the

Shift key while selecting entities. This check box has no effect on Remove mode.

- **Press and Drag.** This check box controls how window selection is made. If this check box is disabled (the default), you pick the point for the first corner, drag the cursor to the desired location, then pick the point for the other corner. If this check box is enabled, you place the cursor at the desired location for the first corner, press and hold the pick button, drag the cursor to the desired location for the other corner, then release the pick button.

- **Implied Windowing.** If this check box is enabled (the default) and you pick a point that is not on an entity, AutoCAD automatically begins a selection window. If this check box is disabled, AutoCAD interprets the first point pick as an attempt to select a single entity and does not automatically begin a selection window. A subsequent pick in empty space will begin a selection window, however.

- **Default Selection Mode.** This button sets up AutoCAD to use its default selection modes: **pick-first** Selection enabled; **U**se Shift to Add disabled; **P**ress and Drag disabled; and **I**mplied Windowing enabled.

- **Pick Box Size.** This scroll bar enables you to change the size of AutoCAD's pick box.

- **Entity Sort Method.** This button displays the Entity Sort Method dialog box, which enables you to control the order in which AutoCAD processes entities in the drawing database. Entity sorting is beyond the scope of *Hands On AutoCAD.*

Unit Review

What You've Learned

- The purpose for selection sets
- The basics of editing
- How to use pick-first selection to build a selection set before issuing an editing command
- How to use pick-after selection to build a selection set within an editing command
- How to remove entities from a set and add entities to a set
- How to control selection settings

Review Questions

True or False

21.01 T F You must hold down the pick button and drag the cursor to select a second window corner if the Press and Drag mode checkbox is enabled.

21.02 T F All commands can be used with pick-first selections.

21.03 T F A window, when used, erases anything it touches.

21.04 T F The Last and Previous options, if used during selection, perform the same function.

21.05 T F It is not possible to begin a selection window automatically without using the Window option.

Multiple Choice

21.06 From which pull-down menu can you access the Selection Settings dialog box? __________

(A) Modify

(B) Draw

(C) Settings

(D) none of the above

Student: ____________________ Date: __________

Instructor: ____________________ Course: ______ Section: ______

21.07 Pick-first editing is done by __________.

(A) selecting entities then issuing a command

(B) issuing a command then selecting entities

(C) holding down the pick button

(D) none of the above

21.08 A crossing selection window can be started by __________.

(A) picking the first point while holding the shift key

(B) picking the first point and moving the crosshairs to the left

(C) picking the first point and moving the crosshairs to the right

(D) none of the above

21.09 Which command activates Entity Section Settings? __________

(A) DDLMODES

(B) DDRMODES

(C) DDSETTINGS

(D) DDSELECT

21.10 The Entity Selection Settings dialog box aids you in __________.

(A) moving the crosshairs across the screen

(B) setting how you will select entities

(C) setting the window of editing entities

(D) setting the extents of your drawing

Student: __________ Date: __________

Instructor: __________ Course: __________ Section: __________

UNIT 22

Introduction to Grips and Autoediting

Grips offer a convenient way to edit entities in AutoCAD. Displayed as squares at key points on entities, grips can be thought of as places to "grab" an entity to modify it. Figure 22.1 shows various types of AutoCAD entities with grips enabled. Although AutoCAD provides other methods for editing entities, grips provide one of the quickest methods for modifying and editing a drawing. Understanding and using grips is an important skill that you should master to become proficient with AutoCAD. This unit will help you begin to develop that skill.

The objectives for this unit are to:

- Understand what grips are and how they can be used
- Become familiar with the autoedit modes associated with grips
- Know how to set grip options

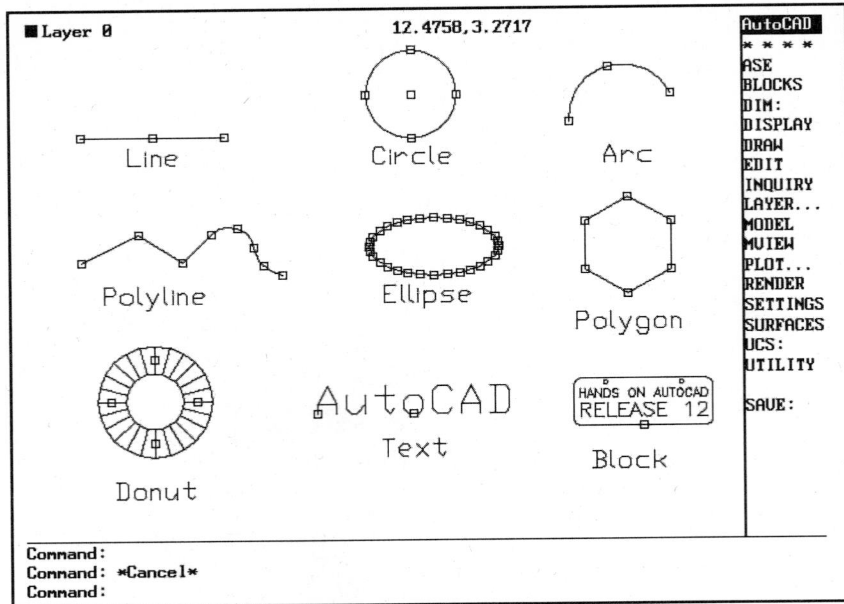

Figure 22.1

Grips displayed on various AutoCAD entities.

Using Grips

As mentioned previously, grips are small squares that appear at specific locations on entities after you select the entities. Grips are by default enabled (turned on) in AutoCAD. A quick way to verify whether grips are enabled is to select an entity while AutoCAD's command prompt is displayed. If small squares (grips) appear on the selected entity, grips are enabled.

NOTE

The presence of a small pickbox on the AutoCAD crosshair cursor does not indicate that grips are enabled. Instead, this cursor pickbox indicates that noun/verb selection is enabled. Noun/verb selection must be enabled for grips to be used. See unit 21, "Introduction to Selection and Editing," for a description of noun/verb selection.

Grips work in conjunction with noun/verb selection, which is explained in unit 21. To give you a brief review of noun/verb selection, recall that there are two methods for selecting entities in AutoCAD. You can issue a command and then select entities in response to the command's prompts. This method is known as pick-after (verb/noun) selection because you specify the verb action that will take place (erase, for example) before specifying the objects you want to change.

You also can configure AutoCAD to enable you to select entities *before* you issue the command that will modify these entities. You can select a group of entities, for example, then issue the ERASE command. The selected entities are then erased without further prompting from AutoCAD. This method of entity selection is referred to as pick-first(noun/verb) selection because the entities are identified before the verb action is specified. Noun/verb selection must be enabled for grips to be used.

Selecting Entities Using Grips

When grips are displayed on an entity, you can select a grip by placing the cursor on it and clicking the pick button. The cursor automatically snaps to the exact center of a grip when the cursor is within a preset range, making it easy to select the grip (the cursor must snap to the grip before you can select the grip).

Picking a grip makes it active, and the grip changes color. If you pick a grip without pressing the Shift key, AutoCAD enters the *stretch autoedit mode*, which you can use to stretch the selected entities based on the selected grip. If you press Shift while selecting your first grip, you can select multiple grips. The use of single and multiple grips is explained a little later in this unit.

The stretch autoedit mode is only one of several autoedit modes. Autoedit modes include:

- **Stretch.** This autoedit mode enables you to stretch entities, and is similar in function to the STRETCH command (explained in unit 55, "Stretching Entities").
- **Move.** This autoedit mode enables you to move entities from one point to another, and is similar to the MOVE command (which is briefly noted in unit 23, "Moving and Stretching Entities").
- **Rotate.** This autoedit mode enables you to rotate entities about a point, and is similar to the ROTATE command (see unit 24, "Rotating, Mirroring, and Scaling Entities").
- **Scale.** This autoedit mode enables you to scale entities larger or smaller, and is similar to the SCALE command (see unit 24, "Rotating, Mirroring, and Scaling Entities").
- **Mirror.** This autoedit mode enables you to mirror entities about an axis, and is similar to the MIRROR command (see unit 24, "Rotating, Mirroring, and Scaling Entities").

In this unit, you will focus on selecting and controlling grips, although you will use some of the autoedit modes in your exercises to learn how grips can be useful. In the next exercise, practice selecting entities and grips.

Using Grips

Selecting Single Grips

1. Begin a new drawing named 022???01 in your assigned directory using 022GRIPS as a prototype.

2. `Command:` *Pick a point at* ① *(see fig 22.2)* — Specifies the first point of a selection window

3. `Command:` *Pick a point at* ② — Specifies the second point of a selection window, selects entities using noun/verb selection, and displays grips on selected entities

Your drawing should resemble figure 22.2.

4. `Command:` *Pick the grip at* ③ *(see fig 22.2)* — Highlights the grip and enters Stretch autoedit mode

   ```
   ** STRETCH **
   <Stretch to point>/Base point/Copy
   /Undo/eXit:
   ```

5. Move the cursor and note that the lines attached to the grip stretch as you move the cursor.

6. `<Stretch to point>/Base point/Copy /Undo/eXit:` *Press* Ctrl+C — Cancels the autoedit mode and returns to the command prompt

7. `Command:` **R** ↵ — Issues the alias for the REDRAW command

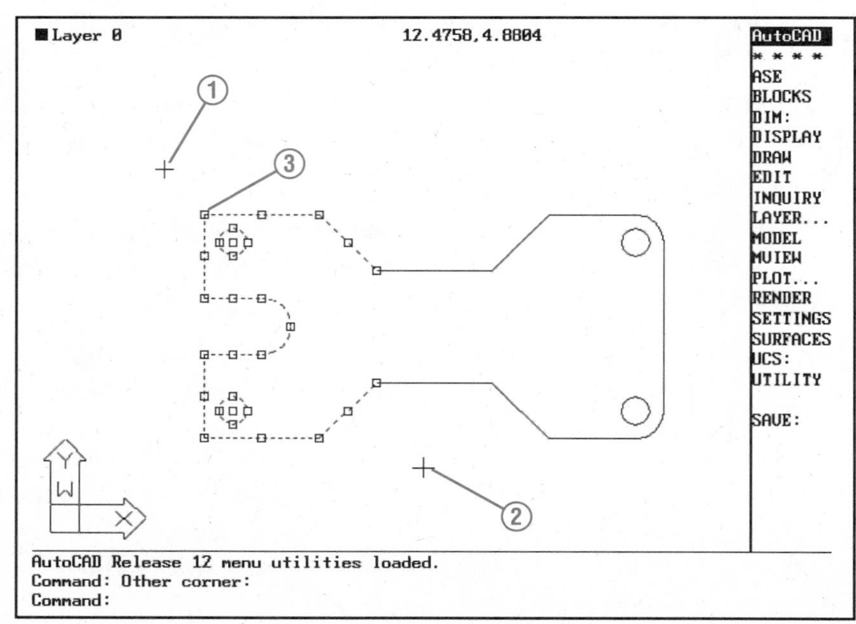

Figure 22.2

Selected entities showing grips enabled.

You can see that the REDRAW command has no effect on displayed grips—any grips that are displayed prior to the redraw are displayed after the redraw. In addition, the REGEN command does not affect grips.

The effect of selecting a grip depends on the location of the grip on the entity and the type of entity. If you select a grip at the midpoint of a line, for example, the line moves during Stretch autoedit mode instead of stretching. You will learn about the effects of grip selection on various types of entities in units 23, 24, and 25.

In the next exercise, hold down the Shift key and select multiple grips to see how it affects the autoedit process.

Selecting Multiple Grips

Continue with your drawing from the previous exercise. The grips that were displayed in the previous exercise should still be visible.

1. `Command:` *Hold down the Shift key, then pick the grips at ①, ②, ③, and ④ (see fig. 22.3)* — Selects and highlights four grips

2. `Command:` *Release the Shift key and pick the grip at ① (see fig. 22.3)* — Enters Stretch autoedit mode

```
** STRETCH **
<Stretch to point>/Base point/Copy
/Undo/eXit:
```

3. Move the cursor and note that the entities attached to all of the selected grips are stretched.

4. `** STRETCH ** <Stretch to point>/Base point/Copy /Undo/eXit:` *Press* Ctrl+C — Cancels Stretch autoedit mode

You can select multiple grips only when AutoCAD is displaying the command prompt (before you enter an autoedit mode). You cannot select multiple grips when an autoedit mode is active. The first grip you select without pressing the Shift key causes AutoCAD to enter Stretch autoedit mode.

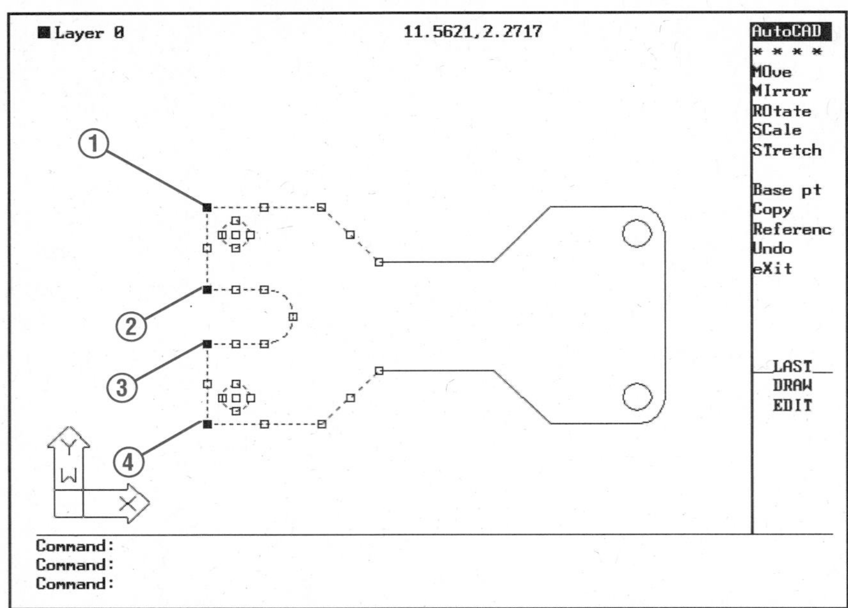

Figure 22.3
Multiple selected grips.

You can see from the exercise that selecting multiple grips affects the selected entities differently. You will learn in other units that multiple grip selection is very useful when you need to edit more than one entity at the same time.

Setting Grip Options

You can control a handful of characteristics of grips. The Settings,Grips command displays the Grips dialog box (see fig. 22.4). You also can enter the DDGRIPS command at the command prompt to display the Grips dialog box. With this dialog box, you can turn grips on and off, set grip size, and specify the colors to be used for selected and unselected grips.

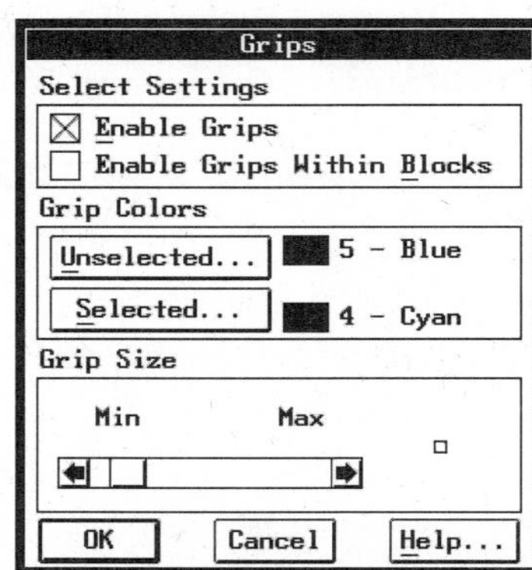

Figure 22.4
The Grips dialog box.

In the following exercise, make a few changes to your grip settings.

Setting Grip Options

Continue with your drawing from the previous exercise.

1. `Command:` *Choose* Settings, *then* Grips — Clears all grips and displays the Grips dialog box
2. *Click on the right arrow of the Grip Size scrollbar five times* — Increases the size of grips
3. *Choose the* Selected *button in the Grip Colors group box* — Displays the Select Color dialog box (see fig. 22.5)
4. *Click on the fourth box in the* Standard Colors *group box, then choose* OK — Specifies cyan as the color for selected grips and closes the Select Color dialog box
5. *Choose* OK — Closes the Grips dialog box
6. `Command:` *Select the line at* ① *(see fig. 22.6)* — Selects the line and displays its grips
7. `Command:` *Pick the grip at* ② *(see fig. 22.6)* — Selects the grip and enters Stretch autoedit mode

   ```
   ** STRETCH **
   <Stretch to point>/Base point/Copy
   /Undo/eXit:
   ```

8. `** STRETCH **` `<Stretch to point>/Base point/Copy /Undo/eXit:` *Press* Ctrl+C — Cancels Stretch autoedit mode

The Grips dialog box also contains an option for enabling grips within blocks so that you can choose grips on entities that comprise a block. This option is discussed in further detail in unit 95.

If you clear the Enable Grips check box in the Grips dialog box, grips will not appear when you select entities. Turning off grips is useful when you want to select entities at the command prompt, but do not want to use autoedit modes on the selection set.

Figure 22.5

The Select Color dialog box.

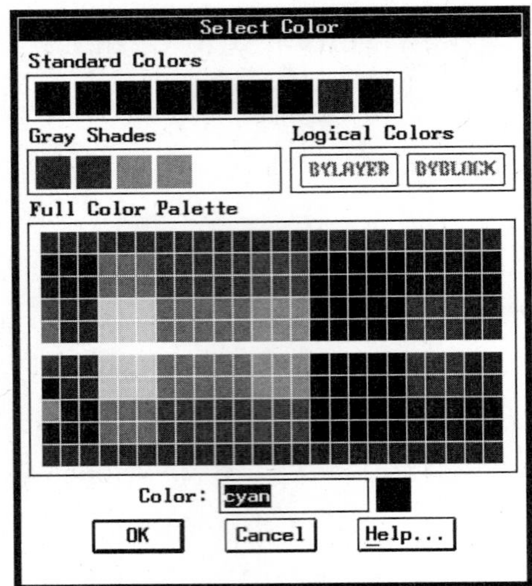

Figure 22.6

The effects of changes in the Grips dialog box.

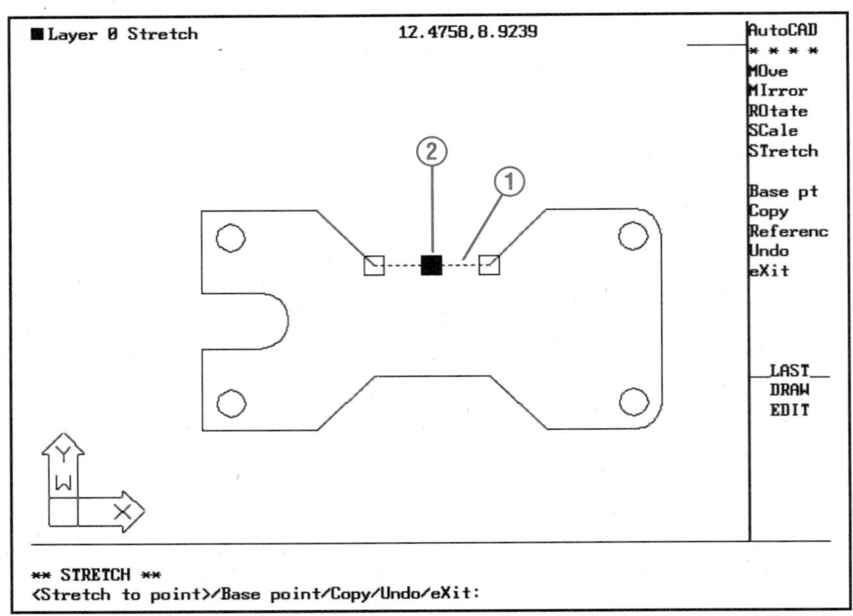

Unit Review

What You've Learned

- How to enable and activate grips
- How to predefine selections sets
- How to set grip options using the Grips dialog box

Review Questions

True or False

22.01 T F The grip locations on a circle are different from the grip locations on a line.

22.02 T F No more than one grip may be active or "hot" at any one time.

22.03 T F The AutoCAD status line indicates whether grips are enabled.

22.04 T F Grips provide the quickest means for modifying entities.

22.05 T F The presence of a pickbox on the crosshair cursor indicates that grips are enabled.

Multiple Choice

22.06 Grips work in conjunction with __________.

(A) layers

(B) the cursor

(C) noun/verb selection

(D) lines and arcs

22.07 When it is near a grip, the cursor automatically snaps to__________.

(A) the center of the grip

(B) the upper left edge of the grip

(C) the midpoint of the line

(D) none of the above

Student: __________ Date: __________

Instructor: __________ Course: __________ Section: __________

22.08 Picking a grip without pressing Shift ________.

(A) enters autoedit mode

(B) selects the grip

(C) makes the grip change color

(D) all of the above

Short Answer

22.09 List the five autoedit modes.

____

____

____

22.10 Describe the effect of clearing the Enable Grips check box in the Grips dialog box.

____

____

____

Student: ______________ Date: ______________

Instructor: ______________ Course: ______________ Section: ______________

Moving and Stretching Entities

nit 22 introduced grips and autoediting modes. Two of the most common operations you can perform with autoedit modes include moving and stretching entities. In this unit, you learn how to use grips along with the Stretch and Move autoedit modes to edit geometry in your drawings.

The objectives for this unit are to:

- Understand the various options of the Stretch autoedit mode
- Use grips to stretch entities
- Understand the various options of the Move autoedit mode
- Use grips to move entities

AutoCAD includes a command called STRETCH that functions very much like the Stretch autoedit mode. The difference is that STRETCH uses pick-after selection (Stretch autoedit mode uses pick-first selection). The STRETCH command is explored in unit 55, "Stretching Entities."

Stretching Entities

One of the most important advantages of AutoCAD compared to manual drafting is the wide range of functions AutoCAD provides for modifying existing entities in a drawing. A common editing operation you will perform often as you prepare drawings is *stretching* entities. Stretching entities generally makes them longer or shorter. With some entities, such as circles, the effects of stretch are somewhat different (the circle's radius becomes larger or smaller). Figure 23.1 shows an example of entities that have been stretched.

Figure 23.1

An example of a stretch operation.

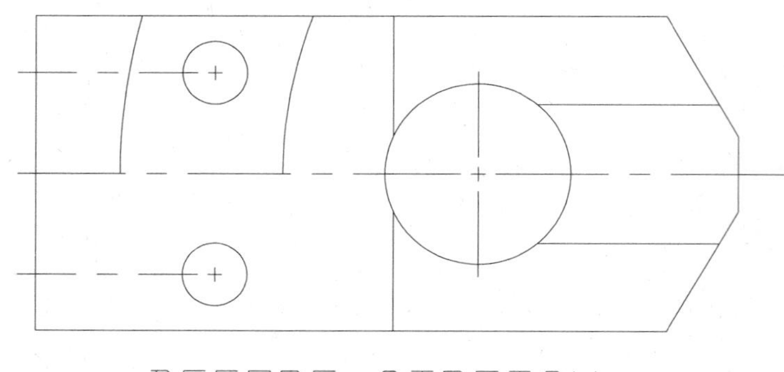

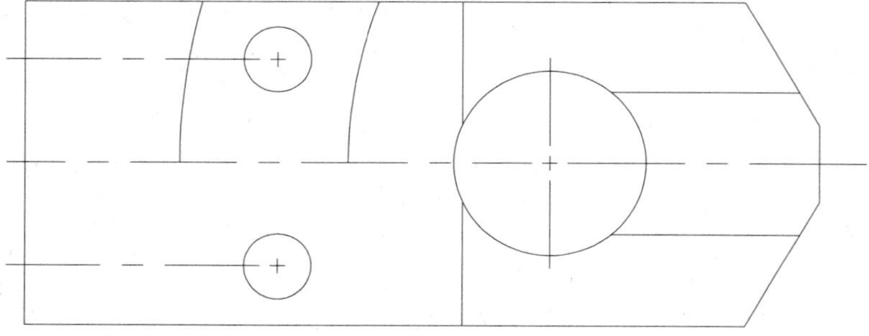

Stretching entities with grips is a fairly straightforward process. If you select the grip at the end point of a line, for example, you can change the location of the end point, which stretches the line. If you select the grip on the quadrant of a circle, you can modify its diameter. There are exceptions to this stretching capability: the stretch command may move an entity rather than stretch it. This happens when you select a grip on an entity that has no valid stretch modification, such as the center of a circle, the midpoint of a line, or insertion point of text.

Some entities cannot be stretched regardless of the grip you select. Blocks, which are introduced in unit 67 ("Introduction to Blocks"), are an example of such an entity. A block can consist of numerous entities, but AutoCAD recognizes them collectively as a single entity. The entities are "locked" into the block and cannot be changed in any way, including stretching. Text is another example: you can move and scale text, but you cannot stretch it.

Using Stretch Autoedit Mode

The first of the autoedit modes is Stretch. You can use Stretch autoedit mode to change entities that are already a part of your drawing. In the following exercises, you will be modifying entities to modify a slide block (see fig. 23.2).

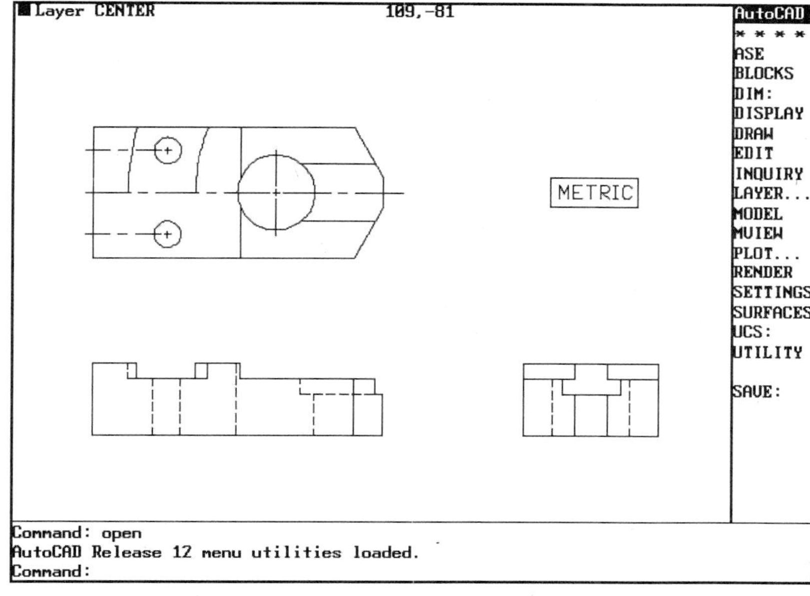

Figure 23.2

Slide block drawing to be modified with autoediting.

First, the length of the slide block must be changed from 108mm to 120mm. Change the block's length in top view; you will edit the front view later. Use figure 23.3 as a guide to select entities and grips.

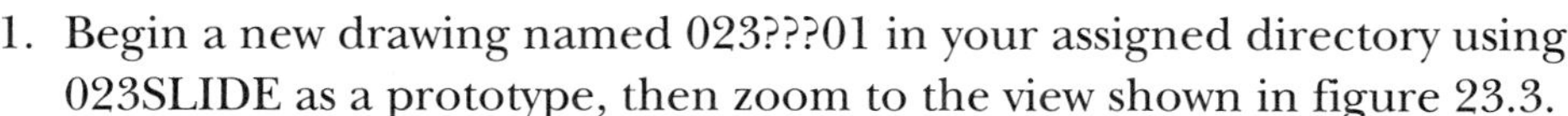

Using Grips to Stretch Entities

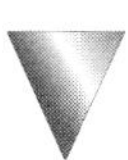

1. Begin a new drawing named 023???01 in your assigned directory using 023SLIDE as a prototype, then zoom to the view shown in figure 23.3.

2. `Command:` *Select the line at* ① *(see fig. 23.3)*	Creates a selection set
3. `Command:` *Select the lines at* ② *and* ③	Adds the lines to the selection set

continues

4. `Command:` *Pick the grip at* ④	Selects the grip and enters Stretch autoedit mode
`** STRETCH **`	
5. `<Stretch to point>/Base point/Copy/ Undo/eXit: @-12,0 ↵`	Stretches the line 12mm to the left

The result should look like figure 23.4.

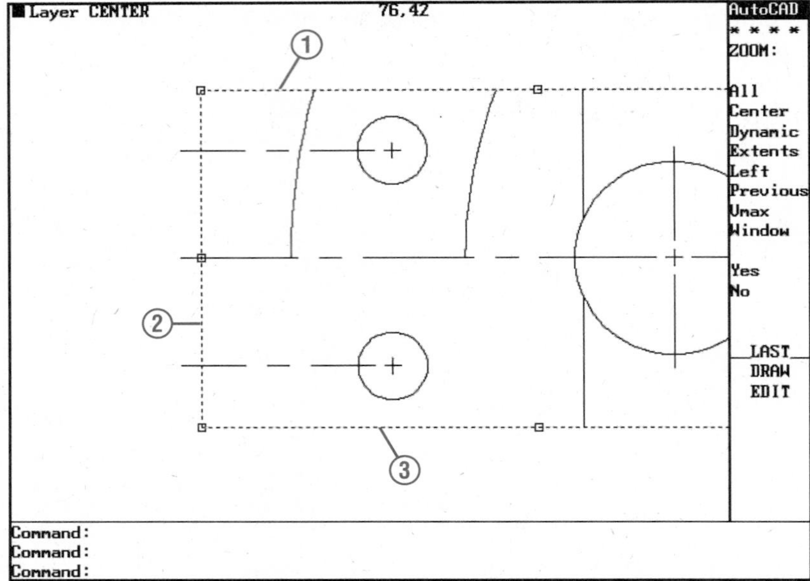

Figure 23.3

Line before stretch.

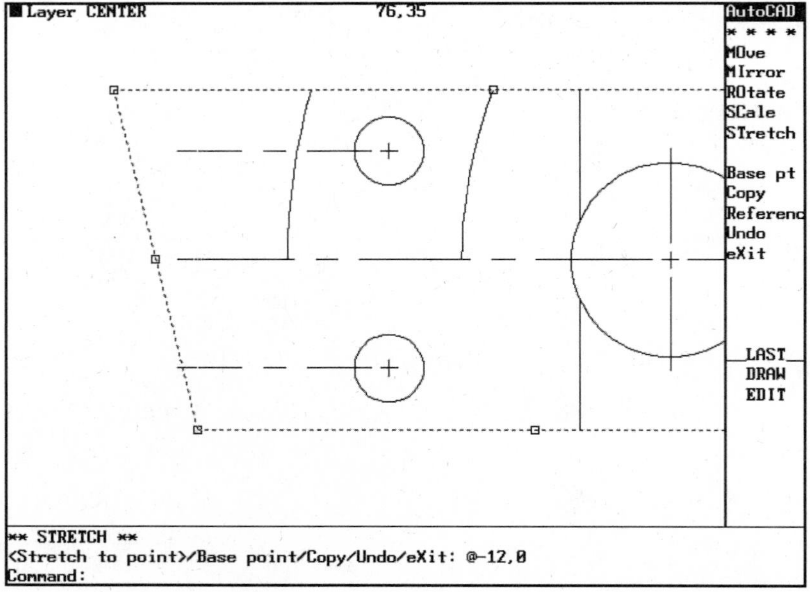

Figure 23.4

Line after stretch.

You can see from the exercise that you can stretch lines one at a time. In this example, however, you also need to stretch the bottom and left-side lines, as well as the centerlines for the two holes. Why not stretch all of them in a single operation? Just select multiple grips before you enter the Stretch autoedit mode. Use figure 23.5 to select entities and grips.

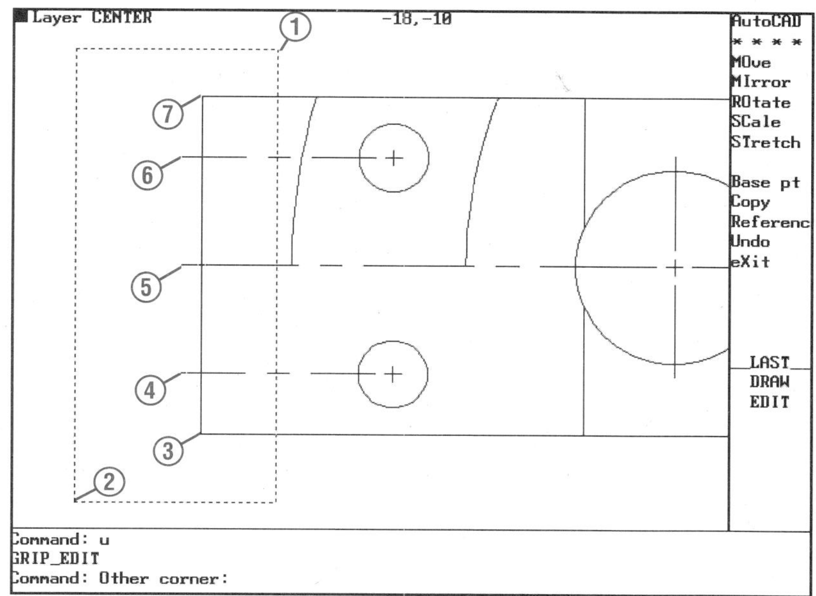

Figure 23.5

Selection points for stretching multiple entities.

Stretching Multiple Entities

Continue with your drawing from the preceding exercise.

1. `Command:` **`U`** ↵ — Undoes the previous stretch operation

   `GRIP_EDIT`

2. `Command:` *Pick points at ① and ② (see fig. 23.5)* — Uses a crossing box to create a selection set containing five lines and displays their grips

3. `Command:` *Hold down the Shift key, then pick the grips at ③, ④, ⑤, ⑥, and ⑦ (see fig. 23.5)* — Selects and highlights multiple grips

4. `Command:` *Release the Shift key and pick the grip at ③* — Enters Stretch autoedit mode

continues

5. Move the cursor on-screen and notice how the entities stretch dynamically to follow the cursor.

   `** STRETCH **`

6. Stretches all selected `<Stretch to point>/Base point/Copy/Undo/eXit:` **`@-12,0`** ↵	Stretches all selected entities 12mm to the left
7. `Command:` *Press* Ctrl+C *twice*	Clears the selection set and clears grips
8. `Command:` **`R`** ↵	Issues the alias for the REDRAW command
9. `Command:` *Choose* File, *then* Save	Saves your drawing

Your drawing should look similar to figure 23.6.

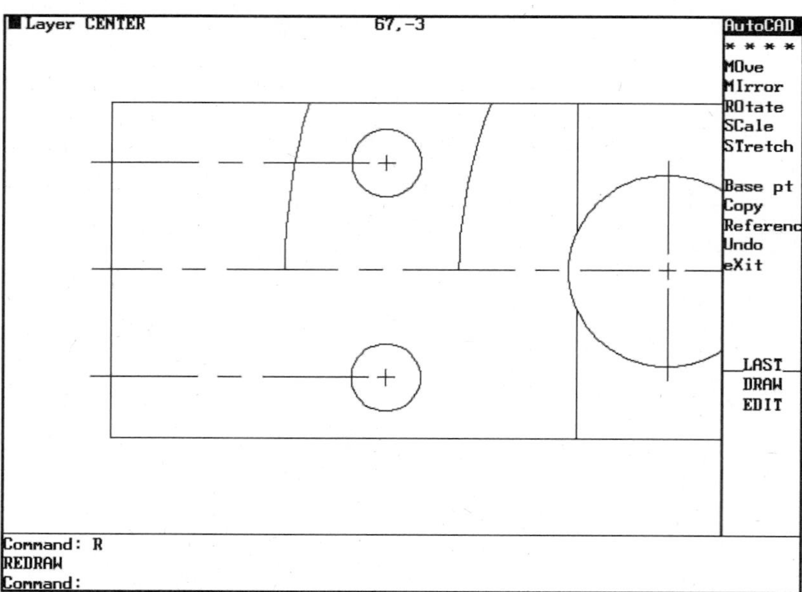

Figure 23.6
Multiple entities stretched using Stretch autoedit mode.

By selecting multiple grips before entering Stretch autoedit mode, you can stretch many entities with a single operation. This is much faster than stretching each of the entities individually.

Next, practice stretching arcs. In the exercise, stretch two arcs from the middle of the slide block to the bottom edge of the slide block (in the top view) to form a curved slot.

You will use a point filter, explained in unit 13 ("Using Absolute and Relative Coordinates"), to select a point in the following exercise. If you are not familiar with point filters, you may want to review unit 13 before continuing.

You also will use an object snap mode *to select a point. Object snap modes are explained in unit 36, "Using Temporary Object Snap Modes." When prompted to do so, select the requested object snap mode from the popup menu, place the center of the crosshairs on the specified line, then click the pick button.*

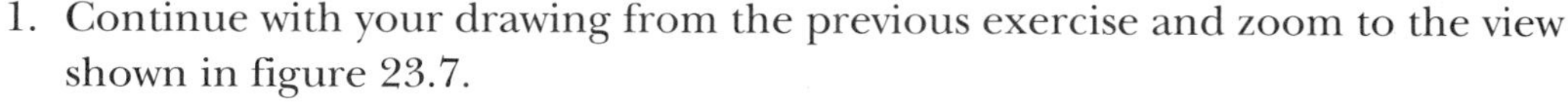

Stretching Arcs

1. Continue with your drawing from the previous exercise and zoom to the view shown in figure 23.7.

2. `Command:` *Select the arc at* ① *(see fig 23.7)*	Creates a selection set and displays grips
3. `Command:` *Pick the grip at* ③ *(see fig 23.7)*	Enters Stretch autoedit mode
`** STRETCH **`	
4. `<Stretch to point>/Base point/Copy/Undo/eXit:` *From the popup menu, choose* .X	Sets object snap mode to .X filter
6. `.X of` *Pick the grip at* ⑤ *(see fig 23.7)*	Specifies the .X ordinate of the new point for the arc
7. `(need YZ):` *From the popup menu, choose* Nearest	Sets object snap mode to NEArest
8. `_nea to` *Pick the line at* ⑥ *(see fig 23.7)*	Locates the new point and stretches the arcs
9. `Command:` *Choose* File, *then* Save	Saves the drawing Repeat the process to stretch the arc at ②down to the bottom edge of the part. Select the grip at ④ to begin the stretch operation.

If you need to need to leave the endpoints of an arc where they are but change the radius of the arc, select the midpoint grip on the arc instead of an end point grip. As you stretch the arc, the radius will change but the end points will remain at their original location.

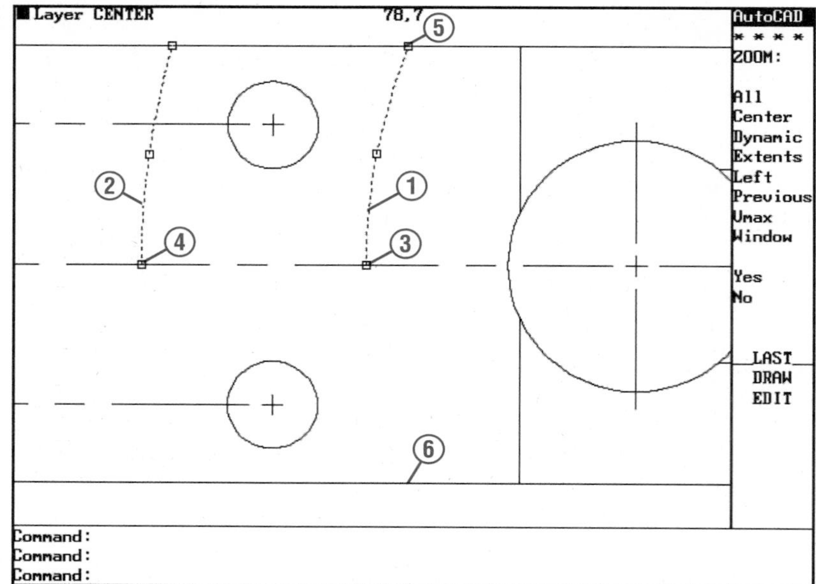

Figure 23.7

Selection points for stretching arcs.

The previous exercise demonstrates an important use for grips: locating points. You do not have to use grips for autoedit modes. You can select an entity to turn on its grips whenever you need to snap to a point that corresponds to the grip. For example, you can select an entity to display its grips, then use the LINE command to draw lines to the grips without using coordinates or object snap modes.

Moving Entities

You read earlier in this unit that you can move certain types of entities with the Stretch autoedit mode. The grip you select on certain entities also determines whether the entity will move or stretch. Moving entities with Stretch autoedit mode does not work in all situations or for all entities, however; AutoCAD includes a Move autoedit mode for explicitly moving entities.

In the following exercise, use the Move autoedit mode to move the two holes in the curved slot 2mm to the left. Use figure 23.8 as a guide.

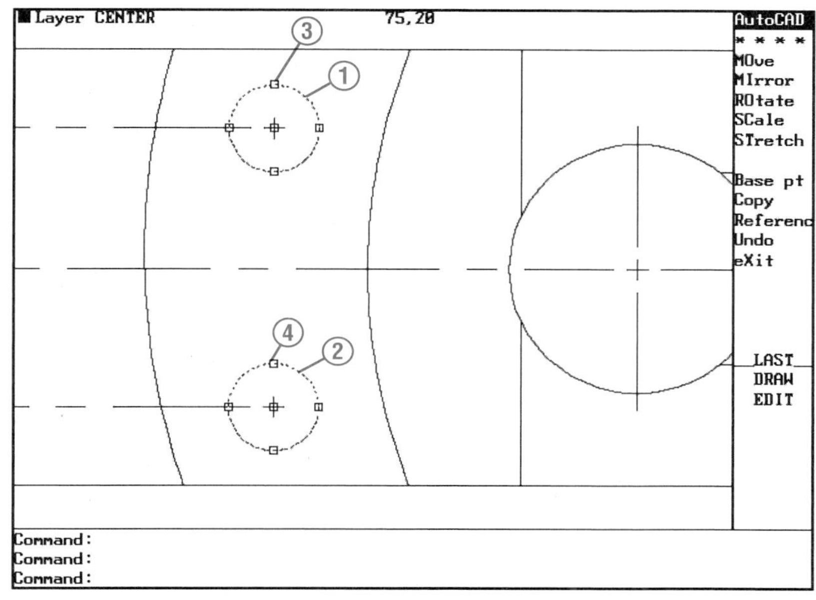

Figure 23.8

Selection points and grips to move circles.

Moving Entities in Move Autoedit Mode

Continue with your drawing from the previous exercise.

1. `Command:` *Select the circles at* ① *and* ② *(see fig. 23.8)* — Creates a selection set and displays grips
2. `Command:` *Hold down the Shift key, then pick the grips at* ③ *and* ④ *(see fig. 23.8)* — Selects multiple grips
3. `Command:` *Release the Shift key and pick the grip at* ③ — Selects the grip and enters Stretch autoedit mode
4. `** STRETCH **` `<Stretch to point>/Base point/Copy/Undo/eXit:` *Press* Enter — Switches to Move autoedit mode
5. `** MOVE **` `<Move to point>/Base point/Copy/Undo/eXit:` **`@2<180`** ↵ — Moves the circles 2mm to the left (at an angle of 180 degrees)

The circles moved, but their center marks did not. In the review exercises you will use Stretch autoedit mode to move the center marks and the holes' centerlines.

AutoCAD includes a command called MOVE that also enables you to move entities. Like the STRETCH command, the MOVE command can use pick-after selection. Unlike STRETCH, however, MOVE also can use pick-first selection. The MOVE command is preferable to Move autoedit mode when you need to define and move a complex selection set.

Unit Review

What You've Learned

- ☞ How to stretch entities using Stretch autoedit mode
- ☞ How to move entities using Move autoedit mode

Review Questions

True or False

23.01 T F Grips that are selected are represented by solid squares.

23.02 T F The Move and Stretch autoedit modes can perform similarly depending on which entity grips are active.

23.03 T F You must use the Tab key to toggle through the autoedit modes.

23.04 T F Autoedit modes require the pick-first selection method.

23.05 T F You cannot stretch an arc.

Multiple Choice

23.06 Which of the following keyboard combinations is used to clear a selection set and clear grips? ____________

(A) Ctrl+Delete

(B) Ctrl+Alt+Delete

(C) Ctrl+D

(D) Ctrl+C

23.07 Which of the following autoedit modes would be used to change the location of a circle? _____________

(A) Move

(B) Base point

(C) Change

(D) Copy

Student: ____________________ Date: ________

Instructor: ____________________ Course: ________ Section: ________

Short Answer

23.08 Explain what happens when you select the midpoint grip of a line, then attempt to stretch the line in Stretch autoedit mode.

23.09 What effect does Stretch autoedit mode have on a circle if you select the circle's center grip?

23.10 Explain the advantage of selecting multiple grips for a stretch operation.

Student: ____________ Date: ____________

Instructor: ____________ Course: ____________ Section: ____________

UNIT 24

Rotating, Mirroring, and Scaling Entities

diting entities using grips is made even more powerful and flexible with AutoCAD's capability of rotating, mirroring, and scaling entities. This unit provides an overview of why these capabilities are important and how you can accomplish these editing tasks using grips and autoedit modes.

The objectives for this unit are to:

- Rotate entities using the Rotate autoedit mode
- Mirror entities using the Mirror autoedit mode
- Scale entities using the Scale autoedit mode

Rotating Entities

AutoCAD enables you to rotate existing entities on a drawing. For example, you may have drawn a feature horizontally because it was easiest to lay out the entities that way, but now need to rotate it to a different angle. Perhaps on another drawing the design has changed and you need to rotate a few entities to suit the new design. AutoCAD makes it easy to rotate the entities using grips and autoediting. Select the entities you want to rotate, pick a point for the center of rotation, then specify the rotation angle graphically or numerically.

The prototype drawing for the exercises in this unit has been set up so that your cursor will snap to most of the points you will need to pick. You will learn about setting and using a snap increment in unit 35, "Using a Snap Increment."

You will use a running object snap mode in the following exercises to pick exact points. Temporary and running object snap modes are explained fully in units 36, "Using Temporary Object Snap Modes," and 37, "Using Running Object Snap Modes."

In the following exercise, position the needle on the gauge by rotating it. Use figure 24.1 as a guide for selecting entities, grips, and points.

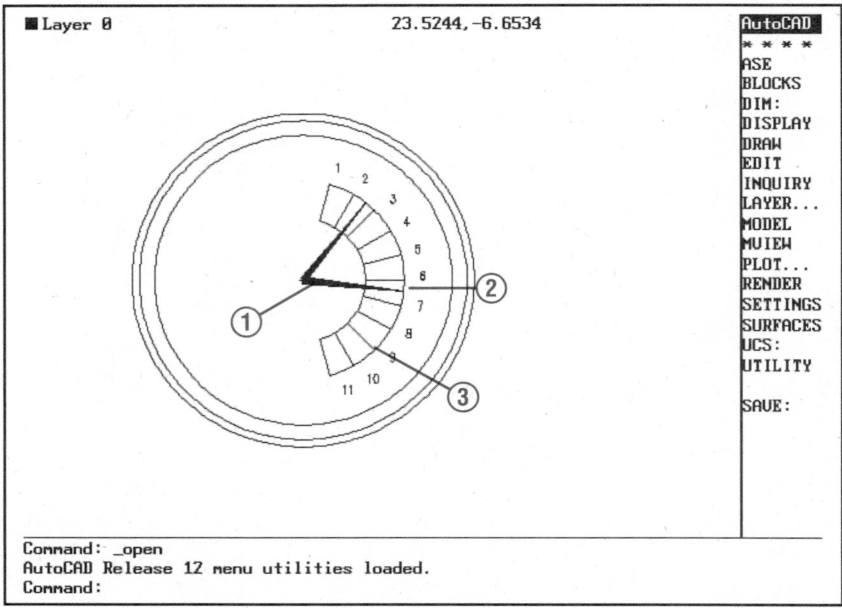

Figure 24.1

Selection points on the gauge drawing.

Rotating Entities Using Grips

1. Begin a new drawing named 024???01 in your assigned directory using 024GAUGE as a prototype.

2. `Command:` *Select the needle at* ① *(see fig. 24.1)*	Selects the needle and displays grips
3. `Command:` *Pick the grip at* ② *(see fig. 24.1)*	Enters Stretch autoedit mode
4. `** STRETCH **` `<Stretch to point>/Base point/Copy/Undo/eXit:` *Press* Enter	Switches to the next autoedit mode
5. `** MOVE **` `<Move to point>/Base point/Copy/Undo/eXit:` *Press* Enter	Toggles to the next autoedit mode
6. `** ROTATE **` `<Rotation angle>/Base point/Copy/Undo/Reference/eXit:` **B** ↵	Specifies the Base point option
7. `Base point:` *Pick a point at the center gauge*	Specifies the center of rotation

8. Move the cursor and note that the needle rotates about the center point you selected. Now set the reference angle for the rotation.

9. `** ROTATE **` `<Rotation angle>/Base point/Copy/Undo/Reference/eXit:` **R** ↵	Specifies the Reference option
10. Reference angle <0>: *Pick a point at the center of the gauge*	Specifies the vertex point of the angle
11. `Second point:` *Pick the grip at* ② *(see fig 24.1)*	Specifies the second point and defines the angle
12. `** ROTATE **` `<New angle>/Base point/Copy/Undo/Reference/eXit:` **ENDP** ↵	Sets a temporary object snap mode
13. *Pick the end point at* ③ *(see fig 24.1)*	Rotates the needle

Your drawing should look similar to figure 24.2.

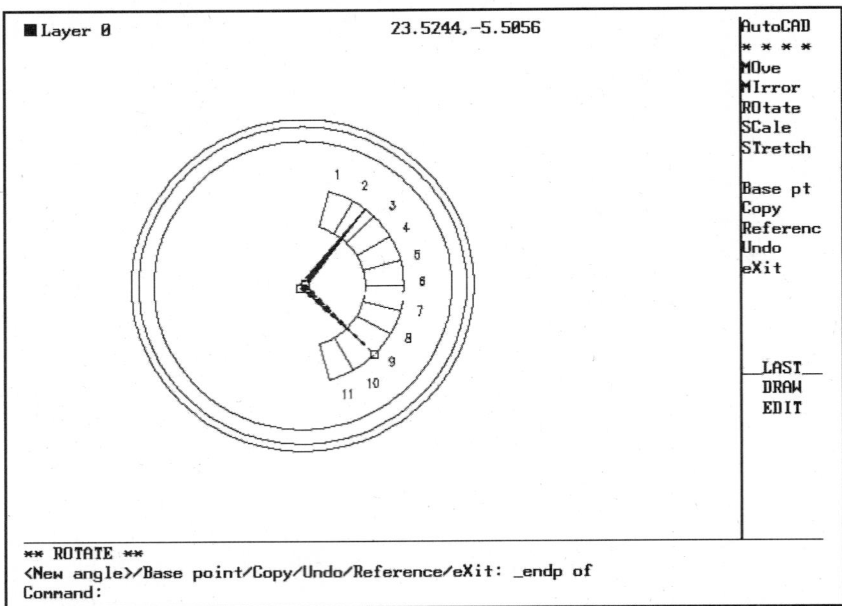

Figure 24.2

Needle rotated to a new location.

You rotated the needle using the Reference option of the rotate command. The Reference option enables you to specify a beginning angle, then specify a new angle or endpoint, and let AutoCAD calculate the necessary amount of rotation. In many cases, you will know the amount of rotation required, and can enter the angle numerically instead of using a reference angle. In such a situation, just enter the rotation angle using the keyboard.

Mirroring Entities

When you *mirror* an object, you make a mirror-image copy of it. You can leave the original intact and make a mirrored duplicate, or remove the original entities. The ability to mirror is particularly useful when you are drawing parts or features that are symmetrical. AutoCAD provides a Mirror autoedit mode that enables you to mirror using grips.

In the following exercise, mirror the gauge entities using grips. Use figure 24.3 as a guide.

Mirroring Entities Using Grips

1. `Command:` **`MIRRTEXT`** ↵	Issues the MIRRTEXT command
2. `New value for MIRRTEXT <1>:` **`0`** ↵	Forces text to maintain proper orientation when mirrored

3. `Command:` *Pick a point at* ① *(see fig. 24.3)*	Specifies first corner of a window selection box
4. `Other corner:` *Pick a point at* ② *(see fig 24.3)*	Specifies the opposite corner of a window selection box
5. `Command:` *Pick the grip at* ③ *(see fig 24.3)*	Activates the grip and enters autoedit mode
6. `** STRETCH **` `<Stretch to point>/Base point/Copy/` `Undo/eXit:` **`MI`** ↵	Switches to Mirror autoedit mode
7. `** MIRROR **` `<Second point>/Base point/Copy/` `Undo/eXit:` **`B`** ↵	Specifies the Base point option
8. `Base point:` *Pick a point at the center of the gauge*	Specifies the starting point of an imaginary line about which to mirror the entities
9. `** MIRROR **` `<Second point>/Base point/Copy/` `Undo/eXit:` *Press* F8, *pick a point above or below the current point, then press* F8	Turns on Ortho, specifies the second point of the mirror line, mirrors the entities, and turns off Ortho
10. `Command:` *Press* Ctrl+C *twice*	Clears the selection set and grips
11. `Command:` **`R`** ↵	Issues the alias for the REDRAW command
12. `Command:` **`U`** ↵ `REDRAW`	Undoes the previous REDRAW command
13. `Command:` **`U`** ↵ `GRIP_EDIT`	Undoes the previous autoedit operation
14. Save your drawing.	

Your drawing should look similar to figure 24.4.

When mirroring entities you must always provide a mirror line about which to mirror the objects. When using grips to mirror entities, AutoCAD assumes the most recent active grip as one endpoint of this line unless another point is specified.

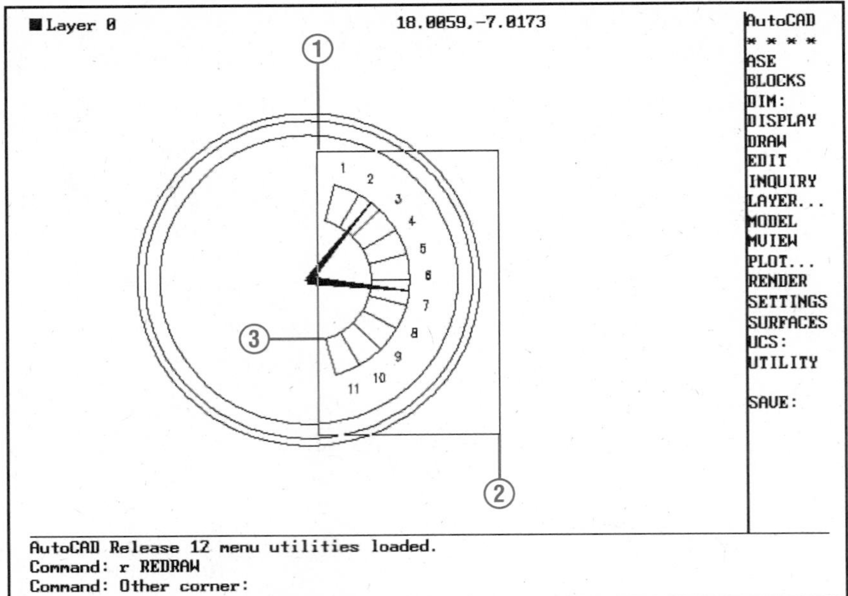

Figure 24.3

Selection points for mirroring.

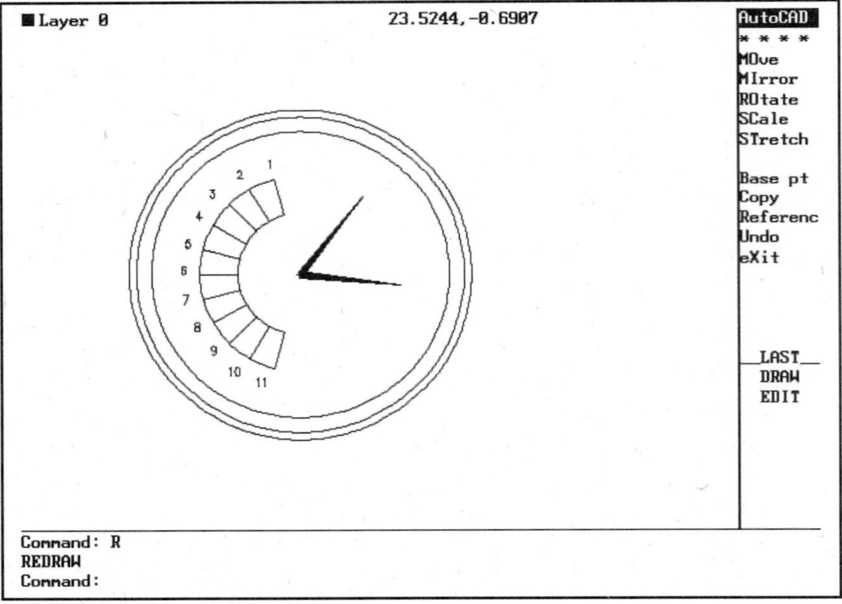

Figure 24.4

Entities mirrored using Mirror autoedit mode.

The imaginary mirror line can be anywhere in 2D space at any angle. It does not have to be either vertical or horizontal, and does not have to be attached to the entities being mirrored. Think of the mirror line as a "pivot point" for the entities being mirrored.

Scaling Entities

Scaling entities means that you change their actual size, smaller or larger, by specifying a scale factor or by using a reference size. Being able to scale entities is useful any time you need to enlarge or reduce the size of one or more entities.

In the following exercise, scale the needle larger in size by defining a reference size.

Scaling Entities Using Grips

1. Continue with your drawing from the previous exercise and zoom to the drawing's extents (use ZOOM Extents).

2. `Command:` *Select the bottom needle*
   Creates selection set and displays grips

3. `Command:` *Pick any grip on the needle*
   Activates the grip and enters Stretch autoedit mode

4. `** STRETCH **`
   `<Stretch to point>/Base point/Copy/Undo/eXit:` **`SC`** ↵
   Switches to Scale autoedit mode

5. `** SCALE **`
   `<Scale factor>/Base point/Copy/Undo/Reference/eXit:` *From the screen menu, choose* Base pt
   Chooses the Base point option

6. `Base point:` *Pick a point at the center of the gauge*
   Specifies the base point for the scale operation

7. `** SCALE **`
   `<Scale factor>/Base point/Copy/Undo/Reference/eXit:` *From the screen menu, choose* Reference
   Chooses the Reference option

8. `Reference length <1.0000>:` *Pick a point at the center of the gauge*
   Specifies the first point

9. `Second point:` *Pick the grip at the tip of the needle*
   Specifies the second point and defines the reference size

10. Move the cursor and note how the entities dynamically change size.

11. `** SCALE **`
    `<New length>/Base point/Copy/Undo/Reference/eXit:` **`ENDP`** ↵
    Sets a temporary object snap mode

continues

12. `of` *Pick the end point at* ① *(see fig. 24.5)*	Specifies the new length and scales the needle
13. Save your drawing.	

When you are scaling, you can just as easily specify a particular scale factor. For example, a scale factor of 2.0 doubles the size of the objects. A scale factor of 0.5 decreases their size by half. A specific scale factor is only useful, however, if you already know the relative size of your objects. The Reference option is useful when you know the relationship between the current size and desired size, but not the actual scale value.

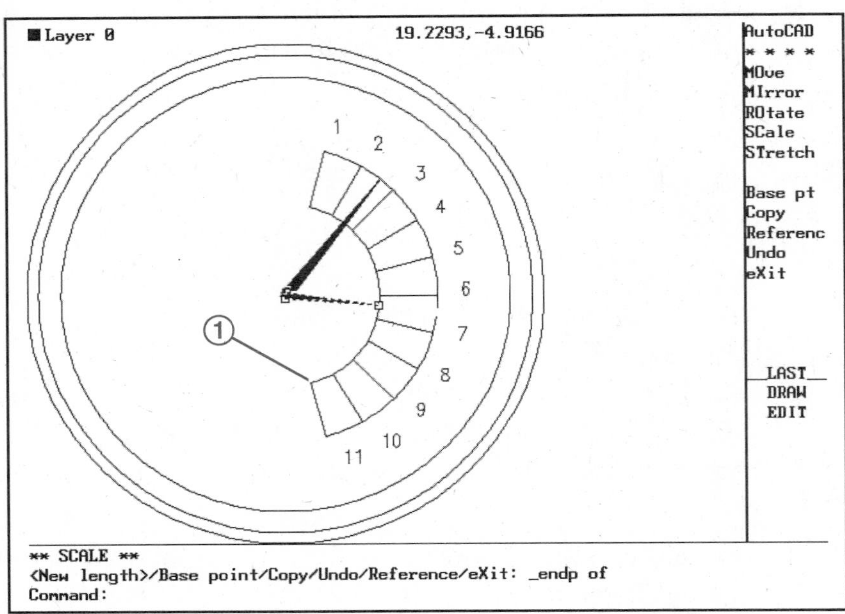

Figure 24.5

Scaling entities with Scale autoedit mode.

Unit Review

What You've Learned

- How to rotate entities using grips and autoediting
- How to mirror objects using grips and autoediting
- How to scale objects using grips and autoediting

Review Questions

True or False

24.01 T F Scaling is the same as stretching.

24.02 T F When you use the Rotate autoedit mode, you can specify a center of rotation (a base point).

24.03 T F You cannot enter a numeric value to rotate the selection set by a specific number of degrees.

24.04 T F The imaginary mirror reference line must be located on one of the entities being mirrored.

24.05 T F Mirror often is useful when you are drawing parts or features that are symmetrical.

24.06 T F The imaginary mirror reference line must be either horizontal or vertical.

24.07 T F Scaling enlarges or reduces the size of the entities in the selection set.

Multiple Choice

24.08 Which of the following is not an autoedit option? __________

(A) Base point

(B) Reference

(C) Undo

(D) Back

Student: ______________________ Date: __________

Instructor: ______________________ Course: __________ Section: __________

24.09 Which of the following autoedit modes can be used to change the size of entities? __________

(A) Rotate

(B) Scale

(C) Mirror

(D) Move

24.10 The __________ option of the Rotate autoedit mode enables you to specify a center point for the rotation.

(A) Reference point

(B) Reference

(C) Center point

(D) Base point

Additional Exercises

24.11 Open the same drawing you worked with in the previous exercises and rotate the smaller needle 15". Be sure to use the center of the circle as your base point.

24.12 Scale the large outer circle by a factor of 1.2. Use the center of the circle as the base point. Zoom to extents when finished.

When you have completed exercises 24.11 and 24.12, your drawing should resemble figure 24.6.

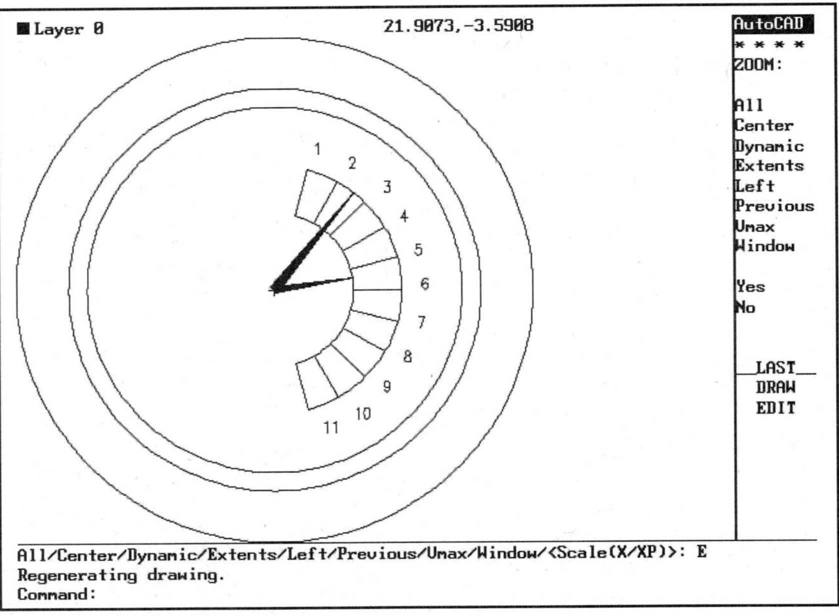

Figure 24.6
Gauge after rotation and scaling.

Student: __________ Date: __________

Instructor: __________ Course: __________ Section: __________

Copying Entities with Autoedit Modes

You may have noticed in previous units that one of the options given during the autoedit modes is Copy. This option provides more flexibility than any other AutoCAD command for editing entities. The Copy option enables you to combine a copy operation with any of the autoedit modes. This capability makes it possible for you to duplicate entities while you also rotate, scale, move, stretch, or mirror the entities. This unit teaches you to copy objects while using each of the autoedit modes.

The objectives for this unit are to:

- ☞ Understand the purpose for copying entities
- ☞ Copy entities during autoedit mode operations

UNIT 25

Understanding the Copy Option

Many drawings contain duplicate data. In the office drawing in figure 25.1, for example, the chairs in the conference room are duplicates of the same set of entities. You could draw each of the chairs separately, but doing so would be a waste of time. One of the main advantages of a CAD application such as AutoCAD is that it enables you to copy entities quickly in the drawing, saving a lot of drawing time. You can draw one chair, for example, then copy, rotate, and move it into position around the table. What would have taken as long as half an hour to do manually you can accomplish in a minute or two by copying.

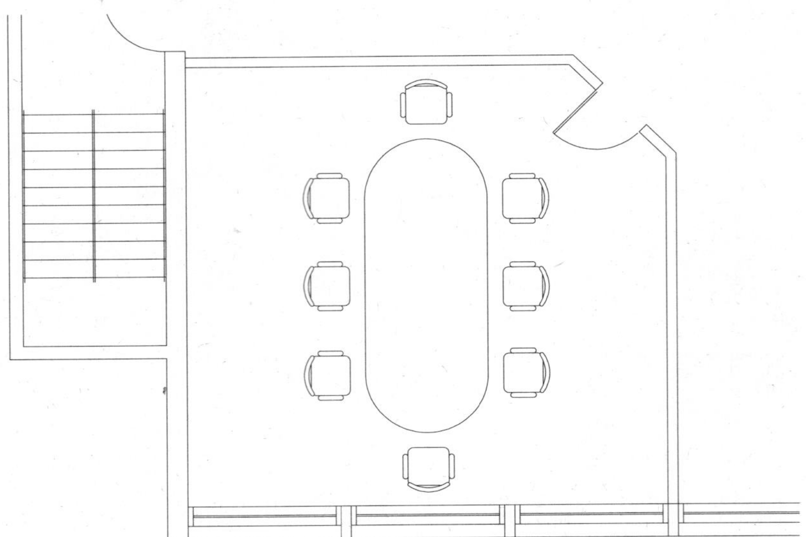

Figure 25.1

Example of a copy operation.

Each of the autoedit modes includes a Copy option. The Copy option differs slightly depending on which autoedit mode you are using. In all cases, however, the original entities are left intact and a copy is made of them. The following list summarizes how the Copy option affects the different autoedit modes:

- **Stretch.** The original entities are not stretched. Instead, the duplicate entities (the copies) are stretched.
- **Move.** The original entities remain in their current location and the copies are moved to the new location(s).
- **Scale.** The original entities are not scaled. Instead, the duplicate entities are scaled.
- **Mirror.** The original entities are not mirrored, but the duplicate entities are mirrored.

- **Rotate.** The original entities are not rotated, but the duplicate entities are rotated.

In all autoedit modes, the Copy option switches the current autoedit mode into a corresponding "multiple" autoedit mode. You can make multiple copies using the current autoedit mode. When using the Rotate multiple autoedit mode, for example, you can create many copies of the original entities, all rotated about the same center point, but at different rotation angles.

The prototype drawing for the exercises in this unit has been set up so that your cursor will snap to most of the points you will need to pick. You will learn about setting and using a snap increment in unit 35, "Using a Snap Increment."

Using Stretch Multiple Autoedit Mode

You can copy and stretch an entity or multiple entities any number of times to any point in 2D space without exiting the autoedit mode. This enables you to create new entities by stretching existing entities.

In the following exercise, create the index marks for your gauge. Use figure 25.2 as a guide to complete the exercise.

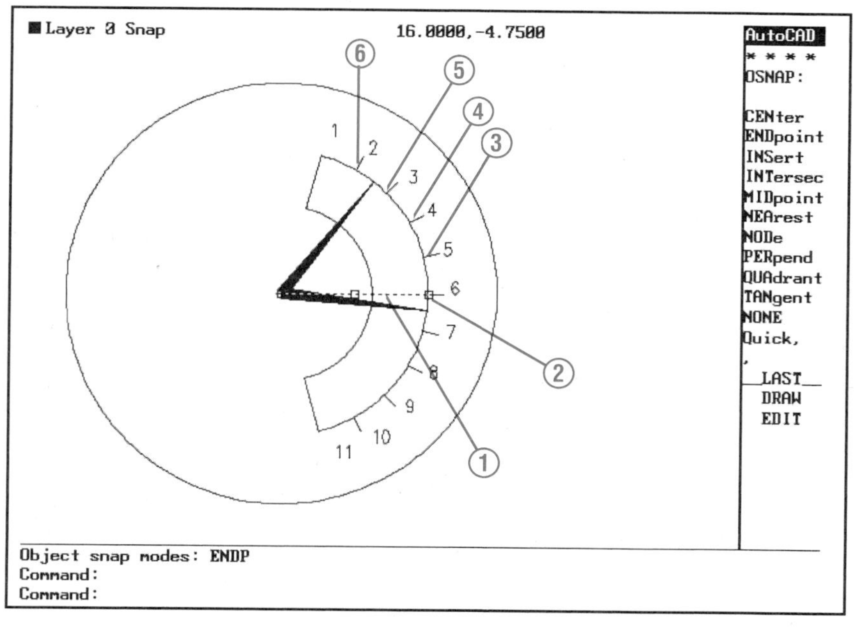

Figure 25.2

Selection points for Stretch multiple autoedit.

You will use a running object snap mode in the following exercise to pick exact points. Temporary and running object snap modes are explained fully in units 36 and 37. When instructed to pick an end point, place the aperture (the square box at the center of the crosshairs) so that it encloses the end point, then press the pick button.

Using Stretch Multiple Autoedit Mode

1. Begin a new drawing named 025???01 in your assigned directory using 025GAUGE as a prototype.

2.	Command: **OSNAP** ↵	Issues OSNAP command
3.	Object snap modes: **ENDP** ↵	Sets running Object Snap to ENDpoint
4.	Command: *Select the horizontal line at ① (see fig. 25.2)*	Selects the line and enables grips
5.	Command: *Pick the grip at ②*	Selects the grip and enters Stretch autoedit mode
	** STRETCH **	
6.	<Stretch to point>/Base point/Copy/Undo/eXit: **C** ↵	Enters the Copy option and switches to Stretch multiple autoedit mode
	** STRETCH (multiple) **	
7.	<Stretch to point>/Base point/Copy/Undo/eXit: *Pick the end point at ③*	Stretches the line to a new location
	** STRETCH (multiple) **	
8.	<Stretch to point>/Base point/Copy/Undo/eXit: *Pick the end points at ④, ⑤, and ⑥*	Stretches the line again to three new points
	** STRETCH (multiple) **	
9.	<Stretch to point>/Base point /Copy/Undo/eXit: *Press* Enter	Exits from autoedit mode

10. Save your drawing.

Your drawing should look like figure 25.3.

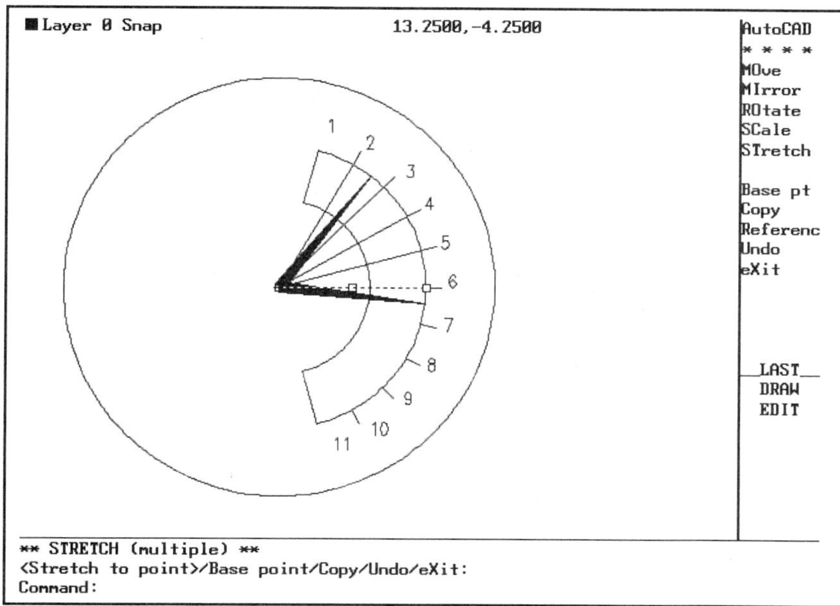

Figure 25.3

Drawing after using Stretch multiple autoedit mode.

You can see that by using the Copy option in the Stretch autoedit mode, you can stretch entities to create new ones, but leave the original entities as they are.

NOTE

The use of Stretch multiple autoedit mode to create all of the index marks is actually not the best method because each of the index lines must now be trimmed to the inner arc. The best method would be to trim the first line, then rotate/copy it into position to create the other index marks. You will use that method in the next section.

Using Rotate Copy Autoedit Mode

By using the Copy option with the Rotate autoedit mode, you can create new entities by rotating an existing entity. The original entity (or entities) stays in its original location, and the copies are rotated to whatever angle you require. As when rotating a selection set without the Copy option, it is important to select the proper center of rotation.

In the following exercise, use the Rotate multiple autoedit mode to re-create the index marks. You will start with a new prototype drawing in which the original index mark has been trimmed to the correct length.

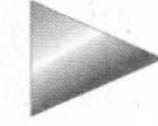

Using Rotate Copy Autoedit Mode

1. Begin a new drawing named 025???02 in your assigned directory using 025TRIM as a prototype.

2.	`Command:` *Pick a point on the line at ① (see fig. 25.4)*	Selects the line and enables grips
3.	`Command:` *Pick the grip at ②*	Selects the grip and enters Stretch autoedit mode
	`** STRETCH **`	
4.	`<Stretch to point>/Base point/Copy/ Undo/eXit:` *From the screen menu, choose* Rotate	Switches to the Rotate autoedit mode
	`** ROTATE **`	
5.	`<Rotation angle>/Base point/Copy/ Undo/Reference/eXit:` **B** ↵	Enters the Base point option
6.	`Base point:` *Pick a point at the center of the gauge*	Specifies the base point
	`** ROTATE **`	
7.	`<Rotation angle>/Base point/Copy/ Undo/Reference/eXit:` **C** ↵	Enters the Copy option
	`** ROTATE **`	
8.	`<Rotation angle>/Base point/Copy/ Undo/Reference/eXit:` **'OSNAP** ↵	Issues the transparent OSNAP command
9.	`>>Object snap modes:` **ENDP** ↵ `Resuming GRIP_ROTATE command.`	Sets running object snap mode to ENDpoint
	`** ROTATE (multiple) **`	
10.	`<Rotation angle>/Base point/Copy/ Undo/Reference/eXit:` *Pick the end points at ③ through ⑩*	Specifies the points to rotate and copy the line
	`** ROTATE (multiple) **`	
11.	`<Rotation angle>/Base point/Copy/ Undo/Reference/eXit:` *Press* Enter	Exits autoedit mode
12.	`Command:` **OSNAP** ↵	Issues OSNAP command
13.	`Object snap modes:` **NONE** ↵	Cancels running object snap modes

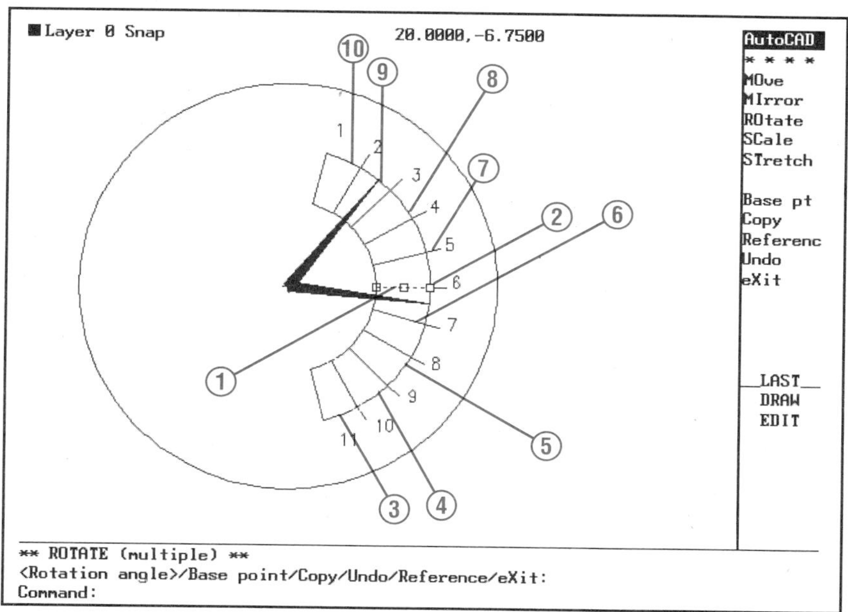

Figure 25.4

Completed drawing after using rotate/copy.

Using Mirror Copy Autoedit Mode

By using the Copy option with the Mirror autoedit mode, you can mirror and duplicate entities in a single operation. The original entities remain intact, and the copies are mirrored about the mirror line that you specify.

Use the mirror copy mode to mirror the gauge markings to the opposite side of the gauge. Use figure 25.5 as a guide to select the entities.

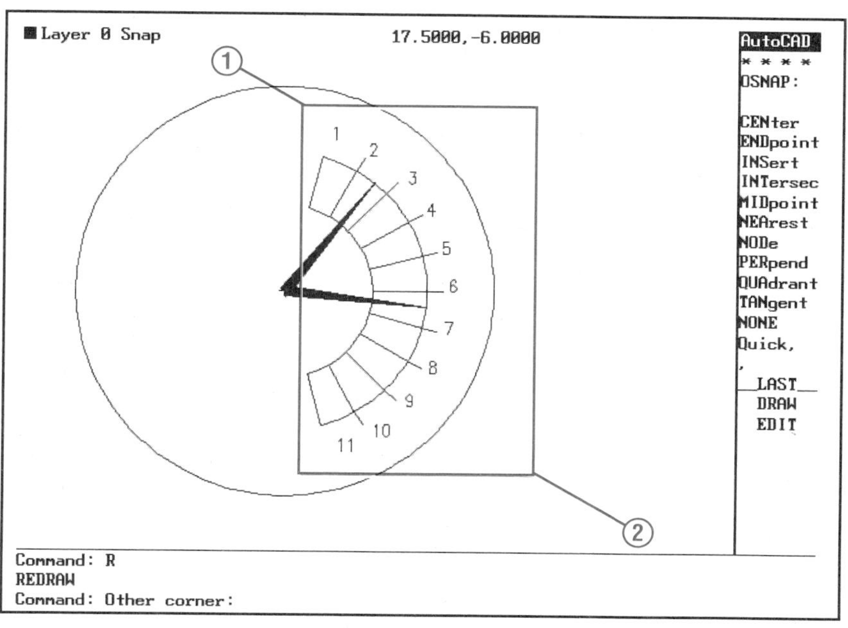

Figure 25.5

Selecting entities to mirror.

Using Mirror Copy Autoedit Mode

Continue with your drawing from the previous exercise

1. `Command:` *Pick points at* ① *and* ② *(see fig. 25.5)*	Selects the entities to be mirrored and displays grips
2. `Command:` *Pick any grip*	Selects the grip and enters Stretch autoedit mode
`** STRETCH **`	
3. `<Stretch to point>/Base point /Copy/Undo/eXit:` **MI** ↵	Switches to Mirror autoedit mode
`** MIRROR **`	
4. `<Second point>/Base point/Copy/ Undo/eXit:` **C** ↵	Enters the copy option
`** MIRROR (multiple) **`	
5. `<Second point>/Base point/Copy/ Undo/eXit:` **B** ↵	Enters the Base point option
6. `Base point:` *Pick a point at the center of the gauge*	Specifies the base point
`** MIRROR (multiple) **`	
7. `<Second point>/Base point/Copy/ Undo/eXit:` *Press* F8, *pick a point above or below the center of the gauge*	Specifies the second point of the mirror line
`** MIRROR (multiple) **`	
8. `<Second point>/Base point/Copy/ Undo/eXit:` *Press* Enter	Exits autoedit mode
9. `Command:` *Press* Ctrl+C *twice*	Deselects entities and removes grips
10. `Command:` **R** ↵	Issues the alias for the REDRAW command

Your drawing should look like figure 25.6.

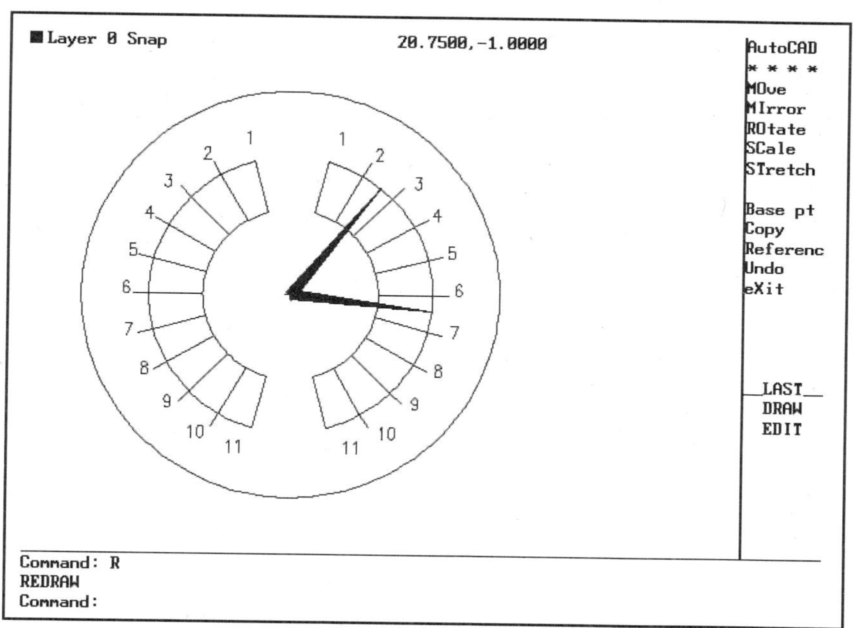

Figure 25.6

Completed drawing after using Mirror multiple.

Using Scale Multiple Autoedit Mode

The Copy option, when used with the Scale autoedit mode, enables you to create duplicates of existing entities that are scaled either larger or smaller than the originals. The original entities remain at their original size, and the copies are scaled by the amount you specify.

Use the Copy option with the Scale autoedit mode in the following exercise to create a bezel or "rim" for your gauge.

Using Scale Copy Autoedit Mode

Continue with your drawing from the previous exercise.

1. `Command:` *Press* F9 — Turns off snap
2. `Command:` *Select the large circle* — Creates a selection set and displays grips
3. `Command:` *Pick the grip at the center of the circle (it may be difficult to see)*

   `** STRETCH **`

4. `<Stretch to point>/Base point/Copy/Undo/eXit:` **SC** ↵ — Switches to the Scale autoedit mode

   `** SCALE **`

continues

	Prompt	Action
5.	`<Scale factor>/Base point/Copy /Undo/Reference/eXit:` **C** ↵	Enters the Copy option
	`** SCALE (multiple) **`	
6.	`<Scale factor>/Base point/Copy/ Undo/Reference/eXit:` **1.1** ↵	Specifies the scale factor and creates scaled copy
	`** SCALE (multiple) **`	
7.	`<Scale factor>/Base point/Copy /Undo/Reference/eXit:` **1.15** ↵	Specifies the scale factor and creates scaled copy
	`** SCALE (multiple) **`	
8.	`<Scale factor>/Base point/Copy /Undo/Reference/eXit:` *Press* Enter	Exits autoedit mode
9.	`Command:` *Press* Ctrl+C *twice*	Deselects entities and removes grips
10.	`Command:` **R** ↵	Issues the alias for the REDRAW command
11.	Save your drawing.	

Your drawing should resemble figure 25.7.

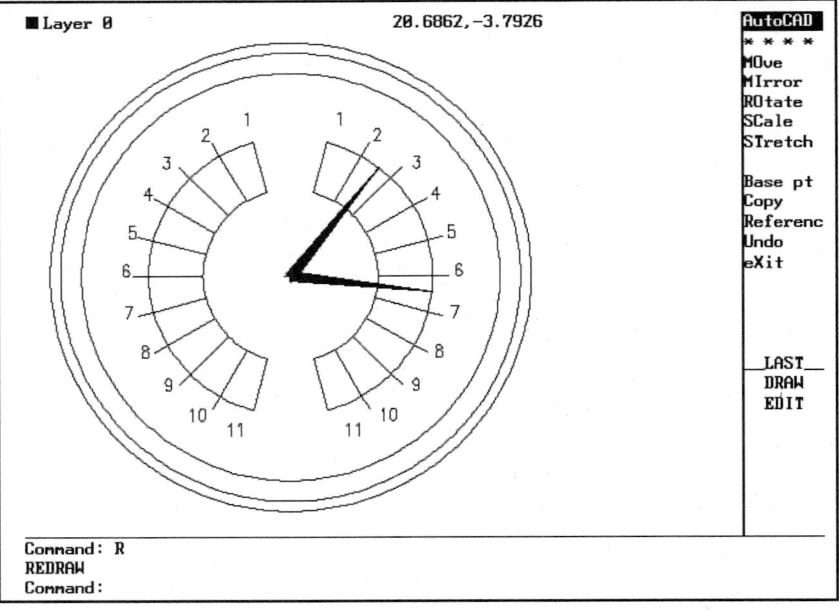

Figure 25.7

Completed drawing after using Scale multiple.

Using Move Multiple Autoedit Mode

The Move autoedit mode enables you to move a selection set from one location to another in the drawing. When you use the Copy option with the Move autoedit mode, the original entities remain at their original locations and copies are made at other locations that you specify. This capability enables you to make many copies quickly of a selection set at various locations in the drawing.

In the following exercise, use the Copy option with the Move autoedit mode to create a total of four gauges. Use figure 25.8 as a guide to select entities and points.

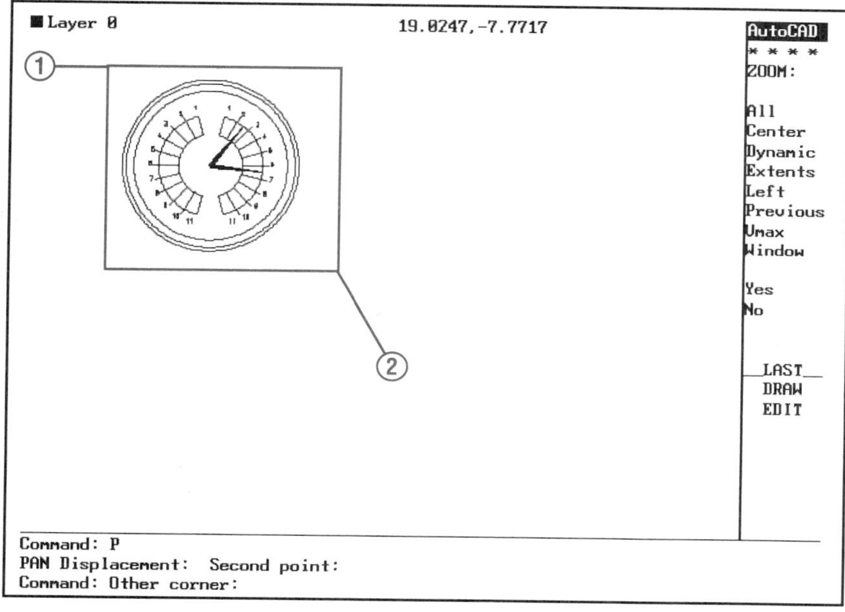

Figure 25.8

Selecting entities for Move multiple operation.

Using Move Multiple Autoedit Mode

1. Continue with your drawing from the previous exercise. Zoom and pan to the view shown in figure 25.8.

2. `Command:` *Pick a point at* ① *(see fig. 25.8)*	Defines first corner of window selection box
3. `Other corner:` *Pick a point at* ②	Defines opposite corner of window selection box
4. `Command:` *Pick any grip*	Selects grip and enters Stretch autoedit mode

`** STRETCH **`

continues

5. <Stretch to point>/Base point /Copy/Undo/eXit: **MO** ↵	Switches to Move autoedit mode
** MOVE **	
6. <Move to point>/Base point /Copy/Undo/eXit: **C** ↵	Enters the Copy option
** MOVE (multiple) **	
7. <Move to point>/Base point /Copy/Undo/eXit: **@8<0** ↵	Specifies a relative coordinate to locate the first copy
** MOVE (multiple) **	
8. <Move to point>/Base point /Copy/Undo/eXit: **@8<-90** ↵	Specifies a relative coordinate to locate the second copy
** MOVE (multiple) **	
9. <Move to point>/Base point /Copy/Undo/eXit: **@8,-8** ↵	Specifies a relative coordinate to locate the third copy
** MOVE (multiple) **	
10. <Move to point>/Base point /Copy/Undo/eXit: *Press* Enter	Exits autoedit mode
11. Command: *Press* Ctrl+C *twice*	Deselects entities and removes grips
12. Command: **R** ↵	Issues the alias for the REDRAW command
13. Save your drawing.	

Your drawing should resemble figure 25.9.

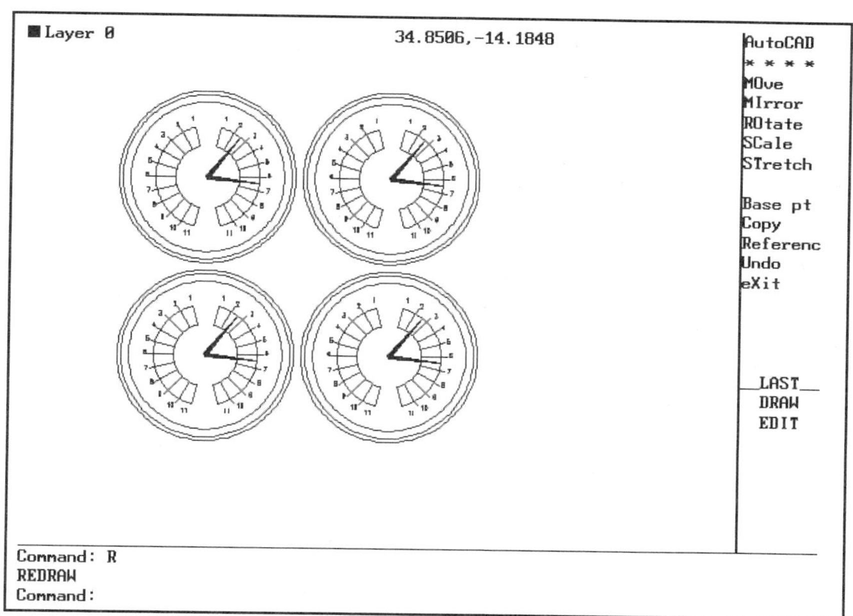

Figure 25.9

Completed drawing after using Move multiple.

Unit Review

What You've Learned

- How to copy using the Stretch autoedit mode
- How to copy using the Move autoedit mode
- How to copy using the Rotate autoedit mode
- How to copy using the Mirror autoedit mode
- How to copy using the Scale autoedit mode

Review Questions

True or False

25.01 T F You can use the Copy option in any of the autoedit modes.

25.02 T F The Copy option enables you to copy entities while performing an autoedit operation on them.

25.03 T F When you use the Copy option in the Scale autoedit mode, the original entities are scaled along with the copy.

25.04 T F The Mirror autoedit mode does not include a Copy option.

25.05 T F The Move multiple autoedit mode is the same as the Stretch multiple autoedit mode.

Multiple Choice

25.06 The __________ multiple autoedit mode enables you to make copies of entities at the same size and rotation, but at different locations.

(A) Rotate

(B) Move

(C) Scale

(D) Mirror

Student: ______________________ Date: __________

Instructor: ______________________ Course: __________ Section: __________

25.07 The points for the mirror line that you specify in Mirror autoedit mode __________.

(A) can be at any location

(B) must be on grips

(C) must be at 90 degrees to the original entities

(D) none of the above

25.08 The __________ option is used to specify the center of rotation when using the Rotate autoedit mode.

(A) Reference

(B) Center

(C) Copy

(D) Base point

Short Answer

25.09 Briefly explain how to copy entities from one location to another in the drawing at the same scale, rotation, and orientation as the original.

____

____

____

25.10 Briefly explain how the Stretch autoedit mode is different from the Move autoedit mode.

____

____

____

Additional Exercises

25.11 Begin a new drawing named 025???11 in your assigned directory using 025GAUG2 as a prototype. Use whichever autoedit modes you prefer to make the gauge on the left look like the gauge on the right. Use figure 25.10 as a guide to complete the exercise. Save your drawing when you are finished.

Student: __________ Date: __________

Instructor: __________ Course: __________ Section: __________

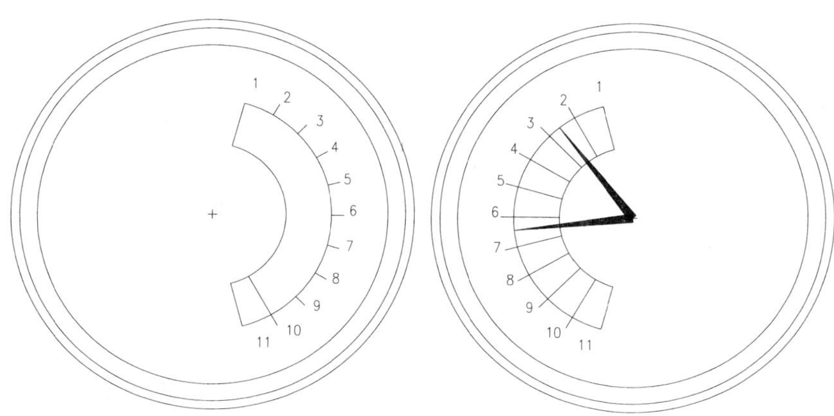

Figure 25.10

Completed gauge drawing.

Student: ____________________ Date: ________

Instructor: ____________________ Course: ________ Section: ________

PART III

Intermediate Drafting and Editing

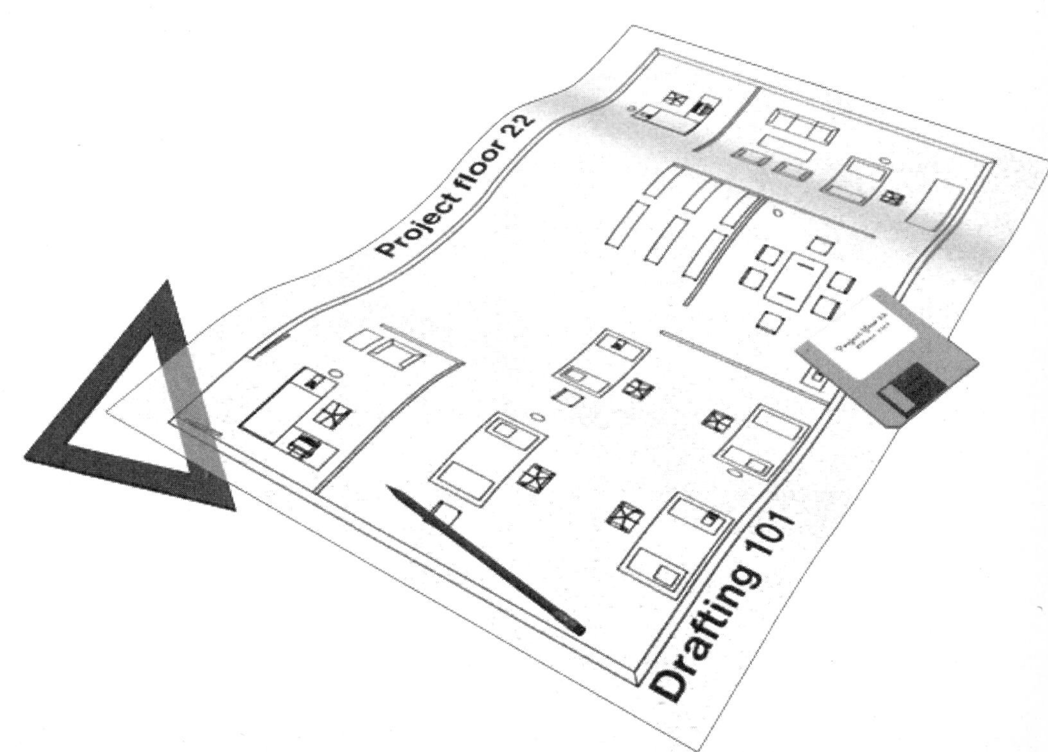

UNIT 26

Drawing Ellipses

Ellipses are used in many different kinds of drawings. An ellipse in AutoCAD is really a series of polyarc segments drawn as a closed polyline. The ELLIPSE command makes creating ellipses simple. This unit explains the function of the ELLIPSE command.

The objectives for this unit are to:

- Understand the function of the ELLIPSE command
- Understand the basic concepts of drawing elliptical entities
- Recognize how ellipses can be used as effective tools to create better looking drawings

Using the ELLIPSE Command

An ellipse consists of a center point, major axis, and minor axis (see fig. 26.1). The ELLIPSE command provides a number of options for creating ellipses based on these three characteristics. The ELLIPSE command also provides an option for creating isometric circles. Instead of specifying the axis points for an isometric ellipse, you specify the center point, circle radius, and rotation angle. AutoCAD then determines the ellipse that results from rotating the circle by the specified rotation angle.

Figure 26.1

Parts of an ellipse.

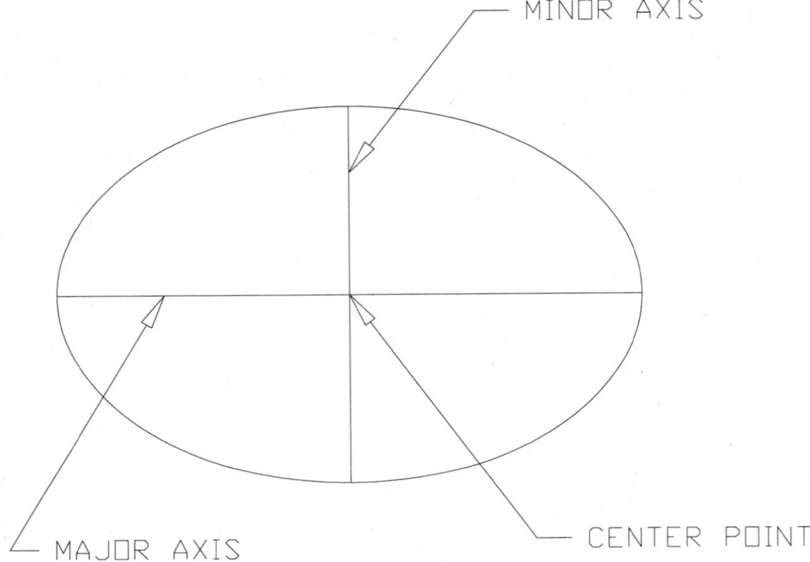

The options available in the ELLIPSE command include:

- **Axis end point 1 and Axis end point 2.** These options enable you to pick the end points of the first axis for the ellipse. You can pick points or enter coordinates to specify the two points.
- **Other axis distance.** This option enables you to specify half of the second axis distance (the radius of the ellipse along the second axis). You can pick a point or enter a value for the distance. The length of the second axis is twice the distance you specify.
- **Center.** This option enables you to specify the center point of the ellipse. You can pick a point or enter a coordinate.
- **Rotation.** This option enables you to specify the rotation angle of the ellipse. To create a 45° ellipse, for example, enter 45 as the rotation value. This option controls the definition of the ellipse; it does not

control the rotation of the ellipse in the XY plane. To rotate an ellipse 30° off of horizontal, for example, you must specify its axis points as 30° from horizontal.

☞ **Isocircle.** This option is used to draw isometric circles. It is used only when isometric snap mode is active. AutoCAD prompts for the center of the circle being drawn, the radius or diameter, then draws the circle as an ellipse on the current isoplane. Unit 98 explains isometric drawing.

The method you use to create an ellipse depends on the type of drawing you are preparing and the construction of the ellipse. Unit 98, "Creating Isometric Drawings," explores the use of the ISOCIRCLE option. The rest of this unit focuses on the other ELLIPSE options.

Specifying End Points and Distances

To draw an ellipse, you can locate two points to define one axis of the ellipse, then pick a point to define the radius of the second axis. This is the default method for the ELLIPSE command. This method is useful when you know the dimensions for the major and minor axis of the ellipse, as well as the end points of the two axes.

In the following exercise, create the outline of an elliptical cam using this ellipse construction method.

Specifying Axis End Points and Radius

1. Begin a new drawing named 026???01 in your assigned directory using 026CAM as a prototype.

2. `Command:` *Choose* Draw, *then* Axis, Eccentricity	Issues the ELLIPSE command
`_ellipse`	
3. `<Axis end point 1>/Center:` *Pick a point at* 3.000,5.000	Specifies first axis end point
4. `Axis end point 2:` *Pick a point at* 9.000,5.000	Specifies second axis end point
5. <Other axis distance>/Rotation: *Pick a point at* 6.000,7.000	Specifies an axis end point for the second axis

Your drawing should look similar to figure 26.2.

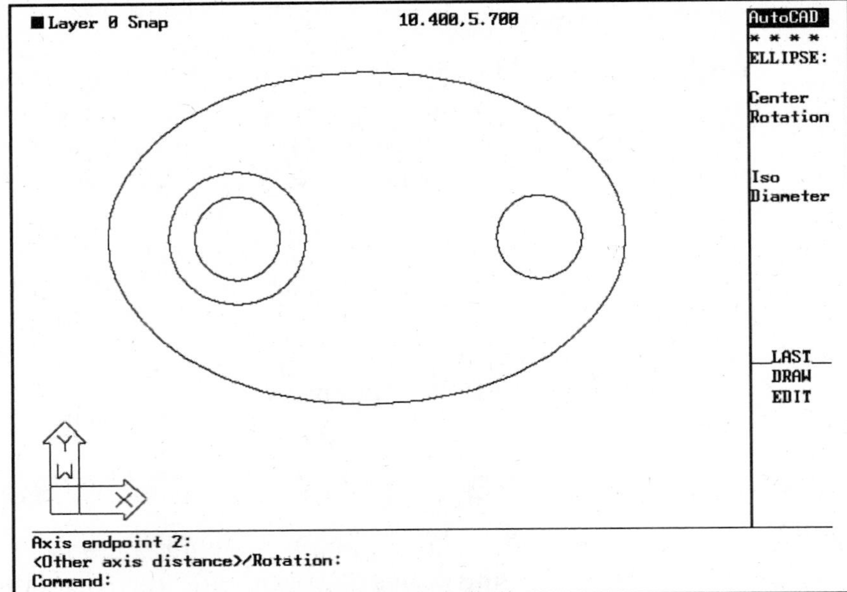

Figure 26.2

Cam outline drawn as an ellipse.

Specifying Center and Axis Points

In addition to specifying the axis end points to draw an ellipse, you can specify the center point and two axis points. This method is useful if you know the location of the center point and the radius of the minor and major axis. In the following exercise, you undo the previous ellipse, then redraw the ellipse by specifying its center point and axis end points.

Specifying Center Point and Axis End Points

Continue with your drawing from the preceding exercise.

1. `Command:` **`U`** ↵ — Undoes the previous ELLIPSE command

   `GROUP`

2. `Command:` *Choose* Draw, *then* Ellipse, *then* Center, Axis, Axis — Issues the ELLIPSE command with the Center option

   `_ellipse`
   `<Axis end point 1>/Center:` **`_c`**

3. `Center of ellipse:` *Pick a point at* 6.000,5.000 — Specifies the center of the ellipse

4. `Axis end point:` **`@3,0`** ↵ — Specifies first axis end point

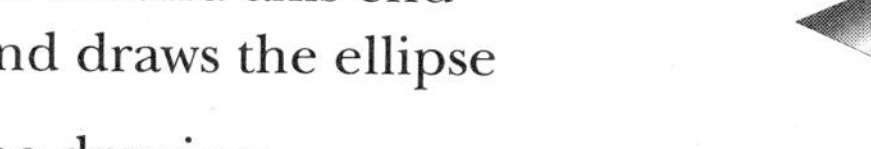

5. `<Other axis distance>/ Rotation:` **`@0,2`** ↵	Specifies second axis end point and draws the ellipse
6. `Command:` *Choose* File, *then* Save	Saves the drawing

The two methods you have used so far to create the ellipse are very similar. In the first method, you specify two axis points to define the center of an ellipse (the center point is midway beween the two axis points). In the second method, you specify the center point directly, then pick the second axis point to define the major axis of the ellipse. You also use point selection and coordinate entry to specify axis end points.

Specifying End Points and Rotation

You also can draw an ellipse by specifying the rotation angle of the ellipse. This rotation angle does not specify the rotation of the ellipse in the XY plane. Instead, it defines the shape of the ellipse by rotating a circle about the ellipse's axis by the specified angle. You can use this method to draw a 45° ellipse, for example. You use this method in the next exercise.

Specifying Center, Axis, and Rotation

Continue with your drawing from the previous exercise.

1. `Command:` **`ELLIPSE`** ↵	Issues the ELLIPSE command
2. `<Axis end point 1>/Center:` **`C`** ↵	Specifies Center option
3. `Center of ellipse:` *Pick a point at* 6.000,3.600	Specifies center point
4. `Axis end point:` **`@0.5,0`** ↵	Specifies axis end point
5. `<Other axis distance>/Rotation:` **`45`** ↵	Creates a 45° ellipse
6. `Command:` *Choose* File, *then* Save	Saves the drawing

Your drawing should look similar to figure 26.3.

If you need to create an ellipse that has a specific rotation angle, use the Rotation option. Although you can create an isometric ellipse using the Rotation option and an angle of 60°, AutoCAD does not define the axis along the isometric axis the way it needs to be. If you need to create an isometric ellipse, use isometric snap and the Isocircle option of the ELLIPSE command (see unit 98, "Creating Isometric Drawings").

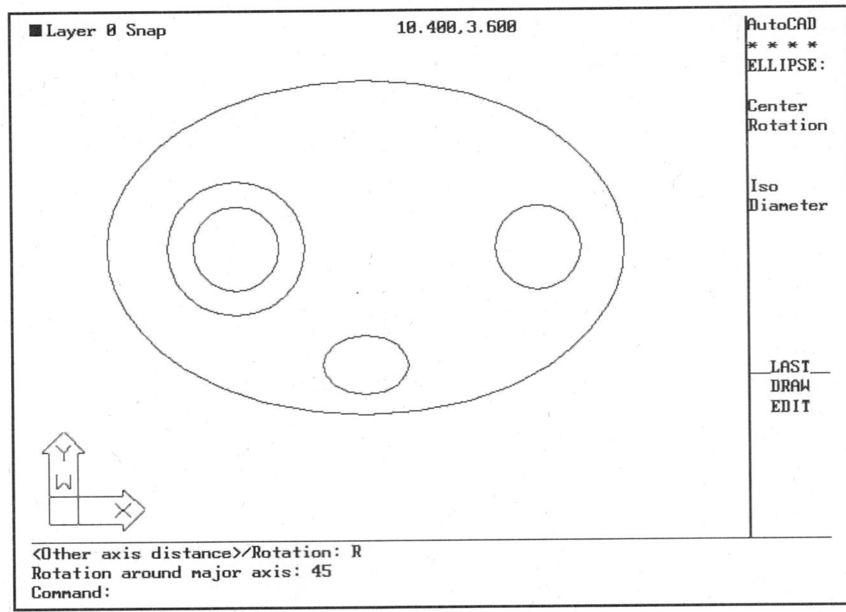

Figure 26.3

A 45-degree ellipse.

Ellipses as Polylines

When AutoCAD creates ellipses, they are formed as a series of polyline arcs (polyarcs). In fact, there is no ellipse entity in AutoCAD. The ELLLIPSE command simply provides a way to create a closed polyline that looks like an ellipse. You can explode the ellipse just like any other polyline, but what you get is many small individual arc entities. So many small, unassociated entities are difficult to edit.

Because they are polylines, however, you can edit ellipses just like any other polyline. You can move, erase, and otherwise edit the ellipse as a single entity. You also can use the PEDIT command (see unit 29, "Editing Polylines") to change the width of the polyline ellipse and make other changes to the ellipse.

To illustrate that ellipses are polylines, you use Stretch autoedit mode in the following exercise to stretch the ellipse.

Stretching an Ellipse

Continue with your drawing from the previous exercise.

1. `Command:` *Select the ellipse at* ① *(see fig. 26.4)*	Creates a selection set
2. `Command:` *Hold down the Shift key and pick the grips at* ② *through* ⑧ *(see fig. 26.4)*	Selects grips

3. `Command:` *Pick the grip at* ⑤ *(see fig. 26.4)* — Enters Stretch autoedit mode

4. `<Stretch to point>/Base point/Copy/Undo/eXit:` *Pick a point at* 8.800,5.000 — Stretches the ellipse (see fig 26.5)

5. `Command:` *Choose* File, *then* Save — Saves the drawing

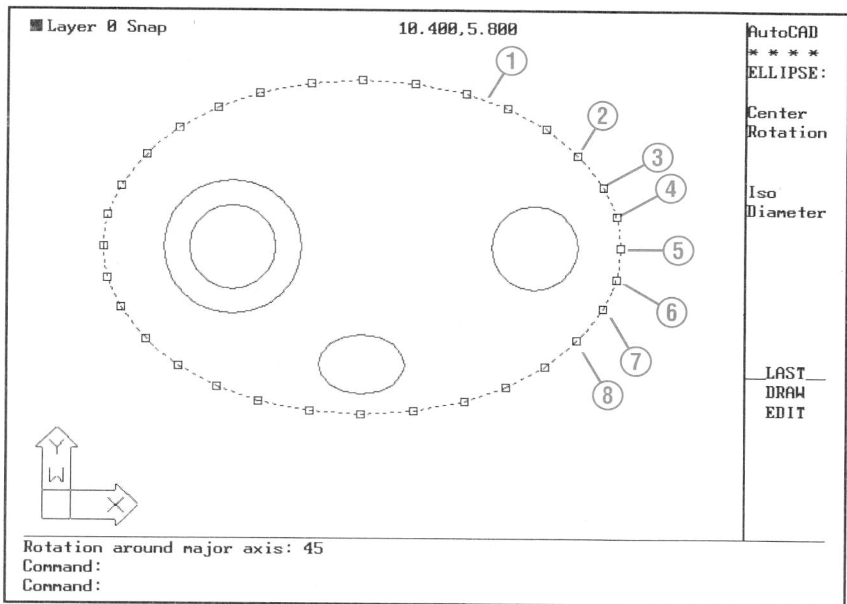

Figure 26.4

Ellipse before stretching.

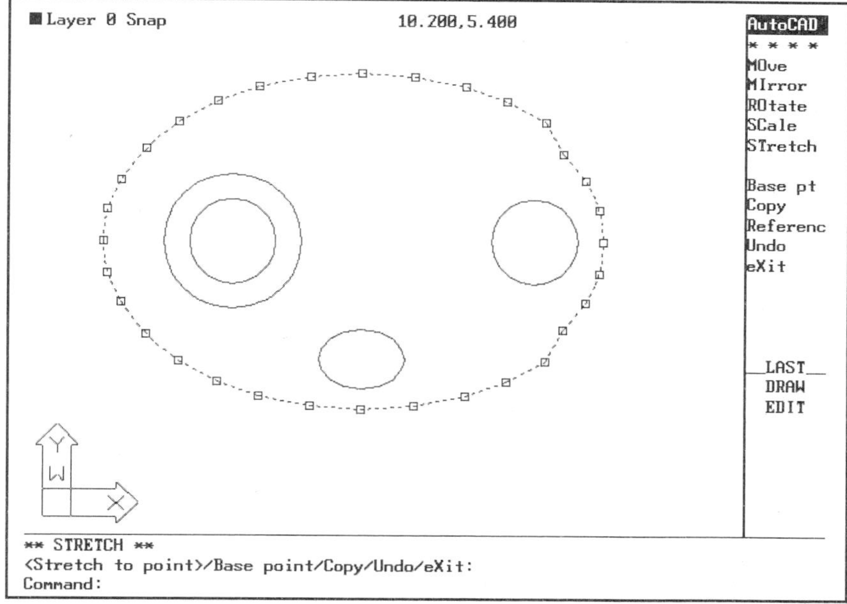

Figure 26.5

Stretched ellipse.

An ellipse, like any polyline, has a grip at each vertex. An ellipse's vertices are located at the end points of the polyarc segments that form the elliptical polyline.

Unit Review

What You've Learned

- ☞ Commands: ELLIPSE
- ☞ How to create ellipses using different options of the ELLIPSE command
- ☞ Ellipses are created as elliptical, closed polylines

Review Questions

True or False

26.01 T F An ellipse is a closed polyline.

26.02 T F The center of an ellipse is located at the intersection of its axes.

26.03 T F The Isocircle option is available only if isometric snap is active.

26.04 T F Ellipses have a major and minor axis.

26.05 T F An ellipse consists of a center point, major axis, and minor axis.

26.06 T F You cannot explode an ellipse.

26.07 T F You can specify points to define one axis of an ellipse, but you must specify a radius to define the other axis.

Multiple Choice

26.08 An ellipse is created from ________.

(A) polyarc segments

(B) arcs

(C) small line segments

(D) ellipse entities

26.09 You can draw an ellipse by specifying ________.

(A) the center point

(B) the axis end points

(C) its rotation angle

(D) all of the above

Student: ________________ Date: ________

Instructor: ________________ Course: ________ Section: ________

Short Answer

26.10 Describe what happens if you attempt to explode an ellipse.

____

____

____

Student: ____________________ Date: ________

Instructor: ____________________ Course: ________ Section: ________

UNIT 27

Drawing Donuts and Rectangles

The DONUT or DOUGHNUT command (AutoCAD accepts both spellings) enables you to construct solid circles that have inner and outer diameters. Donuts are useful for drawing mounting pads on printed circuit boards and for other situations where a donut shape is required. The RECTANG command enables you to draw a rectangular polyline quickly by choosing two opposing corners. This unit explains the DONUT and RECTANG commands.

The objectives for this unit are to:

- Understand the function of the DONUT and RECTANG commands
- Draw donuts with various inner and outer diameters
- Recognize the advantage of using RECTANG to create rectangles

Drawing Donuts

Drawings sometimes require objects that consist of two concentric circles. You can create these circles individually, but AutoCAD provides a DONUT command for creating these donut-shaped objects. The DONUT command prompts you for the inner and outer diameters of the donut, then draws the two circles and fills in the space between them. Figure 27.1 shows a selection of donuts. You can enter the DONUT (or DOUGHNUT) command at the command: prompt or choose Draw, then Donut from the pull-down menu.

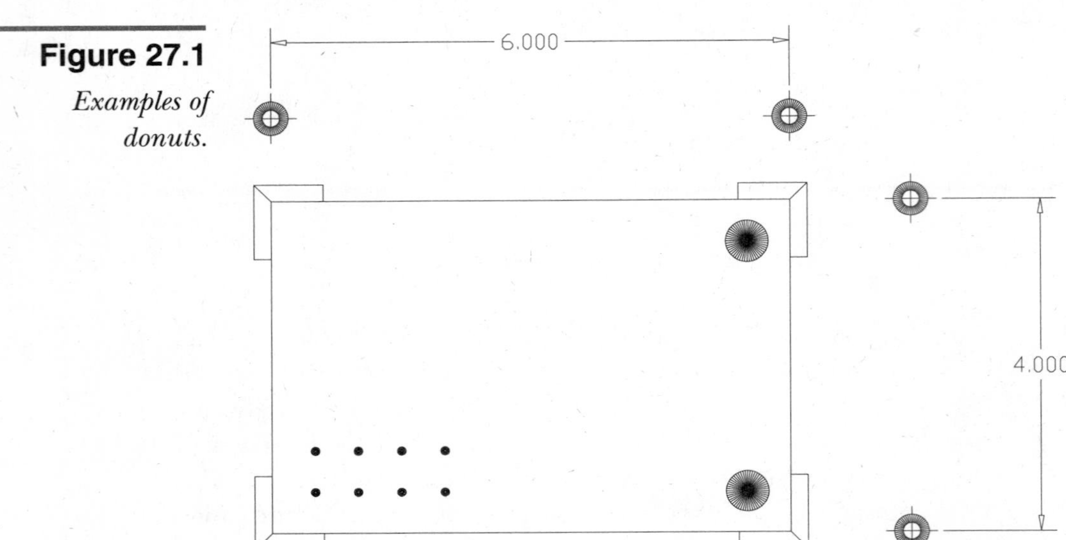

Figure 27.1
Examples of donuts.

In the following exercise, you draw donuts to represent the component mounting pads on a printed circuit board. Your drawing should look similar to figure 27.2 as you begin the exercise.

Drawing Donuts

1. Begin a new drawing named 027???01 in your assigned directory using 027DONUT as a prototype.

2. `Command:` *Choose* Draw, *then* Donut	Issues the DONUT command
`_donut`	
3. `Inside diameter <0.500>:` **`0.02`** ↵	Specifies inside diameter
4. `Outside diameter <1.000>:` **`0.1`** ↵	Specifies outside diameter
5. `Center of doughnut:` *Pick a point at coordinate* 0.500,0.500	Draws a donut

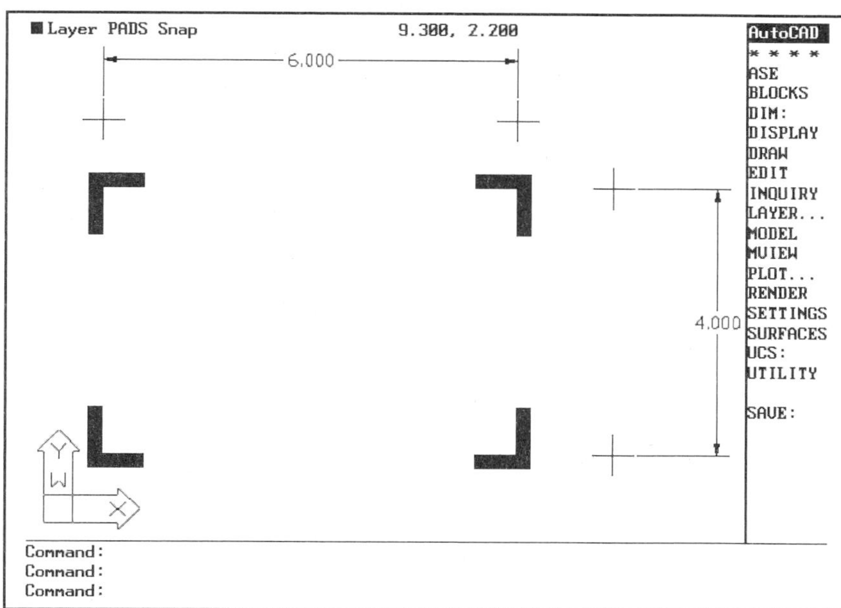

Figure 27.2

Printed circuit board artwork.

6. `Center of doughnut:`
   Pick a point at coordinate 1.000,0.500
7. `Center of doughnut:`
   Pick a point at coordinate 1.500,0.500
8. `Center of doughnut:`
   Pick a point at coordinate 2.000,0.500
9. `Center of doughnut:`
   Pick a point at coordinate 0.500,1.000
10. `Center of doughnut:`
    Pick a point at coordinate 1.000,1.000
11. `Center of doughnut:`
    Pick a point at coordinate 1.500,1.000
12. `Center of doughnut:`
    Pick a point at coordinate 2.000,1.000
13. `Center of doughnut:` *Press* Enter
14. *Zoom to the view shown in figure 27.3*

Figure 27.3

Donuts added to circuit board.

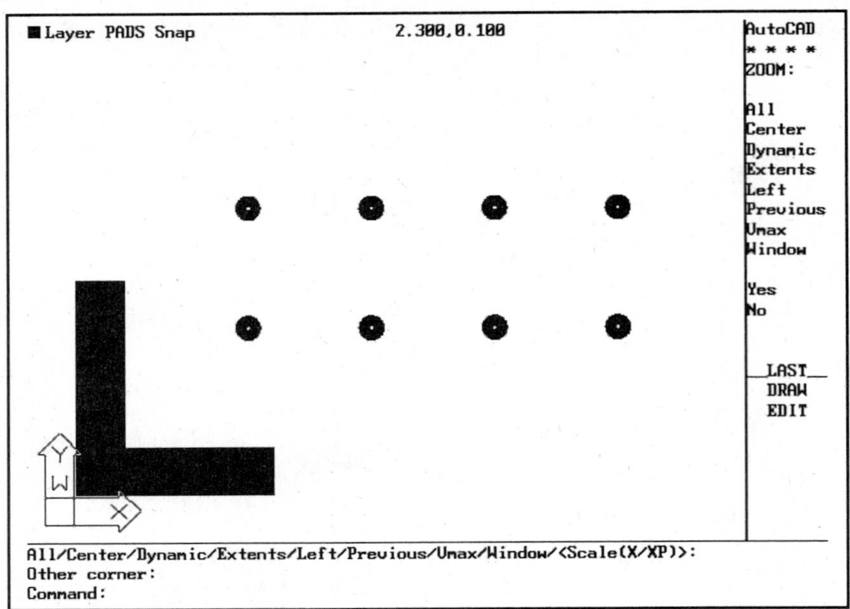

You can see that AutoCAD created filled donuts. The inner diameter of the donuts is 0.02" and the outer diameter is 0.1". Next, zoom to the previous view and add targets to the dimension datum points.

In the remaining exercises in this unit, you use the LAYER command to draw on specific layers. Layers provide a way to organize the information on your drawing. Using layers is explained in detail in unit 59, "Introduction to Layers." For now, just follow the prompts in the exercise to change layers.

Drawing Targets with Donuts

1. Continue with your drawing from the previous exercise, then issue ZOOM with the Previous option.

2. `Command:` **`LAYER`** ↵	Issues the LAYER command
3. `?/Make/Set/New/ON/OFF/Color/Ltype/ Freeze/Thaw/LOck/Unlock:` **`S`** ↵	Specifies the Set option
4. `New current layer <PADS>:` **`REF`** ↵	Specifies the name of the layer to make current
5. `?/Make/Set/New/ON/OFF/Color/Ltype/ Freeze/Thaw/LOck/Unlock:` *Press* Enter	Ends LAYER command

6. `Command:` *Choose* Draw, *then* Donut	Issues the DONUT command
7. `Inside diameter <0.020>:` **`0.2`** ↵	Specifies inside diameter
8. `Outside diameter <0.010>:` **`0.4`** ↵	Specifies outside diameter
9. `Center of doughnut:` *Pick points at* ①, ②, ③, *and* ④ *(see fig. 27.4)*	Draws four donuts
10. `Center of doughnut:` *Press* Enter	Ends DONUT command
11. Save your drawing.	

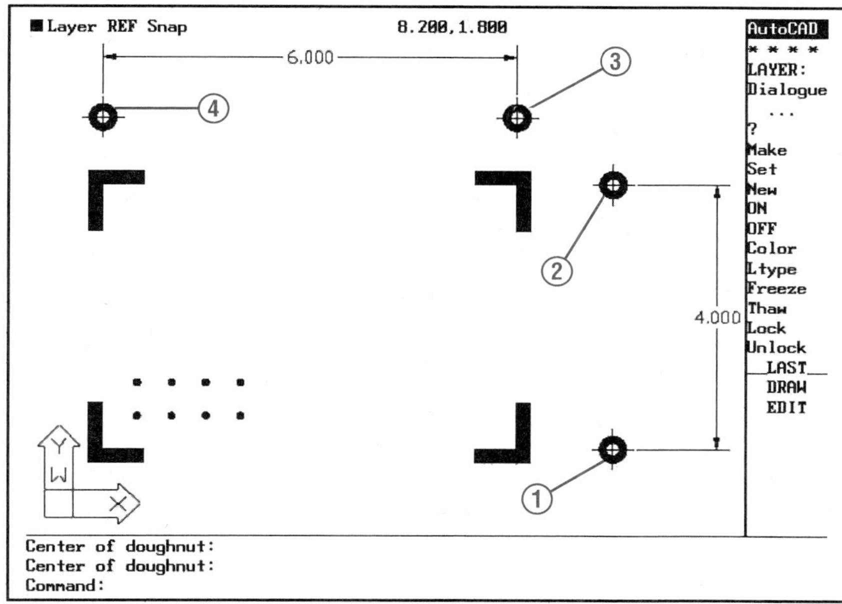

Figure 27.4

Targets added to the drawing.

Drawing a Solid Donut

In addition to drawing donut shapes with the DONUT command, you can draw a filled circle simply by specifying a value of zero for the donut's inner diameter. Any time you need to draw a solid circle, draw it as a donut with an inner diameter of zero.

In the next exercise, you draw two large ground pads on the circuit board. Draw them as donuts with an inner diameter of zero.

Drawing Solid Donuts

Continue with your drawing from the previous exercise.

1. `Command:` **`LAYER`** ↵	Issues the LAYER command
2. `?/Make/Set/New/ON/OFF/Color/Ltype/ Freeze/Thaw/LOck/Unlock:` **`S`** ↵	Specifies the Set option
3. `New current layer <REF>:` **`PADS`** ↵	Specifies the layer to make current
4. `?/Make/Set/New/ON/OFF/Color/Ltype/ Freeze/Thaw/LOck/Unlock:` *Press* Enter	
5. `Command:` *Choose* Draw, *then* Donut `_donut`	Issues the DONUT command
6. `Inside diameter <0.200>:` **`0`** ↵	Specifies inside diameter
7. `Outside diameter <0.400>:` **`0.5`** ↵	Specifies outside diameter
8. `Center of doughnut:` *Pick a point at* 5.500,3.500	Draws solid donut
9. `Center of doughnut:` *Pick a point at* 5.500,0.500	Draws solid donut
10. `Center of doughnut:` *Press* Enter	
11. Save your drawing.	

Your drawing should look similar to figure 27.5.

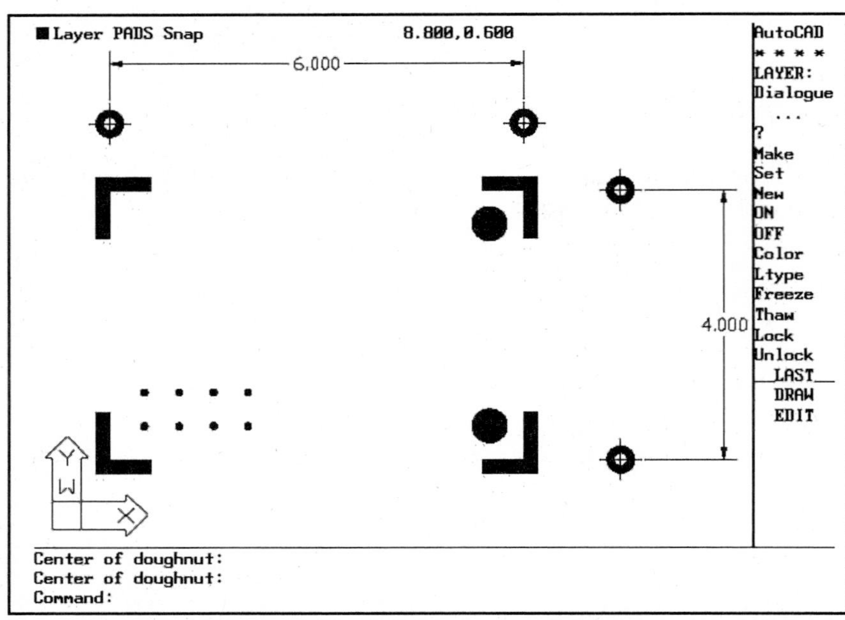

Figure 27.5
Solid donuts.

If you have many donuts in a drawing, the fill in the donuts can take a long time to regenerate. You can temporarily turn off the fill inside the donut by using the FILLMODE command. Enter **`FILLMODE`** *at the* `Command:` *prompt and set FILLMODE to 0. Then, regenerate the drawing. To turn the fill back on, set FILLMODE to 1.*

Drawing a Rectangle

A rectangle is a simple object, and drawing rectangles in AutoCAD is a simple task. Although you can draw rectangles using line segments, the easiest way to draw a rectangle is to use the RECTANG command. RECTANG prompts you for two opposing corners of the rectangle, then draws the rectangle as a closed polyline. You can pick or enter coordinates for the two opposing corner points in any order (left first or right first). You can enter RECTANG at the `Command:` prompt or choose Draw, then Rectangle from the pull-down menu.

In the following exercise, you draw the outline of the circuit board in the drawing from your previous exercise.

Drawing a Rectangle

Continue with your drawing from the previous exercise.

1. `Command:` **`LAYER`** ↵
2. `?/Make/Set/New/ON/OFF/Color/Ltype/Freeze/Thaw/LOck/Unlock:` **`S`** ↵
3. `New current layer <PADS>:` **`BOARD`** ↵ — Makes the BOARD layer current
4. `?/Make/Set/New/ON/OFF/Color/Ltype/Freeze/Thaw/LOck/Unlock:` *Press* Enter
5. `Command:` *Choose* Draw, *then* Rectangle — Issues the RECTANG command

   `rectang`
6. `First corner:` *Pick a point at* 0.000,0.000 — Specifies first corner of rectangle
7. `Other corner:` *Pick a point at* 6.000,4.000 — Specifies second corner of rectangle and draws rectangle
8. Save your drawing.

The rectangle is a standard polyline. It is not recognized as a special rectangle entity. You can edit the rectangle just like any other polyline. In unit 29, "Editing Polylines," you learn to use the PEDIT command to edit polylines such as this one.

Unit Review

What You've Learned

- Commands: DONUT, RECTANG
- How to draw donuts of various sizes using the DONUT command
- How to draw a solid donut
- How to draw rectangles using the RECTANG command

Review Questions

True or False

27.01	T	F	The inner diameter of a donut is always one-half the outer diameter.
27.02	T	F	You cannot draw a donut with an inner diameter of zero.
27.03	T	F	You can pick multiple points to draw donuts with the same inner and outer diameter without exiting the DONUT command.
27.04	T	F	The FILLMODE command controls the color of donuts.
27.05	T	F	The RECTANG command draws a rectangle using lines.
27.06	T	F	You must pick corner points for a rectangle left-to-right.
27.07	T	F	You cannot edit a rectangle after you create it.

Short Answer

27.08 Explain the best way to draw a solid circle.

____

____

____

27.09 How is a donut different from a circle?

____

____

____

Student: ______________________ Date: __________

Instructor: ______________________ Course: __________ Section: __________

27.10 What is the difference between a rectangle drawn with the LINE command and a rectangle drawn with the RECTANG command?

____

____

____

Student: ______________________ Date: __________

Instructor: ______________________ Course: __________ Section: __________

UNIT 28

Drawing Polygons

Polygons are a common shape in many drawings. Triangles, squares, hexagons, and other regular polygons are very much a part of the typical drawing. AutoCAD's POLYGON command enables you to easily draw regular multi-sided, 2D polygons as closed polylines. You only have to specify the number of sides and a few other parameters, and AutoCAD draws the polygons for you. This unit teaches you to use the POLYGON command to draw polygons.

The objectives for this unit are to:

- Understand the function of the POLYGON command
- Draw polygons inscribed within a circle
- Draw polygons circumscribed about a circle
- Draw polygons by specifying the length of an edge

Understanding AutoCAD's Polygons

Drawing polygons using manual drawing methods can be very time-consuming and difficult without a template. You can buy templates for certain types of polygons (such as triangles and hexagons), but these templates are limited in the sizes they offer. With AutoCAD's POLYGON command, however, you can draw polygons at any size.

The POLYGON command first prompts you for the number of sides in the polygon. You then have three methods for specifying the size and orientation of the polygon. The prompts and options of the POLYGON command can help you understand these three methods:

- **Number of sides <4>.** This prompt requests the number of sides in the polygon. You must specify this information regardless of the method you use to determine the size of the polygon. You can enter a number from 3 to 1,024.
- **Center of polygon.** This option enables you to specify the coordinate of the center of the polygon. You can pick a point or enter a coordinate with the keyboard.
- **Edge.** This option enables you to define the size of the polygon by specifying the length of each edge. All edges are of the same length.
- **Inscribed in circle.** This option creates the polygon with the vertices of the polygon's edges touching an imaginary circle. You specify the radius of the circle. The polygon "fits inside" the circle.
- **Circumscribed about circle.** This option creates the polygon with the edges tangent to an imaginary circle. You specify the radius of the circle. The polygon "fits around" the circle.
- **Radius of circle.** This prompt requests the radius of the circle for inscribed and circumscribed polygons.

As mentioned previously, AutoCAD draws polygons as closed polylines. You can edit the polyline so that its segments have a width. Even if you use the PLINE command and set polyline width to anything other than zero, AutoCAD does not draw polylines with a width. The PEDIT command, discussed in unit 29, "Editing Polylines," enables you to change the width of a polyline.

You can issue the POLYGON command at the command prompt. You also can choose Draw, then Polygon to issue the command.

Drawing Inscribed Polygons

Drawing inscribed polygons is one of the three methods of creating polygons in AutoCAD, and is AutoCAD's default option if you issue the POLYGON command from the command prompt. This option creates the polygon with the points (vertices) of the polygon placed on the circumference of an imaginary circle. Use this method when you know the distance from the center of the polygon to a vertex.

In the following exercise, draw two tables with inscribed polygons. Figure 28.1 shows your drawing as you begin the exercise.

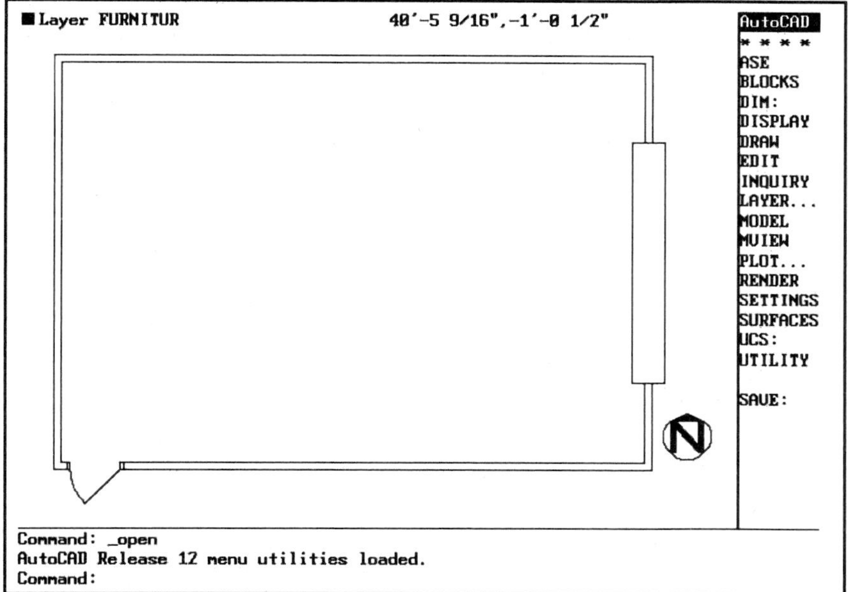

Figure 28.1

A cafe drawing ready for tables.

Drawing Inscribed Polygons

1. Begin a new drawing named 028???01 in your assigned directory, using 028CAFE as the prototype.

2. `Command:` *Choose* Draw, *then* Polygon, *then* Inscribed — Issues the POLYGON command ready to draw polygons using the Inscribed option

   `_polygon`

3. `Number of sides <4>:` *Press* Enter — Accepts the default number of sides

4. `Edge/<Center of polygon>:` *Pick a point near* ① *(see fig. 28.2)* — Specifies the center of the polygon

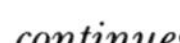

continues

```
Inscribed in
circle/Circumscribed about
circle (I/C) <I>: _inscribed
```

Move the cursor and note how the polygon changes size dynamically.

5. `Radius of circle:` **24** ↵	Specifies the distance from center to a vertex
6. `Command:` *Press* Enter	Repeats the previous command
7. `POLYGON Number of sides <4>:` **8** ↵	Specifies the number of sides to draw an octagon
8. `Edge/<Center of polygon>:` *Pick a point near* ② *(see fig. 28.2)*	Specifies center of polygon
9. `Inscribed in circle/ Circumscribed about circle (I/C) <I>:` *Press* Enter	Accepts default Inscribed option

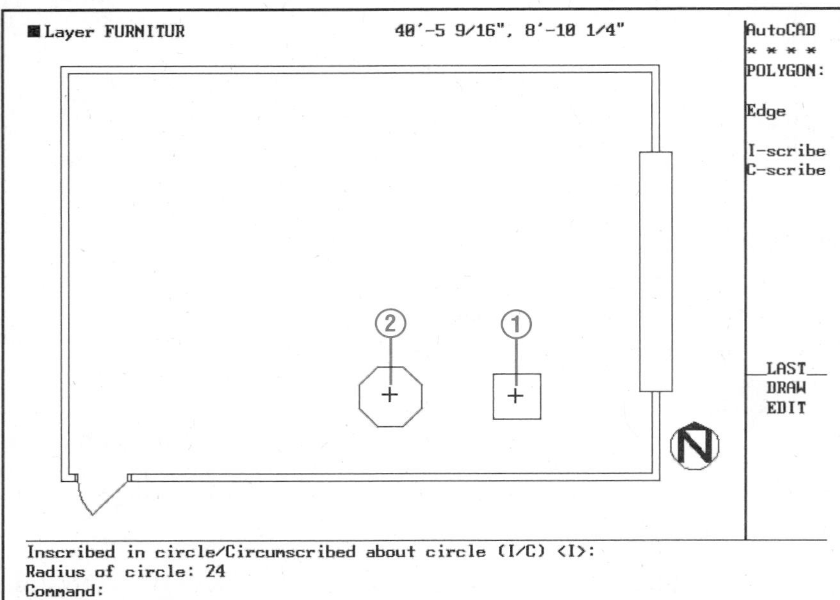

Figure 28.2
Tables drawn as polylines.

10. `Radius of circle:` **24** ↵	Specifies distance from center to vertex

Although the tables are the right shapes, they probably are not the right size. The distance from one edge to another is the determining dimension, not the distance from center to corner. Therefore, you need to use the Circumscribed option in this situation.

Drawing Circumscribed Polygons

Drawing circumscribed polygons is the second of the three methods of creating polygons in AutoCAD. The Circumscribed option creates the polygon with the polygon edges tangent to an imaginary circle. The next exercise shows you how the circumscribed option is used. Erase the two tables you created previously, and then re-create them using the Circumscribed option.

Drawing Circumscribed Polygons

Continue with your drawing from the preceding exercise.

1. Erase the two tables, then zoom to the view shown in figure 28.3.

2. `Command:` *Choose* Draw, *then* Polygon, *then* Circumscribed	Issues the POLYGON command ready to draw using the Circumscribed option
`_polygon`	
3. `Number of sides <8>:` *Press* Enter	Accepts default number of sides
4. `Edge/<Center of polygon>:` *Pick a point near* ① *(see fig. 28.3)*	Specifies center point of polygon
`Inscribed in circle/Circumscribed about circle (I/C) <I>: _circumscribed`	

Move the cursor and note that the radius is now specifying the distance from the center to an edge, not to a corner of the polygon.

5. `Radius of circle:` **`24`** ↵	Creates a polygon that is 48" from edge to edge
6. `Command:` *Press* Enter	Repeats previous command
7. `POLYGON Number of sides <8>:` **`4`**↵	Specifies four sides
8. `Edge/<Center of polygon>:` *Pick a point near* ② *(see fig. 28.3)*	
9. `Inscribed in circle/ Circumscribed about circle (I/C) <C>:` *Press* Enter	Specifies Circumscribed option
10. `Radius of circle:` **`24`** ↵	Draws 48" square table

11. Save the drawing.

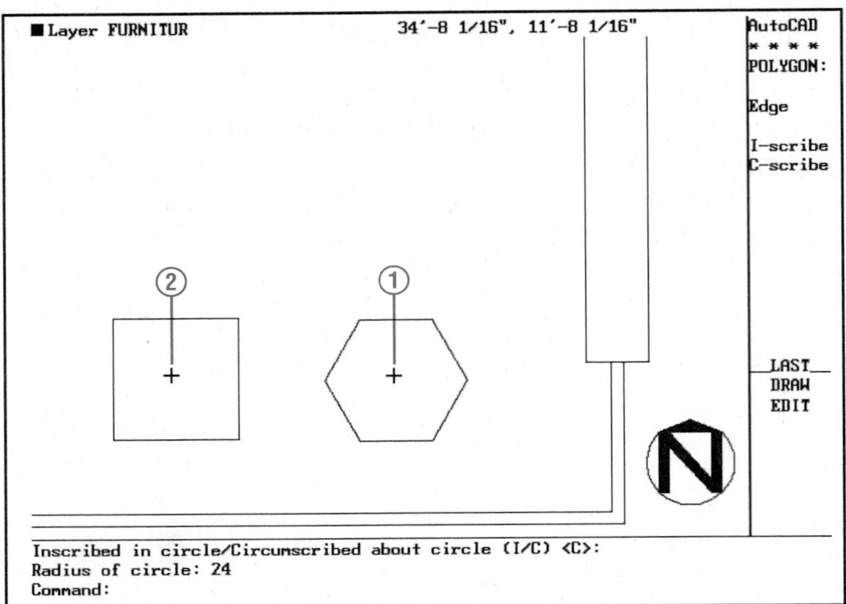

Figure 28.3

Tables drawn using Circumscribed polygons.

You may have noticed that the POLYGON command keeps track of the number of sides you specified in the previous POLYGON command. It also maintains creation method (Inscribed or Circumscribed) last used and offers it as the default.

The Circumscribed option is most useful when you want to draw a polygon of a specific size, because polygons are most often measured from center-to-edge or from edge-to-edge. If you need to draw a polygon with one corner passing through a point, however, you may find the Edge option more useful.

Drawing Polygons by Edges

Sometimes you know the length of each of the polygon's sides, but you do not know the radius of the polygon. The POLYGON command offers an option for handling these situations. By choosing the Edge option, you can specify the length of one of the polygon's sides by picking two points to determine the endpoints of a side (or by entering the coordinates of the two points). AutoCAD draws one edge between these two points, and then constructs the rest of the polygon accordingly.

In the following exercise, draw one more table. This time, draw a hexagonal table with 30"-long edges.

Drawing Polygons by Edges

Continue with your drawing from the preceding exercise.

1. `Command:` *Choose* Draw, *then* Polygon, *then* Edge — Issues the POLYGON command ready to use the Edge option

   `_polygon`

2. `Number of sides <4>:` **`6`** ↵ — Specifies six sides to draw a hexagon

   `Edge/<Center of polygon>: _edge`

3. `First endpoint of edge:` *Pick a point near* ① *(see fig. 28.4)* — Specifies one corner of an edge

   Move the cursor and note that AutoCAD is now determining the polygon based on the length of an edge.

4. `Second endpoint of edge:` **`@30,0`** ↵ — Specifies the length of the edge

5. Save your drawing.

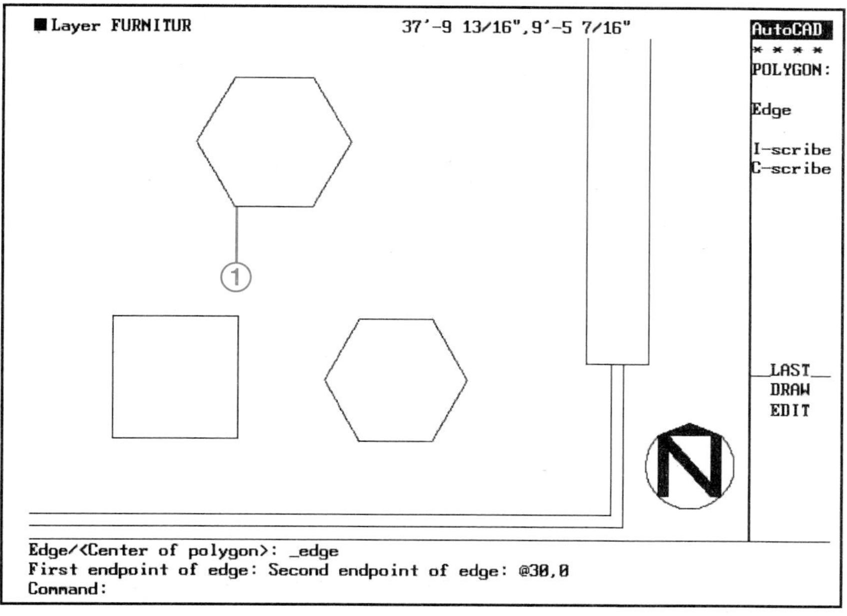

Figure 28.4

Table drawn using the Edge option.

If you need to draw a polygon that is rotated by a certain amount, but are having difficulty specifying axis or edge points to achieve the necessary rotation, draw the polygon at any convenient angle. Then use Rotate autoedit mode to rotate the polygon by the necessary amount.

Unit Review

What You've Learned

- ☞ How to use POLYGON from the pull-down menu/`Command` prompt
- ☞ How you can use POLYGON to create different entities
- ☞ How the POLYGON command can be used with other commands

Review Questions

True or False

28.01 T F A polygon is a zero-width closed polyline.

28.02 T F You can draw a polygon with as few as three sides or as many as 1,024 sides.

28.03 T F Polygons have a major and minor axis.

28.04 T F You can draw a polygon by specifying the length of its major axis.

28.05 T F You can draw a polygon by specifying the length of one edge of the polygon.

28.06 T F A polygon drawn with fewer than three sides is drawn using lines.

Multiple Choice

28.07 Which of the following cannot be drawn using the POLYGON command? __________

(A) square

(B) triangle

(C) hexagon

(D) rectangle

28.08 If you draw a circumscribed polygon, the __________ of the polygon is/are tangent to the defining circle.

(A) corners

(B) edges

(C) corners and edges

(D) center

Student: ____________________ Date: __________

Instructor: ____________________ Course: __________ Section: __________

Short Answer

28.09 Explain the relationship of an inscribed polygon to its defining circle.

____

____

____

28.10 Describe the steps to follow to draw a square with 48" sides whose bottom edge is rotated 30 degrees off of horizontal, without rotating the polygon after it is drawn.

____

____

____

Additional Exercises

28.11 Begin a new drawing named 028???11 in your assigned directory using 028BOLTS as the prototype. Draw the two hex bolts shown in figure 28.5. The bolt on the left is a 1" diameter bolt, and the bolt on the right is a 1/2" diameter bolt. The distance across flats of the head should be 1 1/2 times the diameter of the bolt. Save your drawing.

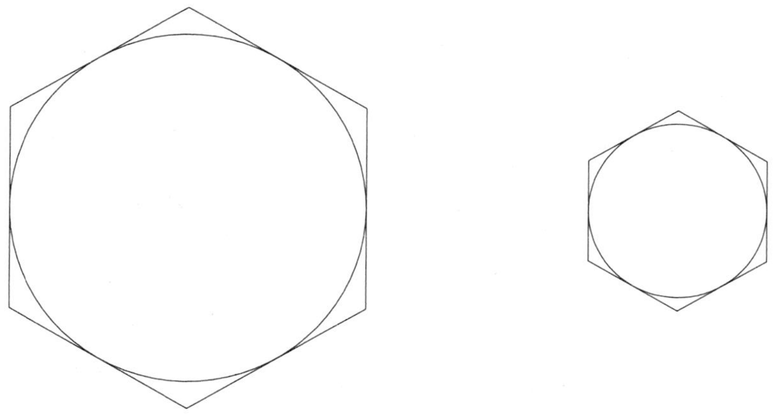

Figure 28.5

Two hex bolt heads.

Student: ______________ Date: ______________

Instructor: ______________ Course: ______________ Section: ______________

28.12 Begin a new drawing named 028???12 in your assigned directory using 028RING as a prototype. Draw the hexagon ring shown in figure 28.6. The hexagons all have 1/2" edges. Do not draw a hexagon in the center of the ring—start with the bottom hexagon and work around the ring.

The order in which you pick edge points determines the orientation of the hexagon. The prototype drawing sets an object snap mode for you. Object snap modes are explained in unit 37, "Using Running Object Snap Modes."

Figure 28.6

A hexagon ring.

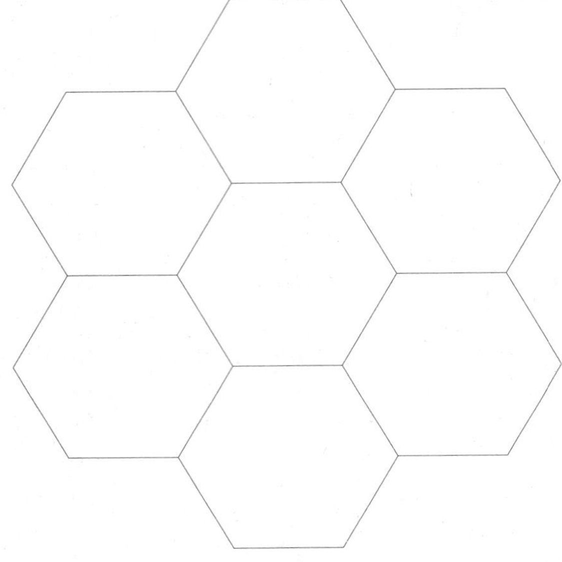

Student: ____________________ Date: ____________

Instructor: ____________________ Course: ____________ Section: ____________

UNIT 29

Editing Polylines

Polylines are one of AutoCAD's most versatile and useful entities. With polylines, you can create complex shapes and objects that you can modify and edit quickly. Because polylines are so useful, and because various commands such as POLYGON create polylines, it is important that you understand how to edit polylines. This unit explains the PEDIT command, which you can use to edit polylines in many different ways. You can issue PEDIT at the command prompt, or choose Modify and then PolyEdit to edit polylines.

The objectives for this unit are to:

- Understand the function of the PEDIT command
- Understand the basic concepts of editing polyline entities
- Modify polylines using PEDIT

Changing the Width of a Polyline

One very common polyline-editing task involves changing the width of segments in the polyline. The Width option enables you to change the width of a polyline. The Width option does not enable you to specify different widths for segments in the same polyline, however. The Width option sets all segments to the width you specify, regardless of their current widths.

You can use the Width option in vertex editing mode to change the starting and ending widths of individual segments in a polyline.

To change the width of a polyline, you only have to pick the polyline, choose the Width option, and then specify the desired width. AutoCAD then changes the width of the polyline accordingly.

In the following exercise, use PEDIT to change the width of some circuit traces on a printed circuit board. The traces are drawn as polylines. Your drawing should look similar to figure 29.1 as you begin the exercise.

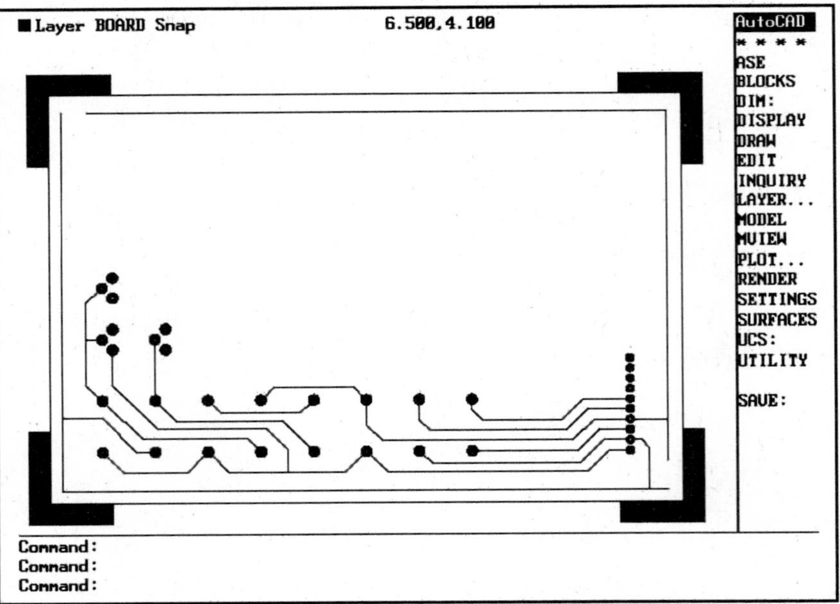

Figure 29.1
A partially completed circuit board.

Changing the Width of Polyline Segments

1. Begin a new drawing named 029???01 in your assigned directory using 029PEDIT as a prototype.

2. `Command:` **`PEDIT`** ↵	Issues the PEDIT command
3. `Select polyline:` *Select the polyline at ① (see fig. 29.2)*	Selects polyline to edit

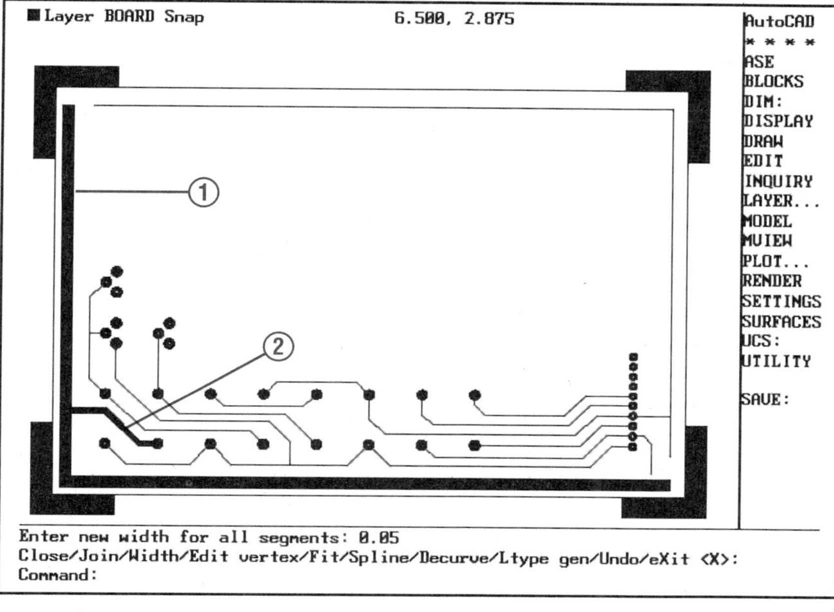

Figure 29.2
Polylines after PEDIT.

4. `Close/Join/Width/Edit vertex/Fit/Spline/Decurve/Ltype gen/Undo/eXit <X>:` **`W`** ↵	Specifies the Width option
5. `Enter new width for all segments:` **`0.2`** ↵	Specifies new width and changes polyline
6. `Close/Join/Width/Edit vertex/Fit/Spline/Decurve/Ltype gen/Undo/eXit <X>:` **`W`** ↵	Specifies Width option
7. `Enter new width for all segments:` **`0.1`** ↵	Specifies new width and changes polyline
8. `Close/Join/Width/Edit vertex/Fit/Spline/Decurve/Ltype gen/Undo/eXit <X>:` *Press* Enter	Ends PEDIT command
9. `Command:` *Press* Enter	Repeats the previous command

continues

10. `PEDIT Select polyline:` *Select the polyline at* ② *(see fig. 29.2)*	
11. `Close/Join/Width/Edit vertex/ Fit/Spline/Decurve/Ltype gen/ Undo/eXit <X>:` **`W`** ↵	Specifies Width option
12. `Enter new width for all segments:` **`0.05`** ↵	Sets width
13. `Close/Join/Width/Edit vertex/ Fit/Spline/Decurve/Ltype gen/ Undo/eXit <X>:` *Press* Enter	
14. Save your drawing.	

In the preceding exercise, PEDIT changes all the segments of the selected polylines to the same width. You can set the polyline's width more than once if you enter the wrong width or a width that does not work well for the design.

PEDIT only uses pick-after selection. If a selection set exists when you issue the PEDIT command, even if the selection set contains only one polyline, AutoCAD clears the selection set and prompts you to select a polyline.

Joining Polyline Segments

Another common polyline-editing task involves joining new segments to an existing polyline. If you draw a polyline and later realize you need to add more segments to it, you can draw the new segments using the LINE command. Then, you can use the Join option of the PEDIT command to join these new line segments to the polyline, creating a single polyline entity. You also can use PEDIT to convert a line segment to a polyline, and then add more segments to it to form a longer polyline.

When you enter the PEDIT command and select an entity, PEDIT first determines if the entity is a polyline. If the entity is a line or arc segment (not a polyline), PEDIT enables you to turn it into a polyline or select a different entity.

Some of the circuit traces on the PC board were drawn using lines rather than polylines. In the following exercise, change one of these traces into a single polyline and also change its width. Use figure 29.3 as a guide to select entities.

Joining Polyline Segments

Continue with your drawing from the preceding exercise.

1. Zoom to the view shown in figure 29.3.
2. `Command:` **`PEDIT`** ↵ — Issues the PEDIT command
3. `Select polyline:` *Select the line at* ① *(see fig. 29.3)* — Selects polyline to edit

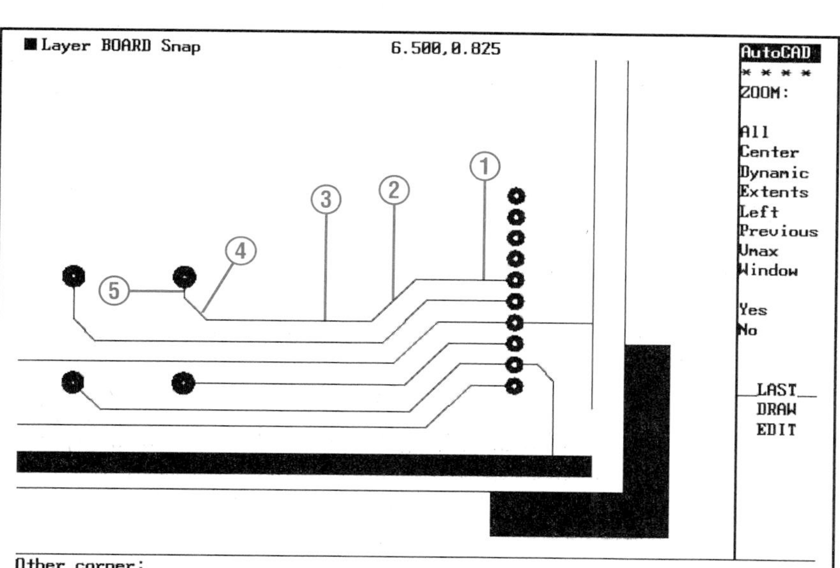

Figure 29.3
Line segments before joining.

4. `Entity selected is not a polyline`
   `Do you want to turn it into one?`
   `<Y>` *Press* Enter — Turns line segment into a polyline
5. `Close/Join/Width/Edit vertex/Fit/`
   `Spline/Decurve/Ltype gen/Undo/`
   `eXit <X>:` **`J`** ↵ — Specifies the Join option
6. `Select objects:` *Select the line at* ② *(see fig. 29.3)*
7. `Select objects:` *Select the lines at* ③, ④, *and* ⑤ *(see fig. 29.3)* — Selects other line segments and adds them to polyline

continues

8.	`Select objects:` *Press* Enter	Ends selection
9.	`Close/Join/Width/Edit vertex/Fit/ Spline/Decurve/Ltype gen/Undo/ eXit <X>:` **`W`** ↵	Specifies the Width option
10.	`Enter new width for all segments:` **`0.025`** ↵	Sets width
11.	`Close/Join/Width/Edit vertex/Fit/ Spline/Decurve/Ltype gen/Undo/ eXit <X>:` *Press* Enter	Ends PEDIT command
12.	Save your drawing.	

Your drawing should resemble figure 29.4.

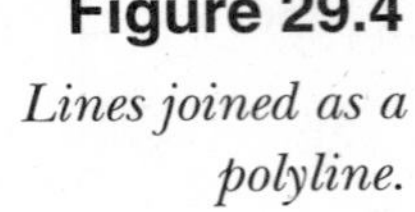

Figure 29.4

Lines joined as a polyline.

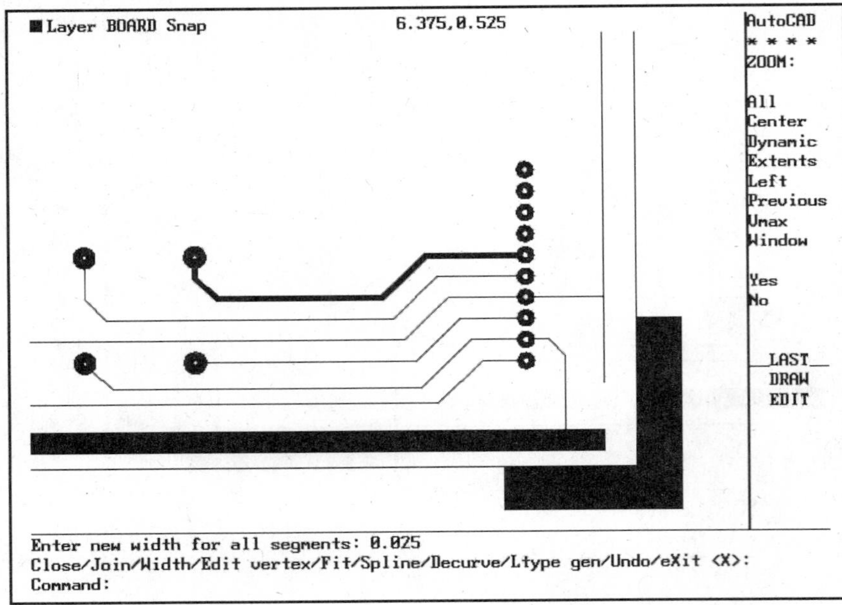

You can use the Join option to join separate polylines into a single polyline, join arc and line segments to an existing polyline, and join line and arc segments to form a new polyline. However, the entities you select must physically join at common vertices. In other words, two adjacent segments must share a common end point for you to be able to join them as a polyline.

Using Other PEDIT Options

The PEDIT command provides many different ways you can modify a polyline. In addition to enabling you to change the width of a polyline and join segments, the PEDIT command also enables you to edit individual vertices, apply curves to a polyline, and perform other polyline-editing tasks.

After you select a polyline or turn an arc or line into a polyline, PEDIT displays the following options:

- **Close.** This option closes an open polyline by connecting the last point with the first point of the polyline using a new polyline segment.
- **Decurve.** This option returns a spline-curved polyline to its original uncurved state. This option undoes a Fit curve to its straightened frame (see the Fit curve option).
- **Edit vertex.** This option enters vertex editing mode. Vertex editing mode enables you to edit individual vertices of an existing polyline. Vertex editing mode provides additional options (see the section later in this unit titled "PEIDT Vertex Editing Options").
- **Fit curve.** This option fits a smooth curve to a polyline by adding vertices to the polyline. The curve is created using a pair of arcs joining each pair of vertices.
- **Join.** This option joins lines, arcs, and polylines to an existing polyline. The result is a single polyline entity created from the selected segments.
- **Ltype gen.** This option determines how linetypes are applied to the segments of a polyline. If this option is turned on, linetype is applied to the polyline in a continuous manner regardless of the location of the vertices in relation to the dashes and spaces in the linetype (which can result in spaces at a vertex). If this option is turned off, the linetype starts and ends with a dash at each vertex.
- **Open.** This option opens a closed polyline by removing the closing segment. This option affects only polylines closed using the Close option of the PLINE command. If you explicitly close the polyline by drawing a segment, the Open option has no visible effect.
- **Spline curve.** This option converts the polyline to a quadratic B-spline or a cubic B-spline, depending on your choice. You can convert a B-spline back into its defining polyline by using the Decurve option.
- **Undo.** This option undoes one edit operation during the PEDIT editing session.
- **Width.** This option sets a uniform width for an existing polyline.
- **eXit.** This option exits the PEDIT session and returns to the AutoCAD command prompt.

PEDIT Vertex Editing Options

If you choose the Edit vertex option of the PEDIT command, AutoCAD provides a new set of polyline-editing options that perform various editing functions on the polyline's vertices. Most of these new options are explained in the following list:

- **Break.** This option enables you to break a polyline. If you select two vertices, AutoCAD removes the segments between the two vertices and breaks the polyline into two separate polylines. If one of the selected vertices is located at the end of the polyline, AutoCAD truncates the polyline. If only one vertex is selected, AutoCAD breaks the polyline into two separate polylines at the selected point.
- **Insert.** This option enables you to insert an additional vertex point after the current vertex.
- **Move.** This option moves the current vertex to a new location.
- **Next.** This option cycles through the vertices in the polyline, making each current. You can use this option to make a specific vertex current so that you can edit the vertex.
- **Previous.** This option performs a function similar to the Next option, but in reverse vertex order.
- **Regen.** This option regenerates the polyline for viewing current changes made to the polyline.
- **Straighten.** This option enables you to straighten a portion of a polyline by removing additional vertices between two vertices that you select.
- **Tangent.** This option sets the tangent direction for current vertex by enabling you to specify the tangent angle. This option generally is used for controlling the way in which a curve is fitted to the polyline.
- **Width.** This option enables you to change the starting and ending widths of a segment.
- **eXit.** This option exits vertex editing, or cancels Break/Straighten command options if they are active.

Consult the AutoCAD manual or ask your instructor for additional help with these PEDIT command options.

If you explode a polyline, AutoCAD separates the polyline into its individual line and arc segments. These segments no longer have any association with one another, although they still share common end points.

Unit Review

What You've Learned

- Commands: PEDIT
- How to change the width of a polyline
- How to join new segments to an existing polyline
- How to create a polyline from an arc or line segment

Review Questions

True or False

29.01 T F PEDIT can taper a polyline segment.

29.02 T F PEDIT can join a circle to a line.

29.03 T F The Join option enables you to join two polylines together if they share a common end point.

29.04 T F The Width option, when in normal polyline editing mode, changes the width of all segments in the polyline.

29.05 T F The Width option, when used in vertex editing mode, changes the starting and ending widths at a vertex.

29.06 T F The Open option can open a closed polyline.

Short Answer

29.07 Explain the function of the Close option.

29.08 Explain the difference between the Width option in normal polyline edit mode and in vertex editing mode.

Student: ______________________ Date: ________

Instructor: ______________________ Course: ________ Section: ________

29.09 What function does the Open option perform?

____

____

____

29.10 Explain the purpose of the Break option.

____

____

____

Additional Exercises

29.11 Continue with your drawing from the preceding exercise. Change the width of all the existing polyline circuit traces to a width of .025". Change the width of the ground and voltage supply strips located at ① and ② in figure 29.5 to .1".

29.12 Continue with your PC board drawing. Change the line segments indicated by ③ in figure 29.5 to polylines. Also change their width to .025".

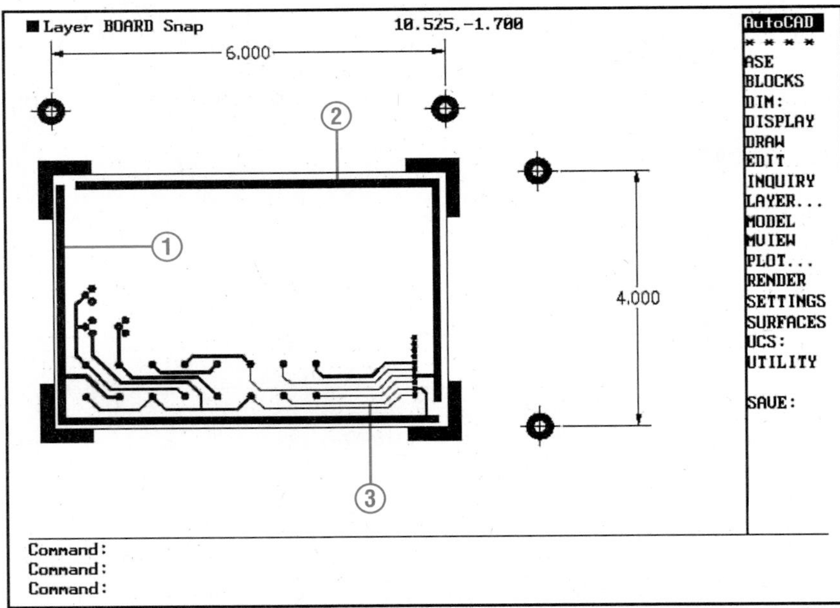

Figure 29.5
Changes to PC board drawing.

Student: __________ Date: __________

Instructor: __________ Course: __________ Section: __________

PART IV

Drawing Accurately

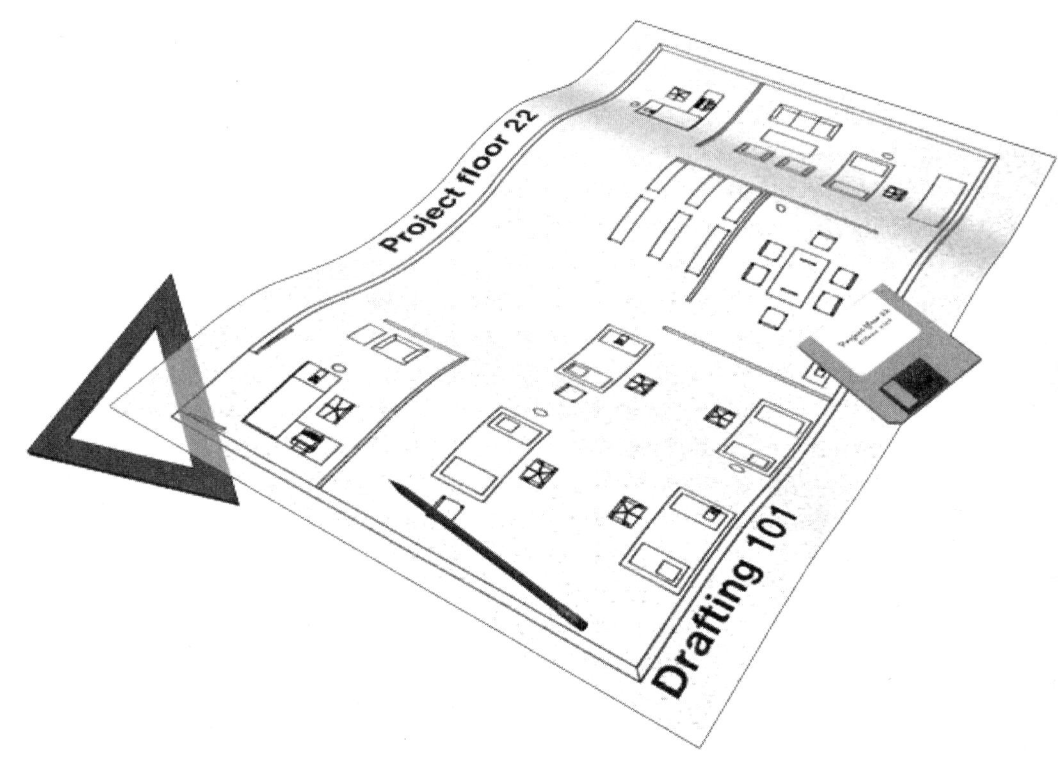

Setting and Working with Units

utoCAD's system of units lets you apply real-world units of measure to your drawings. By default, AutoCAD is set up for input and numeric display in decimal units, but those units can represent anything you like: inches, millimeters, miles, or microns. You must decide the appropriate type of measurement unit for your drawing.

The objectives for this unit are to:

- Understand what units are in AutoCAD and how they are used in different applications
- Use the UNITS command and the Units Control dialog box to set linear and angular unit type and precision
- Enter values at the `Command:` prompt for different linear and angular unit types

Introduction to Units

AutoCAD's UNITS command and the Units Control dialog box let you set the type of units that will be used in a drawing. These options control two types of unit display: linear and angular. You also can control the precision with which the unit values are displayed for each of these two types of measurement.

UNIT 30

AutoCAD unit settings affect three things: the format of the values returned when you query the drawing for an area or distance, the display of coordinates on the status line, and the appearance of the values in dimensions.

AutoCAD provides five types of linear measure:

- **Scientific.** Used when working with very large real numbers. A value in scientific notation consists of a real number raised to a power of 10. Scientific notation can be used to represent any system of measure.
- **Decimal.** Used when working with real numbers in decimal format. AutoCAD can display a maximum of eight decimal places, but is accurate to 14 places for all types of units. Decimal notation can be used to represent any system of measure and is the default type of unit in AutoCAD.
- **Engineering.** Used to represent feet and decimal inches. AutoCAD automatically converts and displays 12 inches as one foot. Engineering notation can be used only if your system of measure is inches.
- **Architectural.** Used to represent feet and fractional inches. The smallest fraction AutoCAD can display is 1/256", but it is accurate to 14 decimal places. Twelve inches is automatically converted to one foot. Architectural notation can be used only if your system of measure is inches.
- **Fractional.** Used when working with real numbers in numerator/denominator format. The smallest fraction AutoCAD can display is 1/256". Fractional notation can be used with any system of measure.

AutoCAD's angular measure options include:

- **Decimal Degrees.** Displays degrees as real numbers with up to eight decimal places. Decimal degrees is the default type of angular measure in AutoCAD.
- **Deg/Min/Sec.** Displays angular measure in degrees-minutes-seconds notation using ASCII characters (that is, 22d14'30"). Measurements of less than one second are shown as decimal places.
- **Grads.** Displays angular measure as grads, with a lowercase g after the value. Ninety degrees is equal to 100 grads.
- **Radians.** Displays angular measure as radians, with a lowercase r after the value. A radian is 180/pi degrees.

- **Surveyor's Units.** Displays angular measure in degrees-minutes-seconds together with quadrant bearings (that is, N22d14'30"E). The circle is divided into four quadrants, so no angular value will be greater than 90 degrees.

AutoCAD will sometimes display coordinates in scientific units if there is not enough room on the status line to show them normally.

You may find that you change your type of linear units from time to time, but, unless you are a surveyor, you probably will not change your angular unit type.

Setting Linear Units

The easiest way to set units in AutoCAD is to use the Units Control dialog box (see fig. 30.1). You can display the Units Control dialog box by entering DDUNITS at the `Command:` prompt, or by choosing Settings, then Units Control.

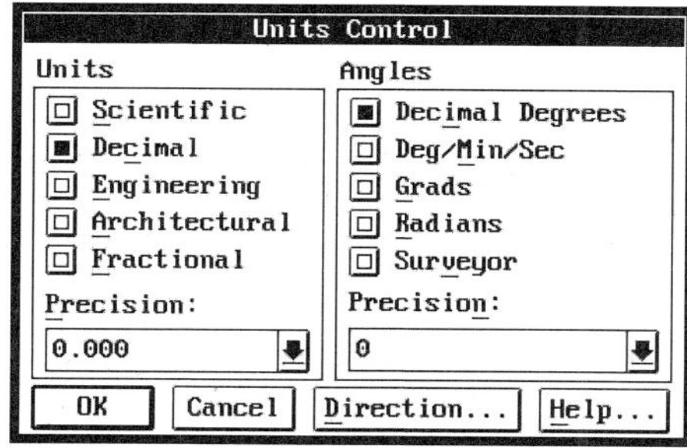

Figure 30.1

The Units Control dialog box.

In the following exercise, use the Units Control dialog box to change the linear units' type and precision.

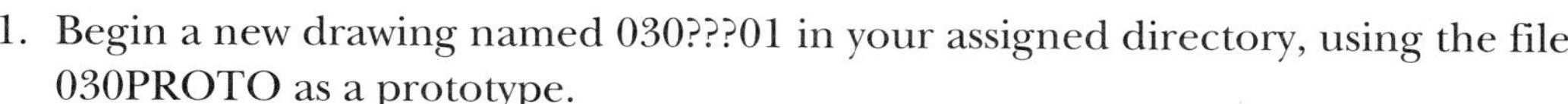

Setting Units

1. Begin a new drawing named 030???01 in your assigned directory, using the file 030PROTO as a prototype.
2. `Command:` *Choose* Settings, *then* Units Control — Displays the Units Control dialog box
3. *Choose the* Architectural *radio button* — Changes the value in the Precision box to 1/16 inch (see fig. 30.2)

continues

Figure 30.2

Setting architectural units in the Units Control dialog box.

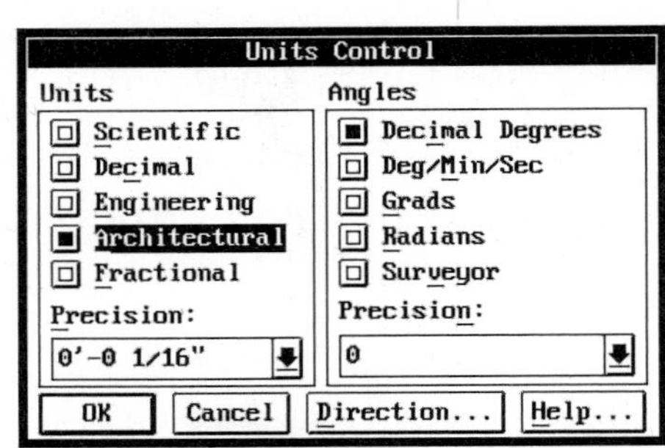

4. *Choose the* Precision *popup list menu button* — Displays a list of precision options (see fig. 30.3)

Figure 30.3

Changing linear precision with the Precision popup list.

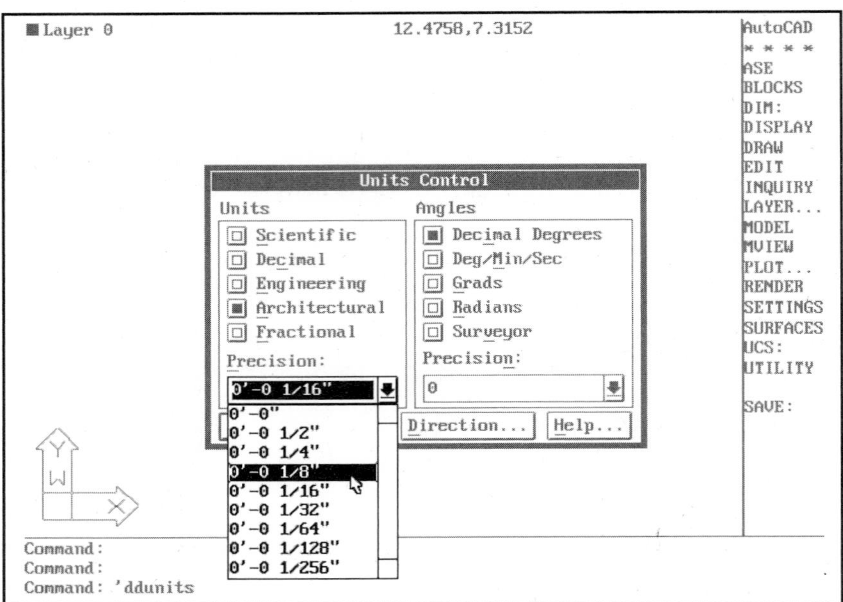

5. *Choose the option* 0'-0 1/8 " — Sets precision to 1/8 "

6. *Choose the* Precision *pull-down menu button* — Displays a list of precision options

7. *Choose the option* 0 '-0 1/16 " — Sets precision back to 1/16 "

8. *Choose* OK — Clears the dialog box from the screen

The coordinate readout at the top of the screen shows your new linear units type.

9. `Command:` *Choose* File, *then* Save — Saves the drawing

You will use your file 030???01 in later units as a prototype.

Working with Linear Values

AutoCAD's units settings control not only the display of values in the coordinate's readout, prompts, and dimensions. As a general principle, however, you can use any type of unit input in any other unit mode.

Change the linear units' type and try entering points under the different units modes to create the rectangle in figure 30.4.

Entering Linear Unit Values

1. `Command:` **`LINE`** ↵ — Starts the line command
2. `From point:` **`0.15E+01,0.15E+01`** ↵ — Enters value in scientific notation and starts line at point ① (see fig. 30.4)
3. `To point:` **`11.25,1.5`** ↵ — Enters value in decimal notation; continues line to ②
4. `To point:` **`11-1/4,5-1/2`** ↵ — Enters value using fractions; continues line to ③

The format for inputting fractional units differs from the way AutoCAD displays them. You must place a dash between your inch value and your fraction; otherwise AutoCAD will not interpret the dimension correctly.

5. `To point:` **`1.5,5-1/2`** ↵ — Enters points combining decimal and fractional entry; continues line to ④
6. `To point:` **`C`** ↵ — Closes the rectangle

You can see that the type of linear units for which AutoCAD is configured does not affect the ways in which you can enter input; AutoCAD will accept any kind of unit format for input. You can even combine types, as in the last example.

You can change units by entering the UNITS command at the `Command:` *prompt, although the UNITS command requires that you respond to a series of prompts, rather than choosing options from a dialog box. If you prefer to type a command to change units, enter the DDUNITS command. This command displays the Units Control dialog box, and has the same effect as choosing Settings, then Units Control.*

Figure 30.4

Rectangle drawn using different linear unit input.

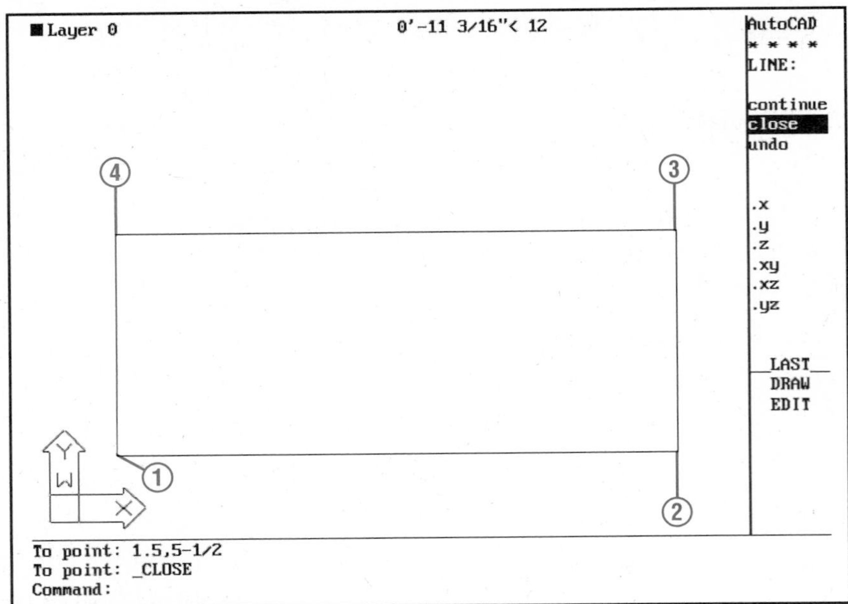

Setting Angular Units

In most cases, you will not have to change your angular unit type. The most common reason to change angular units is if you are entering values from surveyor's notes. You will use the Angular Units side of the Units Control dialog box primarily to change the precision with which your angular units are displayed, and not to change the type of angular measurement.

Changing Angular Units

Continue with your drawing from the previous exercise.

1. `Command:` *Choose* Settings, *then* Units Control	Displays the Units Control dialog box
2. *In the* Units Control *dialog box, choose the* Deg/Min/Sec *radio button*	Selects Degrees/Minutes/Seconds mode and changes the Precision option to 0d
3. *Choose the* Precision *pull-down menu, then choose* 0d00'00"	Changes precision to display angles to the nearest minute (see fig. 30.5)

Although you can change the format of angular measurement by entering the UNITS command at the `Command:` *prompt, the Units Control dialog box is easier.*

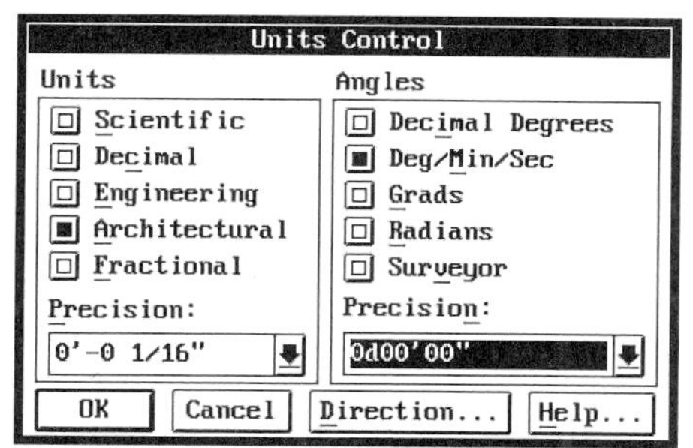

Figure 30.5

Changing angular precision.

Working with Angular Values

Just as you can enter linear unit values in any format, you can do the same with angular values—with one exception. You must have set the angular units' type to Surveyor if you want to input angular values using surveyor's units.

Use the five different types of angular measure to draw the lines shown in figure 30.6.

Inputting Angular Units

1. `Command:` *Choose* Draw, *then* Line, *then* Segments	Starts LINE command
2. `_line From point:` **`10,5`** ↵	Starts the line at ①
3. `To point:` **`@3<240.0`** ↵	Uses decimal degree input to place point at ② (see fig. 30.6)
4. `To point:` **`@3<120d0'0"`** ↵	Uses Degree/Minute/Seconds input to place point at ③
5. `To point:` **`@3<266.6666667G`** ↵	Uses Grads input to place point at ④
6. `To point:` **`@3<2.0944R`** ↵	Uses Radians input to place point at ⑤
7. `To point:` **`@3<S30D0'0"W`** ↵	Attempts to use Surveyor's Units input

AutoCAD does not accept the input and returns an error message because surveyor's units have not been chosen.

```
Point or option keyword required.
```

8. `To point:` *Choose* Settings, *then* Units Control	Displays the Units Control dialog box

```
'ddunits
```

continues

Working with Angular Values

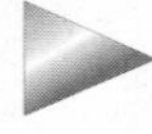

9. *In the* Units Control *dialog box, choose the* Surveyor *radio button, then choose* OK — Sets angular units mode to Surveyor's units and returns to the LINE command

10. `To point:` **`@3<S30D0'W`** ↵ — Draws a line to ⑥

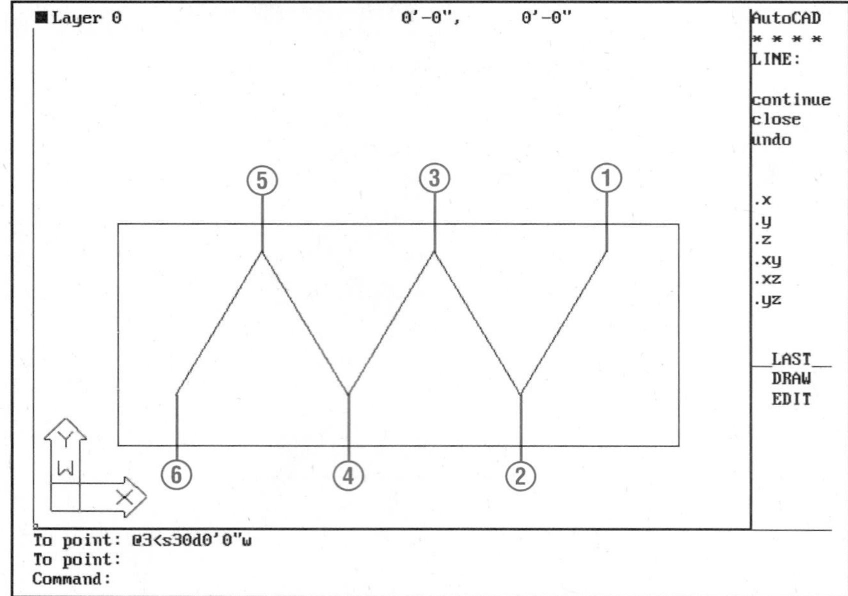

Figure 30.6

Figure drawn using different types of angular unit input.

Changing Directions in Angular Measure

By default, AutoCAD measures angles based on 0 degrees pointing due east (at three o'clock, or to the right of the screen). Also by default, AutoCAD measures angles in a counterclockwise direction. You can change both the location of 0 degrees and the direction of angular measurement through the Units Control dialog box, but you should avoid doing this unless you have a good reason. Surveyors often change these defaults because they typically measure angles clockwise from north instead of counterclockwise from east.

Continue in the same drawing to examine how changing directions works in AutoCAD. Begin with the default settings for angular measure.

Changing Direction of Angular Measure

1. Begin a new drawing using ACAD as a prototype (you do not have to specify a new drawing name).

2. `Command:` *Choose* Draw, *then* Line, *then* Segments

3. `_line From point:` **`3,6`** — Specifies start point

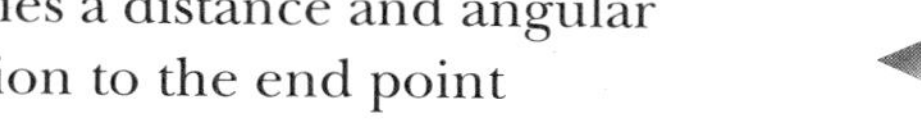

4. `To point:` **`@3<15`**	Specifies a distance and angular direction to the end point
5. `Command:` *Choose* Settings, *then* Units Control	
6. *Choose the* Direction *button*	Displays the Direction Control dialog box (see fig. 30.7)

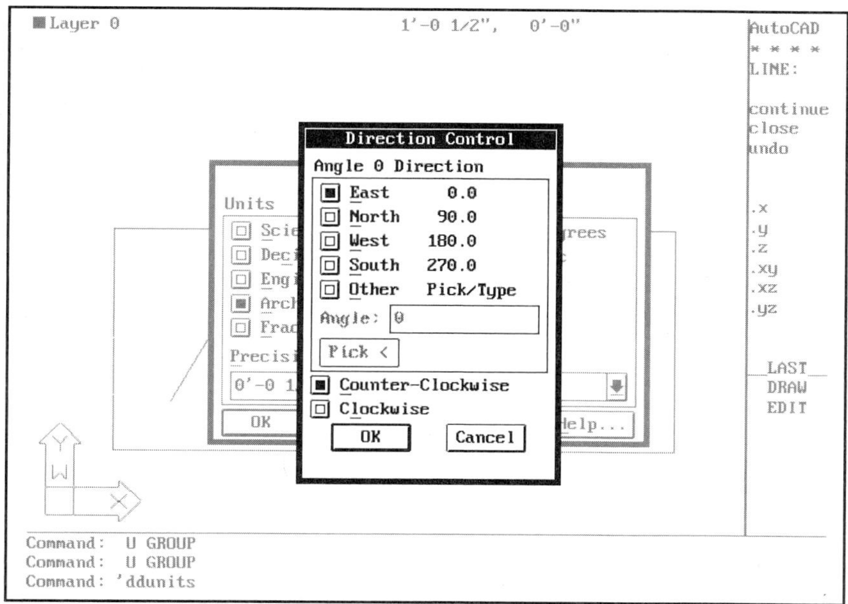

Figure 30.7

Default settings for Direction Control dialog box.

7. *Choose the* North *radio button, then choose the* Clockwise *radio button*	Sets zero degrees to North and specifies clockwise angular measurement (see fig. 30.8)
8. *Choose* OK, *then choose* OK *again*	Closes the Direction Control and Units Control dialog boxes
`Command:` **`LINE`** ↵	
9. `From point:` **`8,6`**	Specifies start point
10. `To point:` **`@3<15`**	Draws a line at 15 degrees from 0
11. `To point:` *Press* Enter	Ends LINE command

AutoCAD drew the first line at 15 degrees counterclockwise from east—its default 0-degree direction. It drew the second line 15 degrees clockwise from north, according to the new settings in the Direction Control dialog box (see fig. 30.9).

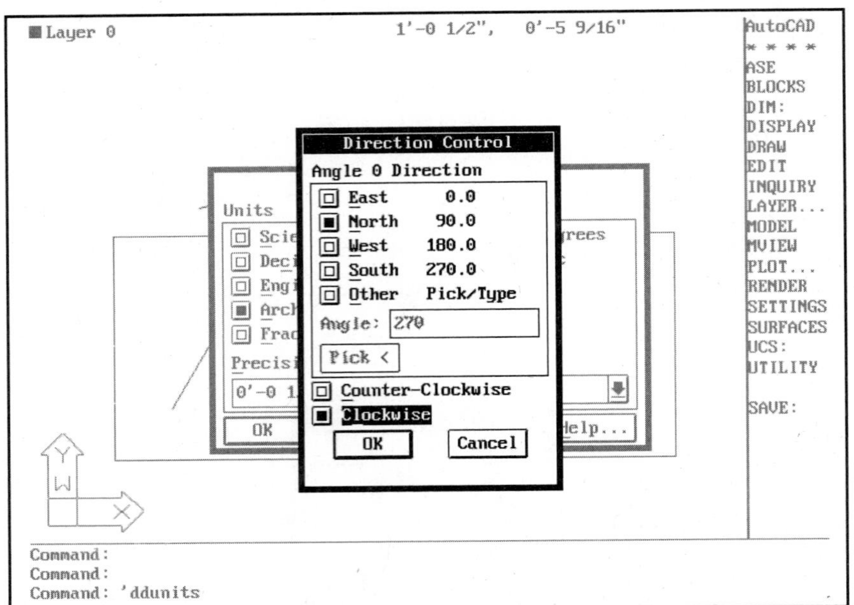

Figure 30.8

Direction Control set to measure clockwise from North.

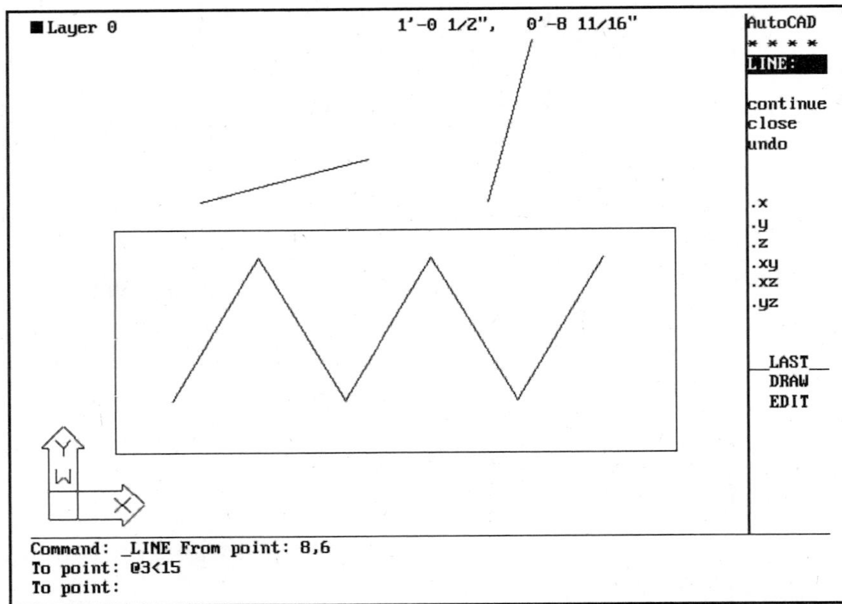

Figure 30.9

Entities created using different angular directions.

Unit Review

What You've Learned

- What units are in AutoCAD
- How to change the active type of linear and angular units
- How to change the precision of linear and angular units
- How to enter linear and angular values for different unit types
- How to change the direction and rotation of angular measure

Review Questions

True or False

30.01 T F By default, in AutoCAD one unit is equal to one inch.

30.02 T F Fractional units can be used only when you work in inches.

30.03 T F The default direction for 0 degrees is east, or to the right of the screen.

30.04 T F METRIC is one of the unit modes in AutoCAD.

30.05 T F In AutoCAD, surveyor's units are always less than 90 degrees.

30.06 T F You can enter a value in decimal inches when Architectural mode is chosen.

30.07 T F You can enter fractional units only if Architectural mode is chosen.

30.08 T F The coordinate output in the status line shows the current unit measurement mode.

30.09 T F A radian is equal to one degree.

30.10 T F A grad is equal to 180/pi degrees.

Student: ______________________ Date: ______

Instructor: ______________________ Course: ______ Section: ______

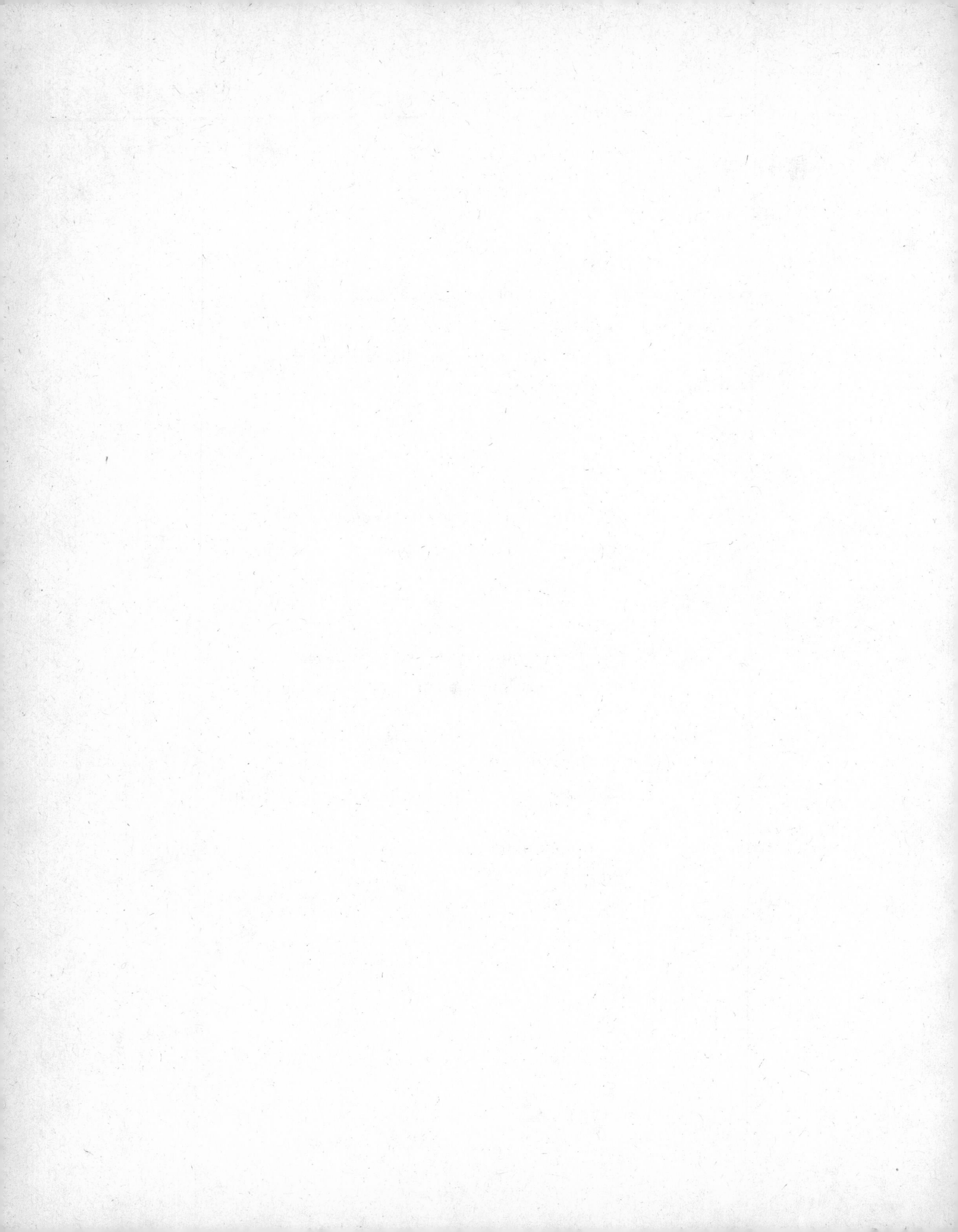

UNIT 31

Setting and Working with Limits

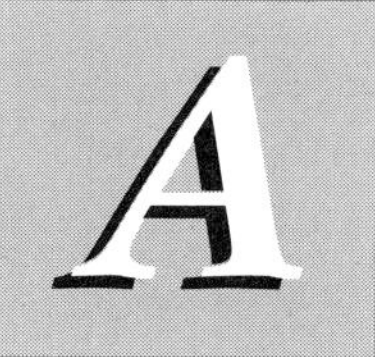

AutoCAD includes a command named LIMITS that enables you to define a boundary in which to draw. Many users find that limits are not very useful, but you might find them useful in a limited number of situations. This unit explains limits and how you can use them.

The objectives for this unit are to:

- Understand limits in AutoCAD and what function they serve
- Understand the relationship between limits and the grid
- Set limits
- Control AutoCAD's automatic limits checking

Understanding Limits

A drawing's limits define an invisible boundary within which you can create the drawing's entities. You can think of limits as representing the boundary of the paper on which you create the drawing, although limits also serve other purposes. One of the primary uses for limits is to provide a boundary to help you contain the drawing within a set sheet size. When configured to do so, AutoCAD prevents you from drawing entities outside the limits, which is much like preventing you from drawing outside the edges of a sheet of paper (drawing on the table, for example). Besides establishing this "virtual drawing sheet," limits also control the area over which the grid is displayed.

You can set limits for model space (the environment in which you have worked in AutoCAD up to this point) as well as in paper space. Paper space is primarily used for composing a drawing for plotting, and is discussed in units 46, "Introduction to Paper Space," and 47, "Composing a Drawing." With the introduction of paper space, limits serve very little purpose in model space. They are useful, however, for defining the size of the grid (which is discussed in unit 34, "Setting and Using a Grid").

Because a drawing's limits are not represented by real entities, and because they can be changed at will, no hard and fast rule dictates the values to which they should be set. There are a few rules of thumb, however, depending on whether you are working in model space or paper space:

☞ **Model space.** Use the limits to define the area covered by the grid. Because you can adjust the sheet size and viewport organization in paper space to accommodate the drawing entities and views, using the limits to control the size of your allowable drawing area in model space serves little purpose.

☞ **Paper space.** Use the limits to define the area in which drawing viewports can be created on the sheet. This helps to prevent you from drawing outside the borders or allowable drawing area on the sheet.

Although limits are covered in *Hands On AutoCAD*, you may find that you seldom use them except to control the size of the grid in model space. In paper space, it is a good idea to insert a title block and sheet border before you begin composing the views on the sheet. Because the title block and border graphically define the boundaries of the drawing sheet, you do not need to set limits for that same purpose.

Setting Drawing Limits

A drawing's limits are represented by two pairs of coordinates that represent the lower left and the upper right corners of the limits area. Often, the lower left corner is set at the origin of the drawing, which is most often located at coordinate 0,0. You set the upper right coordinates to a value appropriate to the sheet size and plot scale of your drawing, or to a value appropriate for sizing your grid.

Any value, positive or negative, can be used to set the limits, but you must always set the lower left corner first and the upper right corner second. If you try to set the second corner below and to the left of the first corner, AutoCAD returns an `Invalid limits` *message.*

In the following exercise, create a new drawing and reset its limits.

Setting Drawing Limits

1. Begin a new drawing named 031???01 in your assigned directory using 031LIMIT as a prototype.

2. `Command:` *Choose* Settings, Drawing Limits	Issues the LIMITS command
`'_limits` `Reset Model space limits:`	
3. `ON/OFF/<Lower left corner> <0.0,0.0>:` *Press* Enter	Accepts the default lower left limit coordinate
4. `Upper right corner <12.0,9.0>:` **17,11** ↵	Specifies the upper right limit coordinate
5. `Command:` *Press* Enter	Repeats the previous command
`'_limits` `Reset Model space limits:`	
6. `ON/OFF/<Lower left corner> <0.0,0.0>:` *Press* Enter	Accepts the current value
7. `Upper right corner <17.0,11.0>:` *Press* Enter	Accepts the current value

The new drawing limits, 17"×11", are now represented in the current system of units.

To have a visual reminder of the drawing limits at all times, you can refer to the grid of dots you see on-screen when you invoke the GRID command. (The GRID command and use of a grid are described in detail in unit 34, "Setting and Using a Grid.") The area covered by the grid is the same area bounded by your drawing limits.

Resetting the Display To Show the New Limits

Continue with your drawing from the preceding exercise.

1. `Command:` **`GRID`** ↵	Issues the GRID command
2. `Grid spacing(X) or ON/OFF/Snap/ Aspect <0.0>:` **`1`** ↵	Sets the grid spacing to 1"
3. `Command:` *Choose* View, *then* Zoom, *then* All	Issues the ZOOM command with the All option

```
_zoom
All/Center/Dynamic/Extents/Left/
Previous/Vmax/Window/<Scale(X/XP)>:
_all Regenerating drawing.
```

The drawing area now displays the limits of the drawing, but zoom out a little to get a clearer understanding of the relationship between grid and limits.

4. `Command:` **`Z`** ↵	Issues alias for ZOOM command
5. `All/Center/Dynamic/Extents/Left/ Previous/Vmax/Window/ <Scale(X/XP)>:` **`0.7X`** ↵	Zooms out by a factor of .7

Your drawing should look similar to figure 31.1.

Another way of checking your current drawing limits that gives you more information is to use AutoCAD's STATUS command.

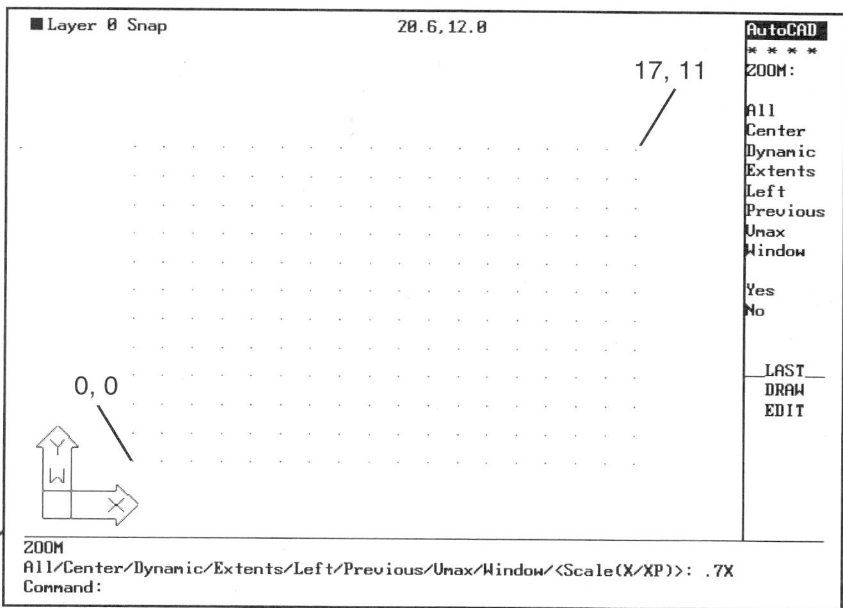

Figure 31.1

The grid fills the area defined by the drawing's limits.

Using STATUS To Check Limits

1. `Command:` *Choose* Assist, *then* Inquiry, *then* Status — Issues the STATUS command

   `'_status`

AutoCAD switches to Text Screen and displays current drawing and system settings. Only the first section is included in the following sample:

```
0 entities in UNNAMED
Model space limits are X:       0.0     Y:    0.0    (Off)
                       X:      17.0     Y:   11.0
Model space uses       *Nothing*
Display shows          X:      -5.1     Y:   -3.6
                       X:      28.6     Y:   20.6
```

The STATUS command confirms the drawing limits you just set.

Working with Limits

By default, AutoCAD does not prevent you from drawing outside the limits. If you use the limits to define the extent of the grid, drawing outside the limits generally is not a problem (except that you are drawing outside the boundaries of the grid, which may defeat the purpose of using a grid).

In the following exercise, try drawing outside your current limits.

Drawing Outside the Limits

Continue with your drawing from the preceding exercise.

1. `Command:` *Choose* Draw, *then* Line, *then* Segments — Issues the LINE command to draw multiple segments
2. `From point:` *Pick a point at* **8,6** — Starts the line inside the limits
3. `To point:` *Pick a point at* **12,6** — Draws a line inside the limits
4. `To point:` *Pick a point at* **14,-2** — Draws a line outside the limits
5. `To point:` *Pick a point at* **20,-2** — Draws a line outside the limits
6. `To point:` *Press* Enter

Your drawing should resemble figure 31.2.

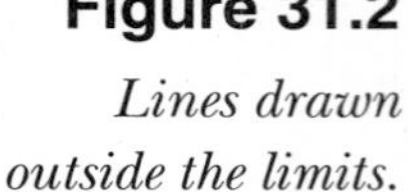

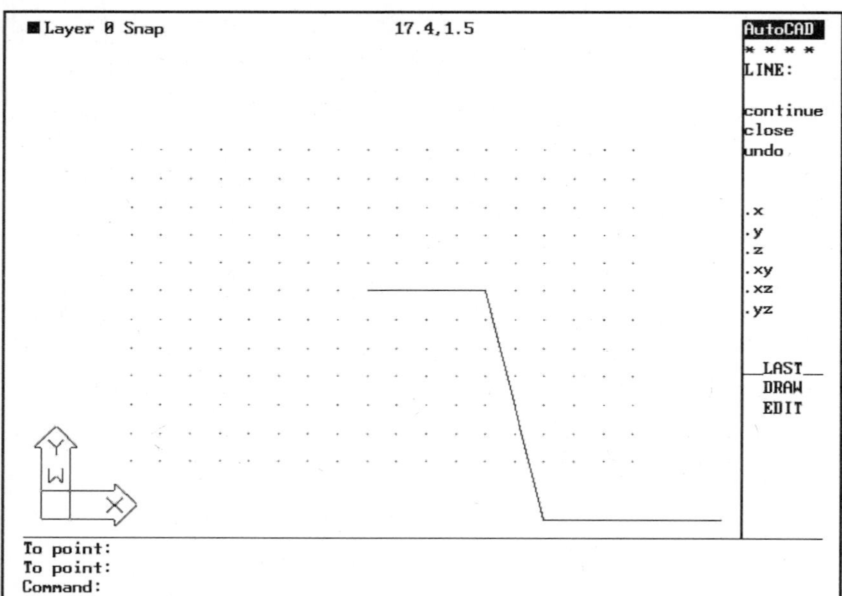

Figure 31.2
Lines drawn outside the limits.

Using Limits Checking

If you are using the limits to provide a boundary outside of which you do not want to draw, you can turn on a feature called *limits checking* to prevent you from drawing outside your preset limits. When limits checking is turned on, AutoCAD does not enable you to draw outside the limits.

Using Limits Checking

Continue with your drawing from the preceding exercise.

1. `Command:` *Choose* Settings, *then* Drawing Limits	Issues the LIMITS command
`'_limits` `Reset Model space limits:`	
2. `ON/OFF/<Lower left corner> <0.00,0.0>:` **ON** ↵	Turns on limits checking
3. `Command:` *Choose* Draw, *then* Line, *then* Segments	Issues the LINE command
4. `_line From point:` *Pick a point at* **8,6**	Starts the line inside the limits
5. `To point:` *Pick a point at* **12,10**	Draws a line inside the limits
6. `To point:` *Pick a point at* **20,6**	Attempts to draw a line outside of the limits
`**Outside limits`	
7. `To point:` *Press* Enter	Ends the LINE command

As you can see from the preceding exercise, when limits checking is on, AutoCAD does not enable you to draw outside of the limits. Turning on limits checking does not affect entities drawn outside the limits when limits checking was turned off.

The main purpose of limits checking is to keep beginners from working outside the drawing area. After you understand how limits work, you probably will prefer to keep limits checking turned off.

Unit Review

What You've Learned

- What limits are and how to use them
- How to set limits
- How limits affect the grid
- How to use limits checking

Review Questions

True or False

31.01 T F Limits must be set before you start drawing.

31.02 T F Limits are always displayed in the current units of measure.

31.03 T F If limits checking is on, you can draw outside the limits but AutoCAD displays an `**OVER` warning message.

31.04 T F You turn limits checking on and off with the LIMITS command.

31.05 T F You must use limits when creating a drawing.

Multiple Choice

31.06 Changing the limits affects __________.

(A) snap setting and ZOOM Extents

(B) units precision and snap setting

(C) extent of the grid

(D) none of the above

31.07 When you are composing a drawing for plotting in paper space, limits are most useful for __________.

(A) controlling the size of the grid

(B) preventing you from drawing or placing views outside the sheet

(C) controlling the sheet size

(D) none of the above

Student: ______________________ Date: __________

Instructor: ______________________ Course: __________ Section: __________

Short Answer

31.08 Which two items of information must you supply to AutoCAD to set the drawing's limits?

____

____

____

31.09 Explain why limits often are not necessary when composing a drawing in paper space.

____

____

____

31.10 Explain what happens when limits checking is turned off, and you try to draw outside the limits.

____

____

____

Student: ________________ Date: ________

Instructor: ________________ Course: ________ Section: ________

UNIT 32

Calculating Scale Factor and Text Height

When you prepare a drawing using manual drawing techniques, you select a blank sheet of the proper size and then begin drawing. To size text, you simply draw it at whatever height is necessary. In AutoCAD, you have to plan your drawing scale, sheet size, and text height a little differently. This unit explains what drawing scale is in an AutoCAD drawing and teaches you how to calculate drawing scale, sheet size, and text height.

The objectives for this unit are to:

- Understand drawing scale
- Calculate the sheet size required for a drawing
- Calculate text height relative to drawing scale

Understanding and Calculating Scale Factor

Production drawings are almost always drawn to a specific scale appropriate to the drawing. House plans often are drawn at a scale of 1/4" = 1'-0", for example. Mechanical drawings are often prepared at scales of 1:1, 2:1, and so on.

When you prepare a drawing in AutoCAD, you usually draw the object full-size. This enables you to enter actual distances and coordinates to prepare an exact drawing without having to scale your numbers up or down according to a specific scale. Scale becomes important when you plot the drawing because you usually want the drawing plotted to a specific scale on a particular sheet size. (Plotting is explained in units 47, 48, and 49.)

Although you usually do not plot a drawing until it is completed, you often must decide on a drawing scale as soon as you start the drawing. This is because text height, dimension height, and other features in the drawing are related directly to the scale at which you plot the drawing. Understanding how to calculate drawing scale, sheet size, and text height is therefore very important.

Understanding Model Space and Paper Space

The environment that you have worked with up to this point is called *model space.* Model space is the primary environment you use when you create a drawing. Think of model space as the "real world" where you create the model using real units, such as inches, feet, millimeters, and so on. Your drawings in model space are usually full-size.

AutoCAD provides a second environment called *paper space.* Paper space is explained in detail in unit 46—"Introduction to Paper Space"—but you need a basic understanding of paper space to understand drawing scale.

You first create your drawing in model space, adding text, dimensions, and so on. After you create a drawing model in model space, you can enter paper space to prepare the drawing for plotting on a plotter or printer. In paper space, one unit equals one unit in the real world, just as it does in model space. The difference from model space is that you can open viewports in paper space that "look into" your model in model space. You can scale these viewports by specifying a ratio between paper-space units and model-space units. You can specify, for example, that 1/4 inch in paper space equals 12 inches in model space—the equivalent of setting a scale of 1/4" =1'-0" for the viewport. Figure 32.1 shows a title block in paper space with a few viewports on it.

Think of paper space as where your drawing sheet and title block are located. You create a drawing in model space, and then switch to paper space to begin laying out the sheet to contain views of your model.

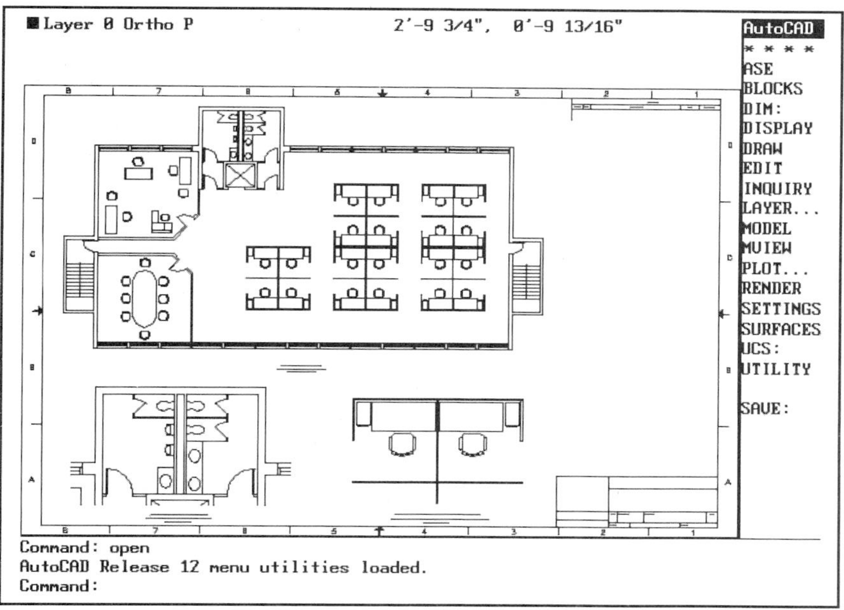

Figure 32.1

A drawing composed in paper space.

Calculating Scale Factor

Even though you usually do not scale the views of your drawing until you compose a plot in paper space, you still need to calculate the drawing scale when you start the drawing, or at the very least, when you begin adding text and dimensions to the drawing. This is because the size you specify for text and dimensions is based on the scale at which your drawing is to be plotted. Calculating drawing scale also is necessary if you intend to plot the drawing from model space.

To calculate a drawing's scale factor, simply determine the ratio between the two values in the drawing's scale. Consider the standard scale 1/2" = 1'-0". The ratio of 1/2 inch to 12 inches is 1:24. This means that one unit in the plot equals 24 units in the model, or real world. This also means that your full-size model must be scaled down by a factor of 24 to make it plot at a scale of 1/2" = 1'-0". To specify a plot scale, take the inverse of the scale factor, or 1/24. If you plot the drawing at a scale of 1/24, or .01466, the resulting scale is 1/2" = 1'-0".

Calculating Text Height

Even if you plan to plot your drawing from paper space, drawing scale still is important to determine text height. For example, assume that you are preparing a house plan. You intend to plot the drawing at a standard scale of

1/4" = 1'-0". The drawing is drawn full-size, and you want the text and dimension values to plot at a height of 1/8 inch. If you place text and dimensions in the drawing with an actual height of 1/8 inch, they will be too small to read when plotted. Imagine it this way: You are perched on a tower 100 feet above your house, trying to read a newspaper lying on the sidewalk. You would never be able to read the newspaper. If the text in the newspaper were six inches tall, however, you should be able to read it without any problems. The drawing text is like the text in the newspaper—you must specify a large enough text size to be readable when the drawing is plotted.

To calculate text height, you must first calculate the drawing's scale. As in the last section on drawing scale, this means determining a ratio between the two numbers in the scale. Using the house plan example of 1/4" = 1'-0", the ratio is 1/4 to 12, 1:48, or .020833. To calculate text height, divide the required text height by the scale factor. If you need 1/8-inch text in this drawing, for example, divide 1/8 inch by .020833. The answer, six, is the size of text you need to use in your drawing to plot the text at 1/8 inch.

What if the drawing is plotted larger than actual size? The same rule still holds true. Consider an example of a mechanical drawing drawn full-size but plotted at a scale of 2:1. The scale factor is two. Assume that the required text size is 3/16 inch. Divide 3/16 inch by two and the answer, 3/32 inch, is the text size you need.

Determining Sheet Size

Whether you plot a drawing in model space or in paper space, you have to determine what size sheet will accommodate the drawing. No set formula for calculating sheet size exists, but you can use trial and error to determine an adequate sheet size for the plotted scale you intend to use.

Consider another plotting example: You have drawn a detail of a structural steel assembly 28 feet long and need to plot it at a standard scale of 1" = 1'-0". The scale ratio is 1 inch to 12 inches, or 1:12. The scale factor is 0.08333 (1/12). First, convert the length of the detail to inches: 28 feet times 12 inches per foot equals 336 inches. Next, calculate the size of the detail when it is plotted. Multiply the actual size of the detail, 336 inches, by the scale factor of 0.08333. The result is 28 inches, which determines the amount of space on the paper required for the detail.

Next, add as much space on either side as you need to accommodate dimensions, text, and other features. In this example, add 10 percent, or about three inches. This means you need a total of 31 inches to accommodate the detail on the sheet. Check the sheet sizes available to you to determine which one is large enough for the drawing. In this example, the best choice is an E-size sheet. Although the detail would fit on a D-size sheet, the detail would extend into the area required by the Bill of Materials and revisions notes. The E-size sheet provides enough space for the detail and other information required on the drawing.

Unit Review

What You've Learned

- ☞ The importance of drawing scale
- ☞ How to calculate drawing scale and scale factor
- ☞ How to determine text size for a drawing
- ☞ How to estimate required sheet size for a drawing

Review Questions

True or False

32.01 T F Text height has no relation to drawing scale in AutoCAD.

32.02 T F Drawings usually are prepared in model space at full-size.

32.03 T F Model space is the primary environment you use to create a drawing.

32.04 T F Paper space is mainly used for composing a plot of a drawing to scale.

32.05 T F To plot text at 1/8 inch on a drawing plotted to scale at 1/4" = 1'-0", the text should be drawn at six inches.

32.06 T F Sheet size is dependent on drawing scale.

Multiple Choice

32.07 To plot text 3/16 inch at a scale of 1/2" = 1'-0", text height should be set to __________.

(A) 3 inches

(B) 4.5 inches

(C) 5 inches

(D) 6 inches

32.08 To plot text 1/8 inch at a scale of 1/4" = 1'-0", text height should be set to __________.

(A) 3 inches

(B) 4 inches

(C) 6 inches

(D) 9 inches

Student: ____________________ Date: __________

Instructor: ____________________ Course: __________ Section: __________

32.09 To plot text 1/8 inch at a scale of 10:1, text height should be set to __________.

(A) 1.25 inches

(B) .125 inch

(C) .0125 inch

(D) 12.5 inches

32.10 To plot text 1/4 inch at a scale of 1/4" = 1'-0", text height should be set to __________.

(A) 3 inches

(B) 6 inches

(C) 9 inches

(D) 12 inches

Student: ____________________ Date: __________

Instructor: ____________________ Course: __________ Section: __________

UNIT 33

Creating and Using Permanent Points

This unit discusses types of points that you can create in a drawing as entities just like lines, circles, and arcs. Point entities, once defined, become an integral part of the drawing. You can use the POINT command to create points in the drawing, and use these points as reference "markers." This unit teaches how to create points and control the way the points display.

The objectives for this unit are to:

- Understand permanent points
- Create point entities
- Control the display of points

Understanding Permanent Points

Although this unit refers to point entities created with the POINT command as *permanent points*, the points are no more permanent than any other AutoCAD entity. You can erase points, just as you can erase lines, circles, and other entities. The term *permanent points* is used to differentiate between point entities and points that you pick in the course of a command. When you pick a point in the LINE command, for example, you simply specify a coordinate for the endpoint of the line—you do not create a point entity. With the POINT command, however, you actually create an entity that by default appears as a dot on the display. When you save the drawing, any points created with the POINT command are saved with the drawing along with all the other entities.

You can issue the POINT command by choosing Draw, then Point. You also can enter **POINT** at the command prompt or choose POINT: from the DRAW screen menu. Regardless of which method you choose, you can enter points with the digitizer or the mouse and by using any coordinate method (absolute, relative, or polar). You can use point filters and object snap modes (explained next) when creating a point.

You can snap to a point entity using an object snap mode. *Object snap modes*, discussed in detail in units 36, "Using Temporary Object Snap Modes," and 37, "Using Permanent Object Snap Modes," enable you to snap the cursor to specific points on entities such as endpoints, midpoints, intersections of entities, and so on. The object snap mode associated with point entities is NODe. You learn how to use the NODe object snap mode later in this unit.

Although points display as a dot by default, you can change the way points appear on the display. Dots can be difficult to see, particularly in a complex drawing, so you often need to change point display mode. The PDMODE and DDPTYPE commands control the display of points. Because it offers a dialog box with graphic options (see fig. 33.1), the DDPTYPE command is easier to use than the PDMODE command. This unit focuses on the use of DDPTYPE to set point display mode.

In the following exercise, place a selection of points in the drawing using the POINT command. You also change the way the points display. When you issue the POINT command using the Draw pull-down menu, AutoCAD automatically continues to repeat the POINT command until you cancel it.

Entering Permanent Points

1. Begin a new drawing named 033???01 in your assigned directory using 033POINT.

2. `Command:` *Choose* Draw, *then* Point — Issues the POINT command

   `_point`

3. `Point:` *Pick a point at* 0.75,0.75 — Draws a point (see fig. 33.2)

   `Command: _point`

4. `Point:` *Pick a point at* 0.75,3.50 — Draws a point (see fig. 33.2)

   `Command: _point`

5. `Point:` *Pick a point at* 5.25,0.75 — Draws a point (see fig. 33.2)

   `Command: _point`

6. `Point:` *Press* Ctrl+C — Cancels the POINT command

   `*Cancel*`

7. `Command:` *Choose* Settings, *then* Point Style — Issues the DDPTYPE command and displays the Point Style dialog box

   `'ddptype`

8. *Choose the icon tile at* ① *(see fig 33.1), then choose* OK — Sets the PDMODE variable to change the way points display

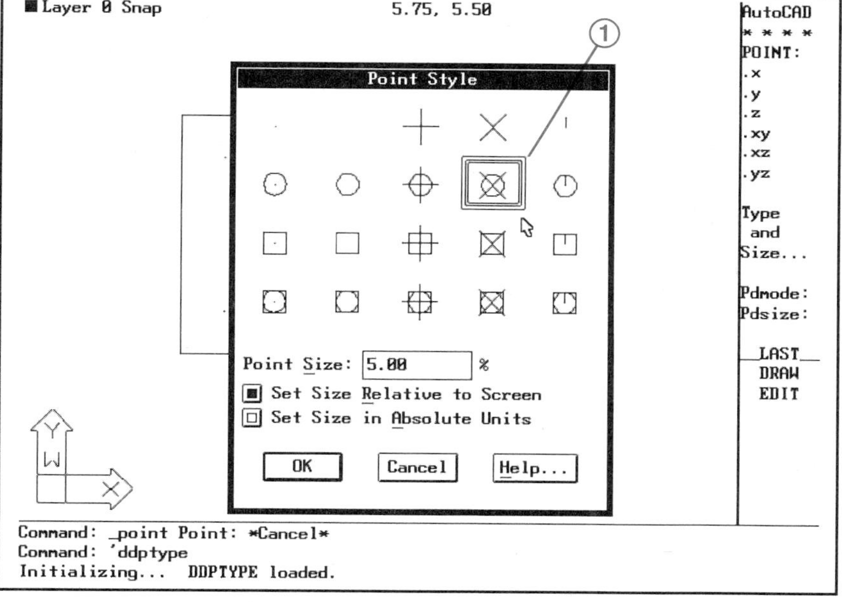

Figure 33.1

The Point Style dialog box.

9. `Command:` **`REGEN`** ↵ — Issues the REGEN command and regenerates the drawing

   `Regenerating drawing.`

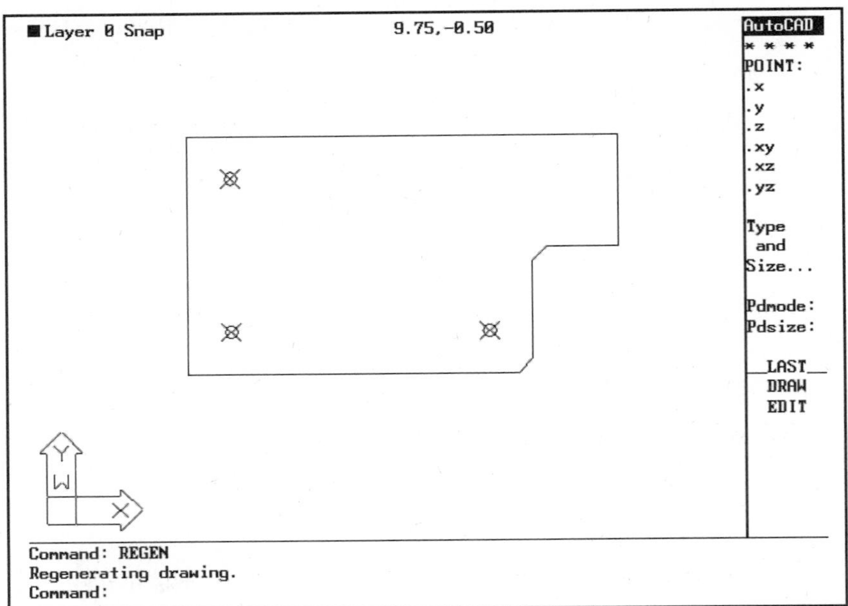

Figure 33.2
Points displayed with new style.

After the drawing regenerates, the display of points changes. New points that you add to the drawing are displayed with the current point display mode. Later in this unit, you learn to change the display of points in other ways.

Selecting Points

By themselves, points are not very useful. They are useful, however, as reference points for drawing other entities. To snap to a point entity, you can use the NODe object snap mode. This locks the point specification exactly to the coordinate of the point entity.

In the following exercise, draw lines between the points you created in the preceding exercise. Use the popup menu to select the NODe object snap mode. To display the popup menu when instructed to do so, press the button on the mouse or digitizer puck that displays the popup menu (which button depends on the configuration of your system).

Snapping to Points

Continue with your drawing from the preceding exercise.

1. `Command:` *Choose* Draw, *then* Line, *then* Segments — Issues the LINE command

   `_line`

2. `From point:` *From the popup menu, choose* Node *(see fig. 33.3)* — Sets NODe object snap mode

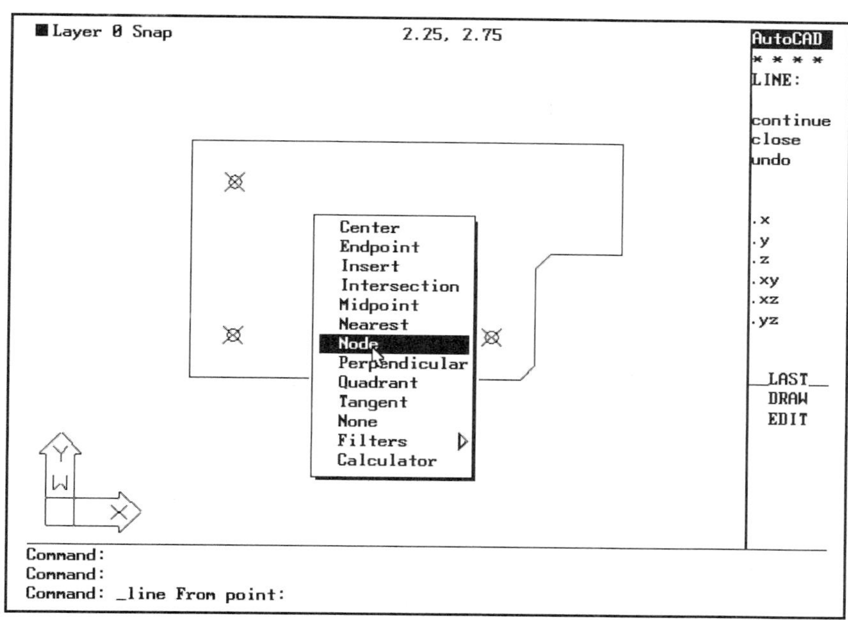

Figure 33.3

Node object snap mode selection in the popup menu.

3. _nod of *Select the point at* ① *(see fig. 33.4)* — Starts the line

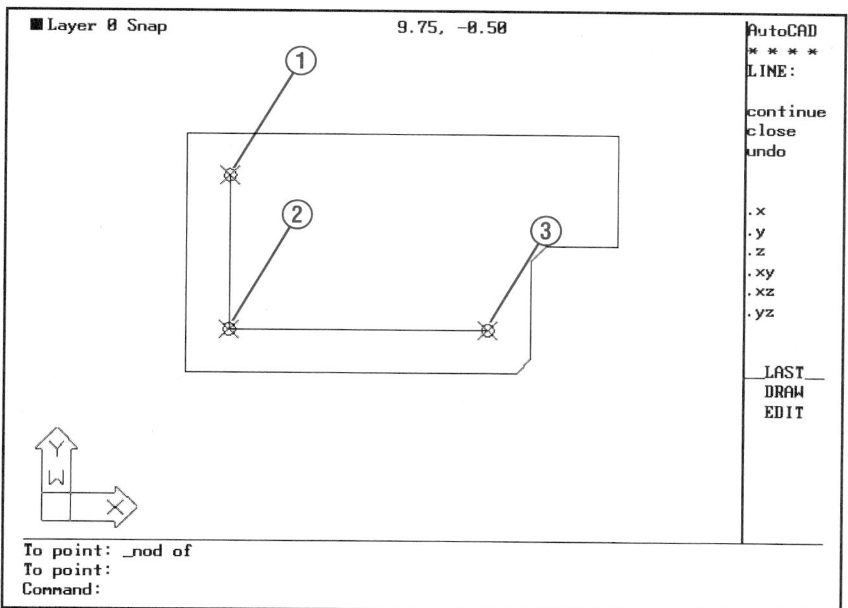

Figure 33.4

Lines drawn using NODe object snap mode.

4. To point: *From the popup menu, choose* Node

5. _nod of *Select the point at* ② *(see fig. 33.4)*

continues

6. `To point:` *From the popup menu, choose* Node	
7. `_nod of` *Select the point at* ③ *(see fig. 33.4)*	
8. `To point:` *Press* Enter	Ends the LINE command

Normally, you do not need to use point entities as references to draw other entities such as lines, circles, and so on. Point entities are useful when you want the points to remain after you draw other entities to them. They also are useful as reference points for creating dimensions without other entities. A drill plan drawing is a good example of the possible use of points—you can specify the drill hole locations with points, rather than with circles.

Changing the Size of Points

It sometimes can be difficult selecting points in a complex drawing, particularly when the points are close together or very near other entities. With the Point Style dialog box, you can change the relative size at which points display. You can make points display at a size relative to the screen size, which causes them to remain consistent in size as you zoom in and out of the drawing. You also can specify that the points display at a set unit size. This causes the points to change size as you zoom in and zoom out, but the point size remains proportional to the rest of the drawing.

The method you choose to display depends on personal preference and on whether you will be zooming the display in and out to select points. If you want the points to always remain the same size, even when you zoom out to a reduced view of the drawing, size points relative to the screen. To keep the points consistent in size with the rest of the drawing, set points to a specific unit size.

In the following exercise, change point display size, and then regenerate the drawing to see the change.

Changing Size of Points

Continue with your drawing from the preceding exercise.

1. `Command:` *Choose* Settings, *then* Point Style	Issues the DDPTYPE command and displays the Point Style dialog box
2. *Choose the* Set Size in Absolute Units *radio button*	Sets points to display using unit size
3. *Type* **1** *in the* Point Size *edit box, then choose* OK	Sets point size to 1 unit

4. `Command:` **`REGEN`** ↵	Issues the REGEN command and regenerates the drawing
`Regenerating drawing.`	

Your drawing should look similar to figure 33.5.

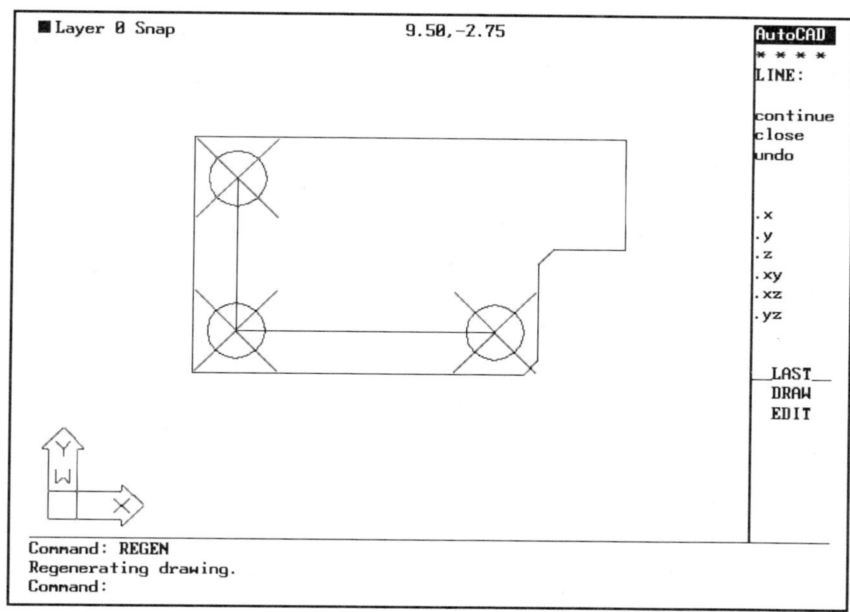

Figure 33.5

Point size changed to one unit.

The point size is now one unit. If you turn on coordinate display and use the cursor to estimate the size of the point, you find that it is one inch in diameter.

You also can change the point style by using the PDMODE command if you know the number of the style. The dot is number zero, and the cross is number two. You can use the PDSIZE command to change the size of points from the command prompt. Because it is difficult to remember the value for each point style, however, it is easier to use the Point Style dialog box to set the point style and size.

Unit Review

What You've Learned

- Commands: DDPTYPE, PDMODE
- The difference between point entities and coordinate points
- How to create point entities
- How to change sizes of points
- How to change point styles
- How to use the NODe object snap mode

Review Questions

True or False

33.01 T F Point entities are the same as coordinate points.

33.02 T F Point entities can be drawn using the absolute coordinate system.

33.03 T F Point sizes can be changed at the command prompt.

33.04 T F Point styles can be changed at the command prompt.

33.05 T F Points become a permanent part of the drawing, but can be erased like other entities.

33.06 T F Each time you draw a line, a point entity also is created at each end of the line.

Multiple Choice

33.07 If you draw several points, change point size, and then regenerate the drawing, the points will __________.

(A) remain the same size

(B) change size to current size entered

(C) disappear

(D) change styles

Student: ____________________ Date: __________

Instructor: ____________________ Course: __________ Section: __________

33.08 Which of the following commands provides a dialog box you can use to select point styles? __________

(A) PDMODE

(B) PDSIZE

(C) DDPTYPE

(D) DDSTYLE

Short Answer

33.09 Explain how point entities are different from coordinates you pick with the cursor when drawing other entities.

____

____

____

33.10 What happens to existing points when you change the current point style, and then regenerate the drawing?

____

____

____

Student: ______________________ Date: __________

Instructor: ______________ Course: __________ Section: ______

UNIT 34

Setting and Using a Grid

Whether you are working with paper drawings or with CAD drawings, drawing on a grid gives you a sense of the size and relationship of the elements in a drawing. The grid assists you in placing lines and other entities accurately on-screen, much like the translucent blue grid lines on engineering paper used with manual drafting methods. This unit teaches you to use AutoCAD's GRID command and options to set up and use an electronic grid when you prepare drawings.

The objectives for this unit are to:

- Understand the function of the grid
- Recognize how the grid provides organization to a drawing
- Locate the grid-related commands in AutoCAD's menus
- Set and use a grid

Setting and Using a Grid

AutoCAD's GRID command enables you to set a rectangular pattern of small dots to any desired spacing on-screen (see fig. 34.1). As you zoom in and out of the drawing, the relationship between the grid points changes because the grid spacing remains constantly associated with the drawings units, not with the drawing area. The grid can be arranged with different X and Y spacing increments, and you can also define an isometric grid.

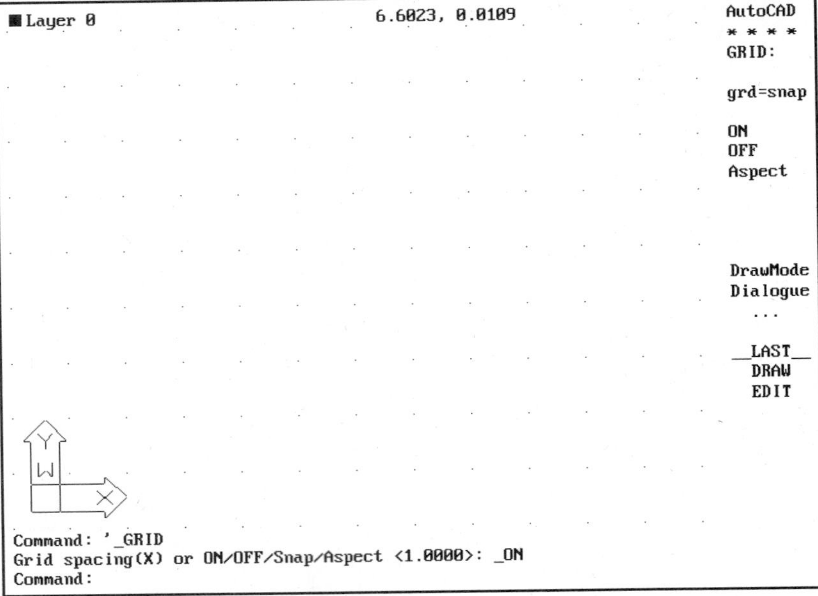

Figure 34.1

A 1" grid displayed in the drawing area.

As figure 34.2 shows, the grid is placed only within the limits of the drawing (drawing limits are explained in unit 31). The grid is not part of the drawing, nor is it ever plotted or erased (see fig. 34.3). The grid also does not control input points. You cannot automatically snap to a grid point, for example, because AutoCAD does not recognize grid points. In this way, the grid is like a transparent overlay on your drawing.

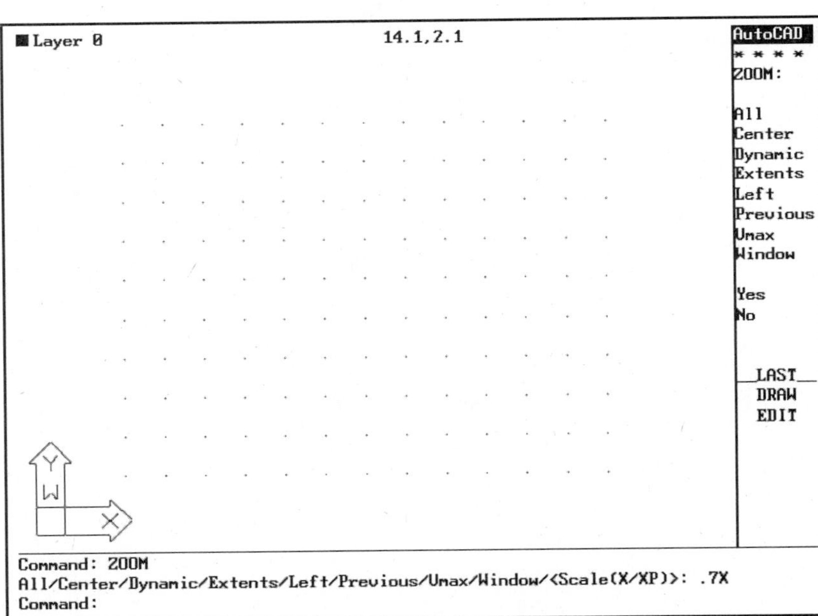

Figure 34.2

Screen zoomed out showing that the grid stops at the defined limits.

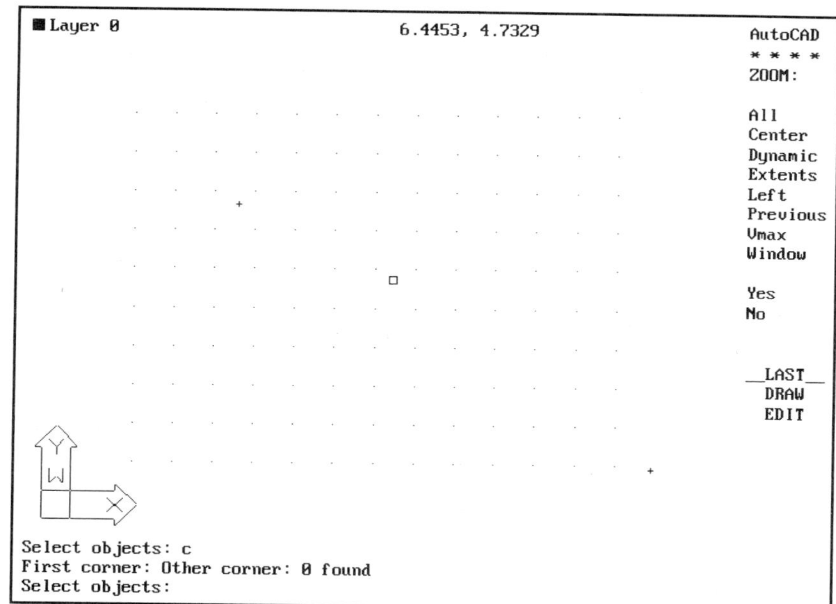

Figure 34.3

Screen showing that grid points cannot be erased.

You can set up a grid by using the GRID command at the `Command:` prompt or the Drawing Aids dialog box. Entering **`GRID`** at the `Command:` prompt starts the GRID command and displays the prompt:

```
Grid spacing(X) or ON/OFF/Snap/Aspect<0.00">:
```

GRID command options include:

- **Grid spacing (X).** The grid spacing is the default option. This option numerically sets X and Y drawing grid unit increments and activates the grid. By setting the grid to 0, AutoCAD makes the grid equal to the snap increment (see Unit 35), changing automatically as the snap value changes. The value may be set to a multiple of the snap increment by entering a numeric value followed by an X. You can set snap to .25, for example, and set grid spacing to 4X. With these settings, AutoCAD will display a 1" grid.
- **ON.** This option activates the grid, using the current grid unit increment setting(s).
- **OFF.** This option deactivates the grid and removes the grid points from the screen.
- **Snap.** This option locks the grid points to the snap increments. It is the same as setting the grid increment to 0. If the snap increment is changed, the grid will change automatically to match.
- **Aspect.** This option enables you to set a grid with differing X and Y grid increments on-screen (see fig. 34.4).

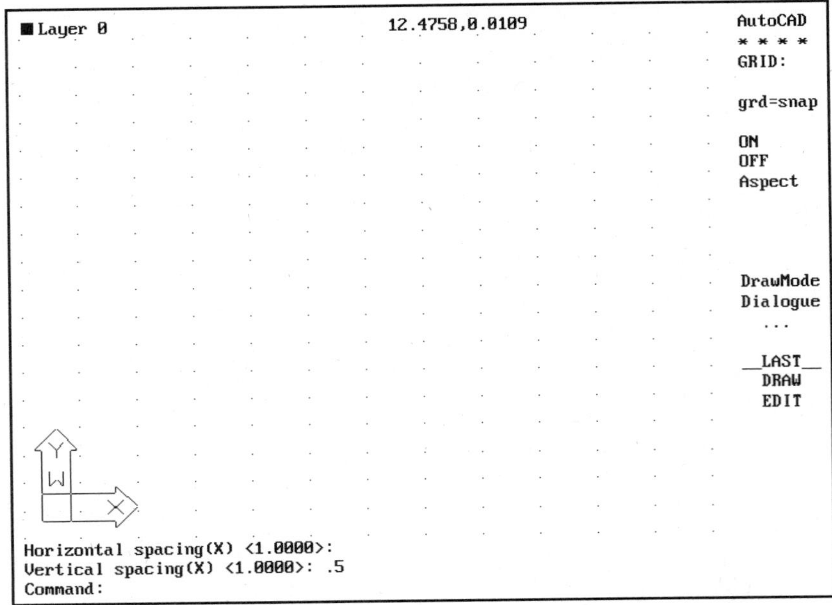

Figure 34.4

Screen showing differing X and Y grid increments.

In addition to using the GRID command and Drawing Aids dialog box to turn the grid on and off, you also can use the F7 function key on the keyboard.

Setting Up a Grid

When you are working on a drawing in which entities are drawn to a given spacing, it is often useful to set the grid to the required spacing, turn on the grid, and use the grid as a guide to place the entities.

In the next exercise, experiment with setting a grid using the Drawing Aids dialog box.

Setting Up a Drawing Grid

1. Begin a new drawing named 034???01 in your assigned directory, using 034GRID as the prototype. Your grid should be set to 1" increments in both the X axis and Y axis.

2. `Command:` *Choose* Settings, *then* Drawing Aids	Displays the Drawing Aids dialog box (see fig. 34.5)
3. *Clear the* On *check box, then choose* OK	Turns off the grid
4. `Command:` *Choose* Settings, *then* Drawing Aids	Displays the Drawing Aids dialog box

5. *Check the* On *check box* — Causes the grid to be turned on after you exit the dialog box
6. *Double-click in the* X Spacing *edit box, type* **0.5**, *then press* Enter — Sets the X and Y grid spacing to .5"
7. *Choose* OK — Displays grid changes
8. `Command:` *Press* F7, *then press* F7 *again* — Turns off the grid, then turns the grid back on

`<Grid off>  <Grid on>`

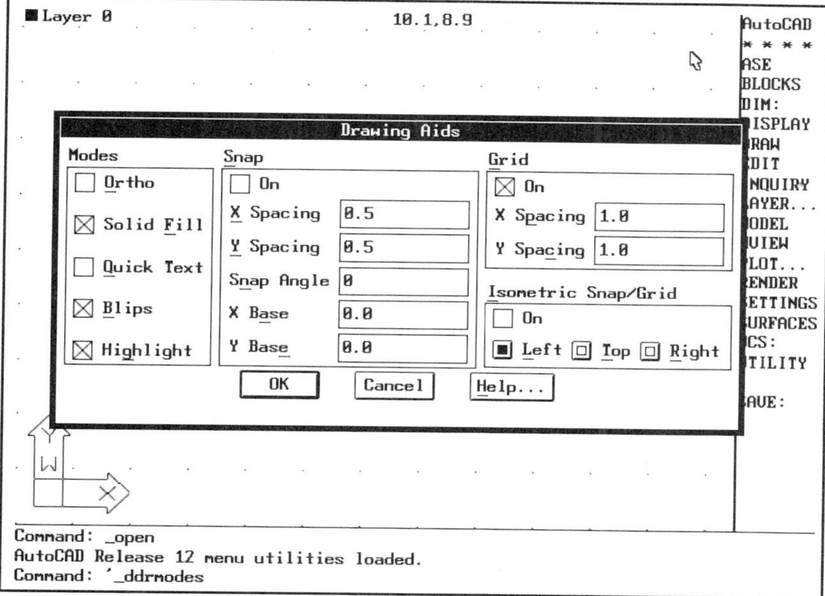

Figure 34.5

The Drawing Aids dialog box.

The F7 function key can be used as a quick way to redraw the screen without using the REDRAW command.

Using a Grid

The use of a grid does not cause accurate point selection, but instead enables you to estimate distances quickly and visually. A grid simply provides a visual frame of reference by which you can estimate distances in the drawing. In the following exercise, set your grid to 1" and draw a rectangle that is approximately 6" wide and 4" high. Do not worry about picking exact points—just use the grid as a visual guide to draw the rectangle.

Working with a Grid

Continue with your drawing from the previous exercise.

1. `Command:` *Choose* Settings, *then* Drawing Aids — Displays the Drawing Aids dialog box
2. *Double-click in the* X Spacing *edit box, type* **1**, *then press* Enter — Sets the X and Y axis spacing to 1"
3. *Choose* OK — Closes the Drawing Aids dialog box
4. `Command:` *Choose* Draw, *then* Rectangle — Starts the RECTANG command

   `rectang`
5. `First corner:` *Pick a point near* ① *(see fig. 34.6)* — Specifies lower left corner of the rectangle
6. `Other corner:` *Pick a point near* ② — Specifies the upper right corner and draws the rectangle

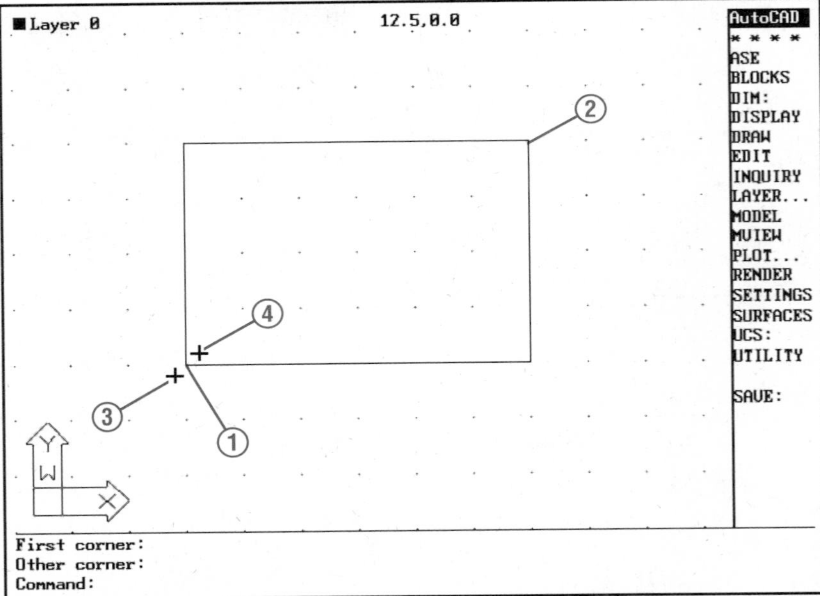

Figure 34.6

A rectangle drawn using grid points as a reference.

Next, zoom in on the lower left corner of the rectangle to see how accurate your point selection was in relation to the grid.

Checking Your Accuracy

1. `Command:` *Choose* View, *then* Zoom, *then* Window — Starts the ZOOM command with the Window option

   ```
   ZOOM
   All/Center/Dynamic/Extents/Left/
   Previous/Vmax/Window/<Scale(X/XP)>:
   _window
   ```

2. `First corner:` *Pick a point at* ③ *(see fig. 34.6), very close to the corner of the rectangle* — Specifies the first corner of the zoom window

3. `Other corner:` *Pick a point at* ④ *(see fig. 34.6), very close to the corner of the rectangle* — Specifies the second corner of the zoom window and zooms in

You should find that the corner of your rectangle does not fall exactly on the grid point (see fig. 34.7).

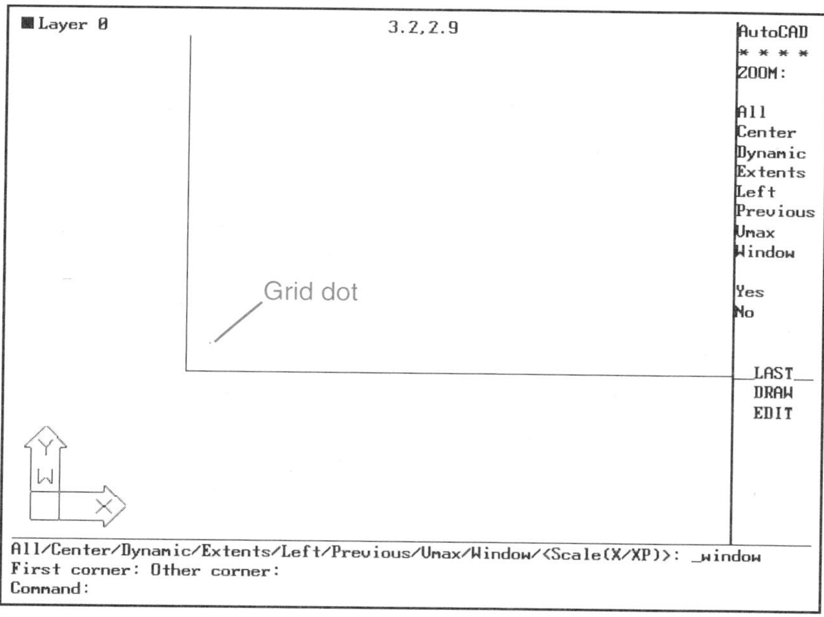

Figure 34.7
Picking does not snap exactly to the grid point.

You can accurately pick a grid point only if you use another command called SNAP in conjunction with the grid. SNAP, which is explained in unit 35. SNAP causes the cursor to *snap* to a specific increment that you specify. If the snap spacing is a multiple of the grid space, or vice versa, you can accurately pick a grid point. A multiple of the grid space, or vice versa, you can accurately pick a grid point. Grid points by themselves, however, are useful only as a visual estimating device.

Setting Grid Options

As mentioned earlier in this unit, you can set unequal X and Y grid spacing, set up an isometric grid, and set the grid equal to the current snap increment. You can set these options either using the GRID command or through the Drawing Aids dialog box. In the following exercise, set the X and Y spacing to different values, then experiment with the Snap option.

Working with Grid Options

Continue with your drawing from the previous exercise.

1. `Command:` *Choose* Settings, *then* Drawing Aids	Displays the Drawing Aids dialog box
2. *Double-click in the* X Spacing *edit box, then enter* **`0.5`**	Sets grid X and Y value to be equal
3. *Double-click in the* Y Spacing *edit box, then enter* **`1.0`**	Sets the Y grid spacing to 1"
4. *Choose* OK	Closes the dialog box and displays grid changes
5. `Command:` **`GRID`** ↵	Starts the GRID command
6. `Grid spacing(X) or ON/OFF/Snap/ Aspect<A>:` **`S`** ↵	Sets the grid spacing equal to the current snap increment

Notice that the screen shows your grid displayed at the last snap setting.

7. `Command:` **`SNAP`** ↵	
8. `Snap spacing/ON/OFF/Aspect/ Rotate/Style <1.000>:` **`0.25`** ↵	Sets new snap spacing

The grid spacing changes to reflect the new snap spacing.

The use of an isometric grid is explained in unit 98.

Unit Review

What You've Learned

- ☞ How you can use grid to estimate distances visually in a drawing
- ☞ How to use the Drawing Aids dialog box to specify the grid spacing
- ☞ How to control grid visibility by turning the grid on and off
- ☞ The effect on the grid when the snap increment spacing is changed

Review Questions

True or False

34.01 T F You must make your grid spacing equal to the snap spacing.

34.02 T F Snap must be on for the grid to display.

34.03 T F The DDRMODES command can used to display the Drawing Aids dialog box.

34.04 T F The GRID command includes an option that enables you to set your grid to the current snap spacing in the drawing.

34.05 T F X and Y grid spacing increments can be set to different values.

Multiple Choice

34.06 Which of the following turns the grid on and off? ________

(A) Freeze

(B) F1

(C) F7

(D) None of the above

34.07 Which of the following is not a grid option? __________

(A) ON

(B) OFF

(C) Snap

(D) Rotated

Student: ______________________ Date: __________

Instructor: ______________________ Course: __________ Section: __________

Short Answer

Answer the following questions.

34.08 Aside from the F7 function key, what is another way to turn the grid on and off?

____

____

____

34.09 Why would you want to set the grid increment spacing different from the snap increment spacing?

____

____

____

34.10 Why are grid points useful as a visual tool?

____

____

____

Student: ______________ Date: ______________

Instructor: ______________ Course: ______________ Section: ______________

UNIT 35

Using a Snap Increment

One of the most useful tools AutoCAD offers to simplify the task of preparing accurate drawings is the *snap increment.* You can set a snap increment and force the cursor to move only by the specified increment. This causes the cursor to "snap" to a specific spacing. By using this snap increment, you can draw entities at specific points and specify lengths simply by picking points. You do not have to enter coordinates. This unit explains the use of snap and helps you understand how snap can be an effective drawing aid.

The objectives for this unit are to:

- Understand the purpose of setting and using a snap increment
- Use SNAP to control snap
- Use the Drawing Aids dialog box to control snap

Understanding Snap

Setting a snap increment and turning on snap forces the cursor to move in specific increments. If snap is set to 0.25", for example, you can quickly draw a line that is 1.25 inches long—just pick a point, move the cursor five snap increments to the right, and then pick another point. You can draw other entities if their defining points correspond to the current snap increment. Snap is like having an automatic ruler that you can use to measure and draw.

You can set the snap increment to any value that fits your needs at the time. You might set snap to many different values during the course of editing a drawing. You might set snap to one inch to draw large features, for example, and then set snap to 0.1" to draw smaller features.

AutoCAD's SNAP command enables you to set the current snap increment and control snap in other ways. When you issue the SNAP command, it displays the following prompt:

```
Snap spacing or ON/OFF/Aspect/Rotate/Style <1.000">:
```

The SNAP command options perform the following functions:

- **Snap spacing.** This default option sets the snap spacing equally for the X and Y axis. You can specify any positive value.
- **ON.** This option activates snap, using the current snap unit increment setting(s).
- **OFF.** This option deactivates snap and allows the crosshairs free movement on the screen.
- **Aspect.** This option enables you to set a snap with differing X and Y axes increments. This option is not available if you are using isometric snap (see the Style option).
- **Rotate.** This option rotates the snap increments in the XY plane. If the snap rotation is changed, the crosshairs change automatically to match the snap orientation. This option is very useful when you need to draw using a specific spacing at angles other than 0 degrees or 90 degrees.
- **Style.** This option provides two choices of snap, either Standard or Isometric. Standard is the default with regular X and Y grid spacing (in which X and Y can be set to different spacing). Isometric snap provides snap increments aligned at 30 degrees off of the horizontal for use in preparing isometric drawings. The axes, crosshairs, grid, and orthographic mode are affected by the Isometric format.

In addition to using the SNAP command to set snap spacing, you can use the DDRMODES command. The DDRMODES command displays the Drawing Aids dialog box shown in figure 35.1. Setting snap with the Drawing Aids dialog box is useful when you also need to set other drawing options.

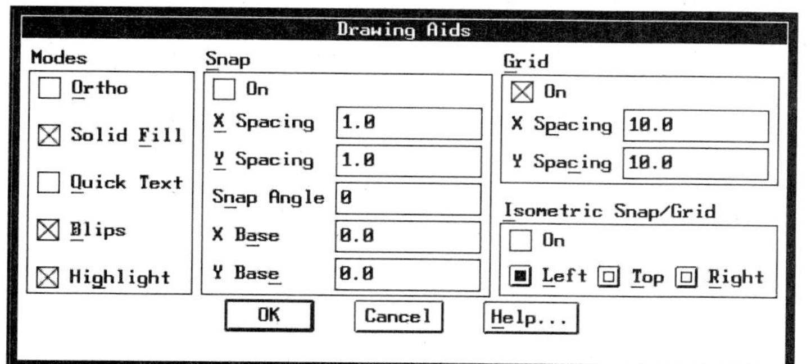

Figure 35.1

The Drawing Aids dialog box.

You can turn SNAP on and off by pressing the F9 function key. If SNAP is on, pressing F9 turns it off. If SNAP is off, pressing F9 turns it on. Pressing Ctrl-B has the same effect as pressing F9.

It is important to understand that the snap increment has no relationship at all to the grid. You can set the snap spacing to match the grid points, but you also can set the snap increment so that the cursor snaps to points other than grid points. If the grid is active but SNAP is turned off, picking a grid point does not place a point exactly at that grid point's coordinate.

Setting and Using a Snap Increment

As explained earlier, you can set the snap increment to any positive value. As you work on a drawing, you can change the snap increment to suit your current needs. When you begin a new drawing, examine the distances and points involved in the drawing. Set SNAP to a spacing that enables you to easily lay out the main features of the drawing. Then, change the snap increment as required as you work with other portions of the drawing.

In the following exercises, lay out the outline of a simple part by using a snap increment. Figure 35.2 shows the part and its overall dimensions. You lay out the entire part without entering any coordinates, lengths, or relative coordinates. First, set the snap increment.

Setting the Snap Increment

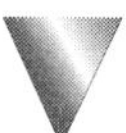

1. Begin a new drawing named 035???01 in your assigned directory using 035SNAP as a prototype.

   Move the cursor and note that it moves freely; it does not snap to grid points.

continues

2. `Command:` *Choose* Settings, *then* Drawing Aids — Issues the DDRMODES command and displays the Drawing Aids dialog box

3. *In the Snap group, place a check in the* On *check box* — Turns on SNAP

4. *Double-click in the* X Spacing *edit box, then enter* **`10`** — Sets snap increment for X and Y axes to 10mm

5. *Choose* OK — Closes the Drawing Aids dialog box

Move the cursor and notice that it snaps to ten millimeter increments, which correspond to the grid points. Also notice that the coordinate display in the status line displays coordinates using the snap increment.

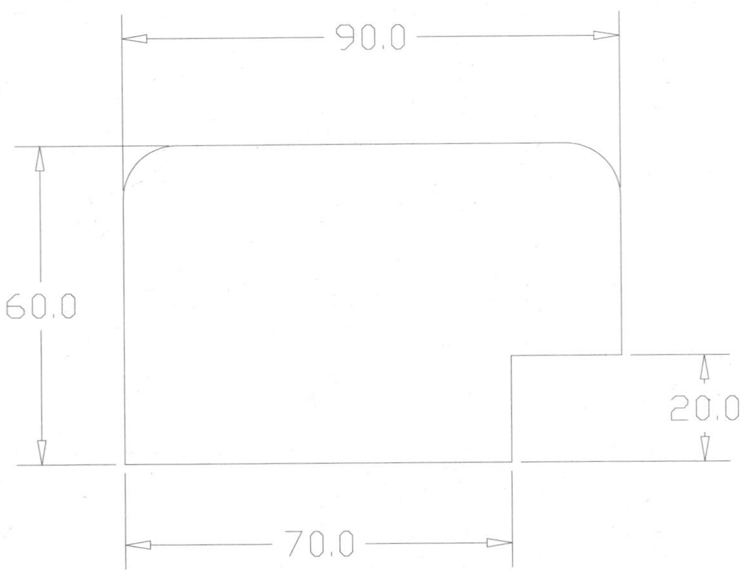

Figure 35.2
Overall dimensions of a single part.

Now that you have set the snap increment to ten units, you can quickly lay out the outline of the part. Use the dimensions shown in figure 35.2 and the following exercise to lay out the part as a polyline.

Using a Snap Increment

Continue with your drawing from the preceding exercise.

1. `Command:` *Choose* Draw, *then* Polyline, *then* 2D — Issues the PLINE command

   `_pline`

2. `From point:` *Pick a point at* 20.0,20.0 *using the coordinate display as a guide* — Specifies the starting point of the polyline

   `Current line-width is 0.0`

3. `Arc/Close/Halfwidth/Length/Undo/Width/<Endpoint of line>:` *Press* F6 *twice to turn on relative coordinate display mode, then draw the outline of the part using polyline and polyarc segments* — Draws the outline of the part (see fig. 35.3)

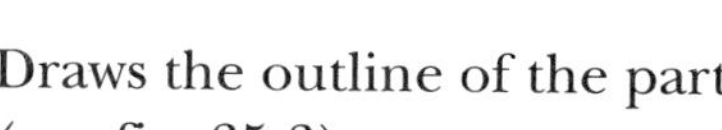

4. Save your drawing.

Your drawing should look similar to figure 35.3.

You now need to set the snap increment to a smaller spacing to draw some of the inner features on the part. Zoom in on the part, set snap increment to 1mm, and then draw the two circles shown in figure 35.4.

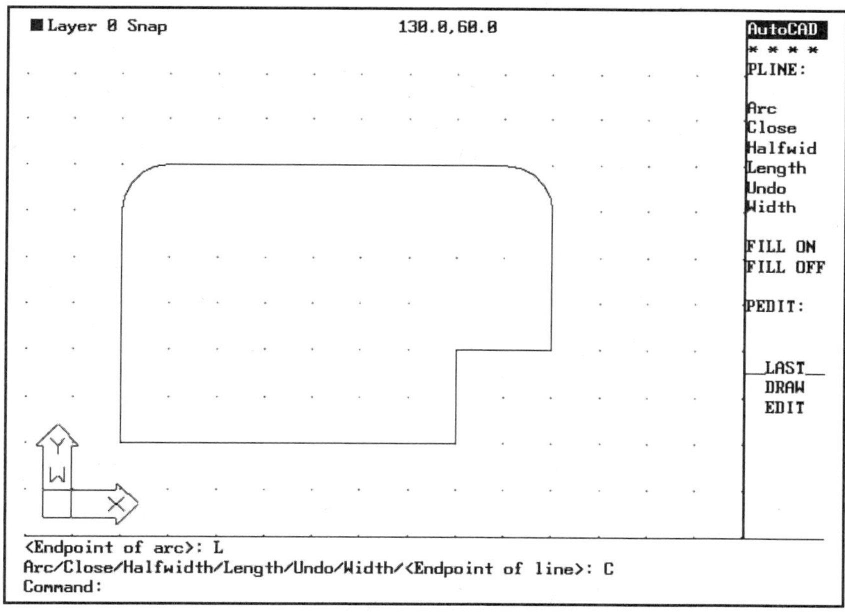

Figure 35.3

The outline of part.

Resetting the Snap Increment

Continue with your drawing from the preceding exercise.

1. `Command:` *Choose* Settings, *then* Drawing Aids — Issues the DDRMODES command and displays the Drawing Aids dialog box

continues

2. *Double-click in the* X Spacing *edit box and enter* **1**	Sets snap increment for X and Y axes to 1 unit
3. *Choose* OK	Closes the dialog box
4. `Command:` *Choose* Draw, *then* Circle, *then* Center, Radius	Issues the CIRCLE command
`_circle`	
5. `3P/2P/TTR/<Center point>:` *Use the coordinate display to locate the center of circle* ① *(see fig. 35.4)*	Specifies the center of the circle 5mm to the right and 5mm above point ②
6. `Diameter/<Radius>:` *Pick a point to specify a 3mm radius*	Defines the radius and draws the circle

7. Repeat the CIRCLE command and draw circle ③ 6 mm to the left and 6 mm above point ④. Specify a radius of 3 mm for the circle.

8. Save your drawing.

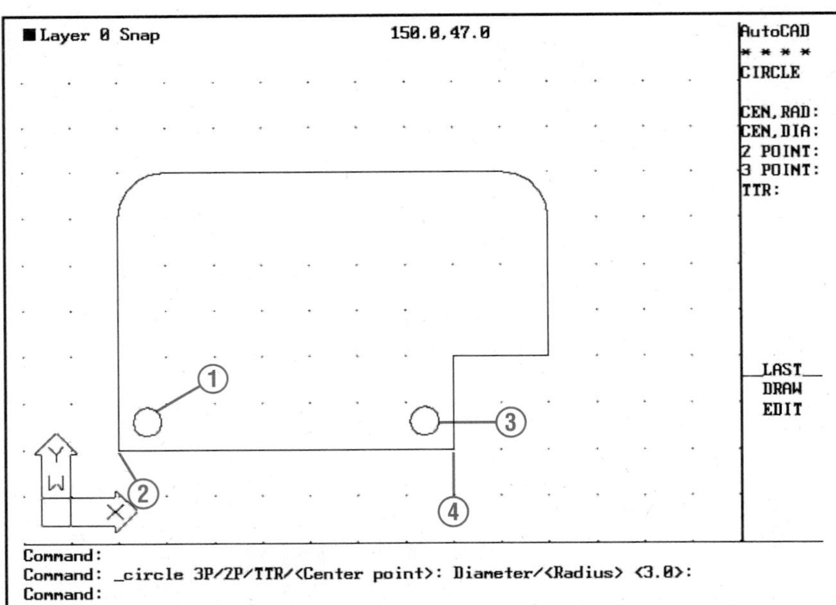

Figure 35.4
Holes added to the part.

It is generally useful to set the grid spacing to a multiple of the snap increment. In the previous exercise, for example, the grid is set to ten, and snap is set to one. If you are drawing in inches, you might set grid to 1" and snap to

.125", or use some other combination that fits the requirements of the drawing. You can use the grid as a visual guide and use the snap increment as a guide to pick exacts points.

You can set the Y axis snap increment different from the X axis snap increment. Doing so causes the cursor to move in different increments along the Y axis than along the X axis. To set the Y increment different from the X increment in the Drawing Aids dialog box, first set X Spacing, and then set Y Spacing. To change the aspect with the SNAP command, use the Aspect option.

Changing the Snap Angle

Occasionally, features in a drawing do not lie along the X or Y axis, but instead are aligned at an angle to one of the two axes. You can rotate the snap angle and move the snap base point to draw features at the necessary angle without using coordinates, just as you can with the normal snap orientation. You can set the snap angle and base point with the SNAP command by using the Rotate option. Or, you can specify the base point and rotation angle in the Drawing Aids dialog box. The base point helps you set up the snap increment to align with the features you are trying to draw.

In the following exercise, draw the slot shown in figure 35.5. Rotate the snap angle and move the base point to the center of the bottom arc. Use the coordinate display as a guide to help you draw the slot to the correct dimensions.

Changing Snap Angle

Continue with your drawing from the preceding exercise.

1. `Command:` **`SNAP`** ↵	Issues the SNAP command
2. `Snap spacing or ON/OFF/Aspect/ Rotate/Style <1.0>:` **`5`** ↵	Sets new snap increment
3. `Command:` *Press* Enter	Repeats previous command
`SNAP`	
4. `Snap spacing or ON/OFF/Aspect/ Rotate/Style <1.0>:` **`R`** ↵	Specifies the Rotate option
5. `Base point <0.0,0.0>:` **`50,40`** ↵	Specifies base point for snap axis orientation

continues

6. `Rotation angle <0>:` **`45`** ↵
7. `Command:` *Choose* Draw, *then* Arc, *then* Cen, Start, End — Issues the ARC command for Center, Start, End method

   `_arc`
8. `Center/<Start point>:` **`_c`**
9. `Center:` *Pick a point at* 50.0,40.0 — Specifies center of the arc
10. Draw the arc with a radius of 5 mm by picking a point above the center (along the Y snap axis), and then picking a point 5 mm below the center (along the Y snap axis).
11. Use the LINE and ARC commands to complete the slot according to the dimensions given in figure 35.5.
12. Save your drawing.

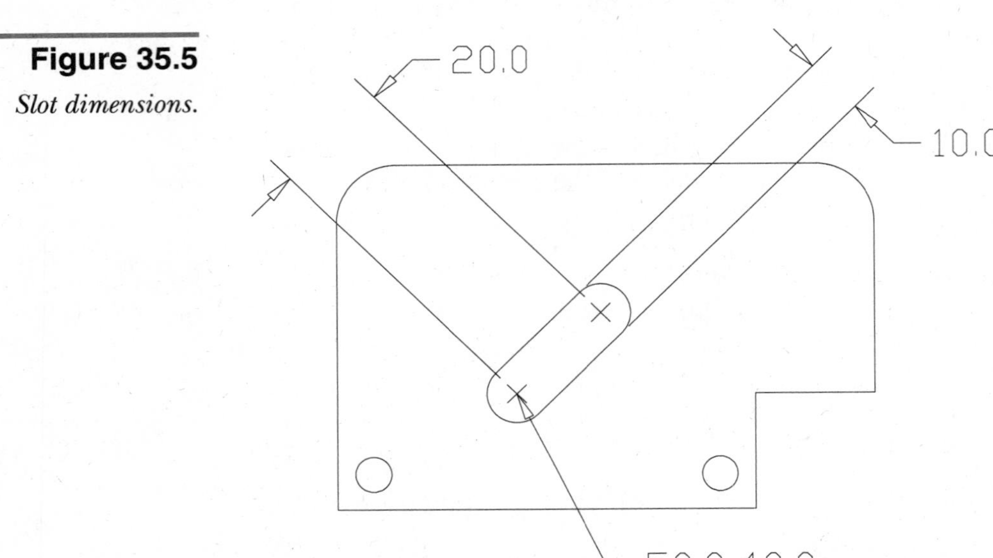

Figure 35.5

Slot dimensions.

Setting the snap base is an important part of using a rotated snap. Setting the snap base makes it possible for you to align the X and Y snap axes with a specific point on the rotated feature that you are trying to draw.

Snap does not have to be turned on for the snap angle to be effective. If you set the snap rotation other than zero, and then turn off snap, the cursor still is rotated according to the snap rotation value. The cursor angle does not return to zero until you set the snap angle to zero.

Using Ortho Mode

Snap can be a useful tool to help you draw horizontal and vertical lines. AutoCAD provides another tool called *ortho mode* that helps you draw straight lines. Ortho mode constrains the rubberband line on the cursor to 90-degree movement when you are picking points. The F8 function key turns ortho mode on and off.

The easiest way to understand ortho mode is to use it. In the following exercise, return the snap angle to zero. Then use ortho mode to draw a punched rectangular slot on the part.

Using Ortho Mode

Continue with your drawing from the preceding exercise.

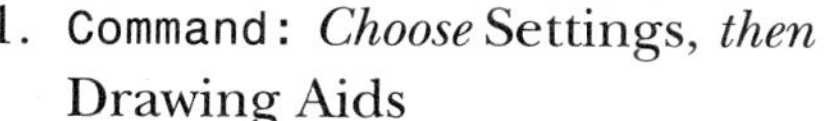

1. `Command:` *Choose* Settings, *then* Drawing Aids	Issues the DDRMODES command and displays the Drawing Aids dialog box
2. *Set* Snap Angle, X Base, and Y Base *to* 0, *then choose* OK	Sets rotation to zero and restores the original snap base point
3. `Command:` *Choose* Draw, *then* Line, *then* Segments	Issues the LINE command
4. `_line From point:` *Pick a point at* 90.0,50.0	Specifies start of line
5. `To point:` *Press* F8	Turns on ortho mode

`<Ortho on>`

Move the cursor and notice that the rubberband line attached to the cursor is constrained to 90-degree movement.

6. `To point:` *Locate the cursor at any point where the coordinate display reads* 10.0<0, *then pick a point*	Draws the bottom line of the slot

Continue drawing the slot. It is 10 mm wide and 20 mm high.

7. Save your drawing.

In many situations, snap duplicates the function of ortho mode. Ortho mode is particularly useful for picking points horizontally or vertically aligned with one another when snap is off. If you need to move an object directly horizontally or vertically, for example, you can pick the base point, turn on ortho mode, and pick virtually any point; and the object moves only horizontally or vertically. You use ortho mode in later units.

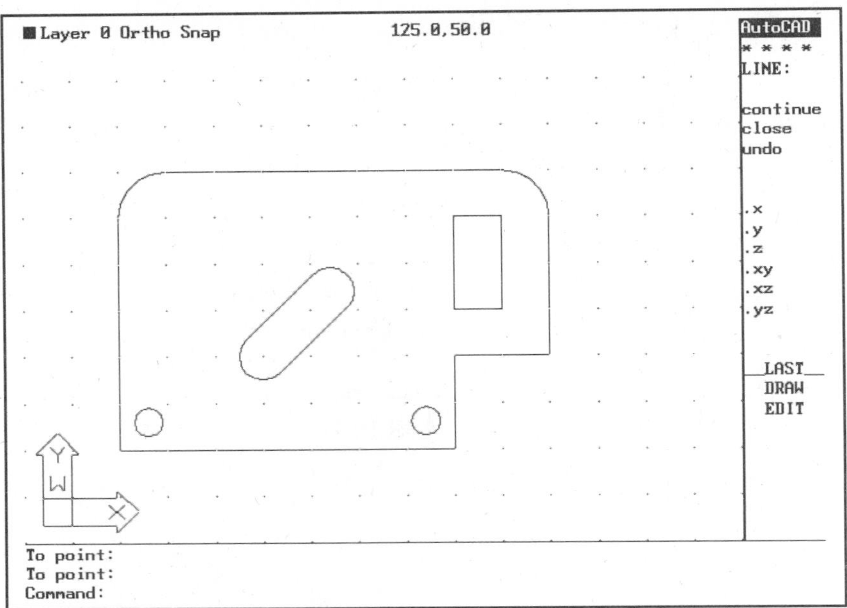

Figure 35.6

Rectangular slot created with ortho mode.

The exercises in unit 36, "Using Temporary Object Snap Modes," assume that you will be using the popup menu to choose object snap modes. If you are using a digitizer and stylus, you can select object snap modes from the digitizer menu instead.

Unit Review

What You've Learned

- Commands: SNAP, DDRMODES
- How you can use snap for uniform spacing and accuracy when picking points
- How to use the Drawing Aids dialog box to specify the snap spacing and other options
- How to control snap with the SNAP command
- How to rotate the snap angle and relocate the snap base point
- How ortho mode constrains point selection to right angles

Review Questions

True or False

35.01 T F The grid cannot be active if the snap angle is set to a value other than zero.

35.02 T F The cursor will only be rotated from its normal orientation if snap is on.

35.03 T F The Rotate option enables you to rotate the snap angle.

35.04 T F The X and Y snap increments can be set to different values.

35.05 T F Snap can be turned on and off by pressing CTRL-B.

Multiple Choice

35.06 Which function key turns snap on and off? __________

(A) F9

(B) F6

(C) F8

(D) None of the above

Student: ______________________ Date: __________

Instructor: ______________________ Course: __________ Section: __________

35.07 How must the grid spacing relate to the snap increment?

____

(A) It must be larger

(B) It must be smaller

(C) It must be equal

(D) There is no relation between grid and snap spacing

35.08 Which of the following sets different X and Y snap axes increments?

(A) ON

(B) Aspect

(C) Style

(D) Rotated

Short Answer

35.09 Briefly explain how snap can speed up the drawing process.

____

____

____

35.10 Briefly explain why the snap base point is important when you use a snap rotation value other than zero.

____

____

____

Student: ______________ Date: ______________

Instructor: ______________ Course: ______________ Section: ______________

UNIT 36

Using Temporary Object Snap Modes

AutoCAD enables you to create extremely accurate drawings with a minimum of effort and time. Along with the coordinate, grip, and snap features discussed in other units, AutoCAD provides *object snap modes,* which allow you to pick specific points on an entity, such as the entity's endpoint or midpoint. Object snap modes are either temporary or permanent (you can have them continually active and then deactivate any or all of them at any time); this unit focuses on temporary object snap modes. The next unit covers permanent object snap modes.

The objectives for this unit are to:

- Understand entity snap points
- Understand temporary object snap modes
- Use temporary object snap modes to improve speed and accuracy

Understanding Entity Points and Object Snap

Before learning to use object snap modes, you need to learn about the objects on which you use object snap modes. You may recall from unit 10 that AutoCAD stores entity data in the form of vectors that define the entity. AutoCAD stores entities in this way so that AutoCAD can perform calculations based on the vector information to produce endpoints, midpoints, intersections, center points and other geometric information. Object snap modes allow you to select these exact points when drafting. Selecting a specific point is called "snapping to a point," and thus the name object snap modes.

Figure 36.1 shows the most common graphics entities and their potential snap points. Note that the snap points are the same as the grip mode edit points discussed in unit 22.

Figure 36.1

Entities and their object snap points.

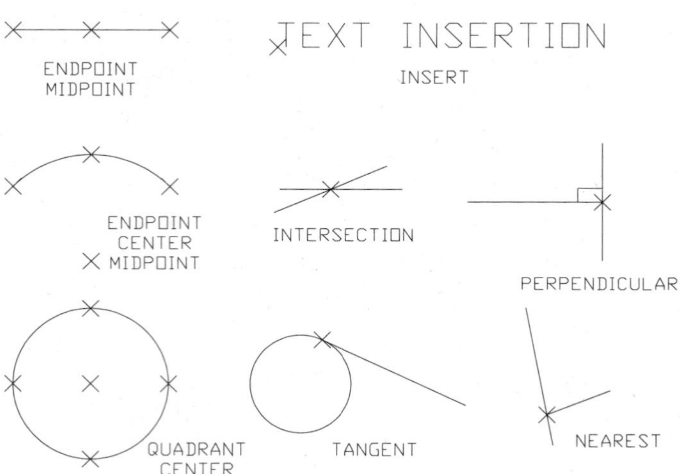

Now that you know what and where snap points are, you can learn about each of the object snap modes. Each object snap can be abbreviated to its first three letters. In this list, which shows you each of the object snap modes and explains the services they provide, the first three letters are capitalized to show you the abbreviations (the letters in uppercase are the only letters you need to type!):

- **CENter.** Snaps to the center of a selected arc or circle.
- **ENDpoint.** Snaps to the closest endpoint of a selected line or arc or the closest corner of a selected trace, solid, or 3D face.
- **INSert.** Snaps to the insertion point of a selected text, block, shape, or attribute.
- **INTersection.** Snaps to the closest intersection of any combination of lines, polylines, arcs, and circles, or to the nearest corner of a trace, solid, or 3D face. For an intersection to work, the entities must intersect in three-dimensional space. The intersection must be inside the aperture box.
- **MIDpoint.** Snaps to a point halfway along a selected line or arc, or to a point halfway along the edge of a selected trace, solid, or 3D face.
- **NEArest.** Snaps to the point on a line, arc, circle, or point that is nearest to the center of the crosshairs.

- **NODe.** Snaps to the nearest point entity or dimension definition point entity. (The DIVIDE and MEASURE commands create NODes.)
- **PERpendicular.** Snaps to a point on a line, arc, or circle that forms a perpendicular from the current point to the selected entity. The resulting point does not have to be located on the selected entity.
- **QUAdrant.** Snaps to the nearest quadrant point of a selected arc or circle. Quadrant points are located at 0, 90, 180, and 270 degrees.
- **QUIck,<object snap mode(s)>.** Forces all object snap modes to accept the first point that satisfies the current snap mode(s). Quick does not necessarily find the best match to the object snap mode. The choice of which point best meets the object snap criteria is based on the entity sort method. Entity sort method is introduced in unit 21 and mentioned again in unit 37.
- **TANgent.** Snaps to a point on an entity to form a tangent between the entity and the previously selected point.
- **NONe.** Temporarily nullifies any running object snap mode settings.

If you choose object snap modes by entering an abbreviation at the `Command:` *prompt, you should get in the habit of using ENDP for endpoint rather than END. This prevents accidental use of the END command which saves your drawing and exits AutoCAD.*

When an object snap mode is active, AutoCAD displays a square box called the *aperture* at the center of the crosshairs. The aperture is displayed in addition to the pickbox, which AutoCAD also displays at the center of the crosshairs.

Each segment of a polyline is treated as a separate line for endpoint and midpoint object snap selections. Each arc in a polyline is treated like a separate arc.

For an entity to be considered in an object snap selection, the entity must cross the aperture box during object selection. In the case of intersection of two entities, the desired intersection must be inside the aperture box. The size of the aperture box during object snap selection is set using the APERTURE command. The APERTURE command is discussed in the next unit.

Drawing with Temporary Object Snap Modes

As the name implies, temporary object snap modes are effective for a limited time. Each object snap mode selected is active for the current object selection or point selection prompt only. Unit 37 addresses permanent object snap modes that remain active for multiple prompts.

Temporary object snap modes are accessed from the pull-down menu, the screen menu, the `Command:` prompt, or from a popup menu. To access temporary object snap modes from the pull-down menu, choose Assist, then Object Snap, then the desired temporary object snap mode. To select a temporary object snap mode from the screen menu, choose * * * *, then the desired object snap mode.

To select an object snap mode at the `Command:` prompt, enter the object snap modes by name or abbreviation at the appropriate object selection or point selection prompt. You can enter multiple object snap modes separated by commas. When you use multiple object snap modes, AutoCAD chooses the point that is closest to the center of the pickbox that meets the criteria of one of the set object snap modes. The Quick object snap mode overrides this method of picking the best point and picks the first point that meets the selection criteria.

You also can display a popup menu of the object snap modes by clicking on the third button of your digitizer. If you have a two-button digitizer, hold down the shift key and click on the second button. The popup menu always appears at your cursor's location, making object snap mode selection faster and reducing the distance you have to move the crosshairs to make a selection.

The following exercises show you how to use temporary object snap modes. The first exercise set uses object snap modes to help you finish drawing a bathroom. The steps use the Center object snap mode to add a rim to the sink.

Using the Center Object Snap Mode

1. Begin a new drawing named 036???01 in your assigned directory, using the file 036PROTO as a prototype.

2. `Command:` *Choose* Draw, *then* Circle, *then* Center, Radius	Starts the CIRCLE command with the Center, Radius option
3. `_circle 3P/2P/TTR/<Center point>:` *Display the popup cursor menu, then choose* Center	Chooses the Center object snap mode

4. `_center of` *Select the circle at* ① *(see fig. 36.2)*	Selects the center of the circle
5. `Diameter/<Radius>:` **`10`** ↵	Sets the radius to 10 and draw the circle

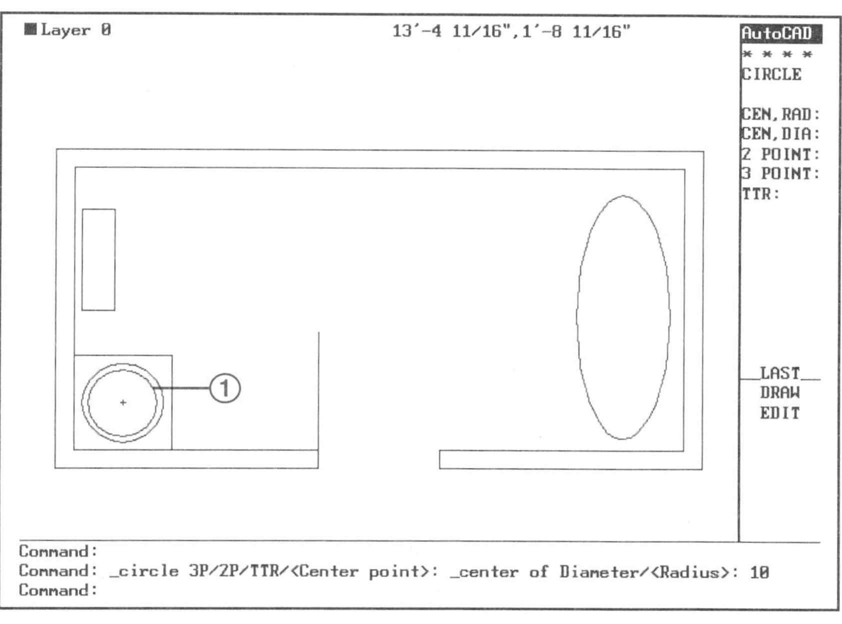

Figure 36.2

Rim added to the sink.

Now use the Midpoint object snap mode to finish the toilet.

Using the Midpoint Object Snap Mode

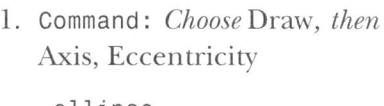

Continue with your drawing from the previous exercise.

1. `Command:` *Choose* Draw, *then* Axis, Eccentricity `_ellipse`	Starts the ELLIPSE command
2. `<Axis endpoint 1>/Center:` *From the screen menu choose,* * * * * *then* MIDpoint	Chooses the Midpoint object snap mode
3. `_MIDpoint of` *Select the line at* ① *(see fig. 36.3)*	Selects the first axis point
4. `Axis endpoint 2:` **`@18<0`** ↵	Specifies the second axis point
5. `<Other axis distance> /Rotation:` **`@7<90`** ↵	

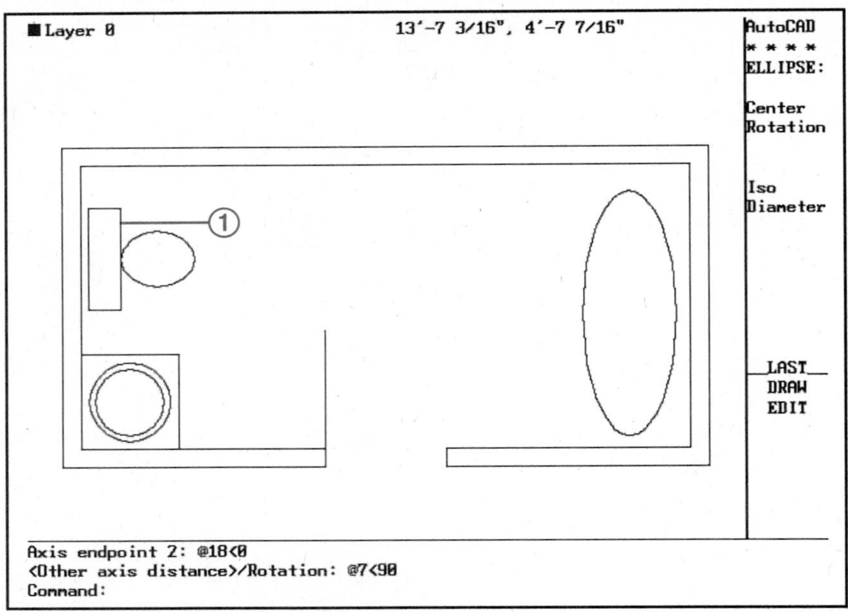

Figure 36.3

The completed toilet.

The following exercise uses the Endpoint and Intersection object snap modes to add a door swing.

Using the Endpoint and Intersection Object Snap Modes

Continue with your drawing from the previous exercise.

1. `Command:` *Choose* Draw, *then* Arc, *then* Start, Cen, End	Starts the ARC command
2. `Center/<Start point>:` *Choose* Assist, *then* Object Snap, *then* Intersection	Chooses the Intersection object snap mode
3. `_int of` *Pick the intersection at* ① *(see fig. 36.4)*	Selects the wall as the start point of the arc
4. `Center/End/<Second point>: _c Center:` **INT** ↵	Chooses the Intersection object snap mode
5. `of` *Pick the intersection at* ②	Selects the intersection of the door and the wall as the center point of the arc
6. `Angle/Length of chord /<Endpoint>:` **ENDP** ↵	Chooses the Endpoint object snap mode
7. `of` *Pick the end point at* ③	Selects the end of the door as the end of the arc

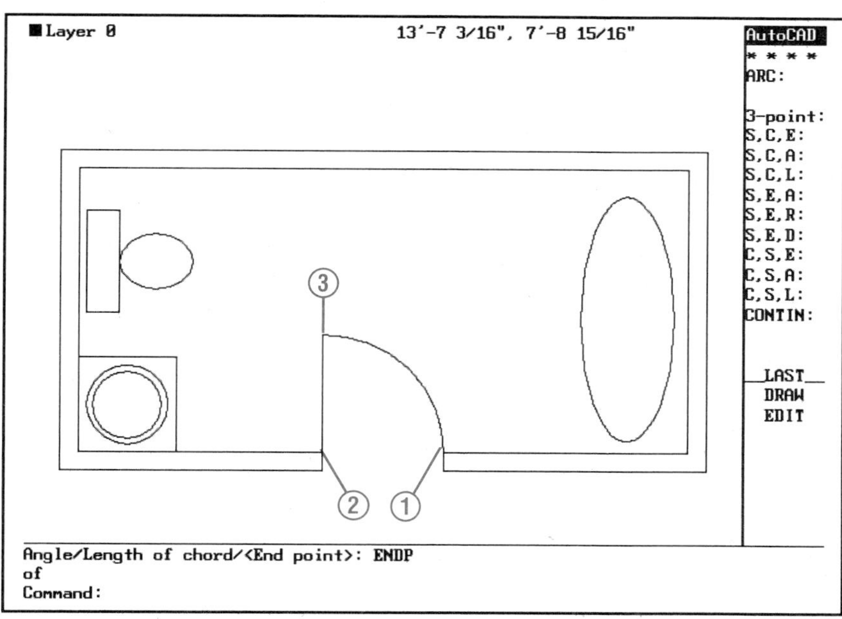

Figure 36.4

A door swing added to the drawing.

The following exercise uses the Nearest and Perpendicular object snap modes to finish the tub.

Using the Nearest and Perpendicular Object Snap Modes

Continue with your drawing from the previous exercise.

1. `Command:` **L** ↵	Starts the LINE command
2. `From point:` *From the popup menu, choose* Nearest	Chooses the Nearest object snap mode
3. `_nea to` *Pick the line at* ① *(see fig. 36.5)*	Starts the border of the tub
4. `To point:` *From the popup menu, choose* Perpendicular	Chooses the Perpendicular object snap mode
5. `_per to` *Pick the line at* ②	Picks a point perpendicular to the wall
6. `To point:` *Press* Enter	Ends the LINE command
7. `Command:` *Choose* File, *then* Save	Saves the drawing

The second exercise set uses the remaining object snap modes to help you draw a belt and pulley system. The first exercise uses the Node option to draw the pulleys.

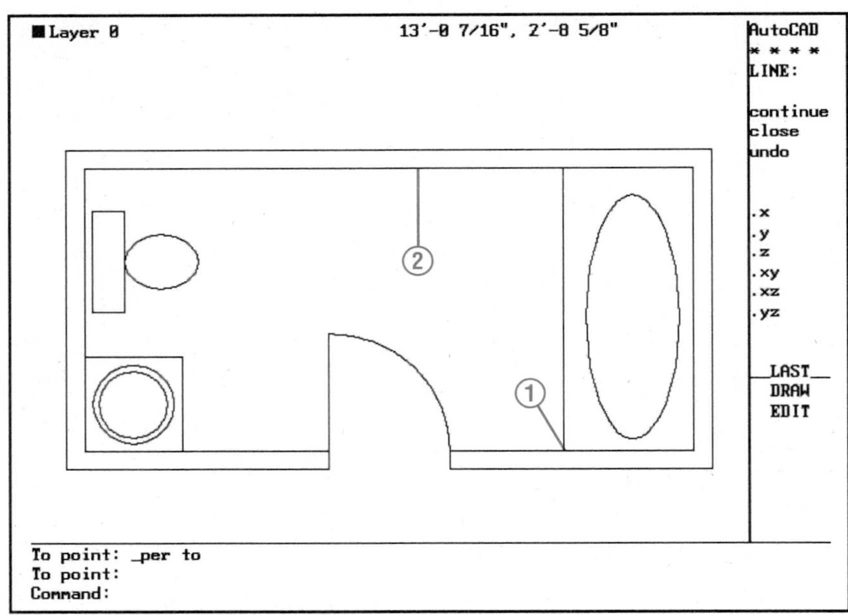

Figure 36.5

Outline added to the tub.

Using the Node Object Snap Mode

1. Begin a new drawing named 036???02 in your assigned directory, using the file 036PROT2 as a prototype.

2. `Command:` *Choose* Draw, *then* Circle, *then* Center Radius — Chooses the CIRCLE command

3. `_circle 3P/2P/TTR/<Center point>:` *From the popup menu, choose* Node — Chooses the Node object snap mode

4. `_nod of` *Pick a point at* ① *(see fig. 36.6)* — Selects the point marking the center of the pulley

5. `Diameter/<Radius>: 1` ↵

The following exercise uses the Tangent and Quadrant object snap modes to draw the belt. Drawing a line from a tangent point to a tangent point is sometimes tricky. This exercise uses two large circles with obvious pick points to make selection more accurate. In your own drawings, you may have to zoom in on circles and arcs during object selection to select the correct tangent point. The ZOOM command is covered in detail in unit 18.

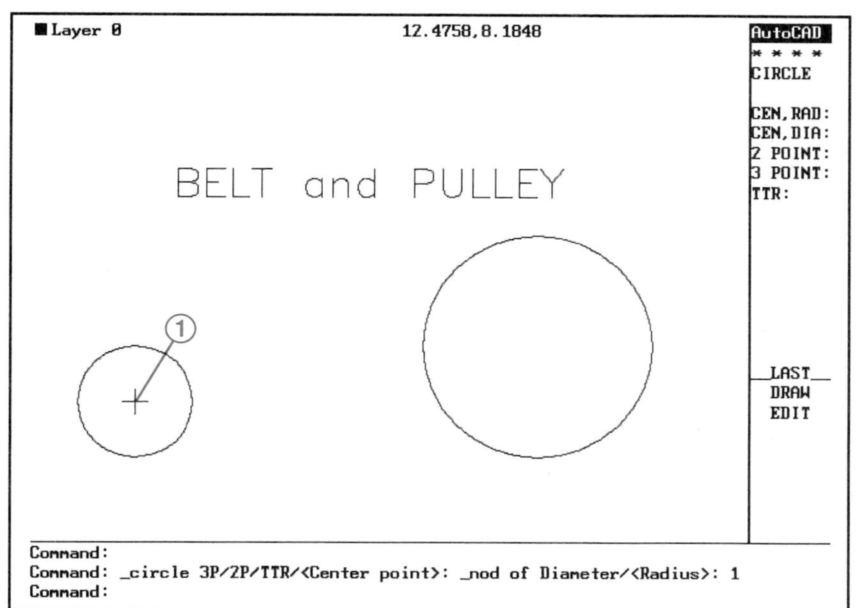

Figure 36.6

Pulleys drawn with the Node object snap mode.

Using the Tangent and Quadrant Object Snap Modes

Continue with your drawing from the previous exercise.

1. `Command:` **`L`** ↵	Starts the LINE command
2. `LINE From point:` *From the popup menu, choose* Tangent	Chooses the Tangent object snap mode
3. `_tan to` *Pick a point at* ① *(see fig. 36.7)*	Selects the first tangent point
4. `To point:` **`TAN`** ↵	Chooses the Tangent object snap mode
5. `to` *Pick a point at* ② *(see fig. 36.7)*	Selects the second tangent point
6. `To point:` *Press* Enter	Ends the LINE command
7. `Command:` *Press* Enter	Repeats the last command
8. `Line From point:` *From the popup menu, choose* Quadrant	Chooses the Quadrant object snap mode
9. `_qua of` *Pick a point at* ③ *(see fig. 36.7)*	Selects the first quadrant point
10. `To point:` **`QUA`** ↵	Chooses the Quadrant object snap mode
11. `of` *Pick a point at* ④ *(see fig. 36.7)*	Selects the second quadrant point
12. `To point:` *Press* Enter	Ends the LINE command

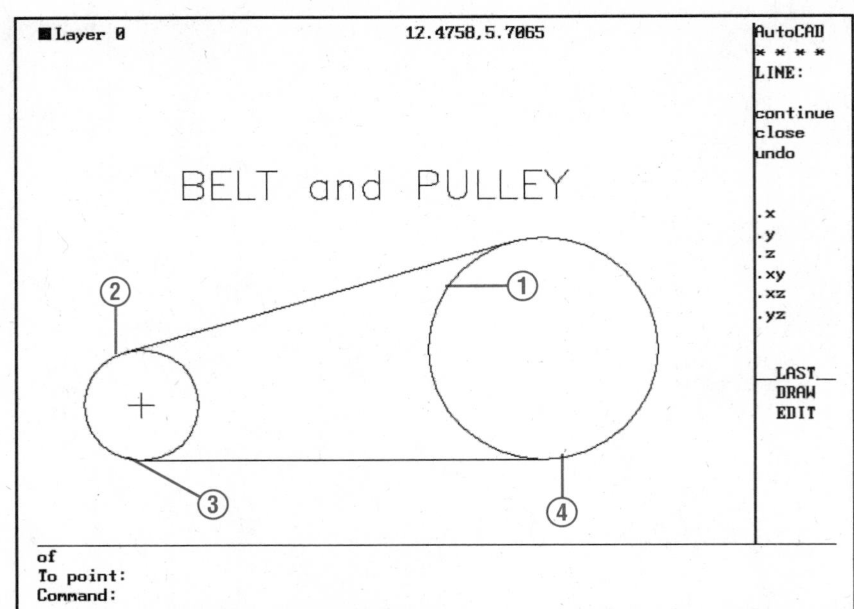

Figure 36.7

The belt added to the pulleys.

Unit Review

What You've Learned

- The object snap points on most common objects
- The object snap modes
- How to access the object snap modes
- How to use the object snap modes to make drafting easier and more accurate

Review Questions

True or False

36.01 T F There are 12 different temporary object snap modes.

36.02 T F Polylines are treated as one entity for Endpoint and Midpoint object snap modes

36.03 T F For the intersection object snap to work, one of the intersecting entities must cross the pickbox

36.04 T F Object snap mode commands can be abbreviated to three letters

36.05 T F Quadrant points are always at 0, 90, 180, and 270 degrees regardless of the orientation of the arc or circle.

Short Answer

36.06 List the four ways to access temporary object snap modes.

____

____

____

36.07 How can you set more than one temporary object snap mode at a time?

____

____

____

Student: __________ Date: ______

Instructor: __________ Course: ______ Section: ______

36.08 How can you force AutoCAD to use the first snap point that meets the snap criteria rather than the best point to meet the object snap mode criteria?

____

____

____

36.09 List the entities that have both Quadrant and Center points:

____

____

____

Student: __________ Date: __________

Instructor: __________ Course: __________ Section: __________

Additional Exercises

36.10 In figure 36.8, identify the following items:

(A) An Intersection object snap __________

(B) A Tangent to Perpendicular object snap __________

(C) A Quadrant object snap __________

(D) An Endpoint to Nearest object snap __________

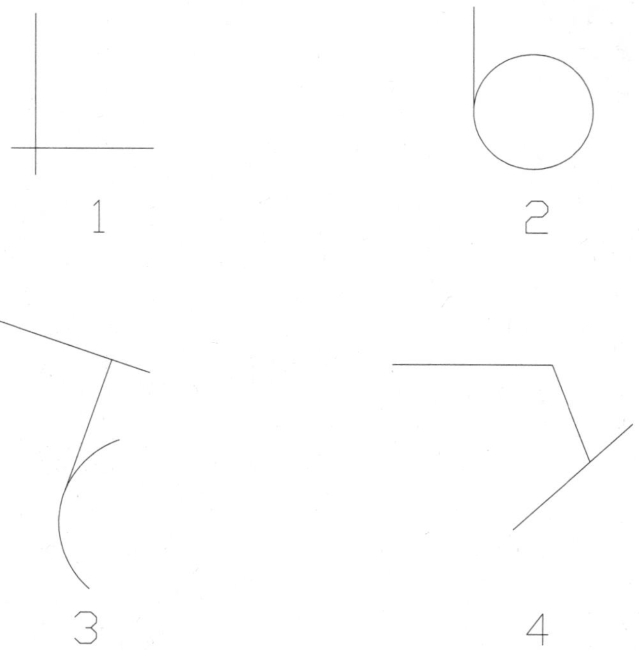

Figure 36.8

Identifying object snap modes.

1

2

3

4

UNIT 37

Using Running Object Snap Modes

Object snap modes provide you with the capability to draw accurately with relatively little effort. Unit 36 introduces each of the object snap modes in the course of discussing temporary object snap modes. This unit discusses running object snap modes that provide all the utility of temporary object snap modes without forcing you to pick an object snap mode at each prompt. The running object snap modes you select stay in effect until you turn them off or pick new object snap modes.

The objectives for this unit are to:

- Understand running object snap modes
- Set running object snap modes with the DDOSNAP and OSNAP commands
- Use a single running object snap mode
- Use multiple running object snap modes
- Understand and set aperture size

The object snap modes discussed in this unit are the same as those discussed in unit 36 with one exception. The only variation is the None object snap, which simply turns off the running object snap modes. For your convenience, the object snap modes are listed here, with the addition of the None object snap mode.

- **CENter.** Snaps to the center of a selected arc or circle.
- **ENDpoint.** Snaps to the closest endpoint of a selected line or arc or the closest corner of a selected trace, solid, or 3D face.
- **INSert.** Snaps to the insertion point of a selected text, block, shape, or attribute.
- **INTersection.** Snaps to the closest intersection of any combination of lines, polylines, arcs, and circles, or to the nearest corner of a trace, solid, or 3D face. For intersection to work, the entities must intersect in three-dimensional space.
- **MIDpoint.** Snaps to a point halfway along a selected line or arc, or to a point halfway along the edge of a selected trace, solid, or 3D face.
- **NEArest.** Snaps to the point on a line, arc, circle, or point nearest the crosshairs.
- **NODe.** Snaps to the nearest point entity or dimension definition point entity.
- **PERpendicular.** Snaps to a point on a line, arc, or circle that is perpendicular from the previous point to the selected entity. The resulting point does not have to be located on the selected entity.
- **QUAdrant.** Snaps to the nearest quadrant point of a selected arc or circle. Quadrant points are located at 0, 90, 180, and 270 degrees.
- **QUIck,<object snap(s)>.** Forces all object snap modes to accept the first point that satisfies the current snap mode(s). Quick does not necessarily find the best match to the object snap mode.
- **TANgent.** Snaps to a point on an arc or circle that forms a tangent between the arc or circle and the previously selected point.
- **NONe.** Turns off any running object snap mode settings.

Temporary object snap modes (discussed in unit 36) take precedence over running object snap modes. If you enter a temporary object snap mode while a running object snap mode is set, the temporary object snap mode is used for that selection, and the running object snap mode is ignored. After the selection, the object snap mode reverts to the running object snap mode.

If no snap points are found while running object snap modes are in effect, the crosshairs pick point is used, and no warnings are displayed.

Running object snap modes are saved with your drawing. Any running object snap modes set when you save and exit your drawing are in effect the next time you edit the drawing.

Unlike temporary object snap modes, running object snap modes are ignored during object selection prompts.

Accessing the DDOSNAP and OSNAP commands

Running object snap modes are set using the DDOSNAP or OSNAP commands. DDOSNAP displays the Running Object Snap dialog box shown in figure 37.1. OSNAP is the command-line equivalent of DDOSNAP.

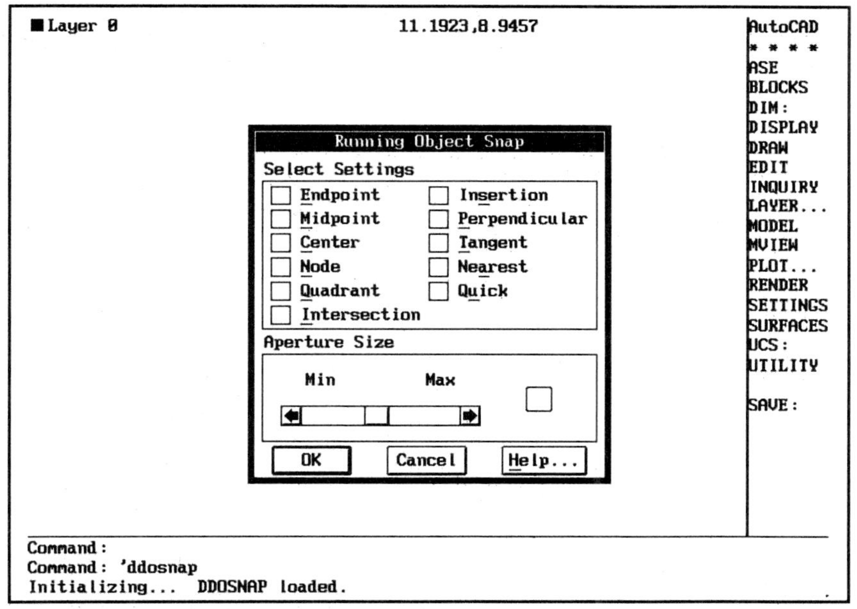

Figure 37.1

The Running Object Snap dialog box.

The DDOSNAP command displays the Running Object Snap dialog box. You can access DDOSNAP from the pull-down menu or the `Command:` prompt. To access DDOSNAP from the pull-down menu, choose Settings, followed by Object Snap, and then click on the desired object snap options. To access DDOSNAP from the `Command:` prompt, simply type **DDOSNAP** and press Enter. DDOSNAP cannot be accessed from the screen menu.

You can access the OSNAP command from the screen menu or the `Command:` prompt. To access OSNAP from the screen menu, choose SETTINGS, next OSNAP, and then choose the desired object snap modes. To access OSNAP from the `Command:` prompt, simply type **OSNAP**, press Enter, and enter the desired object snap modes.

Using a Running Object Snap Mode

The following exercise shows you how to set and use a running object snap mode. In the exercise, use the Running Object Snap dialog box to set the Endpoint running object snap mode to help you draw a pulley and bracket.

Using DDOSNAP and Running Object Snap Modes

1. Begin a new drawing named 037???01 in your assigned directory, using the file 037PROTO as a prototype.

2. `Command:` *Choose* Settings, *then* Object Snap	Displays the Running Object Snap dialog box
`Initializing... DDOSNAP loaded.`	
3. *Choose the* Endpoint *radio button, then* OK	Turns on the Endpoint running object snap and exits the dialog box
4. `Command:` *Choose* Draw, *then* Line, *then* Segments	Starts the LINE command
5. `_line From point:` *Pick* ① *(see fig. 37.2)*	Starts the line at the exact end point
6. `To point:` *Pick a point at* ② *(see fig. 37.2)*	Picks the next point of the line at the exact end point
7. `To point:` *Pick a point at* ③ *(see fig. 37.2)*	Picks the next point of the line at the exact end point
8. `To point:` *Pick a point at* ④ *(see fig. 37.2)*	Picks the next point of the line at the exact end point
9. `To point:` *Press* Enter	Ends the LINE command

Using Multiple Running Object Snap Modes

As with temporary object snap modes, you can set multiple running object snap modes by using the Running Object Snap dialog box (DDOSNAP) or the OSNAP command. If you use the dialog box, simply choose the radio buttons for each of the object snap modes you want to use. If you use the OSNAP command, enter the object snap modes separated by commas in response to the OSNAP command's prompt.

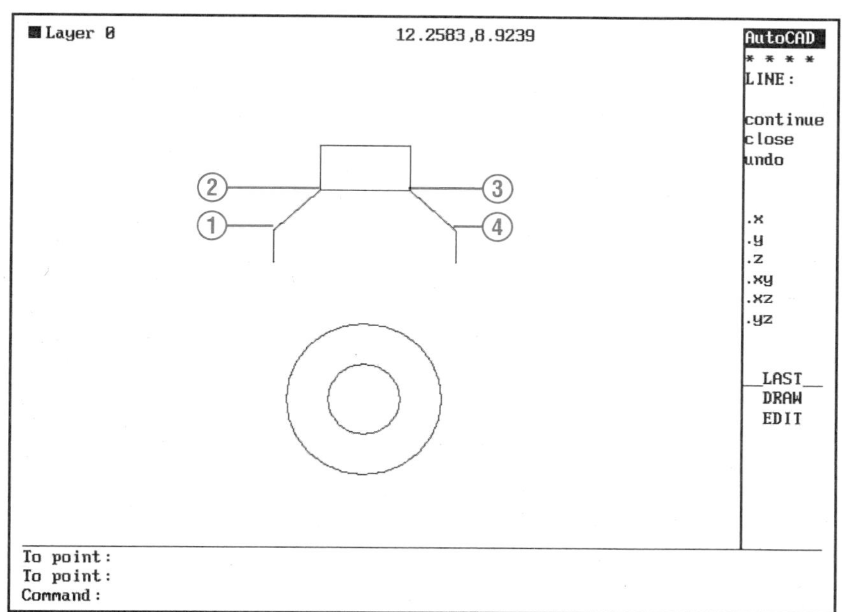

Figure 37.2

Lines drawn using the Endpoint running object snap mode.

When multiple object snap modes are in effect, AutoCAD picks the point that meets the selection criteria closest to the center of the pickbox. The Quick object snap mode overrides this feature and causes AutoCAD to select the first point that meets the selection criteria rather than the best point.

The following exercise shows you how to use multiple running object snap modes to finish the pulley and bracket. The exercise uses the Intersection and Endpoint object snap modes.

Using DDOSNAP and Multiple Running Object Snap Modes

Continue with your drawing from the previous exercise.

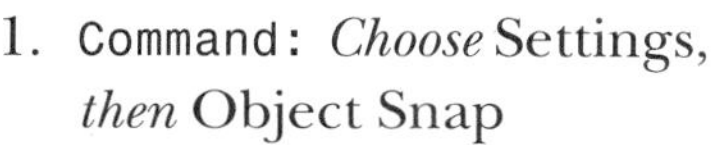

1.	`Command:` *Choose* Settings, *then* Object Snap `'ddosnap`	Displays the Running Object Snap dialog box
2.	*Choose the* Tangent *radio button, then* OK	Adds Tangent running object snap mode and exits the dialog box
3.	`Command:` *Choose* Draw, *then* Line, *then* Segments	Starts the LINE command
4.	`_line From point:` *Pick a point at* ① *(see fig. 37.3)*	Picks the first point of the line at the exact end point

continues

5. `To point:` *Pick a point at* ② *(see fig. 37.3)*	Picks the next point of the line at the exact tangent point
6. `To point:` *Press* Enter	Ends the LINE command
7. `Command:` *Press* Enter	Repeats the last command
8. `LINE From point:` *Pick a point at* ③ *(see fig. 37.3)*	Picks the first point of the line at the exact tangent point
9. `To point:` *Pick a point at* ④ *(see fig. 37.3)*	Picks the next point of the line at the exact end point
10. `To point:` *Press* Enter	Ends the LINE command

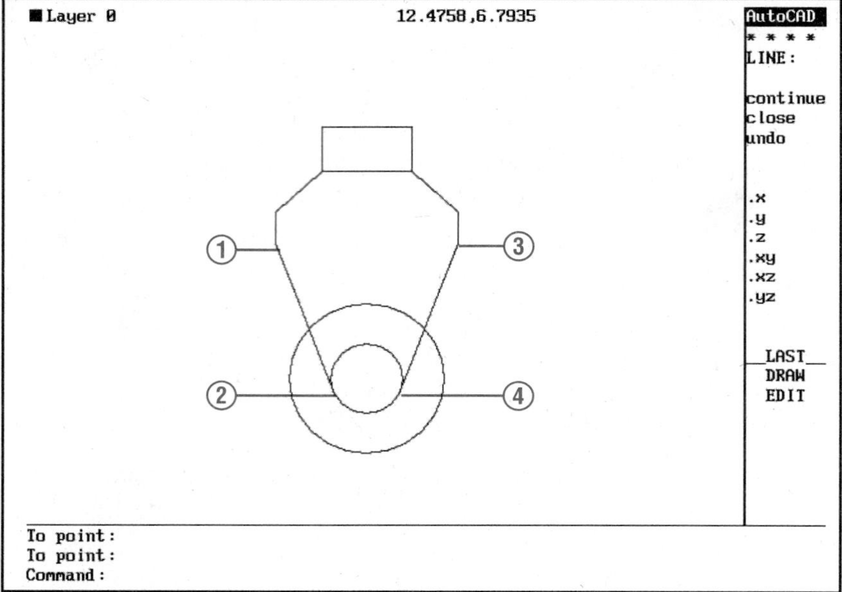

Figure 37.3

Lines drawn using multiple running object snap modes.

Controlling Aperture Size

Whether you are using temporary or running object snap modes, the aperture size determines the accuracy and speed with which you pick points and at which AutoCAD processes the points inside the pick box. Table 37.1 shows the advantages and disadvantages of setting the aperture box to a large or small size.

Table 37.1
Effect of Adjusting the Aperture

Pickbox Size	Advantage/ Disadvantage	Reason
Large	Advantage	The pickbox covers a large area, which makes it easy to place.
	Disadvantage	A large pickbox can cover more potential pick points, forcing AutoCAD to process longer before determining the best possible point.
Small	Advantage	The pickbox covers a small area so AutoCAD has fewer potential pick points to process, speeding AutoCAD's selection of the best pick point. A small pickbox is more accurate, enabling you to pick exactly the point you intend. This also is an issue when you are using temporary object snap modes to select an entity in a dense drawing.
	Disadvantage	A small pickbox covers less area, so it must be placed more precisely to get the correct point.

The size of the pickbox is called the *aperture*. The aperture is set with the APERTURE command. You can access the APERTURE command from the Running Object Snap dialog box, the screen menu, or the `Command:` prompt. In the Running Object Snap dialog box, use the Aperture scroll bar to control the size of the aperture. Experiment on your own with changing the aperture size to see how it affects point selection.

Unit Review

What You've Learned

- How to access DDOSNAP and OSNAP
- How to a set running object snap modes
- How to set multiple running object snap modes
- How to use the running object snap modes to make drafting easier and more accurate
- How to control the size of the pickbox with the APERTURE and DDOSNAP commands

Review Questions

True or False

37.01 T F DDOSNAP is accessed from the pull-down menu only.

37.02 T F All the running object snap modes behave exactly like the temporary object snap modes.

37.03 T F Running object snap modes are saved with your drawing.

37.04 T F When multiple object snap modes are in effect, AutoCAD picks the point that meets the selection criteria closest to the center of the pickbox.

37.05 T F Temporary object snap modes take precedence over running object snap modes.

Short Answer

37.06 Name one effect of setting the aperture to a smaller setting.

____

____

____

37.07 The ______________ object snap causes AutoCAD to accept the first point that meets the selection criteria, rather than the best point.

Student: ______________ Date: ______________

Instructor: ______________ Course: ______________ Section: ______________

37.08 If no pick points are found while using running object snap modes, what does AutoCAD do?

____

____

____

37.09 The aperture size is set with the ____________ or ____________ commands.

Applying the AutoCAD Environment

37.10 Place the number next to the running object snap modes needed to draw figure 37.4. Points are marked with an X; existing lines are shown as continuous lines. The lines to be drawn are shown as hidden lines.

(A) Tangent, Endpoint __________

(B) Endpoint, Endpoint __________

(C) Endpoint, Perpendicular __________

(D) Tangent, Tangent __________

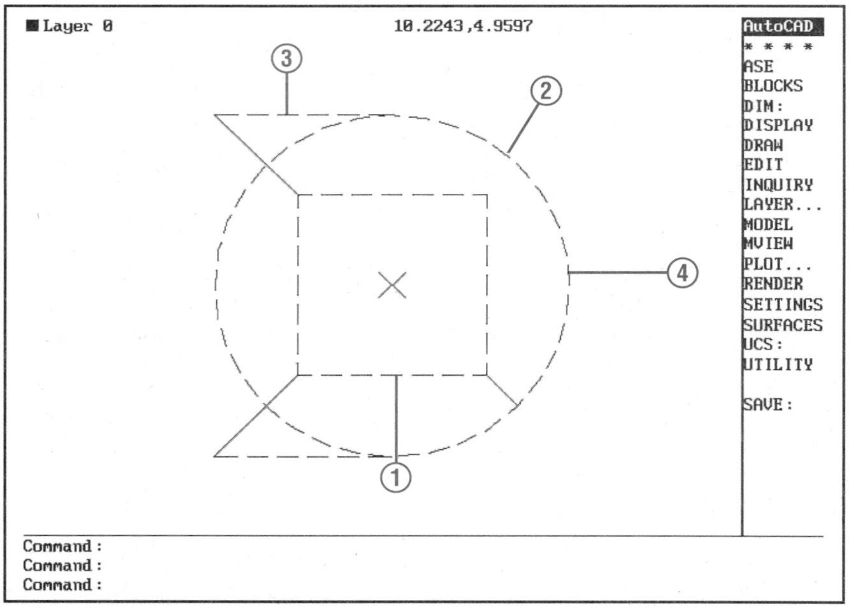

Figure 37.4

Identifying running object snap modes.

Student: ____________ Date: ____________

Instructor: ____________ Course: ____________ Section: ____________

Defining a Coordinate System

UNIT 38

In earlier units, you worked with the default coordinate system provided by AutoCAD. In some situations, you might need to create your own coordinate system. This unit examines such situations and teaches you how to create and use your own coordinate system.

The objectives for this unit are to:

- Understand the WCS (World Coordinate System)
- Understand the UCS (User Coordinate System)
- Move the origin
- Understand and control the UCS icon
- Rotate the UCS to different directions

Understanding the WCS and UCS

The default coordinate system in AutoCAD is called the *World Coordinate System* (WCS). When you begin a new drawing with default settings, AutoCAD places the origin of the WCS in the lower left corner of the screen with the X axis positioned horizontally along the bottom of the screen, and the Y axis positioned vertically on the left side of the screen. As you pan and zoom the drawing, the location of the origin might change on the screen, but it always remains at coordinate 0,0. The WCS is the frame of reference from which AutoCAD measures all points.

You also can create your own coordinate system, called a *User Coordinate System*, or UCS. You can create as many UCSs as you need. You can relocate the origin to a point other than the world 0,0 coordinate, rotate the coordinate system, and make other changes to the coordinate system.

A UCS is most commonly used in 3D modeling, but it also has important uses in 2D drawing. You can create a UCS when you need to place ordinate dimensions on a drawing, for example. *Ordinate dimensions* define points on an object based from a datum point. You can create a UCS with its origin located at the datum point to make dimensioning easier. Figure 38.1 shows a drawing containing ordinate dimensions.

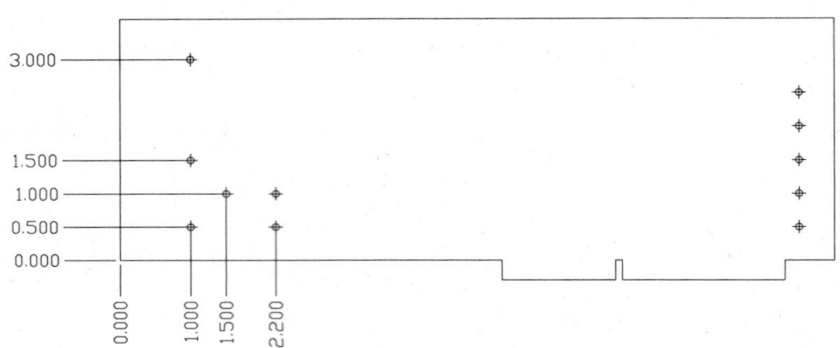

Figure 38.1
Ordinate dimensions are based from a datum point.

A UCS also is very useful when you need to specify a number of points based from a datum point not located at your drawing's world origin of 0,0. You might need to create a UCS in a surveyor's plat that you are creating, for example, to locate points in the plat from different datum points.

It is important to understand that even in a UCS, the origin is located at coordinate 0,0, and all coordinates are based from this origin. The UCS's origin might be at a different location from the WCS origin. The UCS's origin simply identifies the datum point for the current UCS. Think of creating a UCS as simply picking up the X and Y axes and locating them temporarily at a new position. When you switch back to the WCS, the X and Y axes move back to their original positions.

Understanding the UCS Icon

By default, AutoCAD places an icon called the UCS icon in the lower left corner of the display. The UCS icon displays the current orientation of the X and Y axes. It also indicates whether the WCS or a UCS is active. If the UCS icon contains a W, the WCS is active. If the UCS icon does not contain a W, a UCS is active.

By default, the UCS icon remains in the lower left corner of the display. You can set the UCS icon always to be located at the origin. When the UCS icon is located at the origin, a small cross on the icon (see fig. 38.2) marks the location of the origin. This holds true with any coordinate system active.

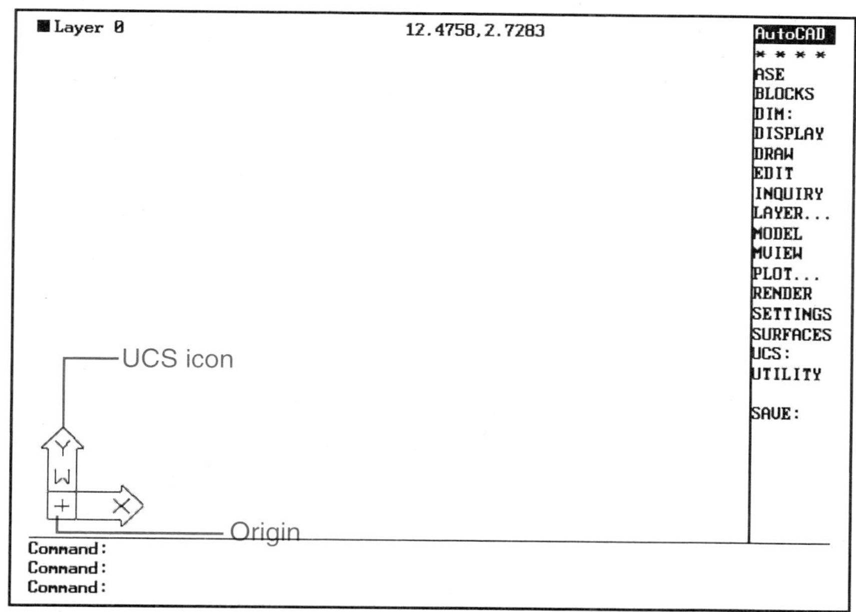

Figure 38.2

UCS icon.

The UCS icon provides a visual indicator of the orientation of the X and Y axes and the location of the origin. The UCS icon is a useful tool when you are working with a UCS. Later in this unit, you learn how to control the UCS icon.

Moving the UCS Origin

On some drawings, like flat pattern layouts for chassis and printed circuit board drawings that have several holes to be drilled, you can use a UCS to simplify the task of locating points and applying dimensions. In the following exercise, use the UCS command to create a UCS and move the origin to locate holes on a printed circuit card.

Moving the UCS Origin

1. Begin a new drawing named 038???01 in your assigned directory using 038BOARD as a prototype.

2. `Command:` *Choose* Settings, *then* UCS, *then* Origin — Issues the UCS command with the Origin option

   ```
   ucs
   Origin/ZAxis/3point/Entity/View/
   X/Y/Z/Prev/Restore/Save/Del/?/
   <World>: _origin
   ```

3. `Origin point <0,0,0>:` *From the popup menu, choose* Endpoint — Sets object snap mode

continues

4. `_endp of` *Pick the end point at* ① *(see fig 38.3)*	Locates the origin of the new UCS
5. `Command:` **`UCSICON`** ↵	Issues the UCSICON command
6. `ON/OFF/All/Noorigin/ORigin <ON>:` **`OR`** ↵	Sets the UCS icon to follow the origin

Your drawing should look similar to figure 38.3.

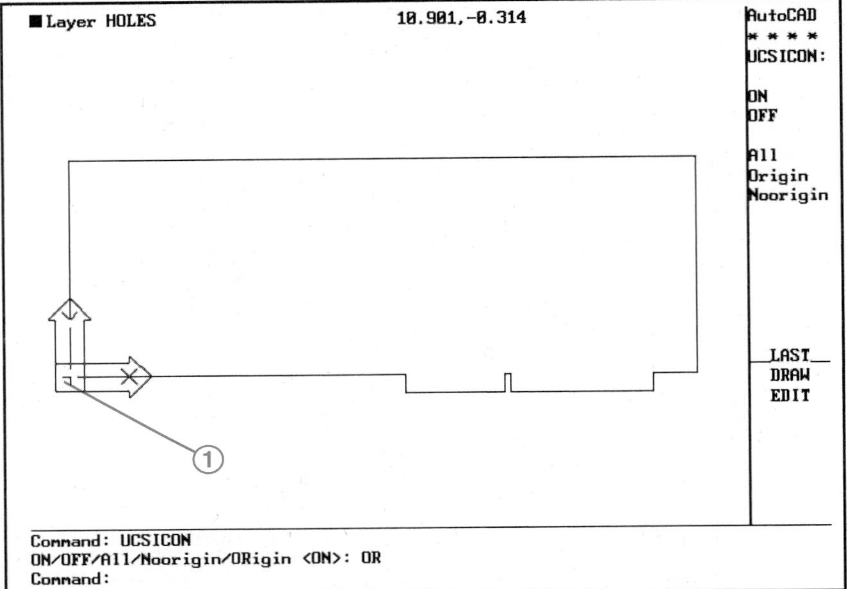

Figure 38.3

New UCS and relocated UCS icon.

Now, all absolute coordinates that you enter are measured from the new origin at the lower left corner of the printed circuit board, not from the world origin.

NOTE

If AutoCAD cannot display the UCS icon at the origin (part of the icon is off the screen), AutoCAD moves the icon to the default location in the lower left corner of the display. AutoCAD moves the icon to the origin when you zoom or pan the display to a view in which AutoCAD can locate the entire icon at the origin.

Next, set point display mode and draw points to locate a few holes.

Drawing in a UCS

Continue with your drawing from the preceding exercise.

1.	`Command:` *Choose* Settings, *then* Point Style	Issues the DDPTYPE command and displays the Point Style dialog box
	`'ddptype`	
2.	*Choose the tile in the second row, third column (cross in a circle)* 3.	Chooses point display type *Choose the* Set Size in Absolute
3.	Sets the size of the points Units *radio button, then enter a point size of* **`0.1`**	to .1 unit (.1")
4.	*Choose* OK	Applies the new point style and closes the dialog box
5.	`Command:` *Choose* Draw, *then* Point	Issues the POINT command
	`_point`	
6.	`Point:` **`1,.5`** ↵	
7.	`Point:` **`1,1.5`** ↵	
8.	`Point:` **`1.5,1`** ↵	
9.	`Point:` **`1,3`** ↵	
10.	`Point:` **`2.2,1`** ↵	
11.	`Point:` **`2.2,.5`** ↵	
12.	`Point:` *Press* Ctrl+C	Ends POINT command
13.	Save your drawing.	

Your drawing should look similar to figure 38.4.

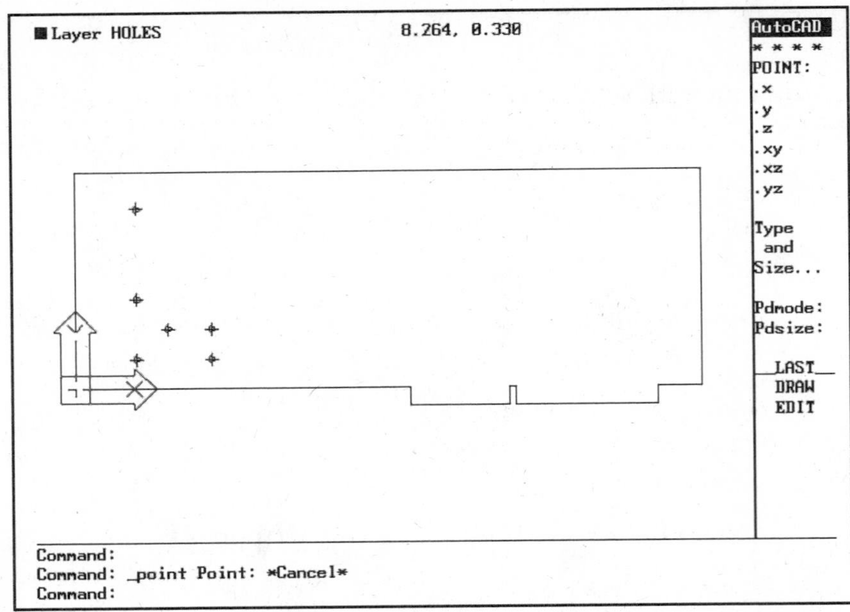

Figure 38.4

Points drawn with a UCS.

Note in the figure that all the points are located relative to the new UCS origin, not the WCS origin.

If you need to draw other points that are most easily located from a different point on the circuit board, you can create another UCS to draw the additional points.

If you want to be able to restore a UCS quickly, use the Save option of the UCS command to save the current UCS by name. You then can use the Restore option to quickly restore the UCS. This makes it possible to define many different coordinate systems and switch among them quickly.

Rotating the UCS

In addition to relocating the UCS origin, you can rotate the UCS. You can rotate it about any of the three axes (X, Y, and Z). You also can rotate the UCS by specifying points to define the orientation of the XY plane, or align the UCS with a specific entity.

In the following exercise, first experiment with the UCS command to rotate the UCS 90 degrees counterclockwise. Then relocate and rotate the UCS by picking points.

When you create a rotated UCS for a 2D drawing, you generally rotate the UCS around the Z axis. The Z axis is perpendicular to the X and Y axes. With the default WCS orientation with the X axis horizontal and the Y axis vertical on the screen, the positive Z axis extends straight out of the screen.

Rotating the UCS about the Z Axis

Continue with your drawing from the preceding exercise.

1.	`Command:` **`UCS`** ↵	Issues the UCS command
2.	`Origin/ZAxis/3point/Entity/View/ X/Y/Z/Prev/Restore/Save/Del/?/ <World>:`**`Z`** ↵	Specifies the Z option
3.	`Rotation angle about Z axis <0>:` **`90`** ↵	Rotates the UCS 90 degrees on the Z axis (see fig. 38.5)
4.	`Command:` **`U`** ↵	Undoes the previous command
5.	`Command:` **`OSNAP`** ↵	Issues OSNAP command
6.	`Object snap modes:` **`ENDP`**	Sets object snap mode
7.	`Command:` **`UCS`** ↵	Issues the UCS command
8.	`Origin/ZAxis/3point/Entity/View/ X/Y/Z/Prev/Restore/Save/Del/?/ <World>:`**`3`** ↵	Specifies the 3-point option
9.	`Origin point <0,0,0>:` *Pick the end point at* ① *(see fig. 38.6)*	Specifies the origin of the UCS
10.	`Point on positive portion of the X-axis <11.100,0.000,0.000>:` *Pick a point at* ② *(see fig. 38.6)*	Specifies the orientation of the X axis relative to the UCS origin
11.	`Point on positive-Y portion of the UCS XY plane <9.100,0.000,0.000>:` *Pick a point at* ③ *(see fig. 38.6)*	Specifies the orientation of the Y axis and defines the coordinate system
12.	`Command:` **`OSNAP`** ↵	Issues OSNAP command
13.	`Object snap modes:` **`NONE`** ↵	Turns off object snap

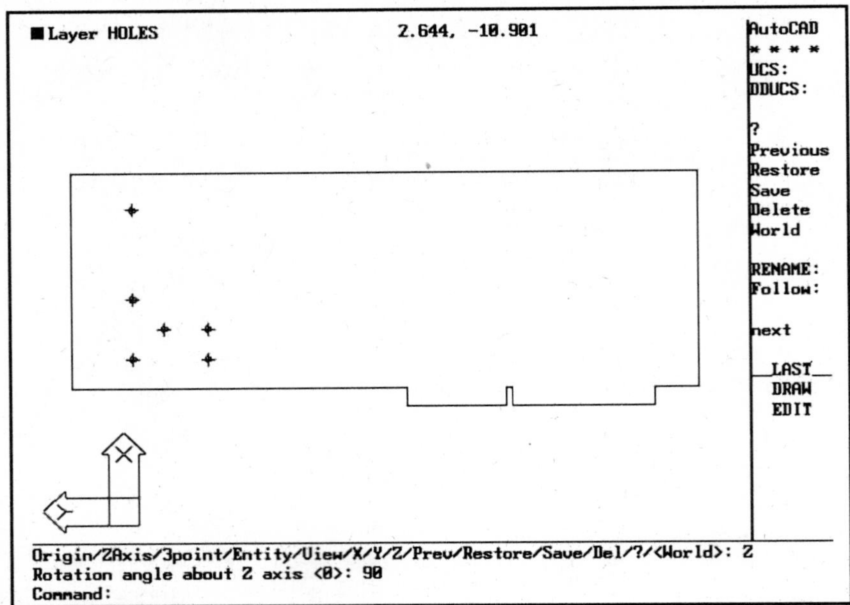

Figure 38.5
UCS rotated 90 degrees on the Z axis.

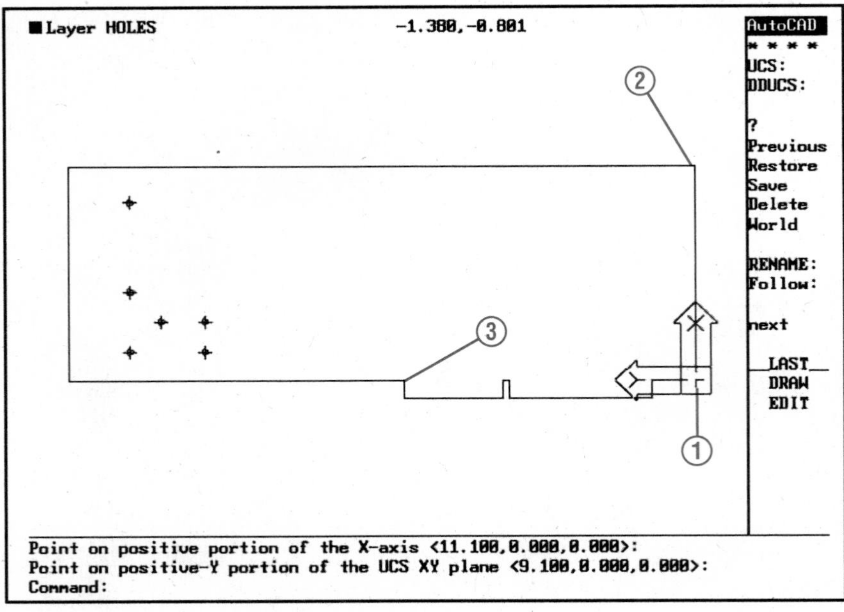

Figure 38.6
UCS rotated and relocated.

Next, locate a few points with the new UCS.

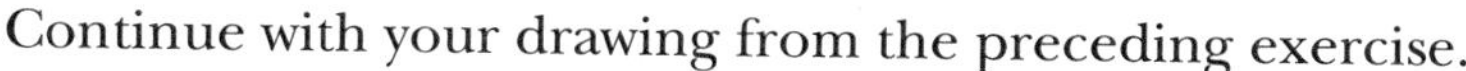

Adding More Points

Continue with your drawing from the preceding exercise.

1. `Command:` *Choose* Draw, *then* Point — Issues the POINT command

   `_point`

2. `Point:` **`0.5,0.5`** ↵
3. `Point:` **`1,0.5`** ↵
4. `Point:` **`1.5,0.5`** ↵
5. `Point:` **`2,0.5`** ↵
6. `Point:` **`2.5,0.5`** ↵
7. `Point:` *Press* Ctrl+C — Ends POINT command
8. Save your drawing

Your drawing should look similar to figure 38.7.

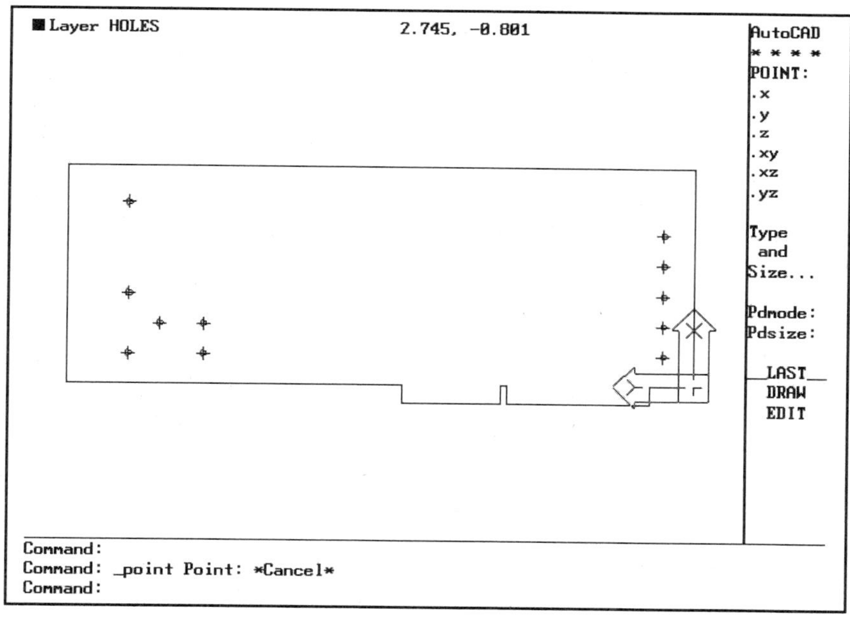

Figure 38.7

Points drawn with rotated UCS.

The X value you specify for each point is measured vertically along the new X axis. The Y spacing remains constant at 0.5", placing all the points at the same Y ordinate.

Changing the View of the UCS

It is often easier to use a UCS if the X and Y axes are oriented on the screen like the default WCS orientation. This places the X axis horizontally and the Y axis vertically on the display, giving you a plan view of the current UCS. To display a plan view of a particular UCS, you can use the PLAN command. PLAN enables you to quickly switch the view to a plan view of the WCS, a named UCS, or the current UCS.

In the following exercise, use the PLAN command to change the view of your circuit board.

Using the PLAN Command

Continue with your drawing from the preceding exercise.

1. `Command:` *Choose* View, *then* Set View, *then* Plan View, *then* Current UCS	Issues the PLAN command with the Current UCS option (see fig. 38.8)

Next, enter the PLAN command at the command prompt and display a plan view of the WCS.

2. `Command:` **`PLAN`** ↵	Issues the PLAN command
3. `<Current UCS>/Ucs/World:` **`W`** ↵	Specifies the World option and displays a plan view of the WCS (see fig. 38.9)

Next, restore the WCS with the UCS command.

4. `Command:` **`UCS`** ↵	Issues the UCS command
5. `Origin/ZAxis/3point/Entity/View/ X/Y/Z/Prev/Restore/Save/Del/?/<World>:` *Press* Enter	Restores the World Coordinate System (WCS)
6. Save your drawing.	

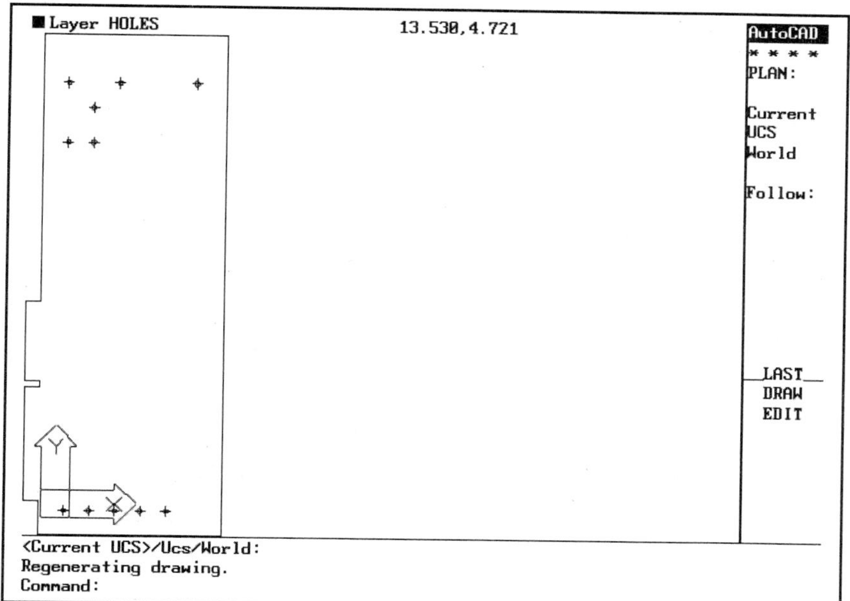

Figure 38.8

Plan view of the current UCS.

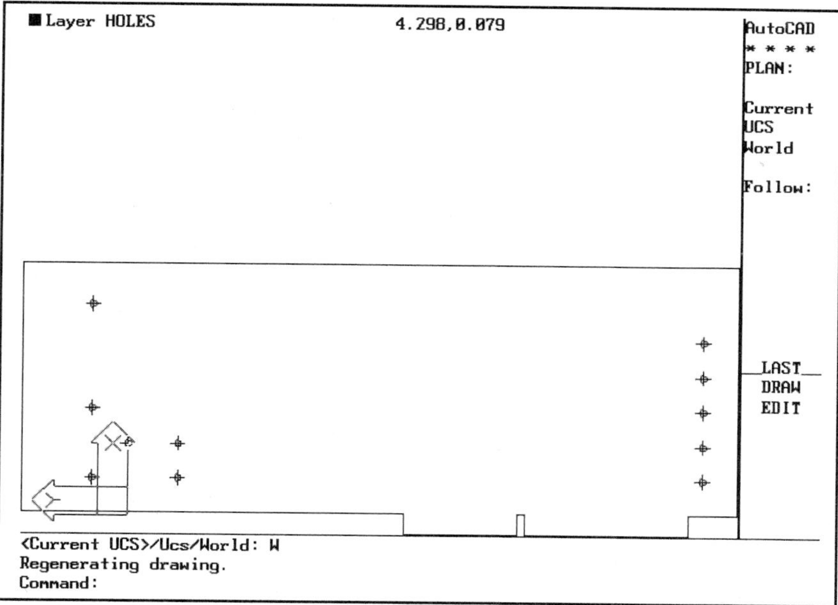

Figure 38.9

Plan view of the WCS.

If your UCS icon is displayed at the origin and you want to switch it back to its default location at the lower left corner of the display, issue the UCSICON command with the Noorigin option.

Use the PLAN command or its associated choices in the View pull-down menu whenver you need to display a plan view based on a particular coordinate system.

Unit Review

What You've Learned

- How to create a User Coordinate System (UCS)
- How to move the origin
- How to move the UCS icon
- How to control the UCS icon

Review Questions

True or False

38.01 T F The UCS icon has a W on it when the WCS is active.

38.02 T F You can turn off the UCS icon.

38.03 T F The UCS icon has a U on it.

38.04 T F The UCS icon has a cross on it when it is located on the origin.

38.05 T F The origin of a UCS cannot be located at a different location from the origin of the WCS.

38.06 T F The UCS command controls the appearance of the UCS icon.

38.07 T F The Z axis is perpendicular to the X and Y axes.

38.08 T F You can align the UCS with an entity such as a line.

Multiple Choice

38.09 The __________ option of the UCS command enables you to relocate the origin by picking one point.

(A) X

(B) Origin

(C) 3-point

(D) Y

Student: ______________________ Date: __________

Instructor: ______________________ Course: __________ Section: __________

38.10 If you rotate the UCS 30 degrees on the Z axis, and then rotate it again 60 degrees on the Z axis, the X axis will be __________.

(A) horizontal on the screen

(B) vertical on the screen

(C) at 60 degrees on the screen

(D) at 30 degrees on the screen

Additional Exercises

38.11 Continue with your drawing 038???01. Locate the origin at ① as shown in figure 38.10. Draw a row of eight points spaced .2" apart at a Y ordinate of 0.5. Place the first point at coordinate 0.5,0.5. Save your drawing.

Figure 38.10

UCS location and orientation.

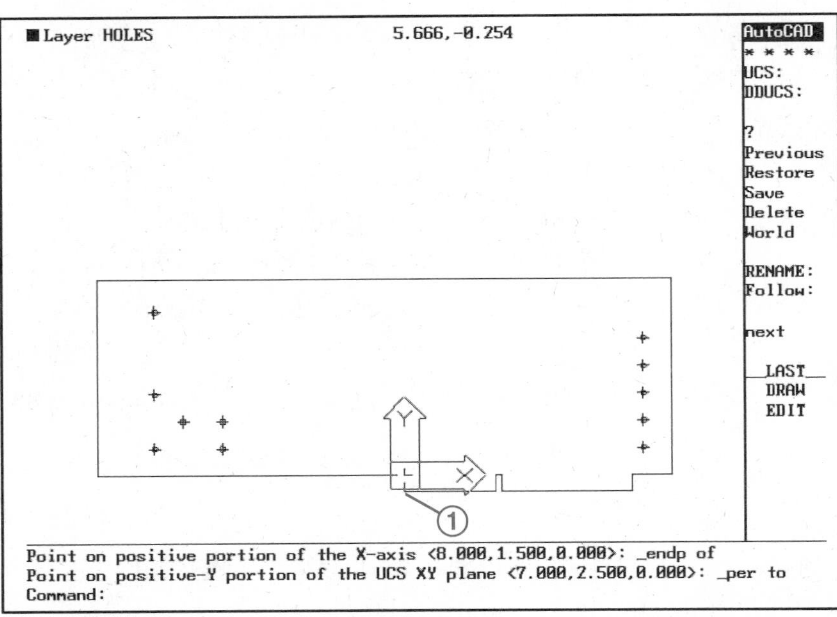

Student: ______ Date: ______

Instructor: ______ Course: ______ Section: ______

PART V

Using Advanced CAD Techniques

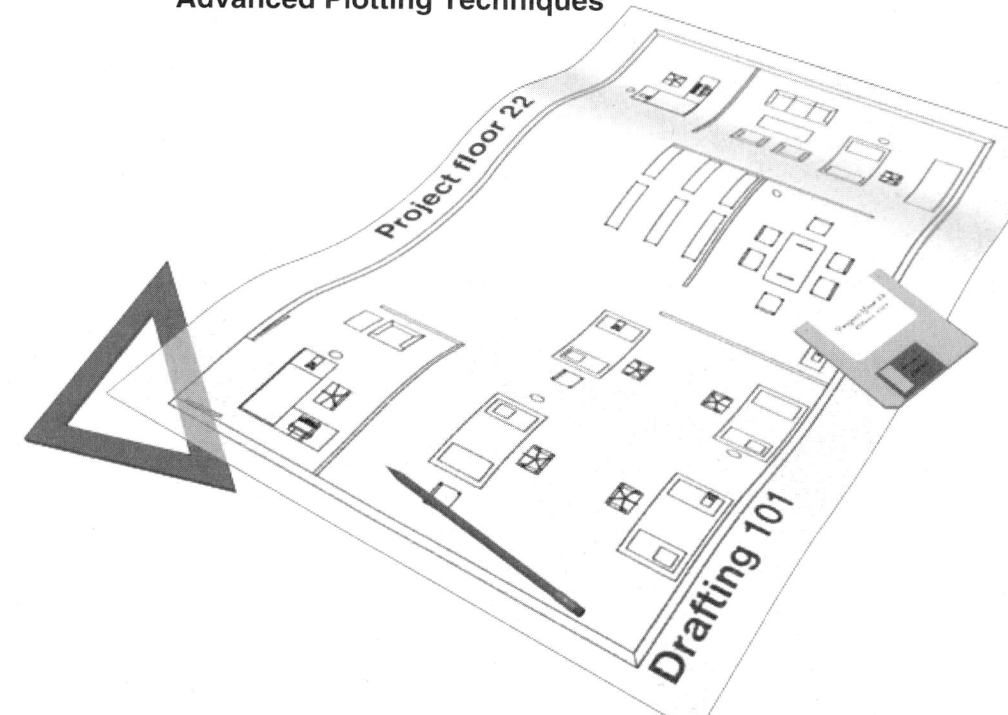

Introduction to Construction Techniques

UNIT 39

s you learned at the end of Part Two: *Using Basic CAD Techniques*, there are ways of creating drawing geometry other than having to create it "from scratch." By modifying existing geometry, you can quickly add to the drawing, tapping into one of the most useful benefits of CAD. Some of the commands used for this purpose are COPY, MIRROR, ARRAY, and OFFSET. The following units introduce these types of construction commands.

The objectives for this unit are to:

- Understand the differences between creating new geometry and modifying existing geometry
- Understand the benefits of specific constructive editing techniques
- Become familiar with the U and UNDO commands

Understanding Drawing Construction

The drawings shown in figure 39.1 and 39.2 illustrate practical examples construction techniques for creating drawing geometry versus creating each entity from scratch.

Figure 39.1

Construction techniques used in an architectural drawing.

Figure 39.2

Construction techniques used in a mechanical drawing.

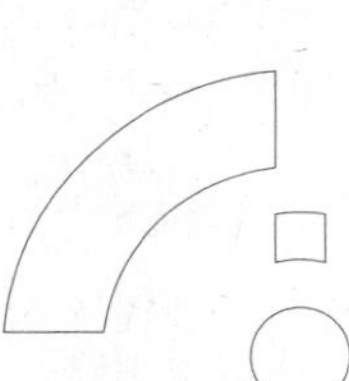

In each figure, the drawing on the left was used as the "skeleton" to create the drawing on the right. By using the commands COPY, MIRROR, ARRAY, OFFSET, and others, the drawing on the right can be completed within a few minutes.

Look at figure 39.1. You see the exterior walls of a building with some doors and windows added. A single door symbol was mirrored to create the final double-door symbol. The door and window frames were constructed by offsetting a line by two inches. The windows and frames were arrayed along the wall to create multiple windows. Some of these windows were then mirrored to the adjacent walls.

Notice in figure 39.1 that only one set of doors and one window needed to be drawn in addition to the walls. The rest of the drawing was created by using construction techniques—duplicating or modifying entities that already exist in the drawing, rather than drawing these entities from scratch.

In Figure 39.2, a few arcs and lines were all that were needed to construct the gear. By arraying the teeth and other geometry, the drawing takes very little time to finish.

Knowledgeable and skillful CAD users are masters of all the time-saving techniques available with CAD. These users think ahead while they use a CAD system. By taking advantage of the power and accuracy of your CAD system, you will also increase your drawing productivity and be more valuable to your employer.

Later units in this book teach you about specific commands and techniques for rapidly constructing a drawing from a few basic entities. The following sections provide a brief overview of some of the most common methods and explain why they are beneficial.

Copying and Arraying

Many drawings contain repetitive information. In the floor plan shown in figure 39.3, each of the windows is identical. Although it is possible to draw each window individually, you can save considerable time by drawing one window, then *copying* it to make the other windows. When you copy entities, you create a duplicate of some existing entities, but place them in a different location. Figure 39.3 illustrates a copy operation. Copying with grips is discussed in unit 25, "Copying Entities with Autoedit Modes."

An *array* operation is very similar to a copy. An array consists of multiple copies. You can define a selection set, then make multiple copies in rows and columns, or created rotated copies about a point. In the gear in figure 39.4, a single gear tooth is arrayed to create the remaining teeth. Working with an array is discussed in unit 42, "Constructing with Array."

Mirroring

The operation behind the term *mirror* is just what its name implies—you use existing entities to create a mirror image of the entities. The original entities might remain, creating a set of mirror-image entities, or the original entities might be erased. Figure 39.5 illustrates a mirror operation.

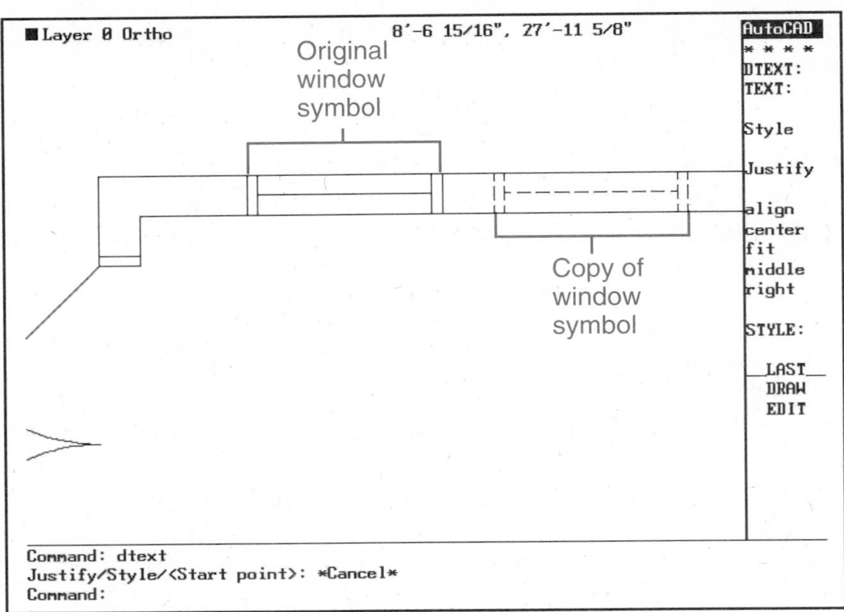

Figure 39.3

Copying existing entities to create new ones.

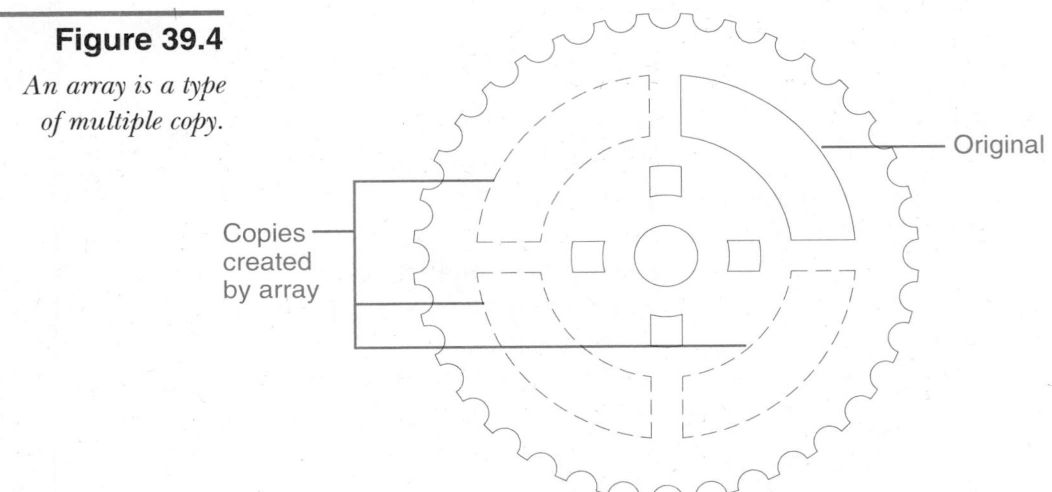

Figure 39.4

An array is a type of multiple copy.

Obviously, the MIRROR command is extremely useful when you need to create a mirror image using entities that already exist in the drawing. Mirroring entities with grips is explained in unit 24, "Rotating, Mirroring, and Scaling Entities." The MIRROR command is discussed in unit 41, "Constructing with MIRROR."

Using Offsets

An *offset* operation is one in which you offset existing entities to form new ones. A good example is a gasket—the outer and inner perimeter of the gasket often follow the same contour. You can create either the inner or outer perimeter, then use an offset operation to duplicate the other contour at a specific distance away. In figure 39.6, the outer perimeter was drawn first, then the OFFSET command was used to duplicate the contour at a specific, consistent distance away from the original.

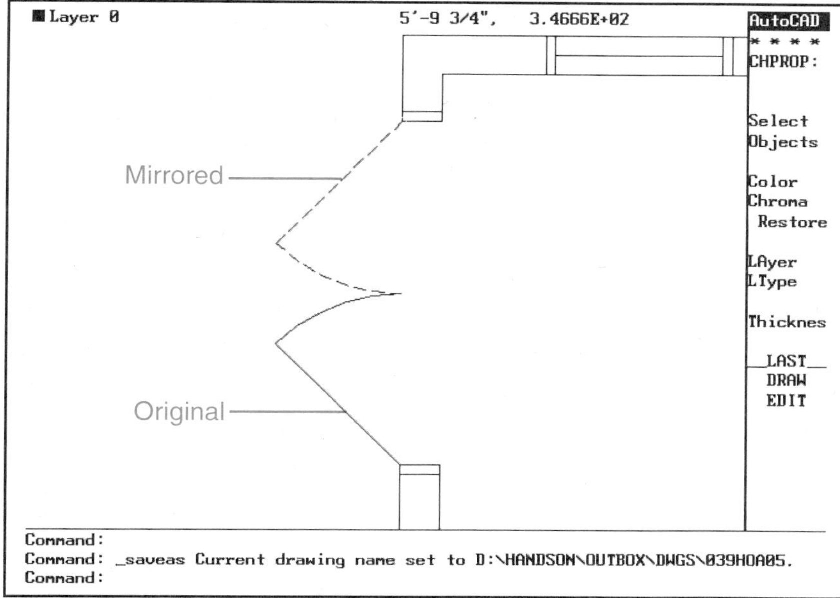

Figure 39.5

A single door mirrored to create a set.

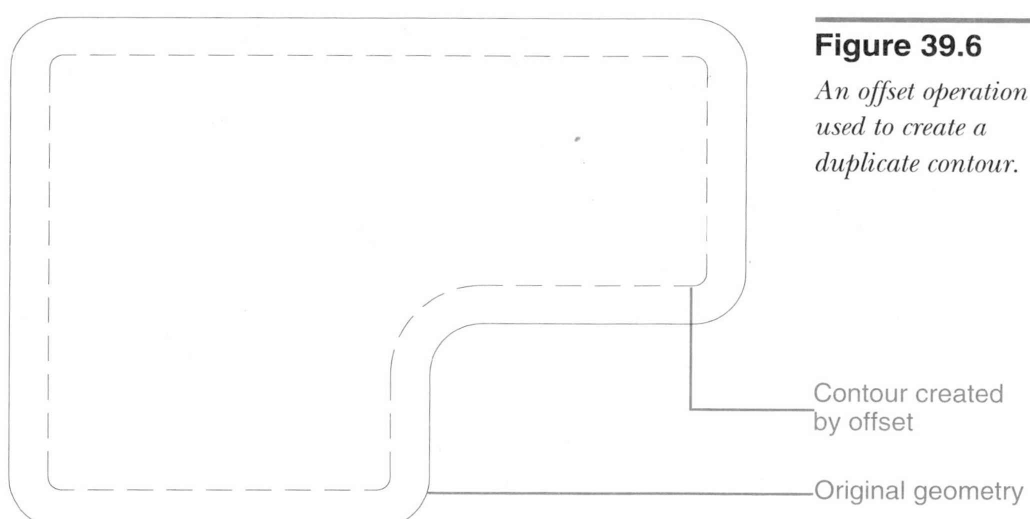

Figure 39.6

An offset operation used to create a duplicate contour.

The OFFSET command is explained in unit 43, "Constructing with OFFSET."

Trimming and Extending

In addition to creating new entities from existing entities by various duplication methods, you can modify existing entities without creating new ones. When defining complex geometry, for example, it often is easiest to create some *construction geometry*, then modify the goemetry to become the finished design. Trimming and extending are examples of operations that use this technique. Figure 39.7 illustrates a typical trim operation.

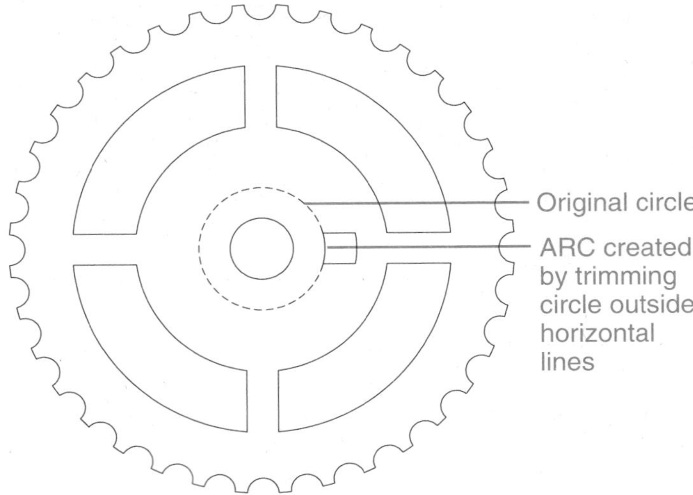

Figure 39.7

A typical trim.

The use of the TRIM command is explained in unit 52, "Trimming Entities"; the EXTEND command is explained in unit 54, "Extending Entities."

Using Grips

As units 22 through 25 explain, grips provide a fast method for modifying existing geometry. In this sense, grips provide a quick mechanism for constructive editing. Most of the other constructive editing operations described earlier in this unit can be performed either with grips and autoedit modes or with individual AutoCAD commands.

A number of constructive editing operations, however, cannot be performed with grips. You cannot create an array using grips, for example. Nevertheless, some operations that can be performed using grips and autoedit modes are easier to accomplish with other commands, as you will learn in later units.

Using Multiple Operations

Often, a single constructive editing technique will not completely suit your needs. In these cases, you must use multiple methods to create the drawing's geometry. Figure 39.8 illustrates one such example. The original window was first copied, then rotated to create the duplicate.

This unit mentions only some of the techniques available in AutoCAD; others are discussed in later units. As you become more proficient with AutoCAD and the many techniques available for creating drawing geometry, you will quickly realize that much of a typical drawing can be created by using these types of constructive editing techniques. Of all the drawing techniques AutoCAD offers, constructive editing is the fastest way to prepare drawings.

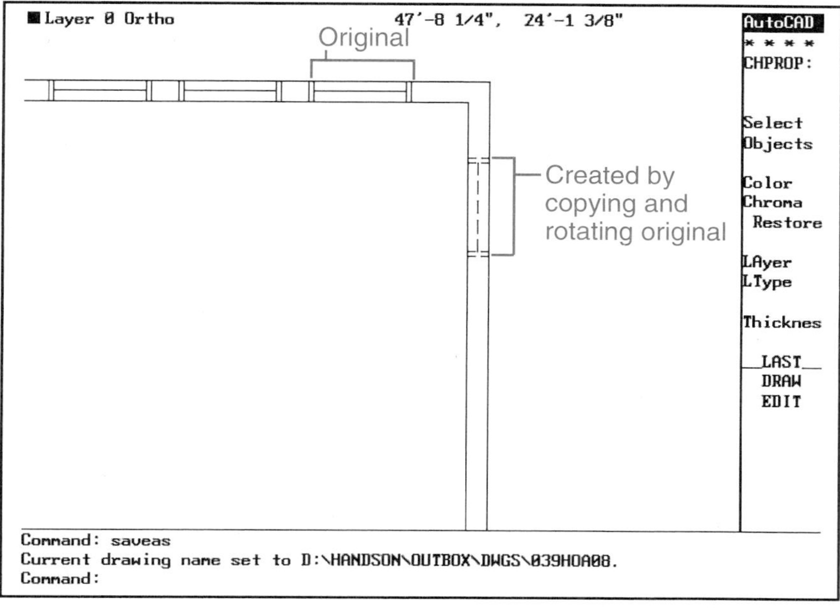

Figure 39.8

A window copied and rotated.

Using the UNDO Command

Two commands that you will most likely use more times than you may care to admit are the U and UNDO commands. These commands are used to undo a command or series of commands. You may need to undo commands because you made a mistake, or perhaps you wanted to try a few things to see how they would look. In many situations, the U and UNDO commands are important when you are using constructive editing to create a drawing. If a construction technique does not work the way you planned, U and UNDO let you "backtrack" to a point before you performed the construction operation(s).

The U command simply backs up one command at a time in your drawing session. If you want to go back five commands, you execute the U command five separate times. The U command has the capability to undo your drawing one step or command at a time until you are completely back at the beginning of your drawing session. When you execute the U command, it shows you on-screen at the command prompt which command it is undoing.

The UNDO command is a more powerful version of the U command. The UNDO command generates the prompt:

```
Auto/Back/Control/End/Group/Mark/<number>:
```

The commonly used options of UNDO include:

- **Back.** Undoes all commands back to the first mark that it finds. See the Mark option for more information.
- **Mark.** Directs AutoCAD to "save this place in my drawing in case I want to UNDO back to here in one step." This is most useful when you are experimenting with various designs in your drawing. You can create a new design, then undo back to the mark and try again. The Mark option also is useful if you are about to begin an editing operation but are not sure it will produce the correct results.
- **<number>.** If you enter a number in response to the UNDO command prompt, AutoCAD undoes the specified number of commands. You can undo the previous six commands, for example, by entering **6** in response to the prompt.

In the following exercise, experiment with the U command.

Using the U Command

1. Begin a new drawing named 039???01 in your assigned directory using 039UNDO as a prototype.

2. `Command:` *Pick points at ① and at ② (see fig. 39.9)*	Selects the center hole and square cutouts in the center of the gear
3. `Command:` **`E`** ↵	Issues the alias for the ERASE command and erases the current selection set
4. `Command:` **`U`** ↵ `ERASE`	Undoes the previous command

Next, use the Mark option to place a mark in the drawing. Perform a few editing operations, then restore the drawing to the mark point by using the Back option of the UNDO command.

Using UNDO Mark and UNDO Back

Continue with your drawing from the previous exercise.

1. `Command:` **`UNDO`** ↵	Issues the UNDO command
2. `Auto/Back/Control/End/Group/Mark/<number>:` **`M`** ↵	Specifies the Mark option

3. Erase the same set of entities that you erased in the previous exercise.
4. Use the move autoedit mode to move the two top cutouts three inches to the right (see fig. 39.10)

5. `Command:` **`UNDO`** ↵	Issues the UNDO command
6. `Auto/Back/Control/End/Group/Mark/<number>:` **`B`** ↵	Specifies the Back option and restores the drawing to the state where the mark was placed

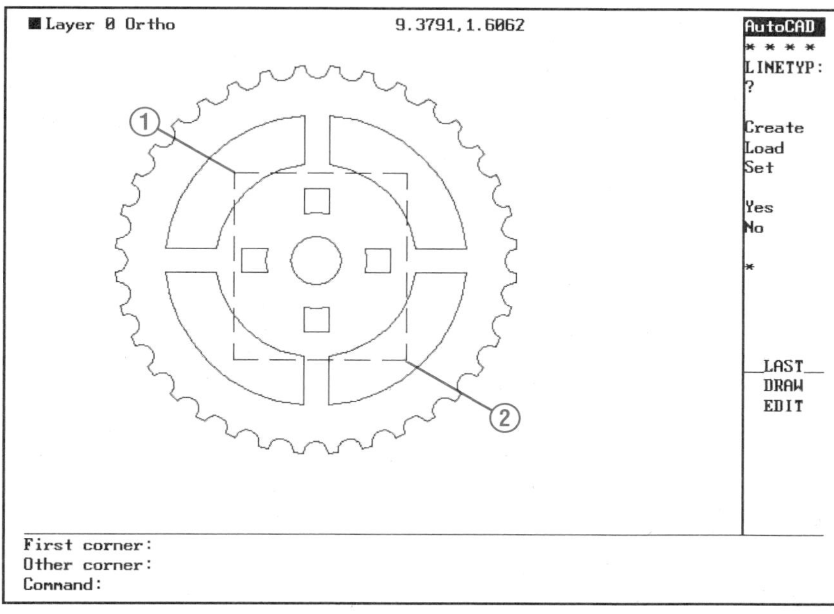

Figure 39.9

Selection points to erase entities.

As your drawings and editing operations become more and more complex, you will come to rely on the U and UNDO commands to test operations and to recover from errors.

If you undo a command or group of commands, use the REDO command to take the drawing back to the state it was in before you used the U or UNDO command.

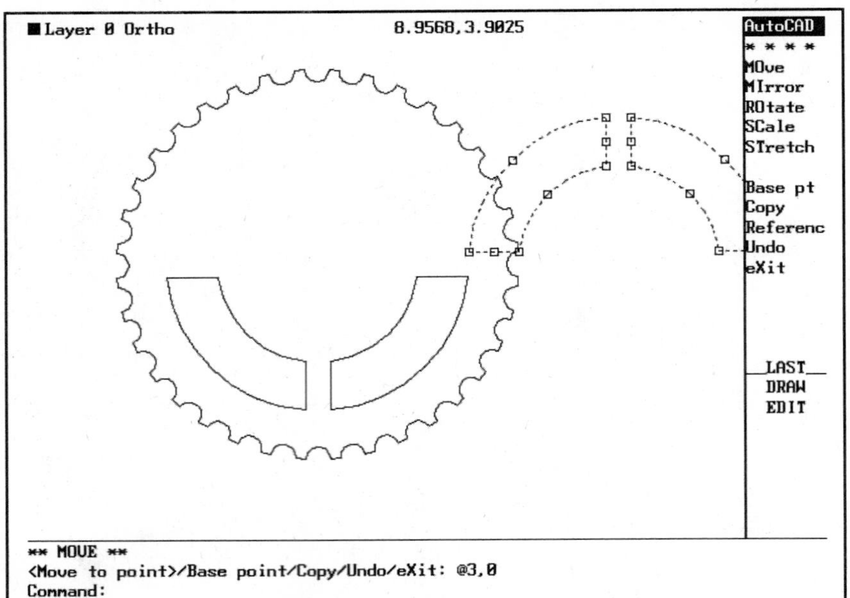

Figure 39.10

Two top cutouts moved three inches to the right.

Unit Review

What You've Learned

- ☞ The importance of using various construction techniques in a drawing
- ☞ The differences between creating new geometry "from scratch" and using construction techniques to modify or create geometry
- ☞ How specific construction techniques speed the drawing process
- ☞ The purpose of the U and UNDO commands

Review Questions

True or False

39.01 T F Using construction techniques to duplicate or modify entities often is faster than drawing "from scratch."

39.02 T F Many drawings contain repetitive information.

39.03 T F A *copy* operation makes a mirror image of the original entities.

39.04 T F You cannot copy entities using grips and autoedit modes.

39.05 T F You cannot array entities using grips and autoedit modes.

39.06 T F You can use the MIRROR command to create a mirror image of a set of entities.

39.07 T F An offset operation copies and rotates entities.

Multiple Choice

39.08 Which of the following cannot be accomplished with grips and autoedit modes? __________

(A) copy

(B) array

(C) stretch

(D) mirror

Student: ______________________ Date: __________

Instructor: ______________________ Course: __________ Section: __________

39.09 Which option of the UNDO command returns the drawing to a previous mark? __________

(A) a number

(B) Mark

(C) Back

(D) End

39.10 A single U command undoes __________ operation(s).

(A) one

(B) two

(C) ten

(D) any number of

Student: ____________________ Date: __________

Instructor: ____________________ Course: __________ Section: __________

UNIT 40

Constructing with COPY

Unit 39 introduced the concept of *constructive editing*, or modifying existing entities to create new ones. Unit 25, "Copying Entities with Autoedit Modes," examines copying entities using autoedit modes. You also can use the COPY command to copy existing entities. This unit teaches you to use the COPY command and explains how it differs from the copy autoedit modes.

The objectives for this unit are to:

- Understand the differences between the COPY command and copy autoedit modes
- Define an appropriate base point with COPY
- Create duplicate entities with COPY
- Use the Multiple option of the COPY command

Understanding COPY

Unit 25 explains the many ways in which you can duplicate entities by using the copy autoedit modes. These modes are very useful when you need to duplicate a limited number of entities, when you can use grips as reference points for the copy operation, or when you need to combine one of the other autoedit modes with your copy operation (such as scaling and copying in a single operation).

The copy autoedit modes are not useful in all situations, however, particularly when you need to copy a complex selection set (see unit 50, "Creating Advanced Selection Sets," for a discussion of complex selection sets). AutoCAD provides a command called COPY that enables you to copy single or multiple entities.

With COPY, you can make a single copy of a selection set, or you can make multiple copies of a single selection set. The primary difference between the COPY command and the copy autoedit modes is that you can define complex selection sets much more easily with the COPY command than you can with Copy autoedit modes' pick-first method of selection. In most other ways, the COPY command and the copy autoedit modes are very similar.

You can use pick-first entity selection with the COPY command. Simply create your selection using pick-first, then issue the COPY command. AutoCAD automatically uses the selection set defined by your pick-first operation and immediately prompts you for a base point. You do not have to make any other entity selections within the COPY command.

Using the COPY Command for Construction

The drawing in figure 40.1 represents a cafeteria with tables and chairs. You will be using this drawing for the next few units to work with COPY and other commands. In the following exercise, copy the rectangular table 8' to the north.

Using One-Point Displacement for the COPY Command

1. Begin a new drawing named 040???01 in your assigned directory using 040CAFE as a prototype.

2. `Command:` *Choose* Construct, *then* Copy — Issues the COPY command

   `_copy`

3. `Select objects:` *Select the rectangular table* — Adds to the selection set for the copy operation

   `1 found`

4. `Select objects:` *Press* Enter	Ends the selection set for the COPY command
5. `<Base point or displacement>/Multiple:` **`0,8'`** ↵	Defines the displacement for the copy
6. `Second point of displacement:` *Press* Enter	Ends the copy operation

Your drawing should look similar to figure 40.2.

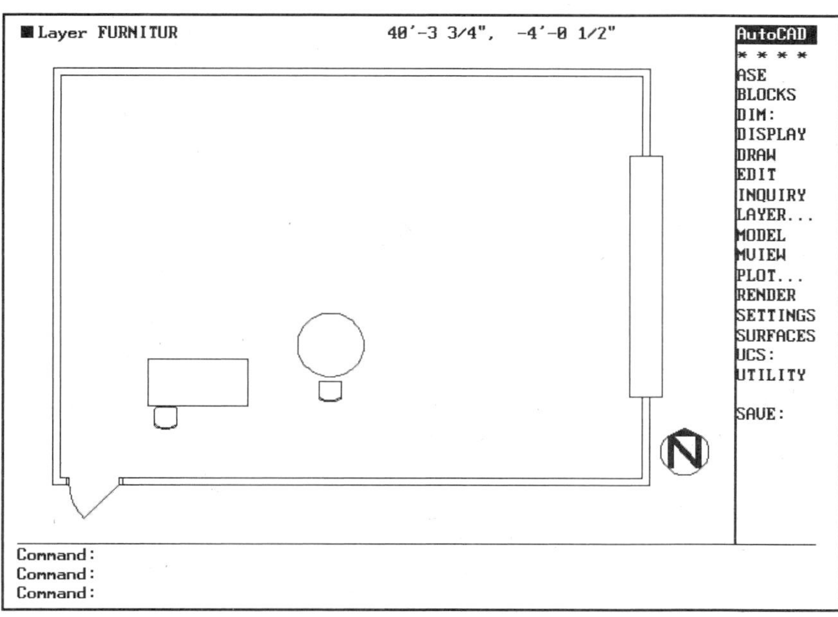

Figure 40.1

Cafeteria drawing.

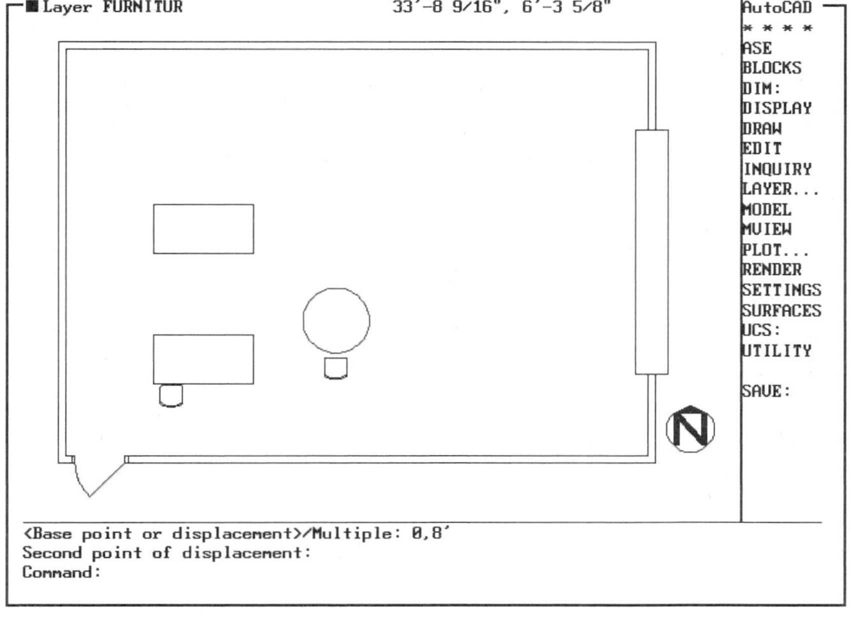

Figure 40.2

A copy of the table.

In this first exercise, you specified a displacement point to tell AutoCAD that you wanted to make a copy 8' in the y-direction from the current location. When you specify a displacement at the `<Base point or displacement>` prompt, you are specifying a relative distance from the original. In other words, the point you specify is not an absolute coordinate but is relative to the selected object's location. Notice that the "@" symbol is not necessary. AutoCAD already assumes that a displacement point you supply for the first prompt is relative.

In the next exercise, copy the table using a two-point displacement method instead.

Using Two-Point Displacement for the Copy Command

1. Use the U command to undo your drawing to its original state.

2. `Command:` **`U`**	Issues the U command and undoes the previous copy
`GROUP`	
3. `Command:` *Select the rectangular table*	Builds a selection set using pick-first
4. `Command:` *Choose* Construct, *then* Copy	Issues the COPY command
`_copy 1 found`	
5. `<Base point or displacement>/Multiple:` *Pick any point on-screen*	Specifies the base point
6. `Second point of displacement:` **`@0,8'`** ↵	Defines the second point of displacement

Your drawing should again look similar to figure 40.2.

In this exercise, you were not particular about where the base point was because you specified a relative displacement. Notice that this time, you had to specify a relative point by using the "@" symbol. Also, you used pick-first selection to select the table to copy. When you issued the COPY command, AutoCAD automatically prompted you to specify a base point without requiring any additional entity selection.

In the next exercise, you are going to be more careful in choosing a base point. You want to copy the rectangular table end-to-end multiple times.

Performing a Multiple Copy

Continue with your drawing from the preceding exercise.

1.	`Command:` *Choose* Construct, *then* Copy `_copy`	Issues the COPY command
2.	`Select objects:` *Select the table at* ① *(see fig. 40.3)* `1 found`	Starts the selection set
3.	`Select objects:` *Press* Enter	Ends the selection set
4.	`<Base point or displacement>/Multiple:` **M** ↵	Specifies the Multiple option
5.	`Base point:` *From the popup menu, choose* Endpoint	
6.	`_endp of` *Pick the end point at* ② *(see fig. 40.3)*	Defines the base point
7.	`Second point of displacement:` *From the popup menu, choose* Endpoint	
8.	`_endp of` *Pick the end point at* ③ *(see fig. 40.3)*	Defines the next point of displacement and creates a copy
9.	`Second point of displacement:` *From the popup menu, choose* Endpoint	
10.	`_endp of` *Pick the end point at* ④ *(see fig. 40.3)*	Defines the next point of displacement and creates a copy
11.	`Second point of displacement:` *From the popup menu, choose* Endpoint	
12.	`_endp of` *Pick the end point at* ⑤ *(see fig. 40.3)*	Defines the next point of displacement and creates a copy
13.	`Second point of displacement:` *Press* Enter	Ends the COPY command

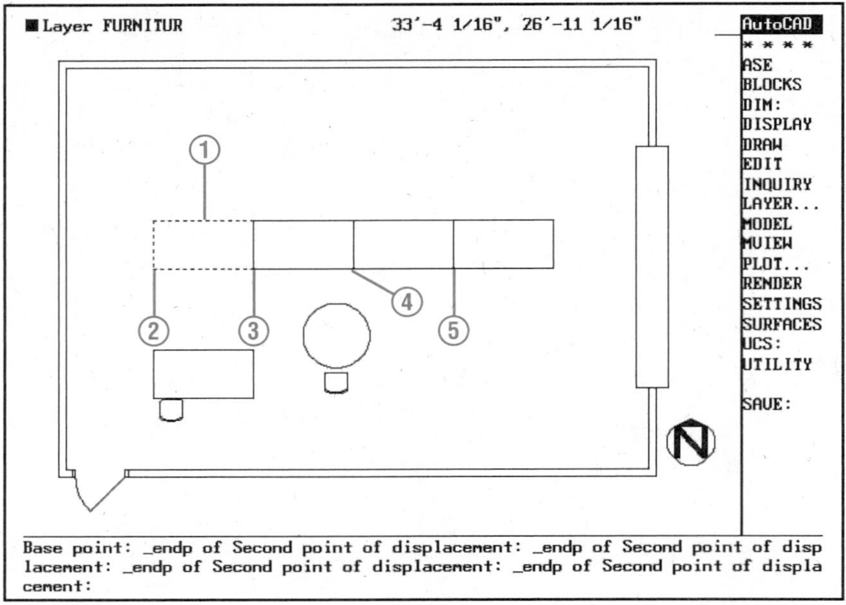

Figure 40.3

Using the Multiple option of the COPY command.

In this exercise, you used the Multiple option to make more than one copy. You also used a specific base point. This is because you wanted to butt the table ends together. Whenever you need to place a copy at a specific point that is not easily defined by a displacement from the original, choose specific points for the base point and for the second point of displacement.

Whenever possible, select a base point that coincides with an end point, center point, or other known point on the original selection set. Then use this specific point to locate the new entities accurately.

Unit 25 introduces the Copy option of the stretch, move, rotate, scale, and mirror autoedit modes. Use these copy autoedit methods when you can use the pick-first method to select entities, or when you want to combine operations such as stretch and copy. Use the COPY command when you need to define a complex selection set or when it is not practical to use pick-first selection (although you also can use pick-first selection with the COPY command).

Unit Review

What You've Learned

- ☞ How to specify a relative base point using the one-point method
- ☞ How to specify a relative base point using the two-point method
- ☞ How to choose a base point strategically
- ☞ How to use the Multiple option

Review Questions

True or False

40.01 T F Constructive editing is the process of modifying existing entities to create new ones.

40.02 T F Copy autoedit modes are useful when you need to combine editing operations such as stretch and copy.

40.03 T F You cannot create a complex selection set with the COPY command.

40.04 T F You can use pick-first selection with the COPY command.

40.05 T F If you enter a displacement in the form X,Y when AutoCAD prompts you for a base point or displacement in the COPY command, you can press Enter at the second point prompt to define a relative displacement.

Multiple Choice

40.06 The COPY command enables you to specify __________ to copy.

(A) autoedit modes

(B) complex selection sets

(C) multiple selection sets

(D) none of the above

Student: ______________________ Date: __________

Instructor: ______________________ Course: __________ Section: __________

40.07 When you specify a coordinate in response to the COPY command's `<Base point or displacement>` prompt, it defines a displacement that is ________.

(A) absolute from the origin

(B) vertical

(C) relative to the original entities

(D) horizontal

40.08 Which symbol can be used to specify a relative displacement?

____

(A) @

(B) <

(C) >

(D) =

Short Answer

40.09 Briefly explain how the Copy option of the autoedit modes is different from the COPY command.

____

____

____

40.10 Briefly explain how to make multiple copies using the COPY command.

____

____

____

Additional Exercises

40.11 Place three chairs along the edge of the lower rectangular table. (One has already been placed for you.) Use the Multiple option and place the chairs at a spacing of 1'3/8"—use figure 40.4 as a guide. Save your drawing.

Student: ________________ Date: ________________

Instructor: ________________ Course: ________________ Section: ________________

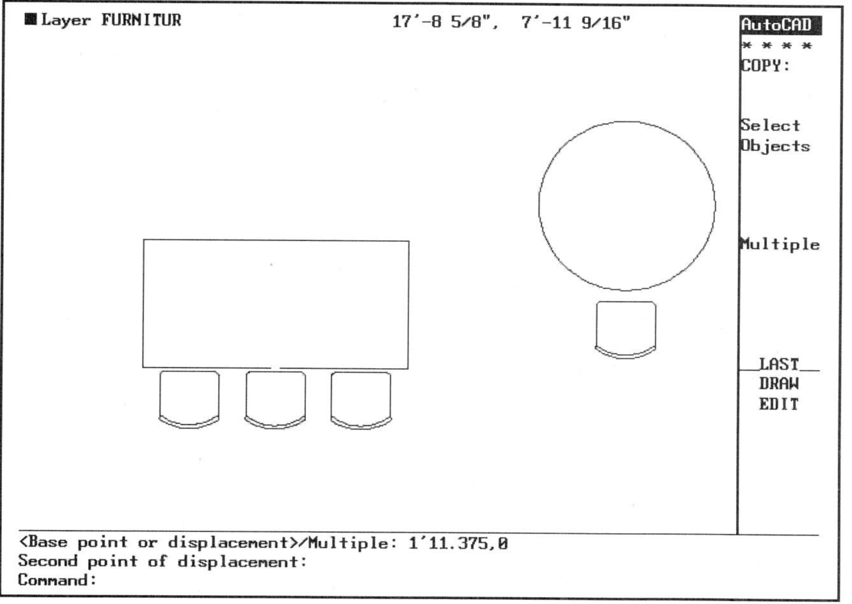

Figure 40.4

Chairs added to one of the tables.

40.12 Make two copies of the round table: one at 8' to the east, and another at 12' to the north (see fig. 40.5). Save your drawing.

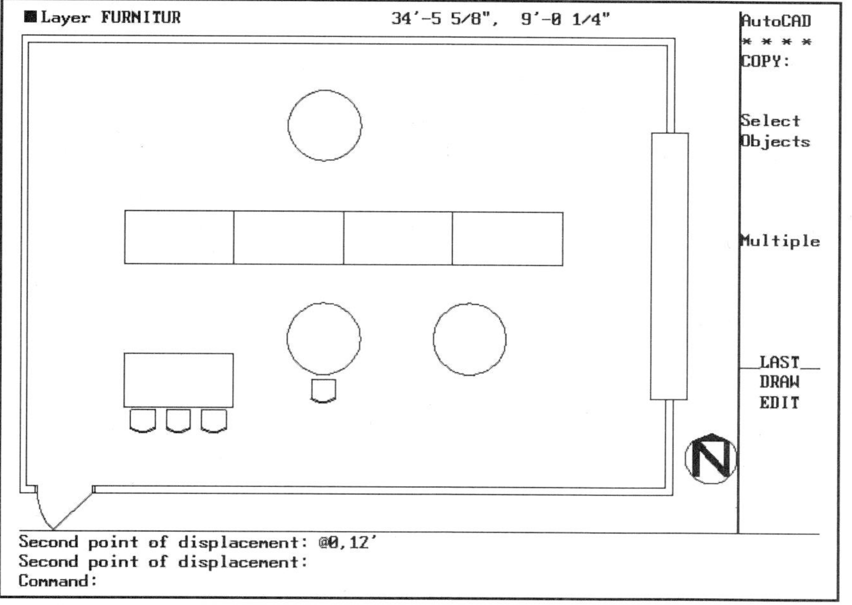

Figure 40.5

Two tables added to the drawing.

Student: ______ Date: ______

Instructor: ______ Course: ______ Section: ______

UNIT 41

Constructing with MIRROR

Another means of constructing geometry is mirroring entities. Unit 24, "Rotating, Mirroring, and Scaling Entities," explains how to use the Mirror autoedit mode to mirror entities. When you mirror entities, you define the two end points of a *mirror line* about which to mirror the entities. In addition to the Mirror autoedit mode, you have another option for mirroring entities. The MIRROR command works very much like Mirror autoedit mode, except it works with both pick-first and pick-after selection.

The objectives for this unit are to:

- ☞ Use the MIRROR command to create new entities
- ☞ Learn the importance of the mirror line

Using the MIRROR Command for Construction

The MIRROR command works virtually the same as Mirror autoedit mode; only a few small differences exist. First, MIRROR works with either pick-first or pick-after selection. If a selection set exists when you issue the MIRROR command, AutoCAD does not prompt you to select additional entities, but immediately prompts you to specify the end points of the mirror line.

Another difference is MIRROR lacks a Copy option. Instead, MIRROR prompts you to specify whether you want to retain the original entities each time you perform the mirror operation. Unlike Mirror autoedit mode, you cannot use MIRROR to create multiple mirrored copies in a single operation.

If you are not familiar with Mirror autoedit mode, you might want to review unit 24 before continuing with this unit.

In the following exercise, use the MIRROR command to create new furniture entities in a cafeteria. Mirror the chair at the rectangular table to the other side of the table. Use figure 41.1 to select entities.

The chairs in the following exercise are blocks. Because of the way AutoCAD recognizes blocks, you can select the entire chair as a single entity. Blocks are explained in unit 67, "Introduction to Blocks."

Using the MIRROR Command

1. Begin a new drawing named 041???01 in your assigned directory using 041CAFE as a prototype.

2. `Command:` *Choose* Construct, *then* Mirror	Issues the MIRROR command
`_mirror`	
3. `Select objects:` *Select the chair at* ① *(see fig. 41.1)*	Defines the selection set
`1 found`	
4. `Select objects:` *Press* Enter	Ends selection

5. `First point of mirror line:` *From the popup menu, choose* Midpoint `_mid of`	
6. *Pick the midpoint at* ②	Defines the first end point of the mirror line
7. `Second point:` *From the popup menu, choose* Midpoint `_mid of`	
8. *Pick the midpoint at* ③ *(see fig. 41.1)*	Specifies the second point of the mirror line
9. `Delete old objects? <N>` *Press* Enter	Accepts default to retain original entities and mirrors the selection set

Your drawing should resemble figure 41.2.

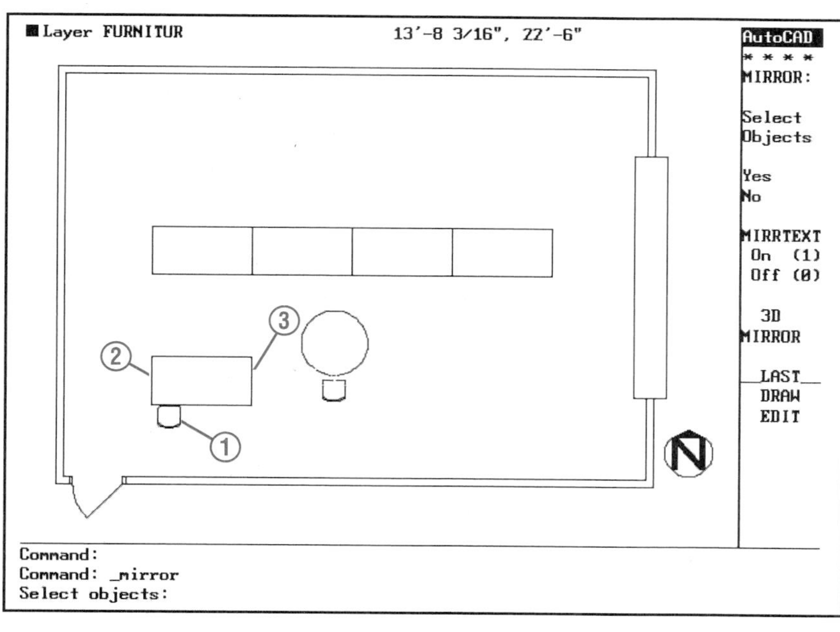

Figure 41.1

Selection points for MIRROR.

In the preceding exercise, you specified that you want to keep the original objects. In the following exercise, mirror the chair at the round table and delete the original object.

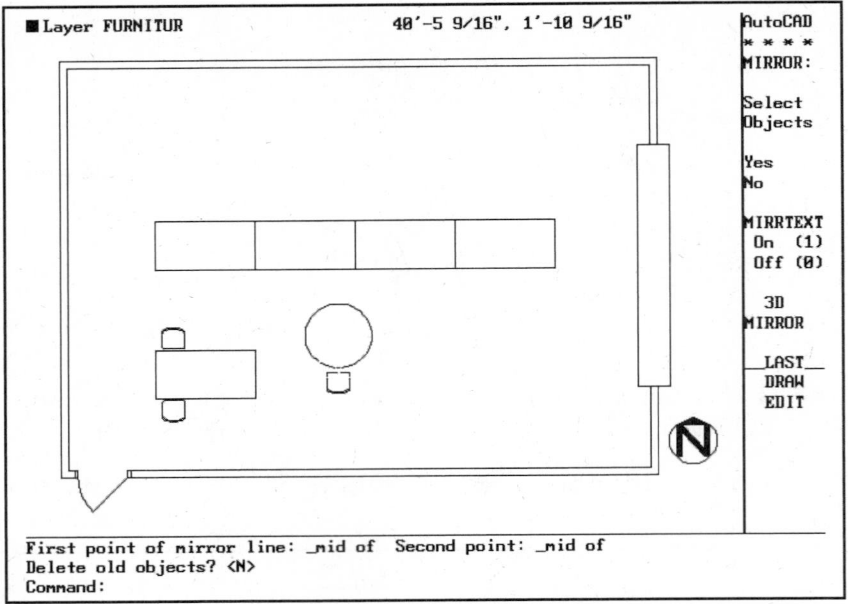

Figure 41.2

Chair created with MIRROR.

Mirroring the chair to move it to the other side of the table is just one method you can use. You also can rotate the chair with ROTATE or with Rotate autoedit mode by using the center of the table as a center point.

Mirroring Objects and Deleting the Originals

Continue with your drawing from the preceding exercise.

1. `Command:` *Choose* Construct, *then* Mirror	Issues the MIRROR command
`_mirror`	
2. `Select objects:` *Select the chair at* ① *(see fig. 41.3)*	Starts a selection set
`1 found`	
3. `Select objects:` *Press* Enter	Ends selection
4. `First point of mirror line:` *From the popup menu, choose* Quadrant	Sets object snap mode
`_qua of`	
5. *Pick the quadrant at* ② *(see fig. 41.3)*	Specifies first point of mirror line

6. `Second point:` *From the popup menu, choose* Quadrant — Sets object snap mode

   `_qua of`

7. *Pick the quadrant at* ③ *(see fig. 41.3)*

8. `Delete old objects? <N>` **Y** ↵ — Directs AutoCAD to delete the original object

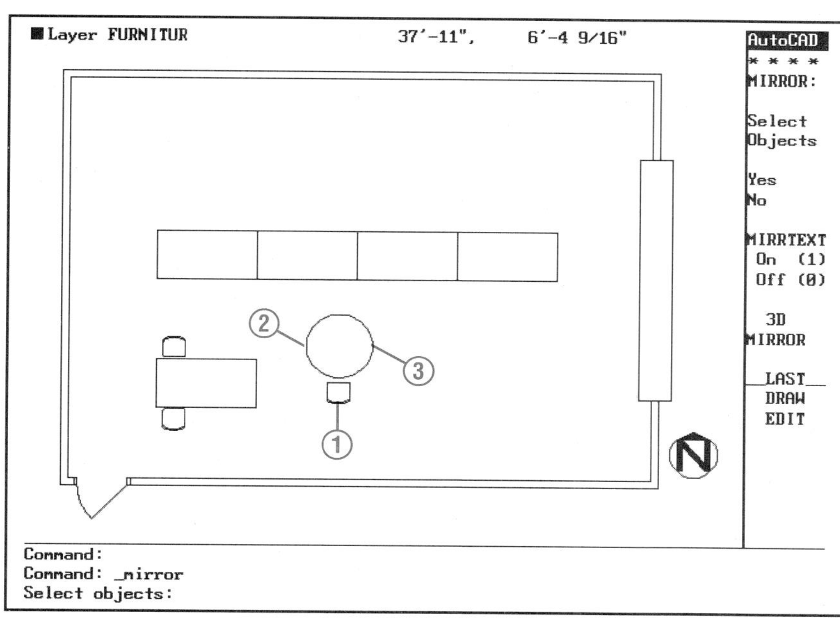

Figure 41.3

Selection points for MIRROR delete.

Your drawing should resemble figure 41.4.

In addition to the absence of a Copy option and its use of pick-after selection, MIRROR has other differences from Mirror autoedit mode. You cannot make multiple copies of entities with a single operation using MIRROR, but you can do so using Mirror autoedit mode. MIRROR does not enable you to specify a base point, but instead prompts you to specify both points of the mirror line. In Mirror autoedit mode, the base point is used as the first point of the mirror line.

If you are mirroring a selection set that contains text, you can use the MIRRTEXT system variable to control whether AutoCAD mirrors the text or retains its original orientation. The default setting for MIRRTEXT is 1. When MIRRTEXT is set to 1, AutoCAD mirrors text in addition to relocating the text according to the location of the mirror line. If MIRRTEXT is set to 0, AutoCAD does not mirror the text, although it relocates the text according to the location of the mirror line.

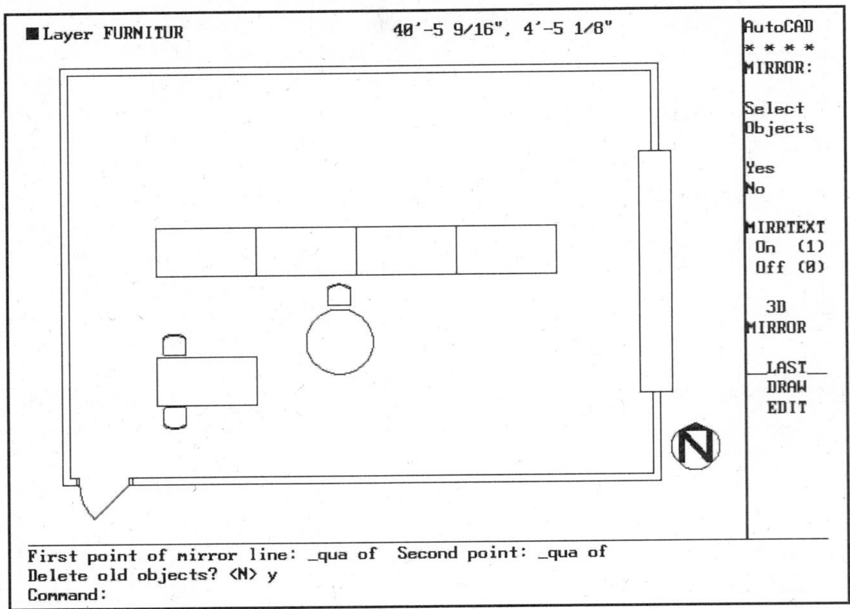

Figure 41.4

Mirroring objects and deleting the original objects.

In many cases, MIRROR and Mirror autoedit mode work equally well for mirroring entities. The advantage to using MIRROR in some cases is that it supports pick-after selection as well as pick-first selection. If you need to use Fence, WPolylgon, CPolygon, or other selection objects to define the selection set when mirroring, use MIRROR. If you need to make multiple mirrored copies, or prefer using grips to edit, use Mirror autoedit mode.

Unit Review

What You've Learned

- How to mirror entities, keeping the original entities
- How to mirror entities, deleting the original entities

Review Questions

True or False

41.01 T F When you mirror entities, you define the two end points of a "mirror line."

41.02 T F If you want to delete the original objects when mirroring a selection set, you must manually erase the original entities.

41.03 T F The mirror line is specified by picking an existing line on your drawing.

41.04 T F When using MIRROR, you must specify a base point.

41.05 T F In the Mirror autoedit mode, you can make multiple copies while mirroring.

Multiple Choice

41.06 When you mirror entities with the MIRROR command, you must define a __________.

(A) mirror line

(B) base point

(C) mirror angle

(D) none of the above

41.07 MIRROR works with __________ selection.

(A) pick-first

(B) pick-after

(C) both A and B

Student: ____________________ Date: __________

Instructor: ____________________ Course: __________ Section: __________

41.08 In Mirror autoedit mode, the __________ is used as the first point of the __________.

(A) selection set, mirror line

(B) base point, selection set

(C) base point, mirror line

(D) none of the above

Short Answer

41.09 List three differences between MIRROR and Mirror autoedit mode.

____

____

____

41.10 Explain why you cannot make multiple mirrored copies with a single MIRROR command.

____

____

____

Additional Exercises

41.11 The safety codes in your area dictate that a room the size of your cafeteria must have at least two exits. Use the MIRROR command to mirror the door and frame to the opposite wall, keeping the original in its place. In a later unit, you learn how to trim the wall lines out between the door frames on your new door. When you complete the exercise, your drawing should resemble figure 41.5. Save your drawing when you are finished.

Student: __________ Date: __________

Instructor: __________ Course: __________ Section: __________

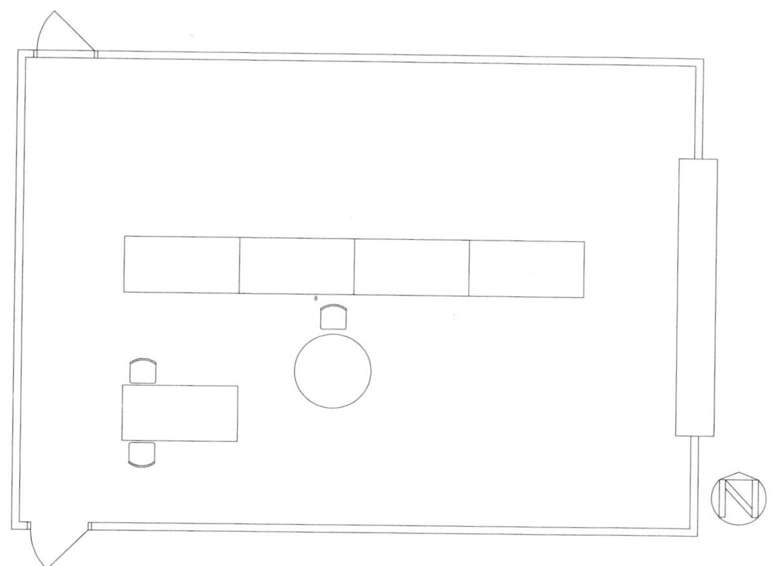

Figure 41.5

Mirroring a door to the opposite wall.

Student: ____________________ Date: __________

Instructor: ____________________ Course: __________ Section: __________

Constructing with ARRAY

In many drawings, a small portion of the drawing can be copied and rotated to create a finished part. The teeth on a gear are an example. In other drawings, you sometimes need to copy one or more objects into rows and columns. AutoCAD provides a single command called ARRAY for performing these tasks.

The objectives for this unit are to:

- Create entities using the Rectangular option of the ARRAY command
- Create entities using the Polar option of the ARRAY command
- Understand how to specify the spacing in arrays

Understanding Arrays

In AutoCAD, objects that you copy into rows and columns are called *rectangular arrays.* The chairs in an auditorium or the desks in a classroom are examples of arrays. Windows equally spaced along a wall are another example of a rectangular array.

AutoCAD also enables you to copy and rotate an object to create a *polar array.* The teeth on a gear are an example of a polar array. By copying and rotating a single tooth, you can quickly draw all the teeth on the gear. Any object that can be created by rotating and copying one or more entities around a point is a polar array.

The ARRAY command enables you to create rectangular and polar arrays. ARRAY works with either pick-first or pick-after selection. If a selection set exists when you issue the ARRAY command, AutoCAD does not prompt for additional entities, but instead prompts you for additional information to create the array. If no selection set exists, AutoCAD prompts you to select objects.

You can issue the ARRAY command by choosing Construct, then Array. You also can enter **ARRAY** at the command prompt or choose it from the EDIT screen menu.

Creating Rectangular Arrays

Rectangular arrays are created by specifying the number of rows and columns in the array and the distances between the rows and columns. The distance between rows and columns is the distance between similar points on the objects and not the empty space between objects.

In the following exercises, modify a drawing of a cafeteria to create rows and columns of chairs and tables.

Creating an Array of Tables

1. Begin a new drawing named 042???01 in your assigned directory using 042ARRAY as a prototype.

2. `Command:` *Choose* Construct, *then* Array — Issues the ARRAY command

   `_array`

3. `Select objects:` *Select the rectangular table* — Defines the selection set

   `1 found`

4. `Select objects:` *Press Enter* — Ends selection

5. `Rectangular or Polar array (R/P) <R>:` **R** ↵ — Specifies the type of array

6. `Number of rows (---) <1>:` **3** ↵ — Specifies the number of rows in the array

7. `Number of columns (|||) <1>:` **3** ↵ — Specifies the number of columns in the array

8. `Unit cell or distance between rows (---):` **7'** ↵ — Specifies the distance between rows at two similar points on the objects

9. `Distance between columns (|||):` **`6'`** ↵	Specifies the distance between columns at two similar points on the objects

Your drawing should look similar to figure 42.1.

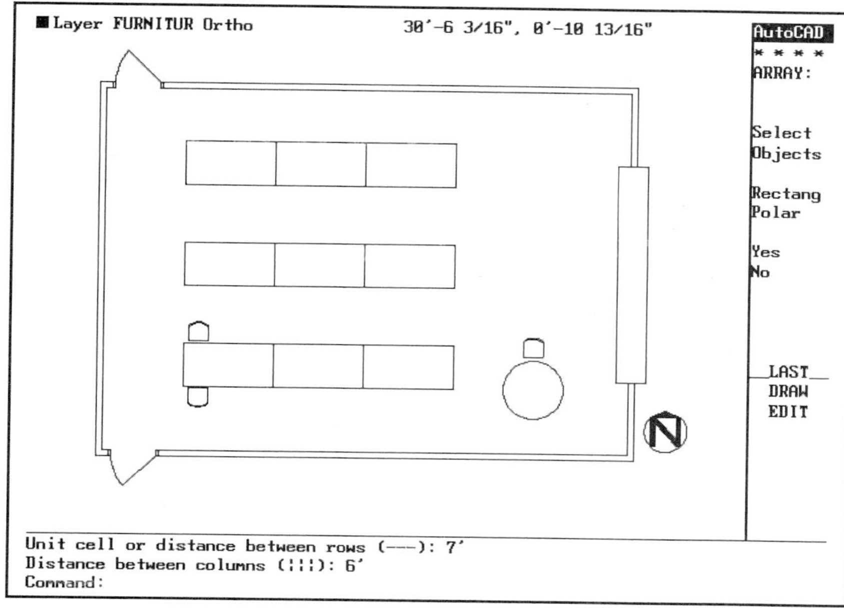

Figure 42.1

Creating a rectangular array.

It is important to note that when you create the rectangular array of tables in the exercise, the distance you specify between rows and columns is not the aisle space between tables. The distances in an array are from one point on the object to a similar point on the object in the next row or column. In the preceding exercise, the distance from one corner of a table to the same corner in the next row is seven feet. Similarly, the distance between columns is six feet, measured from one corner on a table to the same corner in the next column. Because the tables are six feet in length, this setting ensures the tables will butt end-to-end.

NOTE

When specifying the distances between rows and columns, you can use what AutoCAD calls a unit cell. *This is an imaginary rectangle you specify by picking two points. The two points, or opposite corners of the unit cell, show AutoCAD the distances between the rows and columns of the rectangular array. Unit cell specification is useful when you do not know the required distance between rows and columns, but you do have predefined points in the drawing that you can use to define the cell.*

Not every rectangular array consists of rows and columns. In some situations, the array consists only of rows or only of columns. Any time you need to make multiple copies of an object at specific horizontal or vertical spacing, you can use the ARRAY command.

In the following exercise, create a single-row array of chairs.

Creating a Single-Row Array

Continue with your drawing from the preceding exercise.

1. `Command:` **`ARRAY`** ↵	Issues the ARRAY command
2. `Select objects:` *Select the chair at the lower left of the drawing*	Defines the selection set
`1 found`	
3. `Select objects:` *Press* Enter	Ends selection
4. `Rectangular or Polar array (R/P) <R>:` *Press* Enter	Specifies the type of array
4. `Number of rows (---) <1>:` *Press* Enter	Specifies a single-row array
5. `Number of columns (|||) <1>:` **`9`** ↵	Specifies the number of columns in the array
6. `Distance between columns (|||):` **`2'`** ↵	Specifies the distance between similar points on each object

Your drawing should look similar to figure 42.2.

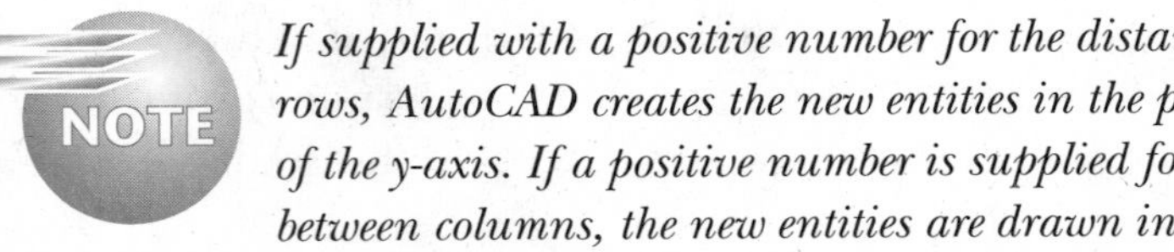

If supplied with a positive number for the distance between rows, AutoCAD creates the new entities in the positive direction of the y-axis. If a positive number is supplied for the distance between columns, the new entities are drawn in the positive direction of the x-axis. To create the array in the opposite direction, specify a negative value for the distance between rows, columns, or both.

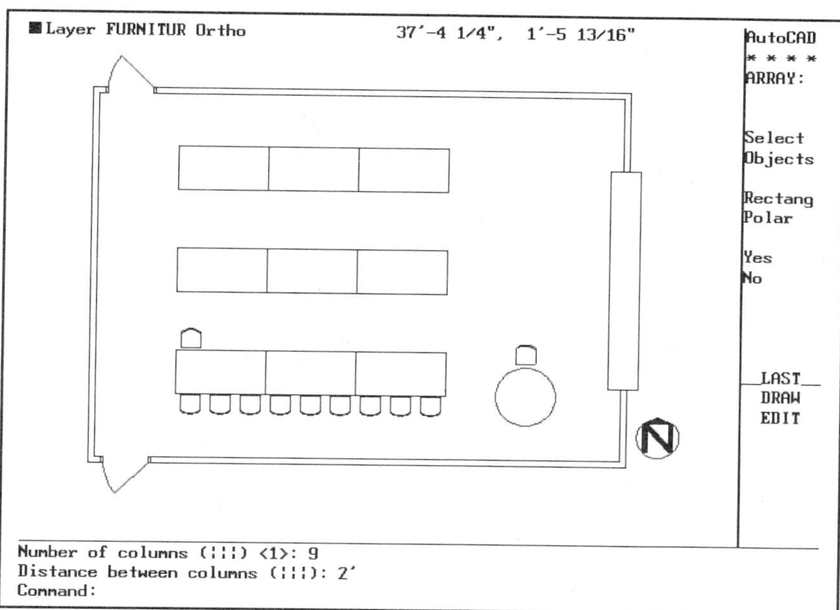

Figure 42.2

A single-row array.

Creating Polar Arrays

To create a polar array, first select the objects to be arrayed, then specify the center point of rotation, the number of copies to be made, and the included angle of the array. The center point specifies the point about which the entities are copied. The number of objects defines how many copies are to be made. The included angle indirectly defines the angle between each copy in the array. If you specify an angle of 360 degrees and 18 copies, for example, the angle between copies in the array will be 20 degrees, which equals 360 degrees divided by 18.

The copies created in a polar array are spaced equally about the center point according to the number of copies and the included angle, as explained earlier. When you create a polar array, you have the option of rotating the entities as they are copied or leaving them in the original orientation. Figure 42.3 illustrates two arrays created using the same geometry. In the array on the left, the objects were rotated as they were copied. In the array on the right, the objects were not rotated.

In the following exercise, use a polar array to place chairs around the round table.

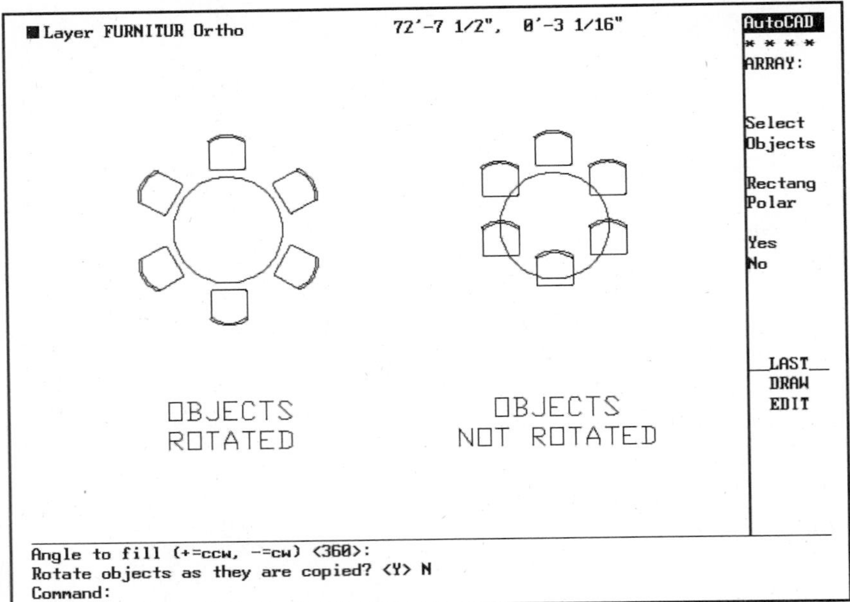

Figure 42.3

Objects rotated and not rotated in an array.

Creating a Polar Array

Continue with your drawing from the preceding exercise.

1. `Command:` *Choose* Construct, *then* Array — Issues the ARRAY command

2. `Select objects:` *Select the chair at ① (see fig. 42.4)* — Starts a selection set

   `1 found`

3. `Select objects:` *Press* Enter — Ends selection

4. `Rectangular or Polar array (R/P) <R>:` **P** ↵ — Specifies the Polar option

5. `Center point of array:` **CEN** ↵ — Sets object snap mode

   `of`

6. *Select the circle at ② (see fig. 42.4)*

7. `Number of items:` **6** ↵ — Defines the number of items in the array, including the original object

8. `Angle to fill (+=ccw, -=cw) <360>:` *Press Enter* — Determines the extent of the polar array (the included angle)

9. `Rotate objects as they are copied? <Y>:` *Press* Enter — Causes AutoCAD to rotate the objects about the center of rotation as it copies them

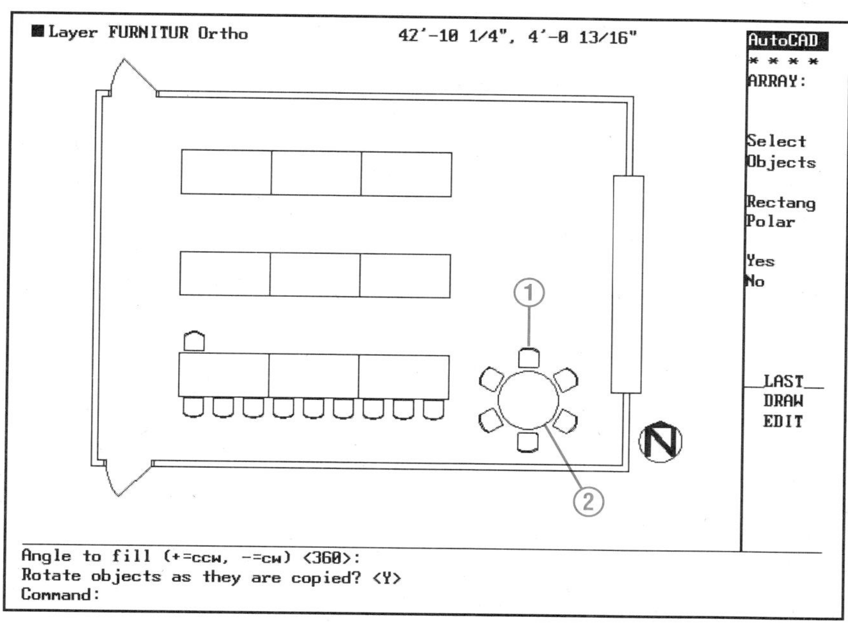

Figure 42.4

Creating a polar array.

In addition to entering a value when prompted for the angle to fill, you can select a point. AutoCAD calculates the angle starting at zero degrees relative to the center of rotation, moving counter-clockwise to an imaginary line that extends from the center of rotation to the selected point. Figure 42.5 illustrates how AutoCAD calculates the angle to fill.

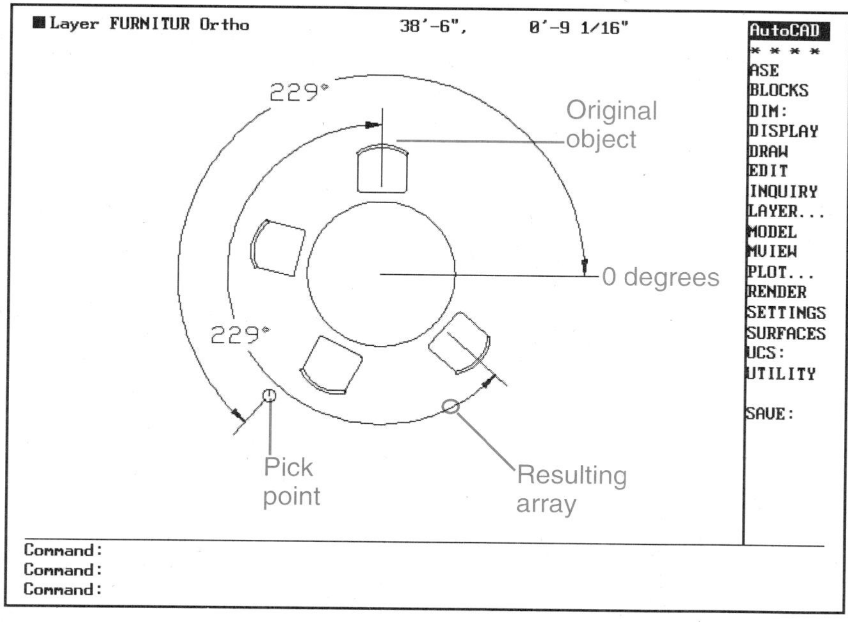

Figure 42.5

Angle calculation by selecting a point.

If you specify a point to define the angle to fill, keep in mind that you are not defining the angle relative to the object being copied. The angle is always measured from zero degrees. If the original object is not located at zero degrees relative to the center of rotation, the resulting array might not be what you expect.

If you need to create multiple copies of an object rotated about the same point, but the objects are not evenly spaced, you can use the Rotate autoedit mode. To do this, select the object(s) you want to array, pick a grip to enter autoedit mode, and then choose the Rotate autoedit mode. Next, specify a new base point that becomes the center of your array. Choose the Copy option, and then pick the new locations for your objects.

Unit Review

What You've Learned

- What is an array
- The difference between a rectangular array and a polar array
- How to specify the distances between rows and columns in a rectangular array
- How to create a polar array

Review Questions

True or False

42.01 T F The ARRAY command is used to copy entities in row-and-column (rectangular) fashion or in a circular (polar) fashion.

42.02 T F A rectangular array can be used to create the teeth on a circular gear.

42.03 T F Rectangular arrays are created by specifying the number of rows and columns and the distances between them.

42.04 T F The distance between rows and columns is specified as the empty space between objects.

42.05 T F A unit cell can be used to specify the distances between rows and columns in a polar array.

42.06 T F When creating a single-row array, you must specify a zero distance between rows.

42.07 T F AutoCAD can accept negative values for distances in a rectangular array.

42.08 T F The center point of a polar array is not always required.

42.09 T F A polar array copies objects in a circular fashion.

42.10 T F A polar array does not always have to be a complete circle.

Student: ____________________ Date: ________

Instructor: ____________________ Course: ________ Section: ________

Additional Exercises

42.11 Use your drawing from the preceding exercise and copy the round table and one of its chairs to a new location in the cafeteria. Use the polar option of the ARRAY command to copy the chair around the table. Specify an angle to fill of 180°. Save the drawing.

42.12 Try the above exercise again but answer "No" when prompted, `Rotate objects as they are copied?` Save the drawing.

42.13 See if you can use the rectangular option of the array command to finish placing chairs along all the rectangular tables in the cafeteria. Save the drawing.

Student: ____________________ Date: ____________

Instructor: ____________ Course: ____________ Section: ____________

Constructing with OFFSET

You use the OFFSET command to create drawing geometry. The OFFSET command enables you to offset certain entities a specified distance from the original object. For example, if you are an architect laying out the outline of a building, you can offset the building outline 6" to represent the wall thickness of your exterior walls. Or perhaps you are a landscape designer, in which case, you could use curve-fit polylines to represent free-form flower beds and offset them 4" to represent the brick used to create the retaining wall. This unit teaches you to perform these types of tasks.

The objectives for this unit are to:

- Understand what OFFSET is
- Create offsets using a specified distance
- Create offsets through a specified point

Using OFFSET and Distance

An important constructive editing tool is the OFFSET command. With OFFSET, you can make a copy of an entity at a specified distance from the original or through a specified point. OFFSET is very useful for laying out construction lines to create drawing geometry. If you need to place lines at a specific distance from both sides of an existing line, for example, the best method is to offset the line. If the entity is a polyline, the OFFSET command offsets the entire polyline.

Figure 43.1 illustrates the various AutoCAD entities that can be offset.

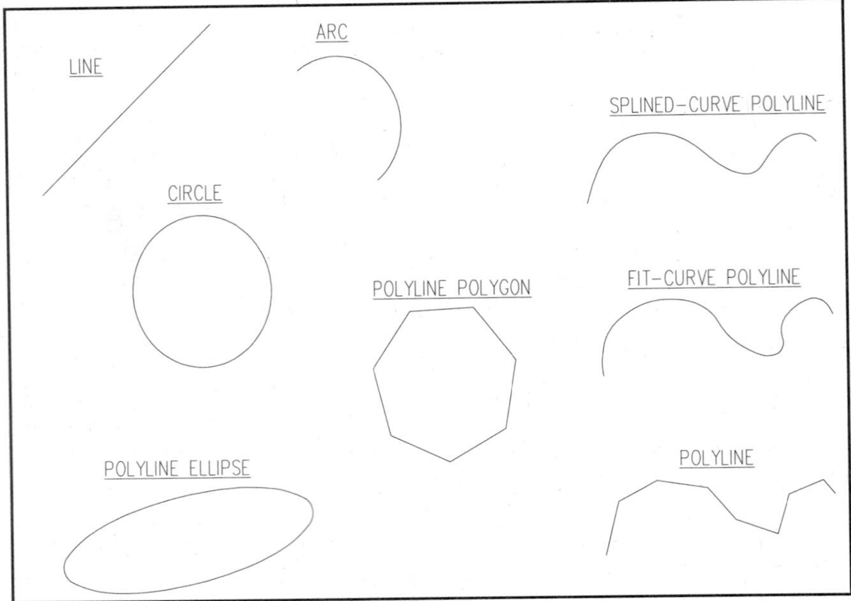

Figure 43.1
Entities that can be offset.

One way to offset an object is to specify a distance for the offset—the wall thickness of a building, for example. You can type this distance explicitly by using the keyboard or define it by picking two points. The OFFSET command then creates a copy of the entity at the specified distance away from the original.

In the following exercises, you create walls by offsetting a selection of polylines.

Using the OFFSET Command

1. Create a new drawing named 043???01 in your assigned directory using 043OFFST as a prototype.

2. `Command:` *Choose* Construct, *then* Offset `_offset`	Issues the OFFSET command
3. `Offset distance or Through <Through>:` **`4.875`** ↵	Specifies the distance from the original for the new entity
4. `Select object to offset:` *Select the polyline at* ① *(see fig. 43.2)*	Specifies the entity to offset

5. `Side to offset?` *Pick a point inside the room*	Determines where to place the offset entity
6. `Select object to offset:` *Select the polyline at* ②	Specifies the entity to offset
7. `Side to offset?` *Pick a point inside the room*	Determines where to place the offset entity
8. `Select object to offset:` *Select the polyline at* ③	Specifies the entity to offset
9. `Side to offset?` *Pick a point inside the room*	Determines where to place the offset entity
10. `Select object to offset:` *Press* Enter	Ends OFFSET command
11. Save your drawing.	

Your drawing should be similar to figure 43.2.

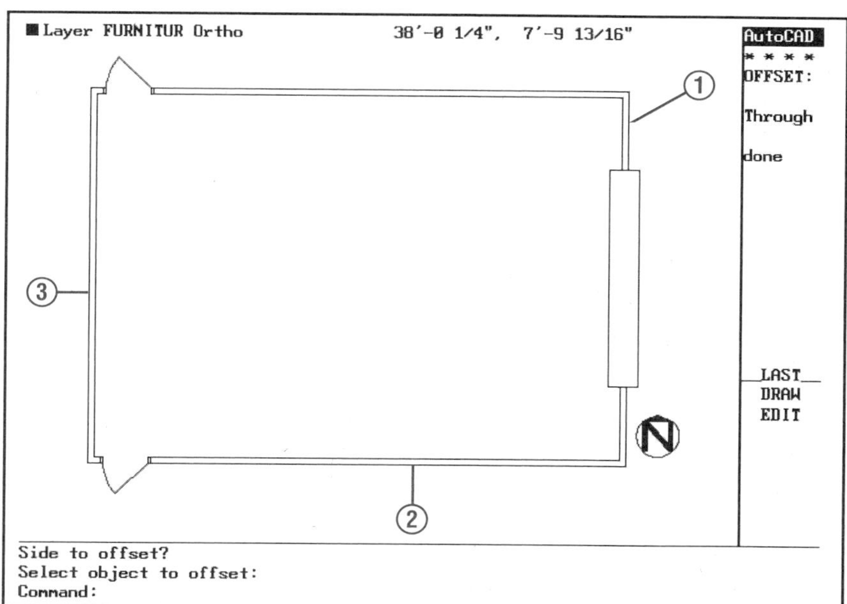

Figure 43.2

Walls created by OFFSET.

You can see that AutoCAD creates a duplicate of the polyline at a distance of 4.875 units away from the original. The new entities inherit the layer, linetype, and color settings of the original entities. In the following exercise, you create multiple offsets of the same entity.

Creating Multiple Offsets

1. Begin a new drawing named 043???02 in your assigned directory using 043OFFS2.
2. `Command:` **`OFFSET`** ↵ — Issues the OFFSET command
3. `Offset distance or Through <0.1500>:` **`0.25`** ↵ — Specifies the distance of the offset
4. `Select object to offset:` *Select the polyline* — Determines the original object to offset
5. `Side to offset?` *Pick a point inside the polyline* — Specifies where to place the offset
6. `Select object to offset:` *Select the original polygon*
7. `Side to offset?` *Pick a point outside the polygon*
8. `Select object to offset:` *Press* Enter — Ends the OFFSET command

Your drawing should now resemble figure 43.3.

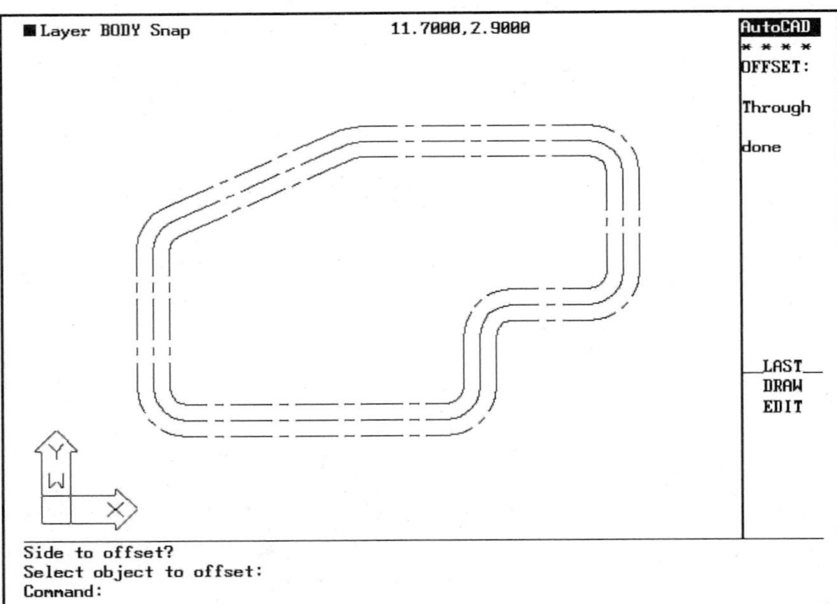

Figure 43.3
Multiple offsets of one entity.

You can create as many offset copies of an entity as you like simply by continuing to select entities and points. To specify a different distance, cancel the OFFSET command and reissue it, specifying a new distance.

The OFFSET command supports only pick-after selection. If a selection set exists when you issue the command, AutoCAD clears the selection set and prompts you to select entities for a new selection set. You can offset only one entity at a time; you cannot select multiple entities with a single selection. You can offset multiple entities in a single OFFSET command, although each offset operation is separate.

The new polylines created in the previous exercise inherit the linetype, layer, and color properties of the original. In this case, the original is the centerline of a gasket. You should place the new entities on the GASKET layer so they assume the proper characteristics. Although changing layer and other entity properties is explained in detail in later units, you can follow the steps in the next exercise to change the layer of the two new polylines.

Changing the Layer of the New Entities

Continue with your drawing from the previous exercise.

1. `Command:` **`CHPROP`** ↵	Issues the CHPROP command
2. `Select objects:` *Select the inside polyline and the outside polyline*	Selects the entities to change
3. `Change what property (Color/LAyer/LType/Thickness) ?` **`LA`** ↵	Chooses the LAyer option
4. `New layer <CENTER>:` **`GASKET`** ↵	Specifies the new layer for the entities
5. `Change what property (Color/LAyer/LType/Thickness) ?` *Press* Enter	Ends the CHPROP command

Your drawing should resemble figure 43.4.

The CHPROP command is just one way to change entity properties. Unit 58, "Modifying Entity Characteristics," explains other ways that you can modify entities.

Figure 43.4

Polylines with new layer properties.

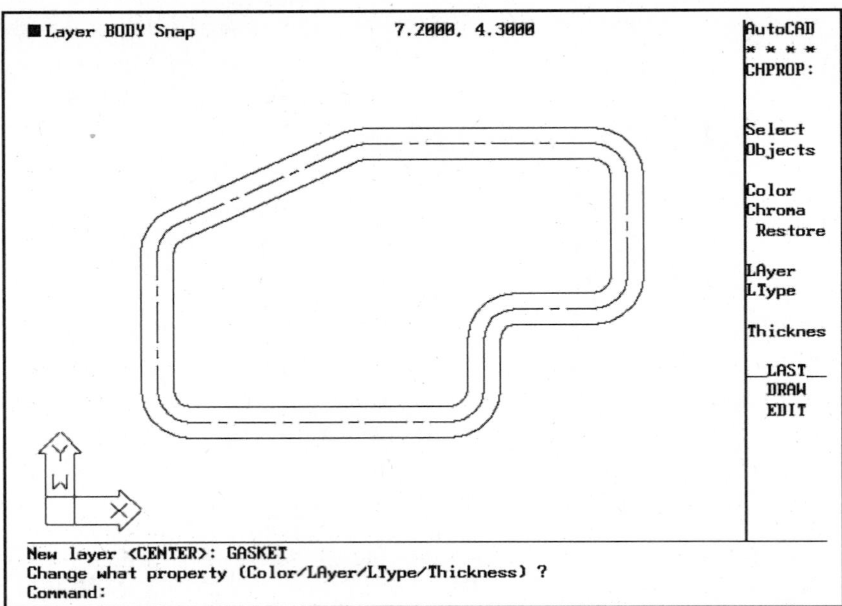

Using OFFSET Through a Point

In addition to specifying a distance for an offset, you can supply a point that the newly created offset entity passes through. You can enter a coordinate using the keyboard or pick a point. You can use any of the point specification methods to pick the point, including object snap modes and filters.

In the following exercise, you create the edges of a pivot plate from construction lines.

Creating an OFFSET Through a Point

1. Begin a new drawing named 043???03 in your assigned directory using 043OFFS3 as a prototype.

2. `Command:` **`OFFSET`** ↵ — Issues the OFFSET command

3. `Offset distance or Through <0.1000>:` **`T`** ↵ — Specifies the Through option

4. `Select object to offset:` *Select the construction line at* ① *(see fig. 43.5)* — Specifies the original object to offset

5. `Through point:` *From the popup menu, choose* Endpoint

6. `_endp of` *Pick the end point at* ② *(see fig. 43.5)* — Determines where to place the offset entity

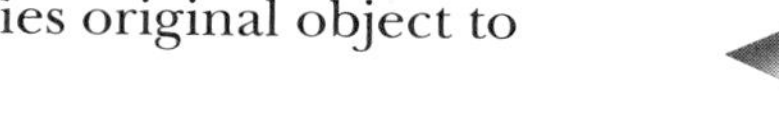

7. `Select object to offset:` *Select the line at ③ (see fig. 43.5)*	Specifies original object to offset
8. `Through point:` *From the popup menu, choose* Endpoint	
9. `_endp of` *Pick the end point at ④ (see fig. 43.5)*	Determines where to place the offset entity
10. `Select object to offset:` *Press* Enter	Ends the OFFSET command

Your drawing should resemble figure 43.5.

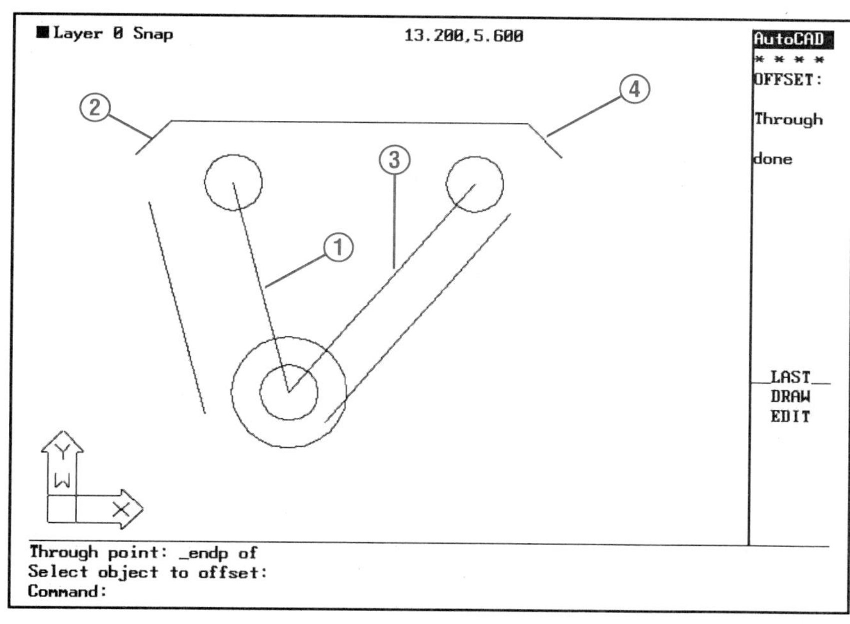

Figure 43.5

Creating an offset through a point.

Offsetting an entity is not always the last step of creating the new entity. In the case of the pivot plate in the previous exercise, you need to extend the new edge lines to complete the edge of the part. By using the OFFSET command, however, you often can quickly lay out geometry from constuction entities, then edit the entities to complete the drawing's geometry. Creating entities in this way usually is faster than drawing the new entities from scratch.

Unit Review

What You've Learned

- What is an offset
- How to create offsets at specified distances
- How to create an offset through a point

Review Questions

True or False

43.01 T F The OFFSET command always creates an exact duplicate of the original object at the same size and orientation.

43.02 T F An offset can be created by specifying a distance from the original object.

43.03 T F OFFSET uses either pick-first or pick-after selection.

43.04 T F An offset can be created by specifying a point for the offset to pass through.

43.05 T F It is possible to offset more than one object at a time.

43.06 T F You cannot offset the same entity twice.

43.07 T F The OFFSET command will offset a line, but will not offset a polyline.

Multiple Choice

43.08 If you attempt to offset a polyline, the OFFSET command will __________.

(A) offset only the selected segment

(B) offset the entire polyline

(C) display an error message

(D) none of the above

43.09 The __________ option of the OFFSET command offsets the entity through a point.

(A) Entity

(B) ID

(C) Point

(D) Through

Student: __________ Date: __________

Instructor: __________ Course: __________ Section: __________

Short Answer

43.10 Explain how the OFFSET command is similar to the Move multiple autoedit mode and the COPY command.

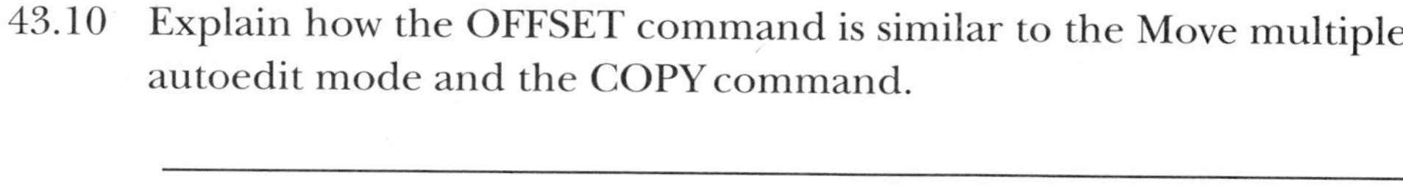

Additional Exercises

43.11 Begin a new drawing named 043???11 in your assigned directory using 043OFFIC as a prototype. Draw a conference room in the lower left corner of the office. The inside dimensions for the room are 22'-4" × 24'-6". The 24'-6" dimension should run horizontally. Draw the walls 6" thick. Use the OFFSET command to create the walls, using the existing inside wall lines. Experiment with the TRIM command to trim the extra portions of the offset lines. Your drawing should look similar to figure 43.6 after you finish. Save your drawing.

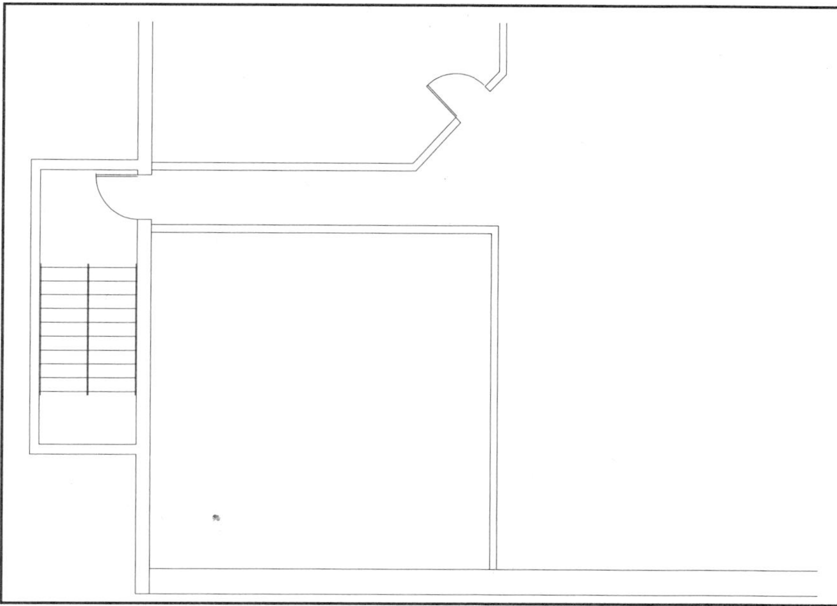

Figure 43.6

Conference room added to the building.

Student: ______ Date: ______

Instructor: ______ Course: ______ Section: ______

UNIT 44

Dividing an Entity

In manual drafting, you sometimes need to divide an entity into equal spaces to lay out lines or other geometry. Although a graphical means of dividing lines, arcs, and circles into equal distances is available, it is sometimes inaccurate and always time consuming. The manual methods also do not work on curves or other entities. With AutoCAD, dividing an entity is simple. AutoCAD maintains a mathematical model of every entity in a drawing, enabling it to calculate the exact length of the entity, regardless of its shape, and then divide it into an equal number of segments. You also can take advantage of AutoCAD's capability to insert an object called a *block* at equal spaces along an entity. This unit teaches you how to perform these tasks.

The objectives for this unit are to:

- Divide entities into equal segments using the DIVIDE command
- Insert a block at equal spaces along an entity
- Use PDMODE to change the display of points in a drawing

Dividing Entities into Equal Segments

Occasionally, you need to divide an entity into an equal number of segments to lay out the geometry of a drawing. Perhaps you need to lay out three windows equally spaced along a wall, or need to lay out shrubs equally spaced along a property line. Rather than calculate the distance yourself, let AutoCAD divide for you.

The DIVIDE command enables you to divide most types of entities into equal-length segments. It works with lines, arcs, circles, donuts, polylines, and other entities made using polylines, such as polygons and ellipses. Unlike manual methods for dividing entities, the DIVIDE command is very accurate. It calculates division points to the same 14-decimal-place accuracy as other AutoCAD functions.

The DIVIDE command does not actually divide an entity into separate segments, however. Instead, DIVIDE places points on the entity at the exact points that locate the segment divisions. You then can use the NODE object snap mode to snap to these division marks. The entity itself is unaffected by the division.

To divide an entity into equal spaces, you only have to select the entity to be divided, and then specify the number of segments. AutoCAD calculates the required distance for each segment and places points along the entity accordingly.

DIVIDE uses only pick-after selection. It does not support pick-first selection.

In the following exercise, use the DIVIDE command to divide a wall into 13 equal sections to locate windows. During the exercise you change the PDMODE variable to define the way points are displayed.

Dividing an Entity

1. Begin a new drawing named 044???01 in your assigned directory using 044OFFIC as a prototype.

2. `Command:` *Choose* Settings, *then* Point Style — Issues the DDPDTYPE command and displays the Point Style dialog box (see fig. 44.1)

   `'ddtype`

3. *Choose the point style tile at* ① *(see fig. 44.1), then choose* OK — Specifies the point display mode (PDMODE variable) and closes the dialog box

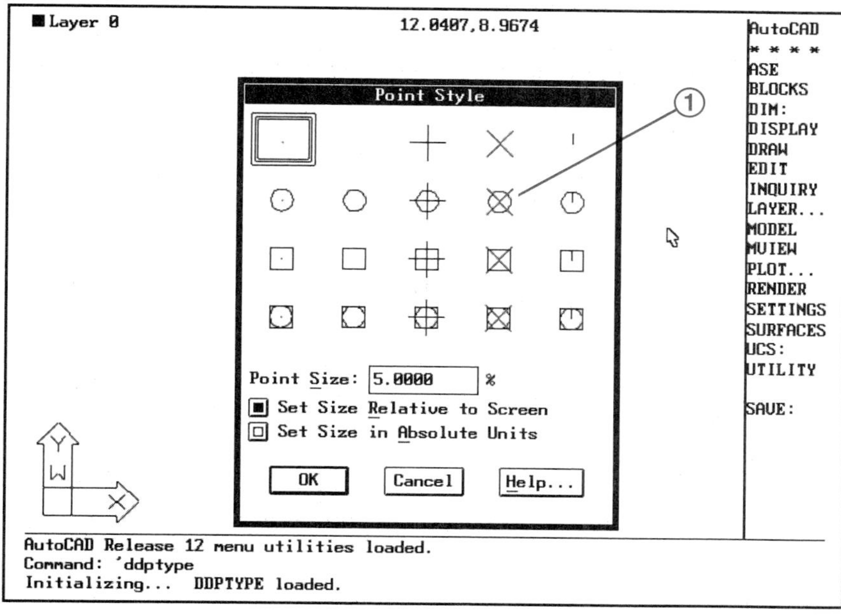

Figure 44.1

The Point Style dialog box.

4. `Command:` *Choose* Construct, *then* Divide — Issues the DIVIDE command

   `_divide`

5. `Select object to divide:` *Select the line at* ② *(see fig. 44.2)* — Specifies which entity to divide

6. `<Number of segments>/Block:` **13** ↵ — Specifies the number of segments in which to divide the entity

7. Save your drawing.

Your drawing should look similar to figure 44.2.

If you prefer, you can use the PDMODE command to set the PDMODE system variable which controls the way points display. When you select a display option from the Point Style dialog box, AutoCAD sets the value of PDMODE according to your selection. The Point Style dialog box is easier to use because it provides a graphical means for selecting the type of point display you want. PDMODE must be set to a numeric value corresponding to the desired display mode.

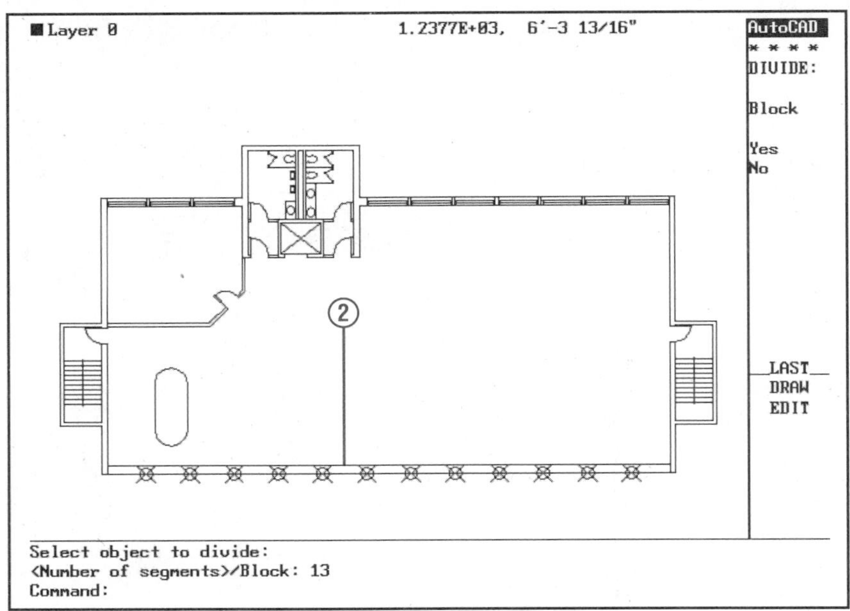

Figure 44.2
Wall line divided into equal segments.

With points located along the wall at equal intervals, you can begin laying out the windows for the wall. One method is to draw the wall studs manually; you also can use the DIVIDE command to insert studs automatically.

Inserting Objects with DIVIDE

In addition to dividing an entity into equal segments, the DIVIDE command optionally inserts a *block* at each division point. Blocks are explained in unit 67, "Introduction to Blocks." For now, you only need to know that blocks are like symbols that you can use repeatedly in a drawing. In your office drawing, the wall studs that separate the windows can be thought of as symbols. Instead of manually drawing each stud, you can have the DIVIDE command insert them for you automatically.

For you to insert a block using DIVIDE, the block must already be defined in the drawing and have a name. Your prototype office drawing contains a block called STUD. In the following exercise, use the DIVIDE command to insert the block STUD automatically at each of the segment division points along the wall.

Inserting Objects with DIVIDE

Continue with your drawing from the preceding exercise.

1. `Command:` **`U`** ↵	Undoes the previous command and removes the points

`GROUP`	
2. `Command:` *Choose* Construct, *then* Divide `_divide`	Issues the DIVIDE command
3. `Select object to divide:` *Select the line at* ② *(see fig. 44.2)*	Specifies which entity to divide
4. `<Number of segments>/Block:` **`B`** ↵	Specifies the Block option
5. `Block name to insert:` **`STUD`** ↵	Specifies the name of the block to insert
6. `Align block with object? <Y>` *Press* Enter	Accepts the default answer to align the block with the object
7. `Number of segments:` **`13`** ↵	Specifies the number of segments
8. Save your drawing.	

Your drawing should resemble figure 44.3.

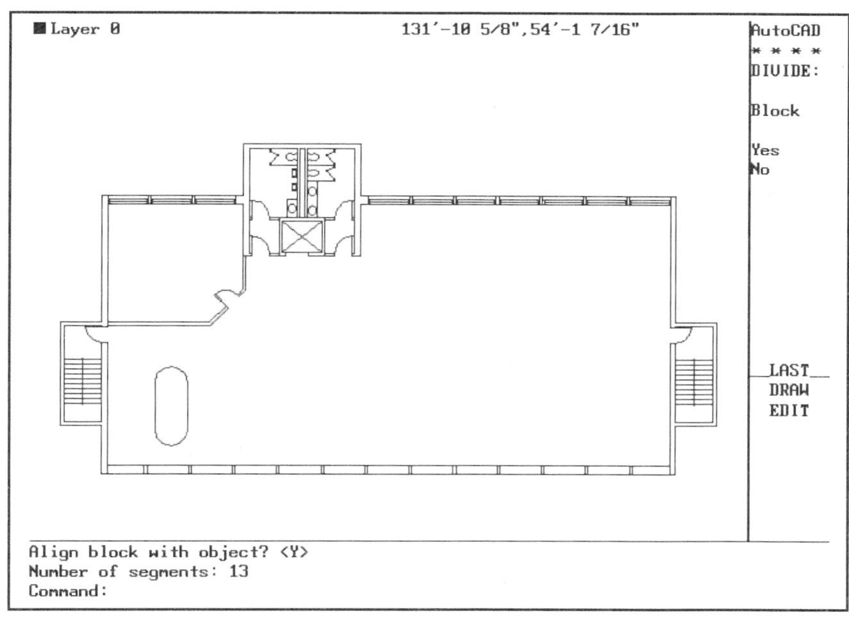

Figure 44.3

Studs inserted along the wall.

You might have guessed the meaning of the prompt `Align block with object`, but the meaning is not clear from the exercise. If you answer with a Y, AutoCAD rotates the block to follow the contour of the entity. If you answer N, AutoCAD does not rotate the block to follow the contour of the entity.

To see the effect this prompt has on the objects, insert a chair around the oblong conference table shown in figure 44.4.

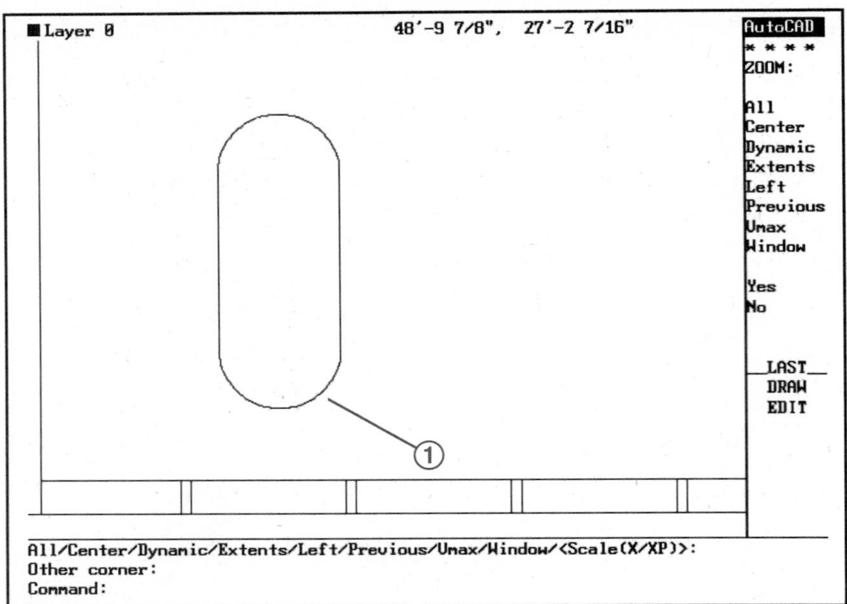

Figure 44.4
Conference table.

Aligning Objects with DIVIDE

1. Continue with your drawing from the preceding exercise and zoom to the view shown in figure 44.4.

2. `Command:` *Choose* Construct, *then* Divide `_divide`	Issues the DIVIDE command
3. `Select object to divide:` *Select the table at* ① *(see fig. 44.4)*	Specifies which entity to divide
4. `<Number of segments>/Block:` **`B`** ↵	Specifies the Block option
5. `Block name to insert:` **`CONCHAIR`** ↵	Specifies the name of the block to insert
6. `Align block with object? <Y>` **`N`** ↵	Directs AutoCAD not to rotate the block during insertion
7. `Number of segments:` **`8`** ↵	Specifies the number of segments

The chair is inserted around the table at the same rotation each time, instead of following the contour of the table (see fig. 44.5).

Next, undo the DIVIDE command and insert the chairs again, this time aligning them with the table.

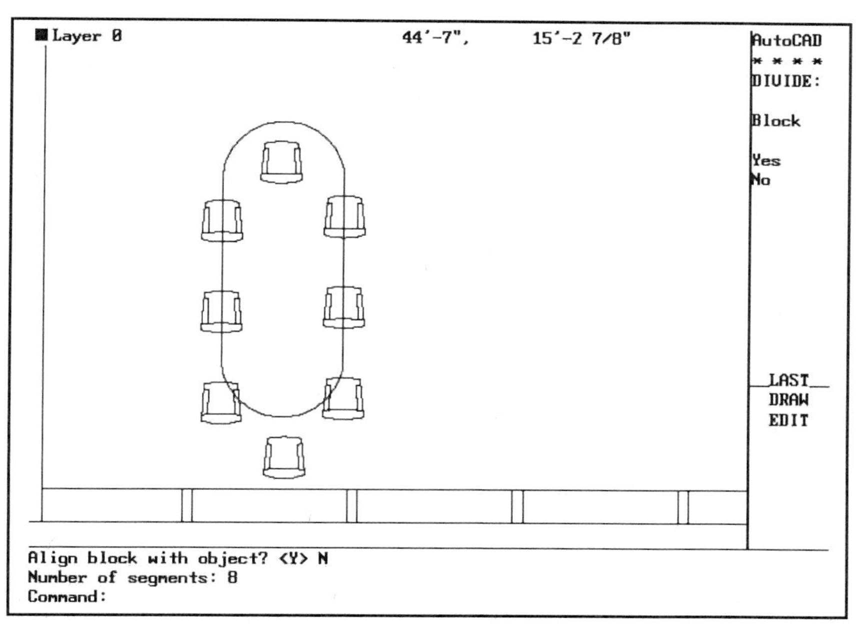

Figure 44.5

Chairs not aligned with the table.

8. `Command:` **`U`** ↵	Undoes the previous command
`GROUP`	
9. `Command:` *Choose* Construct, *then* Divide	Issues the DIVIDE command
`_divide`	
10. `Select object to divide:` *Select the table at* ① *(see fig. 44.4)*	Specifies which entity to divide
11. `<Number of segments>/Block:` **`B`** ↵	Specifies the Block option
12. `Block name to insert:` **`CONCHAIR`** ↵	Specifies the name of the block to insert
13. `Align block with object? <Y>` *Press* Enter	Accepts the default option to rotate the blocks
14. `Number of segments:` **`8`** ↵	Specifies the number of segments
15. Save your drawing.	

Your drawing should look similar to figure 44.6.

The capability to insert blocks using DIVIDE can save time when you must manually lay out the location of objects to insert. Whether you choose to align the objects with the entity depends on the effect you need to achieve. If all the objects require the same orientation, do not align them with the entity.

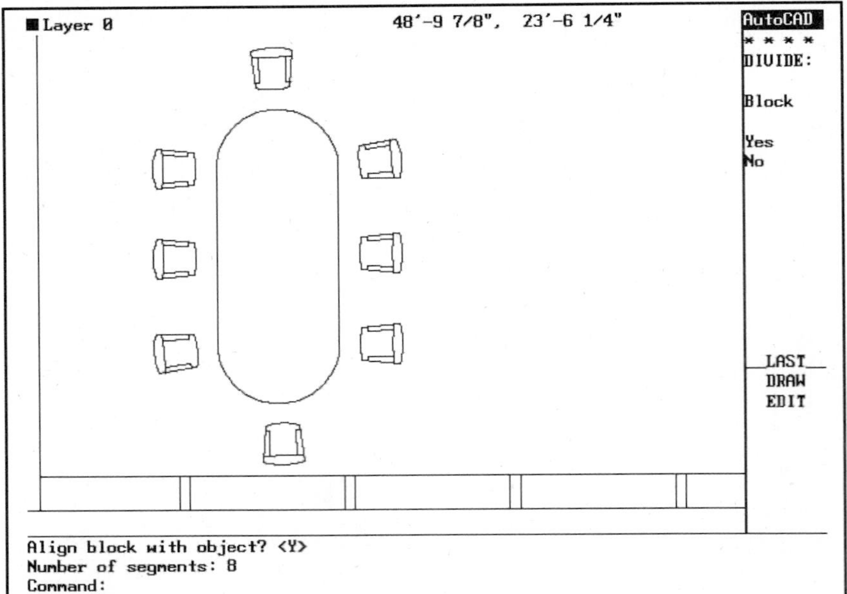

Figure 44.6

Chairs aligned with the table.

You may need to keep other important considerations in mind when designing a block that will be inserted using DIVIDE. One such consideration is to specify the proper base point. Units 67, 68, and 69 explain blocks in much greater detail.

Unit Review

What You've Learned

- Commands: DIVIDE, PDMODE, DDPDTYPE
- How to divide an entity with the DIVIDE command
- How to insert an object called a *block* at equal spaces using DIVIDE
- The effect of aligning blocks with an entity

Review Questions

True or False

44.01 T F DIVIDE breaks an entity into new entities of equal length.

44.02 T F DIVIDE requires that you specify a base point for the start of the division.

44.03 T F DIVIDE only divides lines, arcs, circles, and entities made from polylines.

44.04 T F The PDMODE command specifies how points display in a drawing.

44.05 T F Selecting a point display style from the Point Style dialog box sets the PDMODE system variable.

44.06 T F The DIVIDE command is accurate to six decimal places.

44.07 T F The entity you select to divide is not divided into new entities of equal length.

Multiple Choice

44.08 The DIVIDE command can insert a __________ at equal spaces along an entity.

(A) point

(B) block

(C) both A and B

(D) none of the above

Student: __________ Date: __________

Instructor: __________ Course: __________ Section: __________

44.09 The DIVIDE command uses __________ selection.

(A) pick-first or pick-after

(B) only pick-first

(C) only pick-after

44.10 Which one of the following commands enables you to change the way points display? __________

(A) OSNAP

(B) POINT

(C) PDSTYLE

(D) PDMODE

Student: ____________________ Date: __________

Instructor: __________ Course: __________ Section: __________

UNIT 45

Measuring an Entity

A common design task is to lay out equal distances along an entity. The DIVIDE command, discussed in unit 44, "Dividing an Entity," lays out points along an entity to divide the entity into equal segments. AutoCAD provides another command that places points on an entity. Instead of dividing an entity into equal segments, the MEASURE command measures equal lengths that you specify along the entity, and then places corresponding points along the entity. You can mark off six-inch lengths along a long line, for example. This unit teaches you to use the MEASURE command and offers helpful tips for using it.

The objectives for this unit are to:

- Understand the effect of the MEASURE command
- Measure equal distances along an entity with MEASURE

Measuring an Entity with MEASURE

Occasionally you need to mark off equal graduations on a gauge, mark a wall to locate studs, or locate the pitch points of a thread. AutoCAD's MEASURE command provides an easy means for measuring equal distances on an entity.

The MEASURE command works very much like the DIVIDE command, but the results differ greatly. When you issue the MEASURE command, AutoCAD prompts you to select an entity. MEASURE can measure lines, arcs, circles, donuts, polylines, and other entities created from polylines. After selecting the entity, AutoCAD prompts you to specify a distance or the name of a block. If you specify a distance, AutoCAD measures that distance along the entity, placing points on the entity. You also can specify the name of a block and insert the block at the specified distance along the entity.

Like DIVIDE, MEASURE uses only pick-after selection; it does not support pick-first selection. In addition, MEASURE is accurate to 14 decimal places.

In the following exercise, use MEASURE to measure the thread pitch locations on a threaded shaft. PDMODE already has been set in the prototype so that you can see the points MEASURE creates. Figure 45.1 shows the shaft before points are applied using MEASURE.

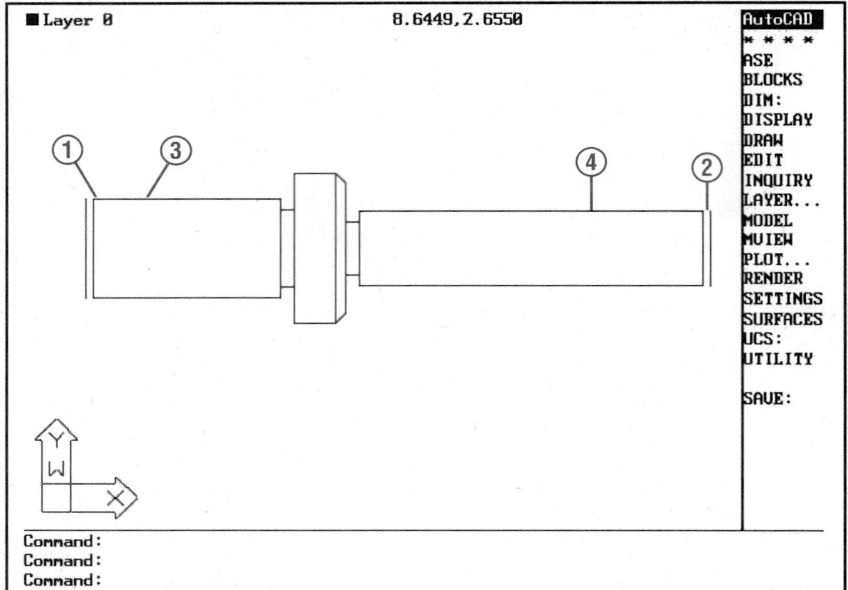

Figure 45.1

Shaft before MEASURE.

The unattached vertical lines at both ends of the shaft represent the end of the shaft. The top horizontal lines that currently represent the outer thread diameters end at a distance of 1/2P (half the pitch distance) from the end of the shaft. The ends of these lines at ① and ② (see fig. 45.1) mark the apex of the first thread.

Measuring an Entity

1. Begin a new drawing named 045???01 in your assigned directory using 045SHAFT as a prototype.

2. `Command:` *Choose* Construct, *then* Measure `_measure`	Issues the MEASURE command
3. `Select object to measure:` *Select the line at* ③ *(see fig. 45.1)*	Specifies the entity to measure
4. `<Segment length>/Block:` **`0.125`** ↵	Specifies the pitch spacing for a 1" thread and locates points on the line
5. `Command:` *Choose* Construct, *then* Measure `_measure`	Issues the MEASURE command
6. `Select object to measure:` *Select the line at* ④ *(see fig. 45.1)*	Specifies the entity to measure
7. `<Segment length>/Block: 0.125 [ ]`	Specifies the pitch spacing for a 3/4" thread and locates points on the line

Your drawing should resemble figure 45.2.

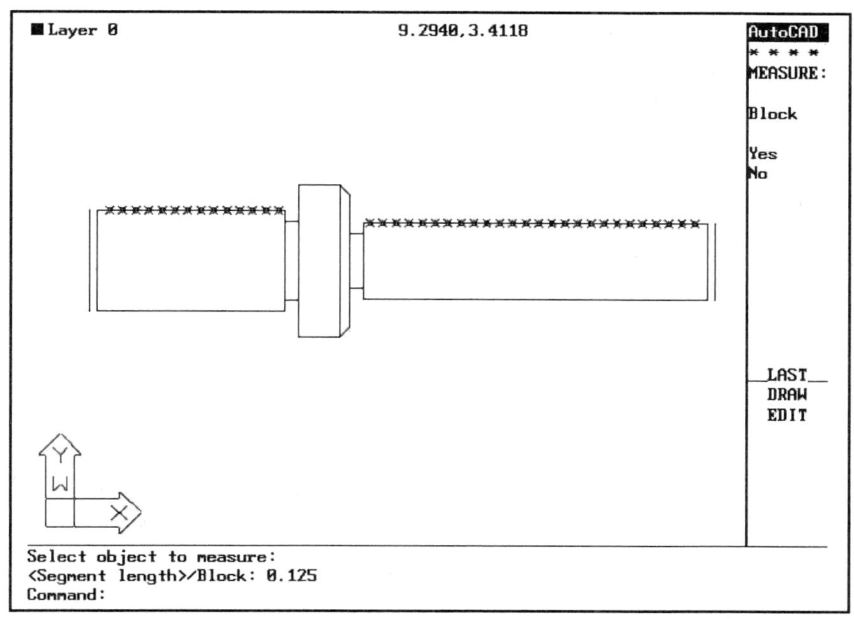

Figure 45.2

Points added using MEASURE.

The location at which you select the line is important because it defines from which end of the line AutoCAD begins measuring. In this example, you must select the lines near the ends of the shaft to locate properly the first thread.

With the pitch points now defined, you can begin drawing the thread geometry. You can do this manually, but a simpler method is to insert the thread lines at each point created by MEASURE. As with the DIVIDE command, you can use MEASURE to insert a block. The next section explains how.

Inserting Objects with MEASURE

In unit 44, "Dividing an Entity," you learned that blocks are symbols you can reuse in a drawing. After you draw a symbol, you can insert it any number of times in the drawing, saving the time that would otherwise be necessary to draw the symbol in each location.

You can use the MEASURE command to insert a block automatically at each of the points it measures on an entity. This provides a means for you to insert blocks along an entity at specific spacings.

In the following exercise, use the MEASURE command to insert a block called THREAD along the top of the threaded ends of the shaft.

Inserting Blocks with MEASURE

Continue with your drawing from the preceding exercise.

1. `Command:` **`U`** ↵ — Undoes the previous MEASURE command

   `GROUP`

2. `Command:` *Choose* Construct, *then* Measure — Issues the MEASURE command

   `_measure`

3. `Select object to measure:` *Select the line at ④ (see fig. 45.1)* — Specifies the entity to measure
4. <Segment length>/Block: **`B`** ↵ — Specifies Block option
5. `Block name to insert:` **`THREAD`** ↵ — Specifies name of block to insert
6. `Align block with object? <Y>` *Press* Enter — Accepts default to align the block with the entity
7. `Segment length:` **`0.125`** ↵ — Specifies the pitch spacing for a 1" thread and locates blocks on the line
8. Save your drawing.

Your drawing should look similar to figure 45.3.

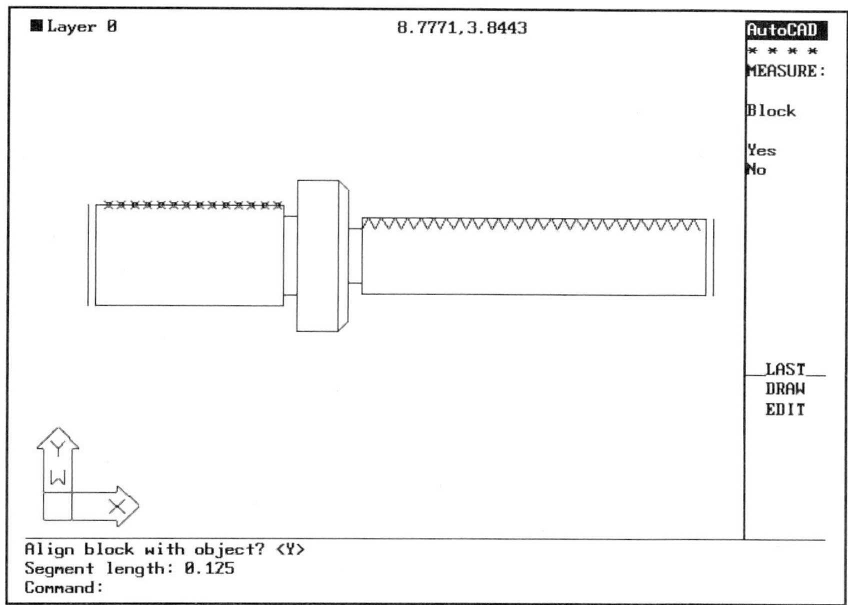

Figure 45.3
THREAD block inserted on line.

If you choose to insert a block using MEASURE, only the blocks are inserted along the entity. MEASURE does not apply points in addition to the blocks.

The MEASURE command is very useful when you need to apply a certain spacing along an entity. Although MEASURE is similar to DIVIDE in the way it works, the results are different. MEASURE places points or blocks at a spacing that you specify along a selected entity. The DIVIDE command places points or blocks on an entity by dividing it into a specific number of segments.

Another way to add the threads to the bolt is to insert the THREAD block, and then use the ARRAY command to create a single-row array of the THREAD block. The ARRAY command is explained in unit 42, "Constructing with ARRAY." Blocks are explained in units 67, "Introduction to Blocks," 68, "Creating a Block," and 69, "Inserting a Block in a Drawing."

Unit Review

What You've Learned

- Commands: MEASURE
- How to place points along an entity at a set spacing using MEASURE
- How to place blocks along an entity at a set spacing using MEASURE

Review Questions

True or False

45.01 T F MEASURE breaks an entity into new entities of equal length.

45.02 T F MEASURE requires that you specify a base point for the start of the measurement.

45.03 T F MEASURE only divides lines, arcs, and circles.

45.04 T F The location at which you select the entity determines from which end of the entity AutoCAD begins measuring.

45.05 T F The MEASURE and DIVIDE commands perform exactly the same function.

45.06 T F The MEASURE command is accurate to 14 decimal places.

45.07 T F The entity you select to measure is not divided into new entities of equal length.

Multiple Choice

45.08 The MEASURE command can insert a __________ at a spacing that you specify along an entity.

(A) point

(B) block

(C) both A and B

(D) none of the above

45.09 The MEASURE command uses __________ selection.

(A) pick-first or pick-after

(B) only pick-first

(C) only pick-after

Student: __________ Date: __________

Instructor: __________ Course: __________ Section: __________

45.10 Which one of the following commands enables you to change the way points display? __________

(A) OSNAP

(B) POINT

(C) PDSTYLE

(D) PDMODE

Additional Exercises

45.11 Continue with your drawing from the preceding exercise. Use MEASURE to lay out the THREAD block along the top of the one inch diameter portion of the shaft. Then, use autoedit modes and other techniques you learned in earlier units to complete the shaft. When completed, your drawing should look similar to figure 45.4. Note that the left end of the shaft is threaded for a left-handed thread, and the right end of the shaft is threaded for a right-handed thread.

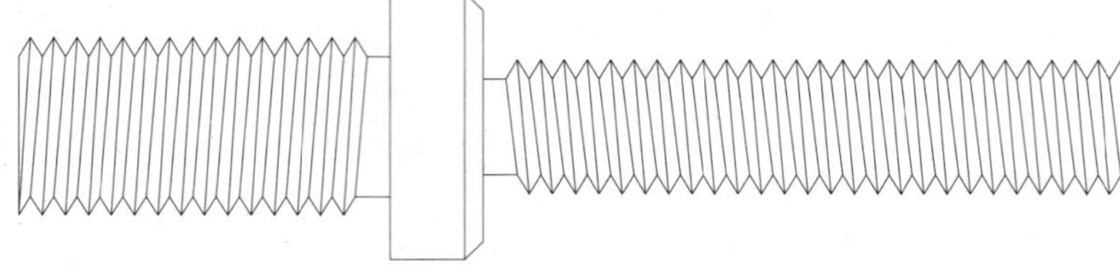

Figure 45.4
The completed shaft.

Student: ______________ Date: ______________

Instructor: ______________ Course: ______________ Section: ______________

UNIT 46

Introduction to Paper Space

Up to now, you have been using AutoCAD's model space environment to prepare drawings. *Model space* is the 3D modeling environment in which you prepare 2D and 3D models. When you need to produce a plot of a drawing, you can use AutoCAD's paper space environment to lay out the plot. This unit introduces paper space and explains a selection of commands that enable you to use paper space.

The objectives for this unit are to:

- Understand the difference between model space and paper space
- Understand the purpose and advantages of paper space
- Use MVIEW to create viewports in paper space
- Use ZOOM XP to specify a scale for a viewport in paper space
- Align views from one paper space viewport to another

Understanding Model Space and Paper Space

Model space is the main environment in which you create a drawing. Think of model space as being a "virtual world" in which you create a full-scale model of a design. The model can be a two-dimensional representation of an object, or it can be a three-dimensional model. Figure 46.1 shows a floor plan created as a 2D model in model space.

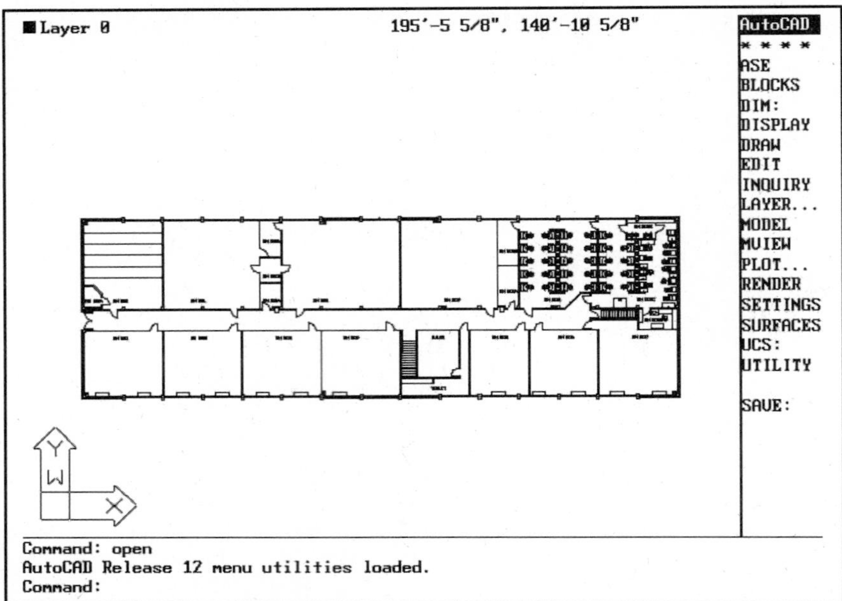

Figure 46.1

2D model in model space.

Preparing the model (2D or 3D) of your design is just the first step toward completion of the drawing. You also must compose a plot of the drawing to add a title block, multiple views of different parts of the model at different scales, details, and other information. Paper space simplifies the task of composing a plot.

Paper space is a 2D-only environment, although most of AutoCAD's commands function in paper space just as they do in model space. Think of paper space as a huge sheet of blank paper. If your drawing model is complete and you are ready to compose the plot, you can enter paper space and insert a title block at full scale. If you work with a D-size drawing, for example, the title block is approximately 36" wide. After you insert the title block, you can open multiple paper space viewports that "look into" model space. These viewports become the different plotted views of your model. Figure 46.2 shows a drawing that was composed in paper space.

When paper space is active, you can select and manipulate paper space viewports. You also can select and manipulate any other entities that you draw in paper space, such as text in the drawing's title block. You cannot, however, select or edit drawing entities that exist in model space, even though you can see them inside a paper space viewport.

Take another look at figure 46.2. Assume that paper space is active. You can see through the viewports into model space, but you cannot select any entities inside the viewport. In a way, working in paper space is like looking through windows onto your drawing. When paper space is active, the windows are "closed" and you cannot reach through them to work on the model space entities that appear in the window. When you switch to model space, you "open" the window; you then can reach through it to work on the drawing. By using the MSPACE and PSPACE commands you can quickly "open and close" these windows to work in the two different environments.

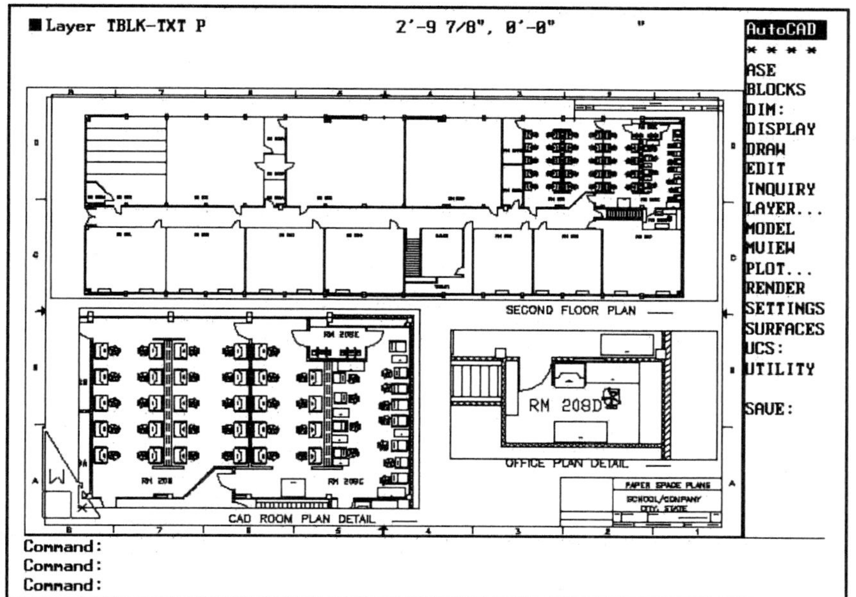

Figure 46.2

A drawing composed in paper space.

TIP

Most often you apply dimensions and text to your drawing in model space, scaling the dimensions and text according to the required plotted scale of the view in which they appear. You also can apply dimensions and text in paper space. If you apply text and dimensions in paper space, they do not have to be sized to match the plotted scale. Paper space represents a 1:1 plotting environment, so if you want 1/8" text in a drawing, you can draw it at 1/8" in paper space.

Moving between Paper Space and Model Space

You cannot work in model space and paper space at the same time; only one of the environments can be active at a time. You can switch quickly back and forth between model space and paper space, however. To understand the difference between model space and paper space, and to understand how to switch between them, you need to understand the TILEMODE command.

TILEMODE On

The TILEMODE system variable controls the types of viewports that AutoCAD displays. You can turn TILEMODE on and off. When TILEMODE is turned on, the following conditions apply:

- You have access only to model space; you cannot work in paper space.
- At least one viewport is always visible on the display.
- Viewports fit neatly together like tiles without overlaps or any spaces left between viewports. The pattern of viewports cover the entire display.
- You can use the VPORTS command and options to divide the current viewport or join it to another viewport to create a larger viewport.

In previous units, you have worked exclusively with TILEMODE turned on.

TILEMODE Off

Before you can enter paper space, you must turn TILEMODE off. The following conditions apply when TILEMODE is turned off:

- You have access to model space and paper space.
- When you turn off TILEMODE for the first time, no viewports are open until you open one using the MVIEW command. The exception is if you use a prototype drawing that already includes paper space viewports.
- Viewports in paper space can overlap, be superimposed on top of each other, and have vacant space (void) between viewports. You also can make the viewport borders invisible by placing the viewports on a layer that is frozen or turned off.
- You can use the MVIEW command and options to open new viewports in paper space.

You must turn off TILEMODE to gain access to paper space. When TILEMODE is turned off, you can switch quickly between model space and paper space by using the MSPACE and PSPACE commands. MSPACE makes model space active and PSPACE makes paper space active.

The following exercise provides a floor plan drawing that includes viewports that have already been set up for you in paper space. You experiment with TILEMODE, MSPACE, and PSPACE to switch between model space and paper space. Figure 46.3 shows your drawing as you begin the exercise.

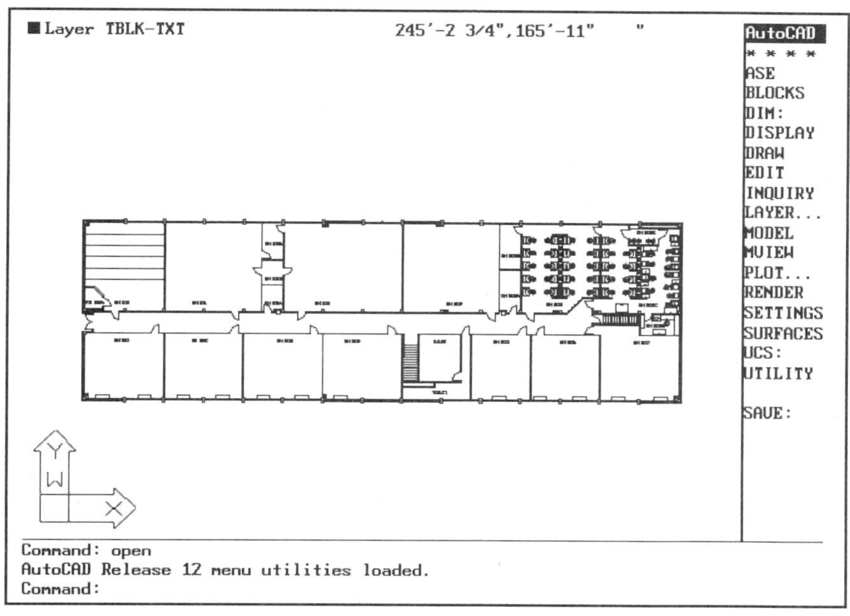

Figure 46.3

A floor plan in model space.

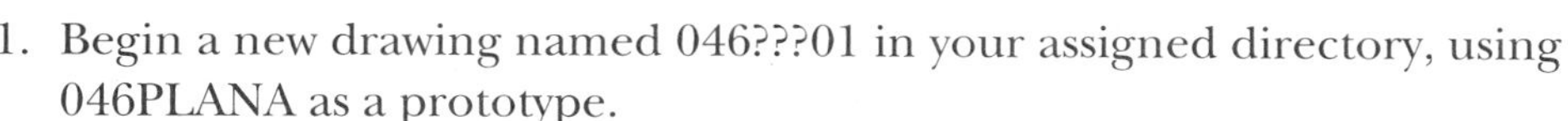

Moving between Paper Space and Model Space

1. Begin a new drawing named 046???01 in your assigned directory, using 046PLANA as a prototype.

2. `Command:` *Choose* View, *then* Tilemode, *then* Off (0) — Turns off the TILEMODE system variable and switches to paper space

   `TILEMODE`

3. `New value for TILEMODE <1>:` **`0`**

   `Regenerating drawing.`

Notice that the cursor (crosshair) now occupies the entire drawing window and is not limited to a current viewport. This indicates that you are in paper space. In addition, a P appears near the left end of the status line, which means paper space is active. Another sure sign that you are in the paper space environment is the appearance of a triangular icon to the lower left of the drawing display.

4. Command: *Choose* View, *then* Model Space — Issues the MSPACE command and activates model space in the current viewport

```
_mspace
```

Move the cursor from one view to the other and observe which view is current. You can click on a non-current view and make it the current view.

5. Command: *Choose* View, *then* Paper Space — Issues the PSPACE command and switches back to paper space

```
_pspace
```

6. Command: *Choose* View, *then* Tilemode, *then* On (1) — Turns on the TILEMODE system variable and returns to tiled viewport display

7.
```
TILEMODE
New value for TILEMODE <0>: 1
Regenerating drawing.
```

TILEMODE controls only the type of viewports that AutoCAD displays and has no direct relationship to paper space or model space. TILEMODE must be off, however, before you can access paper space. When TILEMODE is off, you can work in both paper space and model space by switching between the two environments using the MSPACE and PSPACE commands. If paper space is active, you are working with the entire drawing sheet and viewports. When you switch to model space, you are working only with a specific viewport.

Creating Paper Space Viewports

You can plot all the viewports you open in paper space simultaneously by using different scale and layer control settings. The border of a paper space viewport is a special type of entity; you can stretch them to change the viewport's size, erase them, change their color and linetype, and edit them in other ways. Most important, you can place them on a layer that is frozen or turned off, which makes the viewport border invisible without affecting any of the entities that appear inside the viewport.

Because you can stretch a viewport to any size, you do not need to calculate the size of viewport needed to display a particular view according to its scale. If you decide, after displaying a view, that its viewport is too small or too large, simply stretch the viewport to whatever size you need.

In the following exercise you are provided with the floor plan in model space similar to the previous exercise, but you are not given a paper space layout for the plan. Your task is to turn TILEMODE off and open viewports in paper space to compose the drawing for plotting.

It is a good idea to create separate layers for your title block, viewports, and other paper space entities. The following exercise does not use layers, however. For more information on layers, consult unit 59, "Introduction to Layers."

Opening Paper Space Viewports

1. Begin a new drawing named 046???02 in your assigned directory, using 046PLANB as a prototype.

2. `Command:` *Choose* View, *then* Tilemode, *then* Off (0) — Turns off TILEMODE and switches to paper space

```
TILEMODE
New value for TILEMODE <1>: 0
Regenerating drawing.
```

Draw a simple rectangle to represent the border of your drawing sheet.

3. `Command:` *Choose* Draw, *then* Rectangle — Issues the RECTANG command

```
rectang
```

4. `First corner:` **0,0** ↵ — Specifies 0,0 as the lower left corner

5. `Other corner:` **34,22** ↵ — Specifies upper right corner and draws rectangle

6. Issue the ZOOM command with a zoom factor of 0.9X.

7. `Command:` *Choose* View, *then* Mview, *then* Create Viewport — Issues the MVIEW command

```
_mview
```

8. `ON/OFF/Hideplot/Fit/2/3/4/Restore/<First Point>:` *Pick a point near* ① *(see fig. 46.4)* — Specifies first corner of viewport

9. `Other corner:` **@10,-12.5** ↵ — Specifies the opposite corner of the viewport and draws viewport

```
Regenerating drawing.
```

continues

10. `Command:` *Choose* View, *then* Model Space — Issues the MSPACE command, switches to model space, and makes the viewport active

    `_mspace`

11. `Command:` *Choose* View, *then* Set View, *then* Named View — Displays the View Control dialog box

    `ddview`

12. *Choose* RM212 *from the* View *list box, then the* Restore *button, then* OK — Restores the view RM212 to the viewport

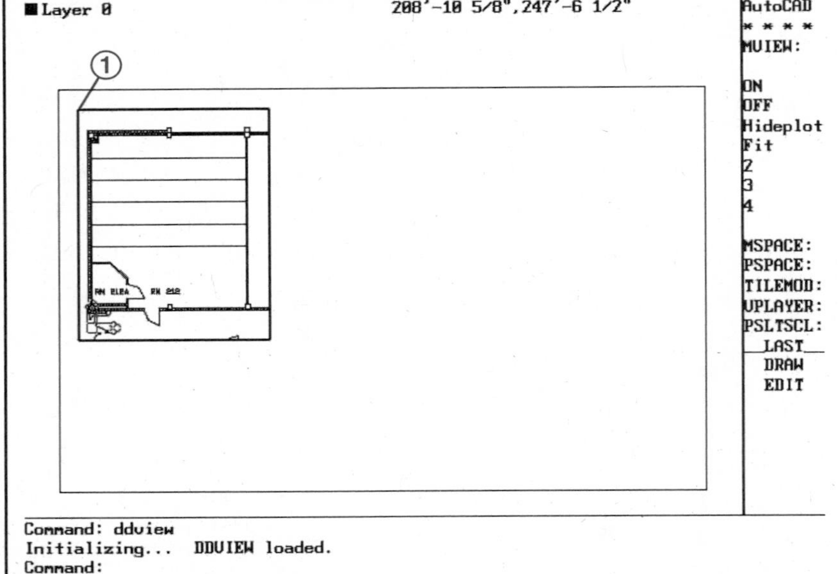

Figure 46.4
A paper space viewport.

You can see that creating a viewport is a simple matter of picking two points to define its border. The MVIEW command provides other options that enable you to quickly create groups of viewports. You use these options in other units. You can set the view in a viewport by panning or zooming the view in model space or by restoring a named view.

Specifying Viewport Scale

The views on a typical plot often use different scales. A detail is generally be shown at a larger scale than the overall plan, for example. To scale a view to a specific scale, use the XP option of the ZOOM command. The XP option, which stands for "times paper space," specifies a ratio between paper space units and model space units. Specifying an XP scale factor is like saying "x units in paper space equals y units in model space."

Consider the example of a view of a floor plan that must be scaled to 1/4" = 1'-0". The ratio of paper space units to real-world model space units is 1:48 (1/4" to 12"). Or, 1/4" on paper equals 12" in the model. You can scale the viewport to 1/48XP to achieve the necessary scale.

In the following exercise, you establish a scale for your new paper space viewport.

Specifying a Paper Space Scale

Continue with your drawing from the preceding exercise.

1. `Command:` **`Z`** ↵ — Issues the alias for the ZOOM command

   `ZOOM`

2. `All/Center/Dynamic/Extents/Left/Previous/Vmax/Window/<Scale(X/XP)>:` **`1/48XP`** ↵ — Sets the scale of the current paper space viewport at 48 model space units for each paper space unit (see fig. 46.5)

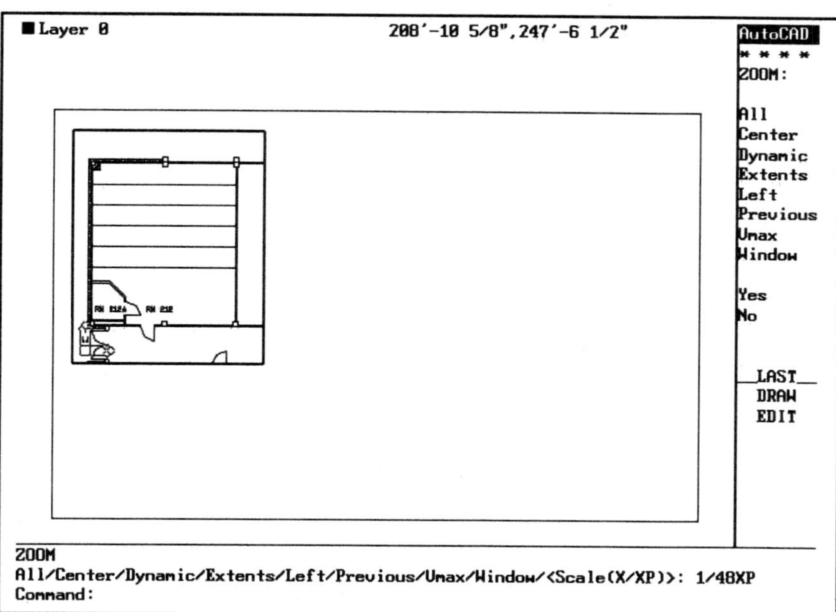

Figure 46.5

Paper space viewport scaled to 1/4" = 1'-0".

After you establish a scale for the viewports in paper space you should not use the ZOOM command during editing because it alters the scale of the viewport. If you do use the ZOOM command, you need to repeat the ZOOM XP procedure to reset the scale of the viewport. If you need to change the view without changing the scale, use the PAN command to move the view within the viewport.

Although it is often unnecessary in an architectural drawing such as the one in the previous exercise, you often do need to align views with one another. This is particularly true with mechanical drawings. You can use the PAN command and point filters to align one view with another. Set one view in its correct location, then pan the second view to align it with the first view. You can use object snap modes to select corresponding points in each view. In addition to using the PAN command, you can use the MVSETUP command to align views. MVSETUP is explained in unit 47, "Composing a Drawing."

Unit Review

What You've Learned

- ☞ Commands: MVIEW, MSPACE, PSPACE, TILEMODE
- ☞ The difference between model space and paper space
- ☞ How to control tiled and non-tiled viewports
- ☞ How to use MVIEW to create paper space viewports
- ☞ How to utilize views from model space in paper space
- ☞ How to set a scale for each viewport in paper space

Review Questions

True or False

46.01 T F Paper space is used mainly in three-dimensional design drafting.

46.02 T F Each viewport in paper space may be plotted at a different scale.

46.03 T F There is very little difference between model space and paper space.

46.04 T F The MVIEW command can be used to create viewports in paper space.

46.05 T F You can edit entities in model space while paper space is active.

Multiple Choice

46.06 More than one view can be plotted from ________.

(A) paper space

(B) model space

(C) TILEMODE

46.07 Tiled viewports on the drawing display indicate that the current environment is _________.

(A) paper space

(B) model space

(C) aligned

(D) non-TILEMODE

Student: ______________________ Date: ________

Instructor: ____________________ Course: ________ Section: ________

46.08 The _________ command allows you to create multiple views of a plan or model in paper space.

(A) VIEW

(B) VPORTS

(C) MVIEW

(D) TILEMODE

Short Answer

46.09 What ZOOM XP factor should you use to scale a view to 1/2" = 1'-0"?

____

____

____

46.10 What happens to a viewport's scale if you zoom in on an area of the viewport in model space?

____

____

____

Additional Exercises

46.11 Continue with your drawing from the previous exercise. Using figure 46.6 as a guide, create additional viewports ①, ②, ③, and ④. Restore view CADSTATN to view ① and scale the view to 1" = 1'-0". Restore view CAD-LABS to view ② and scale the view to 1/4" = 1'-0". Restore view RM-208D to view ③ and scale the view to 1/2" = 1'-0". Scale the key plan in view ④ to 1/360. Pan the views as necessary to achieve the same views as those shown in figure 46.6. Save the drawing.

Student: ______________ Date: ______________

Instructor: ______________ Course: ______________ Section: ______________

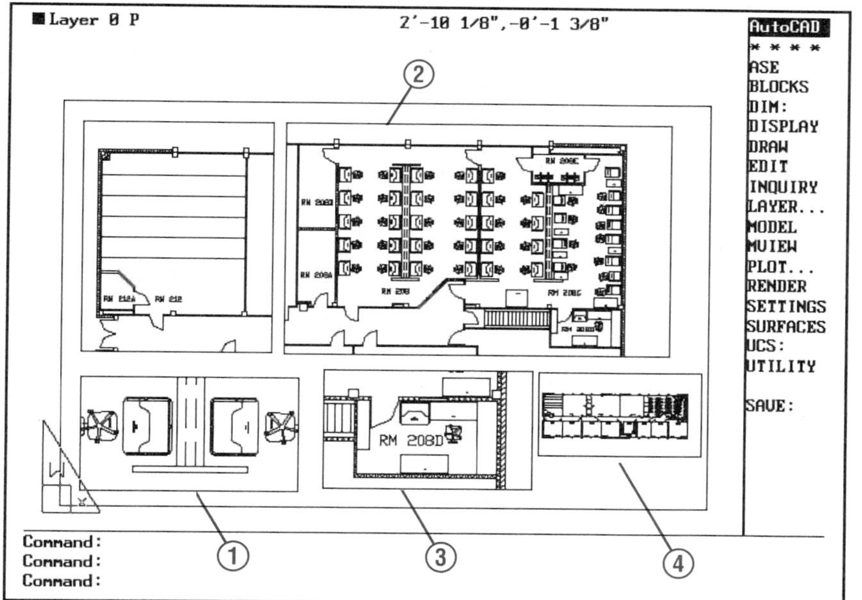

Figure 46.6

Five paper space views.

Student: ________________ Date: ________

Instructor: ________________ Course: ________ Section: ________

UNIT 47

Composing a Drawing

Although you prepare your drawing electronically, you probably still need to produce a copy of the drawing on paper, vellum, or mylar for reproduction or distribution. In AutoCAD, producing a *hard copy* of the drawing is called *plotting* or *printing*, depending on the type of device you use to prepare the hard copy of the drawing. The first step in plotting or printing a drawing is *composing* the drawing. The process of composing a drawing includes inserting a title block, creating viewports and views of the different parts of the drawing, scaling the views, and arranging the views. This unit teaches you how to perform these steps.

The objectives for this unit are to:

- Understand drawing composition
- Insert a title block in paper space
- Set up viewports in paper space
- Organize and align viewports

Starting with a Title Block

Most drawings require a title block that contains your company's name, the name of the design, and other information. You can insert a title block in model space, but paper space (see unit 46, "Introduction to Paper Space") offers a much better environment for setting up views of your drawing. Therefore, you should insert your title block into the drawing in paper space.

After switching to paper space, you could draw your title block and fill in all the necessary information in the title block. Although the information in the title block will probably change from one drawing to another, the title block itself will be the same. In addition, the type of information in the title block will remain the same (the drawing title, company name, and any other information). If you had to add this information every time you composed a drawing, it would take a considerable amount of time. Fortunately, AutoCAD lets you automate the process and reuse a standard title block.

Units 67, 68, and 69 discuss blocks. Think of blocks as symbols that you can insert into a drawing as many times as necessary. The exercise that follows shows you how to insert a standard title block drawing into your current drawing as a block, saving you the time required to draw the title block.

The title block drawing used in the next exercise contains attributes. AutoCAD will prompt you to supply information to fill in these attributes when you insert the title block. These attributes describe the drawing's title, drawing number, and the company name. Unit 91, "Introduction to Symbols and Attributes," introduces attributes.

In the following exercise, insert a title block into your metric drawing of a slide block. The slide block drawing contains only a few dimensions and is not complete. Later units show you how to add additional dimensions and other information to the drawing to complete it. You will learn more about blocks in units 67, 68, and 69. Figure 47.1 shows your drawing as you begin the exercise.

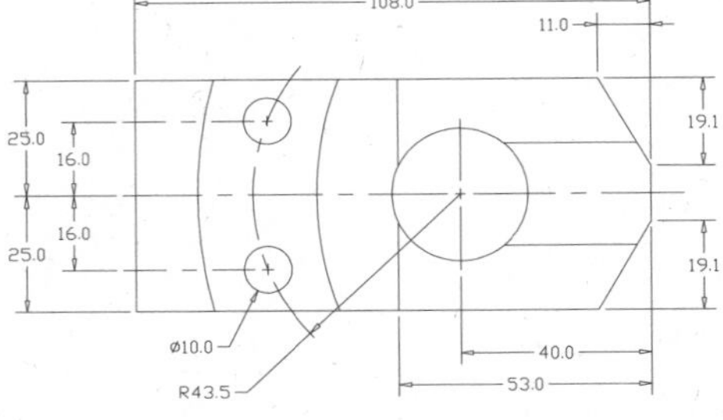

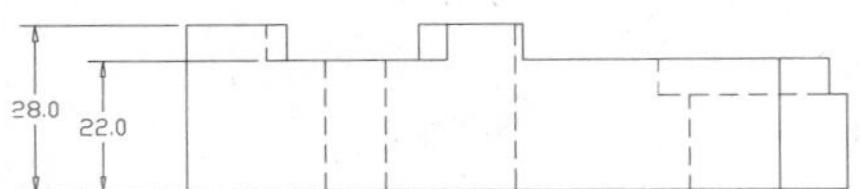

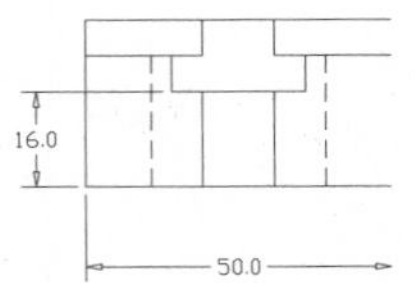

Figure 47.1

A metric slide block drawing.

To insert the title block, first switch to paper space. Then insert the drawing file 047ANSIC as a block into the drawing in paper space.

Inserting a Title Block

1. Begin a new drawing named 047???01 in your assigned directory using 047SLIDE as a prototype.

2. `Command:` *Choose* View, *then* Tilemode, *then* Off (0) — Turns off TILEMODE and switches to paper space

3. `Command:` *Choose* Draw, *then* Insert — Issues the DDINSERT command and displays the Insert dialog box (see fig. 47.2)

   `ddinsert`

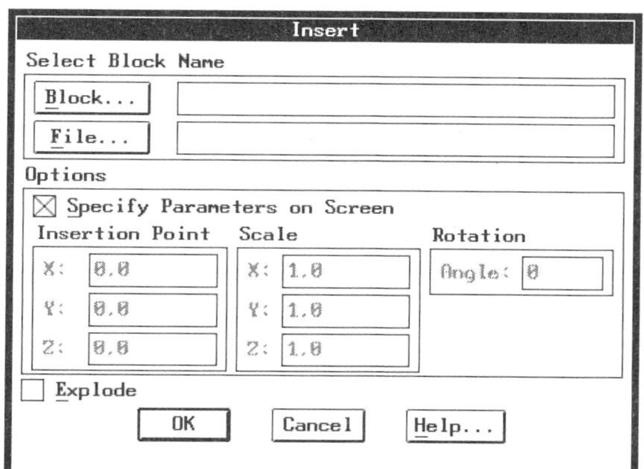

Figure 47.2

The Insert dialog box.

4. *Choose the* File *button* — Displays the Select Drawing File dialog box (see fig. 47.3)

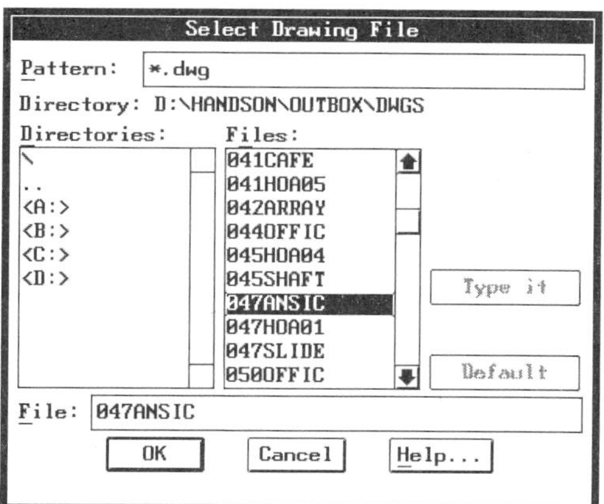

Figure 47.3

The Select Drawing File dialog box.

continues

5. *Locate and select the file* 047ANSIC *in the directory that contains your prototype drawings, then choose* OK	Specifies the name of the file to insert as a block
6. *In the Insert dialog box, clear the* Specify Parameters on Screen *check box*	Accepts default insertion point, scale, and rotation
7. *Choose* OK	Insert the block
8. `Enter drawing title:` **`SLIDE BLOCK`** ↵	Specifies the drawing title
9. `Company or school name:` *Type the name of your school or company and press* Enter	Specifies the company or school name
10. `Enter drawing number:` **`C78231`** ↵	Specifies drawing number
11. Issue the ZOOM command with the All option.	

Your drawing should look similar to figure 47.4.

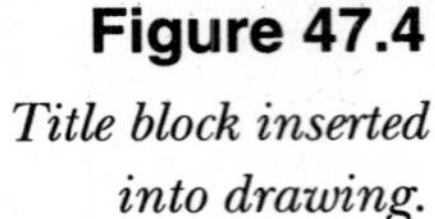

Figure 47.4

Title block inserted into drawing.

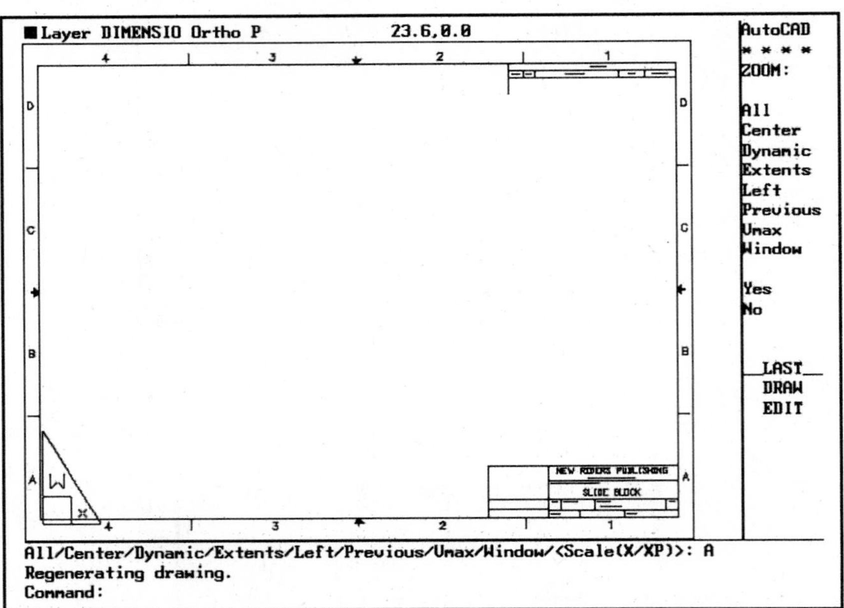

Now that you have a title block, you can begin developing the views of your drawing.

Setting Up Viewports

To bring your drawing from model space into your paper space sheet, you must open *viewports*. MVIEW is the command you use to create viewports in paper space. As you learned in unit 46, MVIEW provides many options for creating viewports in paper space.

In the following exercise, create four viewports to contain the views of your drawing.

Creating Viewports

Continue with your drawing from the previous exercise.

1. `Command:` *Choose* View, *then* Mview, *then* 4 Viewports — Issues the MVIEW command to create four aligned viewports

   `_mview`

   `ON/OFF/Hideplot/Fit/2/3/4/Restore/<First Point>: 4`

2. `Fit/<First Point>:` *Pick a point at* ① *(see fig. 47.5)* — Specifies first corner to locate viewports

3. `Second point:` *Pick a point at* ② *(see fig. 47.5)* — Specifies other corner and creates viewports (see fig. 47.5)

4. Save your drawing.

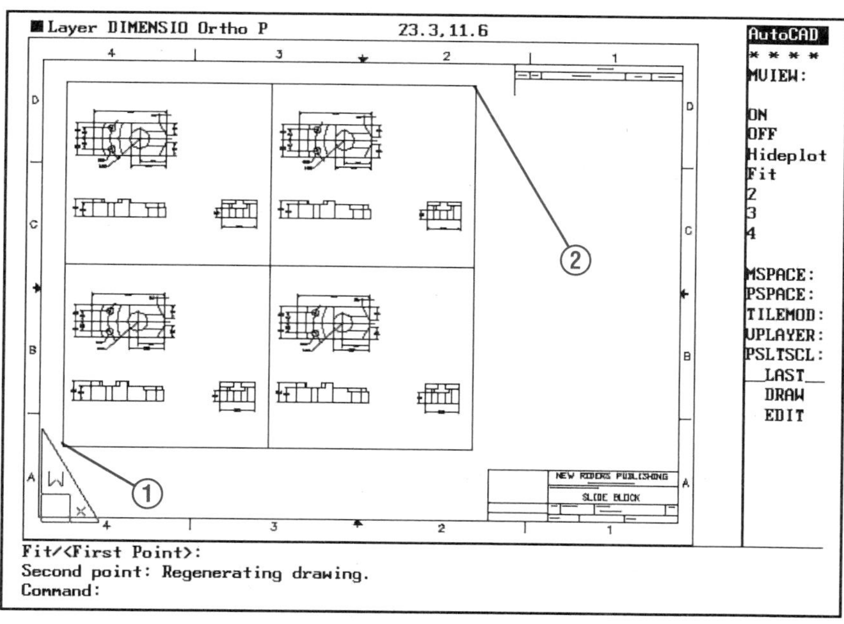

Figure 47.5

Selection points for viewports.

The number and arrangement of viewports in a drawing vary from drawing to drawing. You can create as many viewports as necessary to display the drawing. In many cases, you may need to create additional sheets to contain all of the necessary views and details. You can insert each of these sheets in paper space in the same drawing file, then create and organize the appropriate viewports on each sheet.

Organizing the Views

The next step in composing the drawing is to scale and align the viewports, if necessary. As you learned in unit 46, you can use the ZOOM command with the XP option to scale a viewport relative to paper space. This sets the scale of the view so that it will plot or print to the correct scale.

Your first step in scaling and aligning viewports should be to zoom each of the views as necessary to display the portion of the drawing that will be contained in the viewport. Then, scale the view as necessary. In the following exercise, arrange and scale the upper left viewport to show the top view of the slide block. Figure 47.6 shows the drawing as you begin the exercise.

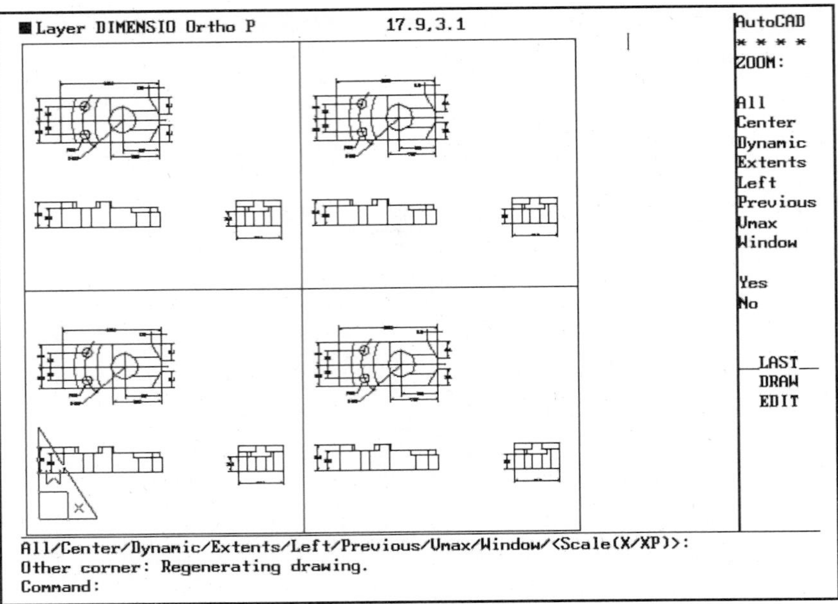

Figure 47.6

Before view setup.

Scaling and Arranging a View

1. Continue with your drawing from the previous exercise, and zoom to the view shown in figure 47.6.

2. `Command:` *Choose* View, *then* Model space	Switches to model space
3. `Command:` *Click in the upper left viewport*	Makes the viewport active
4. `Command:` **`Z`**	
`ZOOM`	
5. `All/Center/Dynamic/Extents/Left/Previous/Vmax/Window/<Scale(X/XP)>:` **`0.03937XP`** ↵	Scales the viewport to the inverse of 25.4 to size the view to a 1:1 scale

6. Pan the upper left view to match the view shown in figure 47.7.

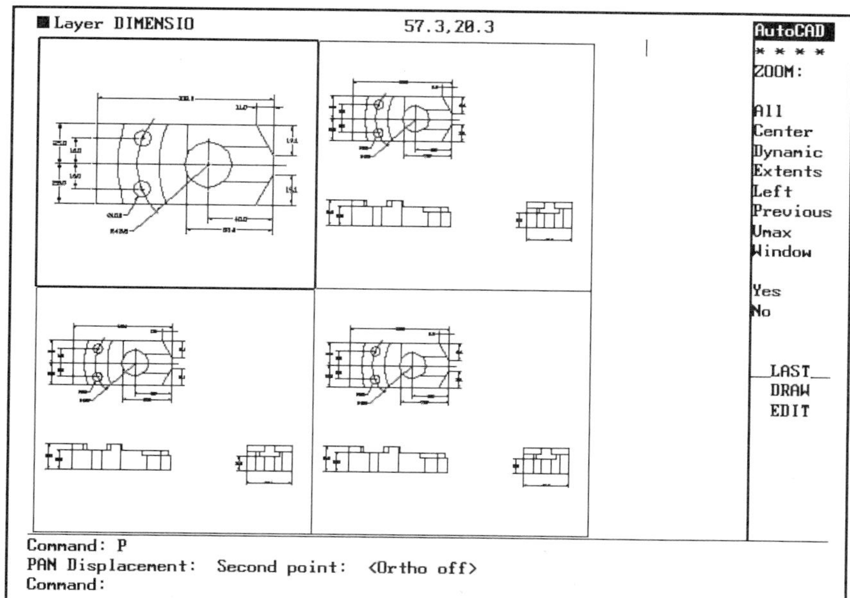

Figure 47.7

View after scaling and panning.

If the viewport is not large enough to display all of your view, you can stretch the viewport to make it larger. To stretch a viewport, enter paper space, then select the viewport. Viewports have a grip at each corner; select a grip, then use Stretch autoedit mode to stretch the viewport. If the viewport is too large and shows too much of the drawing, stretch the viewport to make it smaller.

You will finish arranging your views later in this unit. Next, read about a command that automates drawing setup.

Using MVSETUP

AutoCAD provides a command called MVSETUP that automates the task of inserting a title block. It also automates creating, scaling and aligning viewports. To illustrate MVSETUP's advantages, the exercises use the command to create a standard title block, and to prompt you with the option to save the title block as a separate drawing. Afterward, you can load the title block drawing and customize it, adding your own company logo or other information.

You can issue MVSETUP by choosing View, then MV Setup. The options available in MVSETUP include:

- **Align.** Enables you to align viewports with one another horizontally or vertically. Align also provides options to rotate a view and to rotate the coordinate system in the XY plane.

- **Create.** Automates the process of creating viewports. Create also enables you to delete an object, such as an existing viewport. It is similar in function to the MVIEW command, but offers fewer options for viewport layout.
- **Scale viewports.** Enables you to scale a viewport relative to paper space. Scale viewports duplicates the function of the XP option of the ZOOM command.
- **Options.** Presents even more options for setting the layer on which the title block will be inserted, setting limits, setting drawing units, and specifying whether to insert the title block or attach it as an Xref (Xrefs are explained in unit 70, "Introduction to Xrefs").
- **Title block.** Automates the process of inserting standard title blocks into the drawing.
- **Undo.** Functions like Undo in any other command: the option undoes the previous MVSETUP action.

You can use MVSETUP at any time, even after you have created viewports. To save time you should get in the habit of using MVSETUP because it automates so many drawing composition functions.

In the following exercises, lay out the drawing just as you have in previous exercises, but this time use MVSETUP.

Inserting the Title Block with MVSETUP

1. Begin a new drawing named 047???02 in your assigned directory using 047SLIDE as a prototype.

2. `Command:` *Choose* View, *then* Layout, *then* MV SETUP — Issues the MVSETUP command

```
mvsetup
Initializing...  MVSETUP loaded.
```

3. `Paperspace/Modelspace is disabled. The pre-R11 setup will be invoked unless it is enabled. Enable Paper/Modelspace? <Y>:` *Press* Enter — Switches to paper space

```
Entering Paper space.  Use MVIEW to insert Model space viewports.
Regenerating drawing.
MVSetup, Version 1.15, (c) 1990-1992 by Autodesk, Inc.
```

4. `Align/Create/Scale viewports/Options/ Title block/Undo:` **T** ↵ — Specifies Title block option

Using MVSETUP

5. Delete objects/Origin/Undo/ <Insert title block>: *Press* Enter — Accepts default option to insert title block

```
Available title block options:

   0:        None
   1:        ISO A4 Size(mm)
   2:        ISO A3 Size(mm)
   3:        ISO A2 Size(mm)
   4:        ISO A1 Size(mm)
   5:        ISO A0 Size(mm)
   6:        ANSI-V Size(in)
   7:        ANSI-A Size(in)
   8:        ANSI-B Size(in)
   9:        ANSI-C Size(in)
  10:        ANSI-D Size(in)
  11:        ANSI-E Size(in)
  12:        Arch/Engineering (24 x 36in)
  13:        Generic D size Sheet (24 x 36in)
```

7. Add/Delete/Redisplay/<Number of entry to load>: **9** ↵ — Specifies ANSI-C size title block

8. Create a drawing named ansi-c.dwg? <Y>: *Press* Enter — Creates a standard ANSI-C drawing title block in the specified drawing file

Remain in the MVSETUP command for the next exercise.

MVSETUP automated the process of inserting the title block. Note that AutoCAD did not prompt you to specify information for drawing name, school name, or drawing number. This is because the standard ANSI-C drawing that MVSETUP created does not contain the attributes. Now that ANSI-C.DWG exists, you can open the file and customize it. This includes adding attributes for information within the text area of the title block. The next time you use MVSETUP and select the ANSI-C title block, any changes you have made—including attributes—will be incorporated into the current drawing.

Next, you can use MVSETUP to create some viewports for your drawing.

Creating Viewports with MVSETUP

Continue from the previous exercise.

1. Align/Create/Scale viewports/Options /Title block/Undo: **C** ↵ — Specifies the Create option

2. Delete objects/Undo/<Create viewports>: *Press* Enter — Accepts default option

continues

```
Available Mview viewport layout options:

    0:          None
    1:          Single
    2:          Std. Engineering
    3:          Array of Viewports
```

3. `Redisplay/<Number of entry to load>:` **3** ↵ — Specifies an array of viewports

4. `Bounding area for viewports. Default/ <First point >:` *Pick a point at* ① *(see fig. 47.8)* — Specifies first corner

5. `Other point:` *Pick a point at* ② — Specifies second corner

6. `Number of viewports in X. <1>:` **2** ↵ — Specifies two viewports horizontally

7. `Number of viewports in Y. <1>:` **2** ↵ — Specifies two viewports vertically

8. `Distance between viewports in X. <0.0>:` **0.5** ↵ — Specifies a spacing of 1/2" between viewports horizontally

9. `Distance between viewports in Y. <0.5>:` *Press* Enter — Specifies a spacing of 1/2" between viewports vertically

Remain in the MVSETUP command for the next exercise.

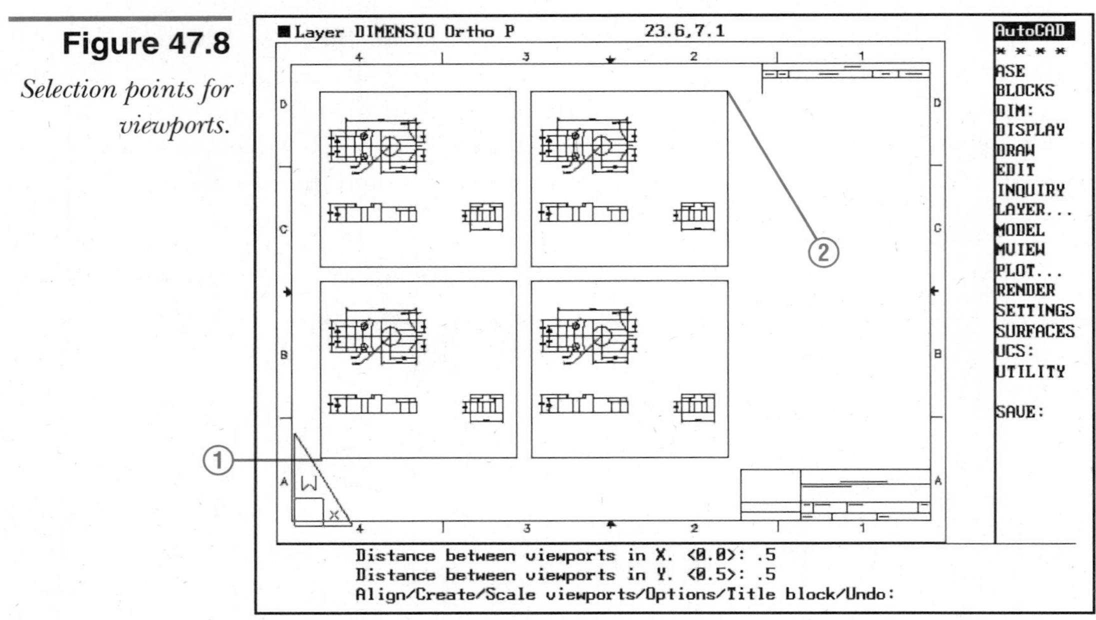

Figure 47.8

Selection points for viewports.

MVSETUP created four viewports spaced 1/2" apart. If you had specified option 2, Std. Engineering, AutoCAD would also have created four viewports. The difference is that the upper-right viewport would have been rotated for a 3D view (rotated off-axis). An advantage to using MVSETUP to create viewports is that it will place a space between the viewports. MVIEW always places viewports adjacent to one another. A space between the viewports can make it easier to select a viewport for editing.

Next, scale all four views to 1:1 relative to paper space. Remember that your drawing is metric.

Scaling Viewports with MVSETUP

1.	`Align/Create/Scale viewports/Options/ Title block/Undo:` **`S`** ↵	Specifies the Scale viewports option
2.	`Select the viewports to scale: Select objects:` *Select each of the four viewports*	Selects all viewports to scale
3.	`Select objects:` *Press* Enter	Ends selection
4.	`Set zoom scale factors for viewports. Interactively/<Uniform>:` *Press* Enter	Accepts default to scale all selected viewports to the same scale
5.	`Enter the ratio of paper space units to model space units...`	
6.	`Number of paper space units. <1.0>:` *Press* Enter	Sets paper space units
7.	`Number of model space units. <1.0>:` **`25.4`** ↵	Sets model space units for metric-to-inch ratio
8.	`Align/Create/Scale viewports/Options/ Title block/Undo:` *Press* Enter	Exits MVSETUP
9.	Save your drawing.	

Your drawing should look similar to figure 47.9.

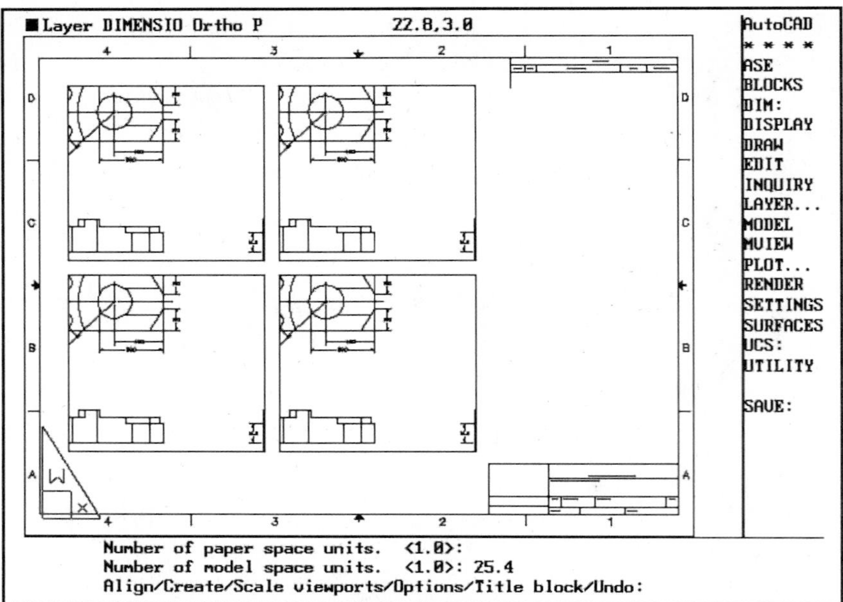

Figure 47.9

Drawing after scaling viewports.

The Scale viewports option in MVSETUP works differently from the XP option of the ZOOM command, although the results are the same. MVSETUP is somewhat easier to use because you do not have to calculate the drawing's scale as a single value as you do with ZOOM. If you are setting a viewport to a scale of 1:10, for example, set paper space units to 1 and model space units to 10. To set a viewport scale to 1/4" = 1'-0", set paper space units to .25 and model space units to 12. You would describe this as a quarter-of-an-inch on paper equals 12 inches in the model. Always set paper space units to the first number in your drawing scale, and set model space units to the second number in the scale.

MVSETUP is a good tool for composing a drawing. It automates virtually all of the tasks you have to perform when composing a drawing. If you want to use your own title blocks, simply insert each of the appropriately sized standard title blocks, direct MVSETUP to save them as drawing files, then modify the drawing files to suit your specifications.

Unit Review

What You've Learned

- Commands: MVIEW, MVSETUP, DDINSERT
- How to insert a title block both manually and with MVSETUP
- How to create viewports both manually and with MVSETUP
- How to scale viewports with ZOOM and with MVSETUP

Review Questions

True or False

47.01 T F A hard copy is a plot or print of a drawing.

47.02 T F *Composing* a drawing includes inserting a title block and creating and organizing views.

47.03 T F You must draw a title block in model space.

47.04 T F You can reuse a standard title block in many drawings.

47.05 T F The MVIEW command creates tiled viewports in model space.

47.06 T F The MVIEW command only works in paper space.

47.07 T F To scale a viewport in paper space to 1/2" = 1'-0" with MVSETUP, set paper space units to 0.5 and model space units to 12.

47.08 T F MVSETUP can organize viewports with a space between the viewports.

47.09 T F The XP option of the ZOOM command and the Scale viewports option of MVSETUP perform the same function.

47.10 T F You cannot insert a title block in model space.

Additional Exercises

47.11 Continue with your drawing 047???02. Pan the top-left viewport to show only the top view of the slide block. Resize the viewport if necessary to show all of the view. Use the Align option of the MVSETUP command to align the viewports so that the bottom-left viewport shows only the front view of the slide block and the bottom-right viewport shows only the side view of the slide block. Make sure the views are properly aligned with one another. Then, delete the upper-right viewport and save your drawing.

Student: ____________ Date: ______

Instructor: ____________ Course: ______ Section: ______

UNIT 48

Plotting a Drawing

Producing a drawing file is seldom the end of the design process. Often, you must produce a copy of the drawing on paper, vellum, or mylar for checking or distribution. Even in operations where drawings are distributed electronically, it is often necessary to produce a hard copy of a drawing. This unit introduces plotting and printing. In it you learn to use AutoCAD's PLOT command to produce a hard copy of a drawing on a printer or plotter.

The objectives for this unit are to:

- Specify plot options such as device, paper size, scale, and plot area.
- Produce a plot on a printer or plotter.
- Review tips on keeping a plotter functioning properly.

About Plotters and Printers

When you create a drawing in AutoCAD, you create a database that represents all the graphic entities and text associated with a drawing. When you plot a drawing, AutoCAD converts the information in the drawing database to instructions that a printer or plotter can reproduce on paper or other media. The printer or plotter can be used to produce a hard copy of the drawing.

The most common output device is the plotter. There are different types of plotters, but all perform the same function: They produce a hard copy of the drawing. Plotters are most commonly used when a large plot of a drawing is required (larger than A-size) or when a final, high-quality plot is required. The most common type of plotter is the pen plotter.

Printers are another means to produce a hard copy of drawings. Printers are useful for small drawings (such as A-size) and for small check plots of drawings to be plotted at their full sheet size on a plotter at a later date. Printers can usually produce hard copy faster than can an ink plotter, which makes them very useful for producing a working copy or a check plot.

In addition to sending a drawing to a plotter or printer, you can plot a drawing to a file. Later, you can copy the file to the printer or plotter, or you can import it into another type of program, such as a desktop publishing program, that can read the plot file.

Choosing a Device

The first step of plotting or printing a drawing is to compose the plot. Composing a plot is discussed in unit 47. If you have not yet worked through the exercises in unit 47, do so before you continue in this unit.

When the drawing is ready to plot, you must specify the device on which the drawing is to be plotted or printed. Before you can plot a drawing to a specific device, that device must be configured in AutoCAD. Your instructor should have already configured AutoCAD on your workstation for at least one plotter or printer.

To select a device, issue the PLOT command when your drawing is ready to plot. AutoCAD displays the Plot Configuration dialog box, shown in figure 48.1. You can use the controls in the Plot Configuration dialog box to specify all of the options for producing a hard copy of your drawing.

To specify an output device, choose the Device and Default Selection button in the Plot Configuration dialog box. AutoCAD then displays the Device and Default Selection dialog box, which lists all of the output devices for which AutoCAD is configured. Figure 48.2 shows the Device and Default Selection dialog box.

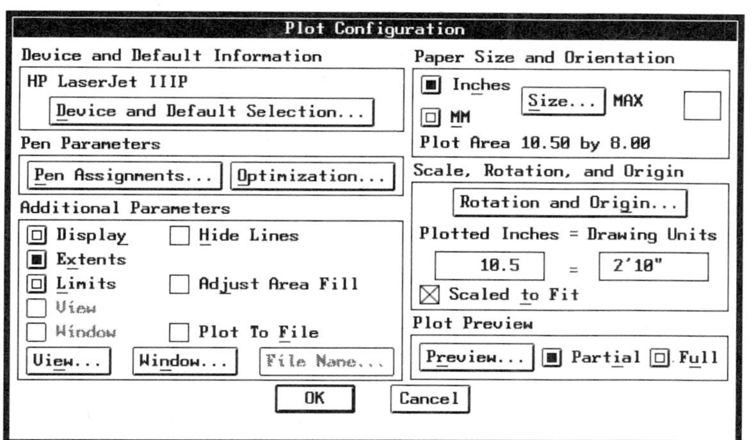

Figure 48.1

The Plot Configuration dialog box.

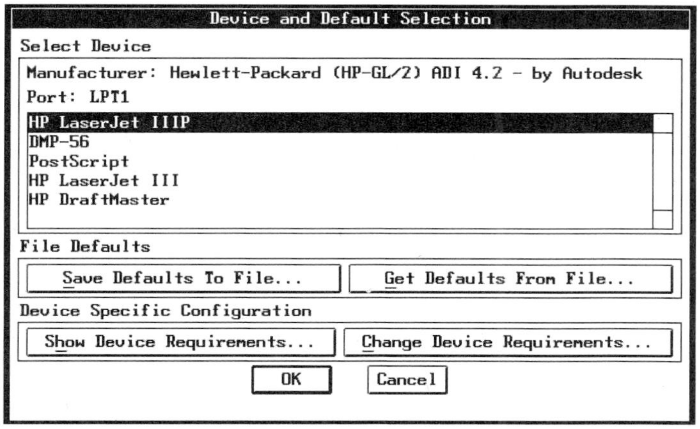

Device and Default Selection
Select Device
Manufacturer: Hewlett-Packard (HP-GL/2) ADI 4.2 - by Autodesk
Port: LPT1
HP LaserJet IIIP
DMP-56
PostScript
HP LaserJet III
HP DraftMaster
File Defaults
Save Defaults To File...
Get Defaults From File...
Device Specific Configuration
Show Device Requirements...
Change Device Requirements...
OK
Cancel

Figure 48.2

The Device and Default Selection dialog box.

The options that you can set depend on the type of device you select. With many plotters, for example, the only option you can specify is the number of copies. With many printers, you can specify the paper source, print resolution, and other options. To specify a device, simply choose it from the list of configured devices.

The following list explains the command buttons that you can use in the Device and Default Selection dialog box to specify device options:

- **Change Device Requirements.** This button displays a dialog box that enables you to specify options such as paper source and number of copies for the device. The options that you can change depend on the type of device you select.
- **Show Device Requirements.** This button displays the current option settings for the device. These are the same options that you can change using the Change Device Requirements button.

- **Save Defaults to File.** You can save your current option settings to a file. This button enables you to store different configurations for the same device, which you can later retrieve, saving you the time of setting the device options again.
- **Get Defaults from File.** This button displays a dialog box that you can use to select a device configuration file and restore settings that you have saved to a file.

Specifying Area, Size, and Scale

After you select a device, you must specify other parameters for the plot. These parameters include the area of the drawing to plot, the paper size to use, and the plot scale.

Specifying Plot Area

You can plot the display, extents, limits, a view, or a window. You control the plot area by choosing one of the radio buttons in the Additional Parameters group in the Plot Configuration dialog box. These options are explained in the following list:

- **Display.** This option plots the view in the current viewport if model space is active. It plots the current view if paper space is active.
- **Extents.** This option plots the area of the drawing defined by its extents.
- **Limits.** This option plots the area of the drawing defined by its limits.
- **View.** This option plots a named view that you specify.
- **Window.** This option plots a window that you define by specifying the corners of the window.

If you want to plot an entire drawing that you have composed in paper space as a single sheet, plot the drawing's extents. All the drawing data should be contained within the title block's borders.

Specifying Paper Size

In addition to specifying which area of the drawing to plot, you also must specify the paper size on which the drawing is to be plotted. To specify paper size, first specify whether you want paper sizes displayed in inches or millimeters. Choose either the Inches or MM radio button in the Paper Size and

Orientation group of the Plot Configuration dialog box. After you specify units of measure, click on the Size button. The Paper Size dialog box appears (see fig. 48.3). The paper sizes displayed in this dialog box vary according to the device you have selected as the plot device.

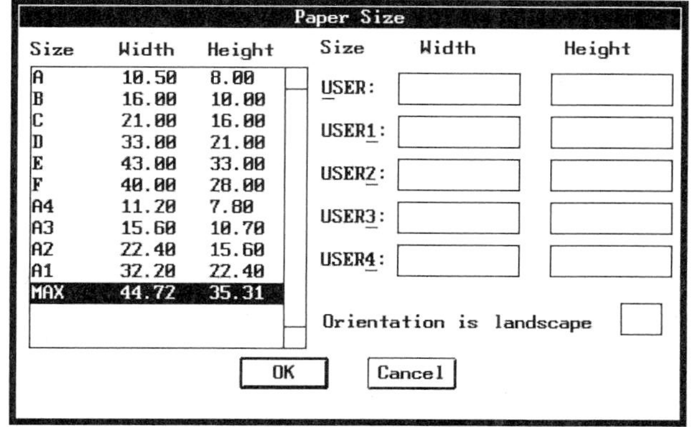

Figure 48.3

The Paper Size dialog box.

To choose a standard size, click on the size in the list at the left of the dialog box. To specify a nonstandard size, enter it in one of the USER edit boxes at the right of the dialog box. Specify both the width and height of your custom paper size. After you specify the paper size, choose OK.

Specifying Plot Scale

AutoCAD plots your drawing to any scale you specify. You can direct AutoCAD to fit the plot to the paper. AutoCAD then plots the area you specify to as large a scale as possible on the paper, essentially filling the paper with the plot. Place a check in the Scale to Fit check box to fit the drawing to the paper.

Fitting a plot to a sheet does not result in a drawing that is plotted to a specific scale. The drawing is proportional to the original, but not to a specific, exact scale.

You also can specify an exact scale for the drawing. Unless you are plotting a check plot that does not have to be to scale, most of your drawings should be plotted to scale. Drawings should always be plotted to scale if they are intended for distribution.

The scale that you specify when plotting depends on how your drawing is composed. If you use paper space to compose your drawing, plot the drawing at a scale of 1:1. If you plot from model space, however, you must determine the correct scale based on the drawing and on the scale at which you want it to plot.

Assume that you want to plot a drawing from model space at a scale of 1/4" = 1'-0". The ratio of this scale is 1:48 (which is the ratio of 1/4" to 12"). This means that your drawing model is 48 times larger than the size at which you want it to plot. To specify the correct scale in this example, enter **1** in the Plotted Inches edit box and enter 48 in the Drawing Units edit box. Both of these edit boxes are located in the Scale, Rotation, and Origin group in the Plot Configuration dialog box.

Making Your First Plot

After you specify the plot device, plot area, paper size, and scale, you are ready to plot your first drawing. In the following exercise, plot a drawing of an office. The drawing has already been composed for you and is ready to plot.

Plotting Your First Drawing

1. Begin a new drawing named 048???01 in your assigned directory using 048OFFIC as a prototype.

2. `Command:` *Choose* File, *then* Plot	Issues the PLOT command and displays the Plot Configuration dialog box
3. *Choose the* Device and Default Selection *dialog box*	Displays the Device and Default Selection dialog box
4. *Choose the proper device for your drawing as directed by your instructor, then choose* OK	Specifies the plot device
5. *Choose the* Size *button*	Displays the Paper Size dialog box
6. *If you are printing to a printer, choose* MAX, *then choose* OK	
7. *If you are printing to a plotter, choose a paper size as directed by your instructor, then choose* OK	
8. *Choose the* Extents *radio button*	Specifies the plot area
9. *Place a check in the* Scaled to Fit *radio button*	Specifies to fit the plot to the paper
10. *Choose* OK	

```
Effective plotting area: 10.50 wide by 6.79 high
Position paper in plotter.
```

Your paper size may vary according to the device and paper size you have specified.

11. `Press Enter to continue or S to Stop for hardware setup` *press* Enter

```
Regeneration done nn%
Plotting viewport 4.
Effective plotting area:  3.15 wide by 1.90 high
Regeneration done nn%
Plotting viewport 3.
Effective plotting area:  3.24 wide by 1.90 high
Regeneration done nn%
Plotting viewport 2.
Effective plotting area:  7.37 wide by 3.84 high
Regeneration done 100%
Plot complete.
```

The output that AutoCAD generates on the screen as it plots varies according to the plot device you select.

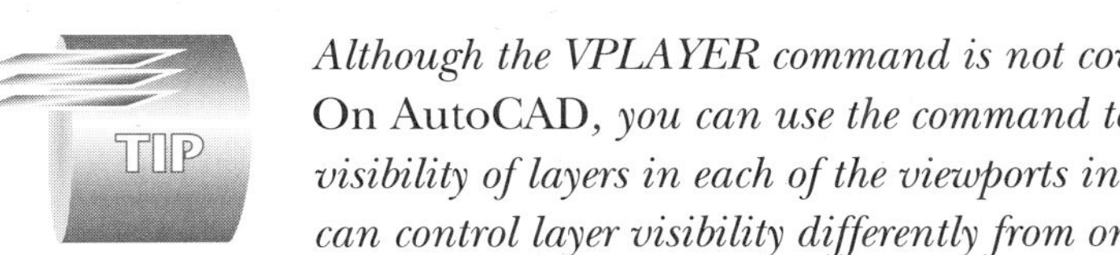

Although the VPLAYER command is not covered in Hands On AutoCAD, *you can use the command to control the visibility of layers in each of the viewports in a drawing. You can control layer visibility differently from one viewport to another, displaying only the information in each viewport that you want plotted as part of that viewport. Essentially, VPLAYER provides the same layer visibility controls as the LAYER and DDLMODES commands, but VPLAYER controls layer visibility on a viewport-by-viewport basis, rather than globally for the entire drawing.*

Unit Review

What You've Learned

- Commands: PLOT
- How to specify plot options
- How to plot a drawing

Review Questions

True or False

48.01 T F A hard copy of a drawing is a copy of the drawing reproduced on paper or other plotter/printer media.

48.02 T F Plotters are often used to produce large copies of drawings.

48.03 T F Printers are often faster than plotters at reproducing a drawing.

48.04 T F Drawings cannot be plotted to a file.

48.05 T F The PLOTCONFIG command controls the options for plotting, such as paper size, scale, etc.

48.06 T F The options you can set for plotting are the same regardless of which device you select.

48.07 T F Plotting the display in paper space plots the current viewport only.

48.08 T F The available paper sizes vary according to the plot device you select.

48.09 T F AutoCAD plots all drawings to scale.

48.10 T F The ratio of the scale 1/2" = 1'-0" is 1:24.

Student: ______________________ Date: __________

Instructor: ______________________ Course: __________ Section: __________

Advanced Plotting Techniques

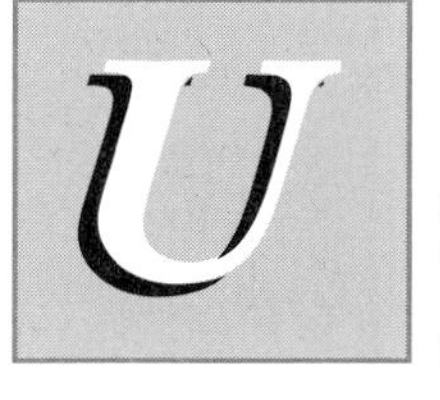

nit 48 explains general techniques for plotting a drawing. This unit explains additional options you can use to control the plot.

The objectives for this unit are to:

- Control plot rotation
- Specify pen color and control other pen parameters
- Plot views and windows
- Plot to a file
- Use plot preview

Controlling Plot Rotation and Origin

Occasionally, it is necessary to rotate a plot. Rotating a plot changes the relationship between the drawing and the sheet on which it is plotted. This is sometimes necessary because of the way in which the paper is inserted in the plotter. It also is useful when you are plotting or printing a drawing to fit the paper and want to plot the drawing as large as possible. The drawing might be taller than it is wide, and rotating it can align the longer edge of the drawing with the longer edge of the paper.

You also can change the origin of a plot. Changing the origin of a plot shifts the drawing on the paper without changing any other orientation (such as rotation). This is useful if you want to center a plot on the sheet or need to move the drawing away from the plotter pinch wheels that hold the paper in place.

To rotate a plot or change its origin, click on the Rotation and Origin button in the Plot Configuration dialog box. The Plot Rotation and Origin dialog box appears (see fig. 49.1).

Figure 49.1

The Plot Rotation and Origin dialog box.

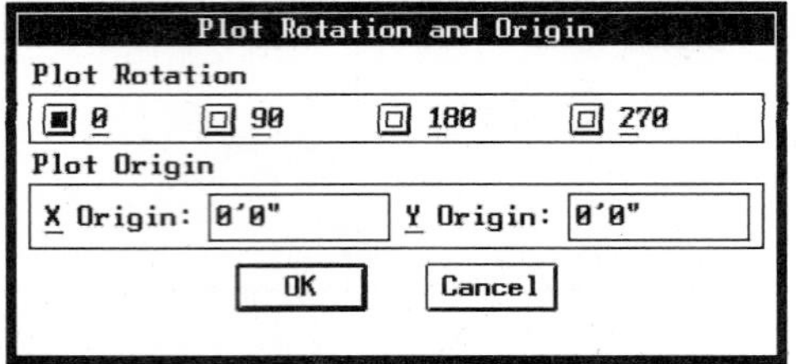

You can rotate the plot in 90-degree increments by choosing the 90 button in the Plot Rotation and Origin dialog box. To change the origin of the plot, specify the X and Y ordinates for the origin in the two edit boxes provided for this purpose.

Controlling Pen Parameters

By default, AutoCAD associates entity color with pen number when you plot a drawing. For example, you can set up your drawing so that everything that appears red in the drawing plots with pen number 2. This makes it possible for you to control pen weight very easily. You can draw entities with a specific color if they need to be plotted with a specific pen. You can assign more than one color to a particular pen number.

NOTE

Pen color and entity color are not directly related. Entities drawn in red are not necessarily drawn with a red pen. Associating entity color with a specific pen can be used to plot certain entities with a certain color of pen, but most often it is used to plot certain entities with a specific pen width. Just remember that you are only associating an entity color with a pen number, and that it is up to you to ensure that the correct pen is inserted in the pen carousel in the correct pen slot.

To control pen and color assignment, click on the Pen Assignments button in the Plot Configuration dialog box. The Pen Assignments dialog box appears (see fig. 49.2).

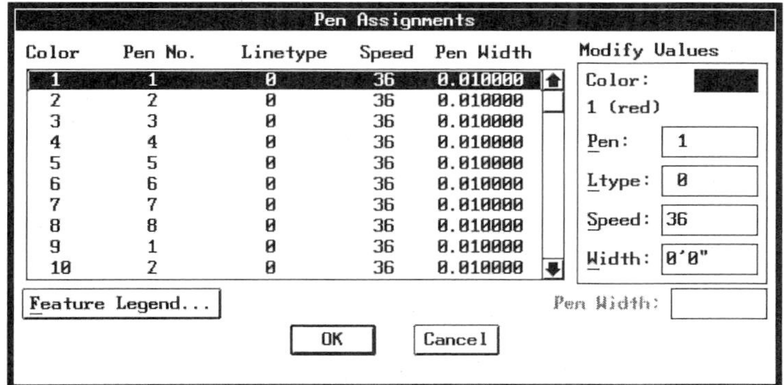

Figure 49.2

The Pen Assignments dialog box.

You can set the pen parameters for a single color or for multiple colors. Just select the colors that you want to change from the list, then enter the parameters in the Modify Values group in the dialog box. When you plot a drawing on a pen plotter, the only parameter you generally change is the Pen parameter. The default pen and plotter assignments vary according to the device you select.

You should rely on AutoCAD's linetypes rather than changing the Ltype parameter, which causes the drawing to plot using the plotter's internally defined linetypes. With a pen plotter, you must use a different width pen to achieve a specific line width, so you should seldom have to change the Width parameter. If you are plotting to a printer, however, the Width parameter offers a way for you to change the width of specific entities on the plot. Simply select the color(s) for which you want to specify a new width, then enter the appropriate line width in the Width edit box.

If your pen plotter supports the feature, you can change the speed at which specific pens operate. If you have problems with a pen not working properly (skipping, for example), you might overcome the problem by slowing down its speed. You also might be able to speed up a plot by speeding up all the pens. Check your plotter manual for tips on setting pen speed according to the type of pen and plot media you use.

Plotting Views and Windows

While you most often plot the display, or plot the limits or extents, of the drawing, you also can plot a named view or a window. Consider an example: You need to compose a drawing with multiple sheets. You can enter paper space and insert each of the sheet title blocks, then compose the necessary views on each sheet. You then can plot each sheet using a window. You do not have to save each sheet in a separate file.

To plot a named view, choose the View button in the Plot Configuration dialog box. Doing so displays the View Name dialog box (see fig. 49.3). Select the view you want to plot, then choose OK. Set any other required options such as scale and paper size, then start the plot.

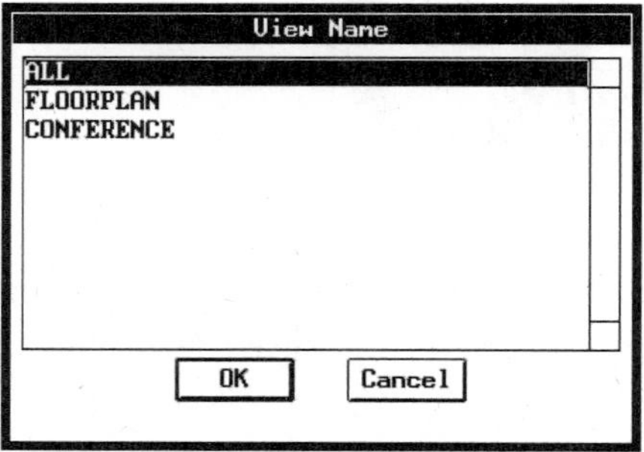

Figure 49.3
The View Name dialog box.

To plot a window, click on the Window button in the Plot Configuration dialog box. The Window Selection dialog box appears (see fig. 49.4). You can specify the X and Y ordinates of the two points that define the opposite corners of the window, or you can click on the Pick button to pick the points graphically from the drawing. After specifying the window, set any other required plot options and start the plot.

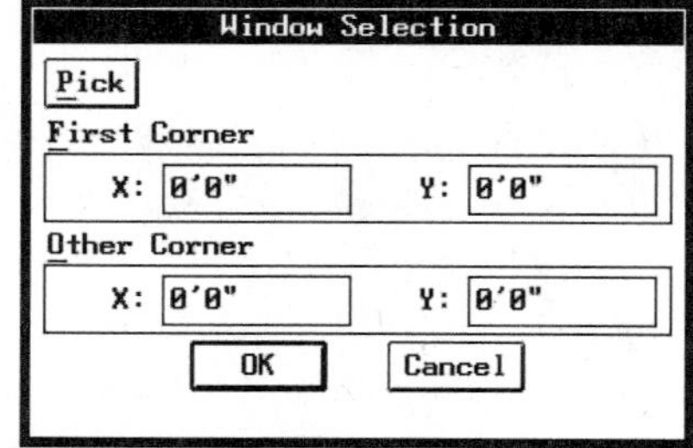

Figure 49.4
The Window Selection dialog box.

Plotting a window is useful when you need to plot only part of a drawing. It is sometimes more useful than plotting a named view because you can usually exclude entities from the window more easily than you can exclude entities from a view.

Plotting to a File

Your system may include a *plot spooler*, a program that handles plotting while you continue to work with your drawing. Normally, you cannot continue to work with AutoCAD while it is plotting a drawing. A plot spooler takes over the task of plotting the drawing, freeing AutoCAD so you can get back to work. Not all plot spoolers function the same, but many require you to first plot the drawing to a file, then turn the file over to the plot spooler. This is one reason to plot a drawing to a file with AutoCAD. Another reason to plot to a file is to incorporate your drawing into another program, such as a desktop-publishing or graphics program. Many such programs can import files in HPGL format, EPS format, or in other of the formats to which AutoCAD can plot.

To plot to a file, first specify all the options you would set when plotting to a device such as a plotter or printer. Select the correct device, paper size, plot area, scale, and other parameters. Then, place a check in the Plot to File check box in the Plot Configuration dialog box. When you plot the drawing, the plot instructions are redirected to a file, instead of to the output device. AutoCAD prompts you for a file name to use for the plot file.

Previewing a Plot

Often, plotting a drawing is time consuming, particularly if you don't use a plot spooler. Also, preprinted sheets that have custom title blocks are generally expensive, so you do not want to waste them with trial-and-error plot setup. To avoid wasting time and other resources plotting a drawing, you can preview the plot. When you preview a plot, AutoCAD shows on-screen what the plot looks like on the paper size and at the scale that you specify.

AutoCAD offers two options for previewing a plot, controlled by two radio buttons in the Plot Preview group in the Plot Configuration dialog box: Partial and Full. Unless yours is a very complex plot, choose the Full radio button to see how your drawing is oriented relative to the paper you selected. Figure 49.5 shows a preview plot generated by AutoCAD.

If the drawing is very complex and takes a long time to regenerate, use the Partial option. Instead of reproducing all of the drawing entities as they would appear on the sheet, AutoCAD represents the sheet with a rectangle and the drawing area with another rectangle, showing the relationship between the two.

Figure 49.5

A full preview plot.

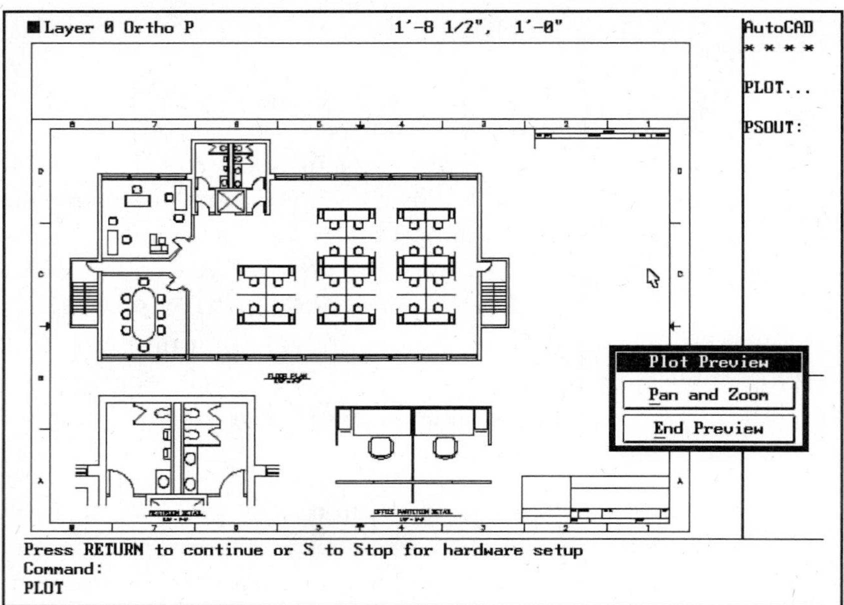

Do a plot preview every time you plot a drawing. This enables you to spot problems with the plot before you actually send it to the plotter or printer.

Unit Review

What You've Learned

- How to control plot rotation and pen assignment
- How to plot a named view or a window
- How to plot a drawing to a file
- How to preview a plot

Review Questions

True or False

49.01 T F Rotating a plot changes the orientation between the drawing and the sheet on which it is plotted.

49.02 T F You cannot change both the origin and rotation of a plot.

49.03 T F Entity layer assignment controls which pen AutoCAD uses to plot an entity.

49.04 T F Pen color and entity color are directly related.

49.05 T F Two entity colors cannot be assigned to the same pen.

49.06 T F You should always use your plotter's linetype definitions rather than AutoCAD's linetype definitions.

49.07 T F Changing the speed at which a pen plots can overcome problems such as skipping.

49.08 T F Multiple sheets of the same drawing must be stored in separate drawing files.

Short Answer

49.09 Why is plotting a window sometimes more useful than plotting a named view?

____

____

____

____

Student: ______________________ Date: __________

Instructor: ______________________ Course: __________ Section: __________

49.10 Briefly explain the function of a plot spooler.

____

____

____

____

Student: ____________________ Date: ________

Instructor: ____________ Course: _______ Section: ______

PART VI

Advanced Editing

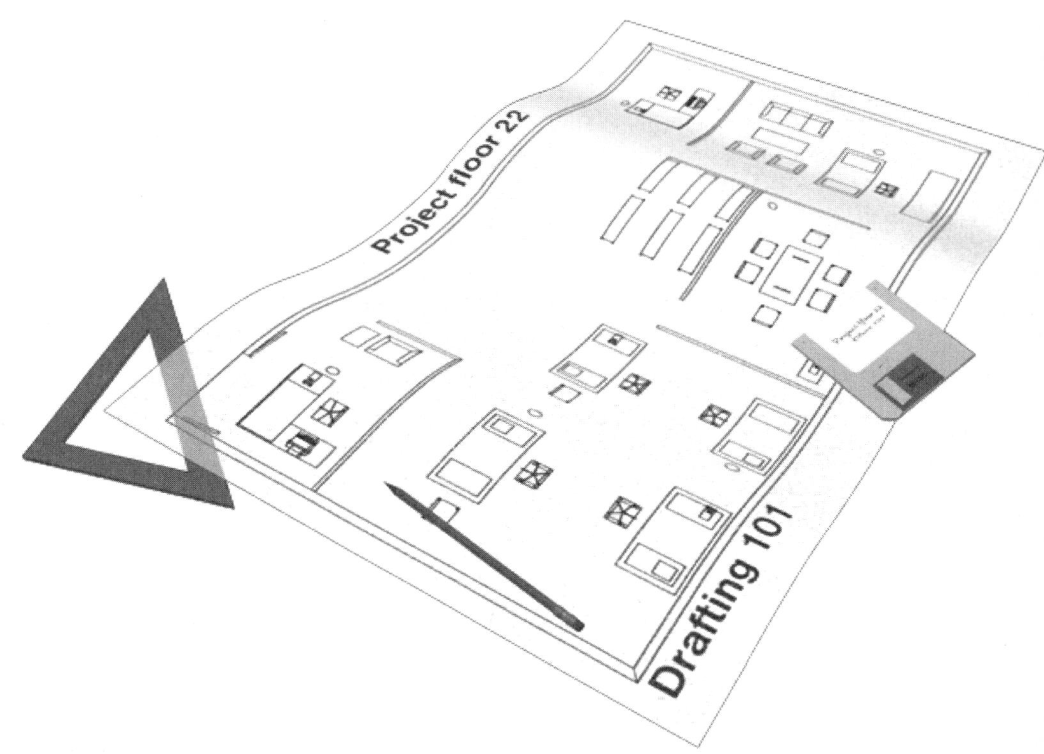

UNIT 50

Creating Advanced Selection Sets

You probably have used pick-first selection in conjunction with autoedit modes and editing commands such as COPY, ERASE, and OFFSET. You might also be familiar with building selection sets using pick-after selection while using many of these same commands. Until now, you have used only a few of the many techniques available for creating selection sets. In addition to individual, window, and crossing selection, AutoCAD provides other selection methods for creating complex selection sets. This unit explains these additional selection methods.

The objectives for this unit are to:

- Understand the different options in the SELECT command
- Create complex selection sets
- Understand how the SELECT command differs from other methods of object selection
- Use advanced selection options

Reviewing Selection Sets

As you already have learned in previous units, a selection set is a single entity or a number of entities that have been grouped together in preparation for an editing operation. You can create selection sets using either the pick-first or the pick-after selection methods (see unit 21, "Introduction to Selection and Editing"). The method you choose depends on the complexity of the selection set.

There can be only one selection set, but you have many options for creating them. When using pick-first selection, you can use a window or crossing selection to select one or more entities. You also can use Shift-pick to add and remove entities from the selection set.

When you are using pick-after selection, you have the same options as those of pick-first selection. You can use a window or crossing selection, you can pick individual entities, and you can add and remove entities from the set. Pick-after selection also offers many other selection options—this unit focuses on the additional methods.

Whichever selection method or options you choose, the end result is the same—a collection of entities is grouped together to form a selection set.

Using the SELECT Command

Whenever you used pick-after selection in previous units, you always did so within a command such as ERASE or COPY. In addition to all of the editing commands that ask you to select objects, a separate command called SELECT does nothing except create a selection set. You can use this selection set in subsequent editing commands by entering P (for Previous) in response to any prompt to select objects. All of the selection options are available with the SELECT command, and unlike the other editing commands, you can see all those options on the screen menu (see fig. 50.1).

The SELECT command is not available from the pull-down menus. You can type it at the command prompt or choose it from the EDIT screen menu.

Although it sometimes is useful to use SELECT to make selection sets, most of the time it is more efficient to invoke the particular edit command you want and build a selection set during the command.

Use the SELECT command in the following exercise to select entities.

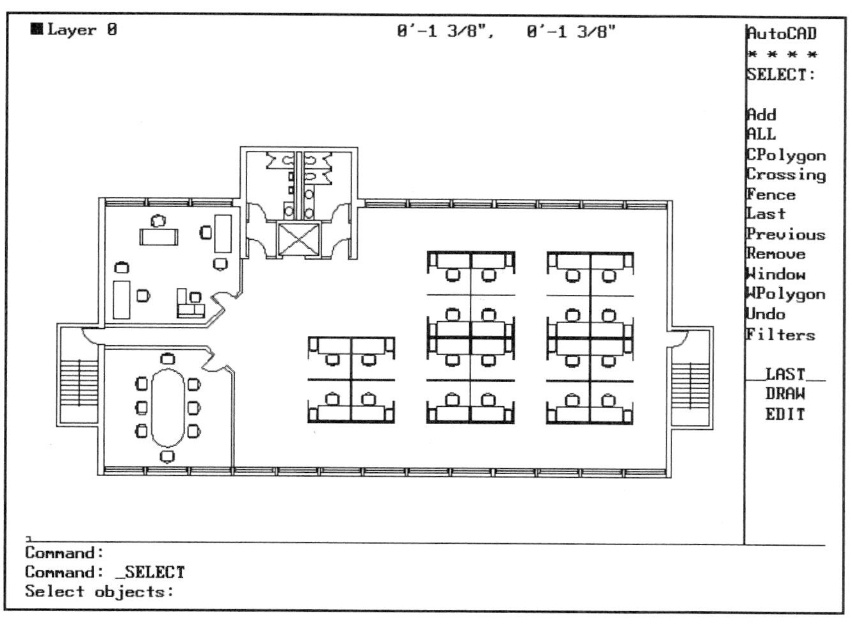

Figure 50.1

The SELECT command displays all its options.

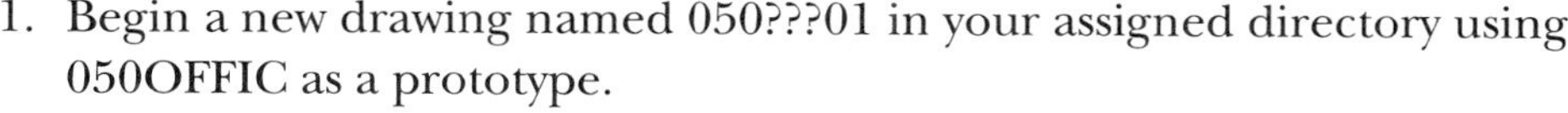

Using the SELECT Command

1. Begin a new drawing named 050???01 in your assigned directory using 050OFFIC as a prototype.

2. `Command:` **`SELECT`** ↵	Issues the SELECT command
3. `Select objects:` **`W`** ↵	Specifies the Window option
4. `First corner:` *Pick a point at* ① *(see fig. 50.2)*	Specifies first corner of the window
5. `Other corner:` *Pick a point at* ②	Specifies other corner and selects entities
`114 found`	
6. `Select objects:` *Press* Enter	Ends the command

Next, use the selection set you just created as the starting point for a new selection set.

7. `Command:` *Press* Enter	Repeats the previous SELECT command
`SELECT`	
8. `Select objects:` **`P`** ↵	Issues the Previous option and selects the previous selection set
`114 found`	

continues

9. `Select objects:` *Pick points at ③ and ④ (see fig. 50.2)* — Specifies a selection window and adds to the selection set

   `61 found`

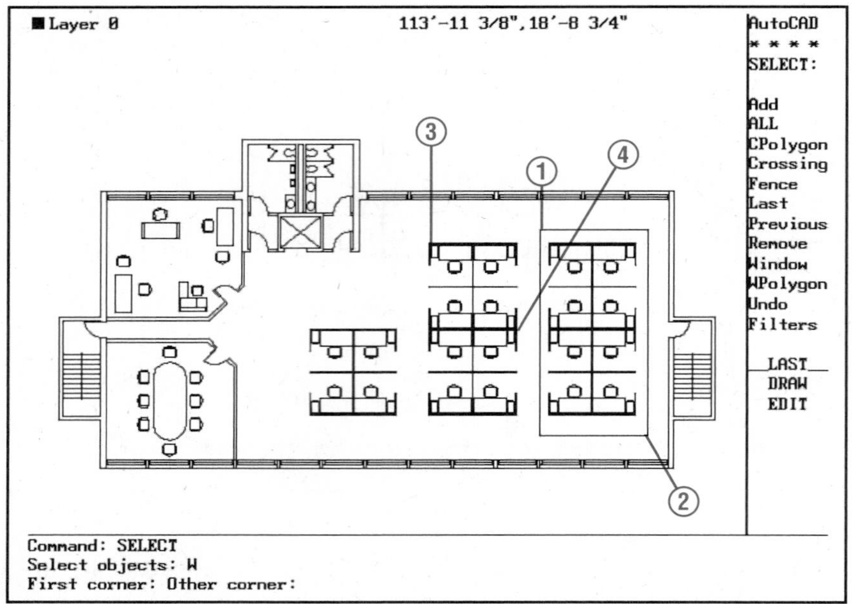

Figure 50.2
Selection points for the SELECT command.

10. `Select objects:` *Press* Enter — Ends the selection set

As you can see from the exercise, the only function of the SELECT command is to create a selection set. You will use the SELECT command in some of the remaining exercises in this unit to create selection sets.

Using Advanced Selection Options

Window and Crossing selection options are useful for grouping several entities into a selection set. In many cases, however, these options have limited use because they are restricted to rectangular selection. Two more selection options, WPolygon and CPolygon, behave similarly to Window and Crossing in what they select, but they allow you to draw non-rectangular boundaries to define the selection set.

Using WPolygon

The WPolygon option is similar to the Window option because it selects any entities that lie completely within the selection boundary. Use WPolygon to select entities in the following exercise.

Object Selection Using WPolygon

1. Pan or zoom to the conference room at the lower left corner of the office plan (see fig. 50.3).

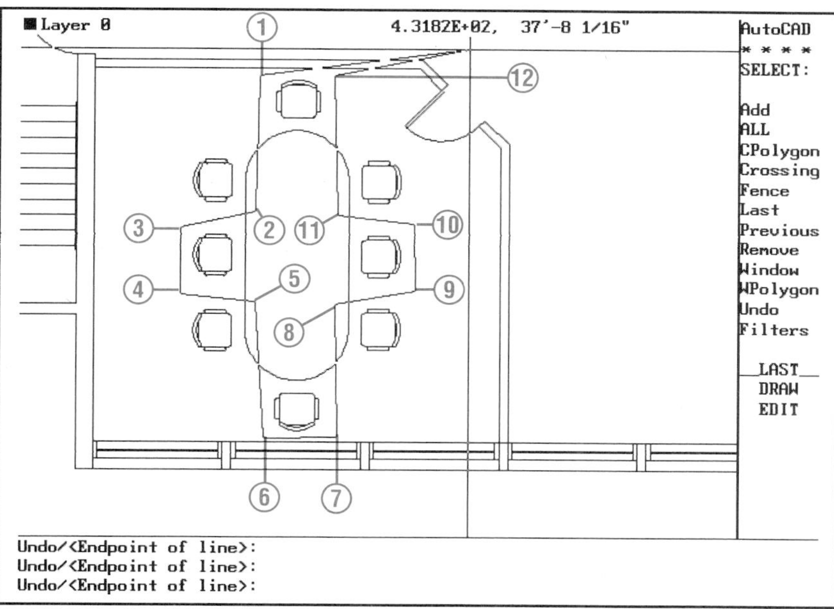

Figure 50.3

WPolygon selects everything completely inside the boundary.

2. `Command:` *From the* EDIT *screen menu, choose* next, *then* SELECT: — Issues the SELECT command

   `_SELECT`

3. `Select objects:` *From the screen menu, choose* WPolygon — Chooses the WPolygon option

   `_WPOLYGON`

4. `First polygon point:` *Pick a point at* ① *(see fig. 50.3)* — Specifies the start point of the boundary

5. `Undo/<Endpoint of line>:` *Pick a point at* ② — Specifies another point in the boundary

Note that after you pick a second point, the boundary shape becomes self-closing.

6. `Undo/<Endpoint of line>:` *Pick a point at* ③

7. *Continue picking points* ④ *through* ⑫ — Completes the polygon

continues

8. `Undo/<Endpoint of line>:` *Press* Enter `4 found`	Ends the WPolygon selection and returns number of entities found

The chair symbols in your drawing are blocks. *AutoCAD recognizes blocks as single entities, even though they comprise multiple entities. Each chair, therefore, represents a single entity. Blocks are discussed in unit 67, "Introduction to Blocks."*

Using CPolygon

Just as WPolygon is a non-rectangular version of the regular Window option, the CPolygon option lets you create a non-rectangular crossing selection. CPolygon selects entities enclosed by and crossed by the polygon.

Use the CPolygon object selection option to select the conference room walls and the door.

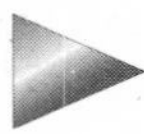

Object Selection Using CPolygon

Continue with your drawing from the previous exercise.

1. `Command:` **`SELECT`** ↵	Issues the SELECT command
2. `Select objects:` *From the* SELECT *screen menu, choose* CPolygon `_CPOLYGON`	Chooses the CPolygon option
3. `First polygon point:` *Pick a point at* ① *(see fig. 50.4)*	Begins the polygon
4. `Undo/<Endpoint of line>:` *Pick a point at* ②	Continues the polygon
5. *Continue picking points* ③ *through* ⑤	Completes the polygon
6. `Undo/<Endpoint of line>:` *Press* Enter `13 found`	Ends the selection set and returns number of entities selected

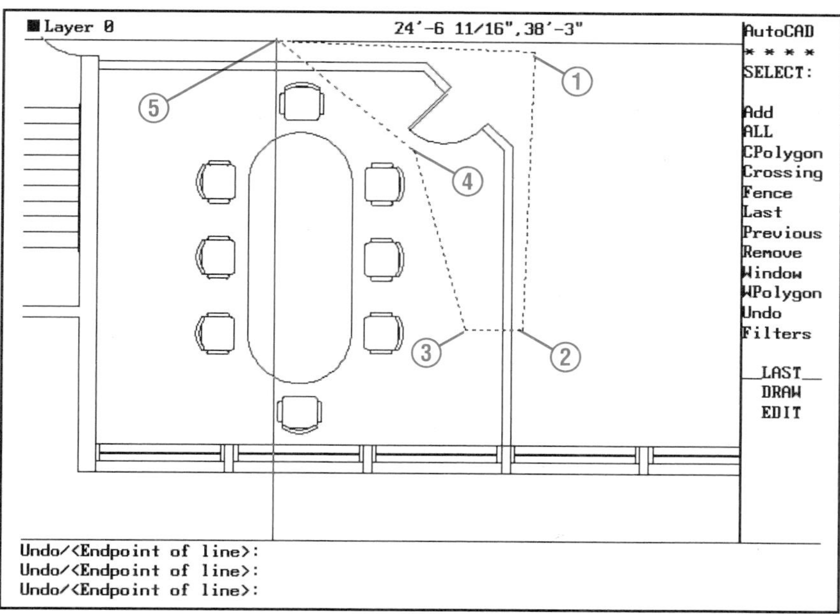

Figure 50.4

CPolygon selects everything within and crossed by the boundary.

Using Fence

CPolygon, like WPolygon, is a self-closing boundary. The last of the three selection modes that uses a polyline-like boundary is called Fence. Unlike WPolygon and CPolygon, Fence does not form a self-closing boundary. In fact, it does not have to be closed at all. If you choose the Fence option, all you have to do is draw a polyline through the objects you want to select. Use the Fence option to select all the chairs in the conference room.

Object Selection Using Fence

Continue with your drawing from the previous exercise.

1. `Command:` **`SELECT`** ↵	Issues the SELECT command
2. `Select objects:` *From the* SELECT *screen menu, choose* Fence	Initiates Fence option
3. `First fence point:` *Pick a point at* ① *(see fig. 50.5)*	Starts the polygon fence
4. `Undo/<Endpoint of line>:` Pick points at ② through ⑥	Defines the fence points
5. `Undo/<Endpoint of line>:` *Press* Enter	Ends selection and returns number of entities found

`8 found`

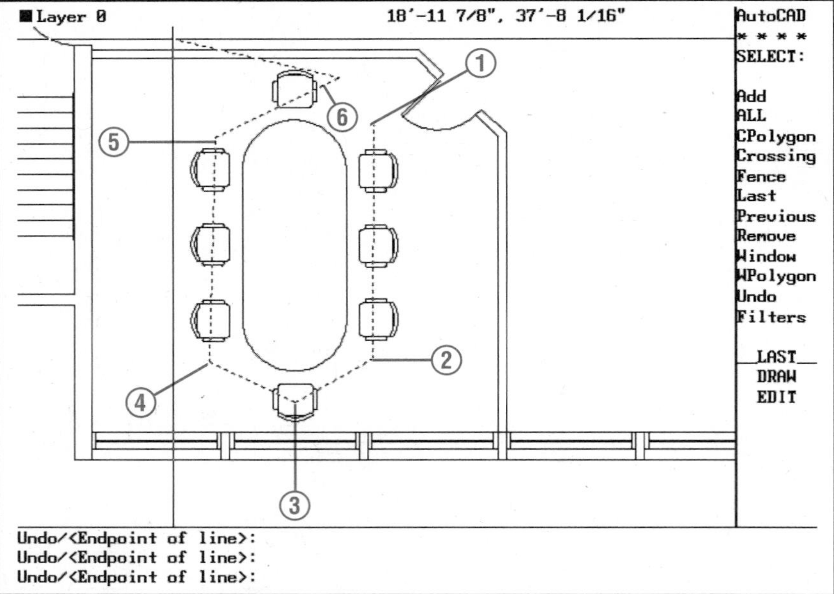

Figure 50.5

Fence selects everything crossed by the fence line.

Using ALL

The last of the advanced selection options is ALL. As its name implies, ALL selects every entity on the drawing with the following exceptions:

- Objects in paper space if model space is active
- Objects in model space if paper space is active
- Objects on layers that are frozen, off, or locked

Unlike the Last option, which finds the newest item in the current display, *ALL will select everything in the drawing except the items listed here. Be sure you really want to edit everything before you use the ALL option.*

Unit Review

What You've Learned

- ☞ Commands: SELECT
- ☞ How to create advanced selection sets
- ☞ How to use the CPolygon, WPolygon, and Fence options to select objects with a polygon/polyline boundary

Review Questions

True or False

50.01 T F Previous finds the most recent entity regardless of whether it is visible on-screen.

50.02 T F The Last entity changes each time a new selection set is made.

50.03 T F The ALL option finds every entity in both paper space and model space, but not entities on locked layers.

50.04 T F The only purpose for the SELECT command is to build a selection set.

50.05 T F There can be only one selection set at a time.

Multiple Choice

50.06 Which selection option enables you to select all entities that lie completely within a boundary? __________

(A) Window

(B) CPolygon

(C) WPolygon

(D) Both A and C

50.07 Which selection option enables you to select all entities that cross or lie inside a boundary? __________

(A) Window

(B) CPolygon

(C) WPolygon

(D) Both A and C

Student: ______________________ Date: __________

Instructor: ______________________ Course: __________ Section: __________

50.08 When you use the Last command as an object selection mode, it finds __________.

(A) the most recently created object in the whole drawing

(B) the most recently created object in the current display

(C) the last selection set you used

(D) None of the above

Short Answer

50.09 When would you use a WPolygon boundary in preference to a Window box?

____

____

____

50.10 Describe the function of the ALL selection option.

____

____

____

Additional Exercises

50.11 Try using WPolygon with SELECT to select all the chairs in the conference room.

50.12 Repeat exercise 50.11, but use CPolygon instead of WPolygon.

Student: ______________ Date: ______________

Instructor: ______________ Course: ______________ Section: ______________

UNIT 51

Introduction to Constructive Editing

A major part of preparing a new drawing is adding new entities using commands such as LINE, CIRCLE, and POLYGON. In manual drafting, you often make use of *construction lines* to lay out a drawing's geometry, then darken the lines and other entities to create the final drawing. You have a similar capability in AutoCAD, but AutoCAD provides many more construction techniques than are available with manual drawing. You can use any graphic entity in AutoCAD as a construction entity.

This unit introduces the concept of *constructive editing*, using existing entities in your drawing as construction entities.

The objectives for this unit are to:

- Understand constructive editing
- Explore methods for constructive editing
- View practical examples of constructive editing

Understanding Editing and Construction

In unit 39, "Introduction to Construction Techniques," and other units, you have probably used various editing commands or autoediting modes. To review, the term *editing* in AutoCAD often refers to modifying existing entities to change their shape or other characteristics, or to creating new entities. Erasing a line, copying a circle, stretching a selection set, and rotating entities are all examples of editing. The term *construction* means using existing entities or new temporary entities to use as a basis to construct the drawing's finished geometry.

Units 21 through 25 explore entity selection, grips, and autoediting. By now you should be familiar with these topics and should be reasonably proficient in editing entities. This unit, along with units 52 through 57, explores techniques you can use to modify existing entities in the drawing to create the drawing's finished geometry. These techniques include trimming, breaking, and extending entities; stretching entities; and applying fillets and chamfers.

Understanding TRIM

AutoCAD provides a TRIM command that enables you to *trim* one entity using another as a *cutting edge*. For example, assume that you have to draw a circular hole that has a flattened edge. The flattened edge is located at a specific distance from the center of the hole. Figure 51.1 shows the hole.

Figure 51.1

A circular hole with a flattened edge.

You could create the geometry manually, but it is much easier to use a combination of commands, including the TRIM command, to create the drawing geometry. Figures 51.2 and 51.3 illustrate how the TRIM command can be used to create the hole. You will learn more about TRIM in unit 52.

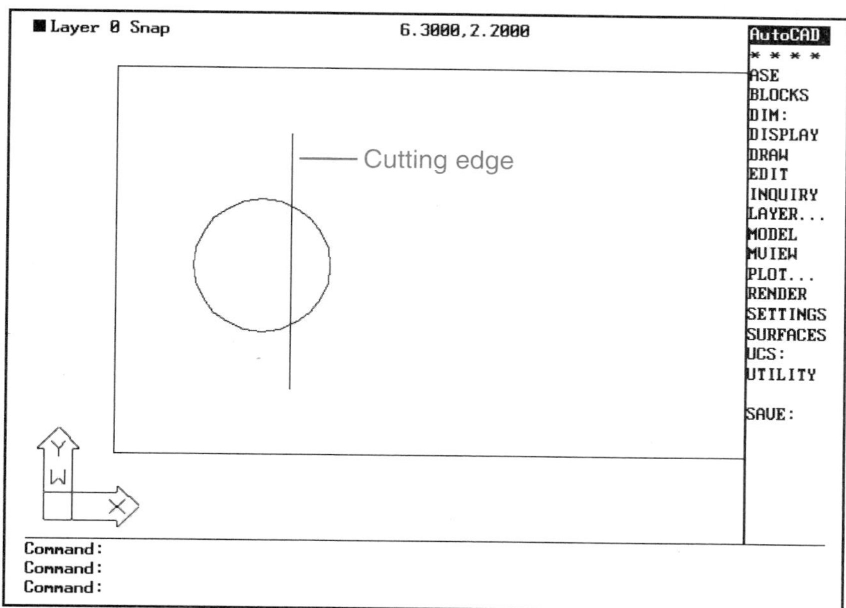

Figure 51.2

Geometry before TRIM.

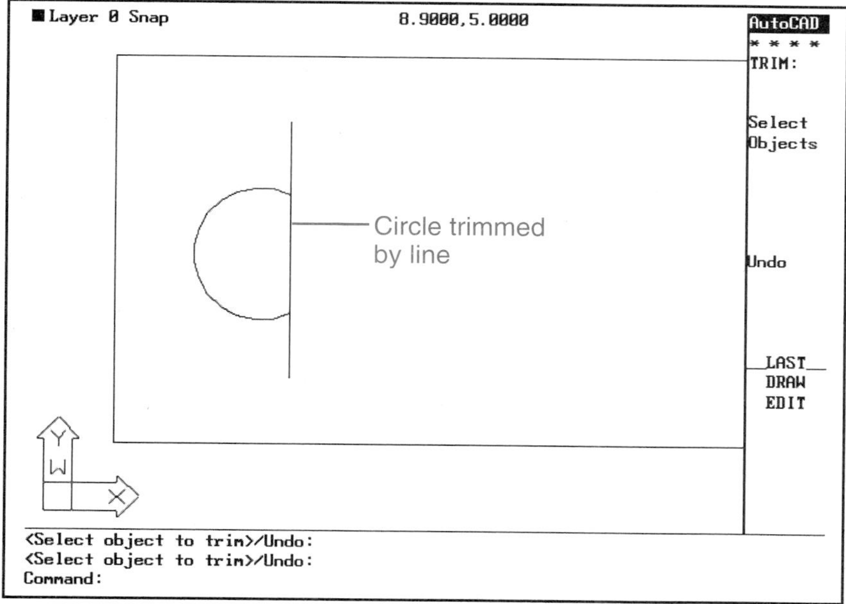

Figure 51.3

Hole partially completed.

You can use TRIM to trim more than one entity in a single command. You can select multiple cutting edges and multiple entities to trim. TRIM works with most graphics entities.

Understanding BREAK

AutoCAD's BREAK command is useful when you need to remove a portion of an entity. With BREAK, you can erase a portion of an entity by *breaking* it at two points. AutoCAD then removes the section between those two points. For example, assume that you need to create a symbol of a door from a line and a circle. Figure 51.4 illustrates how the circle can be broken and the majority of it removed to form the symbol.

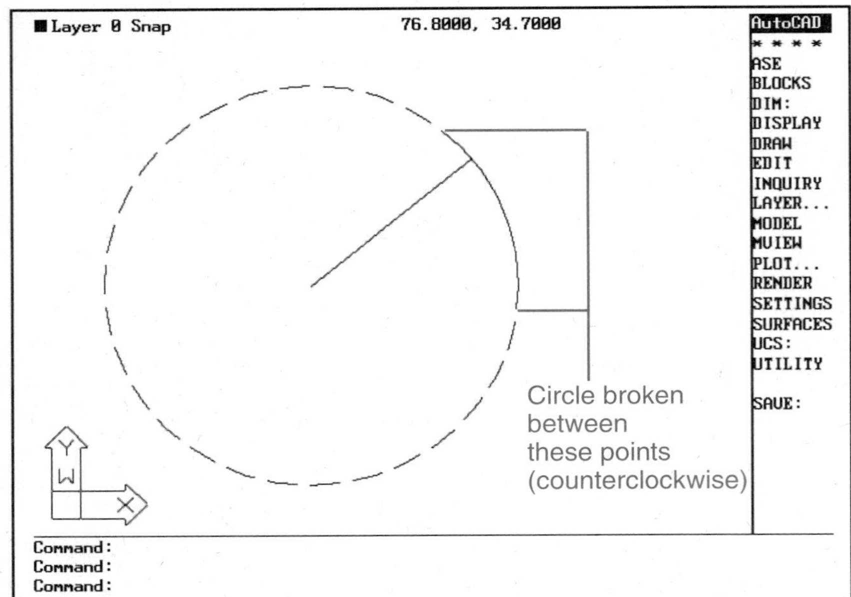

Figure 51.4

A circle broken to create a door symbol.

You can break only one entity at a time with the BREAK command.

Use BREAK when you draw a construction entity and need to remove part of it between two points, but do not have any other geometry to use to trim it. You learn more about the BREAK command in unit 53.

Understanding EXTEND

Another useful constructive editing command is EXTEND, which you can use to *extend* an entity to touch another entity. You first pick a boundary edge, which is the entity to which you want to extend another entity. You then select the entity to extend, and AutoCAD stretches the entities so that they touch the boundary edges.

In many ways, EXTEND is useful as a tool to correct mistakes. You can use it to lengthen a line you drew too short, change an entity you have broken at the wrong location, or fix an entity you have trimmed incorrectly. Figure 51.5 illustrates the EXTEND command.

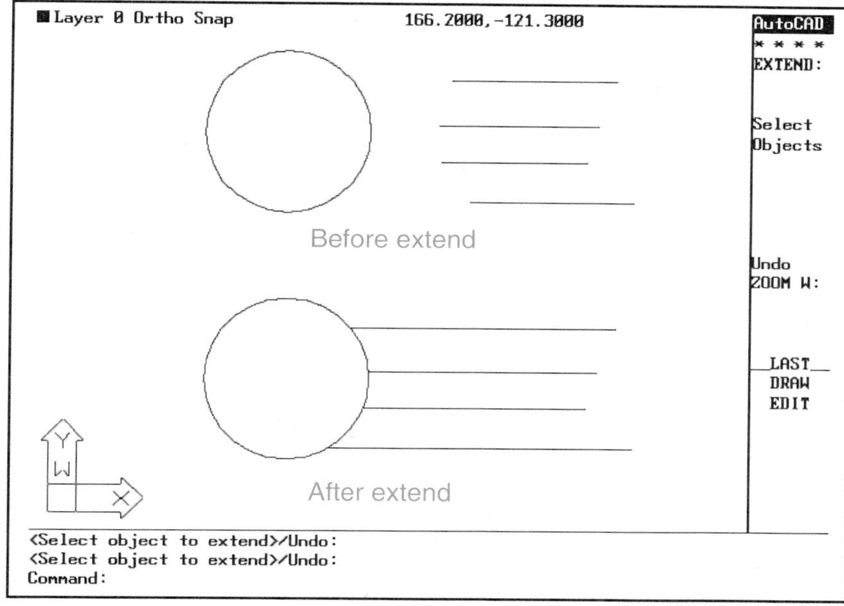

Figure 51.5

Lines lengthened with the EXTEND command.

Use EXTEND when you need to stretch one or more entities to meet or touch another entity. You learn more about EXTEND in unit 54, "Extending Entities."

Within a single EXTEND command, you can choose multiple entities as boundary edges and select multiple entities to extend.

Stretching with STRETCH

You probably know about the Stretch autodedit mode from earlier units. Stretch autoedit mode enables you to change the location of entities' end points so that you can lengthen, shorten, or change the angle of the entities. Stretch autoedit mode uses the pick-first selection method.

The STRETCH command is nearly identical to the Stretch autoedit mode with two exceptions: STRETCH uses pick-after selection, and you cannot duplicate entities using the STRETCH command (it has no Copy or Multiple option).

Use the STRETCH command when you need to stretch entities but require a complex selection set that you can create more easily with the options available with the pick-after selection method. Because of the nature of a stretch operation, however, you will seldom need to stretch a complex selection set. For that reason, Stretch autoedit mode will often be more useful to you. The STRETCH command is explained in unit 55, " Stretching Entities."

Applying Chamfers

A corner that has been cut at an angle is called a *chamfer.* Chamfers are common in mechanical designs. Distances used in a chamfer often are equal, and in a 90° corner result in a 45° chamfer. At other times, however, the edges of the chamfer are not equal. Figure 51.6 illustrates a chamfer.

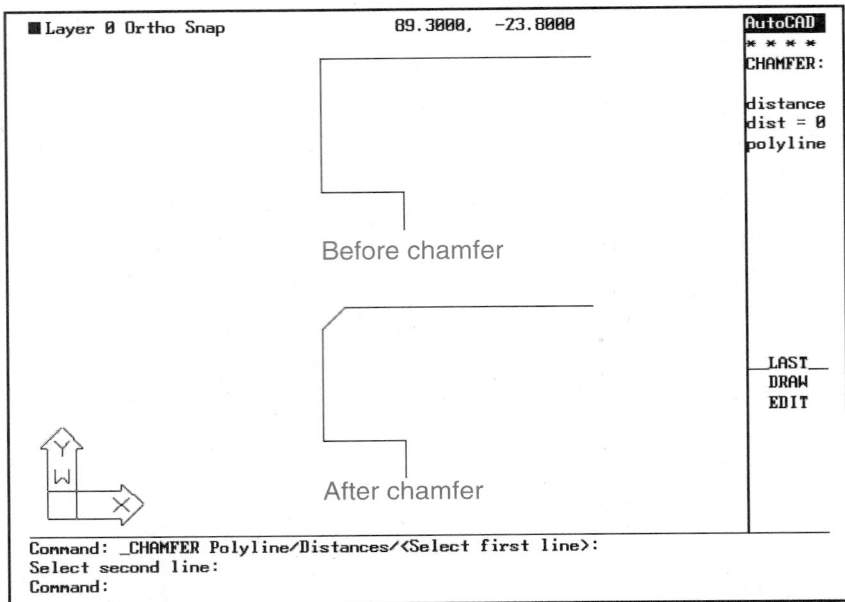

Figure 51.6

A corner before and after a chamfer.

AutoCAD provides a CHAMFER command that you can use to chamfer entities. You specify the length of each leg of the chamfer (setting them equal to achieve a 45° chamfer), then pick the lines or polyline to be chamfered. AutoCAD automatically removes the portions of the lines or polyline to create the chamfer.

You can chamfer all corners of an object with a single CHAMFER command if the object is drawn as a polyline. In addition, you can restore a corner that has been chamfered by setting the chamfer distances to zero.

Applying Fillets

A *fillet* (pronounced fill-it) is a rounded junction of two entities. Fillets are most common in mechanical design, but AutoCAD's FILLET command, which creates fillets automatically, is useful any time you need to create a rounded corner or blend two entities together with a radius. Figure 51.7 illustrates examples of fillets.

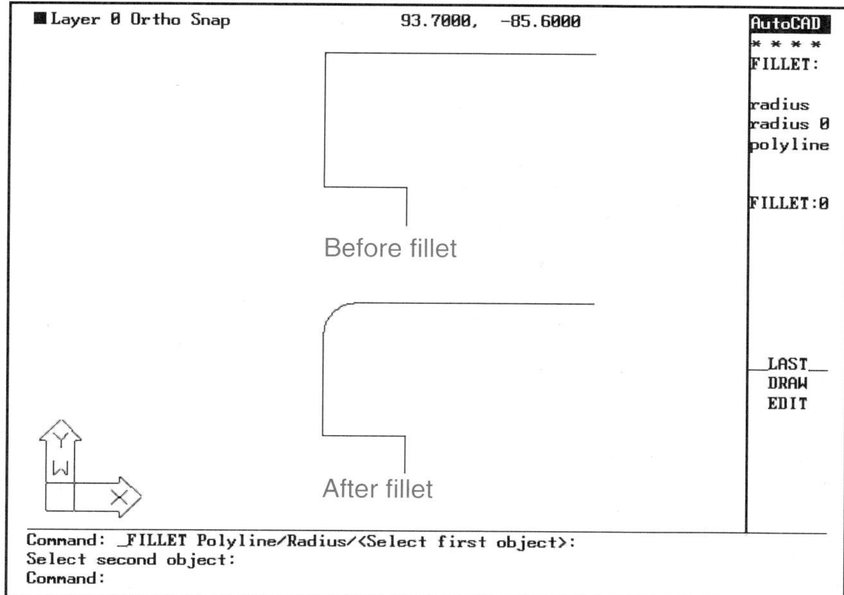

Figure 51.7

Examples of fillets.

When you issue the FILLET command, you specify the radius of the arc, then select the entities to be filleted. The FILLET command blends the two selected entities with an arc of the radius you specify, removing the portions of the entities that extend past the tangent points of the arc.

You can fillet all corners of a polyline with a single FILLET command.

Unit Review

What You've Learned

- What constructive editing is
- Examples of how constructive editing techniques can be applied to create drawing geometry

Review Questions

True or False

51.01 T F You can use almost any graphic entity as a construction entity in AutoCAD.

51.02 T F The term *constructive editing* refers to using existing entities as construction entities to create a finished drawing.

51.03 T F The EXTEND command enables you to move a circle's center point to a new location.

51.04 T F The TRIM command works only with lines, arcs, and circles.

51.05 T F The BREAK command is similar to the ERASE command, but BREAK enables you to erase just a portion of an entity.

51.06 T F You can use the EXTEND command to stretch a line to touch another entity.

51.07 T F The STRETCH command uses pick-first selection.

51.08 T F A *chamfer* is a rounded corner.

51.09 T F A *fillet* is a corner that has been cut at an angle.

51.10 T F You can fillet all corners of a polyline with the FILLET command.

Student: ______________________ Date: ________

Instructor: ______________________ Course: ________ Section: ________

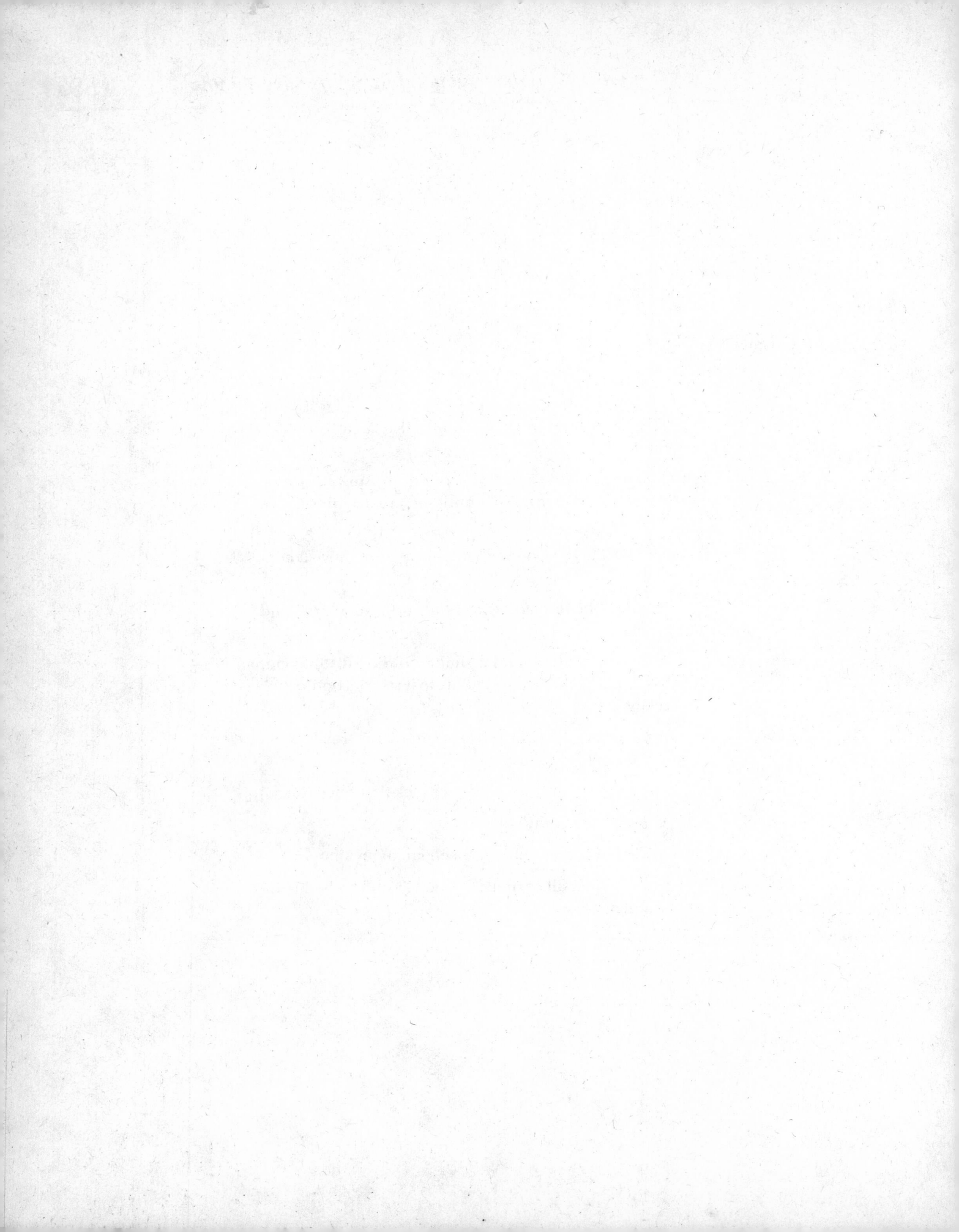

UNIT 52

Trimming Entities

Unit 51 introduced the concept of *constructive editing*, which refers to modifying existing entities to form different or new drawing geometry. One common constructive editing task you will perform often is *trimming* entities. This unit teaches you to use the TRIM command, which enables you to trim, or cut, one or more entities by using another entity as a *cutting edge*. You will find the TRIM command to be a useful tool when you are creating a new drawing or modifying an existing one.

The objectives for this unit are to:

- Understand the purpose of the TRIM command
- Understand uses for constructive trimming
- Trim entities using the TRIM command

Using the TRIM Command

The TRIM command lets you trim one or more entities using another entity as a *cutting edge*. For example, if you need to trim a selection of lines where they pass through a circle, you can use the circle as a cutting edge to trim the lines. Figure 52.1 illustrates this example.

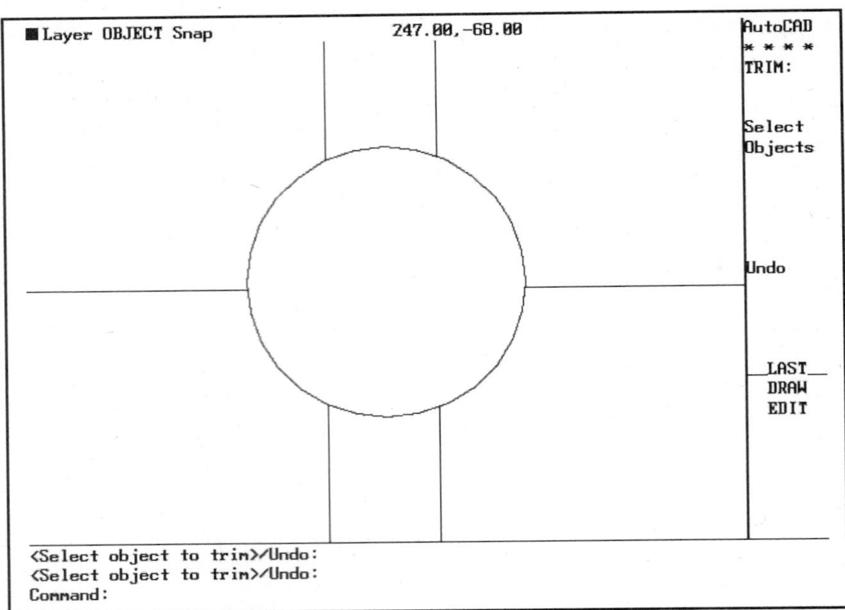

Figure 52.1
Lines trimmed where they cross a circle.

The TRIM command uses pick-after selection. When you first issue the TRIM command, AutoCAD prompts you to select one or more entities to use as cutting edges. AutoCAD uses these entities to determine how the trimming operation will be performed.

After you have selected the cutting edges, you begin selecting the entities to be trimmed. The effect of the TRIM command depends on the relationship between the entities to be trimmed and the cutting edges, as well as the location of the points you select when you specify the entities to be trimmed.

You can access the TRIM command from the Modify pull-down menu, from the second page of the EDIT screen menu, or from the command prompt.

The simplest way to understand the effects of the TRIM command is to use it. In the following exercises, use TRIM to create a V-shaped cutout in a V Block. Much of the drawing's geometry has been completed for you, but you will add other lines and circles to the drawing as construction entities. You then will use the TRIM command to turn these construction entities into parts of the final drawing. When you are finished with the V Block, your drawing should appear similar to figure 52.2.

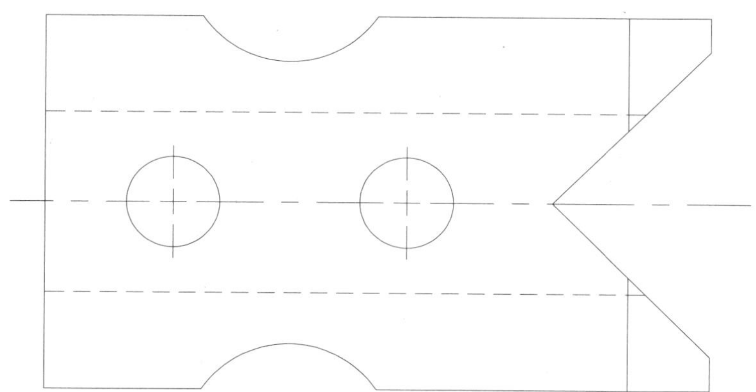

Figure 52.2

A V Block created with TRIM.

In the first exercise, draw the lines that will form the inside edge of the cutout. Because you do not know the exact location for the endpoints of the lines, draw them to extend past the edge of the block.

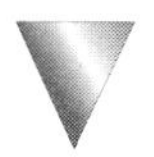

Starting the V Block

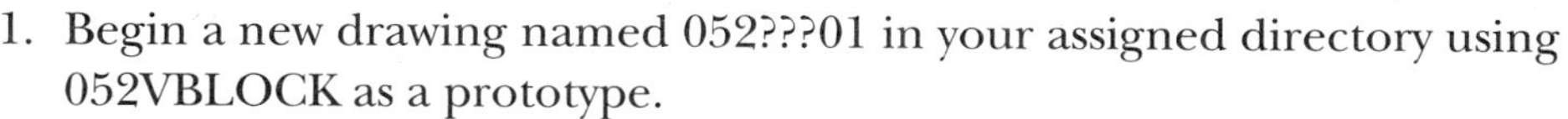

1. Begin a new drawing named 052???01 in your assigned directory using 052VBLOCK as a prototype.

2. `Command:` *Choose* Draw, *then* Line, *then* 1 Segment	Issues the LINE command to draw one segment
`line`	
3. `From point:` *Pick a point at coordinate* 87,33	Starts the line at the vertex of the V-slot
4. `To point:` **`@50<45`** ↵	Draws a line at 45 degrees and ends the LINE command
`To point:`	
5. `Command:` *Choose* Draw, *then* Line, *then* 1 Segment	Issues the LINE command to draw one segment
`line`	
6. `From point:` *Pick a point at coordinate* 87,33	Starts the line at the vertex of the V-slot

continues

7. To point: **@50<-45** ↵ — Draws a line at -45 degrees and ends the LINE command

```
To point:
```

8. Save your drawing.

Your drawing should look similar to figure 52.3.

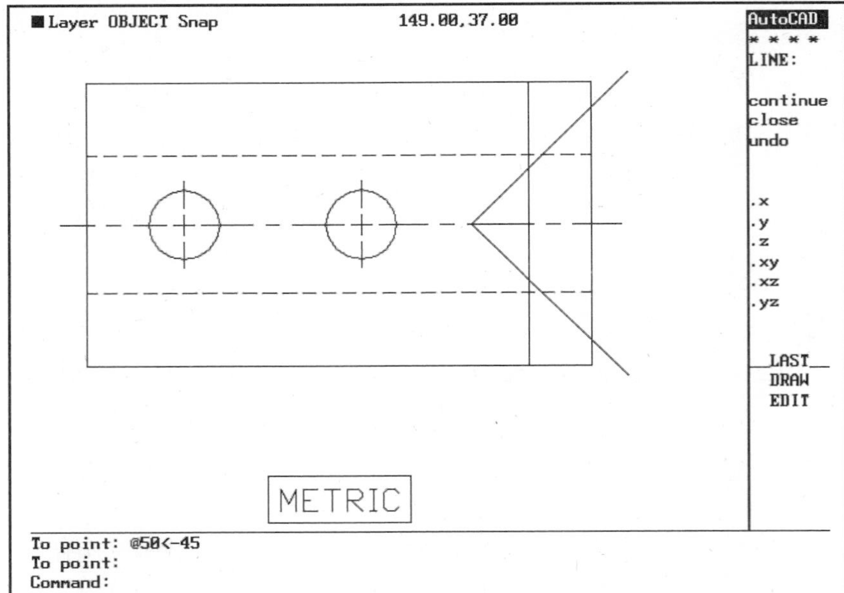

Figure 52.3

Construction lines for the V-slot.

Now you are ready to try the TRIM command. Examine figure 52.2 again. Note that the vertical lines crossing the V-slot need to be trimmed between the two 45-degree lines. The 45-degree lines are the cutting edges in your trim operation, and the vertical lines are the entities to be trimmed. In the following exercise, trim the vertical lines to create the V-slot. Use figure 52.4 as a guide to selecting entities.

Using TRIM to Create the V-Slot

Continue with your drawing from the previous exercise.

1. Command: *Choose* Modify, *then* Trim — Issues the TRIM command

```
_trim
Select cutting edge(s)...
```

2.	Select objects: *Select the line at* ① *(see fig. 52.4)* 1 found	Selects line to use as a cutting edge
3.	Select objects: *Select the line at* ② 1 found	Selects line to use as a cutting edge
4.	Select objects: *Press* Enter	
5.	<Select object to trim>/Undo: *Select the line at* ③	Trims the line to the cutting edges
6.	<Select object to trim>/Undo: *Select the line at* ④	Trims the line to the cutting edges
7.	<Select object to trim>/Undo: *Select the line at* ⑤	Trims the line to the cutting edge
8.	<Select object to trim>/Undo: *Select the line at* ⑥	Trims the line to the cutting edge
9.	<Select object to trim>/Undo: *Press* Enter	Ends the TRIM command
10.	Save your drawing.	

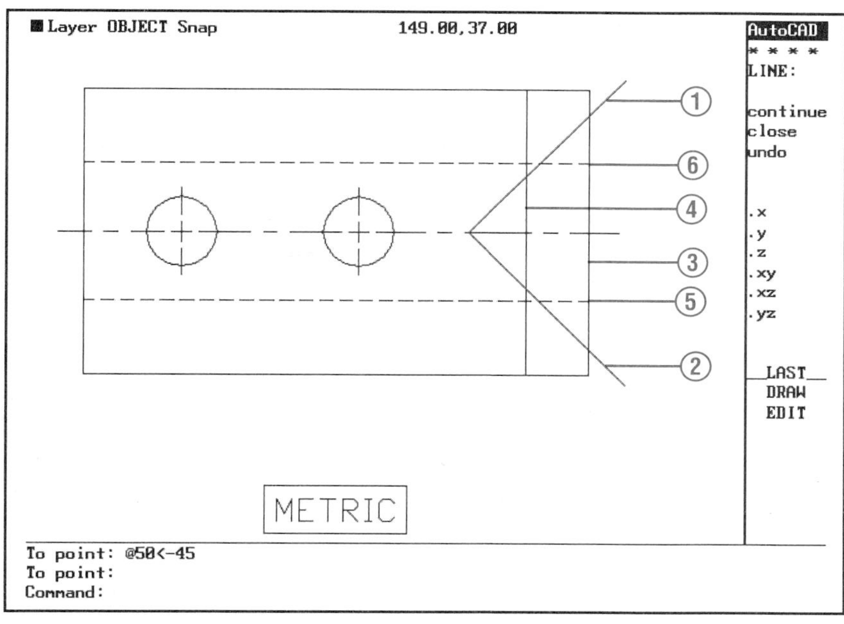

Figure 52.4

Selection points for the TRIM command.

Your drawing should look similar to figure 52.5.

As you can see from the exercise, the way in which TRIM clips the lines depends on whether the line is crossed by a single cutting edge or by multiple cutting edges. In the case of the vertical lines, you selected the line between the two cutting edges, and AutoCAD trimmed out the portion of the line that fell between the two cutting edges. In the case of the horizontal hidden lines, you selected the line to be trimmed on the right side of the cutting edge lines and AutoCAD trimmed the right portion of the lines. If you had selected the horizontal lines to the left of the cutting edge, AutoCAD would have trimmed the portion of the line to the left of the cutting edge.

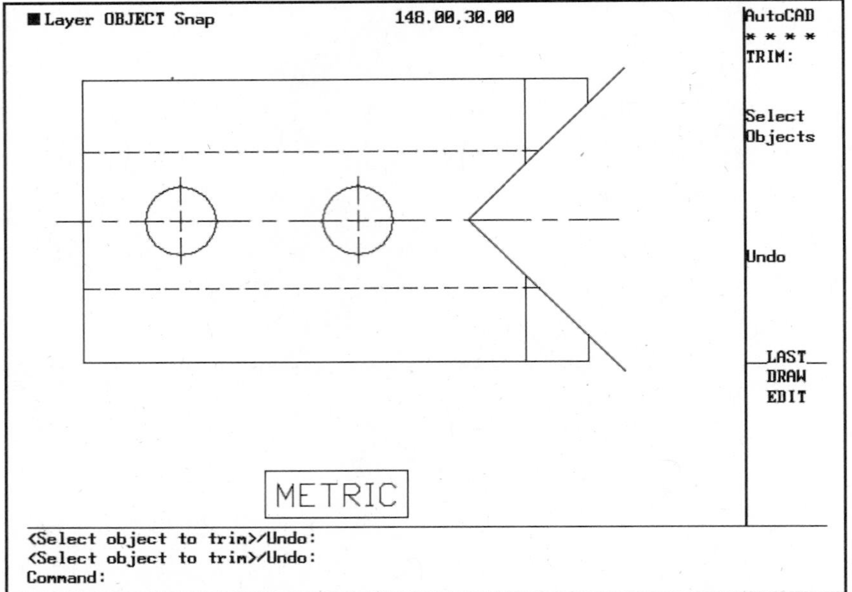

Figure 52.5
Lines after TRIM.

You can use any entity-selection method, such as Fence and WPolygon selection, to select the entities to use as cutting edges. Only lines, arcs, circles, 2D polylines, and paper space viewports can be used as cutting edges, however; all other entities are ignored if they are selected.

Next, complete the V-slot by trimming the remaining lines. Use figure 52.6 as a guide.

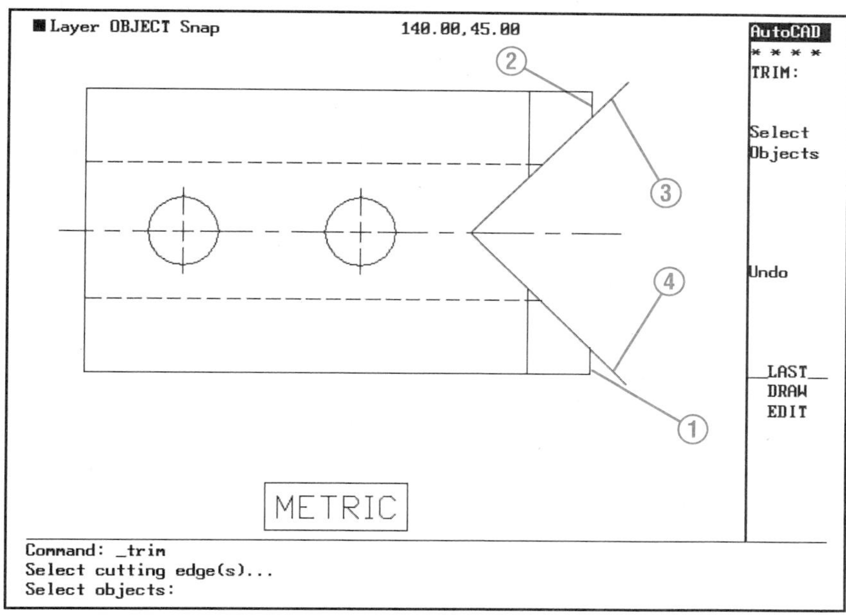

Figure 52.6

Selection points to complete V Block.

Completing the V-Slot

Continue with your drawing from the previous exercise.

1. `Command:` *Choose* Modify, *then* Trim	Issues the TRIM command
`_trim`	
`Select cutting edge(s)...`	
2. `Select objects:` *Select the line at* ① *(see fig. 52.6)*	Selects cutting edge
`1 found`	
3. `Select objects:` *Select the line at* ②	Selects cutting edge
`1 found`	
4. `Select objects:` *Press* Enter	Ends cutting edge selection
5. `<Select object to trim>/Undo:` *Select the line at* ③	Trims the line to the cutting edge
6. `<Select object to trim>/Undo:` *Select the line at* ④	Trims the line to the cutting edge
7. `<Select object to trim>/Undo:` *Press* Enter	Ends the TRIM command
8. Save your drawing.	

Your drawing should look similar to figure 52.7.

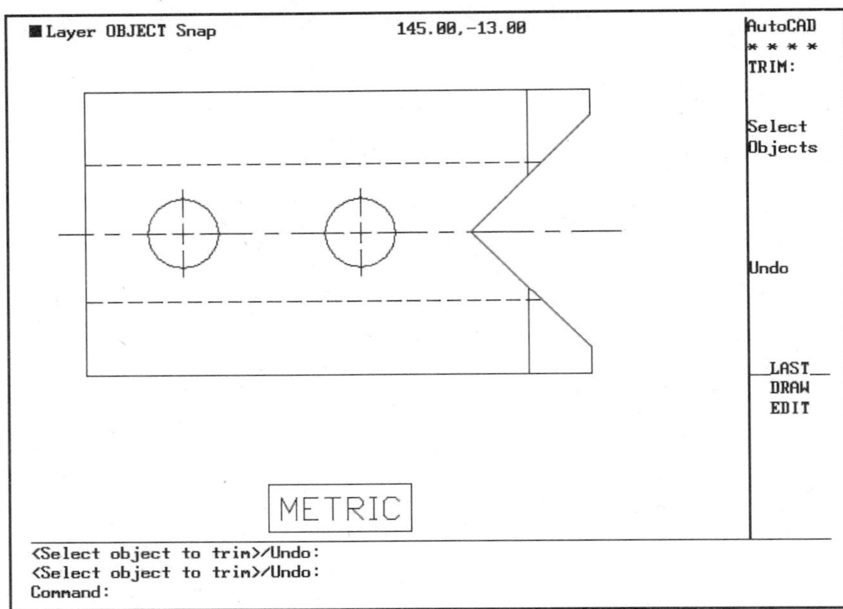

Figure 52.7
The completed V-slot.

You might have noticed that when you selected the outer perimeter of the part, AutoCAD highlighted more than one segment. This is because the outer perimeter of the part was drawn as a closed polyline using the RECTANG command.

You also might have noticed in the exercise that selecting the first two cutting edges did not select the entire outer perimeter of the part—you also had to select the upper cutting edge. This is because the first trim operation you performed, which trimmed out the vertical portion of the rectangle between the 45-degree lines, caused the polyline to be separated into two polylines. The TRIM command sometimes unexpectedly breaks polylines in this manner. Unfortunately, you cannot prevent AutoCAD from breaking the polyline into two segments. You can, however, use the PEDIT command to rejoin the segments into a single polyline (see unit 29, "Editing Polylines").

Performing Complex Trim Operations

You can select entities as cutting edges and as entities to be trimmed in the same trim operation, eliminating the need to issue the TRIM command many times. The location of the selection points determines how and when the entities are trimmed.

In the following exercise, add rounded cutouts to the edges of the V Block by selecting the same entities as both cutting edges and entities to be trimmed. Use figure 52.8 as a guide.

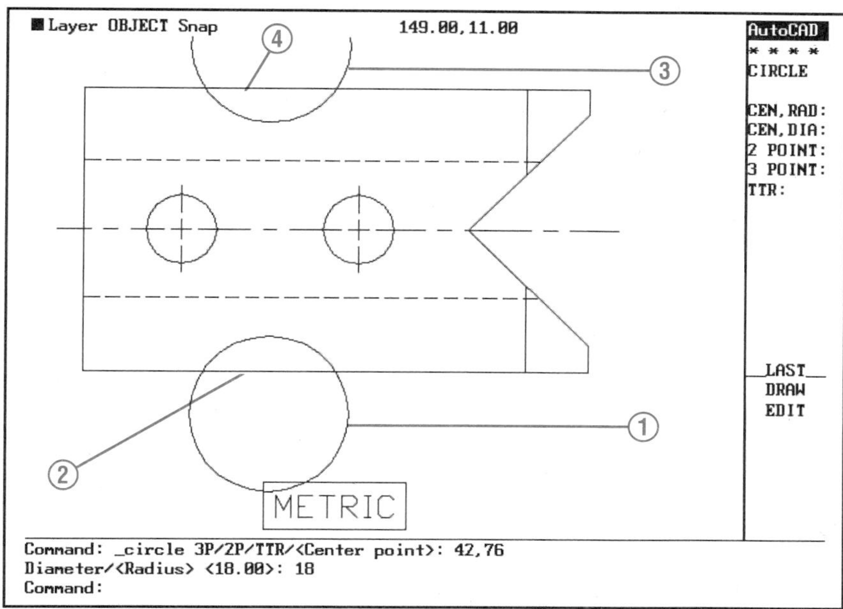

Figure 52.8

Circles and selection points for rounded notches.

Using Entities as Edges and as Entities To Trim

Continue with your drawing from the previous exercise.

1. Draw a circle at coordinate 42,-10 with a radius of 18mm (see fig. 52.8). Draw another circle at coordinate 42,76 with a radius of 18mm.
2. `Command:` *Choose* Modify, *then* Trim — Issues the TRIM command

   `_trim`
   `Select cutting edge(s)...`
3. `Select objects:` *Select the circles and lines at ①, ②, ③, and ④ (see fig. 52.8)* — Selects cutting edges
4. `Select objects:` *Press* Enter — Ends cutting edge selection
5. `<Select object to trim>/Undo:` *Pick the circle at ①* — Trims the circle
6. `<Select object to trim>/Undo:` *Pick the line at ②* — Trims the line
7. `<Select object to trim>/Undo:` *Pick the circle at ③* — Trims the circle
8. `<Select object to trim>/Undo:` *Pick the line at ④* — Trims the line
9. `<Select object to trim>/Undo:` *Press* Enter — Ends the TRIM command
10. Save your drawing.

The results of this exercise appear in figure 52.9.

Including multiple entities in the selection set for cutting edges enables you to combine many different trim operations, which can save a lot of time. An important point to remember is that AutoCAD trims entities based on the point you pick on the entity to be trimmed and its relationship to any selected cutting edges that cross it.

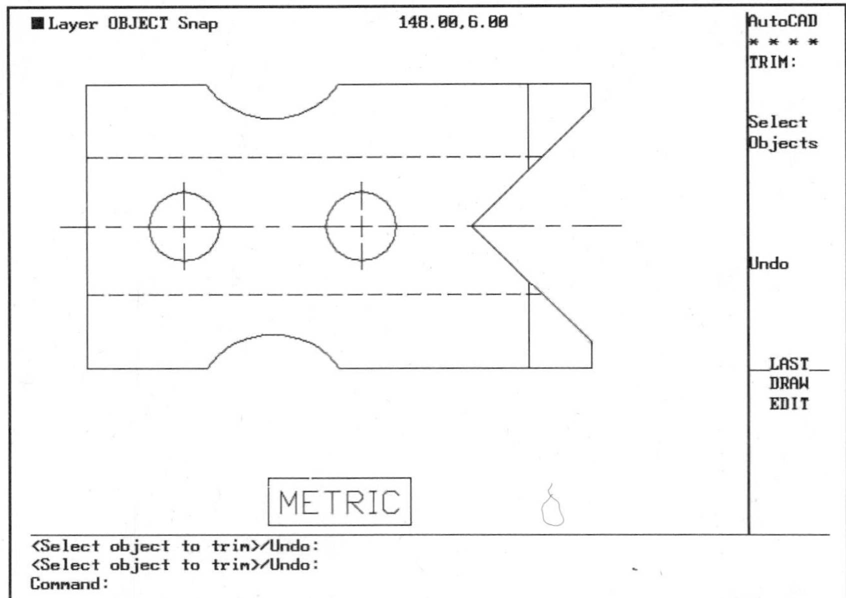

Figure 52.9
Completed circular slots.

Unit Review

What You've Learned

- ☞ Commands: TRIM
- ☞ The purpose of a cutting edge entity
- ☞ The purpose of the TRIM command
- ☞ How to trim entities using TRIM

Review Questions

True or False

52.01 T F You can select only one entity to use as a cutting edge.

52.02 T F The effects of the TRIM command depend partly on the location of the point you pick when specifying the entity to be trimmed.

52.03 T F You can use any selection method, except Fence, to select entities to use as cutting edges.

52.04 T F Only lines, arcs, circles, 2D polylines, and paper space viewports can be used as cutting edges.

52.05 T F AutoCAD sometimes splits a polyline into multiple polylines if you trim it.

Multiple Choice

52.06 Which of the following cannot be used as a cutting edge?

____

(A) line

(B) arc

(C) 3D polyline

(D) paper space viewport

52.07 The TRIM command uses ________ selection.

(A) pick-after

(B) pick-first

(C) either A or B

Student: ________________ Date: ________

Instructor: ________________ Course: ________ Section: ________

52.08 The effect of the TRIM command depends on ________.

(A) the relationship between the cutting edge entities and entities selected for trimming

(B) the location of your selection point on the entity to be trimmed

(C) the size of the current viewport

(D) both A and B

Short Answer

52.09 Explain what can happen to a polyline if you trim it.

____

____

____

52.10 List the three ways to access the TRIM command.

____

____

____

Additional Exercises

52.11 Begin a new drawing named 052???11 in your assigned directory using 052BRAKT as a prototype. Use OFFSET to offset the horizontal line 0.875" above and below the current line. Then, use the TRIM command to complete the top view of the bracket. Your drawing should look similar to figure 52.10 when completed.

Figure 52.10

Completed bracket.

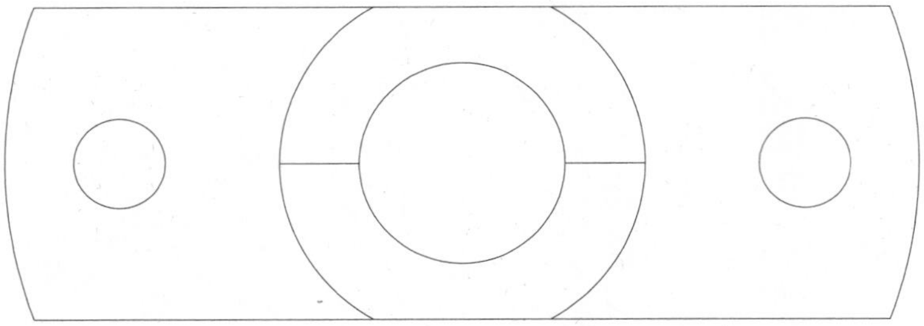

Student: ________________ Date: ________________

Instructor: ________________ Course: ________________ Section: ________________

Breaking Entities

You probably used the ERASE command extensively in earlier units. The ERASE command erases an entire entity. AutoCAD provides another command called BREAK that you can use to erase just part of a line, arc, circle, trace, or 2D polyline. Breaking entities is a common constructive editing task. This unit explains the options available with BREAK and teaches you how to break entities.

The objectives for this unit are to:

- Understand the function of the BREAK command
- Understand the effect of BREAK on different types of entities

Using the BREAK Command

The TRIM command, which is explained in unit 52, "Trimming Entities," enables you to remove a portion of a line exactly at its intersection with one or more other entities. The BREAK command also removes part of an entity, but it does not rely on other entities as cutting edges. Instead, BREAK uses points that you specify on the entity to determine which portion of the entity to remove. In this way, BREAK is like a special ERASE command that enables you to erase part of an entity between two points. Figure 53.1 shows a line broken between two points.

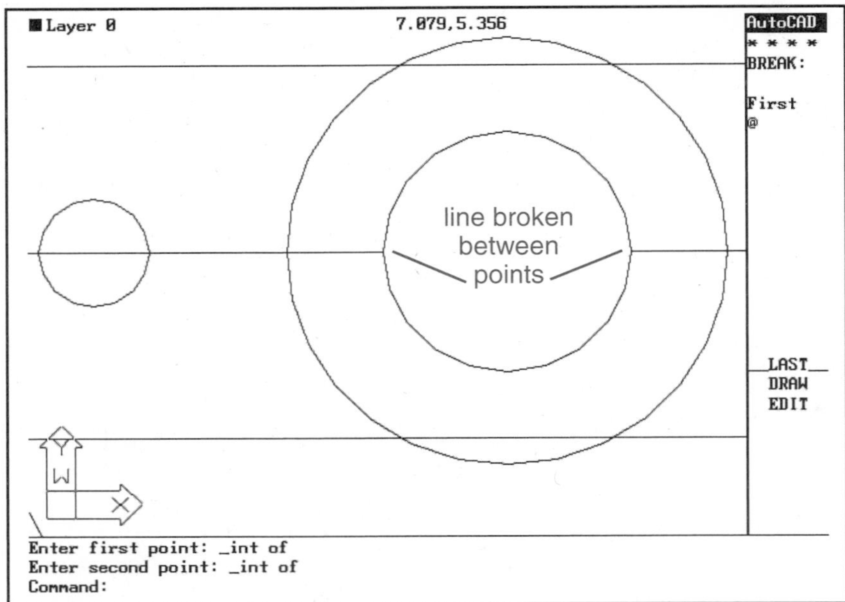

Figure 53.1
A line broken between two points.

You can access the BREAK command from the Modify pull-down menu, the EDIT screen menu, and the command prompt. The pull-down menu items associated with BREAK automatically set BREAK command options that you have to set manually if you use the screen menu or command prompt. The prompts generated by BREAK include:

- `Select object`. This prompt directs you to select the entity to be broken. Unless you specify otherwise, BREAK uses your first pick point on the entity as the start of the break.
- `Enter second point <or F for first point>`. When you pick a second point after this prompt appears, either on the entity or off it, the portion of the entity between the first point and the second point breaks. Entering **`F`** causes AutoCAD to prompt you for a new first point to use as the start of the break rather than the point you originally selected.

If you enter the **`@`** symbol in response to the prompt for a second point, AutoCAD uses the same point as the start and end points for the break. If you use this method on a line, for example, AutoCAD breaks the line at that location, creating two separate lines that share the same end point. It does not actually remove any portion of either line segment.

The cascading menu items for Break in the Modify menu provide three different methods for breaking an entity:

- **Select Object, 2nd Point.** The point on the entity that you use to select the entity is used as the first point, and AutoCAD prompts you for a second point.
- **Select Object, Two Points.** AutoCAD ignores the point by which you select the entity and prompts you to specify the start and end points of the break.
- **At Selected Point.** AutoCAD immediately breaks the entity at the point you pick to select the entity. It does not prompt for additional points. This option breaks the entity into two entities, but does not remove anything.

You can use an object snap mode when you select an entity to break. By using an object snap mode you can specify an exact point to use as the start point of the break. If you are using the menu item At Selected Point, *and you use object snap mode to select the entity, the entity breaks at the exact point corresponding to the object snap mode.*

The review exercise in unit 52 instructs you to use the TRIM command to complete the geometry of a bracket. In the following exercises, use the BREAK command to complete the bracket. Use figure 53.2 as a guide to complete the first exercise.

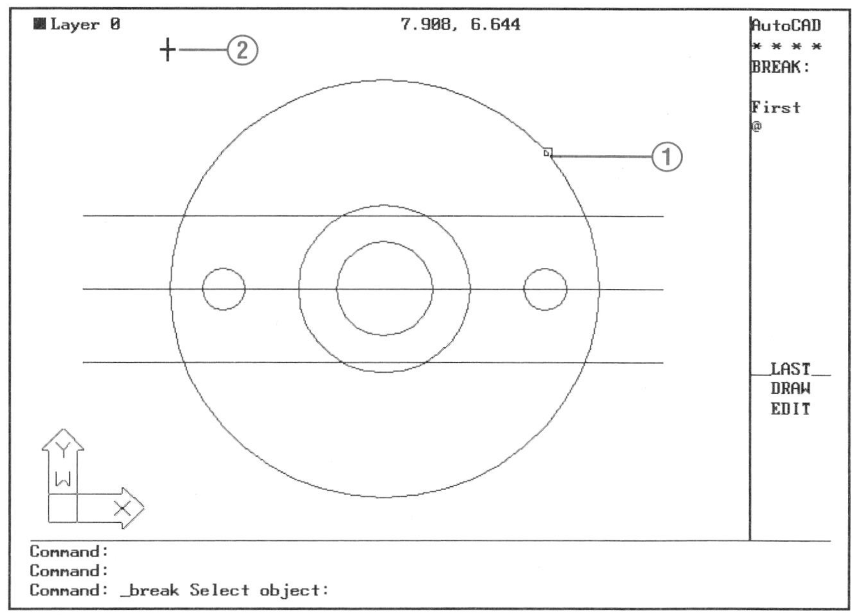

Figure 53.2

Selection points for BREAK.

The TRIM command is actually a better command to use for completing the bracket because it requires fewer steps and fewer point selections. The BREAK command is used here partly for experience, but also to contrast the difference between the BREAK and TRIM commands.

Breaking an Entity

1. Begin a new drawing named 053???01 in your assigned directory using 053BRAKT as a prototype.

2. `Command:` *Choose* Modify, *then* Break, *then* Select Object, 2nd Point `_break`	Instructs the BREAK command to use the pick point as the start of the break
3. `Select object:` *Select the circle at* ① *(see fig. 53.2)*	Selects the entity to break and also specifies the start point of the break
4. Enter second point (or F for first point): *Pick a point near* ② *(see fig. 53.2)*	Specifies the second point of the break and breaks the circle

The circle will appear broken, as shown in figure 53.3.

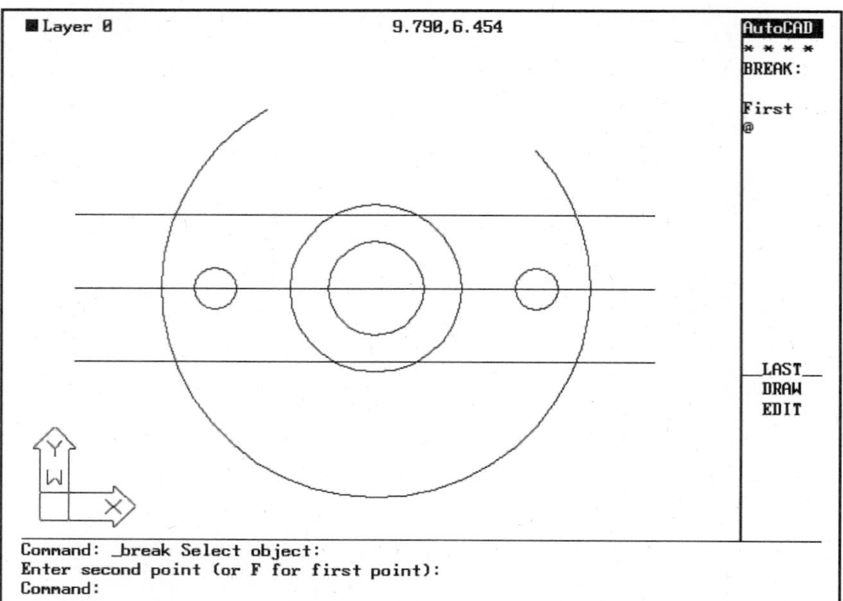

Figure 53.3
Broken circle.

The circle is broken, but not at the correct points. In the next exercise, use the menu item Select Object, Two Points to break the top of the circle at the correct places. Use figure 53.4 as a guide to pick points.

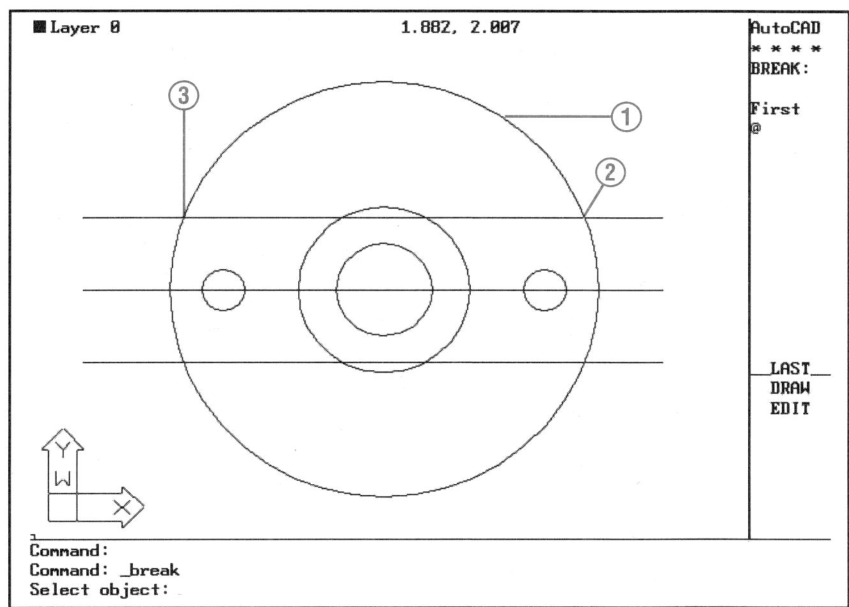

Figure 53.4

Selection points for accurate break.

Breaking Entities at Specific Points

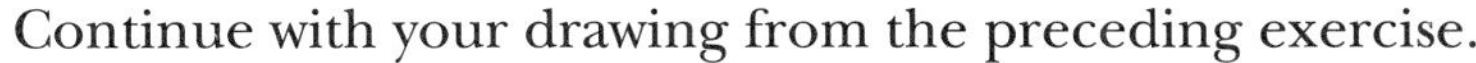

Continue with your drawing from the preceding exercise.

1. `Command:` **`U`** ↵	Undoes the previous BREAK command
2. `Command:` *Choose* Modify, *then* Break, *then* Select Object, Two Points	Issues the BREAK command to break using two points you specify as the break points
`_break`	
3. `Select object:` *Select the circle at* ① *(see fig. 53.4)*	Specifies which entity to break and chooses the F option
`Enter second point (or F for first point): _first`	
4. `Enter first point:` *From the popup menu, choose* Intersection	Sets object snap mode
`_int of`	
5. *Pick the intersection at* ② *(see fig. 53.4)*	Specifies the first point of the break
6. `Enter second point:` *From the popup menu, choose* Intersection	
`_int of`	

continues

7. *Pick the intersection at* ③ *(see fig. 53.4)* — Specifies the second point of the break and breaks the circle

8. Save your drawing.

Your drawing should look similar to figure 53.5.

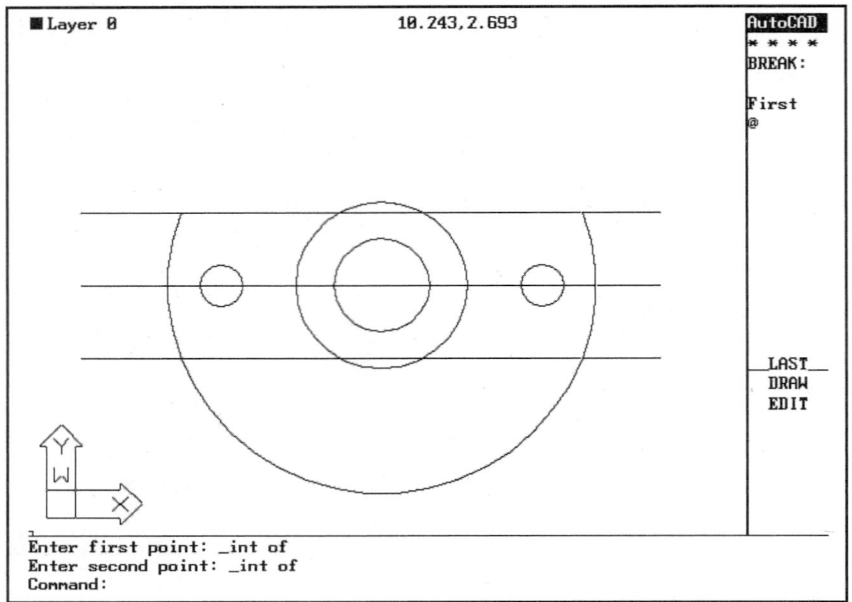

Figure 53.5
Circle broken between two intersections.

Circles and arcs are always broken counter-clockwise. (The second point is always counterclockwise along the arc from the first point.) If you picked the points in reverse order in the preceding exercise, the bottom portion of the circle would be removed.

Next, try breaking an entity at a specific point without removing any portion of an entity. You can do this manually using the @ symbol, but the menu item At Selected Point does it for you automatically. Use figure 53.6 as a guide to select points.

Breaking an Entity at a Point

Continue with your drawing from the preceding exercise.

1. `Command:` *Choose* Modify, *then* Break, *then* At Selected Point — Issues the BREAK command to break using @

```
_break
```

2. `Select object:` *From the popup menu, choose* Intersection — Sets object snap mode

   `_int of`

3. *Pick the intersection at ① (see fig. 53.6)*

Next, erase the outer line segment to show that the line is broken.

4. `Command:` *Select the line at ②, then enter* **E** ↵ — Creates a selection set and issues the alias for the ERASE command

5. Save your drawing.

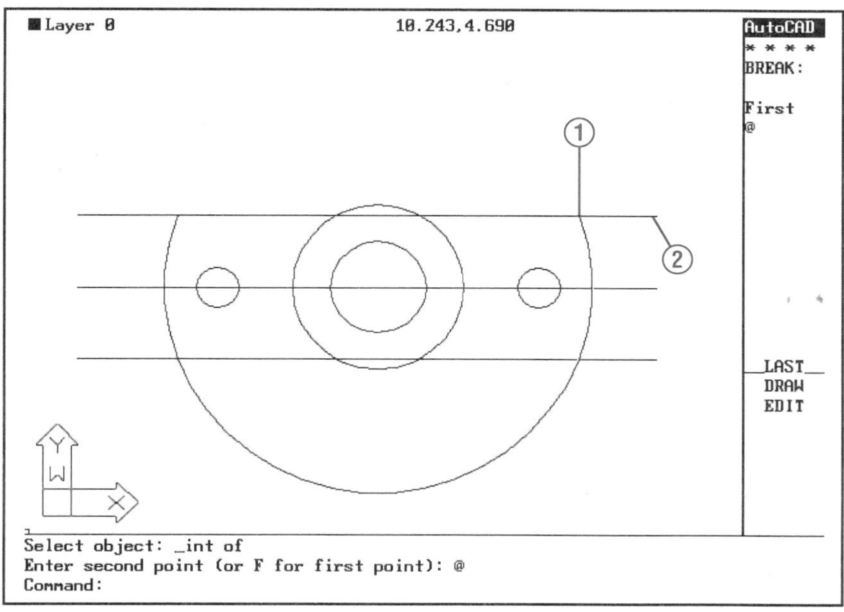

Figure 53.6

Selection points for break using @.

Only the line segment to the right of the specified break point is erased, indicating that the BREAK command broke the line at that point into two separate lines.

You can see from the exercises in this unit that the TRIM command is a faster alternative. Nevertheless, the BREAK command still is very useful, particularly when you need to break an entity at a specific point and no other entities can be used for cutting edges.

Unit Review

What You've Learned

- Commands: BREAK
- How to break entities using BREAK

Review Questions

True or False

53.01 T F The BREAK command uses pick-first selection.

53.02 T F If you enter the @ symbol in response to the BREAK command's prompt for a second point, BREAK uses the same point as the starting and ending points for the break.

53.03 T F Circles are always broken counter-clockwise.

53.04 T F You cannot use object snap modes when selecting an entity to break.

53.05 T F The TRIM command is often a better choice than the BREAK command because TRIM requires fewer steps.

53.06 T F You can select more than one entity to break at a time.

Multiple Choice

53.07 Which of the following is not an entity that the BREAK command can break? __________

(A) line

(B) arc

(C) 2D polyline

(D) A, B, and C can all be broken

53.08 The BREAK command uses __________ that you specify to determine how to break an entity.

(A) lines

(B) points

(C) cutting edges

(D) none of the above

Student: ______________________ Date: __________

Instructor: ______________________ Course: __________ Section: __________

Short Answer

53.09 Explain how the BREAK and TRIM commands are different.

53.10 Explain how the BREAK and ERASE commands are both similar and different.

Additional Exercises

53.11 Continue with your drawing from the previous exercise. Use the BREAK command to complete the bracket drawing as shown in figure 53.7. Save your drawing as 053???11.

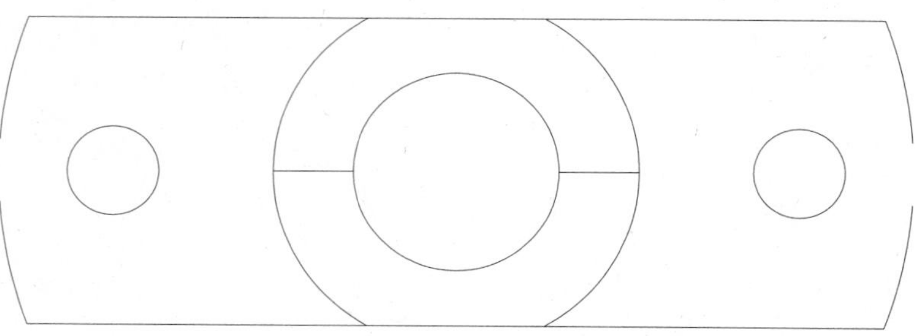

Figure 53.7

Bracket completed using the BREAK command.

Student: ______ Date: ______

Instructor: ______ Course: ______ Section: ______

UNIT 54

Extending Entities

One of the most useful editing commands AutoCAD offers is EXTEND. The EXTEND command enables you to extend (stretch) an entity to touch another entity. In some ways, EXTEND is the opposite of the TRIM command. TRIM cuts an entity using another entity as a cutting edge; EXTEND stretches the entity using another entity as a boundary edge. This unit teaches you how to use the EXTEND command.

The objectives for this unit are to:

- Understand the purpose of the EXTEND command
- Extend or stretch entities using EXTEND

Using the EXTEND Command

By now you certainly are familiar with constructive editing. One editing task you perform often when laying out a drawing is extending entities. *Extending* an entity means stretching one of its end points until it touches another entity. This capability enables you to use lines, arcs, circles, and other entities as construction lines, stretching other entities to touch them. Figure 54.1 shows an example of an extend operation (see ① and ②).

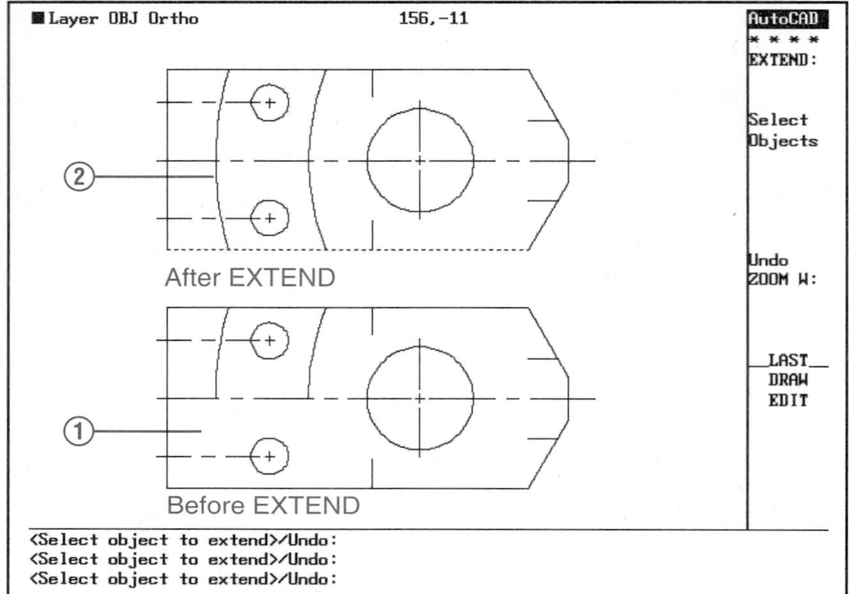

Figure 54.1

Entities before and after EXTEND.

You can issue the EXTEND command by choosing Modify, then Extend. You also can enter EXTEND from the command prompt or choose it from the EDIT screen menu. When you issue the EXTEND command, AutoCAD prompts you to select boundary edges. Boundary edges are the entities you use to stretch other entities. You can select multiple entities to use as boundary edges in a single extend operation. You can select boundaries on either end of a line, for example, and then stretch the line at both ends to touch the two boundaries. The EXTEND command accepts lines, arcs, circles, and 2D polylines as boundary entities.

The EXTEND command uses only pick-after selection. If a selection exists when you issue the EXTEND command, AutoCAD clears the selection set and prompts you to select new entities.

After you finish selecting the boundary edges, AutoCAD prompts you to select the entities to be extended. Only lines, arcs, and open 2D polylines can be extended.

NOTE

If you select an entity other than a line, arc, or open 2D polyline to extend, AutoCAD generates the message `Cannot EXTEND this entity.` *If the selected entity cannot be extended to the boundary because the two cannot intersect, AutoCAD generates the error message* `Entity does not intersect an edge.` *You can select a closed 2D polyline as a boundary edge, but you cannot extend it.*

In the following exercises, use the EXTEND command to modify the same Slide Block drawing that you edited in preceding units. In the first exercise, you stretch two arcs.

Stretching Arcs

1. Begin a new drawing named 054???01 in your assigned directory using 054SLIDE as a prototype.

2. `Command:` *Choose* Modify, *then* Extend	Issues the EXTEND command
`_extend` `Select boundary edge(s)...`	
3. `Select objects:` *Select the line at* ① *(see fig. 54.2)*	Selects a boundary edge
`1 found`	
4. `Select objects:` *Press* Enter	Ends selection of boundary edges
5. `<Select object to extend>/Undo:` *Select the arc at* ② *(see fig. 54.2)*	Extends the arc to the line
6. `<Select object to extend>/Undo:` *Select the arc at* ③ *(see fig. 54.2)*	Extends the arc to the line
7. `<Select object to extend>/Undo:` *Press* Enter	Ends the EXTEND command

Your drawing should look similar to figure 54.3.

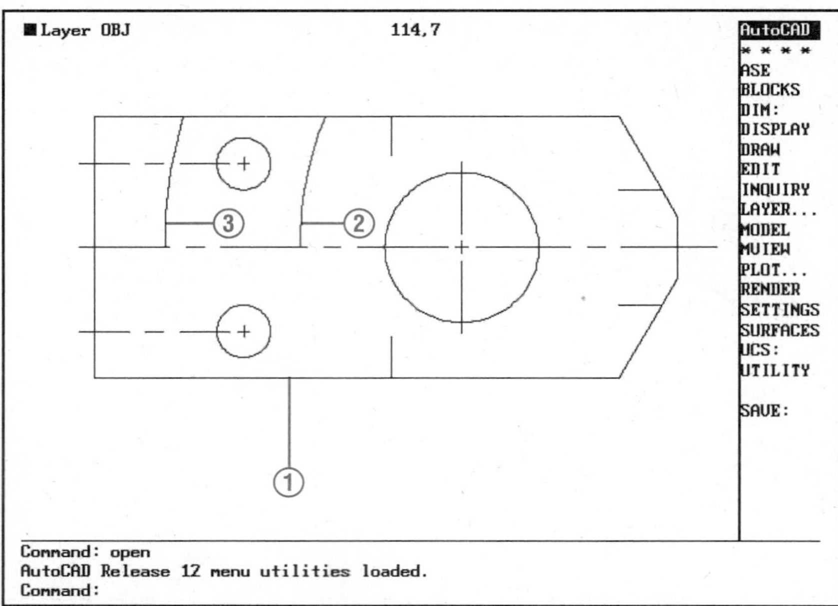

Figure 54.2 *Selection points for stretching arcs.*

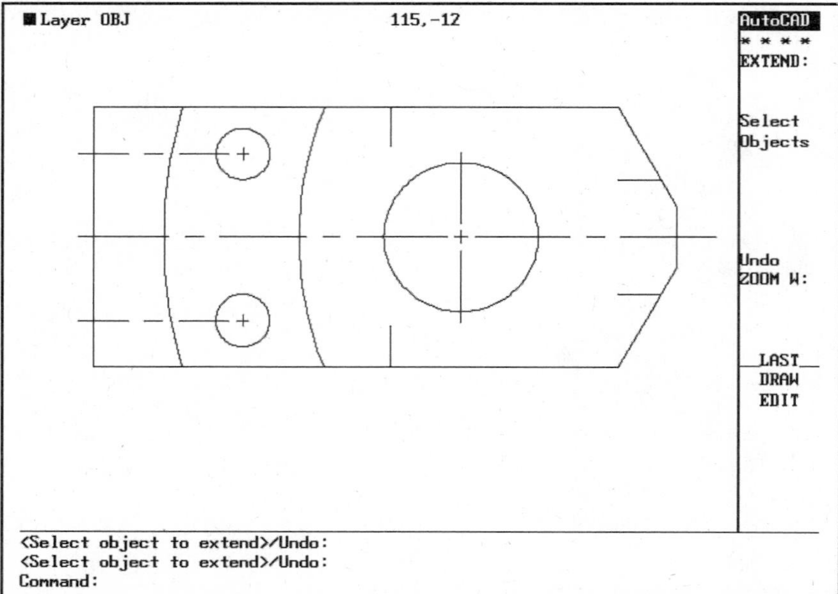

Figure 54.3 *Arcs after EXTEND.*

The arcs retain their original radius and are extended along the arc until they intersect the boundary edge (the line). Next, extend the four lines at the right side of the Slide Block to touch the large circle.

Extending Lines

Continue with your drawing from the preceding exercise.

1. `Command:` *Choose* Modify, *then* Extend   Issues the EXTEND command

`_extend`	
`Select boundary edge(s)...`	
2. `Select objects:` *Select the circle at ① (see fig. 54.4)*	Selects a boundary edge
`1 found`	
3. Select objects: *Press* Enter	Ends selection of boundary edges
4. `<Select object to extend>/Undo:` *Select the line at ② (see fig. 54.4)*	Extends the line to the circle
5. `<Select object to extend>/Undo:` *Select the line at ③ (see fig. 54.4)*	Extends the line to the circle
6. `<Select object to extend>/Undo:` *Select the line at ④ (see fig. 54.4)*	Extends the line to the circle
7. `<Select object to extend>/Undo:` *Select the line at ⑤ (see fig. 54.4)*	Extends the line to the circle
8. `<Select object to extend>/Undo:` *Press* Enter	Ends the EXTEND command
9. Save your drawing.	

Your drawing should look similar to figure 54.5.

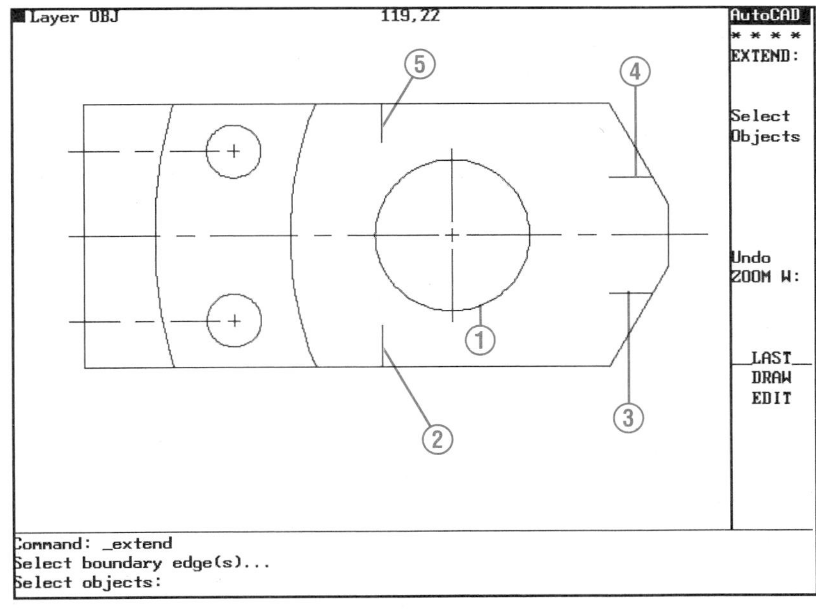

Figure 54.4

Selection points to extend lines.

Figure 54.5

Lines after EXTEND.

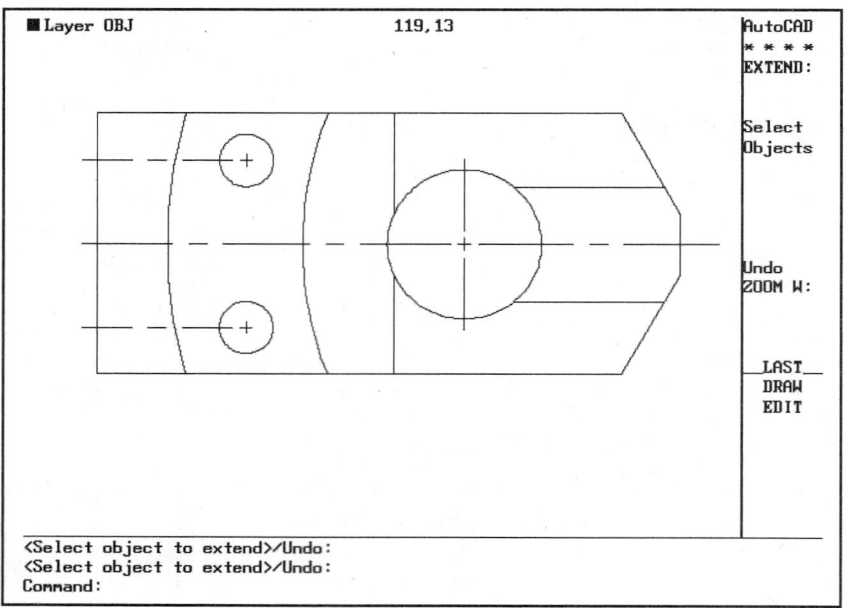

TIP

You can select an entity as a boundary edge and also select it as an entity to be extended. This makes it possible to select a large number of entities with a window or other selection option, and then extend individually as necessary. This also makes it possible to use an entity as a boundary and extend it in the same operation.

Unit Review

What You've Learned

- Commands: EXTEND
- How to extend entities using EXTEND

Review Questions

True or False

54.01 T F The EXTEND command uses pick-first selection.

54.02 T F If a selection set exists when you issue the EXTEND command, AutoCAD clears the selection set and prompts you to select new entities.

54.03 T F You can use any entity as a boundary edge, but you can only extend lines, arcs, and 2D polylines.

54.04 T F You can select multiple entities as boundary edges in the same operation.

54.05 T F You can select a closed 2D polyline as a boundary, but you cannot extend it.

54.06 T F You can extend arcs and circles.

Multiple Choice

54.07 The EXTEND command enables you to stretch an entity by using one or more other entities as __________ edges.

(A) extending

(B) cutting

(C) closed

(D) boundary

54.08 Which of the following cannot be extended? __________

(A) lines

(B) arcs

(C) circles

(D) open 2D polylines

Student: __________ Date: __________

Instructor: __________ Course: __________ Section: __________

Short Answer

54.09 Explain what happens to the radius of an arc if you extend the arc.

54.10 Explain what happens when you select an entity that cannot be extended.

Additional Exercises

54.11 Begin a new drawing named 054???11 in your assigned directory using 054EXTND as a prototype. With figure 54.6 as a guide, use the EXTEND command to extend the lines in the front and right side views to match the views shown in figure 54.6. Save your drawing.

Figure 54.6

Completed Slide Block.

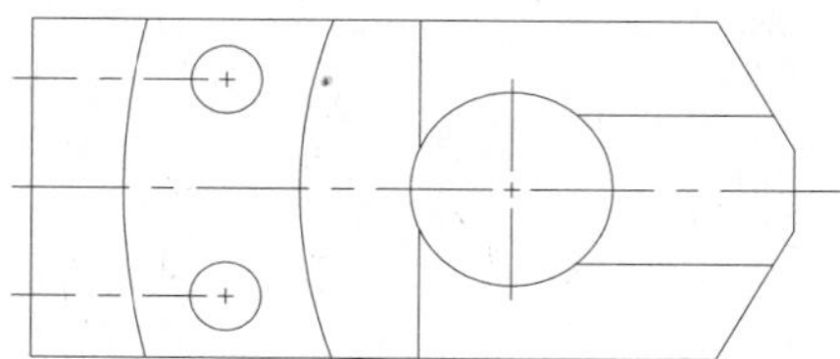

METRIC

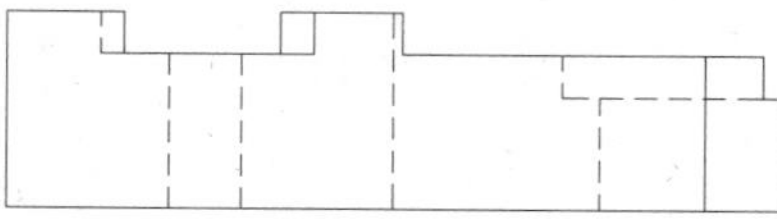

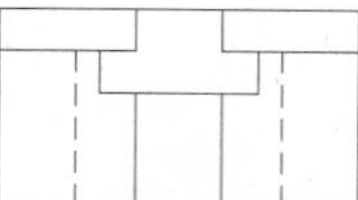

Student: ______ Date: ______

Instructor: ______ Course: ______ Section: ______

UNIT 55

Stretching Entities

Unit 23, "Moving and Stretching Entities," introduced the Stretch autoedit mode and explained how you can use grips and autoediting to stretch entities. AutoCAD also provides another method for stretching entities: the STRETCH command. In most ways, the STRETCH command is very much like Stretch autoedit mode. A few differences exist, however. In some situations, the STRETCH command is more useful than Stretch autoedit mode. This unit teaches you how to use the STRETCH command.

The objectives for this unit are to:

- Understand the similarities and differences between STRETCH and Stretch autoedit mode
- Stretch entities with the STRETCH command

Understanding the STRETCH Command

The STRETCH command functions much like Stretch autoedit mode; even restrictions that apply to Stretch autoedit mode apply to the STRETCH command. For example, you cannot stretch a block with STRETCH. Blocks cannot be stretched by any means.

Unlike Stretch autoedit mode, however, the STRETCH command has no Copy option. Therefore, you cannot copy entities while performing a stretch operation with STRETCH. Other differences also exist. Stretch autoedit mode enables you to change the radius of a circle or arc; the STRETCH command does not stretch circles but it does stretch arcs.

The primary advantage to using STRETCH rather than Stretch autoedit mode is in entity selection: STRETCH uses pick-after selection, which makes it possible to use many more selection options than are available with pick-first selection. For example, you can use the Fence, WPolygon, and CPolygon options when selecting for the STRETCH command. Although these options are helpful, they are useful only in a limited number of situations because the options generally result in moving an entity rather than stretching it.

The most common selection method used with the STRETCH command is Crossing. STRETCH uses crossing mode initially by default. Any entity touched by the initial crossing selection window is stretched, with the exceptions, such as circles. The end points of entities that fall inside the crossing window are relocated, stretching the entities.

Because of the limitations of STRETCH and the additional options available in Stretch autoedit mode, Stretch autoedit mode is often more useful and versatile than STRETCH. Nevertheless, you might encounter situations in which STRETCH is more effective.

Using the STRETCH Command

You can access the STRETCH command by choosing Modify, then Stretch. You also can enter STRETCH from the command prompt or choose it from the second page of the EDIT screen menu. The STRETCH command automatically chooses a crossing option for the first entity selection. Generally, you want to use the crossing window to box in the end points to be stretched.

In the following exercises, complete the same changes accomplished in unit 23 with Stretch autoedit mode. First, stretch the top view of a Slide Block from 108mm to 120mm. Use figure 55.1 as a guide to select points.

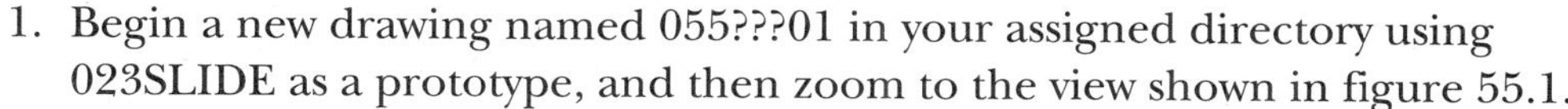

Using STRETCH

1. Begin a new drawing named 055???01 in your assigned directory using 023SLIDE as a prototype, and then zoom to the view shown in figure 55.1.

2.	`Command:` *Choose* Modify, *then* Stretch	Issues the STRETCH command
	`_ stretch`	
	`Select objects to stretch by window or polygon...` `Select objects: _c`	
3.	`First corner:` *Pick a point at* ① *(see fig. 55.1)*	Specifies first corner of crossing window
4.	`Other corner:` *Pick a point at* ②	Specifies second corner of crossing window and selects objects
	`8 found`	
5.	`Select objects:` *Press* Enter	Ends selection
6.	`Base point or displacement:` *Pick any point*	Specifies a base point
7.	`Second point of displacement:` **`@12,0`** ↵	Specifies displacement

Your drawing should look similar to figure 55.2.

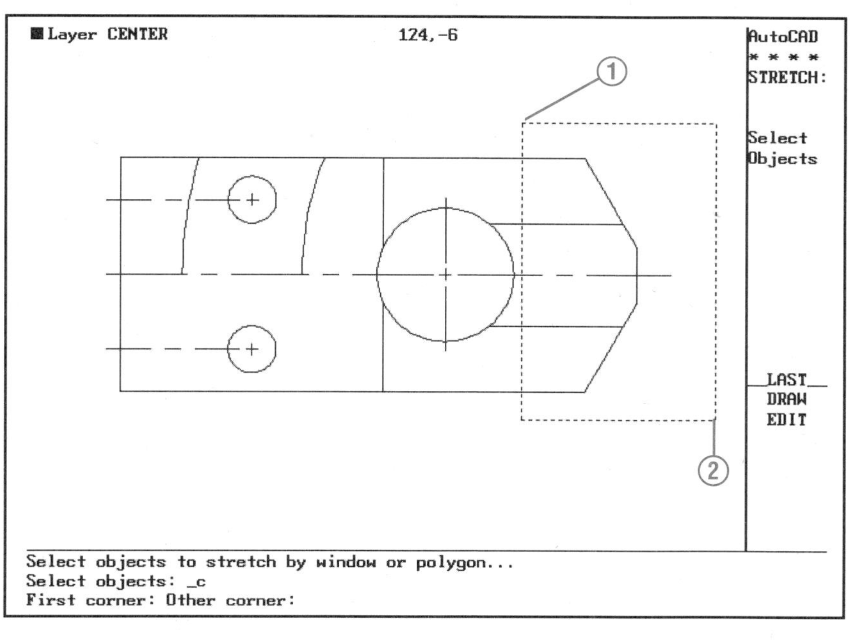

Figure 55.1

Selection points for STRETCH.

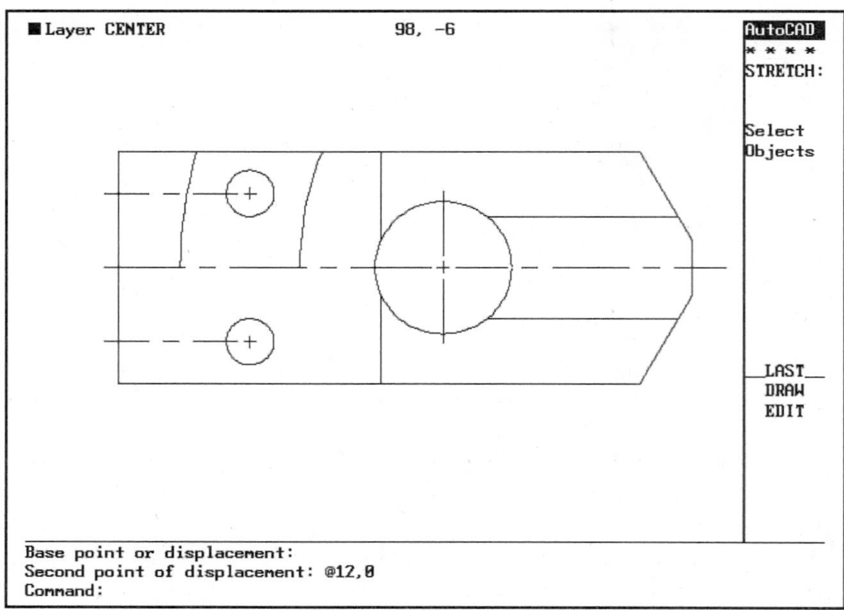

Figure 55.2
Slide block after STRETCH.

Because STRETCH used explicit crossing selection rather than implied crossing selection (these two terms are covered in unit 21, "Introduction to Selection and Editing," you were able to pick the two corner points for the crossing box in left-to-right order. Before ending the selection set, you also could have used any of the selection options, such as Window, Fence, WPolygon, and Remove to modify the selection set.

STRETCH does not use pick-first selection, even if a selection set exists when you issue the command. STRETCH clears any existing selection set when the command starts.

In the next exercise, try to use STRETCH to stretch an arc down to the bottom of the Slide Block. Use figure 55.3 to select points.

Stretching Arcs

Continue with your drawing from the preceding exercise.

1. `Command:` *Choose* Modify, *then* Stretch — Issues the STRETCH command

   `_stretch`

   `Select objects to stretch by window or polygon...`
   `Select objects: _c`

2. `First corner:` *Pick a point at* ① *(see fig. 55.3)* — Specifies first corner of crossing window

3. `Other corner:` *Pick a point at* ② *(see fig. 55.3)* `3 found`	Specifies second corner of crossing window and selects objects
4. `Select objects:` **`R`** ↵	Specifies the Remove option
5. `Remove objects:` *Select the line at* ③ *(see fig. 55.3)*	Removes the line from the selection set
6. `Remove objects:` **`A`** ↵	Specifies the Add option
7. `Select objects:` *Select the circle at* ④ *(see fig. 55.3)*	Adds the circle to the selection set
8. `Select objects:` *Select the circle at* ⑤ *(see fig. 55.3)*	Adds the circle to the selection set
9. `Select objects:` *Press* Enter	Ends selection
10. `Base point or displacement:` *Pick any point*	Specifies a base point
11. `Second point of displacement:` **`@5,-25`** ↵	Specifies displacement

Your drawing should look similar to figure 55.4.

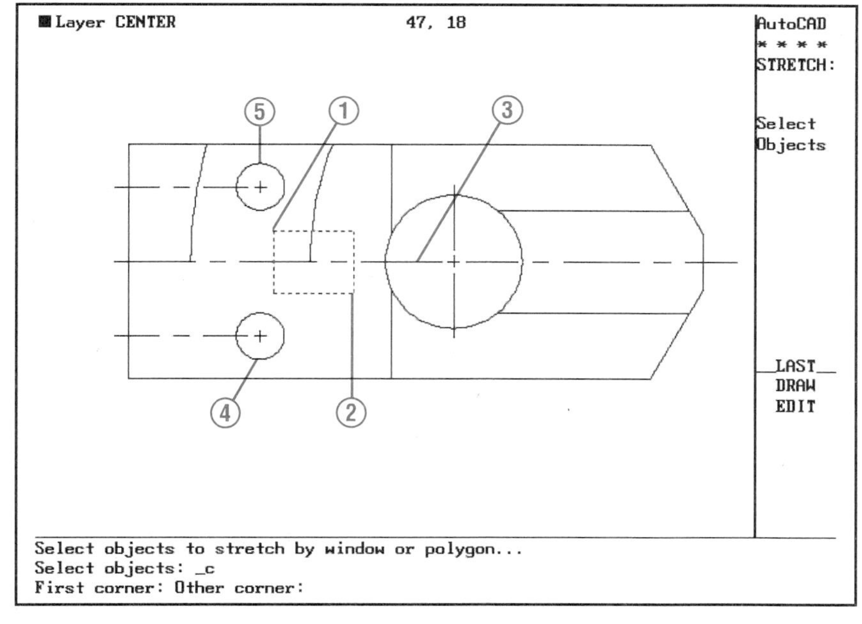

Figure 55.3

Selection points to stretch arc.

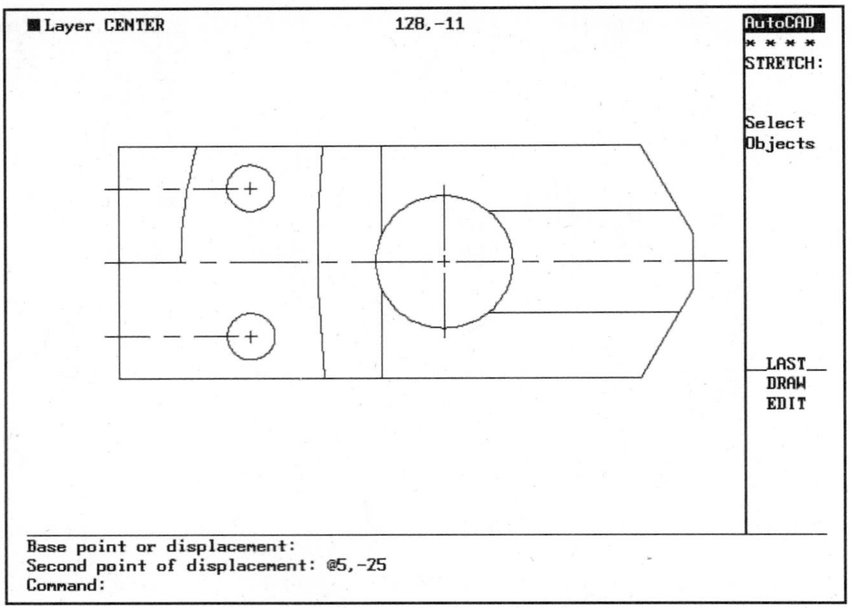

Figure 55.4
Drawing after STRETCH.

The STRETCH command changes the radius of the arc when you stretch it. Because it has this effect, the STRETCH command usually is not useful for stretching arcs. Stretch autoedit mode, however, enables you to stretch an arc and still maintain its original radius. The EXTEND command provides the same benefit.

Another difference with the STRETCH command is that it does not stretch or relocate the two circles that you select in the exercise. This illustrates a major difference between STRETCH and Stretch autoedit mode: STRETCH does not move entities as does Stretch autoedit mode.

You should use Stretch autoedit mode as much as possible when you need to stretch entities because it offers benefits and options STRETCH doesn't have.

Unit Review

What You've Learned

- Commands: STRETCH
- The similarities and differences between Stretch autoedit mode and the STRETCH command
- How to stretch entities using STRETCH
- The limitations of the STRETCH command

Review Questions

True or False

55.01 T F The STRETCH command can use either pick-first or pick-after selection.

55.02 T F If a selection set exists when you issue the STRETCH command, AutoCAD clears the selection set and prompts you to select new entities with a crossing window.

55.03 T F You cannot stretch blocks with STRETCH.

55.04 T F The STRETCH command has a Copy option that functions similar to the Copy option in Stretch autoedit mode.

55.05 T F STRETCH uses a crossing selection window by default.

55.06 T F You cannot stretch a circle to change its radius with STRETCH.

Multiple Choice

55.07 The STRETCH command enables you to stretch an entity by using __________.

(A) a crossing window

(B) pick-after selection

(C) WPolygon

(D) all of the above

Student: ____________________ Date: __________

Instructor: ____________________ Course: ______ Section: ______

55.08 STRETCH offers __________ selection options than/as Stretch autoedit mode.

(A) fewer

(B) more

(C) the same

(D) none of the above

Short Answer

55.09 Explain what happens to the radius of an arc if you stretch an end point of the arc.

____

____

____

55.10 Describe two advantages of using Stretch autoedit mode rather than STRETCH.

____

____

____

Student: ______________________ Date: ______________

Instructor: ______________________ Course: ______________ Section: ______________

UNIT 56

Applying Chamfers

A *chamfer* is a corner cut at a certain angle or with specific distances along each edge of the corner. Chamfers are very common in mechanical design, but also are used in any type of drawing. This unit explains chamfers and teaches you to use AutoCAD's CHAMFER command.

The objectives for this unit are to:

- Understand options for creating chamfers
- Chamfer the intersection of lines with CHAMFER
- Understand the effects of CHAMFER on polylines
- Chamfer all corners of a polyline with CHAMFER

Using the CHAMFER Command

The CHAMFER command trims the intersection of two adjacent lines or polyline segments at specific distances along each segment from the original point of intersection. The segments do not have to end at the intersection; they can extend past (the lines cross one another), or do not have to touch at all. Figure 56.1 shows examples of line segments before and after a chamfer is applied to them.

Often, chamfers are created using a specific angle. Two intersecting lines might be chamfered at a 45-degree angle, for example. AutoCAD does not include an option with CHAMFER to specify a specific angle. Instead, you can specify the length along each segment. Figure 56.2 shows a 1"×2" chamfer. To create a 45-degree chamfer, specify equal distances for both sides of the chamfer.

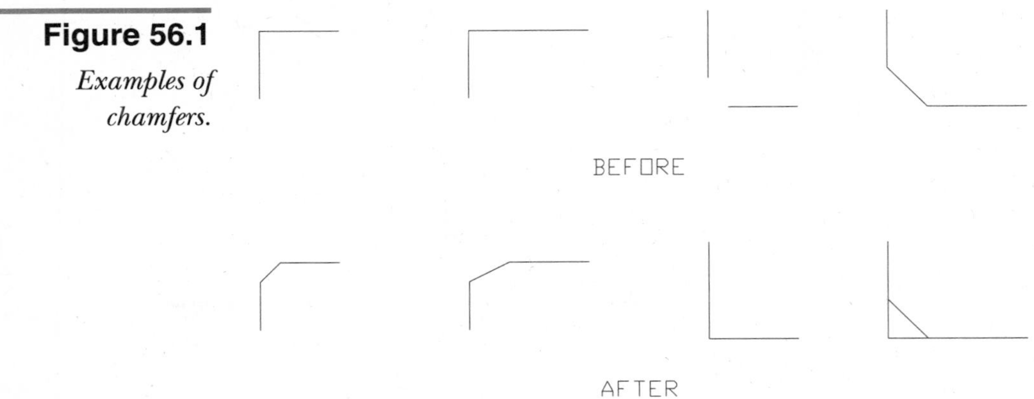

Figure 56.1

Examples of chamfers.

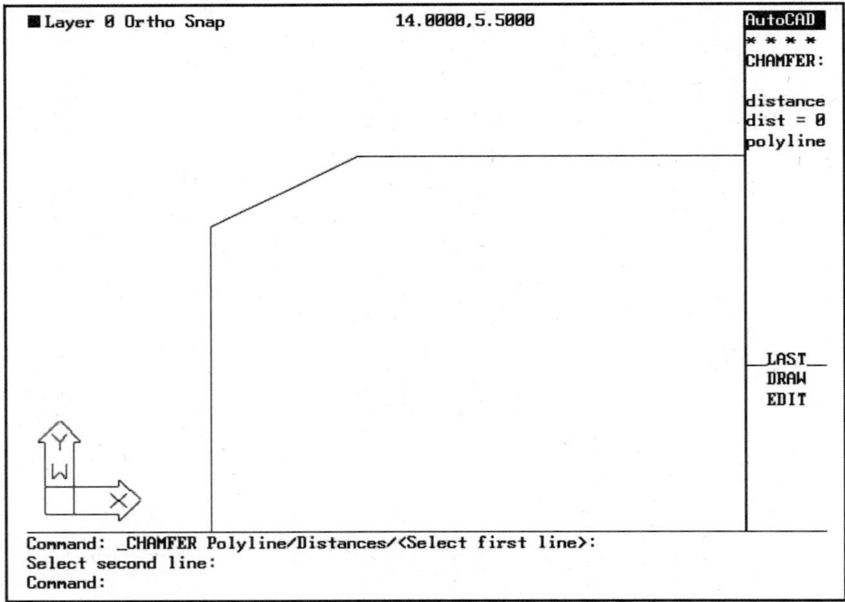

Figure 56.2

A 1"×2" chamfer.

If you need to chamfer an intersection at an angle other than 45 degrees, but do not know both distances, consider drawing a line at the needed angle, and then use TRIM rather than CHAMFER to create the chamfered corner.

You can issue the CHAMFER command by selecting Construct, and then Chamfer. You also can enter the command at the command prompt or select CHAMFER from the EDIT menu.

In the following exercise, use the CHAMFER command to create a 45-degree chamfer at the intersection of the two lines in the upper left corner of the part. Use figure 56.3 to select entities.

Chamfering Lines

1. Begin a new drawing named 056???01 in your assigned directory using 056LINES as a prototype.

2. `Command:` *Choose* Construct, *then* Chamfer — Issues the CHAMFER command

   `_chamfer`

3. `Polyline/Distances/<Select first line>:` **`D`** ↵ — Specifies the Distances option

4. `Enter first chamfer distance <0>:` **`10`** ↵ — Sets the chamfer distance along the first segment

5. `Enter second chamfer distance <10>:` *Press* Enter — Accepts the default, which is equal to the first distance

6. `Command:` *Press* Enter — Repeats the CHAMFER command

   `CHAMFER`

7. `Polyline/Distances/<Select first line>:` *Select the line at* ① *(see fig. 56.3)* — Selects first line of intersection

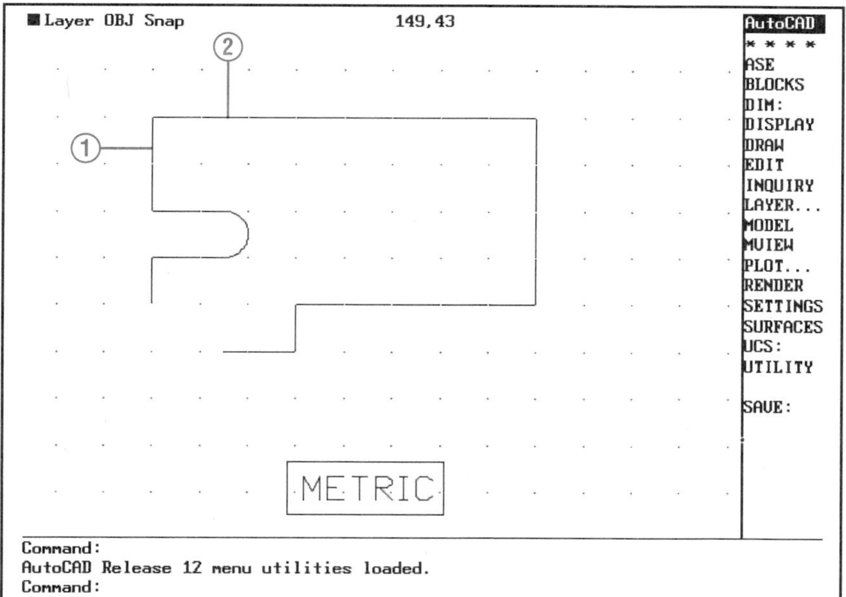

Figure 56.3

Lines to chamfer.

continues

8. Select second line: *Select the line at ② (see fig. 56.3)* — Selects second line and chamfers the lines

Your drawing should resemble figure 56.4.

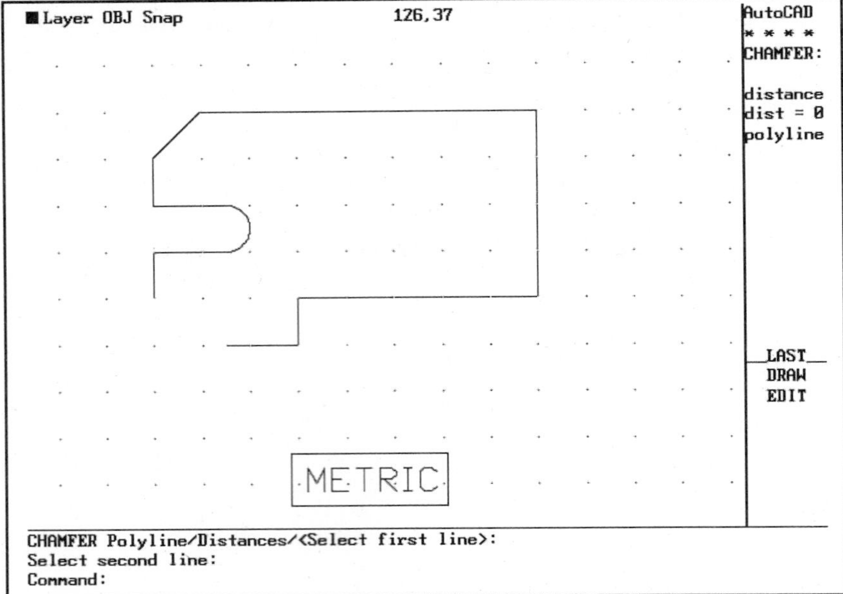

Figure 56.4
Lines after CHAMFER.

AutoCAD trimmed the lines an equal distance on each side of the intersection.

CHAMFER uses pick-after selection only. If a selection set exists when you issue CHAMFER, AutoCAD clears the selection set and prompts you to select new entities.

Applying an Unequal Chamfer

If you specify unequal distances for the chamfer, AutoCAD applies the first distance to the first segment you select and applies the second distance to the second segment you select. To see how CHAMFER handles unequal distances, create a chamfer using unequal distances in the next exercise.

Chamfering with Unequal Distances

Continue with your drawing from the preceding exercise.

1. `Command:` *Choose* Construct, *then* Chamfer — Issues the CHAMFER command

   `_chamfer`

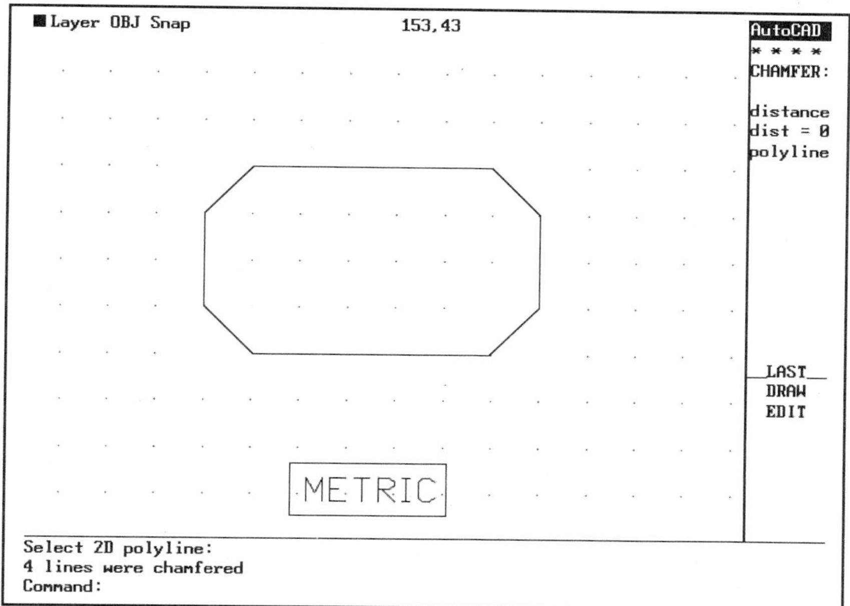

Figure 56.8

The polyline after CHAMFER.

Unit Review

What You've Learned

- Commands: CHAMFER
- How to chamfer lines using equal and unequal distances
- How to chamfer polylines

Review Questions

True or False

56.01 T F The CHAMFER command can use either pick-first or pick-after selection.

56.02 T F If a selection set exists when you issue the CHAMFER command, AutoCAD clears the selection set and prompts you to select new entities.

56.03 T F You can chamfer all corners of a polyline with a single command.

56.04 T F Polyarc segments in a polyline are not affected by CHAMFER.

56.05 T F Chamfer distances must be equal.

56.06 T F You can use CHAMFER to extend two line segments to intersect at a point.

Multiple Choice

56.07 The CHAMFER command trims the __________ of line or polyline segments.

(A) intersection

(B) sides

(C) distances

56.08 If you specify unequal distances, the CHAMFER command applies the first distance to __________.

(A) the first segment selected

(B) the second segment selected

(C) both segments

(D) none of the above

Student: __________ Date: __________

Instructor: __________ Course: __________ Section: __________

Short Answer

56.09 Explain the different methods you must use to chamfer the intersection between two polyline segments, and to chamfer all polyline segments with a single selection.

____

____

____

56.10 Explain what happens if you use a chamfer distance of zero, and then chamfer two lines on either side of an intersection that you already chamfered.

____

____

____

Student: ________________ Date: ________

Instructor: ________________ Course: ________ Section: ________

UNIT 57

Applying Fillets

A *fillet* is a radius that blends two entities, such as two lines, a line and an arc, or two arcs. Fillets are most common in mechanical design, but you can use fillets in virtually any drawing when you need to blend two entities with an arc. AutoCAD's FILLET command enables you to apply fillets. In some ways, FILLET is similar to CHAMFER in the way it works and in its options. If you are familiar with the CHAMFER command (unit 56), you should have no problems with the FILLET command.

The objectives for this unit are to:

- Understand options for creating fillets
- Chamfer the intersection of lines, arcs, and circles with FILLET
- Understand the effects of FILLET on polylines
- Fillet all corners of a polyline with FILLET

Using the FILLET Command

The FILLET command connects two lines, arcs, circles, or polyline segments with a tangent arc of whatever radius you specify. In the case of lines and arcs, the segments do not have to end at a common endpoint. The segments can extend past one another, or not intersect at all. This is similar to the way the CHAMFER command works. Figure 57.1 shows two line segments that have been filleted.

Figure 57.1

Lines before and after FILLET.

If you are filleting arcs, AutoCAD blends the arcs using a tangent arc of the radius you specify and removes the extraneous portion of the original arcs. The sections of the arcs that AutoCAD removes depend on your selection points when you pick the arcs to be filleted and the tangent points of the fillet. For circles, AutoCAD draws the tangent fillet arc between the two circles but does not remove any portion of the original circles.

If you select two polyline segments, AutoCAD fillets the two segments as if they were regular line segments. If you use the Polyline option of the FILLET command, however, AutoCAD fillets all possible vertexes of the polyline.

If the radius you specify does not result in a tangent arc, AutoCAD responds with an error message informing you that there is no valid fillet with the specified radius and AutoCAD does not complete the fillet. You cannot select a polyarc segment to fillet.

FILLET only uses pick-after selection. If a selection set exists when you issue the FILLET command, AutoCAD clears the selection set and prompts for new entities.

In the following exercise, fillet two corners of the V Block that you worked on in unit 52. First, use the FILLET command to fillet the leftmost corners of the part with a 6mm radius fillet.

Applying a Fillet

1. Begin a new drawing named 057???01 in your assigned directory using 057VSTOP as a prototype.

2. `Command:` *Choose* Construct, *then* Fillet — Issues the FILLET command

   `_fillet`

3. `Polyline/Radius/`
   `<Select first object>:` **R** ↵ — Specifies the Radius option

4. `Enter fillet radius <0.00>:` **6** ↵	Specifies the fillet radius
5. `Command:` *Press* Enter `FILLET`	Repeats the previous command
6. `Polyline/Radius/<Select first object>:` *Select the polyline segment at* ① *(see fig. 57.2)*	Specifies the first entity to fillet
7. Select second object: *Select the polyline segment at* ② *(see fig. 57.2)*	Specifies the second entity and applies the fillet

Your drawing should look similar to figure 57.3.

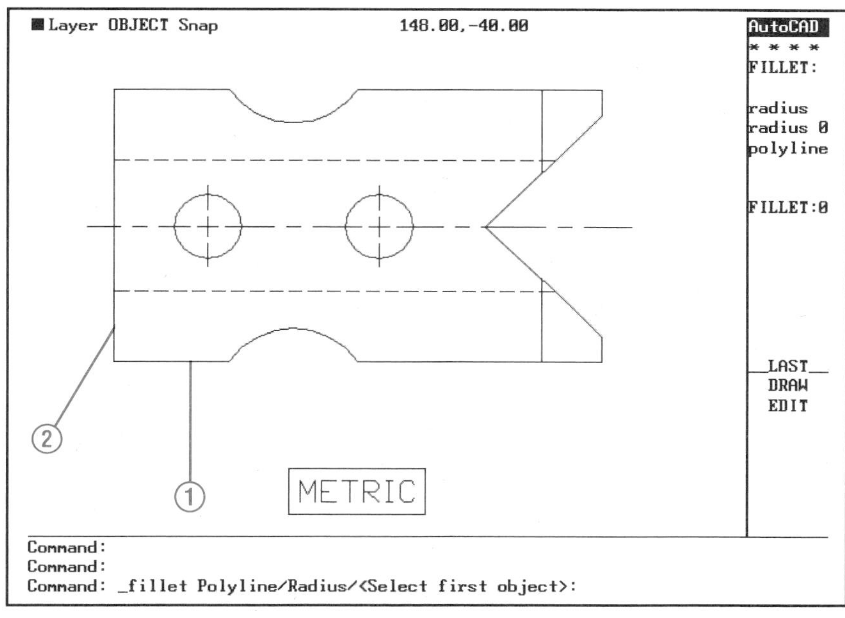

Figure 57.2

Selection points for fillet.

If you do not use the Polyline option, the FILLET command treats polyline segments just like individual line segments, filleting only between the two segments you select. If the two segments you selected in the exercise had been line segments, the resulting fillet would have been the same.

When you fillet a polyline, the fillet arcs become polyarcs. The entire polyline, including the new arc segments, still is recognized by AutoCAD as a single entity.

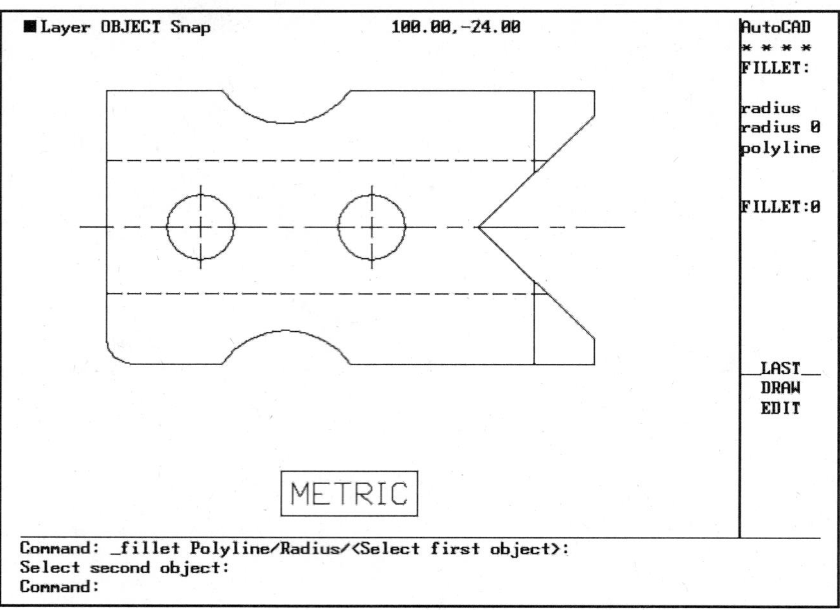

Figure 57.3

Polyline segments after fillet.

There is one limitation of filleting line and polyline segments. You cannot apply a fillet between a line and a polyline segment because doing so would necessitate either adding the line to the polyline or exploding the polyline. If you attempt to fillet the upper left corner of the V Block, for example, AutoCAD will generate an error message and will not apply the fillet. This is because the horizontal segment is a line and the vertical segment is a polyline. To fillet the two entities, you must first explode the polyline.

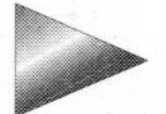

Filleting Lines and Polylines

Continue with your drawing from the previous exercise.

1. `Command:` *Choose* Modify, *then* Explode `_explode`	Issues the EXPLODE command
2. `Select objects:` *Select the polyline at* ① *(see fig. 57.4)* `1 found`	
3. `Select objects:` *Press* Enter	Ends the EXPLODE command and explodes the polyline
4. `Command:` *Choose* Construct, *then* Fillet	Issues the FILLET command
5. `Polyline/Radius/<Select first object>:` *Select the line segment at* ② *(see fig. 57.4)*	Specifies the first entity to fillet
6. `Select second object:` *Select the line segment at* ③ *(see fig. 57.4)*	Specifies the second entity and applies the fillet

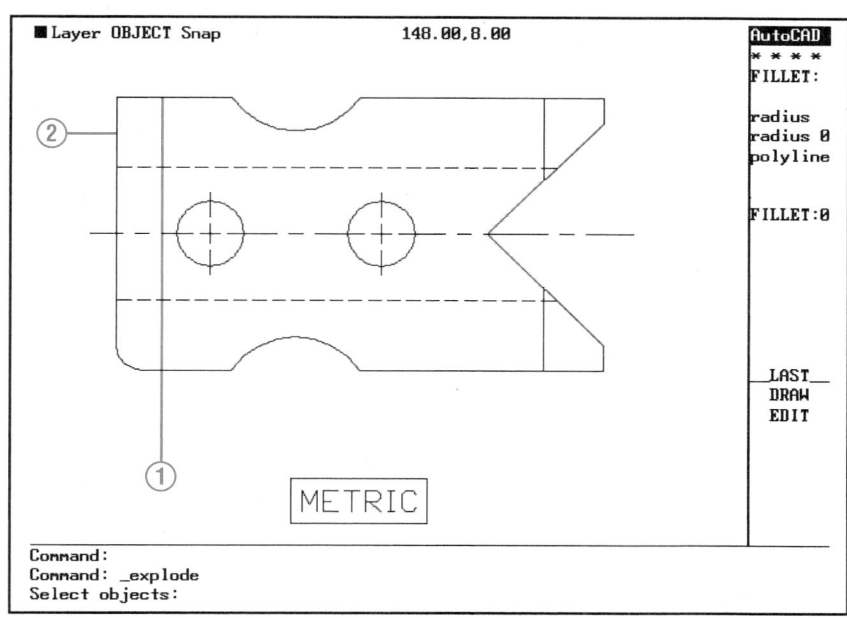

Figure 57.4

Selection points for line and polyline fillet.

Your drawing should look similar to figure 57.5.

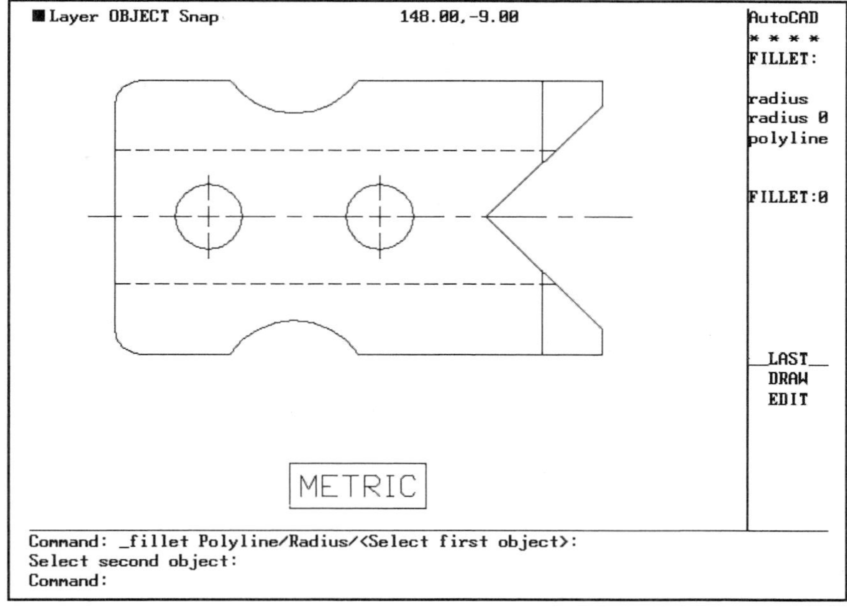

Figure 57.5

Upper corner of V Block after fillet.

The two entities that you select to fillet do not have to be the same type of entity (although the restriction regarding filleting a line and a polyline segment still applies). For example, you can apply a fillet to a line and arc or to a line and a circle. In the following exercise, apply a 3mm fillet to the line and arc at the bottom of the V Block.

Filleting Dissimilar Entities

1. Continue with your drawing from the previous exercise and zoom to the view shown in figure 57.6 (your drawing will not yet show the fillet).

2. `Command:` *Choose* Construct, *then* Fillet — Issues the FILLET command

   `_fillet`

3. `Polyline/Radius/<Select first object>:` **R** ↵ — Specifies the Radius option

4. `Enter fillet radius <6.00>:` **3** ↵ — Specifies the fillet radius

5. `Command:` *Press* Enter — Repeats the previous command

   `FILLET`

6. `Polyline/Radius/<Select first object>:` *Select the line segment at* ① *(see fig. 57.6)* — Specifies the first entity to fillet

7. `Select second object:` *Select the arc at* ② — Specifies the second entity and applies the fillet

8. Save your drawing.

Your drawing should look similar to figure 57.6.

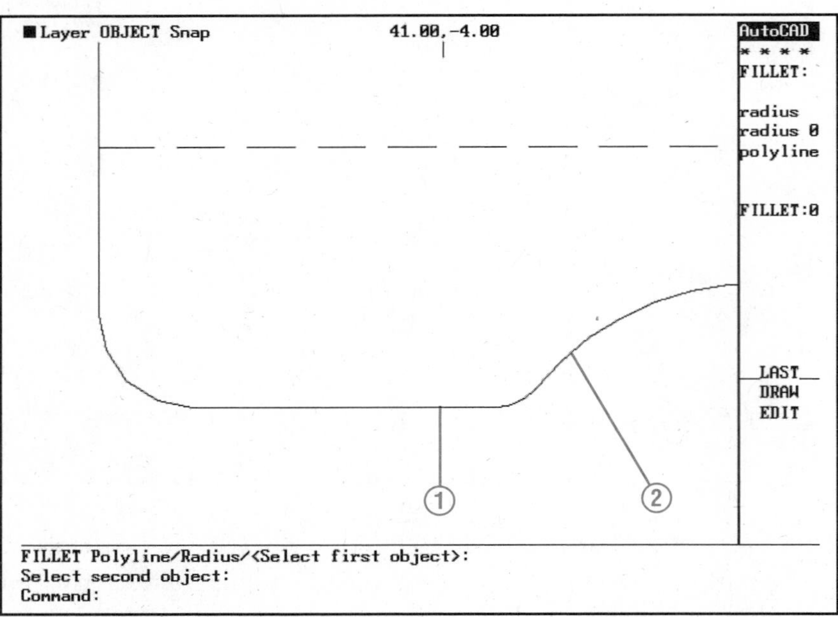

Figure 57.6
Fillet applied to line and arc.

AutoCAD modifies the selected entities according to type. It trims lines and arcs to the tangent point of the fillet, but it does not trim circles.

The portion of a line or arc segment that AutoCAD trims as part of a FILLET operation depends on the length of the entity relative to the fillet and the selection points you use to identify the enitities. In the case of intersecting lines, for example, selecting the lines on a particular side of the intersection retains the line segments on the same side of the intersection. If you have difficulty applying a fillet properly, examine your selection points to determine if they are affecting how AutoCAD trims the entities. In some cases, you may need to use the CIRCLE or ARC commands to draw the fillet manually.

Filleting with Zero Distance

Just as you can chamfer a corner with distances of zero, you also can apply a fillet with a radius of zero between two polyline segments, two line segments, or an arc and a line. The result depends on the types of entities selected. With lines and arcs, AutoCAD does not remove the arc that was created by the previous FILLET command. In the case of polylines, however, the fillet arc is removed.

In the following exercise, apply a fillet with a radius of zero to lines, arcs, and polylines. Use figure 57.7 to select points. Your drawing should look similar to figure 57.8 when you finish.

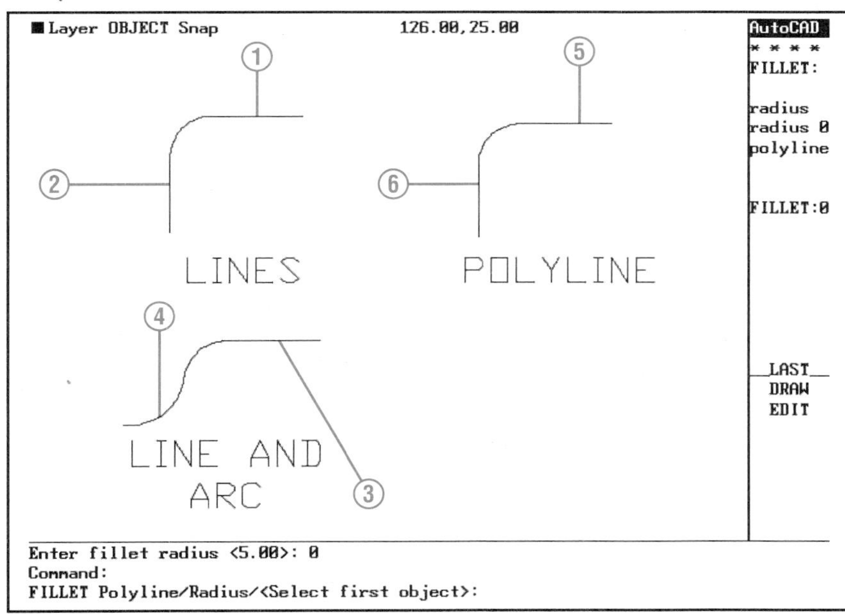

Figure 57.7

Selection points for fillet radius = 0.

Filleting with a Radius of Zero

1. Begin a new drawing named 057???02 in your assigned directory using 057ZERO as a prototype.

2.	`Command:` *Choose* Construct, *then* Fillet `_fillet`	Issues the FILLET command
3.	`Polyline/Radius/<Select first object>:` **R** ↵	Specifies the Radius option
4.	`Enter fillet radius <5.00>:` **0** ↵	Specifies the fillet radius
5.	`Command:` *Press* Enter `FILLET`	Repeats the previous command
6.	`Polyline/Radius/<Select first object>:` *Select the line segment at* ① *(see fig. 57.7)*	Specifies the first entity to fillet
7.	`Select second object:` *Select the line at* ②	Specifies the second entity and applies the fillet
8.	`Command:` *Press* Enter `FILLET`	Repeats the previous command
9.	`Polyline/Radius/<Select first object>:` *Select the line segment at* ③ *(see fig. 57.7)*	Specifies the first entity to fillet
10.	`Select second object:` *Select the arc at* ④	Specifies the second entity and applies the fillet
11.	`Command:` *Press* Enter `FILLET`	Repeats the previous command
12.	`Polyline/Radius/<Select first object>:` *Select the polyline segment at* ⑤	Specifies the first entity to fillet
13.	`Select second object:` *Select the polyline segment at* ⑥	Specifies the second entity and applies the fillet

14. Save your drawing.

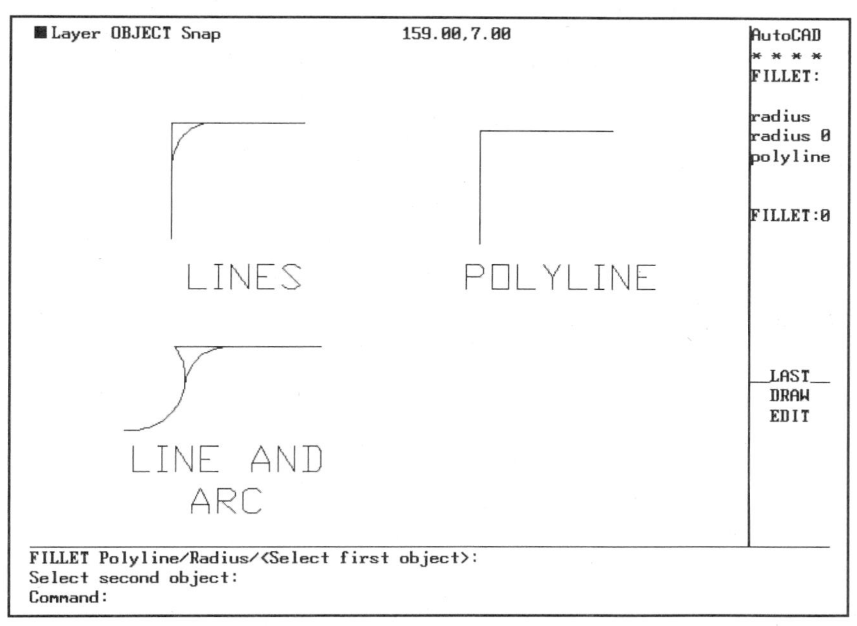

Figure 57.8

Results of fillet radius = 0.

You can see from the exercise and from figure 57.8 that only polylines do not retain the original fillet arc.

Filleting Polylines

In addition to filleting two polyline segments, you can apply a fillet to all possible vertexes in a polyline. This includes all line segments that are long enough to accommodate the fillet, as well as any two nonparallel polyline segments that are separated by a single polyarc segment.

In the following exercise, create the outline of a gasket by applying fillets to a closed polyline.

Applying Fillets to Polylines

1. Begin a new drawing named 057???03 in your assigned directory using 057PLINE as a prototype. The prototype's fillet radius setting is 5.

2. `Command:` *Choose* Construct, *then* Fillet `_fillet`	Issues the FILLET command
3. `Polyline/Radius/` `<Select first object>:` **P** ↵	Specifies the Polyline option
4. `Select 2D polyline:` *Select the polyline at any point*	Applies the fillet (see fig. 57.9)

continues

```
6 lines were filleted
1 was parallel
```

5. Save your drawing.

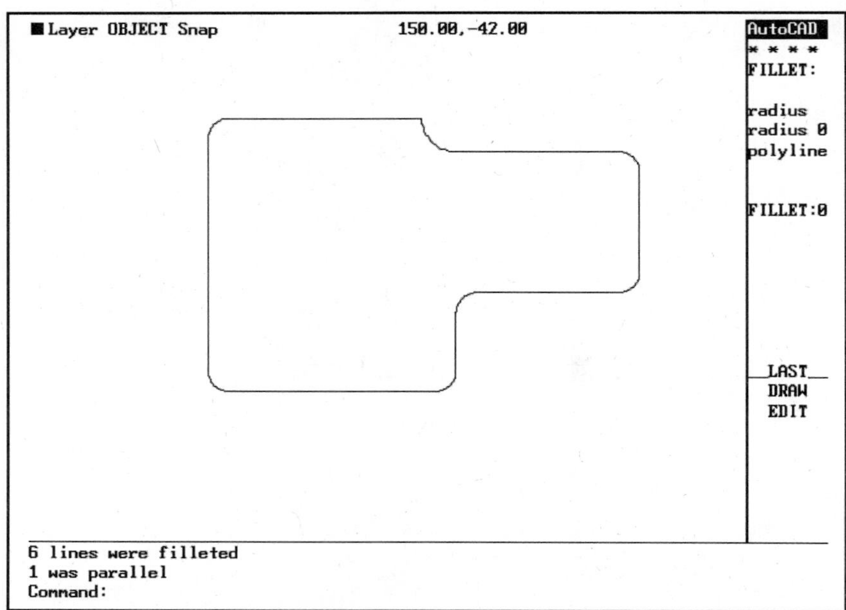

Figure 57.9

Polyline after FILLET.

AutoCAD did not apply a fillet between the two vertical polyline segments at the top of the gasket because they are parallel. It did apply a fillet to the two segments at the lower right corner of the gasket.

Unit Review

What You've Learned

- Commands: FILLET
- How to fillet lines, arcs, circles, and individual polyline vertexes
- How to fillet polylines

Review Questions

True or False

57.01 T F The FILLET command uses only pick-after selection.

57.02 T F If a selection set exists when you issue the FILLET command, AutoCAD clears the selection set and prompts you to select new entities.

57.03 T F You can fillet all corners of a polyline with a single command.

57.04 T F You cannot apply a fillet between a polyline and a polyarc segment.

57.05 T F You can apply a fillet between two different polylines.

57.06 T F You can fillet two lines using a fillet radius of zero.

Multiple Choice

57.07 The FILLET command will not apply a fillet to __________.

(A) lines

(B) arcs

(C) polyarcs

(D) polyline segments

57.08 A fillet is a __________ that blends two entities.

(A) special entity

(B) radius

(C) line segment

(D) polyline

Student: __________ Date: __________

Instructor: __________ Course: __________ Section: __________

Short Answer

57.09 Explain the limitation of applying a fillet between a line and a polyline.

57.10 Briefly explain what happens when you fillet two lines using a radius of zero.

Student: ______________________ Date: ______________

Instructor: ______________ Course: ______________ Section: ______

UNIT 58

Modifying Entity Characteristics

The ability to modify drawings efficiently is one of the most dramatic advantages of computer-aided design and drafting over conventional drafting. Changing the linetype of a line on a manually-prepared drawing means erasing the line, then drawing it again. In AutoCAD, you simply direct AutoCAD to change the line and the change is accomplished. This unit provides instruction on the use of the LIST command to retrieve information about drawing entities. It also covers the DDMODIFY command, which enables you to modify entities quickly in a number of ways.

The objectives of this unit are to:

- ☞ Use LIST to gain information about the properties of drawing entities (color, layer, linetype, etc.)
- ☞ Use LIST to gain information about the geometry of drawing entities (length, coordinate position, and size)
- ☞ Use the DDMODIFY command to alter the properties of drawing entities
- ☞ Use the DDMODIFY command to alter the geometry of drawing entities

Listing Entity Information

AutoCAD includes several commands that enable you to get information about the properties and geometry of entities. The LIST command is one of the most useful of the inquiry commands available in AutoCAD. This command enables you to select one or several entities and have information about the properties and geometry of the entities listed for your reference. The entity properties provided by LIST include:

- ☞ the layer assigned to the entity
- ☞ whether the entity is in model or paper space
- ☞ the entity's coordinate location
- ☞ size of geometry (length, radius, height)
- ☞ other characteristics (angle, scale factors, width, style)

Because one entity type is so different from another, the information provided by LIST varies considerably from one type of entity to another.

The following exercise shows you how to use the LIST command to get information about your drawing entities whether they are in model or paper space. The exercise also uses LIST to indicate the type of information available about several different entity types.

Listing Entity Information

1. Begin a new drawing named 058???01 in your assigned directory, using 047SLIDE as a prototype.

2. Zoom to the view shown in figure 58.1.

3. `Command:` *Choose* Assist, *then* Inquiry, *then* List — Issues LIST command

   `_list`

4. `Select objects:` *Select the line at ① (see fig. 58.1)* — Adds arc entity to selection set

   `1 found`

5. `Select objects:` *Select the circle at ② (see fig. 58.1)* — Add pline entity to selection set

   `1 found`

6. `Select objects:` *Select the dimension at ③ (see fig. 58.1)* — Add pline entity to selection set

   `1 found`

If you press Ctrl+Q after you select entities, but before you press Enter to complete the selection set, the text being output to the screen will be echoed to the line printer. Do not press Ctrl+Q if you do not have a printer connected to your system.

7. `Select objects:` *Press* Enter — Completes the selection set and lists information about the entities

```
                LINE      Layer: OBJ
                          Space: Model space
            from point, X=      0.0  Y=     50.0  Z=      0.0
              to point, X=     97.0  Y=     50.0  Z=      0.0
        Length =     97.0,  Angle in XY Plane =       0
                 Delta X =    97.0, Delta Y =    0.0, Delta Z =     0.0

                CIRCLE    Layer: OBJ
                          Space: Model space
          center point, X=     27.6  Y=     41.0  Z=      0.0
          radius        5.0
     circumference     31.4
            area       78.5

                DIMENSION  Layer: DIMENSIONS
                          Space: Model space
type: vertical
1st extension  defining point: X=    -13.1  Y=     25.0  Z=      0.0
2nd extension  defining point: X=      0.0  Y=     50.0  Z=      0.0
dimension line defining point: X=    -23.0  Y=     50.0  Z=      0.0
default text position: X=    -23.0  Y=     37.5  Z=      0.0
default text
— Press RETURN for more —
dimension style: NO_TOL
```

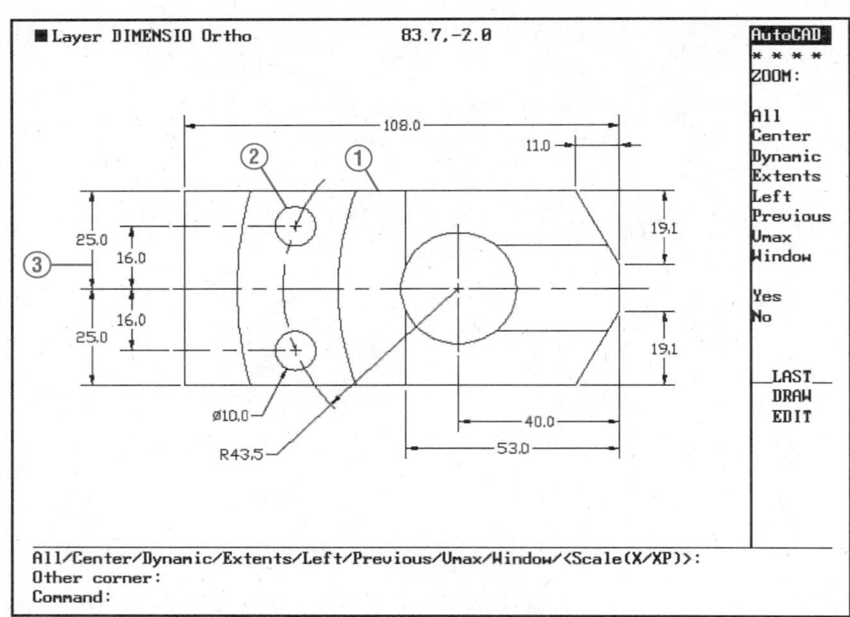

Figure 58.1

Entities selected for LIST.

Notice that the information is different for various types of entities because of the geometric differences between them. There are common data items, however, including layer, linetype, and entity type.

The LIST command is useful for determining the properties of an entity when those properties are not obvious from the entity's appearance. If two layers have been assigned the color red, for example, you cannot be sure which layer is associated with a particular red entity. You can use the LIST command to determine that information.

Another inquiry command, DBLIST, is similar to the LIST command. The difference is that DBLIST lists information about all entities in the drawing. Because the list is generally too lengthy to be useful, the DBLIST command is seldom used.

Modifying Entities

Release 11 and prior releases of AutoCAD relied on the LIST command and on various editing commands to list and edit the properties and geometry of entities. Release 12 offers a Modify dialog box (see fig. 58.2) that enables you to not only retrieve information about entities, but also to edit the entities by changing the entity information displayed in the dialog box. This capability makes editing entities much easier and expands AutoCAD's ability to modify existing entities. The disadvantage of editing with the Modify dialog box is that you can edit only one entity at a time.

Modify Circle
Properties
Color... BYLAYER Layer... OBJ
Linetype... BYLAYER Thickness: 0.0
Center
Pick Point <
X: 27.6
Y: 9.0
Z: 0.0
Radius: 5.0
Diameter: 10.0
Circumference: 31.4
Area: 78.5
Handle: None
OK Cancel Help...

Figure 58.2

An example of the Modify dialog box.

The DDMODIFY command displays the Modify dialog box. The controls that appear in the Modify dialog box change according to the type of entity selected. Some controls simply display a current property or geometry characteristic, but do not give you the option of changing it. Other controls enable you to change the item.

Although you can change the layer assigned to an entity using DDMODIFY, you cannot create new layers or rename existing layers with DDMODIFY. In addition, you cannot assign a linetype using DDMODIFY if the linetype has not yet been loaded.

The following exercise demonstrates the use of DDMODIFY. Use figure 58.3 to define the points.

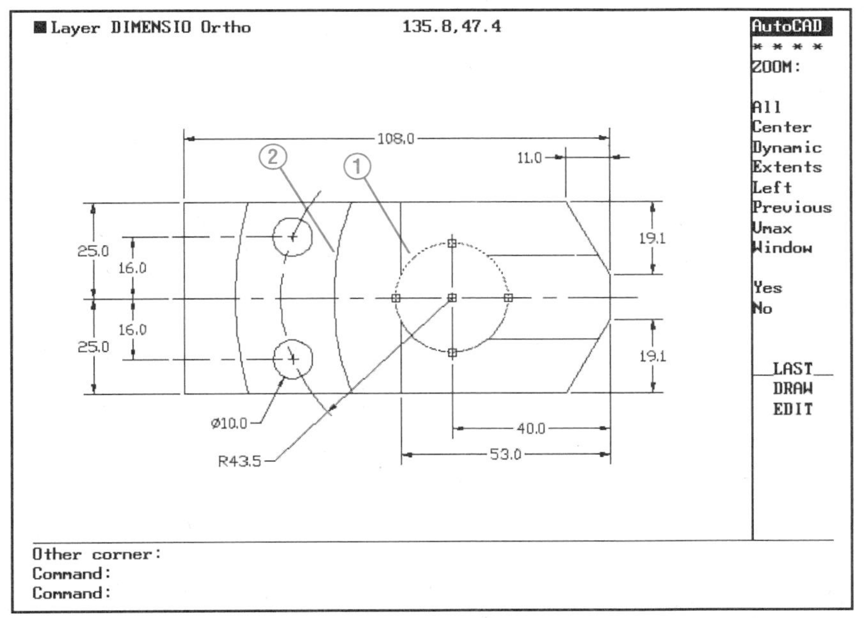

Figure 58.3

Circle to edit.

Using the Modify Entity Dialog Box

Continue with your drawing from the preceding exercise.

1. `Command:` *Select the circle at* ① *(see fig. 58.3)* — Creates a selection set

2. `Command:` *Choose* Modify, *then* Entity — Issues the DDMODIFY command and displays the Modify Circle dialog box (see fig. 58.4)

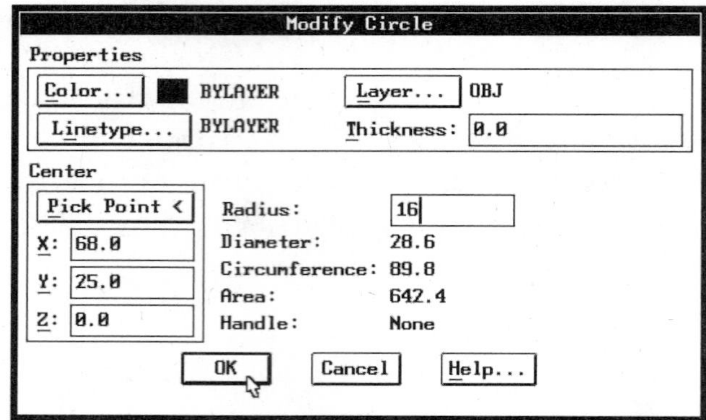

Figure 58.4
The Modify Circle dialog box.

3. *Double-click in the* **R**adius *edit box and enter* **16** — Changes the diameter, circumference, and area information

4. *Choose* OK — Changes the circle's radius

5. `Command:` *Press* Ctrl+C — Clears the selection set

6. `Command:` *Select the arc at* ② *(see fig. 58.3)* — Creates a selection set

7. `Command:` *Choose* Modify, *then* Entity — Issues the DDMODIFY command and displays the Modify Arc dialog box (see fig. 58.5)

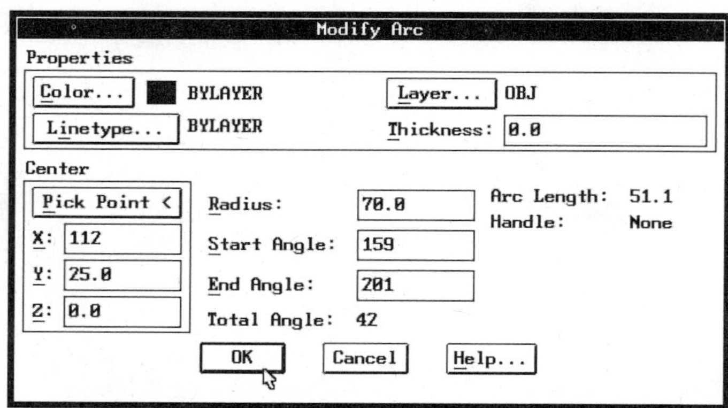

Figure 58.5
The Modify Arc dialog box.

8. *Double-click in the* **X** edit box *and enter* **112**	Changes the X ordinate of the arc's center point
9. *Choose* OK	Relocates the arc (see fig. 58.6)

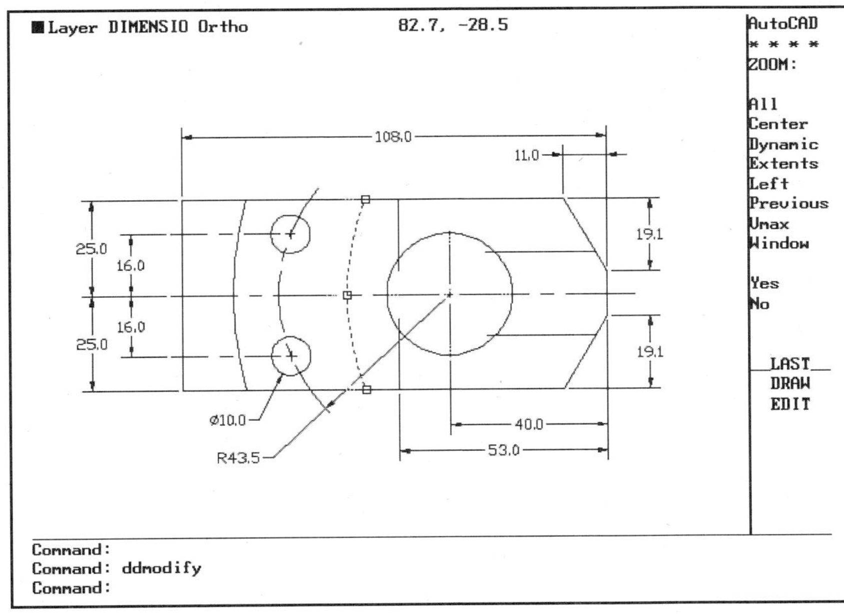

Figure 58.6

Arc relocated with DDMODIFY.

The DDMODIFY command is one of the best methods for modifying entities in a drawing if you need to edit only one entity at a time. Because the properties that can be changed via DDMODIFY vary with each entity type, however, it is not possible to provide examples in this unit of each one. Instead, you now have a basic understanding of how DDMODIFY works. You should be able to use DDMODIFY to edit any entity—just select the entity and then issue the DDMODIFY command. Examine the properties in the dialog box to determine if the change you need to accomplish can be performed using the dialog box. If not, you may have to use autoedit modes or other editing operations to complete the change.

Many of the property and geometry modifications that you can make to an entity with DDMODIFY also can be made using the CHANGE command. CHPROP enables you to change layer, linetype, color, and thickness properties. Neither CHANGE nor CHPROP provides a dialog box, however. All of these commands, including DDMODIFY, work in both paper space and model space.

Unit Review

What You've Learned

- Commands: LIST, DBLIST, DDMODIFY
- How to get information about entity characteristics
- How to get information about entity geometry
- How to edit entity charactistics and geometry with the Modify dialog box

Review Questions

True or False

58.01 T F The LIST command enables you to edit entity properties.

58.02 T F The DDMODIFY (Modify Entity) dialog box will provide information about entity properties and allow you to edit the properties.

58.03 T F The LIST command will only provide information for one entity at a time.

58.04 T F The Modify Entity dialog box performs editing of entity properties that also can be changed with the CHANGE command.

58.05 T F You cannot use the Modify Entity dialog box in paper space.

58.06 T F The Modify Entity dialog box will edit the geometry of entities as well as the properties of entities.

58.07 T F You can make new layer names or rename existing names using Layer button of the Modify Entity dialog box.

Multiple Choice

58.08 The LIST command provides a list for __________ entity(ies) with one execution.

(A) all

(B) one

(C) several

(D) up to 20

Student: ____________ Date: ______
Instructor: ____________ Course: ______ Section: ______

58.09 The Modify Entity dialog box enables you to edit __________ entity(ies) for each execution.

(A) all

(B) one

(C) several

(D) up to 20

58.10 For most entities you can edit __________ using the Modify Entity dialog box.

(A) the layer name

(B) the coordinate location

(C) the size (length, radius, scale, height)

(D) all of the above

Student: ______________________ Date: ______________

Instructor: ____________________ Course: ______________ Section: ______________

PART VII

Organizing a Drawing

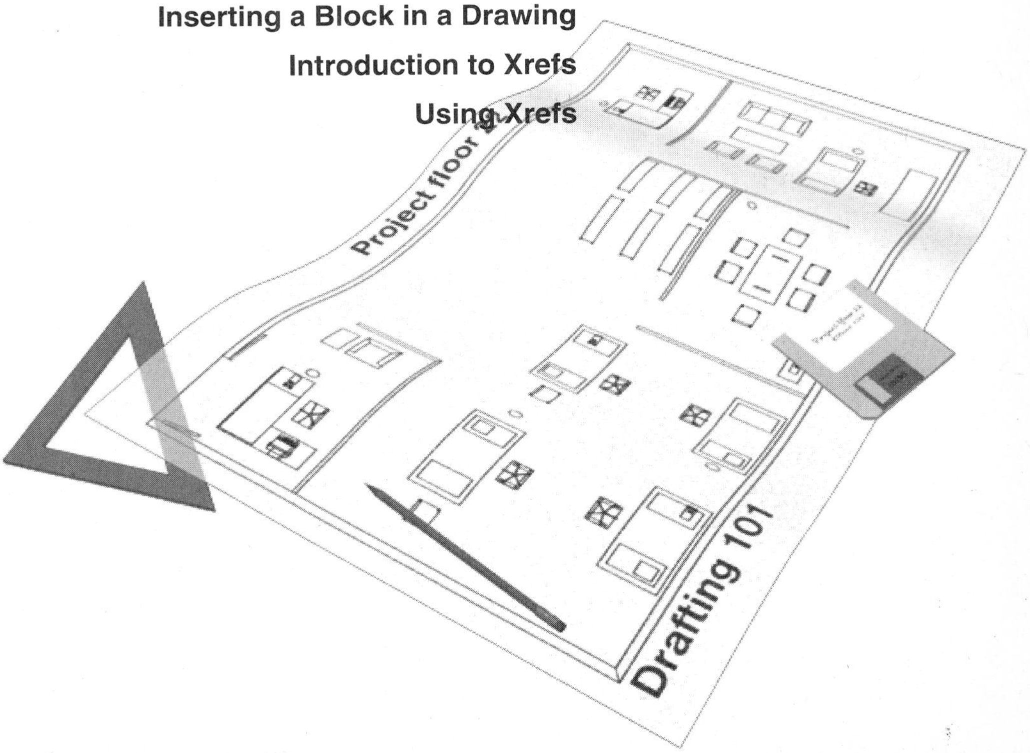

UNIT 59

Introduction to Layers

One important advantage of CAD in comparison to manual drafting techniques is the capability to organize drawing data. AutoCAD provides an infinite number of *layers* or transparent drawing areas on which you can place data. Drawing on layers is like drawing on separate sheets of transparent paper, then overlaying the sheets to form a finished drawing. This unit explains how layers can be helpful in organizing a drawing, and provides an overview of layering in AutoCAD.

This objectives for this unit are to:

- Understand the function of layers
- Recognize how layers provide organization for a drawing
- Identify the characteristics of a layer
- Locate the layer-related commands in AutoCAD's menus

Understanding Layers

The types of information needed to describe a design often cover a broad spectrum. An architectural drawing of a house, for example, may include the outline of the structure, plumbing, electrical, HVAC, landscaping, and other types of information. With manual drafting techniques, you would have to place all of this information on one piece of paper, which is almost impossible.

The many different types of information included in a house design or any other design are related and must be tracked throughout the design process. If a wall is moved, the electrical, plumbing, structural, and HVAC designs often must be changed. If all this information is in one drawing, but is divided into separate overlay drawings that can be viewed together, it is easier to monitor the entire design as changes occur. When all the information is on one drawing, it is also easier to see the effects of a revision on every part of the design. Figure 59.1 illustrates how layers enable you to organize the data on a contour map.

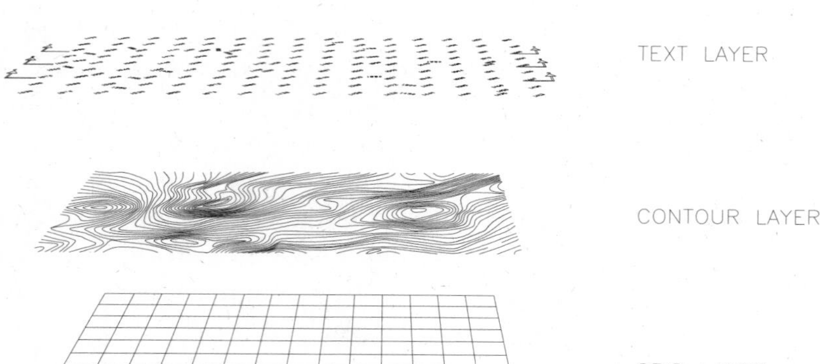

Figure 59.1

Layers enable you to organize different types of information on a drawing.

Understanding AutoCAD's Layers

You can create and use an infinite number of layers in AutoCAD to separate the elements of a design. You can create separate layers for drawing the border, dimensions, notes, text, hidden lines, and object lines. Such a layer structure allows for precise control in display and plotting.

The organization of CAD drawing layers is defined in the drafting standards of a firm. These standards specify the minimum number of layers and the type of information to be placed on each layer. Many firms follow the ANSI Y-14 standards that define CAD layer naming and content when setting up their AutoCAD layering standards.

AutoCAD enables you to control the way layers appear on the display and how they plot. The LAYER command provides options for turning on or off the display of entities on a specific layer. Entities that are displayed are plotted. Each layer of the drawing can also be assigned a pen when plotting. Dashed lines that define hidden planes of a design, for example, can be placed on a layer and plotted with a narrow pen. Object lines can be placed on a layer with the continuous linetype and plotted with a wider pen to make them stand out on the plot.

In addition to controlling pen assignment for layers, you can also turn off the display of layers to decrease the cluttered appearance of a drawing and concentrate on one area of the design. Figures 59.2 and 59.3 display a drawing when the layer containing the hatching is turned on and off.

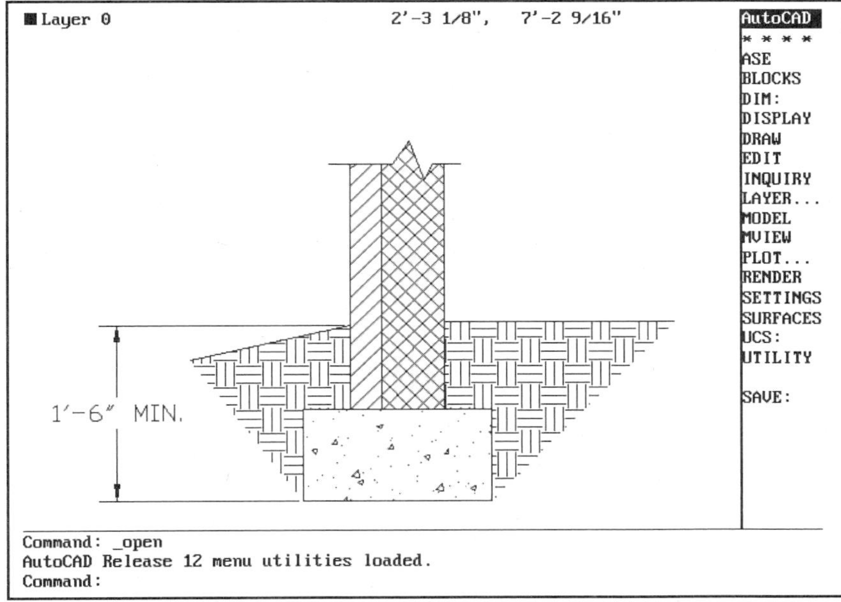

Figure 59.2

A drawing with all layers displayed.

Understanding Layer 0

You can create any number of layers in a drawing. In addition, AutoCAD includes a special layer that is already established when you enter any AutoCAD drawing. AutoCAD assigns the name 0 to this predefined layer. The properties of layer 0 are by default set to On, white color, and continuous linetype; layer 0 may not be renamed or deleted from a drawing. Layer 0 usually is reserved for the creation of blocks; other layers are created for entities other than blocks (Unit 67 introduces blocks). Nevertheless, you can create any entity on layer 0.

The Status line lists the current layer name in the upper left corner of the line. The number zero for layer 0 is displayed when you first enter an AutoCAD drawing. The color of the current layer also is displayed in the box to the left of the current layer name on the status line. Making a different layer active causes the status line to change accordingly.

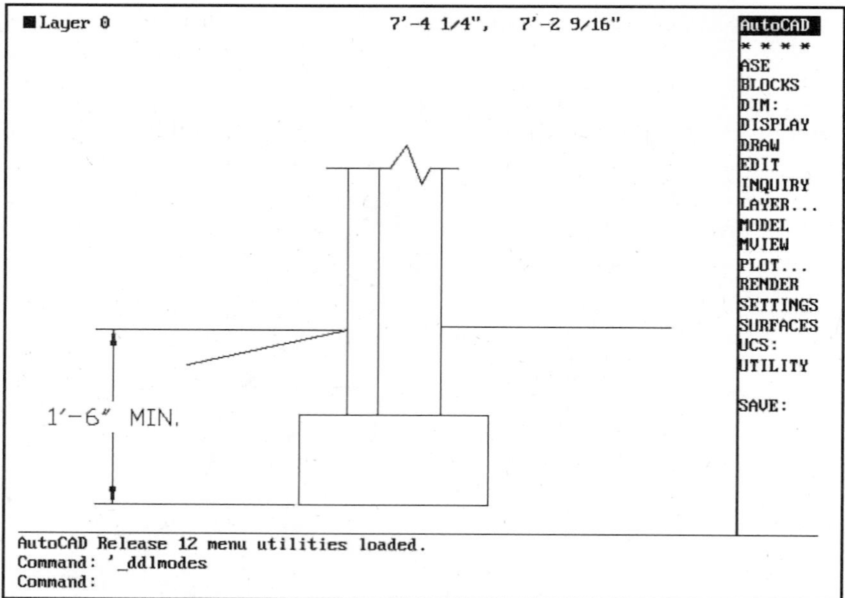

Figure 59.3

The drawing with the layer consisting of hatching turned off.

Locating the LAYER Commands

To control a drawing's layer settings in AutoCAD, choose the Settings pull-down menu, then choose the Layer Control menu item. The Layer Control dialog box then appears. (This dialog box also will appear if you type DDLMODES at the command line.) Figure 59.4 shows the Layer Control dialog box.

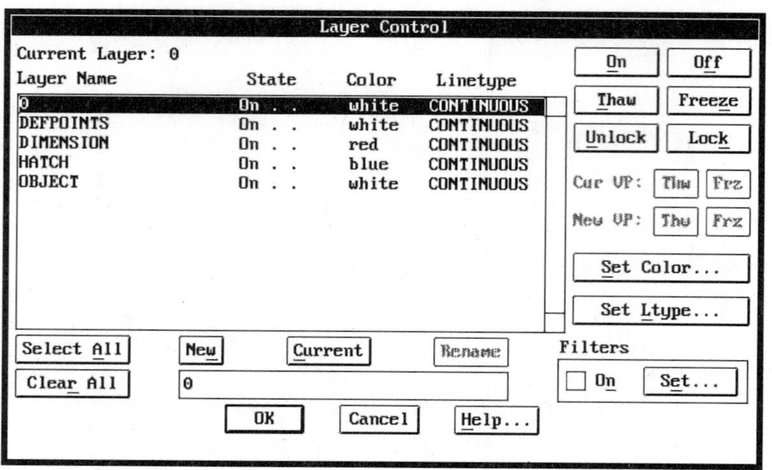

Figure 59.4

The Layer Control dialog box enables you to create and control layers.

The Layer Control dialog box lists all the layers currently defined in the drawing. Each layer has certain *properties* associated with it, which are displayed in the dialog box. Here are the functions of these layer properties:

- **Layer Name.** Specifies the name of the layer.
- **State.** Specifies whether the layer is on, locked, or frozen. These states are explained later in this unit.
- **Color.** Specifies the color assigned to the layer. Any entities drawn on the specified layer will display with the assigned color, unless an explicit entity color is used to override the layer color. AutoCAD has 256-color capability.
- **Linetype.** Specifies the default linetype assigned to the layer. Any entities drawn on the specified layer will display with the assigned linetype, unless an explicit linetype is used to override the layer linetype. Linetypes must first be loaded before they can be assigned to a layer or layers.

The state of a layer determines whether entities on the layer are visible and if they may be edited. These properties are indicated in the State column. Figure 59.5 shows layers with various states indicated in the State column.

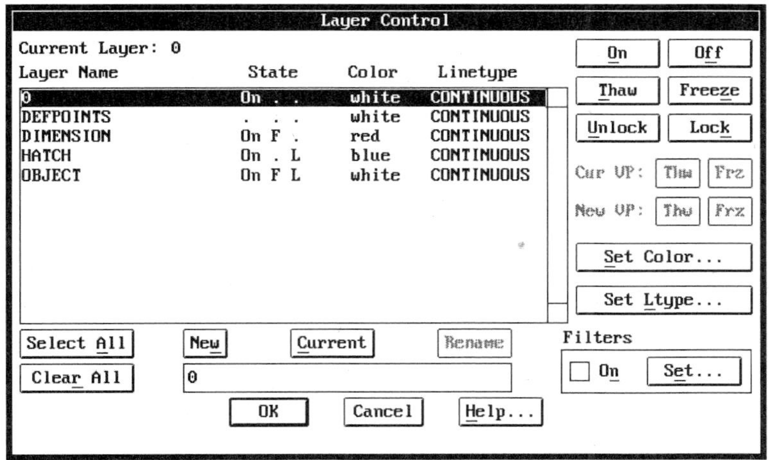

Figure 59.5
Layer Control dialog box indicating property changes in the State column.

The effects of these states on the layers and on the entities associated with a layer are discussed later in this unit and in following units.

The Layer Control dialog box includes a number of controls that let you choose layers and change their properties. Most of these controls are explained in units 60, 61, and 62. Some are explained a little later in this unit.

Using the LAYER Command

In addition to using the Layer Control dialog box, you also can use the LAYER command directly.When the LAYER command is chosen from the root screen menu or `LAYER` is entered at the `Command:` prompt, the LAYER command starts and displays the following prompt:

```
?/Make/Set/New/ON/OFF/Color/Ltype/Freeze/Thaw/LOck/Unlock:
```

These options are used to control the display and properties of entities drawn on each of the drawing's layers. The LAYER command options correspond to the properties and controls in the Layer Control dialog box, which include:

- **?.** AutoCAD prompts you for a name-matching pattern, then displays a list of the name, state, color, and linetype of all defined layers that match your specified pattern. AutoCAD switches to the text screen to display the list.
- **Make.** AutoCAD prompts you for a new layer name, then creates the new layer and makes it current.
- **Set.** AutoCAD prompts you for the layer to make current, then sets the specified layer as the current layer.
- **New.** AutoCAD prompts you for the name(s) of new layers to create; enter multiple new layer names by separating the names with commas.
- **ON.** AutoCAD prompts you for the name(s) of layers to turn on. Entities appear on the display only if their associated layers are turned on.
- **OFF.** AutoCAD prompts you for the name(s) of layers to turn off. Entities do not appear on the display if their associated layers are turned off. Turning layers off does not prevent them from being regenerated.
- **Color.** AutoCAD prompts you for the color to assign to a specific layer; entities drawn on the selected layer will display with the specified color.
- **Ltype.** AutoCAD prompts you for the linetype to assign to a specific layer; entities drawn on the selected layer will display with the specified linetype.
- **Freeze.** AutoCAD prompts you for the name(s) of layers to freeze. Entities on a frozen layer are not regenerated with the REGEN command. Entities on layers that are frozen also do not display.
- **Thaw.** AutoCAD prompts you for the name(s) of layers to thaw. This is the opposite of the Freeze option.

☞ **LOck.** AutoCAD prompts you for the name(s) of layers to lock. Entities on locked layers remain visible but cannot be edited.

☞ **Unlock.** AutoCAD prompts you for the name(s) of layers to unlock. Unlocking a layer allows you to edit entities on the unlocked layer.

Controlling Layers

As you work on a drawing that uses multiple layers, you will perform a number of tasks to control the way the layers appear, which layer is active, and so on. A common task is to specify the current layer.

Specifying the Current Layer

When you are working on a drawing, the current layer is the one on which entities are drawn. If you want to place entities on a layer that is not current, you first must make the layer current, then draw the entities. In the next exercise, experiment with setting a current layer.

Working with the Current Layer

1. Begin a new drawing named 059???01 in your assigned directory, using 059LAYER as the prototype. Note that the status line indicates that layer 0 is the current layer.

2. `Command:` *Choose* Settings, *then* Layer Control — Displays the Layer Control dialog box (see fig. 59.6)

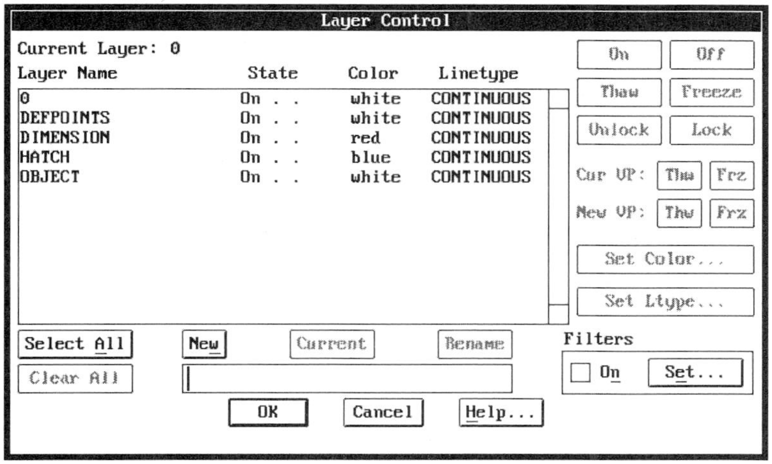

Figure 59.6

The Layer Control dialog box with layers shown.

3. *In the Layer Control dialog box, choose the* HATCH *layer, choose the* Current *button, then choose* OK. — Sets layer HATCH as the current layer

Notice that the status line now indicates that the HATCH layer is current.

You also can set a layer current using the LAYER command. Enter **LAYER** *at the* `Command:` *prompt, enter* **S** *for the Set option, then enter the name of the layer to make current.*

Turning Layers On and Off

It is often necessary to turn off or freeze layers to decrease the clutter of the drawing. Layers may be turned off to hide dimensions, hatching, or other aspects of the design. Layers that are turned off are not plotted. The next exercise introduces you to turning layers on and off.

Controlling Layer Display

Continue with your drawing from the previous exercise.

1. `Command:` *Choose* Settings, *then* Layer Control	Displays the Layer Control dialog box
2. *In the* Layer Control *dialog box, click on the* DIMENSION *layer, then choose the* Off *button, then choose* OK	Turns off the DIMENSION layer and redisplays the drawing

Your drawing should look similar to figure 59.7.

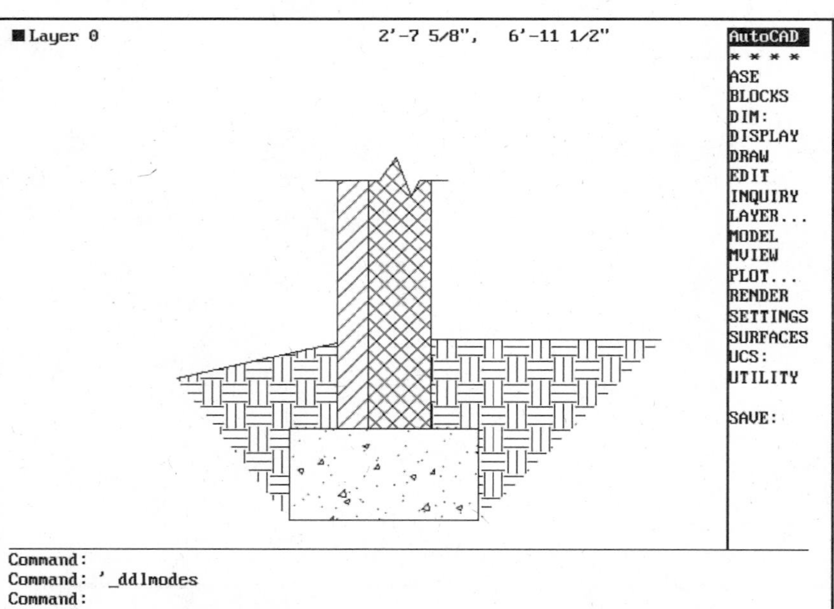

Figure 59.7
The dimension layer disappears when it is turned off.

Next, try using the DDLMODES command instead of using the pull-down menu to open the Layer Control dialog box.

3. Command: DDLMODES	Displays the Layer Control dialog box
4. *In the* Layer Control *dialog box, click on the* DIMENSION *layer, then choose the* On *button, then choose* OK	Turns on the DIMENSION layer and redisplays the drawing

If you attempt to turn off the current layer, AutoCAD displays an error message (see fig. 59.8). Although you can turn off the current layer, you will not be able to see any entities already on it or any new entities that you add to it until you turn on the layer again. In general, there is no reason to turn off the current layer. Any layer can be turned off, including layer 0.

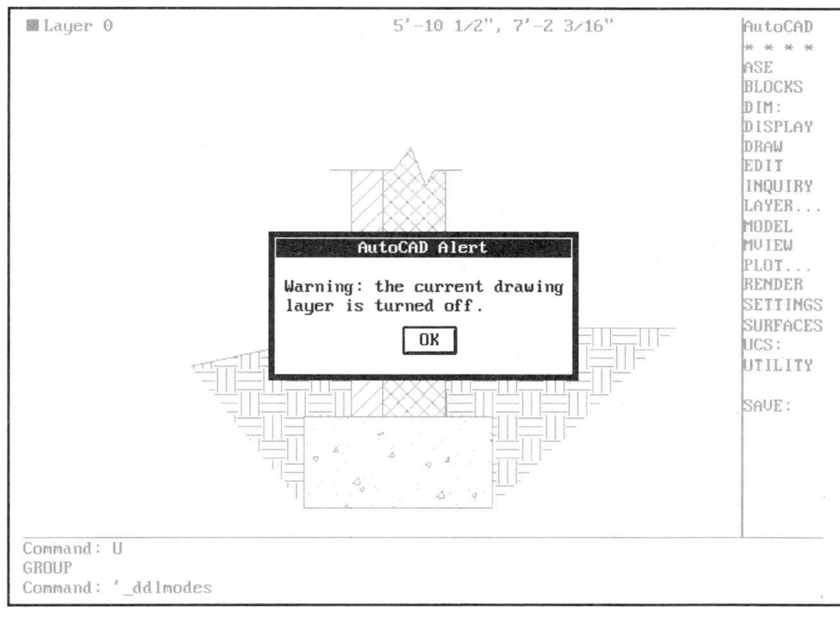

Figure 59.8
AutoCAD generates a warning when you attempt to turn off the current layer.

Freezing a Layer

A frozen layer is much like a layer that is turned off—you cannot see either type of layer. When a layer is turned off, it still regenerates during a drawing regeneration even though it isn't visible. Frozen layers also are not visible. Freezing one or more layers in a complex drawing is a good way to speed up regeneration time. You cannot freeze the current layer.

The Off and Thaw options of the LAYER command also control the way the drawing plots. Any layers that are turned off or frozen do not plot.

Unit Review

What You've Learned

- How you can use layers to organize the data in a drawing
- How to use the Layer Control dialog box to specify the current layer
- How to control layer visibility by turning layers on and off
- The effect of freezing a layer versus turning the layer off

Review Questions

True or False

59.01 T F You must create layer 0 in each drawing when you first begin working on the drawing.

59.02 T F You cannot freeze the current layer.

59.03 T F The DDLMODES command can be used to display the Layer Control dialog box.

59.04 T F The LAYER command includes an option that enables you to list all of the layers in the drawing.

59.05 T F Company standards often define the number and names of layers in a drawing.

Multiple Choice

59.06 Which of the following actions makes the data on a layer disappear from the display?

(A) Freeze

(B) Off

(C) Lock

(D) Either A or B

59.07 Which layer option eliminates the regeneration of entities on a layer?

(A) On

(B) Thaw

(C) Freeze

(D) Off

Student: ______________________ Date: __________

Instructor: ______________________ Course: __________ Section: __________

59.08 A layer will not be plotted if it is:

(A) on

(B) off

(C) thawed

(D) none of the above

59.09 Which of the following is not a layer state?

(A) Off

(B) Frozen

(C) Hidden

(D) Locked

59.10 The current layer is displayed:

(A) in the status line

(B) in the Layer Control dialog box

(C) in the `Command:` prompt

(D) both A and B

Applying the AutoCAD Environment

59.11 Answer the following questions based on the Layer Control dialog box shown in figure 59.9.

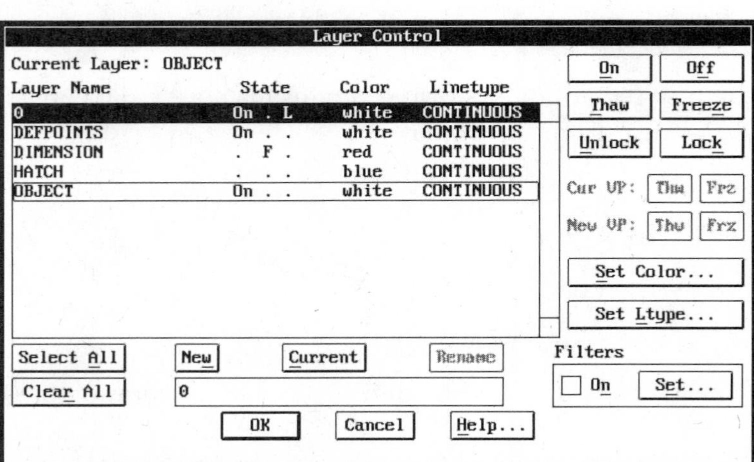

Figure 59.9
The AutoCAD Layer Control dialog box.

1. Name the layer that is current.

____

Student: ______ Date: ______

Instructor: ______ Course: ______ Section: ______

2. List the layers that are frozen.

____

____

____

3. List the layers that are unlocked.

____

____

____

4. List the layers that are off.

____

____

____

5. What procedure would you perform to turn on all layers?

____

____

____

Student: ______________ Date: ______

Instructor: ______________ Course: ______ Section: ______

UNIT 60

Creating Layers

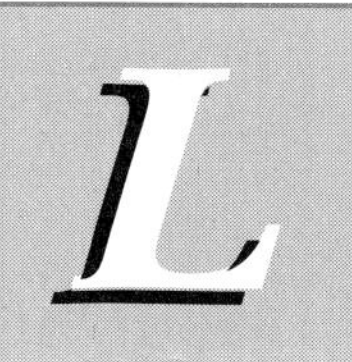

Layers enable you to organize a drawing according to linetype, color, or design disciplines. This unit teaches you to create your own layers in AutoCAD and to assign color and linetype settings to the new layers.

The objectives for this unit are to:

- Create a new layer
- Make a layer current
- Establish the color and linetype for a layer

Creating a New Layer

By default, each new drawing you begin in AutoCAD contains a single layer named 0. You also can create a nearly unlimited number of your own layers. You can create a layer using the LAYER command, but the easiest method is to use the Layer Control dialog box, which was introduced in Unit 59. In the following exercise, use the Layer Control dialog box to create a layer named HIDDEN.

Creating a New Layer

1. Begin a new drawing named 060???01, using 060LAYER as the prototype.

2. `Command:` *Choose* Settings, *then* Layer Control	Displays the Layer Control dialog box
3. *In the edit box above the* OK *button, type* **`HIDDEN`**, *then choose the* New *button*	Creates a new layer named HIDDEN and displays its name in the layer list (see fig.60.1)
4. *Choose* OK	Closes the Layer Control dialog box

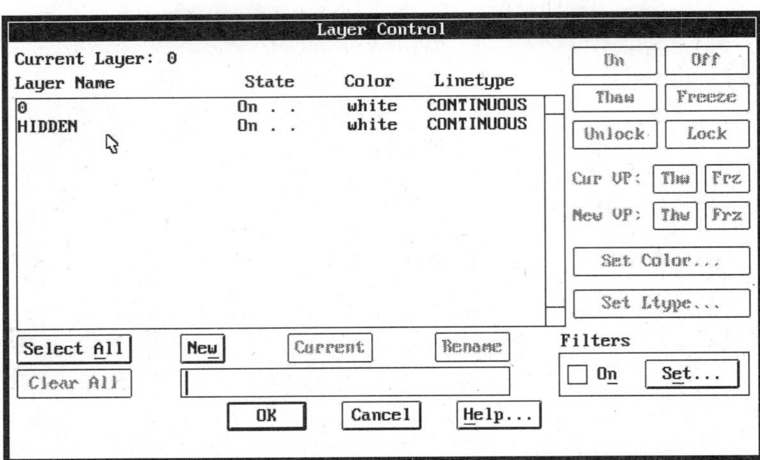

Figure 60.1

HIDDEN layer created in the Layer Control dialog box.

Layer names can consist of 31 characters, including letters, numbers, hyphens, underscores, and special characters. No spaces are permitted within the layer name. Use an underscore to provide the appearance of space in the layer name, such as FLOOR_PLAN (see fig. 60.2).

In addition to using the Layer Control dialog box to create a layer, you also can use the LAYER command to create layers. Create a layer named PLUMBING in the next exercise, using the LAYER command instead of the Layer Control dialog box.

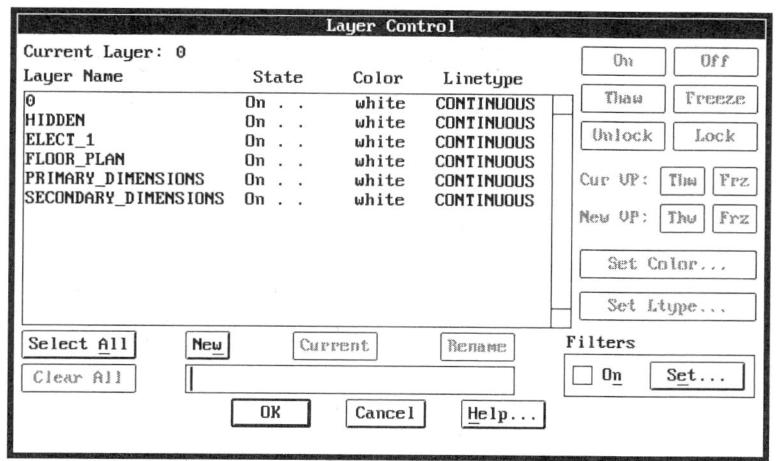

Figure 60.2

Examples of layer names.

Using LAYER To Create a Layer Named PLUMBING

Continue with your drawing from the previous exercise.

1. `Command:` **`LAYER`** ↵ — Starts the LAYER command
2. `?/Make/Set/New/ON/OFF/Color/Ltype/Freeze/Thaw/LOck/Unlock:` **`N`** ↵ — Specifies New option to create a new layer
3. `New layer name(s):` **`PLUMBING`** ↵ — Specifies new layer name
4. `?/Make/Set/New/ON/OFF/Color/Ltype/Freeze/Thaw/LOck/Unlock:` *Press* Enter

In the previous exercise, you did not make layer PLUMBING current. When you return to the drawing editor, the status line still lists layer 0 as the current layer. In addition, you created only one layer. If you need to create more than one layer, you can create them all at the same time.

Creating Multiple Layers

In addition to creating a single layer, you also can create multiple layers at one time. The use of multiple commas enables you to enter multiple layer names. In the following exercise, use the Layer Control dialog box to create four new layers.

Creating Multiple Layers

Continue with your drawing from the previous exercise.

1. `Command:` *Choose* Settings, *then* Layer Control — Displays the Layer Control dialog box

continues

2. *Type* **MECH_1,MECH_2,ELECT,HVAC**, *then choose the* New *button* — Creates four new layers and displays them in the layer list box (see fig 60.3)

3. *Choose* OK — Closes the Layer Control dialog box

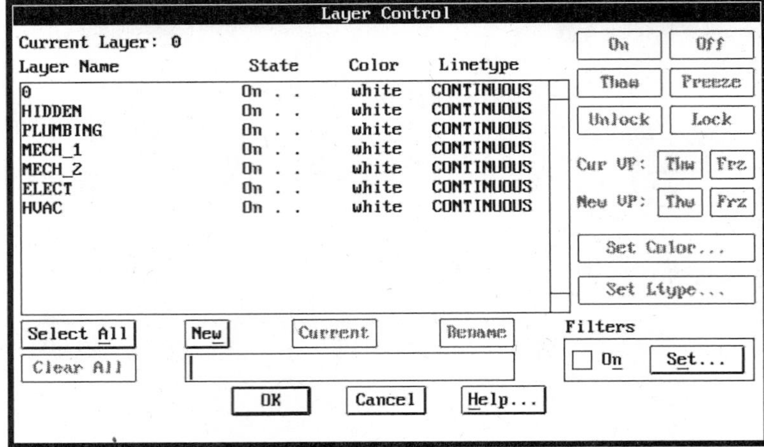

Figure 60.3

Multiple layers added to the drawing.

If you use the LAYER command to create new layers, you can enter multiple layer names, separated by commas, just as you can in the Layer Control dialog box.

Making a Layer Current

To draw entities on a specific layer, you must make the layer the *current layer.* You can make a layer current when you create the layer, or you can use the Layer Control dialog box at any time to make a specific layer current. In the following exercise, make the layer HIDDEN current.

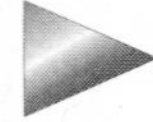

Making a Layer Current

Continue with your drawing from the previous exercise.

1. `Command:` *Choose* Settings, *then* Layer Control

2. *Choose the layer named* HIDDEN *from the layer list* — Highlights the layer name

3. *Choose the* Current *button* — Makes HIDDEN the current layer (see fig. 60.4)

4. *Choose* OK — Returns to the drawing editor and displays HIDDEN as the current layer in the status line

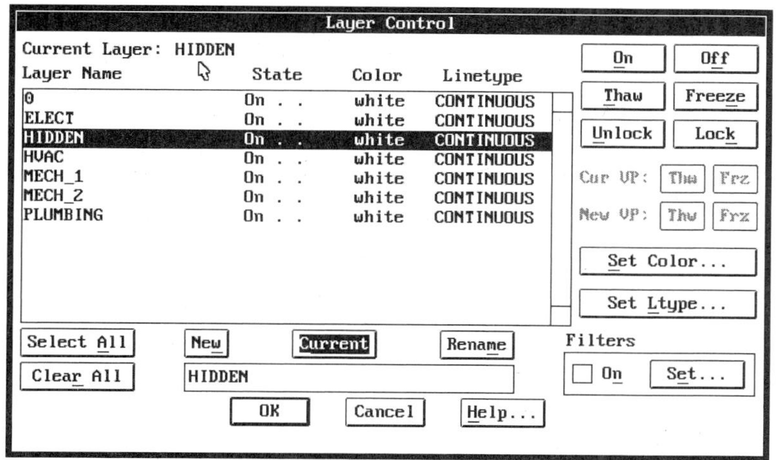

Figure 60.4

The layer named hidden is the current layer.

The LAYER command can also be used to make a layer the current layer. The Set and Make options of the LAYER command set the layer you specify as the current layer. If you use the Set option, the layer must already exist before you try to make it the current layer. If you use the Make option, AutoCAD creates the layer and makes it the current layer.

In the following exercise, use the Make option of the LAYER command to create a layer and make it current.

Using Make To Create and Set a Layer Current

Continue with your drawing from the previous exercise.

1. `Command:` **`LAYER`** ↵	Starts the LAYER command
2. `?/Make/Set/New/ON/OFF/Color/Ltype /Freeze/Thaw/LOck/Unlock:` **`M`** ↵	Chooses the Make option
3. `New current layer <Hidden>:` **`ELECT_2`** ↵	Specifies the name of the new layer
4. `?/Make/Set/New/ON/OFF/Color/Ltype/ Freeze/Thaw/LOck/Unlock:` *Press* Enter	Ends the LAYER command

The status line now indicates that ELECT_2 is the current layer (see fig. 60.5).

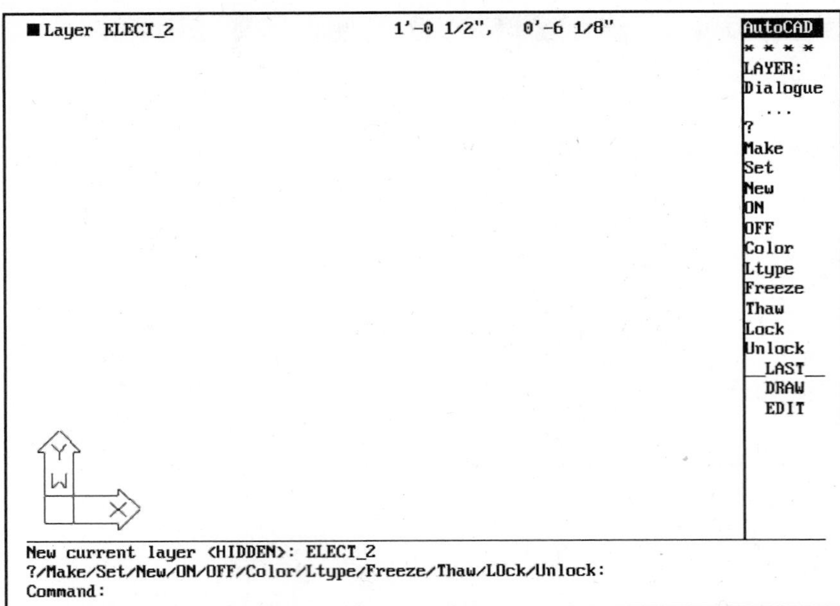

Figure 60.5
The status line indicates that ELECT_2 is the current layer.

You can use the CLAYER command to quickly set the current layer. The CLAYER command's only function is to set the current layer; therefore, the layer must already exist before you try to make it current. Simply enter **CLAYER** *at the* `Command:` *prompt, then enter the name of the layer that you want to make current.*

Controlling Layer Characteristics

Each layer has a color and linetype associated with it. You can draw entities on a specific layer and have those entities automatically assume the color and linetype assigned to that layer. Assigning different colors and linetypes to layers enables you to identify quickly which entities are drawn on which layers. Layers identified by color also help organize visually a drawing's information.

These benefits make the process of setting color and linetype an important part of a drawing. Units 64 and 65 explain the use of linetypes and color in more detail. This unit explains how to assign a specific color and linetype to a layer.

Setting Layer Color

As with all layer options, you can specify linetype and color using either the LAYER command or the Layer Control dialog box. Although you can set the color one layer at a time, you can select multiple layers and assign colors to them with a single color selection. In the next exercise, make a selection of layers red.

Setting Layer Color

Continue with your drawing from the previous exercise.

1. `Command:` *Choose* Settings, *then* Layer Control	Opens the Layer Control dialog box
2. *Choose* PLUMBING *in the layer list*	Highlights the PLUMBING layer
3. *Choose* MECH_1 *in the layer list*	Highlights the MECH_1 layer
4. *Choose* HVAC *in the layer list*	Highlights the HVAC layer
5. *Choose* MECH_2 *in the layer list*	Highlights the MECH_2 layer
6. *Choose* HVAC *in the layer list*	De-selects the HVAC layer
7. *Choose the* **S**et Color *button*	Displays the Select Color dialog box (see fig. 60.6)

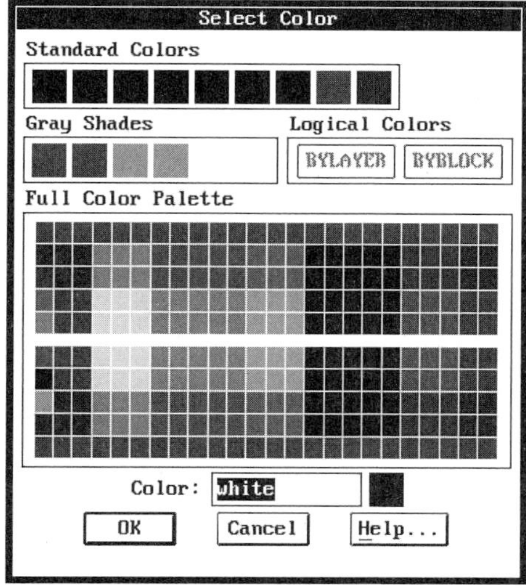

Figure 60.6

The Select Color dialog box.

8. *Click on the red square in the* Standard Colors *group, then choose* OK	Assigns the color red to the layer and changes the color description in the Layer Control dialog box (see fig. 60.7)
9. `Command:` *Choose* File, *then* Save	Saves your drawing

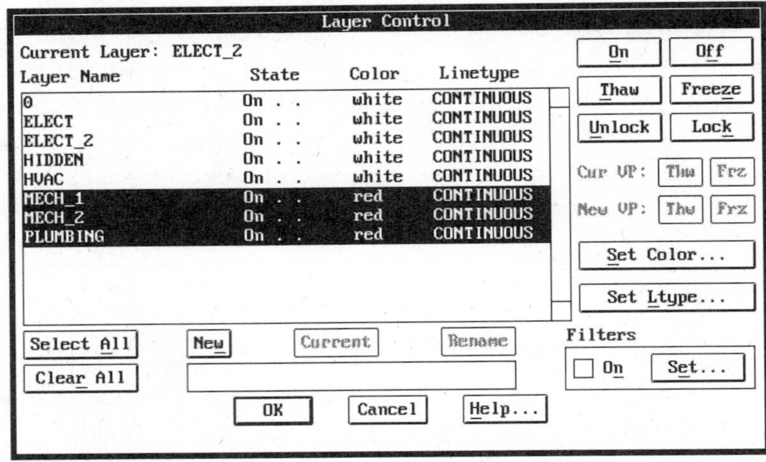

Figure 60.7

The color red assigned to the selected layers.

As you can see from the previous exercise, you can select multiple layers and then set options for all the selected layers with a single command. To de-select a layer, simply select it again after it is highlighted.

In addition to using the Layer Control dialog box to specify a layer's color, you also can use the Color option of the LAYER command to specify its color.

Using Color Numbers

Each color in AutoCAD has a color number associated with it. If you prefer, you can specify the color number in the Select Color dialog box instead of typing the color. You also can specify a color number instead of a color when setting layer color using the Color option of the LAYER command. Table 60.1 lists the color numbers for the first seven AutoCAD colors.

Table 60.1
Standard AutoCAD Color Numbers

Color Number	Color Name
1	Red
2	Yellow
3	Green

Color Number	Color Name
4	Cyan
5	Blue
6	Magenta
7	White

AutoCAD can display up to 256 colors on a system equipped with a video adapter and monitor that is capable of displaying 256 colors.

Setting a Layer's Linetype

Before you can assign a specific linetype to a layer, the linetype must be *loaded* into AutoCAD. After a linetype has been loaded into a drawing and the drawing has been saved, the linetype will be available any time you edit the drawing (Units 63 and 64 explain the use of linetypes in more detail). In the following exercise, use the LINETYPE command to load the linetype HIDDEN into your drawing.

Loading a Linetype

Continue with your drawing from the previous exercise.

1. `Command:` *From the* SETTINGS *screen menu, choose* LINETYP: `'_LINETYPE`	Starts the LINETYPE command
2. `?/Create/Load/Set:` *From the screen menu, choose* Load `_LOAD`	Specifies the Load option
3. `Linetypes to Load:` **`HIDDEN`** ↵	Specifies the name of the linetype to be loaded and displays the Select Linetype File dialog box (see fig. 60.8)
4. *With the file* ACAD *highlighted, choose* OK `Linetype HIDDEN loaded.`	Loads the linetype HIDDEN from the linetype file ACAD.LIN
5. `?/Create/Load/Set:?` *Press* Enter	Ends the LINETYPE command

Figure 60.8

The Select Linetype File dialog box.

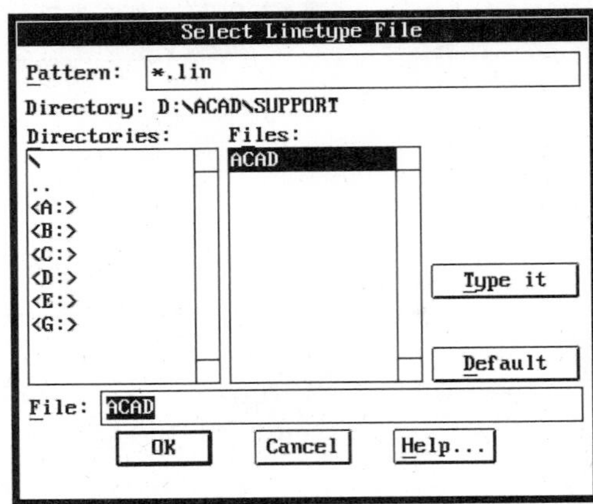

Next, open the Layer Control dialog box and assign the HIDDEN linetype to the HIDDEN layer.

Assigning a Linetype to a Layer

1. `Command:` *Choose* Settings, *then* Layer Control
   Displays the Layer Control dialog box
2. *Choose the* HIDDEN *layer in the layer list, then choose the* Set Ltype *button*
   Selects the HIDDEN layer and displays the Select Linetype dialog box (see fig. 60.9)
3. *Choose* HIDDEN *from the list of linetypes, then choose* OK
   Assigns the linetype HIDDEN to layer HIDDEN
4. `Command:` *Choose* File, *then* Save
   Saves the drawing

Figure 60.9

The Select Linetype dialog box.

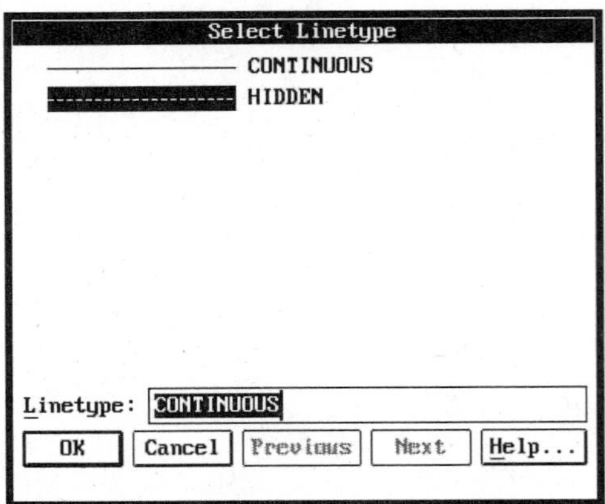

Unit Review

What You've Learned

- How to create and name a layer
- How to make a layer current
- How to specify the color and linetype for a layer
- How to select multiple layers in the Layer Control dialog box and set options for a selection of layers

Review Questions

True or False

60.01 T F The underscore may not be used in the name of a layer.

60.02 T F Color of a layer can be specified by number.

60.03 T F Linetypes other than CONTINUOUS are loaded into a drawing by the LAYER command.

60.04 T F A layer must be current to set its color and linetype.

60.05 T F You can use the Set option of the LAYER command to set the current layer.

60.06 T F You can create multiple layers at one time with the Layer Control dialog box.

60.07 T F A linetype must be loaded into the drawing before you can assign it to a layer.

Short Answer

60.08 List the seven standard color numbers and the name of the color.

____

____

____

60.09 Describe how you can create multiple layers quickly using the LAYER command.

____

____

____

Student: ______________________________ Date: ____________

Instructor: ______________________________ Course: __________ Section: __________

60.10 Describe how you can create multiple layers quickly using the Layer Control dialog box.

____

____

____

Student: ______________________ Date: __________

Instructor: ______________ Course: ________ Section: ______

UNIT 61

Drawing Entities on a Specific Layer

The process of creating layers and setting their characteristics is only the first step in using them in your work. The next step is to begin placing various portions of your drawing on different layers. You can place entities on a layer when you first draw the entities, or you can edit existing entities and change their layers. This unit explains how to draw entities on a specific layer. Unit 66 explains how to change the layer associated with an existing entity.

The objectives for this unit are to:

- Understand how entities are associated with different layers
- Draw entities on specific layers

In the exercises in this unit, you begin a drawing of a gasket. You will create separate layers according to the function of the part, including layers for the layout of the center lines, bolt holes, water circulation holes and the head for which the gasket is being designed. You will create the basic layer structure and geometry of the part in this unit and complete the drawing in future units.

To draw entities on a layer you must create the layer and set the layer current. Once the layer is set current any entity drawn will be placed on the current layer and will normally assume the color and linetype of the current layer. In later units you will learn to draw entities with linetype and color settings different from those of the layer on which the entity is drawn.

In the following exercise, create the layers for your gasket drawing and set their linetype and color characteristics.

Creating Layers for the Gasket Drawing

1. Begin a new drawing named 061???01 in your assigned directory, using the file 061GASKT as a prototype. Verify that SNAP is set to .0625 and GRID is set to .5 in your new drawing.

2. `Command:` *Choose* Settings, *then* Layer Control — Displays the Layer Control dialog box

   `'ddlmodes`

3. *In the edit box above the* OK *button, type* **`BOLT,WATER,GASKET,CENTER,BORDER,DIM,HEAD`** — Specifies layer names

4. *Choose the* New *button* — Creates the layers and displays them in the layer list (see fig. 61.1)

5. *Choose* OK — Closes the Layer Control dialog box

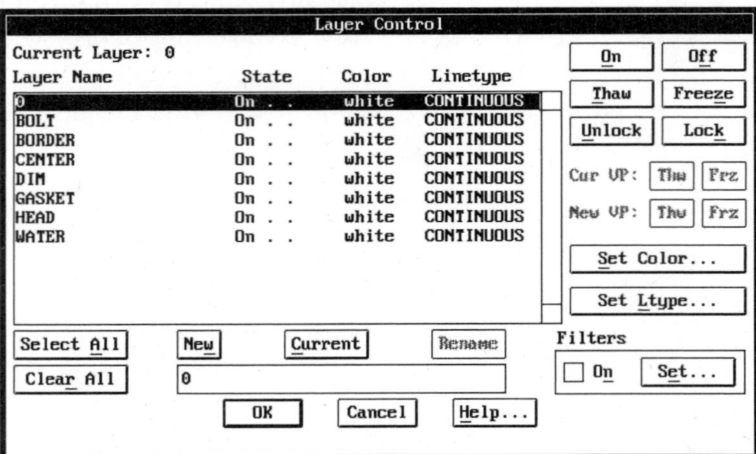

Figure 61.1
New layers in the Layer Control dialog box.

Next, set the color and linetype characteristics for the layers you just created. As you work through the following exercises and create entities on different layers, the layer color and linetype assignments will help you verify visually that the entities have been drawn on the correct layers. Before you set the linetype for layer CENTER, however, you must load the CENTER linetype.

Setting Layer Characteristics for the Gasket Drawing

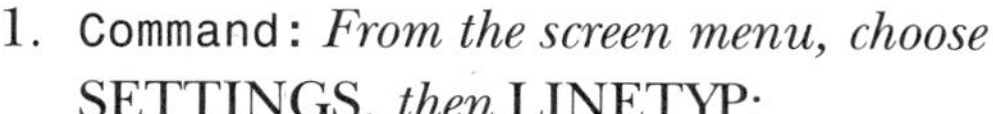

1. `Command:` *From the screen menu, choose* SETTINGS, *then* LINETYP: — Starts the LINETYPE command

   `'_LINETYPE`

2. `?/Create/Load/Set:` *From the screen menu, choose* Load — Chooses the Load option

3. `Linetype(s) to load:` **`CENTER`** ↵ — Specifies linetype to load and displays the Select Linetype File dialog box

4. *In the* Select Linetype File *dialog box, choose* ACAD, *then choose* OK — AutoCAD loads the linetype CENTER from the file ACAD.LIN

   `Linetype CENTER loaded.`

5. `?/Create/Load/Set:` *Press* Enter

6. `Command:` *Choose* Settings, *then* LAYER Control, *and use the* Set Color *and* Set Ltype *buttons to specify the layer settings shown in table 61.1 and in figure 61.2* — Sets the linetype and colors for the layers

Table 61.1
Layer Settings for the Gasket Drawing

Layer Name	Color	Linetype
0	white	CONTINUOUS
BOLT	red	CONTINUOUS
BORDER	cyan	CONTINUOUS
CENTER	green	CENTER
DIM	yellow	CONTINUOUS
GASKET	white	CONTINUOUS
HEAD	blue	CONTINUOUS
WATER	magenta	CONTINUOUS

7. *After you have specified the correct color and linetype settings, choose the* OK *button in the* Layer Control *dialog box* — Closes the Layer Control dialog box and returns to the drawing

8. `Command:` *Choose* File, *then* Save — Saves the drawing

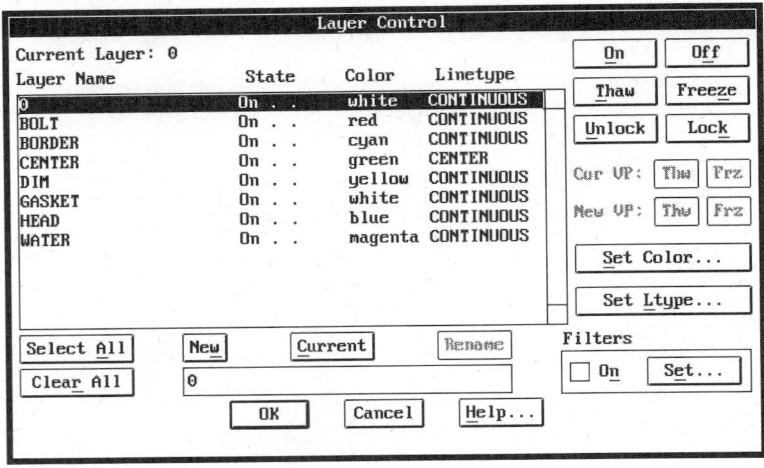

Figure 61.2

Layer settings for the gasket drawing

To begin drawing the gasket, make the layer HEAD current. In the next exercise, draw some of the entities for the outline of the head.

Drawing Entities on a Layer

1. `Command:` **`CLAYER`** ↵	Starts the CLAYER command
2. `New value for CLAYER <"0">:` **`HEAD`** ↵	Sets the layer HEAD current
3. `Command:` *Choose* Draw, *then* Line, *then* Segments	Starts the LINE command
4. `_line From point:` **`2,3`** ↵	Begins horizontal line
5. `To point:` **`@4,0`** ↵	Ends horizontal line
6. `To point:` **`@0,4`** ↵	Ends vertical line
7. `To point:` *Press* Enter	Ends LINE command

To illustrate that the OFFSET command copies the layer settings from the entities you offset, make WATER the current layer.

8. `Command:` *Choose* Settings, *then* Layer Control	
9. *In the* Layer Control *dialog box, choose the* WATER *layer, then choose the* Current *button, then choose* OK	Makes WATER the current layer and returns to the drawing editor
10. `Command:` *Choose* Construct, *then* Offset `_offset`	Starts the OFFSET command
11. `Offset distance or Through <Through>:` **`4`** ↵	Sets offset distance to 4

12. `Select object to offset:` *Select the horizontal line at ① (see fig. 61.3)*	Selects line to offset
13. `Side to offset?` *Pick a point above the line at ②*	Determines direction of offset
14. `Select object to offset:` *Select the vertical line at ③*	Selects vertical line to offest
15. `Side to offset?` *Pick a point to the left of the line at ④*	Determines direction of offset
16. `Select object to offset:` *Press* Enter	Ends OFFSET command
17. `Command:` *Choose* File, *then* Save	

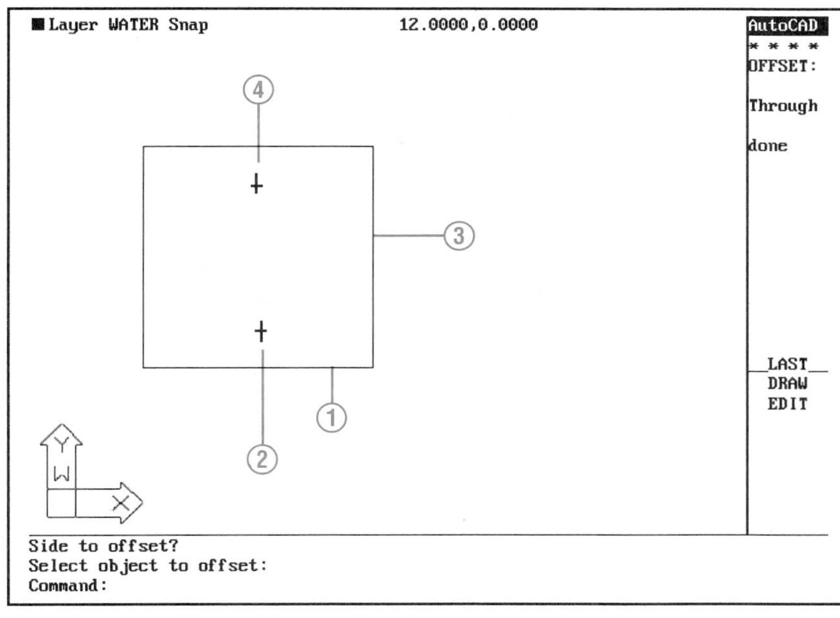

Figure 61.3

Horizontal line of the head to offset.

Copying to Different Layers

Even though WATER was the current layer when you offset the lines, the lines were drawn on the HEAD layer. The OFFSET command (and the COPY command) copy entities onto the same layer as the original entities from which they were created. To copy or offset entities onto a different layer, perform the copy or offset, then modify the layer setting of the newly created entities. Unit 66 explains how to change an entity's properties.

Next, use the FILLET command to fillet the corners of the head outline. Switch back to layer HEAD before continuing to draw.

Editing Entities on the HEAD Layer

1. `Command:` **`CLAYER`** ↵
2. `New value for CLAYER <"WATER">:` **`HEAD`** ↵ — Makes HEAD the current layer
3. `Command:` *Choose* Construct, *then* Fillet — Chooses FILLET command

   `_fillet Polyline/Radius/`
4. `<Select first object>:` *From the screen menu, choose* radius — Selects Radius option
5. `Enter fillet radius <0.0000>:` **`.125`** ↵ — Specifies radius
6. `Polyline/Radius/<Select first object>:` *Fillet all the corners of the square head outline (see fig. 61.4)* — Selects line to fillet
7. `Command:` *Choose* File, *then* Save — Saves the drawing

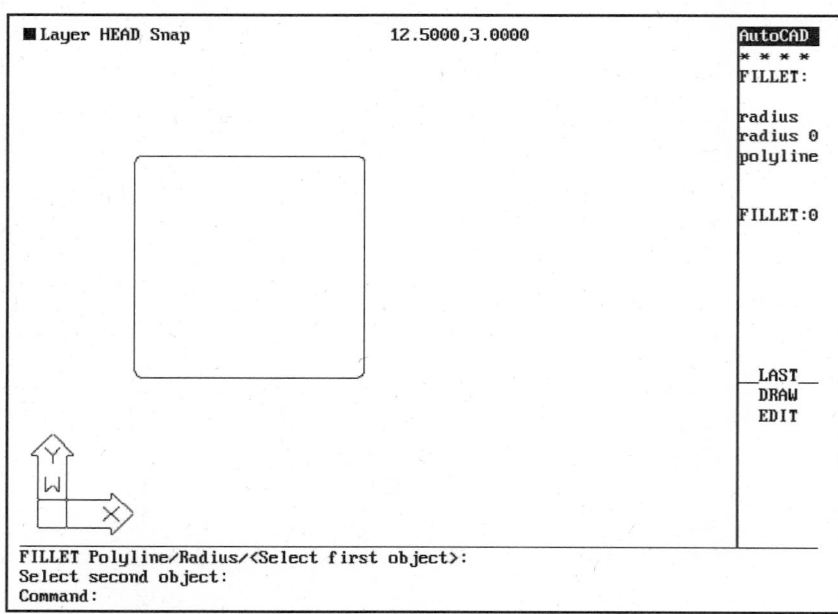

Figure 61.4

Fillets added to each corner of the head outline.

The status line at the top of the screen indicates the current layer and color (the box to the left of the layer name displays the color of the current layer). It is good practice to check the status line for the correct layer name and color whenever you begin working on a different part of the drawing.

Next, begin drawing the gasket. Make the GASKET layer current before you begin drawing.

Drawing Entities on the Gasket Layer

Continue with your drawing from the previous exercise.

1. `Command:` *Use whichever method you prefer to make layer* GASKET *current* — Makes GASKET the current layer and displays GASKET as the current layer in the status line
2. `Command:` *Choose* Draw, *then* Rectangle — Begins the RECTANG command

   `rectang`
3. `First corner:` *Pick a point at* 1.9375,2.9375 — Specifies lower-left corner
4. `Other corner:` *Pick a point at* 6.0625,7.0625 — Draws the rectangle
5. `Command:` *Choose* Settings, *then* Layer Control
6. *In the* Layer Control *dialog box, choose the layer* HEAD, *then choose the* Freeze *button* — Freezes the layer HEAD
7. *Choose* OK — Closes the dialog box and displays the drawing without the HEAD layer

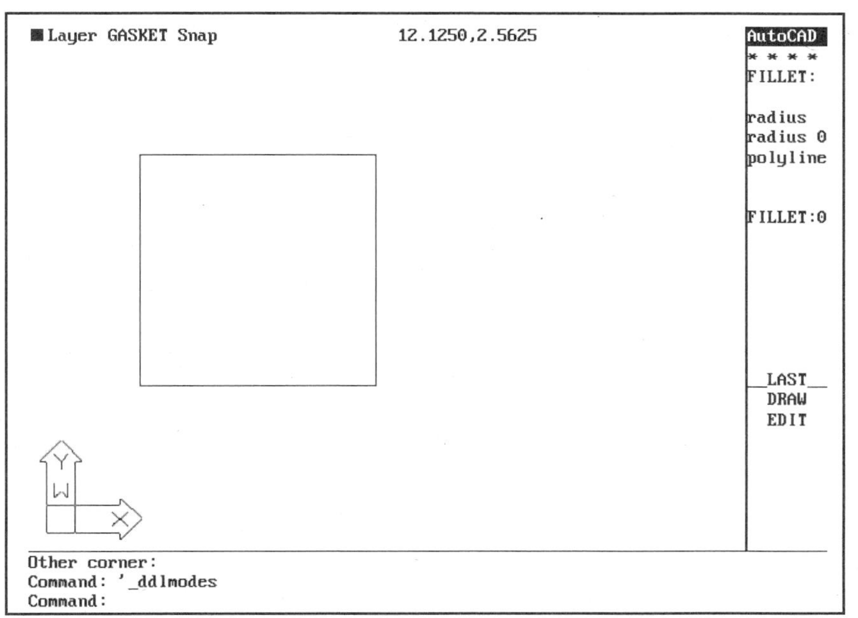

Figure 61.5

Head layer is frozen.

Next, draw the bolt holes on the BOLT layer. Remember to make the BOLT layer current before drawing.

Drawing the Bolt Holes

1. Continue with your drawing from the previous exercise, and set SNAP to .25.
2. `Command:` *Use your preferred method to make layer BOLT current* (LAYER OR DDLMODES commands)
3. `Command:` *Choose* Draw, *then* Circle, *then* Center,Diameter — Starts the CIRCLE command
4. `3P/2P/TTR/<Center point>:` *Pick a point at 2.5,3.5* — Specifies center point
5. `Diameter/<Radius>: _diameter` `Diameter:`**`3/8`** ↵ — Draws 3/8" diameter hole
6. `Command:` *Continue drawing* 3/8" *diameter circles at 2.5,6.5, at 5.5,3.5, and at 5.5,6.5 (see fig. 61.6)* — Completes the bolt holes

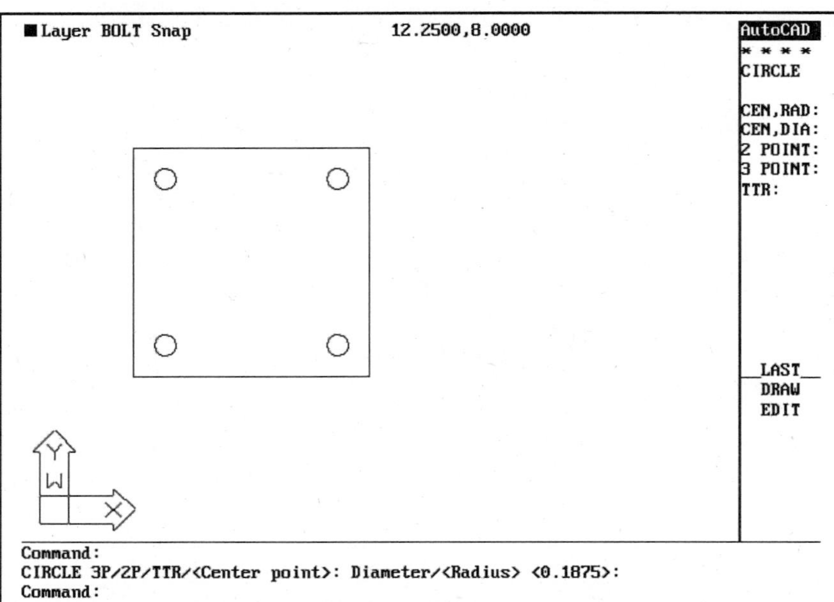

Figure 61.6

Bolt holes added to the gasket drawing.

The bolt holes assumed the layer color and linetype of the BOLT layer because the BOLT layer was current when you drew the circles.

Unit Review

What You've Learned

- How to draw entities on specific layers
- How entities assume the color and linetype characteristics of the layers on which they are drawn

Review Questions

True or False

61.01 T F The current layer is stated in the Layer Control dialog box.

61.02 T F CONTINUOUS linetype is the default for layer 0.

61.03 T F Only one layer may be current at a time.

61.04 T F The status line indicates layers being created.

61.05 T F You must first make a layer current to draw entities on that layer.

Multiple Choice

61.06 The maximum number of characters used to name a layer is ____________.

(A) 31

(B) 21

(C) 7

(D) 10

61.07 If the New option of the Layer command is used to create more than one layer, a(n) _________________.

(A) colon must be placed between names

(B) comma must be placed between names

(C) space must be placed between names

(D) apostrophe must be placed between names

Student: ____________ Date: ______

Instructor: ____________ Course: ______ Section: ______

Short Answer

61.08 How do you know which layer you are drawing on?

61.09 Why do you set a layer current?

61.10 What are the advantages of the Layer Control dialog box in creating layers and setting color and linetype characteristics?

Student: ______ Date: ______

Instructor: ______ Course: ______ Section: ______

UNIT 62

Changing Layer Characteristics

In AutoCAD, you draw on layers that have assigned colors and linetypes (defaults are white and continuous). The entities drawn on a layer adopt the color and linetype settings of that layer unless you override it with explicitly assigned entity settings for the color and linetype properties.

BYLAYER is the default entity setting for color and linetype. BYLAYER causes the entities to use the layer settings. Entities drawn with layer color and linetype settings can be changed by changing the color and linetype settings of their layer. The Layer Control dialog box (DDLMODES command) or the LAYER command can be used to make and modify layer settings.

In the previous unit you drew entities on different layers; in this unit you will change layer settings, see the effects on entities previously drawn on the layers, and draw new entities with other layer colors and linetypes.

The objectives for the unit are to:

- ☞ Modify color and linetype settings for existing layers
- ☞ Set the current layer
- ☞ Draw entities on the layers created with different color and linetype

The exercises in this unit continue the gasket drawing from unit 61. Various entities were drawn on layers that were created according to the function of the part. In this unit, the color and linetype settings of these layers will be changed.

Modifying Layer Settings with the Layer Control Dialog Box

The color or linetype of a layer may be set by the LAYER command or by the DDLMODES command, which is issued by the Layer Control item on the Settings pull-down menu. The DDLMODES command displays the Layer Control dialog box.

Changing Layer Color

To change a layer's color, you select the layer name, then choose the Set Color button, which displays the Select Color dialog box. You then select a color by clicking on one of the colors displayed or by entering the color number or name. The color may be specified by name only if it is one of AutoCAD's seven standard colors, which are 1 (red), 2 (yellow), 3 (green), 4 (cyan), 5 (blue), 6 (magenta), and 7 (white).

The initial layer settings for the gasket drawing are shown in the Layer Control dialog box in figure 62.1.

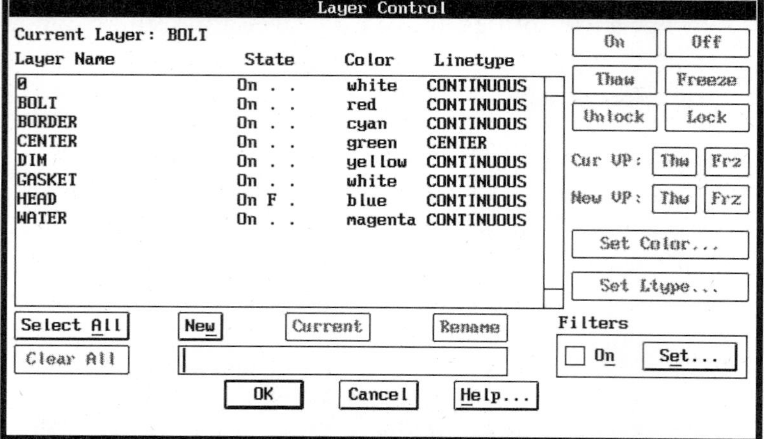

Figure 62.1

Initial settings in the Layer Control dialog box.

In this exercise, you first thaw the HEAD layer, then set it current and change its color to yellow.

Changing Layer Color Using the DDLMODES Command

1. Begin a new drawing named 062???01 in your assigned directory, using the drawing 062GASK as a prototype.

2. `Command:` **`LAYER`** ↵ — Issues LAYER command

3. `?/Make/Set/New/ON/OFF/Color/Ltype/Freeze/Thaw/LOck/Unlock:` **`T`** ↵ — Specifies Thaw option

4.	`Layer name(s) to Thaw: * ↵`	Specifies all layers
5.	`?/Make/Set/New/ON/OFF/Color/Ltype/ Freeze/Thaw/LOck/Unlock:` *Press* Enter	Exits LAYER command and thaws HEAD layer

The entities on the HEAD layer now display as blue lines.

6.	*Choose* Settings, *then* Layer Control	Issues DDLMODES command and opens Layer Control dialog box (see fig. 62.1)
7.	*Select* HEAD *in* Layer Name *list*	Specifies HEAD layer
8.	*Choose* Current	Sets current layer to HEAD
9.	*Choose* Set Color *button*	Opens Select Color dialog box (see fig. 62.2)
10.	*Click on the yellow box at the top or enter* **2** *in the* Color *box at the bottom of the* Select Color *dialog box*	Sets color to yellow
11.	*Choose* OK	Closes Select Color dialog box
12.	*Choose* OK *again*	Closes Layer Control dialog box and displays HEAD layer as yellow

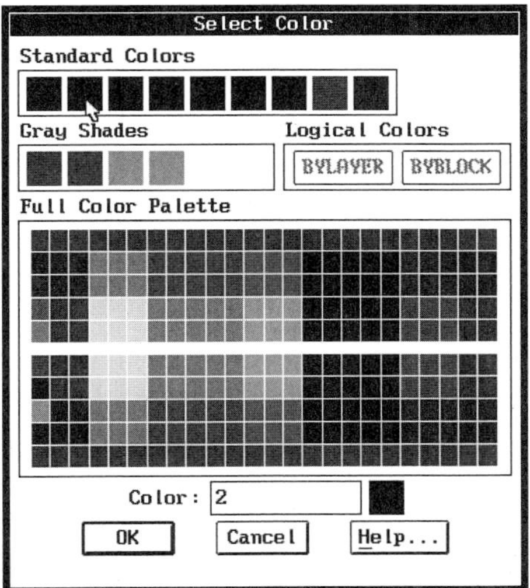

Figure 62.2

Select Color dialog box.

The color 2 (yellow) has been set for the HEAD layer. When the HEAD layer was thawed the entities drawn on that layer appeared blue. The current layer name, HEAD, displays on the status line and the box to the left of the layer name displays the color of the current layer as yellow. When you work with several layers, it is a good practice to check the layer name and color on the status line before drawing each part of the drawing.

Changing Layer Linetype

The Layer Control dialog box (DDLMODES command) is also used to set the layer linetype. Before you set the linetype of a layer using this dialog box, you must first load the desired linetypes into the drawing using the LINETYPE command.

The LINETYPE command prompt appears as `?/Create/Load/Set:`. If you respond to this prompt with an L (Load), you are then asked for the name of the linetype to load. You can specify multiple names with wildcards, such as * for all, or separate names with commas.

After you enter linetype names, AutoCAD displays the Select Linetype File dialog box (see fig. 62.3) with ACAD (the acad.lin file) highlighted as the default. When you press Enter or choose OK, AutoCAD searches the linetype file and loads the linetypes into the drawing. After the linetypes have been loaded, you may select them within the Layer Control dialog box.

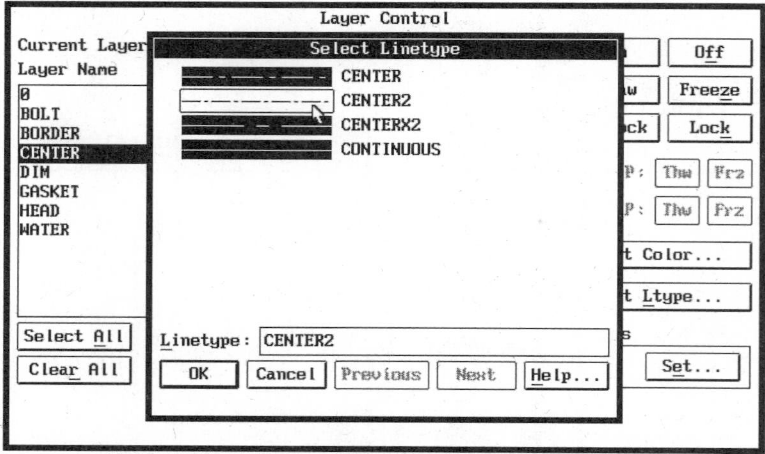

Figure 62.3

Select Linetype dialog box.

To choose a linetype, choose Layer Control from the Settings pull-down menu, then select the layer name to change. Choose the Set Ltype button to open the Select Linetype dialog box and display the available linetypes.

Each standard linetype has three variations, such as CENTER, CENTER2 (half the scale of CENTER), and CENTERX2 (twice the scale of CENTER). In the current gasket drawing, the CENTER layer has a linetype of CENTER. You will load all three CENTER linetypes and change the CENTER layer to CENTER2 in the following exercise.

Changing Layer Linetype with the DDLMODES Command

Continue in the gasket drawing.

1. `Command:` **`LINETYPE`** ↵	Issues LINETYPE command
2. `?/Create/Load/Set:` **`L`** ↵	Selects Load option
3. `Linetype(s) to Load:` **`CEN*`** ↵	Specifies all CENTER linetypes and opens Select Linetype File dialog box
4. *Choose* OK	Closes dialog box and loads linetypes

5. `Linetype CENTER is already loaded. Reload it? <Y>` *Press* Enter
`Linetype CENTER reloaded.`
`Linetype CENTER2 loaded.`
`Linetype CENTERX2 loaded.`
	Reloads CENTER

6. `?/Create/Load/Set:` *Press* Enter	Exits LINETYPE command
7. *Choose* Settings, *then* Layer Control	Issues DDLMODES command
8. *Select* CENTER *from* Layer Name *list*	Specifies layer name
9. *Choose* Set Ltype *button*	Opens Select Linetype dialog box (see fig. 62.4)

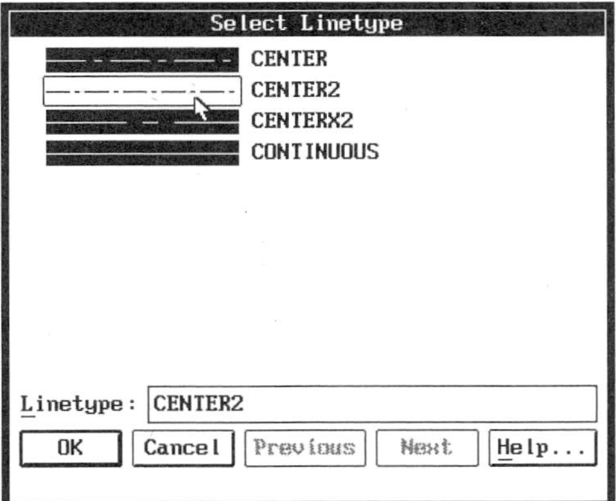

Figure 62.4

Select Linetype dialog box.

10. *Click on the* CENTER2 *linetype, or enter* **CENTER2** *in the* Linetype *field*	Selects CENTER2 linetype
11. *Choose* OK	Accepts setting and closes Select Linetype dialog box
12. *Choose* OK *again*	Closes Layer Control dialog box; redisplays CENTER layer with CENTER2 linetype

`Regenerating drawing.`

Changing a linetype setting causes an automatic drawing regeneration, even if the layer has no entities on it. If you are making several changes or just want to suppress the regeneration or both, you can first use the REGENAUTO command to turn automatic regeneration off. The linetype settings will take effect, but won't be visible on existing entities until the drawing is regenerated by a zoom, the REGEN command, or by turning REGENAUTO on again.

To list the linetypes in the default ACAD.LIN file, you can enter ? (a question mark) at the LINETYPE command's `?/Create/Load/Set:` *prompt. This opens the Select Linetype File dialog box. Press Enter to accept the default ACAD.LIN file and the linetypes will be displayed on the text screen. Another method is to load all linetypes with the * wildcard so that the Select Linetype dialog box displays them all.*

Changing Layer Color and Linetype with the LAYER Command

The LAYER command provides another way to set the layer color or linetype, and to set the current layer. Unlike the Layer Control dialog box, the LAYER command automatically loads the linetypes you specify. You do not need to load the desired linetypes first into the drawing using the LINETYPE command.

In the next exercise, you will use the LAYER command, which can be abbreviated as LA, to change the color of the GASKET layer from white to red, to set the CENTER layer color to blue, to set its linetype back to CENTER, and to set the CENTER layer current so that you can draw center lines.

Changing Layer Color and Linetype with the LAYER Command

Continue in the gasket drawing.

1. `Command:` **`LA`** ↵	Issues LAYER command
2. `?/Make/Set/New/ON/OFF/Color/Ltype/Freeze/Thaw/LOck/Unlock:` **`C`** ↵	Specifies Color option
3. `Color:` **`1`** ↵	Specifies red
4. `Layer name(s) for color 1 (red) <HEAD>:` **`GASKET`** ↵	Specifies layer name to change
5. `?/Make/Set/New/ON/OFF/Color/Ltype/Freeze/Thaw/LOck/Unlock:` **`S`** ↵	Specifies Set option

6.	`New current layer <GASKET>:` **CENTER** ↵	Sets CENTER current
7.	`?/Make/Set/New/ON/OFF/Color/Ltype/Freeze/Thaw/LOck/Unlock:` **C** ↵	Specifies color option
8.	`Color:` **5** ↵	Specifies color blue
9.	`Layer name for color 5 (blue) <CENTER>:` *Press* Enter	Accepts current layer for color assignment
10.	`?/Make/Set/New/ON/OFF/Color/Ltype/Freeze/Thaw/LOck/Unlock:` **L** ↵	Specifies Ltype option
11.	`Linetype (or ?) <CONTINUOUS>:` **CENTER** ↵	Specifies CENTER linetype
12.	`Layer name(s) for linetype CENTER <CENTER>:` ↵	Accepts current layer for linetype assignment
13.	`?/Make/Set/New/ON/OFF/Color/Ltype/Freeze/Thaw/LOck/Unlock:` *Press* Enter	Exits command and makes changes

The status line now indicates CENTER as the current layer name, (see fig. 62.5) and shows blue in the color box.

With the Ltype option, the LAYER command offers CONTINUOUS, not the current linetype, as a default.

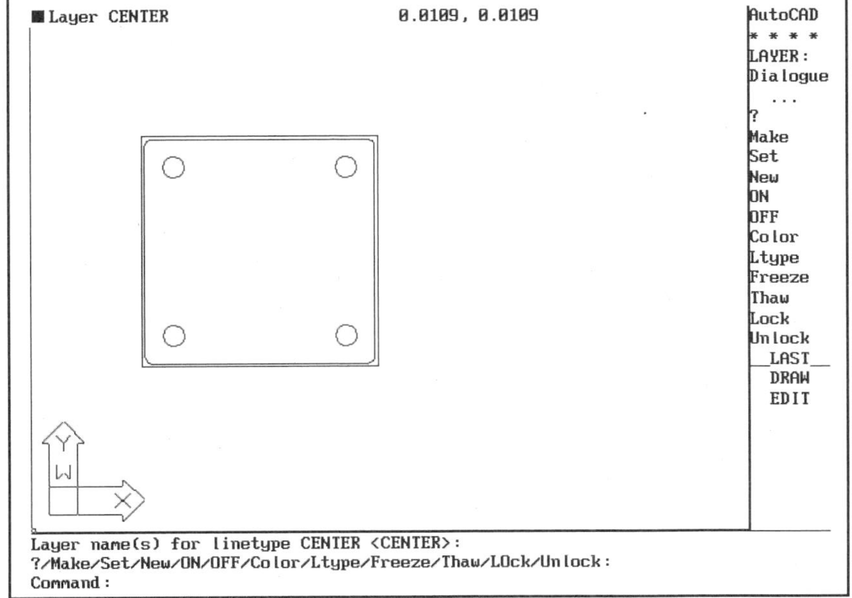

Figure 62.5

CENTER layer current, ready to draw.

The drawing is now ready to draw centerlines on the layer CENTER, with color blue. Use the L abbreviation for the LINE command. Make sure ortho mode is on and use the coordinate display and snap increment to pick the points for the center lines. After drawing two lines, you will offset them to create the bolt center lines. However, you will first set the BOLT layer current to demonstrate that OFFSET creates new lines on the same layer as the original lines, not the current layer.

In the LAYER command (but not in the Layer Control dialog box), you can abbreviate the seven standard color names by entering only the first letter for each.

Drawing Center Lines

Continue in the gasket drawing, with CENTER in the current layer name box and blue in the color box on the status line.

1. `Command:` **`L`** ↵	Issues LINE command
2. `From point:` *Pick* ① *at 1.5,5 (see fig. 62.6)*	Starts line
3. `To point:` *Pick* ② *at 6.5,5*	Draws horizontal center line
4. `To point:` *Press* Enter	Ends LINE command
5. `Command:` *Press* Enter	Repeats LINE command
6. `LINE From point:` *Pick* ③ *at 4,2.5 (see fig. 62.6)*	
7. `To point:` *Pick* ④ *at 4,7.5*	Draws vertical center line
8. `To point:` *Press* Enter	Ends LINE command

Before offsetting the center lines, use either the Layer Control dialog box or LAYER command to set the BOLT layer current and change its color to cyan.

9. `Command:` *Choose* Construct, *then* Offset	Issues OFFSET command
10. `_offset` `Offset distance or Through <Through>:` **`1.5`** ↵	Sets distance for OFFSET

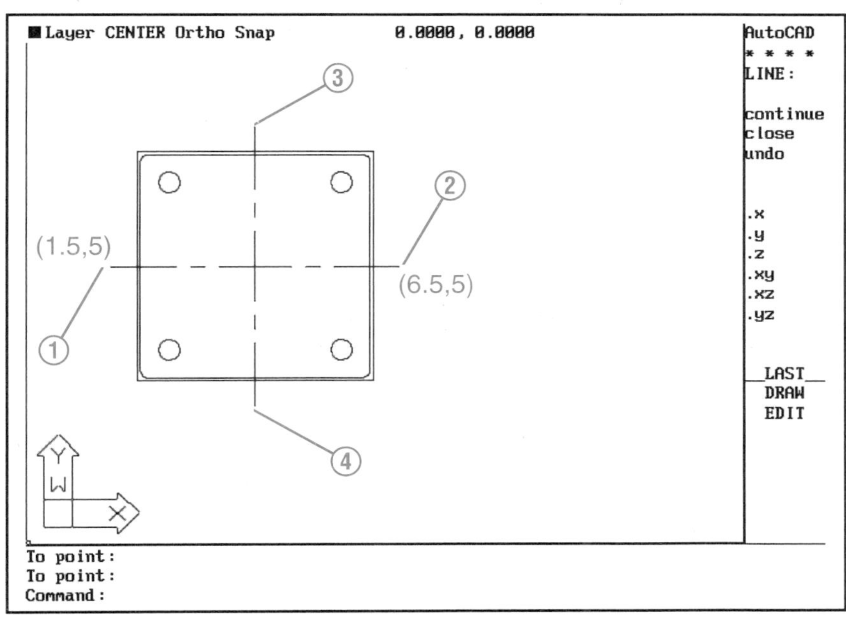

Figure 62.6

Center lines in progress.

11. `Select object to offset:` *Pick vertical center line*	Selects line to be offset
12. `Side to offset?` *Pick any point to the left*	Indicates side to offset and draws line at ① (see fig. 62.7)
13. `Select object to offset:` *Pick vertical center line again*	Selects line to be offset
14. `Side to offset?` *Pick any point to the right*	Draws offset line
15. `Select object to offset:` *Repeat process to offset horizontal center line as shown in figure 62.7, then press* Enter *to end OFFSET command*	

The lines created by OFFSET are blue and have a CENTER linetype; they are on the CENTER layer, not the current BOLT layer. Regardless of this capability, the most common way to do this is to change layers and work on the current layer.

Figure 62.7

Center lines placed with OFFSET.

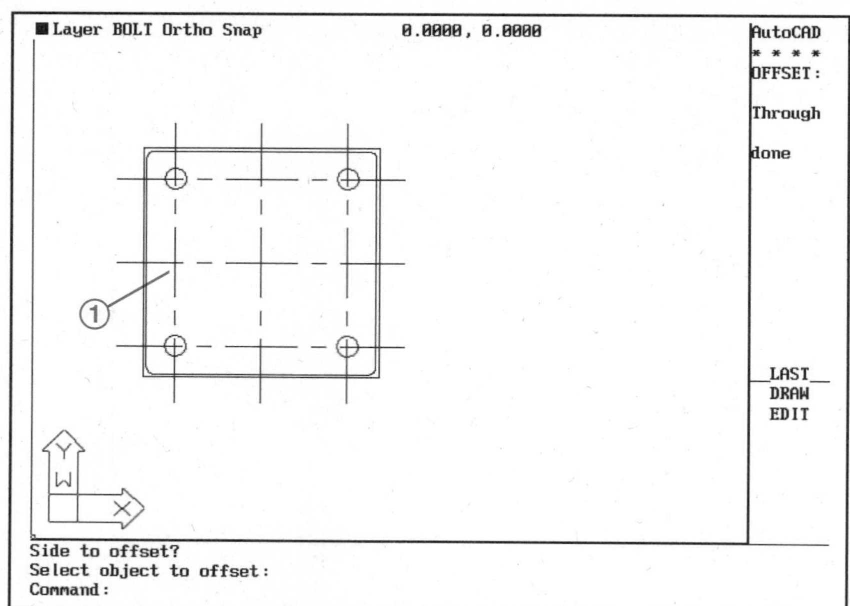

Unit Review

What You've Learned

- ☞ How to change the color and linetype for a layer using the Layer Control dialog box (DDLMODES command) and the LAYER command
- ☞ How to draw on various layers with preset layer colors and linetypes

Review Questions

True or False

62.01 T F The color of the current layer will always be shown on the Status line.

62.02 T F The linetype of a layer is shown in the status line.

62.03 T F Continuous linetype is loaded in all drawings.

62.04 T F Only one color may be assigned to a layer.

62.05 T F Colors may only be defined by number in the Layer Control dialog box.

Multiple Choice

62.06 When using the LINETYPE command, which of the following options can be used to display all linetypes in a linetype file?

(A) ?

(B) Create

(C) Load

(D) Set

Short Answer

62.07 How do you change the settings of a layer on which you are drawing?

____

____

____

Student: ____________________ Date: __________

Instructor: ____________ Course: ______ Section: ______

62.08 What does "current layer" mean? How do you set a layer current?

62.09 What are the advantages of the Layer Control dialog box versus the LAYER command in setting color for a layer? What disadvantage does it have for setting linetypes?

Applying the AutoCAD Environment

62.10 Refer to figure 62.8: what is the color and linetype of the current layer?

62.11 Refer to figure 62.8: how would you change the color of the GASKET layer using the Layer Control dialog box?

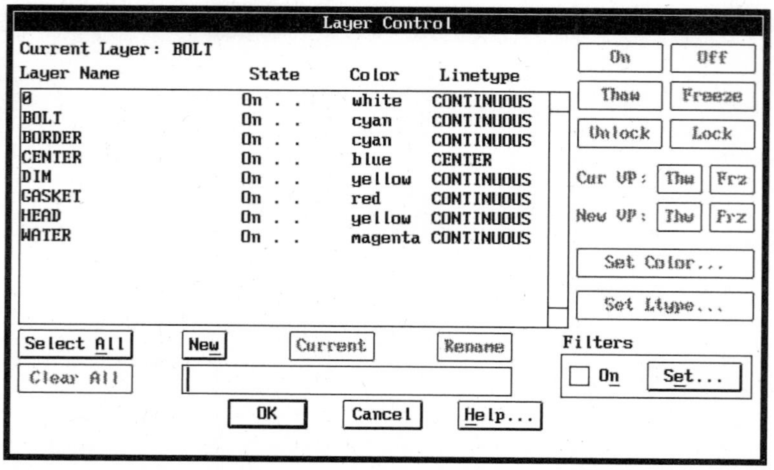

Figure 62.8

Layer Control box for questions 62.10 and 62.11.

Layer Control

Current Layer: BOLT

Layer Name	State	Color	Linetype
0	On . .	white	CONTINUOUS
BOLT	On . .	cyan	CONTINUOUS
BORDER	On . .	cyan	CONTINUOUS
CENTER	On . .	blue	CENTER
DIM	On . .	yellow	CONTINUOUS
GASKET	On . .	red	CONTINUOUS
HEAD	On . .	yellow	CONTINUOUS
WATER	On . .	magenta	CONTINUOUS

On Off
Thaw Freeze
Unlock Lock
Cur VP: Thw Frz
New VP: Thw Frz
Set Color...
Set Ltype...
Select All New Current Rename
Clear All
Filters
On Set...
OK Cancel Help...

Student: ____ Date: ____

Instructor: ____ Course: ____ Section: ____

UNIT 63

Introduction to Linetype and Color

In previous units you controlled the display of entities by setting the color or linetype of layers. The layer upon which an entity resides is only one of the properties an entity can possess. Color, linetype, and thickness are other properties that entities possess. Although you can assign color and linetype by layers, AutoCAD provides the additional flexibility of assigning colors and linetypes directly to entities, regardless of their layer.

The objectives for this unit are to:

- Explain entity color and linetype properties
- Explain explicit, BYBLOCK, and BYLAYER entity color and linetype settings
- Describe how to use the Entity Creation Modes dialog box (DDEMODES command) to set entity color and linetype
- Describe how to use the COLOR and LINETYPE commands to set entity color

Understanding Entity Properties

Every entity has color, linetype, thickness, and layer properties. Generally, the entity inherits the property settings current at the time the entity is created. To create an entity with a specific property setting, change the current setting for the property, then draw the entity as you did for the layer property in the previous unit. The current entity properties are displayed in the Entity Modes dialog box (see fig. 63.1), and the current color and layer are also displayed on the status line.

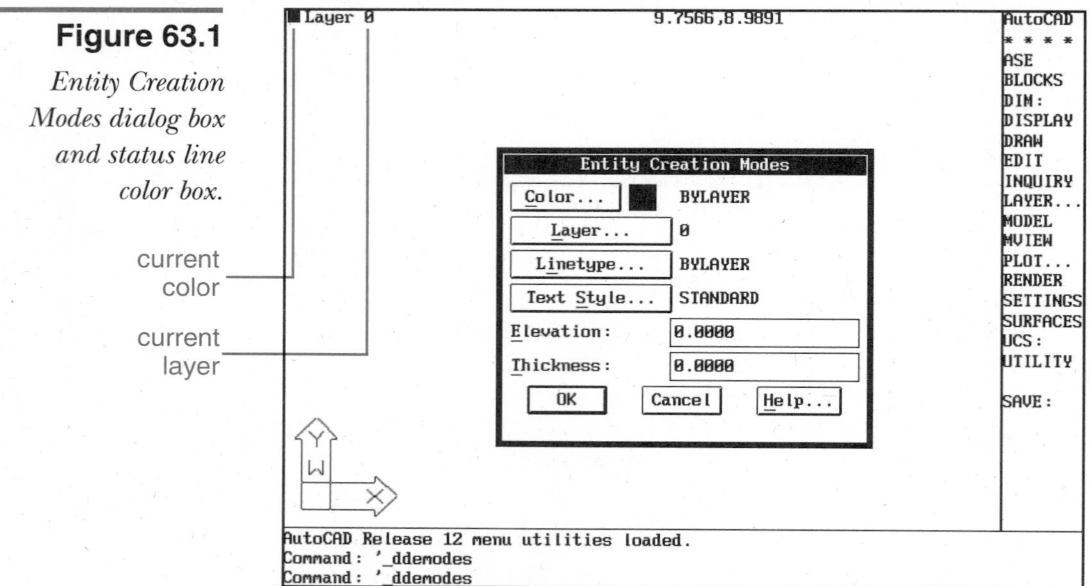

Figure 63.1
Entity Creation Modes dialog box and status line color box.

The dialog box shows settings for color, layer, linetype, text style, elevation, and thickness. The text style is not a general entity setting, but all entities have color, layer, linetype, elevation and thickness properties. The default settings for these settings are shown in figure 63.1. The current color and linetype can be set to explicit settings such as red and dashed, or set to BYLAYER (the default), or to BYBLOCK.

BYLAYER is the default color and linetype property setting. It means that entities adopt the color and linetype settings of the layer upon which they are drawn. If you make explicit entity color or linetype property settings, they override the layer settings. The BYBLOCK setting is a special setting used in blocks. See unit 67 for details on blocks. If an entity is created with current color or linetype properties of BYBLOCK, and the entity is then made part of a block, the entity inherits the settings that are in effect at the time the block is inserted.

AutoCAD's FILTER command can select entities by their color, linetype, layer, or any combination of properties. For example, the FILTER command can create a selection set of all text of a given color, enabling you to edit that text.

Using Color in AutoCAD

Color in AutoCAD is not included for making pretty drawings. The primary purpose of color is to control how objects will plot. Plotter pens, linetype, speed, and line widths can be assigned to different colors to control the plotted appearance of lines. The primary purpose of color assignment is for lineweight control. Laser, PostScript, and ink jet plotters usually use imaginary logical pens; you do not need a pen plotter to use this means of lineweight control.

A second use of color is in 3D applications, in which material properties for rendering are sometimes assigned to colors. The third, and least significant, purpose of color is to differentiate objects on-screen.

Using Linetypes in AutoCAD

The reasons why linetypes are used in CAD are more commonly known than the uses for color. The obvious purpose of linetypes is their visual appearance in the plotted drawing. For this reason, you should set a drawing's linetype scale for the plotted appearance, not the screen appearance. Linetype scaling is discussed further in unit 64. Linetypes are also used to identify materials or wall types in third-party AutoCAD applications.

Although many plotters offer plotter-defined linetypes, you usually have better control of linetypes by defining them in AutoCAD.

When applied to polylines (see unit 29), linetype patterns can be drawn per segment or drawn across the length of the entire polyline. This is controlled by the PLINEGEN system variable (default value 0, off). When approximating curves with short polyline segments, a linetype may appear continuous or irregular because the segemnts are too short to fit the linetype pattern between their vertices unless PLINEGEN is set to 1 (on). When PLINEGEN is on, linetype patterns are generated across the length of the entire polyline, ignoring intervening vertices.

Using Explicit versus Layer Settings

By setting explicit entity color or linetype for entities, entities with various colors or linetypes can reside on a single layer. For example, you can draw the hatching of one component in red and hatch another part in blue. All the hatching resides on one layer that can be turned off or frozen, yet the presentation and plotted lineweight of the hatching are enhanced and controlled by the color. You might also want to group all annotation, such as notes and drawing titleblock data, on a single text layer, and then use color to plot the text with various lineweights.

It is often easier to change the current color and linetype settings as you work rather than plan ahead and create a complete and well-organized set of layers with preset colors and linetypes. Prototyping involves planning ahead, however, and is most advantageous. Just because you can set explicit entity colors and linetypes as you work does not make it a good practice. It is easier to reset and modify color and linetype after entities are drawn if they are set by layer. It can be more tedious and difficult to reset them if they are set by entity, particularly when the entities are within blocks.

Explicit settings for entities can become a big problem when giving drawings to and receiving drawings from clients and consultants who may need to modify settings to suit their standards. Use explicit settings sparingly, and take the time to set up a complete and well-organized system of layers for most drawing tasks.

When you set an explicit color or linetype, future entities will be drawn in that color or linetype regardless of the layer on which they reside. If you change the current entity color or linetype property or the color or linetype of a layer, the color or linetype of the entities that were created using a previous explicit color or linetype will not change.

Use the CHPROP command or Modify Entity dialog box (DDMODIFY command) to change the properties of existing entities.

Setting Properties with the Entity Creation Modes Dialog Box

The Entity Creation Modes dialog box is opened by selecting Entity Modes from the Settings pull-down menu or by entering the DDEMODES command at the command line. The dialog box controls the current entity settings for color, layer, linetype, text style, elevation, and thickness.

Setting Color with the Entity Creation Modes Dialog Box

The Select Color dialog box, shown in figure 63.2, is opened by selecting the Color button.

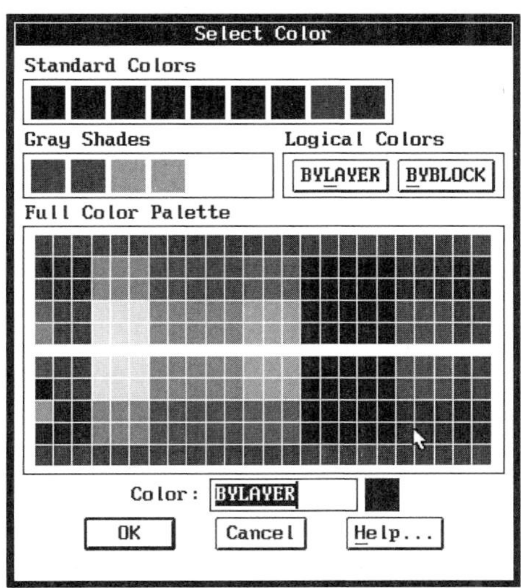

Figure 63.2

Select Color dialog box.

This dialog box is identical to the one opened from the Layer Control dialog box. When opened from the Entity Creation Modes dialog box, the Select Color dialog box sets the current entity color. To set the color, you can click on any of the displayed colors or on the buttons BYLAYER and BYBLOCK, or enter a color name or number in the Color box.

Setting Linetype with the Entity Creation Modes Dialog Box

Linetype is the other entity property that is controlled BYLAYER, BYBLOCK, or explicitly. The default current linetype in a new drawing is BYLAYER, which causes entities to adopt the linetype of the current layer. If entity linetypes are assigned explicitly, they override the layer linetype. The DDEMODES command, which displays the Entity Creation Modes dialog box, enables you to change the current linetype setting for subsequently drawn entities. The Linetype button opens the Select Linetype dialog box, which displays the linetypes that have been previously loaded into the drawing, and the BYBLOCK, BYLAYER, and CONTINUOUS selections. Figure 63.3 shows the Select Linetype dialog box with all standard linetypes loaded.

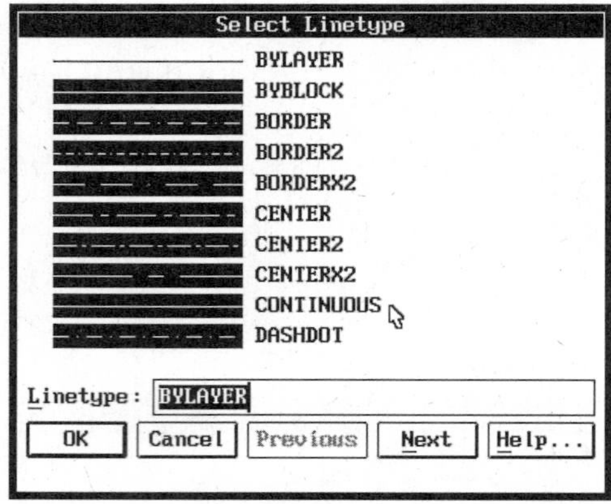

Figure 63.3
Select Linetype dialog box.

Each standard linetype has three variations, such as CENTER, CENTER2 (half the scale of CENTER), and CENTERX2 (twice the scale of CENTER).

This dialog box is identical to the one opened from the Layer Control dialog box. When opened from the Entity Creation Modes dialog box, the Select Linetype dialog box sets the current entity linetype. To set the current entity linetype you can click on any of the displayed linetypes or enter a linetype name in the Linetype box.

You must load linetypes before you can select them in the Select Linetype dialog box.

Loading Linetypes

You can load the desired linetypes into the drawing using the LINETYPE command. The LINETYPE command displays the prompt `?/Create/Load/Set:`. If you respond to this prompt with an L (Load), you are prompted for the name of the linetype to load. You can specify multiple names with wildcards, such as * for all, or separate the names with commas. After you enter linetype names, AutoCAD displays the Select Linetype File dialog box (see fig. 63.4) with ACAD (the ACAD.LIN file) highlighted as the default. When you press Enter or choose OK, AutoCAD searches the linetype file and loads the linetypes into the drawing. After the linetypes have been loaded, you can select them within the Layer Control dialog box. The loaded linetypes will then be available in the Select Linetype dialog box.

*It is easier to load all linetypes with the * wildcard, but that adds all their definitions to the drawing and increases size of the drawing file by about 4500 bytes. After you use the linetypes you need, you can use the PURGE command to purge unused linetypes. To do so, you must close the drawing and use PURGE before any drawing commands after reopening the drawing.*

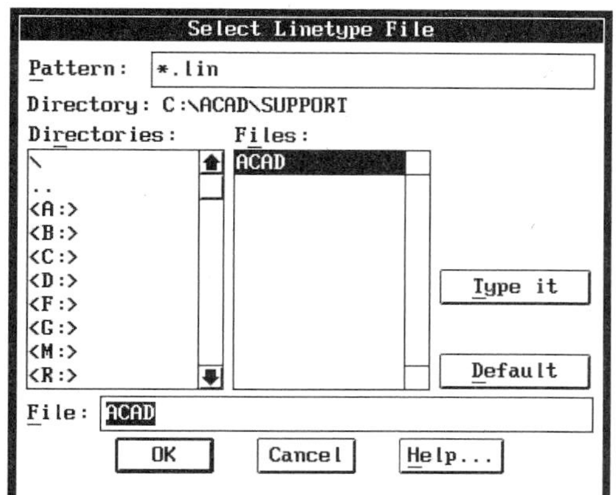

Figure 63.4

Select Linetype File dialog box.

Setting Properties with the COLOR and LINETYPE Commands

The current entity color can also be set by using the COLOR command, by choosing COLOR from the SETTINGS screen menu, or by entering COLOR at the command line. To set the entities color using the COLOR command, you respond to the COLOR prompt with the name or number of a color or with BYBLOCK or BYLAYER.

In the color command, you can abbreviate color names by entering only the first letter of each name. You can also abbreviate BYLAYER and BYBLOCK as BYL and BYB.

In addition to loading linetypes, the LINETYPE command can also be used to set the current entity linetype to an explicit linetype or by layer or by block (BYLAYER or BYBLOCK).

LINETYPE command options include:

- **?.** Displays a list of the available linetypes defined in a specified linetype file
- **Create.** Enables you to define new linetypes
- **Load.** Loads linetypes from a file
- **Set.** Sets the current entity linetype

The Set option performs the same function as selecting the Linetype from the Entity Modes dialog box. You can set the current entity linetype to BYLAYER, BYBLOCK, or to an explicit linetype by name. If the linetype you set has not previously been loaded, the Set option automatically loads it from the default ACAD.LIN linetype file.

Unit Review

What You've Learned

- Properties of entities
- Setting explicit color and linetype
- Setting color and linetype by layer and by block using the BYLAYER and BYBLOCK options
- How the DDEMODES, COLOR, and LINETYPE commands can be used to set entity properties
- How to load linetypes

Review Questions

True or False

63.01 T F The color of an entity always depends on its layer color.

63.02 T F The Entity Creation Modes dialog box is opened by selecting Entity from the Settings pull-down menu.

63.03 T F Setting the current color entity property can only be accomplished by using the COLOR command.

63.04 T F Several entity colors can be set at one time using the COLOR command.

Multiple Choice

63.05 The __________________ command opens the Entity Creation Modes dialog box.

(A) Modes

(B) DDENTITY

(C) DDEMODES

(D) DDEDIT

63.06 To set entity color without regard to its layer color is the process of setting color ________________.

(A) BYLAYER

(B) BYBLOCK

(C) Explicitly

(D) None of the above

Student: ____________________ Date: __________

Instructor: ____________________ Course: __________ Section: __________

63.07 The default for the entity color property is ________________.

(A) BYLAYER

(B) BYBLOCK

(C) White

(D) Black

63.08 To set the current linetype entity property, the command ____________________ is used.

(A) DDEMODES

(B) Entity Creation

(C) DDENTITY

(D) None of the above

Applying the AutoCAD Environment

63.09 Refer to figure 63.5: name the command that was used to load the CENTER and HIDDEN linetypes.

Figure 63.5

Select Linetype dialog box.

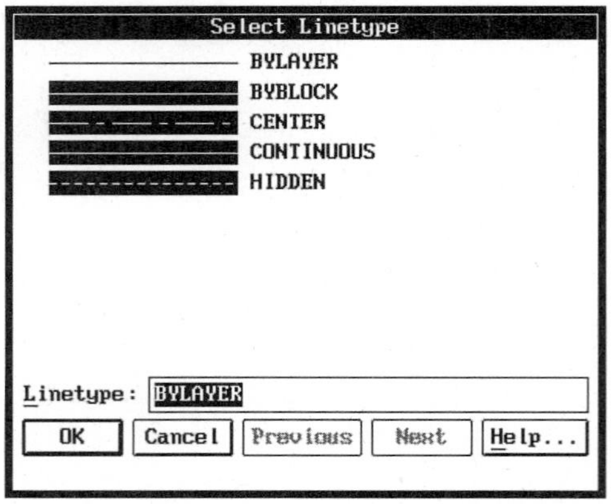

63.10 Refer to figure 63.6: what are the current entity properties set for:

color________________

layer________________

linetype_____________

Student: ____________ Date: ____________

Instructor: ____________ Course: ____________ Section: ____________

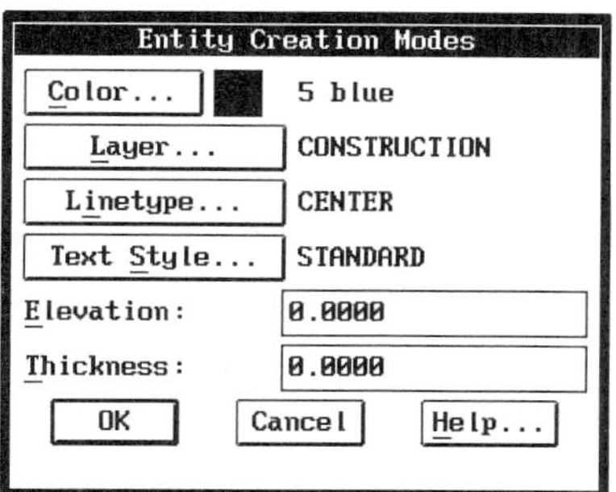

Figure 63.6

Entity Creation Modes dialog box.

Additional Exercises

63.11 Why would you draw an entity with explicit properties instead of using layer color or linetype?

____

____

____

63.12 Can you visually distinguish the display or plot if entities have been drawn with layer settings versus explicit entity properties?

____

____

____

Student: ________________ Date: ________

Instructor: ________________ Course: ________ Section: ________

UNIT 64

Drawing Entities with Linetypes

You learned in units 61 through 63 that entities can automatically inherit the linetype assigned to a layer. Although linetype control by layer is generally preferable, you may sometimes prefer to use *explicit* entity linetypes for simple drawings or where a linetype is only used once or twice in a drawing. You use the LINETYPE command to control entity linetypes.

Preliminary planning of the drawing should include listing the linetypes required for the drawing. Usually a design requires only three or four linetypes, which are generally found among the 24 linetypes in the ACAD.LIN file that AutoCAD provides. These linetypes do not exactly conform to the ANSI Y14.2M standard line alphabet. You can create new linetypes if you must use ANSI standard linetypes or if your drawing conventions, such as for civil and architectural drawings, require additional linetypes not included in the ACAD.LIN file.

The objectives for the unit are to:

- Load linetypes and set the current entity linetype
- Draw entities with explicit entity linetypes
- Create special new linetypes and a linetype library file
- Understand the scaling of linetypes using the LTSCALE command

Setting Up Linetypes

To draw entities with entity linetypes, you must first load linetypes from an AutoCAD linetype library file, such as the default ACAD.LIN file. You use the LINETYPE command to load linetypes.

As discussed in unit 63, "Introduction to Linetype and Color," you should only load necessary linetypes, or for convenience load all linetypes and later purge the unneeded ones. Limiting the number of linetypes loaded decreases the file size. A drawing with the loaded linetypes CENTER and HIDDEN is approximately 4000 bytes smaller than the same drawing with all linetypes loaded. The PURGE command is used to limit linetypes in a drawing and is discussed in unit 69, "Inserting a Block in a Drawing."

The preliminary planning of a drawing should include the decision to assign various linetypes explicitly or with the BYLAYER command. The default linetype assignment is BYLAYER, which applies linetypes to each entity according to the linetype setting of the layer upon which the entity resides. In contrast, an explicit entity linetype setting applies the current linetype to an entity regardless of the linetype assigned to its layer.

The use of explicit linetypes is convenient if a drawing contains only a few entities that require a particular linetype. For example, if an entire drawing only includes one or two center lines, you may choose to draw them explicitly rather than to create a separate layer for the center linetype.

By contrast, a drawing that includes several different linetypes should utilize layers to increase control, flexibility, and ease of assigning line weights when plotting.

Entity linetypes are set using the LINETYPE command, which offers the following options:

- **?.** This option displays a list of linetypes in a linetype file. There are 24 linetypes defined in the standard ACAD.LIN file.
- **Create.** This option enables you to create new linetypes.
- **Load.** This option prompts you to load linetypes from a linetype library file.
- **Set.** This option prompts you to set the current entity linetype.

Linetypes defined in custom linetype files must be preloaded before you can make them current.

Using Linetypes Properly in Drawings

For the exercises in this unit, continue with the gasket drawing from unit 62, "Changing Layer Characteristics" (see fig. 64.1).

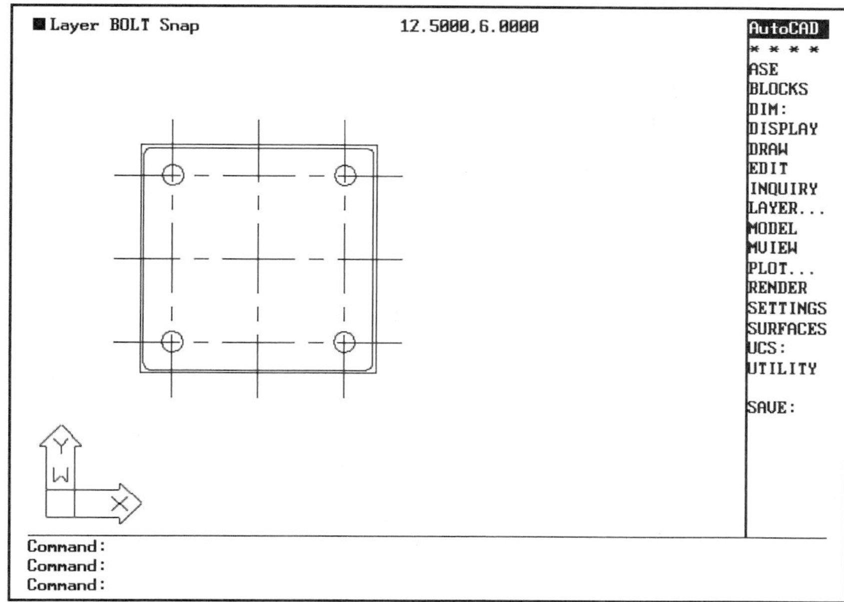

Figure 64.1

The gasket drawing.

The linetypes in the gasket drawing are not applied according to standard drafting practices, but are used as examples only. Correct application would be to apply center marks to the circles, then draw center lines between the center marks. Applying center marks is explained in unit 75, "Adding Diameter and Radius Dimensions."

The CENTER linetype used in this drawing has approximately twice the segment size that an ANSI standard center line should have at a 1:1 scale. (You could use LTSCALE, discussed later in this unit, to adjust it, but it is best to reserve LTSCALE for linetype-plot scale setting.) The 24 linetypes in the ACAD.LIN file provide three sizes for each of eight linetypes. For example, in addition to the linetype CENTER there is also a CENTER2 (half the size of CENTER) and a CENTERX2 (twice the size of CENTER). The CENTER2 and HIDDEN2 linetype are close to the ANSI standard.

In the following exercises, you erase one of the existing center lines, which were drawn by layer, and replace it with an explicit CENTER entity linetype, drawn on the current BOLT layer. First, load the CENTER2 and HIDDEN2 linetype.

Loading Linetypes

1. Begin a new drawing named 064???01 in your assigned directory, using 064GASK as a prototype.

2. `Command:` **`LINETYPE`** ↵	Issues LINETYPE command
3. `?/Create/Load/Set:` **`L`** ↵	Specifies Load option
4. `Linetype(s) to load:` **`CENTER2,HIDDEN2`** ↵	Specifies linetypes and opens Select Linetype File dialog box
5. *Choose* OK	Accepts default ACAD.LIN file and closes Select Linetype File dialog box
6. `Linetype CENTER2 loaded` `Linetype HIDDEN2 loaded`	Loads CENTER2 and HIDDEN2 linetypes
7. `?/Create/Load/Set:` *Press* Enter	Ends LINETYPE command

Using Entity Linetypes

Whether you use the LINETYPE Set option or the Select Linetype dialog box, you can set the current linetype to BYLAYER (see units 60-62), BYBLOCK (see units 67-69), or to an explicit linetype such as DASHED, CENTER, or CONTINUOUS. When the current linetype is set to an explicit linetype, it is applied to all subsequently created entities until reset.

In the following exercise, erase one of the existing center lines and replace it with a line drawn with an explicit linetype on the current BOLT layer. Use the Entity Creation Modes dialog box to set the current linetype.

Drawing with Explicit Linetypes

1. Continue with the gasket drawing from the previous exercise and erase the center line at ① (see fig. 64.4).

2. `Command:` *Choose* Settings, *then* Entity Modes	Issues DDEMODES command and opens Entity Creation Modes dialog box (see fig. 64.2)

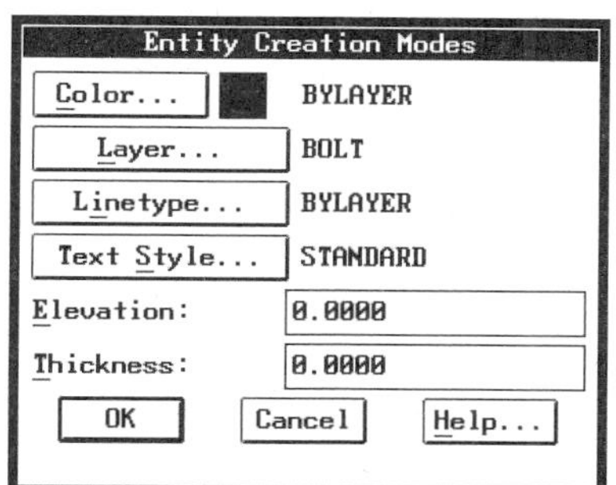

Figure 64.2

Entity Creation Modes dialog box.

3. *Choose* Linetype	Opens Select Linetype dialog box (see fig. 64.3)

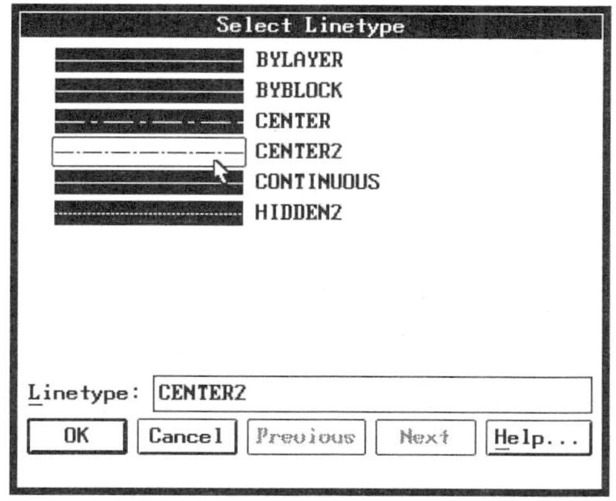

Figure 64.3

Select Linetype dialog box.

4. *Click on* CENTER2	Selects linetype
5. *Choose* OK	Accepts selection and closes Select Linetype File dialog box
6. *Choose* OK *again*	Closes Entity Creation Modes dialog box and sets current linetype explicitly to CENTER2
7. *Draw a line from* ② *to* ③ *(see fig. 64.4).*	

Your drawing should look similar to figure 64.4.

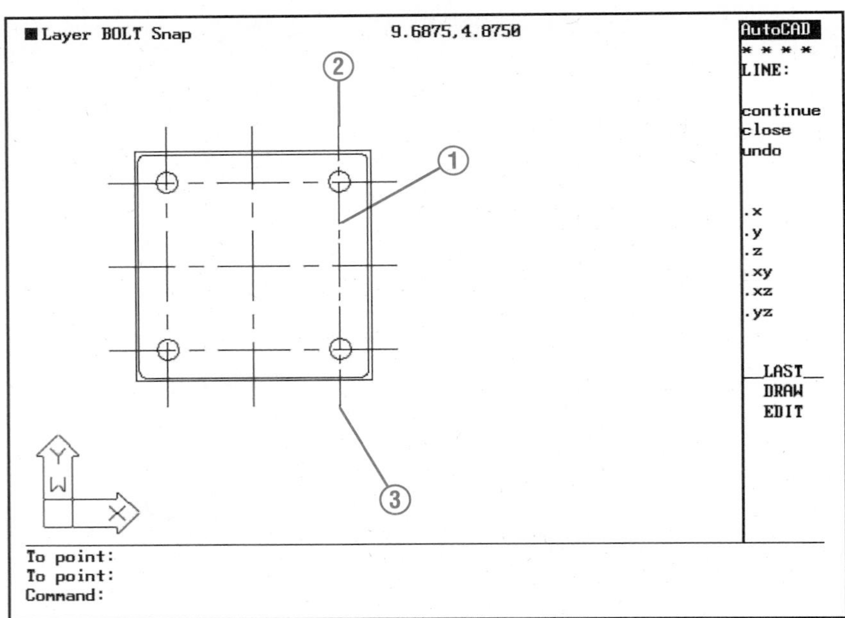

Figure 64.4
Drawing with explicit linetype CENTER2.

The new center line appears different from the other center lines located on the CENTER layer because it was drawn with the CENTER2 explicit linetype. The layer CENTER has the linetype CENTER assigned to it.

Controlling Linetype Scale

The appearance of the dashes and spaces of linetypes depends on the size of the drawing and the magnification of the viewport. As you increase the magnification of the viewport with the ZOOM command, the spaces and dashes of the linetypes increase in size.

AutoCAD provides a command called LTSCALE that enables you to control the relative scale of a linetype (the size of dashes and spaces, for example). In AutoCAD's default prototype drawing, LTSCALE is set to 1. Increasing LTSCALE increases the relative size of the linetype. Decreasing LTSCALE decreases the relative size of the linetype.

Because most drawings are drawn full-size and later scaled for plotting, you must often use LTSCALE to achieve the correct linetype scale in your finished drawing. A good rule of thumb to use for LTSCALE is to set it equal to the working scale of your drawing. A drawing that will be plotted at 1/4" = 1'-0" is reduced 48 times its actual size, so you should set LTSCALE for the drawing to 48.

Although the gasket drawing will not need to be reduced when plotted, you can still use it to experiment with LTSCALE.

Changing LTSCALE

Continue with your drawing from the previous exercise.

1. `Command:` **`LTSCALE`** ↵	Issues LTSCALE command
2. `New scale factor <1.0000>:` **`.5`** ↵	Specifies LTSCALE factor (see fig. 64.5)
3. `Regenerating drawing`	
4. `Command:` *Press* Enter	Repeats previous command
5. `LTSCALE New scale factor <0.5000>:` **`1.5`** ↵	Specifies LTSCALE factor (see fig. 64.6)

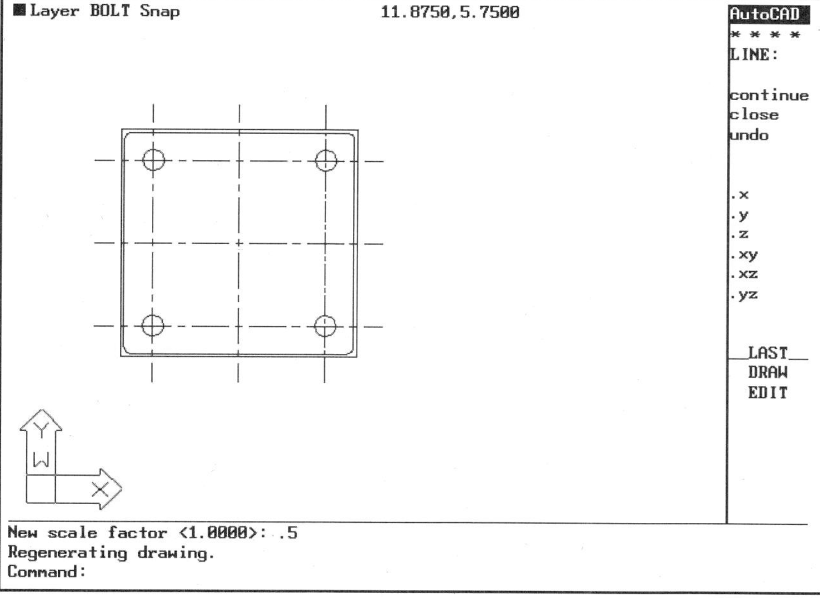

Figure 64.5

LTSCALE set to .5.

Figure 64.6

LTSCALE set to 1.5.

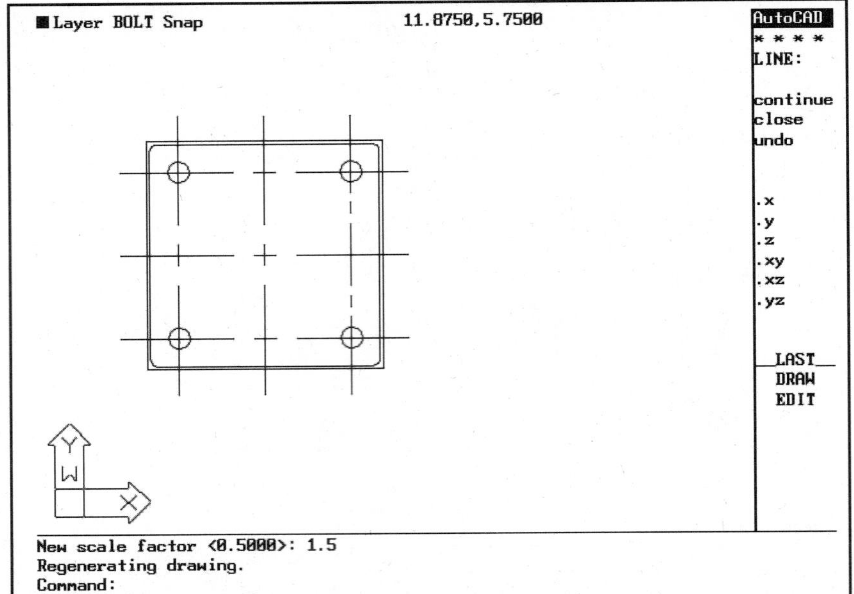

Unit Review

What You've Learned

- How to draw entities with explicit linetype
- How to draw entities with linetype controlled according to layer
- How to create linetypes in a linetype library file
- How to set the LTSCALE for drawings of various sizes

Review Questions

True or False

64.01 T F All linetypes must be loaded into a drawing with the LINETYPE command.

64.02 T F Explicit linetypes will be displayed on the Layer Control dialog box.

64.03 T F Changing to explicit linetype must be done at the beginning of the drawing.

64.04 T F Only one explicit linetype can be used in a drawing.

Multiple Choice

64.05 The maximum number of linetypes available in a drawing is ________.

(A) 24

(B) 8

(C) 1

(D) No limit

64.06 The ________ command is used to load linetypes into a drawing.

(A) Load

(B) Set

(C) LINETYPE

(D) None of the above

Student: ________________ Date: ________

Instructor: ________________ Course: ________ Section: ________

64.07 The LINETYPE scale of a drawing should be set to ________:

(A) four times its scale when plotted

(B) one half its reduction size when plotted

(C) 1 regardless of size

(D) the save value as the scale factor

Short Answer

64.08 What linetype scale is equivalent in a metric drawing to a linetype scale of 1 in an English units drawing?

____

____

____

64.09 Explain how an explicit linetype is different from a linetype set with BYLAYER.

____

____

____

64.10 To magnify the linetype spaces and dashes to twice their linetype definition in a drawing, what should be the LTSCALE factor?

____

____

____

Student: ______________ Date: ______________

Instructor: ______________ Course: ______________ Section: ______________

UNIT 65

Drawing Entities with Color

In unit 63 you learned that entities can automatically inherit the color assigned to the layer on which they are drawn. By assigning different colors to the layers in your drawing, you can switch from layer to layer and draw in different colors. With colors you can organize your drawing data visually. Color also is extremely useful for placing entities on their proper layers because you can verify the entity's layer by its color.

As with linetype, you also can draw entities with an explicit color. Entities drawn in this way inherit the current color setting rather than the color assigned to the entity's layer. You can draw a blue circle, for example, on a layer that has been assigned the color red. In this unit you learn to set and use explicit colors.

The objectives for the unit are to:

- Use the COLOR and DDEMODES commands to set the current color
- Draw entities with explicit color and BYLAYER color

Setting Entity Color

The DDEMODES and COLOR commands are used to set color. Choose Settings, Entity Modes to display the Entity Creation Modes dialog box. Choose the Color button in the Entity Creation Modes dialog box to display the Select Color dialog box shown in figure 65.1.

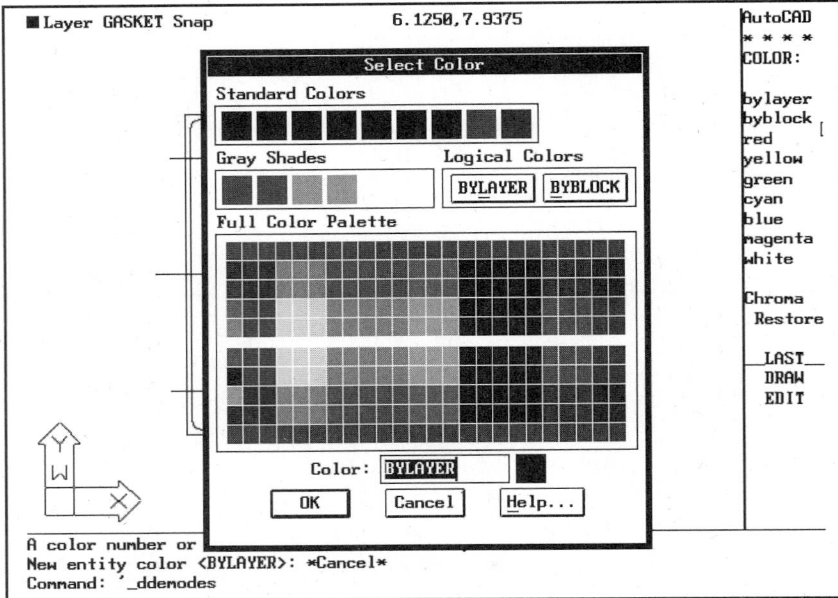

Figure 65.1

The Select Color dialog box.

By default, the current color is set to BYLAYER, which means that any entities you draw will inherit the color assigned to the current layer. You can set color to one of the following three settings:

- **BYLAYER.** This setting causes entities to inherit the color assigned to the current layer.
- **BYBLOCK.** When this setting is used, new entities are drawn in white until they are grouped into a block. When the block is inserted into a drawing, the entities will inherit the current color assigned by the COLOR command.
- **Explicit color.** This can be a color name, such as red or blue, or a number from 1 to 255. Entities drawn with an explicit color inherit that color, regardless of the color assigned to the current layer.

Table 65.1 lists the basic colors and their numeric values (these seven colors are the only ones that you can specify by name). AutoCAD supports up to 255 colors, but you may not be able to view all of them on your display. Color 8 usually is black or gray, and colors 9 through 15 usually are intensified versions of colors 1 through 7.

Table 65.1
Common Color Assignments

Color Value	Color Name
1	Red
2	Yellow
3	Green
4	Cyan
5	Blue
6	Magenta
7	White

The Select Color dialog box enables you to select BYLAYER and BYBLOCK, as well as the 255 AutoCAD colors. The number of different *shades* you see in the dialog box depends on the capability of your computer video adapter and display driver.

You can select an explicit color by entering its color value or color name (1 or Red, for example) in the Color edit box. Another option is to select a color by clicking on a square in the Standard Colors, Gray Shades, or Full Color Palette groups. To select either BYLAYER or BYBLOCK, choose the appropriate button. When you select a color, its color name or value appears in the Color edit box.

In the next exercise you will continue working with the gasket drawing used in previous units. You will begin drawing on the HEAD layer. The color property of the HEAD layer is yellow, but you will set the current color explicitly to green. Entities you draw on layer HEAD will inherit the current color green, rather than the layer color yellow.

The center lines in the prototype for the next exercise have been changed to reflect correct drafting practices. Note that center marks also have been added to the circles.

Setting a Color

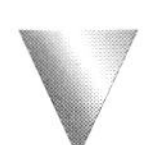

1. Begin a new drawing named 065???01 in your assigned directory, using 065GASK as the prototype.

continues

2. *Choose* Settings, *then* Layer Control `'_ddlmodes`	Issues DDLMODES command and displays the Layer Control dialog box
3. *Choose* HEAD *layer, then* Current, *then* OK	Sets HEAD as current layer
4. `Command:` *Choose* Settings, *then* Entity Modes `'_ddemodes`	Issues DDEMODES command and displays Entity Creation Modes dialog box
5. *Choose* Color	Displays the Select Color dialog box
6. *In the* Standard Colors *group, click on the green square*	Specifies explicit color green
7. *Choose* OK	Closes the Select Color dialog box
8. *Choose* Linetype	Displays the Select Linetype dialog box
9. *Choose* BYLAYER, *then* OK	Specifies linetype BYLAYER and closes Select Linetype dialog box
10. *Choose* OK	Closes the Entity Creation Modes dialog box

Drawing by Color

Now that you have set an explicit color, any new entities that you draw will inherit the current explicit color. If you set the current color back to BYLAYER, entities will once again inherit the color setting of the current layer. There is nothing you have to do other than set the current color to draw entities with a specific color.

Draw some new entities to see how they are affected by the color and layer settings.

Drawing with an Explicit Color

Continue with your drawing.

1. `Command:` *Choose* Draw, *then* Circle, *then* Center, Diameter

   `_circle`

2. `3P/2P/TTR/<Center point>:` *From the popup menu, choose* Intersection — Sets temporary object snap mode

3. `_int of` *Pick the intersection of lines at* ① *(see fig. 65.2)*

   `Diameter/<Radius>: _diameter`

4. `Diameter:` **2** ↵ — Specifies diameter

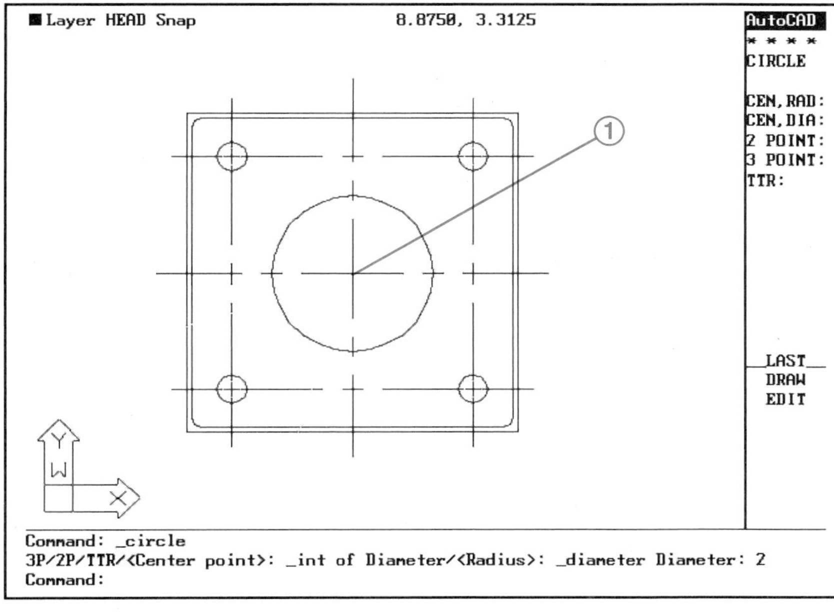

Figure 65.2

Center location for circle.

Even though the circle was drawn on a layer that has been assigned the color yellow, the circle is green because it inherited the current explicit color setting.

Next, set color back to BYLAYER and draw on the GASKET layer.

Using BYLAYER Color

Continue with your drawing from the preceding exercise.

1. Use the Layer Control dialog box or the LAYER command to set GASKET as the current layer.

2. `Command:` *Choose* Settings, *then* Entity Modes — Issues DDEMODES command

   `_ddemodes`

3. *Choose* Color — Displays the Select Color dialog box

continues

4. *Choose* BY LAYER, OK, *then* OK *again* — Specifies BYLAYER color and exits dialog boxes

Notice that the color indicator in the status line now changes to red (see fig. 65.3).

5. `Command:` *Choose* Draw, *then* Circle, *then* Circle, Diameter
6. `3P/2P/TTR/<Center point>:` **`CEN`** ↵ — Sets CENter object snap
7. `of` *Pick the green circle (see fig. 65.3)* — Specifies location of center point

   `Diameter/<Radius><1.000>:_diameter`
8. `Diameter<2.000>:` **`2.125`** ↵ — Specifies diameter for circle

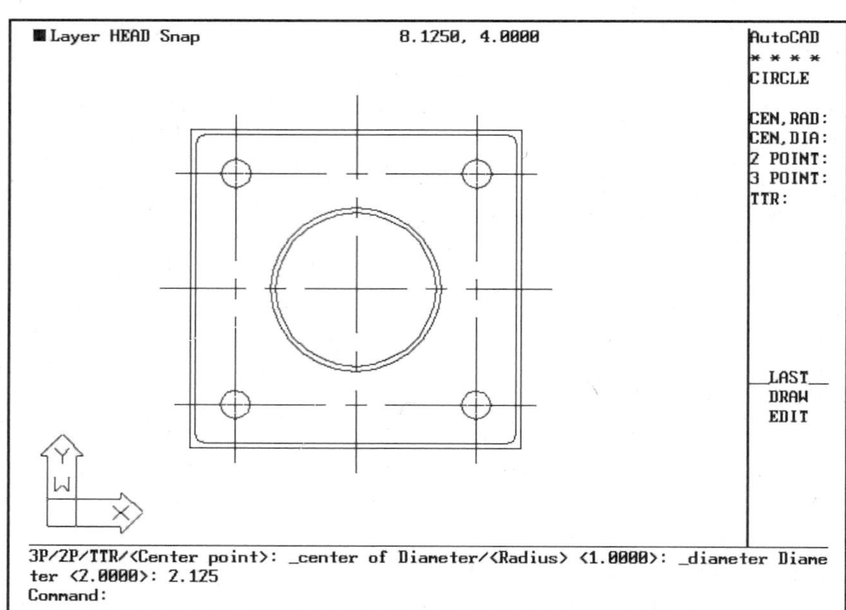

Figure 65.3

New circle added to the gasket.

Entity color can also be set by the COLOR command. When you issue the COLOR command, the existing color setting is shown in brackets in the prompt. This command does not control the color property of a layer. If a color number or name is displayed in brackets, the color is explicit. You can issue the COLOR command from the keyboard or choose it from the SETTINGS screen menu.

Using the COLOR Command To Set Color

Continue with the drawing used in the preceding exercise.

1. `Command:` **`COLOR`** ↵ — Issues COLOR command

2. `New entity color<BYLAYER>:` **`GREEN`** ↵	Specifies color explicitly
3. `Command:` **`CIRCLE`** ↵	Issues CIRCLE command
4. `3P/2P/TTR/<Center point>:` **`2,2`** ↵	Specifies center location
5. `Diameter/<Radius> <0.5>:` *Press* Enter	Specifies radius of circle
6. `Command:` *Press* Enter	

Notice a green circle is drawn on the GASKET layer that has a red layer property. The color green has been set explicitly.

7. `Command:` **`COLOR`** ↵	Issues COLOR command
8. `New entity color <3 (green)>:` **`BYLAYER`** ↵	Specifies color BYLAYER
9. `Command:` **`CIRCLE`** ↵	Issues CIRCLE command
10. `3P/2P/TTR/<Center point>:` **`3,2`** ↵	Specifies center location
11. `Diameter/<Radius><0.5000>:` *Press* Enter	Specifies radius for circle

Although it may be difficult at this stage to understand how valuable color can be, you should make a habit now of using color extensively in your drawings. Structure your layers to separate data such as basic part geometry, text, dimensions, center lines, and hidden lines. Assign a distinct color to each layer and draw using BYLAYER as much as possible. The use of BYLAYER makes it easier for you to identify entities quickly that have been drawn on the wrong layer, and this setting also makes color selection automatic. Simply select the correct layer and draw—the entities will inherit the correct color automatically.

Unit Review

What You've Learned

- How to set the color of a drawing to BYLAYER or BYBLOCK
- The explicit use of the COLOR and DDEMODES commands
- How to draw entities with an explicit entity color

Review Questions

True or False

65.01 T F The upper left corner of the status line indicates the explicit entity color if an explicit color is set.

65.02 T F The upper left corner of the status line indicates the layer color property if color is set to BYLAYER.

65.03 T F You cannot enter a color number instead of a color name in the Select Color dialog box.

65.04 T F When you are setting the current color, picking a color in the Select Color dialog box changes all selected entities to the specified color.

65.05 T F You can enter a color value as a number only for the first eight colors.

65.06 T F Colors 1 through 7 are the only colors that you can specify by name rather than number.

65.07 T F Setting an explicit color has no effect on linetype.

Multiple Choice

65.08 The maximum number of colors that are allowed in a drawing is ________.

(A) 24

(B) 255

(C) 8

(D) no limit

Student: ______________________ Date: __________

Instructor: ______________________ Course: __________ Section: __________

65.09 The __________ option of the Color command causes new entities to inherit the color property of the layer on which they are drawn.

(A) Color

(B) BYLAYER

(C) BYENTITY

(D) BYBLOCK

65.10 Entering __________ in response to the COLOR command will set the color of entities drawn to that color regardless of layer.

(A) a color

(B) BYLAYER

(C) BYBLOCK

(D) BYENTITY

Student: ______________________ Date: __________

Instructor: ______________________ Course: __________ Section: __________

UNIT 66

Changing an Entity's Properties

In previous units you learned how to draw entities on layers with various linetype and color properties. In addition, you drew entities with explicit linetype and color. How do you change the layer assigned to an entity? What if you have made a mistake in color or linetype assignments? Or, what if the design has changed and you need to change the color or linetypes of some of the existing entities in the drawing? Instead of forcing you to erase and redraw the entities, AutoCAD provides commands that make changing these entity properties a simple process. This unit teaches you to use these commands.

The objectives for the unit are to:

- Change entities with explicit color and linetype
- Change entities with color and linetype BYLAYER and BYBLOCK
- Change the layer of an entity
- Use the DDCHPROP and DDMODIFY commands

Changing Entity Color

For any number of reasons, you will sometimes need to change the color assigned to one or more existing entities. You may need to change the color from BYLAYER to an explicit color or vice versa, or maybe you have drawn some entities using red and now want them to be yellow.

You can use the DDCHPROP command to change the color of an entity. You can access this command from the pull-down menus by selecting Modify, Change, Properties. AutoCAD will then prompt you to select the object to change. Create a selection set consisting of one or more entities, then press Enter. The Change Properties dialog box appears (see fig. 66.1).

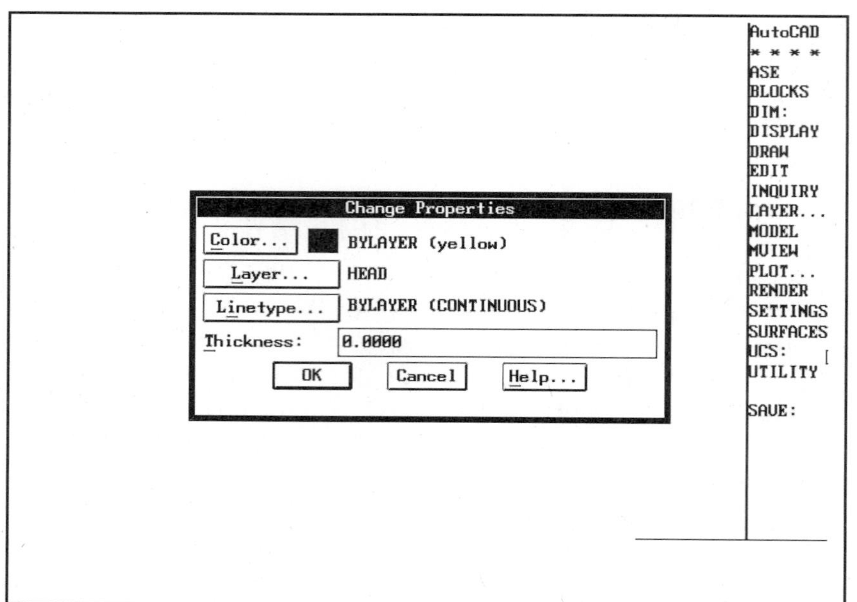

Figure 66.1
The Change Properties dialog box.

If you prefer, you can use pick-first selection to create the selection set of entities to be changed. If a selection set exists when you issue the DDCHPROP command, AutoCAD does not prompt for additional entity selection. Instead, it performs the change you specify on the existing selection set.

The Change Property dialog box displays the existing color, linetype, layer, and thickness properties of the entity. If you want to change the Color of entities in the selection set, pick the Color button. The Select Color dialog box will appear, as shown in figure 66.2.

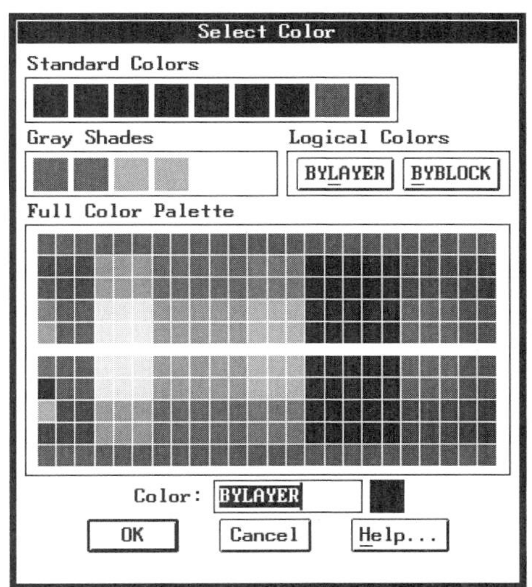

Figure 66.2

The Select Color dialog box.

This dialog box is identical to the Select Color dialog box used with the DDEMODES command. You can specify a color by number, by name, BYLAYER, BYBLOCK, or pick one of the colored squares to select a color. If you choose Cancel in the Change Properties dialog box, no changes are made to the selection set.

In the following exercise, change the 2" circle on the HEAD layer from green to BYLAYER.

Changing Entity Color

1. Begin a new drawing named 066???01 in your assigned directory using 065GASK as a prototype.

2. `Command:` *Choose the* Modify *pull-down menu, then* Change, *then* Properties — Issues DDCHPROP command and displays the Change Properties dialog box

   `ddchprop`
   `Initializing...DDCHPROP loaded.`

3. `Select objects:` *Select the circle at ① (see fig. 66.3)* — Creates selection set

   `1 found`

4. `Select object:` *Press* Enter — Ends object selection

   Notice that the Change Properties dialog box displays an explicit color (green).

continues

5. *Choose* Color	Displays the Select Color dialog box
6. *Choose* BYLAYER, *then* OK	Specifies BYLAYER color property and closes Select Color dialog box
7. *Choose* OK *in the* Change Properties *dialog box*	Ends DDCHPROP command and changes the circle's color

Next, use pick-first to select entities, then use DDCHPROP to change their color.

8. `Command:` *Select the four bolt holes*	Creates a selection set and displays grips
9. `Command:` *Choose* Modify, *then* Change, *then* Properties	Issues DDCHPROP command and displays the Change
10. *Choose* Color	Displays the Select Color dialog box
11. *Type* **`Red`** *in the* Color *edit box and press* Enter	Specifies explicit color
12. *Choose* OK	Closes dialog box and changes color or bolt holes

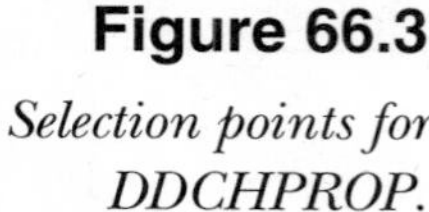

Figure 66.3

Selection points for DDCHPROP.

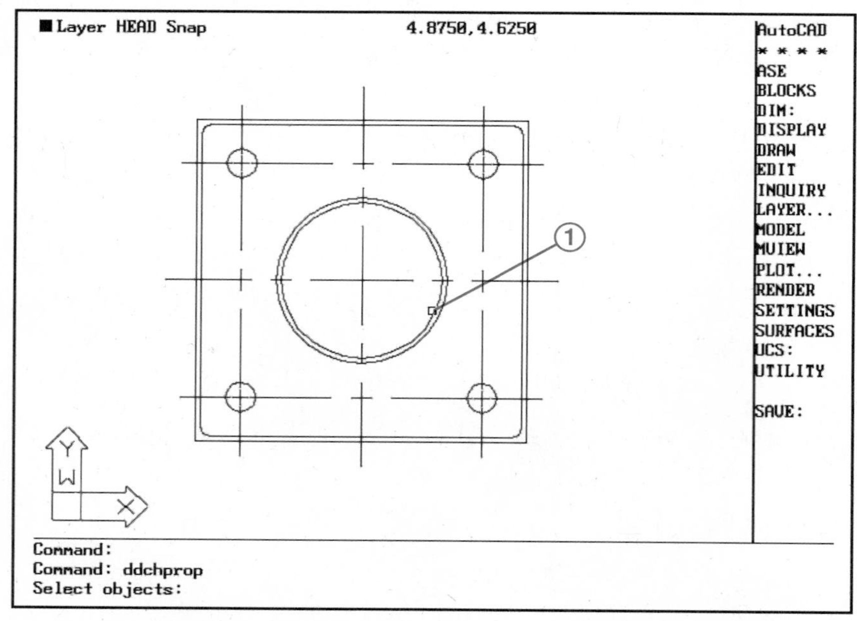

You can use the CHPROP command to change layer, color, and linetype properties of entities. CHPROP displays a prompt with options, rather than use a dialog box like the DDCHPROP command. Like DDCHPROP, the CHPROP command works with both pick-first and pick-after selections.

Changing Entity Linetype

You often will need to change the linetype assigned to one or more entities because of design changes or errors. As you may have guessed, you can use the DDCHPROP command (or the CHPROP command) to change the linetype assigned to an entity. In the Change Properties dialog box, choose the Linetype button. AutoCAD displays the Select Linetype dialog box shown in figure 66.4.

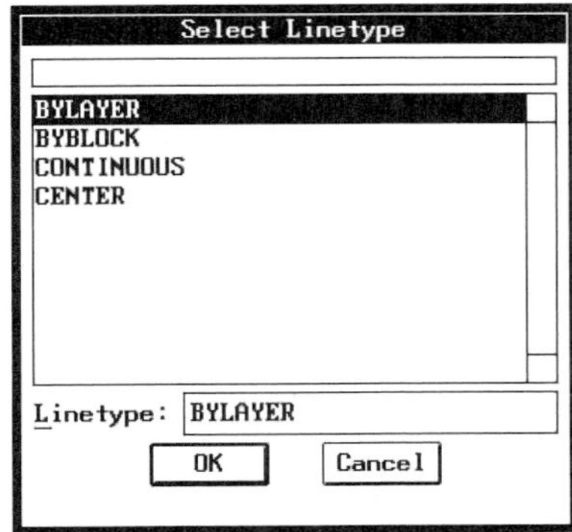

Figure 66.4

The Select Linetype dialog box.

You can change the selection set's linetype to an explicit linetype, to BYLAYER, or to BYBLOCK. If BYLAYER is selected, the entities will inherit the linetype property assigned to their layers. If BYBLOCK is selected, the entity's linetype will be displayed according to the linetype setting of the drawing at the time the entities are inserted as a block. The current linetype of the entity will be stated in the linetype edit box. If the desired linetype is not displayed for you to select, use the LINETYPE command to load the desired linetype into the drawing, then issue the DDCHPROP command.

Changing Linetype

Continue with your drawing from the previous exercise.

1. `Command:` *From the* SETTINGS *screen menu, choose* LINETYP:	Issues the LINETYPE command
2. `?/Create/Load/Set:` **`L`** ↵	Specifies Load option

continues

3. `Linetype(s) to load:` **`PHANTOM`** ↵ — Specifies linetype to load and displays Select Linetype File dialog box

4. *Click on* ACAD, *then choose* OK — Specifies linetype file and loads linetype PHANTOM

5. `?/Create/Load/Set:` *Press* Enter — Ends LINETYPE command

6. `Command:` *Choose* Modify, *then* Change, *then* Properties — Issues DDCHPROP command and displays the Change Properties dialog box

   `ddchprop`

7. `Select objects:` *Select the circle at* ① *(see fig. 66.5)* — Starts a selection set

   `1 found`

8. `Select objects:` *Press* Enter — Ends object selection and displays Change Properties dialog box

9. *Choose the* Linetype *button* — Displays the Select Linetype dialog box

10. *Click on* PHANTOM, *choose* OK, *then* OK *again* — Specifies new linetype and changes circle's linetype

11. Save your drawing.

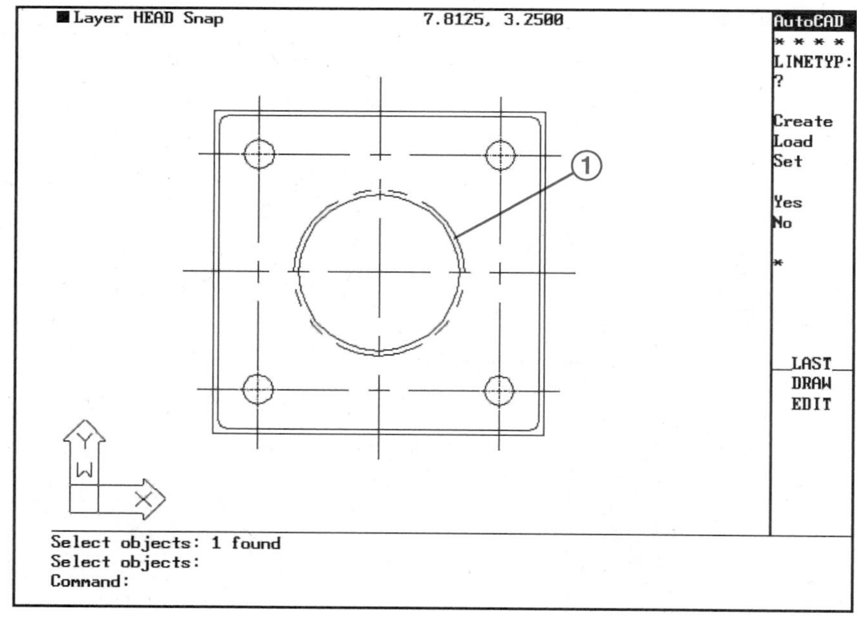

Figure 66.5

Circle linetype changed to PHANTOM.

Changing Entity Layer

The Change Properties dialog box also enables you to change the layer assigned to the entities in a selection set. You may need to move entities onto a new layer to organize your drawing, or you might have made a mistake and drawn the entities on the wrong layer. Rather than erase them and draw them on the correct layer, just change their layer assignments.

In addition to using the Change Properties dialog box (DDCHPROP), you also can use the Modify Entity dialog box displayed by the DDMODIFY command. Like DDCHPROP, DDMODIFY enables you to change the layer, linetype, and color assigned to an entity. DDMODIFY also enables you to change other characteristics of the entity depending on the type of entity selected. With a circle selected, for example, you can change the center point and radius of the circle. You cannot modify more than one entity at a time with DDMODIFY, however.

In the following exercise, use DDMODIFY and the Select Layer dialog box (see fig. 66.6) to change the layer of an entity.

Select Layer

Current Layer: HEAD

Layer Name	State	Color	Linetype
0	On	white	CONTINUOUS
BOLT	On	cyan	CONTINUOUS
BORDER	On	cyan	CONTINUOUS
CENTER	On	blue	CENTER
DIM	On	yellow	CONTINUOUS
GASKET	On	red	CONTINUOUS
HEAD	On	yellow	CONTINUOUS
WATER	On	magenta	CONTINUOUS

Set Layer Name: HEAD

OK Cancel

Figure 66.6

The Select Layer dialog box.

Changing Entity Layer

Continue with your drawing from the previous exercise.

1. `Command:` *Select the circle at* ① *(see fig. 66.7)* — Creates a selection set

2. `Command:` *Choose* Modify, *then* Entity — Issues the DDMODIFY command and displays the Modify Circle dialog box

   `ddmodify`

continues

3. *Choose the* Layer *button* — Displays the Select Layer dialog box
4. *Choose the* GASKET *layer* — Specifies new layer
5. *Choose* OK, *then* OK *again* — Sets new layer property and changes entity layer
6. Save your drawing.

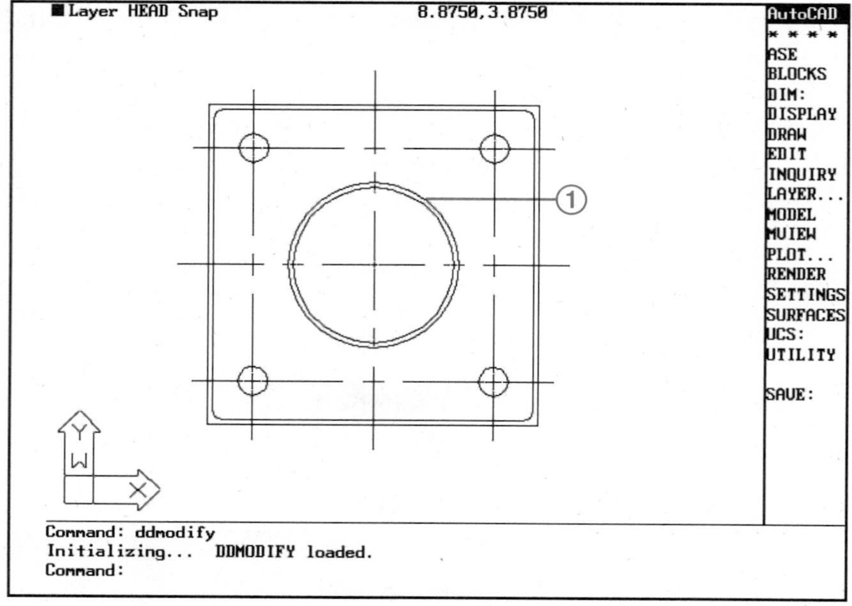

Figure 66.7
Circle to change layer assignment.

Because the entities are now on the GASKET layer, they inherit the color and linetype of their new layer.

You could also have used DDCHPROP to change the layer of the circle. If you need to change the properties of multiple entities, or if you only need to change the layer, linetype, or color of an entity, use DDCHPROP.

If you need to edit the entity (change the value of text, radius of a circle, etc.), use DDMODIFY. Note that many of the editing functions available in DDMODIFY also can be accomplished using autoedit modes.

Unit Review

What You've Learned

- How to change entity color, linetype, and layer using the DDCHPROP command
- How to use the DDMODIFY command to change entity properties

Review Questions

True or False

66.01 T F To change an entity to a different layer you must make that layer current.

66.02 T F The Layer button in the Change Properties dialog box enables you to view the properties of all layers in the drawing.

66.03 T F The DDMODIFY and DDCHPROP commands enable you to change the layer property of an entity.

66.04 T F Linetypes can be loaded into a drawing using the DDMODIFY command.

66.05 T F Layers can be created using the DDMODIFY command.

Multiple Choice

66.06 The __________ command enables you to change the color of an entity.

(A) Color

(B) DDCHPROP

(C) Entity

(D) BYLAYER

66.07 To determine the coordinates of the beginning of a line and its color, use the __________ command.

(A) LINE

(B) COLOR

(C) DDMODIFY

(D) DDCHPROP

Student: __________ Date: __________

Instructor: __________ Course: __________ Section: __________

66.08 If an entity has its color BYLAYER, the color property of a layer is stated in the __________ dialog box.

(A) Linetype

(B) Change Properties

(C) DDENTITY

(D) Change Line

Short Answer

66.09 What pull-down menus are used to select the DDCHPROP and DDMODIFY commands?

____

____

____

66.10 What linetypes are automatically loaded in all drawings?

____

____

____

Student: ______________________ Date: ________

Instructor: ______________ Course: __________ Section: ______

UNIT 67

Introduction to Blocks

Many drawings contain symbols that are repeated throughout the drawing. Components or parts of a drawing also are often repeated in a design. In manual drafting, these symbols are often placed with a design template. One type of design template is an Architectural design template, which might contain symbols for plumbing fixtures, door openings, kitchen appliances, and electrical outlets. AutoCAD includes a feature called BLOCKS that serve much the same purpose in an AutoCAD drawing that templates serve for manually-prepared drawings. In AutoCAD, design templates are divided into *blocks*, which are groups of symbols that you might want to use often. In this unit you learn about blocks, which are a useful tool for adding symbols and standard parts to your drawing.

The objectives for this unit are to:

- Understand how blocks can increase design productivity
- Recognize how the COLOR and LINETYPE commands can be used to control the display of blocks
- Identify the special properties of blocks created on layer 0

Using Blocks To Organize a Drawing

The BLOCK command in AutoCAD enables you to create parts and symbols that can be used repetitively in a drawing. The BLOCK command links together entities and defines them with a name. Entities linked together are redefined as one entity (a block) rather than as multiple entities that make up the block. Every time you need to insert the symbol in the drawing, you specify it by name and AutoCAD adds it to the drawing at the location you specify.

For example, assume that you are creating an electrical schematic (see fig. 67.1). You can define each of the symbols for resistors, capacitors, transistors, and other components as blocks. You give each block a name, and the name for the resistor block might be RESISTOR. When you need to add a resistor to the schematic, you simply insert the block named RESISTOR. Inserting the block takes only a few seconds, and saves you the time required to redraw each symbol individually. In many cases, you can increase your productivity considerably by using blocks.

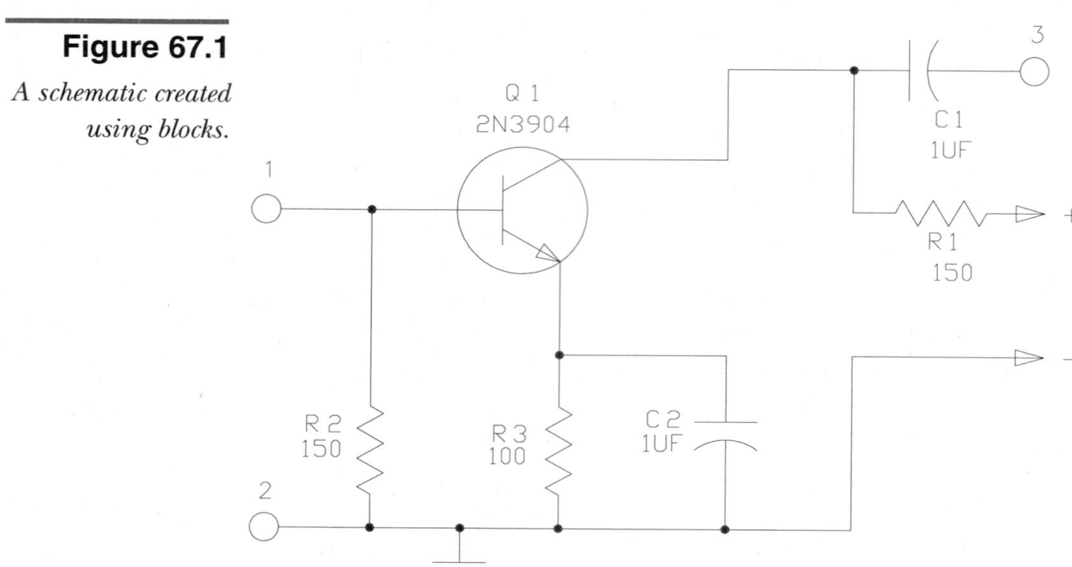

Figure 67.1
A schematic created using blocks.

Not only do you save time by using blocks, but your drawings are more uniform. Because each RESISTOR symbol is based on the same block definition, each one is identical to the others. Another advantage to using blocks is a decrease in the amount of disk space required to store a drawing, along with a decrease in the amount of memory needed to load and edit the drawing.

To illustrate how blocks save disk space and memory, assume that you have a standard part in a drawing that consists of 100 entities (lines, circles, etc.). If you copy the part using one of the autoedit modes or the COPY command, you duplicate the entities. If you copy it 10 times, you have added 1000 new entities to the drawing. If you make the part a block, and then insert it 10 times, you create only 110 entities—100 for the original block definition and 10 for the blocks. When you use blocks extensively, you can save a large amount of disk space.

When you begin a new drawing, review it and prepare a list of potential blocks to be used in a design. Review the sketch and other design information to identify parts or symbols that will be used often, then create the blocks before you begin the main drawing.

Understanding AutoCAD's Blocks

A *block reference* is a table that AutoCAD creates in memory to contain a description of the entities that make up a block. A drawing contains a reference for each different block. When you save a drawing, these block references are stored in the drawing file along with the other information that describes the drawing.

When you need to use a block, you *insert* it into the drawing. If the block definition exists in memory, AutoCAD places a block in the drawing at the location you specify, and the entities contained in the block appear at that location.

You can create a block from entities that are already in your drawing. If you draw a transistor symbol, for example, you later can use the BLOCK command to create a block from its entities. The block definition is then stored in memory and the original entities disappear from the drawing. After the block is created you can insert it into the drawing as many times as necessary.

In addition, you also can insert *any* AutoCAD drawing file as a block. When you insert a file in a drawing, AutoCAD first creates a block reference and copies all of the entities in the file into the block reference. Then, AutoCAD inserts the block at the location you specify.

A drawing stored on disk is not a block. When you insert a drawing as a block, the drawing being inserted does not change in any way. The entities do not become a block until you insert the file into another drawing. The source file from which the block definition is created does not change in any way when you use it to create a block definition in another drawing.

AutoCAD enables you to place the block into the drawing at various scales and rotations. You can change the size of a block by setting its scale factor. Blocks are placed into the drawing using the INSERT or DDINSERT command, from which you specify the X-scale, Y-scale, and Z-scale factors and the rotation angle to insert the block into the drawing. One block may be used to represent several components of a design with the same shape but of different sizes. Designers often create a *one-unit block* and insert it with multiple scale factors.

As an example, mechanical designers may use several sizes of nuts in a design. The nut consists of a hexagon circumscribed around a circle. Two inner circles represent the inner and outer diameter of the thread. The distance across flats of the hexagon is 1-1/2 times the diameter of the bolt. If you create a block for a 1" nut, you can insert it at larger or smaller scales to represent smaller or larger nuts. To represent a 5/16" nut, for example, insert the block at 0.3125 scale.

Figure 67.2

One-unit nut and 5/16" nut.

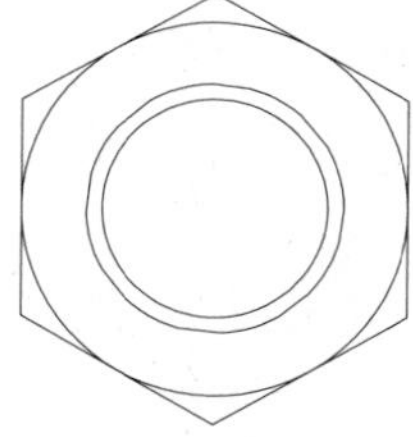

Throughout the design a single block can be used to represent all top views of nuts regardless of their size, which greatly decreases the time required to finish an assembly drawing. It also significantly reduces the amount of disk space and memory needed to store the drawing.

A block can be rotated when it is inserted, and a single block can be used to represent a single component in various positions. The architectural designer can use a single block for receptacles located on walls of various orientations (see fig. 67.3).

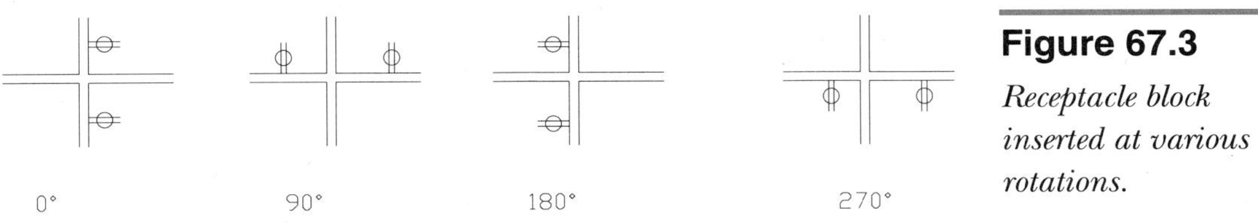

Figure 67.3

Receptacle block inserted at various rotations.

Another advantage to using blocks is the capability to redefine *a block. When you redefine a block, all occurrences of the block in the drawing also change. You can quickly change a number entities in the drawing in one operation. Redefining blocks is explained in unit 95, "Editing Blocks."*

Blocks and Layers

Entities that are linked together to form a block may be drawn on various layers or with unique color and linetype. The entity properties of the components of the block are retained when the block is inserted. If the block for the receptacle symbol shown in figure 67.3 is drawn with red explicit color, for example, it will be displayed in red color when it is inserted, regardless of its destination layer. Blocks retain the color, linetype, and layer properties of their source entities. If a block contains entities that were created on a layer that does not exist in the current drawing, AutoCAD adds the new layer to the drawing to contain those block entities.

The Entity Creation Modes settings for color, linetype, and layer of the entities of the block determine the properties of the block when inserted. You can insert blocks on layers that may have properties that differ from the blocked entities and the block will still be displayed with its unique properties. If you insert a block containing red lines onto a layer with a yellow color assignment, for example, the lines will still appear red.

Using BYBLOCK

There are two exceptions that prevent a block from retaining its original linetype and color properties: if the entities of the block were created with BYBLOCK color and BYBLOCK linetype, or are created on layer 0, the entities may not retain the same color and linetype properties with which they originally were drawn. If the entities of the block were created with BYBLOCK color and BYBLOCK linetype, they will be inserted into the drawing with the color and linetype of the drawing at the time of insertion. The drawing in figure 67.4 consists of entities created with color and linetype BYBLOCK.

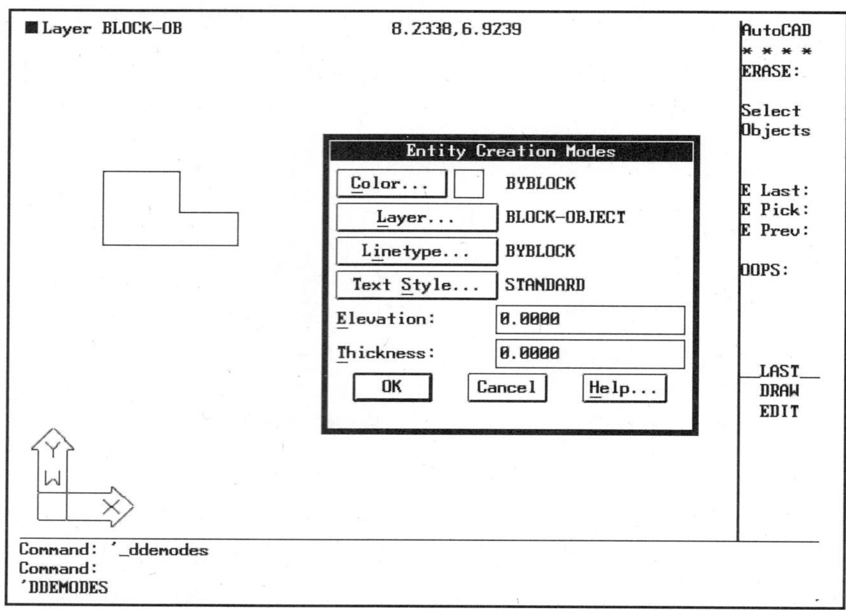

Figure 67.4

Entity Creation Modes of blocked entities.

When these entities are blocked and inserted back into the drawing they will take on the color and linetype property of the drawing at the time of insertion, regardless of the color or linetype that was used to create the original entities. Figure 67.5 shows the same entities inserted as a block below the original entities.

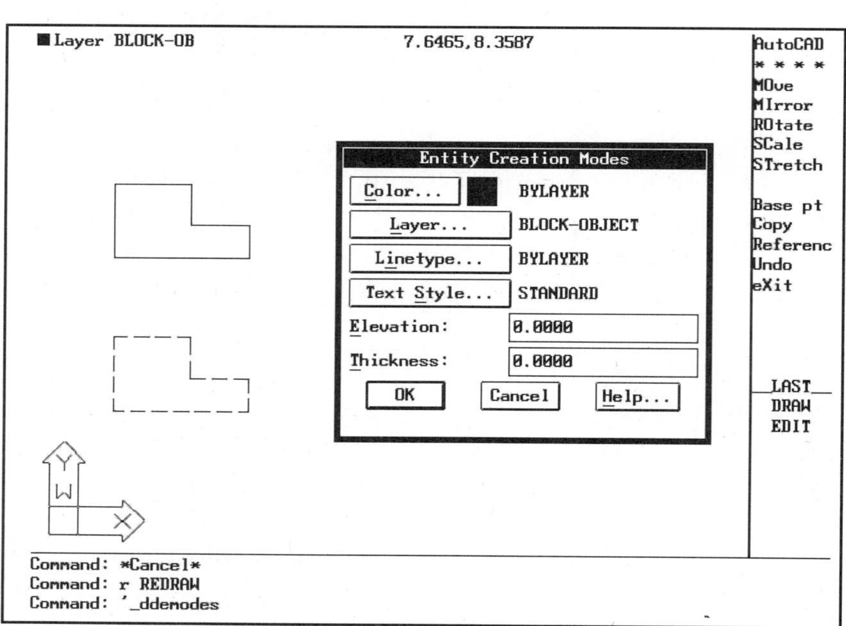

Figure 67.5

Entity Creation Modes when block is inserted.

The Entity Creation Modes at the time the block was inserted are both BYLAYER. The block has taken on the properties of the layer upon which it was placed. You can insert the same block in the drawing with color set explicitly to yellow and linetype set explicitly to hidden. The new occurrence of the block will then take on these explicit properties.

Using Layer 0 for Blocks

If you create a block from entities on layer 0, then insert the block, the entities retain their original color and linetype properties if they were set explicitly. If the entities were originally created on layer 0 with BYLAYER, however, these entities "float through" to the current layer and inherit the color and linetype properties of the current layer. Therefore, some of the entities in the block might retain their original color and linetype, but others may inherit the color and linetype of the current layer.

If an explicit color or linetype is set when you insert the block, the layer 0 entities in the block will not inherit the current explicit settings. They only inherit the color and linetype properties associated with the current layer.

With so many different options, the way you decide to structure the properties of entities in your blocks can be confusing. A few tips on the use of layers and blocks may help:

- **Explicit color and linetype, any layer.** Draw the entities with explicit color and linetype when you want those entities to retain their original color and linetype regardless of the layer, color, or linetype that is current when you insert the block. You can draw the entities on any layer.
- **Layer 0 and BYLAYER.** Draw the entities on layer 0 with linetype and color set to BYLAYER if you want the entities to inherit the color and linetype properties of the layer on which you insert the block.
- **Any color or linetype, and non-0 layers.** Draw the entities on any layer other than 0 and use either BYLAYER or explicit color and linetype settings whenever you want the entities to retain their original layer, color, and linetype settings.
- **BYBLOCK color.** Draw the entities with color set to BYBLOCK if you want the entities to inherit the current color when the block is inserted (regardless of the color property assigned to the current layer).
- **BYBLOCK linetype.** Draw the entities with linetype set to BYBLOCK if you want the entities to inherit the current linetype when the block is inserted (regardless of the linetype property assigned to the current layer).

Unit Review

What You've Learned

- ☞ Symbols and components of a drawing repeated in a design can be blocked and inserted thoughout the design to increase productivity, improve consistency, and reduce disk and memory requirements.
- ☞ Entities of blocks retain their layer, linetype, and color properties when inserted into a drawing if the entities were created with explicit linetype or color or were created on a layer other than 0 (unless BYBLOCK is used).
- ☞ Entities created with BYBLOCK color and BYBLOCK linetype will inherit the current color and linetype when the block is inserted.

Review Questions

True or False

67.01 T F All blocks must be created on layer 0.

67.02 T F Blocks may not be created with entities of explicit color.

67.03 T F The color of enitities within a block must be set the same as they are to appear when inserted.

67.04 T F All entities in a block must have the same color.

Multiple Choice

67.05 You can change the __________ scale of a block when you insert it into a drawing.

(A) X-

(B) Y-

(C) Z-

(D) all of the above

Student: ______________________ Date: __________

Instructor: ______________________ Course: __________ Section: __________

67.06 If entities are set to __________ color, they will be assigned color according to the color setting of the drawing at the time of insertion.

(A) BYLAYER

(B) BYBLOCK

(C) explicit

(D) white

67.07 If you insert a block consisting of entities drawn on five layers using __________ color and linetype, the entities will retain their original layer properties for linetype and color.

(A) BYLAYER

(B) BYBLOCK

(C) white/continuous

(D) 0

67.08 Entities created on layer 0, when inserted into a drawing as part of a block, inherit __________.

(A) BYBLOCK color and linetype

(B) BYLAYER color and linetype of the current layer

(C) explicit color and linetype

(D) white color

Short Answer

67.09 What are the advantages of creating a one-unit block?

____

____

____

67.10 Explain what happens to entities created on layer 0 with color and linetype set to BYLAYER when the entities are inserted as part of a block.

____

____

Student: __________ Date: __________

Instructor: __________ Course: __________ Section: __________

UNIT 68

Creating a Block

Before you can begin to use a block in a drawing, you must create the block. With the BLOCK command you can define the block's name, its insertion base point, and the entities to be included in the block. This unit teaches you to use the BLOCK command to create blocks.

The objectives for this unit are to:

- Recognize how the BLOCK and WBLOCK commands are used to create blocked entities.
- Use the BASE command to change the base of drawings used as blocks.

Creating a Full-Size Block

Block definitions are created by using the BLOCK command. This command defines the entities that are grouped and gives you the opportunity to name the block. The block name should be descriptive of the entities representing the block. A block name such as BLK1 or BLK2 does not describe the contents. A block name such as SINK2132 or SINK18, however, would remind you that the blocks represent sinks that are 21"×32" and 18" in diameter, respectively. Block names may be up to 31 characters long and include underscores, hyphens, letters, numbers, and the dollar symbol.

Using a name that describes the block's contents is particularly important if you are creating a library of standard parts. These parts will be used on many different drawings and may be used by other users, making a recognizable name very important.

The BLOCK command is located in the root screen menu as BLOCKS and under the Construct pull-down menu as Block. The BLOCK command prompts you for the block name. You can insert the name or review a list of block names that have already been created by entering a question mark. In addition to the list of blocks, a summary of the quantity and type of blocks used in the drawing is presented. There are four categories of blocks:

- **User Blocks.** Blocks created by you (the user)
- **External Reference.** Reference drawings that are attached to your file
- **Dependent Blocks.** Blocks of the reference file that have been attached to the drawing
- **Unnamed Blocks.** Internally created blocks that are created by AutoCAD to perform crosshatching, associative dimensioning, and solid modeling operations

After defining the name of the block, you are prompted for the insertion base point. You can specify an absolute coordinate or pick a point in the drawing (that is, a point on one of the entities on the block or off it). The insertion point will become the handle by which you insert the block. Insertion points are usually established using one of the object snap modes to ensure the block is inserted precisely. When you are creating a block, think about how you will use it. Pick an insertion point that will make it easy for you to insert the block in the correct location. Figure 68.1 shows some sample block insertion points.

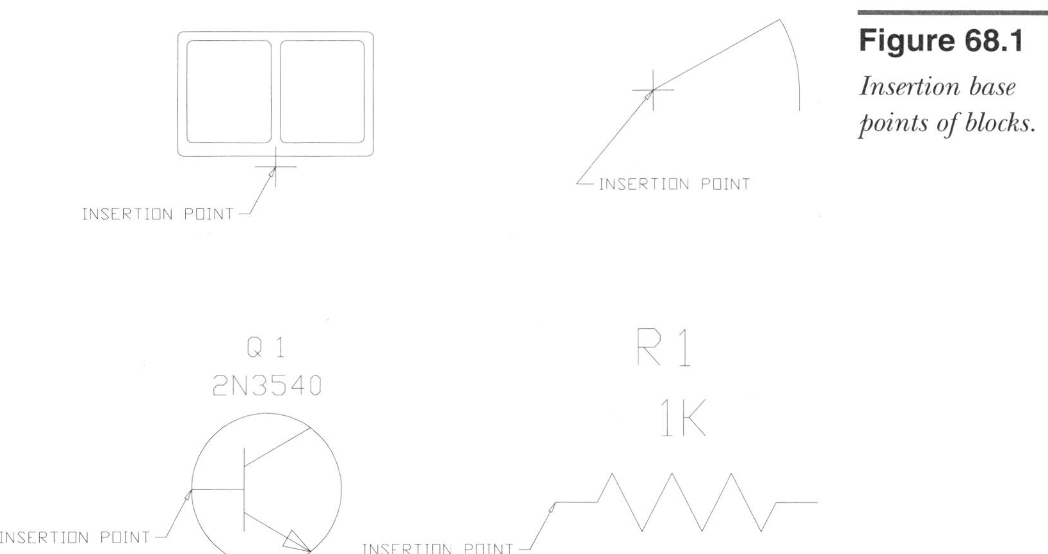

Figure 68.1

Insertion base points of blocks.

After you name the block and define the insertion base point, AutoCAD prompts you to select the objects to become the block. The entities do not have to have any relationship with one another (they need not be connected to one another). Continue to select the objects until you have selected all the entities for the block, then press Enter to terminate the selection process. The selected entities will then disappear from the screen. The entities that disappear are now named as a block and can be inserted into the current drawing with the INSERT or DDINSERT commands (see unit 69, "Inserting a Block in a Drawing").

If you want to keep the block definition but also want to bring back the original entities that defined the block, use the OOPS command. OOPS will place the entities back in the drawing (not as a block), but will also retain the block definition in memory. The use of the U or UNDO commands to bring back the entities also reverses the block definition.

In the following exercise, create a block of the diagonal slot at the lower left quadrant of the gasket.

Creating a Block

1. Begin a new drawing named 068???01 in your assigned directory using 068GASK as a prototype.

2. `Command:` *Select the four entities that make up the slot (see fig. 68.2)* — Creates a selection set and displays grips

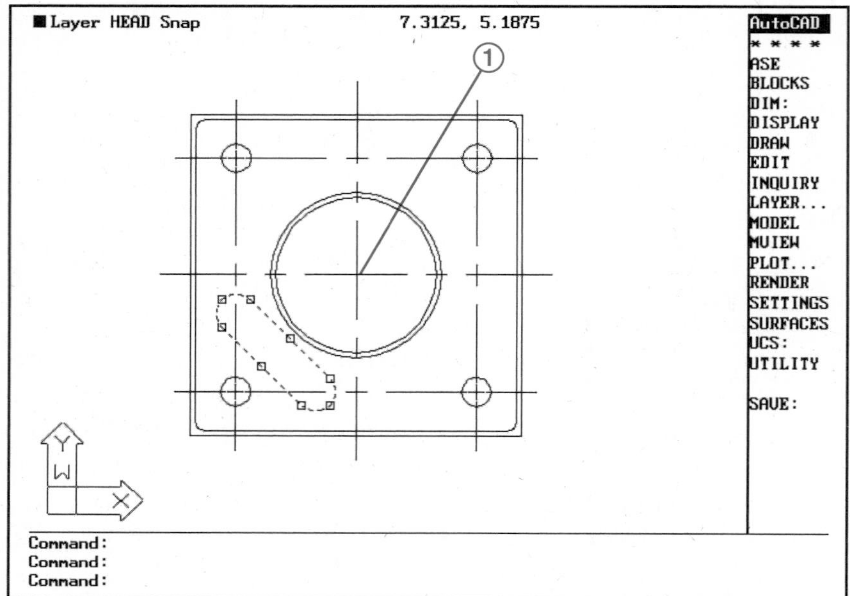

Figure 68.2
Entities to create block SLOT.

3. `Command:` *Choose* Construct, *then* Block — Issues BLOCK command

   `_block`

4. `Block name (or ?):` **`WATERGATE`** ↵ — Specifies name of block

5. `Insertion base point:` **`INT`** ↵ — Sets object snap mode

6. `of` *Pick the intersection at* ① *(see fig. 68.2)* — Specifies the insertion base point of the block

The newly created WATERGATE block will disappear into the drawing's memory. Next, view a list of all the blocks stored in your drawing.

7. `Command:` *Choose* Draw, *then* Insert — Displays the Insert dialog box (see fig. 68.3)

8. *Choose* Block — Displays the Blocks Defined in This Drawing dialog box

Notice that the block SLOT now appears in the dialog box.

9. *Choose* Cancel, *then* Cancel *again* — Closes the dialog boxes and cancels the block insertion

10. Save your drawing. — Block disappears into drawing's memory

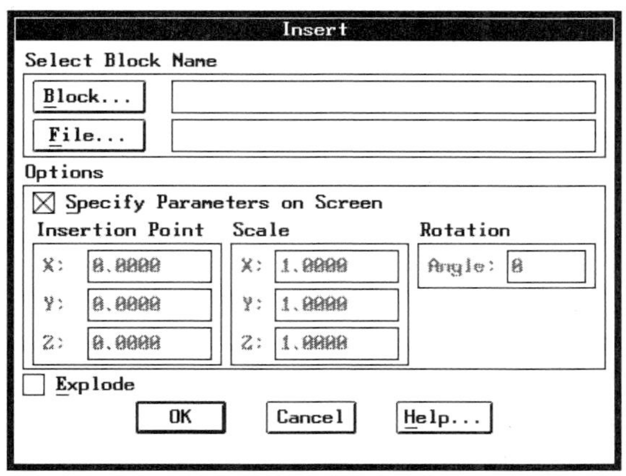

Figure 68.3

The Insert dialog box.

In unit 69 you will complete the block insertion process that you started in the previous exercise. For now, you have created a block called SLOT. When you saved your drawing, the block was saved along with the rest of the data in the drawing file.

You used an object snap mode in the previous exercise to specify the insertion base point of the SLOT block. Although you can pick any point for a base point (even without an object snap mode), you should get in the habit of using exact points for insertion base points. The use of exact points makes it possible for you to place the block accurately.

Creating a Unit Block

A unit block can be created to represent several objects that have the same shape but vary in size or rotation. This capability enables you to insert one block at different scales and rotations that represents several components or symbols. In the following exercise, you will create the symbol for a nut that is used in unit 69 to represent nuts of various sizes. Create the nut for a 1" diameter bolt.

Drawing a One-Unit Nut

1. Create a new drawing named 068???02 in your assigned directory using 068NUT as a prototype.

continues

2. Use LINETYPE or DDEMODES to set the current linetype to HIDDEN.

Next, draw a circle to represent the outside thread diameter.

3. `Command:` *Choose* Draw, *then* Circle, *then* Center, Diameter	Issues the CIRCLE command
`_circle`	
4. `3P/2P/TTR/<Center point>:` **`0,0`** ↵	Specifies center of circle
5. `Diameter/<Radius>: _diameter` `Diameter:` **`1`** ↵	Specifies diameter of circle

6. Use LINETYPE or DDEMODES to set the current linetype to CONTINUOUS.

Next, draw the circle for the inside thread diameter.

7. `Command:` *Choose* Draw, *then* Circle, *then* Center, Radius	Issues the CIRCLE command
`_circle`	
8. `3P/2P/TTR/<Center point>:` *With snap on, pick point* 0,0	
9. `Diameter/<Radius> <0.5000>:` **`0.45`** ↵	

Next, draw the outer circle to define the hexagonal shape of the nut.

10. `Command:` *Choose* Draw, *then* Circle, *then* Center, Diameter	Issues the CIRCLE command
`_circle`	
11. `3P/2P/TTR/<Center point>:` *Pick a point at* 0,0	
12. `Diameter/<Radius> <0.4000>:` `_diameter` `Diameter <0.8000>:` **`1.5`** ↵	

To complete the nut, draw the hexagon.

13. `Command:` *Choose* Draw, *then* Polygon, *then* Circumscribed	Issues the POLYGON command
`_polygon`	
14. `Number of sides <4>:` **`6`** ↵	
15. `Edge/<Center of polygon>:` *Pick a point at* 0,0	
`Inscribed in circle/Circumscribed about circle (I/C) <I>: _circumscribed`	

16. `Radius of circle:` *From the popup menu, choose* Quadrant

17. `_qua of` *Pick the circle at* ① *(see fig. 68.4)*

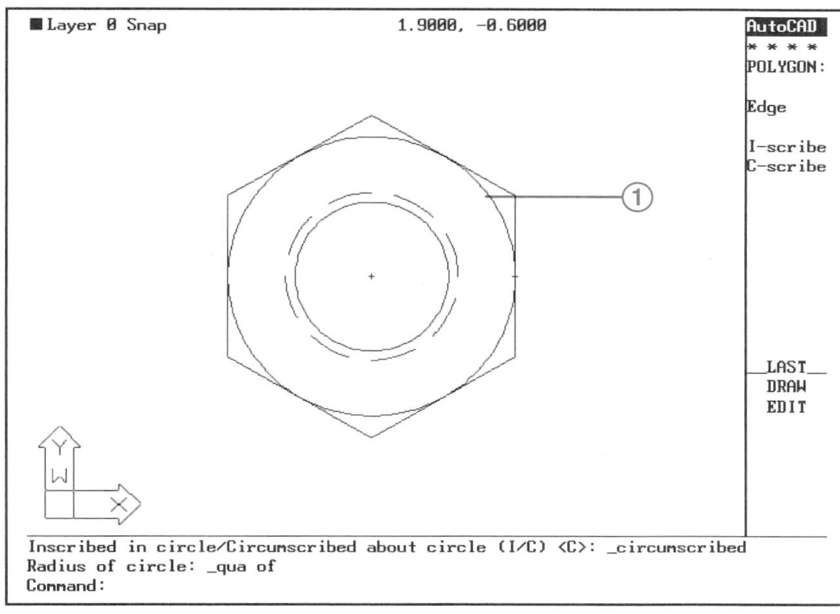

Figure 68.4

A nut symbol.

The outer thread diameter of the symbol is 1". The hexagonal body of a nut is typically 1 1/2 times the size of the thread size. Therefore, the hexagon was drawn at 1 1/2". You can insert this nut symbol into a drawing at full size for a 1" nut, but you also can use it for other size nuts. Because it is drawn at 1", it is easy to scale it to other sizes. To insert a 1/2" nut, for example, just scale the 1" nut by 0.5. In unit 69 you will experiment with inserting the nut at different sizes.

The inner thread diameter of 0.9" is an approximation. When the nut block is inserted at different sizes, the circle representing the inner thread diameter may not be sized exactly to scale. In most situations, the inner thread circle displayed out of scale is not a problem.

Next, create a block called NUT using the geometry you just created. Use pick-after selection this time.

Creating the NUT Block

Continue with your drawing from the preceding exercise.

1. `Command:` *Choose* Construct, *then* Block `_block`	Issues BLOCK command
2. `Block name (or ?):` **`NUT`** ↵	Specifies name of block
3. `Insertion base point:` **`0,0`** ↵	Specifies the insertion base point of the block
4. `Select objects:` **`ALL`** ↵	Selects all entities in the drawing
5. `Select objects:` *Press* Enter	Ends selection and creates the block
6. Save the drawing.	

Writing a Block to Disk

Block definitions are used within a drawing, but you also can write a block to a file using the WBLOCK command. Essentially, this means that you copy the block to a new drawing file on disk. The new drawing file is no different from any other drawing file that you create and save using the SAVE or SAVEAS commands.

Once the block definition is written to a file, you can use it outside of the current drawing. This technique enables you to export symbols you create in a drawing so that you can use them in other drawings.

When you enter the WBLOCK command, the Create Drawing File dialog box appears and prompts you for the name of the file you want to create. The file name should be descriptive of the entities represented by the block, just as the block name represents the purpose for the block. After you enter the file name, AutoCAD prompts you for the block name; enter the name of the block in memory that you want to write to disk.

In the following exercise, write the block NUT to disk as a file called NUT1.

Creating a WBLOCK file

Continue with your drawing from the previous exercise.

1. `Command:` **`WBLOCK`** ↵	Issues the WBLOCK command and displays the Create Drawing File dialog box
2. *In the* File *edit box, enter* **`NUT1`** ↵	Specifies the name of the file to create and closes the dialog box

3. `Block name:` **`NUT`** ↵	Specifies the name of the block to write to disk
4. Save the drawing.	

In addition to entering the name of a block in response to the block name prompt, you can enter = or *. The equal sign (=) can be used when the output file name is the same as the block name of the current drawing. AutoCAD will recognize the block based on the file name you assign as the WBLOCK output file name. The asterisk (*) will cause the current drawing to be written as the output file, which will include all used blocks. AutoCAD will drop unused blocks, layers, linetypes, textstyles, and dimension styles from the drawing. It will use coordinate 0,0 as the insertion base point.

If you press Enter without entering a name when AutoCAD prompts you to supply the block name, the WBLOCK command prompts you to select objects. This means that you can write a selection set of entities to disk without first making them into a block with the BLOCK command.

The drawing file NUT1 now exists in your assigned directory. If you want to view it, load the drawing. You will use NUT1 in unit 69.

WBLOCK creates standard AutoCAD drawing files. There is no difference between a drawing that you create and save with the QSAVE or SAVE commands and a drawing created with WBLOCK.

Unit Review

What You've Learned

- Commands: BLOCK, WBLOCK
- How to use the BLOCK command to define a block
- The importance of selecting an insertion point
- How to write a block to disk using WBLOCK

Review Questions

True or False

68.01 T F A blank may be used as a block's name.

68.02 T F User blocks are blocks that you create.

68.03 T F You cannot create a block from entities on layer 0.

68.04 T F Block names can be a maximum of 30 characters long.

68.05 T F The insertion base point of a block must be placed using object snap modes.

68.06 T F If you press Enter when prompted for a block name in the WBLOCK command, you can write a selection set of entities directly to a file without saving them as a block in the current drawing.

Multiple Choice

68.07 Blocks can be saved to a file by the __________ command.

(A) BLOCK

(B) Base

(C) WBLOCK

(D) File

68.08 To save the file and block with the same name, the _____ sign can be used as the block name in the WBLOCK command.

(A) *

(B) =

(C) /

(D) ^

Student: ____________________ Date: ________

Instructor: ____________________ Course: ________ Section: ________

68.09 The insertion base point of drawings written to disk with WBLOCK using * as the block name is located at ______________.

(A) 1,1

(B) 0,0

(C) the lower left corner

(D) the lower left corner of the limits

68.10 The command that will restore the entities of a block back to the drawing after you define the block is __________.

(A) BLOCK

(B) OOPS

(C) RESTORE

(D) Base

Additional Exercises

68.11 Create a one-unit block for the door symbol shown in figure 68.5. Draw the arc at 1" radius and at a center point of 0,0. The end point of the line should be located at 0,0. Afterward, use the BLOCK command to define a block called DOOR.

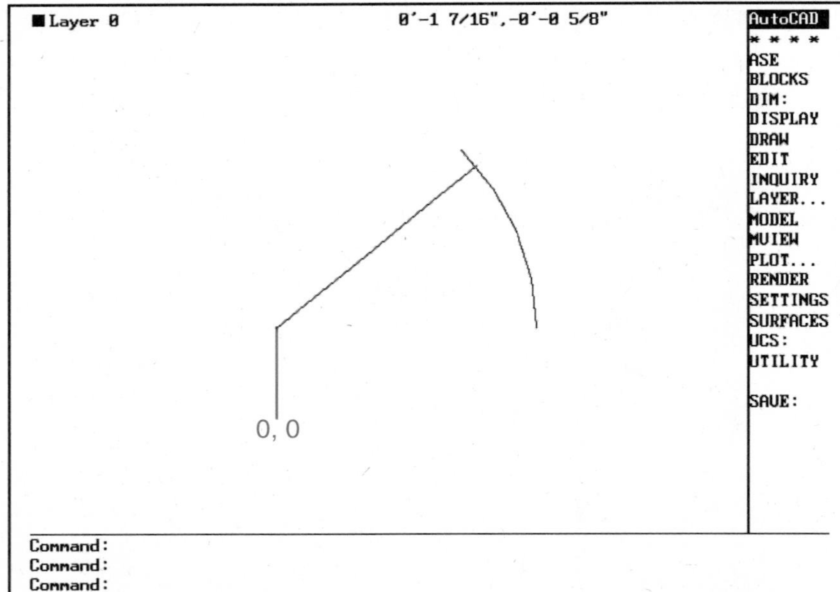

Figure 68.5

A one-unit door symbol.

68.12 Use WBLOCK to create a file called DOOR1 in your assigned directory using the block you created in exercise 68.11.

Student: ______ Date: ______

Instructor: ______ Course: ______ Section: ______

UNIT 69

Inserting a Block in a Drawing

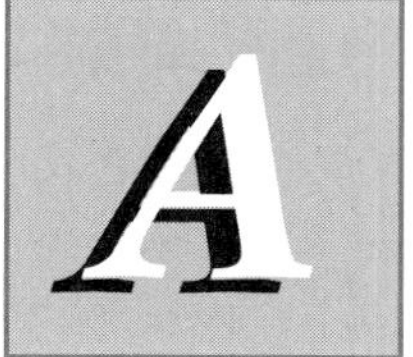

After you define a block in a drawing, you can insert it into the current drawing. You also can insert any drawing file into a drawing as a block. AutoCAD provides three commands for inserting blocks into a drawing: INSERT, DDINSERT, and MINSERT. This unit teaches you to use these commands to insert blocks.

The objectives for this unit are to:

- Use the INSERT, DDINSERT, and MINSERT commands to insert blocks and drawing files (as blocks) into a drawing
- Redefine a block using INSERT
- Explode blocks inserted into a drawing

Inserting a Block

To insert a block in a drawing, you must specify the name of the block or file to be inserted, the point at which you want the block to be inserted, the rotation of the block, and its scales in the X, Y, and Z axes. If you issue the INSERT command to insert a block, AutoCAD prompts you at the command line for this information. The DDINSERT command functions similarly to the INSERT command in the way it inserts blocks into a drawing, but DDINSERT provides a dialog box that you can use to locate the block or file to be inserted and specify the insertion parameters. Because the DDINSERT command is in some ways simpler to use, it is the one used in this unit.

You can access DDINSERT by choosing Draw, then Insert. This menu combination invokes the DDINSERT command, which displays the Insert dialog box shown in figure 69.1.

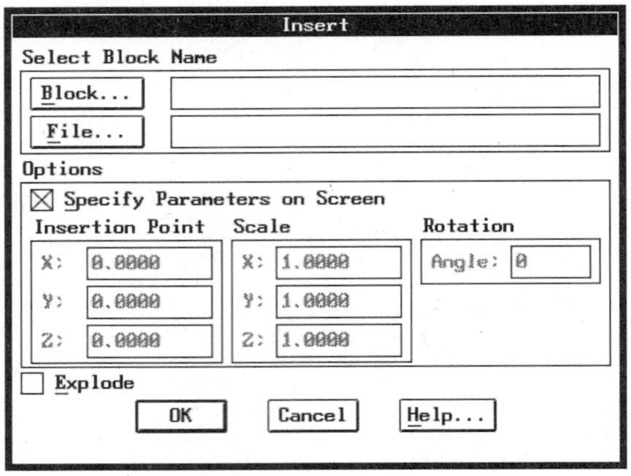

Insert
Select Block Name
Block...
File...
Options
Specify Parameters on Screen
Insertion Point Scale Rotation
X: 0.0000 X: 1.0000 Angle: 0
Y: 0.0000 Y: 1.0000
Z: 0.0000 Z: 1.0000
Explode
OK Cancel Help...

Figure 69.1

The Insert dialog box.

To select a block for insertion that is already defined in the drawing, choose the **B**lock button. This causes the Blocks Defined in this Drawing dialog box to appear as shown in figure 69.2.

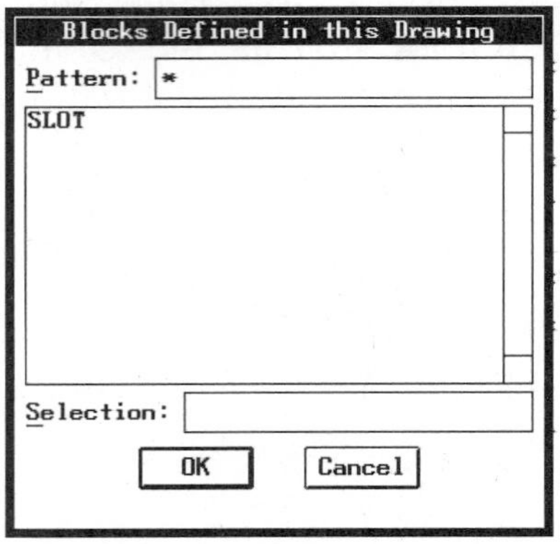

Blocks Defined in this Drawing
Pattern: *
SLOT
Selection:
OK Cancel

Figure 69.2

Block dialog box of the DDINSERT command.

To insert a file into the drawing as a block, choose the **F**ile button. The Select Drawing File dialog box appears (see fig. 69.3), enabling you to select the directory and the desired file.

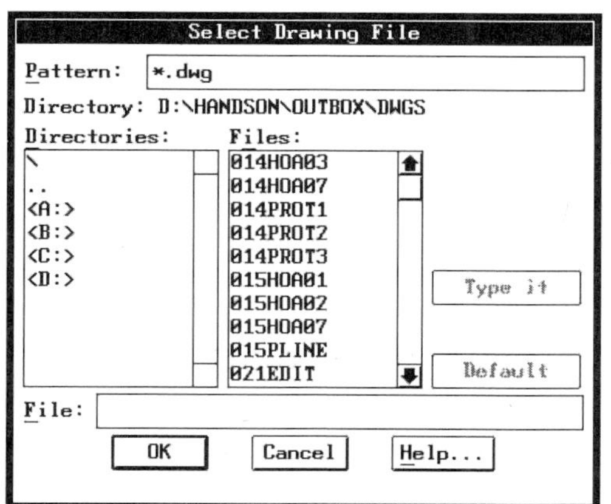

Figure 69.3

The Select Drawing File dialog box of the DDINSERT command.

The insertion base point that you specify when you create a block is the point by which the block is inserted. When you pick a point to insert a block, AutoCAD locates the block's insertion base point at the point you specify. If you are inserting a drawing file that has not had a specific base point set, the origin (0,0,0) becomes the insertion base point by default.

Setting Initial Block Parameters

You can specify the insertion point, scale, and rotation of the block at the command prompt or in the edit boxes in the Options group of the Insert dialog box. To set the insertion point, scale, and rotation in these boxes, place a check in the checkbox labeled Specify Parameters on Screen. To specify the parameters at the command prompt, clear this checkbox. If you specify the parameters at the command prompt, AutoCAD dynamically changes the appearance of the block as you specify rotation and scale values. This gives you a graphical means of verifying your settings.

In the following exercise, insert a block by presetting its parameters.

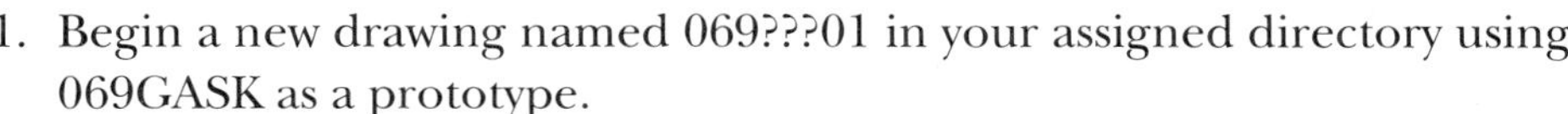

Using DDINSERT and Presets when Inserting a Block

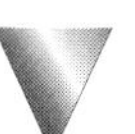

1. Begin a new drawing named 069???01 in your assigned directory using 069GASK as a prototype.

2. `Command:` *Choose* Draw, *then* Insert — Issues DDINSERT command and displays the Insert dialog box

3. *Choose the* Block *button*	Displays the Blocks Defined in this Drawing dialog box
4. *Select* SLOT *from the list, then choose* OK	Specifies name of block to be inserted
5. *Clear the* Specify Parameters on Screen *check box*	Enables preset controls
6. *Enter* **4** *in the* X insertion point *edit box (see fig. 69.4)*	Specifies X-ordinate of insertion point
7. *Enter* **5** *in the* Y insertion point *edit box*	Specifies Y-ordinate of insertion point
8. *Choose the* OK *button*	Ends preset specifications and inserts the block (see fig. 69.5)

9. Save your drawing.

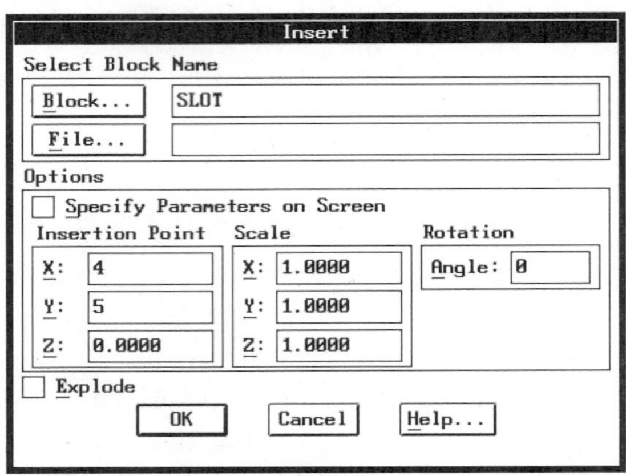

Figure 69.4

The Insert dialog box with preset values.

The block is inserted based on the preset values entered in the Insert dialog box. The use of preset scales and rotation when inserting a block does not enable you to see the size and orientation of the block prior to insertion. In addition, you might not know the absolute coordinate position where you want to insert the block. Therefore, you can use the Insert dialog box just to select the block, and then specify the other parameters at the command prompt and graphically when you insert the block.

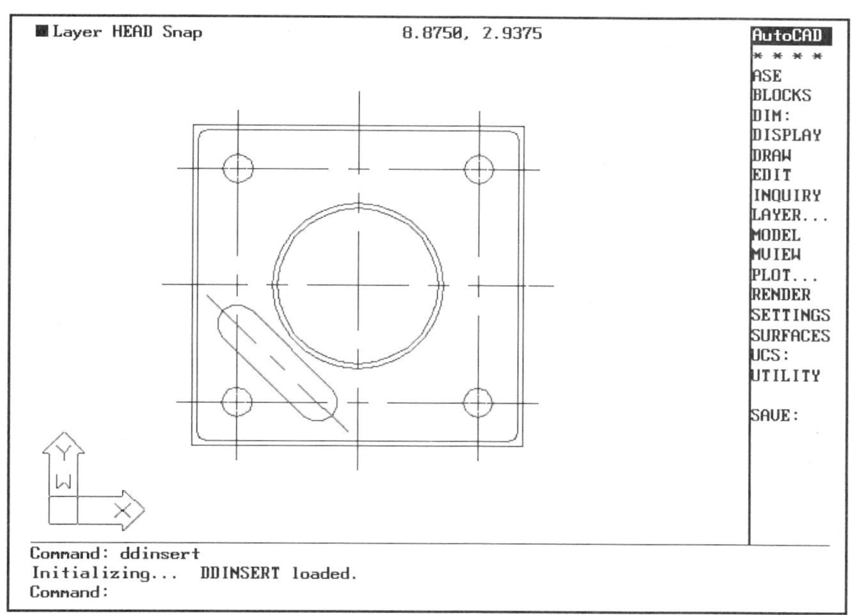

Figure 69.5

SLOT block inserted drawing.

Inserting a Block without Presets

Continue with your drawing from the preceding exercise.

1. `Command:` *Choose* Draw, *then* Insert `_ddinsert`	Issues the DDINSERT command
2. *Choose the* Block *button*	Displays the Blocks Defined in this Drawing dialog box
3. *Enter* **`SLOT`** *in the* Selection *edit box*	Specifies name of block to insert
4. *Place a check in the* Specify Parameters on Screen *check box*	Enables entry of parameters at the command prompt
5. *Choose* OK	Exits dialog box
6. `Insertion point:` **`INT`** ↵ `of`	Sets object snap mode
7. *Pick the intersection of center lines at* ① *(see fig. 69.6)*	Specifies insertion point of the block
8. `X scale factor <1>/ Corner / XYZ:` *Press* Enter	Accepts default of 1 for X scale
9. `Y Scale factor (default = x):` *Press* Enter	Accepts default of 1 for Y scale
10. `Rotation angle <0>:` **`180`** ↵	Specifies rotation angle and inserts the block
11. Save your drawing.	

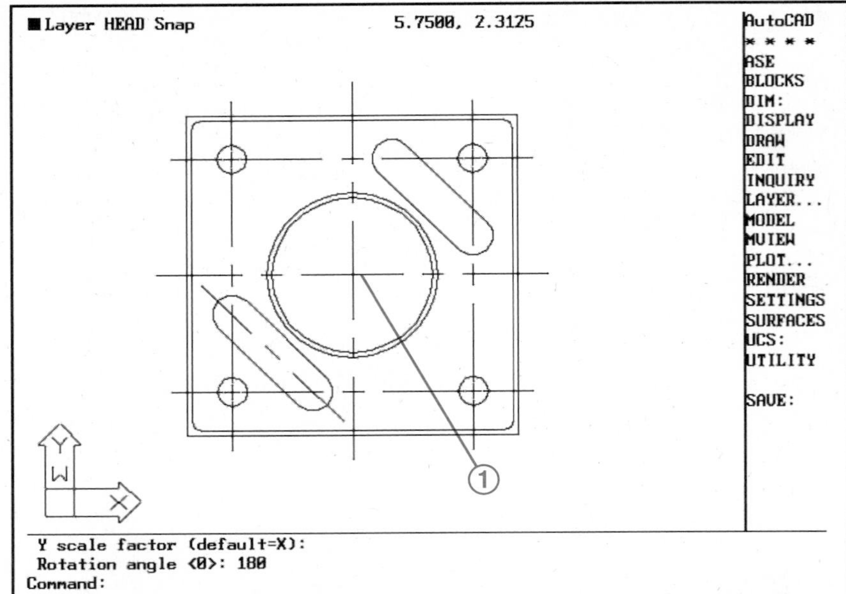

Figure 69.6

Location for insertion point.

Presetting Values from the Command Prompt

You can preset the scale and rotation of the block without using the Insert dialog box. After you select the block and specify the insertion point, you can use one of 10 options to preset scale and rotation values:

- **Scale.** Presets scale factors for X, Y, and Z.
- **Xscale.** Presets X scale only.
- **Yscale.** Presets Y scale only.
- **Zscale.** Presets Z scale only.
- **Rotate.** Presets rotation angle.
- **Pscale.** Presets scale factors for X, Y, and Z, but prompts you for verification prior to insertion.
- **PXscale.** Presets X-scale factor, but prompts for verification prior to insertion.
- **PYscale.** Presets Y-scale factor, but prompts for verification prior to insertion.
- **PZscale.** Presets Z-scale factor, but prompts for verification prior to insertion.
- **PRotate.** Presets rotation angle, but prompts for verification prior to insertion.

Inserting a Drawing File

Any drawing file can be inserted into another drawing as a block. Instead of selecting the Block button to list the available blocks in the drawing, choose the File button. AutoCAD displays the Select Drawing File dialog box, which you can use to locate and select the file to be inserted.

If you want to use the INSERT command to insert a file, but want to choose the file from a dialog box, enter a tilde (~) in response to AutoCAD's prompt for a block name to insert.

If you use the INSERT command rather than DDINSERT, AutoCAD prompts you at the command prompt for the name of block to be inserted. If you specify a name that does not match the name of a block defined in the drawing, AutoCAD searches the current drawing directory for a drawing file of the same name. You can enter a full path along with the file name to insert a block from a specific directory or disk. When AutoCAD locates the file, it creates a block from the drawing and names the block with the same name as the file.

If you need to change the insertion base point of a drawing before inserting it into another drawing as a block, first load the drawing to be inserted. Use the INSBASE command to change the coordinate of the insertion base point. You cannot change the insertion base point of a block during the INSERT command.

Redefining a Block with INSERT

In unit 68, "Creating a Block," you learned that you can use the BLOCK command to redefine a block and change it throughout the drawing. You also can use the INSERT command to redefine a block. Assume that you have a block named OLDBLOCK inserted in the drawing, and you want to replace it with a block or a drawing file named NEWBLOCK. You can issue the INSERT command and specify OLDBLOCK=NEWBLOCK as the block name. AutoCAD redefines all occurrences of OLDBLOCK using the block or file NEWBLOCK.

In the following exercise, redefine SLOT with the drawing 069SLOT2. The prototype for the next exercise contains block definitions for SLOT and 069SLOT2.

Your drawing should look similar to figure 69.7.

Redefining a Block with INSERT

1. Begin a new drawing named 069???02 in your assigned directory using 069GASK2 as a prototype.

2. `Command:` **`INSERT`** ↵	Issues the INSERT command
3. `Block name (or ?) <SLOT>:` **`SLOT=069SLOT2`** ↵	Redefines the block
4. `Insertion point:` *Press* Ctrl+C	Cancels the command

Your drawing should look similar to figure 69.7.

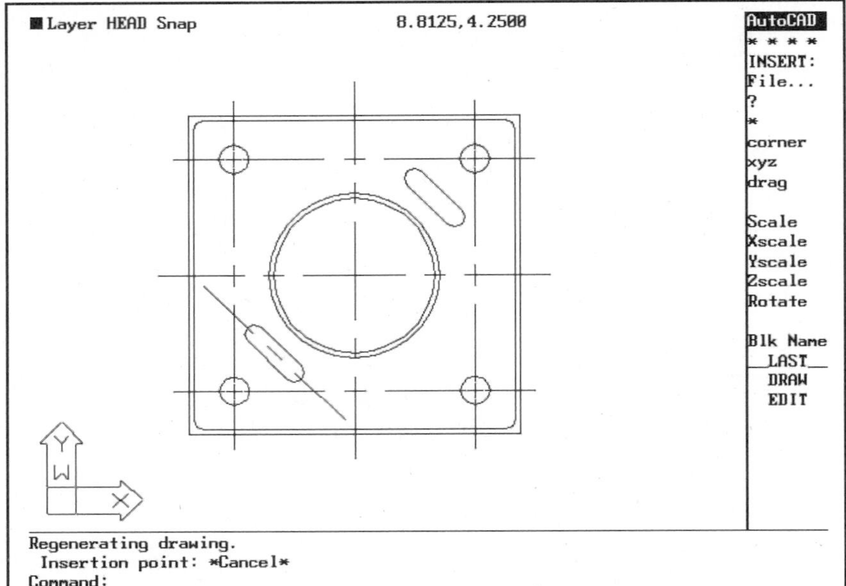

Figure 69.7
SLOT redefined with 069SLOT2.

Use this technique any time you need to redefine a block based on another block in the drawing or on a drawing file.

Exploding a Block

You learned that AutoCAD treats all entities in a block definition as a single entity. You cannot edit individual entities in a block definition.

Exploding a block removes the block definition and breaks the block into its constituent entities. The EXPLODE command is used to explode an existing block. The EXPLODE command is located in the EDIT screen menu and under the Modify pull-down menu. After a block is exploded, you can edit any entities that were formally part of the block. Exploding a block affects only the selected block insertion and does not affect all blocks of the same name.

The EXPLODE command uses both pick-first and pick-after selection. If a selection set exists when you issue the EXPLODE command, AutoCAD explodes all appropriate entities in the selection set (blocks and polylines). It ignores all entities in the selection set that cannot be exploded.

Exploding a Block

Continue with your drawing from the preceding exercise.

1. `Command:` *Select the slot at the lower left of the gasket*	Selects the entire block
2. `Command:` *Choose* Modify, *then* Explode	Issues the EXPLODE command and explodes the selected block
`1 found`	
3. `Command:` *Select any one entity on the exploded slot*	Selects the single entity rather than all entities in the slot

Now that the slot is exploded, you can change the linetype, color, and layer of any of the entities individually, or use other editing techniques to modify the slot.

*If you know that you need to explode a block before you insert it, use the DDINSERT command and place a check in the Explode check box. AutoCAD automatically explodes the block on insertion. You also can explode a block on insertion with the INSERT command. Just precede the block name with an asterisk, such as *NUT.*

Inserting an Array of Blocks with MINSERT

The MINSERT command is used to place a rectangular array of blocks in a drawing. All blocks in the array are recognized as a single entity. If you select any block in the array, all blocks in the array are selected.

In the following exercise, insert a nut symbol at each of the four small holes on the gasket. The nut is a 1" unit-scale symbol. Scale it to 0.375 for a 3/8" nut.

Inserting a Block with MINSERT

1.	Begin a new drawing named 069???03 in your assigned directory using 069NUTS as a prototype.	
2.	`Command:` **`MINSERT`** ↵	Issues the MINSERT command
	`_MINSERT`	
3.	`Block name (or ?):` **`NUT`** ↵	Specifies NUT as block
4.	`Insertion point:` **`2.5,3.5`** ↵	Specifies insertion point
5.	`X scale factor <1> / Corner / XYZ:` **`0.375`** ↵	Specifies X scale to .375
6.	`Y scale factor (default = X):` *Press* Enter	Accepts default Y scale equal to X scale
7.	`Rotation angle <0>:` *Press* Enter	Accepts default rotation of 0
8.	`Number of rows (---) <1>:` **`2`** ↵	Specifies 2 rows in the array
9.	`Number of columns (¦¦¦) <1>:` **`2`** ↵	Specifies 2 columns in the array
10.	`Unit cell or distance between rows (---):` **`3`** ↵	Specifies distance between rows
11.	`Distance between columns (¦¦¦):`**`3`** ↵	Specifies distance between columns and inserts array of nuts(see fig. 69.8)
12.	Save your drawing.	

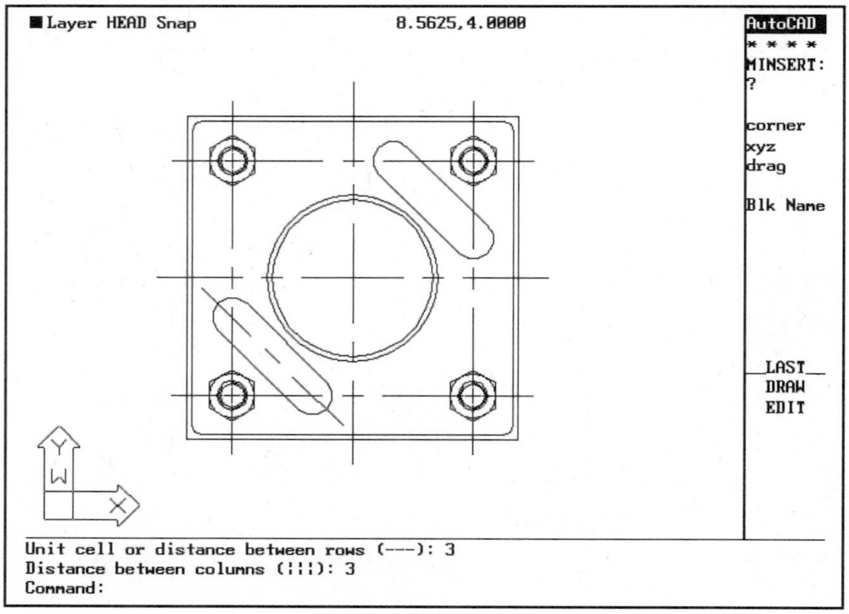

Figure 69.8

Array of nuts.

Blocks inserted with the MINSERT command cannot be exploded. In addition, all blocks of the array will have the same scale and rotation.

Unit Review

What You've Learned

- How to use the INSERT and DDINSERT commands to insert a block and a drawing file into a drawing
- How to insert a block array using the MINSERT command
- How to modify the entities of an inserted block using the EXPLODE command

Review Questions

True or False

69.01 T F The BLOCK command is used to insert a drawing file into a drawing.

69.02 T F The block's insertion base point can be changed when a block is inserted into a drawing.

69.03 T F The scale and rotation of the block can be set when the block is inserted.

69.04 T F You can insert a drawing as a block using the DDINSERT command.

69.05 T F A block can be exploded when it is inserted into a drawing.

69.06 T F Blocks inserted with MINSERT can be exploded.

69.07 T F If a block is exploded, all blocks with that same definition are exploded in the drawing.

Multiple Choice

69.08 An array of blocks can be inserted into the drawing using the __________ command.

(A) INSERT

(B) MINSERT

(C) BLOCK

(D) EXPLODE

Student: __________ Date: __________

Instructor: __________ Course: __________ Section: __________

69.09 To insert a block and explode it at the same time, a __________ is entered as a prefix to the block name.

(A) *

(B) =

(C) /

(D) ^

69.10 To preset the rotation of a block when inserting it, you respond to the Insertion point prompt by entering __________.

(A) Scale

(B) X-scale

(C) Rotate

(D) Angle

Student: ______________________ Date: __________

Instructor: ______________ Course: __________ Section: __________

UNIT 70

Introduction to Xrefs

When you insert a block, the block becomes a permanent part of the drawing. You can erase the block and redefine it, but the entities that make up the block still are contained in the drawing. AutoCAD provides another mechanism for inserting one drawing into another drawing. *External references,* also referred to as *Xrefs,* appear in a drawing but do not actually become a part of the drawing. As you learn in this unit, Xrefs are extremely useful for *workgroup design*—working on a design as part of a team.

The objectives for this unit are to:

- Understand what a workgroup is and how it can apply in design and drafting
- Understand the advantages of workgroup design
- Understand the purpose of externally referenced drawings (Xrefs)
- Understand the advantages of using Xrefs rather than blocks
- Recognize the options of the XREF command

Understanding External References (Xrefs)

An *external reference,* or *Xref,* is simply a drawing that appears within another drawing, similar to the way a block appears in a drawing in which it is inserted. You can select an Xref, move it around in the drawing, rotate it, and perform other editing operations on it, just as you can with blocks.

Xrefs are very different from blocks, however. The entities that make up a block definition are stored within the drawing that contains the block definition. If you insert one drawing into another drawing as a block, the entities that make up the inserted drawing are copied into the destination drawing. The entities that appear in a drawing as part of an Xref do not become part of the drawing, however. These entities exist only in the external source file from which they are read. Xrefs can be considered "ghost images" because the entities are not really in the drawing, although they appear as if they are.

Xrefs are not inserted into a drawing in the same manner as blocks, although the process is very similar. An Xref is attached to a drawing. The XREF command enables you to attach an Xref to a drawing. Although the two operations sound different, attaching an Xref is very similar to inserting a block. You specify the insertion point (which is actually the *attachment* point), the scale factor for the Xref, and its rotation. The Xref then appears in the drawing at the specified point. Like blocks, you can attach a file in a drawing at many locations and at different scales and rotations.

Understanding the Advantages of Xrefs

If Xrefs are so much like blocks, what purpose do they serve? The primary benefit of Xrefs is that they make workgroup design possible. The term *workgroup design* means to work as part of a team on a single project. Consider a commercial building as an example. The design has many aspects—floor plan, electrical, plumbing, HVAC, equipment layout, office layout, facilities planning, and more. Complex jobs like this often are designed by a team of designers rather than a single person. The team of designers is considered a *workgroup.*

Coordinating a complex project such as a commercial building is difficult. Each designer in the workgroup must rely on other members for information about the design. One person might be responsible for designing the floor plan, another might be responsible for electrical layout, and so on.

All these areas are related, however. For example, everyone in the workgroup needs to know what the floor plan for the building is so that they can design their part of the building. For example, the person laying out the plumbing needs a copy of the building's floor plan to determine the location of pipes and other fixtures.

Each designer could insert the floor plan into his or her drawing as a block. If the floor plan is inserted as a block, however, the piping designer has no way of knowing if the floor plan changes because the block does not update automatically. The person designing the floor plan would have to inform everyone else on the project that the design changed. The piping designer might suddenly discover fixtures she located in a restroom are now located in a hall. Her design then has to be changed.

Xrefs can help keep all these different drawings up to date. If the floor plan is attached to each designer's drawing as an Xref, it does not actually become a part of these other drawings. If a change occurs to the original reference drawing, the change occurs automatically each time the other designers load their drawings, regenerate the drawing, plot the drawing, or specifically direct AutoCAD to update the Xrefs in the drawing. Any changes to one aspect of the design can be reflected automatically in other areas of the design. When a change occurs, each designer in the workgroup knows almost immediately and can change his or her area of the design accordingly.

You can use object snap modes to snap to points in an Xref. This makes it possible to use the geometry in the Xref as if it were a real part of your drawing.

Saving Memory and Disk Space

Another advantage of Xrefs is that they enable you to place a lot of information in a drawing without substantially increasing the drawing's file size or the amount of memory it requires to edit. The reason: entities in the Xref do not become a part of the drawing.

If you attach an Xref that contains 1,000 entities to a drawing, you add only one entity to the drawing—the reference itself. All the other entities remain in the original reference file. Whenever necessary, AutoCAD reads the entities from the source file to update its display. The use of Xrefs also reduces disk space requirements because the data in the Xref is not duplicated in each drawing to which it is attached.

Other Uses for Xrefs

Xrefs are not just for workgroup design. Any time you want to add information to a drawing but do not want to make the information a permanent part of the drawing, you can attach it as an Xref. The title block for a drawing is a good example. The title block itself never changes, although the information in the title block does change. Instead of inserting the title block as a block, attach it as an Xref.

You also can use Xrefs to attach temporary reference information to your drawing. Suppose you are designing a mechanical part that attaches to another part, which already has been designed. You can attach this other part to your drawing to provide a basis for your design. By doing so, you ensure that your part matches perfectly with the other part.

An Xref can contain nested Xrefs. *If you attach an Xref to a drawing, save the drawing, and then attach this new drawing in another as an Xref, the new Xref contains the nested Xref.*

Understanding Layers and Named Objects

Several drawings can be attached to a drawing as Xrefs, and each Xref can have unique or similar layer characteristics as the drawing to which it is attached. If you attach an Xref that has unique layers named in it, those new layers appear in the drawing, but are prefixed with the name of the Xref. If you attach an Xref named FPLAN and it contains a layer called WALLS, the WALLS layer is renamed FPLAN|WALLS and appears with that new name in the Layer Control dialog box. Layer names in the Xref that match layers in the drawing to which it is attached also are renamed in the same way. If your new drawing contains a layer called WALLS and you attach the FPLAN drawing, you have two different layers—one named WALLS and another named FPLAN|WALLS.

Although you can change the color and linetype characteristics of Xref layers, freeze and thaw them, and turn them on and off, you cannot make these layers current. This prevents you from drawing on these layers. This is necessary because the layers do not really exist, and are only "borrowed" from the Xref. Figure 70.1 shows the Layer Control dialog box for a drawing to which an Xref has been attached.

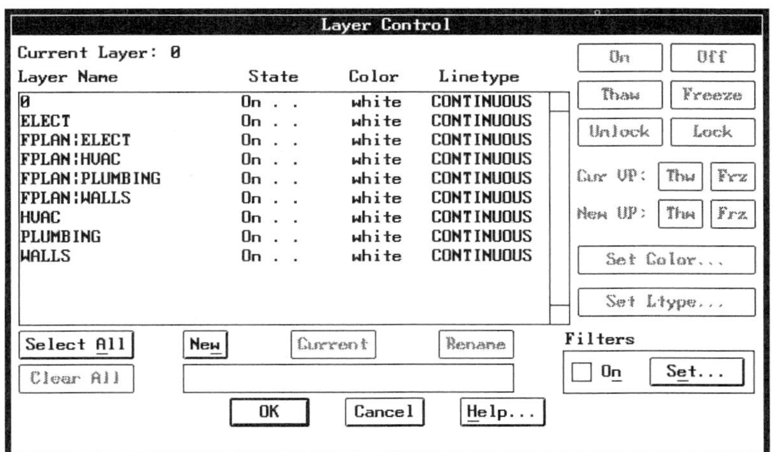

Figure 70.1

Layer Control of a drawing with attached Xrefs.

Other named objects of the externally referenced drawings also are brought into the current drawing. Named objects include blocks, dimensions styles, layers, linetypes, text styles, named user coordinate systems, named views, and named viewport configurations. These named objects become dependent upon the externally referenced drawing and are renamed within the current drawing. As with layers, these objects are prefixed by the name of the Xref, such as FPLAN|MYLINETYPE.

AutoCAD does not retain the layers in an Xref as part of the current drawing when you save it. AutoCAD enables you to retain the layer visibility changes by turning on the VISRETAIN system variable. The VISRETAIN system variable, when set to one, causes the layer visibility of Xrefs to be saved with the current drawing and to be retained when the reference drawing is reloaded into the drawing. If you turn off an Xref's layer, it will be turned off the next time you load the drawing.

Named objects of an Xref can become part of the current drawing by using the Bind option of the XREF command. *Binding* the Xref causes its named objects to become a permanent part of the current drawing; binding a reference drawing transforms it into a block. Dependent named objects that are part of the reference drawing are bound to a current drawing and renamed with the drawing file name and *$number$* prefixing the original object name (see fig. 70.2). AutoCAD attempts to use the number zero in the object name. If that name already exists, AutoCAD continues to increase the number by one until it determines a new, unused name. Unit 96, "Editing Xrefs," explains Xref binding in more detail.

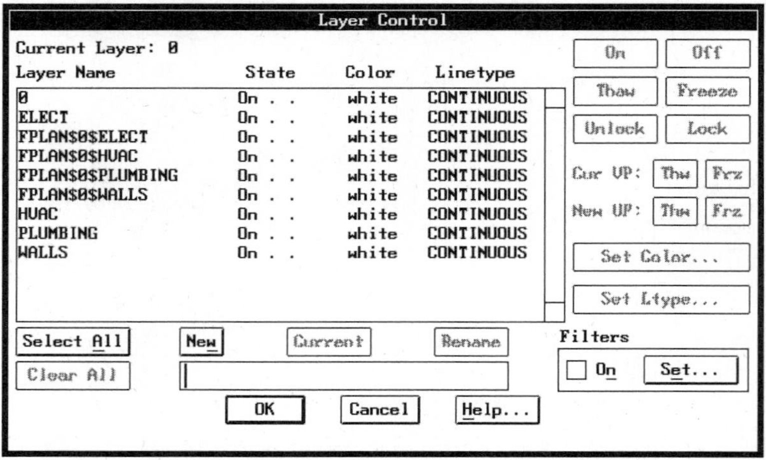

Figure 70.2

Layer Control dialog box when layers are bound to a drawing.

NOTE

The XBIND command enables you to select specific named objects to bind to the current drawing without binding all named objects. The XBIND command is located in the BLOCKS screen menu. AutoCAD prompts you to select the following named objects to bind: Block, Dimstyle, Layer, Ltype, and Style. You can use these named objects in your current drawing. The named objects are renamed with the number and dollar sign to signify their sources.

Understanding Xref Command Options

The XREF command is located in the File pull-down menu and in the BLOCKS screen menu. The XREF command provides several options:

- **?.** Entering a question mark displays a list of Xrefs attached to the current drawing.
- **Attach.** This option prompts you for the name of a drawing to attach as an Xref to the current drawing.
- **Bind.** This option prompts you for the name of one or more Xrefs to bind to the current drawing as a block.
- **Detach.** This option prompts you for the name of one or more Xrefs to detach from the drawing. Detaching an Xref removes it and its reference from the drawing.
- **Path.** This option enables you to change the path where an Xref can be found. Use this option when an Xref moves to a different disk or directory.
- **Reload.** This option enables you to reload one or more Xrefs, updating any changes that occurred in the reference drawing(s).

Unit Review

What You've Learned

- Xrefs can be attached to a drawing file to reduce the file size and memory required to display the design
- Xrefs facilitate workgroup design
- Xrefs are attached using the XREF command
- You can bind an Xref to the drawing, making it a block

Review Questions

True or False

70.01 T F The layers of an Xref cannot be frozen.

70.02 T F The entities in Xrefs are saved as part of the current drawing.

70.03 T F Entities in an Xref must be bound to the current drawing before object snap modes can be applied to the entities.

70.04 T F Only drawings in the same directory can be used as Xrefs.

70.05 T F Layers of Xrefs are renamed when attached to a drawing.

70.06 T F Named objects of an Xref are discarded when it is attached to the current drawing.

Multiple Choice

70.07 A list of Xrefs can be obtained using the XREF command and by entering __________ at the XREF prompt.

(A) Bind

(B) Path

(C) List

(D) ?

70.08 The Path option of the XREF command enables you to change __________.

(A) the directory of the Xref

(B) the drive of the Xref

(C) the path of the named objects

(D) A and B

Student: ______________________ Date: __________

Instructor: ______________________ Course: __________ Section: __________

70.09 To remove an Xref from a drawing, use the __________ option of the XREF command.

(A) Bind

(B) Attach

(C) Detach

(D) Remove

70.10 Xrefs that are bound to the current drawing become a __________.

(A) new drawing

(B) block

(C) detached reference file

(D) bound entity

Student: ______________________ Date: __________

Instructor: ______________________ Course: __________ Section: __________

Using Xrefs

The XREF command attaches drawings to the current drawing as Xrefs. This unit includes several exercises that use Xrefs. The exercises demonstrate attach Xrefs, change the path to an Xref, and list the Xrefs that are attached to the drawing.

The objectives for this unit are to:

- Use the XREF command to attach an Xref to a drawing
- Use the XREF command to change the path of a reference drawing and to change which drawings are used as reference
- Use the List option of the XREF command to obtain a list of attached Xrefs

Attaching an Xref to a Drawing

The XREF command is located in the File pull-down menu and in the BLOCKS screen menu. The default option, Attach, enables you to select the drawing to attach to your current drawing. The Select File to Attach dialog box appears with options to select the drive, directory and file name of the drawing you want to use as an external reference. The path to the selected file is saved and each time the drawing is opened, regenerated, or plotted, that path will be followed to reload the Xref. When attaching an Xref, you also must supply the insertion point, scale, and rotation to attach the reference drawing, just as you do when inserting a block.

In the following exercise, begin a new drawing using the prototype of a computer lab. Then, attach a drawing of a desk as an Xref. The drawing of the desk, 071DESK, is located on the same drive and directory as your prototype drawings.

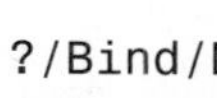

Attaching a Reference Drawing

1. Begin a new drawing named 071???01 in your assigned directory, using 071LAB as a prototype.
2. `Command:` *Choose* File, *then* Xref, *then* Attach — Issues the XREF command with the Attach option and displays the Select File to Attach dialog box (see fig. 71.1)

```
?/Bind/Detach/Path/Reload/<Attach>:
_attach
Xref to Attach: ~
```

3. *Locate and select the file* 071DESK, *then choose* OK — Specifies the name of the drawing to attach

```
Attach Xref 071DESK: 071desk.dwg
071DESK loaded.
```

4. `Insertion point:` *Pick a point at* ① *(see fig. 71.2)* — Specifies the point at which the Xref will be attached
5. `X scale factor <1> / Corner / XYZ:` *Press* Enter — Accepts the default X scale of 1
6. `Y scale factor (default=X):` *Press* Enter — Accepts default Y scale equal to X scale
7. `Rotation angle <0>:` *Press* Enter — Accepts default rotation of zero degrees
8. Save your drawing.

Your drawing should resemble figure 71.2.

The XREF command does not provide a dialog box that you can use to preset insertion point, scale, and rotation values for the Xref. You must enter these values at the command prompt.

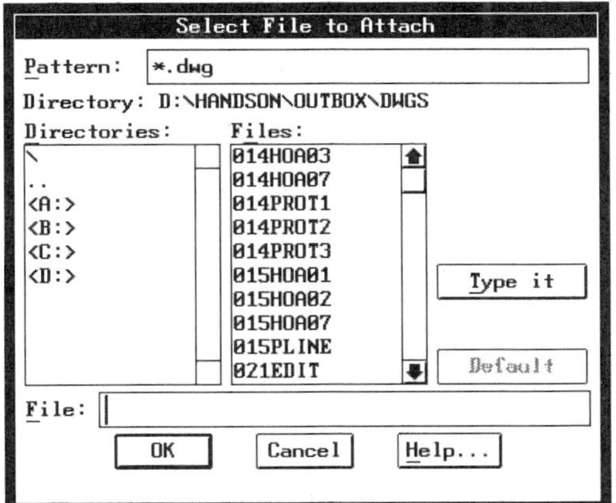

Figure 71.1

The Select File to Attach dialog box.

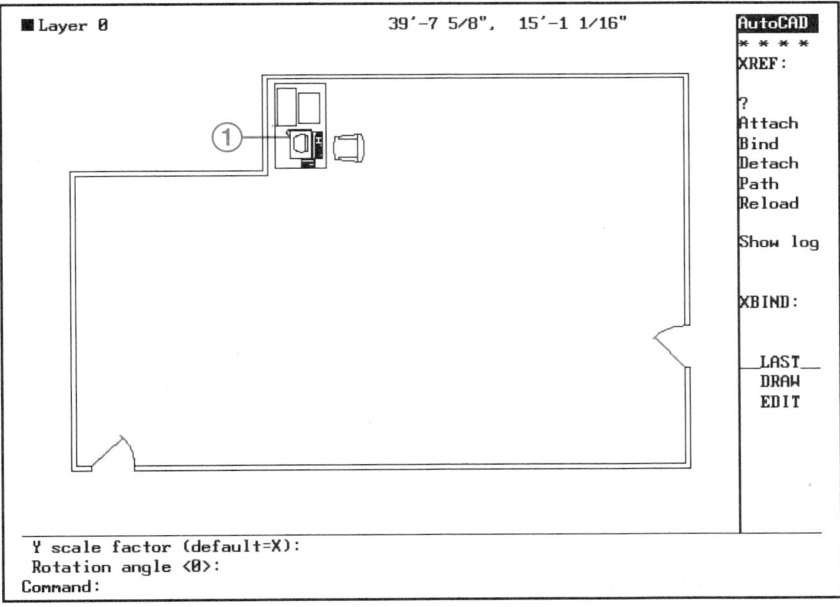

Figure 71.2

Desk attached as an Xref.

The Xref has been attached to the drawing. If you select it, you will discover that it has only one grip, located at its insertion point, just like a block. You can select the grip and use any of the autoedit modes to modify the Xref. As with blocks, you cannot stretch the Xref; stretching the Xref only moves it.

If the source drawing for the Xref changes, you will see the change reflected in your drawing when you load the drawing, regenerate it, or plot it. You will see an example of this in unit 96, "Editing Xrefs."

Xrefs are useful when you need to view a different drawing without closing the drawing that is currently open. You can attach the other drawing as an Xref, view it as necessary, then detach it from your drawing to remove it.

This unit does not cover scaling and rotating Xrefs on insertion because the process is identical to scaling and rotating blocks. If you are not familiar with this process, refer to unit 69, "Inserting a Block in a Drawing."

Unlike a block, you cannot explode an Xref because the entities in the Xref are not a part of the current drawing. You must first bind the Xref to the drawing to make it a block, then explode it if you want to edit entities in the Xref. Rather than bind an Xref, a much better option is to save the current drawing, load the source file for the Xref, and make the changes directly to the source file. Then reload the original drawing and the changes will be reflected in the Xref.

Changing the Xref's Path

When you attach a drawing as an Xref, AutoCAD stores the insertion base point, scale, and rotation of the Xref with your drawing. It also stores the path of the file that is attached, including the disk, directory, and file name of the Xref's source drawing. Occasionally, the source drawing for the Xref may move to a different drive or directory. You may be working with preliminary drawings, for example. When the drawings are finalized, they might be moved to a different location. You need some way to direct AutoCAD to look in this new location for the Xref's source drawing. The Path option solves this problem.

In the following exercise, copy the 071DESK drawing from your prototype directory to your assigned directory. Make a small modification to the new copy of the desk drawing, then open your lab drawing and change the path of the Xref.

Changing an Xref's Path with the Path Option

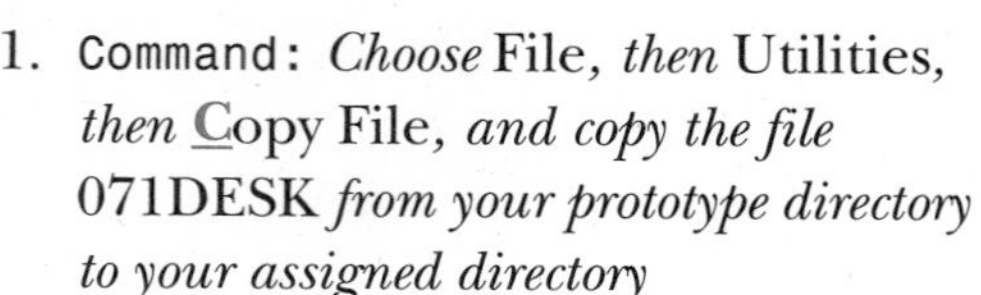

1. `Command:` *Choose* File, *then* Utilities, *then* Copy File, *and copy the file* 071DESK *from your prototype directory to your assigned directory* — Creates a copy of 071DESK in your own directory

2. Open the file 071DESK from your assigned directory, then use ERASE to modify the drawing as shown in figure 71.3. Save the changes.

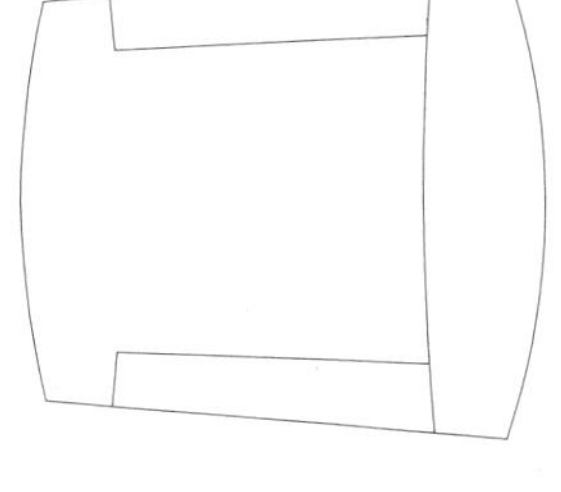

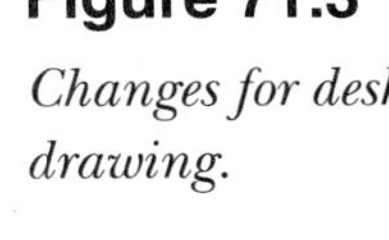

Figure 71.3

Changes for desk drawing.

3. Open the drawing 071???01 from your assigned directory.

4. `Command:` *Choose* File, *then* Xref, *then* Change Path — Issues the XREF command with the Path option

   `?/Bind/Detach/Path/Reload/<Attach>:`
   `_path`

5. `Edit path for which Xref(s):` **`071DESK`** ↵ — Specifies the name of the Xref to change path

   `Scanning...`
   `Xref name: 071DESK`
   `Old path:` *prototype-dir*\\`071desk.dwg`

6. `New path:` *Enter the path to your assigned directory, including the file name* 071desk.dwg, *then press* Enter — Specifies the new path to the file

   `Reload Xref 071DESK: 071DESK.DWG`
   `071DESK loaded. Regenerating drawing.`

Because of the change you made to the desk drawing, your current drawing should resemble figure 71.4.

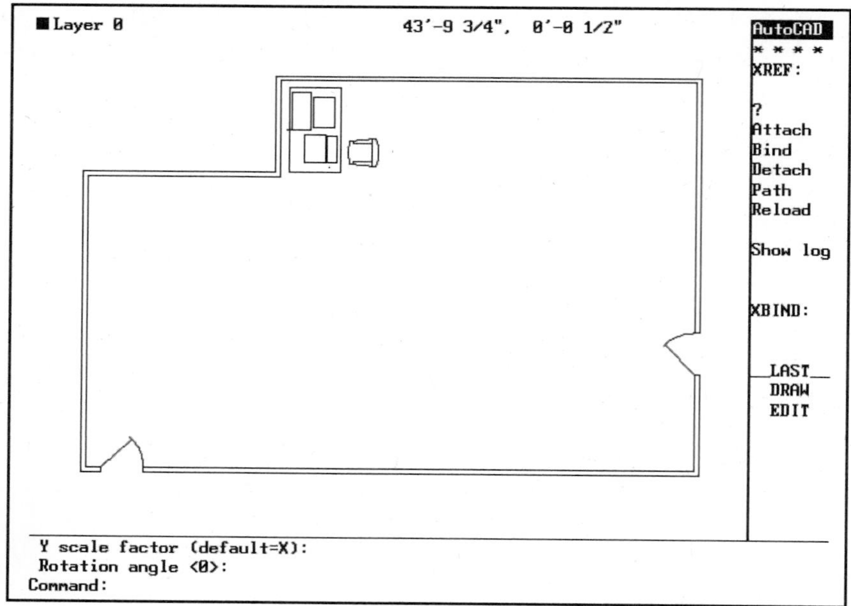

Figure 71.4 *Drawing after changing path.*

The Path option may also be used to change the name of the drawing file to attach. When AutoCAD prompts you for the new path, you can enter the path and file name of a different drawing. This technique enables you to attach a new drawing without having to detach the old one, and then attach a new one. You may, however, have to change the location and rotation of the new Xref.

Listing Xrefs

The List option of the XREF command provides you with a list of the drawings that have been attached to the current file. The path to the reference file also is stated.

In the following exercise, use the List option to list the Xrefs currently attached to your drawing.

Listing Attached Xrefs

1. `Command:` *Choose* File, *then* Xref, *then* List — Issues the XREF command with the List option

```
_xref
?/Bind/Detach/Path/Reload/<Attach>: ?
Xref(s) to list <*>: *

      Xref Name                  Path
---------------------      ---------------
   071DESK                  071DESK.DWG

Total Xref(s): 1
```

2. `Command:` *Press* F1 — Switches to the graphics screen

In this example, there is only one Xref attached to the drawing. If the drawing had contained additional Xrefs, these would also have been listed.

Unit Review

What You've Learned

- How to attach a drawing as an Xref
- How to use the Path option to change the path and the drawing file name used as a reference drawing
- How to list the Xrefs that are attached to a drawing

Review Questions

True or False

71.01 T F The List option of the XREF command provides a list of Xrefs that have been attached to the current drawing.

71.02 T F The Path option of the XREF command renames the current drawing file.

71.03 T F The Path option of the XREF command cannot be used to change the drive in the path for an Xref.

71.04 T F Several drawings may be used as Xrefs in a single drawing.

71.05 T F You cannot explode an Xref.

Multiple Choice

71.06 To attach a reference drawing at half size, the X scale factor and Y scale factor should be set to __________.

(A) 0.5

(B) 2

(C) 1

(D) 0.2

71.07 Which of the following can be used to change the source file used for an Xref?

(A) Path

(B) List

(C) Layer

(D) LAYER

Student: __________ Date: __________

Instructor: __________ Course: __________ Section: __________

Applying the AutoCAD Environment

Refer to figure 71.5 to answer questions 71.08, 71.09, and 71.10.

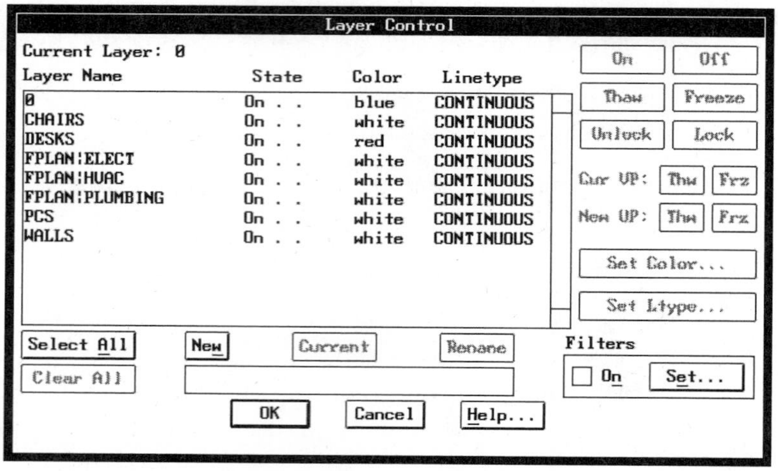

Figure 71.5

Layer Control dialog box with a reference drawing.

71.08 List the layers that loaded with an Xref in the drawing.

____

____

____

71.09 List the name of the Xref.

____

____

____

71.10 If the Xref were bound to the current drawing, which layer names would change and what would the new names be?

____

____

____

Student: ________________ Date: ________

Instructor: ______________ Course: ________ Section: ________

PART VIII

Annotating a Drawing

Setting Text Options

AutoCAD provides great flexibilty in adding notes or text to a drawing. This unit introduces you to the TEXT and DTEXT commands. DTEXT is the command most commonly used for creating text entities.

The objectives for this unit are to:

- Understand the TEXT command—the forerunner to the DTEXT command
- Use the DTEXT command to place text in a drawing
- Set the text height and rotation angle of text
- Understand text justification when placing text in a drawing

Adding Text to a Drawing

Suppose that you are working on a drawing that must be dimensioned in metric units. You want to add the following note to your drawing: "NOTE: ALL DIMENSIONS ARE METRIC UNLESS OTHERWISE NOTED." Use the TEXT command to place this line of text in a drawing.

Using the TEXT Command

1. Start AutoCAD and begin a new drawing.
2. `Command:` **`TEXT`** ↵
3. `Justify/Style/<Start point>:` *Pick a point near the left edge of the drawing area* — Specifies the start point for the text
4. `Height <0.2000>:` *Press* Enter — Specifies text height
5. `Rotation angle <0>:` *Press* Enter — Specifies rotation angle of text
6. `Text:` **`NOTE: ALL DIMENSIONS ARE METRIC UNLESS NOTED OTHERWISE`** ↵ — Specifies text to be placed in the drawing

Your drawing should look similar to figure 72.1.

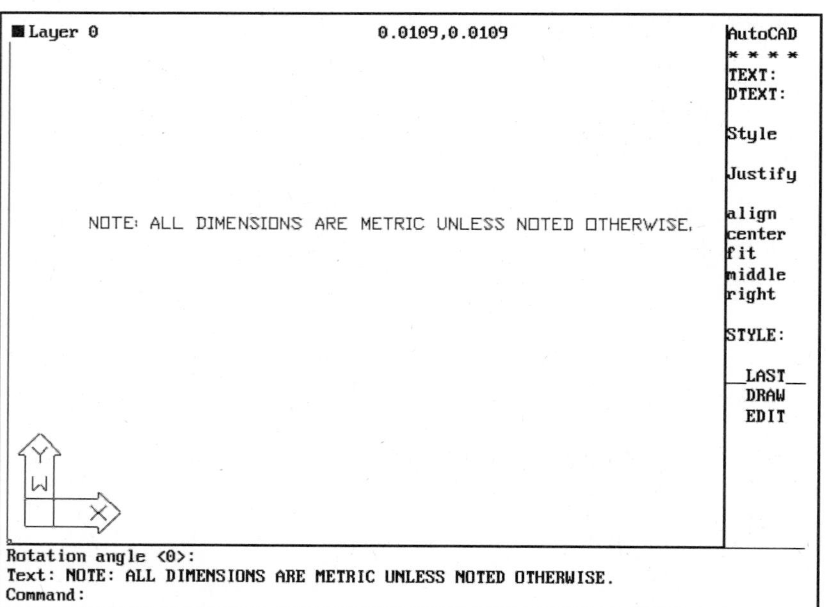

Figure 72.1
A note added to a drawing.

As you can see from the preceding exercise, the TEXT command inserts only a single line of text into the drawing. The DTEXT command, however, enables you to insert multiple lines of text with one command.

Now try the same exercise using DTEXT rather than TEXT. As you work with the DTEXT command, notice that AutoCAD dynamically shows the text as it will appear in your drawing. DTEXT gets its name from ***Dynamic*** TEXT. When you press Enter after typing the text, DTEXT assumes you want to type another line below it. Notice that the box cursor drops to the next line. If you have no other text to type, simply press Enter at the `Text:` prompt to end the DTEXT command.

Using the DTEXT command

Continue with the drawing from the preceding exercise.

1. `Command:` *Choose* Draw, *then* Text, *then* Dynamic	Starts the DTEXT command
2. `_dtext Justify/Style/<Start point>:` *Pick a point near the left edge of the drawing area*	Specifies the start point for the text
3. `Height <0.2000>:` *Press* Enter	Specifies text height
4. `Rotation angle <0>:` *Press* Enter	Specifies rotation angle of text
5. `Text:` **`NOTE: DO NOT SCALE THIS DRAWING`** ↵	Specifies text to be placed in the drawing
6. `Text:` *Press* Enter	Ends the DTEXT command

AutoCAD treats each line of text as a single text entity in its drawing database. If you try to erase or pick a single letter from a line of text, the entire line of text is selected. In addition, each line of text you enter with the DTEXT command is treated as a single entity even if you enter multiple lines of text with one DTEXT command. Editing text is discussed in unit 73.

Understanding Justification

By default, AutoCAD prompts you for a start point when you enter the DTEXT or TEXT command. Unless you specify otherwise, the start point is the lower-left point of the text. The location of the start point of text in relation to the text itself is called the text's *justification*. Although lower-left justification is AutoCAD's default, you can use many other text justifications to place text. Figure 72.2 illustrates the various justifications or alignment options and their abbreviations.

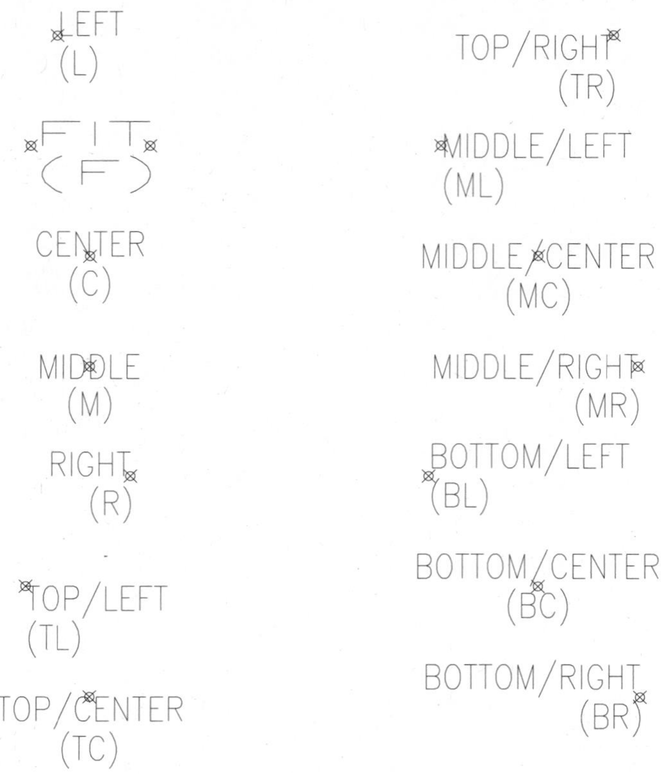

Figure 72.2
Justification options and their abbreviations.

You can specify any of the justification options shown in figure 72.2 in response to the following DTEXT or TEXT prompt (enter the letters shown in parentheses):

```
Justify/Style/<Start point>: Enter the alignment option here
```

Alignment options are useful for creating tables of data, such as bills of materials or schedules. Use DTEXT to create a column of quantities in the following exercise.

Creating a Table of Text

1. Begin a new drawing named 072???01 in your assigned directory, using 072BILL1 as a prototype drawing.
2. `Command:` *Zoom to the view shown in figure 72.3.*
3. `Command:` *Choose* Draw, *then* Text, *then* Dynamic — Starts the DTEXT command
4. `_dtext Justify/Style/<Start point>:` **R** ↵ — Specifies right justification
5. `End point:` *Pick a point at* ① *(see fig. 72.3)* — Specifies the end point for the text

6.	`Height <0.2000>:` **.15** ↵	Specifies the text height
7.	`Rotation angle <0>:` *Press* Enter	Specifies the default rotation
8.	`Text:` **23** ↵	Enters a line of text
9.	`Text:` **1** ↵	
10.	`Text:` **45** ↵	
11.	`Text:` **4** ↵	
12.	`Text:` **46** ↵	
13.	`Text:` **77** ↵	
14.	`Text:` **12** ↵	
15.	`Text:` *Press* Enter	Ends the DTEXT command and draws the text right-justified

Your drawing should look similar to figure 72.3.

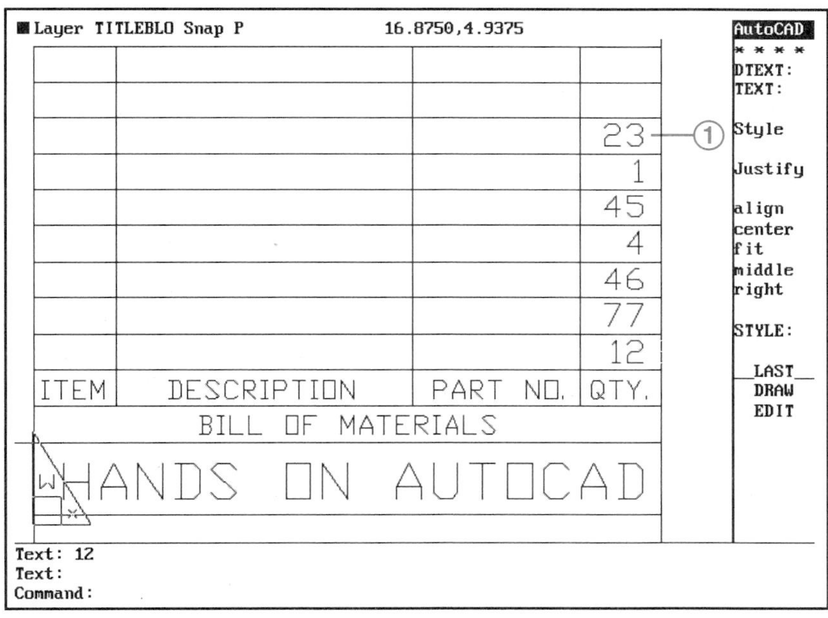

Figure 72.3

Quantities added to a bill of materials.

Setting Text Height, Justification, and Rotation

You might have noticed by now that AutoCAD provides a way to specify the text height and rotation angle of text, adding great flexibility to drawing annotation.

The text height can be entered in AutoCAD as any *real number* (a number containing a decimal value, such as 1.25). The *text height value* specifies the distance from the bottom to the top of a capital letter. Text height does not include descenders of lowercase letters such as g, q, or y. *Descenders* are the portions of these letters that extend below the bottom of capital letters on the same line. Figure 72.4 illustrates how text height is measured.

Figure 72.4
Text height is measured from the bottom to the top of a capital letter.

Text height must be calculated according to the required final plotted scale of your drawing. For a review of calculating text height relative to plotted scale, refer to unit 32.

Using Text Rotation

In addition to a value for height, you also can specify a value for rotation of text when placing text in a drawing. The rotation angle can be entered as any real number in the active AutoCAD angle format. AutoCAD's capability to rotate text is useful for aligning text with objects for labeling purposes.

In the next exercise, place text in your drawing at 45°. Use figure 72.5 as a guide to place the text.

Placing Rotated Text in a Drawing

1. Begin a new drawing named 072???02 using 072ANGLE as a prototype drawing.

2. `Command:` *Choose* Draw, *then* Text, *then* Dynamic	Starts the DTEXT command
3. `_dtext Justify/Style/<Start point>:` *Pick a point at* ① *(see fig. 72.5)*	Starts the text using left justification
4. `Height <0.2000>:` **`.1`** ↵	Specifies text height
5. `Rotation angle <0>:` **`45`** ↵	Specifies rotation angle

6. Text: **ALIGN THIS EDGE WITH PART 24589** ↵ — Specifies text
7. Text: *Press* Enter — Ends the DTEXT command

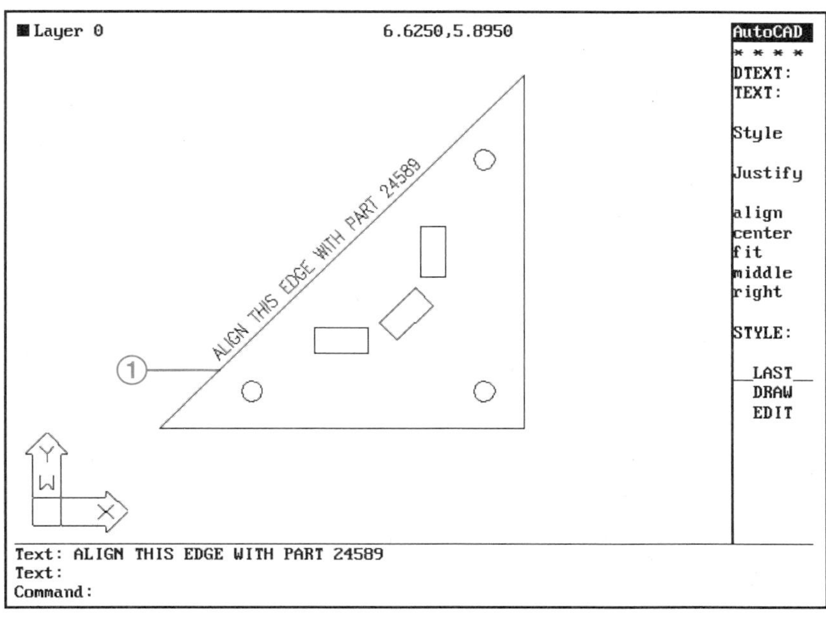

Figure 72.5

Rotated text added to the drawing.

Next, add some more text to the drawing, this time using 90 degrees and 0 degrees to place the text. Use figure 72.6 as a guide to place the text.

Placing Text Orthogonally

Continue with the drawing from the preceding exercise.

1. `Command:` **DTEXT** ↵ — Starts DTEXT command
2. `Justify/Style/<Start point>:` **J** ↵ — Specifies Justify option
3. `Align/Fit/Center/Middle/Right /TL/TC/TR/ML/MC/MR/BL/BC/BR:` **TL** — Specifies top/left justification
4. `Top/left point:` *Pick a point at* ① *(see fig. 72.6)*
5. `Height <0.1000>:` *Press* Enter — Uses same text height as previous text
6. `Rotation angle <45>:` **90** ↵ — Specifies rotation angle
7. `Text:` **ALIGN THIS EDGE WITH PART NO. 24587** ↵
8. `Text:` *Press* Enter — Ends the DTEXT command

continues

9.	`Command:` **DTEXT** ↵	
10.	`Justify/Style/<Start point>:` **J** ↵	Specifies Justify option
11.	`Align/Fit/Center/Middle/Right /TL/TC/TR/ML/MC/MR/BL/BC/BR:` **TC**	Specifies top/center justification
12.	`Top/center point:` *Pick a point at* ② *(see fig. 72.6)*	
13.	`Height <0.1000>:` *Press* Enter	Uses same text height as previous text
14.	`Rotation angle <90>:` **0** ↵	Specifies rotation angle
15.	`Text:` **ALIGN THIS EDGE WITH PART NO. 24588** ↵	
16.	`Text:` *Press* Enter	Ends the DTEXT command
17.	`Command:` *Choose* View, *then* Redraw	

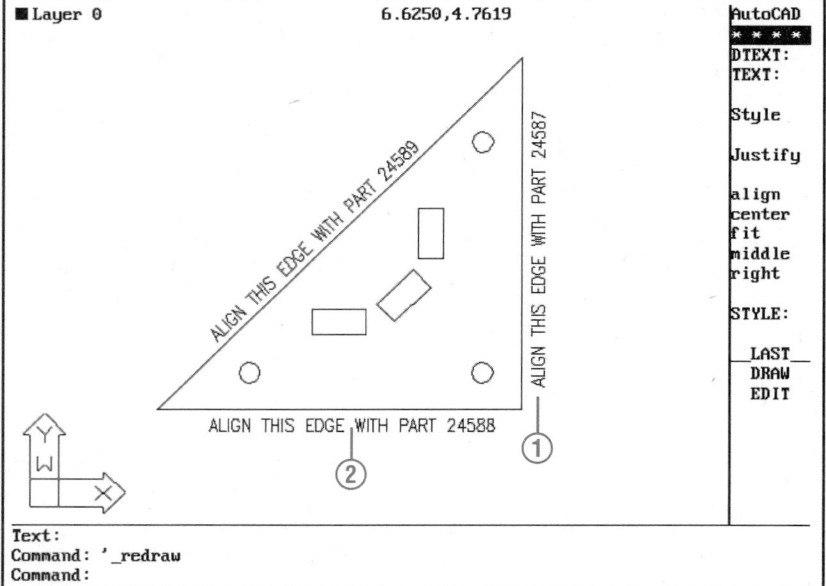

Figure 72.6
Text added to a drawing at 90 degrees and 0 degrees.

TIP

If you have many lines of text to enter at various locations within your drawing, you do not have to use DTEXT several times. When the DTEXT command prompts for text, you can pick a point anywhere in the drawing to place the text. When you press Enter twice to end the command, DTEXT then places the text in your drawing. If you must place a lot of text, you might want to use DTEXT more than once, restarting the command occasionally. This avoids deleting all the text entered while within the DTEXT command if you mistakenly press Ctrl+C.

Unit Review

What You've Learned

- ☞ Commands: TEXT, DTEXT
- ☞ How to enter text in a drawing using the TEXT and DTEXT commands
- ☞ Where the start point is in relationship to text for each of the justification options
- ☞ How to specify text height, justification, and rotation

Review Questions

True or False

72.01 T F The DTEXT command is the most common method for adding text to a drawing.

72.02 T F The TEXT command inserts multiple lines of text into a drawing.

72.03 T F The DTEXT command inserts multiple lines of text into a drawing.

72.04 T F The default justification for text is upper-left.

72.05 T F You can use three different types of text justification in AutoCAD.

72.06 T F Text height is measured from the bottom of a capital letter to its top.

72.07 T F Text can be placed in the drawing at any rotation.

Multiple Choice

72.08 The ____________ command can be used to insert multiple lines of text into a drawing.

(A) STYLE

(B) TEXT

(C) DTEXT

(D) either B or C

Student: ____________________ Date: __________

Instructor: ____________________ Course: __________ Section: __________

72.09 AutoCAD treats each line of text in a drawing as __________.

(A) one part of a multi-line entity

(B) a single entity

(C) individual characters

(D) none of the above

72.10 The default text justification is __________.

(A) left

(B) TL (Top/Left)

(C) center

(D) TR (Top/Right)

Additional Exercises

72.11 Begin a new drawing named 072???X1 in your assigned directory, using the file 072BILL2.DWG as a prototype. In the Bill of Materials section in your drawing, add the following items:

ITEM	QTY	DESCRIPTION	REM
1	12	BOLT, 3/8-16NC-2A	GP
2	12	WASHER, FLAT, 3/8	GP
3	12	NUT, HEX, 3/8-16NC-2B	GP
4	1	SN2087-A	
5	1	SN2087-B	
6	1	SN2992	

Use Center justification for text in the ITEM field. Use Right justification for text in the QTY field. Use Bottom/Left justification for text in the DESCRIPTION and REM fields. Use a text height of .15" for all text. Save your drawing when you are through.

Student: __________ Date: __________

Instructor: __________ Course: __________ Section: __________

72.12 Load your drawing 072???X1, which you worked on in exercise 72.11. Add the following text to the appropriate locations in the title block:

TITLE: ASSY, COVER PLATE
SIZE: A
DWG NO.: SA3901
REV: 0
SHEET: 1 OF 4
SCALE: N/A

Fill in a company name or school name as directed by your instructor.

Student: ______________________ Date: __________

Instructor: ______________________ Course: __________ Section: __________

UNIT 73

Advanced Text Techniques

Standards for drawing text vary from company to company. Each company prefers a particular font style in the drawings it produces. With AutoCAD, you can create many different styles of text in a drawing. Some examples of special text styles include architectural signage for a building, panel layouts for electrical boxes, dial faces for custom gauges, and silk-screening for printed circuit boards. A variety of fonts also can be useful for creating attractive, professional-looking title sheets for your projects.

AutoCAD also comes with utilities for importing large amounts of text into your drawings from ASCII text files. This is most useful for adding to a drawing specifications, coded notes, or other text typed in a file.

The objectives for this unit are to:

- Understand text styles
- Create and use text styles
- Change text characteristics
- Understand ASCII text files and how to import text from them

Understanding Text Styles

AutoCAD includes many font files, and you can purchase other font files from third parties. A *font file* contains a description of how to draw each vector for each character in the font. These files are commonly referred to as *shape* files, or .SHP files. SHP files are compiled by AutoCAD into a file with an .SHX extension. This is the file AutoCAD uses when it draws the characters on-screen.

When AutoCAD is installed, by default it places the .SHX files in a FONTS directory under the main AutoCAD directory, such as C:\ACAD\FONTS. When you create or change a text style, AutoCAD searches this directory first for the specified font file.

A *text style* is a style you define that uses a particular font file. A text style defines such things as preset text height, character width factors, oblique angles of the characters, and other characteristics. You can define any number of text styles for any particular font file. Figure 73.1 shows a selection of different text styles.

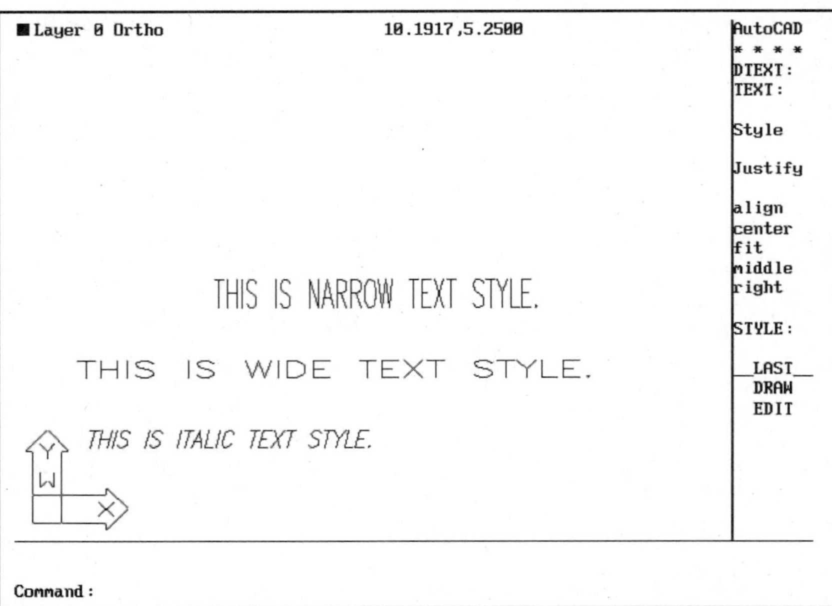

Figure 73.1
A selection of different text styles in a drawing.

In the following exercises, create and use three text styles, which all use the ROMANS.SHX font file. Then, place some text in your drawing using your newly defined text styles.

Defining a Text Style

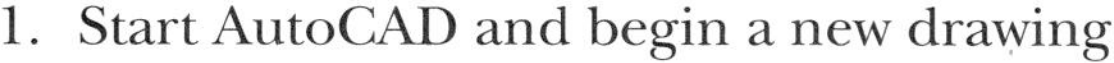

1. Start AutoCAD and begin a new drawing.

2. `Command:` **`STYLE`** ↵	Starts the STYLE command
3. `Text style name (or ?) <STANDARD>:` **`NARROW`** ↵	Specifies the name of the new text style

`New style.`

In the Select Font File dialog box (see fig. 73.2), AutoCAD prompts you for the name of the font file to use for the text style NARROW.

4. Type **ROMANS** (for Roman Simplex) in the File edit box, or locate the file ROMANS.SHX using the Directories and Files list boxes. Then choose OK.

5. `Height <0.0000>:` *Press* Enter	Allows text height to be entered during text insertion
6. `Width factor <1.0000>:` **`.5`** ↵	Specifies width of text relative to height of text
7. `Obliquing angle <0>:` *Press* Enter	Specifies obliquing angle
8. `Backwards?` **`<N>`** *Press* Enter	Specifies text to be read left-to-right
9. `Upside-down?` **`<N>`** *Press* Enter	Specifies text to be drawn right-side-up
10. `Vertical?` **`<N>`** *Press* Enter	Specifies characters to be oriented side-by-side

NARROW is now the current text style.

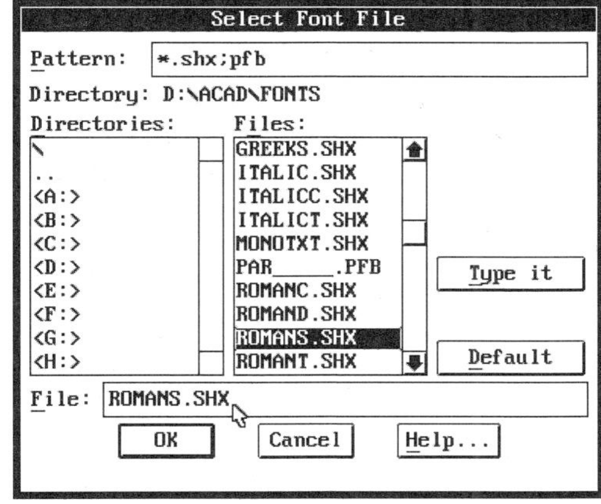

Figure 73.2

Choose or enter the font file name in the Select Font File dialog box.

Next, try using your NARROW text style in a drawing. When you add the text, your drawing should look similar to figure 73.3.

Using a Text Style

Continue with your drawing from the preceding exercise.

1. Command: **DTEXT** ↵	Starts the DTEXT command
2. Justify/Style/<Start point>: *Pick a point at* ① *(see fig. 73.3)*	Specifies start point for text
3. Height <0.2000>: **.5**	Specifies text height of .5"
4. Rotation angle <0>:	Specifies text rotation of 0
5. Text: **THIS IS NARROW TEXT STYLE** ↵	Specifies text
6. Text: *Press* Enter	Ends the DTEXT command

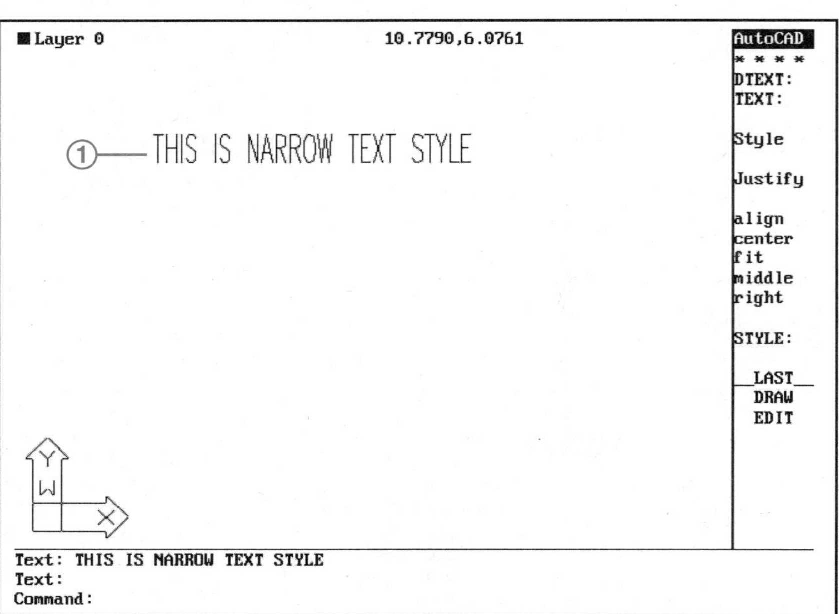

Figure 73.3

Text added to a drawing using the NARROW style.

You can create many styles that use the same font file, but have different height, width, obliquing, and rotation characteristics. In the following exercise, create a new style called WIDE using the same ROMANS font you used to create the NARROW font style.

Creating Additional Text Styles

1. `Command:` *From the* SETTINGS *screen menu choose* Next, *then choose* STYLE: ↵	Starts the STYLE command
2. `'_STYLE Text style name (or ?) <NARROW>:` **`WIDE`** ↵	Specifies the name of the new text style
`New style.`	

AutoCAD displays the Select Font File dialog box.

3. Locate and choose ROMANS.SHX or enter **ROMAN** in the File edit box, and then choose OK.

4. `Height <0.0000>:` *Press* Enter	Allows text height entry during text insertion
5. `Width factor <1.0000>:` **`1.5`** ↵	Specifies width-to-height ratio of 1.5:1
6. `Obliquing angle <0>:` *Press* Enter	
7. `Backwards?` **`<N>`** *Press* Enter	
8. `Upside-down?` **`<N>`** *Press* Enter	
9. `Vertical?` **`<N>`** *Press* Enter	

WIDE is now the current text style.

10. `Command:` *Choose* Draw, *then* Text, *then* Dynamic	Starts the DTEXT command
11. `_dtext Justify/Style/<Start point>:` *Pick point* ① *(see fig. 73.4)*	Specifies start point of text
12. `Height <0.5000>:` **`.3`** ↵	
13. `Rotation angle <0>:` *Press* Enter	
14. `Text:` **`THIS IS WIDE TEXT STYLE`** ↵	
15. `Text:` *Press* Enter	

Create one more style using the ROMANS font file. This time, create an italic style by specifying an obliquing angle.

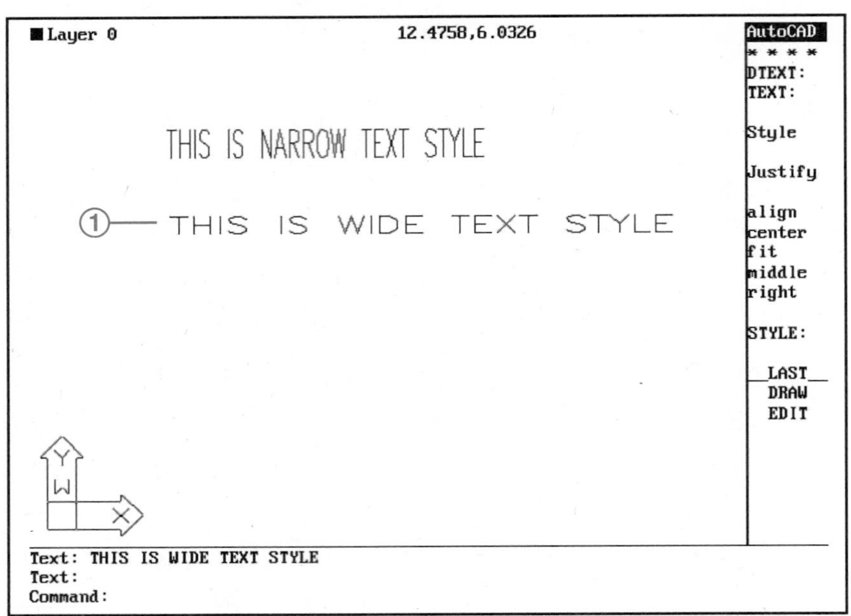

Figure 73.4

Text added to the drawing using the WIDE text style.

Creating a Style with an Obliquing Angle

1. `Command:` **`STYLE`** ↵
2. `Text style name (or ?) <WIDE>:` **`ITALIC`** ↵

   `New style.`

AutoCAD displays the Select Font File dialog box.

3. Locate and choose ROMANS.SHX or enter **ROMAN** in the File edit box, and then choose OK.
4. `Height <0.0000>:` **`.3`** ↵ — Specifies an explicit text height
5. `Width factor <1.0000>:` **`.8`** ↵ — Specifies width factor
6. `Obliquing angle <0>:` **`15`** ↵ — Specifies an obliquing angle
7. `Backwards? <N>` *Press* Enter
8. `Upside-down? <N>` *Press* Enter
9. `Vertical? <N>` *Press* Enter

ITALIC is now the current text style.

10. `Command:` **`DTEXT`** ↵
11. `Justify/Style/<Start point>:`
    Pick a point at ① *(see fig. 73.5)* — Specifies start point of text

Understanding Text Styles

12. `Rotation angle <0>:` *Press* Enter

13. `Text:` **`THIS IS ITALIC TEXT STYLE.`** ↵

    `Text:`

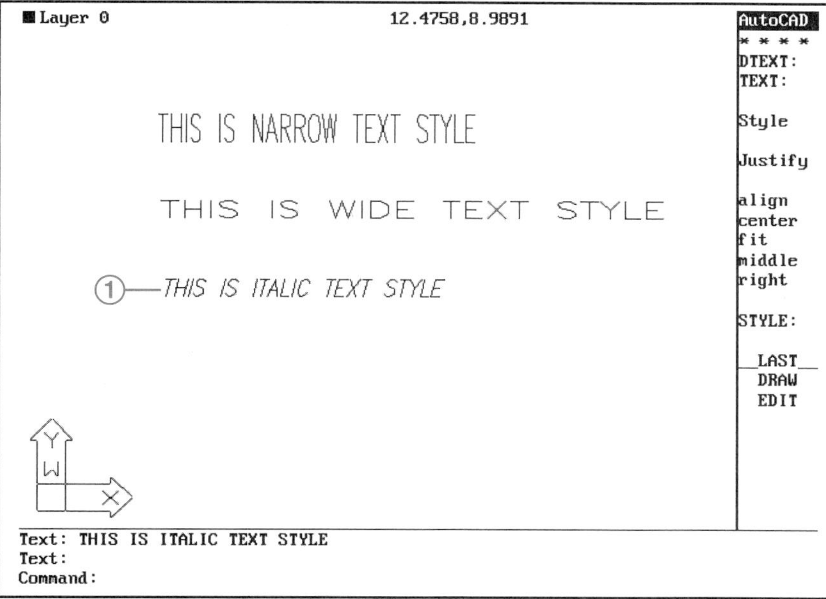

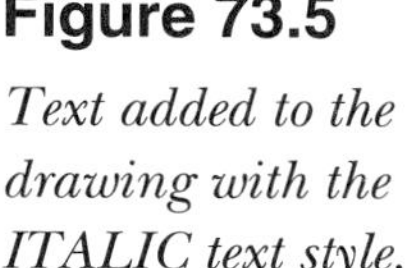

Figure 73.5

Text added to the drawing with the ITALIC text style.

NOTE

When you defined the ITALIC text style, you specified a fixed text height of .3. If you specify a text height other than zero in the STYLE command, AutoCAD does not prompt for a text height when you use that style in the DTEXT command. If you want to be able to specify any text height while placing text, use a text height of zero when defining the style.

In addition to specifying text height, width factor, and obliquing angle, the capability to specify whether your text is generated backwards, upside-down, or vertically adds to the variety of text styles you can create. The backward and upside-down options are useful in applications in which the drawing might be reverse-printed or printed on the reverse side of the paper. Labels or circuit masks for electronics are examples of uses for backward and upside-down lettering.

Choosing a Style Graphically

In addition to defining a style with the technique you used in the preceding exercises, you also can select a font style graphically in AutoCAD, as the following exercise illustrates.

Graphically Selecting a Font Style

1. `Command:` *Choose* Draw, *then* Text, *then* Set Style — Displays the Select Text Font dialog box (see fig. 73.6)
2. In the Select Text Font dialog box, click on Roman Triplex in the list box at the left, or click on the ROMAN TRIPLEX tile (see fig. 73.6), and then choose OK.
3. `Height <0.0000>:` *Press* Enter
4. `Width factor <1.0000>:` *Press* Enter
5. `Obliquing angle <0>:` *Press* Enter
6. `Backwards? <N>` *Press* Enter
7. `Upside-down? <N>` *Press* Enter
8. `Vertical? <N>` *Press* Enter

ROMANT is now the current text style.

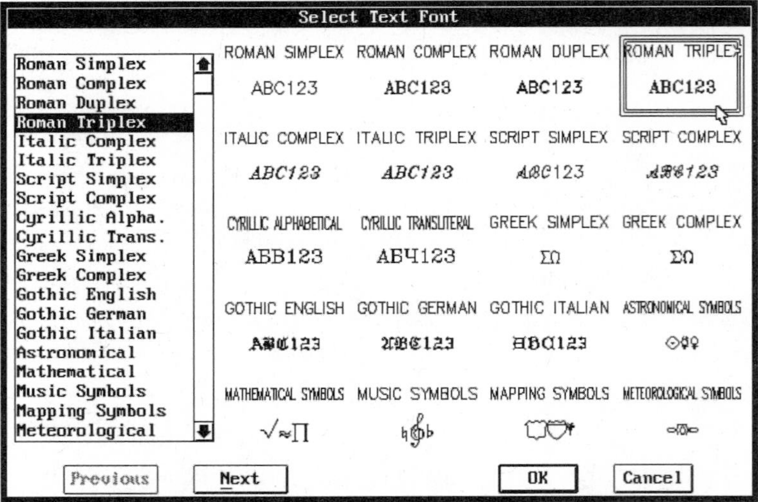

Figure 73.6
The ROMAN TRIPLEX tile in the Select Text Font dialog box.

Changing Text

Because nobody is perfect and people often change their minds, AutoCAD provides a way to modify text already placed in a drawing. The DDMODIFY command offers the best method for changing text. Access DDMODIFY by choosing Entity from the Modify pull-down menu, or by entering **DDMODIFY** at the `Command:` prompt. Then pick the text entity you want to modify. A dialog box appears similar to the one shown in figure 73.7.

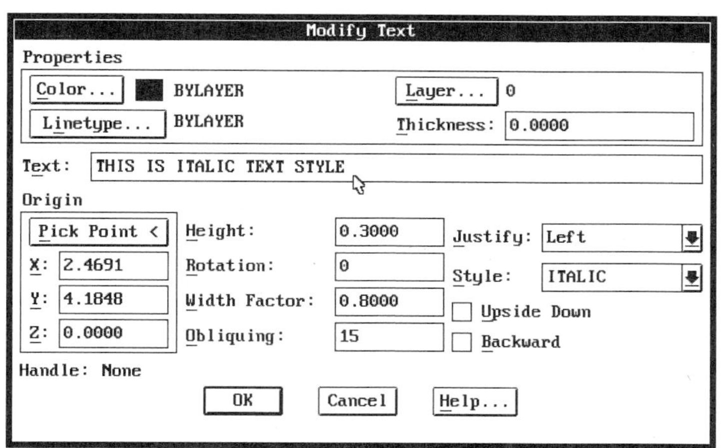

Figure 73.7

The Modify Text dialog box.

Change the text height and obliquing angle of the Italic style text from the preceding exercise. The new text height will be 0.5 units and the oblique angle will be 20°.

Changing Text Height and Obliquing Angle

1. `Command:` *Choose* Modify, *then* Entity — Starts the DDMODIFY command
2. `Select object to modify:` *Pick the italic-style text* — Selects the text and displays the Modify Text dialog box
3. Modify the value for height to 1" and for obliquing to 5°, and then choose OK.

Your selected text line should change to reflect the new height and obliquing values you specified.

Experiment with the other DDMODIFY options for text. As you can see in the Modify Text dialog box, an enormous amount of flexibility is available for annotating your drawing.

Importing Text

An *ASCII (American Standard Code for Information Interchange) text file* is a file containing text without any formatting codes normally used by word processors. It primarily consists of alphanumeric characters (letters and numbers), spaces, punctuation symbols, and an end-of-file marker.

Because ASCII text files contain only basic text, they are useful for many purposes, such as importing their contents into AutoCAD. AutoCAD ships with an AutoLISP utility for importing ASCII text into drawings. This utility—ASCTEXT.LSP—is located in AutoCAD's SUPPORT directory.

Assume that you need to insert a list of specifications into your drawing as text. In the following exercise, insert text into a new drawing from an ASCII text file named 073SPECS.TXT.

Inserting Text from an ASCII Text File

1. Begin a new drawing in AutoCAD.
2. `Command:` **`(LOAD "ASCTEXT")`** ↵ — Loads the file ASCTEXT.LSP

   `ASCTEXT loaded.`
3. `Command:` **`ASCTEXT`** ↵ — Starts the ASCTEXT command

AutoCAD displays the File to Read dialog box, prompting you for the file name of the ASCII text file to import.

4. Locate and choose 073SPECS.TXT in the dialog box, or type its correct path and file name, and then choose OK. (Ask your instructor if you are not sure where to find the file 073SPECS.TXT.)
5. `Start point or Center/Middle/Right/?:` *Pick a point near the upper left of the drawing area*
6. `Height <0.2000>:` **`.1`** ↵
7. `Rotation angle <0>:` *Press* Enter
8. `Change text options? <N>:` **`Y`** ↵

View the options, but do not change any of them.

9. `Distance between lines/<Auto>:` *Press* Enter
10. `First line to read/<1>:` *Press* Enter
11. `Number of lines to read/<All>:` *Press* Enter
12. `Underscore each line? <N>:` *Press* Enter
13. `Overscore each line? <N>:` *Press* Enter
14. `Change text case?  Upper/Lower/<N>:` *Press* Enter
15. `Set up columns? <N>:` *Press* Enter

Your screen should resemble figure 73.8.

Some companies store specifications and notes in ASCII files to eliminate tedious typing within drawings. The ASCTEXT command is used to format that text data in the drawing.

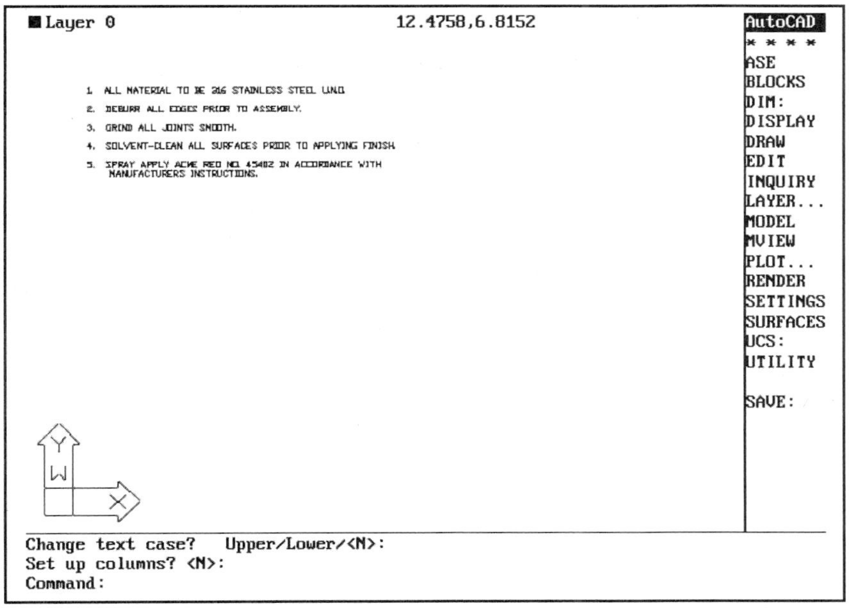

```
Layer 0                              12.4758,6.8152        AutoCAD
                                                           * * * *
                                                           ASE
  1. ALL MATERIAL TO BE 316 STAINLESS STEEL U.N.O.         BLOCKS
  2. DEBURR ALL EDGES PRIOR TO ASSEMBLY.                   DIM:
  3. GRIND ALL JOINTS SMOOTH.                              DISPLAY
  4. SOLVENT-CLEAN ALL SURFACES PRIOR TO APPLYING FINISH.  DRAW
  5. SPRAY APPLY ACME RED NO. 45402 IN ACCORDANCE WITH     EDIT
     MANUFACTURERS INSTRUCTIONS.                           INQUIRY
                                                           LAYER...
                                                           MODEL
                                                           MVIEW
                                                           PLOT...
                                                           RENDER
                                                           SETTINGS
                                                           SURFACES
                                                           UCS:
                                                           UTILITY

                                                           SAVE:
  Y
  W
     X
Change text case?  Upper/Lower/<N>:
Set up columns? <N>:
Command:
```

Figure 73.8

Specifications added to a drawing from a text file.

Unit Review

What You've Learned

- ☞ Commands: STYLE, DDMODIFY, ASCTEXT
- ☞ The purpose of font files
- ☞ How to create and modify text styles
- ☞ How to import ASCII text into a drawing

Review Questions

True or False

73.01 T F To define a text style, you must specify the text file to be used for the style.

73.02 T F AutoCAD includes only three text styles.

73.03 T F A text style definition includes the width factor of the text.

73.04 T F If you define a text style with a height other than 0, AutoCAD does not prompt you for the text height when you use the style.

73.05 T F You cannot create a style that uses backwards text.

Multiple Choice

73.06 The DDMODIFY command enables you to change the ____________ of an existing text entity.

(A) height

(B) text

(C) color

(D) all of the above

73.07 A(n) ____________ file contains text without any formatting codes.

(A) style

(B) character

(C) ASCII

(D) alpha

Student: ______________________ Date: __________

Instructor: ______________________ Course: __________ Section: __________

Short Answer

73.08 What effect does setting an explicit height have when you define a text style?

____

____

____

73.09 List four special uses for text styles in different types of drawings.

____

____

____

73.10 Describe a use for a text style that uses backward text.

____

____

____

Student: ______________ Date: ______

Instructor: ______________ Course: ______ Section: ______

UNIT 74

Adding Linear Dimensions

dding dimensions to a drawing is perhaps the most time-consuming and frustrating part of completing a drawing, but it also is the most important. Accurate dimensions facilitate production or construction of the subject of your drawing.

AutoCAD provides a flexible—though sometimes complicated—method of dimensioning. The next few units clarify the steps needed to produce meaningful dimensions in AutoCAD.

The objectives for this unit are to:

- Understand dimensioning variables and their purposes
- Apply horizontal dimensions
- Apply vertical dimensions
- Apply aligned dimensions

Understanding AutoCAD Dimensioning

Although dimensioning is included with AutoCAD, the dimensioning environment is somewhat removed or separated from the drawing environment. In fact, the AutoCAD `Command:` prompt changes to a `Dim:` prompt while the dimensioning commands are active. In AutoCAD's early days, the dimensioning module was a separate, add-on option. Today, dimensioning is integrated into the AutoCAD environment, but still maintains its own subset of commands.

The key to effective dimensioning in AutoCAD is a thorough understanding of the dozens of dimensioning system variables used to control the appearance and behavior of the dimensions. Although you certainly are not expected to memorize all the variables and their functions, becoming familiar with their names and functions makes it much easier for you to use AutoCAD's dimensioning commands effectively. Unit 79 introduces dimensioning variables and covers them in detail. This unit explains only a few of the dimension variables and their effects.

To dimension a drawing in AutoCAD and to understand the effect dimension variables have on dimensions, you first must understand the various components of a dimension entity, as shown in figure 74.1.

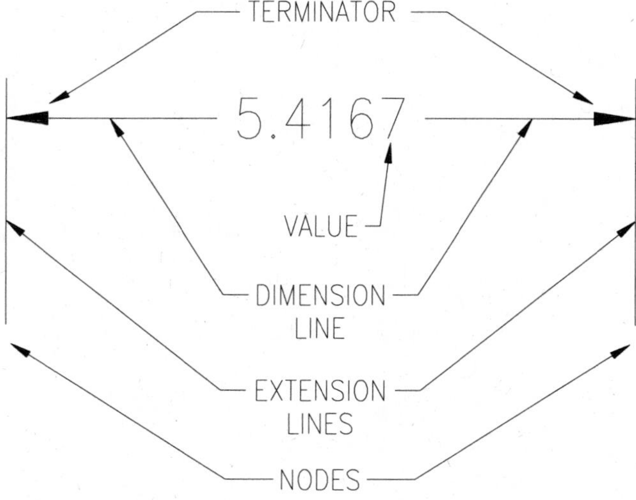

Figure 74.1

The main components of a dimension entity.

Perhaps the two most important dimension variables are DIMSCALE and DIMTXT. DIMSCALE is used to determine the relative size of the features (arrowheads, text values, and so on). DIMSCALE must be set to a scale appropriate for the final plotted scale of the drawing. When DIMSCALE is set properly, dimension text and other dimension features are plotted at the proper size in your drawing.

If you mastered unit 32 and know how to calculate your drawing scale factor, set your DIMSCALE to the same factor. For example, a drawing to be plotted at 1/4"=1'-0" has a DIMSCALE of 48, which is derived from the ratio of 1/4":1'-0", or 1:48. Likewise, a drawing plotted at 1=10 has a DIMSCALE of 10.

DIMTXT controls the size of the text values in all dimensions. This setting should reflect the size of the desired text height of dimension values when your drawing is plotted to scale. The default AutoCAD DIMTXT value is 0.1800. Two commonly used values are 0.100" and 1/8". Generally, your DIMTXT value should be consistent with the plotted text height of the text throughout your drawing. This gives your drawing a consistent appearance, with all dimension text values and text entity heights plotting at the same height.

Figure 74.2 illustrates the dimension features controlled by the DIMTXT and DIMSCALE dimension variables.

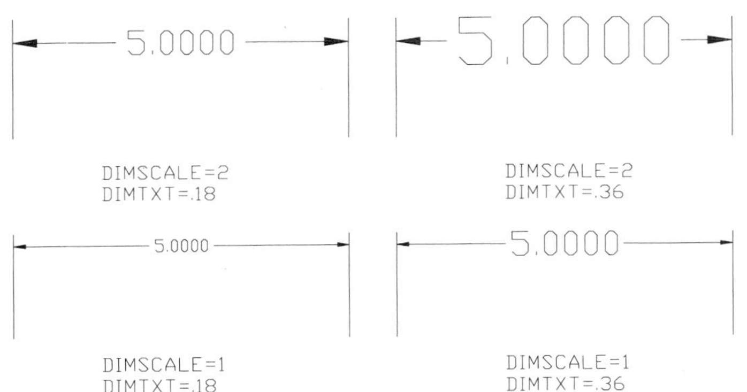

Figure 74.2

The effect of the DIMTXT and DIMSCALE dimension variables.

Applying Horizontal Dimensions

When adding horizontal, vertical, or aligned dimensions to your drawing, AutoCAD provides two ways to specify the distance or object to be dimensioned. The first method requires you to specify the location of the *node points*, which are the two points to be dimensioned. The second option enables you to select the entity to be dimensioned. Each method has a specific use, and sometimes one method is more appropriate than the other.

AutoCAD's dimensioning features do not preclude good drafting practices. Although CAD is a tremendous tool for producing drawings, it is not a replacement for a general knowledge of drafting principles. A good and marketable CAD user knows how to produce drawings that meet generally accepted standards.

In the next few exercises, you add dimensions to a tool plate. Use figure 74.3 as a guide to add your dimensions.

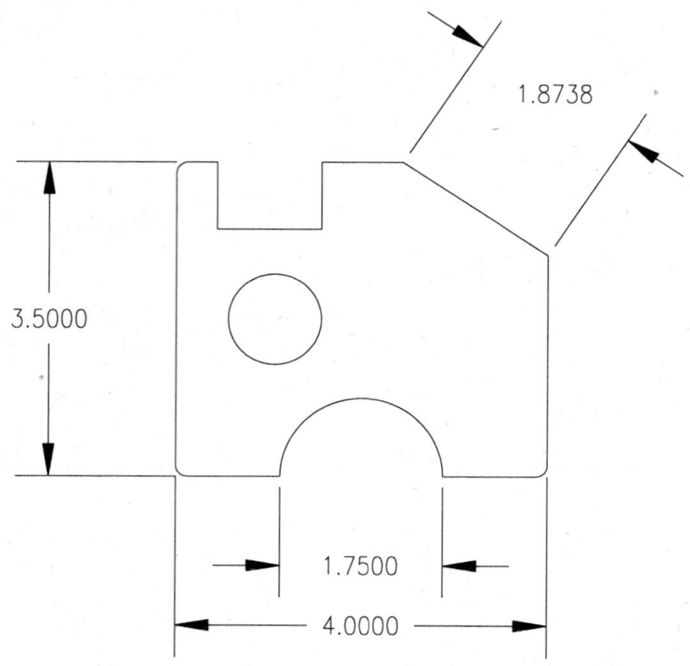

Figure 74.3

Dimensions added to a drawing of a tool plate.

Dimensioning by Selecting an Entity

1. Begin a new drawing named 074???01 in your assigned directory and use drawing 074TOOLP as a prototype.
2. Use the STYLE command to create a text style named ROMANS using the ROMANS.SHX font file. Change the width factor to 0.8.
3. Use the LAYER or Layer Control dialog box to make layer DIMENSIONS current.
4. `Command:` **`DIMTXT`** ↵
5. `New value for DIMTXT <0.1800>:` **`.1`** ↵ Sets size of text to .1"
6. `Command:` **`DIMSCALE`** ↵

7. `New value for DIMSCALE <1.0000>:` **`2`** ↵	Sets dimension scale to 2
8. `Command:` **`DIMTIX`** ↵	
9. `New value for DIMTIX <0>:` **`1`** ↵	Forces dimension text inside dimension line

Next, dimension the semicircular notch at the bottom of the part by entity selection. Use figure 74.3 as a guide.

10. `Command:` *Choose* Draw, *then* Dimensions, *then* Linear, *then* Horizontal `Dim: _horizontal`	Enters dimensioning mode and starts horizontal dimensioning
11. `First extension line origin or RETURN to select:` *Press* Enter	Specifies to dimension by selecting an entity
12. `Select line, arc, or circle:` *Select the semicircle at* ① *(see fig. 74.4)*	Generates a dimension
13. `Dimension line location (Text/Angle):` *Drag the cursor down and pick a point at* ② *(see fig. 74.4)*	Specifies location for dimension line
14. `Dimension text <1.750>:` *Press* Enter	Verifies the dimension value

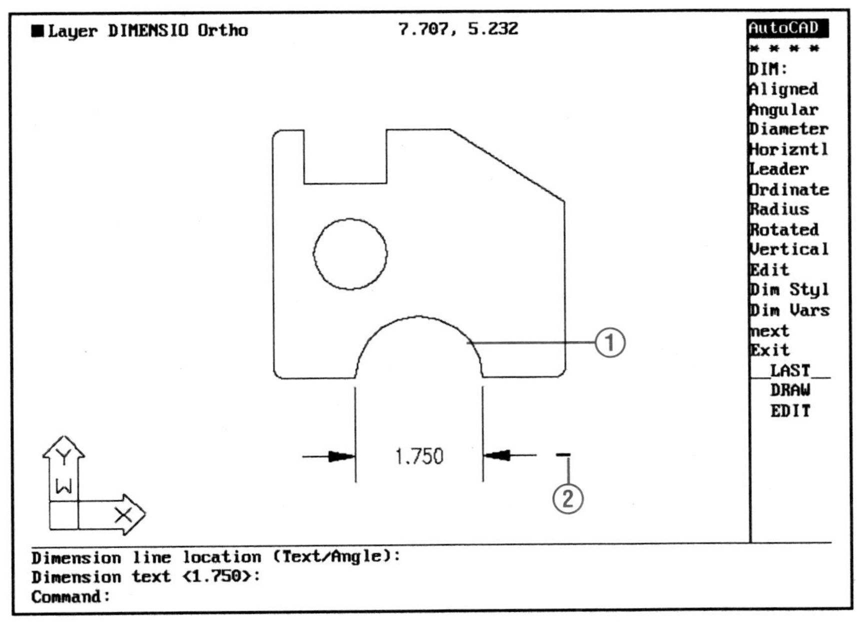

Figure 74.4

A horizontal dimension added to the tool plate.

When DIMTIX is set to 1, AutoCAD places dimension values inside the dimension line, even when they do not fit. When DIMTIX is set to 0, AutoCAD places the dimension inside the dimension line only when it fits properly. Otherwise, AutoCAD moves the dimension value outside the dimension line.

Next, dimension the bottom length of the part by specifying two points. Use the object snap mode ENDP to locate the points to be dimensioned.

Dimensioning by Specifying Points

Continue with your drawing from the preceding exercise.

1. `Command:` *Choose* Draw, *then* Dimensions, *then* Linear, *then* Horizontal — Enters dimensioning mode and starts horizontal dimensioning

   `Dim: _horizontal`

2. `First extension line origin or RETURN to select:` *From the popup menu, choose* Endpoint

3. `_endp of` *Select the line at* ① *(see fig. 74.5)* — Specifies first dimension point

4. `Second extension line origin:` *From the popup menu, choose* Endpoint

5. `_endp of` *Select the line at* ② — Specifies second dimension point

6. `Dimension line location (Text/Angle):` *Drag the cursor down and pick a point at* ③ — Specifies dimension line location

7. `Dimension text <4.0000>:` *Press* Enter

Applying Vertical Dimensions

The same dimensioning variables and principles of horizontal dimensions also apply for vertical dimensions. You can place a vertical dimension by selecting an entity or by selecting two points.

In the following exercise, dimension the overall height of the tool plate at the left edge of the part. Instead of using the pull-down menu to enter dimension mode, use the DIM command. Before you place the dimension, examine the part carefully. Decide what type of dimensioning—by entity selection or point specification—is best in this situation.

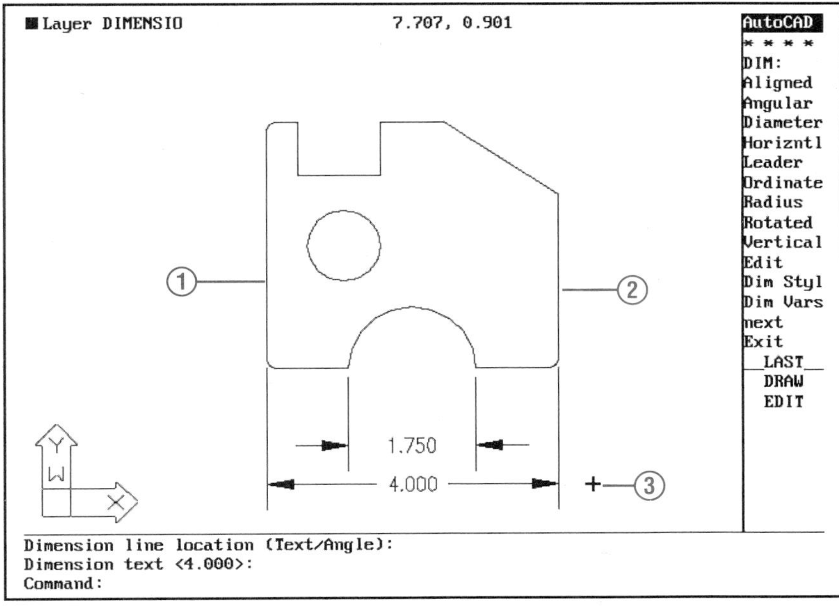

Figure 74.5

Overall horizontal dimension added to the tool plate.

Placing a Vertical Dimension

Continue with your drawing from the preceding exercise.

1. `Command:` **`DIM`** ↵ — Enters dimensioning mode
2. `Dim:` **`VER`** ↵ — Specifies vertical dimension
3. `First extension line origin or RETURN to select:` *From the popup menu, choose* Endpoint
4. `_endp of` *Select the horizontal line at* ① *(see fig. 74.6)*
5. `Second extension line origin:` *From the popup menu, choose* Endpoint
6. `_endp of` *Select the horizontal line at* ② *(see fig. 74.6)*
7. `Dimension line location (Text/Angle):` *Pick a point at* ③ *(see fig. 74.6)*
8. `Dimension text <3.500>:` *Press* Enter — Places dimension
9. `Dim:` *Press* Ctrl+C — Ends dimensioning mode

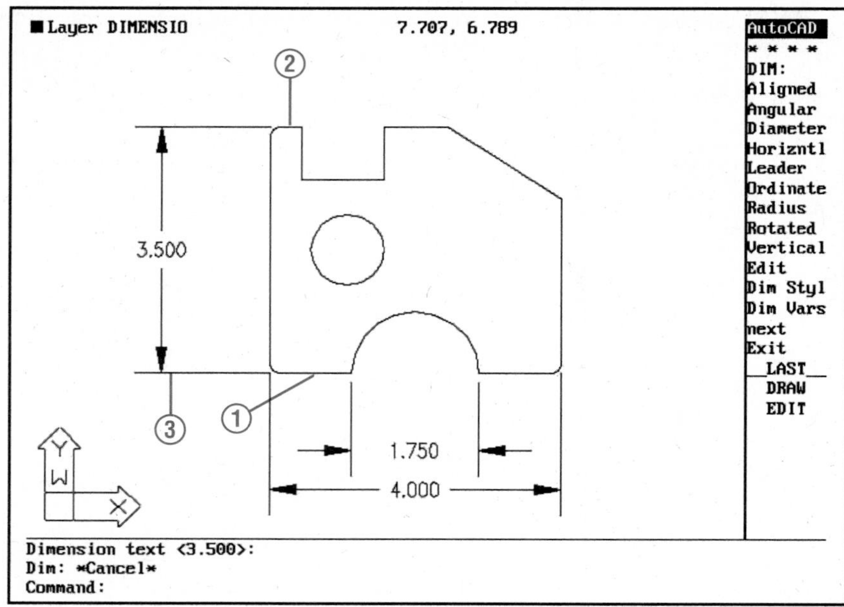

Figure 74.6
Vertical dimension added to the tool plate.

Applying Aligned Dimensions

In *aligned dimensions,* the dimension line is parallel to the two points selected for the extension line origin (nodes). In all other respects, an aligned dimension is just like a horizontal or vertical dimension. Use aligned dimensions when you must dimension a feature on a part not vertical or horizontal.

In the following exercise, dimension the angled portion at the top right of the tool plate.

Using Aligned Dimensions

1. `Command:` *Choose* Draw, *then* Dimensions, *then* Linear, *then* Aligned — Enters dimension mode and starts aligned dimensioning

   `Dim: _aligned`

2. `First extension line origin or RETURN to select:` *Press* Enter

3. `Select line, arc, or circle:` *Select the angled line at* ① *(see fig. 74.7)*

4. `Dimension line location (Text/Angle):` *Pick a point at* ② *(see fig. 74.7)*	Locates the dimension line
5. `Dimension text <1.874>:` *Press* Enter	Accepts dimension value
6. `Dim:` *Press* Ctrl+C	Ends dimension mode

Your finished drawing should look similar to figure 74.7.

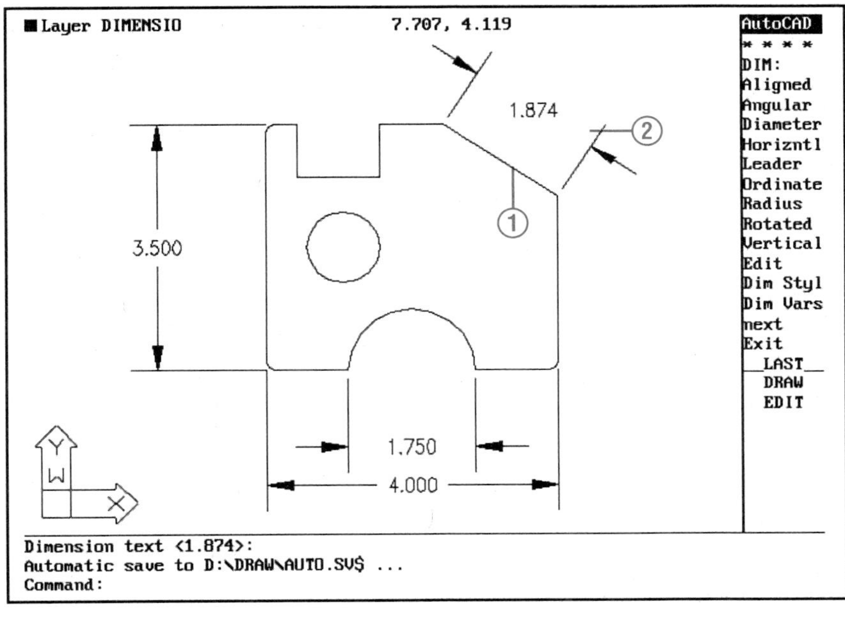

Figure 74.7

Aligned dimension added to tool plate drawing.

Unit Review

What You've Learned

- ☞ Commands: DIMTXT, DIMTIX, DIMSCALE, HORIZONTAL, VERTICAL, ALIGNED
- ☞ How to set DIMSCALE and DIMTXT according to drawing scale
- ☞ How dimension variables such as DIMSCALE and DIMTXT can control dimension characteristics
- ☞ How to apply horizontal, vertical, and aligned dimensions

Review Questions

True or False

74.01 T F Dimensioning mode uses the `Dim:` prompt rather than the `Command:` prompt.

74.02 T F The DIMSCALE variable controls only the size of dimension text.

74.03 T F The DIMTXT variable controls the size of the dimension, including arrowheads.

74.04 T F If a drawing is to be plotted at a scale of 48, DIMSCALE should be set to 12.

74.05 T F When applying a linear dimension, you can pick two points for the dimension or select an entity to dimension.

Multiple Choice

74.06 The ___________ dimension variable controls the size of dimension text.

(A) DIMSCALE

(B) DIMTIX

(C) DIMTXT

(D) DIMSIZE

Student: ______________________ Date: __________

Instructor: ______________________ Course: __________ Section: __________

74.07 The __________ dimension variable controls the overall size of the dimension, relative to the drawing scale.

(A) DIMSCALE

(B) DIMTXT

(C) DIMTIX

(D) DIMSIZE

74.08 Increasing the value of DIMSCALE makes a dimension appear __________.

(A) smaller

(B) at the same scale as the drawing

(C) bigger

(D) in no way different

Short Answer

74.09 When placing linear dimensions by picking points, which three points does AutoCAD prompt you to pick?

____

____

____

74.10 Calculate the value of DIMSCALE for a drawing to be plotted at a scale of 1/2"=1'-0".

____

____

____

Additional Exercises

74.11 Begin a new drawing named 074???X1, using the file 074TBLOK as a prototype. Create a new layer called DIMENSIONS to contain all your dimensions. Set DIMTIX=1 to force dimension text inside the dimension lines. Then, using figure 74.8 as a guide, add linear dimensions to the tool block. Save your drawing when you are finished.

Student: __________ Date: __________

Instructor: __________ Course: __________ Section: __________

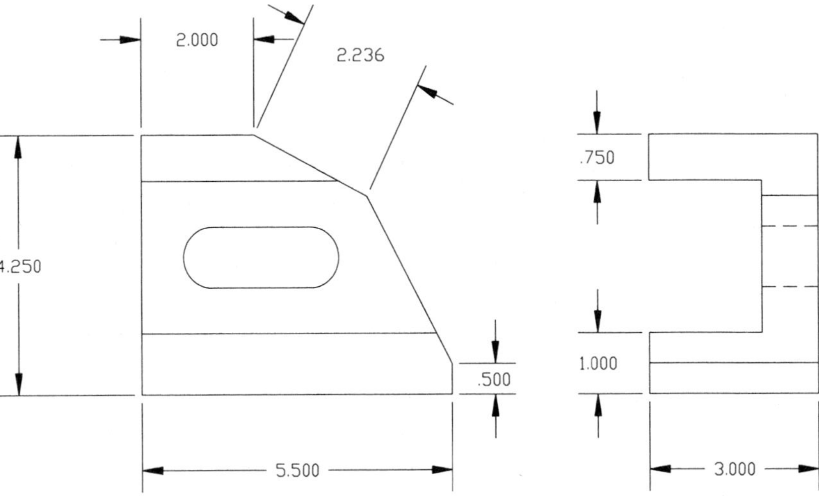

Figure 74.8

Tool block with linear dimensions.

Student: ____________ Date: ______

Instructor: ____________ Course: ______ Section: ______

UNIT 75

Adding Diameter and Radius Dimensions

utoCAD provides the capability to add many types of dimensions to a drawing. Unit 74 explains how you can add linear dimensions (horizontal, vertical, and aligned) to a drawing. AutoCAD also enables you to add radius and diameter dimensions to a drawing's arcs and circles. In many cases, you only have to select the arc or circle, and then pick a location for the dimension line; AutoCAD does the rest. This unit shows you how to add radius and diameter dimensions to a drawing.

The objectives for this unit are to:

- Apply radius dimensions to arcs and circles
- Apply diameter dimensions to circles
- Understand text placement options for radius and diameter dimensions
- Add center marks to circles and arcs
- Control the size of center marks

Applying Diameter Dimensions

To apply a diameter dimension in AutoCAD, start the appropriate dimensioning command, and then select the circle to be dimensioned. The point you use to select the circle is the point at which AutoCAD places the tip of the dimension or leader line. The extension line is drawn at an angle equal to that from the center of the circle to the tip of the leader. If the DIMTIX dimension variable is off, AutoCAD also prompts you for the placement of the dimension text by asking you to specify the length of the leader line.

In the following exercise, add inside and outside diameter dimensions to a radial gauge face.

Applying Diameter Dimensions

1. Begin a new drawing named 075???01, using the file 075GFACE as a prototype.
2. Create a DIMENSION layer and make it the current layer.
3. `Command:` **`DIMTIX`** ↵
4. `New value for DIMTIX <0>:` **`1`** ↵ — Forces text inside the dimension line
5. `Command:` *Choose* Draw, *then* Dimensions, *then* Radial, *then* Diameter — Starts diameter dimension mode

   `Dim: _diameter`
6. `Select arc or circle:` *Select the large circle at* ① *(see fig 75.1)* — Specifies start point of dimension line
7. `Dimension text <4.00>:` *Press* Enter — Accepts dimension value and places dimension
8. `Command:` **`DIMTIX`** ↵
9. `New value for DIMTIX <1>:` **`0`** ↵ — Causes AutoCAD to place dimension value outside dimension line
10. `Command:` **`DIM`** ↵ — Enters dimensioning mode
11. `Dim:` **`DIA`** ↵ — Starts diameter dimensioning command
12. `Select arc or circle:` *Select the small circle at* ② *(see fig 75.1)* — Selects circle to dimension

13. `Dimension text <.12>:` *Press* Enter	Accepts dimension value
14. `Enter leader length for text:` *Pick a point at* ③ *(see fig 75.1)*	Places the dimension
15. Dim: EXIT ↵	Exits dimensioning mode

Your drawing should look similar to figure 75.1.

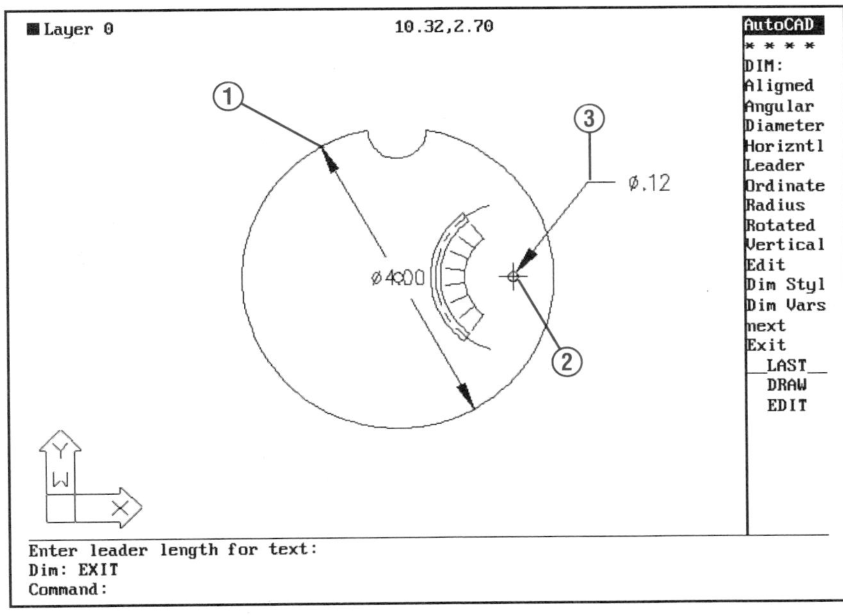

Figure 75.1

Two diameter dimensions added to the gauge face.

Notice that AutoCAD prompts for text/leader placement for diameter dimensions when DIMTIX is set to 1 (On). AutoCAD by default places the diameter symbol as a prefix in the dimension text. Also note that you can use the EXIT command to end dimensioning mode. You also can press Ctrl+C to end dimensioning mode.

Another dimension variable that controls the appearance of diameter dimensions is DIMTOFL (DIMension Text Outside, Force Line inside). This causes AutoCAD to draw a dimension line through the diameter of the circle at the point you pick. Place a diameter dimension with DIMTOFL on.

Placing an Outside Diameter Dimension

1. Continue with your drawing from the preceding exercise, and erase the 4.00" diameter dimension.
2. `Command:` **`DIMTOFL`** ↵
3. `New value for DIMTOFL <0>:` **`1`** ↵

continues

4. `Command:` *Choose* Draw, *then* Dimensions, *then* Radial, *then* Diameter	Starts diameter dimensioning command
`Dim: _diameter`	
5. `Select arc or circle:` *Select the large circle at* ① *(see fig. 75.2)*	
6. `Dimension text <4.00>:` *Press* Enter	Accepts dimension value
7. Enter leader length for text: *Pick a point at* ② *(see fig. 75.2)*	Places dimension

Your drawing should look like figure 75.2.

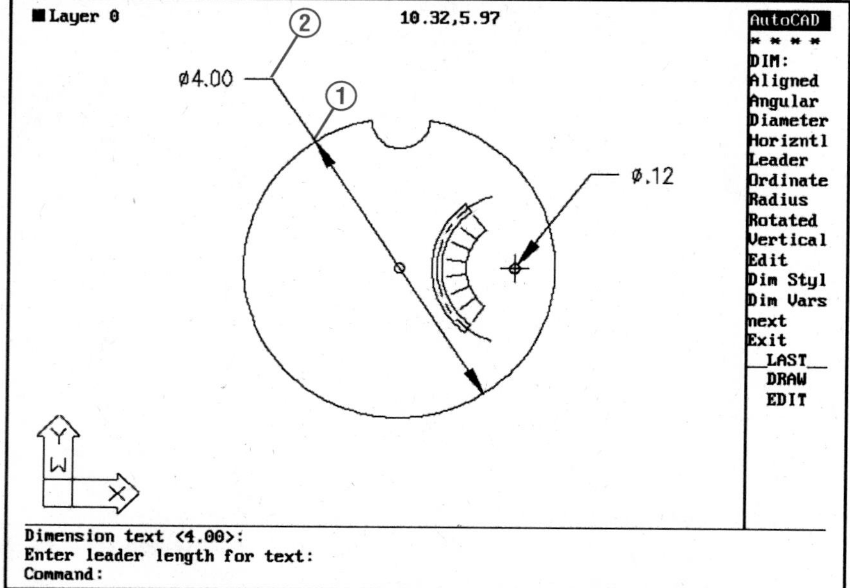

Figure 75.2

Outside diameter dimension added to the gauge face.

If you want to draw an outside diameter dimension with the dimension leader on the outside of the circle, set DIMTIX and DIMTOFL both to 0. To place the dimension value outside the circle and the dimension line inside the circle, set DIMTOFL to 1. To place the dimension text inside the circle, set DIMTIX to 1.

Applying Radius Dimensions

The steps used to place a radius dimension are very similar to placing a diameter dimension. DIMTIX still is used to control where the dimension text is placed. If DIMTIX is set to 1, the text is placed inside the radius. If DIMTIX is set to 0, the text is placed outside the radius.

In the following exercise, replace the 4.00" outside diameter dimension with an inside radius dimension.

Placing a Radius Dimension

1. Erase the 4.00" diameter dimension from the preceding exercise.
2. `Command:` **`DIMTIX`** ↵
3. `New value for DIMTIX <0>:` **`1`** ↵ — Turns DIMTIX on
4. `Command:` *Choose* Draw, *then* Dimensions, *then* Radial, *then* Radius — Starts radius dimensioning command

   `Dim: _radius`
5. `Select arc or circle:` *Pick a point on the large circle at* ① *(see fig. 75.3)* — Locates dimension line start point
6. `Dimension text <2.00>:` *Press* Enter — Accepts dimension value and places dimension

Next, place an outside radius dimension for the notch at the top of the part.

7. `Command:` **`DIMTIX`** ↵
8. `New value for DIMTIX <1>:` **`0`** ↵ — Causes AutoCAD to place dimension value outside dimension line
9. `Command:` **`DIM`** ↵ — Enters dimensioning mode
10. `Dim:` **`RAD`** ↵ — Starts radius dimension command
11. `Select arc or circle:` *Pick a point on the semicircular notch at* ② *(see fig. 75.3)*
12. `Dimension text <0.38>:` *Press* Enter — Accepts dimension value
13. `Enter leader length for text:` *Pick a point at* ③ *(see fig. 75.3)* — Locates the dimension text
14. `Dim: EXIT`↵ — Exits dimensioning mode

Your drawing should look similar to figure 75.3.

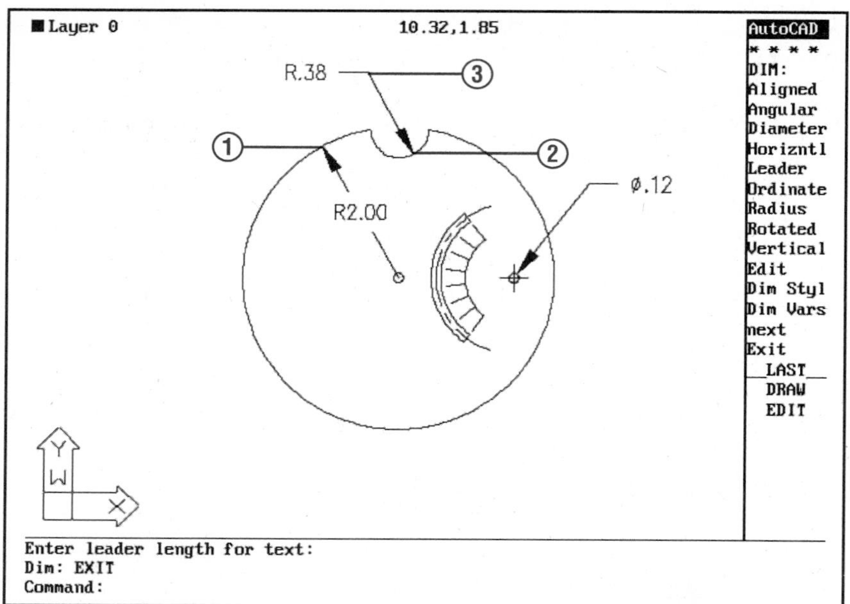

Figure 75.3

Radius dimensions added to the gauge face.

Occasionally, you may want to move the dimension text in a radius or diameter dimension to another location out of the way of other features in the drawing. Unit 85 explains how to edit dimensions, including moving a dimension's text.

Placing Center Marks

Center marks—crosses at the center of arcs and circles—are useful for layout purposes in most drafting disciplines. When you dimension a drawing in AutoCAD, you can have AutoCAD place center marks for you automatically.

AutoCAD controls the size and appearance of center marks through the dimensioning variable DIMCEN. DIMCEN can be set to any real number. A positive value controls the size of the center marks, a zero value means that center marks will not be drawn, and a negative value means that center lines rather than center marks are drawn. The absolute value of a negative DIMCEN value specifies the size of the center mark portion of the center line. Figure 75.4 illustrates the effect of the DIMCEN dimensioning variable.

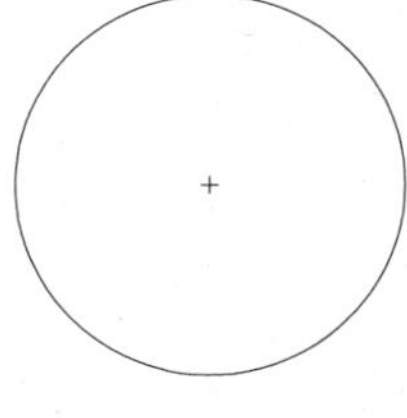

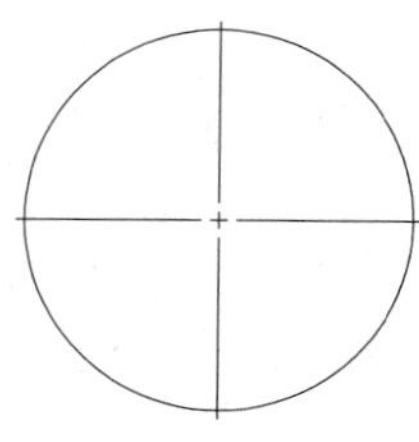

Figure 75.4

The effect of the DIMCEN dimensioning variable on center marks.

The dimensioning command CEN places center marks on the drawing by prompting for an arc or circle. Diameter and radius dimensions also are affected by the value of DIMCEN; AutoCAD applies a center mark to diameter and radius dimensions according to the value of DIMCEN.

In the following exercise, place some center marks on the circles and arcs on the gauge face.

Placing Center Marks

1. Continue with your drawing from the preceding exercise and erase all the dimensions in the drawing.

2.	`Command:` **`DIMCEN`** ↵	
3.	`New value for DIMCEN <0.09>:` *Press* Enter	Verifies that DIMCEN is set to .09"
4.	`Command:` *Choose* Draw, *then* Dimensions, *then* Radial, *then* Center Marks `Dim: _center`	Starts CEN dimensioning command
5.	`Select arc or circle:` *Pick the small hole at* ① *(see fig. 75.5)*	Places center mark

Next, add a center mark to the notch at the top of the gauge face.

6.	`Command:` **`DIM`** ↵	
7.	`Dim:` **`CEN`** ↵	Starts CEN dimensioning command
8.	`Select arc or circle:` *Pick the notch at* ② *(see fig. 75.5)*	Places center mark
9.	`Dim:` **`DIMCEN`** ↵	
10.	`Current value <0.05> New value:` **`-.09`** ↵	Reset DIMCEN to draw center lines
11.	`Dim:` **`CEN`** ↵	
12.	`Select arc or circle:` *Pick the large circle at any point*	Draws center lines
13.	`Dim: EXIT` ↵	Exits dimensioning mode

Your drawing should look like figure 75.5.

Figure 75.5

Center marks added to the gauge face drawing.

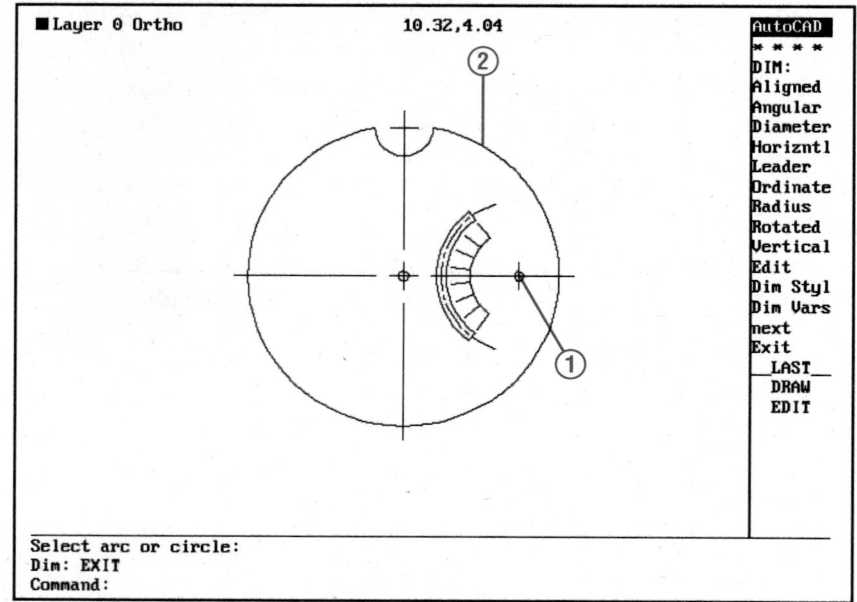

Experiment with different values for DIMTOFL, DIMTIX, and DIMCEN to add radius and diameter dimensions to your drawing.

Unit Review

What You've Learned

- Commands: DIMTOFL, DIMCEN, DIM:DIAMETER, DIM:RADIUS, DIM:CENTER
- How to place diameter dimensions
- How to place radius dimensions
- How to control the location of dimension text with DIMTOFL
- How to control the location of dimension lines with DIMTIX

Review Questions

True or False

75.01 T F If DIMTIX is off, dimension text is drawn inside a circle.

75.02 T F DIMTOFL controls the location of text relative to the dimension extension lines.

75.03 T F If DIMCEN is set to a negative number, the CEN dimensioning command draws center lines on a circle.

75.04 T F The EXIT command can be used to exit dimensioning mode.

75.05 T F You cannot control the location of text in a diameter dimension.

Multiple Choice

75.06 AutoCAD prompts you to select ________________ when you use the DIA dimensioning command.

(A) the center of a circle

(B) the size of center marks

(C) a circle or arc

(D) none of the above

75.07 A positive value for DIMCEN specifies ______________.

(A) the center mark size

(B) center line length

(C) text-to-center distance

(D) none of the above

Student: ______________________ Date: ________

Instructor: ____________ Course: ______ Section: ______

75.08 Setting DIMCEN to 0 causes AutoCAD to draw ____________.

(A) center lines just to the edge of circles

(B) no center mark

(C) a default .1" center mark

(D) center marks on layer 0

Short Answer

75.09 Briefly explain the effect of positive, negative, and zero values for DIMCEN.

____

____

____

75.10 Describe two ways to end dimensioning mode.

____

____

____

Student: ______________ Date: ______________

Instructor: ______________ Course: ______________ Section: ______________

UNIT 76

Adding Chain Dimensions

nit 74 explains how to add linear dimensions to a drawing in AutoCAD. In addition to singular linear dimensions, AutoCAD enables you to place *continued,* or *chain* dimensions in a drawing. This unit explains this type of dimension and teaches you how to place them in a drawing.

The objectives of this unit are to:

- Place a linear dimension to be continued
- Place a continued dimension using the last linear dimension as a reference
- Place a continued dimension by specifying a linear dimension to use as a reference.

Applying Chain Dimensions

Chain (or *continued*) dimensions are used when you must draw a series of linear dimensions. Continued dimensions will work only with AutoCAD's horizontal, vertical, aligned, and rotated linear dimensions. Continued dimensions are sometimes refered to as "stacked" dimensions, meaning that one dimension is stacked on top of or next to another. Figure 76.1 illustrates continued dimensioning.

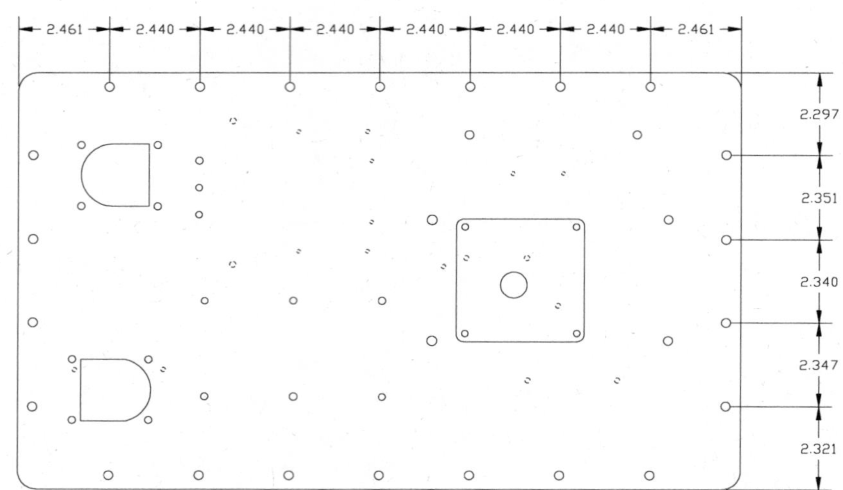

Figure 76.1
An example of continued dimensions.

Continued dimensions must have a base or starting linear dimension as a reference. To begin a series of continued dimensions, use a horizontal, vertical, aligned, or rotated dimension as the first dimension in the set. Duplicate figure 76.1 in the following exercise.

Drawing a Starting Dimension

1. Begin a new drawing named 076???01 in your assigned directory, using 076CONT.DWG as a prototype.

2. Place a horizontal dimension as a starting point for your continued dimensions.

3. `Command:` *Choose* Draw, *then* Dimensions, *then* Linear, *then* Horizontal — Starts DIM:HOR command

   `Dim: _horizontal`

4. `First extension line origin or RETURN to select:` *From the popup menu, choose* Endpoint — Sets object snap mode

5. `_endp of` *Select the line at* ① *(see fig. 76.2)* — Specifies the first extension line origin for the dimension

6. `Second extension line origin:` *From the popup menu, choose* Center	Sets object snap mode
7. `_center of` *Select the circle at* ② *(see fig. 76.2)*	Specifies the next point for the linear dimension
8. `Dimension line location (Text/Angle):` *Pick a point at* ③ *(see fig. 76.2)*	Specifies the location for the dimension line and arrowheads
9. `Dimension text <2.461>:` *Press* Enter	Accepts dimension value determined by AutoCAD

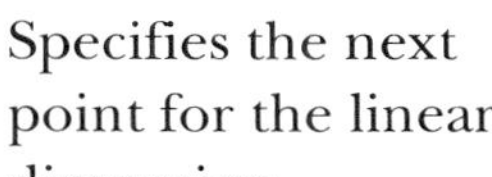

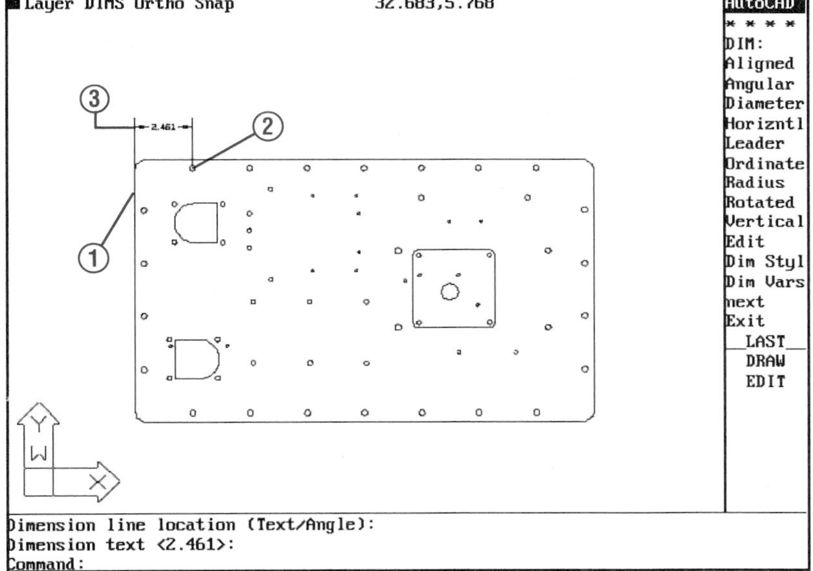

Figure 76.2

A starting horizontal dimension added to the drawing.

The horizontal dimension you just entered will serve as the start of your continued dimensions. Next, place a few continued dimensions in the drawing.

Placing a Continued Dimension

Continue with your drawing from the previous exercise.

1. `Command:` *Choose* Draw, *then* Dimensions, *then* Linear, *then Continue*	Starts the DIM:CONT command

```
Dim: _continued
```

continues

2. `Second extension line origin or RETURN to select:` *From the popup menu, choose* Center	Sets object snap
3. `_center of` *Select the circle at ① (see figure 76.3)*	Specifies second dimension point
4. `Dimension text <2.440>:` *Press* Enter	Accepts dimension value determined by AutoCAD
5. `Command:` **`DIM`** ↵	Enters dimensioning mode
6. `Dim:` **`CONT`** ↵	Starts continued dimensioning
7. `Second extension line origin or RETURN to select:` *From the popup menu, choose* Center	
8. `_center of` *Select the circle at ②*	Specifies second point of next dimension
9. `Dimension text <2.440>:` *Press* Enter	Accept the default dimension value
10. `Dim:` **`EXIT`** ↵	Exits dimensioning mode
11. `Command:` *Choose* File, *then* Save	Saves the drawing

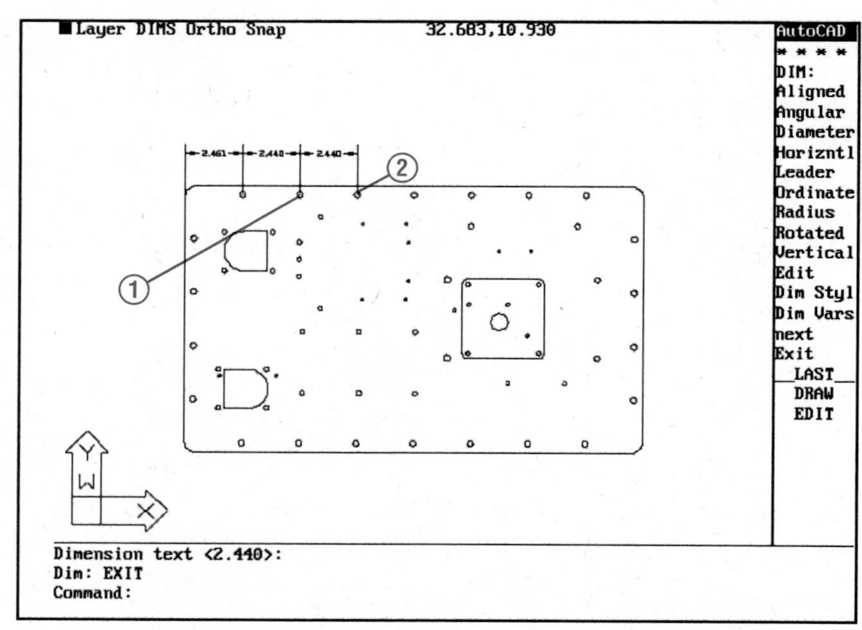

Figure 76.3

Continued dimensions added to the drawing.

AutoCAD automatically uses the last linear dimension placed on your drawing as the dimension from which to continue the next dimension. AutoCAD places the dimension line and arrowheads of the continued dimensions in line with the previous linear dimension. Continue the exercise by placing additional continued dimensions until your drawing resembles figure 76.4.

Finishing the Horizontal Continued Dimensions

1. `Command:` *Choose* Settings, *then* Object Snap	Displays the Running Object Snap dialog box
2. *Check the* Center *check box, then choose* OK	Sets running object snap to Center and closes the dialog box
3. `Command:` *From the root screen menu, choose* DIM: `DIM`	Enters dimensioning mode
4. `Dim:` *From the* DIM: *screen menu, choose* next, *then* Continue `Dim: _CONTINUE`	Starts DIM:CONT command
5. `Second extension line origin or RETURN to select:` *Select the circle at* ① *(see fig. 76.4)*	Draws continued dimension
6. `Dimension text <2.440>:` *Press* Enter	Accepts dimension value
7. `Dim:` *Press* Enter	Repeats the DIM:CONT command
8. `Second extension line origin or RETURN to select:` *Select the circle at* ②	Draws continued dimension
9. `Dimension text <2.440>:` *Press* Enter	Accepts dimension value
10. `Dim:` *Press* Enter	Repeats the DIM:CONT command
11. `Second extension line origin or RETURN to select:` *Select the circle at* ③	Draws continued dimension
12. `Dimension text <2.440>:` *Press* Enter	Accepts dimension value
13. `Dim:` **`EXIT`** ↵	Exits dimensioning mode
14. `Command:` *Choose* File, *then* Save	

Figure 76.4

Multiple horizontal continued dimensions added to the drawing.

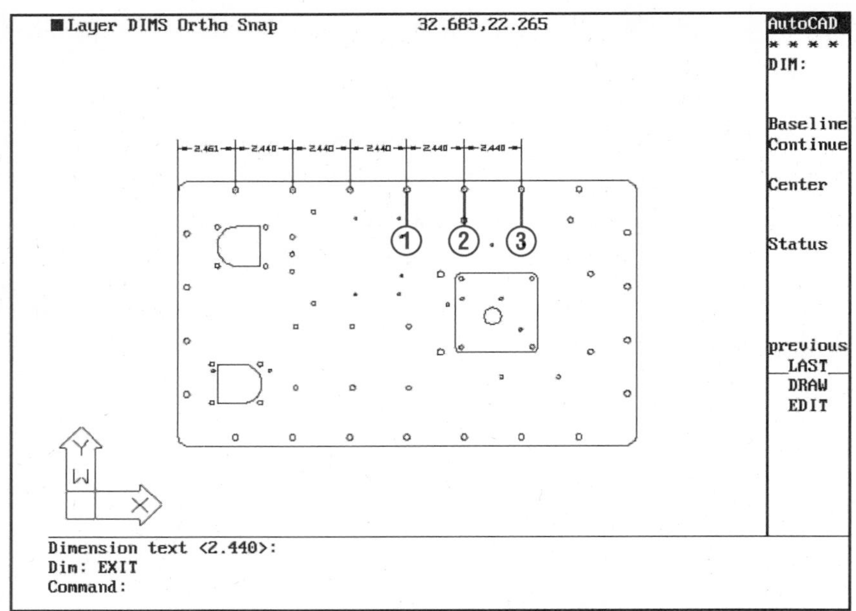

Specifying an Existing Starting Dimension

There may be occasions when you place a starting dimension, but intend to place continued dimensions afterward. Or, perhaps you make other changes in your drawing before you place the continued dimensions. When you decide to go back and place continued dimensions, AutoCAD may not use the same starting dimension from which you want to work. Instead of letting AutoCAD choose which starting dimension to use, you can specify the starting dimension.

To learn how you can specify the starting dimension, place a vertical dimension on your drawing as shown in figure 76.5.

Adding a Vertical Dimension

Continue with your drawing from the previous exercise. Center running object snap should still be active.

1. `Command:` *Choose* Draw, *then* Dimensions, *then* Linear, *then* Vertical	Starts DIM:VER command
`_dim1`	
2. `Dim: _vertical`	
3. `First extension line origin or RETURN to select:` *From the popup menu, choose* Endpoint	Sets object snap to Endpoint

4. `_endp of` *Select the line at* ① *(see fig. 76.5)*	Specifies first point of dimension
5. `Second extension line origin:` *Select the circle at* ②	Specifies second point of dimension
6. `Dimension line location (Text/Angle):` *Pick a point at* ③	Specifies dimension line location
7. `Dimension text <2.321>:` *Press* Enter	Accepts the dimension value

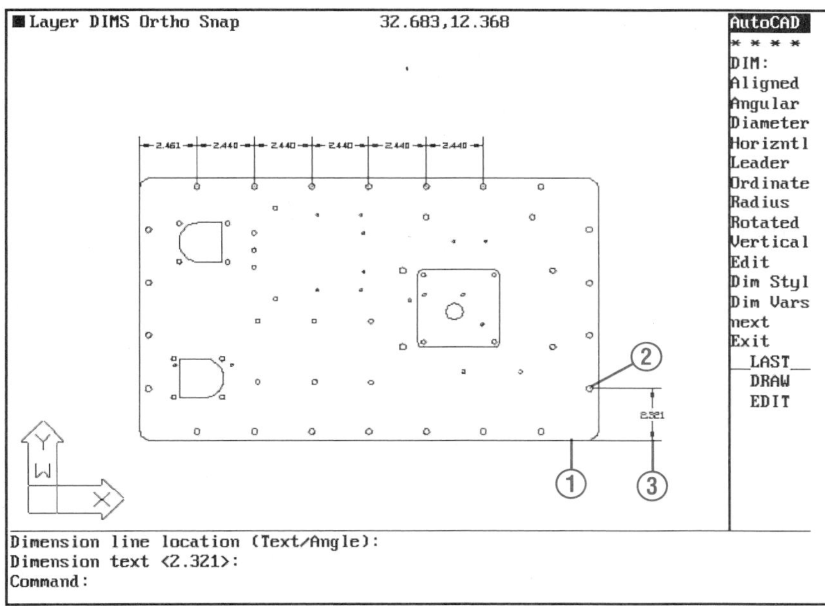

Figure 76.5

Vertical dimension to be continued.

Now return to the top of the part to place a continued dimension by specifying the dimension to use as a reference.

Specifying the Starting Dimension

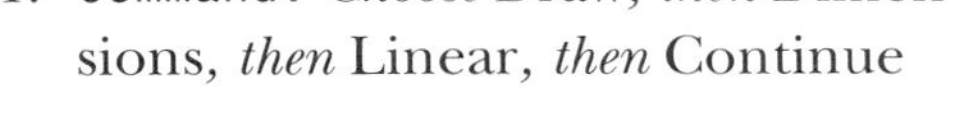

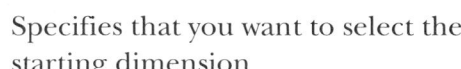

1. `Command:` *Choose* Draw, *then* Dimensions, *then* Linear, *then* Continue	
2. `Second extension line origin or RETURN to select:` *Press* Enter	Specifies that you want to select the starting dimension
3. `Select continued dimension:` *Select the dimension at* ① *(see fig. 76.6)*	AutoCAD determines the first *horizontal* point of the continued dimension

continues

4. `Second extension line origin or RETURN to select:` *Select the circle at* ② — Specifies second point of dimension
5. `Dimension text <2.440>:` *Press* Enter — Accepts default dimension value
6. `Command:` *Choose* File, *then* Save — Saves the drawing

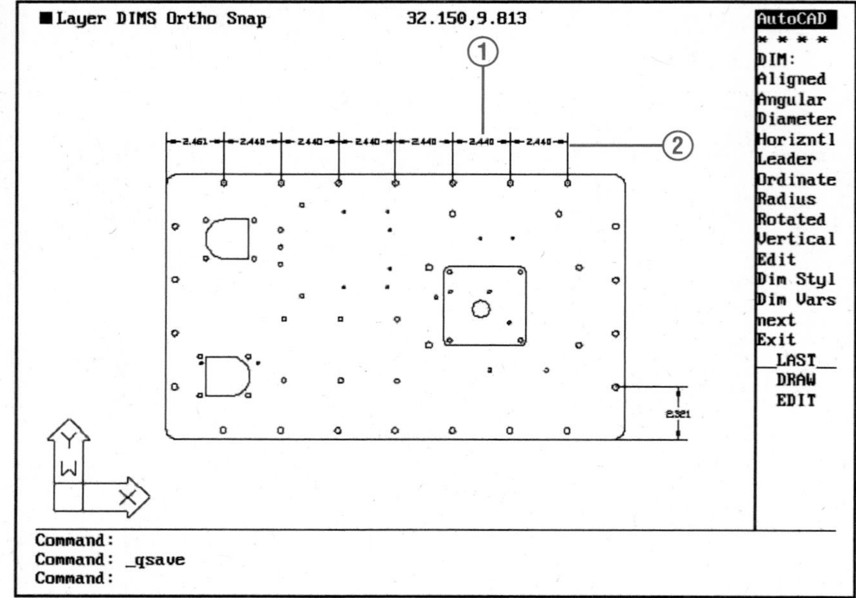

Figure 76.6
Final horizontal continued dimension added to the drawing.

Next, return to the right side of the part and complete the vertical continued dimensions. This will give you another opportunity to select the starting dimension.

Placing the Vertical Continued Dimensions

Continue with your drawing from the previous exercise. Center running object snap mode should still be active.

1. `Command:` **`DIM`** ↵ — Enters dimensioning mode.
   `Dim:` *From the* DIM: *screen menu, choose* next, *then* Continue — Starts the DIM:CONT command
   `CONTINUE`
2. `Second extension line origin or RETURN to select:` *Press* Enter — Specifies that you want to select the starting dimension
3. `Select continued dimension:` *Select the dimension at* ① *(see fig. 76.7)* — Specifies the starting dimension

4. `Second extension line origin or RETURN to select:` *Select the circle at* ② — Specifies second point for dimension
5. `Dimension text <2.347>:` *Press* Enter — Accepts dimension value and places dimension
6. `Dim:` *Press* Enter — Repeats DIM:CONT command

   `_CONTINUE`
7. `Second extension line origin or RETURN to select:` *Select the circle at* ③ — Specifies second point for dimension
8. `Dimension text <2.347>:` *Press* Enter — Accepts dimension value and places dimension
9. `Dim:` *Press* Enter — Repeats DIM:CONT command

   `_CONTINUE`
10. `Second extension line origin or RETURN to select:` *Select the circle at* ④ — Specifies second point for dimension
11. `Dimension text <2.347>:` *Press* Enter — Accepts dimension value and places dimension
12. `Dim:` **`EXIT`** ↵ — Exits dimensioning mode
13. `Command:` *Choose* File, *then* Save

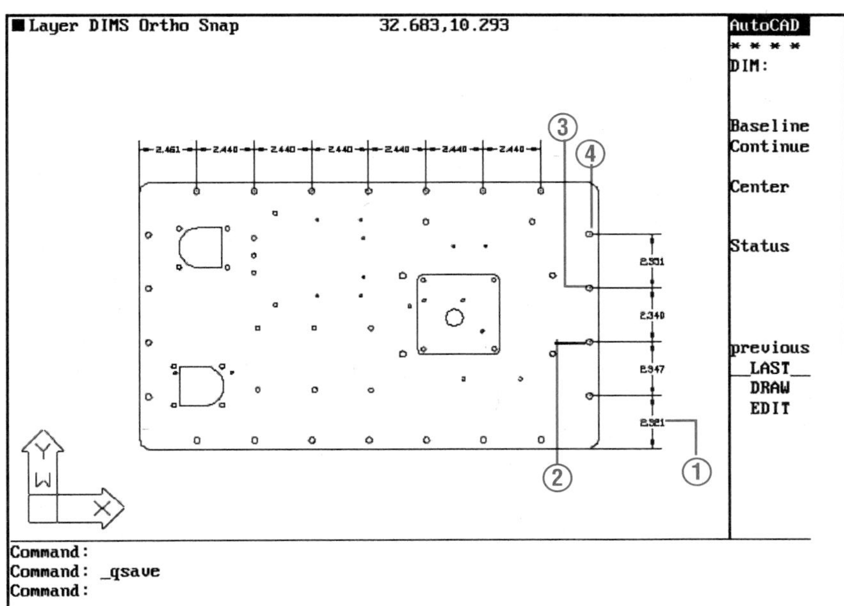

Figure 76.7

Vertical continued dimensions added to the drawing.

Unit Review

What You've Learned

- Command: DIM:CONTINUE
- How to place continued linear dimensions using the last linear dimension as a reference
- How to place continued linear dimensions by selecting a dimension to use as a reference

Review Questions

True or False

76.01 T F The CONTINUE command is used to continue (chain) any type of dimension.

76.02 T F CONTINUE can be used to dimension the radius of arcs.

76.03 T F CONTINUE assumes the last linear dimension as a reference starting point.

76.04 T F Pressing Enter at the `Dim:` prompt repeats the previous dimensioning command.

76.05 T F You can specify the starting reference dimension when drawing continued dimensions.

76.06 T F Continued dimensions also are known as baseline dimensions.

76.07 T F Continued dimensions also are known as chain dimensions.

76.08 T F The CONTINUE command automatically locates the dimension line and text for a continued dimension in line with the starting dimension.

76.09 T F CONTINUE does not prompt you to accept the default dimension value.

76.10 T F The EXIT command exits AutoCAD.

Student: ______________________ Date: ____________

Instructor: ______________________ Course: ____________ Section: ____________

Additional Exercises

The file 076CONCR.DWG on the Hands-On disk contains a partial drawing of a building with CMU (Concrete Masonry Units), also known as concrete block walls. Continued dimensions are commonly used on drawings such as this to assist the masonry conractor in the proper placement of window and door openings. Begin a new drawing named 076???02 in your assigned directory, using the file 076CONCR as a prototype. Dimension the exterior window and door openings as shown in figure 76.8.

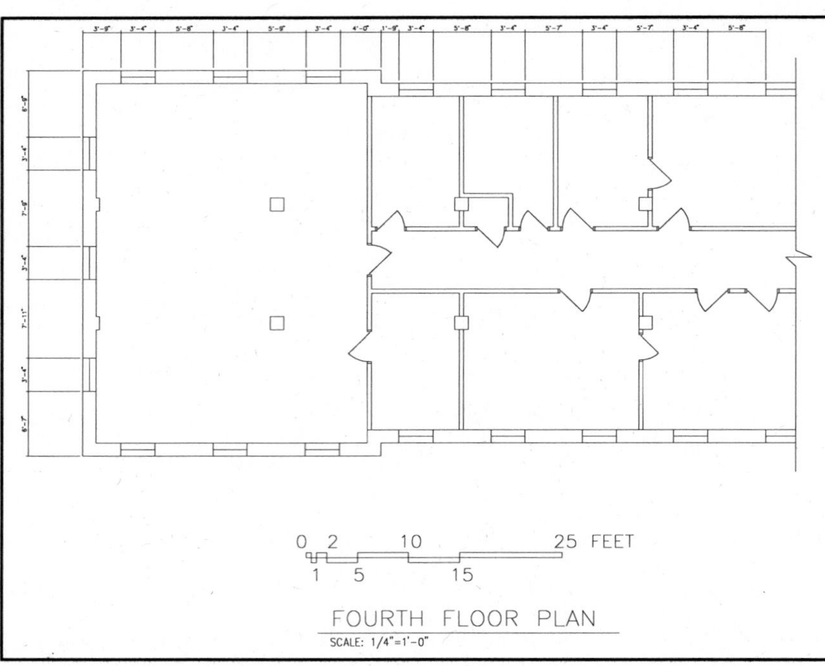

Figure 76.8

Architectural drawing using Continued dimensions to show placement of exterior window and door openings.

Student: ______ Date: ______

Instructor: ______ Course: ______ Section: ______

UNIT 77

Adding Baseline Dimensions

Baseline dimensions are very similar to chain dimensions (also known as continued dimensions). In fact, the methods of applying both are nearly the same. This unit teaches you to place baseline dimensions in a drawing by using the drawing from unit 76.

The objectives of this unit are to:

- Differentiate between a continued and baseline dimension
- Place baseline dimensions using the last default linear dimension as a reference
- Place baseline dimensions using a selected linear dimension as a reference
- Control the distance between consecutive baseline dimensions

Understanding Baseline Dimensions

Baseline dimensions derive their name from the requirement that all measurements are made from one reference point, which is called a *baseline*. Baseline dimensions are inherently more accurate over the length of a string of dimensions than are continued dimensions. This is due to a lack of tolerance error accumulation that can occur from the start of the dimension string to the end.

To illustrate the errors possible with chain dimensions, suppose that in the architectural drawing in unit 76, you used continued dimensions to measure the wall and door openings in a concrete block wall. What if the first dimension had an error of 1" and the next dimension was off by 1/2"? You can see that by the end of the dimension string, each error accumulation adds up to a major error at the end. This is because each subsequent dimension in continued dimensions is referenced from the previous dimension string. Therefore, if the reference dimension contains an error, each subsequent dimension will reflect this error plus additional errors that may accumulate. Continued dimensions are satisfactory in this real-world example because they serve only as a rough guideline for the contractor to lay out the walls for your building.

Baseline dimensions avoid this error accumulation by only referencing the same start point for each dimension (see fig. 77.1).

Because each dimension references the same point, errors are localized to a particular feature and do not affect other features throughout the dimension string.

The drafting discipline, type of drawing, and office standards will dictate which method—whether continued or baseline—is best suited for your particular application. Parts requiring close tolerance, for example, generally use some form of baseline dimensioning.

Like continued dimensions, baseline dimensions require a reference dimension to begin. You can let AutoCAD assume the last linear dimension as the default reference dimension or select the dimension to reference.

Applying Baseline Dimensions

In the following exercises, use drawing 077BASE.DWG from the Hands-On disk as a prototype for a new drawing. First, place a horizontal linear dimension for AutoCAD to use as a reference.

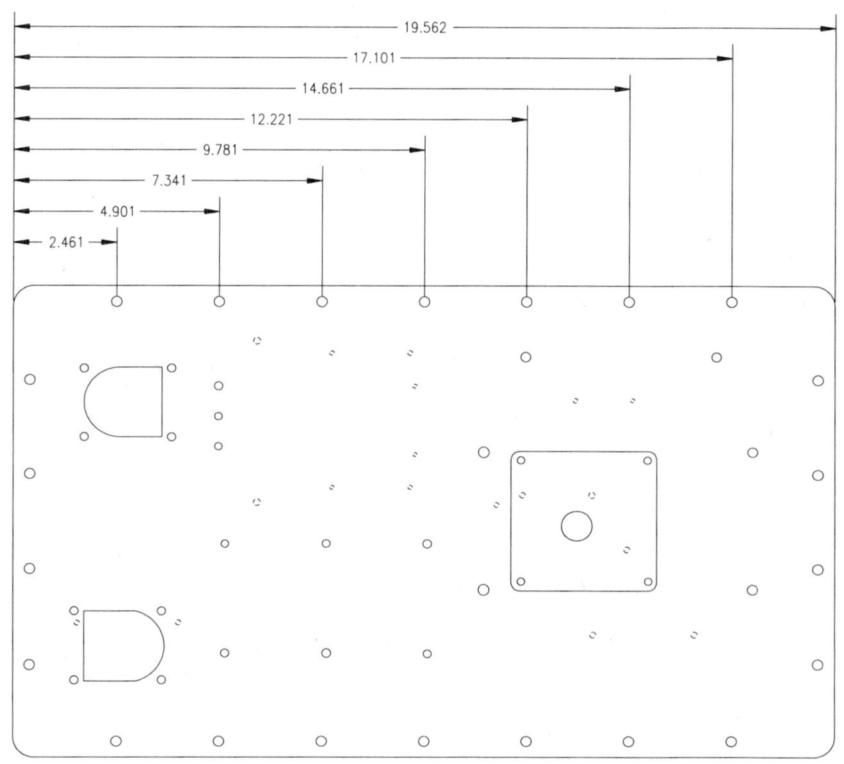

Figure 77.1

An example of baseline dimensioning.

Placing a Starting Dimension for Baseline Dimensioning

1. Begin a new drawing named 077???01 in your assigned directory, using 077BASE as a prototype.

2. `Command:` *Choose* Draw, *then* Dimensions, *then* Linear, *then* Horizontal	Enters dimensioning mode and starts horizontal dimensioning
`_dim1`	
`Dim: _horizontal`	
3. `First extension line origin or RETURN to select:` *From the popup menu, choose* Endpoint	Specifies object snap mode
4. `_endp of` *Select the line at* ① *(see fig. 77.2)*	Specifies start of dimension
5. `Second extension line origin:` *From the popup menu, choose* Center	

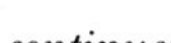

continues

Figure 77.2

Starting dimension added to the drawing.

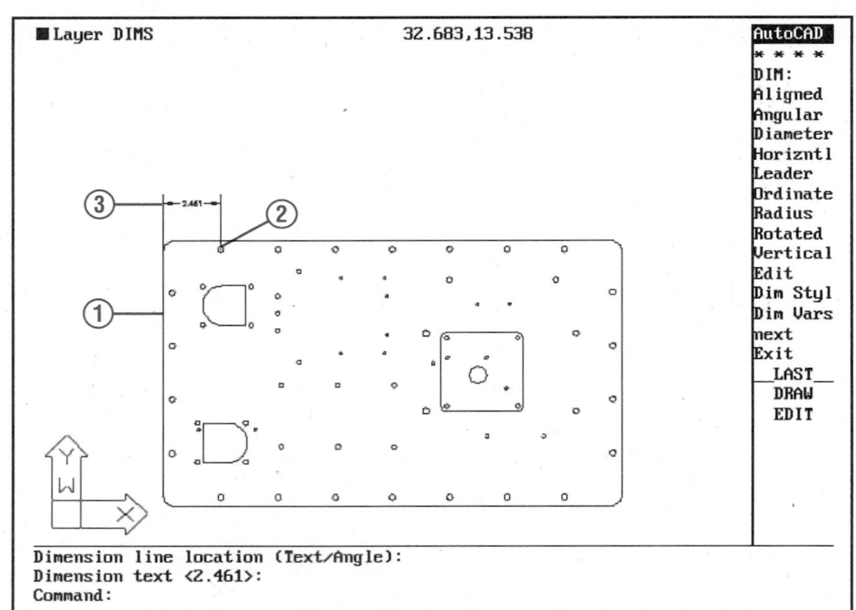

6. `_center of` *Select the circle at* ② *(see fig. 77.2)* — Specifies the second node point

7. `Dimension line location (Text/Angle):` *Pick a point at* ③ *(see fig. 77.2)* — Specifies the location of the dimension line

8. `Dimension text <2.461>:` *Press* Enter — Accepts default value

This dimension will serve as the reference for your baseline dimensions. AutoCAD will use the first node point (extension line origin) of the linear dimension for its calculations of subsequent baseline dimensions.

Now continue the dimension string using baseline dimensions.

Placing Horizontal Baseline Dimensions

1. `Command:` *Choose* Draw, *then* Dimensions, *then* Linear, *then* Baseline

   `_dim1`

   `Dim: _baseline`

2. `Second extension line origin or RETURN to select:` *From the popup menu, choose* Center — Specifies object snap mode

3. `_center of` *Select the circle at* ① *(see fig. 77.3)* — Specifies second point for dimension

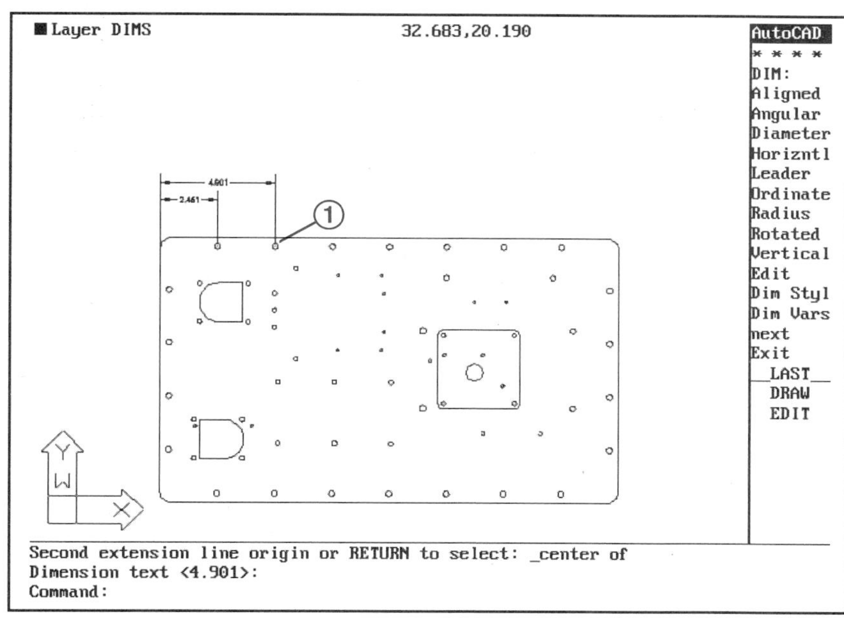

Figure 77.3

Point selection to place the baseline dimension.

4. `Dimension text <4.901>:` *Press* Enter	Accepts default value

AutoCAD automatically places the dimension a set distance away from the previous dimension. This offset distance is controlled by the dimension variable DIMDLI. To increase the distance between dimensions, increase the value of DIMDLI. To change the value of DIMDLI, enter **`DIMDLI`** at the `Command:` prompt. You will use DIMDLI in an exercise in the unit review.

Continue baseline dimensioning until your drawing resembles figure 77.1.

Completing the Horizontal Baseline Dimensions

1. `Command:` *Choose* Settings, *then* Object Snap, *then check the* Center *checkbox, then choose* OK	Sets running object snap mode to Center
2. `Command:` **`DIM`** ↵	Enters dimensioning mode
3. `Dim:` **`BASE`**	Starts DIM:BASE command
4. `Second extension line origin or RETURN to select:` *Select the circle at* ① *(see fig. 77.4)*	Specifies the second node of the dimension
5. `Dimension text <7.341>:` *Press* Enter	Accepts default value
6. `Dim:` *Press* Enter `BASE`	Repeats DIM:BASE command

continues

Figure 77.4

Completed horizontal baseline dimensions.

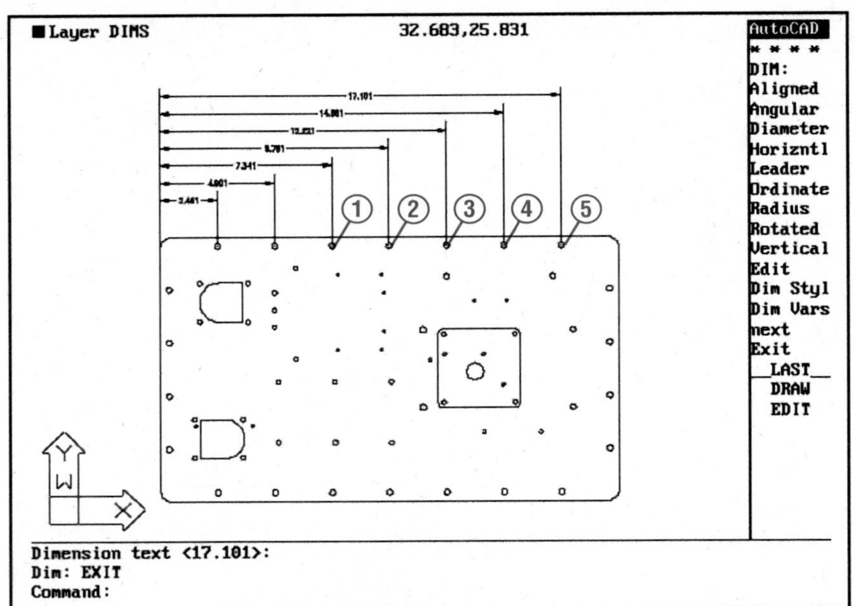

7. `Second extension line origin or RETURN to select:` *Select the circle at* ②	Specifies the second node of the dimension
8. `Dimension text <9.781>:` *Press* Enter	Accepts default value
9. `Dim:` *Press* Enter `BASE`	Repeats DIM:BASE command
10. `Second extension line origin or RETURN to select:` *Select the circle at* ③ *(see fig. 77.4)*	Specifies the second node of the dimension
11. `Dimension text <12.221>:` *Press* Enter	Accepts default value
12. `Dim:` *Press* Enter `BASE`	Repeats DIM:BASE command
13. `Second extension line origin or RETURN to select:` *Select the circle at* ④ *(see fig. 77.4)*	Specifies the second node of the dimension
14. `Dimension text <14.661>:` *Press* Enter	Accepts default value
15. `Dim:` *Press* Enter `BASE`	Repeats DIM:BASE command
16. `Second extension line origin or RETURN to select:` *Select the circle at* ⑤ *(see fig. 77.4)*	Specifies the second node of the dimension

17. `Dimension text <17.101>:` *Press* Enter	Accepts default value
18. `Dim:` **`EXIT`** ↵	Exits dimensioning mode
19. `Command:` *Choose* File, *then* Save	

You also will want to dimension the right side of the part using the bottom edge as a reference point for the baseline dimensions. Apply a vertical linear dimension to start.

Placing the First Vertical Dimension

Continue with your drawing from the previous exercise. Running object snap mode still should be set to Center (it was set in the preceding exercise).

1. `Command:` **`DIM`** ↵	Enters dimensioning mode
2. `Dim:` **`VER`** ↵	Starts DIM:VER command
3. `First extension line origin or RETURN to select:` *Select the circle at* ① *(see fig. 77.5)*	Specify the first node point

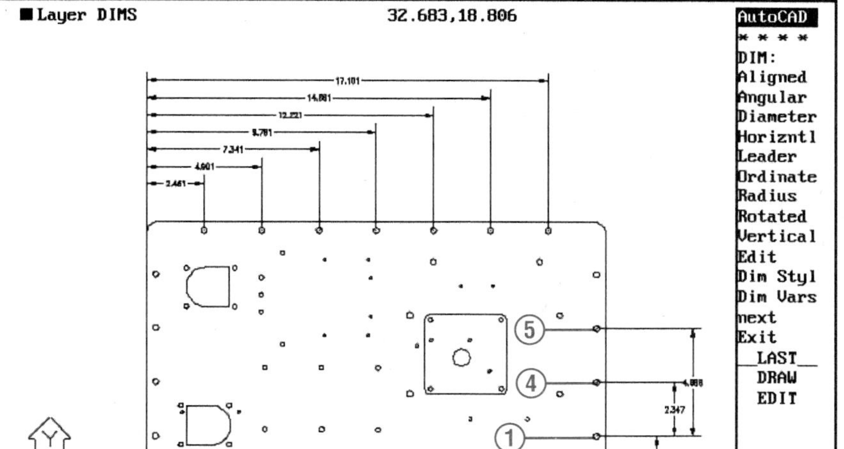

Figure 77.5

Adding vertical baseline dimensions.

4. `Second extension line origin:` *From the popup menu, choose* Endpoint	Temporarily overrides Center object snap with Endpoint
5. `_endp of` *Select the line at* ② *(see fig. 77.5)*	Specifies start point of dimension

continues

6. `Dimension line location (Text/Angle):` *Pick a point at* ③	Specifies the location for the dimension line
7. `Dimension text <2.321>:` *Press* Enter	Accepts default value

Remain in dimensioning mode for the next exercise.

Notice that you picked the dimension points in the previous exercise from top to bottom, rather than starting from the bottom of the part. In the next exercise, you will see the effect that selection order has on baseline dimensions.

Placing a Vertical Baseline Dimension

Continue with your drawing from the previous exercise. Running object snap mode still should be set to Center.

1. `Dim:` **`BASE`** ↵	Specify a baseline dimension
2. `Second extension line origin or RETURN to select:` *Select the circle at* ④ *(see fig. 77.5)*	Specifies point to dimension
3. `Dimension text <2.347>:` *Press* Enter	Accepts default value
4. `Dim:` *Press* Enter `BASE`	Repeats DIM:BASE command
5. `Second extension line origin or RETURN to select:` *Select the circle at* ⑤	Specifies point to dimension
6. `Dimension text <4.686>:` *Press* Enter	Accepts default value

Notice that you did not get the expected results when you placed the first baseline dimension. You wanted to use the bottom edge of the part as the baseline. Instead, AutoCAD used the center of the circle, or the first extension line origin at ① for the vertical dimension. When AutoCAD places continued and baseline dimensions, it uses the *first* extension line origin of the starting dimension as its reference point.

If you want to baseline dimension from the bottom of the part to the top of the part, you must pick the extension line origin points of the reference linear dimension in that order. In other words, it would have been better to start your initial vertical dimension from ② rather than ① to indicate to AutoCAD the direction you intended to go with the baseline dimensions.

Fortunately, you can show AutoCAD which extension line of your starting dimension you want to use as the baseline for your dimension string.

Specifying the Baseline Reference

1. Erase the previous two vertical dimensions.

2. `Command:` **`DIM`** ↵

3. `Dim:` **`BASE`** ↵

4. `Second extension line origin or RETURN to select:` *Press* Enter

5. `Select base dimension:` *Select the extension line at* ① *(see fig. 77.6)* — Specifies the reference point for subsequent baseline dimensions

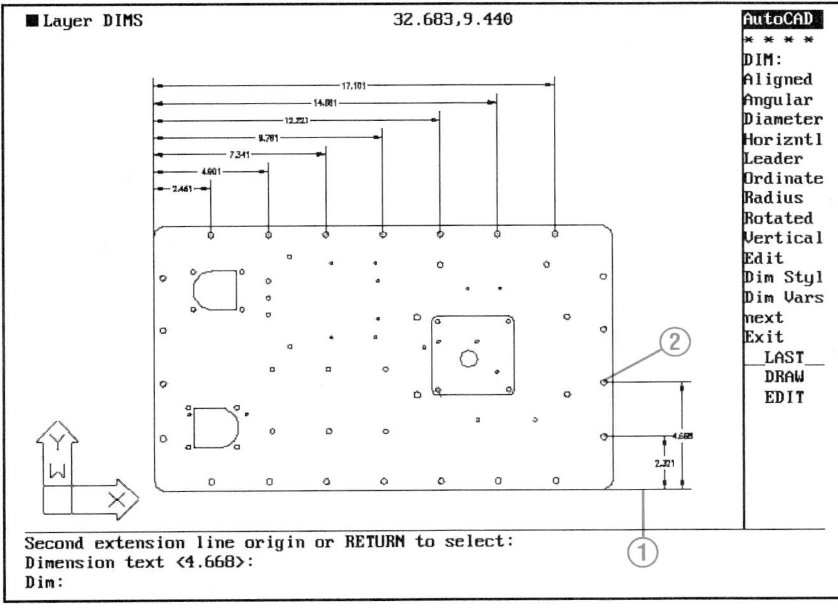

Figure 77.6

Corrected vertical baseline dimension.

6. `Second extension line origin or RETURN to select:` *Select the circle at* ② — Specifies point to dimension

7. `Dimension text <4.668>:` *Press* Enter — Accepts default value

Unit Review

What You've Learned

- The differences between a continued and a baseline dimension
- How to apply a baseline dimension using the last linear dimension as a reference
- How to apply a baseline dimension by selecting a dimension to use as a reference
- The importance of point selection order when drawing a starting baseline dimension

Review Questions

True or False

77.01 T F A set of baseline dimensions in a drawing also are known as continued dimensions.

77.02 T F Baseline dimensions in a drawing always reference the same baseline.

77.03 T F The order in which points are picked for the starting baseline dimension does not affect the other dimensions.

77.04 T F You can control the distance between baseline dimensions by picking the location for the dimension line.

77.05 T F DIMDLI controls the distance between baseline dimensions.

77.06 T F Baseline dimensions help avoid tolerance and error accumulation.

77.07 T F Some types of drawings are better suited to continued dimensions than to baseline dimensions.

77.08 T F AutoCAD always will prompt you to select the reference baseline dimension when you begin baseline dimensioning.

77.09 T F The distance between baseline dimensions is set automatically according to the distance between points being dimensioned.

77.10 T F Chain and baseline dimensions are the same thing.

Student: __________ Date: __________

Instructor: __________ Course: __________ Section: __________

Additional Exercises

77.11 Begin a new drawing named 077???12, using the file 077MOUNT as a prototype. Add continued and baseline dimensions to the drawing as shown in figure 77.7. After you have completed all the horizontal dimensions, set DIMDLI to .5, then place the vertical baseline dimensions. When you are finished, save the drawing.

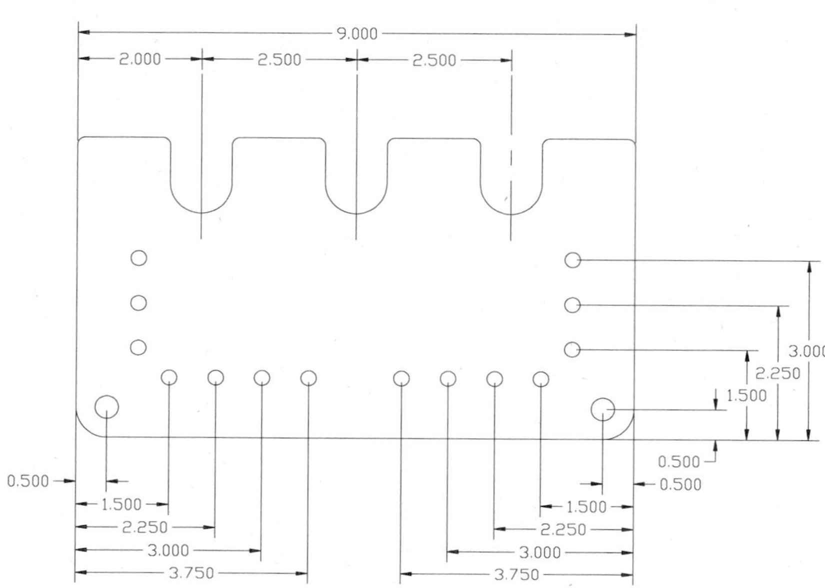

Figure 77.7

Dimension the mount plate as shown.

Student: ____________ Date: ____________

Instructor: ____________ Course: ____________ Section: ____________

UNIT 78

Adding Ordinate Dimensions

Previous units discuss types of dimensioning that measure the relative distance between two points. Another type of dimension measures the location of a feature's coordinates relative to a common point of reference. These dimensions are called *ordinate dimensions.* This unit explains ordinate dimensions and teaches you how to apply them using AutoCAD.

The objectives for this unit are to:

- Understand ordinate dimensions
- Apply ordinate dimensions using AutoCAD
- Understand how the origin applies to ordinate dimensions
- Create a frame of reference using the UCS command

Because ordinate dimensions are measurements of x- and y-values that are orthogonal (at 90 degrees to one another), you should always have AutoCAD's ORTHO mode ON to facilitate the placement of ordinate dimensions.

Understanding Ordinate Dimensions

A *coordinate* is a pair of x,y values; an *ordinate* is a single x- or y-value. Ordinate dimensioning is simply a matter of specifying the x or y location of a feature relative to the origin of the coordinate system. The origin point is considered the *datum* point for the dimension value. *x-datum* and *y-datum* points are specified, indicating along which axis the dimensions are being placed.

Ordinate dimensioning is used primarily in mechanical engineering environments, often for specifying the locations of holes or features to be drilled, punched, or machined in sheet metal or plate steel. Figure 78.1 illustrates one form of ordinate dimensioning.

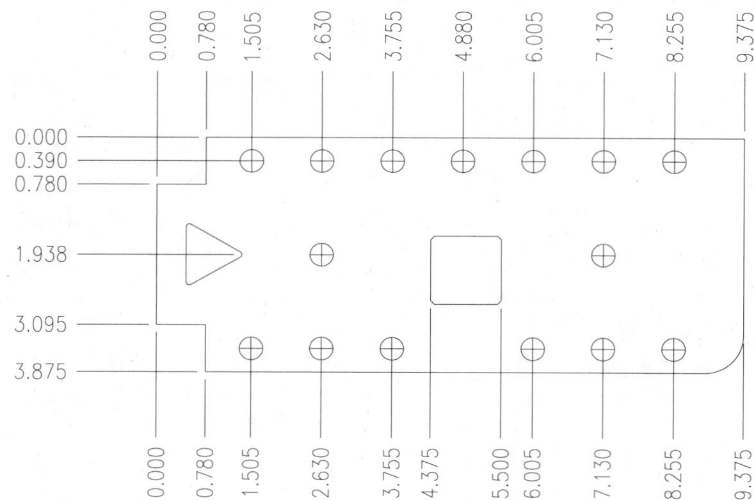

Figure 78.1

An example of ordinate dimensioning.

Unlike many types of linear dimensions, ordinate dimensions are not subject to error accumulation because all the dimensions in a drawing reference a common datum.

Applying Ordinate Dimensions

The datum point for ordinate dimensions always is the origin of the drawing, or coordinate 0,0. For AutoCAD to calculate properly the ordinate dimension value, the drawing geometry must be oriented so that the correct datum point of the geometry is located at 0,0. You can create a User Coordinate System (UCS) with its origin at the desired datum location, and place the x-y axis in the proper orientation (unit 38 explains how to define a coordinate system). If you are using the World Coordinate System, the World origin becomes the datum point.

In figure 78.1, the UCS is set so that the origin is at the lower left corner of the part. By default, the x-axis is east and the y-axis is north. When you are applying ordinate dimensions, you may find it helpful to turn on the UCS icon and have it display at the origin of your UCS.

Set up a UCS and the UCSICON, then apply ordinate dimensions to the features along the top edge of the part in the following exercise. Use figure 78.1 as a reference.

Setting Up a UCS for Ordinate Dimensioning

1. Begin a new drawing named 078???01 in your assigned directory, using the file 078ORDIN as a prototype. ORTHO should be on.

2. `Command:` **`UCSICON`** ↵	Starts UCSICON command
3. `ON/OFF/All/Noorigin/ORigin <OFF>:` **`ON`** ↵	Turns the UCS icon on
4. `Command:` *Press* Enter `UCSICON`	Repeats the UCSICON command
5. `ON/OFF/All/Noorigin/ORigin <ON>:` **`OR`** ↵	Displays the UCS icon at the origin of the UCS
6. `Command:` **`UCS`** ↵	Starts the UCS command
7. `Origin/ZAxis/3point/Entity/View /X/Y/Z/Prev/Restore/Save/Del /?/<World>:` **`O`** ↵	Specifies the Origin option
8. `Origin point <0,0,0>:` *From the popup menu, choose* Filters, *then* .X	Uses .X point filter
9. `.X of` *From the popup menu, choose* Endpoint	Specifies object snap mode
10. `_endp of` *Pick the end point at* ① *(see fig. 78.2)*	Specifies X value of origin
11. `(need YZ):` *From the popup menu, choose* Filters, *then* .YZ	Selects the .YZ point filter
12. `.YZ of` *From the popup menu, choose* Endpoint	Specifies object snap mode
13. `_endp of` *Pick the end point at* ② *(see fig. 78.2)*	Specifies YZ value of origin

continues

Figure 78.2

A User Coordinate System must be created before placing ordinate dimensions.

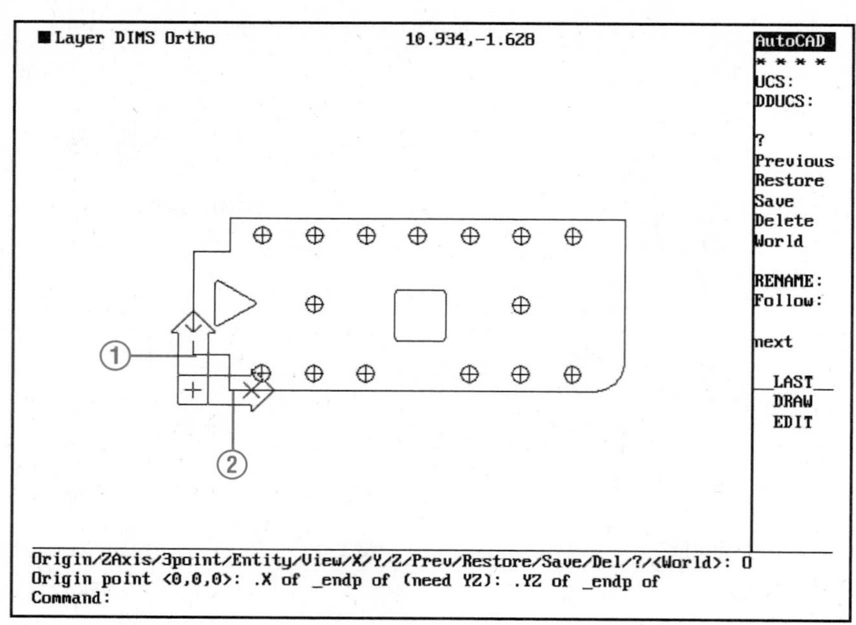

At this point your drawing should resemble figure 78.2.

You have just created a coordinate system with the origin (0,0) at the lower left corner of the plate. The new UCS has been added before any machining or drilling has been done. This UCS origin will serve as the basis (datum) for your ordinate dimensions.

Continue with the next exercise and place the x-datum ordinate dimensions.

Applying X-Datum Ordinate Dimensions

1. `Command:` *Choose* Draw, *then* Dimensions, *then* Ordinate, *then* X-Datum	Starts ordinate dimensioning for X-datum
2. `Select Feature:` **`0,0`** ↵	Places a dimension at 0,0
`Leader endpoint (Xdatum/Ydatum): _X`	Specifies X-datum dimension
3. `Leader endpoint:` *Pick a point at* ① *(see fig. 78.3)*	Specifies the length of the leader
4. `Dimension text <0.000>:` *Press* Enter	Accepts default value

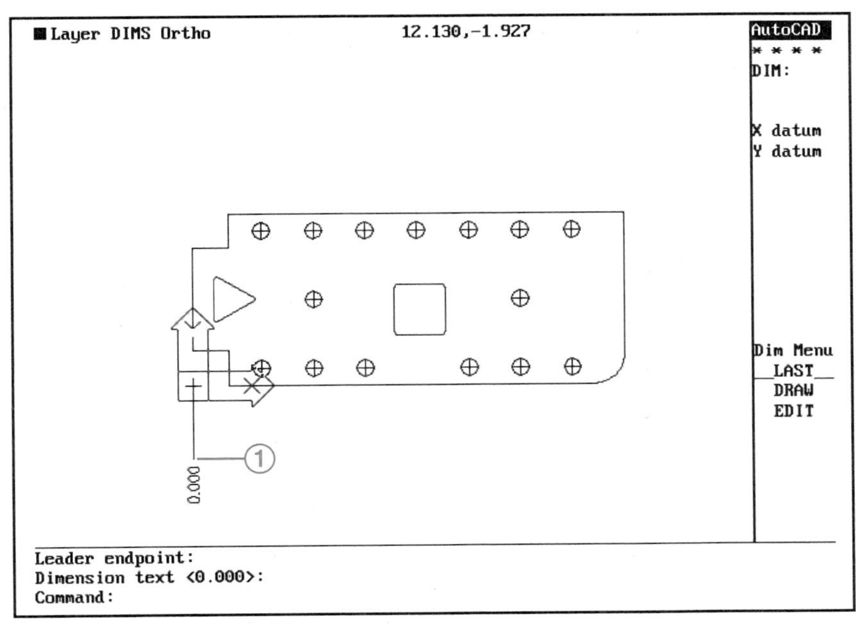

Figure 78.3

Placing ordinate dimensions.

To make it easier for you to specify the lengths of the leaders and to make your drawing neater, draw a temporary line from the endpoint of your first ordinate dimension in the direction you are dimensioning. When prompted to specify the leader endpoint, use the perpendicular object snap mode to specify a point on your temporary line. Figure 78.4 illustrates the placement of this line.

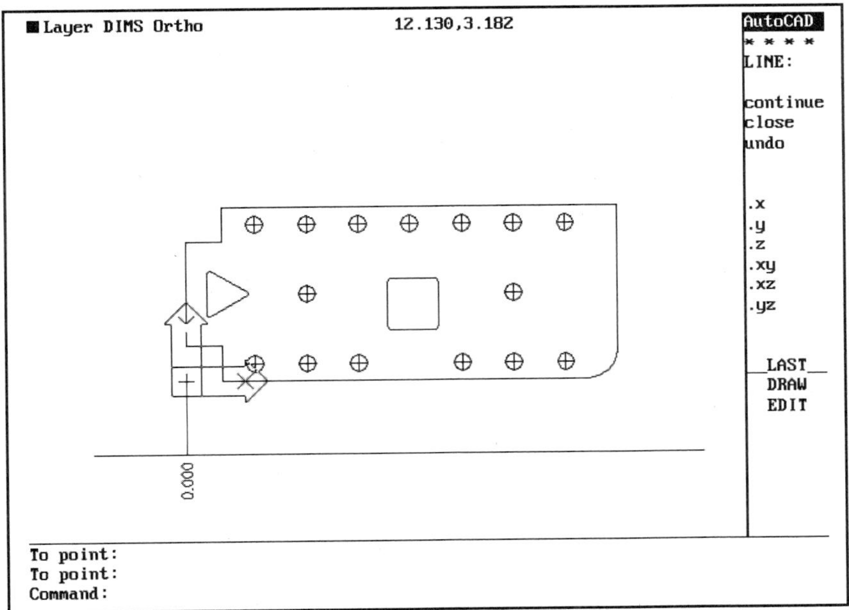

Figure 78.4

Use a temporary line as a guide for lining up ordinate dimensions.

Choosing a Datum by Default

When placing ordinate dimensions, you can explicitly specify a datum direction (X or Y) as in the previous exercise. It is generally faster, however, to let AutoCAD determine the datum direction. When you are prompted for the leader endpoint, the direction given by your cursor (assuming ORTHO is ON) will determine the datum direction. In the exercises in this unit, an up or down direction for the leader indicates to AutoCAD an x-datum dimension. A horizontal direction for the leader indicates a y-datum dimension.

Continue by finishing the x-datum ordinate dimensions. The following exercise gets you started.

Completing the X-Datum Dimensions

Continue with your drawing from the previous exercise.

1. `Command:` **`DIM`** ↵ — Enters dimensioning mode
2. `Dim:` **`ORD`** ↵ — Specifies ordinate dimensions
3. `Select Feature:` *From the popup menu, choose* Endpoint
4. `_endp of` *Select the center mark line at* ① *(see fig. 78.5)* — Specifies dimension point datum point

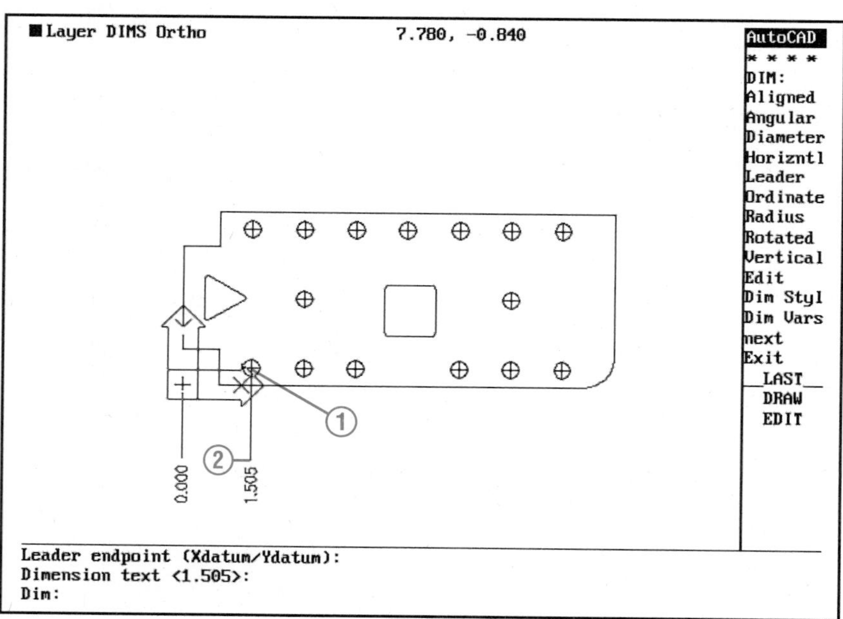

Figure 78.5

X-datum dimension added to the drawing.

5. `Leader endpoint (Xdatum/Ydatum):` *Pick a point at* ② *(see fig. 78.5)* — Specifies location of the dimension

6. `Dimension text <1.505>:` *Press* Enter	Accepts default value
7. `Dim:` **`EXIT`** ↵	Exits dimensioning mode

Applying Y-Datum Ordinate Dimensions

Next, place a few y-datum ordinate dimensions. You may reset the UCSICON to Noorigin if you find that it is in the way. Do not change the actual User Coordinate System (UCS), however. Remember to draw a temporary guide line for your leader lengths.

Applying Y-Datum Ordinate Dimensions

1. `Command:` *Choose* Draw, *then* Dimensions, *then* Ordinate, *then* Y-datum
`_dim1`
`Dim: _ordinate`
	Starts dimensioning for Y-datum ordinate dimension

2. `Select Feature:` **`0,0`** ↵	Specifies dimension point
3. `Leader endpoint (Xdatum/Ydatum):` *Pick a point at* ① *(see fig. 78.6)*	Specifies the length of the leader

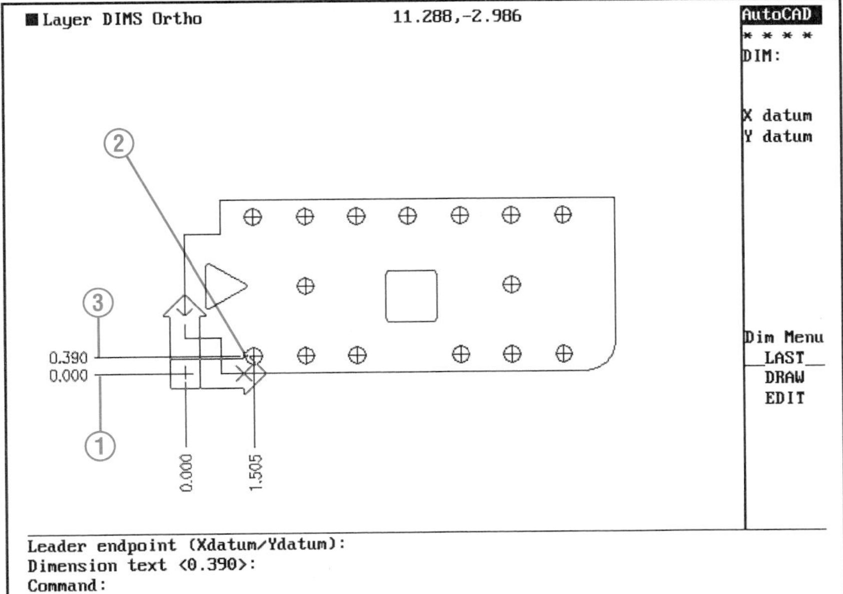

Figure 78.6

Y-datum dimension added to the drawing.

continues

4. `Dimension text <0.000>:` *Press* Enter	The default dimension value

5. `Command:` *Choose* Draw, *then* Dimensions, *then* Ordinate, *then* Automatic
`_dim1`
`Dim: _ordinate`	

6. `Select Feature:` *From the popup menu, choose* Endpoint	Specifies object snap mode
7. `_endp of` *Pick a point at* ② *(see fig. 78.6)*	Specifies dimension point
8. `Leader endpoint (Xdatum/Ydatum):` *Pick a point at* ③	Specifies the leader length
9. `Dimension text <0.390>:` *Press* Enter	Accepts default value

Unit Review

What You've Learned

- Commands: ORD
- What is an ordinate dimension
- What are X-datum and Y-datum dimensions
- How to apply ordinate dimensions

Review Questions

True or False

78.01 T F Ordinates are the node points placed by AutoCAD's dimensions.

78.02 T F The ordinate datum points are the origin of the UCS.

78.03 T F The UCS icon must be displayed at the origin of the UCS for ordinate dimensioning to work properly.

78.04 T F Orthogonal means that the x and y values are always 90 degrees to each other

Multiple Choice

78.05 Ordinate dimensioning is used primarily in what field?

(A) Architecture

(B) Mechanical design

(C) Civil Engineering/Surveying

(D) Electrical Engineering

78.06 Which of the following is useful for proper ordinate dimensioning?

(A) Temporary guide line for leader lengths

(B) UCS

(C) ORTHO mode

(D) All of the above

78.07 Ordinate dimensioning deals with how many ordinates?

Student: ____________________ Date: __________

Instructor: ____________________ Course: __________ Section: __________

(A) Three

(B) Four

(C) Two

(D) Any number

78.08 Ordinate dimensions are useful for the measurement and placement of:

(A) Drilled holes

(B) Punched shapes

(C) Notches

(D) All of the above

Short Answer

78.09 Describe the purpose of a User Coordinate System (UCS) for ordinate dimensioning.

____

____

____

78.10 Describe how the UCS origin and the x- and y-datum are related.

____

____

____

Additional Exercises

78.11 Continue with your drawing from the previous exercise. Add X-datum and Y-datum ordinate dimensions to the drawing as shown in figure 78.7. Save the drawing as 078???11.

Student: ______________ Date: ______________

Instructor: ______________ Course: ______________ Section: ______________

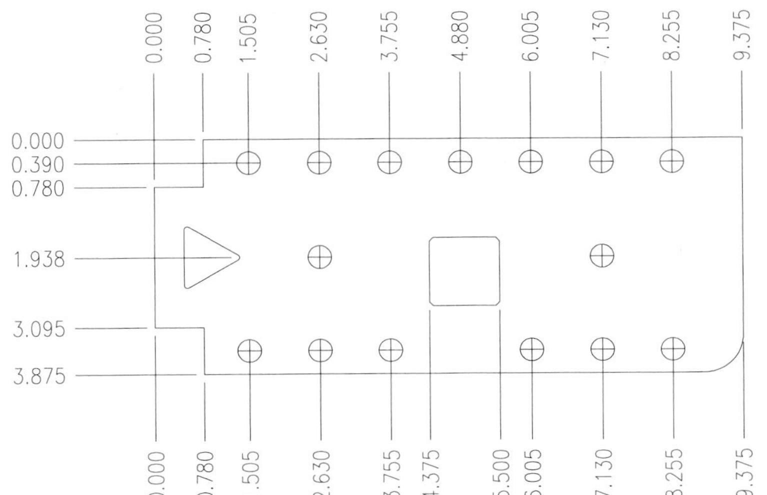

Figure 78.7

Final ordinate dimensions added to the drawing.

Student: ______________________ Date: ________

Instructor: ______________ Course: ______ Section: ______

UNIT 79

Adding Angular Dimensions

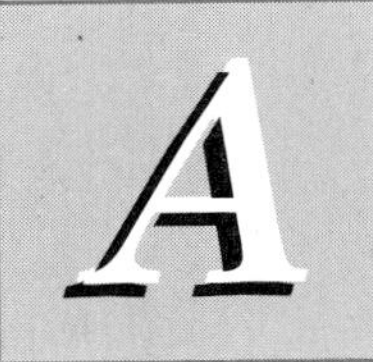

ngular dimensions are used to dimension the angle between two non-parallel lines, the included angle of an arc, or the angle defined by any three points. This unit teaches you to apply angular dimensions.

The objectives for this unit are to:

- Place angular dimensions between two non-parallel lines
- Dimension an arc
- Control the placement of dimension text in angular dimensions

Applying Angular Dimensions

As with other types of dimensions in AutoCAD, you can apply angular dimensions very easily. After you select a few entities or points, AutoCAD automatically calculates the necessary angle, and draws the dimension. AutoCAD provides four methods for applying an angular dimension. You can dimension:

- The included angle of an arc
- A portion of a circle
- The angle between two lines
- Three points to define an angular dimension

Whichever method you choose, it is important to understand that AutoCAD actually uses the same underlying information to calculate the angle. This underlying information includes a vertex point for the angle, a start point, and an end point. The start point and end point define the included angle. Each of the methods simply provides a different way to select these points, either manually or automatically.

Dimensioning Angles Using Lines

In the following exercise, place angular dimensions to lay out the faceplate of a gauge. Use lines to define the angular dimension. Figure 79.1 shows how your drawing should appear before you add any dimensions to it.

Figure 79.1

Placing angular dimensions.

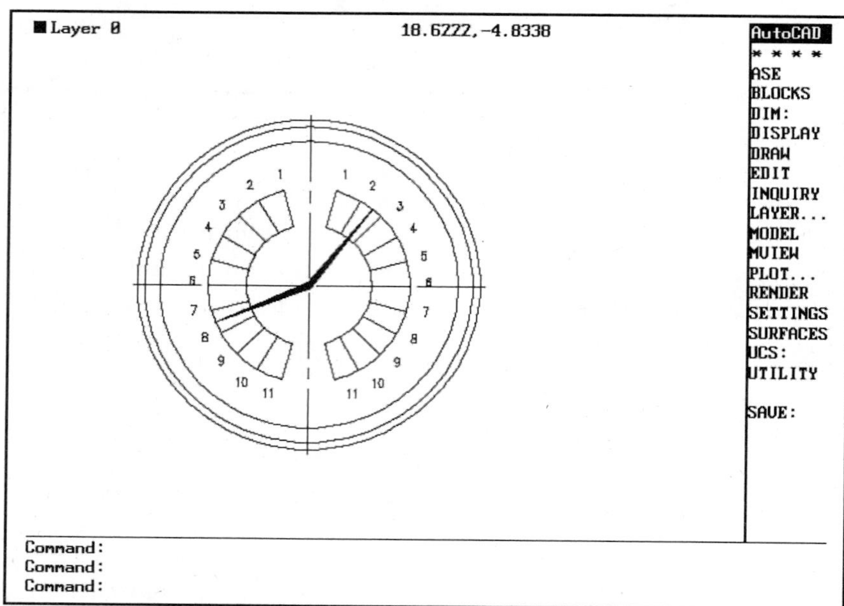

For clarity, center marks and center lines have been omitted from the gauge drawing.

Applying Angular Dimensions with Lines

1. Begin a new drawing named 079???01 in your assigned directory; use the drawing 079GAUGE as a prototype.

2. `Command:` *Choose* Draw, *then* Dimensions, *then* Angular — Issues the ANG dimension command

```
_dim1
Dim: _angular
```

3. `Select arc, circle, line, or RETURN:` *Select the line at* ① *(see fig. 79.2)*	Specifies the first line to define the angle
4. `Second line:` *Select the line at* ② *(see fig. 79.2)*	Specifies the second line to define the angle
5. `Dimension arc line location (Text/Angle):` *Pick a point at* ③ *(see fig. 79.2)*	Specifies the location for the dimension arc
6. `Dimension text <15>:` **`<> TYP.`** ↵	Accepts the default dimension value and appends the text TYP. to the dimension text
7. `Enter text location (or RETURN):` *Press* Enter	Accepts the default dimension location calculated by AutoCAD

8. Save your drawing.

Your drawing should look similar to figure 79.2.

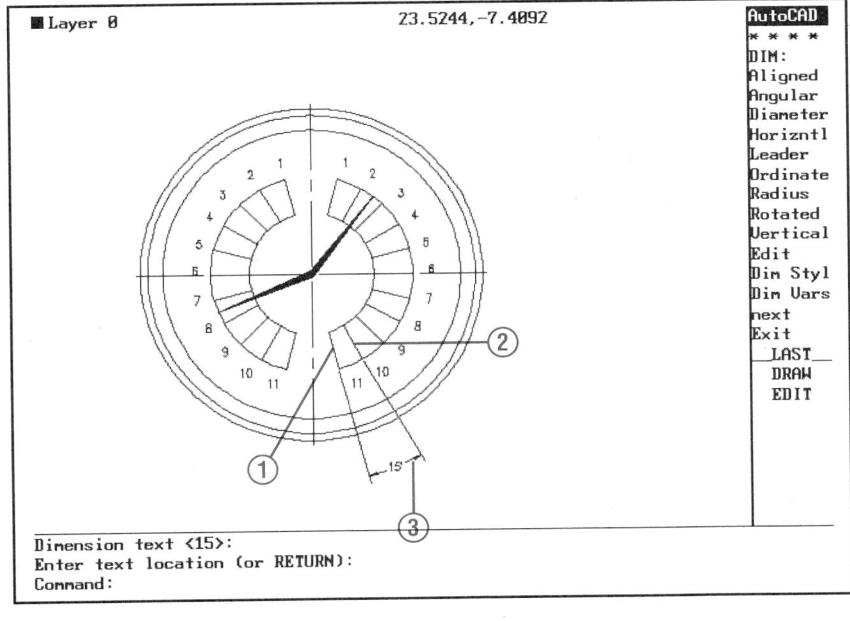

Figure 79.2

An angular dimension added to the gauge drawing.

AutoCAD calculated the angle between the two lines. Rather than accept the default value for the dimension text, you directed AutoCAD to use the calculated value (by entering `<>` as part of the dimension text) and add "TYP." to the dimension text. You also may have noticed that you could have picked a specific point for the placement of the dimension text. By instead pressing Enter in response to AutoCAD's prompt to locate the dimension text, you caused AutoCAD to place the dimension text in its default position.

Dimensioning Angles Using Arcs

If you select an arc when AutoCAD prompts you to select an entity for angular dimensioning, AutoCAD automatically calculates the included angle of the arc using the center of the arc as the vertex, and the two end points of the arc to define the angle. This feature is very useful for quickly dimensioning the included angle of an arc.

If you select a circle at the ANG dimension command's first prompt, AutoCAD automatically selects the center point of the circle as the vertex of the angle to be measured. You then must select two points to define the angle.

In the next exercise, dimension an arc using an angular dimension.

Placing an Angular Dimension by Specifying an Arc

Continue with your drawing from the previous exercise.

1. `Command:` *Choose* Draw, *then* Dimensions, *then* Angular
`_dim1`
`Dim: _angular`
	Issues the ANG dimension command

2. `Select arc, circle, line, or RETURN:` *Select the arc at* ① *(see fig. 79.3)*	Selects the arc to dimension
3. `Dimension arc line location (Text/Angle):` *Pick a point at* ② *(see fig. 79.3)*	Defines the dimension arc location
4. `Dimension text <150>:` *Press* Enter	Accepts the default dimension text value
5. `Enter text location (or RETURN):` *Press* Enter	Determines the text location

Your drawing should look similar to figure 79.3.

In this instance, AutoCAD used the center of the arc as the vertex of the angle. The two imaginary lines connecting the center of the arc to the end points of the arc define the included angle of the arc. This is the measurement that AutoCAD calculated for you.

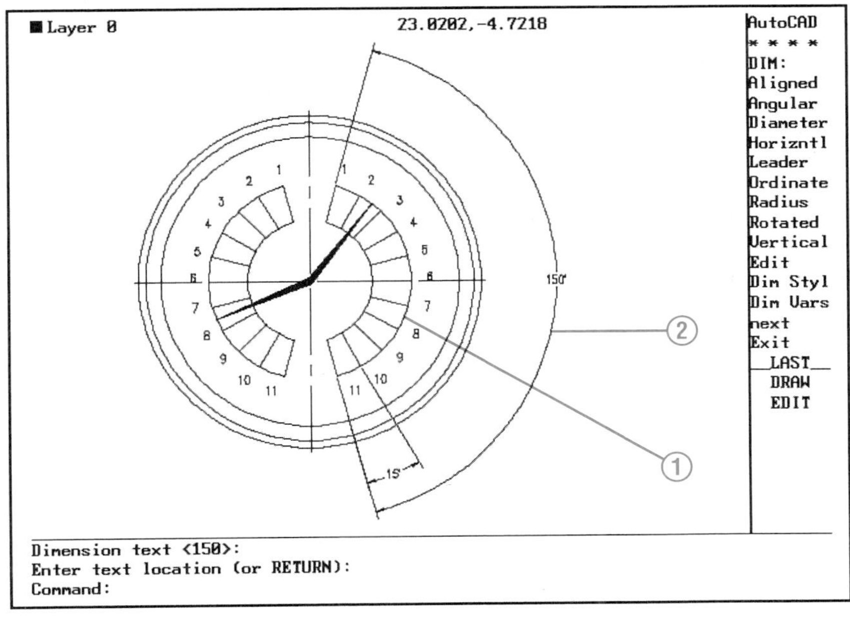

Figure 79.3

An arc used to dimension an angle.

The location of the cursor when you pick a point to locate the dimension arc determines whether AutoCAD calculates an inside angle or outside angle. The two angle endpoints are examined counterclockwise. If the point you select for the location of the dimension arc lies between the first and second points in a counterclockwise order, AutoCAD calculates the inside angle. If the selected point lies between the second and first points in counterclockwise order, AutoCAD calculates the outside angle.

Dimensioning Angles Using Points

Occasionally it is necessary to dimension an angle that is not defined by two lines, by an arc, or that is part of a circle. AutoCAD enables you to apply an angular dimension by using three points instead of existing entities. The first point defines the vertex of the angle, and the second and third points define the included angle.

In the next exercise, place an angular dimension by specifying three points.

Placing an Angular Dimension Based on Three Points

1. Use the same drawing as the previous exercise and zoom to the view shown in figure 79.4.

continues

Step	Action	Result

2.	`Command:` *Choose* Draw, *then* Dimensions, *then* Angular
	
	`_dim1`
	`Dim: _angular`
		Issues the ANG dimension command

3.	`Select arc, circle, line, or RETURN:` *Press* Enter	Specifies the option for three-point input
4.	`Angle vertex:` *From the popup menu, choose* Center	
5.	`_center of` *Select any arc or circle*	Specifies the vertex point
6.	`First angle endpoint:` *From the popup menu, choose* Quadrant	
7.	`_qua of` *Pick the circle at* ① *(see fig. 79.4)*	Specifies the second point for angle measurement
8.	`Second angle endpoint:` *From the popup menu, choose* Endpoint	
9.	`_endp of` *Pick the end point at* ②. *(see fig. 79.4)*	Specifies the third point for angle measurement
10.	`Dimension arc line location (Text/Angle):` *From the popup menu, choose* Endpoint	
11.	`_endp of` *Pick a point at* ③ *(see fig. 79.4)*	Locates the dimension arc
12.	`Dimension text <90>:` *Press* Enter	Accepts default dimension text value
13.	`Enter text location (or RETURN):` *Press* Enter	Accepts default dimension text location
14.	Save your drawing.	

Your drawing should resemble figure 79.4.

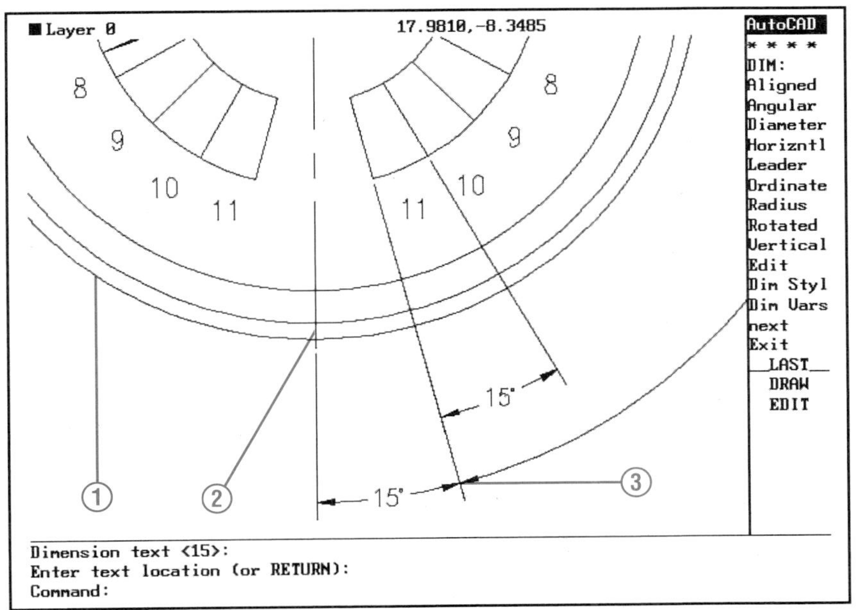

Figure 79.4

Angular dimension added using points.

It is important to remember that regardless of the method of angular dimensioning you use, AutoCAD still relies on three points to define the angular dimension:

- **An angle vertex.** This could be a point you specify, the center of an arc or circle, or the point in space where two existing non-parallel lines would intersect.
- **First angle end point and second angle end point.** These points may be specific points you choose, the endpoints of two existing lines, or the end points of an arc.

Unit Review

What You've Learned

- How to apply angular dimensions by selecting two lines
- How to apply angular dimensions by selecting an arc
- How to apply angular dimensions by specifying three points
- How AutoCAD calculates and places an angular dimension

Review Questions

True or False

79.01 T F An angular dimension can be used to dimension the angle defined by any three points.

79.02 T F The method that AutoCAD uses to calculate an angular dimension is different for each of the entity selection methods in the ANG dimension command.

79.03 T F Entering <> as part of a dimension text string causes AutoCAD to replace the <> characters with the calculated dimension value.

79.04 T F You cannot control the location of the dimension text in an angular dimension.

79.05 T F You can select arcs, circles, or lines to dimension an angle.

Multiple Choice

79.06 You can select __________, __________, and __________ when dimensioning an angle.

(A) polylines, arcs, and lines

(B) polylines, arcs, and circles

(C) lines, arcs, and circles

(D) none of the above

79.07 AutoCAD calculates angles __________.

(A) clockwise

(B) counterclockwise

(C) to single decimal place precision

(D) both B and C

Student: __________ Date: __________

Instructor: __________ Course: __________ Section: __________

79.08 The location of the cursor when you pick a point to locate a dimension arc determines ________.

(A) the location of the dimension text

(B) the location of the center cross

(C) the position of the dimension arrows

(D) whether AutoCAD calculates an inside or an outside angle value

Short Answer

79.09 Briefly describe a situation in which AutoCAD will calculate an outside angle based on your dimension arc point selection.

79.10 Explain how selecting an arc differs in result from selecting a circle when dimensioning an angle.

Additional Exercises

79.11 Begin a new drawing named 079???11 using 079ANGLE as a prototype. Dimension the drawing as shown in figure 79.5.

79.12 Begin a new drawing named 079???12 using 079ANG2 as a prototype. Dimension the drawing as shown in figure 79.6.

Student: ________ Date: ________

Instructor: ________ Course: ________ Section: ________

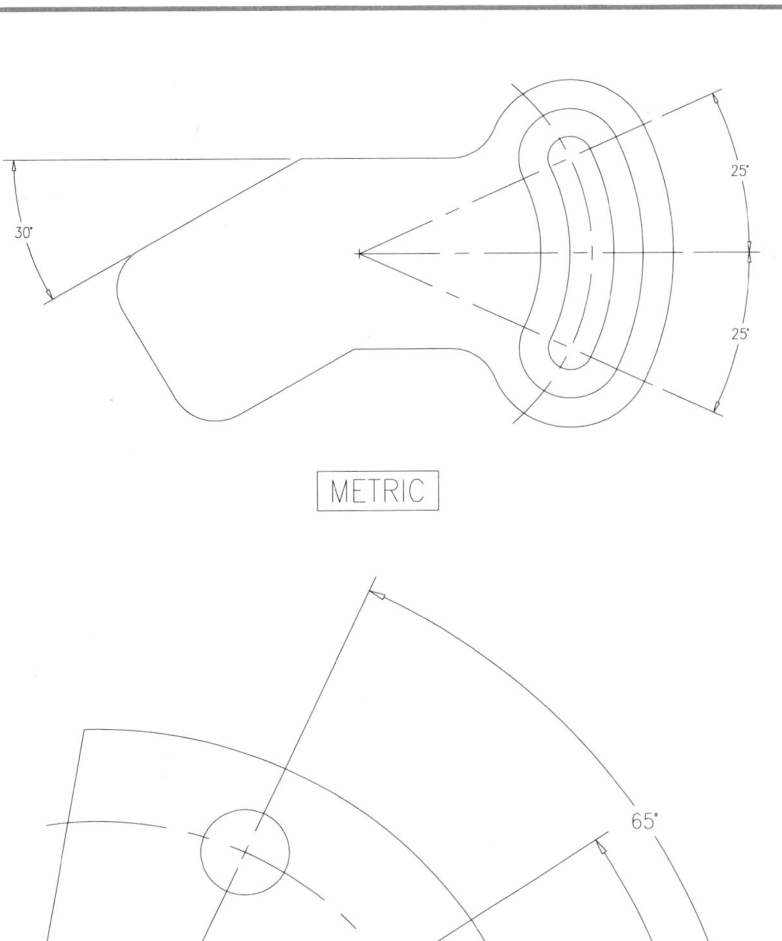

Figure 79.5

Applying angular dimensions.

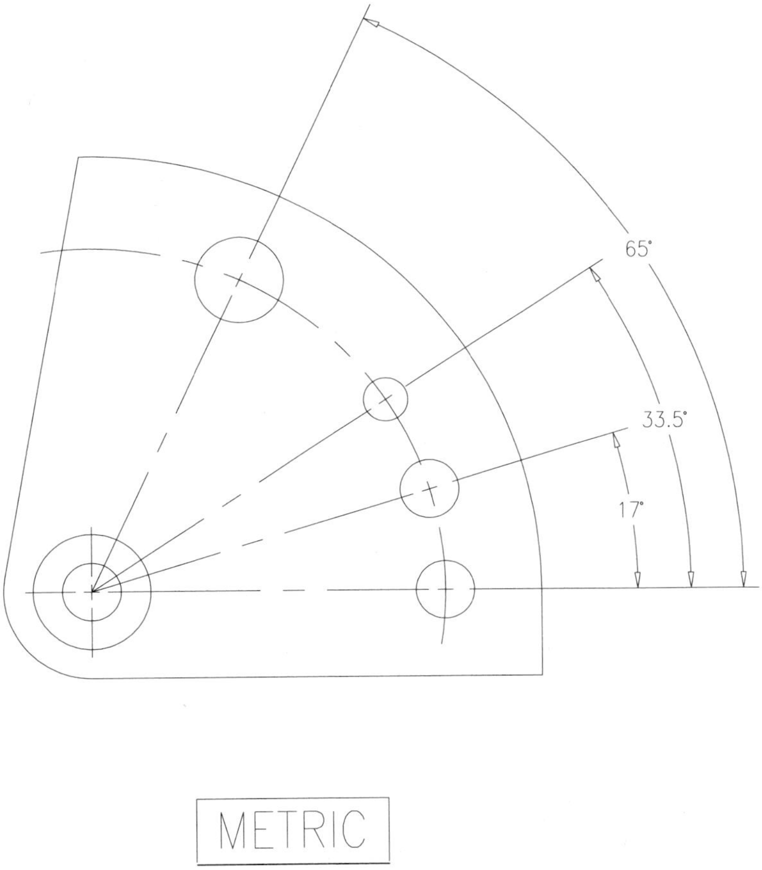

Figure 79.6

Applying angular dimensions.

Student: ______________________ Date: ________

Instructor: ______________________ Course: ________ Section: ________

UNIT 80

Introduction to Dimension Variables

In preceding dimensioning units, you used dimension variables to a small degree to control the way dimensions were applied to your exercise drawings. This unit explains dimension variables in more detail and explains why they are so important to effective dimensioning.

The objectives for this unit are to:

- Understand the importance of dimension variables for applying dimensions
- Gain an overall familiarity with the various dimension variables and their purposes
- Examine the effect of setting dimension variables
- Understand the use of the Dimension Styles and Variables dialog box

Understanding Dimension Variables

Unlike simple entities such as lines and circles, dimensions have many different features. A dimension typically includes a text value, a dimension line with arrows or other terminators, and extension lines. With some types of dimensions, such as those that contain tolerances, there are even more features. In addition, the text location, text size, and arrowhead size often may vary.

To avoid including many different types of dimension entities, AutoCAD uses dimension variables to control the appearance of dimensions. By changing the value of AutoCAD's dimension variables, you can modify the size of a dimension's features, create tolerance values, use alternate units, change terminator types, and more. Figure 80.1 shows a selection of dimensions created by using different dimension variable values.

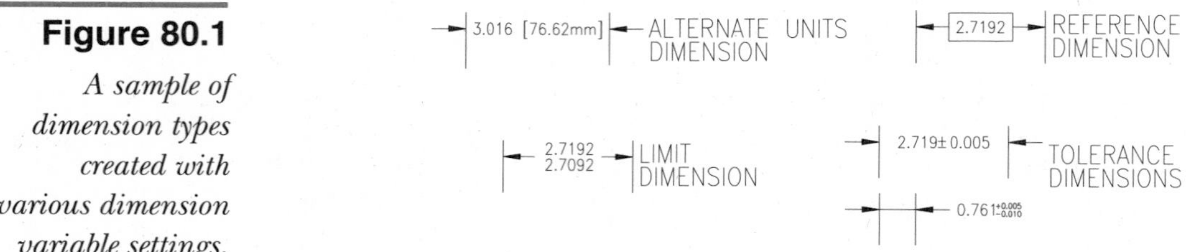

Figure 80.1

A sample of dimension types created with various dimension variable settings.

AutoCAD has 42 dimension variables that control the appearance of dimensions on your drawing. This unit and the remainder of the dimensioning units discuss only a selection of these dimension variables. Table 80.1 explains the use of some of the more commonly used dimension variables; Appendix D provides a complete list of AutoCAD's dimensioning variables.

Table 80.1

Common Dimension Variables

Variable	Description
DIMALT	Allows for dual dimensioning (inches/millimeters, for example).
DIMALTD	Specifies the number of decimal places in an alternate unit.
DIMALTF	Specifies the amount to scale the alternate units. For example, to dimension in inches/millimeters, set DIMALTF to 25.4 (one inch equals 25.4 millimeters).
DIMAPOST	The suffix to use on alternate dimensions. "mm" can be used for millimeter alternate units.

Variable	Description
DIMASO	Controls whether the dimensions you apply are associated to an object by its node points. When you modify an object that contains associative dimensions, the dimensions change automatically. AutoCAD applies associative dimensions by default. Unit 85 examines associative dimensions in detail.
DIMCEN	Controls the size of center marks ("crosshairs") for marking the centers of circles and arcs.
DIMDLE	Controls how far the dimension line extends beyond the extension lines.
DIMDLI	Controls the spacing of dimension lines for baseline dimensions.
DIMEXE	Controls how far the extension line extends beyond the dimension line.
DIMEXO	Controls the size of the gap between the object, or node point, and the extension line.
DIMGAP	Controls the spacing between the text and dimension line.
DIMLFAC	Enables you to dimension items not drawn at a 1:1 scale. This variable is used to apply a scale factor to all calculated dimensions.
DIMLIM	Enables you to apply limit dimensions. Limit dimensions are common in the mechanical engineering field. They specify that a particular dimension must fall between two values (upper and lower limits).
DIMPOST	Enables you to supply a prefix, suffix, or both to a dimension value.
DIMSCALE	Determines the overall scale factor for all dimension "subentities" (text, lines, arrowheads, and so on).
DIMSOXD	Controls whether the dimension line is drawn outside the extension lines.
DIMSTYLE	Enables you to specify a style name used to store the values of various dimension variables.
DIMTAD	Controls whether the text value is drawn above or breaks the dimension line.

continues

Table 80.1, Continued
Common Dimension Variables

Variable	Description
DIMTFAC	Controls the text size for text values in a tolerance dimension.
DIMTIH	Controls whether the text drawn between the extension lines is always horizontal or aligned with the dimension line.
DIMTIX	Places the dimension text between the extension lines even when AutoCAD normally places the text outside the dimension lines.
DIMTM	Sets minus tolerance value. Used in limits and tolerance dimensions.
DIMTP	Sets plus tolerance value.
DIMTOFL	Places text outside the extension lines, but draws a dimension line between the extension lines.
DIMTOH	Controls whether the text drawn outside the extension lines is always horizontal or aligned with the dimension line. Similar to DIMTIH.
DIMTOL	Turns on and off tolerance dimensioning.
DIMTXT	Controls the height of the dimension text.
DIMZIN	Controls whether zero feet or zero inches or both is diplayed in a dimension value.

Table 80.1 is not intended to be a detailed explanation of each AutoCAD dimension variable. Rather, the table gives you an idea of some dimension characteristics that you can control and suggests how you can draw different types of dimensions in AutoCAD. By simply changing a few dimension variables, for example, you can switch from standard linear dimensions to toleranced linear dimensions.

Some dimension variables are real numbers. For example, you can set DIMDLI, which specifies the spacing between baseline dimensions, to .38 units. Other dimension variables act as toggles, turning features on or off. DIMTOL is an example: it turns on and off tolerance dimensions. With these types of variables, a value of 1 or ON turns the feature on; a value of 0 or OFF turns off the feature.

To experiment with dimension variables, create a few dimensions in the following exercise with different dimension variable settings.

Experimenting with DIMSCALE

1. Begin a new drawing without a name using the file 080DIMV as a prototype.

2. `Command:` **`DIMSCALE`** ↵

3. `New value for DIMSCALE <1.0000>:` **`2`** ↵ — Sets DIMSCALE to 2

4. `Command:` *Choose* Draw, *then* Dimensions, *then* Linear, *then* Horizontal — Starts the DIM:HOR command

   `_dim1`

   `Dim: _horizontal`

5. `First extension line origin or RETURN to select:` *From the popup menu, choose* Endpoint — Sets object snap mode

6. `_endp of` *Select the line at* ① *(see fig. 80.2)* — Specifies first dimension point

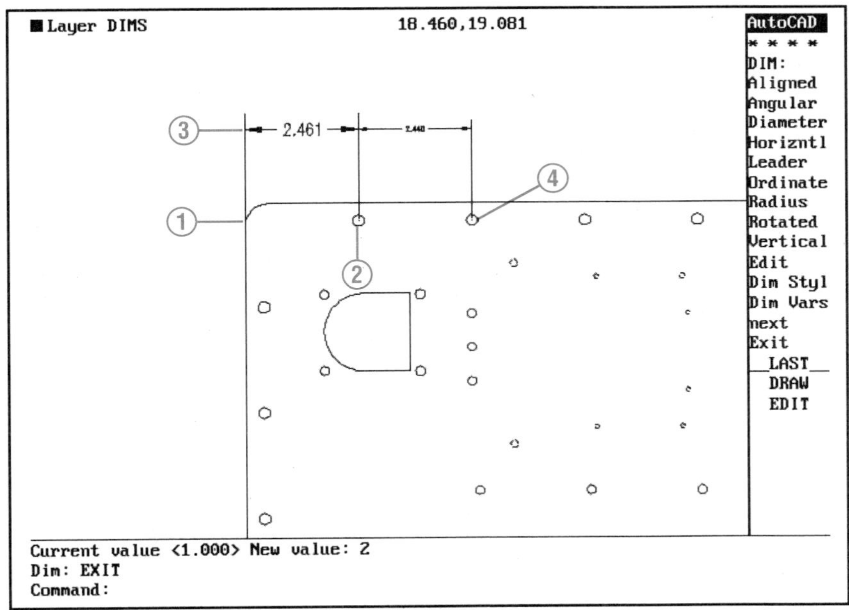

Figure 80.2

A few dimensions applied using different DIMSCALE values.

7. `Second extension line origin:` *From the popup menu, choose* Center — Sets object snap mode

8. `_center of` *Select the circle at* ② *(see fig. 80.2)* — Specifies second dimension point

continues

9. `Dimension line location (Text/ Angle):` *Pick a point at* ③ *(see fig. 80.2)*	Specifies dimension line location
10. `Dimension text <2.461>:` *Press* Enter	Accepts default value
11. `Command:` **`DIMSCALE`** ↵	
12. `New value for DIMSCALE <2.0000>:` **`1`** ↵	Sets DIMSCALE to 1
13. `Command:` **`DIM`** ↵	
14. `Dim:` **`CONT`** ↵	
15. `Second extension line origin or RETURN to select:` *From the popup menu, choose* Center	Sets object snap mode
16. `_center of` *Select the circle at* ④ *(see fig. 80.2)*	Specifies second dimension point
17. `Dimension text <2.440>:`	Accepts default value
18. `Dim:` **`DIMSCALE`** ↵	
19. `Current value <1.000> New value:` **`2`** ↵	Sets DIMSCALE back to 2
20. `Dim:` **`EXIT`** ↵	

You can see that DIMSCALE controls the overall relative size of dimension features. Next, try experimenting with the DIMTIX dimension variable.

Experimenting with DIMTIX

1. `Command:` *Choose* Draw, *then* Dimensions *then* Radial, *then* Radius
`_dim1`
`Dim: _radius`
	Starts DIM:RAD command

2. `Select arc or circle:` *Select the arc at* ① *(see fig. 80.3)*	Specifies the arc to dimension
3. `Dimension text <0.863>:` *Press* Enter	Accepts default value
4. `Enter leader length for text:` *Pick a point at* ② *(see fig. 80.3)*	Locates the dimension leader and text
5. `Command:` **`DIMTIX`** ↵	
6. `New value for DIMTIX <0>:` **`1`** ↵	Turns DIMTIX on

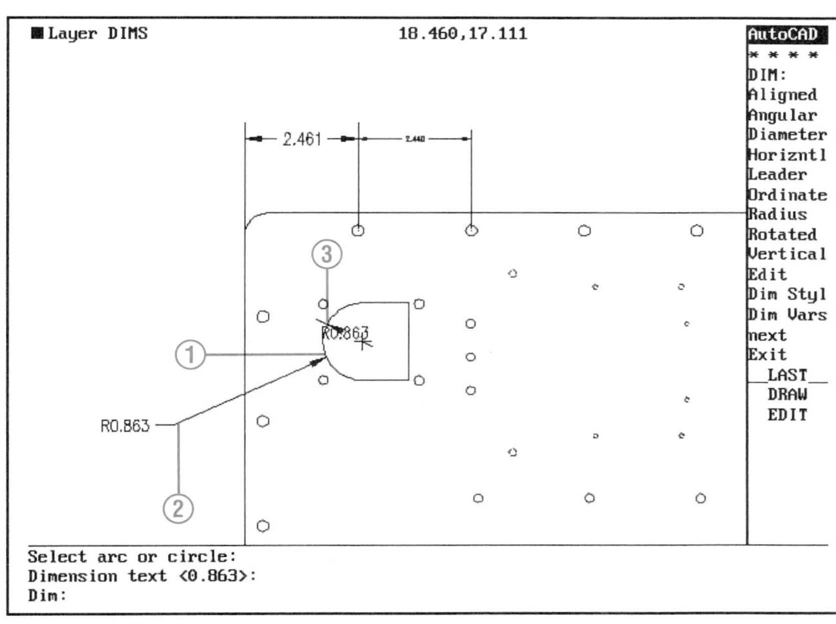

Figure 80.3

The effects of different values for DIMTIX.

7. `Command: DIM` ↵ — Enters dimensioning mode
8. `Dim:` **`RAD`** ↵ — Starts DIM:RAD command
9. `Select arc or circle:` *Pick the arc at* ③ *(see fig. 80.3)* — Selects the arc to dimension
10. `Dimension text <0.863>:` *Press* Enter — Accepts default value

In the last exercise, AutoCAD calculated that no room was between the extension lines for both the text and arrowheads. With DIMTIX set to 0, AutoCAD placed the text outside the arc automatically. If DIMTIX is set to 1, however, AutoCAD forces the text inside the arc, even when it does not fit.

Try one more dimension variable experiment. Create a dimension with tolerance values just by changing a few dimension variables.

Creating a Tolerance Dimension

1. `Command:` **`DIMTP`** ↵
2. `New value for DIMTP <0.000>:` **`.002`** ↵ — Sets the plus dimension tolerance
3. `Command:` **`DIMTM`** ↵
4. `New value for DIMTM <0.000>:` **`.001`** ↵ — Sets the minus dimension tolerance

continues

5. `Command:` **`DIMTOL`** ↵

6. `New value for DIMTOL <0>:` **`1`** ↵ — Turns on tolerance dimension mode

7. `Command:` **`DIM`** ↵ — Enters dimensioning mode

8. `Dim:` **`CONT`** ↵ — Starts DIM:CONT command

9. `Select continued dimension:` *Select the dimension at* ① *(see fig. 80.4)* — Specifies the starting base dimension

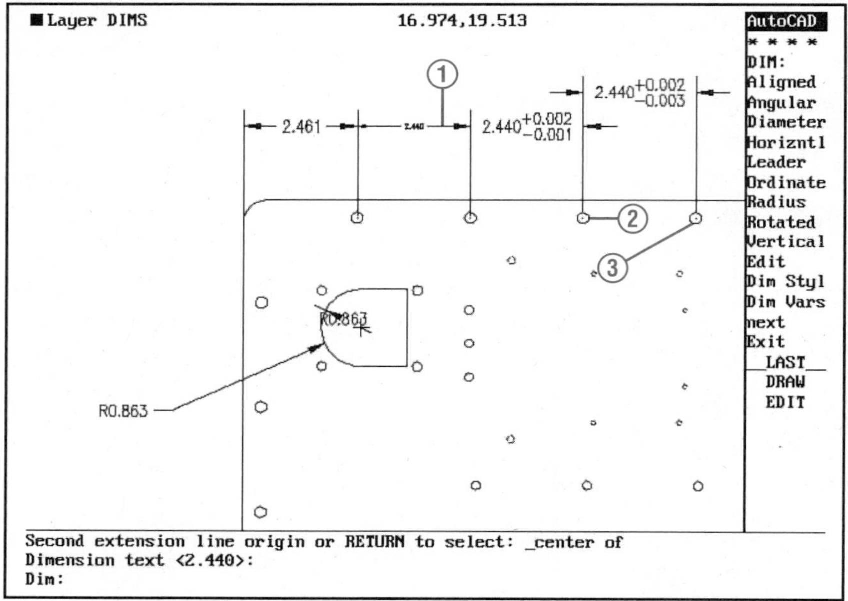

Figure 80.4

Tolerance dimensions applied by changing DIMTP, DIMTM, and DIMTOL.

10. `Second extension line origin or RETURN to select:` *From the popup menu, choose* Center — Sets object snap mode

11. `_center of` *Select the circle at* ② *(see fig. 80.4)* — Specifies the point to dimension

12. `Dimension text <2.440>:` *Press* Enter — Accepts default value

    `Dim:` **`DIMTM`** ↵

13. `Current value <0.001> New value:` `.003` ↵ — Changes minus dimension tolerance

14. `Dim:` **`CONT`** ↵ — Starts DIM:CONT command

15. `Second extension line origin or RETURN to select:` *From the popup menu, choose* Center — Sets object snap mode

16. `_center of` *Select the circle at* ③ *(see fig. 80.4)*	Specifies the point to dimension
17. `Dimension text <2.440>:` *Press* Enter	Accepts default value

Setting Dimension Variables with DDIM

To change dimension variables, you can enter any of the dimension variable names at the `Command:` prompt. With so many different variables and so many cryptic names, it is difficult to remember each variable's function. Fortunately, AutoCAD provides a better method to set dimensioning options—the Dimension Styles and Variables dialog box (see. fig. 80.5). You can display the Dimension Styles and Variables dialog box by entering **DDIM** at the `Command:` prompt, or by choosing Settings, and then Dimension Style.

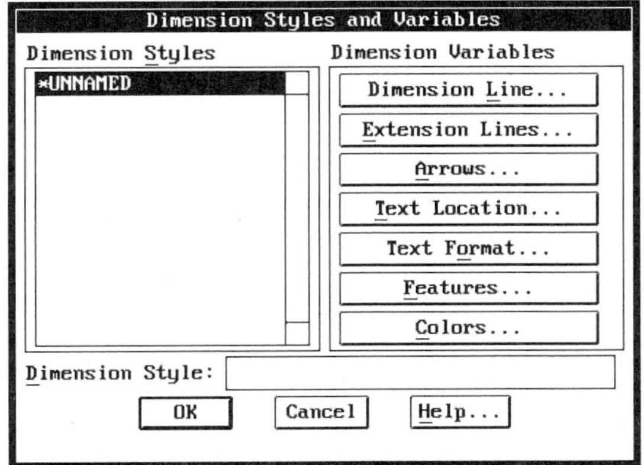

Figure 80.5

Dimension Styles and Variables dialog box.

The Dimension Styles and Variables dialog box prevents you from having to memorize dozens of variables and settings for dimensioning. All the dialog box really does is set the values for you as you make intuitive selections from the dialog box.

You use the Dimension Styles and Variables dialog box in upcoming units to set dimension variables and create dimension styles.

Other factors in your drawing besides dimension variables affect the appearance of dimensions. Four system variables, LUPREC (Linear Units PRECision), AUPREC (Angular Units PRECision), LUNITS (Linear UNITS), and AUNITS (Angular UNITS) affect the number of decimal places displayed in your dimensions as well as what units (architectural, engineering, decimal, and so on) are used.

continues

In addition to the changes these variables make, also remember that your dimension always inherits the current active text style for the dimension text. Later, when dimension styles are discussed, remember that these factors are not stored in a dimension style.

Unit Review

What You've Learned

- The importance of dimension variables in controlling the appearance of dimensions
- How changing a dimension variable can affect the appearance of subsequent dimensions
- The purpose of the Dimension Styles and Variables dialog box is to control the values of dimension variables

Review Questions

True or False

80.01 T F DIMSCALE is used primarily to control the size of dimension text.

80.02 T F DIMTIX forces the dimension text between the extension lines.

80.03 T F DIMALTF is one variable you must set if you are creating dual English/Metric dimensions.

80.04 T F DIMTAD is one variable that controls the location of dimension text.

80.05 T F DIMTOH sets the plus tolerance value for a tolerance dimension.

80.06 T F When you apply a tolerance dimension, AutoCAD does not automatically add the minus (-) or plus (+) signs beside each tolerance value.

80.07 T F AutoCAD has a total of 20 dimension variables.

80.08 T F DIMTXT controls dimension text height.

80.09 T F DIMTXT controls the location of dimension text.

Short Answer

80.10 Describe associative dimensioning and its advantages over non-associative dimensions.

____

____

____

Student: ________________ Date: ________

Instructor: ________________ Course: ________ Section: ________

UNIT 81

Adding Limit Dimensions

A limit dimension is one type of tolerance dimension that you can apply to a drawing in AutoCAD. This unit explains limit dimensions and teaches you how to apply them in a drawing simply by changing a few dimension variables.

The objectives for this unit are to:

- Understand what are limit dimensions
- Apply limit dimensions in AutoCAD
- Understand which dimension variables control the appearance of limit dimensions
- Understand how AutoCAD calculates the upper and lower values of limit dimensions
- Use LUPREC to control the number of decimal places displayed in a dimension value

Understanding Limit Dimensions

Limit dimensions are used to tell the manufacturer of a part that a particular dimension must fall between two limits. Limit dimensions are drawn with an upper limit and lower limit, one on top of another. Figure 81.1 shows a portion of a drawing that includes limit dimensions.

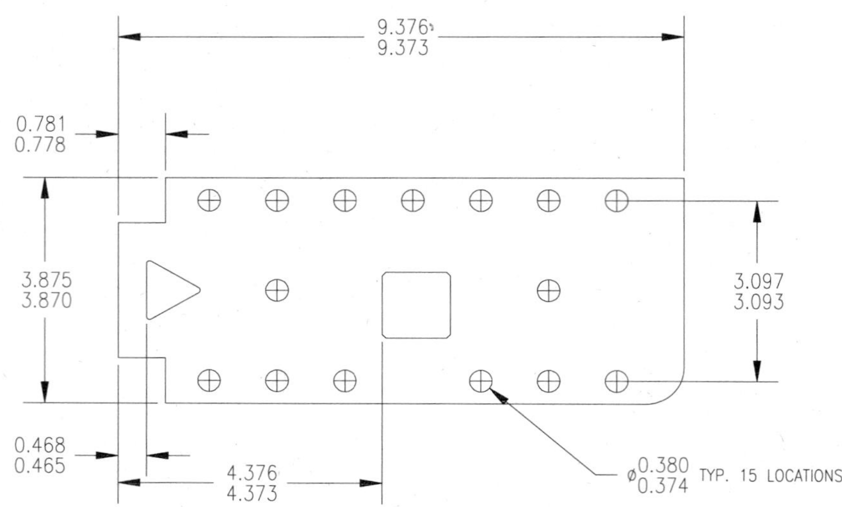

Figure 81.1

A portion of a drawing containing limit dimensions.

To apply a limit dimension in AutoCAD, you must set a few dimension variables. This unit emphasizes the use of the Dimension Styles and Variables dialog box to set up AutoCAD for limit dimensioning. The use of this dialog box eliminates the need for you to remember which dimension variables control the limit dimension characteristics. You also will set the LUPREC system variable, which controls the precision of linear dimensions in AutoCAD.

Setting and Applying Limit Dimensions

In the following exercise, set LUPREC to three decimal places. Then, use the Dimension Styles and Variables dialog box to set up AutoCAD to create a limit dimension.

Setting Up for Limit Dimensioning

1. Begin a new drawing without a name, using 081LIMIT.DWG as a prototype.

2. `Command:` **`LUPREC`** ↵	Starts LUPREC command
3. `New value for LUPREC <4>:` **`3`** ↵	Sets precision to 3 decimal places
4. `Command:` *Choose* Settings, *then* Dimension Style	Displays the Dimension Styles and Variables dialog box (see fig. 81.2)

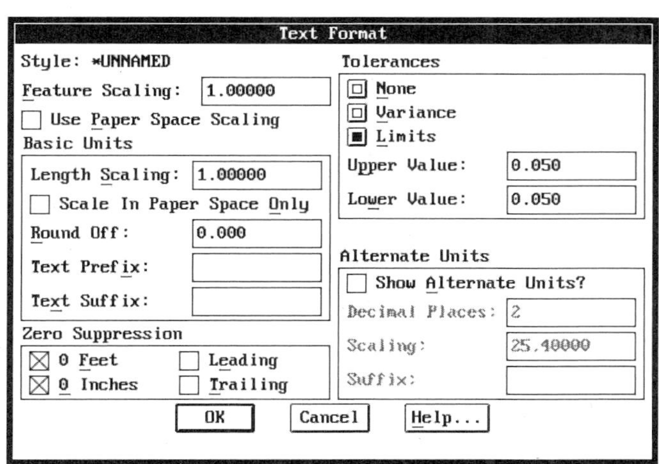

Figure 81.2

DDIM Text Format dialog box.

5. *Choose* Text Format	Displays the Text Format dialog box
6. *Choose the* Limits *radio button*	
7. *Double-click in the* Upper Value *edit box, then enter* .050	Highlights the current value and sets upper limit to .050
8. *Double-click in the* Lower Value *edit box, then enter* .050	Highlights the current value and sets lower limit to .050
9. *Choose* OK	Closes the Text Format dialog box
10. *Choose* OK	Closes the Dimension Styles and Variables dialog box

When you set LUPREC, it has the same effect as using the Units Control dialog box or the UNITS command to set linear precision. If you set LUPREC, then open the Units Control dialog box, you will see that the value for linear precision has changed to match the value of LUPREC.

Now that you have configured AutoCAD for limit dimensions, apply a limit dimension in the following exercise. Use figure 81.3 as a guide to complete the exercise.

Applying a Limit Dimension

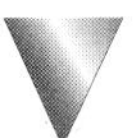

1. `Command:` **`OSNAP`** ↵	Starts OSNAP command
2. `Object snap modes:` **`ENDP`**	Sets running object snap mode

continues

3. `Command:` *Choose* Draw, *then* Dimensions, *then* Linear, *then* Horizontal
`_dim1`
`Dim: _horizontal`
	Starts the DIM:HOR command

4. `First extension line origin or RETURN to select:` *Select the line at* ① *(see fig. 81.3)*	Specifies the first point of dimension

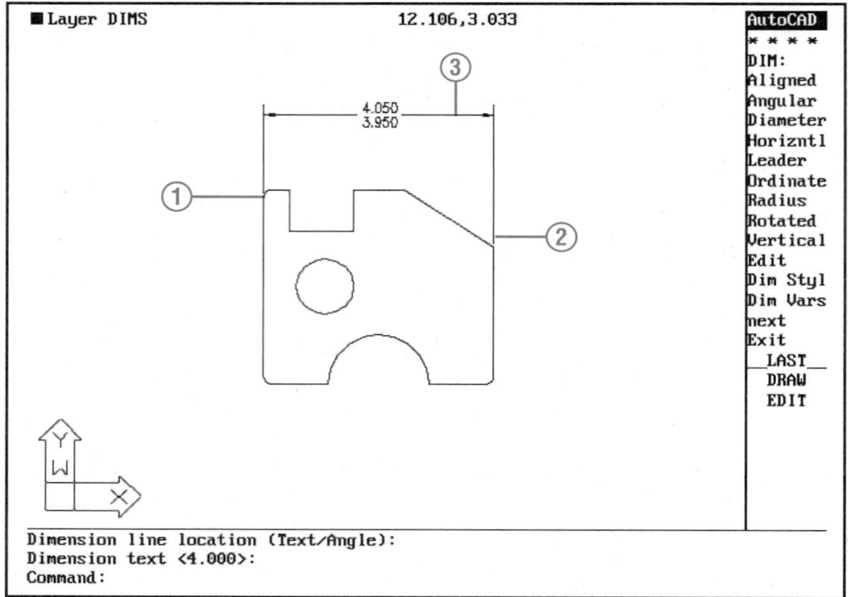

Figure 81.3
A limit dimension applied to a drawing.

5. `Second extension line origin:` *Select the line at* ② *(see fig. 81.3)*	Specifies second point of dimension
6. `Dimension line location (Text/Angle):` *Pick a point near* ③ *(see fig. 81.3)*	Specifies dimension line location
7. `Dimension text <4.000>:` *Press* Enter	Accepts default value

When you applied the horizontal limit dimension, AutoCAD calculated the actual dimension of 4.000, added the Upper Value to the dimension for a value of 4.050, and subtracted the lower value from the dimension for a value of 3.950. When this piece is manufactured, the final dimension must fall between these two values.

Now apply a vertical limit dimension with different values.

Applying a Vertical Limit Dimension

1. `Command:` *Choose* Settings, *then* Dimension Style ↵ — Displays the Dimension Styles and Variables dialog box

2. *Choose the* Text Format *button* — Displays the Text Format dialog box

Notice that the Limits radio button still is selected.

3. *Double-click in the* Upper Value *edit box, then enter* **`.000`** — Highlights the value and sets an upper limit of .000

4. *Double-click in the* Lower Value *edit box, then enter* **`.030`** — Highlights the value and set a lower limit of .030

5. *Choose* OK, *then choose* OK *again* — Closes the Text format dialog box and the Dimension Styles Variables dialog box

6. `Command:` *Choose* Draw, *then* Dimensions, *then* Linear, *then* Vertical — Starts the DIM:HOR command

   `_dim1`

   `Dim: _vertical`

7. `First extension line origin or RETURN to select:` *Select the end point at* ① *(see fig. 81.4)* — Specifies the first point of dimension

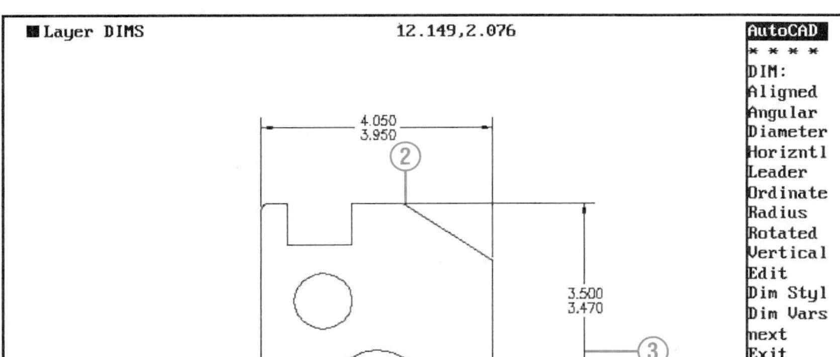

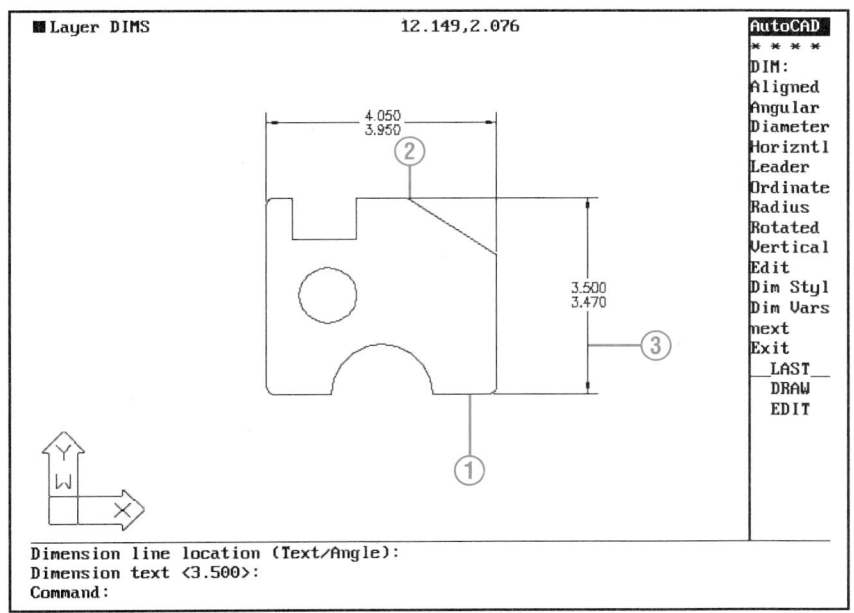

Figure 81.4

A vertical limit dimension added to the drawing.

continues

8. `Second extension line origin:` *Select the end point at* ② *(see fig. 81.4)*	Specifies second point of dimension
9. `Dimension line location (Text/Angle):` *Pick a point near* ③ *(see fig. 81.4)*	Specifies dimension line location
10. `Dimension text <3.500>:` *Press* Enter	Accepts default value

Notice that AutoCAD used the actual dimension for the upper limit since you specified 0.000 for the Upper Value. AutoCAD subtracted the lower value of 0.030 from the actual dimension of 3.500 for a lower limit of 3.470. The manufactured dimension for the overall height of this part must be within 3.500 and 3.470.

What really happens when you select options from the Dimension Styles and Variables dialog box is that AutoCAD changes the values of dimension variables to create the limit dimensions. When you select the Limits radio button in the Text Format dialog box, AutoCAD sets DIMLIM to 1 and DIMTOL to 0. When you specify a value in the Upper Value edit box, AutoCAD sets DIMTP (Tolerance Plus value). When you specify a value in the Lower Value edit box, AutoCAD sets DIMTM (Tolerance Minus value). You used the system variable LUPREC (Linear Units PRECision) to control the number of decimal places displayed in the dimension value.

The dimension variables DIMTM and DIMTP can be set to negative values either directly or through the Dimension Styles and Variables dialog box. Because AutoCAD adds the limit value and subtracts the minus value from the calculated dimension automatically, setting DIMTP or DIMTM to a negative value serves little purpose.

To illustrate how dimension variables control the appearance of limit dimensions, change DIMTP and DIMTM from the keyboard and apply another limit dimension.

Setting Limit Dimension Options with Dimension Variables

1. `Command:` **`DIMTP`** ↵	Starts DIMTP command
2. `New value for DIMTP <0.000>:` **`.010`** ↵	Sets upper tolerance value
3. `Command:` **`DIMTM`** ↵	Starts DIMTM command
4. `New value for DIMTM <0.030>:` **`.010`** ↵	Sets lower tolerance value

5. `Command:` *Choose* Draw, *then* Dimensions, *then* Linear, *then* Horizontal — Starts the DIM:HOR command

   `_dim1`

   `Dim: _horizontal`

6. `First extension line origin or RETURN to select:` *Select the end point at* ① *(see fig. 81.5)* — Specifies the first point of dimension

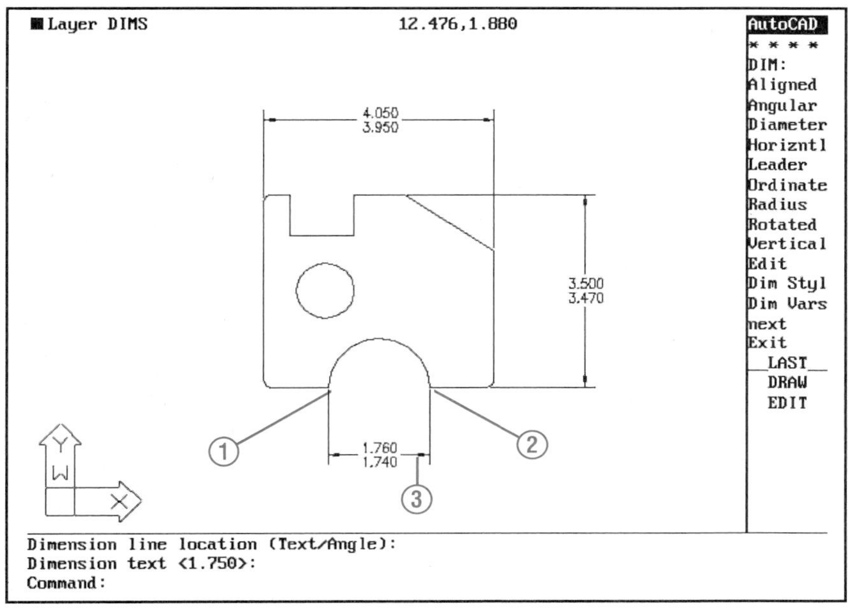

Figure 81.5

Arc dimensioned with a limit dimension.

7. `Second extension line origin:` *Select the end point at* ② *(see fig. 81.5)* — Specifies second point of dimension

8. `Dimension line location (Text/Angle):` *Pick a point near* ③ *(see fig. 81.5)* — Specifies dimension line location

9. `Dimension text <1.750>:` *Press* Enter — Accepts default value

For quick dimensioning, sometimes it is faster to set only one or two variables using the keyboard rather than wade through dialog boxes to find the area you need to change. Unfortunately, this requires that you remember the name of the dimension variable and its use. The Dimension Styles and Variables dialog box frees you from having to remember these dimension variables.

Unit Review

What You've Learned

- ☞ How the Dimension Styles and Variables dialog box controls the values of dimension variables
- ☞ How to control the upper and lower values of a limit dimension
- ☞ How LUPREC controls the number of decimal places in a dimension value
- ☞ How to apply limit dimensions by setting DIMTOL, DIMLIM, DIMTP, and DIMTM dimension variables by keyboard entry or through the Dimension Styles and Variables dialog box

Review Questions

True or False

81.01 T F LUPREC is a dimension variable that must be set each time a dimension is placed in the drawing.

81.02 T F DIMTP and DIMTM must be non-zero values.

81.03 T F The Text Format button in the Dimension Styles and Variables dialog box enables you to set variables that control the appearance of limit dimensions.

81.04 T F AutoCAD adds the user-specified DIMTP value to the actual dimension value.

81.05 T F DIMLIM controls the actual upper and lower values within a limit dimension.

81.06 T F Limit dimensions and tolerance dimensions cannot be used in the same drawing.

Multiple Choice

81.07 Which of the following are used by AutoCAD to create a limit dimension?

(A) DIMTOL

(B) DIMLIM

(C) DIMPREC

(D) A and B

Student: ______________________ Date: __________

Instructor: ______________________ Course: __________ Section: __________

81.08 Which of the following dimension variables are not *required* for AutoCAD to create a limit dimension?

(A) DIMTP

(B) DIMTOL

(C) DIMLIM

(D) DIMASO

(E) DIMTM

Short Answer

81.09 Discuss the advantages and disadvantages of the DDIM dialog box versus setting dimension variables via the keyboard.

____

____

____

Student: __________ Date: __________

Instructor: __________ Course: __________ Section: __________

Additional Exercises

81.10 Begin a new drawing named 081???10, using the file 081LIMEX as a prototype. Add the dimensions to the drawing as shown in figure 81.6. Use the ID command to determine the actual distance between dimension points, then set the necessary dimension variables to achieve the dimensions displayed in figure 81.6. Save your work when you are finished.

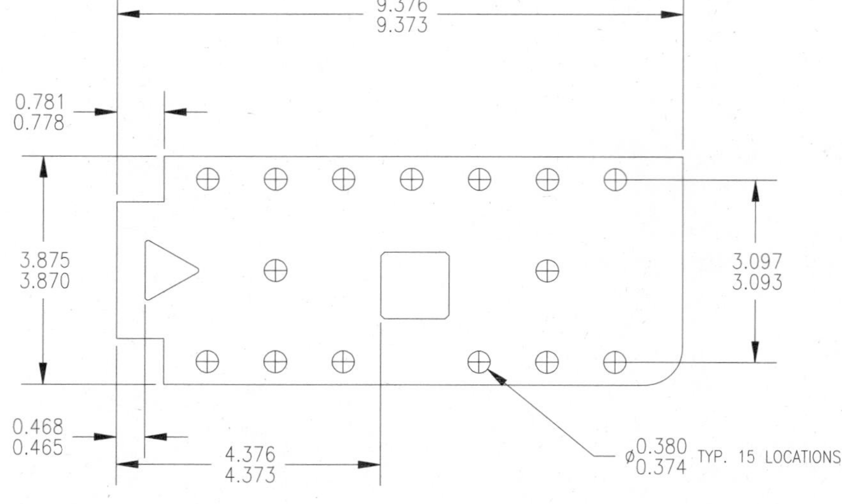

Figure 81.6

Add limit dimensions to the part as shown.

UNIT 82

Using Alternate Units

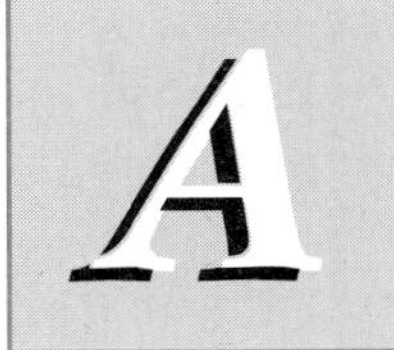

lternate-units dimensioning offers the capability to specify and place dimension values for units other than those in which your drawing was created. For example, one of the most common applications for alternate units is the use of millimeters (mm) in addition to feet and inches. This unit teaches you to add dimensions using alternate units.

The objectives for this unit are to:

- Place dimensions using DIMLFAC to scale the dimension value
- Place dimensions using alternate units via the Dimension Styles and Variables dialog box
- Understand which dimension variables control the appearance and function of alternate-units dimensioning

Applying a Linear Dimension Factor

AutoCAD provides a way to apply a linear dimension scale factor to your dimensions. This means that every dimension you place on your drawing is multiplied by a scale factor that you set. For example, suppose that you insert a detail block into your drawing at one-fourth scale to fit on the sheet. If you apply dimensions to this detail normally, all your dimension values read and display at one-fourth their actual value. A 12-inch line, for example, dimensions at three inches. AutoCAD corrects this situation through the DIMLFAC (Linear FACtor) variable. In this example, you can set DIMLFAC to 4 so that AutoCAD can properly calculate and display the desired dimension. AutoCAD multiplies the actual dimension by the value in DIMLFAC.

Figure 82.1 shows a partial floor plan of a building with a detail blow-up of a window plan view. The floor plan is full size to be plotted at 1/4" = 1' 0". The window detail geometry was scaled to plot at 1" = 4". Both the floor plan and detail were drawn in model space. This means that the detail is twelve times larger than real life units. You calculate this by dividing the floor plan scale factor of 48 by the detail scale factor of four. If you dimension the detail using the AutoCAD default values for dimension variables, all the dimension values are twelve times the actual value. Verify this in the following exercise.

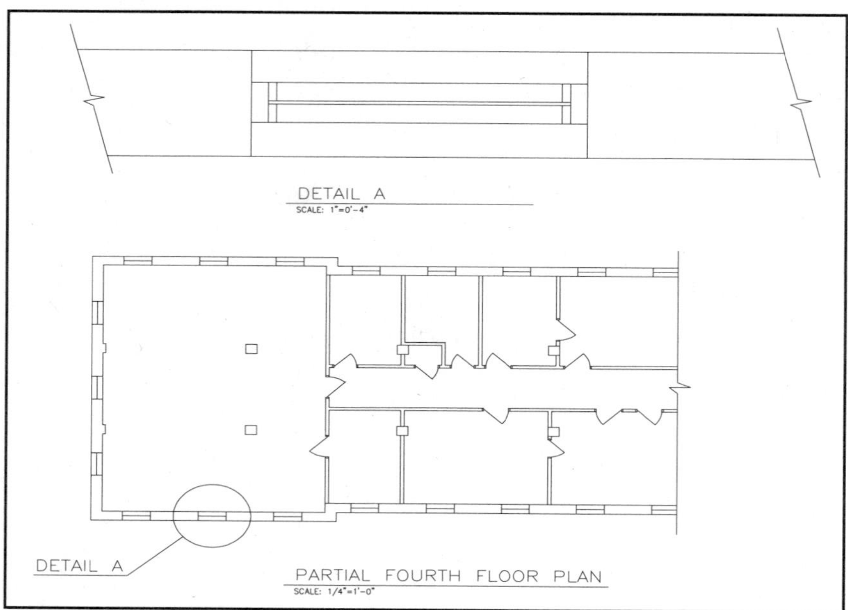

Figure 82.1
Partial floor plan to be dimensioned.

Applying Dimensions without a Linear Scale Factor

1. Begin a new drawing named 082???01 in your assigned directory, using the file 082FLOOR as a prototype.
2. Zoom to the window area circled and labeled Detail A on the floor plan (see fig. 82.2), and then set running object snap to ENDP.

Step	Description
3. `Command:` **`DIMLFAC`** ↵	
4. `New value for DIMLFAC <1.0000>:` *Press* Enter	Verifies DIMLFAC setting
5. `Command:` **`DIMSCALE`** ↵	
6. `New value for DIMSCALE <48.0000>:` *Press* Enter	Verifies DIMSCALE setting
7. `Command:` *Choose* Assist, *then* Inquiry, *then* Distance	Starts the DIST command
8. `'_dist First point:` *Pick the end point at* ① *(see fig. 82.3)*	Specifies start point for distance inquiry
9. `Second point:` *Pick the end point at* ②	Specifies second point for DIST command

```
Distance = 3'-4",  Angle in XY Plane = 0,  Angle from XY Plane = 0
Delta X = 3'-4",  Delta Y = 0'-0",   Delta Z = 0'-0"
```

Next, apply a horizontal dimension to the window.

Step	Description

10. `Command:` *Choose* Draw, *then* Dimensions, *then* Linear, *then* Horizontal
`_dim1`
`Dim: _horizontal`
	Starts DIM:HOR command

11. `First extension line origin or RETURN to select:` *Pick the end point at* ①	Specifies start of dimension
12. `Second extension line origin:` *Pick the end point at* ②	Specifies second dimension point
13. `Dimension line location (Text/Angle):` *Pick a point at* ③	Specifies location of dimension text
14. `Dimension text <3'-4">:` *Press* Enter	Accepts default value

Zoom to the previous view.

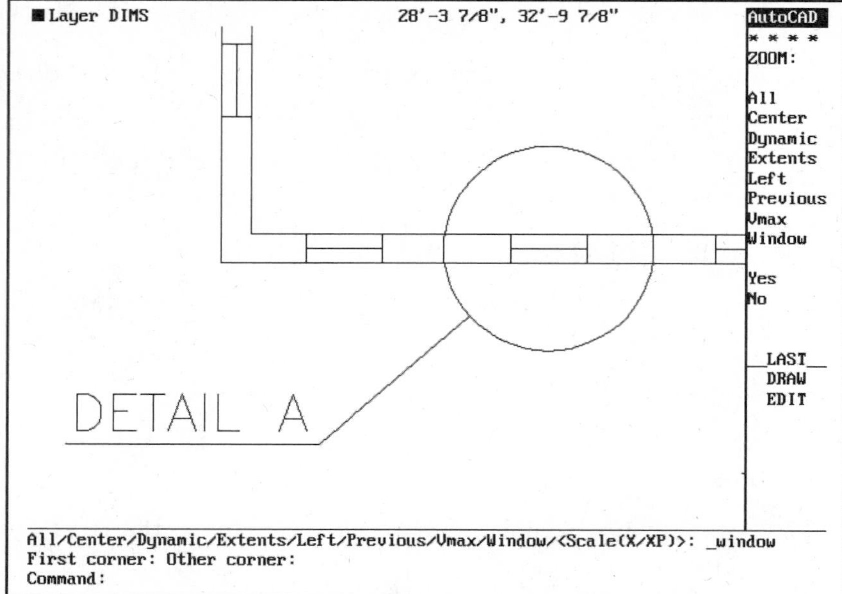

Figure 82.2
View ready for dimensioning.

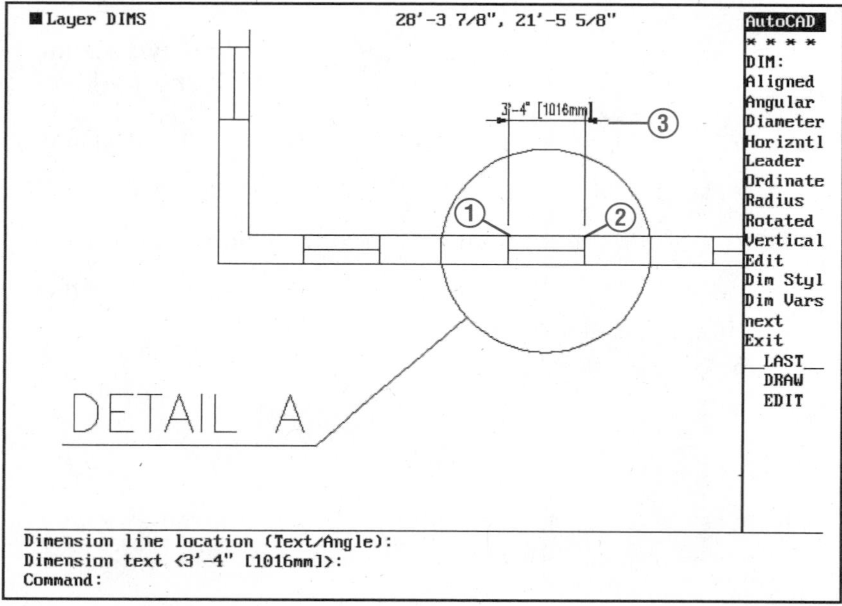

Figure 82.3
Dimension added to the window.

Detail A on your drawing is a copy of the area circled on the floor plan with some added details such as the window frame and glass. Zoom to Detail A and, without changing any dimension variables, apply a horizontal dimension for the rough opening as before. What happens?

Checking the Detail Dimension

1. Zoom to the view shown in figure 82.4.	

2. `Command:` *Choose* Draw, *then* Dimensions, *then* Linear, *then* Horizontal
`_dim1`
`Dim: _horizontal`
	Starts DIM:HOR command

3. `First extension line origin or RETURN to select:` *Pick the end point at* ① *(see fig. 82.4)*	Specifies start of dimension
4. `Second extension line origin:` *Pick the end point at* ② *(see fig. 82.4)*	Specifies second dimension point
5. `Dimension line location (Text/Angle):` *Pick a point at* ③ *(see fig. 82.4)*	Specifies location of dimension text
6. `Dimension text <40'-0">:` *Press* Enter	Accepts default value

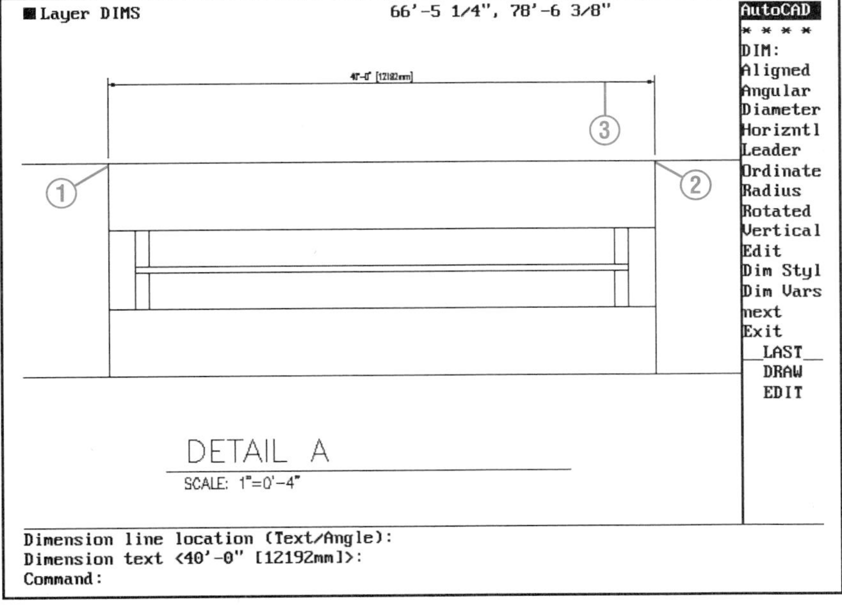

Figure 82.4

Detail dimension added to the drawing.

Notice that the dimension value is 40'-0" instead of 3'-4". Why is this? The detail is a copy of the window plan scaled by 12, which explains the 40'-0" value: 3'-4" × 12 = 40'-0".

If the objects you are dimensioning are not drawn full size or to the same scale as the rest of the drawing, you must use DIMLFAC to properly dimension those objects. In this case, you must set DIMLFAC to 1 divided by 12 or 1/12 or 0.8333 because AutoCAD gives you a value twelve times larger than you want. This forces AutoCAD to divide the actual dimension by 12 to display the desired value.

Using DIMLFAC To Display a Proper Dimension Value

1. Erase the horizontal dimension you applied in the previous exercise.

2. `Command:` *Choose* Settings, *then* Dimension Style	Displays the Dimension Styles and Variables dialog box
3. *Choose* Text Format	Displays the Text Format dialog box
4. *Double-click in the* Length Scaling *edit box, and then enter* **1/12**	Sets the DIMLFAC variable to 1/12 (.08333)
5. *Choose* OK, *then choose* OK *again*	Closes dialog boxes and returns to drawing editor

6. `Command:` *Choose* Draw, *then* Dimensions, *then* Linear, *then* Horizontal
`_dim1`
`Dim: _horizontal`
	Starts DIM:HOR command

7. `First extension line origin or RETURN to select:` *Pick the end point at* ① *(see fig. 82.5)*	Specifies start of dimension
8. `Second extension line origin:` *Pick the end point at* ② *(see fig. 82.5)*	Specifies second dimension point
9. `Dimension line location (Text/Angle):` *Pick a point at* ③ *(see fig. 82.5)*	Specifies location of dimension text
10. `Dimension text <3'-4">:` *Press* Enter	Accepts default value

Your dimension value should be 3'-4" this time. AutoCAD reads the real value of 40'-0" and multiplies it by the DIMLFAC (.08333) value to get the desired value of 3'-4".

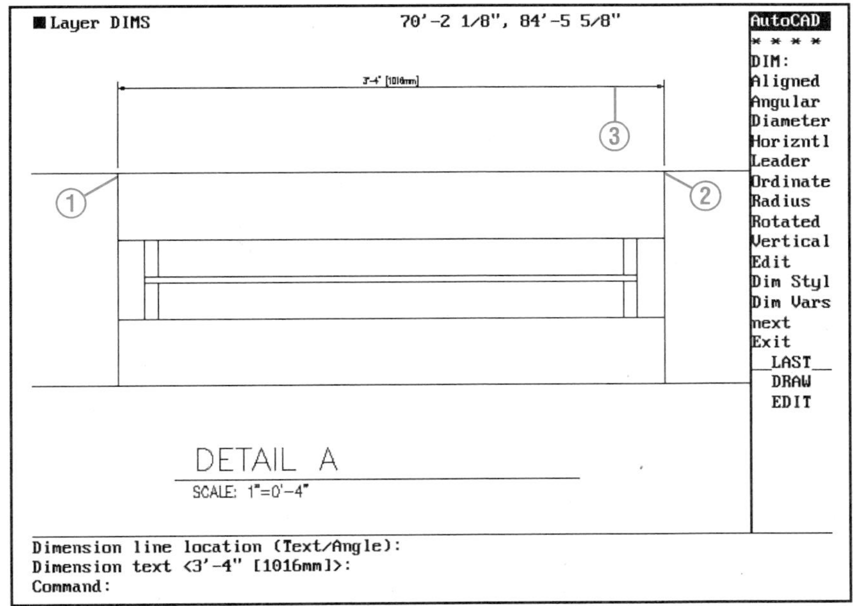

Figure 82.5

Dimension applied with correct DIMLFAC value.

Applying Dual Dimensions

Suppose that your building design is to be used for a federal courthouse facility in Seattle, Washington. The government requires all construction documents to use the metric system of measurement. Your office is in the preliminary design stages, and not all your staff is comfortable with the metric system. You decide to use dual dimensions for preliminary documents so that your staff can see both units of measure at the same time.

You want to dimension your floor plan using inches and millimeters. You want your dimensions to show no decimal places on the millimeters value, and you want to use "mm" as a suffix to the dimension. For example, your dimensions would look similar to the following:

```
1" [25mm]
```

Dimension the wall of the floor plan using alternate units. Use continued dimensions.

Applying Alternate-Units Dimensions

1. Begin a new drawing named 082???02 in your assigned directory, using the file 082COURT as a prototype.

2. Zoom to the view shown in figure 82.6.

3. `Command:` *Choose* Settings, *then* Dimension Style — Displays the Dimension Styles and Variables dialog box

continues

4. *Choose* Text Format, *then check the* Show Alternate Units? *check box*	Turns on alternate unit display
5. *Double-click in the* Decimal Places *edit box, then enter* **0**	Causes AutoCAD to display whole numbers only
6. *Verify that the value in the* Scaling *edit box is set to 25.4*	Sets linear factor for alternate units
7. *Double-click in the* Suffix *edit box,then enter* **mm**	Causes AutoCAD to apply the mm suffix to alternate dimensions
8. *Choose* OK	Closes the Text Format dialog box
9. *Choose* OK	Closes the Dimension Styles and Variables dialog box

10. `Command:` *Choose* Draw, *then* Dimensions, *then* Linear, *then* Horizontal
`_dim1`
`Dim: _horizontal`
	Starts DIM:HOR command

11. `First extension line origin or RETURN to select:` *From the popup menu, choose* Endpoint	
12. `_endp of` *Pick the end point at* ① *(see fig. 82.6)*	Specifies first dimension point
13. `Second extension line origin:` *From the popup menu, choose* Endpoint	
14. `_endp of` *Pick the end point at* ② *(see fig. 82.6)*	Specifies second dimension point
15. `Dimension line location (Text/Angle):` *Pick a point at* ③ *(see fig. 82.6)*	Locates dimension line
16. `Dimension text <5'-8" [1727mm]>:` *Press* Enter	Accepts default value

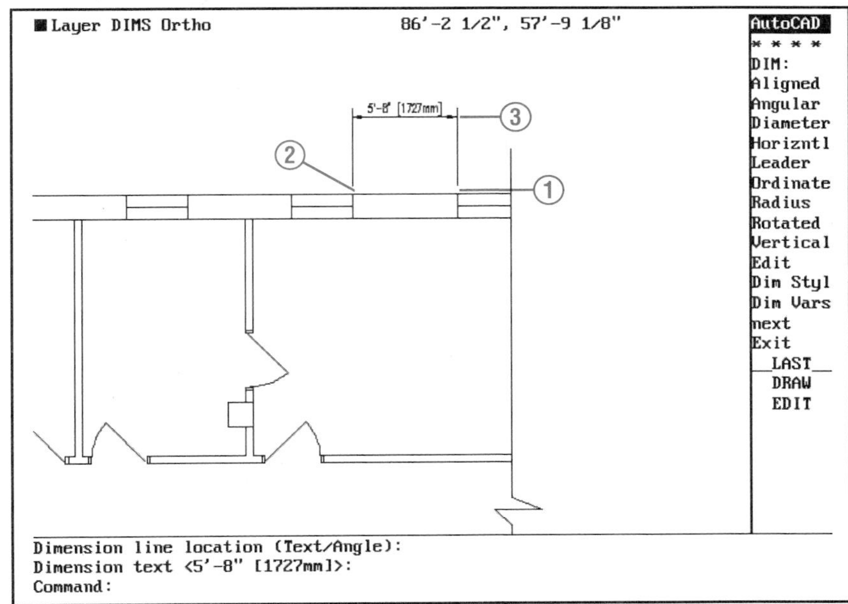

Figure 82.6

Alternate-units dimensioning.

It is often difficult to maintain good dimension appearance when using alternate units. The width of the dimension value is sometimes difficult to place on the drawing exactly where you want because the text often is too wide to fit within the dimension line and the dimension contains both units of measure. Unfortunately, you cannot automatically place the primary units dimension above the line and the alternate dimension below the line. If necessary, you can simulate alternate-units dimensions by placing the alternate dimension under the dimension line as text.

Unit Review

What You've Learned

- ☞ The purpose of the DIMLFAC dimension variable
- ☞ How to apply dimensions using DIMLFAC
- ☞ How to apply dimensions using alternate units

Review Questions

True or False

82.01 T F DIMLFAC controls the size of the dimension text.

82.02 T F DIMLFAC is used primarily for details drawn at a scale other than that of the base drawing.

82.03 T F Alternate units are used only for inch/millimeter dimensioning.

82.04 T F When applying alternate-units dimensions, AutoCAD always places the mm suffix at the end of the dimension.

82.05 T F DIMALT specifies whether to use alternate units.

82.06 T F AutoCAD automatically places alternate dimensions within square brackets [ ].

Multiple Choice

82.07 Which of the following is used by AutoCAD to calculate the proper alternate-units value based on the actual dimension value?

(A) DIMALT

(B) DIMASO

(C) DIMASZ

(D) DIMALTF

82.08 If your drawing was created to be plotted at 1/8"=1'-0", but you create a detail at 1/2"=1'-0", what DIMLFAC value would you use to dimension the detail?

(A) 1/24

(B) 96/24

(C) 24/96

(D) 24

Student: ____________ Date: ____________

Instructor: ____________ Course: ____________ Section: ____________

Short Answer

82.09 Describe how AutoCAD uses the value stored in DIMLFAC when placing dimensions.

____

____

____

82.10 Describe how DIMLFAC and DIMSCALE differ in their functionality.

____

____

____

Additional Exercises

82.11 Begin a new drawing named 082???11 in your assigned directory, using the file 082COURT as a prototype. Place alternate-unit (mm) dimensions across the top of the drawing, dimensioning the window openings and spacings. Use figure 82.7 as a reference.

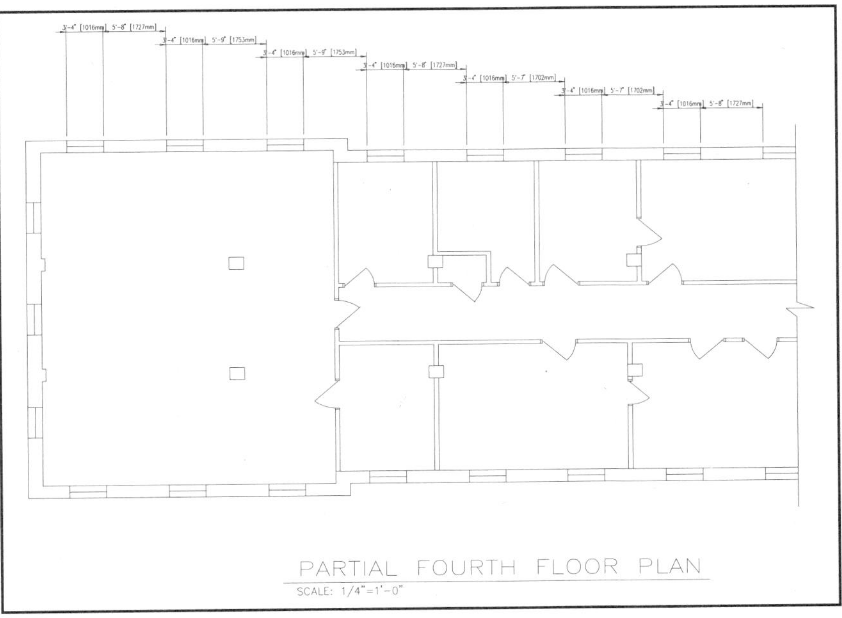

Figure 82.7
Alternate-units dimensions added to the courthouse drawing.

Student: ______________ Date: ______________

Instructor: ______________ Course: ______________ Section: ______________

82.12 Begin a new drawing named 082???12 in your assigned directory, using 082HOA02.DWG as a prototype. This drawing is similar to the one used in previous exercises in this unit. The major difference is that the window detail is drawn full-size in model space. Two model space viewports are used to show the two views. Set TILEMODE=1 to see the difference. Set TILEMODE back to zero when you are finished.

Dimension the detail in paper space using DIMLFAC. When dimensioning from paperspace, DIMLFAC asks for a new value, or asks you to specify a viewport to set the DIMLFAC value. Use the Viewport option to set the DIMLFAC scale. Place the dimensions on the DIMS layer and freeze the VPORTS layer.

Student: ______________________ Date: __________

Instructor: ______________________ Course: __________ Section: __________

UNIT 83

Adding Tolerance Dimensions

Tolerance dimensions are very similar to limit dimensions in that they are used primarily in mechanical design fields. With limit dimensions, only the limits of the dimension are shown. With tolerance dimensions, an "ideal" or base dimension value is given with the tolerances or limits following it. The tolerance or limit values define the amount that the actual manufactured dimension is allowed to vary from the theoretical base dimension.

The objectives for this unit are to:

- Understand tolerance dimensions
- Apply tolerance dimensions using AutoCAD
- Understand which dimension variables control the appearance of tolerance dimensions

Setting Tolerance Variables

As with other types of dimensions in AutoCAD, tolerance dimensions are controlled by a few dimension variables. The dimensioning variables that control the appearance of tolerance dimensions include:

- **DIMTOL.** This variable turns on and off dimension tolerancing. If DIMTOL is set to 0, AutoCAD places standard dimensions. If DIMTOL is set to 1, AutoCAD places tolerance dimensions.
- **DIMLIM.** This variable controls limit dimensioning. If DIMTOL is set to 1, DIMLIM is automatically set to 0.
- **DIMTP.** This variable stores the upper value, or plus tolerance, of the tolerance dimension.
- **DIMTM.** This variable stores the lower value, or minus tolerance, of the tolerance dimension.
- **DIMTFAC.** This variable stores the scaling factor to use for the text height of the tolerance values. AutoCAD multiplies the default text height by this value to obtain the text height for the tolerance value text.

Some dimensioning standards dictate that dimensions in inch units not have a leading zero for values less than one inch. For example, .142 is preferred over 0.142. With metric drawings, however, leading zeros are included. Therefore, you also will use DIMZIN to control the display of leading zeroes in your dimension values in this unit.

As always, you can set these values from the keyboard, but in these exercises, you will use the Dimensions Styles and Variables dialog box.

Figure 83.1 illustrates tolerance dimensioning in which DIMTP (Tolerance Plus value) and DIMTM (Tolerance Minus value) are the same. Duplicate a few of the dimensions in figure 83.1 by using the Dimension Styles and Variables dialog box (see fig. 83.2) to set the proper values for the dimension variables.

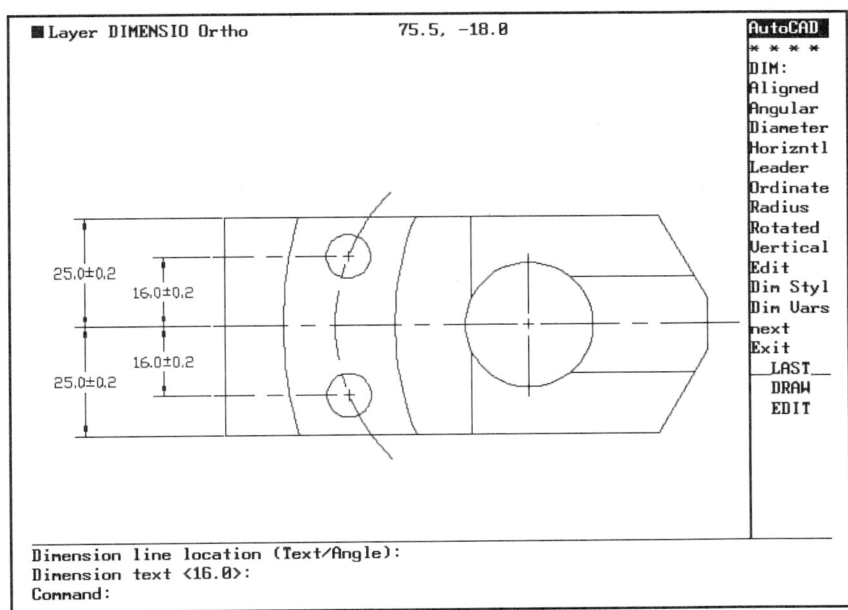

Figure 83.1

Tolerance dimensions with DIMTP and DIMTM set to equal values.

Layer DIMENSIO Ortho 116.9,-10.2
AutoCAD
* * * *
ASE
BLOCKS
DIM:
DISPLAY
DRAW
EDIT
INQUIRY
LAYER...
MODEL
MVIEW
PLOT...
RENDER
SETTINGS
SURFACES
UCS:
UTILITY
SAVE:
Dimension Styles and Variables
Text Format
Style: *UNNAMED
Feature Scaling: 12.70000
Use Paper Space Scaling
Basic Units
Length Scaling: 1.00000
Scale In Paper Space Only
Round Off: 0.0
Text Prefix:
Text Suffix:
Zero Suppression
0 Feet
0 Inches
Leading
Trailing
Tolerances
None
Variance
Limits
Upper Value: 0.2
Lower Value: 0.2
Alternate Units
Show Alternate Units?
Decimal Places: 3
Scaling: 0.03937
Suffix:
OK
Cancel
Help...
Command:
Command:
Command: ddim

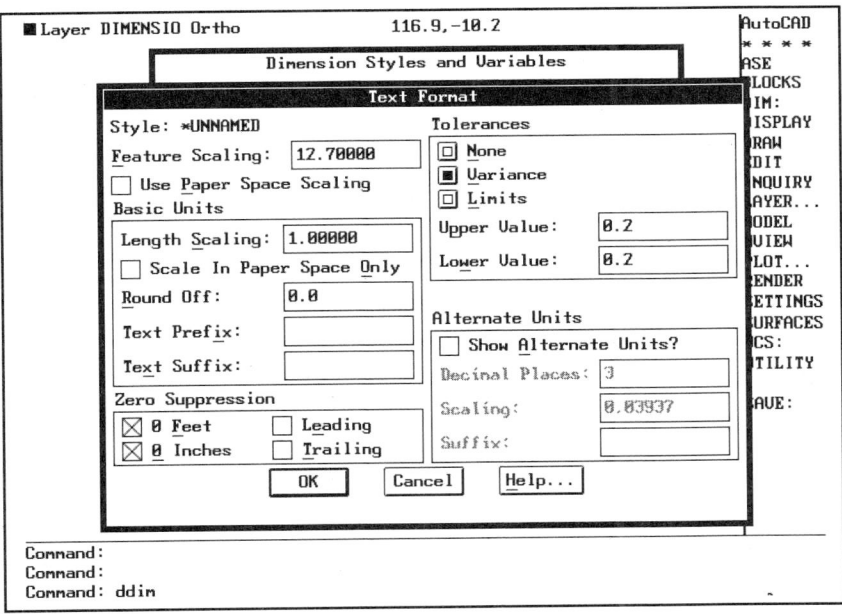

Figure 83.2

The Text Format dialog box.

Placing Tolerance Dimensions with Equal Tolerance Values

1. Begin a new drawing named 083???01 using 083SLIDE as a prototype, then zoom to the view shown in figure 83.3.

2. `Command:` *Choose* Settings, *then* *Dimension Style* — Displays the Dimension Styles and Variables dialog box

continues

3. *Choose* Text Format	Displays the Text Format dialog box
4. *Choose the* Variance *radio button*	Turns on tolerance dimensioning by setting DIMTOL to 1 or ON, and enables the Upper Value and Lower Value edit boxes
5. *Set* Upper Value *to* 0.1	Sets upper tolerance value (sets DIMTP dimension variable)
6. *Set* Lower Value *to* 0.1	Sets lower tolerance value (sets DIMTM dimension variable)
7. *Choose* OK	Closes Text Format dialog box
8. *Choose* OK	Closes Dimension Styles and Variables dialog box
9. *Set* running OSNAP *to* ENDpoint.	
10. `Command:` *Choose* Draw, *then* Dimensions, *then* Linear, *then* Vertical	Starts the VER dimensioning command

11. Apply the two overall outside vertical dimensions as shown in figure 83.3. Remember to align the dimensions properly.

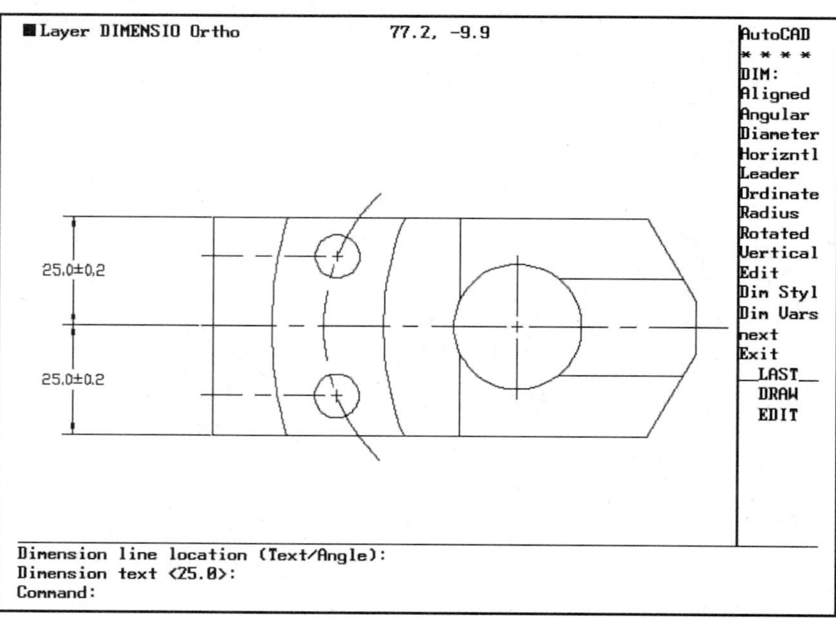

Figure 83.3

Tolerance dimensions added to the slide block drawing.

Because the Upper Value and Lower Value (DIMTP and DIMTM variables) are the same, AutoCAD automatically places a ± sign before the tolerance value. This means that the tolerance for the dimension is +.02mm (DIMTP) and -.02mm (DIMTM).

Now place tolerance dimensions with differing plus and minus values.

Placing Tolerance Dimensions with Differing Tolerance Values

Continue with your drawing from the previous exercise.

1. `Command:` **`DDIM`** ↵	Displays the Dimension Styles and Variables dialog box
2. *Choose* Text Format	Displays the Text Format dialog box
3. *Set* Upper Value *to* 0.2	Sets DIMTP dimension variable
4. *Set* Lower Value *to* 0.3	Sets DIMTM dimension variable
5. *Choose* OK, *then* OK *again*	Closes the dialog boxes and returns to the drawing editor

6. Apply the overall horizontal tolerance dimension as shown in figure 83.4.

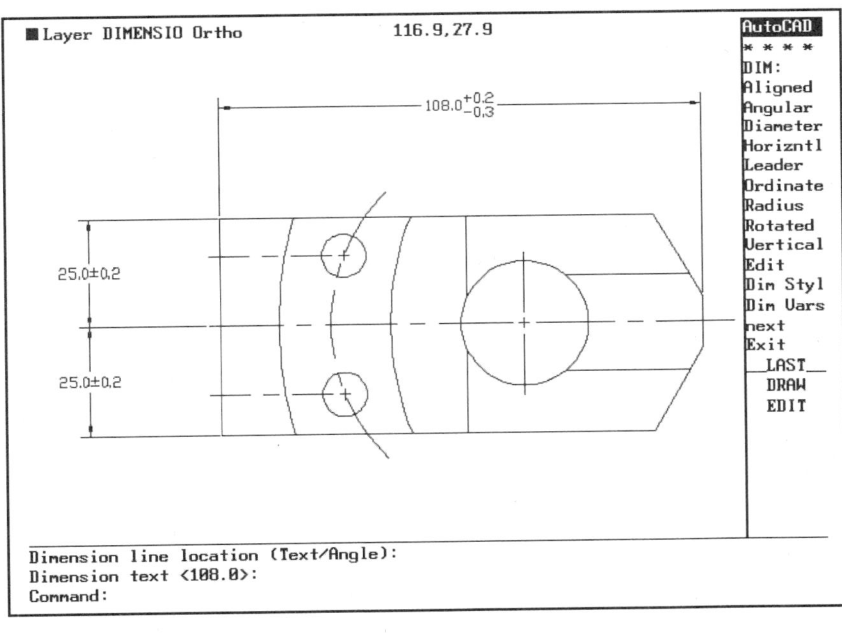

Figure 83.4

A tolerance dimension with differing DIMTP and DIMTM values.

This time, DIMTP (Upper Value) and DIMTM (Lower Value) are different. To display these values, AutoCAD places one value on top of another with a corresponding (+) sign or (-) sign.

If a plus or minus tolerance value is zero, AutoCAD does not insert a leading plus or minus sign in front of the zero tolerance.

Using Alternate Units with Tolerances

In many situations, it is necessary to use dual dimensioning as well as tolerancing. If alternate dimensions are enabled with tolerance dimensions, AutoCAD places both for you automatically. In the following exercise, turn on alternate units, then place an overall horizontal dimension to compare it with the others you have already placed.

It is not accepted drafting practice to mix single and dual dimensions on a drawing, nor is it acceptable to dimension the same feature twice. It is done here only to illustrate the difference between the types of dimensions you are working with in this unit. Also, in a dual dimensioned drawing, inches generally are the primary unit of measure and metric is secondary.

Using Dual Dimension Tolerances

Continue with your drawing from the previous exercise.

1. `Command:` *Choose* Settings, *then* Dimension Style	Displays the Dimension Styles and Variables dialog box
2. *Choose* Text Format	Displays the Text Format dialog box
3. *Place a check in the* Show Alternate Units *check box*	Enables alternate units
4. *Set* Decimal Places *to 3*	Specifies precision of alternate units
5. *Set* Scaling *to 0.03937*	Sets scaling to convert from millimeters to inches
6. *Choose* OK, *then* OK *again*	Closes the dialog boxes and returns to the drawing editor

7. Draw another overall horizontal dimension as shown in figure 83.5, then save your drawing.

When you are working on a drawing that includes many toleranced dimensions (whether single- or dual-dimensioned), you probably will need to change the upper and lower limits many times to accommodate differences in tolerance requirements within the drawing. You can issue the DIMTM command to set the minus tolerance value quickly, and issue the DIMTP command to set the plus tolerance value.

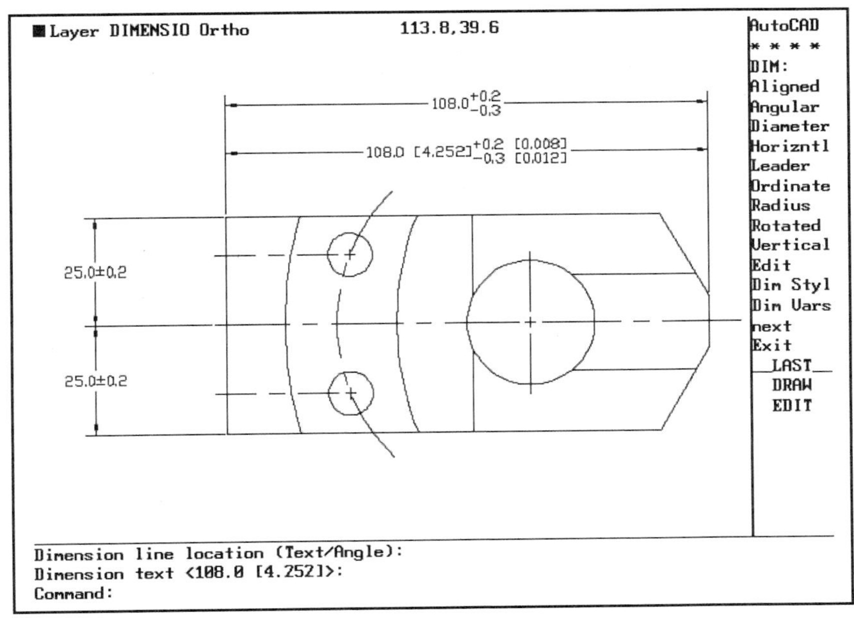

Figure 83.5

A tolerance dimension using dual-dimensioning.

Unit Review

What You've Learned

- Commands: DIMTOL, DIMLIM, DIMTP, DIMTM
- What is a tolerance dimension
- What are plus and minus tolerance values
- How to apply tolerance dimensions

Review Questions

True or False

83.01 T F Tolerance dimensions specify how close a dimension must be to an ideal dimension.

83.02 T F DIMZIN controls the number of decimal places displayed in a dimension.

83.03 T F DIMTP is added to the calculated dimension value in a tolerance dimension.

83.04 T F AutoCAD displays a ± sign in front of the tolerance values only if they are the same.

83.05 T F DIMTXT is used to control the size of the main dimension value in a tolerance dimension.

83.06 T F AutoCAD's Dimension Styles and Variables dialog box uses the word "Variance" to denote tolerance dimensions.

Multiple Choice

83.07 Tolerance dimensioning is used primarily in which field?

____

(A) civil engineering

(B) architectural design

(C) mechanical design

(D) semiconductor engineering

Student: __________ Date: __________

Instructor: __________ Course: __________ Section: __________

83.08 Which of the following dimension variable settings must be used for tolerance dimensioning? __________

(A) DIMLIM=0 / DIMTOL=ON

(B) DIMLIM=0 / DIMTOL=1

(C) DIMLIM=OFF / DIMTOL=OFF

(D) DIMTP=ON / DIMLIM=OFF

83.09 DIMTP controls which of the following? __________

(A) upper tolerance value

(B) lower tolerance value

(C) minus tolerance value

(D) plus tolerance value

83.10 Tolerance dimensions are most similar to __________.

(A) baseline dimensions

(B) limit dimensions

(C) linear dimensions

(D) ordinate dimensions

Additional Exercises

83.11 From the DDIM dialog box, choose Features. From the Features dialog box, find the Text Position group in the lower right. Enter 0.1 for Tolerance Height. This sets DIMTFAC to a scale factor of 0.5 (one-half of 0.2 is 0.1). Erase the dimensions from the previous exercises and dimension again using the new DIMTFAC setting. Save your drawing as 083???11.

Student: __________ Date: __________

Instructor: __________ Course: __________ Section: __________

UNIT 84

Introduction to Dimension Styles

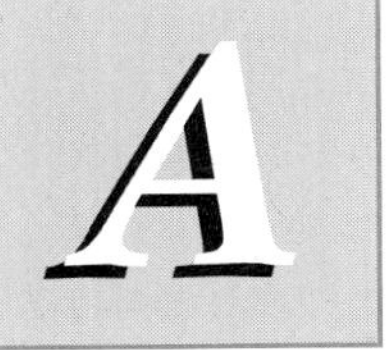

As you have seen in previous units, dimensioning in AutoCAD requires a certain mastery of dozens of dimension variables. Imagine a drawing with many different types of dimensions (see fig. 84.1). Each type requires different settings for the dimension variables. It is extremely difficult and time-consuming to try to remember and manipulate all of the dimension variables for each type of desired dimension. Dimension styles make the process of managing dimension variables easier. This unit explains how you can use dimension styles to simplify dimensioning in AutoCAD.

The objectives for this unit are to:

- Understand the purpose of dimension styles
- Create and use a dimension style
- Restore and use a previously defined dimension style

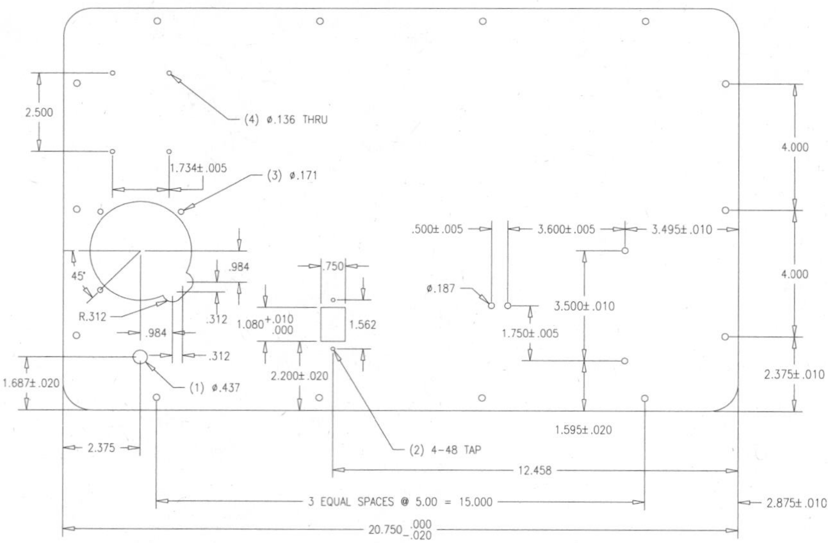

Figure 84.1

Dimensions created using dimension styles.

Understanding Dimension Styles

Dimension styles were devised to make it easier to manipulate and place dimensions in AutoCAD. You can think of dimension styles as a named group of dimension-variable values for a particular style of dimension. When you assign a dimension style and give it a name, AutoCAD reads the values of all the dimension variables and stores them with the style name you assign. When you want to place a particular style of dimension, you simply restore it using its name.

Restoring a dimension style assigns all of its variable values to the appropriate dimension variables. Placing a dimension with a particular style active causes the dimension to assume the characteristics of that dimension style. If you have created a dimension style for toleranced dimensions, for example, restoring that style and placing a dimension results in toleranced dimensions.

Some AutoCAD system variables affect the display of dimensions but are not stored in dimension styles. These variables include LUPREC, LUNITS, AUPREC, and AUNITS.

The dimension variables DIMSHO and DIMASO are not stored within dimension styles.

In the following exercise, list the variable settings for a selected dimension style.

Listing the Dimension Variable Settings for a Dimension Style

1. Begin a new drawing named 084???01 in your assigned directory using 084STYLE as a prototype.

2. `Command:` **`DIM`** ↵	Enters dimensioning mode
3. `Dim:` **`VAR`** ↵	Issues the VAR dimensioning command
4. `Current dimension style: T02 ?/Enter dimension style name or RETURN to select dimension:` *Press* Enter	Specifies to select dimension by picking rather than by name
5. `Select dimension:` *Pick the radius dimension at* ① *(see fig. 84.2)*	Specifies which dimension to list the variables for

```
Current dimension style: RADIUS

Status of RADIUS:

DIMALT   Off          Alternate units selected
DIMALTD  2            Alternate unit decimal places
DIMALTF  25.400       Alternate unit scale factor
DIMAPOST              Suffix for alternate text
DIMASO   On           Create associative dimensions
DIMASZ   0.180        Arrow size
DIMBLK                Arrow block name
DIMBLK1               First arrow block name
DIMBLK2               Second arrow block name
DIMCEN   0.000        Center mark size
DIMCLRD  BYBLOCK      Dimension line color
DIMCLRE  BYBLOCK      Extension line & leader color
DIMCLRT  BYBLOCK      Dimension text color
DIMDLE   0.000        Dimension line extension
DIMDLI   0.250        Dimension line increment for
                      continuation
DIMEXE   0.130        Extension above dimension line
DIMEXO   0.060        Extension line origin offset
DIMGAP   0.090        Gap from dimension line to text
DIMLFAC  1.000        Linear unit scale factor
DIMLIM   Off          Generate dimension limits
DIMPOST               Default suffix for dimension
                      text
DIMRND   0.000        Rounding value
DIMSAH   Off          Separate arrow blocks
DIMSCALE 2.000        Overall scale factor
DIMSE1   Off          Suppress the first extension
                      line
DIMSE2   Off          Suppress the second extension
                      line
```

continues

DIMSHO On	Update dimensions while dragging
DIMSOXD Off	Suppress outside extension dimension
DIMSTYLE RADIUS	Current dimension style (read-only)
DIMTAD Off	Place text above the dimension line
DIMTFAC 1.000	Tolerance text height scaling factor
DIMTIH On	Text inside extensions is horizontal
DIMTIX Off	Place text inside extensions
DIMTM 0.005	Minus tolerance
DIMTOFL Off	Force line inside extension lines
DIMTOH On	Text outside extensions is horizontal
DIMTOL Off	Generate dimension tolerances
DIMTP 0.005	Plus tolerance
DIMTSZ 0.000	Tick size
DIMTVP 0.000	Text vertical position
DIMTXT 0.125	Text height
DIMZIN 4	Zero suppression

6. `Dim:` *Press* Ctrl+C — Exits dimensioning mode

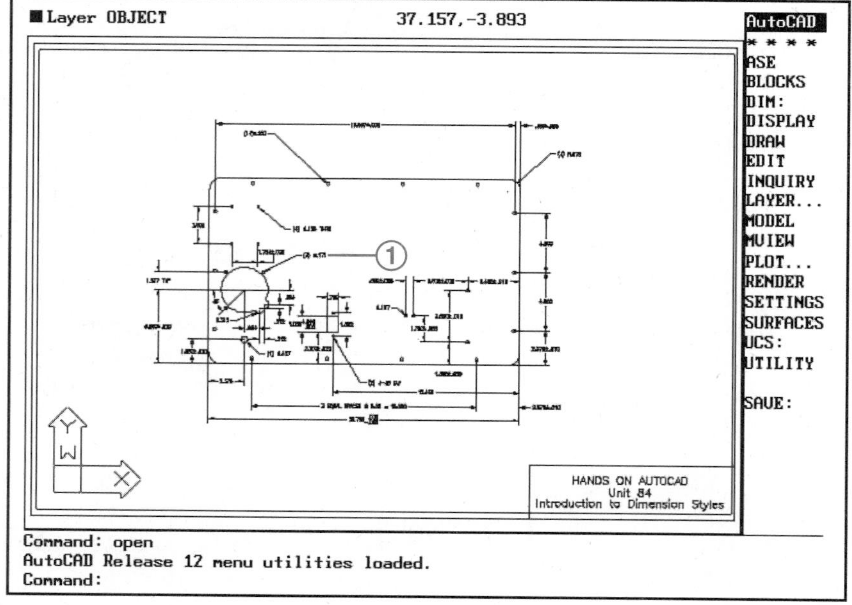

Figure 84.2

A dimension associated with the RADIUS dimension style.

Dimension styles are in no way related to text styles used for text.

The VAR dimensioning command is a handy way to see what the various dimension variable settings are for a particular style. The convenience of being able to assign a dimension style name to a group of variable settings makes dimensioning in AutoCAD a much simpler task.

You also have used the VAR dimensioning command to see how a group of dimension variable settings can be associated with a dimension style name. The radius dimension you selected in the previous exercise used a dimension style named RADIUS. In the following exercise, look at a list of the other dimension styles that are defined in your prototype drawing.

Viewing Defined Dimension Styles

1. `Command:` *Choose* Settings, *then* Dimension Style — Displays the Dimension Styles and Variables dialog box (see fig. 84.3)
2. Examine the names of the 10 defined dimension styles, then choose the Cancel button to close the dialog box.

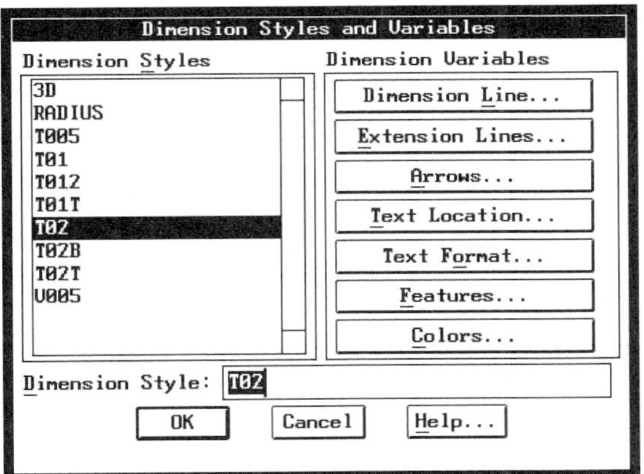

Figure 84.3

Dimension styles shown in the Dimension Styles and Variables dialog box.

Now that you know about saving a group of dimension variables settings with a name, you are ready to create a few dimension styles of your own.

Defining a Dimension Style

Your drawing contains several predefined dimension styles. Create a new dimension style named DIAMETER. You want the diameter dimensions to read something like "3.295 DIA." instead of the AutoCAD default of "∅3.295."

When you create a dimension style, AutoCAD bases the new style on another selected style. If no styles are defined in a drawing, AutoCAD stores the current dimension variable values under the new name you specify. For this exercise, the RADIUS dimension style is close to what you want in the DIAMETER dimension style.

Defining a Dimension Style

Continue with your drawing from the preceding exercise.

1. `Command:` **`DDIM`**	Activates the Dimension Styles and Variables dialog box
2. *Choose* RADIUS *in the list of Dimension Styles*	Makes the RADIUS style the active dimension style
3. *Enter* **`DIAMETER`** *in the* Dimension Style *edit box, then press* Enter	Creates a new dimension style named DIAMETER using the style RADIUS as a basis

The new style named DIAMETER inherits all of the dimension variable settings found in the style RADIUS. You want to make some changes by having AutoCAD add a "DIA." suffix to all diameter dimensions instead of the ∅ symbol prefix.

4. *Choose the* Text Format *button*	Displays the Text Format dialog box
5. *Enter* `%%` *in the* Text Prefix *box (see fig. 84.4)*	Specifies a "null" character for the text prefix
6. *Enter* **`DIA.`** *in the* Text Suffix *box (include a leading space before the* DIA. *text)*	Specifies a suffix of DIA. for diameter dimensions
7. *Choose* OK	Exits the Text Format dialog box
8. *Choose* OK	Exits the DDIM dialog box
9. Save your drawing.	

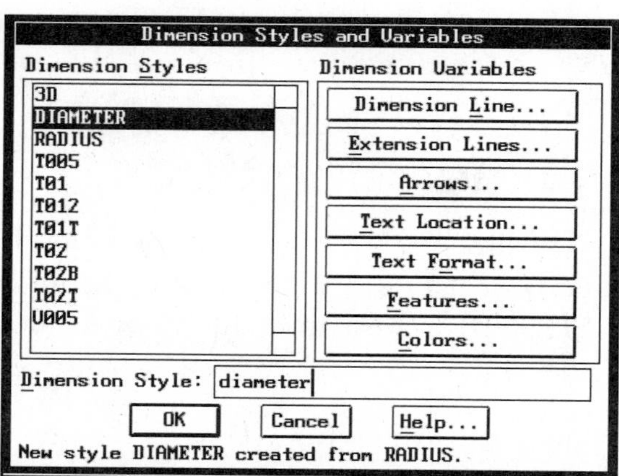

Figure 84.4
Changing variables for a new dimension style.

You created a new dimension style named DIAMETER based on an existing dimension style. You modified the DIMPOST variable by specifying a text prefix and suffix for the diameter dimension value. Now, use this new dimension style.

Dimension style names can be up to 31 characters long. This means that you can assign meaningful names to your styles. For example, a style for tolerance dimensions might read "TOL_P003_M003," meaning "Tolerance - Plus value 0.003, Minus value 0.003." This takes the guesswork out of cryptic names like "T33."

Dimensioning with Style

The advantages of using dimension styles are evident when it comes to placing dimensions on your drawing. Whether you have a number of styles already predefined or create them as you need them, the use of dimension styles is simple: choose the appropriate style at the time you need to place a particular dimension. Use your newly created DIAMETER style to place diameter dimensions on your drawing.

Applying Dimensions Using a Dimension Style

Continue your drawing from the preceding exercise.

1. `Command:` *Choose* View, *then* Tilemode, *then* On — Turns on TILEMODE and switches to a single tilemode viewport
2. Zoom to the view shown in figure 84.5.
3. `Command:` **`DDIM`** ↵ — Displays the Dimension Styles and Variables dialog box
4. *Choose* DIAMETER *from the* Dimension Styles *list, then choose* OK — Sets the DIAMETER style as the active dimension style and exits the dialog box
5. `Command:` **`DIM`** ↵ — Enters dimensioning mode
6. `Dim:` **`DIA`** ↵ — Specifies Diameter dimensioning
7. `Select arc or circle:` *Pick the arc at* ① — Specifies the arc or circle to dimension

continues

8. `Dimension text <3.125>:` *Press* Enter	Accepts the default dimension value
9. `Enter leader length for text:` *Pick a point near* ② *(see fig. 84.5)*	Specifies the leader length
10. `Dim:` *Press* Enter	Reenters the DIAMETER dimension command

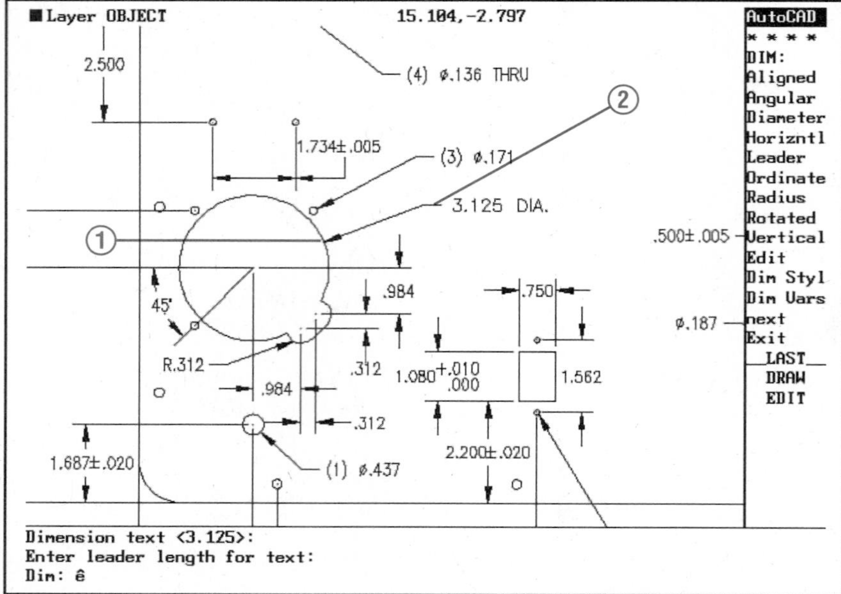

Figure 84.5

Diameter dimension placed using a dimension style.

You can see from the exercise that placing a particular type of dimension is a simple process when you use dimension styles. To place a dimension, you need only select the desired style, then place the dimension. AutoCAD uses the variables defined for the selected style to create the dimension.

Dimension Styles and Prototype Drawings

As you become more experienced with AutoCAD, you will use the same types of dimensions over and over again. Save time and use dimension styles instead. As you create these styles, you are building a personal "library" of styles to choose from without having to memorize dozens of variables and their settings.

The prototype drawing used in the exercises already had several dimension styles defined. This drawing just as well could have contained no geometry at all. A drawing can contain nothing other than the dimension styles and other settings that you would need when creating a new drawing. This eliminates the need to create new dimension styles for each new drawing session because the new drawing inherits the styles and settings that are present in the prototype. When you need to use a particular type of dimension style, you can simply select it from the Dimension Styles and Variables dialog box, rather than define it in each drawing in which it is required.

Unit Review

What You've Learned

- The purpose of dimension styles
- How dimension styles store variable settings
- How to define a dimension style
- How to dimension using a dimension style

Review Questions

True or False

84.01 T F Dimension styles are very similar to text styles.

84.02 T F Dimension styles store all of the values of every dimension variable except DIMSHO and DIMASO.

84.03 T F Dimension style names must be eight characters or less.

84.04 T F The VARIABLES command resets all of the dimension variables to their default values.

84.05 T F New dimension styles inherit the values stored in the active dimension style or current settings if no style is defined.

Multiple Choice

84.06 Dimension styles are most useful for which one of the following fields? ____________

(A) Architecture

(B) Retail store planning and design

(C) Civil engineering

(D) Mechanical design

84.07 A dimension style name can comprise up to _________ characters.

(A) 8

(B) 12

(C) 31

(D) 10

Student: ____________ Date: ____________

Instructor: ____________ Course: ____________ Section: ____________

84.08 Dimension styles can be stored with __________ drawings.

(A) prototype

(B) detail

(C) all

(D) some

Short Answer

84.09 Describe how to change the variable settings within a predefined dimension style.

____

____

____

84.10 Explain the advantages of using dimension styles in a prototype drawing.

____

____

____

Additional Exercises

84.11 Using the drawing from the previous exercises, create a new dimension style named RADIUS_CEN based on the preexisting RADIUS style. This style will place center marks at the center of the selected arcs. In the Dimension Styles and Variables dialog box, choose Features. For Center Mark Size, enter 0.090. Choose OK to exit the Feature dialog box. Choose OK to exit the DDIM dialog box. Place some radius dimensions on the drawing, then save your drawing as 084???11.

84.12 The RESTORE dimension command is used to make a dimension style current. It can also be used to list the differences in variable settings between two styles. With the RADIUS_CEN style active, type **RESTORE** at the Dim: prompt. When the following prompt appears, enter **~RADIUS**:

```
?/Enter dimension style name or RETURN to select dimension:
```

The tilde (~) tells AutoCAD to list the differences in variable settings between the styles RADIUS_CEN and RADIUS.

UNIT 85

Working with Associative Dimensions

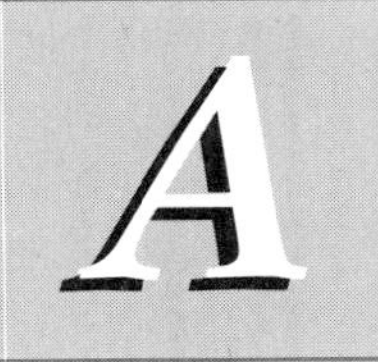

An *associative dimension* entity is associated with another entity or group of entities by its definition points. In previous units you have worked with associative dimensions. When you erased or selected dimensions, all the features of the dimension entity—arrows, dimension lines, extension lines, definition points, and text—were grouped together and selected as a single dimension entity.

One of the advantages of associative dimensions is that they can automatically update when geometry changes. In other words, if you stretch a line that has been dimensioned associatively, the dimension will automatically update to reflect the new dimension. Another advantage is that because all of the components of a dimension (arrows, lines, text, etc.) are grouped together into a dimension entity, you can quickly select, erase, or otherwise edit dimensions.

The objectives for this unit are to:

- Understand the purpose of associative dimensions
- Modify associative dimensions by modifying their related geometry
- Understand the advantages and disadvantages of associative dimensions

Understanding Associative Dimensions

Associative dimensioning in AutoCAD is controlled by the dimension variable DIMASO. If DIMASO is set to one or ON, AutoCAD creates associative dimensions. If DIMASO is set to zero or OFF, AutoCAD creates the dimension using separate line, text, and solid entities.

Create associative and non-associative dimensions in the following exercise to learn how they differ.

Placing an Associative Dimension

1. Begin a new drawing named 085???01 in your assigned directory using 085ASSOC as a prototype.

2. `Command:` *Choose* Settings, *then* Dimension Style	Displays the Dimension Styles and Variables dialog box
3. *Choose the style* TOLERANCE_P2_M1, *then choose* OK	Sets the current dimension style
4. `Command:` **`DIMASO`**	Issues the DIMASO command
5. `New value for DIMASO <1>:` *Press* Enter	Sets up AutoCAD to create associative dimensions
6. `Command:` **`DIM`** ↵	Enters dimensioning mode
7. `Dim:` **`DIMSHO`** ↵ `Current value <On> New value:` *Press* Enter	Allows dragging of the dimension as you place or update an associative dimension

8. Place a horizontal dimension as shown in figure 85.1.

Now place a non-associative dimension.

Placing a Non-Associative Dimension

Continue with your drawing from the preceding exercise.

1. `Command:` **`DIM`** ↵	
2. `Dim:` **`DIMASO`** ↵ `Current value <On> New value:` **`OFF`**	Turns off associative dimensioning

3. Place a vertical dimension as shown in figure 85.2.

Your drawing should resemble figure 85.2.

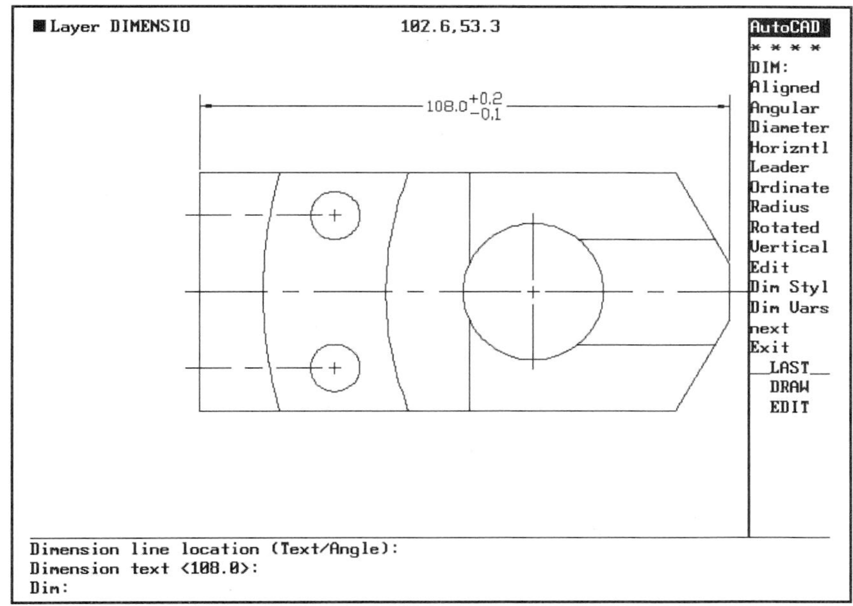

Figure 85.1

Associative dimension added to the drawing.

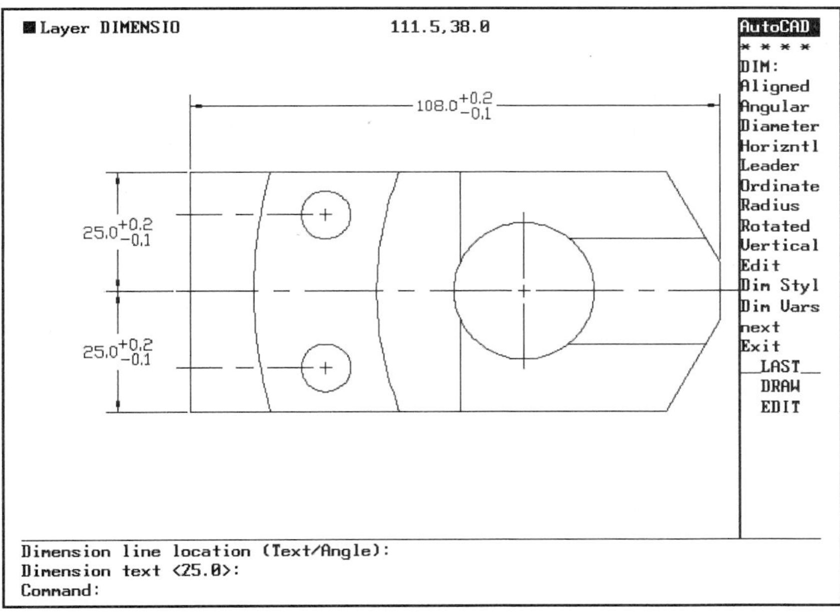

Figure 85.2

Placing non-associative dimensions.

Now that you have placed associative dimensions and non-associative dimensions, what happens when you change the geometry affecting a dimension? Continue with the next section to find out.

Working with Associative Dimensions

Suppose you want to make some design changes to your drawing. The length needs to increase by 2mm and the height needs to decrease by 3mm on both sides of the centerline. Modify the drawing from the previous exercise and note what happens to the dimensions.

Modifying Geometry Tied to Associative Dimensions

1. `Command:` *Choose* Modify, *then* Stretch — Issues the STRETCH command for automatic crossing selection

```
_stretch
Select objects to stretch by window or polygon...
Select objects: _c
```

2. `First corner:` *Pick a point at* ① *(see fig. 85.3)* — Specifies the first corner of the crossing box

3. `Other corner:` *Pick a point at* ② *(see fig. 85.3)* — Specifies the opposite corner of the crossing box and selects entities

```
9 found
```

4. `Select objects:` *Press* Enter — Ends the object-selection process

5. `Base point or displacement:` *Pick a point anywhere on-screen* — Specifies the reference point for the STRETCH command

Notice what happens to the dimension as you drag your cursor around the screen. The dimension dynamically updates to reflect the current value.

6. `Second point of displacement:` **`@2,0`** ↵ — Specifies 2mm displacement to the right

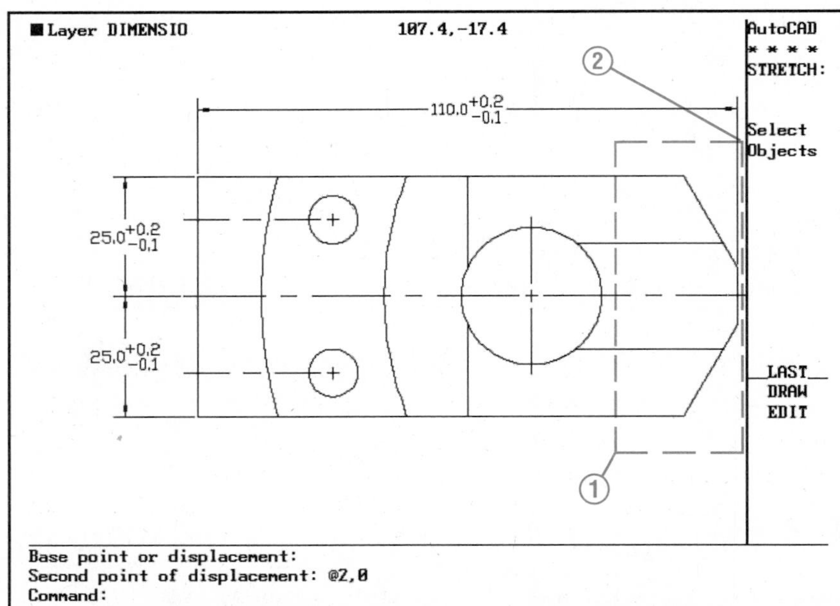

Figure 85.3
Updating an associative dimension by stretching.

Your dimension value should have increased by 2mm to 110mm. It is important to remember that if you want a dimension value to update when stretching the associated geometry, you must include the definition point of the dimension in your selection set. This point is used by AutoCAD to calculate the new dimension value.

Remember that the vertical dimension you applied in the drawing was not associative. Try shrinking the vertical dimension by 3mm using the STRETCH command.

Modifying Geometry of Non-Associative Dimensions

1. `Command:` *Choose* Modify, *then* Stretch — Issues the STRETCH command

   ```
   _stretch
   Select objects to stretch by window or polygon...
   Select objects: _c
   ```

2. `First corner:` *Pick a point at* ① *(see fig. 85.4)* — Specifies the first corner of the crossing box

3. `Other corner:` *Pick a point at* ② *(see fig. 85.4)* — Specifies the opposite corner of the crossing box

   ```
   21 found
   ```

4. `Select objects:` *Press* Enter — Ends the object-selection process

5. `Base point or displacement:` *Pick a point anywhere on-screen* — Specifies the reference point for the STRETCH command

   Notice what happens to the dimension as you drag your cursor around the screen. It does not automatically update as the associative dimension did in the previous exercise.

6. `Second point of displacement:` **`@0,3`** — Specifies 3mm vertical displacement

7. Save your drawing.

Your drawing should look similar to figure 85.4.

The dimension value did not change as you stretched the geometry. Your new dimension value should read 22.0mm instead of 25.0mm. You want the dimension to reflect the actual value; to do so, you now must manually edit the text value for the dimension. Remember that you can do this with non-associative dimensions because they consist of separate text and line entities.

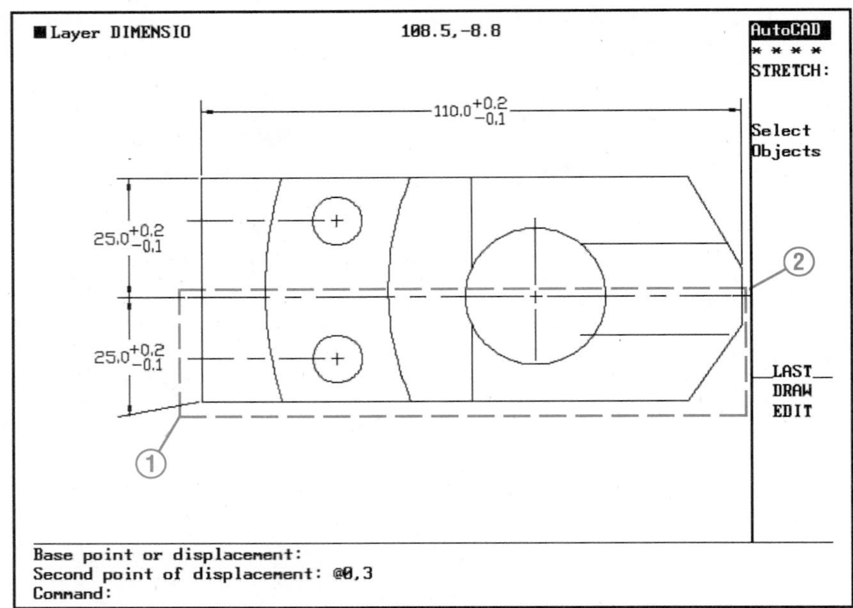

Figure 85.4
Updating a non-associative dimension by stretching.

If you want dimension values to always reflect the correct value, you should use associative dimensions. With associative dimensions, you do not have to remember to update the text value every time you modify a drawing's geometry.

Using EXTEND with Associative Dimensions

The EXTEND command has a unique effect on associative dimensions. You can use the EXTEND command to change the value of an associative dimension simply by extending the dimension entity. This can be useful when you need to change the dimension separately from the drawing geometry.

Assume that you need to increase the length of the slide block used in the previous exercises to match an existing line on the drawing, but you do not know the distance by which the length must increase. One method for changing the geometry is to use the EXTEND command to extend the object's lines. In the following exercise, begin the modification by extending the outer slide block lines and the horizontal dimension.

Extending Associative Dimensions

1. Begin a new drawing named 085???02 in your assigned directory using 085EDIT as a prototype.

2. `Command:` *Choose* Modify, *then* Extend — Issues the EXTEND command

   `_extend`
   `Select boundary edge(s)...`

3. `Select objects:` *Pick the line at* ① *(see fig. 85.5)* — Specifies the boundary for the EXTEND command

   `1 found`

4. `Select objects:` *Press* Enter — Ends selection

5. `<Select object to extend>/Undo:` *Select the line at* ② *(see fig. 85.5)* — Extends the top line to the boundary

Notice in figure 85.5 that the dimension does not extend automatically. You must select the dimension entity to extend it.

6. `Select objects:` *Select the dimension entity at* ③ *(see fig. 85.5)* — Extends the dimension and changes its value

7. `Select objects:` *Press* Enter — Ends the command

Your drawing should look similar to figure 85.6.

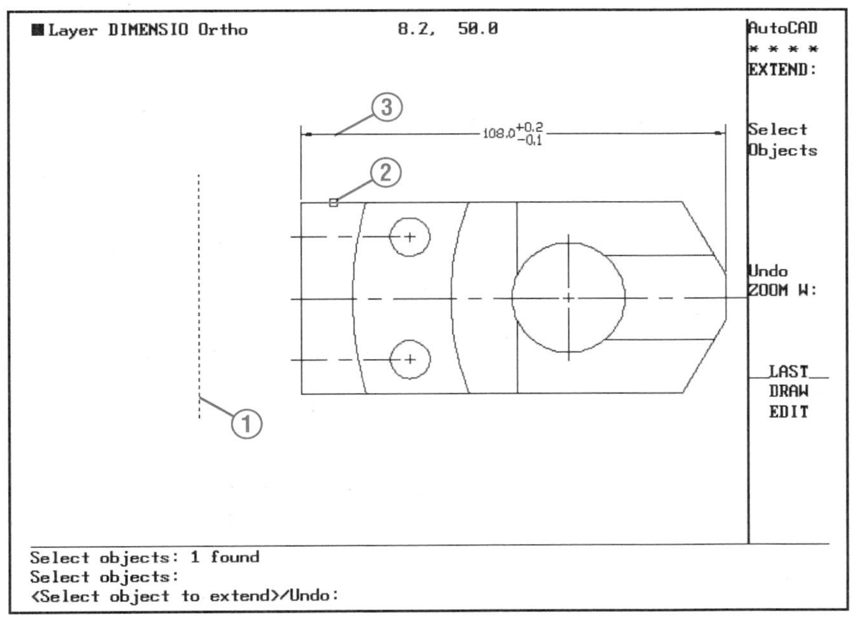

Figure 85.5

Top line extended without dimension.

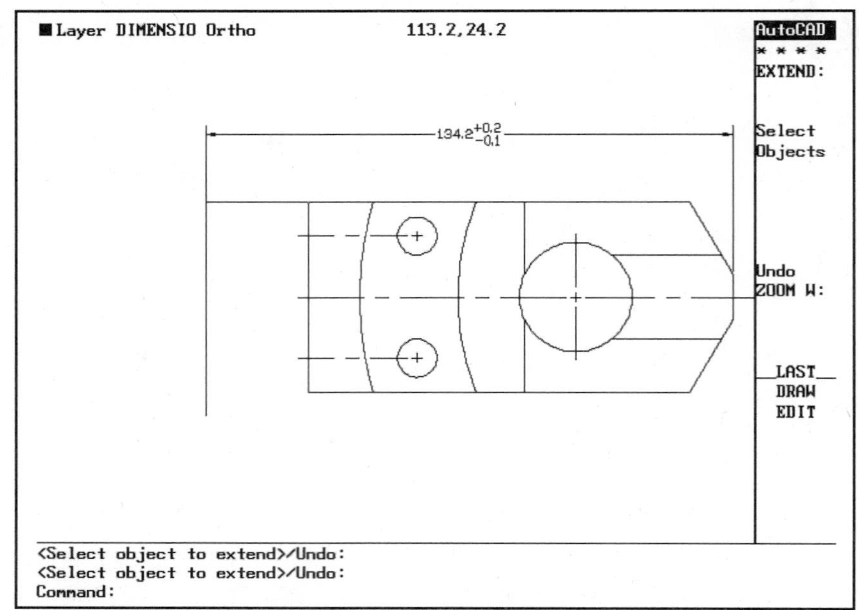

Figure 85.6
Extended associative dimension.

AutoCAD calculates the extension point for a dimension based on the tip of the terminator (such as the arrow), not on the dimension's association point with the drawing geometry. In some cases, this can lead to unexpected results when you extend a dimension.

In many situations, you may find it easier to use the STRETCH command to modify geometry and associative dimensions. In some drawings, however, the EXTEND command is easier when you need to extend entities and their associated dimensions.

You can use the TRIM command to trim dimension lines of a non-associative dimension. You also can use TRIM to change the value of an associative dimension. Simply select a trimming boundary, then select a dimension. The dimension will be trimmed to the boundary.

Unit Review

What You've Learned

- The definition of associative dimensions
- The differences between associative and non-associative dimensions
- The advantages of associative dimensions
- How to apply associative dimensions

Review Questions

True or False

85.01 T F DIMSHO enables you to see associative dimensions dynamically updated on the screen as you modify them.

85.02 T F DIMSHO has to be ON to place associative dimensions.

85.03 T F The term *associative dimensions* means that the dimensions are associated with the drawing geometry.

85.04 T F Non-associative dimensions are stored in the AutoCAD drawing database as anonymous blocks.

85.05 T F Associative dimensions cannot be erased with a single pick.

85.06 T F Non-associative dimensions comprise individual, separate text, line, and other entities.

Short Answer

85.07 List some advantages and disadvantages of using associative dimensions.

____

____

____

85.08 Give a description of an associative dimension.

____

____

____

Student: _______________ Date: _______________

Instructor: _______________ Course: _______________ Section: _______________

85.09 Describe the importance of definition points in an associative dimension.

____

____

____

Additional Exercises

85.10 Use the EXPLODE command to explode an associative dimension. Now try to stretch or modify the dimension. What happens? When you explode an associative dimension, it becomes a non-associative dimension. The only way to restore the dimension entity (other than UNDO) is to apply a new dimension.

85.11 Begin a new drawing named 085???11 in your assigned directory using 085EDIT2 as a prototype. Decrease the length of the part by moving the left vertical line to the right by 4mm (use autoedit modes or the MOVE command to do this). Use the TRIM command to trim the lines and dimension back to the new edge line.

Student: __________ Date: __________

Instructor: __________ Course: __________ Section: __________

UNIT 86

Editing Dimensions

Associative dimensions can be great productivity enhancers, but sometimes they can be difficult to modify to get the desired appearance. Fortunately, other ways are available to edit the appearance and text value of dimensions. This unit explains how you can modify associative dimensions without modifying drawing geometry.

The objectives for this unit are to:

- ☞ Change the value and position of associative dimension text
- ☞ Use grips to edit associative dimensions
- ☞ Use the OBLIQUE dimension command to modify the appearance of an associative dimension

Editing Dimensions

You can edit dimensions in a number of ways, including modifying the dimension text value, relocating the text, reinstating the text in its original location, and more. Editing the value of a dimension is one of the most common changes you will make.

Changing Dimension Text (NEWTEXT)

Occasionally, you may need to change the text value of a dimension after you have placed the dimension. Perhaps you need to add a prefix or suffix, such as R1.25 TYP, or change a design that will require a new dimension value. In the latter case, you normally would modify the geometry to update the dimension automatically. Sometimes, though, this is impractical because of deadlines or difficulties in editing the geometry. In addition, the modifications could be so extensive that it would be more cost-effective to change the dimension value than to change the geometry to match the actual desired value. In this situation, it is more practical to change the dimension text rather than the defining geometry.

In the following exercise, change the 3'-4" dimensions to read 3'-4" TYP.

Changing Dimension Text Values

1. Begin a new drawing named 086???01 in your assigned directory using 086TEXT as a prototype.

Step	Description

2. `Command:` *Choose* Modify, *then* Edit Dims, *then* Dimension Text, *then* Change Text
`_dim1`
`Dim: _newtext`
	Issues the NEWTEXT dimensioning command

3. `Enter new dimension text:` **`<> TYP.`** ↵	Specifies the new text to substitute for the dimension value
4. `Select objects:` *Select the three 3'-4" dimensions*	Selects the dimensions to modify
5. `Select objects:` *Press* Enter	Ends selection and modifies dimension text

Your drawing should look similar to figure 86.1.

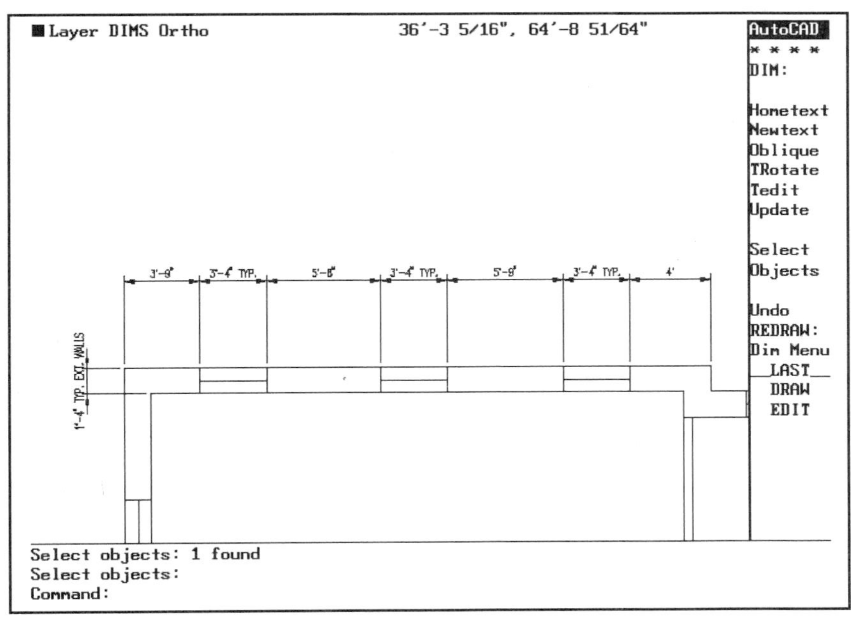

Figure 86.1

Text added to existing dimensions.

The dimensions you picked should have the "TYP." suffix after their values. Any time you type in the characters "<>" for a dimension text value, AutoCAD substitutes the actual value for these characters. You also can do this when you place dimensions and are prompted to accept the calculated dimension value or enter a new dimension value.

Moving Dimension Text (TEDIT)

Another common editing task is to relocate a dimension's text. This often is necessary because the text does not fit properly in the location at which AutoCAD placed it. You also may need to add a new dimension when an existing dimension is in the new dimension's way.

In the next exercise, move the dimension text to reposition it.

Moving Dimension Text

Continue with your drawing from the previous exercise.

1. Zoom to the view shown in figure 86.2.

2. `Command:` *Choose* Modify, *then* Edit Dims, *then* Dimension Text, *then* Move Text — Issues the TEDIT dimensioning command

```
_dim1
Dim: _tedit
```

3. `Select dimension:` *Select the dimension at* ① *(see fig. 86.2)* — Specifies which dimension to edit

continues

4. `Enter text location (Left/Right/Home /Angle):` *Pick a point to locate the text, as shown in figure 86.2* — Specifies new position for the dimension text

5. `Command:` **U** ↵ — Undoes the text relocation

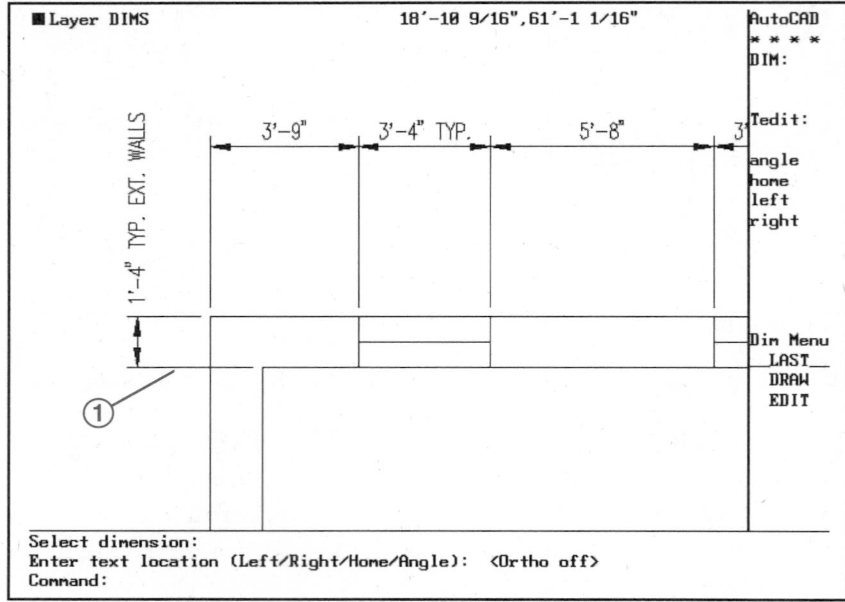

Figure 86.2
Dimension text moved to a new location.

Use the TEDIT command in situations where the text value may be conflicting with some drawing geometry or overlapping the extension lines.

Rotating Dimension Text (TROTATE)

In addition to moving the text, TEDIT enables you to rotate the text as well. TEDIT, however, will only allow you to modify one dimension at a time. TROTATE, on the other hand, will allow you to change the angle of text on multiple dimensions at a time. Try using TROTATE in the following exercise.

Using TROTATE To Rotate Dimension Text

Continue with your drawing from the previous exercise.

1. Zoom to the view shown in figure 86.3.

2. `Command:` *Choose* Modify, *then* Edit Dims, *then* Dimension Text, *then* Rotate Text — Issues the TROTATE dimensioning command

```
_dim1
Dim: _trotate
```

3. `Enter text angle:` **45** ↵ — Specifies a rotation angle

4. `Select objects:` *Pick each of the horizontal dimensions (you can use a crossing box to select them)* — Specifies dimensions for text rotation
5. `Select objects:` *Press* Enter — Ends the command
6. Save your drawing.

Your drawing should look similar to figure 86.3.

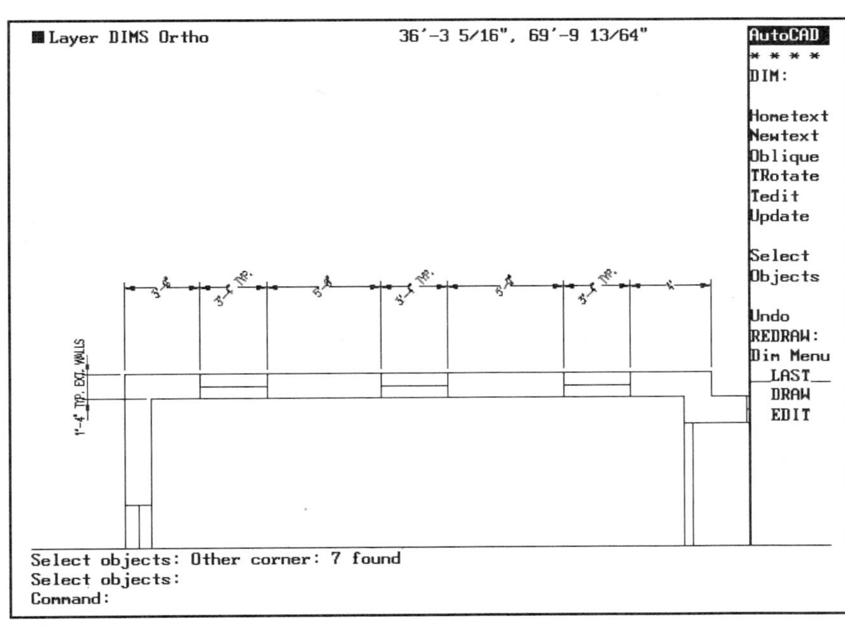

Figure 86.3

Dimension values rotated to 45 degrees.

Restoring Dimension Text (HOMETEXT)

Suppose that you have moved some dimension text and want to restore it to its original location and angle. For example, assume that you want to restore all of the horizontal dimensions to their standard text locations. Use the HOMETEXT dimensioning command to do this rather than try to guess at the text's original location when moving it.

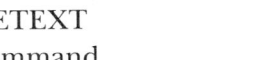

Using HOMETEXT To Restore Dimension Text Position

Continue with your drawing from the previous exercise.

1. `Command:` *Choose* Modify, *then* Edit Dims, *then* Dimension Text, *then* Home Position — Issues the HOMETEXT dimensioning command

```
_dim1
Dim: _trotate
```

continues

2. `Select objects:` *Select all of the horizontal dimensions*	Specifies which dimensions to modify
3. `Select objects:` *Press* Enter	Ends selection process and moves the dimensions

Your drawing should look similar to figure 86.4.

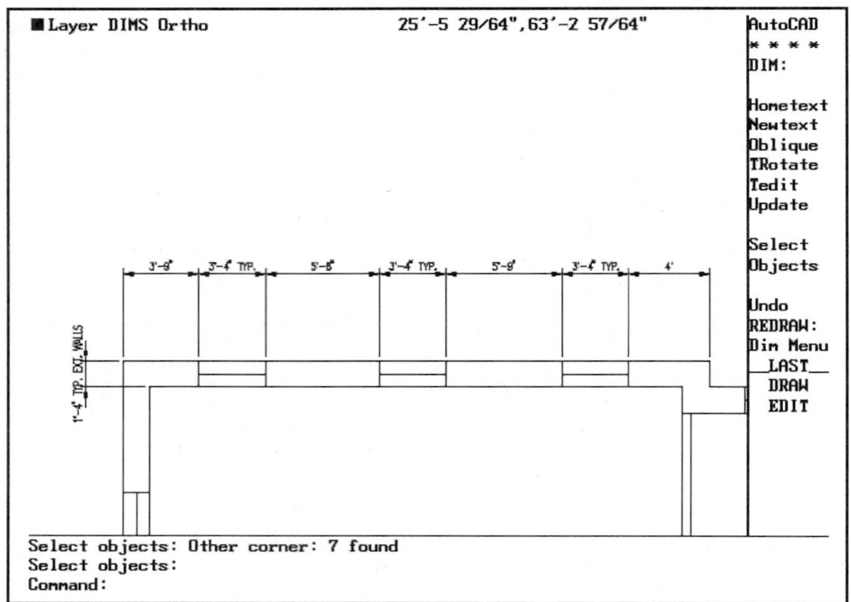

Figure 86.4
Dimension text restored to its original location and angle.

The HOMETEXT dimensioning command not only moves the text back to its default position, but it also resets the text angle to its default value.

Editing Dimensions with Grips

One of the most powerful ways to edit associative dimensions is by using grips. When you select a dimension to activate grips, grips appear at key points in the dimension. Figure 86.5 illustrates several types of dimension entities. Figure 86.6 illustrates the same dimensions with grips activated.

As you can see in figure 86.6, AutoCAD places grips at the following locations on the dimension:

- **Definition points.** You can use the grips at the definition points to reposition the definition point, decrease or increase the distance from the object to the extension line, or actually move the definition point to change the value of the dimension.

- **Endpoints of the dimension line.** Use these grips to relocate the dimension line, dimension arrows, and dimension text in a single operation.
- **Insertion point of the text.** Use this grip to relocate the dimension text. If you move the text onto the dimension line, the dimension line breaks for the text. If you move the text away from the dimension line, the break in the dimension line will "heal" itself.

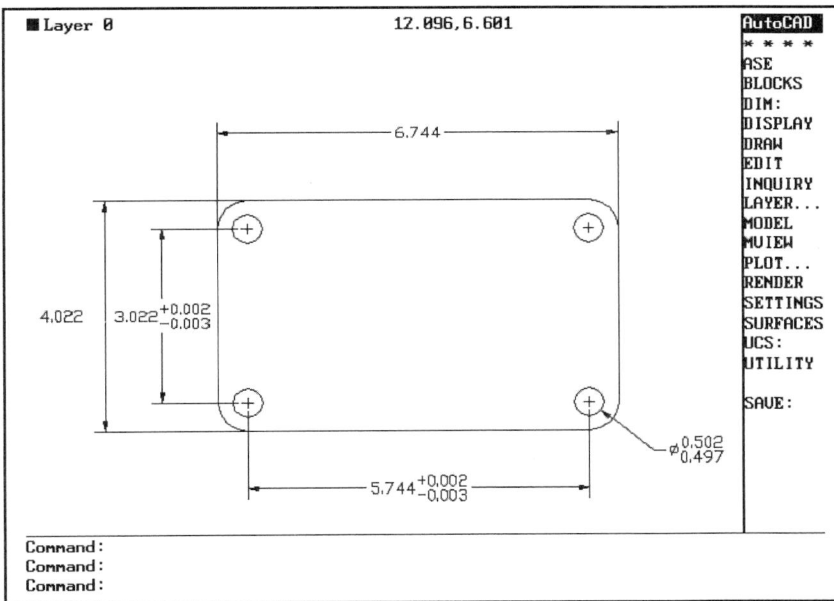

Figure 86.5

Dimension entities without grips.

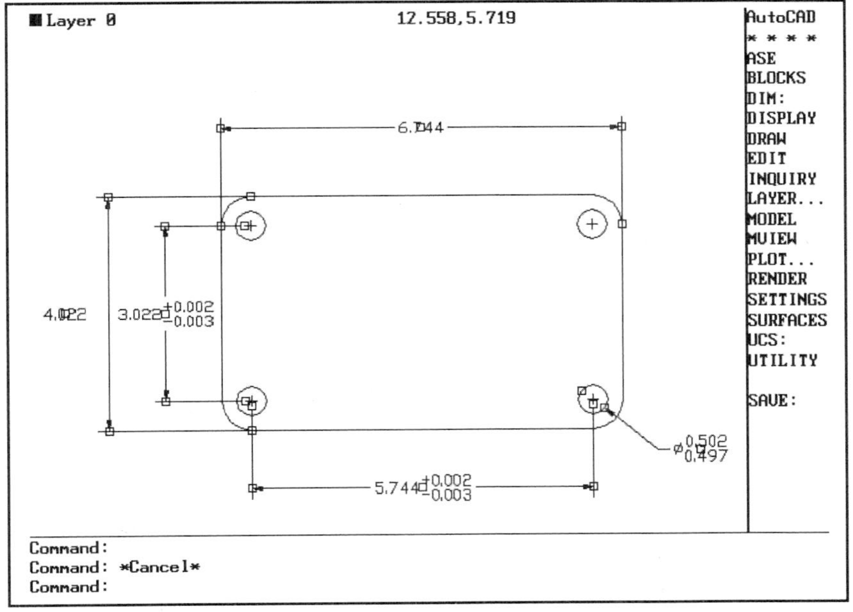

Figure 86.6

Dimension entities with grips.

Use grips in the following exercise to modify a few dimensions.

Using Grips To Modify Dimensions

Continue with your 086???01 drawing that you started in the beginning of this chapter.

1. Zoom to the view shown in figure 86.7.
2. `Command:` *Select the text at* ① *(see fig. 86.7)* — Displays the dimension's grips
3. `Command:` *Select the grip at the middle of the dimension text* — Enters stretch autoedit mode
4. `<Stretch to point>/Base point/Copy/Undo/eXit:` *Relocate the dimension text to* ② *(see fig. 86.7)*

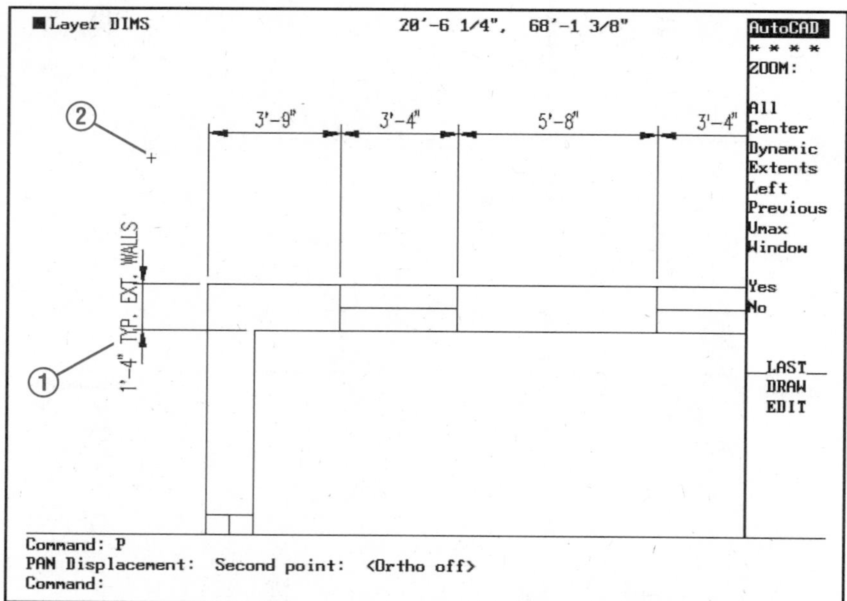

Figure 86.7

Dimension text moved using grips.

5. `Command:` *Select the dimension at* ① *(see fig. 86.8)* — Displays the dimension's grips
6. `Command:` *Pick the grip at* ② — Enters stretch autoedit mode
7. `<Stretch to point>/Base point/Copy/Undo/eXit:` *From the popup menu, choose* Endpoint
8. `_endp of` *Pick the end point at* ③ *(see fig. 86.8)* — Relocates the dimension definition point and changes the dimension (see fig. 86.8)

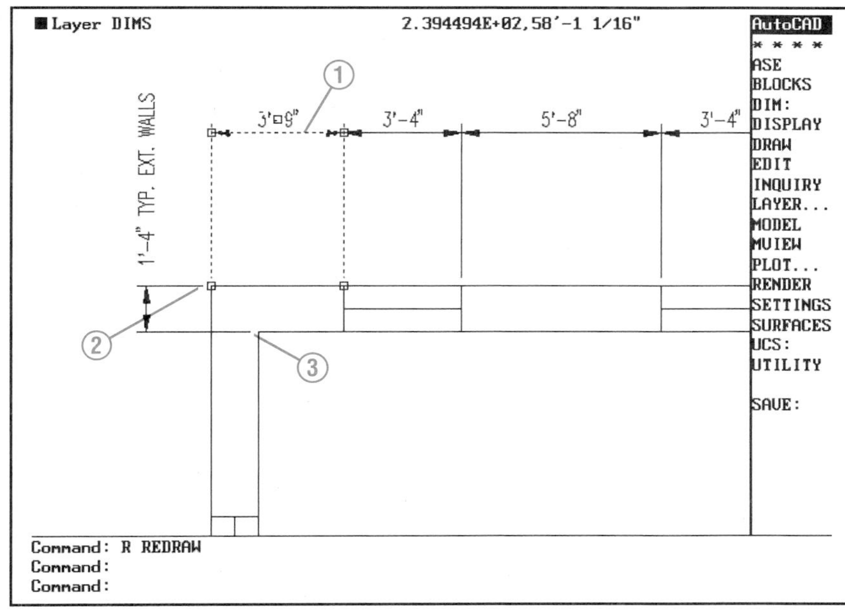

Figure 86.8

Dimension moved using grips.

Updating Dimensions (UPDATE)

Another powerful way to modify dimensions is the UPDATE dimensioning command. The UPDATE command takes the current dimension style (if any) and the values of every dimension variable and applies them to the selected dimension. The dimension is updated with the new settings.

In the next exercise, change the style of a dimension by using the UPDATE command.

Modifying Dimension Styles with UPDATE

1. Begin a new drawing named 086???02 in your assigned directory using 086UPDAT as a protoype.

2. `Command:` *Choose* Settings, *then* Dimension Style	Displays the Dimension Styles and Variables dialog box
3. *Choose the* T005 *dimension style, then choose* OK	Sets the current dimension style
4. `Command:` *Choose* Modify, *then* Edit Dims, *then* Update Dimension	Issues the UPDATE dimensioning command
5. `Select objects:` *Select the dimension entities at* ① *and* ② *(see fig. 86.9)*	Specifies the dimensions to modify
6. `Select objects:` *Press* Enter	Ends the command and updates the dimensions

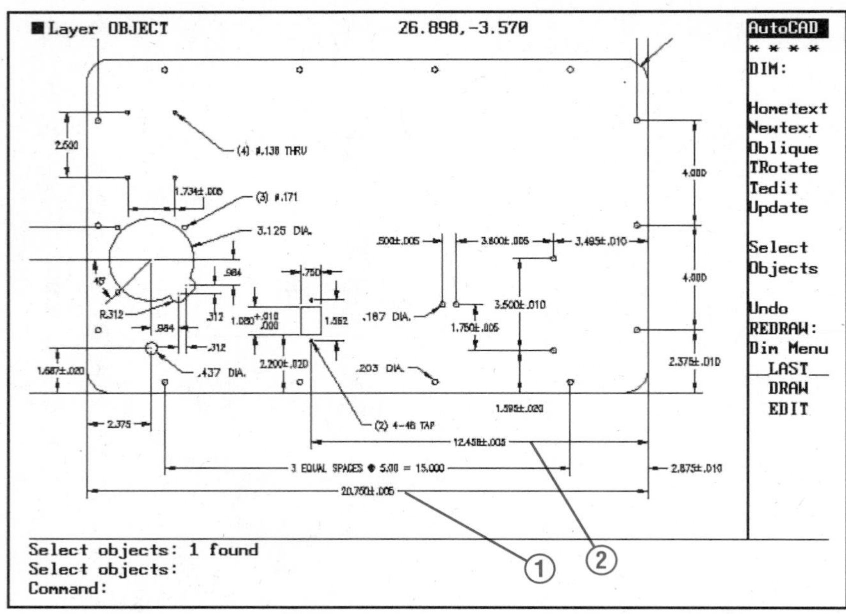

Figure 86.9

Dimensions modified using UPDATE.

As you can see from the exercise, the UPDATE command gives you a way to change the appearance of an existing dimension. Rather than change a dimension's style, you can change a single dimension variable, then update the dimension to use the new variable value.

Making Dimensions Oblique (OBLIQUE)

Oblique dimensions are used in situations in which a normal horizontal or vertical dimension would not fit properly. AutoCAD enables you to quickly change standard dimensions to oblique dimensions.

Creating Oblique Dimensions

1. Begin a new drawing named 086???03 in your assigned directory using 086OBLIQ as a prototype.

2. `Command:` *Choose* Modify, *then* Edit Dims, *then* Oblique Dimension — Issues the OBLIQUE dimensioning command

```
_dim1
Dim: _oblique
```

3. `Select objects: ALL ↵` — Specifies all entities in the drawing

```
21 found
```

4. `Select objects:` *Press* Enter	Ends selection
5. `Enter obliquing angle (RETURN for none): -45` ↵	Specifies oblique angle

Your drawing should resemble figure 86.10.

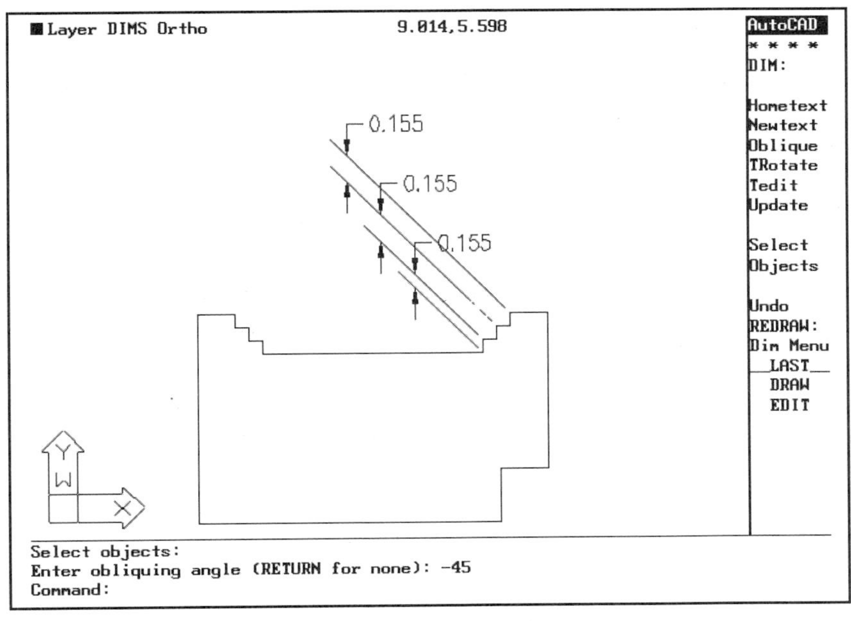

Figure 86.10

Oblique dimensions.

Unit Review

What You've Learned

- Commands: NEWTEXT, TROTATE, TEDIT, HOMETEXT, OBLIQUE, UPDATE
- How to modify associative dimensions with dimensioning edit commands
- How to update dimensions

Review Questions

True or False

86.01 T F When you use TROTATE, you can rotate the text within a dimension.

86.02 T F When you use TEDIT, you can change the value of dimension text.

86.03 T F NEWTEXT is used for changing the value of dimension text.

86.04 T F HOMETEXT sets the User Coordinate System at the definition point of the dimension text.

86.05 T F OBLIQUE is used to offset dimensions by a user-specified angle to make them easier to read.

86.06 T F The DIMSTYLE command can be used to change styles assigned to a dimension.

86.07 T F You cannot change the text location of an associative dimension.

86.08 T F You can relocate dimension text using grips.

86.09 T F You can change a dimension from one style to another by using the UPDATE dimensioning command.

86.10 T F You cannot enter a negative angle in response to the OBLIQUE dimensioning command.

Additional Exercises

86.11 Begin a new drawing named 086???11 in your assigned directory using 086SLIDE as a prototype. Create a dimension style named TOL_P1_M3 with a DIMTP value of 0.1 and a DIMTM value of 0.3.

Student: ____________________ Date: ________

Instructor: ____________________ Course: ________ Section: ________

Use the UPDATE dimensioning command to update all of the dimensions to the new TOL_P1_M3 style. Save your drawing.

86.12 Begin a new drawing named ???SLIDE in your assigned directory using 086SLD2 as a prototype. Make the dimension style DUAL current, then completely dimension the drawing using dual dimensioning. Use the correct dimensioning technique when applying the dimensions.

When you have finished dimensioning the drawing, insert a title block in paper space and compose the drawing for plotting. Save your drawing. Next, save the drawing to a new file named ???STD in your assigned directory. Make the STD dimension style current, then update all of the dimensions to use the STD style. Save your drawing. You should have two drawings: one using the STD style, and one using the DUAL style.

Student: ____________ Date: ________

Instructor: ____________ Course: ________ Section: ________

PART IX

Working with Boundaries, Inquiry, and Areas

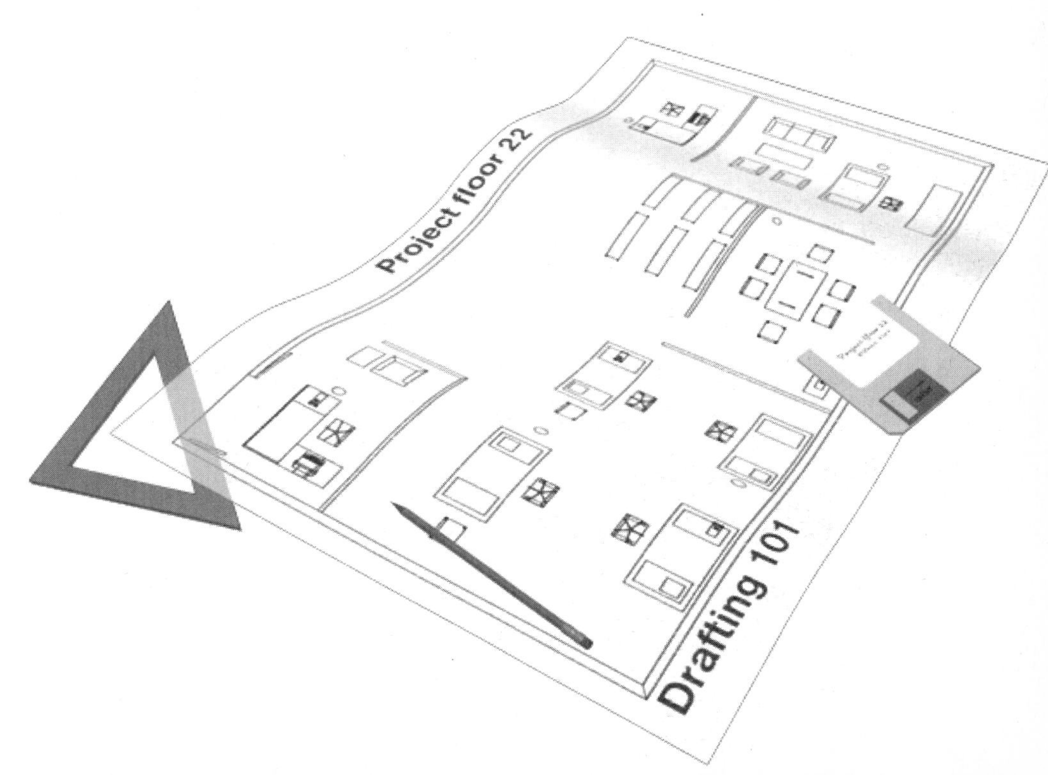

UNIT 87

Introduction to Hatching

An important part of many drawings is *crosshatching* (also called *hatching* or *section lining*). Hatching is used in sectional views to denote material cut by a cutting plane. Various types of standard hatch patterns are used to denote specific types of materials. Hatching also is used in other types of drawings to fill areas with a pattern.

While hatching a drawing using manual techniques is time-consuming, AutoCAD makes it a simple task. AutoCAD provides a wide range of standard hatch patterns and makes it possible to hatch an area in a matter of seconds. This unit teaches you to use a selection of AutoCAD's command to hatch areas.

The objectives for this unit are to:

- Understand how hatching (section lining) is applied to a drawing in AutoCAD
- Set hatch options for hatch pattern, scale, and angle
- Apply a hatch using BHATCH

Understanding Hatching

AutoCAD provides two methods to apply a hatch to a drawing. The HATCH command and the BHATCH command both enable you to apply a hatch to the drawing (see fig. 87.1). The HATCH command is limited in its capability to recognize hatch boundaries, and often does not work very well. The BHATCH command is a much better alternative because it works well, offers options not available in the HATCH command, and provides dialog boxes that you can use to set hatch options. This unit teaches you to hatch using the BHATCH command. The HATCH command is not covered in *Hands On AutoCAD.*

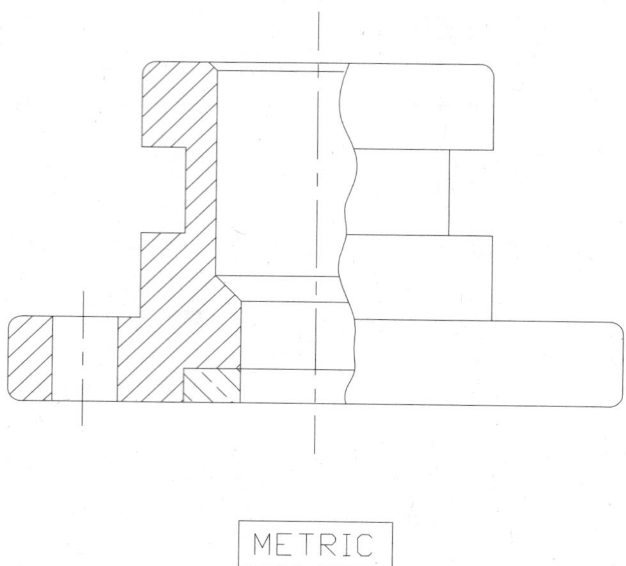

Figure 87.1
Hatch created in AutoCAD.

To hatch an area in AutoCAD, you must specify a few parameters, including the pattern to be used for the hatch, the scale of the pattern, and its angle. After you specify these parameters, you have two ways to define the area to be hatched. The easiest method is to pick a point inside the area and let AutoCAD automatically determine where the hatch should be applied. The second method is to pick the entities that enclose the area to be hatched. This second method is sometimes more time consuming, but is necessary in some situations in which AutoCAD is cannot properly detect the area to be hatched. It also is useful when you need to define a complex boundary for your hatch.

Regardless of the method you choose, AutoCAD automatically applies the hatch to the area you specify. A *hatch* is a special kind of block (blocks are explained in unit 67, "Introduction to Blocks"). AutoCAD recognizes an entire hatch as a single entity. You can select it with a single pick, erase it, and perform other editing options on the hatch without having to select individual lines in the hatch. If you explode a hatch, it breaks down into its constituent line segments. You then can erase or modify individual lines in the hatch.

It is generally not a good idea to explode a hatch because it can be very difficult to edit the entire hatch to change color, linetype, layer, and so on, or to erase the hatch. If you cannot make the necessary change to the hatch, consider erasing the hatch, rehatching the area, and applying the necessary change as you do so.

Working with Hatch Options

One of the steps in applying a hatch is to set the parameters that determine how the hatch looks when you apply it. This includes specifying the pattern, scale, and angle for the hatch. The *pattern* determines the arrangement and type of lines used for the hatch. AutoCAD provides 53 predefined hatch patterns. You can change the scale and angle of these patterns to achieve exactly the style of hatch you need. You also can define your own hatch patterns, although doing so can be difficult and is beyond the scope of *Hands On AutoCAD*.

The angle of a hatch pattern determines the rotation of the pattern relative to its original orientation. Specifying an angle of zero degrees does not necessarily result in a horizontal pattern. This is because the pattern may have been defined at a specific angle. Figure 87.2 shows the same pattern in two different areas. The pattern at the left is applied with an angle of zero degrees, and the pattern on the right is applied with an angle of 45 degrees.

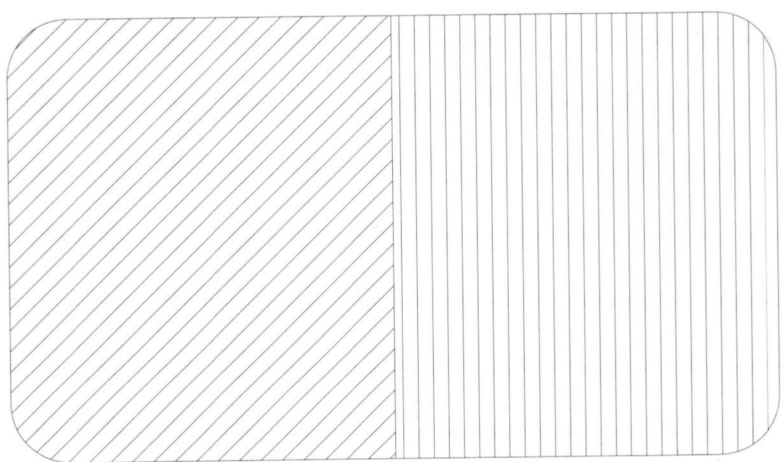

Figure 87.2

The same pattern at zero and 45 degrees.

Note that the lines in the pattern at the left are at 45 degrees, even though the pattern was applied with an angle of zero degrees. This is because the original pattern defines the lines at 45 degrees. By rotating the pattern by 45 degrees (example at the right in fig. 87.2), the lines rotate from 45 degrees to 90 degrees.

The scale of the pattern affects the relative spacing between lines and spaces in the pattern. Figure 87.3 shows two areas hatched with the same pattern. The example at the left was applied with a scale of one, and the pattern at the right was applied with a scale of two.

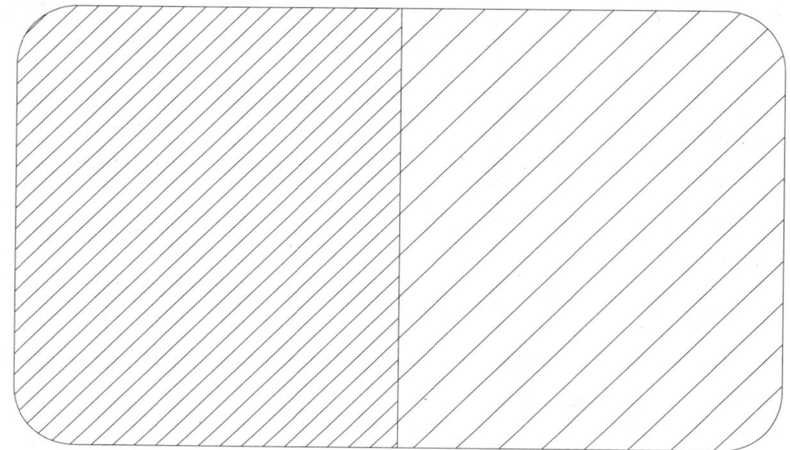

Figure 87.3

Pattern at scale of one and scale of two.

The patterns are defined such that you can use the scale of the drawing to determine the correct pattern scale. For a full-size standard drawing, for example, a scale of one generally works well. For a full-size metric drawing, a scale of 25.4 maintains a good spacing for the pattern.

AutoCAD's standard set of hatch patterns is stored in the file ACAD.PAT. If you create your own hatch pattern, it is stored in a file with a name that matches the name of the pattern. A pattern named FLOOD, for example, would be stored in a file named FLOOD.PAT

Setting Hatch Options

The BHATCH command provides a selection of dialog boxes that you can use to specify hatch options such as pattern, scale, and angle. In the following exercises, you work with a drawing of a bearing, and eventually will apply hatching to the section view. First, set the pattern, scale, and angle of the hatch.

Setting Hatch Options

1. Begin a new drawing named 087???01 in your assigned directory using 087BEARG as a prototype.

2. `Command:` *Choose* Draw, *then* Hatch — Issues the BHATCH command and displays the Boundary Hatch dialog box (see fig. 87.4)

   `bhatch`

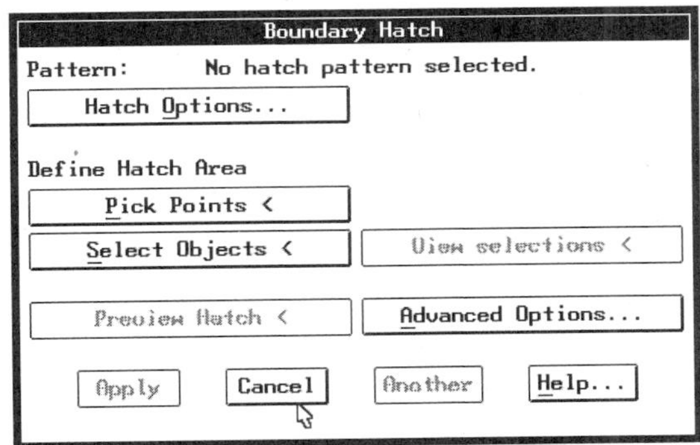

Figure 87.4

The Boundary Hatch dialog box.

3. *Choose the* Hatch Options *button* — Displays the Hatch Options dialog box (see fig. 87.5)

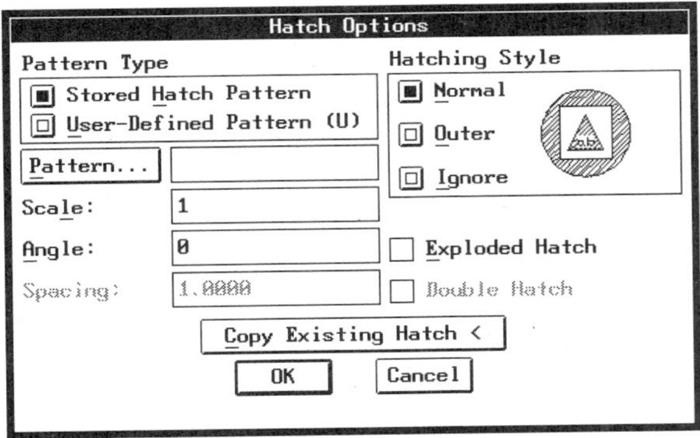

Figure 87.5

The Hatch Options dialog box.

4. *Enter* **25.4** *in the* Scale *edit box* — Specifies the scale of the pattern, setting it for a metric drawing

5. *Choose the* Pattern *button* — Displays the Choose Hatch Pattern dialog box (see fig. 87.6)

6. *Click on the* ANSI31 *tile* — Selects a standard general hatch pattern and returns to the Hatch Options dialog box

continues

Figure 87.6

The Choose Hatch Pattern dialog box.

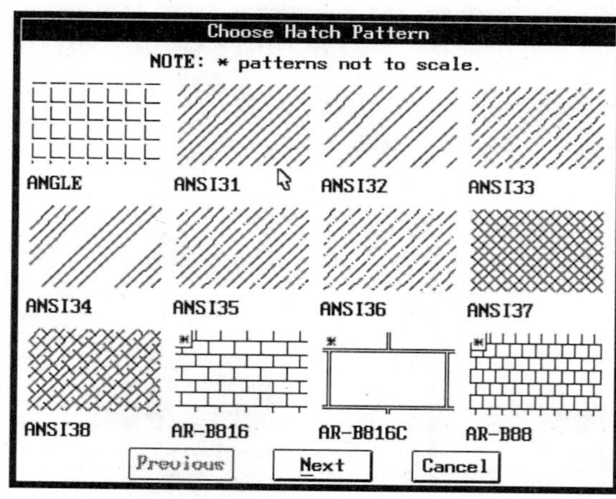

7. *Choose* OK — Returns to the Boundary Hatch dialog box

Do not exit the Boundary Hatch dialog box. You continue with it in the next exercise.

To choose a hatch pattern that does not appear on the current page of the Choose Hatch Pattern dialog box, choose the Next or Previous buttons as appropriate to locate the pattern you require.

Applying a Simple Hatch

The easiest way to apply a hatch is to pick a point inside the area to be hatched and let AutoCAD calculate where the hatch should be applied. In the following exercise, use this method to hatch the bearing. Figure 87.7 shows selection points for defining the hatch boundaries.

Applying a Simple Hatch

Continue with your drawing from the preceding exercise. The Boundary Hatch dialog box should still be displayed.

1. *Choose the* Pick Points *button*

2. `Select internal point` *Pick a point at ① (see fig. 87.7)* — Specifies a point inside the boundary to be hatched

```
Selecting everything...
Selecting everything visible...
Analyzing the selected data
```

3. `Select internal point` *Pick a point at ② (see fig. 87.7)* — Specifies another boundary to include in the hatch

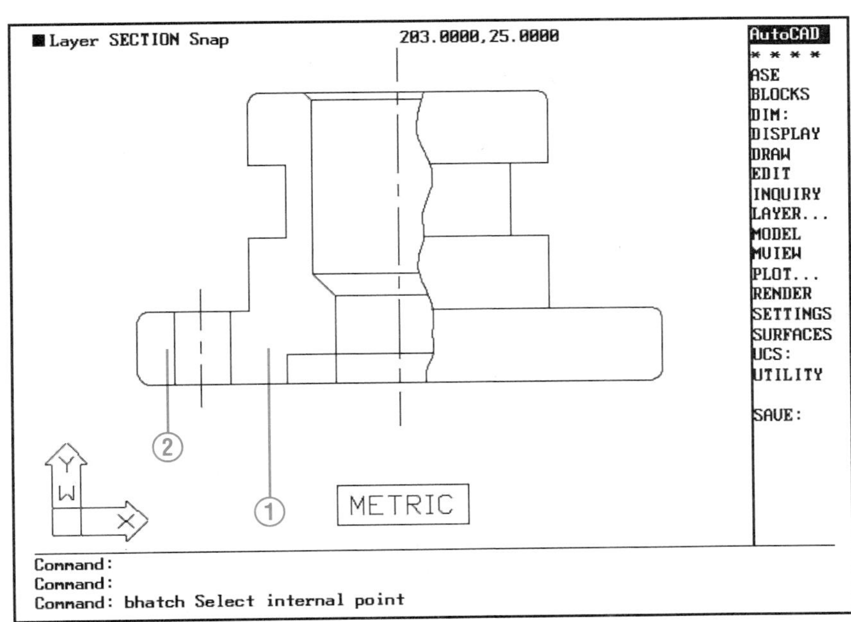

Figure 87.7

Selection points for BHATCH.

4. `Select internal point` *Press* Enter	Ends selection and redisplays the Boundary Hatch dialog box
5. *Choose the* Apply *button*	Applies the hatch
6. Save your drawing.	

Your drawing should resemble figure 87.8.

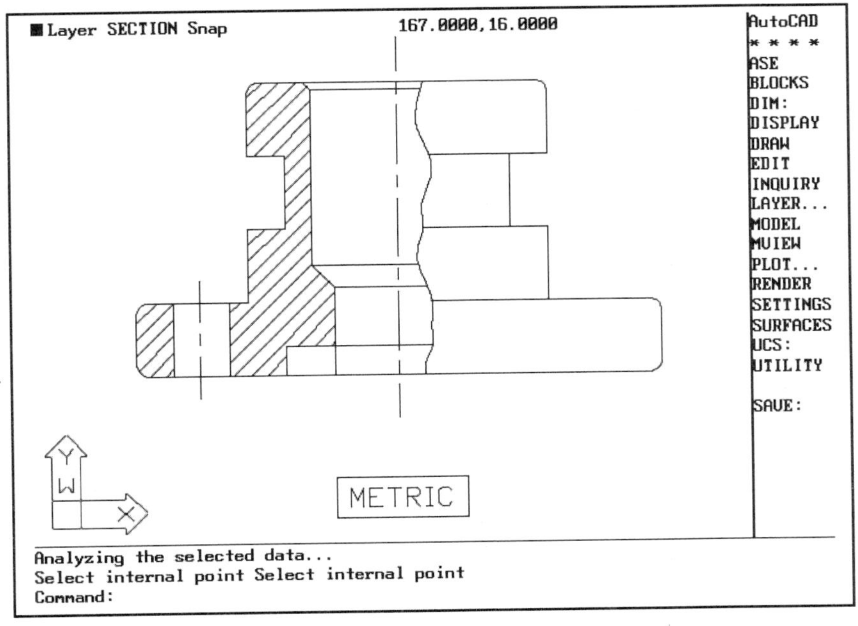

Figure 87.8

Results of BHATCH.

Applying a hatch is a simple process if the boundary you are attempting to hatch is closed (make sure you pay attention for this). If the boundary is open, AutoCAD displays a Boundary Definition Error dialog box informing you that the boundary is open. If you select the button labeled Look at it, AutoCAD displays the boundary and draws a line indicating the general location of the break in the boundary. Choosing OK enables you to select a different boundary.

If the boundary is not closed, you can use the Select Objects method to define the entities to be hatched, but this still may not result in a correct hatch. The best solution in most cases is to cancel the hatch operation and correct the drawing geometry to form a closed boundary. Another good way to create a boundary is with the PLINE command.

Unit Review

What You've Learned

- Commands: BHATCH
- How to specify pattern, scale, and angle options for a hatch
- How to apply a hatch to an area using the BHATCH command

Review Questions

True or False

87.01 T F Hatching also is referred to as section lining.

87.02 T F Hatching is used in sectional views to denote material cut by a cutting plane.

87.03 T F You can edit the individual lines in a hatch as soon as you apply the hatch.

87.04 T F Exploding a hatch breaks it into its individual line segments.

87.05 T F A hatch is a special type of Xref.

87.06 T F The BHATCH command is often a better choice than the HATCH command for applying a hatch.

Multiple Choice

87.07 The __________ affects the spacing between lines and segments in a hatch pattern.

(A) pattern scale

(B) pattern angle

(C) BHATCH variable

(D) location of the boundary points

87.08 To apply an ANSI31 hatch so that the hatch lines will be vertical, the angle should be set to __________ degrees.

(A) 0

(B) 45

(C) 90

Student: __________________ Date: __________

Instructor: __________________ Course: __________ Section: __________

87.09 A hatch is a special kind of __________.

(A) linetype

(B) block

(C) fill mode

87.10 Before you can edit individual line segments in a hatch, you must use the __________ command on the hatch.

(A) EXPLODE

(B) DDCHPROP

(C) HATCH

(D) HATCHEDIT

Additional Exercises

87.11 Continue working with your bearing drawing. Apply another hatch using the BRASS pattern. Specify an angle that gives you a hatch that matches the one shown in figure 87.9. Use a scale of 25.4 for the BRASS hatch. Save your drawing.

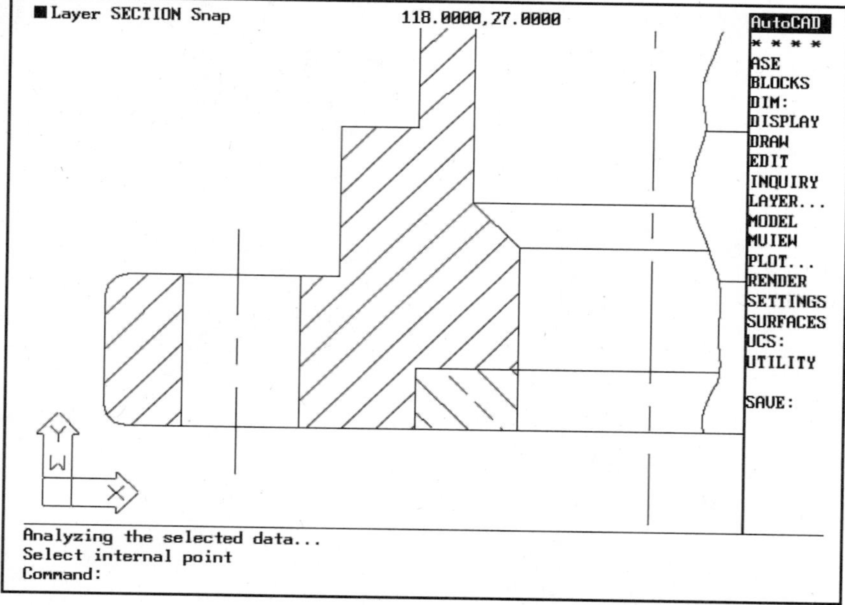

Figure 87.9 *BRASS hatch applied to the drawing.*

87.12 Begin a new drawing named 087???12 in your assigned directory using 087WHEEL as a prototype. Apply the ANSI31 pattern in the proper locations on the section view. Save your drawing when you are finished. Consult with your instructor if you are unsure of where to apply the hatching.

Student: ______ Date: ______

Instructor: ______ Course: ______ Section: ______

UNIT 88

Advanced Hatch Options

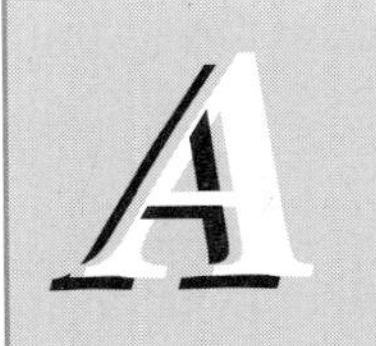

A hatch does not always fill an entire area. Sometimes the area includes voids (such as holes) or text that should not be covered by the hatch. Or, you may want to hatch over interior features. AutoCAD provides advanced features to handle these situations. This unit teaches you how to apply hatches correctly in these situations.

The objectives for this unit are to:

- ☞ Hatch around voids and text
- ☞ Define a boundary set
- ☞ Retain a boundary during hatching

Hatching around Voids and Text

Unit 87, "Introduction to Hatching," explained how you can use the BHATCH command to quickly hatch one or more closed boundaries. In most situations, you can simply pick points inside the boundaries where you want the hatch to be applied, and AutoCAD correctly applies the hatch. In some cases, however, you must use other selection and hatch methods to apply the hatch. If a boundary contains text, for example, you cannot simply pick a point inside the boundary to apply the hatch. If you do, AutoCAD hatches over the text.

In other situations, you may want to hatch over interior features. AutoCAD provides hatching options that enable you to control the way BHATCH handles interior features. You can cause BHATCH to hatch every other boundary, only the outermost boundary, or hatch everything inside the outer boundary. Figure 88.1 shows the same object hatched with each of these three options.

Figure 88.1

Internal boundary hatch options.

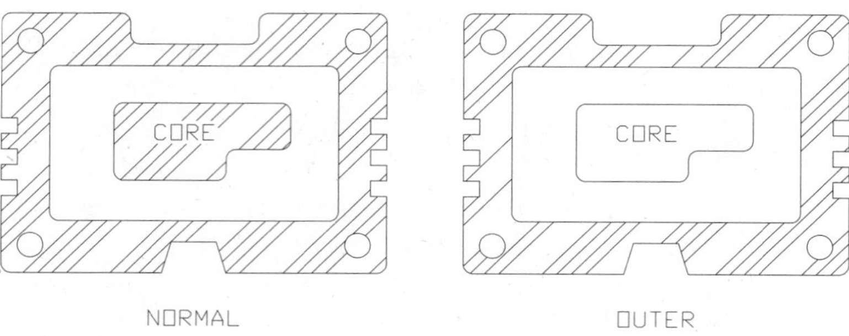

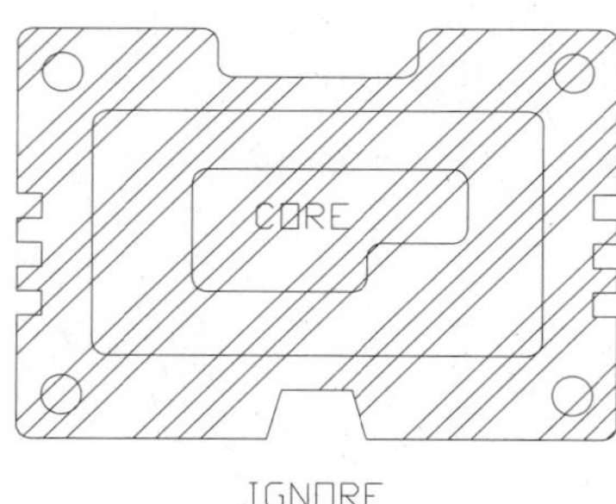

In the following exercises, hatch the molded rubber part shown in figure 88.2. First, try hatching the core boundary by picking an internal point.

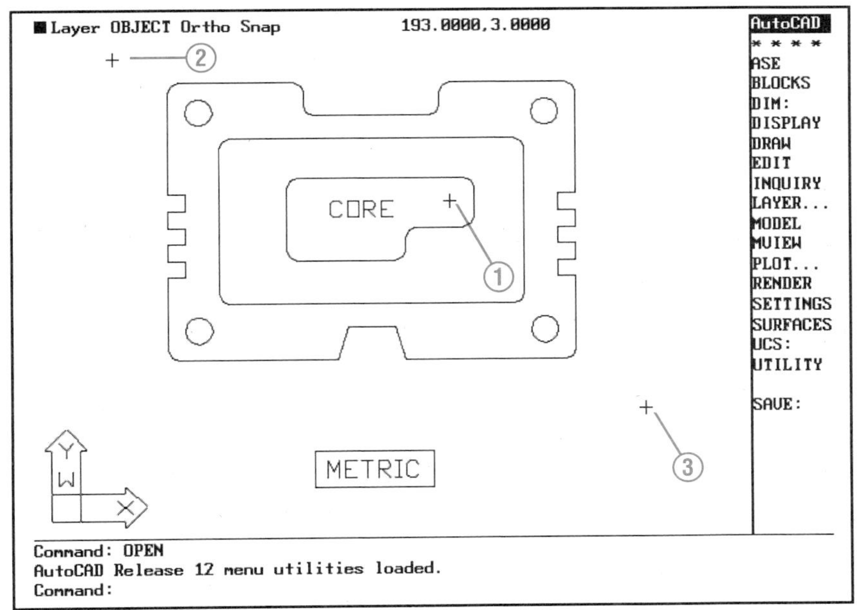

Figure 88.2

Selection points for hatch.

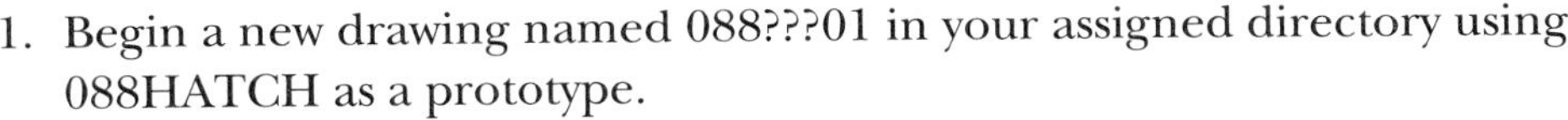

Hatching Embedded Voids

1. Begin a new drawing named 088???01 in your assigned directory using 088HATCH as a prototype.

2. `Command:` *Choose* Draw, *then* Hatch	Issues the BHATCH command and displays the Boundary Hatch dialog box
`bhatch`	
3. *Choose the* Hatch Options *button and set the hatch pattern to* ANSI34, Scale *to* 25.4, *and* Angle *to* 0, *then choose* OK	Sets hatch pattern, scale, and angle
4. *In the* Boundary Hatch *dialog box, choose the* Pick Points *button*	Chooses the pick point to define boundary
5. `Select internal point` *Pick a point at* ① *(see fig. 88.2)*	Specifies internal point

`Selecting everything...`
`Selecting everything visible...`
`Analyzing the selected data`	

6. `Select internal point` *Press* Enter	Ends selection
7. *In the* Boundary Hatch *dialog box, choose the* Preview Hatch *button*	Displays the hatch (see fig. 88.3)

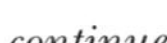
continues

8. `Press RETURN to continue.` *Press* Enter	Redisplays the Boundary Hatch dialog box
9. *Choose* Cancel	Cancels the hatch operation

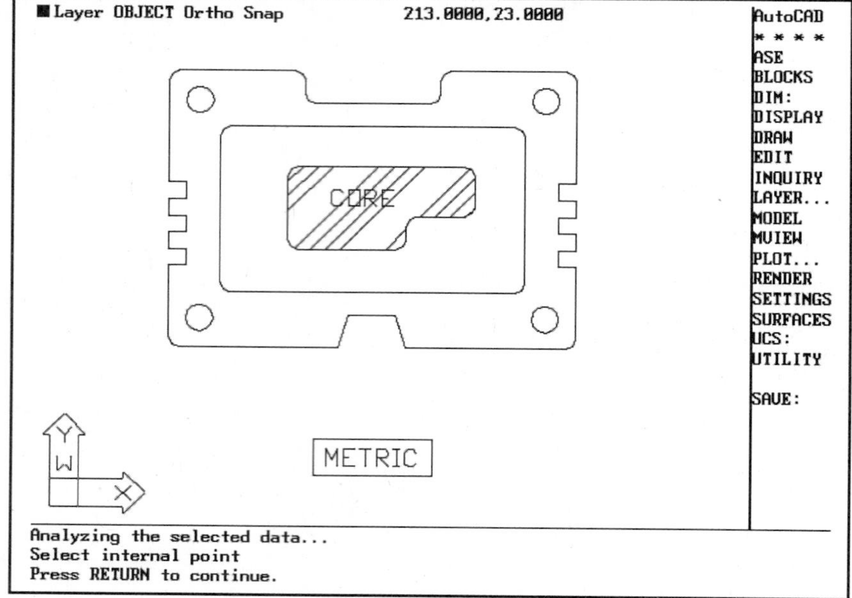

Figure 88.3
First hatch applied.

In the preceding exercise, AutoCAD hatches over the text. To prevent AutoCAD from hatching over internal features, you often need to use entity selection rather than point selection to define the boundary to be hatched. In the following exercise, use entity selection to hatch the object. You use each of the three boundary recognition options to see how they work.

Hatching Over Interior Features

Continue with your drawing from the preceding exercise.

1. `Command:` *Choose* Draw, *then* Hatch	Issues the BHATCH command and displays the Boundary Hatch dialog box
`bhatch`	
2. *Choose the* Hatch Options *button*	Displays the Hatch Options dialog box
3. *Choose the* Ignore *radio button, then* OK	Sets BHATCH to ignore interior features when hatching and returns to Boundary Hatch dialog box

4. *Choose the* Select Objects *button*	Chooses to select entities to define the boundary
5. `Select objects:` *Pick points at* ② *and* ③ *(see fig. 88.2)* `69 found`	Selects all the entities in the part
6. `Select objects:` *Press* Enter	Ends selection and redisplays the Boundary Hatch dialog box
7. *Choose the* Preview Hatch *button*	Displays the hatch (see fig. 88.4)
8. `Press RETURN to continue.` *Press* Enter	Redisplays Boundary Hatch dialog box

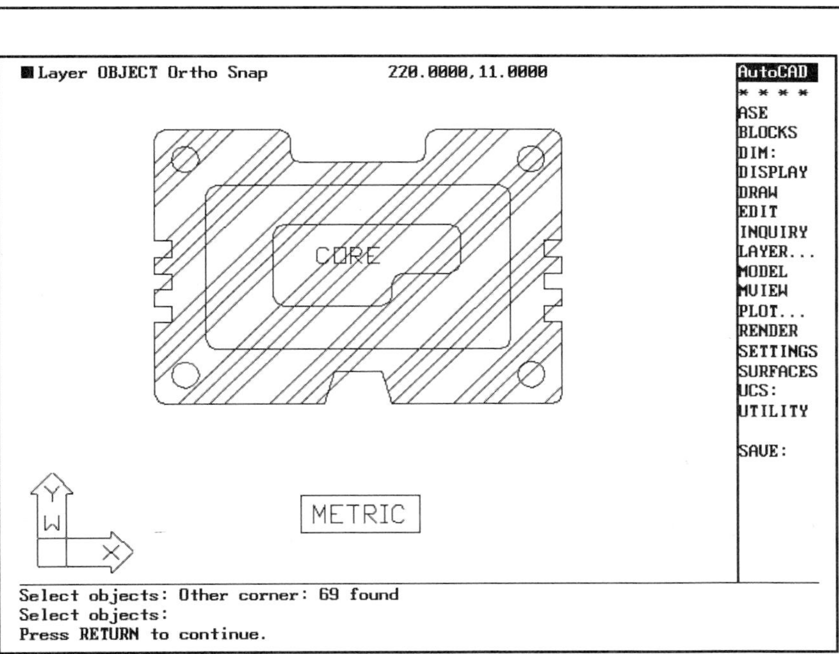

Figure 88.4

Results of Ignore option.

In the preceding exercise, AutoCAD hatches everything inside the outer boundary, ignoring all inner boundaries and features. Note also that AutoCAD did not correctly hatch the part. The hatch extends outside the boundary at the bottom and sides of the part.

Next, use the Outer option to hatch just the outermost boundary.

Hatching Outermost Boundary Only

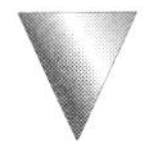

Continue with your drawing from the preceding exercise. The Boundary Hatch dialog box should still be displayed.

continues

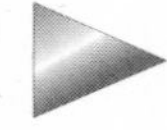

1. *Choose the* Hatch Options *button, choose the* Outer *radio button, then choose* OK	Displays the Hatch Options dialog box, sets boundary recognition option, and returns to Boundary Hatch dialog box
2. *Choose the* Preview Hatch *button*	Displays the hatch (see fig.88.5)
3. `Press RETURN to continue.` *Press* Enter	Redisplays Boundary Hatch dialog box

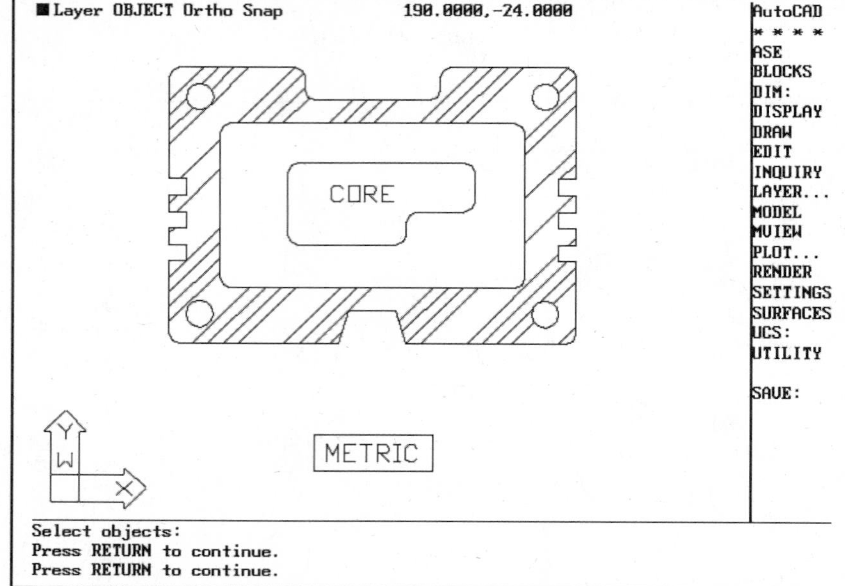

Figure 88.5
Results of Outer option.

AutoCAD changes the hatch to include only the outermost boundary. Note that the boundary is now hatched correctly—the hatch does not extend outside the boundary. However, the inner boundary still is not hatched. Use the Normal option to change the hatch.

Hatching with the Normal Option

Continue with your drawing from the preceding exercise. The Boundary Hatch dialog box should still be displayed.

1. *Choose the* Hatch Options *button, choose the* Normal *radio button, then choose* OK	Displays the Hatch Options dialog box, sets boundary recognition option, and returns to Boundary Hatch dialog box
2. *Choose the* Apply *button*	Applies the hatch (see fig. 88.6)
3. Save your drawing.	

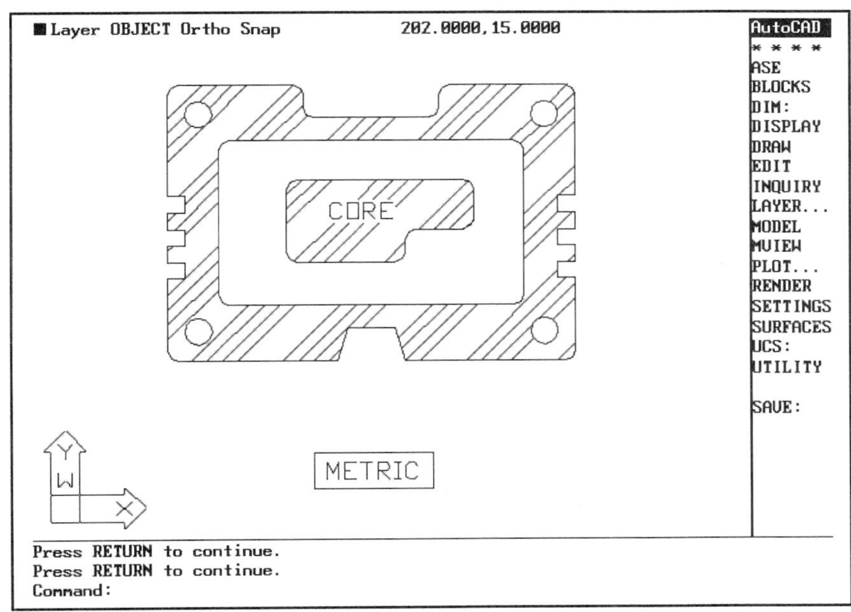

Figure 88.6

Results of Normal option.

When you use the Normal option and select entities to define the hatch, AutoCAD usually recognizes correctly the interior features and hatches accordingly. In this case, AutoCAD hatches around the text inside the core boundary.

Whether you choose the Normal, Outer, or Ignore option depends on the results you need to achieve. Use Normal to hatch embedded voids and boundaries. Use Outer to hatch only the outermost boundary. Use Ignore to hatch everything inside the outer boundary.

Defining a Boundary Set

AutoCAD provides features for defining and retaining boundaries as part of the BHATCH command. This unit focuses on one of these features: the capability to retain a boundary.

When AutoCAD analyzes a drawing to define a hatch boundary, it creates the boundary as a polyline. AutoCAD then uses this polyline to apply the hatch. By default, AutoCAD deletes the polyline when it completes the hatch. You can, however, direct AutoCAD to retain the polyline. This capability is useful if you want to duplicate the boundary to use elsewhere.

In the following exercise, delete the hatch you have now and reapply it, this time retaining the boundary.

Retaining a Boundary

1. Begin a new drawing named 088???02 in your assigned directory using 088POLY as a prototype.

2. Command: *Choose* Draw, *then* Hatch — Issues the BHATCH command and displays the Boundary Hatch dialog box

   `bhatch`

3. On your own, set the hatch pattern to ANSI34 and scale to 25.4.

4. *Choose the* Advanced Options *button* — Displays the Advanced Options dialog box (see fig. 88.7)

5. *Place a check in the* Retain Boundaries *check box, then choose* OK — Sets BHATCH to retain the boundary it creates for the hatch and redisplays the Boundary Hatch dialog box

6. *Choose the* Pick Points *button* — Chooses to pick point to define boundary

7. `Select internal point` *Pick a point inside the boundary* — Specifies internal point

   ```
   Selecting everything...
   Selecting everything visible...
   Analyzing the selected data
   ```

8. `Select internal point` *Press* Enter — Ends selection

9. *In the* Boundary Hatch *dialog box, choose the* Apply *button* — Applies the hatch (see fig. 88.8)

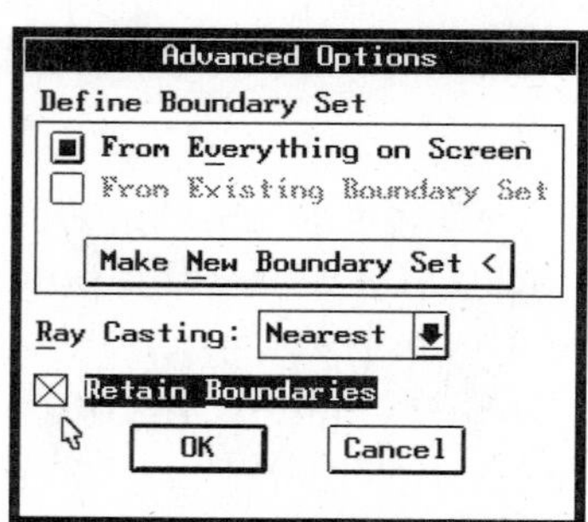

Figure 88.7

The Advanced Options dialog box.

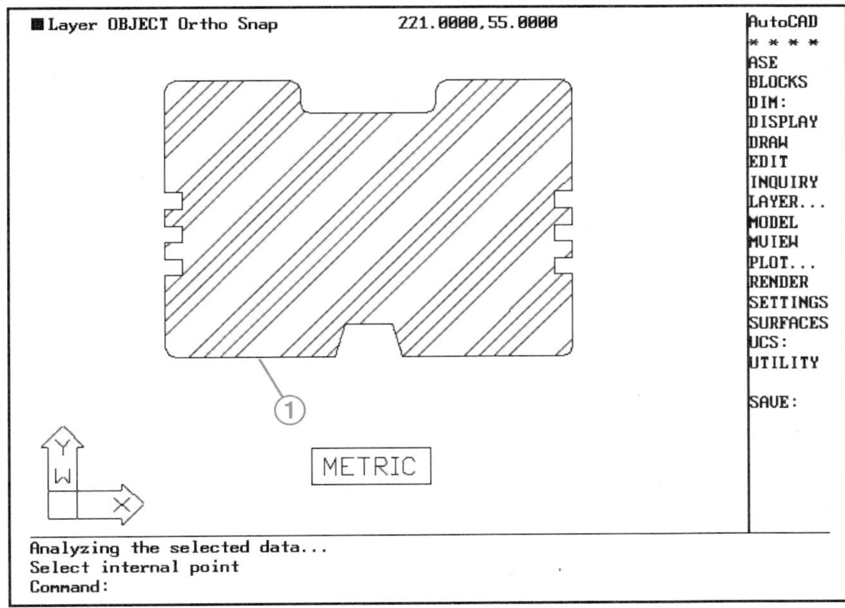

Figure 88.8

Hatch applied to boundary.

Although you cannot tell at this point, AutoCAD creates a polyline around the perimeter of the part. In the following exercise, move the boundary polyline off of the part.

Moving the Boundary Polyline

Continue with your drawing from the preceding exercise.

1. `Command:` *Pick a point at* ① *(see fig. 88.8)*	Selects the polyline boundary
2. `Command:` **`M`** ↵	Issues the alias for the MOVE command
`MOVE 1 found`	
3. `Base point or displacement:` *Pick any point*	Specifies base point
4. `Second point of displacement:` **`@130,0`** ↵	Specifies displacement

5. Issue ZOOM with the Extents option. Your drawing should look similar to figure 88.9.

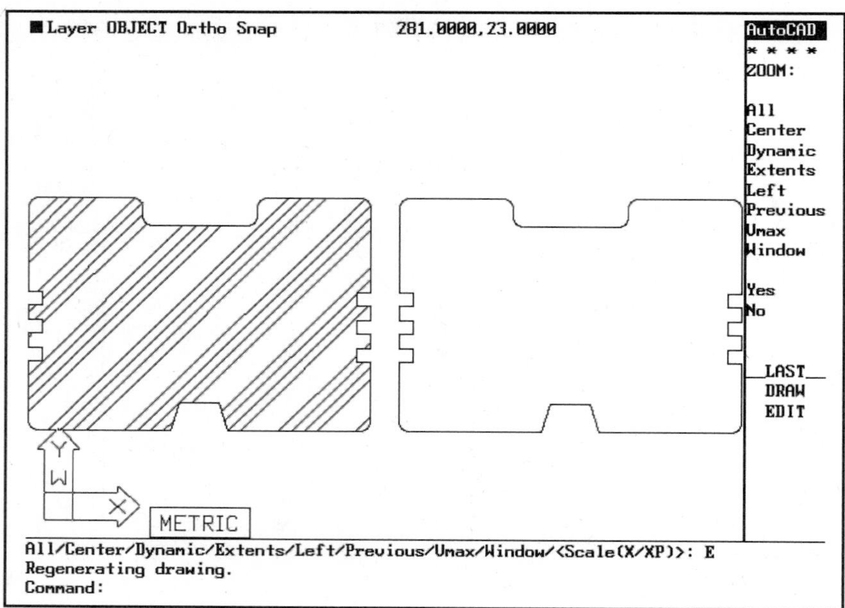

Figure 88.9

Boundary moved away from part.

TIP

Retaining the boundary in this way provides a means to form a polyline from existing non-polyline entities. The BPOLY command also enables you to define a polyline boundary, but does so outside the BHATCH command. You can use BPOLY in place of PEDIT to convert entities into a polyline. BPOLY is explained in unit 89, "Working with Areas."

Unit Review

What You've Learned

- Commands: BHATCH
- How to hatch around text
- How to hatch inner voids
- How to retain a boundary during hatching

Review Questions

True or False

88.01 T F BHATCH always hatches around text.

88.02 T F You can select entities to define a boundary instead of picking an internal point.

88.03 T F You cannot select entities to hatch with a window.

88.04 T F The Normal option causes BHATCH to hatch only the outermost boundary.

88.05 T F The Ignore option causes BHATCH to hatch over internal features.

88.06 T F The Outer option causes BHATCH to apply the hatch outside the boundary, rather than inside.

88.07 T F When AutoCAD creates a hatch boundary, it creates the boundary as a polyline.

88.08 T F By default, AutoCAD retains the polyline boundaries it creates during BHATCH, placing them on a special layer.

88.09 T F You cannot edit a polyline boundary created by BHATCH.

88.10 T F BHATCH never applies hatch lines outside a boundary.

Student: ____________________ Date: ________

Instructor: ____________________ Course: ________ Section: ________

UNIT 89

Working with Areas

Many design disciplines require that you calculate the area of boundaries. For example, you might need to determine the number of square feet in a room or building to estimate building cost. Or, perhaps you need to figure the surface area of a part to determine its weight or the amount of protective coating required to cover it. Whatever the situation, it is a fairly easy task to determine the area of a boundary in AutoCAD. This unit teaches you to use the AREA and BPOLY commands to work with areas.

The objectives for this unit are to:

- Calculate the area of a simple boundary
- Correctly calculate the area of a boundary containing voids
- Determine the perimeter of a boundary
- Create a boundary polyline using the BPOLY command

Determining Area and Perimeter

The AREA command enables you to determine the area and perimeter of a boundary. The boundary can be either open or closed, depending on the method you use to calculate the area. The AREA command displays the results of its calculation at the command prompt area, and also stores the area and perimeter in two system variables, AREA and PERIMETER. Both of these variables are read-only, which means that you cannot change them directly. They can be changed only as the result of a calculation by the AREA command.

The AREA command provides three methods for defining the boundary, and these methods are described in the following list:

- **Point selection.** You can pick points to define a boundary and AutoCAD calculates the area and perimeter of the boundary. This method is somewhat limited, because you can only define a boundary that has corners—you cannot create a complex boundary that is curved or contains curved segments. This method is useful for deriving a quick estimate of an area or for working with simple boundaries.
- **Entity selection.** You can select a circle or a polyline to include in a boundary. This enables you to select fairly complex boundary sets, but they must consist of these two types of entities.
- **Add and subtract options.** The AREA command offers two modes for selecting entities for the area calculation. The default option adds to the set. You also can subtract areas, which is useful for subtracting voids from inside a larger boundary.

To see how the AREA command works, use it to calculate the area of a simple steel plate. In the following exercise, calculate the overall area of the part, but do not subtract the holes or slot from the area. Snap is turned on in the prototype to make it easy for you to select points without using object snap modes.

Calculating a Simple Area

1. Begin a new drawing named 089???01 in your assigned directory using 089AREA as a prototype.

2. `Command:` *Choose* Assist, *then* Inquiry, *then* Area — Issues the AREA command

   `_area`

3. `<First point>/Entity/Add/Subtract:` *Pick a point at* ① *(see fig. 89.1)* — Specifies the first point of the boundary

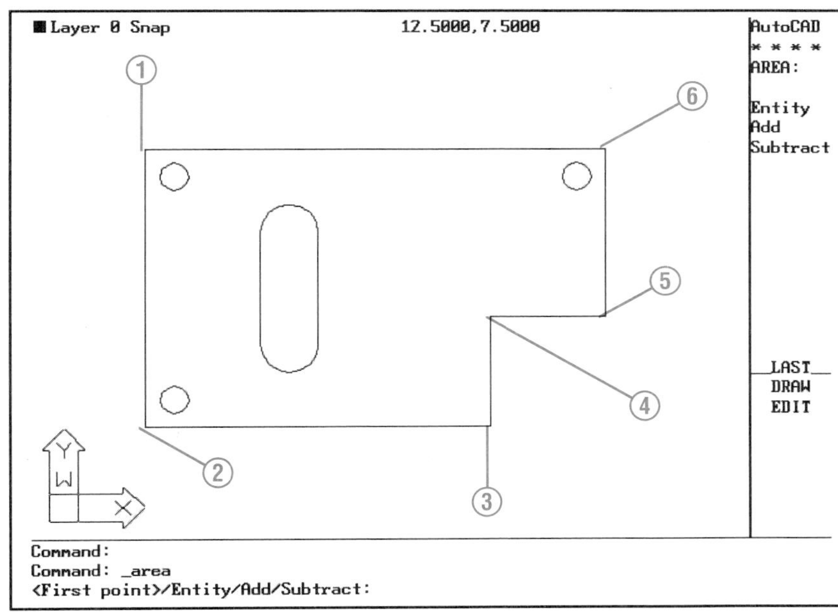

Figure 89.1

Selection points for AREA.

4. `Next point:` *Pick points at* ② *through* ⑥ *(see fig. 89.1)*
5. `Next point:` *Press* Enter — Ends selection and displays the area and perimeter

```
Area = 36.0000, Perimeter = 26.000
```

AutoCAD calculates the area and perimeter and displays the values in the command prompt area. The area is correct only if you want the overall area of the part and do not want to subtract the interior holes and slot. To calculate the true area of the part, you must subtract these interior features.

One method to subtract the interior features is to calculate their areas separately, and then subtract them manually from the overall area using a calculator. In the following exercise, take the first step in that process and calculate the area of the slot.

Calculating the Area of the Slot

Continue with your drawing from the preceding exercise.

1. `Command:` *Choose* Assist, *then* Inquiry, *then* Area — Issues the AREA command

   `_area`

2. `<First point>/Entity/Add/Subtract:` **`E`** ↵ — Chooses the Entity option

continues

3. Select circle or polyline: *Select the slot* — Selects the polyline and displays its area and perimeter

   Area = 2.7854, Perimeter = 7.1416

Calculating and subtracting each interior feature manually is time-consuming and introduces the possibility of error. To simplify the task, use AutoCAD's capability to add and subtract entities from the calculation. The next section explains how.

Subtracting Interior Features

The outer perimeter of the part and the interior slot are drawn as polylines. The holes are drawn as circles. Because the AREA command works with polylines and circles, you can accurately determine the area of the part, subtracting the holes and slot. To do so, you must use the Entity option in combination with the Add and Subtract options.

In the following exercise, enter Add mode, and then select the outer polyline. Enter Subtract mode, and then subtract the holes and the slot. AutoCAD handles the calculation, subtracting the interior features from the overall area.

Using Add and Subtract Modes

Continue with your drawing from the preceding exercise.

1. Command: *Choose* Assist, *then* Inquiry, *then* Area — Issues the AREA command

   _area

2. <First point>/Entity/Add/Subtract: **A** ↵ — Enters Add mode

3. <First point>/Entity/Subtract: **E** ↵ — Specifies the Entity option

4. (ADD mode) Select circle or polyline: *Select the polyline at* ① *(see fig. 89.2)* — Starts the area calculation and displays the area of the boundary

   Area = 36.0000, Perimeter = 26.0000
   Total area = 36.0000

5. (ADD mode) Select circle or polyline: *Press* Enter — Exits Add mode

6. <First point>/Entity/Subtract: **S** ↵ — Enters Subtract mode

7. <First point>/Entity/Add: **E** ↵ — Specifies the Entity option

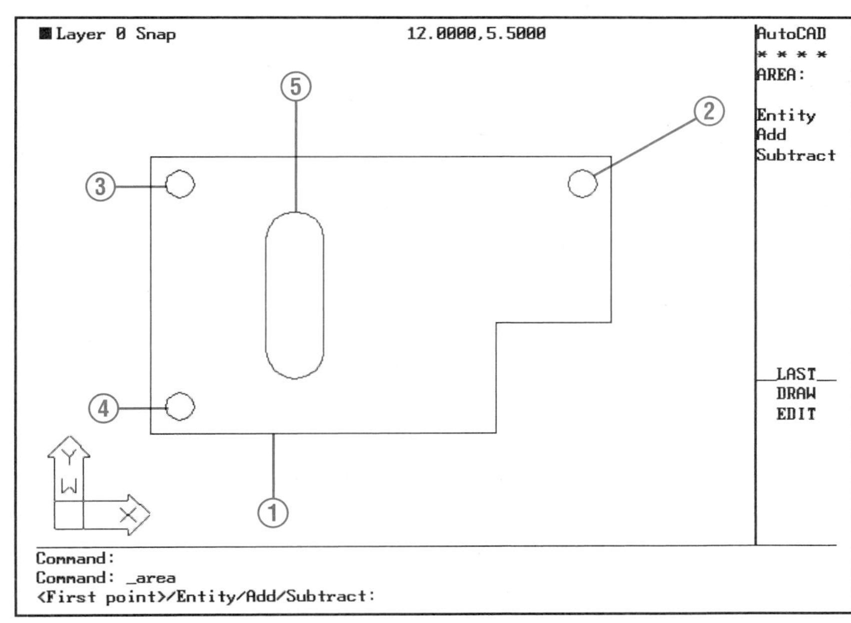

Figure 89.2

Selection points for total area.

8. `(SUBTRACT mode) Select circle or polyline:` *Select the circle at* ② *(see fig. 89.2)*
`Area = 0.1963, Circumference = 1.5708`
`Total area = 35.8037`
	Subtracts the area of the circle from the overall area

9. `(SUBTRACT mode) Select circle or polyline:` *Select the circle at* ③ *(see fig. 89.2)*
`Area = 0.1963, Circumference = 1.5708`
`Total area = 35.6073`
	Subtracts the area of the circle from the overall area

10. `(SUBTRACT mode) Select circle or polyline:` *Select the circle at* ④ *(see fig. 89.2)*
`Area = 0.1963, Circumference = 1.5708`
`Total area = 35.4110`
	Subtracts the area of the circle from the overall area

11. `(SUBTRACT mode) Select circle or polyline:` *Select the slot at* ⑤
`Area = 2.7854, Perimeter = 7.1416`
`Total area = 32.6256`
	Subtracts the area of the slot from the overall area

12. `(SUBTRACT mode) Select circle or polyline:` *Press* Enter	Exits Subtract mode
13. `<First point>/Entity/Add:` *Press* Enter	Ends the AREA command

The area of the object is 32.6256, which AutoCAD calculated by subtracting the area of the three circles and the slot from the overall area of the outer polyline.

You can switch back and forth between Add and Subtract modes as necessary. You also can mix point selection with entity selection to define the boundary to be calculated.

Developing a Boundary with BPOLY

If you already worked through unit 88 "Advanced Hatch Options," you know that the BHATCH command includes an option that automatically generates a polyline boundary when you hatch an area. The BPOLY command provides the same function without generating a hatch. BPOLY enables you to create a polyline that bounds an area. BPOLY can be very useful in helping you calculate the area of complex boundaries.

Assume that you need to calculate the square footage of rooms in a building so that you can order the proper amount of flooring. In the following exercise, use the BPOLY command to quickly generate a polyline that you can use to calculate the area of a room. Figure 89.3 shows the drawing of the building with which you will be working. Figure 89.4 shows the room requiring the area calculation.

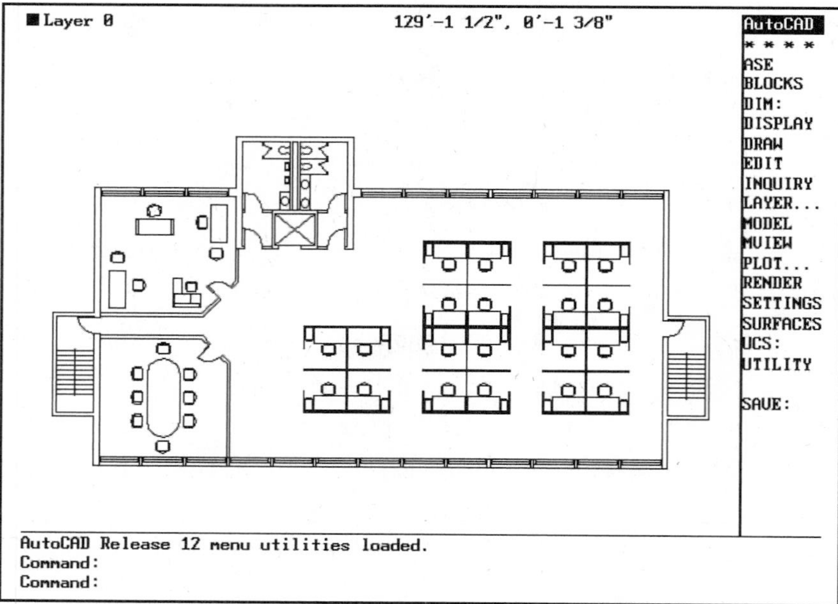

Figure 89.3

Office building for area calculation.

Because the BPOLY command does not automatically close a boundary for you, you must draw a line across the door opening to enable BPOLY to correctly define the polyline boundary.

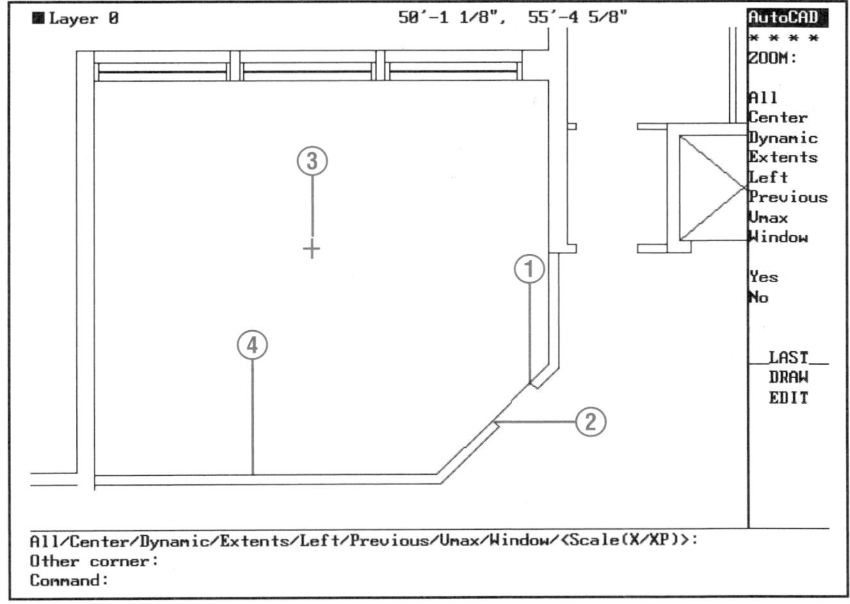

Figure 89.4

Room for calculation.

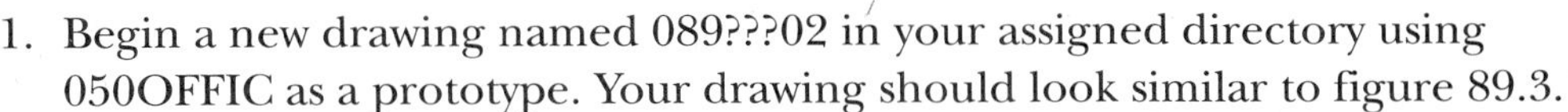

Using the BPOLY Command

1. Begin a new drawing named 089???02 in your assigned directory using 050OFFIC as a prototype. Your drawing should look similar to figure 89.3.

2. Issue the DDLMODES command and freeze layers DOOR, FIXT, FURN, and PARTITION. Then, zoom to the view shown in figure 89.4.

3. Draw a line from ① to ② (see fig. 89.4). Use object snap modes to snap to the endpoints of the existing lines.

4. `Command:` **`BPOLY`** ↵ — Issues the BPOLY command and displays the Polyline Creation dialog box (see fig. 89.5)

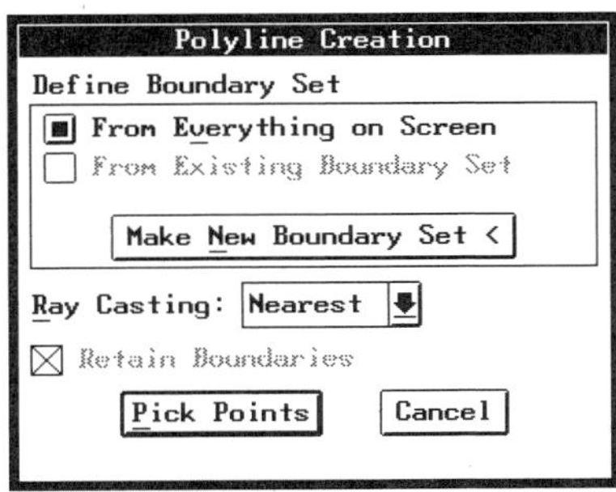

Figure 89.5

The Polyline Creation dialog box.

5. *Choose the* Pick Points *button*

continues

6. `Select internal point` *Pick a point at*③ *(see fig. 89.4)*	Specifies a point inside the boundary

`Selecting everything...`
`Selecting everything visible...`
`Analyzing the selected data...`	

7. `Select internal point` *Press* Enter	Ends selection and creates the polyline
8. `Command:` *Choose* Assist, *then* Inquiry, *then* Area	Issues the AREA command
`_area`	
9. `<First point>/Entity/Add/` **`Subtract: E`** ↵	Chooses the Entity option
10. `Select circle or polyline:` *Select the polyline at*④ *(see fig. 89.4)*	Selects the polyline and displays its area and perimeter
`Area = 77625.97 square in. (539.0692 square ft.), Perimeter = 91'-0 3/8"`	

AutoCAD uses the polyline to calculate the area and displays the results using the current units setting of feet and inches. It reports the area in square inches and in square feet.

BPOLY works well in many situations. In some cases, you must draw the polyline yourself because the geometry of the boundary is too complex. Simply draw the polyline over the existing entities, and then use the new polyline to calculate the area of the boundary. Place the polyline on a frozen layer or erase it when you are finished with it.

Unit Review

What You've Learned

- Commands: AREA, BPOLY
- How to calculate the area of a boundary
- How to add and subtract areas to determine a total area
- How to use BPOLY to create a polyline boundary

Review Questions

True or False

89.01 T F You can calculate the area of an open boundary by picking points around the perimeter of the boundary.

89.02 T F The AREA command stores calculated area and perimeter values in the AREA and PERIMETER system variables.

89.03 T F You can define a complex boundary with curves by picking points with the area command.

89.04 T F The AREA command accepts selection of circles, lines, and polylines.

89.05 T F To calculate the correct area of an object that contains holes or other voids, you must subtract the interior features manually.

89.06 T F You can mix point selection and entity selection to define a boundary for area calculation.

89.07 T F The BPOLY command applies a hatch inside a polyline boundary.

89.08 T F The AREA command optionally calculates the weight of an object based on its area.

Multiple Choice

89.09 The AREA command accepts selection of __________ and circles.

(A) lines

(B) arcs

(C) polylines

Student: ______________________ Date: __________

Instructor: ______________________ Course: __________ Section: __________

89.10 The __________ option of the AREA command makes it possible to calculate the true area of a boundary that contains voids.

(A) Bpoly

(B) Void

(C) Pick

(D) Subtract

Additional Exercises

89.11 Continue with your office drawing from the preceding exercise. Draw a polyline boundary around the main work area and hallway, and then determine the area. Enter the result in square feet: __________. Figure 89.6 shows the area to be calculated.

Figure 89.6

The area to be calculated.

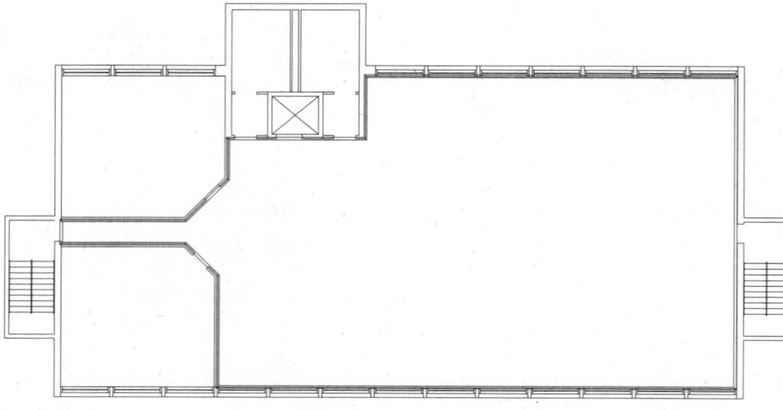

Student: __________ Date: __________

Instructor: __________ Course: __________ Section: __________

UNIT 90

Using ID and DIST

AutoCAD provides two inquiry commands that you will find very useful. The ID command enables you to identify the coordinates of a point. The DIST command calculates the distance and angle between two points. Both commands are helpful for laying out a drawing's geometry and for checking the design. This unit teaches you to use the ID and DIST commands.

The objectives for this unit are to:

- Use ID to identify the coordinates of a point
- Understand the function of the LASTPOINT variable
- Use ID to set the LASTPOINT variable
- Use DIST to calculate the distance and angle between two points

Locating Points with ID

As you work on a drawing, it often is necessary for you to determine the coordinates of a point. For example, you may need to identify a reference point in a surveyor's plat. Or, you may need to identify a point so that you can use it as a reference for entering other coordinates. The ID command helps by displaying information about a point, including its coordinates.

The ID command also performs another function. As you enter points, the coordinates of the last point entered are stored in the LASTPOINT variable. Think of LASTPOINT as the location where your imaginary pen is resting, ready to draw more entities. Using the ID command stores the coordinates of the point you select in the LASTPOINT variable. This is useful when you want to begin drawing not at a point you pick, but rather at a set distance from a specific point. It is like picking up your pen and putting it down at a new point without drawing anything.

Later in this unit, you see how you can use ID to change LASTPOINT. First, however, you should experiment with ID to learn how it works. In the following exercise, use ID to list the coordinate values of the centers of two circles.

Using the ID Command

1. Begin a new drawing named 090???01 in your assigned directory using 090PLATE as a prototype.

2. `Command:` *Choose* Assist, *then* Inquiry, *then* ID Point	Issues the ID command
`'_id`	
3. `Point:` *From the popup menu, choose* Center	Sets temporary object snap mode
4. `_center of` *Select the circle at* ① *(see fig. 90.1)*	Specifies the point to identify and displays the coordinates of the point
`X = 50.0000     Y = 60.0000     Z = 0.0000`	
5. `Command:` *Press* Enter	Repeats the previous command
6. `'ID Point:` *From the popup menu, choose* Center	Sets object snap mode
7. `_center of` *Select the circle at*② *(see fig. 90.1)*	Specifies the point to identify and displays the coordinates of the point
`X = 80.0000     Y = 60.0000     Z = 0.0000`	

Unless you are specifically trying to find the coordinates of a point, the ID command is not overly useful. It is most useful for setting the LASTPOINT variable as a tool for drawing. You can set LASTPOINT using ID, and then begin drawing relative to that point.

For example, assume that you want to draw a line that starts at the end of the line at ① in figure 90.2. The line must be drawn to a point that is 10 mm to the left and 12 mm above point ②. It would be extremely difficult to begin drawing the line at ①. Because you know the relative distance from ② to the end of the new line, however, it is a simple task to draw the line. Setting ② as the LASTPOINT is the key to solving the problem.

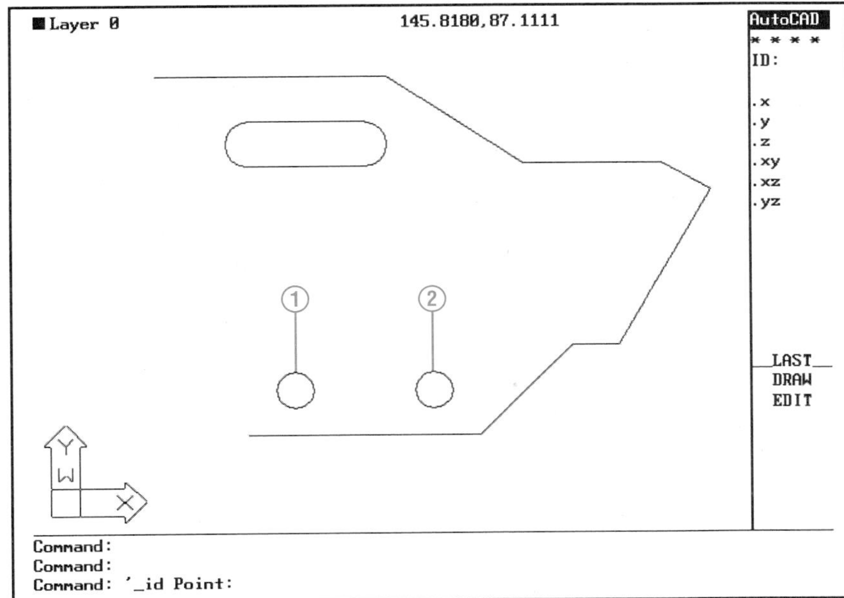

Figure 90.1

Selection points for ID.

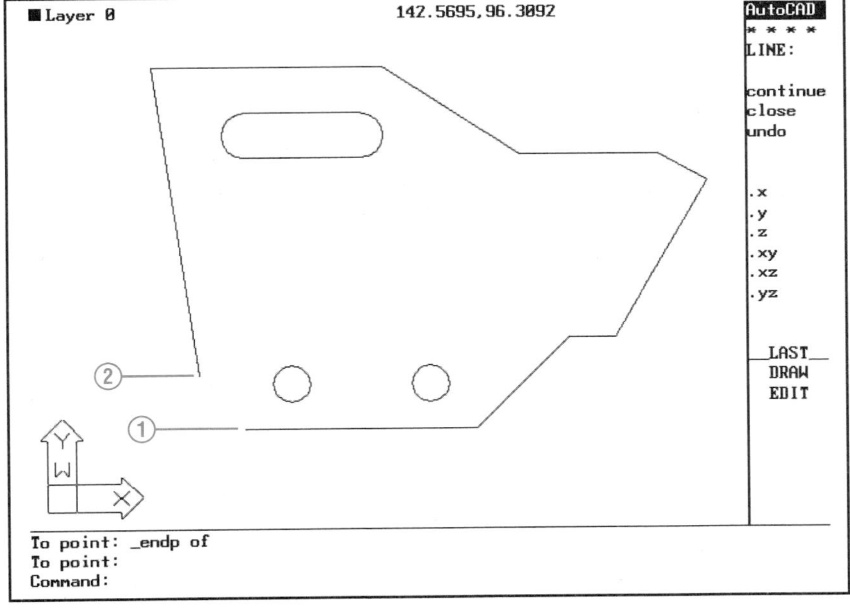

Figure 90.2

Reference points for line.

In the next exercise, draw the line described previously.

Setting LASTPOINT with ID

Continue with your drawing from the preceding exercise.

1. `Command:` *Choose* Assist, *then* Inquiry, *then* ID Point	Issues the ID command
`'_id`	
2. `Point:` *From the popup menu, choose* Endpoint	Sets temporary object snap mode
3. `_endp of` *Pick the end point at* ① *(see fig. 90.2)*	Specifies the point to identify and displays the coordinates of the point
`X = 40.0000     Y = 50.0000     Z = 0.0000`	
4. `Command:` **`L`** ↵	Issues the alias for the LINE command
5. `LINE From point:` **`@-10,12`** ↵	Locates the start of the line relative to LASTPOINT
6. `To point:` *From the popup menu, choose* Endpoint	Sets object snap mode
7. `_endp of` *Pick the end point at* ② *(see fig. 90.2)*	
8. `To point:` *Press* Enter	
9. Save your drawing.	

You can set the value of LASTPOINT by entering the LASTPOINT command at the command prompt, and then typing or picking a coordinate.

Relative point specification always is based from the LASTPOINT coordinates. Using ID to set LASTPOINT is a useful means of locating the starting point of a new entity as a specific distance from an existing point.

When you enter the @ symbol in response to a point selection prompt, you actually are specifying the point defined by LASTPOINT. In fact, you can think of @ as meaning "use the coordinates stored in LASTPOINT."

You can enter **ID** at the command prompt to issue the ID command. You also can choose ID: from the INQUIRY screen menu to issue the ID command.

Checking Distances and Angles

Another inquiry function you often will perform is checking the distance and angle between two points. You may need to check the length of a line, the size of a room, the angle between one edge of a part and another edge, and so on. You can determine these distances and angles by using AutoCAD's dimensioning commands, but often you need to know only the distance or angle, and do not want to apply a dimension to the drawing.

The DIST command enables you to check the distance and angle between two points. You can issue DIST by choosing Assist, then Inquiry, and then Distance. You also can enter **DIST** at the command prompt or choose DIST: from the INQUIRY screen menu.

In the following exercise, use the DIST command to check the length of some edges of the plate you worked on earlier in this unit. Use figure 90.3 as a reference.

Using the DIST Command

Continue with your drawing from the preceding exercise.

1. Draw a line from ① in fig. 90.3 to @2,0 (which is ③), and then to ②. Use ENDP object snap to snap the lines to ① and ②. Your drawing should look similar to figure 90.3 when you complete this step.

2. `Command:` **`OSNAP`** ↵	Issues OSNAP command
3. `Object snap modes:` **`ENDP`** ↵	Sets running object snap mode
4. `Command:` *Choose* Assist, *then* Inquiry, *then* Distance `'_dist`	Issues the DIST command
5. `First point:` *Pick the end point at ③ (see fig. 90.3)*	Specifies first point
6. `Second point:` *Pick the end point at ② (see fig. 90.3)*	Specifies second point and displays the distance and angle between the two points

```
Distance = 14.4222,  Angle in XY Plane = 304,  Angle from XY Plane = 0
Delta X = 8.0000,  Delta Y = -12.0000,   Delta Z = 0.0000
```

continues

7. `Command:` *Press* Enter — Repeats the previous command
8. `'DIST First point:` *Pick the end point at ④ (see fig. 90.3)* — Specifies first point
9. `Second point:` *Pick the end point at ⑤ (see fig. 90.3)* — Specifies second point and displays distance and angle

```
Distance = 28.2843,  Angle in XY Plane = 45,  Angle from XY Plane = 0
Delta X = 20.0000,  Delta Y = 20.0000,   Delta Z = 0.0000
```

10. Save your drawing.

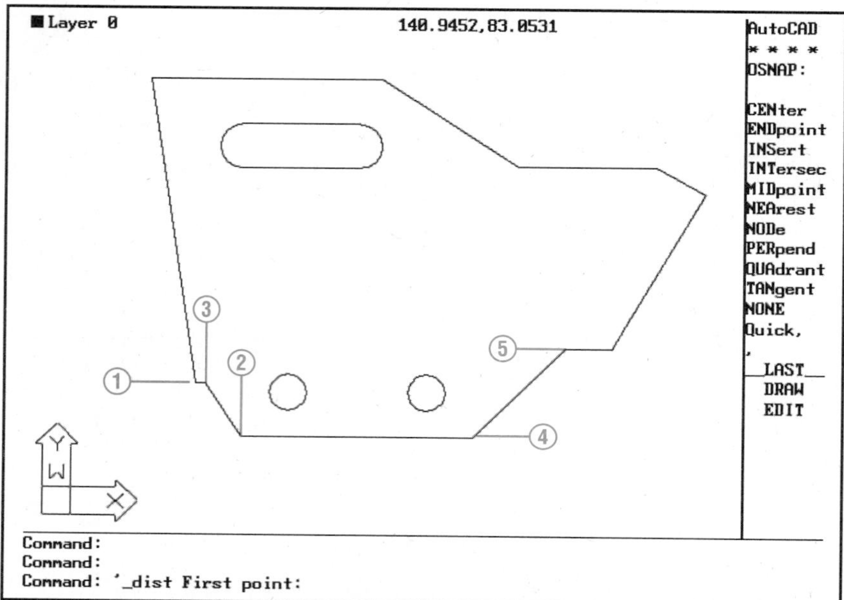

Figure 90.3

Selection points for DIST.

You can see that DIST provides the actual distance between the two points. The distance between points ④ and ⑤, for example, is 28.2843. In addition to providing the actual point-to-point distance, DIST also provides the angle between the two points in the XY plane; the angle from the XY plane; and the delta values for each ordinate. The following list explains these items of information:

- **Angle in XY Plane.** This is the angle between the first point and the second point measured in the XY plane. In a 2D drawing, such as the one in the preceding example, this is the angle between the two points relative to zero degrees.

- **Angle from XY Plane.** This is the angle between the first point and the second point measured from the XY plane. This value is zero for all 2D drawings (assuming that you do not enter a Z value other than zero for a coordinate). Unit 99, "Introducing the Third Dimension," explains the 3D coordinate system.
- **Delta X.** This is the relative distance along the X axis between the two points.
- **Delta Y.** This is the relative distance along the Y axis between the two points.
- **Delta Z.** This is the relative distance along the Z axis between the two points.

You can enter a coordinate value at the keyboard in response to the DIST command's prompt to specify a point. You can enter the first point using the keyboard, for example, and then pick a point.

Unit Review

What You've Learned

- Commands: ID, DIST
- How to determine the coordinates of a point with ID
- How to set the LASTPOINT variable with ID
- How to draw relative to a point by using LASTPOINT
- How to determine the distance and angle between two points

Review Questions

True or False

90.01 T F ID displays the angle between two points.

90.02 T F The ID command lists the X, Y, and Z ordinates of a point.

90.03 T F Selecting a point with the ID command stores the coordinate of the point in the LASTPOINT variable.

90.04 T F You can set the value of LASTPOINT by issuing the LASTPOINT command.

90.05 T F The @ symbol can be used to enter the coordinate stored in the LASTPOINT variable.

90.06 T F The @ symbol can only be entered in response to the ID command.

90.07 T F The DIST command displays the actual distance between two points.

90.08 T F DIST measures the angle between two lines.

90.09 T F You can only pick points in response to the DIST command; you cannot enter the coordinates of a point.

90.10 T F The distance reported by DIST is the same distance reported by ID.

Student: ____________________ Date: ________

Instructor: ____________________ Course: ________ Section: ________

Additional Exercises

90.11 Continuing with your drawing from the preceding exercise, determine the following information. Use figure 90.4 as a reference to identify entities and points:

Delta X distance from ① to ②: __________

Delta Y distance from ③ to ④: __________

Length of line ⑤: __________

Length of the slot from ⑥ to ⑦: __________

Distance between the two holes: __________

The angle in the XY plane of line ⑧: __________

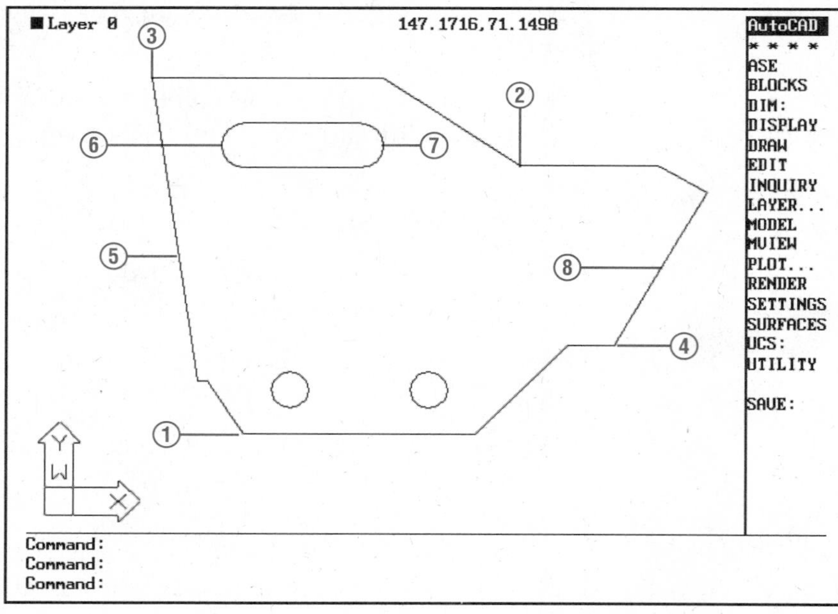

Figure 90.4

Points for determining distance.

Student: __________ Date: __________

Instructor: __________ Course: __________ Section: __________

PART X

Using Symbols

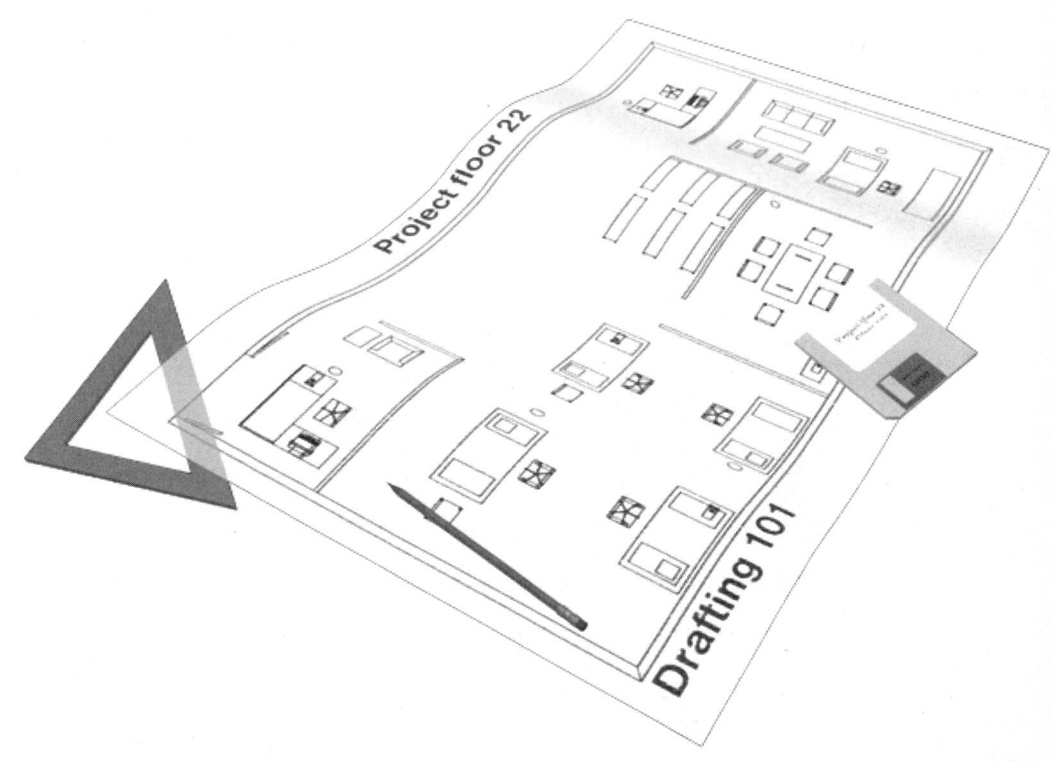

UNIT 16

Introduction to Symbols and Attributes

In manual drafting, you commonly use templates to draw repetitive features, such as architectural or electrical symbols. This not only reduces drawing time, but also ensures the accuracy and consistency of common drawing elements. These symbols are usually further identified by a note on the drawing. For example, a door on a floor plan might be accompanied by a call-out relating it to a door schedule for size and material information.

You also can create and use symbols in AutoCAD. In fact, the functions available in AutoCAD for creating and working with symbols offer capabilities that cannot be duplicated in manual drafting. For this reason, being able to work with symbols in AutoCAD is an extremely important skill. This unit provides a brief overview of the options you have for creating symbols and their associated notes in AutoCAD.

The objectives of this unit are to:

- Understand the use of scaled and unit-size symbols
- Understand the use of attributes to attach textual information to your drawing
- Understand how the use of symbols can increase drawing speed and accuracy while decreasing drawing size

Understanding Symbols in AutoCAD

Symbols and standard parts can be used to a much greater degree in AutoCAD than in a manual drawing. For example, you probably use symbols common to your design discipline for which templates are not available. In AutoCAD, you can create a symbol and store it for use on any other drawing, essentially creating your own symbol "templates." Any change made to standard symbols or parts may be instantly applied to all drawings containing the symbol. Part numbers, prices, etc., may also be attached to your symbols for automatic generation of bills of materials, cost reports, and other documents.

AutoCAD supports two types of entities—blocks and Xrefs—for use as symbols and standard parts. Unit 67 introduces blocks, and unit 70 introduces Xrefs. You probably have already used blocks and Xrefs in exercises in previous units. Blocks and Xrefs are most commonly used in AutoCAD to represent common symbols and parts.

Anything drawn repeatedly on the same drawing or on different drawings should be considered a standard symbol. By creating blocks or Xrefs of these symbols, you ensure their uniformity and accuracy throughout all drawings. Your drawings will be more accurate, and your drawing time and drawing file size will be greatly reduced. Most important, however, is the time you will save by using common symbols instead of drawing new objects.

Working with Symbols

There are two ways to use symbols on a drawing. Symbols may be *standard scale parts* or *unit-size blocks.* First, consider standard scale symbols.

Using Standard Scale Symbols

An architectural drafter would use a symbol template to manually draw doors, windows, bathroom fixtures, etc., on a floor plan. These are standard scale parts—their size remains the same throughout the drawing. A symbol for a 36" door, for example, would always be 36". A standard plumbing fixture such as a toilet would always be drawn the same size. You typically do not scale these types of symbols larger or smaller than their standard sizes.

With blocks and Xrefs, you have the same ability to create a symbol once and use it again as needed on the same drawing or other drawings. This saves much time and ensures the uniformity and accuracy of the symbol because the same symbol is being used each time. Therefore, any symbol drawn to the same size each time you use it is a standard scale part. Figure 91.1 illustrates several standard scale parts.

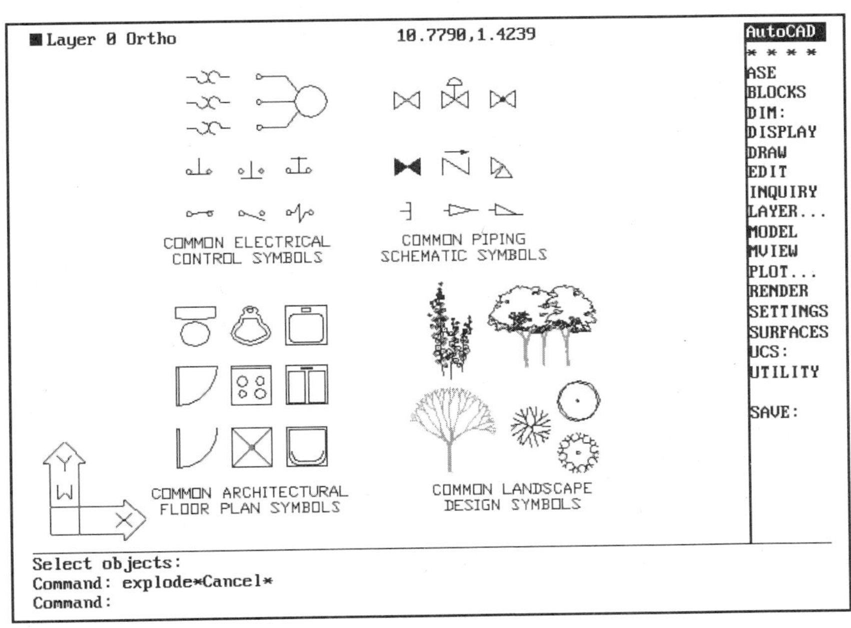

Figure 91.1

Standard scale drawing symbols.

Whether you insert a standard scale symbol as a block or as an Xref depends on how the symbol is used. In most cases, you will insert symbols as blocks. If the symbol is used in more than one drawing, and you want to be able to change it quickly in all drawings where it is used, consider attaching the symbol as an Xref instead of inserting it as a block.

To create a standard scale symbol, simply create a drawing of the part, fixture, or symbol full-size. When you insert the symbol in a drawing, it will be inserted at actual size to match the scale of the rest of the drawing (because you generally create a drawing full size, then scale it during plotting).

Using Unit-Size Blocks

The unit-size block gives you much more power over the appearance of symbols than is possible in manual drafting. Many symbols consist of the same geometry with different proportions. For example, a threaded hole is a very common symbol for mechanical drafters. Although the geometry is always consistent, the size of the circles change for each different hole size. You can use a single, one-unit-size block at different scales to represent different hole sizes. By scaling the block to different sizes, you vary the size of the block, but not its proportions. Figure 91.2 illustrates the use of unit-size blocks.

Figure 91.2

Unit-size block used to show different sizes of threaded holes.

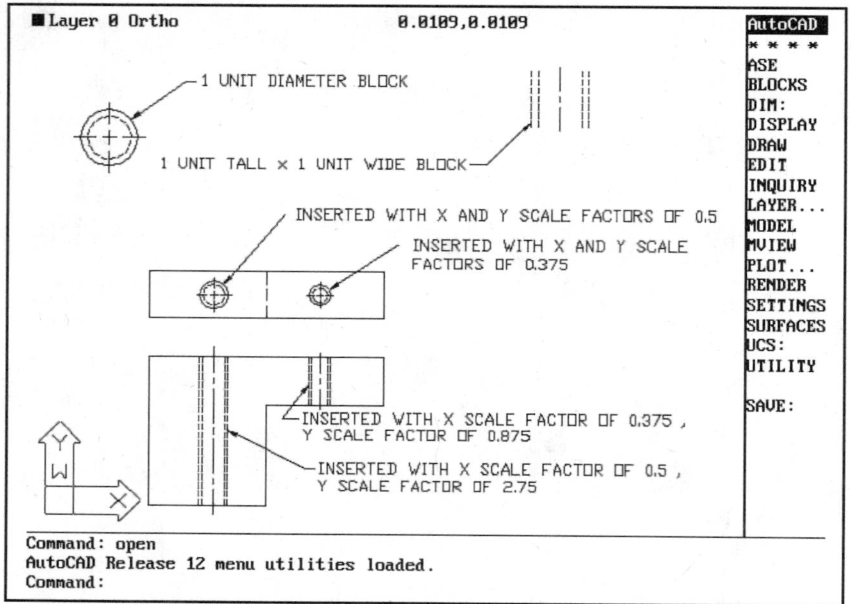

Any time you need to create a symbol that varies in size, such as threaded holes, bolts, trees, or any other object whose size varies, create the symbol as a unit-size block. For more information on creating unit size blocks, refer to unit 68.

Conserving Disk Space and Memory

Another aspect of using blocks and Xrefs for symbols in a drawing is decreased drawing size. Some symbols can be quite complex, consisting of many entities. Each of these entities must be defined in the drawing file, so more entities mean a larger drawing file. When you use a block AutoCAD considers it to be one entity, saving valuable drawing space. If each symbol were created individually, and not as a block, each of the entities in the symbol would be duplicated in the drawing's database, requiring more disk space to store and more memory when you edit the drawing. Keeping drawing size and memory requirements to a minimum speeds the process of loading and saving drawings.

Xrefs are particularly useful for keeping drawing size and memory requirements to a minimum because Xrefs do not become a part of the drawing in which they are inserted. Xrefs exist only once—in the source drawing file that contains the Xref's geometry. This single file can be referenced in any number of other drawings, but the entities that make up the Xref exist only in the source drawing.

The use of Xrefs also helps you automatically update drawings when a symbol or part changes. If a standard part changes, you simply change the source drawing, and any other drawings in which the source drawing is referenced will be updated automatically the next time they are loaded.

Understanding Attributes

Other information in the form of text is often needed to accompany a drawing symbol. Examples are the reference designators for electronic components on a schematic, the door and window specifications on a floor plan, equipment numbers on a facilities plan, and so on. Sometimes this additional text is displayed on the drawing with the symbol, but at other times the text is only needed as reference data and does not have to be visible on the plotted drawing.

AutoCAD includes an entity called an *attribute* that is meant specifically for adding this type of associative text to a symbol. You can attach an attribute to a symbol, or even have a symbol consisting only of attributes. This text can be the same each time you use the symbol (referred to as having a set value), or the value of the attribute can be assigned as you place the symbol (a variable value). Figure 91.3 illustrates some common uses of attributes. All the text in this drawing are attributes. See if you can determine which attributes have set values and which have variable values.

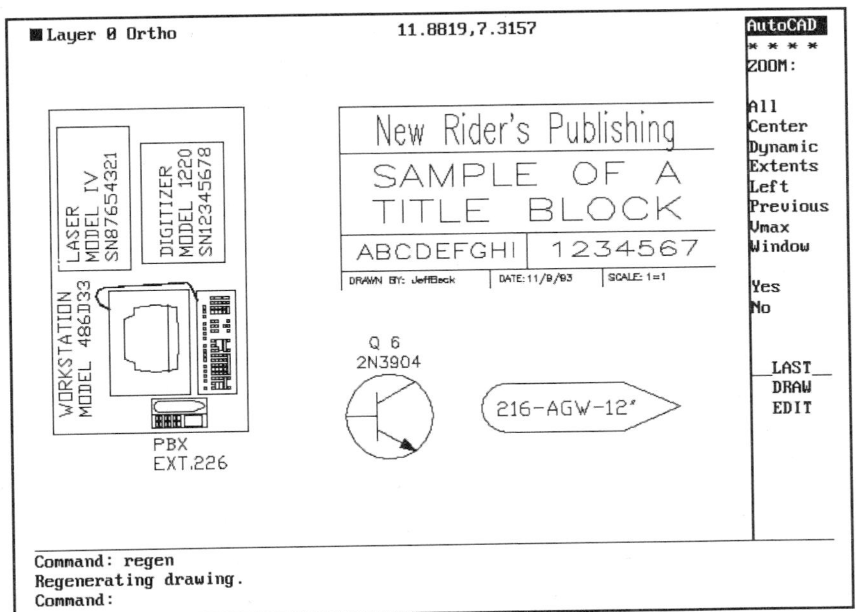

Figure 91.3

Common uses of set and variable attributes.

Attributes used in this manner contain the reference information commonly associated with a symbol on your drawing. Attributes have another use, however, that has no equal in manual drafting. Information about your symbol can be attached with an *invisible attribute,* which is not displayed on your drawing. Imagine attaching price, manufacturer, and model number information to a resistor symbol. You will see in unit 97 how you can extract this information from the drawing to generate a parts list, cost sheet, or any type of tabular data. When using attributes in this manner, you can create an *intelligent drawing,* a drawing containing much more information than would be possible or practical to display, but information that is very useful.

In the units that follow you will learn how to create and use symbols that contain attributes. You also will learn how to extract information from the attributes in a drawing.

Unit Review

What You've Learned

- ☞ Definition and purpose of standard scale part symbols
- ☞ Definition and purpose of unit-size symbols
- ☞ Use of symbols to increase drawing speed and accuracy
- ☞ Use of symbols to decrease drawing size
- ☞ Definition and purposes of attributes

Review Questions

True or False

91.01 T F The use of standard scale symbols is similar to the use of a drafting template in manual drafting.

91.02 T F Unit-sized blocks can be scaled along one axis only.

91.03 T F Any attribute information attached to a symbol will always be displayed.

91.04 T F The use of Xrefs in place of blocks decreases the amount of disk space required to store a drawing.

Multiple Choice

91.05 Using an Xref in place of a block will __________ the drawing file size.

(A) decrease

(B) increase

(C) double

(D) not affect

91.06 The use of blocks or Xrefs will increase the speed and __________ of your drawing.

(A) size

(B) cost

(C) accuracy

(D) all of the above

Student: ______________________________ Date: __________

Instructor: ______________________________ Course: __________ Section: __________

91.07 A (an) ________ is textual information attached to a symbol.

(A) block

(B) attribute

(C) external reference file

(D) variable

Short Answer

91.08 Give an example of three common uses of standard scale symbol in an architectural drawing.

____

____

____

91.09 Give an example of a common use of unit-size blocks in a mechanical drawing.

____

____

____

91.10 Briefly explain why Xrefs are useful in a design in which parts or systems will change during the design cycle.

____

____

Student: ____________ Date: ____________

Instructor: ____________ Course: ____________ Section: ____________

UNIT 92

Creating an Attribute

Many types of information are associated with a drawing besides the graphical drawing entities themselves. An electrical schematic includes notes about component part numbers and values; a piping plan needs pipeline numbers and sizes; a mechanical drawing requires thread callouts; and so on. There also is other information associated with a drawing that does not necessarily become a part of the plotted drawing. For example, the electrical schematic is linked to a parts list; the piping plan makes use of a pipeline list; and the mechanical drawing references a bill of materials.

In this unit, you will learn how to use attributes to add these types of information to your drawing.

The objectives for this unit are to:

- Create attributes with the DDATTDEF command
- Use the BLOCK command to create symbols with attributes
- Use the WBLOCK command to write symbols with attributes to disk
- Understand practical applications of attribute information

Creating Attributes

Attributes are special types of entities that look like text, but which behave very differently from text. Usually, attributes are used in symbols along with graphic entities. A symbol also can consist only of attributes (and contain no graphical entities). You can think of attributes as containers in which you can store data. An attribute can have a value assigned to it when you create the attribute, or you can fill the attribute with data when you insert its symbol into a drawing. As you read through this unit, you will see some practical examples of attributes.

Attributes perform two primary functions. They provide a consistent means for you to add text information to graphical symbols. They also make it possible for you to store reference information in the drawing, then extract and correlate that information for later use.

The easiest way to create attributes is to use the Attribute Definition dialog box (see fig. 92.1). You can display this dialog box by issuing the DDATTDEF command. You also can display it by choosing Draw, then Text, then Attributes, then Define.

Figure 92.1

The Attribute Definition dialog box.

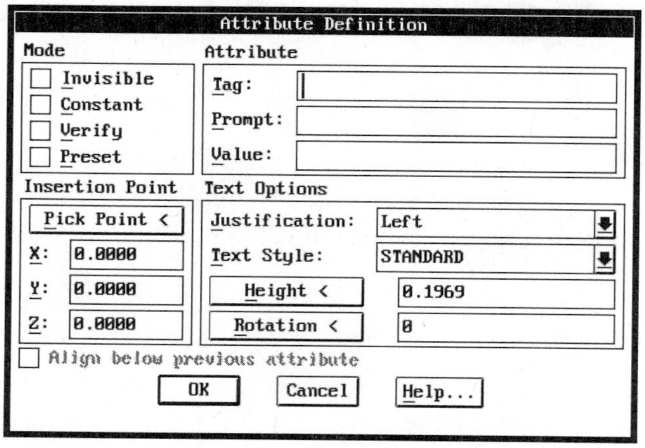

As you can see in figure 92.1, the Attribute Definition dialog box is separated into four sections; Mode, Attribute, Insertion Point, and Text Options. The following sections examine each of those control groups separately.

Mode Settings

Remember that an attribute is information attached to a symbol. This may be information you want displayed on the drawing, such as a reference number relating the symbol to a parts list. You also may want to attach information such as cost or manufacturer's catalog number to a symbol, but do not want that information displayed on the drawing. The information might be the same each time the symbol is used or might change with each occurrence of the symbol. For example, each resistor in an electrical schematic would be labeled with an R, but each one would have a different sequence number (R1, R2, R3, and so on). These properties of an attribute are set with the Mode options, as shown in the following list:

- **Invisible.** The attribute normally will be displayed on your drawing. Placing a check in this box tells AutoCAD not to display the attribute.
- **Constant.** The attribute normally will be assigned a value as the symbol is placed on your drawing (AutoCAD prompts you for the value when you insert the symbol). Placing a check in this box specifies that the attribute will always be the same, and will not be set when the symbol is inserted into the drawing. Selecting Constant disables the Verify and Preset options.

If the Constant mode is selected, the attribute cannot be modified after the symbol is placed.

- **Verify.** Placing a check in this box tells AutoCAD you want to verify the information you type for an attribute before it is placed on the drawing. This gives you an opportunity to correct any typographical errors.
- **Preset.** Placing a check in this box produces the same result as the Constant mode described above (the value is preset), except a Preset attribute may be modified after the symbol is placed.

Attribute Settings

With the Attribute group of controls in the Attribute Definition dialog box, you give the attribute a name, define the prompt that AutoCAD will display when the symbol is placed, and supply default values for the attributes. These properties are described in the following list:

- **Tag.** This is the name of your attribute, such as part number, model number, or cost. Spaces are not permitted in the tag; use a hyphen or an underscore character if a space is desired, such as Part_Number. All attributes *must* be given a tag.
- **Prompt.** This is the prompt you wish AutoCAD to issue when you place the symbol in your drawing. For example, **Enter Cost of Item:** would prompt the user to enter the cost of the item. If no prompt is specified, AutoCAD will use the Tag setting for a prompt.

If the Constant mode is set, the Attribute Prompt is disabled.

Although you may enter an attribute tag and an attribute prompt with up to 256 characters, the Enter Attributes dialog box (described in unit 93) will truncate the entry prompt to 24 characters. Therefore, you should try to keep your prompts to a minimum number of characters, also make the prompt as understandable as possible.

- **Value.** This section allows you to enter default attribute text. AutoCAD will display this text when placing your symbol, but will also allow you the option of replacing it. You can accept the default value without having to type it each time. This setting may be left blank, but can save a lot of typing when you use it.

Insertion Point Settings

In the Insertion Point group of the Attribute Definition dialog box, you specify where to place your attribute text on the drawing. The following list explains these controls:

- **Pick Point <.** This button allows you to select a point on the drawing screen as you normally place text with the DTEXT command.
- **X:, Y:, and Z.** These allow you to specify text location by supplying coordinates.
- **Align below previous attribute.** If this check box is selected, the above options are disabled and the attribute text is automatically placed just below the last attribute defined. This is similar to pressing Enter at the Start point option of the DTEXT command.

If no Insertion Point settings are specified, AutoCAD will place attribute text at the origin point (0,0,0).

Text Option Settings

In the Text Options group of the Attribute Definition dialog box, you specify the text style, justification, height, and rotation angle to use for the attribute. These options are described in the following list:

- **Justification.** These are the same options you are given with the DTEXT command to justify text (see unit 72).
- **Text Style.** This control lets you select from a popup list of all text styles *currently loaded*. It does not allow you to load a text style—this must be done with the STYLE command before using the DDATTDEF command.

The current text style is the default option for this setting.

- **Height <.** This button allows you to specify a text height from the command prompt, or to pick points on the drawing screen. You may also specify text height by typing it in the edit box to the right of this button.
- **Rotation <.** This button allows you to specify the text rotation angle from the command prompt or to pick points on the drawing screen. You may also specify the rotation angle by typing it in the edit box to the right of this button.

If a text style with a predefined height and rotation angle is selected with the Text Style option, the Height and Rotation options are not available.

To practice creating attributes, complete the following exercise. You will be defining attributes for a transistor symbol for an electrical schematic. At the end of this unit, you will define attributes for several other electrical components. These will be used later to create a fully annotated schematic.

Using the Attribute Definition Dialog Box

1. Begin a new drawing named 092???01 in your assigned directory, using the drawing 092ADEF1 as a prototype.

2. `Command:` *Choose* Draw, *then* Text, *then* Attributes, *then* Define	Issues the DDATTDEF command and displays the Attribute Definition dialog box
3. *Place a check in the* Preset *check box in the* Mode *section*	Specifies that the attribute's value is preset

continues

4. *Fill in the edit boxes for* Tag *and* Value *in the* Attribute *group as shown in figure 92.2.* — Sets the tag name for the attribute and its default value

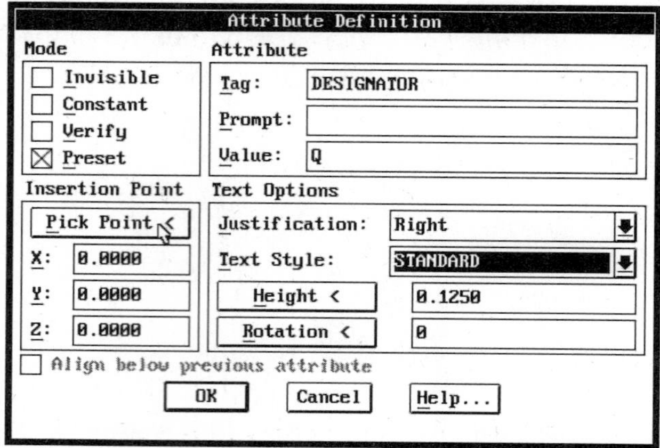

Figure 92.2

The Attribute Definition dialog box for Designator attribute.

5. *Choose the* Justification *popup list in the* Text Options *group and choose* Right — Sets the justification of the attribute text

6. *In the* Height *edit box, set text height to 0.125* — Sets the text height for the attribute

7. *Click on the* Pick Point *button in the* Insertion Point *group and select the insertion point at* ① *(see figure 92.3)* — Specifies the insertion point of the attribute

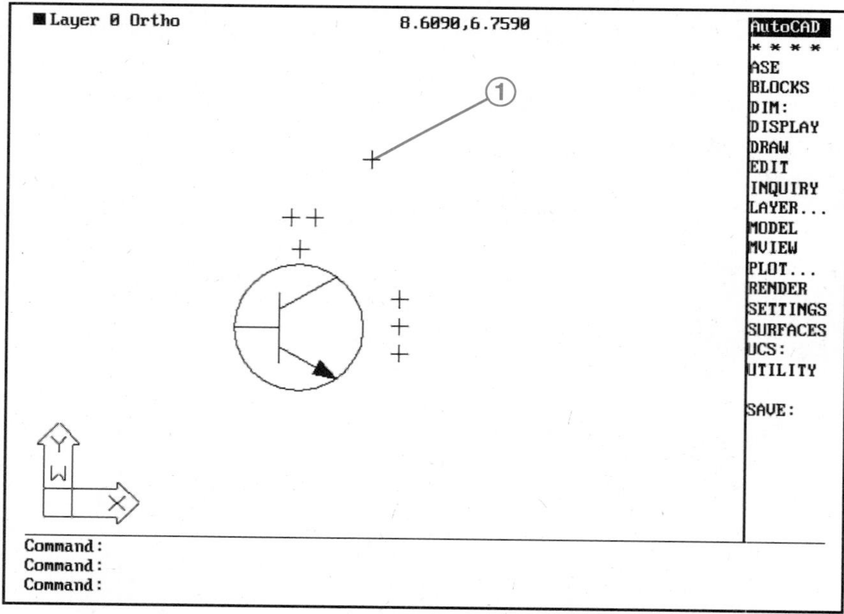

Figure 92.3

Insertion points for transistor attributes.

8. *Choose* OK	Exits the dialog box and creates the attribute

You have just created an attribute. Next, use the Attribute Definition dialog box again to create more attributes.

Creating More Attributes

Continue with your drawing from the preceding exercise.

1. Command: *Choose* Draw, *then* Text, *then* Attributes, *then* Define	Issues the DDATTDEF command and displays the Attribute Definition dialog box
2. *Clear the* Preset *check box*	Turns off the Preset option

Create an attribute for Reference_Number using figure 92.4 as a guide. Use the Pick Point button to locate the attribute just to the right of the Designator attribute as shown in figure 92.9.

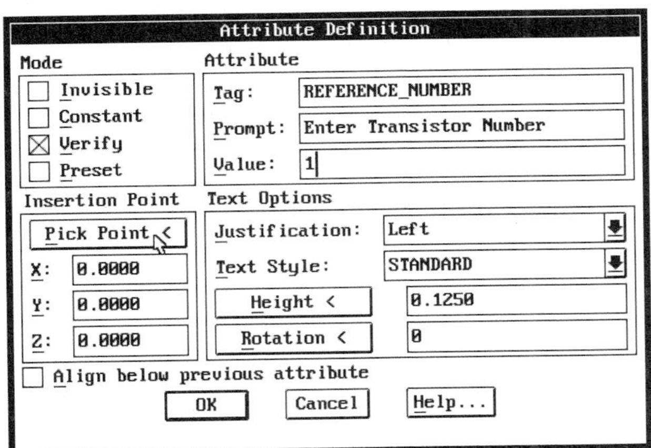

Figure 92.4

The Attribute Definition dialog box for Reference_Number attribute.

3. Command: *Choose* Draw, *then* Text, *then* Attributes, *then* Define	Issues the DDATTDEF command and displays the Attribute Definition dialog box

4. Create an attribute for Value using figure 92.5 and locate the attribute as shown in figure 92.9.

5. Command: **DDATTDEF** ↵	Issues the DDATTDEF command and displays the Attribute Definition dialog box
6. *Place a check in the* Align below previous attribute *check box*	Causes the new attribute to be aligned below the previous attribute and disables the Insertion Point and Text Options controls

continues

7. Create attributes for Cost, Manufacturer, and Catalog_Number as shown in figures 92.6 through 92.8.

8. Save your drawing when you have completed all of the attributes.

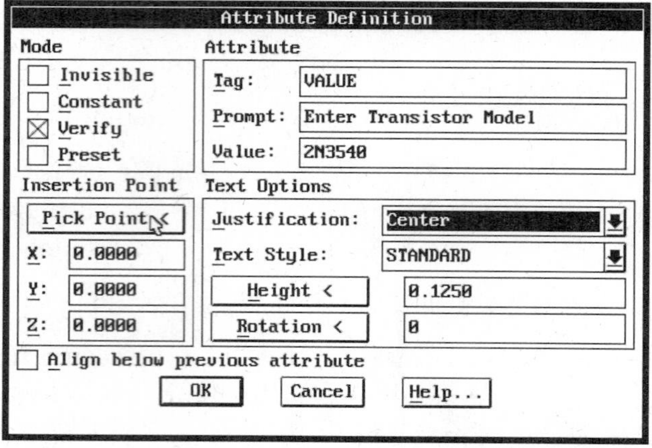

Figure 92.5

The Attribute Definition dialog box for Value attribute.

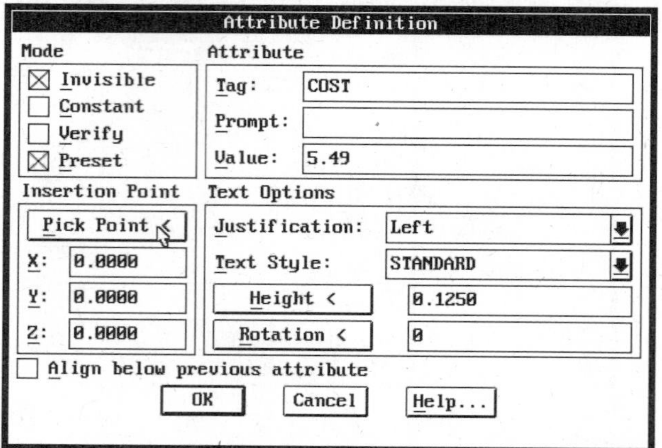

Figure 92.6

The Attribute Definition dialog box for Cost attribute.

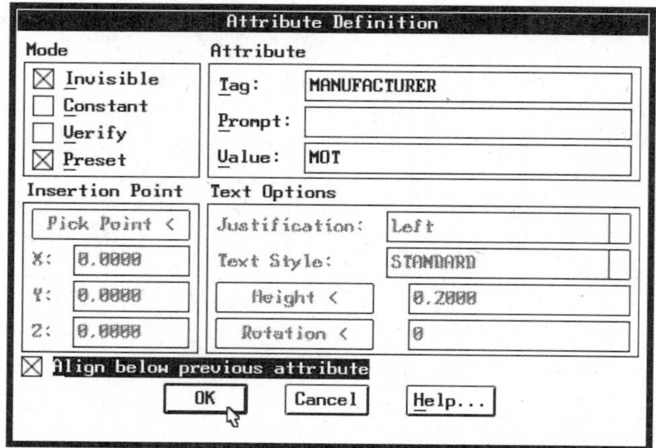

Figure 92.7

The Attribute Definition dialog box for Manufacturer attribute.

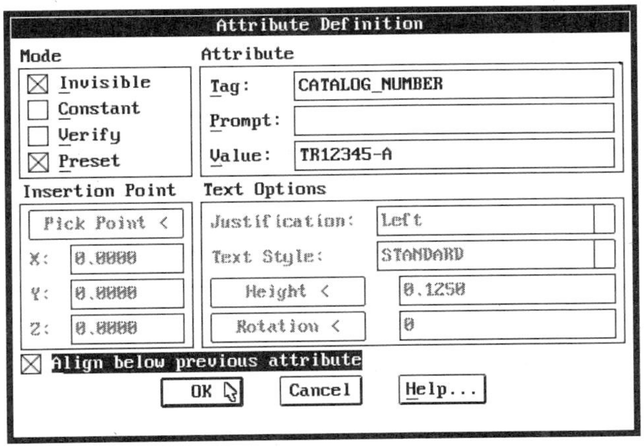

Attribute Definition
Mode: Invisible [x], Constant [ ], Verify [ ], Preset [x]
Attribute — Tag: CATALOG_NUMBER; Prompt: ; Value: TR12345-A
Insertion Point — Pick Point <; X: 0.0000; Y: 0.0000; Z: 0.0000
Text Options — Justification: Left; Text Style: STANDARD; Height < 0.1250; Rotation < 0
[x] Align below previous attribute
OK | Cancel | Help...

Figure 92.8

The Attribute Definition dialog box for Catalog_Number attribute.

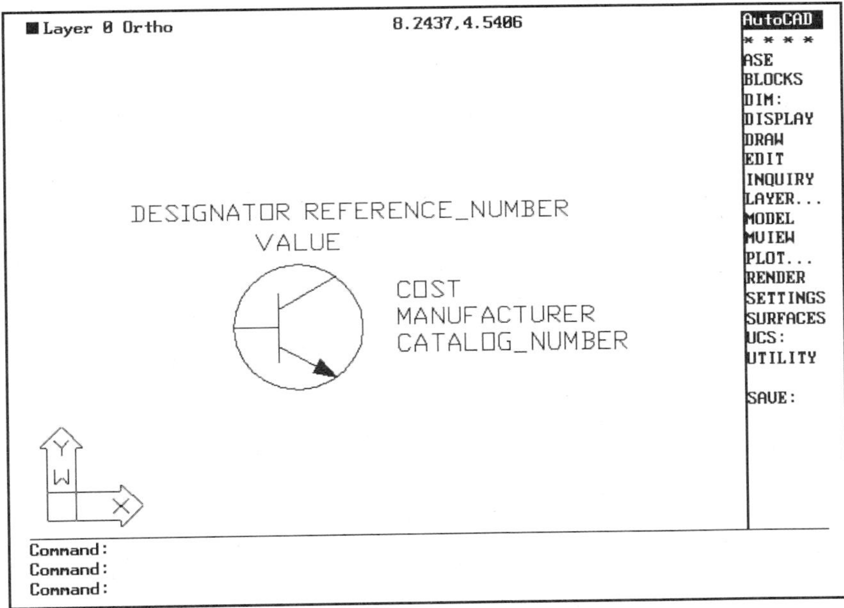

Figure 92.9

The completed attributes.

Defining attributes is just the first step in putting them to work for you. Often, you will use attributes in conjunction with blocks. The next section explains how to use attributes with blocks.

Using Attributes in Blocks

In the previous exercise, you created some symbol attributes. When created, attributes simply show their attribute tag. In order to supply individual attribute values, you must create a block that contains the attributes. When this block is inserted into a drawing, you will be prompted to supply the attribute values. You may want to review the information on creating blocks in units 67 and 68 before proceeding.

In the following exercise, you will use the BLOCK command to create a symbol with attributes. You will then use the WBLOCK command to write the block to disk so it may be used in future drawings.

Creating Blocks with Attributes

1. If you completed and saved the previous exercise, you can continue with the same drawing. Otherwise, begin a new drawing in your assigned directory named 092???02 using the drawing 092ADEF2 as a prototype.

2. `Command:` *Choose* Construct, *then* Block	Issues the BLOCK command
`_block`	
3. `Block name (or ?):` **`TRANSISTOR`** ↵	Names the block
4. `Insertion base point:` **`ENDP`** ↵	Sets temporary object snap
5. `of` *Pick the transistor base at* ① *(see figure 92.10)*	Specifies base point of block

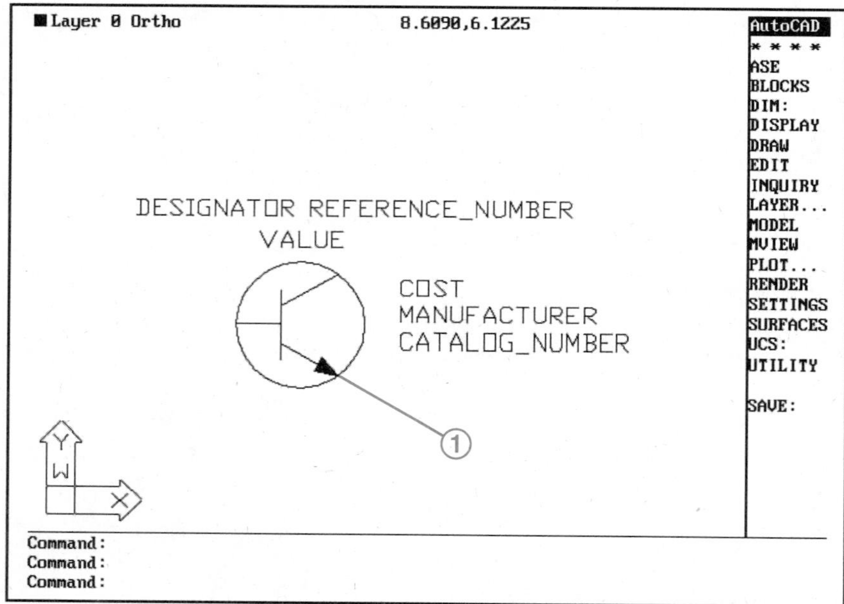

Figure 92.10

Transistor and attributes.

6. `Select objects:` **`ALL`** ↵	Adds all entities to the selection set
`13 found`	
7. `Select objects:` *Press* Enter	Ends object selection and creates the block
8. `Command:` **`OOPS`** ↵	Places object back on screen

9. `Command:` **`WBLOCK`** ↵ Issues the WBLOCK command

10. The Save File dialog box will open on your screen to prompt you for a file name. Enter TRANSIST for the file name and press Enter or choose OK.

11. `Block name:` **`TRANSISTOR`** ↵ Specifies the entities in the transistor block to write to disk

AutoCAD places no limit on the number of attributes that may be attached to a block.

You have created blocks with attribute definitions linked to them. In unit 93, you will use these blocks to complete an electrical schematic.

Unit Review

What You've Learned

- The parts of the DDATTDEF dialog box
- How to create an attribute
- How to create an attribute with a preset value
- How to create an attribute with a constant value
- How to use the BLOCK command to place an attribute in a symbol
- How to use the WBLOCK command to store your symbol with attributes to disk

Review Questions

True or False

92.01 T F Attributes are normally invisible unless you change the Invisible setting in the DDATTDEF dialog box.

92.02 T F If no attribute prompt is defined, AutoCAD will prompt for attribute information with the attribute tag.

92.03 T F If no insertion point is specified, attribute text is placed at 0,0,0.

92.04 T F You may load a new text style from the DDATTDEF dialog box.

Multiple Choice

92.05 The DDATTDEF command is used to ______________ .

(A) create a block

(B) write a block to disk

(C) create an attribute

(D) write an attribute to disk

92.06 A block may contain ____________ attributes.

(A) 24

(B) 36

(C) 256

(D) an unlimited number of

Student: ______________________ Date: __________

Instructor: ______________________ Course: __________ Section: __________

92.07 An attribute defined as ____________ cannot be modified after it is placed.

(A) invisible

(B) constant

(C) preset

(D) permanent

92.08 An attribute prompt should be limited to __________ characters to avoid being truncated.

(A) 8

(B) 24

(C) 36

(D) 256

Short Answer

92.09 What is the purpose of using the WBLOCK command?

____

____

____

92.10 List the four parts of the DDATTDEF dialog box and briefly describe the purpose of each.

____

____

____

Additional Exercises

92.11 Begin a new drawing named 092???03 in your assigned directory using 092ADEF3 as a prototype. Define attributes for the resistor and the capacitor using the information from the following tables. When all attributes are defined, use the BLOCK and WBLOCK commands to save each symbol and its attributes. Name your symbols RES and CAP. Figure 92.11 shows the insertion base points and the resistor and capacitor with all attributes defined.

Student: ____________________ Date: ____________

Instructor: ____________________ Course: ____________ Section: ____________

Attribute Settings for Resistor

Mode settings: I=Invisible, C=Constant, V=Verify, P=Preset

Tag	Mode	Prompt	Value
Designator	P	N/A	R
Reference_Number	V	Enter Resistor Number	1
Value	V	Enter Resistor Rating	1K
Cost	I,P	(Leave blank)	1.55
Manufacturer	I,P	(Leave blank)	MOT
Catalog_Number	I,P	(Leave blank)	R12345

Attribute Settings for Capacitor

Mode settings: I=Invisible, C=Constant, V=Verify, P=Preset

Tag	Mode	Prompt	Value
Designator	P	N/A	C
Reference_Number	V	Enter Capacitor Number	1
Value	V	Enter Capacitor Rating	.01UF
Cost	I,P	(Leave blank)	2.13
Manufacturer	I,P	(Leave blank)	MOT
Catalog_Number	I,P	(Leave blank)	C213

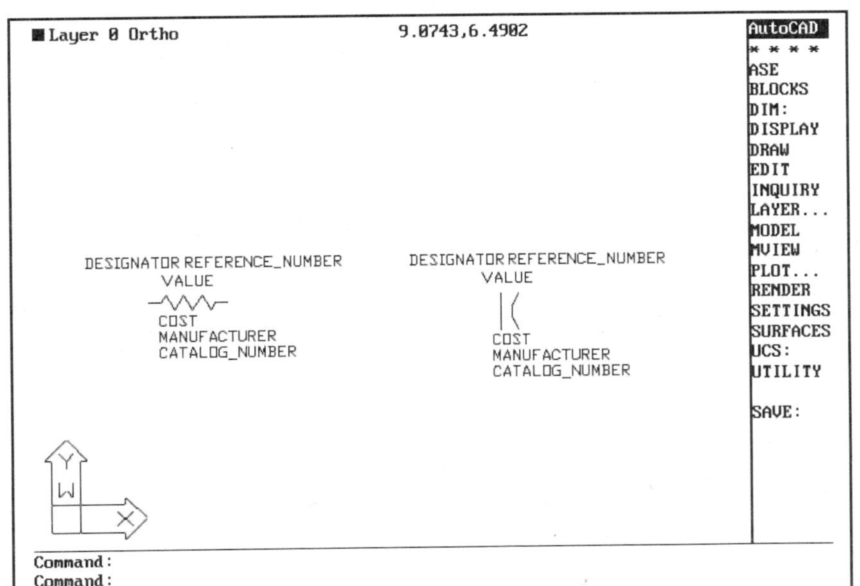

Figure 92.11

Insertion base points for Resistor and Capacitor blocks.

Student: ______ Date: ______

Instructor: ______ Course: ______ Section: ______

Inserting a Block with Attributes

UNIT 93

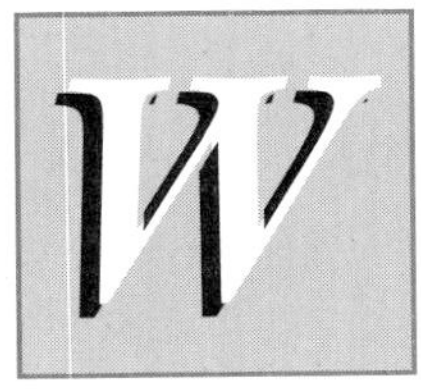

When you insert a block with attributes into a drawing, AutoCAD prompts you to supply data for the attributes. This gives you a chance to "fill" the attributes with data. You can enter attribute information at the command prompt or in a dialog box. This unit explores both methods of supplying this information while inserting a block. For more information on block insertion, you may want to review unit 69.

The objectives for this unit are to:

- Review the use of DDINSERT to insert a block or a drawing into the current drawing
- Insert a block with attributes using the Enter Attributes dialog box to supply attribute information
- Insert a block with attributes using the command prompt to supply attribute information
- Describe the settings of the ATTDIA system variable and use them to control attribute entry methods

Inserting a Block with Attributes

When inserting blocks with attributes, you must supply the attribute information to be associated with the block. Supplying this information is called "defining the attribute's value." Attributes defined as constant, however, do not allow you to supply this information during block insertion.

AutoCAD enables you to define the attribute's value from a dialog box or from the command prompt. The method of defining the attribute's value is controlled by the system variable ATTDIA. This variable has only two settings: a setting of 0 (the default) directs AutoCAD to use the command prompt to request information about attribute values. A setting of 1 directs AutoCAD to display a dialog box to request this information.

When ATTDIA is set to 1, AutoCAD ignores the VERIFY setting established with the DDATTDEF command because values entered are displayed in the dialog box for verification.

Figure 93.1 shows the Enter Attributes dialog box. This is the dialog box you will see when inserting a block with attributes if the system variable ATTDIA is set to 1.

Figure 93.1

The Enter Attributes dialog box.

Enter Attributes

Block name: DESK

Enter Extension Number	
Enter Phone Type	PBX
Enter Desk Type	WORKSTATION
Enter Monitor Type	SVGA
Enter Computer Model	486D33
Enter Keyboard Type	101K
Enter Employee's Salary	
Enter Office Number	
Employee's Supervisor	
Enter Employee Name	

OK | Cancel | Previous | Next | Help...

Along the left side of the dialog box are the attribute prompts that were defined with the DDATTDEF command. To the right of each prompt is an edit box containing the default values that were defined also with the DDATTDEF command. This edit box is empty if no default value was supplied with the DDATTDEF command. If no attribute prompt was defined, the attribute tag is used in its place.

Note in figure 93.1 that the dialog box displays only ten attributes. More attributes are defined, which means that the Next and Previous buttons at the bottom of the dialog box are enabled. The Cancel button cancels the block insertion. When all attributes have been set to their proper values, the OK button directs AutoCAD to complete the block insertion.

In the following exercise, you will insert a block with attributes using the Enter Attributes dialog box. To do so, you first must set the system variable ATTDIA to 1. This exercise inserts the first component in an electrical schematic which will be completed later in this unit.

Using the Enter Attributes Dialog Box

1. Begin a new drawing named 093???01 in your assigned directory, using the drawing 093ATTDB as a prototype.

2. `Command:` **`ATTDIA`** ↵ `New value for ATTDIA <0>:` **`1`** ↵	Sets the ATTDIA system variable to 1
3. `Command:` *Choose* Draw, *then* Insert	Displays the Insert dialog box
4. *In the* Insert *dialog box, choose* File, *locate and select the file named* TRANSIST, *then choose* OK	Selects the file to insert as a block
5. `Insertion point:` **`ENDP`** ↵ `of` *Pick the end point at* ① *(see fig. 93.2)*	Use endpoint object snap
6. `X scale factor <1> / Corner / XYZ:` *Press* Enter	Accepts default X-scale factor
`Y scale factor (default=X):` *Press* Enter	Accepts default Y-scale factor
`Rotation angle <0>:` *Press* Enter	Accepts default rotation angle

After you specify the rotation angle, the Enter Attributes dialog box appears on-screen.

7. Change the attribute values in the edit boxes to the values shown in figure 93.3, then click on OK.

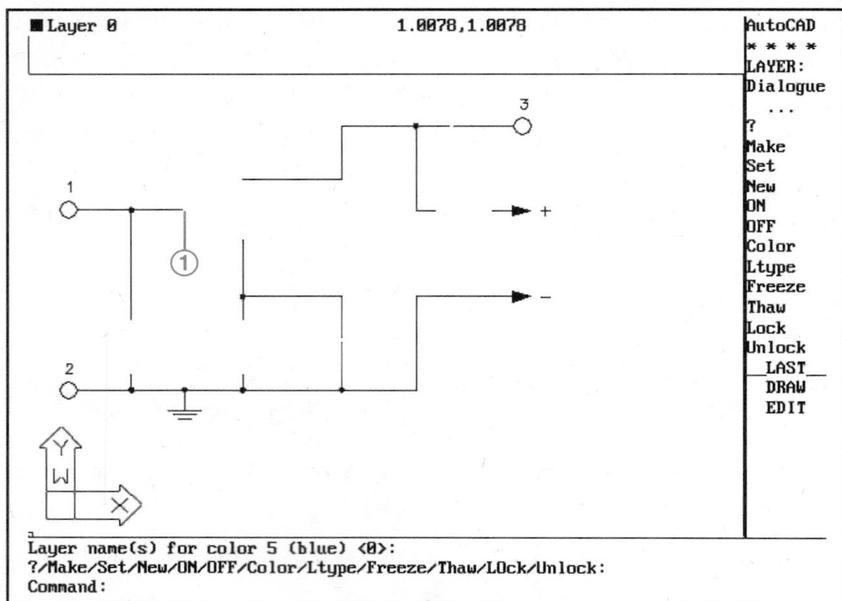

Figure 93.2

Insertion point for transistor block.

Enter Attributes	
Block name: TRANSIST	
Enter Transistor Number	1
MANUFACTURER	MOT
CATALOG_NUMBER	TR12345-B
DESIGNATOR	Q
Enter Transistor Model	2N3540
COST	6.76

OK | Cancel | Previous | Next | Help...

Figure 93.3

Values for transistor attributes.

You can see that AutoCAD automatically prompts you to supply information for any of the attributes contained in the block, which do not have preset values. You only have to enter the information in the appropriate edit box in the Enter Attributes dialog box, and AutoCAD takes care of inserting the data into the drawing.

Working with ATTDIA=0

As stated earlier, AutoCAD enables you to define attribute values from the command prompt and in the Enter Attributes dialog box. When inserting a block with attributes in this manner, you will be prompted to supply the value for each attribute individually. If the Verify option was used in the attribute definition, the values you input will be redisplayed at the command prompt for verification. You will not be prompted to supply values for attributes defined as Constant or Preset.

In the following exercise, insert blocks with attributes by defining the attribute values in the command prompt. This means you must first set the system variable ATTDIA to 0.

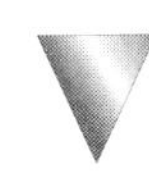

Using the Command Prompt To Enter Attribute Information

1. If you completed and saved the previous exercise, you can continue with the same drawing. Otherwise, begin a new drawing named 093???02 in your assigned directory using the drawing 093ATTCP as a prototype.

2. `Command:` **`ATTDIA`** ↵ `New value for ATTDIA <1>:` **`0`** ↵	Changes ATTDIA to 0 (off)
3. `Command:` **`DDINSERT`** ↵	Displays the Insert dialog box
4. *Choose* File, *locate and select the file named* RES, *then click on OK*	Selects the file RES for insertion
5. `Insertion point:` **`ENDP`** ↵ of *Select at* ① *(see fig. 93.4)*	Use endpoint object snap tool
6. `X scale factor <1> / Corner / XYZ:` *Press* Enter	Accepts default X-scale factor
7. `Y scale factor (default=X):` *Press* Enter	Accepts default Y-scale factor
8. `Rotation angle <0>:` **`270`** ↵	Specifies a new rotation angle
9. `Enter attribute values` `Enter Resistor Rating <1K>:` **`150`** ↵ `Enter Resistor Number <1>:` **`2`** ↵	 Changes the attribute value Changes the attribute value
10. `Verify attribute values`	
11. `Enter Resistor Rating <150>:` *Press* Enter	Accepts default value
12. `Enter Resistor Number <2>:` *Press* Enter	Accepts default value
13. `Command:` *Press* Enter `DDINSERT`	Repeats the DDINSERT command
14. *Choose* File, *locate and select the file named* CAP, *then click on* OK	Selects the file CAP for insertion

continues

15. `Insertion point:` **`ENDP`** ↵ — Uses end point object snap tool
    `of` *Select at* ② *(see fig. 93.4)*
16. `X scale factor <1> / Corner / XYZ:` *Press* Enter — Accepts default X-scale factor
17. `Y scale factor (default=X):` *Press* Enter — Accepts default Y-scale factor
18. `Rotation angle <0>:` **`270`** ↵ — Specifies a new rotation angle

    `Enter attribute values`
19. `Enter Capacitor Rating <.01UF>:` **`1UF`** ↵ — Changes the attribute value
20. `Enter Capacitor Number <1>:` **`2`** ↵ — Changes the attribute value

    `Verify attribute values`
21. `Enter Capacitor Rating <1UF>:` *Press* Enter — Accepts default value
22. `Enter Capacitor Number <2>:` *Press* Enter — Accepts default value

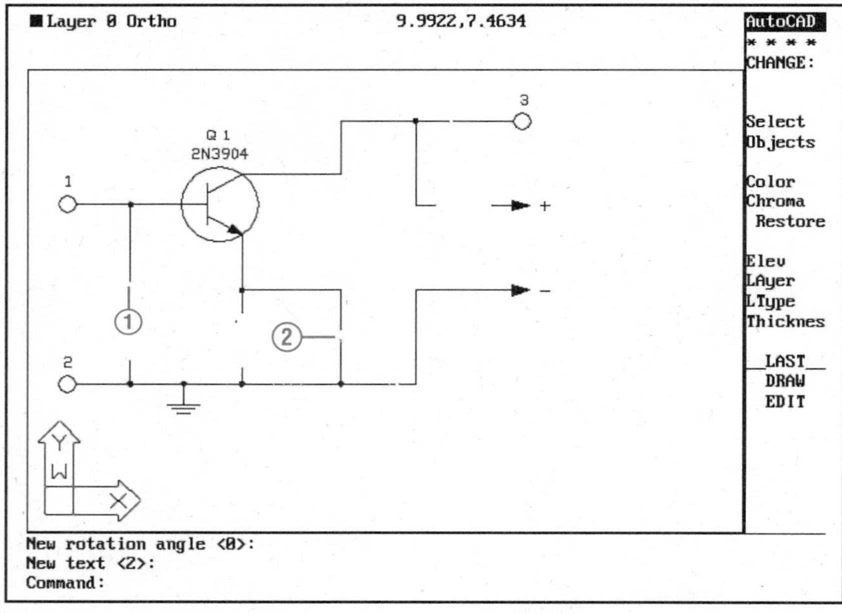

Figure 93.4

Insertion point for resistor and capacitor blocks.

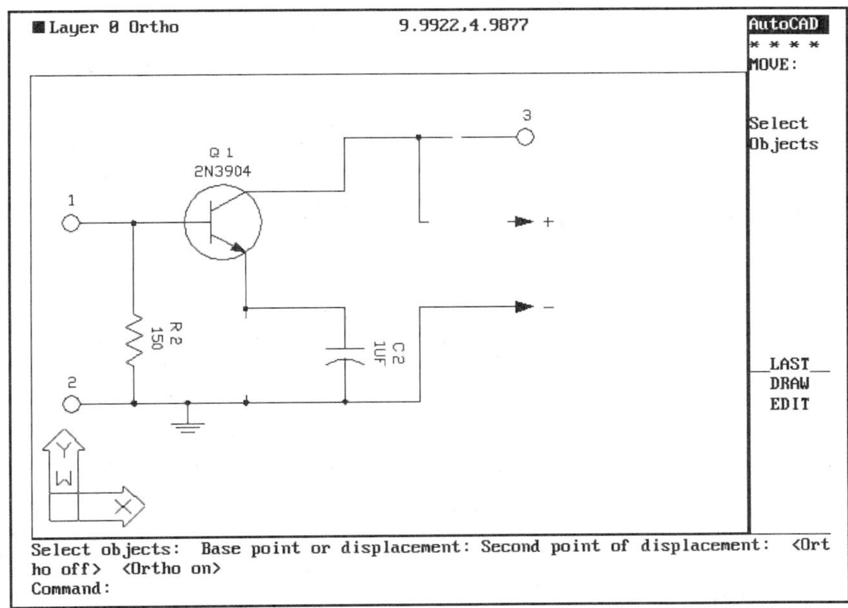

Figure 93.5

Resistor and capacitor blocks at 270-degree rotation.

As you can see in figure 93.5, inserting the resistor and capacitor blocks at a rotation angle other than zero could cause problems with your attribute positions. In unit 94, you will learn how to orient your attributes to any position and make other changes to them after they have been inserted.

Unit Review

What You've Learned

- ☞ How to insert a block with attributes using the DDINSERT command
- ☞ The function and use of the ATTDIA system variable
- ☞ The function and use of the Enter Attributes dialog box
- ☞ The use of the command prompt to enter attribute information

Review Questions

True or False

93.01 T F The DDINSERT command enables you to insert blocks or drawing files.

93.02 T F Attribute values are always entered in a dialog box.

93.03 T F To supply attribute values during block insertion, the system variable ATTDIA must be set to 1.

93.04 T F The Enter Attributes dialog box enables you to change attributes defined as constant.

Multiple Choice

93.05 To supply attribute values at the command prompt, ATTDIA must be set to __________.

(A) 0

(B) 1

(C) On

(D) Off

93.06 The Enter Attributes dialog box can display up to __________ attributes at a time.

(A) 8

(B) 10

(C) 24

(D) 36

Student: __________ Date: __________

Instructor: __________ Course: __________ Section: __________

93.07 If no attribute prompt is specified when an attribute is created, AutoCAD uses the attribute's __________ for a prompt.

(A) default value

(B) tag

(C) mode setting

(D) block name

93.08 When a block is inserted with a rotation angle, its attributes are __________.

(A) left at their original angles

(B) deleted

(C) rotated to the same angle as the block

(D) rotated 90 degrees from the block's rotation angle

Short Answer

93.09 Describe what happens when the verify mode of an attribute is turned on and you can supply attribute values from the command prompt.

____

____

____

93.10 Why is the Verify setting of an attribute ignored when entering attribute values from the dialog box?

____

____

____

Additional Exercises

93.11 If you completed and saved the previous exercise, you can continue with the same drawing. Otherwise, begin a new drawing named 093???03 in your assigned directory by using the drawing 093ATTAE as a prototype. Insert the remaining resistors and capacitor to complete the schematic (see fig. 93.6). Use the information in table 93.1 for attribute settings.

Student: ______________ Date: ______________

Instructor: ______________ Course: ______________ Section: ______________

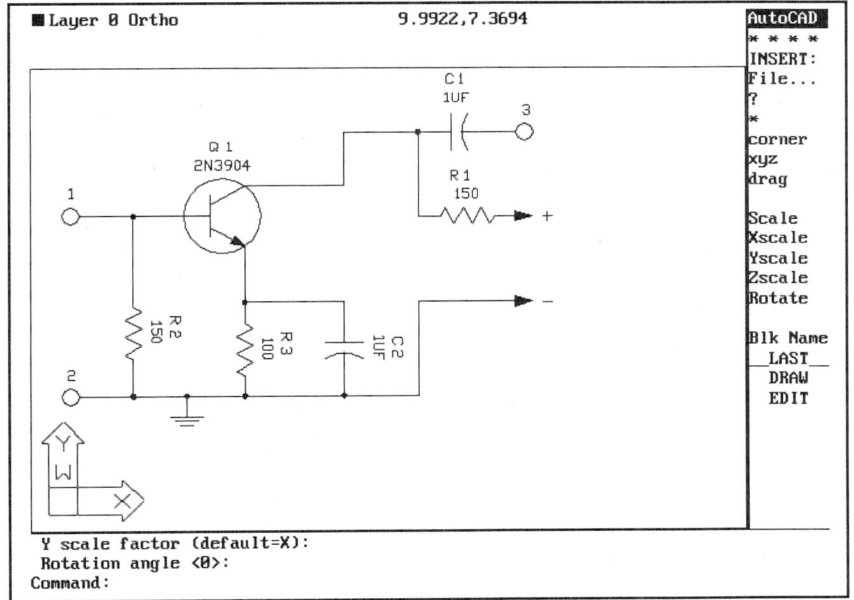

Figure 93.6

The completed schematic.

Table 93.1

Attribute Values for Resistor R1

Prompt	Value
Enter Resistor Rating	150
Enter Resistor Number	1
Manufacturer	MOT
CATALOG_NUMBER	R6759
COST	1.38

Attribute Values for Resistor R3

Prompt	Value
Enter Resistor Rating	100
Enter Resistor Number	3
Manufacturer	MOT
CATALOG_NUMBER	R7437
COST	0.95

Student: ______________________ Date: __________

Instructor: ____________________ Course: ________ Section: ________

Attribute Values for Capacitor C1

Prompt	Value
Enter Capacitor Rating	1UF
Enter Capacitor Number	1
Manufacturer	MOT
CATALOG_NUMBER	C714
COST	2.13

Student: ______________________ Date: __________

Instructor: ____________________ Course: ________ Section: ________

Editing Attributes

The use of attributes would be severely limited if you could not change attributes after you create them. As an example, suppose you buy transistors from Bob's Electronics for $1.62 each, and add this information to each transistor. Eventually Bob will raise his prices, requiring you to change the transistor's price attribute. You can change attribute text using two different methods. In this unit you learn when to use each method, and also examine a command for changing the position, rotation angle, and other properties of attribute text.

The objectives for this unit are to:

- Determine whether to use DDEDIT or DDATTE to change attribute text
- Change attribute text with DDEDIT
- Change attribute text with DDATTE
- Change attribute text position and rotation angle with ATTEDIT
- Summarize the uses of ATTEDIT

Editing Attribute Definitions

Two commands can be used to edit attribute text. One of these, DDEDIT, may only be used to edit attribute text *before* the attribute is linked to a symbol with the BLOCK command. DDEDIT is useful when changes occur during attribute setup. You can correct any misspelled words or make other changes to the attributes before the attribute is linked to the object.

You can enter the DDEDIT command at the command prompt or select it from the EDIT screen menu. When you issue the DDEDIT command, you will be prompted with:

```
<Select a TEXT or ATTDEF object>/Undo:.
```

AutoCAD only allows selection of one text or attribute entity at a time. The cursor crosshairs are replaced with a pick box for entity selection, or you can type **L** to select the last entity drawn. When an attribute is selected, the Edit Attribute Definition dialog box appears (see fig. 94.1). As you can see from the illustration, you are given the opportunity to change the attribute's tag, prompt, and default value. If the text is too long to be displayed in the edit box, you can use your keyboard's right arrow to scroll the text into the edit box.

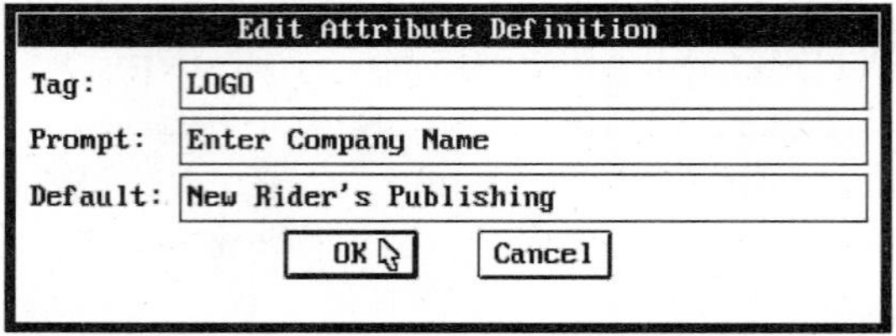

Figure 94.1

The DDEDIT command's Edit Attribute Definition dialog box.

Aside from attributes, the DDEDIT command can be used to edit text created with the TEXT or DTEXT commands.

After an attribute definition has been changed, AutoCAD will continue to prompt for text or attribute selection. When you are finished editing, press the Enter key on your keyboard to return to the command prompt.

In the following exercise, change attributes to create a custom title block that can be inserted in future drawings. You can use this or a similar title block to automate the creation of title blocks. You will use the DDEDIT command to make changes to the title block attributes. You will then use BLOCK and WBLOCK to create a symbol of the title block and write the symbol to disk.

Customizing Title Block Attributes with DDEDIT

1. Begin a new drawing named 094???01 in your assigned directory using the drawing 094TITLE as a prototype.

2. `Command:` *From the* EDIT *screen menu, choose* DDEDIT `_DDEDIT:`	Issues the DDEDIT command
3. `<Select a TEXT or ATTDEF object>/ Undo:` *Select the attribute* LOGO *from the title block*	Displays the Edit Attribute Definition dialog box for LOGO
4. *Change the* Default *edit box from New Riders Publishing to your school or company name, then choose* OK	
5. `<Select a TEXT or ATTDEF object>/ Undo:` *Select the attribute* TITLE_LINE_ONE *from the title block*	Displays the Edit Attribute Definition dialog box for TITLE_LINE_ONE
6. *Enter* **`HANDS ON AUTOCAD`** *in the* Default *edit box, then choose* OK	Changes the value of the attribute
7. `<Select a TEXT or ATTDEF object>/ Undo:` *Select the attribute* TITLE_LINE_TWO *from the title block*	Displays the Edit Attribute Definition dialog box for TITLE_LINE_TWO
8. *Enter* **`RELEASE 12`** *in the* Default *edit box, then choose* OK	Changes the value of the attribute
9. `<Select a TEXT or ATTDEF object>/Undo:` *Select the attribute* NAME	Displays the Edit Attribute Definition dialog box for NAME
10. *Enter your name in the* Default *edit box, then choose* OK	Changes the value of the attribute
11. `<Select a TEXT or ATTDEF object>/Undo:` *Select* DWG.SCALE	Displays the Edit Attribute Definition dialog box for DWG.SCALE
12. *Change the* Prompt *edit box from* Enter Dwg.Scale *to* Enter Drawing Scale, *then choose* OK	Changes the prompt for the attribute
13. `<Select a TEXT or ATTDEF object>/Undo:` *Press* Enter	Ends attribute editing

Now that you have edited the attributes, create a block of the title block and use WBLOCK to save it to disk.

Creating a Block of the Title Block

Continue with your drawing from the preceding exercise.

1.	`Command:` **`ATTDIA`** ↵ `New value for ATTDIA <0>:` **`1`** ↵	Sets ATTDIA to 1
2.	`Command:` *Choose* Construct, *then* Block	Issues the BLOCK command
3.	`_block Block name (or ?):` **`TITLE`** ↵	Specifies the block name
4.	`Insertion base point:` **`NODE`** ↵ `of` *pick the node point at the lower right corner of the title block*	Uses the node object snap and specifies the base point
5.	`Select objects:` **`ALL`** ↵ `20 found`	Chooses all entities for block
6.	`Select objects:` *Press* Enter	Ends block object selection
7.	`Command:` **`WBLOCK`** ↵	Issues the WBLOCK command

8. The Create Drawing File dialog box appears. Type the file name TITLE in the edit box, then choose OK.

9.	`Block name:` **`TITLE`** ↵	Selects the block TITLE for the WBLOCK file
10.	`Command:` *Choose* Draw, *then* Insert `ddinsert`	Issues the DDINSERT command
11.	`Block name (or ?):` **`TITLE`** ↵	Selects the block to insert
12.	`Insertion point:` *Pick a point at the lower right corner of your screen*	
13.	`X scale factor <1> / Corner / XYZ:` *Press* Enter	Accepts the default X scale
	`Y scale factor (default=X):` *Press* Enter	Accepts the default Y scale
	`Rotation angle <0>:` *Press* Enter	Accepts the default rotation

14. Because ATTTDIA is set to 1, the Enter Attributes dialog box appears. Enter the attribute settings shown in figure 94.2, then save your drawing.

As you can see from this exercise, editing attribute definitions is a simple process if you do it before the BLOCK command is used on the attribute.

Enter Attributes

Block name: TITLE

Enter Drawing Scale	N/A
Enter Dwg.Number	1234567
Line 2 of Dwg.Title	RELEASE 12
Line 1 of Dwg.Title	HANDS ON AUTOCAD
Enter Company Name	New Rider's Publishing
Enter Dwg.Filename	094TITLE
Enter Date	(enter current date)
Drawn By :	(enter your name)

OK Cancel Previous Next Help...

Figure 94.2

Attribute values for title block.

Editing Attribute Entities in a Block

If you need to make changes to attribute information after the BLOCK command has been used on the attribute, you will use either the DDATTE command or the ATTEDIT command.

Editing Attributes with DDATTE

After a block is created and the symbol containing your attributes has been inserted into a drawing, you can use the DDATTE command to change the attribute values.

Attribute values can only be changed if they are variable attributes. This means if the attribute was defined as Constant with the DDATTDEF command (unit 92), it cannot be modified after being inserted.

You can issue the DDATTE command at the command prompt or select it from the EDIT screen menu. After you issue the DDATTE command, the Edit Attributes dialog box appears, as shown in figure 94.3.

Does this dialog box look familiar? It is the same dialog box used in unit 93—"Inserting a Block with Attributes"—to enter the attribute information if ATTDIA is set to 1. The only difference is the dialog box title, which has changed from Enter Attributes to Edit Attributes. The DDATTE command does not require the ATTDIA variable to be set to 1. Its use is the same as the Enter Attributes dialog box. Along the left side the attribute prompt is diplayed, but cannot be changed. In the edit box to the right of each prompt is the current attribute value, which may be changed.

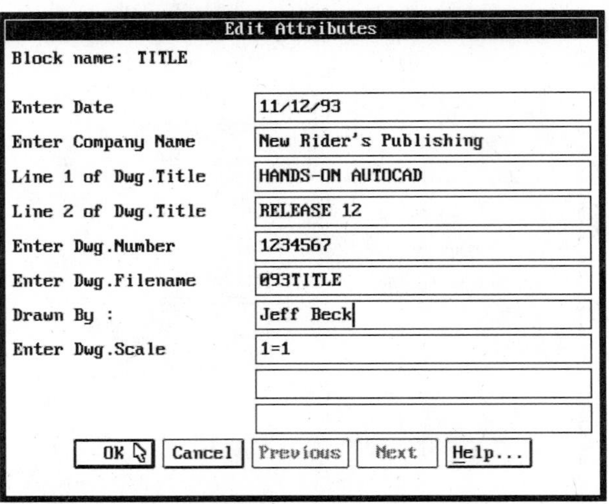

Figure 94.3

The DDATTE command's Edit Attributes dialog box.

Attributes defined as Constant are not displayed in the Edit Attributes dialog box.

In the next exercise, continue adding information to the electrical schematic you started in unit 92 ("Creating an Attribute"). Use the information in table 94.1 to change the new attributes.

Table 94.1
New Values for Electrical Schematic

Part designation	Cost	Manufacturer
Q	17.33	Radio Shack
C1	1.33	Circuit Barn
C2	1.33	Circuit Barn
R1	1.55	No change needed
R2	1.55	No change needed
R3	1.15	No change needed

Editing Block Attributes with DDATTE

1. If you completed and saved the final exercise from unit 92, you can continue with the same drawing. Otherwise, begin a new drawing named 094???02 in your assigned directory using the drawing 094ATTE as a prototype.

2. `Command:` *From the* EDIT *screen menu, choose* DDATTE: — Issues the DDATTE command

3. `Select block:` *Select the transistor block by picking on the symbol or the attribute text* — Displays the Edit Attributes dialog box

4. *Change the* COST *and* MANUFACTURER *attributes as shown in Table 94.1.*

5. `Command:` *Press* Enter — Repeats the DDATTE command

   `DDATTE`

6. `Select block:` *Select the C1 capacitor block and edit as shown in table 94.1*

7. Continue editing attributes for components C2, R1, R2, and R3, changing their values to match the values given in table 94.1.

Editing Attributes with ATTEDIT

As you have seen, DDEDIT lets you change an attribute's values easily before the attribute is added to a block. You have also changed these values after block insertion with DDATTE.

Another command enables you to edit attributes after they have been inserted as blocks. The ATTEDIT command is used to change more than the attribute information; it also is used to change the way attribute information is presented. With ATTEDIT, you can change the position, height, angle, style, layer, and color of attribute text. The ATTEDIT command can be entered from the command prompt or selected from the EDIT screen menu.

The final exercise in unit 93 created a drawing with attribute text positioned at incorrect angles. Compare figure 94.4, which shows the exercise completed in unit 93, with figure 94.5. The attribute text was given unidirectional alignment in figure 94.5 using the ATTEDIT command.

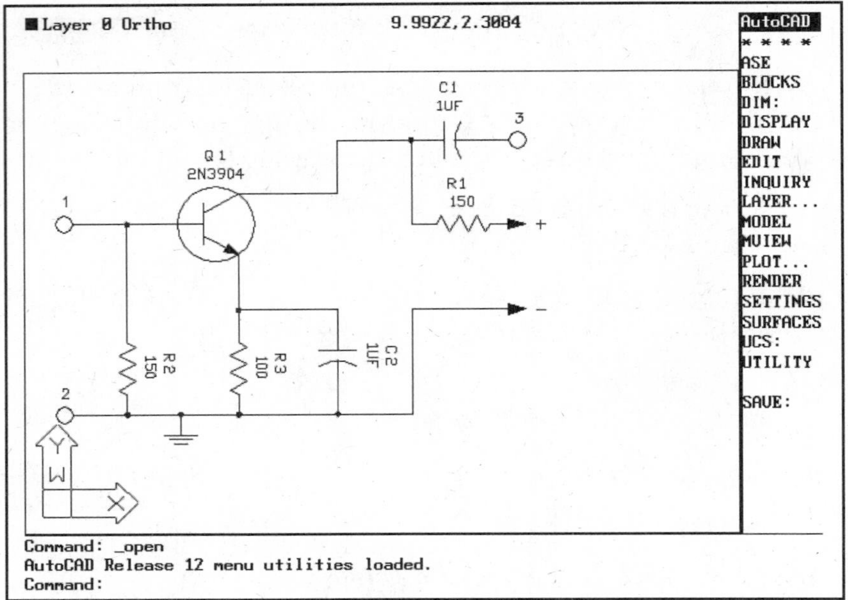

Figure 94.4

Attribute text incorrectly positioned on the drawing.

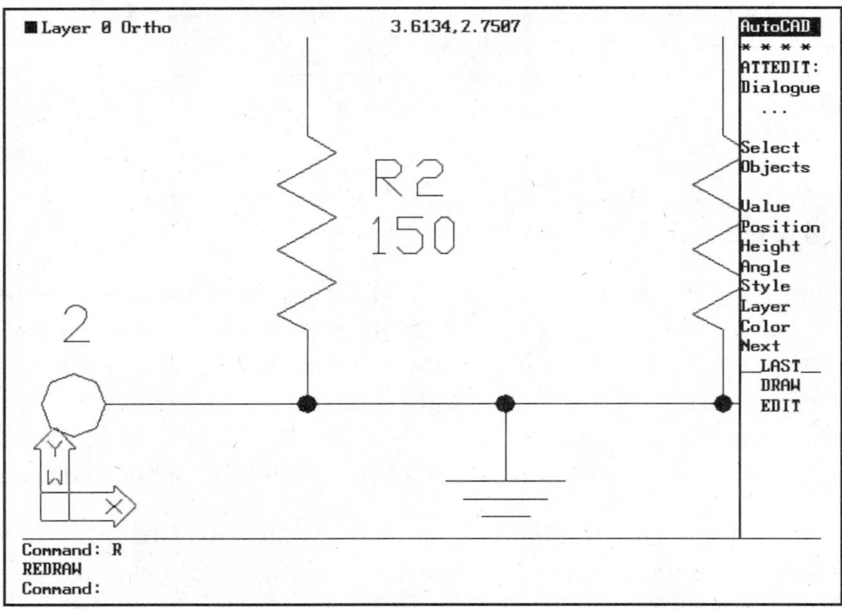

Figure 94.5

Text positions for R2 adjusted using ATTEDIT.

In the following exercise, modify the drawing in figure 94.4 to correct the text orientation using ATTEDIT. Refer to figure 94.5 for appropriate location and orientation of attribute text.

Editing Block Attributes with ATTEDIT

1. If you completed and saved the previous exercise, you may continue with the same drawing. Otherwise, begin a new drawing named 094???03 in your assigned directory, using the drawing 094ATTED as a prototype.

2. *Zoom in on resistor R2 (see fig. 94.5)*

3. `Command:` *From the* EDIT *screen menu, choose* ATTEDIT:	Issues the ATTEDIT command
4. `Edit attributes one at a time? <Y>` *Press* Enter	Accepts the default of Y (yes)

If N (no) is specified, attribute positions cannot be changed.

5. `Block name specification <*>:` *Press* Enter	Accepts the default (any block selected)

You can supply a block name to edit only those blocks with a name that matches the one you specify.

6. `Attribute tag specification <*>:` *Press* Enter	Accepts the default (any tag selected)

You can supply a tag to edit only those attributes with the specified tag.

7. `Attribute value specification <*>:` *Press* Enter	Accepts the default (any value selected)

You can supply an attribute value to edit attributes that have the specified value.

8. `Select Attributes:` *Select the attributes with the values* R, 2, *and* 150 *for component R2*	Selects attributes

`3 attributes selected.`

Attributes are NOT highlighted when selected with this command.

At this point, an X will appear on the first selected attribute, and you will be prompted for the attribute properties you want to modify.

9. `Value/Position/Height/Angle/Style /Layer/Color/Next <N>:` **`A`** ↵	Specifies Angle option
10. `New rotation angle <270>:` **`0`** ↵	Specifies new angle

continues

11. `Value/Position/Height/Angle/Style/ Layer/Color/Next <N>:` **P** ↵	Specifies Position option
12. `Enter text insertion point:` *Pick a point to position the text, as shown in figure 94.5*	Specifies a new text insertion point
13. `Value/Position/Height/Angle/Style/ Layer/Color/Next <N>:` *Press* Enter	Selects next attribute

At this point, the X will move to the next selected attribute.

14. `Value/Position/Height/Angle/Style/ Layer/Color/Next <N>:` **A** ↵	Specifies Angle option
15. `New rotation angle <270>:` **0** ↵	Specifies new angle
16. `Value/Position/Height/Angle/Style/ Layer/Color/Next <N>:` **P** ↵	Specifies Position option
17. `Enter text insertion point:` *Pick a point to position the text, as shown in figure 94.5*	Relocates the text
18. `Value/Position/Height/Angle/Style/ Layer/Color/Next <N>:` *Press* Enter	Selects the next attribute
19. `Value/Position/Height/Angle/Style/ Layer/Color/Next <N>:` **A** ↵	Specifies the Angle option
20. `New rotation angle <270>:` **0** ↵	Specifies new angle
21. `Value/Position/Height/Angle/Style/ Layer/Color/Next <N>:` **P** ↵	Specifies the Position option
22. `Enter text insertion point:` *Pick a point to position the text, as shown in figure 94.5*	Relocates the text
23. `Value/Position/Height/Angle/Style/ Layer/Color/Next <N>:` *Press* Enter	

After the last selected attribute has been modified, the default <N> (for Next) will return you to the command prompt.

24. Pan to component R3 and use ATTEDIT to correct its attribute positions and angles. Do the same for component C2. When completed, your drawing should look similar to figure 94.6.

As you can see, the ATTEDIT command allows you to change almost any property of an attribute. Editing attributes with ATTEDIT is a much longer and more difficult process than using DDATTE, however. Use DDATTE when you need to edit the value of an attribute, and use ATTEDIT when you need to edit the attribute's other characteristics.

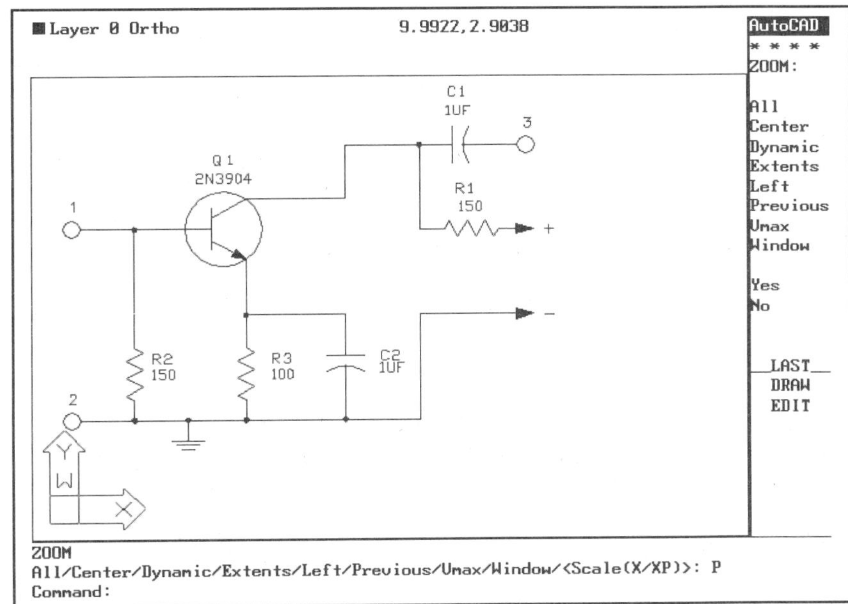

Figure 94.6

Attributes modified with ATTEDIT.

So far in Part 10, you have learned how to attach text to your blocks and make the text constant, variable, and visible or invisible. You also have seen how to modify anything about these text attributes. But what about adding more attributes to the symbol or modifying the symbol itself? These questions are addressed in units 95 and 96.

Unit Review

What You've Learned

- ☞ When and how to use the DDEDIT command to modify attribute tags, prompts, and values
- ☞ When and how to use the DDATTE command to modify attribute values
- ☞ Use of the ATTEDIT command to change the angle and position of attribute text
- ☞ An overview of the many attribute properties that can be changed with the ATTEDIT command

Review Questions

True or False

94.01 T F The DDEDIT command can be used to edit attributes after the attributes have been inserted.

94.02 T F The DDEDIT command can also be used on text created with the TEXT or DTEXT commands.

94.03 T F The DDATTE command can be used to modify attributes defined as Constant.

94.04 T F The DDATTE command can be used to change the rotation angle of attribute text.

Multiple Choice

94.05 The DDEDIT command can be typed at the command prompt or selected from the __________ screen menu.

(A) DRAW

(B) EDIT

(C) BLOCKS

(D) UTILITY

Student: ____________________ Date: __________

Instructor: ____________________ Course: __________ Section: __________

94.06 The DDEDIT command allows you to change an attribute's Prompt, Value, and __________.

(A) Mode

(B) Rotation angle

(C) Text Style

(D) Tag

94.07 The __________ command is the easiest way to change an attribute value after insertion as a block.

(A) DDATTE

(B) DDEDIT

(C) ATTEDIT

(D) EXPLODE

94.08 The __________ command allows you to change an attribute's color.

(A) DDATTE

(B) DDEDIT

(C) ATTEDIT

(D) EDIT

Student: ______________________ Date: ______________

Instructor: ______________________ Course: ______________ Section: ______________

UNIT 95

Editing Blocks

s with other entities you draw in AutoCAD, blocks often need to be edited. This might mean repositioning or resizing the block. It might also mean copying, moving, scaling, or mirroring the block. Or you may need to change completely the appearance of all occurrences of a block within a drawing (called *redefining* the block). In any of these situations, AutoCAD enables you to edit blocks easily. This unit teaches you to edit blocks and to use blocks more effectively.

The objectives for this unit are to:

- ☞ Understand how to substitute an existing block with a different block using the INSERT command
- ☞ Understand how to create a new block from an existing block with the INSERT command
- ☞ Understand how to explode a block to modify it, then redefine the modified block
- ☞ Understand how to edit blocks and their attributes with grips
- ☞ Understand the use of the GRIPBLOCK system variable
- ☞ Understand how using block redefinition and substitution can increase your drawing speed and efficiency

Redefining Blocks

Because AutoCAD recognizes a block as a singular entity, you cannot directly edit the individual entities contained in the block. You can, however, *redefine* the block. There are several methods and uses of block redefinition. Blocks can be redefined to change the appearance of all occurrences of a block throughout a drawing. Blocks can be exploded, edited, and then redefined to reflect a change in the original block. You may want to replace an existing block with a different block, or use an existing block to define a new block.

Redefining Blocks with EXPLODE

One way to edit the individual entities in a block is to *explode* the block. The EXPLODE command converts a block into its individual entities. You can edit the individual entities, then use the BLOCK command again to redefine the block.

In the following exercise, a chair has been added to the workstation at the top of the drawing. This chair is not part of the DESK block, but needs to be placed at each desk to give you a better idea of space requirements. Redefine the block DESK to include the chair.

Block Redefinition and Substitution

1. Begin a new drawing named 095???01 in your assigned directory using the drawing 095REDEF as a prototype, then zoom to the view shown in figure 95.1.

2. Command: *Choose* Modify, *then* Explode	Issues the EXPLODE command
3. Select objects: *Select the desk with the chair by it*	Selects a block
4. Select objects: *Press* Enter	Ends object selection

Note that the desk's attribute tags are displayed when it is exploded.

5. Command: *Choose* Construct, *then* Block	Issues the BLOCK command
6. block Block name (or ?): **DESK** ↵	Specifies the BLOCK name
7. Block DESK already exists. Redefine it? <N> **Y** ↵	Directs AutoCAD to redefine block DESK
8. Insertion base point: **MID** ↵ of *Pick a point at* ① *(see fig. 95.1)*	Specifies insertion point

9. `Select objects:` *Use a window to select the desk, its attributes and the chair (be careful not to select the wall behind the desk)* — Selects entities for the block

   `133 found`

10. `Select objects:` *Press* Enter — Ends selection and redefines the block

   `Block DESK redefined`
   `Regenerating drawing.`

11. Zoom to the previous view.

Because all the desks in the drawing are occurrences of the block DESK, all of them are redefined automatically to include the chair.

12. On your own, use the INSERT command to insert the block DESK to replace the one you removed. Use default values for all attributes.

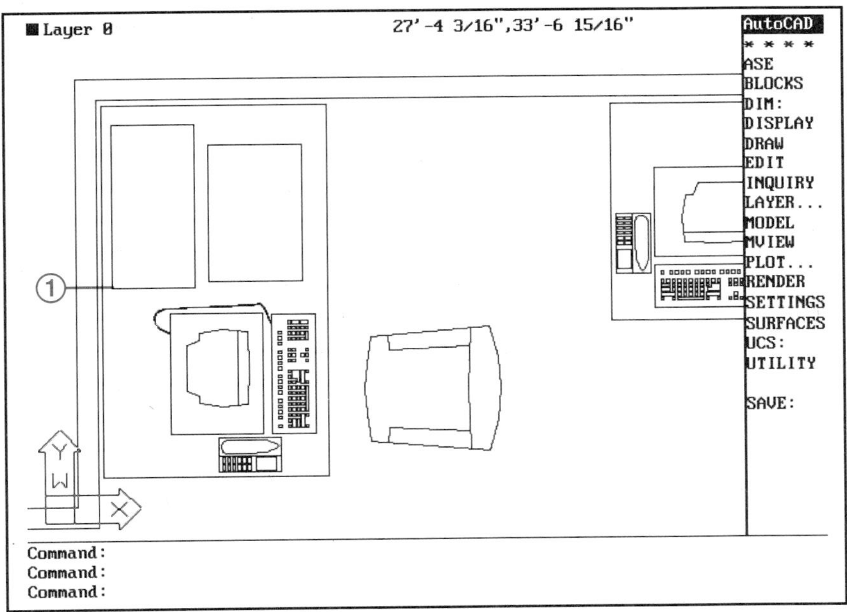

Figure 95.1

Insertion point for block DESK redefinition.

The EXPLODE command also explodes polylines into their individual line and arc segments. Because polygons and ellipses are created as polylines, the EXPLODE command has the same effect on these types of entities as on polylines.

Using = To Redefine Blocks

To speed up regeneration and redraw, you can replace the complex DESK block with a simple representation while you are working on the drawing, then redefine the complex block when the drawing is finished. You can replace the complex block by setting it *equal* to a simple block.

In the following exercise, replace the DESK block with a simpler one. Zoom to the view shown in figure 95.1 and draw an outline around the desk and chair with the PLINE command.

Replacing a Complex Block with a Simple Block

1. Continue with your drawing from the previous exercise and zoom to the view shown in figure 95.2.
2. Draw a polyline from ① to points ② through ⑥, then close the polyline (see fig. 95.2). Use object snap modes where appropriate to snap to the existing desk.

3. `Command:` *Choose* Construct, *then* Block	Issues the BLOCK command
4. `_block Block name (or ?):` **`DESKBOX`** ↵	Names the simplified block
5. `Insertion base point:` **`INS`** ↵ `of` *Pick any point on the DESK block*	Specifies insertion point with INSert object snap
6. `Select objects:` **`L`** ↵	Specifies Last object drawn
`1 found`	
7. `Select objects:` *Press* Enter	Ends object selection and defines the block
8. `Command:` **`WBLOCK`** ↵	Issues the WBLOCK command

The Create Drawing dialog box will appear on-screen. Create a drawing file named DESKBOX.

9. `Block name:` **`DESKBOX`** ↵	Specifies the block DESKBOX to define the simplified WBLOCK

10. Issue the ZOOM command with the All option and note the amount of time your drawing takes to regenerate the complex blocks.

11. `Command:` **`INSERT`** ↵	Issues the INSERT command
12. `Block name (or ?) <DESK>:` **`DESK=DESKBOX`** ↵	Replaces block DESK with block DESKBOX

```
Block DESK redefined
Regenerating drawing.
```

13. `Insertion point:` *Press* CTRL+C — Cancels the block insertion
14. Issue the ZOOM command with the All option.

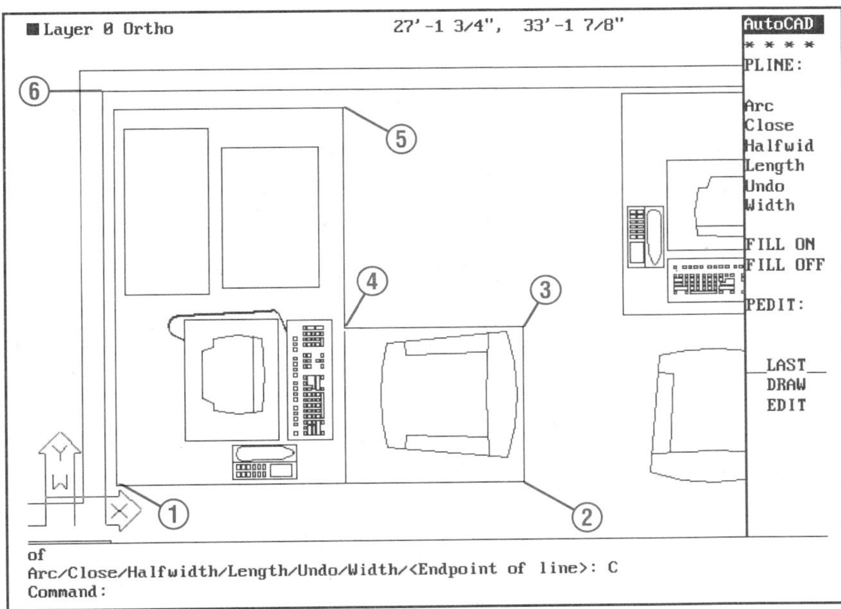

Figure 95.2

Pick points for simplified desk outline block.

Your drawing should resemble figure 95.3.

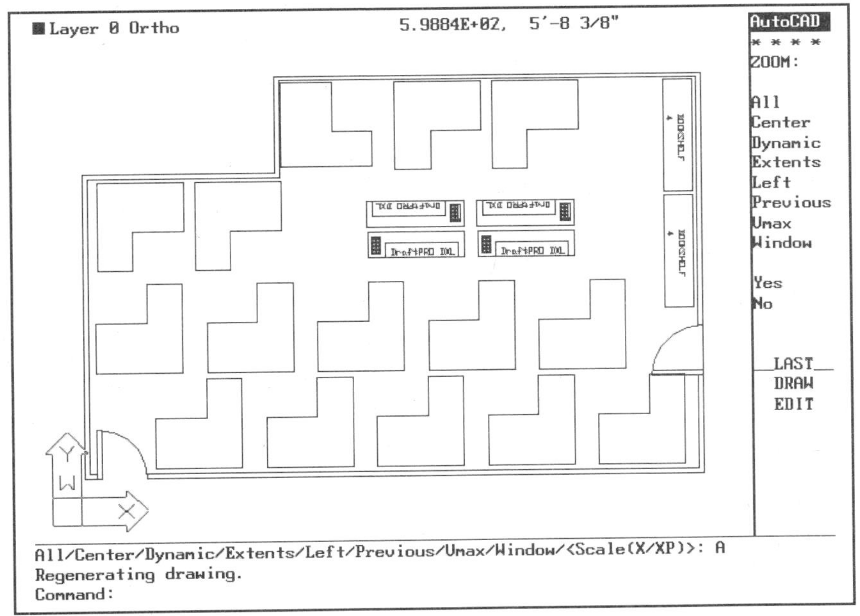

Figure 95.3

Complex block replaced by a simple block.

Did you notice how quickly the drawing regenerated? You can rearrange the furniture and try new layouts with much greater speed than was possible with the complex blocks. When you are satisfied with the layout, replace the original desk block.

Restoring the Original Block

Continue with your drawing from the preceding exercise.

1. `Command:` **`INSERT`** ↵ — Issues the INSERT command
2. `Block name (or ?) <DESK>:` **`DESK=`** ↵ — Redefines the block DESK to its original state

   `Block DESK redefined`
   `Regenerating drawing.`
3. `Insertion point:` *Press* CTRL+C — Cancels the block insertion
4. Save your drawing.

As you can see, drawing speed can be greatly increased with intelligent use of block substitution and redefinition.

In addition to redefining blocks to simplify them and speed up drawing regeneration and redraw, you can use the same method outlined in the previous exercise to create new blocks. Assume you need to create a new block called NEWBLOCK that is similar to an existing block called OLDBLOCK. Use the INSERT command to insert a new block using the existing block as a reference (NEWBLOCK=OLDBLOCK, for example). Then, explode NEWBLOCK, make whatever changes are necessary, and use BLOCK to turn it into a block again.

The EXPLODE and INSERT commands are not the only methods you have for editing blocks. As with other types of entities, you can edit blocks using grips.

Editing Blocks with Grips

Because AutoCAD recognizes a block as a single entity regardless of the number of entities it contains, blocks usually display only one grip. This single grip is located at the insertion point of the block. You can use the grip to perform autoedit functions such as move and copy on the block. If the block contains attributes, it also will display a grip for each attribute in the block.

AutoCAD supplies a system variable called GRIPBLOCK to control the method of displaying grips within a block. The easiest way to control the value of GRIPBLOCK is to use the check box labeled Enable Grips Within Blocks in the Grips dialog box (choose Settings, then Grips to display this dialog box). You also can enter GRIPBLOCK at the command prompt to set this variable directly.

The default setting for GRIPBLOCK is 0. When GRIPBLOCK is set to 0 (the default), a block displays a single grip for the block itself and a grip for each attribute in the block (as described previously). This setting is useful if you are interested in moving, copying, or rotating the block. You can reposition attributes in the block with the attribute grips, although you cannot change their angle without rotating the entire block. Figure 95.4 shows a block with its grips highlighted and GRIPBLOCK set to 0.

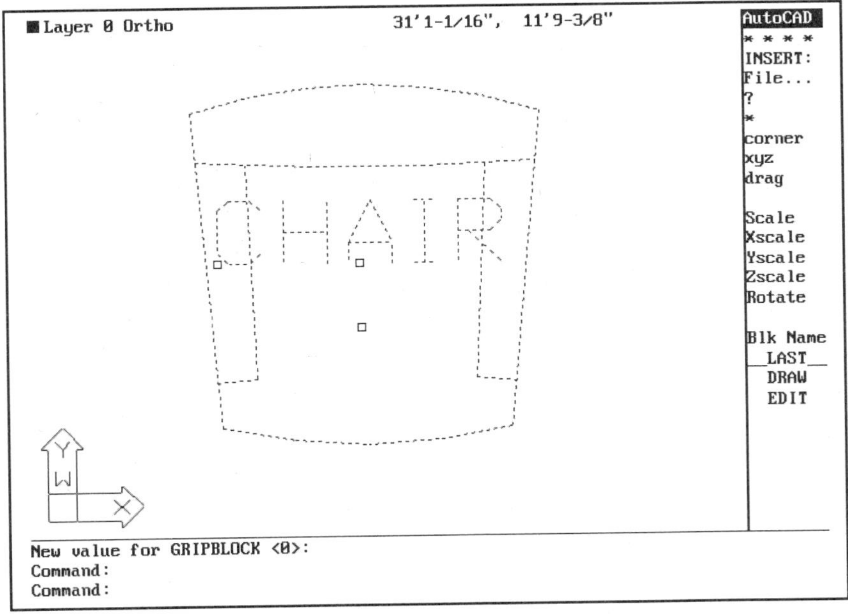

Figure 95.4

Chair block grips with GRIPBLOCK set to 0.

With GRIPBLOCK set to 1, all entities within the block display grips as if they were individual entities. This is useful when you need to edit using a base point in the block other than the block's insertion point. Figure 95.5 shows a block with its grips highlighted and GRIPBLOCK set to 1.

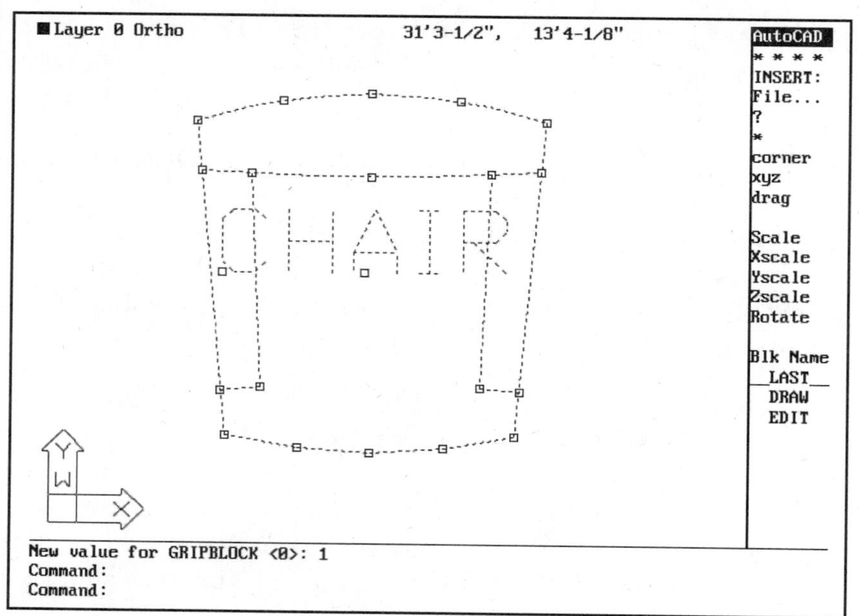

Figure 95.5

Chair block grips with GRIPBLOCK set to 1.

Even though each of the entities displays its grips when GRIPBLOCK is set to 1, you cannot use the grips to edit individual entities within the block. You must explode the block to change individual entities other than attributes.

The following exercise demonstrates the use of grips to edit a block. You will see how the computer room layout in the previous exercise might have been originally designed.

Editing Blocks with Grips

1. Begin a new drawing named 095???02 in your assigned directory using 095GRIPS as a prototype. Zoom to the view shown in figure 95.6.

2. `Command:` **`GRIPBLOCK`** ↵ `New value for GRIPBLOCK <0>:` **`0`** ↵	Verifies that GRIPBLOCK is set to zero
3. `Command:` *Select any part of the desk at* ① *(see fig. 95.6)*	Creates a selection set and displays the block's grips
4. `Command:` *Select the grip at* ② *(see fig. 95.6)*	Selects the grip and enters Stretch autoedit mode
`** STRETCH **`	
5. `<Stretch to point>/Base point/Copy /Undo/eXit:` *Press* Enter	Switches to the Move autoedit mode

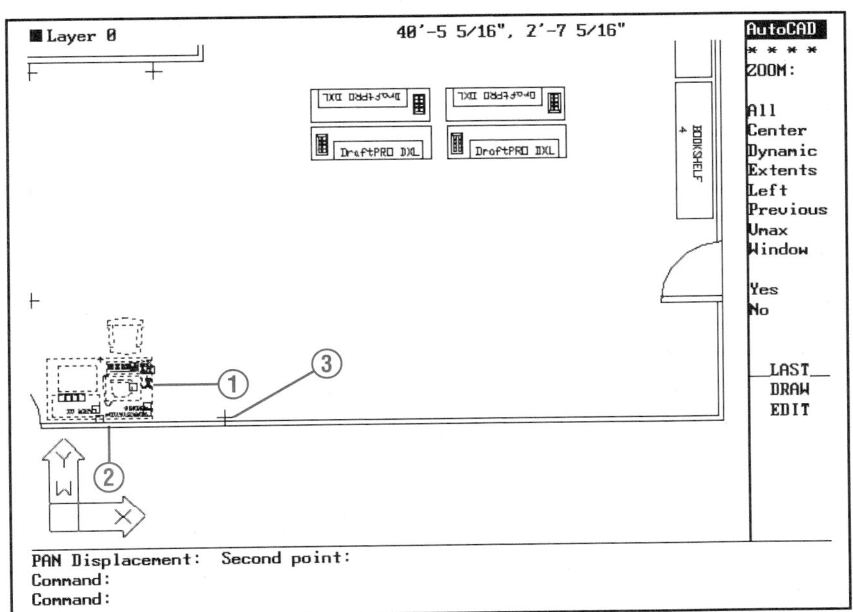

Figure 95.6

Pick points for desk autoedit operation.

`** MOVE **`

6. `<Move to point>/Base point UndoeXit:` **C** ↵ — Specifies the Copy option//Copy/

`** MOVE (multiple) **`

7. `<Move to point>/Base point/Copy /Undo/eXit:` **INT** ↵ of *Pick a point at* ③ *(see fig. 95.6)* — Uses the Intersection object snap to specify new location

`** MOVE (multiple) **`

8. `<Move to point>/Base point/Copy /Undo/eXit:` *Hold down the Shift key, continue to drag the crosshairs to the right, then select the next location at an equal space as the first desk*

`** MOVE (multiple) **`

9. `<Move to point>/Base point/Copy /Undo/eXit:` *Repeat the previous step, inserting two more desks at equal spacing*

`** MOVE (multiple) **`

10. `<Move to point>/Base point /Copy/Undo/eXit:` **X** ↵ — Exits autoedit mode

11. Zoom all and save your drawing.

Your drawing should resemble figure 95.7.

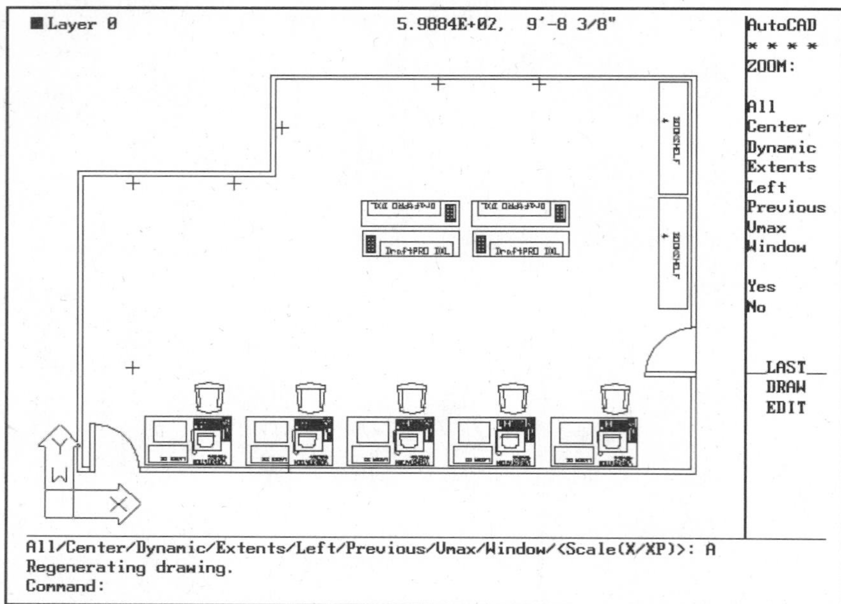

Figure 95.7

Desk blocks copied with grips.

Blocks behave much like any other type of entity when you use the Move, Scale, Mirror, and Rotate autoedit modes to edit them. The use of the Stretch autoedit mode on a block has the same effect as using the Move autoedit mode because blocks cannot be stretched.

Editing Attributes with Grips

You can see how grip editing of blocks can be useful, but what about attributes? In the next exercise, the location of the attributes for a capacitor and resistor are not correct. Move them into the correct location using grips and autoediting.

Editing Attributes with Grips

1. Begin a new drawing named 095???03 in your assigned directory, using 095SCHEM as a prototype.

2. `Command:` *Select the capacitor block*	Creates a selection set and displays grips
3. `Command:` *Hold down the Shift key and pick the grips at* ① *through* ⑤ *(see fig. 95.8)*	Selects all the grips in the capacitor

4. `Command:` *Release the Shift key and pick the grip at* ① (see fig. 95.8) — Enters Stretch autoedit mode

   `** STRETCH **`

5. `<Stretch to point>/Base point /Copy/Undo/eXit:` *Drag the attributes to the position shown in figure 95.8 and pick a point* — Moves the attributes to the correct location

6. Repeat the previous step to move the resistor's attributes into the correct position (above the symbol).

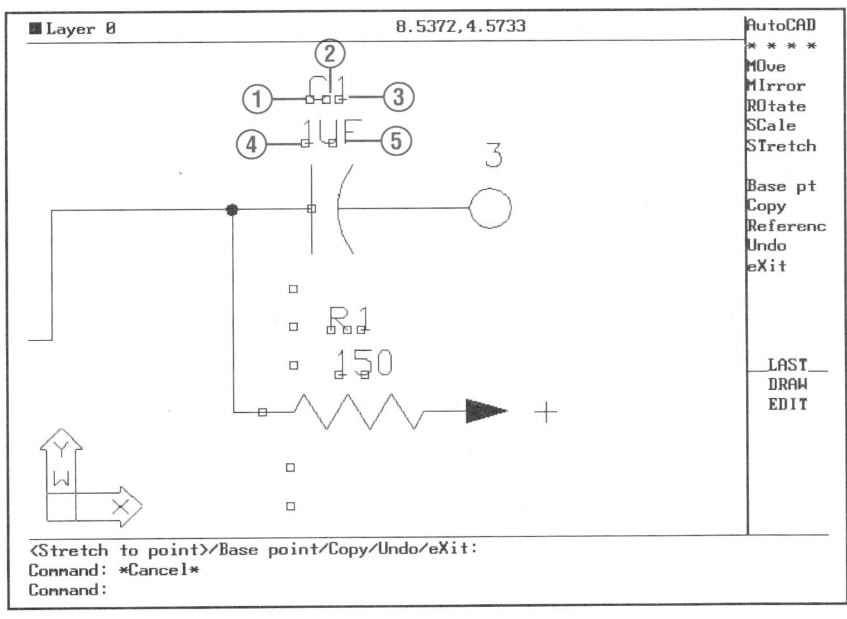

Figure 95.8

Attributes moved using grips.

You can move attributes within a block only with Stretch autoedit mode. The Move, Rotate, Mirror, and Scale autoedit modes affect the entire block, not just the attributes.

The capability to edit, substitute, and redefine blocks provides a large amount of control over drawings that use blocks. If you are using symbols that are likely to change, however, an even more productive method is to use Xrefs instead of blocks. The methods for editing Xrefs are described in the next unit.

Unit Review

What You've Learned

- ☞ How to explode, modify, then redefine a block with the BLOCK command
- ☞ How to substitute an existing block with a new block using INSERT *block1=block2*
- ☞ How to return a substituted block to its original state using INSERT *block1=*
- ☞ How to create a new block from an existing block using INSERT *block2=block1*
- ☞ How to edit blocks and attributes with grips
- ☞ The function of the system variable GRIPBLOCK

Review Questions

True or False

95.01 T F When a block is redefined, all occurrences of the block within the drawing are automatically changed.

95.02 T F A block's attributes values are lost when the block is exploded.

95.03 T F Attributes cannot be repositioned when GRIPBLOCK is set to 0.

95.04 T F A block will move with its attributes when you edit attributes with grips.

Multiple Choice

95.05 The GRIPBLOCK setting can be changed by selecting Grips from the __________ pull-down menu.

(A) Modify

(B) Settings

(C) Draw

(D) Assist

Student: ______________________ Date: __________

Instructor: ______________________ Course: ______ Section: ______

95.06 To enable all grips for entities within a block, GRIPBLOCK should be set to ________

(A) 0

(B) 1

(C) On

(D) Off

95.07 If BLOCKA and BLOCKB are both existing blocks, specifying BLOCKA=BLOCKB for the INSERT command will ________.

(A) replace BLOCKA with BLOCKB

(B) replace BLOCKB with BLOCKA

(C) create a new block containing both BLOCKA and BLOCKB

(D) cause an error message to appear

95.08 If BLOCKA is an existing block but BLOCKB does not exist, specifying BLOCKB=BLOCKA for the INSERT command will ________.

(A) rename BLOCKA to BLOCKB

(B) rename BLOCKB to BLOCKA

(C) create a BLOCKB identical to BLOCKA

(D) cause an error message to appear

Short Answer

95.09 What is the advantage of substituting a simple block for a complex block?

____

____

____

95.10 Explain what happens when you hold the Shift key while dragging entities during a multiple Move autoedit operation.

____

____

____

Student: ________ Date: ________

Instructor: ________ Course: ________ Section: ________

Additional Exercises

95.11 Begin a new drawing named 095???11 in your assigned directory using 095REDEF as a prototype. Modify the drawing so that only one of every four desks has a laser printer. Define a new desk block (DESKA) from the existing desk (DESK), then explode DESKA and erase the laser printer. After editing it, make it a block again. Use DESKA to replace three of every four desks by erasing them and copying the new block in their place. Save your drawing when you are finished.

Student: ______________________________ Date: __________

Instructor: ____________________________ Course: __________ Section: __________

UNIT 96

Editing Xrefs

In units 70 and 71, you learned how Xrefs differ from blocks and reduce the amount of data in a drawing. You also saw practical examples showing how Xrefs are well-suited to workgroup environments, in which more than one person might be working on separate drawings that are later combined. In unit 71, "Using Xrefs," you saw how to attach an Xref to your drawing, how to change the path of the Xref, and how to list Xrefs in a drawing. You may want to review this information before proceeding.

In this unit, you will see how changes to an Xref are reflected in the drawing to which the Xref is attached. You also will examine other issues related to modifying Xrefs.

The objectives for this unit are to:

- ☞ Understand that Xrefs update automatically when a drawing containing an Xref is loaded or plotted
- ☞ Update an Xref while editing the drawing containing the Xref
- ☞ Make an Xref file a permanent part of a drawing
- ☞ Remove an Xref from a drawing

Updating Xrefs

You can update an Xref in your drawing in one of two ways. The first method is handled automatically—Xrefs update automatically when the drawing containing them is loaded or plotted. For example, if you were working on a plumbing plan for a house and another user in your workgroup moved a wall on the floor plan (which was attached to your drawing as an Xref), this change would show up the next time you loaded or plotted your plumbing plan. You might suddenly realize that some of your pipes, which were located in a wall, are now in the middle of a doorway because of the change the other user made to the building's floorplan.

Because you may have no control over someone else editing a drawing attached as an Xref to your drawing, the source drawing for the Xref can change unexpectedly. To keep your Xrefs as up-to-date as possible, AutoCAD provides the Reload option to update an Xref while you are working on your drawing.

In the following exercises, use the Reload option of the XREF command to update an Xref.

Attaching a Desk as an Xref

1. Begin a new drawing named 096???01 in your assigned directory, using 096XREF1 as a prototype.

2. `Command:` *Choose* File, *then* Utilities, *and copy the file* DESK2.DWG *from your class's master directory to your assigned directory*	Creates a copy of DESK2 in your assigned directory
3. `Command:` *Choose* File, *then* Xref, *then* Attach	Issues the XREF comand with the Attach option and displays the Select File to Attach dialog box
4. *Select the file* DESK2 *from your assigned directory, then choose* OK	Selects the file to attach
5. `Insertion point:` **`INT`** ↵ `of` *Pick the intersection of lines at* ① *(see fig. 96.1)*	Uses intersection object snap
6. `X scale factor <1> / Corner / XYZ:` *Press* Enter	Accepts default X scale factor
7. `Y scale factor (default=X):` *Press* Enter	Accepts default Y scale factor
8. `Rotation angle <0>:` *Press* Enter	Accepts default rotation angle

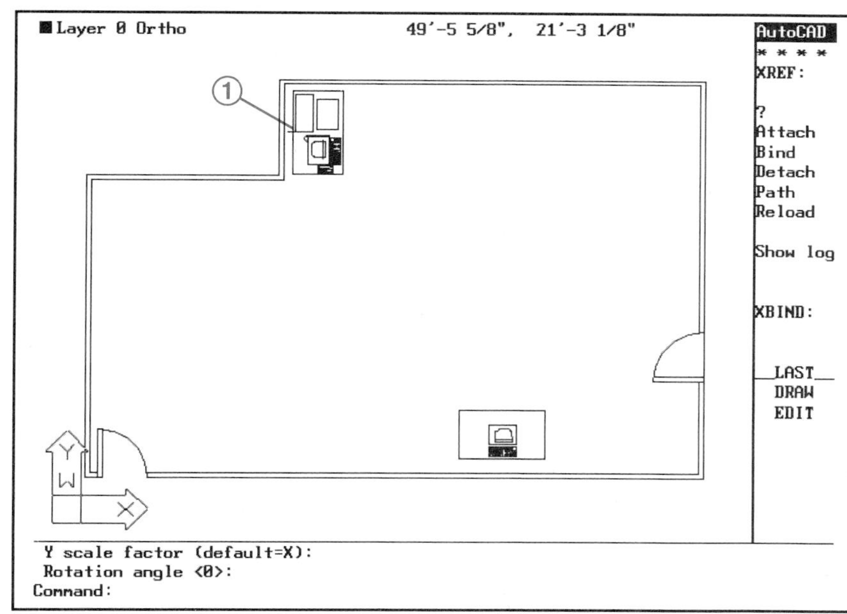

Figure 96.1

Insertion point for Xref DESK2.

Next, use WBLOCK to replace the source drawing for DESK2. This will simulate another user modifying DESK2 while you are working with your layout drawing.

Replacing DESK2

Continue with your drawing from the previous exercise.

1. `Command:` **`WBLOCK`** ↵	Issues the WBLOCK command and displays the Create Drawing File dialog box
2. *Enter* **DESK2** *in the* File *edit box*	Specifies the name of the file to create

AutoCAD informs you that the file DESK2 already exists and asks you if you want to replace it.

3. *Choose* Yes	Causes AutoCAD to replace the existing DISK2
4. `Block name:` *Press* Enter	
5. `Insertion base point:` *From the popup menu, choose* Midpoint	
6. `_mid of` *Pick the line at* ① *(see fig. 96.2)*	Specifies the insertion point for the new DESK2 drawing

continues

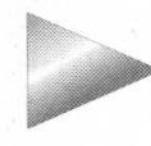

7. `Select objects:` *Pick points at* ② and ③ *(see fig. 96.2)* — Selects the desk entities with a window

Next, forget about the steps you just took and assume that another user has recently edited the drawing DESK2. Reload the Xref to see the changes.

8. `Command:` *Choose* File, *then* Xref, *then* Reload

```
_xref ?/Bind/Detach/Path/Reload/
<Attach>: _reload
```

9. `Xref(s) to reload:` **DESK2** ↵ — Specifies the name of the Xref to reload

```
    Scanning...
Reload Xref DESK2: DESK2.dwg
DESK3 loaded. Regenerating drawing.
```

Your drawing should resemble figure 96.3.

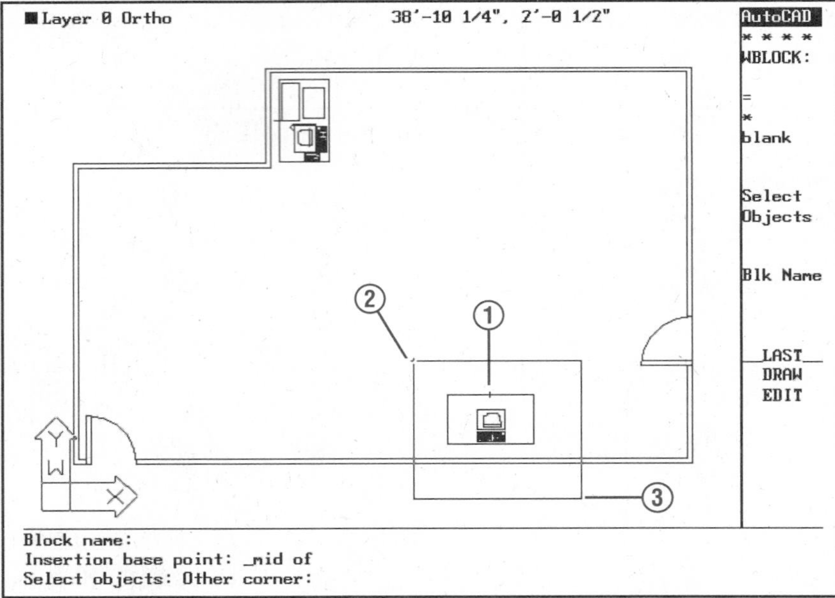

Figure 96.2
Selection points for WBLOCK command.

Instead of entering the name of a single Xref to reload, you can enter * *as the Xref name and AutoCAD will reload all Xrefs that are attached to the drawing. To reload only some of the Xrefs, enter their names separated by commas.*

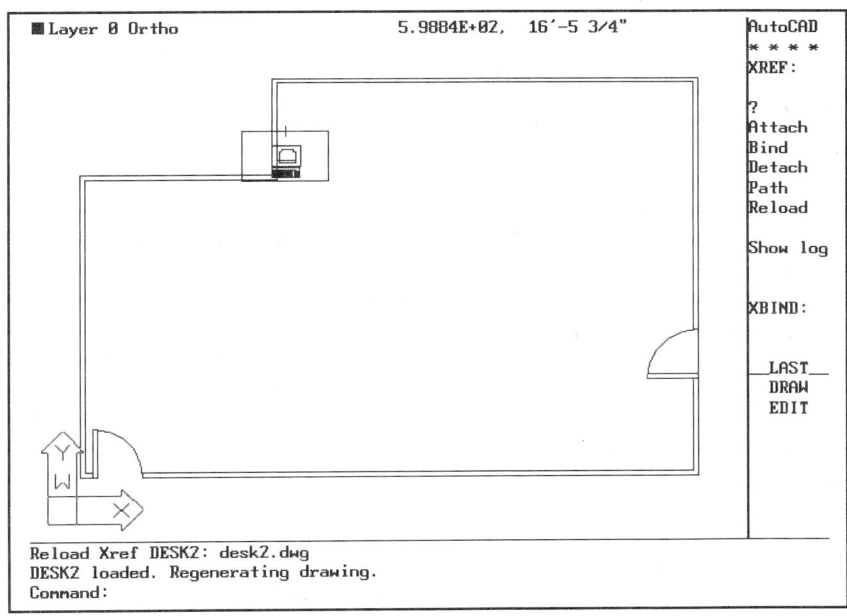

Figure 96.3

Drawing after reloading Xref.

When you are working on a drawing containing Xrefs, and the source drawings of the Xrefs might be modified by another user, use the Reload option of the XREF command occasionally. This command ensures that your design uses the most current version of the source file.

Binding an Xref

Although the use of Xrefs has obvious advantages, occasionally you may need to make the Xref a permanent part of the drawing. For example, if you send a drawing file containing Xrefs to a customer, you also must send all the Xref files associated with it. Not only must these files be present, the Xrefs also must be in the same directories they were in when they were attached to the drawing. Unless the customer creates the same directory structure and keeps all Xref files in their proper original directories, the Xrefs will not load when the drawing containing them is loaded. These requirements can make the transfer of drawing files inconvenient and difficult.

In this situation, it may be better to *bind* the Xref to your drawing to make the Xref a permanent part of the drawing file. *Binding* an Xref makes the Xref a block in your drawing and eliminates the need for external files. The next exercise shows the procedure for binding an Xref to your drawing.

Binding the Desk Xref to the Computer Room Layout

1. Begin a new drawing named 096???02 in your assigned directory, using the drawing 096XREF2 as a prototype. As the drawing loads, note the command prompts indicate that AutoCAD is searching for and loading the external files DESK and CHAIR.

   ```
   Resolve Xref DESK: DESK
   DESK loaded.
   Resolve Xref CHAIR: CHAIR
   CHAIR loaded.
   AutoCAD Release 12 menu utilities
   loaded.
   ```

2. `Command:` **`XREF`** ↵ — Issues the XREF command
3. `?/Bind/Detach/Path/Reload/<Attach>:` **`B`** ↵ — Specifies the Bind option
4. `Xref(s) to bind:` **`DESK`** ↵ — Specifies the Xref name to bind

   `Scanning...`

You can enter an asterisk (*) when prompted for the Xref name to bind all Xrefs contained in the drawing. If you want to bind more than one, but not all, enter the Xref names separated by commas.

The Xref has been converted to a block and is now a part of your drawing. You can insert it as a block in other locations in the drawing or perform any other operations for editing blocks.

Detaching an Xref

Occasionally, you will want or need to remove one or more Xrefs from your drawing. This is called *detaching* the Xref. Detaching an Xref is necessary when you have attached the wrong source file, when the Xref is no longer needed in the drawing, and in other situations when you want to eliminate the Xref completely from the drawing. The Detach option of the XREF command detaches Xrefs from the drawing.

Detaching an Xref from your drawing deletes all occurrences of the Xref in the drawing. Note that if you only want to delete one occurrence of an Xref, you can simply erase it. When you choose the Detach option of the XREF command, you are prompted for the name or names of the Xrefs to detach.

You can respond with an individual Xref name, more than one name separated by commas, or an asterisk (*) to detach all Xrefs from your drawing.

If Xrefs are erased but not detached, AutoCAD will continue to search for them when the drawing is loaded or plotted, and will display an error message if the Xref files are not found. To avoid this search, the Xrefs must be detached from your drawing.

If you attempt to detach an Xref that is part of another Xref in the drawing (a nested Xref), AutoCAD will not detach it unless the Xref in which it is nested also is detached.

In the following exercise, detach the nested Xref CHAIR. Then detach the Xref DESK, in which CHAIR is nested.

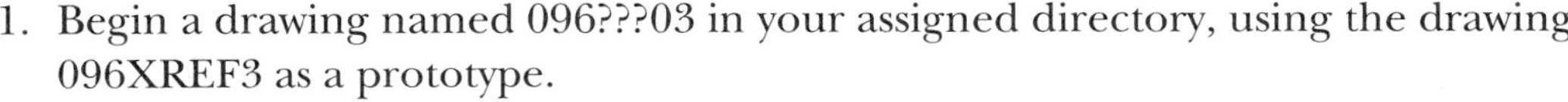

Detaching the Desk and Chair Xrefs

1. Begin a drawing named 096???03 in your assigned directory, using the drawing 096XREF3 as a prototype.

2. `Command:` *Choose* File, *then* Xref, *then* Detach — Issues the XREF command with the Detach option

   ```
   ?/Bind/Detach/Path/Reload/
   <Attach>: _detach
   ```

3. `Xref(s) to Detach:` **`CHAIR`** ↵ — Specifies Xref to detach

   ```
       Scanning...
   Xref CHAIR has multiple references.
   Not Detached.
   ```

   The Xref CHAIR was not detached because it is nested in the Xref DESK.

4. `Command:` *Press* Enter — Repeats the last command

   ```
   XREF
   ```

5. `?/Bind/Detach/Path/Reload/<Attach>:` **`D`** ↵ — Specifies the Detach option

6. `Xref(s) to Detach:` **`DESK3`** ↵ — Specifies Xref to detach

   ```
       Scanning...
   ```

   The Xref DESK3 is detached, along with the Xref CHAIR that was nested in it.

You can see that when an Xref is detached, it is removed from the drawing.

Unit Review

What You've Learned

- ☞ When AutoCAD automatically updates Xrefs
- ☞ How and why to force AutoCAD to reload a drawing's Xrefs when the drawing is already loaded
- ☞ How and why to make an Xref a permanent part of a drawing
- ☞ How to remove all occurrences of an Xref from a drawing
- ☞ What a nested Xref is and when it occurs
- ☞ Special considerations when removing nested Xrefs
- ☞ Use of an asterisk (*) when specifying all Xref names for editing
- ☞ Use of a comma to specify more than one Xref name for editing

Review Questions

True or False

96.01 T F Erasing all Xrefs from a drawing is the same as detaching them with the XREF command.

96.02 T F The bind option of the XREF command makes an XREF a block in the drawing to which it is bound.

96.03 T F A "nested" Xref can be detached from the drawing without detaching the XREF in which it is nested.

Multiple Choice

96.04 An Xref that contains another Xref is called a __________ Xref.

(A) double

(B) nested

(C) stacked

(D) layered

Student: ______________________ Date: __________

Instructor: ______________________ Course: __________ Section: __________

96.05 When the XREF command prompts for names of Xrefs to bind to your drawing, entering an asterisk (*) will __________ .

(A) show a list of names

(B) cause an error message

(C) abort the command

(D) bind all Xrefs contained in the drawing

96.06 An Xref is updated automatically when loading or __________ a drawing.

(A) regenerating

(B) redrawing

(C) ending

(D) saving

Short Answer

96.07 Give an example of when it is better to use an Xref than a block.

96.08 Give an example of when binding an Xref to your drawing might be useful.

96.09 Explain briefly how detaching an Xref is different from erasing it.

96.10 Explain why it is important to use Xrefs when you are working with other people on a project.

Student: __________ Date: __________

Instructor: __________ Course: __________ Section: __________

UNIT 97

Extracting Data with Attributes

In unit 91 you learned that you could use attributes to create an *intelligent drawing*. This means your drawing can contain much more information than the usual graphic and dimensional information normally associated with drawings. In units 92, 93, and 94 you developed a schematic drawing with several invisible attributes containing information such as cost, manufacturer, and price. In this unit, you will see how this information can be used to generate a parts list automatically with pricing and ordering information.

The objectives for this unit are to:

- Understand the purpose and advantage of generating reports from attribute data
- Understand the different file formats for extracting attribute data
- Design a template file for extracting attribute data
- Use the DDATTEXT command to generate a report from attribute data

Understanding Data Extraction

The first step in using attributes effectively is determining the appropriate use of attribute report generation. You must decide what types of tabular data will be needed to accompany drawings containing your attributes. For instance, if the drawing is a mechanical assembly it will be accompanied by a parts list showing the name of each item, the type of material the item is made of, a drawing number where each item is detailed and/or a vendor from whom each item should be purchased. If the drawing is a facilities management layout, it might be accompanied by a report showing locations and types of office furniture, names and extension numbers for telephones throughout the facility, location and service dates for fire extinguishers, or any number of other types of information about the facility.

The major advantage of using attributes to create these types of reports is the simultaneous updating of drawings and reports. If the electrical schematic you developed in earlier units undergoes a design change, the drawing can be updated and a new report generated from the revised drawing. This method of linking drawings and information not only saves time but virtually eliminates the chance of having an outdated parts list, a cost estimate sheet, or other reports based on attached information.

Information extracted from the drawing may be used in many different ways by different departments. The manager of Information Systems might need information stored in your attributes to incorporate into a report generated in the FORTRAN programming language. The Purchasing Department manager might need other attribute information linked to a database program. The CAD department programmers might need more detailed information to design programs for automatic drawing creation.

Although these disciplines are beyond the scope of this book, you should understand that AutoCAD allows you to extract your attribute data in three different formats—CDF (comma delimited format), SDF (space delimited format), or DXF (drawing interchange file). The format you need to use depends on how the information is to be used. To link attribute information to reports generated from custom programs, database programs, spreadsheets, or word processors, the CDF or SDF formats are most useful.

CDF simply means the attributes in the report will be separated by a comma—SDF means the attributes are separated by a space. When you use either of these formats, you first must create a *template file* that tells AutoCAD which attributes to list and in what order. The DXF method generates a rather complex file with attributes listed on separate lines, the block's geometry defined, and other information about the blocks and attributes. In the next section, you will create a template file to generate the report shown in table 97.1 from the electrical schematic shown in figure 97.1.

Table 97.1
Electrical Schematic Attribute Extract File

TRANSIST	Q	1	2N3904	Rodeo Shack	TR12543-B	7.33
RES	R	2	150	Bob's Electronics	R12345	1.55
CAP	C	2	1UF	Circuit Barn	C213	1.33
CAP	C	1	1UF	Circuit Barn	C714	1.33
RES	R	1	150	Bob's Electronics	R6579	1.55
RES	R	3	100	Bob's Electronics	R7437	1.15

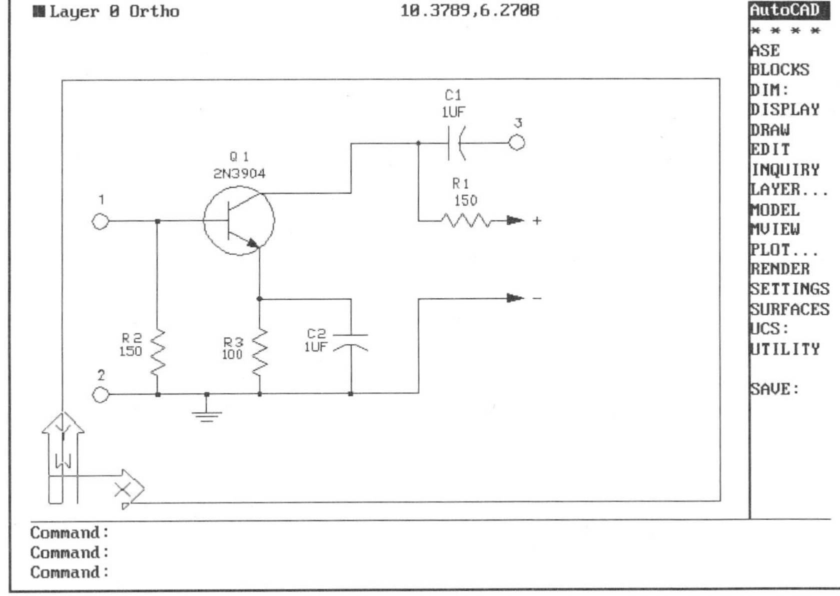

Figure 97.1
Electrical schematic used to generate the report in table 97.1

Creating a Report Template File

To create a report from attributes in either CDF or SDF formats, you must first create a report template file. A *report template file* is simply a text file that tells AutoCAD which attributes to include in the report and how to arrange them. You also can include information about the block that the attributes are attached to, such as the block's name, coordinates, number of blocks used, layer, and scale factors used for block insertion. This template file must be created from either a text editor, such as the MS-DOS Editor or Windows Notepad, or from a word processor capable of saving an ASCII file.

Each item of the template file is called a *field*, and each block from which attributes are extracted forms a *record* containing all fields. For instance, in table 97.1 the text "TRANSIST" is the information in a field showing the block's name, and the entire row of information about the transistor is a record containing seven different fields. AutoCAD places no limit on the number of fields contained in a record or the number of records contained in a file.

When defining a field in the template file, first enter the field name. This can be a property of the block or an attribute tag. If a block property is used it must begin with BL:, as you will see in the following exercise.

AutoCAD recognizes two types of fields—character and numeric. The next step in defining a field is to specify which type it is. After the field name enter a space (or any number of spaces) with the spacebar (DO NOT use the TAB key), then either a C to specify a character field or an N to specify a numeric field. This is immediately followed by six digits; the first three digits specify the width of the field (the number of characters) and the second three specify the number of decimal places for a numeric field. These last three digits must always be 000 for a character field.

You can perform the following exercise in any word processor if you save the information as an ASCII file. If you do, you *must* type ↵ after entering the last line of the report template.

If you are using a version of MS-DOS earlier than 5.0, you do not have the MS-DOS Editor on your system. You can use the EDLIN program to create your TEMPLATE.TXT file. Ask your instructor for help if you do not know how to use EDLIN.

Creating a Report Template File

1. *Start AutoCAD.*
2. `Command:` **`SHELL`** ↵ — Issues the SHELL command to run an external program
3. `OS Command:` **`EDIT TEMPLATE.TXT`** ↵ — Starts the MS-DOS Editor to edit a file named TEMPLATE.TXT (MS-DOS 5.0 and 6.*x* users only)
4. *In the MS-DOS Editor, enter the following lines of text:*

```
BL:NAME C008000
DUMMY1 C002000
DESIGNATOR C003000
REFERENCE_NUMBER N004000
DUMMY2 C002000
VALUE C010000
```

```
DUMMY3 C002000
MANUFACTURER C018000
DUMMY4 C002000
CATALOG_NUMBER C010000
DUMMY5 C002000
COST N006002
```

5. *Press* Alt, *then* F, *then* S — Saves the file
6. *Press* Alt, *then* F, *then* X — Exits the MS-DOS Editor and returns to AutoCAD

Be sure to supply a field width in the template file long enough to accommodate the value to be placed in it. If the value is longer than the field width, AutoCAD will truncate the value and display a `Field overflow` *message.*

Extracting Attribute Data

Now that you have generated a report template file to tell AutoCAD how to format the report, you are ready to extract the information stored in the electrical schematic to generate a formal report. You will do this with the DDATTEXT command. This is the easiest part of the procedure—all you need to do is specify the type of report, the template file's name, and the name for the report file.

If AutoCAD finds any blocks that have no value supplied for a field in the report, it will leave a character field blank or will fill a numeric field with zeros. If attributes exist that are not specified in any field in the template file, they will be omitted from the report.

In the following exercise, use the template file you just wrote to format a report for the electrical schematic in figure 97.1.

Extracting Attribute Data from the Electrical Schematic

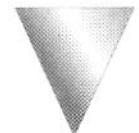

1. Begin a new drawing named 097???01 in your assigned directory, using the drawing 097ATTEX as a prototype.
2. `Command:` **`DDATTEXT`** ↵ — Issues the DDATTEXT command and displays the Attribute Extraction dialog box (fig. 97.2)

continues

3. *Choose the* Space Delimited File *radio button* — Sets output file delimiter type

4. *Choose the* Template File *button and select the report template file named* TEMPLATE.TXT *you created in the previous exercise* — Selects the source template file

The default Output File name will be the same as your drawing file name, except with a file extension of .TXT instead of .DWG.

Do not give the output file the same name as the template file because this will overwrite the template file.

5. *Choose the* Select Objects *button* — Switches to the drawing editor to select objects to include in the report

6. `Select objects:` **`ALL`** — Specifies all objects in the drawing

   `46 found`

All entities selected that are not blocks are ignored.

7. Select objects: *Press* Enter — Ends object selection

   `6 records in extract file.`

Figure 97.2

The Attribute Extraction dialog box.

Attribute Extraction
File Format
Comma Delimited File (CDF)
Space Delimited File (SDF)
Drawing Interchange File (DXF)
Select Objects < Number found: 0
Template File...
Output File... C:\AUTHOR\UNITS\DWGS
OK Cancel Help...

Your report is done. Next, you can issue the TYPE command to view the contents of the file on your text screen. You also can load the report into the MS-DOS Editor or a word processor to view it.

Viewing Your Report

Continue with your drawing from the preceding exercise.

1. `Command:` **`TYPE`** ↵ — Issues the DOS TYPE command
2. `File to list:` **`097???01.TXT`** — Substitute your drawing name, but with the extension .TXT

```
TRANSIST Q  1 2N3904  Rodeo Shack          TR12543-B      7.33
RES         R          2 150  Bob's Electronics      R12345  1.55
CAP         C          2 1UF  Circuit Barn           C213    1.33
CAP         C          1 1UF  Circuit Barn           C714    1.33
RES         R          1 150  Bob's Electronics      R6579   1.55
RES         R          3 100  Bob's Electronics      R7437   1.15
```

Attribute extraction enables you to organize and pull information from a drawing that you can use in other applications and reports. Generally, one person in your department will be responsible for extracting information from drawings and generating reports or exporting the data to other applications. If your organization is small, however, each drafter or designer may have that responsibility.

Unit Review

What You've Learned

- The types of reports that can be generated from attributes
- The purpose and advantage of generating reports from attributes
- The three different file formats used for generating reports
- What a template file is and how to design one with DOS EDIT or a word processor
- The meaning of the terms field, record, and file in report generation
- Use of the DDATTEXT command

Review Questions

True or False

97.01 T F To generate a report in a Comma Delimited File (CDF), you first must create a template file.

97.02 T F AutoCAD will display an error message if an attribute exists that is not specified in any field of the template file.

97.03 T F If an attribute's value is longer than the field that contains the value, it will be truncated.

97.04 T F In the DDATTEXT dialog box, the Template file name is used as the default name for the Output file.

97.05 T F Invisible attributes will not be extracted by the DDATTEXT command.

Multiple Choice

97.06 Generating reports from attributes __________.

(A) increases speed of drawings and associated reports

(B) increases accuracy of drawings and associated reports

(C) is rarely done

(D) both A and B

Student: ________________ Date: ________

Instructor: ________________ Course: ________ Section: ________

97.07 Attributes extracted in the __________ format do not require a template file.

(A) CDF

(B) SDF

(C) DXF

97.08 If entities other than blocks are selected in the DDATTEXT command, AutoCAD will __________ .

(A) ignore them

(B) include them in the report

(C) cancel the command

(D) generate an error message

97.09 The first three digits after the C in the field definition C015000 indicate the __________.

(A) number of attributes to place in the field

(B) field width

(C) number of decimal places for the field

(D) field number

Short Answer

97.10 Show the line of text needed in a template file to specify a field for the attribute tag EXTENSION_NUMBER. The information will be stored to be stored as a three-digit number with no decimal places.

____

____

____

97.11 Give an example of a type of report that might be generated from attributes in the architectural field.

____

____

____

Student: __________ Date: __________

Instructor: __________ Course: __________ Section: __________

PART XI

Working in 3D

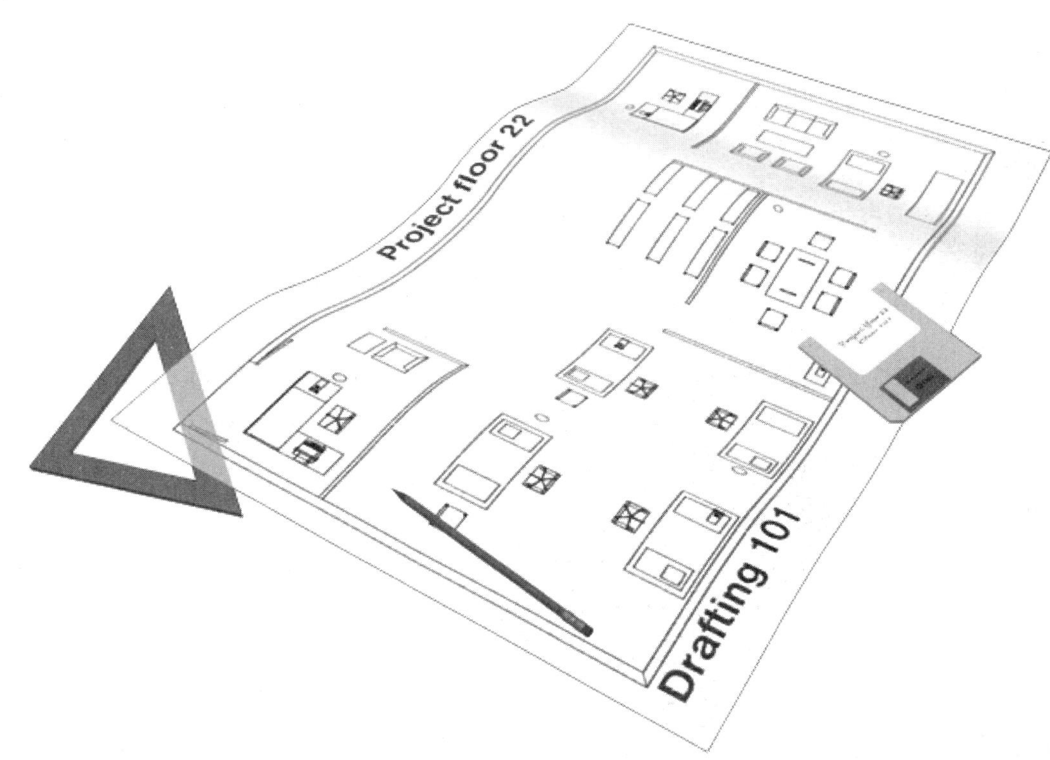

Creating Isometric Drawings

UNIT 98

Many drafters and designers use AutoCAD only to create two-dimensional drawings. You also can use AutoCAD to create true three-dimensional solids and surface models. These three-dimensional models can be used to generate two-dimensional drawings, often saving drawing time. In many applications, however, a two-dimensional isometric drawing is more useful than a true 3D model. AutoCAD provides a handful of tools that simplify the task of creating isometric drawings. This unit teaches you to use those tools to create your own isometric drawings in AutoCAD.

The objectives for this unit are to:

- Understand how isometric drawings created in AutoCAD differ from true 3D models
- Set and use ISOPLANE modes
- Set and use isometric grid and snap
- Create a simple isometric drawing

Creating an Isometric Drawing in AutoCAD

To create an isometric drawing, AutoCAD provides special grid options specifically for isometric drawing. Essentially, AutoCAD enables you to display an isometric grid and align the snap increment to the grid. When you are using a standard grid with the WCS (World Coordinate System), the X axis is horizontal on the display, and the Y axis is vertical. The grid dots follow that horizontal/vertical alignment.

When you turn on AutoCAD's isometric grid, however, the grid dots align along the isometric axes, not along the X and Y axes (see fig. 98.1), and the cursor also changes to reflect this new alignment. Just as a standard grid provides a visual frame of reference by which you can create orthographic drawings, the isometric grid provides a frame of reference by which you can create isometric drawings. The isometric grid does not by itself provide for accurate isometric point selection. For that, you must use snap.

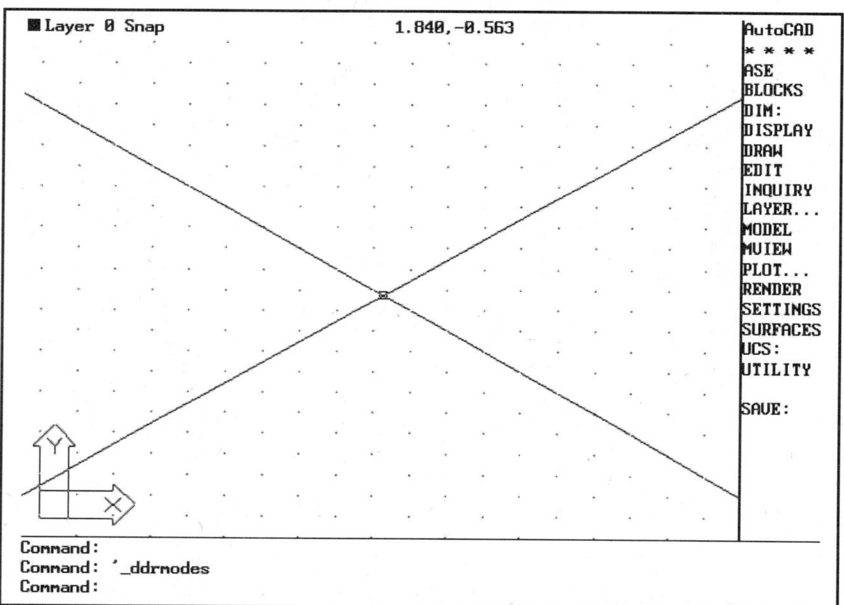

Figure 98.1

An isometric grid in AutoCAD (Top ISOPLANE mode).

AutoCAD provides three different isometric grid/snap orientations that are controlled by the ISOPLANE system variable: Top, Left, and Right. Figure 98.1 shows the grid with the Top ISOPLANE mode. Figure 98.2 shows Left ISOPLANE mode, and figure 98.3 shows Right ISOPLANE mode.

As you learn in upcoming exercises, you can work in different areas of the drawing according to the orientation of that part of the drawing by selecting a particular ISOPLANE mode.

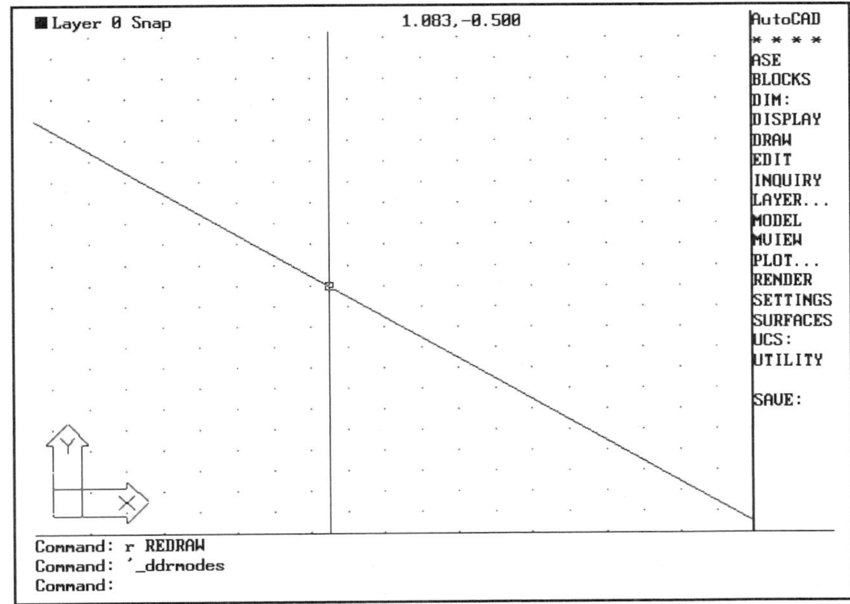

Figure 98.2
Left ISOPLANE mode.

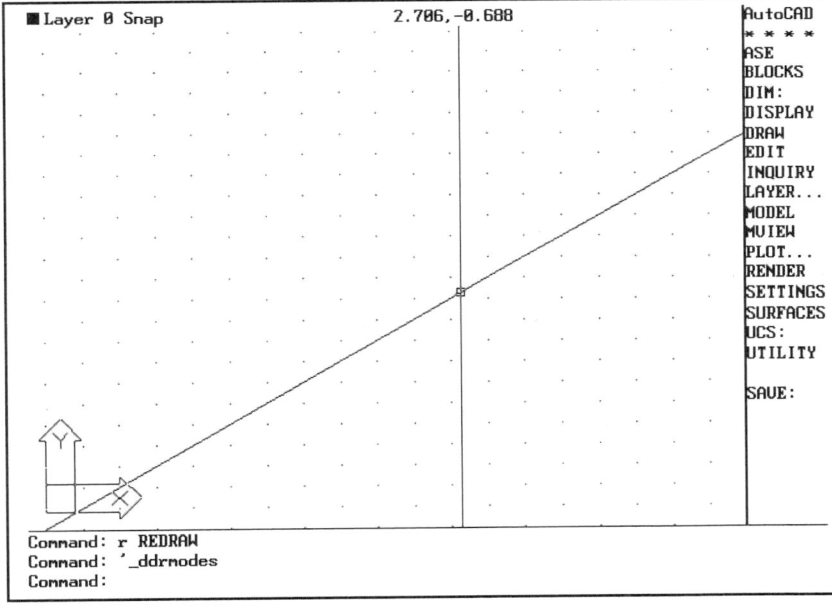

Figure 98.3
Right ISOPLANE mode.

Controlling Snap for Isometric Drawing

When you turn on the isometric grid, and then turn on snap, the snap increment aligns itself with the current ISOPLANE mode. Instead of snapping to .25" increments horizontally, for example, the cursor snaps to .25" increments at a 30-degree angle to horizontal. This makes it possible to create an isometric drawing quickly because you can pick points with the cursor rather than enter points and relative coordinates with the keyboard.

Drawing Isometrics

When you are ready to begin drawing in isometric mode, first set up your grid and snap accordingly. The easiest way to control the isometric grid and snap is to use the Drawing Aids dialog box from the Settings pull-down menu. In the following exercise, set the grid to .5" and set snap to .125". Then, turn on the isometric grid in the Top ISOPLANE mode.

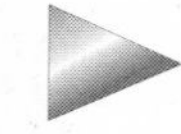

Setting Isometric Grid and Snap

1. Begin a new drawing named 098???01 in your assigned directory, using the file 098ISO as a prototype.

2. `Command:` *Choose* Settings, *then* Drawing Aids	Displays the Drawing Aids dialog box
3. *In the* Isometric Snap/Grid *group box, check the* On *check box*	Turns on isometric grid option and dims the X Spacing edit boxes for Snap and Grid
4. *Choose the* Top *radio button*	Sets the isometric grid orientation to the Top ISOPLANE mode
5. *Double-click in the* Y Spacing *edit box in the* Snap *group, then enter* **`0.125`**	Sets snap to .125"
6. *Double-click in the* Y Spacing *edit box in the* Grid *group, then enter* **`0.5`**	Sets the grid spacing to .5"
7. *Check the* On *check box in the* Snap group	Turns on snap
8. *Choose* OK	Closes the dialog box and displays the isometric grid

Now, you are ready to begin drawing in isometric. Use figure 98.4 as a guide to work through the following exercises.

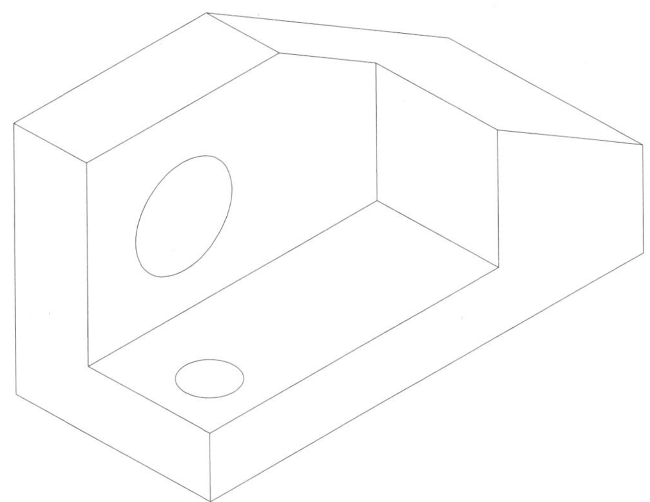

Figure 98.4

Dimensions for wedge block drawn in isometric.

Starting the Wedge Block

Continue with your drawing from the previous exercise.

1. `Command:` *Choose* Draw, *then* Line, *then* Segments	Starts the LINE command
2. `_line From point:` *Pick a point at* ① *(see fig. 98.5)*	Starts the line
3. `To point:` *Press* F6, *then press* F6 *again*	Turns off coordinate display, then turns it on with relative display mode
`<Coords off>  <Coords on>`	
4. `To point:` *Using the coordinate, display grid, and snap as a guide, pick a point* @2.000<330	Draws a line to ②
5. `To point:` *Pick a point* @4.500<30	Draws a line to ③
6. `To point:` *Pick a point* @1.000<90	Draws a line to ④
7. `To point:` *Press* Enter	Ends the LINE command
8. `Command:` *Press* Enter	Repeats the LINE command
9. `LINE From point:` *Pick a point at* ② *(see fig. 98.5)*	
10. `To point:` *Pick a point* @0.625<90	Draws a line to ⑤
11. `To point:` *Pick a point* @3.000<30	Draws a line to ⑥

continues

12. `To point:` *Pick a point* @1.250<150 — Draws a line to ⑦
13. `To point:` *Pick a point* @3.000<210 — Draws a line to ⑧
14. `To point:` *Pick a point at* ⑤ *(see fig. 98.5)*
15. `To point:` *Press* Enter

Figure 98.5

The first few lines of the wedge block drawn.

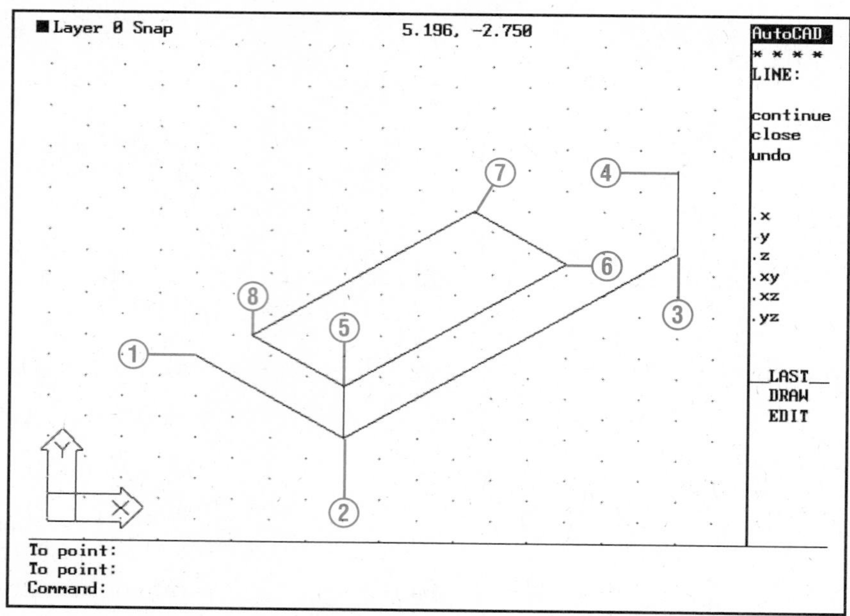

Next, set the grid for the Left ISOPLANE mode, and then draw the left edge of the wedge block.

You can enter the ISOPLANE command at the `Command:` *prompt to change between Top, Left, and Right ISOPLANE modes.*

Drawing the Left Edge of the Wedge Block

1. `Command:` *Choose* Settings, *then* Drawing Aids
2. *In the* Isometric Snap/Grid *group, choose the* Left *radio button, then choose* OK — Sets grid to the Left ISOPLANE mode and exits the dialog box
3. `Command:` *Choose* Draw, *then* Line, *then* Segments

4. `_line From point:` *From the popup menu, Choose* End point
5. `_endp of` *Pick the line at* ① *(see fig. 98.6)*
6. `To point:` *Pick a point* @2.500<90 — Draws a line to ②
7. `To point:` *Pick a point* @0.750<330 — Draws a line to ③
8. `To point:` *Pick a point at* ④ *(see fig. 98.6)*
9. `To point:` *Press* Enter

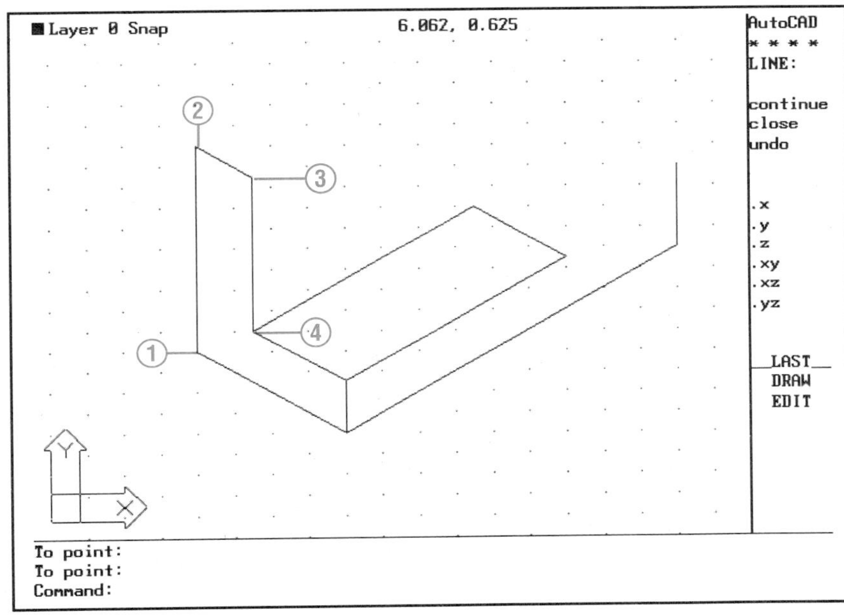

Figure 98.6

The completed left edge of the wedge block.

Next, draw the top surface of the wedge block, and then add some construction lines to the right edge of the wedge block.

Drawing the Top and Right Side

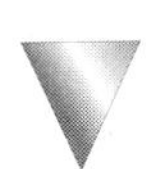

Use the Drawing Aids dialog box to select the Top ISOPLANE mode.

1. `Command:` **L** ↵
2. `From point:` *Pick a point at* ① *(see fig. 98.7)*
3. `To point:` *Pick a point* @2.000<30 — Draws a line to ②

continues

4. `To point:` *Pick a point* @0.750<210 — Draws a line to ③
5. `To point:` *Pick a point at* ④ *(see fig. 98.7)*
6. `To point:` *Press* Enter
7. `Command:` *Press* Enter — Repeats the LINE command
8. `LINE From point:` *Pick a point at* ⑤ *(see fig. 98.7)*
9. `To point:` *Pick a point* @2.00<150
10. `To point:` *Pick a point at* ② *(see fig. 98.7)*
11. `To point:` *Press* Enter

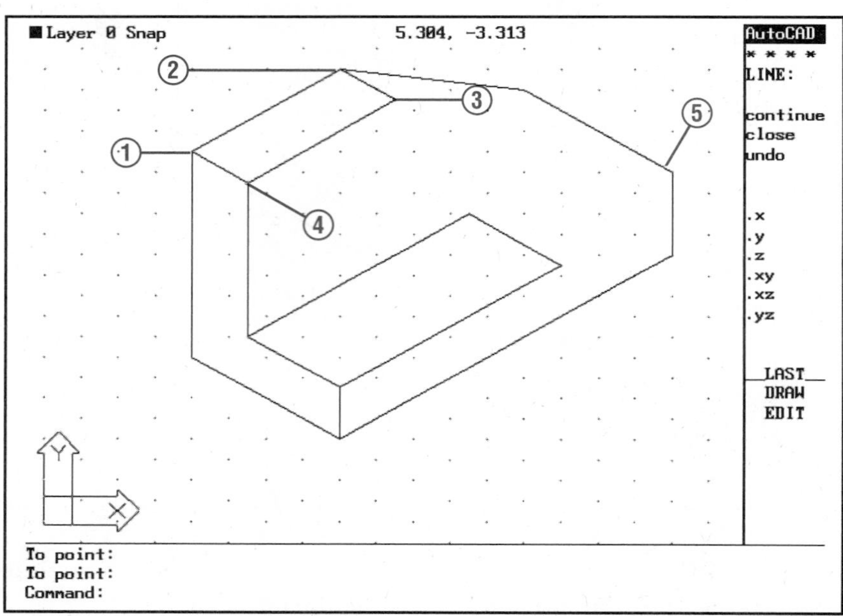

Figure 98.7

Top completed and right side laid out.

To complete the main body of the part, add the lines for the inside right edge of the notch. Because you do not know the exact dimensions for the height of the notch, you must create some construction geometry to locate all the points.

Completing the Main Body

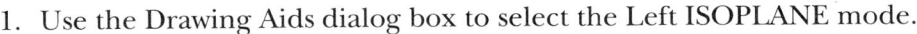

1. Use the Drawing Aids dialog box to select the Left ISOPLANE mode.	
2. `Command:` **L** ↵	Starts the LINE command
3. `LINE From point:` *Pick a point at* ① *(see fig. 98.8)*	
4. `To point:` *Pick a point* @2.000<90	
5. `To point:` *Press* Enter	
6. `Command:` *Select the line at* ②, *then pick a point at* ③ *(see fig. 98.8)*	Selects the line and enters autoedit mode
`** STRETCH **`	
7. `<Stretch to point>/Base point/Copy/Undo/eXit:` **MO** ↵	Chooses Move autoedit mode
`** MOVE **`	
8. `<Move to point>/Base point/Copy/Undo/eXit:` **C** ↵	Chooses Copy/Move autoedit mode
`** MOVE (multiple) **`	
9. `<Move to point>/Base point/Copy/Undo/eXit:` *Pick a point at* ④ *(see fig. 98.8)*	Copies the line
`** MOVE (multiple) **`	
10. `<Move to point>/Base point/Copy/Undo/eXit:` *Press* Enter	Exits autoedit mode
11. `Command:` *Choose* Modify, *then* Trim	
12. *Trim the two construction lines as shown in figure 98.8*	

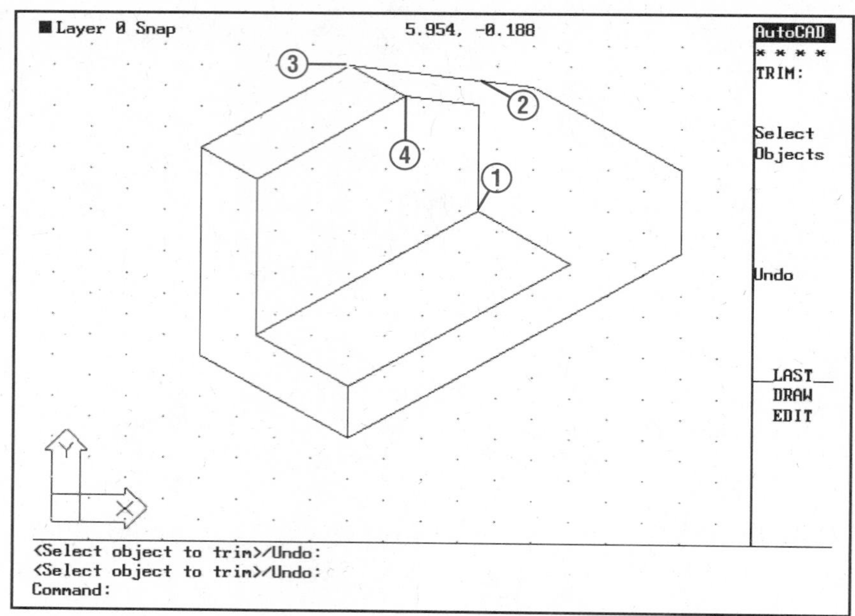

Figure 98.8
Notch lines trimmed.

Now you are ready to complete the drawing.

Completing the Isometric Drawing

1. Using the COPY command or the Move/Copy autoedit mode, copy the vertical line from ① to ② (see fig. 98.9). Then, use the LINE command to draw lines ③ and ④.
2. Use the Drawing Aids dialog box to select the Right ISOPLANE mode.
3. Next, add the ellipse for the hole in the back of the notch.
4. To make the grid align with the inside face of the notch, use the UCS command to move the origin to the top of the notch face.

5. `Command:` **`UCS`** ↵	Starts the UCS command
6. `Origin/ZAxis/3point/Entity/View/X/Y/Z/ Prev/Restore/Save/Del/?/<World>:` **`O`** ↵	Chooses the Origin option
7. `Origin point <0,0,0>:` *Pick a point at* ⑤ *(see fig. 98.9)*	Causes the grid to align with the back face of the notch
8. `Command:` *Choose* Draw, *then* Ellipse, *then* Axis, Eccentricity	Starts the ELLIPSE command
9. `<Axis endpoint 1>/Center/Isocircle:` **`I`** ↵	Chooses Isocircle option
10. `Center of circle:` *Pick the grid point at* ⑥ *(see fig. 98.9)*	

11.	`<Circle radius>/Diameter:` **`0.5`** ↵	Specifies .5" radius
12.	Use the Drawing Aids dialog box to select the Top ISOPLANE mode.	
13.	`Command:` **`UCS`** ↵	Starts the UCS command
14.	`Origin/ZAxis/3point/Entity/View/X/Y/Z/ Prev/Restore/Save/Del/?/<World>:` **`O`** ↵	Chooses the Origin option
15.	`Origin point <0,0,0>:` *Choose* Endpoint *object snap, then pick a point at* ⑦ *(see fig. 98.9)*	Causes the grid to align with the back face of the notch
16.	`Command:` *Choose* Draw, *then* Ellipse, *then* Axis, Eccentricity	Starts the ELLIPSE command
17.	`<Axis endpoint 1>/Center/Isocircle:` **`I`** ↵	Chooses Isocircle option
18.	`Center of circle:` *Pick the grid point at* ⑧ *(see fig. 98.9)*	
19.	`<Circle radius>/Diameter:` **`0.25`** ↵	Specifies .25" radius
20.	`Command:` *Save your drawing*	

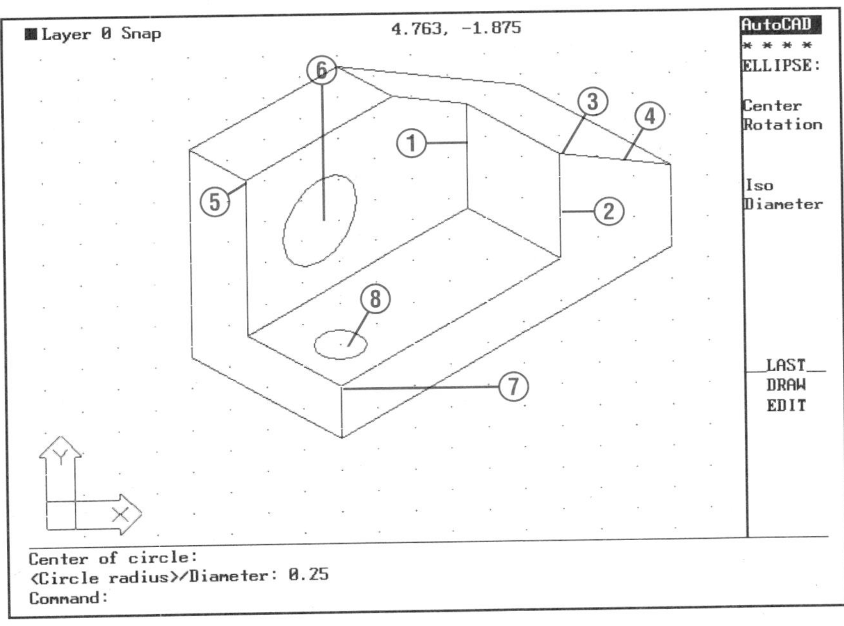

Figure 98.9

The completed wedge block isometric drawing.

Unit Review

What You've Learned

- How to set an isometric grid and snap
- How ISOPLANE modes change the orientation of the grid and cursor
- How to create an isometric drawing

Review Questions

True or False

98.01 T F The snap increment has no relationship to the isometric grid.

98.02 T F You can use the UCS command to realign the grid with features in the drawing.

98.03 T F The four ISOPLANE modes are Top, Bottom, Left, and Right.

98.04 T F You can set unequal X and Y axis grid spacing when using an isometric grid.

98.05 T F In some situations it is easier to create an isometric drawing than a 3D model.

98.06 T F When the isometric grid is displayed and snap is turned on, the cursor can snap to points 30 degrees off of horizontal.

98.07 T F You can change the current ISOPLANE mode by entering ISOPLANE at the `Command:` prompt.

98.08 T F Snap turns on automatically when you turn on the isometric grid.

98.09 T F Unlike the standard grid, the isometric grid allows accurate point selection without using snap.

98.10 T F The X and Y values for the isometric grid always are equal.

Additional Exercises

98.11 Begin a new drawing named 098???11 in your assigned directory using no prototype. Create an isometric drawing of the object shown in figure 98.10.

Student: ____________________ Date: __________

Instructor: ____________________ Course: __________ Section: __________

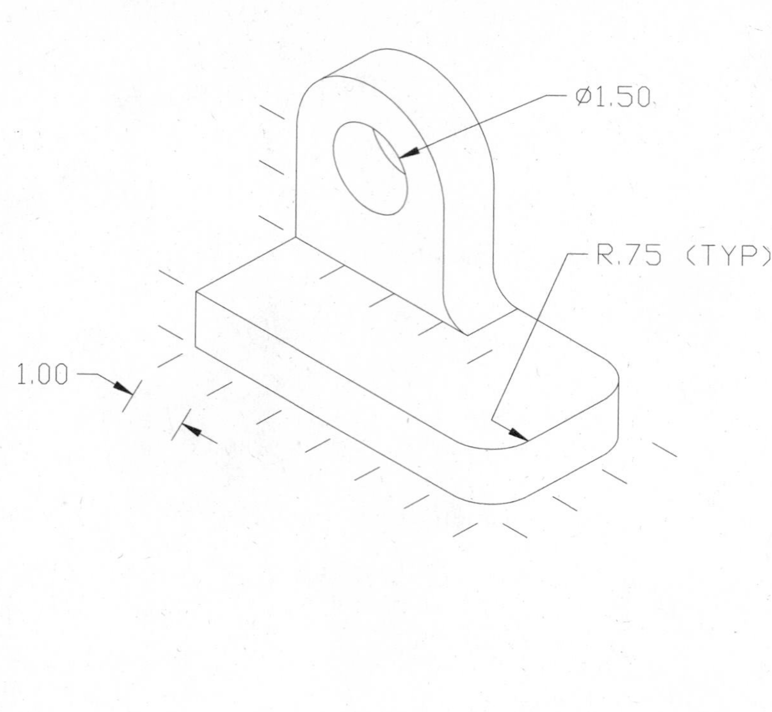

Figure 98.10

Control bracket drawn as an isometric.

Student: ____________________ Date: ____________

Instructor: ____________________ Course: ____________ Section: ____________

UNIT 99

Introducing the Third Dimension

In its standard configuration, AutoCAD provides the capability to create three-dimensional models. With the addition of the Advanced Modeling Extension (AME), you can use AutoCAD to produce 3D solids models. This unit introduces you to some of the features and concepts you need to understand to create three-dimensional drawings in AutoCAD. The unit prepares you to begin creating your own 3D models.

The objectives for this unit are to:

- Understand the relationship of the X, Y, and Z axes
- Use the VPOINT command to display an off-axis view of a 3D drawing
- Use the UCS (User Coordinate System) command to rotate the coordinate system and relocate the origin

Displaying a 3D View

An important part of working in 3D in AutoCAD is the ability to manipulate the views of the object on which you are working. Although you can draw in 3D while using orthographic views, it is much easier to use "3D" views, or off-axis views of the object. These views enable you to see the three-dimensional relationships between entities in the model.

Using the VPOINT Command

The VPOINT command enables you to move your viewpoint to any location in the 3D model and generate a view of the model based on that viewpoint. Think of using VPOINT in this way as simply "walking" around the model to look at it from different viewpoints.

AutoCAD provides some predefined VPOINT views that you can use to view the model, or you can define your own view. In the following exercise, use the VPOINT command to view a 3D cube from different viewpoints.

Using the VPOINT Command

1. Begin a new drawing named 099???01 in your assigned directory, using 099CUBE as a prototype.

2. `Command:` *Choose* View, *then* Set View, *then* Viewpoint, *then* Presets	Displays the Viewpoint Presets dialog box (see fig. 99.1)
3. *Choose* 315 *in the* X Axis *selector, then choose* 30 *in the* XY Plane *selector*	Sets up the viewpoint
4. *Choose* OK	Displays the new view (see fig. 99.2)

As you can see in figure 99.2, the cube model you are working with is a true 3D cube. As you move the viewpoint to different locations in the model, the view and orientation of the cube change.

Next, use the Axes option to specify a new viewpoint.

Using the Axes Option To Choose a Viewpoint

1. `Command:` *Choose* View, *then* Set View, *then* Viewpoint, *then* Axes	Displays the viewpoint globe (see fig. 99.3)
2. *Move the cursor in the viewpoint globe until the axes are oriented as shown in figure 99.3, and then click on the* Select *button*	Chooses a viewpoint by orienting the axes and displays the view shown in figure 99.4

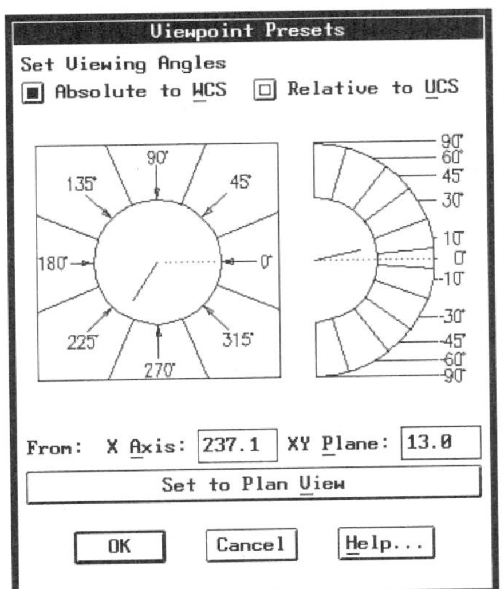

Figure 99.1

The Viewpoint Presets dialog box.

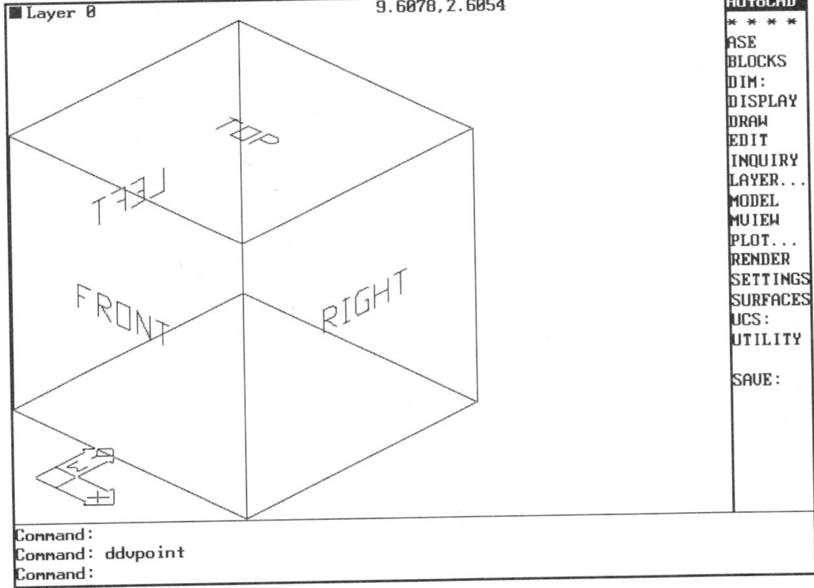

Figure 99.2

View at 315 degrees X Axis, 30 degrees XY Plane.

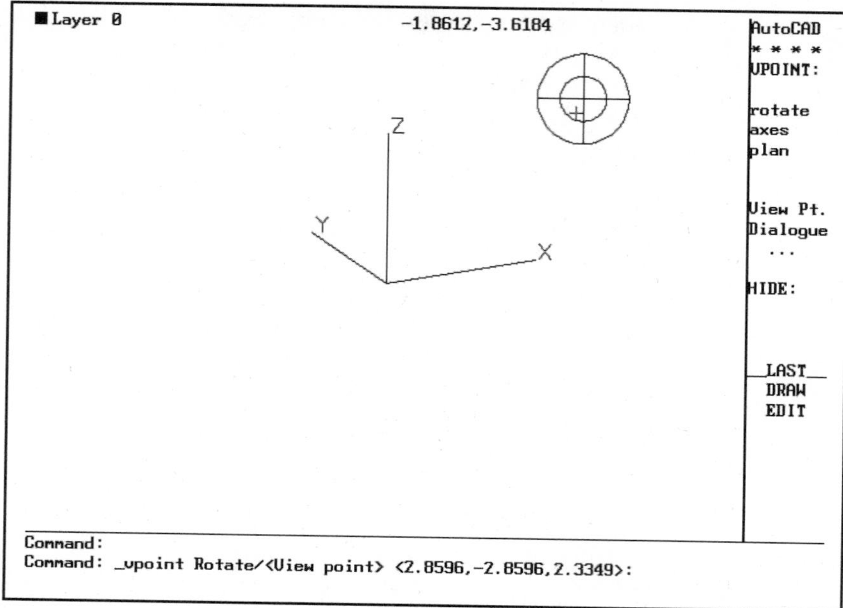

Figure 99.3

The VPOINT globe and axes.

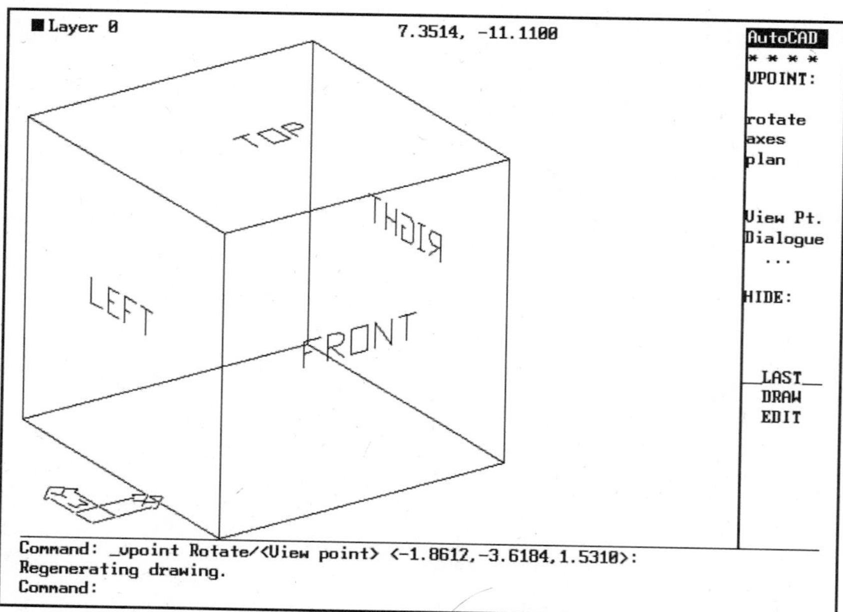

Figure 99.4

View resulting from selecting a viewpoint with the VPOINT globe.

If you select a point on the VPOINT globe inside the globe's inner circle, the resulting viewpoint is above the XY plane. If you select a point on the VPOINT globe between the inner and outer circle, the resulting viewpoint is below the XY plane.

Now that you are familiar with two ways to display a 3D view of a model, you are ready to begin working in 3D.

Rotating the UCS in 3D

Unit 38 explains how to define a coordinate system to facilitate some types of 2D design and dimensioning. Another use for the UCS command is to define coordinate systems that you can use to create 3D models. Using the UCS command in this way requires that you understand the relationship between the X, Y, and Z axes.

Understanding Axis Relationships

Up to this point, you probably have worked exclusively with the X and Y axes in AutoCAD, and are familiar with their relationship to one another. 3D modeling has another axis, called the Z axis, which is perpendicular to the X and Y axes. Figure 99.5 shows the default relationship between the three axes and the display when you begin a new drawing.

As you can see in figure 99.5, the Z axis is perpendicular to the X and Y axes. When you begin a new drawing, the Z axis points toward you. As you move the viewpoint and UCS, however, the orientation of the Z axis relative to your viewpoint changes. The relationship of the X, Y, and Z axes to one another never changes, however.

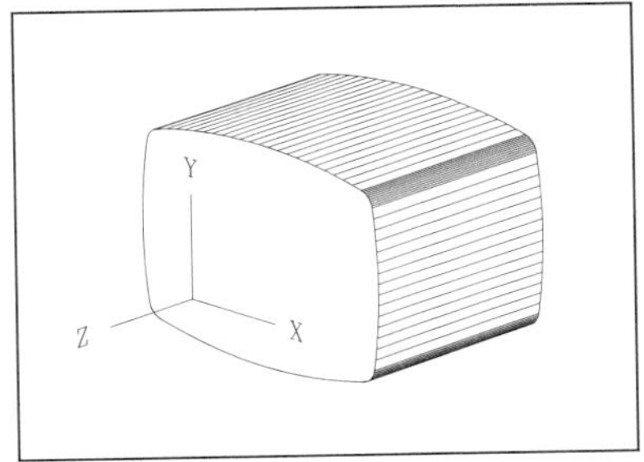

Figure 99.5

The relationship between the axes and the display.

Controlling the UCS Icon

The UCS icon is a valuable tool that enables you to keep track of the orientation of the axes relative to the 3D model. The UCS icon does not indicate the Z axis directly as it does the X and Y axes, but it does provide an indication of the direction of the positive Z axis.

Figure 99.6 illustrates how the UCS icon provides visual clues to the orientation of the coordinate system and your viewpoint. The UCS icon displays the letter W when you are using the World Coordinate System (WCS). The W disappears from the icon when you begin using a User Coordinate System (UCS).

In addition, the UCS icon changes according to the position of the viewpoint's relationship to the XY plane. If the viewpoint is above the XY plane, the UCS icon displays lines at the center of the icon (see fig. 99.6). If the viewpoint is below the XY plane, the lines do not appear.

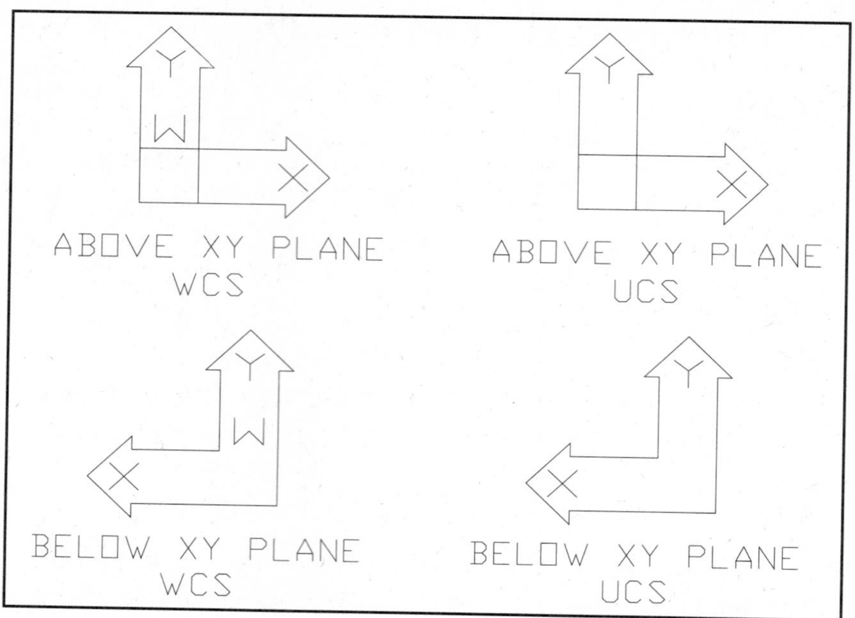

Figure 99.6

The UCS icon provides visual clues about the orientation of the axes and viewpoint.

It often is helpful to move the UCS icon to the origin when you are working with multiple coordinate systems in a 3D model. To move the UCS icon to the origin, use the Origin option of the UCSICON command.

Rotating the UCS

Unlike most 2D drawing, you often must define multiple User Coordinate Systems when creating a 3D model. In addition to relocating the origin of the UCS, you often will rotate the UCS about its axes, relative to the WCS. Although not required, it is extremely helpful to keep the UCS icon turned on when you are working in a UCS to keep track of the orientation of the axes relative to your model.

In the following exercise, rotate the UCS on each of the three axes. Keep the UCS icon turned on to see the effect of your UCS change.

Rotating the UCS

1. Continue with your drawing from the previous exercise and zoom to the view shown in figure 99.7.

2. `Command:` **`UCS`** ↵ — Starts the UCS command

3. `Origin/ZAxis/3point/Entity /View/X/Y/Z/Prev/Restore/Save/Del /?/<World>:` **`X`** ↵ — Chooses the X option

4. `Rotation angle about X axis <0>:` **`90`** ↵	Rotates the UCS 90 degrees on the Y axis
5. `Command:` *Press* Enter	Repeats the UCS command
`UCS`	
6. `Origin/ZAxis/3point/Entity /View/X/Y/Z/Prev/Restore/Save/Del /?/<World>:` **`Y`** ↵	Chooses the Y option
7. `Rotation angle about Y axis <0>:` **`90`** ↵	Rotates the UCS 90 degrees on the Y axis
8. `Command:` *Press* Enter	
`UCS`	
9. `Origin/ZAxis/3point/Entity /View/X/Y/Z/Prev/Restore/Save/Del /?/<World>:` **`Z`** ↵	Chooses the Z option
10. `Rotation angle about Z axis <0>:` **`90`** ↵	Rotates the UCS 90 degrees on the Z axis
11. `Command:` *Press* Enter	
`UCS`	
12. `Origin/ZAxis/3point/Entity /View/X/Y/Z/Prev/Restore/Save/Del /?/<World>:` **`W`** ↵	Restores the WCS
13. `Command:` *Press* Enter	
`UCS`	
14. `Origin/ZAxis/3point/Entity /View/X/Y/Z/Prev/Restore/Save/Del /?/<World>:` **`X`** ↵	Chooses the X option
15. `Rotation angle about X axis <0>:` **`30`** ↵	Rotates the UCS 30 degrees on the X axis (see fig. 99.7)
16. `Command:` *Press* Enter	
`UCS`	
17. `Origin/ZAxis/3point/Entity /View/X/Y/Z/Prev/Restore/Save/Del /?/<World>:` **`W`** ↵	Restores the WCS

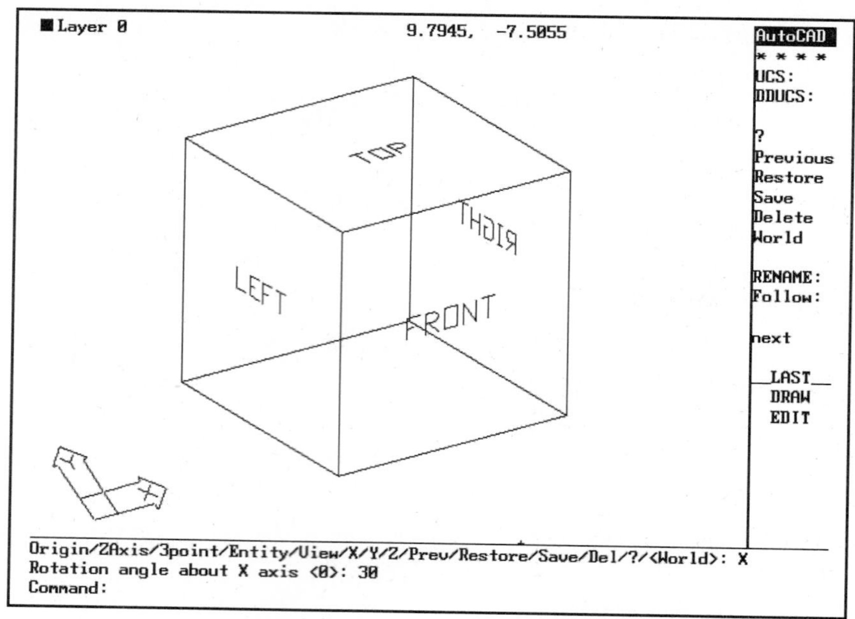

Figure 99.7

The UCS rotated 30 degrees along the X axis.

In addition to rotating the UCS, you also often move the origin of the UCS, just as you do in some types of 2D design. The following section explains a few methods for moving the UCS in 3D.

Moving the Origin

Often you must move the UCS to a new location in a 3D model to position new entities relative to a particular feature or point. When you move the origin of the UCS, you also can rotate it and align it with various features in the model at the same time. In the following exercise, set up the UCS icon to follow the origin, and then move and rotate the UCS to align it with the left face of the cube.

Moving the UCS Origin

1. `Command:` **`UCSICON`** ↵	
2. `ON/OFF/All/Noorigin/ORigin <ON>:` **`OR`** ↵	Sets the UCS icon to follow the origin
3. `Command:` **`UCS`** ↵	Starts the UCS command
4. `Origin/ZAxis/3point/Entity /View/X/Y/Z/Prev/Restore/Save/Del /?/<World>:` **`O`** ↵	Chooses the Origin option
5. `Origin point <0,0,0>:` *From the popup menu, choose* Endpoint	Relocates the origin

6. `_endp of` *Pick the end point at ① (see fig. 99.8)*

7. `Command:` **`UCS`** ↵ — Starts the UCS command

8. `Origin/ZAxis/3point/Entity /View/X/Y/Z/Prev/Restore/Save/Del /?/<World>:` **`O`** ↵ **`ZA`** ↵ — Chooses the ZAxis option

   `Origin point <0,0,0>:`

9. `Point on positive portion of Z-axis <0.0000,0.0000,1.0000>:` **`@-1,0,0`** ↵ — Specifies the positive direction of the Z axis

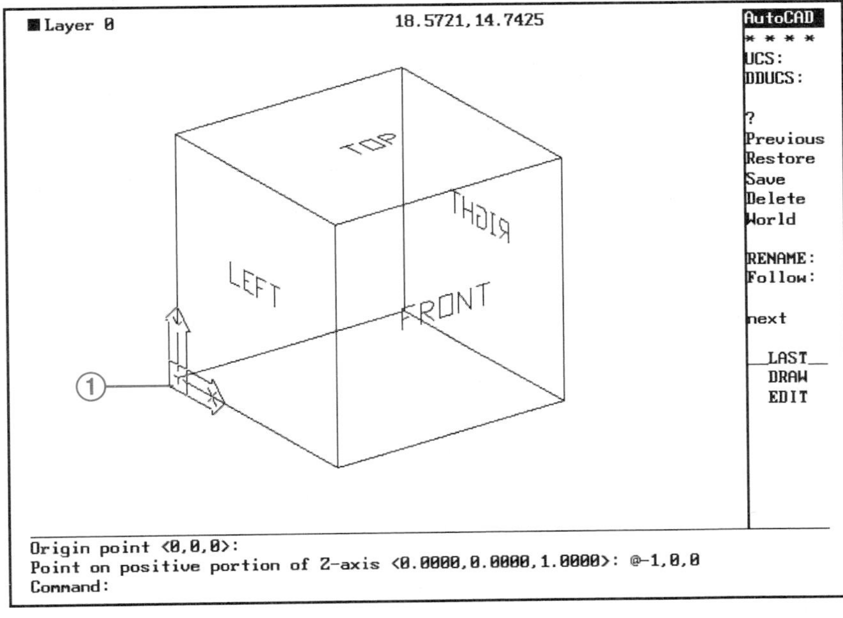

Figure 99.8

The UCS relocated and rotated.

In the preceding exercise, you relocated the origin and rotated the UCS in two separate steps. You also can move the origin and rotate the UCS in a single step by specifying the points that define the XY plane of the UCS. In the following exercise, relocate the UCS to the front of the cube, with the origin at the lower left corner of the front face.

Using the 3point Option

1. `Command:` **`UCS`** ↵ — Starts the UCS command

2. `Origin/ZAxis/3point/Entity /View/X/Y/Z/Prev/Restore/Save/Del /?/<World>:` **`3`** ↵ — Chooses the 3point option

continues

3. `Origin point <0,0,0>:` *From the popup menu, choose* Endpoint

4. `_endp of` *Pick the end point at* ① *(see fig. 99.9)* — Specifies the origin point of the UCS

5. `Point on positive portion of the X-axis <7.0000,0.0000,0.0000>:` *From the popup menu, choose* Endpoint

6. `_endp of` *Pick a point at* ② *(see fig. 99.9)* — Defines the direction of the X axis

7. `Point on positive-Y portion of the UCS XY plane <6.0000,1.0000,0.0000>:` *From the popup menu, choose* Endpoint

8. `_endp of` *Pick a point at* ③ *(see fig. 99.9)* — Defines the direction of the Y axis

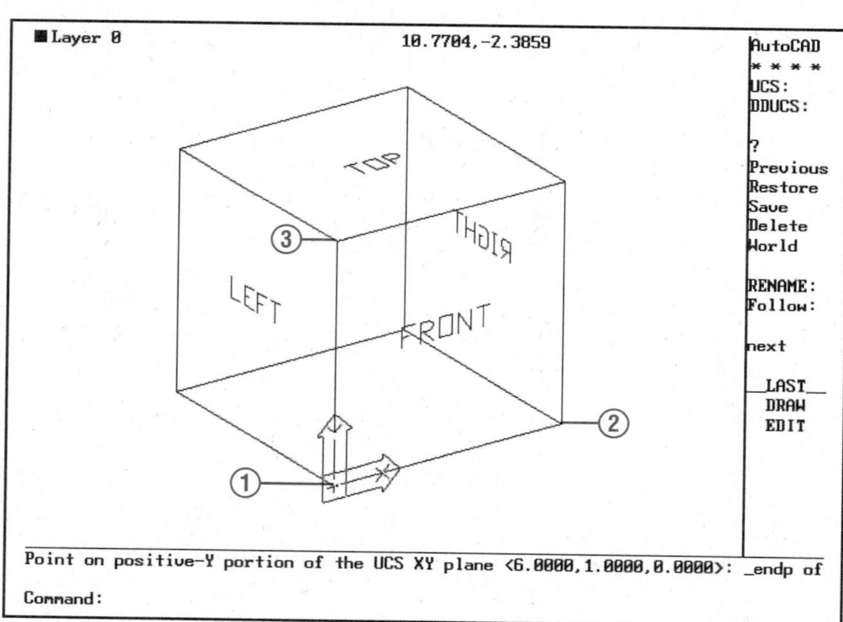

Figure 99.9

The UCS relocated and rotated to the front face.

The capability to move the UCS origin to a new location and to rotate the UCS is very important because it creates a local frame of reference by which you can locate entities in the model. When creating three-dimensional models with AutoCAD, you will use the UCS command often.

Unit Review

What You've Learned

- Commands: UCS, UCSICON, VPOINT
- How to display an off-axis view with VPOINT
- How to rotate the UCS
- How to relocate the origin of the UCS

Review Questions

True or False

99.01 T F You cannot create three dimensional drawings without the Advanced Modeling Extension.

99.02 T F The VPOINT command enables you to display an off-axis view.

99.03 T F The VPOINT globe displays a set of predefined views.

99.04 T F The Z axis is perpendicular to the X axis and parallel to the Y axis.

99.05 T F The Z axis is perpendicular to both the X and Y axes.

99.06 T F The relationship between the X, Y, and Z sometimes changes.

99.07 T F The UCS icon is a good means for tracking the location and orientation of the UCS.

99.08 T F You can rotate the UCS only in 90 degree increments.

99.09 T F You can move the origin and rotate the UCS in a single operation.

99.10 T F The 3point option of the UCS command enables you to relocate the origin and rotate the UCS in one step.

Student: ______________________ Date: ________

Instructor: ______________________ Course: ________ Section: ________

UNIT 100

Drawing Wireframes

ne type of 3D model is the wireframe model. This unit explains what a wireframe model is and teaches you how to create them. When you have completed this unit, you will be ready to experiment with other methods, such as surfaces, to create a 3D model.

The objectives for this unit are to:

- Understand wireframes
- Understand and use 3D coordinates
- Draw 2D entities in 3D space
- Create a simple wireframe model

Understanding Wireframe Models

A *wireframe model* is the simplest type of 3D model to create. A true wireframe model consists only of entities that connect points in 3D space. Wireframe models do not contain information about any of the surfaces in the model, nor do they contain any information about solids in the model. Figure 100.1 shows a typical wireframe model—you might recognize it if you completed the isometric drawing in unit 98.

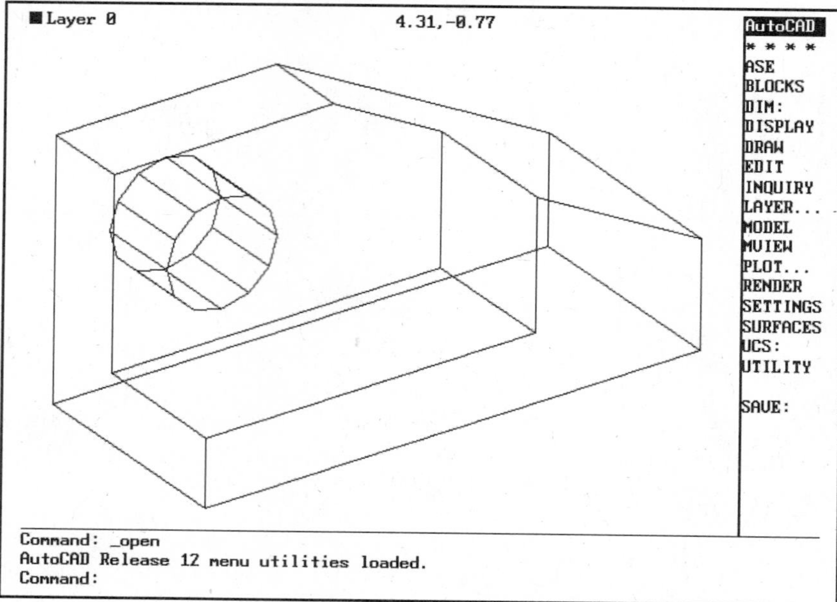

Figure 100.1
A wireframe model.

With simple objects, wireframe models are easier to create than surface or solids models. Wireframe models also take up less memory and disk space because they do not contain the same level of information as surface models and solids models. Often, this is a disadvantage; you typically cannot have the system create a solid-looking view of the wireframe (called hidden line removal). You also cannot determine surface intersections, centers of gravity, or other information about a design from a wireframe model.

Wireframe models do have uses, however, and one use is to teach the concepts behind 3D model construction. For that reason, and because you can create wireframe models without the AME module, *Hands On AutoCAD Release 12* concentrates on wireframe modeling.

Using 3D Coordinates

As you learned to use AutoCAD, you no doubt used coordinates extensively for accurate drawing. You now know that you can pick points from the display while grid and snap are turned on, enter absolute coordinates at the keyboard, and enter relative coordinates. Up to this point, however, you dealt exclusively with 2D coordinates—coordinates that only include X and Y ordinates.

In 3D modeling, however, you need to use three-dimensional coordinates. All the coordinates you entered in the past were 3D coordinates, but you might not have known it. Each coordinate in AutoCAD consists of three ordinates: X, Y, and Z. If you enter a coordinate but include only the X and Y ordinates, AutoCAD assumes a Z ordinate of 0. Therefore, entering the coordinate 1,1 is the same as entering the coordinate 1,1,0. The last value specifies the Z ordinate of the point.

As with 2D coordinates, you can enter 3D coordinates in response to most AutoCAD point prompts (although some commands do not accept 3D coordinates). This includes specifying absolute and relative Cartesian points, as well as polar points.

In the following exercises, experiment with 3D point entry. Create a wireframe model of a cube, and then draw a line from one corner of the cube using polar point specification. Start by setting up a 3D view using VPOINT.

Setting Up a 3D View

1. Begin a new drawing named 100???01 in your assigned directory using 100WIRE as a prototype.

2.	Command: **VPOINT** ↵	Starts the VPOINT command
3.	Rotate/<View point> <0.0000,0.0000, 1.0000>: **-1,-2,.75** ↵ Regenerating drawing.	Specifies the viewpoint
4.	Command: *Choose* Settings, *then* Drawing Aids	
5.	*Turn on snap and set it to .25, then choose* OK	Sets snap and returns to the drawing
6.	Command: **L** ↵	Starts the LINE command
7.	LINE From point: **0,0,0** ↵	Starts the line at the origin
8.	To point: *Pick a point at 6,0*	Draws the first segment
9.	To point: **6,6,0** ↵	Draws a line to ① (see fig. 100.2)
10.	To point: **0,6,0** ↵	Draws a line to ② (see fig. 100.2)

continues

11. `To point:` **`@0,-6,0`** ↵	Draws a line to ③ (see fig. 100.2)
12. `To point:` **`@0,0,6`** ↵	Draws a line to ④ (see fig. 100.2)
13. `To point:` **`@6,0`** ↵	Draws a line to ⑤ (see fig. 100.2)
14. `To point:` **`6,6`** ↵	Draws a line to ① (see fig. 100.2)
15. `To point:` **`U`** ↵	Undoes the segment
16. `To point:` **`6,6,6`** ↵	Draws a line to ⑥ (see fig. 100.2)
17. `To point:` *Press* Enter	Ends the LINE command

18. Zoom and pan to the view shown in figure 100.2.

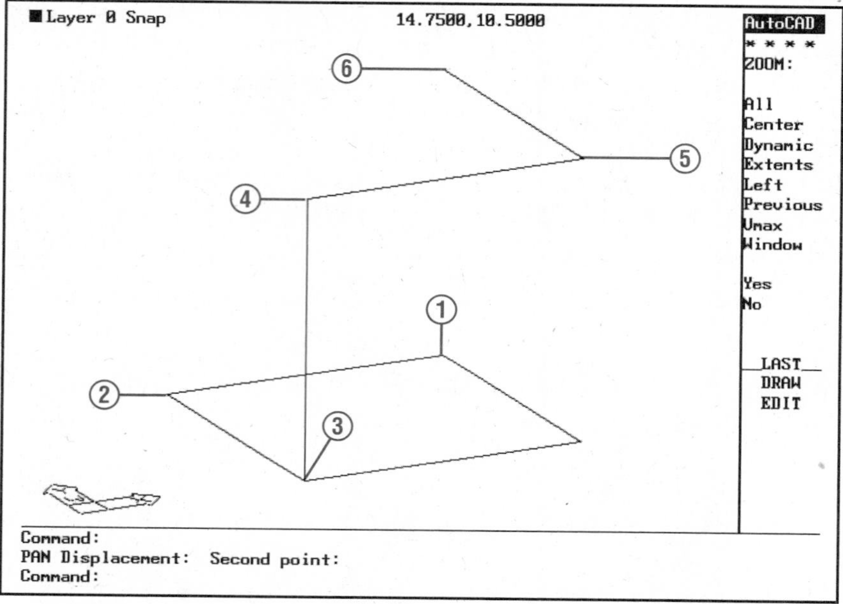

Figure 100.2
Part of a wireframe cube.

If you closely followed your point input in the preceding exercise, you might have noticed that AutoCAD assumes the same Z ordinate as the previous point whenever you use relative (@) point specification. If you use absolute point specification and omit the Z ordinate, however, AutoCAD does not use the same Z ordinate as the previous point. When you enter absolute points in a 3D model, get in the habit of entering all three ordinate values. If you are entering a relative point, you can omit the Z ordinate unless your relative point does not have the same Z ordinate as the previous point.

Drawing in 3D

As in 2D drawing, you can use constructive editing to create entities. You also can use object snap modes to snap to points in the model. In many situations, you also can use editing tools such as TRIM and EXTEND to modify existing entities in the drawing.

In the following exercise, use the Move/Copy autoedit mode to copy some of the lines from the bottom of the cube to the top of the cube. Then, use End point running object snap to draw the remaining vertical lines.

Completing the Cube

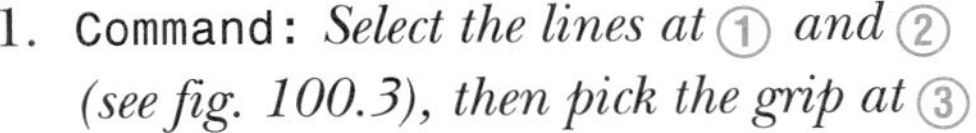

1. `Command:` *Select the lines at ① and ② (see fig. 100.3), then pick the grip at ③* — Selects the lines and enters Stretch autoedit mode

   `** STRETCH **`

2. `<Stretch to point>/Base point/Copy/Undo /eXit:` **`MO`** ↵ — Enters Move autoedit mode

   `** MOVE **`

3. `<Move to point>/Base point/Copy/Undo /eXit:` **`C`** ↵ — Enters Move/Copy autoedit mode

   `** MOVE (multiple) **`

4. `<Move to point>/Base point/Copy/Undo /eXit:` *From the popup menu, choose* Endpoint

5. `_endp of` *Pick the end point at ④ (see fig. 100.3)*

   `** MOVE (multiple) **`

6. `<Move to point>/Base point/Copy/Undo /eXit:` *Press* Enter — Exits autoedit mode

7. Set running object snap to Endpoint, then draw lines from ③ to ④, from ⑤ to ⑥, and from ⑦ to ⑧ (see fig. 100.3).

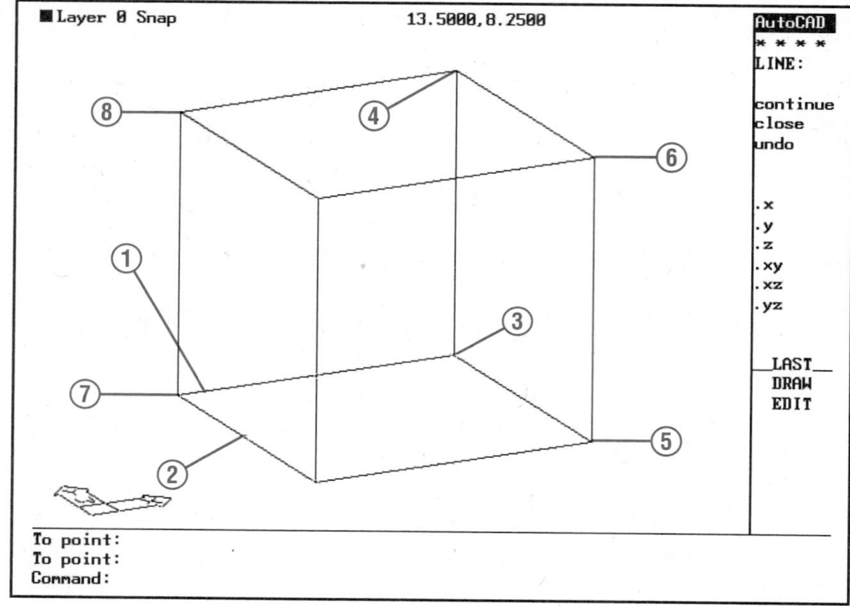

Figure 100.3

The completed wireframe cube.

In an upcoming exercise, you create multiple views of the cube. To keep the views straight, add a label to the front and top faces of the cube. Use the UCS and DTEXT commands to place the text, and use figure 100.4 as a guide to select points.

Adding Labels to the Cube

1. Turn off snap, but leave the End point running object snap mode active.
2. `Command:` **`UCS`** ↵ — Starts UCS command
3. `Origin/ZAxis/3point/Entity /View/X/Y/Z/Prev/Restore/Save/Del /?/<World>:` **3** ↵ — Chooses 3-point option
4. `Origin point <0,0,0>:` *Pick the end point at ① (see fig. 100.4)*
5. `Point on positive portion of the X-axis <1.0000,0.0000,0.0000>:` *Pick the end point at ② (see fig. 100.4)*
6. `Point on positive-Y portion of the UCS XY plane <0.0000,1.0000,0.0000>:` *Pick the end point at ③ (see fig. 100.4)*
7. `Command:` **`DTEXT`** ↵
8. `Justify/Style/<Start point>:` **`C`** ↵

9. `Center point:` **`NONE`** ↵

   Turns off running object snap for the next point selection

10. **`3,1`** ↵

    Specifies the location of the text

11. `Height <0.2000>:` **`.5`** ↵
12. `Rotation angle <0>:` *Press* Enter
13. `Text:` **`FRONT`** ↵
14. `Text:` *Press* Enter
15. `Command:` **`UCS`** ↵

    Starts UCS command

16. `Origin/ZAxis/3point/Entity /View/X/Y/Z/Prev/Restore/Save/Del /?/<World>:` **`3`** ↵

    Chooses 3-point option

17. `Origin point <0,0,0>:` *Pick the end point at ③ (see fig. 100.4)*
18. `Point on positive portion of the X-axis <1.0000,0.0000,0.0000>:` *Pick the end point at ④ (see fig. 100.4)*
19. `Point on positive-Y portion of the UCS XY plane <0.0000,1.0000,0.0000>:` *Pick the end point at ⑤ (see fig. 100.4)*
20. `Command:` **`DTEXT`** ↵
21. `Justify/Style/<Start point>:` **`C`** ↵
22. `Center point:` **`NONE`** ↵

    Turns off running object snap for the next point selection

23. **`3,1`** ↵

    Specifies the location of the text

24. `Height <0.5000>:` *Press* Enter
25. `Rotation angle <0>:` *Press* Enter
26. `Text:` **`TOP`** ↵
27. `Text:` *Press* Enter
28. Save your drawing.

Your drawing should now look similar to figure 100.4.

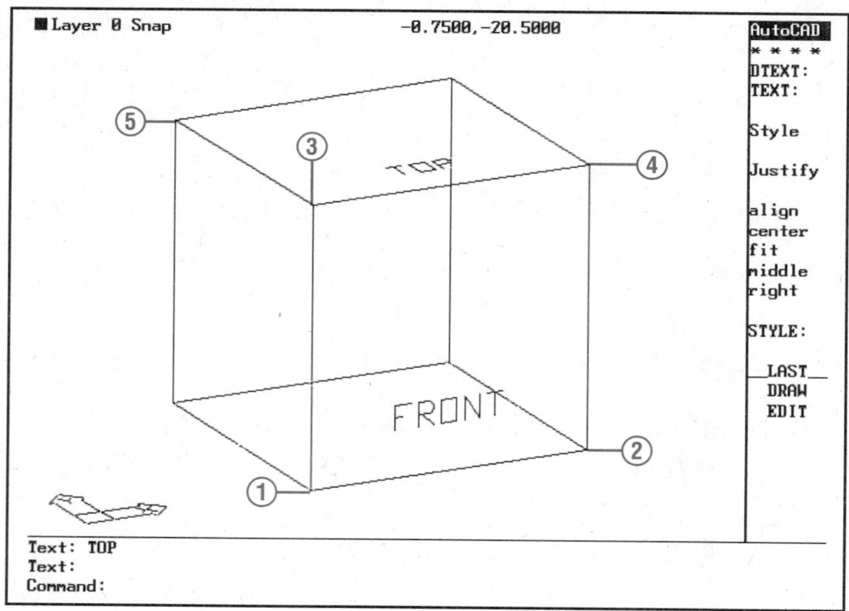

Figure 100.4

Labels added to the cube.

Using Multiple Viewports

Before you experiment with polar point specification, set up a few viewports so that you can view your wireframe model from different viewpoints at the same time. You can set up MVIEW viewports, but the following exercise uses tiled viewports instead. If you prefer to set up MVIEW viewports, you can do so on your own.

Setting Up Multiple Views

1. `Command:` *Choose* View, *then* Layout, *then* Tiled Vports	Displays the Tiled Viewport Layout dialog box
2. *Choose the* Three: Left *option, then choose* OK	Creates three tiled viewports with the larger viewport to the left of the display (see fig. 100.5)
3. `Command:` *Click in the upper right viewport*	Makes the viewport active
4. `Command:` **`PLAN`** ↵	Starts the PLAN command
5. `<Current UCS>/Ucs/World:` *Press* Enter	Sets the viewport to display a plan view of the current UCS
6. `Command:` *Click in the lower right viewport*	Makes the viewport active
7. `Command:` *Choose* View, *then* Set View, *then* Viewpoint, *then* Presets	Displays the Viewpoint Presets dialog box

8. *Choose 270 in the* X Axis *selector,* 0 *in the* XY Plane *selector, then choose* OK — Sets the viewport to display a front view of the cube (see fig. 100.5)

9. Zoom the two right viewports to .8X, set running object snap to NONE.

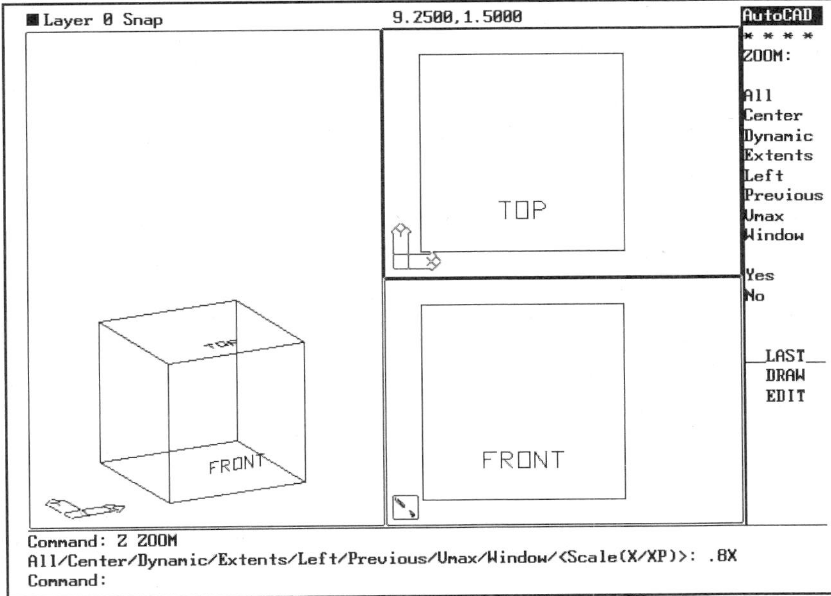

Figure 100.5

Multiple tiled viewports.

Working with Polar 3D Points

Now you are ready to try drawing some lines using polar coordinates. With the multiple viewports you just created, you can see the relationship between the points you specify.

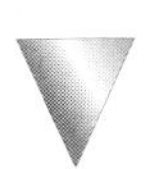

Using Polar 3D Coordinates

1. Continue with your drawing from the preceding exercise, and set the UCS back to World. Running object snap mode should be set to NONE.

   First, draw a line flat on the bottom of the cube at a 45° angle to the front face.

2. `Command:` **`L`** ↵

3. `LINE From point:` **`0,0,0`** ↵ — Starts line at front left corner of cube

4. `To point:` **`@3<45`** ↵ — Draws line to ① (see fig. 100.6)

5. `To point:` *Press* Enter

continues

Next, draw a line 4" long, 60° off the front face, and 10° off the bottom face by specifying two angles in a single point specification.

6. `Command:` *Press* Enter
7. `LINE From point:` **`0,0,0`** ↵ — Draws line to ② (see fig. 100.6)
   `To point:` **`@4<60<10`** ↵
8. `To point:` *Press* Enter

Next, check the distance from one corner of the cube to the opposite corner.

9. `Command:` **`DIST`** ↵
10. `First point:` **`0,0,0`** ↵
    `Second point:` *From the popup menu, choose* Endpoint
11. `_endp of` *Pick the end point at* ③ *(see fig. 100.6)*

```
Distance = 10.3923,  Angle in XY Plane = 45,  Angle from XY Plane = 35
Delta X = 6.0000,  Delta Y = 6.0000,   Delta Z = 6.0000
```

Finally, draw a line from one corner of the cube to the opposite corner using the information you derived from the DIST command.

12. `Command:` **`L`** ↵
13. `LINE From point:` **`0,0,0`** ↵
14. `To point:` **`@10.3923<45<35`** ↵
15. `To point:` *Press* Enter

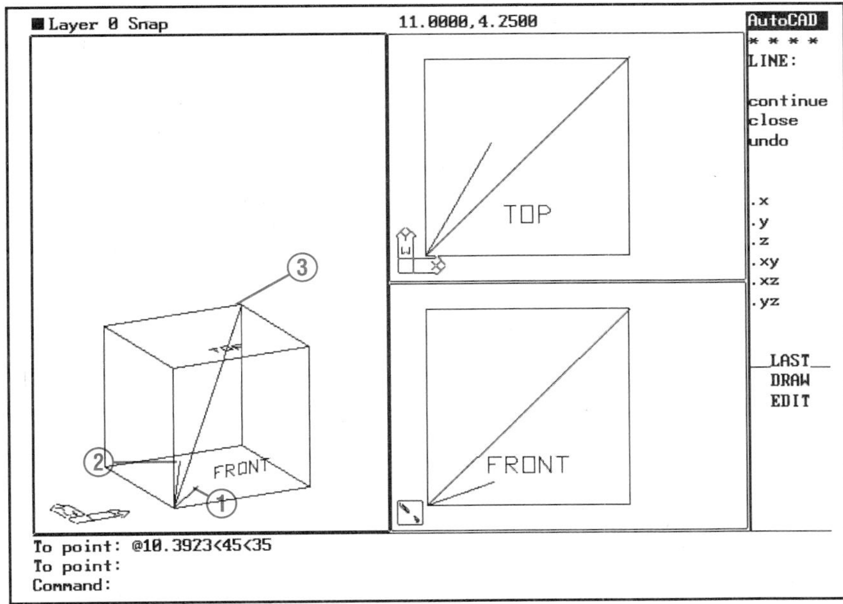

Figure 100.6

Lines added with polar point specification.

You can see from the preceding exercise that you can enter dual angles when specifying polar coordinates. The first angle value specifies the angle of the line in the XY plane, and the second angle value specifies the angle of the line out of (above or below) the XY plane.

The exercises in this unit are very simple, but they familiarize you with entering 3D coordinates. They also provide you with some experience in defining multiple viewports and relocating the UCS.

Unit Review

What You've Learned

- How to enter 3D coordinates
- The effect of adding a Z ordinate to a coordinate value
- How to enter 3D polar coordinates
- How to set up multiple views for 3D display

Review Questions

True or False

100.01 T F A wireframe model can be used to model surfaces.

100.02 T F A wireframe model can be used to model solids.

100.03 T F All points entered in AutoCAD include a Z ordinate, even if you enter only the X and Y ordinates.

100.04 T F Entering the coordinate 1,0 is the same as entering 1,0,0.

100.05 T F Some commands do not accept a 3D coordinate.

100.06 T F If you enter an absolute point but omit the Z ordinate, AutoCAD uses the same Z ordinate as the previous point.

100.07 T F If you enter a relative point but omit the Z ordinate, AutoCAD uses the same Z ordinate as the previous point.

100.08 T F You cannot use the COPY command or autoedit modes to copy an entity to a different Z ordinate.

100.09 T F Text cannot be rotated normal to a UCS; all text in a drawing has the same orientation.

100.10 T F You can enter two angles in a 3D polar point specification.

Student: ____________ Date: ______

Instructor: ____________ Course: ______ Section: ______

Menu Map

One of the most convenient and helpful new features of AutoCAD Release 12 is its extensive menu system. AutoCAD Release 12 takes advantage of a detailed menu system to provide you with numerous options that were only available from the `Command:` line in earlier versions of AutoCAD. New AutoCAD users often had trouble taking full advantage of AutoCAD's capabilities because of the need to remember hundreds of commands and subcommands. With the latest release of AutoCAD Release 12, extensive menus open up new levels of CAD features that were once only used by seasoned CAD professionals.

The following pages provide you with a road map to the Release 12 menus. The menu map in this appendix will help you become familiar with the location of commands that no longer are the domain of the experienced CAD veteran.

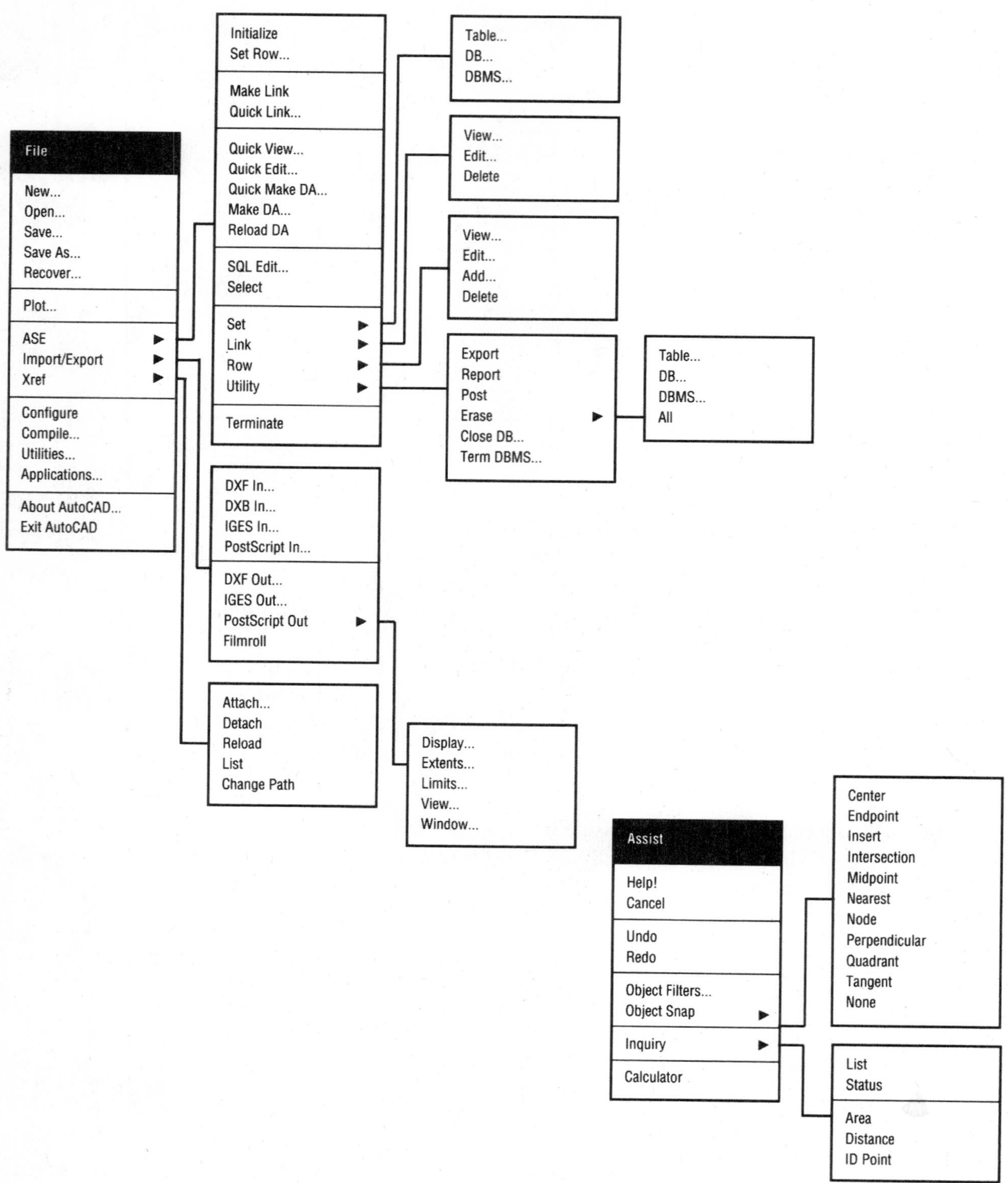
File
New...
Open...
Save...
Save As...
Recover...
Plot...
ASE
Import/Export
Xref
Configure
Compile...
Utilities...
Applications...
About AutoCAD...
Exit AutoCAD
Initialize
Set Row...
Make Link
Quick Link...
Quick View...
Quick Edit...
Quick Make DA...
Make DA...
Reload DA
SQL Edit...
Select
Set
Link
Row
Utility
Terminate
Table...
DB...
DBMS...
View...
Edit...
Delete
View...
Edit...
Add...
Delete
Export
Report
Post
Erase
Close DB...
Term DBMS...
Table...
DB...
DBMS...
All
DXF In...
DXB In...
IGES In...
PostScript In...
DXF Out...
IGES Out...
PostScript Out
Filmroll
Attach...
Detach
Reload
List
Change Path
Display...
Extents...
Limits...
View...
Window...
Assist
Help!
Cancel
Undo
Redo
Object Filters...
Object Snap
Inquiry
Calculator
Center
Endpoint
Insert
Intersection
Midpoint
Nearest
Node
Perpendicular
Quadrant
Tangent
None
List
Status
Area
Distance
ID Point

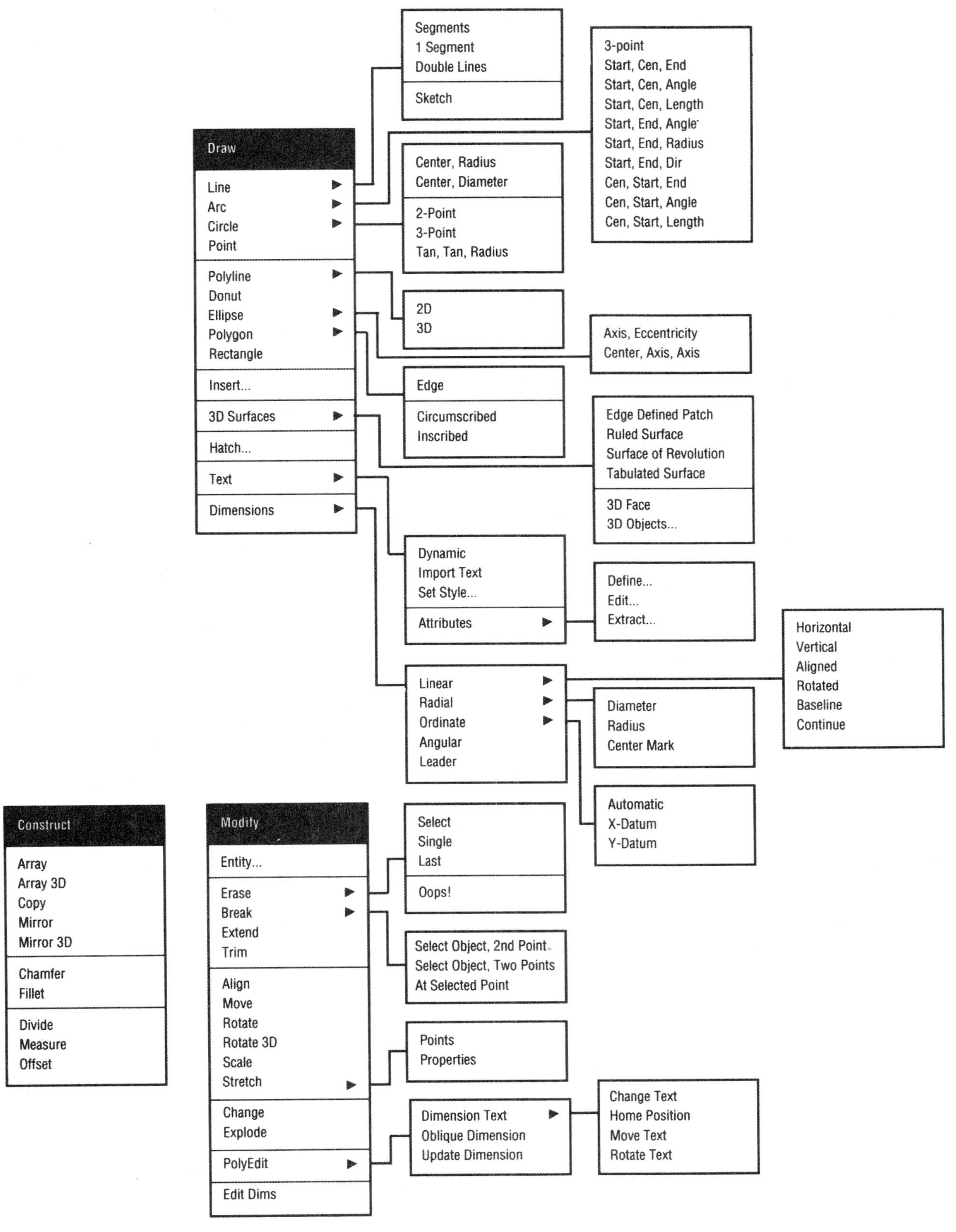
Segments
1 Segment
Double Lines
Sketch
3-point
Start, Cen, End
Start, Cen, Angle
Start, Cen, Length
Start, End, Angle
Start, End, Radius
Start, End, Dir
Cen, Start, End
Cen, Start, Angle
Cen, Start, Length
Draw
Line
Arc
Circle
Point
Polyline
Donut
Ellipse
Polygon
Rectangle
Insert...
3D Surfaces
Hatch...
Text
Dimensions
Center, Radius
Center, Diameter
2-Point
3-Point
Tan, Tan, Radius
2D
3D
Axis, Eccentricity
Center, Axis, Axis
Edge
Circumscribed
Inscribed
Edge Defined Patch
Ruled Surface
Surface of Revolution
Tabulated Surface
3D Face
3D Objects...
Dynamic
Import Text
Set Style...
Attributes
Define...
Edit...
Extract...
Horizontal
Vertical
Aligned
Rotated
Baseline
Continue
Linear
Radial
Ordinate
Angular
Leader
Diameter
Radius
Center Mark
Automatic
X-Datum
Y-Datum
Construct
Array
Array 3D
Copy
Mirror
Mirror 3D
Chamfer
Fillet
Divide
Measure
Offset
Modify
Entity...
Erase
Break
Extend
Trim
Align
Move
Rotate
Rotate 3D
Scale
Stretch
Change
Explode
PolyEdit
Edit Dims
Select
Single
Last
Oops!
Select Object, 2nd Point
Select Object, Two Points
At Selected Point
Points
Properties
Dimension Text
Oblique Dimension
Update Dimension
Change Text
Home Position
Move Text
Rotate Text

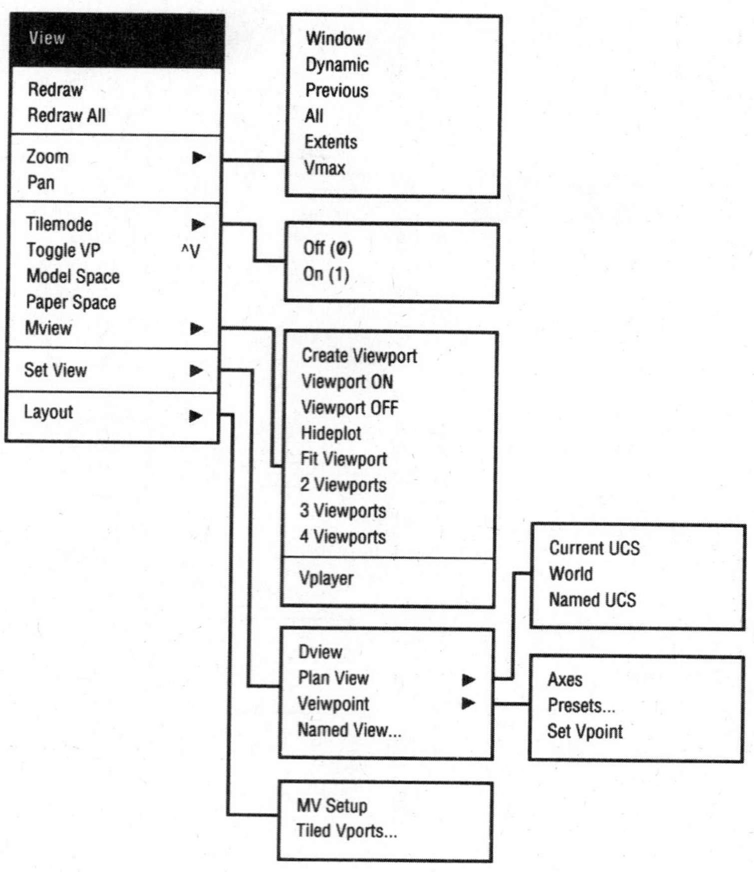
View
Redraw
Redraw All
Zoom
Pan
Tilemode
Toggle VP ^V
Model Space
Paper Space
Mview
Set View
Layout
Window
Dynamic
Previous
All
Extents
Vmax
Off (Ø)
On (1)
Create Viewport
Viewport ON
Viewport OFF
Hideplot
Fit Viewport
2 Viewports
3 Viewports
4 Viewports
Vplayer
Current UCS
World
Named UCS
Dview
Plan View
Veiwpoint
Named View...
Axes
Presets...
Set Vpoint
MV Setup
Tiled Vports...

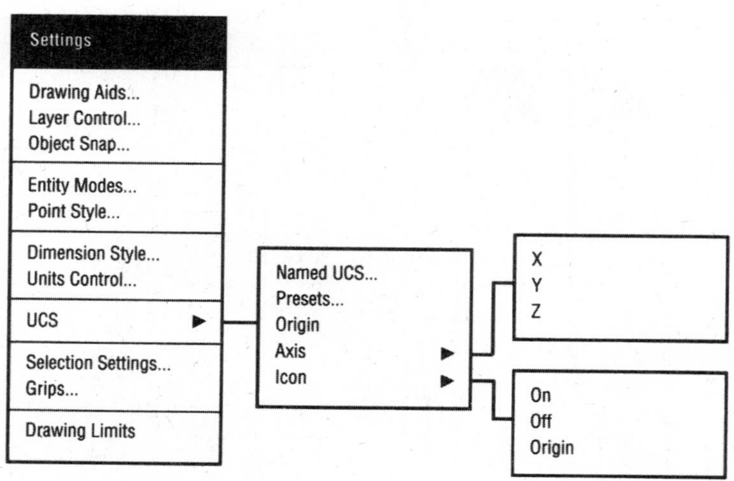
Settings
Drawing Aids...
Layer Control...
Object Snap...
Entity Modes...
Point Style...
Dimension Style...
Units Control...
UCS
Selection Settings...
Grips...
Drawing Limits
Named UCS...
Presets...
Origin
Axis
Icon
X
Y
Z
On
Off
Origin

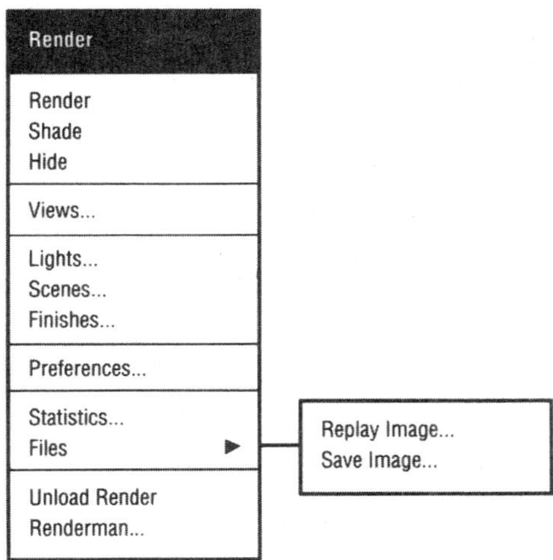
Render
Render
Shade
Hide
Views...
Lights...
Scenes...
Finishes...
Preferences...
Statistics...
Files
Unload Render
Renderman...
Replay Image...
Save Image...

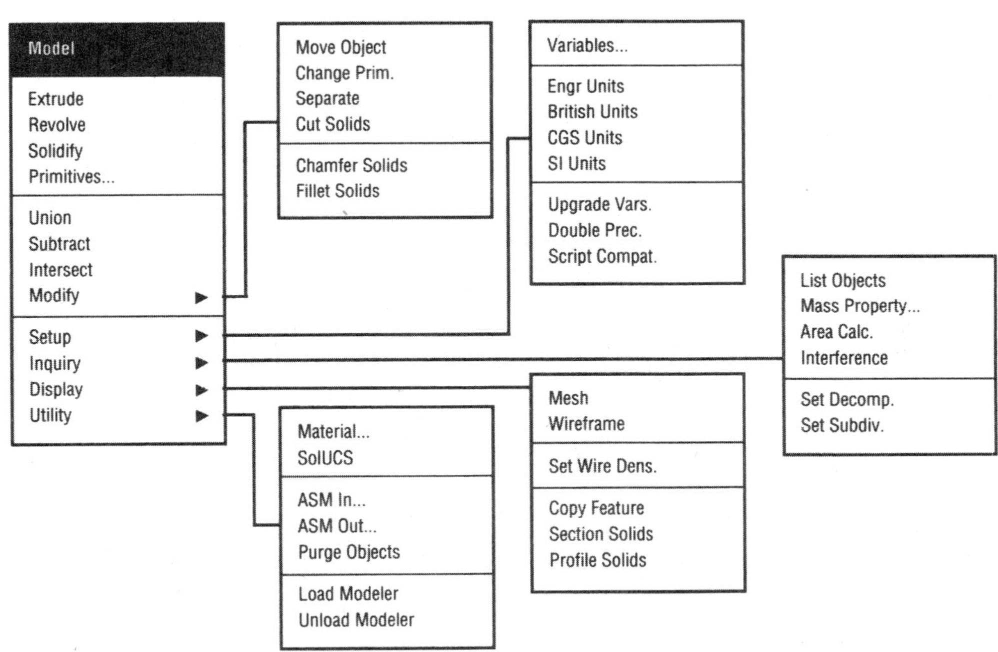
Model
Extrude
Revolve
Solidify
Primitives...
Union
Subtract
Intersect
Modify
Setup
Inquiry
Display
Utility
Move Object
Change Prim.
Separate
Cut Solids
Chamfer Solids
Fillet Solids
Variables...
Engr Units
British Units
CGS Units
SI Units
Upgrade Vars.
Double Prec.
Script Compat.
List Objects
Mass Property...
Area Calc.
Interference
Set Decomp.
Set Subdiv.
Mesh
Wireframe
Set Wire Dens.
Copy Feature
Section Solids
Profile Solids
Material...
SolUCS
ASM In...
ASM Out...
Purge Objects
Load Modeler
Unload Modeler

APPENDIX B

AutoCAD System Variables

This appendix contains a table of AutoCAD system variables. You can use the following table to look up AutoCAD's environment settings and their values. Table B.1 presents all the variables available through AutoCAD, AutoLISP, or the AutoCAD Development System (ADS). Each system variable's name and the default AutoCAD prototype drawing (ACAD.DWG) settings for the variable are shown. A brief description is given for each variable, and the meaning is given for each code. Some variable names appear in italic; you use the SETVAR command to set their values. You can set all other variables directly by entering their names at the `Command:` prompt or indirectly through AutoLISP, ADS, or by using the command shown in the *Command Name* column.

Variable names and features shown in bold are new to Release 12. All values are saved with the drawing unless noted with (CFG) for ConFiGuration file, or (NS) for Not Saved. Variables marked (RO) are read only; you cannot change them.

Table B.1
AutoCAD System Variables

Variable Name	Default Setting	Command Name	Variable Description
ACADPREFIX	C:\ACAD;C:\ACAD\SAMPLE;...		Directory search path set by DOS environment variable ACAD (NS),(RO)
ACADVER	12		The release number of your copy of AutoCAD
AFLAGS	0	**DDATTDEF**, ATTDEF	Current state of ATTDEF modes. The value is the sum of the following: 1 = Invisible 2 = Constant 4 = Verify 8 = Preset
ANGBASE	0	**DDUNITS**, UNITS	The direction of angle 0 in the current UCS
ANGDIR	0	**DDUNITS**, UNITS	The direction of angle measure: 1 = Clockwise 0 = Counterclockwise
APERTURE	10	**DDOSNAP**, APERTURE	Half the OSNAP target size in pixels (CFG)
AREA	0.0000	AREA, LIST	The last computed area in square drawing units

Variable Name	Default Setting	Command Name	Variable Description
ATTDIA	0		Controls the attribute-entry method: 1 = DDATTE dialog box 0 = Attribute prompts
ATTMODE	1	ATTDISP	Attribute display: 1 = Normal=1 2 = On 3 = Off
ATTREQ	1		Attribute values used by Insert: 1 = Prompts for values 0 = Uses defaults
AUDITCTL	**0**		**Controls the creation of an ADT log file containing AUDIT results:** **0 = No file** **1 = ADT file** **(CFG)**
AUNITS	0	**DDUNITS**, UNITS	The angular unit display code: 0 = Decimal deg. 1 = Degrees/min/sec 2 = Grads 3 = Radians 4 = Surveyors
AUPREC	0	**DDUNITS**, UNITS	The number of angular units in decimal places

continues

Table B.1, Continued
AutoCAD System Variables

Variable Name	Default Setting	Command Name	Variable Description
BACKZ	0.0000	DVIEW	The DVIEW back clipping plane offset in drawing units *See VIEWMODE* (RO)
BLIPMODE	1	BLIPMODE	Controls blip display: 1 = Blips 0 = No Blips
CDATE	19881202.144648898	TIME	Current date and time in YYYYMMDD.HHMMSSmsec format (NS),(RO)
CECOLOR	BYLAYER	DDEMODES, COLOR	The current entity color (RO)
CELTYPE	BYLAYER	DDEMODES, LINETYPE	The current entity linetype (RO)
CHAMFERA	0.0000	CHAMFER	The first chamfer distance
CHAMFERB	0.0000	CHAMFER	The second chamfer distance
CIRCLERAD	**0.0000**		**The default radius value for new circle entities:** **0 = None (NS)**
CLAYER	0	DDLMODES, LAYER	The current layer (RO)

Variable Name	Default Setting	Command Name	Variable Description
CMDACTIVE	**1**	**CMDACTIVE**	**Indicates that an AutoCAD command is active (used primarily by ADS):** **1 = None** **2 = Transparent** **4 = Script** **8 = Dialog box** **(NS),(RO)**
CMDECHO	1		Controls AutoCAD `Command:` prompt echoing by AutoLISP: 1 = Echo 0 = No Echo (NS)
CMDDIA	**1**		**Controls whether the PLOT command issues dialog boxes or prompts; a nonzero setting issues dialog boxes, and 0 issues prompts (CFG)**
CMDNAMES	""		**Names of any active commands**
COORDS	0	[^D] [F6]	Controls the updating of the coordinate display: 0 = Absolute upon picks 1 = Absolute continuously 2 = Relative only during prompts

continues

Table B.1, Continued
AutoCAD System Variables

Variable Name	Default Setting	Command Name	Variable Description
CVPORT	1	VPORTS	The current viewport's number
DATE	2447498.61620926	TIME	The current date and time in Julian format (NS),(RO)
DBMOD	**4**	**Most**	**Describes modifications to the current drawing database:** **0 = None** **1 = Entities** **2 = Symbol table** **4 = Database variable** **8 = Window** **15 = View** (**RO**)
DIASTAT	0	DD?????	The last dialog box exit code: 0 = Canceled 1 = OK button (RO)
DIMALT	0	**DDIM,** DIMALT	Controls the drawing of additional dimension text in an alternative-units system: 1 = On 0 = Off
DIMALTD	2	**DDIM,** DIMALTD	The decimal precision of dimension text when alternative units are used

Variable Name	Default Setting	Command Name	Variable Description
DIMALTF	25.4000	**DDIM,** DIMALTF	The scale factor for dimension text when alternate units are used
DIMAPOST	""	**DDIM,** DIMAPOST	The user-defined suffix for alternative dimension text (RO)
DIMASO	1	DIMASO	Controls the creation of associative dimensions: 1 = On 0 = Off
DIMASZ	0.1800	**DDIM,** DIMASZ	Controls the size of dimension arrows and affects the fit of dimension text inside dimension lines when DIMTSZ is set to 0
DIMBLK	""	**DDIM,** DIMBLK	The name of the block to draw rather than an arrow or tick (RO)
DIMBLK1	""	**DDIM,** DIMBLK	The name of the block for the first end of dimension lines *See DIMSAH* (RO)
DIMBLK2	""	**DDIM,** DIMBLK2	The name of the block for the second end of dimension lines *See DIMSAH* (RO)

continues

Table B.1, Continued
AutoCAD System Variables

Variable Name	Default Setting	Command Name	Variable Description
DIMCEN	0.0900	**DDIM,** DIMCEN	Controls center marks or center lines drawn by radial DIM commands: Mark size = value Draw center lines = negative (mark size = absolute value)
DIMCLRD	0	**DDIM,** DIMCLRD	The dimension line, arrow, and leader color number: 0 = BYBLOCK 256 = BYLAYER
DIMCLRE	0	**DDIM,** DIMCLRE	The dimension extension line's color
DIMCLRT	0	**DDIM,** DIMCLRT	The dimension text's color
DIMDLE	0.0000	**DDIM,** DIMDLE	The dimension line's extension distance beyond ticks when ticks are drawn (when DIMTSZ is nonzero)
DIMDLI	0.3800	**DDIM,** DIMDLI	The offset distance between successive continuing or baseline dimensions
DIMEXE	0.1800	**DDIM,** DIMEXE	The length of extension lines beyond dimension lines

Variable Name	Default Setting	Command Name	Variable Description
DIMEXO	0.0625	**DDIM,** DIMEXO	The distance by which extension lines originate from dimensioned entity
DIMGAP	0.0900	**DDIM,** DIMGAP	The space between text and a dimension line; determines when text is placed outside a dimension **(Creates reference dimension outlines if negative)**
DIMLFAC	1.0000	**DDIM,** DIMLFAC	The overall linear dimensioning scale factor; if negative, acts as the absolute value applied to paper space viewports
DIMLIM	0	**DDIM,** DIMLIM	Presents dimension limits default text: 1 = On 0 = Off *See DIMTP and DIMTM*
DIMPOST	""	**DDIM,** DIMPOST	The user-defined suffix for dimension text, such as "mm" (RO)
DIMRND	0.0000	**DDIM,** DIMRND	The rounding interval for linear dimension text

continues

Table B.1, Continued
AutoCAD System Variables

Variable Name	Default Setting	Command Name	Variable Description
DIMSAH	0	**DDIM,** DIMSAH	Enables the use of DIMBLK1 and DIMBLK2, rather than DIMBLK or a default terminator: 1 = On 0 = Off
DIMSCALE	1.0000	**DDIM,** DIMSCALE	The overall scale factor applied to other dimension variables except tolerances, angles, measured lengths, or coordinates 0 = Paper space scale
DIMSE1	0	**DDIM,** DIMSE1	Suppresses the first extension line: 1 = On 0 = Off
DIMSE2	0	**DDIM,** DIMSE2	Suppresses the second extension line: 1 = On 0 = Off
DIMSHO	0	DIMSHO	Determines whether associative dimension text is updated during dragging: 1 = On 0 = Off

Variable Name	Default Setting	Command Name	Variable Description
DIMSOXD	0	**DDIM,** DIMSOXD	Suppresses the placement of dimension lines outside extension lines: 1 = On 0 = Off
DIMSTYLE	*UNNAMED	**DDIM,** `Dim:` SAVE	Holds the name of the current dimension style (RO)
DIMTAD	0	**DDIM,** DIMTAD	Places dimension text above the dimension line, rather than within: 1 = On 0 = Off
DIMTIH	1	**DDIM,** DIMTIH	Forces dimension text inside the extension lines to be positioned horizontally, rather than aligned: 1 = On 0 = Off
DIMTIX	0	**DDIM,** DIMTIX	Forces dimension text inside extension lines: 1 = On 0 = Off
DIMTM	0.0000	**DDIM,** DIMTM	The negative tolerance value used when DIMTOL or DIMLIM is on

continues

Table B.1, Continued
AutoCAD System Variables

Variable Name	Default Setting	Command Name	Variable Description
DIMTOFL	0	**DDIM,** DIMTOFL	Draws dimension lines between extension lines, even if text is placed outside the extension lines: 1 = On 0 = Off
DIMTOH	1	**DDIM,** DIMTOH	Forces dimension text to be positioned horizontally, rather than aligned when it falls outside the extension lines: 1 = On 0 = Off
DIMTOL	0	**DDIM,** DIMTOL	Appends tolerance values (DIMTP and DIMTM) to the default dimension text: 1 = On 0 = Off
DIMTP	0.0000	**DDIM,** DIMTP	The positive tolerance value used when DIMTOL or DIMLIM is on
DIMTSZ	0.0000	**DDIM,** DIMTSZ	When assigned a nonzero value, forces tick marks to be drawn (rather than arrowheads) at the size specified by the value; affects the placement of the dimension line and text between extension lines

Variable Name	Default Setting	Command Name	Variable Description
DIMTVP	0.0000	**DDIM,** DIMTVP	Percentage of text height to offset dimension vertically
DIMTXT	0.1800	**DDIM,** DIMTXT	The dimension text height for non-fixed text styles
DIMZIN	0	**DDIM,** DIMZIN	Suppresses the display of zero inches or zero feet in dimension text 0 = Feet & Inches = 0 1 = Neither 2 = Inches only 3 = Feet only
DISTANCE	0.0000	DIST	The last distance computed by the DISTANCE command (NS) (RO)
DONUTID	**0.5000**		**The default inner diameter for new DONUT entities; may be 0 (NS)**
DONUTOD	**1.0000**		**The default outer diameter for new DONUT entities; must be nonzero (NS)**
DRAGMODE	2	DRAGMODE	Controls object dragging on screen: 0 = Off 1 = If requested 2 = Auto
DRAGP1	10		The regen-drag sampling rate (CFG)

continues

Table B.1, Continued
AutoCAD System Variables

Variable Name	Default Setting	Command Name	Variable Description
DRAGP2	25		The fast-drag sampling rate (CFG)
DWGCODEPAGE	**ascii**		**The code page used for the drawing**
DWGNAME	UNNAMED		The current drawing name supplied by the user when the drawing was begun (RO)
DWGTITLED	**0**	**NEW**	**Indicates whether the current drawing has been named or not: 1 = Yes 0 = No (RO)**
DWGPREFIX	C:\ACAD\		The current drawing's drive and directory path (NS) (RO)
DWGWRITE	**1**	**OPEN**	**Indicates that the current drawing is opened as read-only: 0 = No 1 = Yes**
ELEVATION	0.0000	ELEV	The current elevation in the current UCS for the current space
ERRNO	0		An error number generated by AutoLISP and ADS applications (See the *AutoLISP Reference Manual* or the *ADS Programmer's Reference Manual*)

Variable Name	Default Setting	Command Name	Variable Description
EXPERT	0		Suppresses successive levels of `Are you sure?` warnings: 0 = None 1 = REGEN/LAYER 2 = BLOCK/WBLOCK/SAVE 3 = LINETYPE 4 = UCS/VPORT 5 = DIM
EXTMAX	-1.0000E+20,-1.0000E+20		The X,Y coordinates of the drawing's upper right extents in the WCS (RO)
EXTMIN	1.0000E+20,1.0000E+20		The X,Y coordinates of the drawing's lower left extents in the WCS (RO)
FILEDIA	1		Controls the display of the dialog box for filename requests: 0 = Only when a tilde (~) is entered 1 = On (CFG)
FILLETRAD	0.0000	FILLET	The current fillet radius
FILLMODE	1	FILL	Turns on the display of fill traces, solids, and wide polylines: 1 = On 0 = Off

continues

Table B.1, Continued
AutoCAD System Variables

Variable Name	Default Setting	Command Name	Variable Description
FRONTZ	0.0000	DVIEW	The DVIEW front clipping plane's offset, in drawing units; *see VIEWMODE* (RO)
GRIDMODE	0	DDRMODES, GRID	Controls grid display in the current viewport: 1 = On 0 = Off
GRIDUNIT	0.0000,0.0000	DDRMODES, GRID	The X,Y grid increment for the current viewport
GRIPBLOCK	**1**	**DDGRIPS**	**Controls the display of grips for entities in blocks:** **1 = On** **2 = Off** **(CFG)**
GRIPCOLOR	**5**	**DDGRIPS**	**The current color code of unselected grips; can be a value of 0 to 255 (CFG)**
GRIPHOT	**1**	**DDGRIPS**	**The current color code of selected grips; can be a value of 0 to 255 (CFG)**

Variable Name	Default Setting	Command Name	Variable Description
GRIPS	**1**	**DDSELECT**	**Controls the display of entity grips and grip editing** **1 = On** **0 = Off** **CFG)**
GRIPSIZE	**5**	**DDGRIPS**	**The size of grip box in pixels; equals PICKBOX = 0 (CFG)**
HANDLES	0	HANDLES	Controls the creation of entity handles for the current drawing: 1 = On 0 = Off (RO)
HELPFILE	**""**	**HELP**	**The default help filename; also set by the ACADHELP environment variable (NS)**
HIGHLIGHT	1		Determines whether the current object selection set is highlighted: 1 = On 2 = On (NS)
HPANG	**0**	**BHATCH, HATCH**	**The default angle for new hatch patterns (NS)**

continues

Table B.1, Continued
AutoCAD System Variables

Variable Name	Default Setting	Command Name	Variable Description
HPDOUBLE	**0**	**BHATCH, HATCH**	**Controls user-defined hatch pattern doubling: 1 = On 0 = Off (NS)**
HPNAME	**""**	**BHATCH, HATCH**	**The default name for new hatch patterns (NS)**
HPSCALE	**1.0000**	**BHATCH, HATCH**	**The default scale factor for new hatch patterns; must be nonzero (NS)**
HPSPACE	**1.0000**	**BHATCH, HATCH**	**The default spacing for user-defined hatch patterns; must be nonzero (NS)**
INSBASE	0.0000,0.0000BASE		Insertion base point X,Y coordinate of current drawing in current space and current UCS
INSNAME	**""**	**DDINSERT, INSERT**	**The default block name for new insertions (NS)**
LASTANGLE	0	ARC	The end angle of the last arc in the current-space UCS (NS) (RO)
LASTPOINT	0.0000,0.0000,0.0000		The current space and UCS coordinate of the last point entered (recall with "@") (NS)

Variable Name	Default Setting	Command Name	Variable Description
LENSLENGTH	50.0000	DVIEW	The current viewport perspective view lens length, in millimeters (RO)
LIMCHECK	0	LIMITS	Controls limits checking for current space: 1 = On 0 = Off
LIMMAX	12.0000,9.0000	LIMITS	The upper right X,Y limit of current space, relative to the WCS
LIMMIN	0.0000,0.0000	LIMITS	The lower left X,Y limit of current space, relative to WCS
LOGINNAME	""	**CONFIG**	**The name entered by the user or configuration file during login to AutoCAD (CFG)(RO)**
LTSCALE	1.0000	LTSCALE	The global scale factor applied to linetypes
LUNITS	2	**DDUNITS**, UNITS	The linear units format: 1 = Scientific 2 = Decimal 3 = Engineering 4 = Architectural 5 = Fractional
LUPREC	4	**DDUNITS**, UNITS	Units precision decimal places or fraction denominator

continues

Table B.1, Continued
AutoCAD System Variables

Variable Name	Default Setting	Command Name	Variable Description
MACROTRACE	**0**		**Controls the DIESEL macro-debugging display** **1 = On** **0 = Off**
MAXACTVP	16		The maximum number of viewports to regenerate (NS) (RO)
MAXSORT	200		The maximum number of symbols and filenames sorted in lists, up to 200 (CFG)
MENUCTL	**1**		**Command-line input-sensitive screen menu-page switching:** **1 = On** **0 = Off** **(CFG)**
MENUECHO	0		Suppresses the display of menu actions on the command line; the value is the sum of the following: 1 = Menu input 2 = Command prompts 4 = Disable ^P toggling (NS)
MENUNAME	ACAD	MENU	The current menu name, plus the drive/path, if entered (RO)

Variable Name	Default Setting	Command Name	Variable Description
MIRRTEXT	1		Controls reflection of text by the MIRROR command: 0 = Retain text direction 1 = Reflect text
MODEMACRO	""		**A DIESEL language expression to control status-line display**
OFFSETDIST	**-1.0000**	**OFFSET**	**The default distance for the OFFSET command; negative values enable the Through option (NS)**
ORTHOMODE	0	[^O] [F8]	Sets the current Ortho mode state: 1 = On 0 = Off
OSMODE	0	**DDOSNAP,** OSNAP	The current object snap mode; the value is the sum of the following: 1 = Endp 2 = Mid 4 = Cen 8 = Node 16 = Quad 32 = Int 64 = Ins 128 = Perp 256 = Tan 512 = Near 1024 = Quick

continues

Table B.1, Continued
AutoCAD System Variables

Variable Name	Default Setting	Command Name	Variable Description
PDMODE	0		Controls the graphic display of point entities
PDSIZE	0.0000		Controls the size of point graphic display
PERIMETER	0.0000	AREA, DBLIST, LIST	The last computed perimeter (NS) (RO)
PFACEVMAX	4		The maximum number of vertices per face in a PFACE mesh (NS) (RO)
PICKADD	**1**	**DDSELECT**	**Controls whether selected entities are added to, or replace (added with Shift+select) the current selection set: 0 = Added 1 = Replace (CFG)**
PICKAUTO	**0**	**DDSELECT**	**Controls the implied (AUTO) windowing for object selection: 1 = On 0 = Off (CFG)**

Variable Name	Default Setting	Command Name	Variable Description
PICKDRAG	**0**	**DDSELECT**	**Determines whether the pick button must be depressed during window-corner picking in set selection (MS Windows style):** **1 = On** **0 = Off** **(CFG)**
PICKFIRST	**0**	**DDSELECT**	**Enables entity selection before command selection (noun/verb paradigm):** **1 = On** **0 = Off** **(CFG)**
PICKBOX	3		Half the object-selection pick box size, in pixels (CFG)
PLATFORM	*Varies*		Indicates the version of AutoCAD in use: a string such as "386 DOS Extender," "Sun 4/SPARCstation," "Apple Macintosh," etc.
PLOTID	""	**PLOT**	**The current plotter configuration description (CFG)**
PLOTTER	**0**	**PLOT**	**The current plotter configuration number (CFG)**

continues

Table B.1, Continued
AutoCAD System Variables

Variable Name	Default Setting	Command Name	Variable Description
PLINEGEN	**0**		**The control points for polyline generation of noncontinuous linetypes:** **0 = Vertices** **1 = End points**
PLINEWID	**0.0000**	**PLINE**	**The default width for new polyline entities**
POLYSIDES	**4**	**POLYGON**	**The default number of sides (3 to 1024) for new polygon entities (NS)**
POPUPS	1		Determines whether the Advanced User Interface (dialog boxes, menu bar, pull-down menus, icon menus) is supported: 1 = Yes 0 = No (NS) (RO)
PSPROLOG	**""**		**The name of the PostScript post-processing section of ACAD.PSF to be appended to the PSOUT command's output**
PSQUALITY	**75**	**PSQUALITY**	**The default quality setting for rendering of images by the PSIN command**

Variable Name	Default Setting	Command Name	Variable Description
PSLTSCALE	**1**		**Paper-space scaling of model space linetypes:** **1 = On** **0 = Off** **(DWG)**
QTEXTMODE	0	QTEXT	Sets the current state of Quick text mode: 1 = On 0 = Off
REGENMODE	1	REGENAUTO	Indicates the current state of REGENAUTO: 1 = On 0 = Off
SAVEFILE	**AUTO.SV$**	**CONFIG**	**The default directory and file-name for automatic file saves (CFG)(RO)**
SAVETIME	**120**	**CONFIG**	**The default interval between automatic file saves, in minutes:** **0 = None** **(CFG)**
SAVENAME	**""**	**SAVEAS**	**The drawing name specified by the user to the last invocation of the SAVEAS command in the current session (NS) (RO)**

continues

Table B.1, Continued
AutoCAD System Variables

Variable Name	Default Setting	Command Name	Variable Description
SCREENBOXES	**25**	**CONFIG**	**The number of available screen menu boxes in the current graphics screen area (RO)**
SCREENMODE	**0**	**[F1]**	**Indicates the active AutoCAD screen mode or window:** **0 = Text** **1 = Graphics** **2 = Dual screen** **(RO)**
SCREENSIZE	572.0000,414.0000		The size of current viewport, in pixels, X and Y (RO)
SHADEDGE	3		Controls the display of edges and faces by the SHADE command: 0 = Faces shaded, edges unhighlighted 1 = Faces shaded, edges in background color 2 = Faces unfilled, edges in entity color 3 = Faces in entity color, edges in background
SHADEDIF	70		Specifies the ratio of diffuse-to-ambient light used by the SHADE command; expressed as a percentage of diffuse reflective light

Variable Name	Default Setting	Command Name	Variable Description
SHPNAME	""	**SHAPE**	**The default shape name (NS)**
SKETCHINC	0.1000	SKETCH	The recording increment for SKETCH segments
SKPOLY	0		Controls the type of entities generated by SKETCH: 1 = Polylines 0 = Lines
SNAPANG	0	**DDRMODES,** SNAP	The angle of SNAP/GRID rotation in the current viewport, for the current UCS
SNAPBASE	0.0000,0.0000	**DDRMODES,** SNAP	The X,Y base point of SNAP/GRID rotation in the current viewport, for the current UCS
SNAPISOPAIR	0	**DDRMODES,** SNAP [^E]	The current isoplane for the current viewport: 0 = Left 1 = Top 2 = Right
SNAPMODE	0	**DDRMODES,** SNAP	Indicates the state of [^B] [F9] snap for the current viewport: 1 = On 0 = Off

continues

Table B.1, Continued
AutoCAD System Variables

Variable Name	Default Setting	Command Name	Variable Description
SNAPSTYL	0	**DDRMODES,** SNAP	The snap style for the current viewport: 1 = Isometric 0 = Standard
SNAPUNIT	1.0000,1.0000	**DDRMODES**, SNAP	The snap X,Y increment for the current viewport
SOLAMEVER	**2.1**		**The Region Modeler software's version number**
SOLAREAU	**sq cm**		**The unit system for area calculations**
SOLAXCOL	**3**		**The color number of the SOLMOVE MCS icon**
SOLDELENT	**3**	**SOLIDIFY**	**Controls prompting for original entity deletion by the SOLIDIFY command.** **1 = Don't delete** **2 = Ask** **3 = Delete**
SOLDISPLAY	**WIRE**	**SOLMESH, SOLWIRE**	**Controls the default display mode for new solids**
SOLHANGLE	**45.000000**	**SOLIDIFY**	**The default angle of new solid entity hatch patterns**
SOLHPAT	**U**	**SOLIDIFY**	**The default pattern name for new solid entity hatching**

Variable Name	Default Setting	Command Name	Variable Description
SOLHSIZE	1.000000	SOLIDIFY	The default scale for new solid entity hatch patterns
SOLLENGTH	cm	SOLLIST, SOLMASSP	The unit system for perimeter calculations
SOLMATCURR	MILD_STEEL	SOLMAT	The default material assigned to new solid entities
SOLPAGELEN	25	SOLLIST, SOLMASSP SOLMAT	The length of message pages, in lines
SOLRENDER	CSG	SHADE, SOLMESH SOLWIRE	The display type for solids CSG = By primitive UNIFORM = As composite
SOLSERVMSG	3	MANY	The level of details displayed by Region Modeler messages 0 = None 1 = Errors 2 = Errors+progress 3 = All
SOLSOLIDIFY	3	MANY	Controls prompting for entity conversion to solid regions 1 = Don't convert 2 = Ask 3 = Convert

continues

Table B.1, Continued
AutoCAD System Variables

Variable Name	Default Setting	Command Name	Variable Description
SOLWDENS	**4**	**MANY**	**Controls the number of edges used to represent curved solid surfaces displayed as wire frames (SOLWDENS*4)**
SORTENTS	**0**	**DDSELECT**	**The optimization codes for oct-tree spatial database organization; the value is the sum of the following:** **0 = Off** **1 = Object selection** **2 = OSNAP** **4 = REDRAW** **8 = MSLIDE** **16 = REGEN** **32 = PLOT** **64 = PSOUT** **(CFG)**
SPLFRAME	0		Controls the display of control polygons for spline-fit polylines, defining meshes of surface-fit polygon meshes, invisible 3D face edges: 1 = On 0 = Off
SPLINESEGS	8		The number of line segments in each spline curve

Variable Name	Default Setting	Command Name	Variable Description
SPLINETYPE	6		Controls the spline type generated by the PEDIT command's Spline option: 5 = Quadratic B-Spline 6 = Cubic B-Spline
SURFTAB1	6		The number of RULESURF and Tabsurf tabulations, also the REVSURF and EDGESURF M-direction density
SURFTAB2	6		The REVSURF and EDGESURF N-direction density
SURFTYPE	6		Controls type of surface generated by Pedit smooth option: Quadratic B-Spline=5 Cubic B-Spline=6 Bezier=8
SURFU	6		The M-direction surface density of 3D polygon meshes
SURFV	6		The N-direction surface density 3D polygon meshes
SYSCODEPAGE	**ascii**		**The code page used by the system**
TABMODE	**0**	**TABLET, [F10]**	**Controls tablet mode:** **1 = On** **0 = Off**

continues

Table B.1, Continued
AutoCAD System Variables

Variable Name	Default Setting	Command Name	Variable Description
TARGET	0.0000,0.0000,0.0000	DVIEW	The UCS coordinates of the current viewport's target point (RO)
TDCREATE	2447498.61620031	TIME	The date and time of the current drawing's creation, in Julian format (RO)
TDINDWG	0.00436285	TIME	The total amount of editing time elapsed in the current drawing, in Julian days (RO)
TDUPDATE	2447498.61620031	TIME	The date and time when the file was last saved, in Julian format (RO)
TDUSRTIMER	0.00436667	TIME	User-controlled elapsed time in Julian days (RO)
TEMPPREFIX	""		The directory configured for placement of AutoCAD's temporary files; defaults to the drawing directory (NS) (RO)
TEXTEVAL	0		Controls the checking of text input (except by DTEXT) for AutoLISP expressions: 0 = Yes 1 = No (NS)

Variable Name	Default Setting	Command Name	Variable Description
TEXTSIZE	0.2000	TEXT	The height applied to new text entities created with nonfixed-height text styles
TEXTSTYLE	STANDARD	TEXT, STYLE	The current text style's name (RO)
THICKNESS	0.0000		The current 3D extrusion thickness
TILEMODE	1	TILEMODE	Release 10 VPORT compatibility setting; enables/disables paper space and viewport entities: 1 = On 0 = Off
TRACEWID	0.0500	TRACE	The current width of traces
TREEDEPTH	**3020**	**DDSELECT**	**The maximum number of node subdivisions for oct-tree spatial database organization in model space and paper space for the current drawing**
TREEMAX	?	**TREEMAX**	**The maximum number of nodes for oct-tree spatial database organization for the current AutoCAD configuration (CFG)**

continues

Table B.1, Continued
AutoCAD System Variables

Variable Name	Default Setting	Command Name	Variable Description
UCSFOLLOW	0		Controls automatic display of the plan view in the current viewport when switching to a new UCS: 1 = On 0 = Off
UCSICON	1	UCSICON	Controls the UCS icon's display; the value is the sum of the following: 0 = Off 1 = On 2 = At origin
UCSNAME	""	**DDUCS**, UCS	The name of the current UCS for the current space: "" = Unnamed (RO)
UCSORG	0.0000,0.0000,0.0000	**DDUCS**, UCS	The WCS origin of the current UCS for the current space (RO)
UCSXDIR	1.0000,0.0000,0.0000	**DDUCS**, UCS	The X direction of the current UCS (RO)
UCSYDIR	0.0000,1.0000,0.0000	**DDUCS**, UCS	The Y direction of the current UCS (RO)

Variable Name	Default Setting	Command Name	Variable Description
UNDOCTL	**5**	**UNDO**	**The current state of UNDO; the value is the sum of the following:** **1 = Enabled** **2 = Single command** **4 = Auto mode** **8 = Group active** **(RO)(NS)**
UNDOMARKS	**0**	**UNDO**	**The current number of marks in the UNDO command's history (RO) (NS)**
UNITMODE	0		Controls the display of user input of fractions, feet and inches, and surveyor's angles: 0 = Per LUNITS 1 = As input
USERI1 - 5	0		User integer variables USERI1 to USERI5
USERR1 - 5	0.0000		User real-number variables USERR1 to USERR5
VIEWCTR	6.2518,4.5000	ZOOM, PAN, VIEW	The X,Y centerpoint coordinate of the current view in the current viewport (RO)
VIEWDIR	0.0000,0.0000,1.0000	DVIEW	The camera point offset from target in the WCS (RO)

continues

Table B.1, Continued
AutoCAD System Variables

Variable Name	Default Setting	Command Name	Variable Description
VIEWMODE	0	DVIEW, UCS	The current viewport's viewing mode; the value is the sum of the following: 1 = Perspective 2 = Front clipping on 4 = Back clipping on 8 = UCSFOLLOW On 16 = FRONTZ offset in use (RO)
VIEWSIZE	9.0000	ZOOM, VIEW	The current view's height, in drawing units (RO)
VIEWTWIST	0	DVIEW	The current viewport's view-twist angle (RO)
VISRETAIN			Controls retention of XREF file-layer settings in the current drawing 0 = Off 1 = On
VSMAX	12.5036,9.0000,0.0000	ZOOM,PAN,VIEW	The upper right X,Y coordinate of the current viewport's virtual screen for the current UCS (NS) (RO)

Variable Name	Default Setting	Command Name	Variable Description
VSMIN	0.0000,0.0000,0.0000	ZOOM,PAN,VIEW	The lower left X,Y coordinate of the current viewport's virtual screen for the current UCS (NS) (RO)
WORLDUCS	1	UCS	The current UCS, equivalent to WCS: 1 = True 0 = False (RO)
WORLDVIEW	1	DVIEW,UCS	Controls the automatic changing of a UCS to the WCS during the DVIEW and VPOINT commands: 1 = On 0 = Off
XREFCTL	0		Controls the creation of an XLG log file that contains XREF results: 0 = No file 1 = XLG file (CFG)

INDEX

Symbols

A

INDEX

INDEX

INDEX

INDEX

INDEX

INDEX

E

G

INDEX

H

I

J–K

L

INDEX

M

INDEX

INDEX

INDEX

S

INDEX

INDEX

INDEX

W

INDEX

Hands On AutoCAD

REGISTRATION CARD

Fill out this card to receive information about future AutoCAD books and other New Riders titles!

Name ______________________ **Title** ______________________

Company ______________________

Address ______________________

City/State/ZIP ______________________

I bought this book because: ______________________

____

I purchased this book from:

☐ A bookstore (Name ______________________)

☐ A software or electronics store (Name ______________________)

☐ Mail order (Name of Catalog ______________________)

I purchase this many computer books each year:

☐ 1–5 ☐ 6 or more

I currently use these applications: ______________________

____

____

____

I found these chapters to be the most informative: ______________________

____

I found these chapters to be the least informative: ______________________

____

Additional comments: ______________________

____

☐ I would like to see my name in print! You may use my name and quote me in future New Riders products and promotions. My daytime phone number is: ______________________

New Riders Publishing 201 West 103rd Street • Indianapolis, Indiana 46290 USA

Fold Here

PLACE
STAMP
HERE

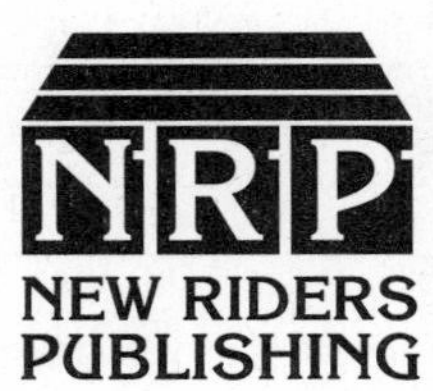

New Riders Publishing
201 West 103rd Street
Indianapolis, Indiana 46290
USA